KU-772-804

The **Rough Guide** to

England

written and researched by

Robert Andrews, Jules Brown, Phil Lee and Rob Humphreys

with additional contributions by
Kate Hughes

ROUGH
GUIDES

NEW YORK • LONDON • DELHI

www.roughguides.com

Contents

Coastal England colour section following p.216

Festivals and events colour section following p.728

◄◄ Salisbury Cathedral ◄ Bamburgh Castle

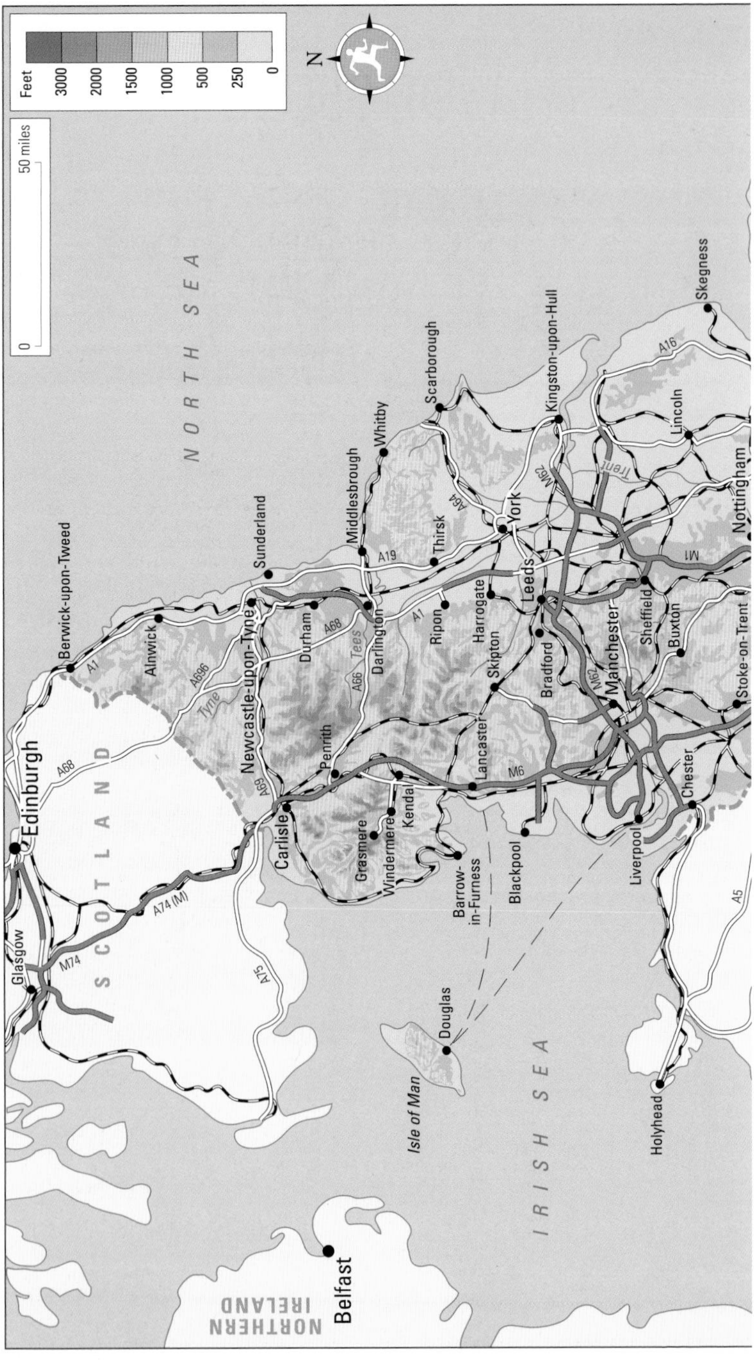
Feet
3000
2000
1500
1000
500
250
0
0
50 miles
N
NORTH SEA
IRISH SEA
SCOTLAND
NORTHERN IRELAND
Belfast
Isle of Man
Douglas
Edinburgh
Glasgow
Berwick-upon-Tweed
Alnwick
Newcastle-upon-Tyne
Sunderland
Durham
Middlesbrough
Darlington
Whitby
Scarborough
Thirsk
Ripon
Harrogate
York
Leeds
Bradford
Skipton
Kingston-upon-Hull
Lincoln
Skegness
Nottingham
Sheffield
Manchester
Buxton
Stoke-on-Trent
Chester
Liverpool
Holyhead
Blackpool
Lancaster
Barrow-in-Furness
Kendal
Windermere
Grasmere
Penrith
Carlisle
Tyne
Tees
Trent
A1
A5
A16
A19
A64
A66
A68
A69
A75
A696
A74 (M)
M1
M6
M62
M74

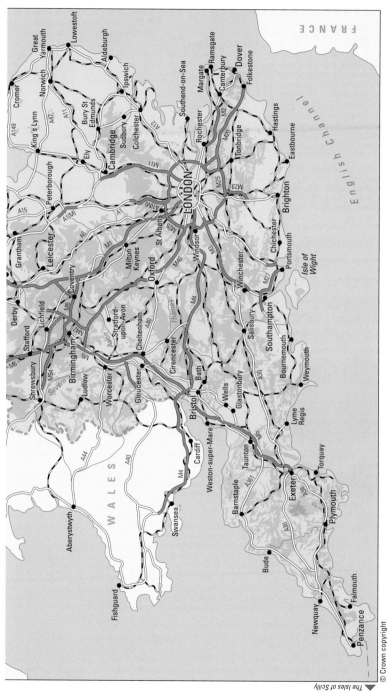

▲ The Isles of Scilly

© Crown copyright

Introduction to

England

Of the two hundred-plus destinations across the world that Rough Guides cover, there is none so fascinating, beautiful and culturally diverse, yet as insular, self-important and irritating, as England. You may share the same language, and you might think you already know the country well (after all, even the world's most remote communities are on first-name terms with its princes, footballers and pop stars). But there's far more to England than its famous buildings, landscapes, history and monuments – more, in truth, than even a 1000-page guidebook can hope to cover in detail. We'll tell you what's worth seeing and why, but we won't pull our punches.

Just a few examples. There are English landmarks that every schoolchild knows – from the Houses of Parliament to Stonehenge – but to reach them you have to endure the country's overcrowded roads and risible public transport system. There are national parks, from the Lake District to Dartmoor, that are the equal in beauty of anything in Europe, yet the English countryside faces crisis on an almost annual basis. And while there are hundreds of atmospheric hotels and celebrated restaurants across the country, you may find yourself served with a sneer instead of a smile.

Should this stop you visiting? Not a chance, for England is also an endlessly surprising country. England may have a notorious taste for nostalgia, but its cities have a restless energy and a talent for reinvention. So for every tourist who wants to stand outside the gates of Buckingham Palace or visit Stratford-upon-Avon, there's another who makes a beeline for the latest show at Tate Modern or the cityscape of downtown Manchester. Contemporary England is a deeply conservative place which at the same time has a richly multi-ethnic culture. Famously, fish and chips gave way some years ago to chicken tikka masala as the country's favourite dish, and while the nation

Fact file

- As part of the United Kingdom of Great Britain and Northern Ireland ("the UK"), **England** is a parliamentary democracy, with Queen Elizabeth II as its head of state. Its traditional **industries** – fishing, farming, mining, engineering, shipbuilding – are all in decline and business today is dominated by banking and finance, the media and technology, steel production, oil and gas, and tourism.

- Bordered by Scotland to the north and Wales to the west, England is the largest country in Great Britain, occupying an area of 50,085 sq miles (129,720 sq km). The **terrain** is diverse, from plains to peaks, cliffs to beaches, though the superlatives are all modest on a world scale – the largest lake, Windermere, is 10 miles (16km) long, the highest mountain, Scafell, just 3205ft (978m) above sea level.

- The **population** of just over 50 million is dense for a country of its size, but settlement is concentrated in the southeast around London, and in the large industrial cities of the Midlands and the North.

- This is one of the world's most **multi-ethnic** countries, made up largely of people of Anglo-Saxon, Scots, Welsh and Irish descent, but with sizeable communities from the Caribbean, Africa, the Indian subcontinent, China, Southeast Asia and Eastern Europe.

tends to distrust all things European, the English increasingly embrace a continental lifestyle.

Ask an English person to define their country in terms of what's worth seeing and you're most likely to have your attention drawn to

> **It's impossible to overstate the bucolic attractions of the various English regions, from Cornwall to the Lake District, or the delights they provide.**

England's golden rural past. The classic images are found in every brochure – the village green, the duckpond, the country lane and the farmyard. And it's true that it's impossible to overstate the bucolic attractions of the various English regions, from Cornwall to the Lake District, or the

The national game

Football, footie, call it what you will (no English fan ever says "soccer") – the English invented it and subsequently appropriated it as an expression of (often misguided) national pride. The country has the oldest league and cup competitions in the world, the best-known club on the planet in Manchester United and  players who are more famous than pop stars. For outsiders, though, the nuances of supporting a team can be difficult to unravel. The city of Manchester, like Liverpool and Sheffield, has two teams; London has thirteen (none of them called London). Supporters of geographically adjacent teams (Newcastle and Sunderland, say, or Southampton and Portsmouth) hate each other; while everyone despises Chelsea with its ruthless purchase of success. And once you've got to the bottom of this, you still might never get to see a live game as tickets for the famous teams can sell out a year in advance, even at very high prices. You could watch football on TV (between August and May), but for the real experience you have to visit the unfashionable provincial clubs inhabiting the lower divisions. Macclesfield Town against Rochdale on a wet Tuesday night in February – that's a proper football match. Everything else is just entertainment.

delights they provide – from walkers' trails and prehistoric stone circles to traditional pubs and obscure festivals. But despite celebrating their rural heritage, the modern-day English have an ambivalent attitude towards "the countryside". Farming today forms only a tiny proportion of the national income and there's a real dislocation between the population of the burgeoning towns and suburbs and the small, struggling rural communities.

So perhaps the heart of England is found in its towns and cities instead? The shift towards urban living and working has been steady since the Industrial Revolution, and industry – and the Empire it inspired – has provided a framework for much of what you'll see as you travel around. Virtually every English town bears a mark of former wealth and power, whether it be a magnificent Gothic cathedral financed from a monarch's treasury, a parish church funded by the tycoons of the medieval wool trade, or a triumphalist civic building raised on the back of the slave and sugar trade. In the south of England you'll find old dockyards from which the navy patrolled the oceans, while in the north there are mills that employed entire

town populations. England's museums and galleries – several of them ranking among the world's finest – are full of treasures trawled from its imperial conquests. And in their grandiose stuccoed terraces and wide esplanades, the old seaside resorts bear testimony to the heyday of English holiday towns, at one time as fashionable as any European spa.

In short, England isn't just one place, but a perpetual collision of culture, class and race – the product of multiple identities adapting and somehow fitting together. Its political philosophies and institutions have influenced the most diverse Western societies; its idiosyncrasies and prejudices have left their mark across the English-speaking world, and its inventions and creative momentum, from the Industrial Revolution to the Turner Prize, continue to inspire. But the only certainty for visitors is that however long you spend in England and however much you see, it still won't be enough to understand the place.

Where to go

To begin to get to grips with England, **London** is the place to start. Nowhere else in the country can match the scope and innovation of the metropolis, a colossal, frenetic city, perhaps not as immediately attractive as its European counterparts, but with so much variety that lack of cash is the only obstacle to a great time. It's here that you'll find England's best spread of nightlife, cultural events, museums, galleries, pubs and restaurants. However, each of the other large cities – **Birmingham**,

Understanding the English

The English are the most contradictory people imaginable, and however long you spend in the country you'll never figure them out. As a glance at the tabloid newspapers will confirm, England is a nation of overweight, binge-drinking reality TV addicts, obsessed with toffs and C-list celebs. But it's also a country of animal-loving, tea-drinking, charity donors, where queuing remains a national pastime and bastions of civilization, like Radio 4, are jealously protected. It's a country where accent and vocabulary can stamp a person's identity like a brand, but it's also a genuine haven for refugees, with immigrants from more than 100 ethnic backgrounds. It's a nation that prides itself on its patriotism – yet has a Scottish prime minister, an Italian football coach and a Greek royal consort. Ask any English person to comment on all of this and you'll get an entertaining range of views. Try to make sense of these, and the resulting picture might suggest something akin to a national identity crisis.

Perhaps the only thing that unites the English is their sense of humour. The English are devoted to sarcasm on a gigantic scale. Tell the average English person how well they dress or how much you value their friendship and, more often than not, you'll be confronted by a blank stare and forced half-smile. If pushed, expect a self-deprecating remark or a tongue-in-cheek response. They won't be offended, but they simply won't believe you and they'll wonder why on earth you said something that was best kept to yourself. Canny celebrities appreciate this need for diffidence very well, avoiding any hint of boastfulness at any cost and attributing their success to their mother, teacher, agent, cat ... pretty much anyone will do in the flight from risibility. Visitors to England often take this reserve – and accompanying sarcasm – as coldness or even hostility, but in fact it very rarely is – it's just the way they are: the warmth is in the humour, a sort of national solidarity that is bred in the bone. If you are included in the banter, you have been accepted ... but they certainly won't tell you that.

Bristol, **Newcastle**, **Leeds**, **Sheffield**, **Manchester** and **Liverpool** – makes its own claim for historic and cultural diversity, and you certainly won't have a representative view of England's cities if you venture no further than the capital. It's in these regional centres that the most exciting architectural and social developments are taking place, though for many visitors they rank a long way behind ancient cities like **Lincoln**, **York**, **Salisbury**, **Durham** and **Winchester** – to name just those with the most celebrated of England's cathedrals. Most beguiling of all, though, are the long-established **villages** of England, hundreds of which amount to nothing more than a

> **The warmth [of the English] is in the humour, a sort of national solidarity that is bred in the bone.**

pub, a shop, a gaggle of cottages and a farmhouse offering bed and breakfast. **Devon**, **Cornwall**, the **Cotswolds** and the **Yorkshire Dales** harbour some especially picturesque specimens, but every county can boast a decent showing of photogenic hamlets.

Evidence of England's pedigree is scattered between its settlements as well. Wherever you're based, you're never more than a few miles from a **ruined castle**, a majestic **country house** or a **monastery**, and in many parts of the country you'll come across the sites of civilizations that thrived here before England existed as a nation. In the southwest there are remnants of a **Celtic** culture that elsewhere was all but eradicated by the **Romans**, and from the south coast to the northern border you can find traces of **prehistoric** settlers, the most famous being the megalithic circles of Stonehenge and Avebury.

Then of course there's the English **countryside**, an extraordinarily diverse terrain from which Constable, Turner, Wordsworth, Emily Brontë and a host of other native luminaries took inspiration. Most dramatic and best known are the moors and uplands – **Exmoor**, **Dartmoor**, **Bodmin Moor**, the **North York Moors** and the **Lake District** – each of which has its over-visited spots, though a brisk walk will usually take you out of the throng. Quieter areas are tucked away in every corner of England, from the lush vales of **Shropshire** near the border with Wales to the flat wetlands of the eastern **Fens** and the chalk downland of **Sussex**. It's a similar story on the **coast**, where the finest sands and most rugged cliffs have long been discovered, and sizeable resorts have grown to exploit many of the choicest locations. But again, if it's peace you're after, you can find it by heading for the exposed strands of **Northumberland**, the pebbly flat horizons of **East Anglia** or the crumbling headlands of **Dorset**.

When to go

Considering the temperateness of the English **climate**, it's amazing how much mileage the locals get out of the subject – a two-day cold snap is discussed as if it were the onset of a new Ice Age, and a week above 25°C (upper 70s °F) starts rumours of drought. However, on the whole, English summers rarely get very hot and the winters don't get very cold, and there's not a great deal of regional variation, as the chart shows. That said, extreme weather patterns are becoming more frequent and recent years have seen summer temperatures well into the 30s (over 90°F) and catastrophic winter and spring flooding in many parts of the country. Usually though, rainfall is fairly even over all of England, though in general the south gets more **hours of sunshine** than the north. Differences between the regions are slightly more marked in **winter**, when the south tends to be appreciably milder and wetter than the north.

▲ Bournemouth beach

The bottom line is that it's impossible to say with any degree of certainty that the weather will be pleasant in any given month. May might be wet and grey one year and gloriously sunny the next, and the same goes for the autumnal months. November stands an equal chance of being crisp and clear or foggy and grim. Obviously, if you're planning to camp or go to the beach, you'll want to visit between June and September – a period when you shouldn't go anywhere without booking your accommodation well in advance. Elsewhere, if you're balancing the likely fairness of the weather against the density of the crowds, the

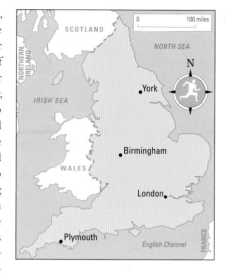

best time would be between **April and early June** or in **September** or **October**.

Average temperatures and rainfall

	Jan	Feb	Mar	Apr	May	Jun	Jul	Aug	Sep	Oct	Nov	Dec
Birmingham												
(°F)	42	43	48	54	60	66	68	68	63	55	48	44
(°C)	5	6	9	12	16	19	20	20	17	13	9	7
(inches)	3	2.1	2	2.1	2.5	2	2.7	2.7	2.4	2.7	3.3	2.6
(mm)	74	54	50	53	64	50	69	69	61	69	84	67
London												
(°F)	43	44	50	56	62	69	71	71	65	58	50	45
(°C)	6	7	10	13	17	20	22	21	19	15	10	7
(inches)	2.1	1.6	1.5	1.5	1.8	1.8	2.2	2.3	1.9	2.2	2.5	1.9
(mm)	54	40	37	37	46	45	57	59	49	57	64	48
Plymouth												
(°F)	47	47	50	54	59	64	66	67	64	58	52	49
(°C)	8	8	10	12	15	18	19	19	18	15	11	10
(inches)	3.9	2.9	2.7	2.1	2.5	2.1	2.8	3	3.1	3.6	4.5	4.3
(mm)	99	74	69	53	63	53	70	77	78	91	113	110
York												
(°F)	43	44	49	55	61	67	70	69	64	57	49	45
(°C)	6	7	10	13	16	19	21	20	18	14	10	7
(inches)	2.3	1.8	1.5	1.6	2	2	2.4	2.7	2.2	2.2	2.6	2
(mm)	59	46	37	41	50	50	62	68	55	55	65	50

35

things not to miss

It's not possible to see everything England has to offer in one trip – and we don't suggest you try. What follows is a selective taste of the country's highlights: architecture, dramatic landscapes and even good things to eat and drink. They're arranged in five colour-coded categories, which you can browse through to find the very best things to see, do and experience. All highlights have a page reference to take you straight into the guide, where you can find out more.

01 Avebury stone circle Page **286** • Stonehenge might get all the publicity, but the stones at nearby Avebury have a raw appeal and are far more accessible.

02 Shopping in Leeds Page 782 • The thriving commercial capital of the north mixes designer stores and bustling markets.

03 Lake District National Park Page 725 • England's largest national park is also many peoples' favourite, boasting sixteen major lakes, including Wast Water (pictured here) and scores of mountains, not least the country's highest peak, Scafell Pike.

04 Blackpool Page 698 • The British seaside's best-known landmark provides the Blackpool skyline with a touch of grace.

05 A pint down the pub Page 44 • From trendy micro-breweries to ancient coaching inns, England's pubs are an essential part of any visit to the country. The best brews to sample, and the best places to try them, are listed in the Guide.

| ACTIVITIES | CONSUME | EVENTS | NATURE | SIGHTS |

07 Newcastle nightlife Page **888** • Lock up your inhibitions, leave your coat at home and hit the Toon.

06 York Minster Page **820** • Britain's biggest Gothic church has a thousand-year history and treasures to match, including the world's largest medieval stained-glass window.

08 Dartmoor Page **407** • Southern England's greatest expanse of wilderness is perfect for hikers, riders and pony fans.

ACTIVITIES | CONSUME | EVENTS | NATURE | SIGHTS |

17

13 **A ride on the Snaefell Mountain Railway** Page **715** • Take a tramcar to the Isle of Man's highest point for a view over four countries.

14 **Eden Project** Page **434** • With its strong ecological thrust, the West Country's most spectacular attraction presents a refreshing alternative to the hard-sell, commercial edge of most of the region's crowd-pullers.

15 **Liverpool** Page **686** • England's City of Culture for 2008, Liverpool may surprise first-time visitors with its breadth of attractions – and there's no more handsome cityscape in the country.

16 Alnwick Castle and Garden

Page **910** • To discover more of England's long and turbulent past, pay a visit to one of the country's many castles – like Alnwick in Northumberland, which also boasts England's most enterprising modern garden.

17 Fish and chips

Page 42 • There's nothing better than fish and chips, nor any better way to eat them than wrapped in paper and eaten on the beach.

18 Durdle Door

Page **266** • One of the highlights of the Dorset coast, this spectacular limestone arch has an immediate appeal, and is close to both the marine wildlife reserve of Kimmeridge Bay and some choice beaches.

19 Ely

Page **515** • An isolated Cambridgeshire town in the heart of the eerie fenland landscape, Ely is noted for its magnificent cathedral.

20 **Castle Howard** Page **827** • England's grandest stately home? It will take you the best part of a day to decide, as there's much to see and do at any time of the year.

21 **Canterbury Cathedral** Page **179** • Mother Church of the Church of England, this cathedral is famous for its shrine to the murdered Archbishop, Thomas à Becket, and the tales that Chaucer weaved round a fictitious pilgrimage to the martyr's tomb.

22 **Surfing, Newquay** Page **456** • The beaches strung along the northern coast of Devon and Cornwall offer some great breaks, with Newquay the place to see and be seen.

23 **Bath** Page **364** • Visit the Roman baths, admire England's most elegant Georgian terrace or do some serious shopping in one of the country's most beautiful cities.

24 **Lizard Point, Cornwall**
Page **422** • This headland has none of the razzmatazz of Land's End, which is all to its favour, yet still has the views; there are some great beaches within a short coastal hike, too.

25 **Southwold** Page **490** • George Orwell didn't like the place, but everyone else does: Southwold is perhaps the most beguiling of England's seaside towns.

26 **Tate Modern** Page **121** • Housed in a spectacular former power station, the world's largest modern art gallery is simply awesome.

27 The Royal Pavilion, Brighton Page 209 •

George IV's pleasure dome, designed by Nash, is the supreme example of Oriental-Gothic architecture.

28 Northumberland National Park Page 902 •

Explore the wilds of England's least-known and most remote national park.

29 Hadrian's Wall Page 895 •

The most enduring and atmospheric reminder of the 350-year Roman period is this 76-mile-long wall, stretching from coast to coast through dramatic northern English countryside.

30 **The Peak District** Page **588** • The Peak District offers great walking countryside and some of England's most appealing landscapes.

31 **St Ives, Cornwall** Page **449** • Bustling seaside resort with great beaches and the southwest's best arts collection.

32 **Scilly Isles** Page **446** • England's most stunning offshore islands offer majestic beaches and crystal-clear waters.

33 **White Cliffs of Dover**
Page **188** • The famous white cliffs, dominating the Channel port of Dover, have been used as the very emblem of England in verse and song.

34 **Books, Hay-on-Wye** Page **561** • An outpost on the English–Welsh border, Hay-on-Wye may be remote, but it does cut a dash with the size and the variety of its second-hand bookshops.

35 **Oxford** Page **301** • The famous old university town is a gorgeous ensemble of honey-coloured buildings and dreaming spires.

Basics

Basics

Getting there

London is one of the world's busiest transport hubs, and stiff competition between the airlines ensures good deals on flights. Heathrow and Gatwick airports take the bulk of transatlantic and long-haul flights, though several airlines also fly into Manchester in the northwest. Low-cost flights from mainland Europe tend to fly into London's other three airports – Stansted, Luton and City – as well as regional airports, including Birmingham, Bristol, Leeds/Bradford, Liverpool and Newcastle.

Airfares to England are highest from early June to mid-September, at Easter, and at Christmas and New Year; fares drop during the "shoulder" seasons – mid-September to early November and mid-April to early June – and are usually cheapest during the low season, November through to April. Note that flying at **weekends** is generally more expensive.

Tickets are available either direct from the airlines or from a **discount travel agent**, which sometimes offers student and youth fares as well as a range of other travel-related services. Many airline and **travel websites** can now also book package holidays, accommodation and car rental. You can turn up some great online deals, but always check the small print as many purchases are non-changeable and non-refundable.

Coming from mainland Europe or Ireland, you'll find a range of **ferry** routes to ports which offer good bus and train connections to England's major centres. Alternatively, you can reach London from France and Belgium on direct Eurostar **trains** using the Channel Tunnel – and if you're planning to see much of England (or Europe) by train, you may want to investigate rail passes, some of which must be purchased in advance of your trip (see p.33 for more). Finally, **drivers** who choose not to use the ferries can load their vehicles on Eurotunnel trains running between Calais and Folkestone.

Package tours of England, where all flights, accommodation and ground transport are arranged for you, take the hassle out of travel and can sometimes be cheaper than organizing things yourself. All-inclusive **city breaks** from North America can provide a good introduction to England, though in most cases England simply means London. Many outfits in the UK and overseas offer standard **coach-tour** itineraries of England's historic highlights, or help you explore some aspect of the country's heritage, such as art and architecture, gardens and stately homes, culture and sports. Some companies offer budget versions of their holidays, staying in hostels or B&Bs, as well as hotel packages. For activity holidays, see p.53.

Flights from the US and Canada

Many airlines fly direct **from the US** to London, and some also to Manchester. New York has the most non-stop services, though there are also non-stop flights from Washington DC, Boston, Chicago, Miami, Orlando, Las Vegas, San Francisco and Los Angeles. Flights with a connection, usually on mainland European airlines, are often cheaper but tend to route through their European hubs, adding (sometimes significantly) to your journey time. Depending on the airline, low-season midweek fares from New York cost under US$500, from Los Angeles more like US$600–700, but bear in mind that the very cheapest deals tend to have little or no flexibility, and that taxes and fees can add up to US$100 to any quoted price.

From **Canada**, airlines like Air Canada and bmi fly non-stop from the gateway cities of Toronto, Montréal and Vancouver to London and Manchester. Low-season fares from Toronto start at around CAN$550 return, from Vancouver more like CAN$900. Zoom

Airlines offer budget fares to London and Manchester from Ottawa, Montréal, Toronto, Halifax, Winnipeg, Calgary, and Vancouver, while the charter operator Air Transat has good-value flights to London, Manchester, Newcastle, Birmingham and Exeter, mainly from Toronto, but also from Vancouver.

Flying time to any British airport from New York or Toronto is around seven hours, and from LA or Vancouver more like ten hours (it's an hour extra coming the other way, due to headwinds).

Flights from Ireland

Stiff competition on routes between Ireland and England keeps the cost of flights low. **From the Republic**, Ryanair generally has the cheapest tickets – special deals sometimes even offer free flights, with passengers paying just the taxes (around €30). Otherwise, you can usually expect to pay from around €70 return. Ryanair flies to fourteen airports in England from Dublin, Cork, Kerry, Knock and Shannon, while fellow budget airline bmibaby flies from Cork and Knock to Birmingham and Manchester. Aer Lingus and British Airways also offer cut-price deals, and fly from Dublin, Cork and Shannon to Birmingham, Manchester, Newcastle and London.

The cheapest options **from Belfast** are easyJet to Bristol, Liverpool, London and Newcastle; Flybe, which serves eight English airports; and bmibaby to Manchester, East Midlands and Birmingham. Return flights cost from around £50, though much cheaper deals are possible.

Flights from Australia, New Zealand and South Africa

The route **from Australia and New Zealand** to London is highly competitive, with the lowest return fares usually in the range of A$1500–2500 from Australia, NZ$2000–3000 from New Zealand. The main departure points are Sydney, Melbourne, Perth and Auckland. The very cheapest tickets rarely have much, if any, flexibility and you might want to pay more to be able to change your dates or to travel with one of the major airlines like Qantas, British Airways, Air New Zealand or Singapore Airlines. These airlines also tend to be able to arrange things like fly-drive and accommodation packages or onward travel to other British destinations – flights to Manchester, for example, are sometimes available at no extra cost.

Travel time from Australia or New Zealand to England is over twenty hours, even with the best connections, so you might want to consider a stopover – most airlines will let you do this for no extra charge, and many of the cheaper flights, for example with Asian or Middle Eastern carriers, involve a stop in any case. Most New Zealand flights involve a connection, whether in Asia or the US; there's little to choose between the two routes in terms of journey time.

Flights from Johannesburg in **South Africa** usually cost ZAR6000–8000 return and take over eleven hours non-stop, though some of the cheapest, operated by Emirates, involve lengthy connections in Dubai. There are fewer direct flights from Cape Town, and they take slightly longer and cost a bit more.

Flights from mainland Europe

Low-cost airlines have not only reduced the cost of flying to England considerably, but have opened up access to many regional airports, so you don't necessarily have to start your trip in London. Ryanair, easyJet, bmibaby, Flybe, VLM, Brussels Airlines and others fly to regional English airports from all over the continent. Airports at Manchester, Liverpool, Newcastle, Durham Tees Valley and Leeds/Bradford open up the north of the country, while you'll also find flights to Bournemouth and Southampton (for the south coast), Nottingham (East Midlands), Stansted and Norwich (for East Anglia), and Bristol and Exeter (for the southwest).

Ferries from mainland Europe and Ireland

Ferries cross from several European countries to ports in England. The quickest, cheapest services are on the traditional cross-Channel routes **from France** (Calais, Boulogne, Dieppe and Dunkerque) to Dover, Folkestone and Newhaven in the southeast. However, other services might

Fly less – stay longer! Travel and climate change

Climate change is the single biggest issue facing our planet. It is caused by a build-up in the atmosphere of carbon dioxide and other greenhouse gases, which are emitted by many sources – including planes. Already, flights account for around 3–4 percent of human-induced global warming: that figure may sound small, but it is rising year on year and threatens to counteract the progress made by reducing greenhouse emissions in other areas.

Rough Guides regard travel, overall, as a global benefit, and feel strongly that the advantages to developing economies are important, as are the opportunities for greater contact and awareness among peoples. But we all have a responsibility to limit our personal "carbon footprint". That means giving thought to how often we fly and what we can do to redress the harm that our trips create.

Flying and climate change

Pretty much every form of motorized travel generates CO_2, but planes are particularly bad offenders, releasing large volumes of greenhouse gases at altitudes where their impact is far more harmful. Flying also allows us to travel much further than we would contemplate doing by road or rail, so the emissions attributable to each passenger become truly shocking. For example, one person taking a return flight between Europe and California produces the equivalent impact of 2.5 tonnes of CO_2 – similar to the yearly output of the average UK car.

Less harmful planes may evolve but it will be decades before they replace the current fleet – which could be too late for avoiding climate chaos. In the meantime, there are limited options for concerned travellers: to reduce the amount we travel by air (take fewer trips, stay longer!), to avoid night flights (when plane contrails trap heat from Earth but can't reflect sunlight back to space), and to make the trips we do take "climate neutral" via a carbon offset scheme.

Carbon offset schemes

Offset schemes run by **climatecare.org**, **carbonneutral.com** and others allow you to "neutralize" the greenhouse gases that you are responsible for releasing. Their websites have simple calculators that let you work out the impact of any flight. Once that's done, you can pay to fund projects that will reduce future carbon emissions by an equivalent amount (such as the distribution of low-energy light bulbs and cooking stoves in developing countries). Please take the time to visit our website and make your trip climate neutral.

Ⓦ**www.roughguides.com/climatechange**

---

be more convenient, depending on your departure point and destination: you can reach Ramsgate in northern Kent from **Belgium** (Ostend); Portsmouth, Poole and Weymouth in the south and Plymouth in the southwest from Brittany (Roscoff, St Malo), Normandy (Caen, Cherbourg) and **Spain** (Bilbao and Santander); Harwich in Essex from **Denmark** (Esbjerg) and **Holland** (Hook of Holland); Hull in Yorkshire from Belgium (Zeebrugge) and Holland (Rotterdam); or Newcastle in the northeast from Holland (Amsterdam), **Norway** (Stavanger, Bergen) and **Sweden** (Gothenburg). As an alternative to the ferry crossing, drivers can load their cars aboard trains at Calais for the Eurotunnel crossing to Folkestone (see p.30).

Unless you're bringing your own vehicle to tour England, there's little incentive in coming by ferry from either the **Republic or Northern Ireland**, as crossings tend to take longer and are often pricier than flying. Direct services run from Dublin and Belfast to Liverpool and Douglas (Isle of Man), and from Larne to Fleetwood. Otherwise, crossings are via Wales, which can be relatively convenient for the English northwest, Midlands and southwest.

Fares on all routes vary according to the time of year, time and type of crossing, while sleeping accommodation is often obligatory on night crossings from the continent. Consult ⓦ www.directferries.com for more information.

Trains from mainland Europe and Ireland

Direct **Eurostar trains** run roughly hourly through the Channel Tunnel to London St Pancras International from Lille (1hr 25min), Paris (2hr 20min) and Brussels (2hr). Return fares start from around €75 from Paris or Lille, €95 from Brussels, though these rates come with many restrictions. More flexible tickets can cost around €200 return, though discounted flexible youth (for under-26s) and senior (over-60s) fares are available. If you are intending to tour Kent, you might consider disembarking at Ashford (for mid-Kent) or Ebbsfleet (for North Kent) rather than London.

For drivers, **Eurotunnel** operates drive-on-drive-off shuttle trains through the Channel Tunnel from Calais to Folkestone. The 24-hour service runs every 20–30 minutes throughout the day (every 90min or so at night) and takes 35 minutes. Although you can just turn up, booking is advised, especially at weekends, or if you want the best deals. Off-peak return fares for a car and passengers booked at least 14 days in advance start at around €140 though fully flexible fares allowing changes cost much more than this.

From Ireland, you can book integrated train and ferry services from almost any station in Ireland to any English station. The quickest Dublin–London route takes 7hr 20min, with one-way fares around €44; contact Irish Ferries (see p.32) for details.

Buses from mainland Europe and Ireland

Eurolines is Europe's largest international bus network, coordinating independent coach services to London from dozens of **mainland European cities**, including Amsterdam, Brussels, Frankfurt, Hamburg, Madrid, Paris and Rome. Prices are around €70 return from Paris, though this often offers no saving over a low-cost airline. Eurolines also operate bus and ferry services **from Dublin** (connections can be booked from other major towns in Ireland),

to a number of English cities, from €35 return. National Express offers a bus/ferry route **from Belfast** to London (around £50 return). The downside is that from both north and south the trip involves an overnight ferry crossing to Holyhead, arriving at the crack of dawn.

Airlines, agents and operators

Online booking

ⓦ www.expedia.com (in US),
ⓦ www.expedia.ca (in Canada)
ⓦ www.orbitz.com (in US)
ⓦ www.travelocity.com (in US)
ⓦ www.travelocity.ca (in Canada)
ⓦ www.zuji.com.au (in Australia),
ⓦ www.zuji.co.nz (in New Zealand)

Airlines

Air Canada US and Canada ☎ 1-888/247-2262, ⓦ www.aircanada.com.
Air New Zealand Australia ☎ 0800/132 476, US ☎ 1800-262/1234, New Zealand ☎ 0800/737000; ⓦ www.airnz.co.nz.
Air Transat Canada ☎ 1-866/847-1112, ⓦ www.airtransat.com.
American Airlines US and Canada ☎ 1-800/433-7300, ⓦ www.aa.com.
bmi US ☎ 1-800/788-0555, Republic of Ireland ☎ 01/407 3036; ⓦ www.flybmi.com.
Bmibaby Republic of Ireland ☎ 1890/340 122, ⓦ www.bmibaby.com.
British Airways US and Canada ☎ 1-800/AIRWAYS, Republic of Ireland ☎ 1890/626 747, Australia ☎ 1300/767 177, New Zealand ☎ 09/966 9777, South Africa ☎ 114/418 600; ⓦ www.ba.com.
Brussels Airlines Belgium ☎ 0902/51600, ⓦ www.brusselsairlines.com.
Continental Airlines US and Canada ☎ 1-800/523-3273, Republic of Ireland ☎ 1890/925 2520, Australia ☎ 02/9244 2242, New Zealand ☎ 09/308 3350; ⓦ www.continental.com.
Delta US and Canada ☎ 1-800/221-1212, ⓦ www.delta.com.
easyJet ⓦ www.easyjet.com.
Flybe Republic of Ireland/International ☎ +44/1392 268529, ⓦ www.flybe.com.
Qantas Airways US and Canada ☎ 1-800/227-4500, Australia ☎ 13 13 13, New Zealand ☎ 0800/808 767 or 09/357 8900; ⓦ www.qantas.com.
Ryanair Republic of Ireland ☎ 0818/303030, ⓦ www.ryanair.com.

Singapore Airlines Australia ☎ 13 10 11, New Zealand ☎ 0800/808 909; ⊛ www.singaporeair.com.

South African Airways South Africa ☎ 11/978 1111, ⊛ www.flysaa.com.

United Airlines US ☎ 1-800/UNITED-1, ⊛ www.united.com.

Virgin Atlantic US ☎ 1-800/821-5438, South Africa ☎ 11/340 3400; ⊛ www.virgin-atlantic.com.

VLM Airlines Belgium ☎ 032/878080, Holland ☎ 0900/450 5050; ⊛ www.flyvlm.com.

Zoom Airlines US and Canada ☎ 1-866/359-9666, ⊛ www.flyzoom.com.

Agents and operators

Abercrombie & Kent US ☎ 1-800/554-7016, ⊛ www.abercrombiekent.com. Classy travel specialist, with no-expense-spared escorted and independent trips.

British Airways Holidays US ☎ 1-877/428 2228, ⊛ www.baholidays.com. Flight-inclusive vacations and sightseeing itineraries, including London city breaks.

British Travel International US ☎ 1-727/643-5710, ⊛ www.britishtravel.com. Agent for all independent arrangements: rail and bus passes, car rental, hotels and a comprehensive accommodation reservation service.

Carry On Tours +44 20/8748 9197, ⊛ www.carryontours.com. One-, two- and three-day minibus tours out of London on a variety of themes, from Eccentric Britain to Harry Potter locations.

CIE Tours International US ☎ 1-800/243-8687, ⊛ www.cietours.com. Long-established operator offering escorted coach tours and self-drive B&B holidays.

Contiki Holidays UK ☎ 020/8290 6422, ⊛ www.contiki.com. Lively adventure tours for 18–35s, in particular 3- and 5-day London trips or an 8-day all-Britain tour.

Delta Vacations US ☎ 1-800/654-6559, ⊛ www.deltavacations.com. General tour operator with London and Manchester city breaks.

ebookers Republic of Ireland ☎ 01/488 3507, ⊛ www.ebookers.ie. Low fares on an extensive selection of scheduled flights and package deals.

English Experience US ☎ 1-800/892-9317, ⊛ www.english-experience.com. Small-group, customized tours in B&Bs or hotels, covering the historic sights in Sussex, Kent, the Cotswolds, Lake District, Yorkshire Dales, Devon and Cornwall, or East Anglia.

Explore Holidays Australia ☎ 02/9423 8080, ⊛ www.exploreholidays.com.au. Organizes customized London packages and tours all over England that include accommodation, passes to sights, car rental and the like.

Flightcentre US ☎ 1-866/967 5351, ⊛ www.flightcentre.us; Canada ☎ 1-877/967 5302, ⊛ www.flightcentre.ca; Australia ☎ 133 133, ⊛ www.flightcentre.com.au; New Zealand ☎ 0800/243 544, ⊛ www.flightcentre.co.nz.

Martin Randall Travel UK ☎ 020/8742 3355, ⊛ www.martinrandall.com. All-inclusive historical and cultural tours led by experts – for example, tours of West Country churches, or concert tours of the north.

Maupintour US ☎ 1-800/255-4266, ⊛ www.maupintour.com. Quality, all-inclusive, themed escorted tours – London at Christmas, or lakes and literature, for example.

Road Trip UK ☎ 0845/200 6791, ⊛ www.roadtrip.co.uk. Inclusive, activity-filled budget bus tours, departing from London, using mainly hostel accommodation. Two- or three-day weekend tours to Bath and Stonehenge; Cornwall; Devon (murder mystery), or York and Sherwood Forest; or longer tours touching on Scotland, Wales and Ireland.

STA Travel US and Canada ☎ 1-800/781 4040, Australia ☎ 134 STA, New Zealand ☎ 0800/474 400, South Africa ☎ 0861/781 781; ⊛ www.statravel.com. Worldwide specialists in independent travel; also student IDs, travel insurance, car rental, rail passes, and more. Good discounts for students and under-26s.

Thomas Cook UK ☎ 0870/750 5711, ⊛ www.thomascook.co.uk. Wide range of UK breaks, plus hotel and theatre-ticket bookings.

Trailfinders UK ☎ 0845/058 5858, Republic of Ireland ☎ 01/677 7888, Australia ☎ 1300/780 212; ⊛ www.trailfinders.com.au. One of the best-informed and most efficient agents for independent travellers.

Travel Cuts US ☎ 1-800/592-CUTS, Canada ☎ 1-800/246-9762; ⊛ www.travelcuts.com. Efficient, easy-to-use flight finder for budget and student travel.

Rail contacts

BritRail Travel US ☎ 1-866/BRITRAIL, Canada ☎ 1-514/733 5247; ⊛ www.britrail.com.

Europrail International Canada ☎ 1-888/667-9734, ⊛ www.europrail.net.

Eurostar outside UK ☎ +44 1233/617575, ⊛ www.eurostar.com.

Eurotunnel Belgium ☎ 070/223210, France ☎ 0810/630304; ⊛ www.eurotunnel.com.

The Man in Seat Sixty-One ⊛ www.seat61.com. The world's finest train travel website. It's nerdishly comprehensive, with more detail than you ever wanted to know about train travel in the UK (and worldwide), but full of useful tips and links.

Megatrain ☎ 0900/160 0900, ⊛ www.megatrain.com. Cheap fares on limited routes.

National Rail UK ☏ 08457/484950, outside UK ☏ +44 20/7278 5240; ⓦ www.nationalrail.co.uk. Advice on timetables, routes, tickets and services throughout the country.

Rail Europe US ☏ 1-877/257-2887, ⓦ www.raileurope.com/us; Canada ☏ 1-800/361-RAIL, ⓦ www.raileurope.ca; Australia ⓦ www.railplus.com.au; New Zealand ⓦ www.railplus.co.nz.

Bus contacts

Eurolines UK ☏ 0870/580 8080, ⓦ www.nationalexpress.com/eurolines.
National Express UK ☏ 0870/580 8080, ⓦ www.nationalexpress.com.

Ferry contacts

Brittany Ferries UK ☏ 0870/366 5333, Republic of Ireland ☏ 021/4277 801; ⓦ www.brittanyferries.co.uk.
DFDS Seaways UK ☏ 0870/252 0524, ⓦ www.dfdsseaways.co.uk.

Irish Ferries Northern Ireland ☏ 0818/300 400, Republic of Ireland ☏ 0818/300 400, UK ☏ 0870/517 1717; ⓦ www.irishferries.com.
Isle of Man Steam Packet UK ☏ 0871/222 1333, ⓦ www.steam-packet.com.
Norfolkline France ☏ 03.28.59.01.01, Republic of Ireland ☏ 01/819 2999, UK ☏ 0871/870 1020 for English Channel, ☏ 0870/600 4321 for Irish Sea; ⓦ www.norfolkline.com.
P&O Ferries France ☏ 02.85.12.01.56, Spain ☏ 902 020 461, UK ☏ 0870/598 0333; ⓦ www.poferries.com.
Sea France France ☏ 08.25.08.25.05, UK ☏ 0871/663 2546; ⓦ www.seafrance.com.
SpeedFerries France ☏ 03.21.10.50.00, UK ☏ 0870 220 0570; ⓦ www.speedferries.com.
Stena Line Northern Ireland ☏ 0870/520 4204, Republic of Ireland ☏ 01/204 7777, UK ☏ 0870/570 7070; ⓦ www.stenaline.co.uk.
Transmanche France ☏ 0800/650 100, UK ☏ 0800/917 1201; ⓦ www.transmancheferries.com.

Getting around

Just about every place in England is accessible by train or bus. However, public transport costs are among the highest in Europe and cross-country travel can eat up a large part of your budget. It pays to investigate all the special deals and passes, some of which are only available outside England, and for long distances it may be worth considering an internal flight. It's often cheaper to drive yourself around the country (certainly if you're sharing costs), though fuel and car-rental tariffs again are among the highest in Europe. Congestion around the main cities can be bad, and even the motorways (most notoriously the M25, London's orbital road) are liable to sporadic gridlocks, especially on public holidays.

By rail

The British **rail network** links all major cities and towns in England. Although privatization and chronic under-investment has resulted in a severe decline in services over the years, overall reliability is still fairly good compared to other European countries. Main-line routes out of London especially have fast and frequent services – York or Exeter, for instance, can be reached in around two hours – though travelling across the country can be a lengthy business, often involving connections and several different services.

Ticket prices are relatively high. The various train-operating companies offer a bewildering variety of ticket options, all with Byzantine restrictions and weird anomalies (for instance, two single tickets are often cheaper than a return, and it can be cheaper to travel return from the north to London, rather than from London to the north). As a rule, the earlier you book, the cheaper your ticket will be. Just turning up and buying

Mileage chart

	Birmingham	Bristol	London	Manchester	Newcastle	Nottingham	Penzance	York
Birmingham		90	121	89	207	51	274	133
Bristol	90		120	171	298	142	193	224
London	121	120		204	285	129	310	211
Manchester	89	171	204		145	71	356	71
Newcastle	207	298	285	145		161	482	89
Nottingham	51	142	129	71	161		326	87
Penzance	274	193	310	356	482	326		408
York	133	224	211	71	89	87	408	

a ticket at the station is the most expensive way to go, especially during peak periods or at any time on a Friday. An open, fully flexible London–Manchester return ticket can cost up to £220, while booking at least one day in advance, travelling off-peak and accepting certain restrictions (no refund, no amendments) can bring the return fare as low as £25. However, as only limited numbers of the cheapest tickets are issued, they sell out quickly, and should be booked one to four weeks in advance. **Megatrain** (☎0900/160 0900, ⓦwww.megatrain.com) offer a limited number of budget fares on certain routes, though you'll need to be fairly flexible regarding departure time and journey time (trains on these routes tend to be slower) to take advantage of these.

A **seat reservation** is usually included with the ticket – vital if you want to ensure a seat and not a perch in the corridor next to the toilets. At weekends and on public holidays, many long-distance services let you upgrade your ticket by buying a **first-class supplement** for around £15, worth paying if you're facing a five-hour journey on a popular route. If the station's ticket office is closed or does not have a vending machine, you may buy your ticket on the train. Otherwise, **boarding without a ticket** will render you liable to paying the full fare to your destination.

You can buy through tickets at any station, though advance credit-card **reservations** can also be made through the rail companies themselves (National Rail Enquiries can supply the necessary contact name and number), or through an **online booking** service, such as ⓦwww.thetrainline.com. In all instances, **National Rail Enquiries'** information line or website (☎08457/484950, ⓦwww.nationalrail.co.uk) is an essential first call for timetable and route information.

Rail passes

For overseas visitors planning to travel widely by train, a **Britrail pass** might be a wise investment. It gives unlimited travel in England (and throughout Britain) and is valid for varied periods of up to one month (consecutive days travel) or two months (flexi-travel). The pass is available in a wide variety of types, with first- and second-class versions, discounted Youth Passes and Senior Passes (first-class only). Other BritRail combo passes are tailored to families or small groups. Note that BritRail passes have to be bought before you enter England. Any good travel agent or tour operator can supply up-to-date information, or consult any of the BritRail or Rail Europe websites listed under Rail contacts, p.31.

Eurail passes (ⓦwww.eurail.com) are not valid in the UK, though they do provide discounts on the Eurostar service to England and some ferry routes. However, European residents (proof of residency required) can buy an **InterRail** pass (ⓦwww.raileurope .co.uk/inter-rail), which provides free, unlimited train travel in the UK, as well as discounts on Eurostar and certain cross-Channel ferries.

In Britain itself, a variety of **regional rail "Rover" passes** can be purchased by both locals and visitors, offering unlimited travel in multi-day or flexi-day formats, from around £40 for four days' train travel. You need to check restrictions and validity carefully before buying – all the information is on ⓦwww .nationalrail.co.uk.

Alternatively, there's a whole raft of UK **discount passes** including the **Young Person's Railcard** (£20), available to full-time students and those aged between 16 and 25, and **Senior Railcard** for people over 60 (£20), both of which give a third off most fares. Locals and visitors can buy the passes from most UK stations – take along two passport photographs and proof of age or status. Those with children can buy a **Family Railcard** (£20), which entitles up to four adults to a 33 percent discount, and up to four children to a sixty percent reduction of the child's full fare. No photos are needed, and not all adults and children need to be related.

By bus

Long-distance bus services duplicate many rail routes, very often at half the price of the train or less. Services between major towns and cities are frequent and the buses – often referred to as coaches – are modern and comfortable. However, journeys take much longer than the equivalent train ride, partly due to traffic congestion.

By far the biggest countrywide operator is **National Express** (℡0870/580 8080, ⊛www.nationalexpress.com), whose network extends to every corner of England. On busy routes, and on any route at weekends and during holidays, it's advisable to book ahead, rather than just turn up. Fares are very reasonable, with big discounts for under-26s, over-60s and families, while advance-purchase fares and special deals are common – "fun fares" from £1 from London to other major cities, for example. Overseas passport holders can buy a **BritXplorer** pass (in 7-, 14- or 28-day versions) in the UK, from National Express travel shops or at major ports and airports, though you'd have to do a lot of bus travelling to make it pay.

Megabus (℡0900/160 0900, ⊛www.megabus.com) also operates low-budget coach services between some 35 towns in England. Some routes have frequent services, for example up to twelve daily between Oxford and Cambridge, though most have 1–3 departures a day, often at inconvenient times – there is just one departure daily from Plymouth to

London, leaving at 7.45am. Again, fares are generally cheaper the further in advance you book them.

Local bus services are run by a huge array of companies. In many cases, timetables and routes are well integrated, but it's increasingly the case that private companies duplicate the busiest routes in an attempt to undercut the commercial opposition, leaving the more remote spots neglected. As a rule, the further away from urban areas you get, the less frequent and more expensive bus services become, but there are very few rural areas which aren't served by at least an occasional minibus.

In the spring and summer, many national park areas support a network of **weekend and bank holiday buses**, taking visitors to beauty spots, villages and hiking trailheads. In addition, some rural areas not covered by other forms of public transport are served by inexpensive weekday **Postbus** minibuses (℡0845/774 0740, ⊛www.royalmail.com /postbus), that carry mail and fare-paying passengers, usually early in the morning.

For up-to-date information, the website and phone service **Traveline** (℡0871/200 2233, ⊛www.traveline.org.uk) has details of all national and local bus routes and schedules.

By air

For longer journeys across the country such as London–Newcastle or Manchester–Newquay, you might consider using **domestic flights**, operated by such airlines as easyJet, Ryanair, Flybe and bmibaby. You can often find lower prices than the equivalent train fares, though you won't always save much on total travel time.

By car or motorbike

In order to drive in England you need a current full driving licence. If you're bringing your own vehicle into the country you should also carry your vehicle registration, ownership and insurance documents at all times. Motorcyclists and their passengers are obliged to wear a helmet while riding.

In England you **drive on the left**. Motorways – "M" roads – and main "A" roads may have up to four lanes in each direction, but even these can get very

Distances, weights and measures

Distances (and speeds) on English signposts are in miles, and beer is still served in pints. For everything else – money, weights and measures – a mixture of metric and imperial systems is used: fuel is dispensed by the litre, while meat and vegetables may be sold by the pound or the kilo, or both.

congested, with long tailbacks a regular occurrence, especially at peak travel times and on public holidays. In the country, on "B" roads and minor roads, there might only be one lane (single track) for both directions. Keep your speed down, and be prepared for abrupt encounters with tractors, sheep, ponies and other hazards in remote spots.

Don't underestimate the English weather – snow, ice, fog and wind cause havoc every year, and driving conditions on motorways as much as in rural areas can deteriorate quickly. Local radio stations and national Radio Five Live (693/909 MW) feature constantly updated traffic bulletins.

Speed limits are 20–40mph in built-up areas, 70mph on motorways and dual carriageways (freeways) and 60mph on most other roads. As a rule, assume that in any area with street lighting the speed limit is 30mph unless otherwise stated. England has so far resisted toll roads (apart from one or two minor examples), but the principle has been broached by the success of **congestion charging** in London – if you intend to drive a car into central London, it will cost you (see p.82 for more).

Fuel is expensive – unleaded petrol (gasoline) and diesel cost a little over £1 per litre. Out-of-town supermarkets usually have the lowest prices, while the highest prices are charged by motorway service stations.

The AA (Automobile Association; ⓦwww .theaa.com), RAC (ⓦwww.rac.co.uk) and Green Flag (ⓦwww.greenflag.co.uk) all operate **24-hour emergency breakdown** services, and offer useful online route plans. You may be entitled to free assistance through a reciprocal arrangement with a motoring organization in your home country – check before setting out. You can make use of these emergency services if you are not a member of the organization, but you will need to join at the roadside and will incur a hefty surcharge too.

Parking

Car parking in towns, cities and popular tourist spots can be a nightmare and often costs a small fortune. If you're in a tourist city for a day, look out for **park-and-ride schemes** in which you park on the outskirts and take a cheap or free bus to the centre. Parking in long- or short-stay **car parks** will be cheaper than using on-street meters, which often restrict parking time to one or two hours at the most. As a rule, the smaller the town, the cheaper the parking. Some towns operate free **disc-zone parking**, which allows limited-hours town-centre parking in designated areas: if that's what roadside signs indicate, you need to pick up a cardboard disc from any local shop and display it in your windscreen. A yellow line along the edge of the road indicates **parking restrictions**; check the nearest sign to see exactly what they are. A double-yellow line means no parking at any time, though you can stop briefly to unload or pick up people or goods, while a red line signifies no stopping at all.

Vehicle rental

Car rental is usually cheaper arranged in advance from home through one of the large multinational chains or through your tour operator as part of a fly-drive package.

If you rent a car from a company in England (see p.37), expect to pay around £30 per day, £50 for a weekend or from £120 per week. You can sometimes find last-minute or web fares of under £20 per day, though you'll need to book well in advance for the cheapest rates and be prepared for extra charges (like cleaning fees). Otherwise, small **local agencies** often undercut the major chains – we've highlighted some in the "Listings" sections of certain towns and cities. Few companies will rent to drivers with less than one year's

Open spaces and sporting places

Lee Valley Regional Park
A unique destination

The Lee Valley Regional Park stretches 26 miles along the banks of the River Lee, from Ware in Hertfordshire, through Essex, to the Thames at East India Dock Basin. Providing leisure activities suiting all ages, tastes and abilities, you can find sports centres, urban green spaces, heritage sites, country parks, nature reserves and riverside trails. So whatever you do in your leisure time, whether it's golf, horse riding, ice skating, fishing, cycling, bird watching, camping or simply exploring the countryside, you'll find it in Lee Valley Regional Park.

With an incredible eight Sites of Special Scientific Interest (SSSI), four Special Protection Areas (SPA) and four nature reserves and centres of sporting excellence, there is a great deal to discover. Why not bring a picnic and visit our Dragonfly Sanctuary in Waltham Abbey or see how an old munitions testing ground has been transformed into a wildlife oasis at Gunpowder Park?

There is a range of accommodation available in the Regional Park, including a top class youth hostel and ideally situated caravan and campsites providing reasonably priced accommodation for the perfect weekend away.

For more information visit our website
www.leevalleypark.org.uk or call **01992 702 200**.

experience and most will only rent to people between 21 and 75 years of age.

For **camper van** rental, Just Go (☎0870/240 1918, from outside UK ☎+44 1582/842888, ⊛www.justgo.uk.com), can supply quality vehicles sleeping four to six people, equipped with CD/DVD, full bathrooms, kitchenette and bike racks. Rates range from £300 to £950 per week, depending on the vehicle and season; minimum hire is five days (winter) or seven days (summer).

Car rental agencies

Avis UK ☎0870/606 0100, Republic of Ireland ☎021/428 1111, US and Canada ☎1-800/331-1212, Australia ☎13 63 33 or 02/9353 9000, New Zealand ☎09/526 2847 or 0800/655 111; ⊛www.avis.com.
Budget UK ☎0870/156 5656, US ☎1-800/527-0700, Canada ☎1-800/268-8900, Australia ☎1300/362 848, New Zealand ☎0800/283 438; ⊛www.budget.com.
easyCar UK ☎0871/050 0444, ⊛www .easycar.com.
Europcar UK ☎0870/607 5000, Republic of Ireland ☎01/614 2800, US and Canada ☎1-877/940 6900, Australia ☎393/306 160; ⊛www.europcar.com.
Hertz UK ☎020/7026 0077, Republic of Ireland ☎01/870 5777, US and Canada ☎1-800/654-3131, Australia ☎133 039, New Zealand ☎0800/654 321; ⊛www.hertz.com.
National UK ☎0870/400 4581, US ☎1-800/CAR-RENT, Australia ☎0870/600 6666, New Zealand ☎03/366 5574; ⊛www.nationalcar.com.
Suncars UK ☎0870/902 8021, Republic of Ireland ☎1850/201 416; ⊛www.suncars.com.

Thrifty UK ☎01494/751 500, Republic of Ireland ☎01/844 1950, US and Canada ☎1-800/847-4389, Australia ☎1300/367 227, New Zealand ☎09/256 1405; ⊛www.thrifty.com.

Cycling

No one would choose to get around England by **cycling** on the main "A" roads – there's simply too much traffic and cyclists are given scant regard by many motorists. If you have to use the roads, it's far better to stick to the quieter "B" roads and country lanes; best of all, however, is to follow one of the **traffic-free trails** of the extensive National Cycle Network (see Sports and outdoor activities, p.52).

Surprisingly, **cycle helmets** are not compulsory in the UK – but if you're hell-bent on tackling the congestion, pollution and aggression of city traffic, you're well advised to wear one. You do have to have a **rear reflector** and front and back **lights** when riding at night, and you are not allowed to carry children without a special **child seat**. It is also illegal to cycle on pavements, and in most public parks, while **off-road** cyclists must stick to bridleways and byways designated for their use.

Bike rental is available at cycle shops in most large towns, and at villages within national parks and other scenic areas; contact details are given in the Guide. Expect to pay around £10–15 per day, with discounts for longer periods; you may need to provide credit card details, or leave a passport as a deposit.

Accommodation

Accommodation in England ranges from motorway lodges to country retreats, and from budget guesthouses and hostels to swish boutique hotels. There are plenty of characterful and well-refurbished old buildings – former coaching inns in towns, converted mansions and manor houses in rural areas – with heaps of historic atmosphere.

Nearly all tourist offices will **reserve rooms** for you. In some areas you pay a deposit that's deducted from your first night's bill (usually ten percent); in others the office will take a percentage or flat-rate commission – usually around £3. Also useful is the "Book-a-bed-ahead" scheme, which reserves accommodation in your next destination – again for a charge of about £3.

A nationwide **grading system** awards stars to hotels (five stars is the top rank),

guesthouses and B&Bs. There's no hard and fast correlation between rank and price, but the grading system does lay down minimum levels of standards and service. On the whole, British people don't tend to insist on **seeing a room before taking it** (unlike, say, in France or Spain), but you shouldn't be afraid to ask – any place worth its salt, be it designer hotel or humble B&B, should have no objection.

Accommodation price codes

Throughout this guide, accommodation is graded on a scale of ❶ to ❾, the number indicating the lowest price you could expect to pay per night in that establishment for a **double room in high season**. Breakfast is included unless otherwise stated. We've given the actual price (at the time of writing) for **dorm accommodation** in youth and backpackers' hostels, as well as price codes for those hostels that have private rooms.

❶ £40 or under	❹ £61–70	❼ £111–150
❷ £41–50	❺ £71–90	❽ £151–200
❸ £51–60	❻ £91–110	❾ over £200

At the lower end of this scale (❶–❸) – almost always B&Bs rather than hotels – you'll normally experience small rooms, spartan facilities and shared bathrooms, though even in the most basic of places, you should get a washbasin, a TV and a kettle in the room, and the use of a guest lounge. You'll pay a few pounds more for en-suite shower and toilet facilities – but don't expect a great deal of space (or indeed a bath) in these "bathrooms". Above £50 you can expect a little more space and comfort all round, though some properties located in rural or unfashionable localities will have cheaper rates without sacrificing comfort.Most accommodation in England falls into categories ❹–❻, which usually guarantees a good location, decent en-suite rooms, and a few trimmings. Parking should be available, and often dining facilities too. Credit-card payments will often be accepted at these establishments. At the higher end of the scale you can expect a range of services and facilities such as fresh flowers, gourmet breakfasts, king-sized beds and quality bathrooms. Many top-notch B&Bs in this category offer more luxury and better value pound for pound than more impersonal hotels. Paying the top rates (❼–❾), usually in superior hotels in city centres, in seaside villas or in rural mansions, you can expect to be properly pampered, with first-class facilities – there may be a gym, pool and other leisure activities on hand – and spacious rooms. Almost always, there will be a good restaurant on the premises.

Hotels

Hotels vary wildly in size, style, comfort and price. The starting price for a one-star establishment is around £60 per night for a double/twin room, breakfast usually included; two- and three-star hotels can easily cost £100 a night, while four-and five-star properties may charge around £200 a night, often considerably more in London or in resort or country-house hotels. Many city hotels offer cut-price **weekend rates** to fill the rooms vacated by the weekday business trade. It's worth noting, however, that many upper-end urban hotels charge a room-rate only – breakfast can be another whopping £10 or £15 on top.

Several **budget hotel chains** – including Premier Travel Inn (ⓦwww.premierinn.com), Holiday Inn Express (ⓦwww.hiexpress.com), Jurys Inn (ⓦwww.jurysinns.com), Ibis (ⓦwww.ibishotel.com), Ronada (ⓦwww.ronada.com); Norstel (ⓦwww.norstel.com); Canpanile (www.canpanile.com); Comfort Inn, Sleep Inn and Quality Hotels (all ⓦwww.choicehotelsuk.co.uk) – have properties usefully located in city centres across the country. Their style tends towards the no-frills (with breakfast charged extra), but with rates starting at £60–70 for an en-suite room (often sleeping up to four), they're a good deal for families and people travelling in small groups.

B&Bs and guest houses

At its most basic, the typical English **bed-and-breakfast (B&B)** is an ordinary private house with a couple of bedrooms set aside for paying guests. Larger establishments with more rooms, particularly in resorts, style themselves **guesthouses**, but they are pretty much the same thing. Many B&Bs and guest houses have raised their game in recent years – some are truly excellent – and we've highlighted the best choices in every area.

Single travellers tend not to get as good a deal as couples, since many B&Bs and small hotels don't have single rooms – establishments often charge well over half the room rate for sole occupancy of a double/twin room. Don't assume that a B&B is no good if it's ungraded: many places choose not to enter into a grading scheme, and in the rural backwaters some of the best accommodation is to be found in **farmhouses** and other properties whose facilities may technically fall short of official standards.

In towns and villages, many **pubs** also offer B&B, again often not graded. Standards vary wildly – some are great, others truly awful – but at best you'll be staying in a friendly spot with a sociable bar on hand, and you'll rarely pay more than £70 a room.

Useful contacts

B&B My Guest ☎0870/444 3840, ⓦwww.beduk.co.uk. Online bookings at 300 traditional or historic B&B properties.
Distinctly Different ☎01225/866842, ⓦwww.distinctlydifferent.co.uk. Stay the night in converted buildings across the country, from old brothel to Baptist chapel, windmill to lighthouse.
Farm Stay UK ☎024/7669 6909, ⓦwww.farmstay.co.uk. The largest network of farm-based accommodation in the UK.
Wolsey Lodges ☎01473/822058, ⓦwww.wolseylodges.com. Superior B&B in inspected properties across England, from Elizabethan manor houses to Victorian rectories.

Hostels, camping barns and student halls

The **Youth Hostels Association** (YHA; ℡0870/770 8868, ⊛www.yha.org.uk) has over 220 properties, ranging from mansions to thatched cottages, offering bunk-bed accommodation in single-sex dormitories and smaller rooms of two, four or six beds. Some hostels also offer tipi accommodation, and some have pitches for camping. In cities, resorts and national park areas the facilities are often every bit as good as some budget hotels. Indeed, most hostels have moved well away from the old-fashioned, institutional ambience, and many boast laundry facilities, Internet access, a sitting room, cycle stores, cafés and bike rental.

You no longer have to be a member to use a YHA hostel, though non-members pay a £3 supplement (under-18s, £1.50). Otherwise, adult **membership** costs around £16 per year, £23 for joint/family, or £10 for under-26s. Overseas members of **International Youth Hostel Federation** (IYHF) have automatic membership of the YHA; if you aren't an IYHF member, you can join the YHA in person at any affiliated hostel on your first night's stay.

Prices at YHA hostels are calculated according to season and demand, with most charging around £14–21 for members, a little less in simpler places and slightly more in cities such as York, Bristol and London. Many hostels also have private twin/double and family rooms available (£35–65). Length of stay is normally unlimited and the hostel will provide bed linen, pillows and duvet. Hostel **meals** – breakfast, packed lunch or dinner – are always good value (around £5), while nearly all hostels also have self-catering kitchens.

It's always best to book well in advance, and essential during school holidays (Easter, late July to early Sept and the Christmas period, plus half-terms). Note that very few hostels are open year-round, with some only open to group bookings for long periods of the year, and many closed at least one day a week, even in high season. You can book online, and most places accept payment by credit card.

A growing number of independent **backpacker hostels** offer similar facilities to the YHA, generally at lower prices. They tend to attract a more youthful, backpacking (rather than the YHA's family/hiker) crowd, and they usually don't have membership requirements or curfews. A useful publication is the annually updated **Independent Hostel Guide** (Backpackers Press; ⊛www.backpackerspress.com). The website ⊛www.backpackers.co.uk also gives the lowdown on independent hostels and budget accommodation.

More institutional **YMCAs** (⊛www.ymca.org.uk) are often good options in towns and cities – they're usually well maintained, with dormitories (£13–18) and private rooms (around £40 for two), plus good sports facilities. Not all are suitable for short-term holiday accommodation however – check first.

In the wilder parts of England, such as the north Pennines, Lake District, Peak District, Dartmoor and Exmoor, walkers and other hardy types can book accommodation in **camping barns**, mostly administered by the YHA (and members get discounts), but open to all. Conditions are very basic, but they are weatherproof and extremely good value (from £5 a night); the thirteen Lake District barns have their own website, ⊛www.lakelandcampingbarns.co.uk. Many areas also have privately run barns, often called **bunkhouses**, with prices starting at around £10–12 per person, per night.

In England's university towns you can find out-of-term accommodation (Easter & Christmas hols, plus July–Sept) in **student halls of residence**, in one-bedded rooms either with their own or shared bathrooms, or in self-contained flats with self-catering facilities. Prices start at around £20 per night, not always including breakfast. For a list of everything that's on offer, contact the Summer Village (℡0870/712 5002, ⊛www.thesummervillage.com) or Venuemasters (℡0114/249 3090, ⊛www.venuemasters.co.uk).

Camping and caravanning

There are hundreds of **campsites** in England, charging from £6 per tent per night in simple, family-run places in low season to around £18 a night on large sites with laundries, shops and sports facilities. You can also camp in the grounds (and use the facilities) of around 18 YHA hostels (details on ⓦwww.yha.org.uk) for half the adult overnight price per person.

Between October and Easter, you'll often have to travel several miles to find a campsite that's open, though if you're desperate it's always worth asking at places nominally closed – they'll sometimes give you a pitch with minimal facilities for a small fee. In addition to official sites, **farmers** may offer pitches for as little as £5 per night, but don't expect tiled bathrooms and hair dryers for that kind of money. Even farmers without a reserved camping area may let you pitch in a field if you ask first; setting up a tent without asking will not be well received. **Camping rough** is illegal in national parks and nature reserves.

Campervans and caravans are well served at sites throughout the country. Many campsites in the most popular parts of rural and coastal England have caravans to rent, usually by the week, the majority of them large, fully-equipped units permanently stationed at their sites. If you've got a tent, however, you may prefer to look for a site that's exclusively for tents.

Detailed, annually revised **guides** to England's camping and caravan sites include the official *Caravan and Camping Parks in Britain*, available in all major bookshops. The website ⓦwww.ukcampsite.co.uk lists thousands of sites, and includes helpful user-written reviews.

Self-catering accommodation

Holiday properties for rent in England range from city penthouses to secluded cottages. **Studios and apartments**, available by the night in an increasing number of English cities, offer an attractive alternative to hotel stays, with prices from around £100 a night, or from £140 in London. Rural self-catering **cottages and houses** work out cheaper, though the minimum rental period is usually a week. The least you can expect to pay for a small cottage sleeping four people in mid-winter would be around £250 per week, but in summer for a sizeable house near the Cornwall coast or in the Lake District you should budget for £650 and upwards.

We've listed the main **agencies** below, but every regional tourist board has details of cottage rentals in its area. Otherwise, Stilwell's (☎0870/197 6964, ⓦwww.stilwell.co.uk) can send you their free annual guide, *Cottages Direct*, where you select your property and then book direct with the cottage owners.

Houses and cottages

Cornish Cottage Holidays ☎01326/573808, ⓦwww.cornishcottageholidays.co.uk. Lots of thatched cottages and seaside places.
Country Holidays ☎0870/078 1200, ⓦwww.country-holidays.co.uk. A range of graded properties all over the UK.
Heart of the Lakes ☎01539/432321, ⓦwww.heartofthelakes.co.uk. Excellent choice of over 300 quality properties in the Lake District.
Helpful Holidays ☎01647/433593, ⓦwww.helpfulholidays.com. Everything from cottage rentals to a castle, throughout the West Country.
Hoseasons Holidays ☎01502/502588, ⓦwww.hoseasons.co.uk. Holiday lodges and country cottages throughout Britain.
Landmark Trust ☎01628/825925, ⓦwww.landmarktrust.org.uk. Their handbook (£11.50 – refundable on first booking) lists over 180 converted historic properties, ranging from restored forts and Martello towers to a tiny radio shack used in World War II.
National Trust ☎0870/458 4422, ⓦwww.nationaltrustcottages.co.uk. The NT owns 350 cottages, houses and farmhouses, most set in their own gardens or grounds.
Rural Retreats ☎01386/701177, ⓦwww.ruralretreats.co.uk. Upmarket accommodation in restored old buildings, many of them listed.

Studios and apartments

Apartment Service ☎020/8944 1444, ⓦwww.apartmentservice.com. Studios and apartments in towns and cities all over England.
Holiday Serviced Apartments ☎0845/470 4477, from overseas +44 1923/820077, ⓦwww.holidayapartments.co.uk. Available in London, Cambridge and Manchester.
Serviced Stays ☎0871/226 1902, from overseas +44 29/2079 5800, ⓦwww.servicedstays.com. Apartments in London, Manchester and Bristol.

Food and drink

There's no longer any excuse for eating badly in England, provided you have the money. Changing popular tastes have transformed both supermarket shelves and café menus over the last decade, and there's an increasing importance placed on "ethical" eating, whether free-range, organic, humanely produced or locally sourced. London continues to be the gourmet's main destination, while good, moderately priced restaurants and, increasingly, "gastropubs" can be found across the country. Thankfully, some more traditional pubs remain, and for tourists and locals alike the old-fashioned English "local" remains an enduring social institution, and is often the best introduction to town or village life.

English food

England's best known traditional dish is **fish and chips**. Sampled by every overseas visitor at least once, it's often destined to disappoint – crisp and light at its best (traditionally using fresh cod or haddock), it can also be limp, greasy and very heavy-going. Local knowledge is the key: most towns, cities and resorts have an acclaimed fish and chip shop/restaurant, with some – like Whitby's *Magpie Café* or *Stein's Fish & Chips* in Padstow – becoming destinations in themselves.

Other **traditional English dishes** are just as ubiquitous – steak and kidney pie, liver and onions, lamb chops, roast beef and roast chicken all figure on menu after menu in cafés, pubs and restaurants across the land. Unfortunately, though, far too many places churn out very average examples that conform to every negative stereotype about English cooking – overcooked meat, soggy veg, frozen chips and lumpy gravy. However, for every dismal meal served, there's a local café or restaurant somewhere providing excellent food at reasonable prices, from fresh soup using local, seasonal ingredients to home-made ice cream. There's also been a revival of traditional English cuisine in the more fashionable restaurants, with some of England's top chefs presenting their own versions of British working-class classics.

There's a new emphasis, too, on the importance of local growers and suppliers, and many cafés and restaurants now boast locally sourced or organic ingredients. Partly as a result, **regional specialities** are increasingly found in simple cafés and top restaurants alike, from something as basic as a proper Cornish pasty (just steak, turnip and potatoes) to Lancashire hot-pot (lamb and potato stew).

Many mid-range and top-end restaurants present what, for the want of a better term,

The Full English

The **English breakfast**, or "Full English" – mainstay of every B&B and hotel – usually kicks off with a choice of cereals, followed by eggs, sausage, bacon, tomatoes and mushrooms, plus toast and tea or coffee. Places offering a vegetarian version might substitute soya/tofu sausages or similar for the meat, while travellers in northern England may be offered black pudding, a blend of onions, pork fat, oatmeal and congealed blood. If you don't want a big fry-up every morning you can generally ask for scrambled, boiled or poached eggs instead, while the better establishments might offer dishes like home-made muesli and yoghurt, fresh fruit salad, pancakes, kippers (smoked herring) or smoked haddock and other delights. Increasingly available, even in B&Bs, is a "continental" breakfast, or croissants and fruit.

A guide to English dishes

Bubble-and-squeak – fried leftover potato and cabbage (and sometimes other veg).

Chip butty – a chip sandwich.

Crumble – a dessert of stewed fruit topped with a crunchy cooked mix of butter, flour and sugar. Can also refer to savoury, usually vegetable, dishes (without the sugar).

Faggot – an offal meatball.

Mushy peas – soaked and boiled marrowfat peas, almost a paste, served with fish and chips.

Piccalilli – a mustard pickle.

Ploughman's lunch – plate of bread, cheese (or sometimes ham), pickle and salad.

Shepherds' pie – savoury minced lamb topped with mashed potato (made with minced beef, it's a cottage pie).

Spotted dick – suet pudding with currants or sultanas (a dessert).

Toad-in-the-hole – sausages baked in Yorkshire pudding.

Yorkshire pudding – baked batter, usually served as part of a traditional Sunday roast.

---

is generally known as **Modern British** (or Modern English) cuisine. This can be code for "mix and match", sometimes to disastrous effect, but at its best this inventive feel for food marries local, seasonal produce with Mediterranean, Asian or even Pacific Rim ingredients and techniques.

Vegetarians are fairly well catered for in England. Away from London and the big cities, specialist vegetarian places are thin on the ground, but most restaurants and pubs have at least one vegetarian option on their menus, while Italian, Indian and Chinese restaurants usually provide a decent choice of meat-free dishes. For a list of vegetarian establishments across England, check The Veg Dining website (Ⓦwww.vegdining.com). Gluten-free options on menus are still rare.

Cafés and restaurants

Every town, city and resort has a plethora of cheap **cafés**, characteristically unassuming places offering non-alcoholic drinks, all-day breakfasts, snacks and meals. Most are only open during the daytime (roughly 8am–5pm), and tend to be cash-only establishments with few airs and graces. **Teashops** or **tearooms** tend to be more genteel, and serve a range of sandwiches, cakes and light meals throughout the day, as well, of course, as tea.

Old-fashioned chrome-and-formica **coffee bars** – almost always Italian in origin – still cling on in London and a few other towns. Most, however, have been replaced by American-style chain coffee shops, such as Starbucks, Costa and Caffè Nero.

Licensed **café-bars** on the European model are now increasingly commonplace, too – although primarily places to drink, an increasing number serve reasonably priced food. Given the challenge posed by the newcomers, **pubs** that serve food have had to raise their game over the last few years. While many still firmly stick to crisps, sandwiches and chips-with-everything, or lean heavily on the microwave and deep-fat fryer, others have embraced the change in British tastes – indeed, the **gastropub** (more of an informal restaurant) is now a recognized fixture in many villages, towns and cities.

It's surprisingly hard to find a true English **restaurant** that serves only traditional English food. Asian restaurants, on the other hand, are ubiquitous. England's postwar immigrant communities have contributed greatly to the country's dining experience and even the smallest town these days boasts an Indian (more properly Bangladeshi or Pakistani, in most cases) or Chinese (mostly Cantonese) restaurant. The majority

Restaurant prices

Unless specific prices are given, restaurants listed in this Guide have been assigned one of four price categories:

Inexpensive under £12.50
Moderate £12.50–20
Expensive £20–35
Very expensive over £35

This is the price you can expect to pay per person for a three-course meal or equivalent, *excluding* drinks and service.

are relatively inexpensive, with the best – and most authentic examples – in ethnic enclaves in London and the industrial cities of the Midlands (Birmingham, Leicester), north Bradford and the northwest (Manchester, Liverpool). Indeed, in many ways, the curry house is now the quintessential English restaurant.

Other budget stand-bys are Italian restaurants and pizza places – again, there's rarely a small town without one – while Spanish tapas bars, Thai restaurants and French chain bistros are pretty well represented too.

It goes without saying that London has the best selection of **top-class restaurants**, and the widest choice of cuisines, but visitors to Manchester, Birmingham, Bristol, Leeds and other major cities hardly suffer these days. Indeed, wherever you are in England you're never more than half an hour's drive from a really good meal – and some of the very best dining experiences are just as likely to be found in a suburban back street or quiet village rather than a metropolitan hotspot. Heston Blumenthal's Michelin-starred *Fat Duck*, for example – often touted as the world's best restaurant – is in the small Berkshire village of Bray.

The biggest deterrent to enjoying England's gastronomic delights is the expense. While a great curry in London's Brick Lane or a Cantonese feast in Manchester's Chinatown can still be had for under £15 a head, the going rate for a full meal with drinks in most modest restaurants in the country is more like £20–25 per person. Even in a decent pub, with main courses averaging £8–10, the price soon mounts up. If a restaurant has any sort of reputation, you can expect to be spending £30–40 each, and much, much more for the services of a top chef – tasting menus at England's best-known Michelin-starred restaurants cost £75–100 per person.

Restaurants usually open for **lunch** (usually noon–2/3pm) and **dinner** (7–10/11pm); in the reviews in the Guide we've stated any significant variations from this rule. Pub kitchens often close in the afternoon – between about 2pm and 6pm – and on one or two evenings a week, often Sunday and Monday; few serve after about 9pm. **Reservations** are recommended for all popular restaurants, especially at weekends – and the most celebrated places will require advance reservations weeks (or months) in advance. **Credit cards**, in particular American Express and Diners, are not always accepted, especially at small places or out in the sticks.

Pubs and bars

Originating as wayfarers' hostelries and coaching inns, **pubs** have outlived the church and marketplace as the focal points of many an English town and village. They are as varied as the country's townscapes: in larger market towns you'll find huge oak-beamed inns with open fires and polished brass fittings; in remoter upland villages there are stone-built pubs no larger than a two-bedroomed cottage. At its best, the pub can be as welcoming as the full name – "public house" – suggests. Sometimes, particularly in the more inward-looking parts of industrial England, you might have to dig deeper for a welcome, especially in those no-nonsense pubs where something of the old division of the sexes still holds sway. In such places, the "spit and sawdust" **public bar** is where working men can bond over a pint or two; the plusher **saloon bar**, with a separate entrance, is the preferred haunt of couples and women.

In many towns and cities, and especially in areas with a younger population, the traditional pub faces a challenge from the contemporary **bar and café-bar**. The majority are owned and operated by chains – for example All Bar

No smoking

In the UK, the vast majority of hotels and B&Bs no longer allow **smoking**. In all public buildings and offices, restaurants and pubs, and on all public transport, it is now banned outright.

One and Pitcher & Piano – though there are a few honourable independent exceptions, many of which we've listed in the Guide.

After almost a century, English **licensing hours** have been liberalized, with pubs and bars in theory now able to open 24 hours a day, provided they have the necessary permission. In practice, hours in most pubs are still 11am to 11pm, though cities and resorts all now have a growing number of places with extended licences, especially at weekends – it isn't that difficult these days to get a drink after 11pm somewhere, at least in urban areas.

Beer and wine

The most widespread type of English beer is **bitter**, which should be pumped by hand from the cellar and served at cellar temperature. If it comes out of an electric pump (and especially if it's labelled "smoothflow" or similar), it isn't the real thing. Many pubs are owned by large breweries

who favour their own beers, though there should also be one or two "guest ales" available. For the best choice, however, you generally need a to a find a **free house** – an independently run pub that can sell whichever brand of beer it pleases.

The big breweries do distribute some good bitters – Boddington's, Directors, John Smith's, Tetley's and Bass are commonplace – but the real glory of English beer is in the local detail. Hundreds of medium-sized and small breweries still produce what are known as **"real ales"** to traditional recipes. Alongside beer, you'll also find **cider**, made from fermented apples, and – particularly in the West Country and Shropshire – scrumpy, a potent and cloudy beverage, usually flat, dry and very apple-y.

The English also consume an enormous and ever-increasing quantity of **wine**, but although restaurants (and supermarkets) commonly stock a good to excellent range, wine sold in pubs can vary enormously in quality. Recent years have seen a significant improvement in home-produced wines, the product of better knowledge and management. The majority of England's vineyards are located in the southern half of the country, where conditions can be similar to those in Germany and northern France – however the variable climate means that some years produce far better crops than others.

The media

The English are fond of their daily newspapers and there are a lot to choose from, though most are drearily conservative in tone and substance. As well as the nationals, most regions have their own local titles, and newsagents' shelves are stacked high with magazines of every description. As regards TV, broadcasting standards are not as high as they used to be, though they still compare favourably with most of the rest of the world. There are five terrestrial channels – three commercial, and two run by the British Broadcasting Corporation (BBC) and funded by a licence fee – as well as a plethora of digital, satellite and cable channels. The BBC also runs an extensive network of radio stations, with the speech-based Radio 4 serving as its political and contemporary affairs flagship.

Newspapers and magazines

From Monday to Saturday, four **daily newspapers** occupy the "quality" end of the market: the Rupert Murdoch-owned *Times*, the staunchly Conservative *Daily Telegraph*, and the left-of-centre *Independent* and *Guardian*. Among the high-selling **tabloid titles**, the most popular is the *Sun*, an inventive, muck-raking right-wing Murdoch paper whose chief rival is the traditionally left-leaning *Daily Mirror*. The middlebrow daily tabloids – the *Daily Mail* and the *Daily Express* – are noticeably (some would say rabidly) xenophobic and right-wing. England's oldest **Sunday newspaper** is *The Observer*, now in the same stable as the *Guardian* and with a similar stance, while all the other major papers all publish their own Sunday editions. Meanwhile, an army of **local newspapers** – at least one in every major town and city – provides intriguing insights into English life, with local news, events and personalities to the fore.

Newsagents offer a range of **specialist magazines and periodicals** covering just about every subject, with motoring, music, sport, computers, gardening and home improvements leading the way. *The Economist* is essential reading in many a boardroom; the left-wing *New Statesman* concentrates on social issues, while the satirical bi-weekly *Private Eye* prides itself on printing the stories the rest of the press won't touch, and on riding the consequent stream of libel suits.

Australians, New Zealanders and South Africans in London should look out for the weekly free magazine, *TNT*, which provides a résumé of news from home as well as jobs, accommodation and events in the capital. Otherwise, the *Wall Street Journal*, *USA Today* and the *International Herald Tribune* are widely distributed, as are the magazines *Time* and *Newsweek*.

Television

There are five main terrestrial **television channels** in the UK. These are divided between the BBC (ⓦwww.bbc.co.uk), through BBC1 and BBC2, and three independent commercial channels, ITV, Channel 4 and Channel 5 (the latter still not available everywhere in England). Broadcasting standards leave a lot to be desired, with much of the output imported from the US, but despite regular complaints about falling standards and periodic mutterings about the licence fee (paid by all British viewers), there's still more than enough quality to keep the **BBC** in good repute both at home and abroad. Of the two BBC channels, BBC2 is the more offbeat and heavyweight, BBC1 more avowedly populist. Various regional companies together form the **ITV** network, and they're united by a more tabloid approach to programme-making – necessarily so, because if they don't get the advertising they don't survive. **Channel 4** is similarly influenced, but is the home of hit (and hip) US comedies and serials, and has some of the best investigative news programmes, with a more internationalist view. The newer **Channel 5** is slowly offering a better range of programmes following sustained mockery.

The UK's **satellite** and **cable** TV companies are mounting a strong challenge to the erstwhile dominance of the terrestrial channels. Live sport, in particular, is increasingly in the hands of Rupert Murdoch's Sky, the major satellite provider, whose 24-hour rolling Sky News programme rivals that of CNN. In response, both the BBC and the other commercial channels have launched their own digital ventures, including the BBC's News 24 (rolling news), BBC3 (young adult) and BBC4 (arts and culture), ITV's entertainment channel ITV2, and Channel 4's film channel Film4, entertainment channel E4 and more serious More4.

Radio

The BBC's **radio network** (@www.bbc.co.uk/radio) has five nationwide stations. These are **Radio 1**, which is almost exclusively devoted to new chart and urban music, and specialist DJs; **Radio 2** (Britain's most listened-to radio station), a combination of light pop and specialist music, with a sprinkling of arts programmes and documentaries; **Radio 3**, which focuses on classical music; **Radio 4**, a blend of current affairs, arts and drama; and **Five Live**, a 24-hour rolling sports and news channel.

All have faced tough challenges for market share in recent years, the hardest hit being Radio 1, whose rivals include a range of local commercial stations, most notably London's **Capital Radio** (95.8 FM) and **Heart** (106.2 FM), though Radio 3 has had to struggle hard against **Classic FM** (100 to 102 FM). The BBC also operates a full roster of **local radio stations**, mostly featuring local news, chat and mainstream pop.

Festivals and events

Many of the showpiece events marketed to tourists – Trooping the Colour, Chelsea Flower Show, the Lord Mayor's Show and the like – say little about contemporary England and nothing about the country's regional folk history. Better to catch London's exuberant Notting Hill Carnival or a wacky village celebration for a more instructive idea of what makes the English tick. Every major town and city has at least one prime event, some dating back centuries, others more recent concoctions, but everywhere there's a general willingness to revive the traditional and experiment with the new – from medieval jousting through to the performing arts. The festival and events calendar below picks out some of the best – and we highlight some of our personal favourites in the Festivals colour section – but for exhaustive lists of events you'll need to contact local tourist offices. The May and August bank holiday weekends, and the summer school holidays (July and Aug) are the favoured times for events to be held.

January/February

London Parade (Jan 1). A procession of floats, marching bands, clowns, American cheerleaders and classic cars wends its way from Parliament Square at noon, through the centre of London, to Berkeley Square.

Chinese New Year (Jan 26, 2009; Feb 14, 2010). Processions, fireworks and festivities in the country's two main Chinatowns in London and Manchester.
Shrove Tuesday (47 days before Easter Sunday, so usually in Feb). The last day before Lent is also known as "Pancake Day" – eating them and racing

Stunning Countryside
Northamptonshire is Natures Way

Save up to
£370
on Country House
Hotels*

Only an hour from London, Birmingham,
Oxford and Cambridge, yet situated in the
very middle of prime English countryside.

For more information:

Visit: www.explorenorthamptonshire.co.uk
Email: info@explorenorthamptonshire.co.uk
Or call: **01604 609393**

Txt **GUIDE** to **84880** for your free 2008
visitor guide

*Subject to availability

Northamptonshire
let yourselfgrow.com

with them are traditional pastimes. The most famous race is held in Olney (Buckinghamshire).

Shrovetide Football (Shrove Tuesday & Ash Wednesday). The world's oldest, largest, longest, maddest football game takes place in and around Ashbourne, Derbyshire.

Easter

British and World Marbles Championship (Good Friday). Held at Tinsley Green, near Crawley, Sussex.

Bacup Nutters Dance (Easter Saturday). Blacked-up Lancashire clog dancers mark the Bacup town boundaries.

Hare Pie Scramble and Bottle-Kicking (Easter Monday). Barmy and chaotic village bottle-kicking contest at Hallaton, Leicestershire. See p.636.

World Coal-Carrying Championship (Easter Monday). Gawthorpe, near Ossett, West Yorkshire, sees an annual race to carry 50kg of coal a mile through the village and be crowned "King of the Coil Humpers".

Easter Parade (Easter Monday). One of England's largest parades (since 1885) is held in London's Battersea Park.

April

Ulverston Walking Festival (1st week). Cumbria's "Festival Town" celebrates the great outdoors with hikes and events.

May

Padstow Obby Oss (May 1). Processions, music and dancing through the streets of Padstow, Cornwall; an equally raucous Obby Oss festival takes place in Minehead, Somerset. See p.457.

Helston Furry Dance (May 8). A courtly procession and dance through the Cornish town by men in top hats and women in formal dresses. See p.442.

Bath International Music Festival (mid-May to 1st week June). Arts jamboree, with a concurrent fringe festival. See p.369.

Glyndebourne Opera Festival (mid-May to end-Aug). One of the classiest arts festivals in the country, in East Sussex. See p.207 and *Festivals and events* colour section.

Brockworth Cheese Rolling (late May bank holiday Mon). Pursuit of a cheese wheel down a murderous Gloucestershire incline – one of the weirdest knees-ups in England.

Chelsea Flower Show (3rd or 4th week). Essential event for England's green-fingered legions at the Royal Hospital, Chelsea, in London.

Hay Festival of Literature and the Arts (last week). The nation's literary types descend on this Welsh border town for a big bookish shindig. See p.562.

June

Aldeburgh Festival (June). Suffolk jamboree of classical music, established by Benjamin Britten. See p.488.

Beating Retreat (early June) Soldiers on foot and horseback provide a colourful, very British ceremony on Horse Guards Parade in London over three evenings, marking the old military custom of drumming and piping the troops back to base at dusk.

Strawberry Fair (1st Sat). Free festival of music, arts and crafts held on Midsummer Common in Cambridge.

Appleby Horse Fair (2nd week). The country's most important gypsy gathering at Appleby-in-Westmorland, Cumbria. See p.761.

Trooping the Colour (2nd Sat). Massed bands, equestrian pageantry, gun salutes and fly-pasts for the Queen's Official Birthday on Horse Guards Parade, London.

Glastonbury Festival (last week). Top-class music and comedy line-up – the rain nearly always turns it into a mud bath, but nothing dampens the trippy-hippy vibe. See p.374 and *Festivals and events* colour section.

World Worm-Charming Championships (end of June). Annual world championships of worm-charming and other zany pastimes, held at Willaston, Cheshire.

July

Urban Games (dates vary June/July). Skater-chic comes to Clapham Common, London, for a weekend of boarding, BMXing and freestyling.

Rushbearing Festival (1st week). Symbolic procession of crosses and garlands at Ambleside in the Lake District, dating back centuries.

York Early Music Festival (1st/2nd week). The country's premier early music festival, spread out over 10 days. See p.826.

Great Yorkshire Show (2nd week). England's biggest region celebrates its heritage, culture and cuisine in a huge three-day agricultural bash at Harrogate, North Yorkshire. See p.812.

Swan Upping (3rd week). Ceremonial registering of the River Thames cygnets, from Sunbury to Pangbourne, during which liveried rowers search for swans, marking them as belonging to either the Queen, the Dyers' or the Vintners' City liveries. At Windsor, all the oarsmen stand to attention in their boats and salute the Queen.

Cambridge Folk Festival (last week). Biggest event of its kind in England, with lots more than just folk music. See p.531.

Whitstable Oyster Festival (late July). Oysters are washed down with champagne and Guinness, with parades and diverse musical accompaniments. See p.174.

WOMAD (late July). Renowned three-day world music festival at Charlton Park, outside Malmesbury, Wiltshire.

The Proms (July to early Sept). Top-flight international classical music festival at the Royal Albert Hall, London, with very cheap standing-room tickets, ending in the famously patriotic Last Night of the Proms. See p.158.

Pride London (dates vary). Encompassing a rally in Trafalgar Square, a whistle-blowing march through the city streets, plus cabaret stage and Drag Idol contest in Leicester Square.

August

Brighton Pride (1st week). A week of events celebrating lesbian, gay, bisexual and transgender culture, culminating in the country's biggest gay carnival parade on the final Sat. See p.215.

Cowes Week (1st week). Full-blown sailing extravaganza in the Isle of Wight, with partying aplenty and star-studded entertainment for land lubbers. See p.245.

Sidmouth Folk Week (1st week). Folk and roots performers at a variety of venues, plus theatre and dance. See p.394.

Whitby Regatta (1st week). The country's oldest regatta – sea races, funfair and fireworks on the windy North Yorkshire coast. See p.854.

Grasmere Lakeland Sports and Show (3rd/4th week). Wrestling, fell-running, ferret-racing and other curious Lake District pastimes.

Notting Hill Carnival (last Sun and bank holiday Mon). Vivacious celebration led by London's Caribbean community but including everything from Punjabi drummers to Brazilian salsa, plus music, food and floats. See *Festivals and events* colour section.

Leeds West Indian Carnival (bank holiday Mon). England's oldest carnival, featuring processions, dancing and barbecues.

Whitby Folk Week (bank holiday week). One of England's most traditional folk meets, a week's worth of morris and sword dancing, finger-in-your-ear singing, storytelling and more. See p.853.

Reading Festival (bank holiday weekend). Berkshire's annual three-day rock and contemporary music jamboree.

September

Blackpool Illuminations (early Sept to early Nov). Five miles of extravagantly kitsch light displays on the Blackpool seafront. See p.699.

Abbots Bromley Horn Dance (1st Mon after Sept 4). Vaguely pagan mass dance in mock-medieval costume – one of the most famous of England's ancient customs, at Abbots Bromley, Staffordshire.

St Ives September Festival (2 weeks mid-Sept). Eclectic Cornish festival of art, poetry, literature, jazz, folk, rock and world music. See p.450.

Open House (3rd weekend). A once-a-year opportunity to peek inside hundreds of buildings, many of which don't normally open their doors to the public. Takes place in London and, to a lesser extent, elsewhere in the country.

October

World Conker Championship (2nd Sun). Thousands flock to Ashton, Northamptonshire, to watch modern-day gladiators fight for glory armed only with a nut and twelve inches of string.

State Opening of Parliament (late Oct). The Queen arrives in a fancy coach accompanied by the Household Cavalry to give a speech in the House of Lords and officially open Parliament at 11am. It also takes place whenever a new government is sworn in.

Halloween (Oct 31). Last day of the Celtic calendar and All Hallows Eve: pumpkins, plus a lot of ghoulish dressing-up, trick-or-treating and parties.

November

London to Brighton Veteran Car Rally (1st Sunday). Ancient machines lumbering the 57 miles down the A23 to the seafront.

Guy Fawkes Night/Bonfire Night (Nov 5). Nationwide fireworks and bonfires commemorating the foiling of the Gunpowder Plot in 1605 – most notably at York (Fawkes' birthplace), Ottery St Mary in Devon, and at Lewes, East Sussex (see p.205) and *Festivals and events* colour section.

Lord Mayor's Show (2nd Sat). Celebrations held since 1215, featuring a daytime cavalcade and nighttime fireworks, to mark the inauguration of the new Lord Mayor of the City of London.

December

Tar Barrels Parade (Dec 31). Locals in Allendale Town, Northumberland turn up with trays of burning pitch on their heads to parade round a large communal bonfire. See p.875.

New Year's Eve (Dec 31). The biggest celebration takes place in London, with a massive fireworks display over the Thames, and thousands of inebriates in Trafalgar Square. Also a huge bash on Newcastle's Quayside.

Sports and outdoor activities

As the birthplace of football, cricket, rugby and tennis – to name just four sports – England can boast a series of sporting events that attract a world audience. If you prefer participating to spectating, the country caters for just about every outdoor activity, too: we've concentrated below on walking, cycling and water sports, but there are also opportunities for anything from rock climbing to pony-trekking. The Guide highlights recommended operators in every region, or contact any local tourist office.

Spectator sports

Football is the national game, with a wide programme of professional league matches across four divisions taking place every Saturday afternoon from early August to early May, with plenty of Sunday and midweek fixtures too. It's very difficult to get tickets to Premier League matches involving the most famous teams (Chelsea, Arsenal, Manchester United, Liverpool), but tours of their grounds are feasible – the Guide has the details – or you can try one of the lower-league games. The annual showpiece is the **FA Cup Final**, the biggest domestic football competition (and the world's oldest knock-out football competition), though again, tickets are virtually unobtainable – find a lively bar and watch it on TV with the rest of the country.

Rugby comes in two codes – 15-a-side **Rugby Union** and 13-a-side **Rugby League**, both fearsomely brutal contact sports that can make entertaining viewing even if you don't understand the rules. In general, it's much less popular than football, with Union particularly still seen as an upper-class game (it originated in English public, ie private, schools). Seeing a top game should present few problems, either in the weekly Premiership (Union; matches Sept–May) or Super League (League; matches Feb–Sept).

The game of **cricket** is English idiosyncrasy at its finest. Foreigners – and most Brits – marvel at a game that can last five days and still end in a draw, while few people have the faintest idea about its rules or tactics. A plethora of competitions and matches between the 18 "first-class" English counties (played April–Sept) means visitors can easily experience the sport – if the four-day County Championship matches seem like too much of a commitment, there are also one-day National League matches, a one-day knockout cup competition (the C&G Trophy) and the highly popular three-hour matches of the Twenty20 Cup.

For something even more peculiarly English, you don't have to look any further than the **University Boat Race**, a rowing contest on the Thames in west London between crews from Oxford (the "Dark Blues") and Cambridge ("Light Blues") universities. First raced in 1829, and once a major event, it barely registers with the general public these days, though it still makes a good day out – be warned, the best riverside vantage-spots fill early.

Finally, if you're in England at the end of June or early July, you won't be able to miss the country's annual fixation with **tennis** in the shape of the Wimbledon championships. No one gives a hoot about the sport for the other fifty weeks of the year, but as long as one plucky Brit endures, the entire country gets caught up with tennis fever.

Sporting events calendar

National Hunt Festival, Cheltenham (mid-March). The country's premier steeplechase (fence-jumping) meeting, including the Cheltenham Gold Cup. See p.340.

University Boat Race (Sat in late March/early April). Two eight-man crews race down the Thames in London.

Grand National, Aintree (1st Sat in April). Thrills and lots of spills in the steeplechase to end them all.

London Marathon (April). The country's biggest running race, as vicars and people dressed as teapots trail in behind the speedy pros.

FA Cup Final (mid-May). Football's greatest day out at London's new Wembley Stadium.

Derby week, Epsom (1st week June). The world's most expensive horseflesh competing in the 200-year-old Derby, the Coronation Cup and the Oaks.

Wimbledon Lawn Tennis Championships (last week June & 1st week July). England's annual bout of tennis fever.

Henley Royal Regatta (1st week in July). Glamorous Oxfordshire rowing tournament, with tons of toffs and strawberries.

Twenty20 Cup Finals Day (early Aug). Two semi-finals and the final take place in one fast-and-furious day of cricket.

Rugby League Challenge Cup Final (last Sat in Aug). Held since 1896, this is the culmination of the biggest knock-out competition for rugby league clubs.

Walking

England's finest **walking areas** are the granite moorlands and spectacular coastlines of Devon and Cornwall in the southwest, and the highlands of the north – notably the Peak District, the Yorkshire Dales, the North York Moors, and the Lake District. We've highlighted local walks, climbs, rambles and trails throughout the Guide, but it goes without saying that even for short hikes you need to be **properly equipped**, follow local advice and listen out for local weather reports. England's climate may be relatively benign, but the weather is changeable in any given season and people die on the moors and mountains every year. For details of operators specializing in **organized walking holidays** in England (see opposite).

Keen hikers might want to tackle one of England's dozen or so **National Trails** (www.nationaltrail.co.uk), which amount to some 2500 miles of waymarked path and track. Perhaps the most famous – certainly the toughest – is the **Pennine Way** (268 miles; usual walking time: 16 days), stretching from the Derbyshire Peak District to the Scottish Borders, while the challenging **South West Coast Path** (630 miles; 56 days) through Somerset, Devon, Cornwall and Dorset tends to be tackled in shorter sections. Other trails are less gung-ho in

character, like the **South Downs Way** (101 miles; 8 days) or the fascinating **Hadrian's Wall Path** (84 miles; 7 days). You'll find more details on all these walks in the Guide; excellent guides to all National Trails are published by Aurum Press.

Cycling

The **National Cycle Network** is made up of 10,000 miles of signed cycle route, a third on traffic-free paths (including disused railways and canal towpaths), the rest mainly on country roads. You're never very far from one of the numbered routes, all of which are detailed on the Sustrans website (☎0845/113 0065, ⊛www.sustrans.org.uk), a charitable trust devoted to the development of environmentally sustainable transport.

Major routes include the well-known **C2C** (Sea-to-Sea), 140 miles between Whitehaven/Workington on the northwest coast and Newcastle/Sunderland on the northeast. There's also the **Cornish Way** (123 miles), from Bude to Land's End, and routes that cut through the very heart of England, such as from Derby to York (154 miles) or along the rivers Severn and Thames (128 miles; Gloucester to Reading).

Most local tourist offices and good bookshops stock a range of **cycling guides**, with maps and detailed route descriptions. You can also get maps and guidance (some free) from Sustrans and from the Cyclists Touring Club (☎0870/873 0060, ⊛www.ctc.org.uk).

Water sports

With hundreds of miles of coastline and inland waterways, not to mention an entire district of lakes, it's hardly surprising that England offers excellent water sports opportunities.

Sailing and **windsurfing** are especially popular along the south coast (particularly the Isle of Wight and Solent) and in the southwest (around Falmouth in the Carrick Roads estuary, Cornwall, and around Salcombe and Dartmouth, both in South Devon). Here, and up in the Lake District, on Windermere, Derwent Water and Ullswater, you'll be able to rent boards, dinghies and boats, either by the hour or for longer periods of instruction – from around £25 for a couple of hours' of windsurfing to around £140 for a two-day non-residential sailing course. The UK Sailing Academy (☎01983/294941, ⓦwww.uk-sail.org.uk) in Cowes on the Isle of Wight is England's finest instruction centre for windsurfing, dinghy sailing, kayaking and kitesurfing and offers non-residential and residential courses.

Newquay in Cornwall is the country's undisputed **surfing** centre, whose main break, Fistral, regularly hosts international contests. But there are quieter spots all along the north coast of Cornwall and Devon, as well as a growing scene on the more isolated northeast coast from Yorkshire to Northumberland. In the southwest (less so in the northeast) there are plenty of places where you can rent or buy equipment, which means that prices are kept down to reasonable levels, say around £10 per day each for board and wetsuit.

Activity holiday operators

Most operators offering **activity holidays** tend to have two types of trip: escorted (or guide-led) and self-guided, the latter usually slightly cheaper. On all holidays you can expect luggage transfer each night, pre-booked accommodation, detailed route instructions, a packed lunch and back-up support. Some companies offer budget versions of their holidays, staying in hostels or B&Bs, as well as hotel packages.

Boating and sailing

Blakes Holiday Boating ☎0870/220 2498, ⓦwww.blakes.co.uk. Cruisers, yachts and narrowboats on the Norfolk Broads, the River Thames and various English canals.

Classic Sailing ☎01872/580022, ⓦwww.classic-sailing.co.uk. Hands-on sailing holidays on traditional wooden boats and tall ships, including Devon, Cornwall and the Isles of Scilly. Women-only weekends available.

Hoseasons Holidays ☎01502/502588, ⓦwww.hoseasons.co.uk. Self-drive cruisers on the Norfolk Broads and River Thames, as well as traditional narrowboats on inland waterways.

Le Boat US ☎1-800/992-0291, ⓦwww.leboat.com. Hire a hotel-barge or self-drive cruiser on the River Thames (3 days or 1 week) or the Norfolk Broads (1 week).

Cycling

Capital Sport ☎01296/631671, ⓦwww.capital-sport.co.uk. Gentle self-guided cycling tours in Kent, Oxford and the Cotswolds, in either B&B or "fine" accommodation.

Country Lanes ☎01425/655022, ⓦwww.countrylanes.co.uk. Ranging from day-trips to week-long outings, mainly in the Lake District and New Forest.

Holiday Lakeland ☎01697/371871, ⓦwww.holiday-lakeland.co.uk. Offers 3- to 5-day tours in Northumberland and the Pennines, including coast-to-coast, Pennine Cycleway and Hadrian's Wall Cycleway routes; also a four-day, self-guided Lake District tour.

Saddle Skedaddle ☎0191/265 1110, ⓦwww.skedaddle.co.uk. Biking adventures and classic road rides – includes guided and self-guided tours in Cornwall, the Cotswolds, Northumberland and the New Forest, from a weekend to a week.

Surfing

Big Friday ☎01637/872512, ⓦwww.bigfriday.com. Surf weekend packages from London to Newquay, with accommodation, travel and tuition laid on. Also women-only weekends.

Global Boarders ☎0845/330 9303, ⓦwww.globalboarders.com. Tailor-made surf packages in Cornwall, with a variety of accommodation options and transport to wherever the best breaks are.

Surfers World ☎01271/871224, ⓦwww.surfersworld.co.uk. Short breaks with surfing courses in Woolacombe, North Devon, or on the north Cornwall coast.

Walking

Above The Line ☎019467/26229, ⓦwww.wasdale.com. Mountain courses (hill walking for softies, guided ascents, navigation and so on), with accommodation in the *Wasdale Head Inn*, the Lake District birthplace of British mountaineering.

Contours Walking Holidays ☎01768/480451, ⓦwww.contours.co.uk. Short breaks or longer walking holidays and self-guided hikes in every region, north and south, from famous trails to little-known local routes.

English Lakeland Ramblers US ☎800/724-8801, ⓦwww.ramblers.com. Escorted walking tours in the Lake District or the Cotswolds (May–Sept), either inn-to-inn or based in a country hotel.

Footpath Holidays ☎01985/840049, ⓦwww.footpath-holidays.com. Guided and self-guided

outward bound   inner peace

the lake district
Cumbria

Where there are two
sides to every story

for information and to book online
visit **golakes.co.uk**

order your free brochure on
0844 888 5188

experience
englandsnorthwest

walking packages to various hill and coastal areas, from the Yorkshire Dales to Cornwall, most with 5 or 7 nights B&B.

Ramblers Countrywide Holidays
℡01707/386800, ⓦwww.ramblersholidays .co.uk. Sociable guided walking tours (scenic, themed or special interest) all over the UK, graded from "leisurely" to "challenging".

Sherpa Expeditions ℡020/8577 2717, ⓦwww .sherpa-walking-holidays.co.uk. At-your-own-pace, self-guided walks (and cycle tours) between country pubs, mainly in Yorkshire, the Lakes and the southwest. Most trips last 8–10 days and run between April and Oct.

Walking Women ℡0845/644 5335, ⓦwww .walkingwomen.co.uk. Popular, year-round women-only walking breaks in such areas as the Lake District, the Yorkshire Dales, the Cotswolds and the South Downs, mainly 3–5 days.

Wilderness Travel US ℡1-800/368-2794, ⓦwww.wildernesstravel.com. Inn-to-inn hiking packages, either taking in the Lake District and Yorkshire Dales (10 days), or coast-to-coast (2 weeks).

Miscellaneous

Doone Valley Trekking ℡01598/741234, ⓦwww.doonevalleytrekking.co.uk. Short breaks and week-long holidays on Exmoor, for all ages and levels, with self-catering farmhouse accommmodation.

Explore Britain ℡01740/650900, ⓦwww .xplorebritain.com. Escorted and independent walking and cycling holidays including coast-to-coast, the Thames Valley, the Cotswolds and the Lake District.

Mountain Water Experience ℡01548/550675, ⓦwww.mountainwaterexperience.com. Kayaking, caving, coasteering and other adventure pursuits, based in Dartmoor and south Devon.

Outward Bound ℡0870/242 3028, ⓦwww .outwardbound-uk.org. Residential courses and activity holidays in the Lake District, including climbing, caving, sailing and canoeing, geared towards under-25s, but family weekends also available.

YHA ℡0870/770 8868, ⓦwww.yha.org.uk. Huge range of good-value hostel-based activity weekends and holidays, from walking, climbing and biking to surfing, kayaking and caving.

Shopping

Although it is now one of the chief leisure activities of the English, shopping can be a rather soulless experience in towns and cities. High streets up and down the country feature the same bland chain stores selling very similar ranges of mass-produced items. But while out-of-town shopping centres and supermarkets have sucked much of the life out of town centres, it is still possible to track down neighbourhoods, stores and the occasional oddity that make for a more enjoyable retail experience.

Most places, for example, have a **market** at least once a week, which may vary from a sprawling sea of stalls, as in London's Camden, Portobello and Spitalfields (see p.117), to sedate local village affairs. Street markets or covered markets are often the best places to pick up craft items, though you may have to wade among a proliferation of candles, t-shirts and twee bric-a-brac to find anything truly original. Markets are also the only places (apart from antique shops and some second-hand shops) where **haggling** is acceptable. Look on ⓦwww.country -markets.co.uk to find where and when a market takes place close to you. Many towns also have a weekly or monthly **farmers' market** (see ⓦwww .farmersmarkets.net), where local foodstuffs and artisan products are offered – the biggest of these is in Winchester, with over 90 producers. You'll also find similarly authentic local items in rural **farmshops**, usually signposted by the side of the road.

Clothing and shoe sizes

Women's dresses and skirts

American	4	6	8	10	12	14	16	18
British	8	10	12	14	16	18	20	22
Continental	38	40	42	44	46	48	50	52

Women's blouses and sweaters

American	6	8	10	12	14	16	18
British	30	32	34	36	38	40	42
Continental	40	42	44	46	48	50	52

Women's shoes

American	5	6	7	8	9	10	11
British	3	4	5	6	7	8	9
Continental	36	37	38	39	40	41	42

Men's suits

American	34	36	38	40	42	44	46	48
British	34	36	38	40	42	44	46	48
Continental	44	46	48	50	52	54	56	58

Men's shirts

American	14	15	15.5	16	16.5	17	17.5	18
British	14	15	15.5	16	16.5	17	17.5	18
Continental	36	38	39	41	42	43	44	45

Men's shoes

American	7	7.5	8	8.5	9.5	10	10.5	11	11.5
British	6	7	7.5	8	9	9.5	10	11	12
Continental	39	40	41	42	43	44	44	45	46

If you're looking for specific items, you'll want to seek out particular districts and towns which specialize in them: Birmingham's Jewellery Quarter (see p.581) for silver and gold, for example, or Hay-on-Wye (see p.561) for books, while almost every Cotswold hamlet sports an antiques shop or two.

On the whole, though, England is not an especially cheap place to shop. Most goods in the UK, with the chief exceptions of books and food, are subject to 17.5-percent **Value Added Tax** (VAT), which is included in the marked price of goods. Visitors from non-EU countries can save a lot of money through the **Retail Export Scheme** (tax-free shopping), which allows a refund of VAT on goods to be taken out of the country. (Savings will usually be minimal for EU nationals because of the rates at which the goods will be taxed upon import to the home country.) Note that not all shops participate in this scheme (those doing so will display a sign to this effect), and that you cannot reclaim VAT charged on hotel bills or other services.

Travel essentials

Costs

England is an expensive place to visit. Even if you're camping or hostelling, using public transport, buying picnic lunches and eating in pubs and cafés your minimum expenditure will be around £35/US$70/€50 per person per day. Couples staying in B&Bs, eating at unpretentious restaurants and visiting a fair number of tourist attractions, are looking at £60–70/US$125–145/€85–100 per person, while if you're renting a car, staying in hotels and eating well, budget for at least £120/US$245/€170 each. This last figure, of course, won't even cover your accommodation if you're staying in stylish city or grand country-house hotels, while on any visit to London work on the basis that you'll need an extra £25/US$50/€35 per day to get the best out of the city.

Many of England's **historic attractions** – from castles to stately homes – are owned and/or operated by either the **National Trust** (℡0870/458 4000, Ⓦwww.nationaltrust.org.uk) or **English Heritage** (℡0870/333 1181, Ⓦwww.english-heritage.org.uk), whose properties are denoted in the Guide with "NT" or "EH". Both organizations charge entry fees for most of their sites (usually £4–8), though some are free. If you plan to visit more than half a dozen places owned by either, it's worth considering an annual membership (around £40), which allows unlimited entry to each organization's respective properties – and you can join on your first visit to any attraction. US members of the Royal Oak Foundation (Ⓦwww.royal-oak.org) get free admission to all National Trust properties.

Many **stately homes** remain privately owned, in the hands of the landed gentry, who tend to charge £8–12 for admission to edited highlights of their domain. Other old buildings are owned by local authorities, which generally charge lower admission charges or allow free access.

Municipal **art galleries and museums** across England often have free admission, as do the great state museums in London and the provinces, such as the British Museum, National Gallery, National Railway Museum and Royal Armouries. Private museums and other collections usually charge for entrance, but rarely more than £6. Several of the country's **cathedrals** charge admission – of around £4 – but most ask for voluntary donations, as do many churches.

The admission charges given in the Guide are the full adult rate, unless otherwise stated. Concessionary rates for **senior citizens** (over 60), under-26s and **children** (from 5 to 17) apply almost everywhere, from fee-paying attractions to public transport, and typically give around fifty percent discount; you'll need official identification as proof of age. The unemployed and full-time students are

Tipping

Although there are no fixed rules for **tipping**, a ten to fifteen percent tip is anticipated by restaurant waiters and expected by taxi drivers. Some restaurants levy a "discretionary" or "optional" **service charge** of 10 or 12.5 percent. If they've done this, it should be clearly stated on the menu and on the bill. However, you are not obliged to pay the charge, and certainly not if the food or service wasn't what you expected. It is not normal to leave tips in pubs, but the bar staff are sometimes offered drinks, which they may accept in the form of money. The only other occasions when you'll be expected to tip are in hairdressers, and in upmarket hotels where porters, bell boys and table waiters expect and usually get a pound or two.

England on a budget

Faced with another £2.50 pint, a £30 theatre ticket and a twenty-quid taxi ride back to your £100-a-night hotel, England might seem like the most expensive country in Europe. However, there are ways to stick to a **budget** and still get the most out of your stay.

- Entry is free to many of England's showpiece **museums and galleries**, including some of the world's finest art and historical collections in London, Leeds, York, Birmingham, Manchester, Liverpool and Bristol.
- **Beer** is cheaper in the north of England, and cheapest of all in Lancashire, according to the peerless *Good Pub Guide*.
- Take every **discount card/ID** you're entitled to, as students, young travellers, youth hostellers and seniors all get free or discounted entry to many sights and attractions.
- Go to the **cinema** during the day; it's nearly always cheaper before 5pm.
- Set meals can be a real steal, even at the poshest of **restaurants**, where a limited-choice two- or three-course lunch or a "pre-theatre" menu might only cost 40 percent of the usual price.
- Book **transport** tickets as far in advance as possible, and always ask about Day Rovers and other special deals.
- Don't drive – **walk**. In places like the Yorkshire Dales, the Lake District, or along the Cornish coastal path, the easiest and most enjoyable way to get from village to village is on your own two feet.
- Give the big-ticket **festivals** (Glastonbury, Glyndebourne) a miss; there are thousands of others throughout the year that are free and fun, from Derbyshire well-dressing to the Notting Hill Carnival.
- Visit the **markets** – from grungy Camden in London to Northumberland farmers' markets, you can browse for free and pick up some bargains along the way.

often entitled to discounts too, and under-5s are rarely charged.

Students and under-26s can benefit from an International Student ID Card or International Youth Travel Card, while teachers qualify for the **International Teacher Card**, all giving special air, rail and bus fares and discounts at museums, theatres and other attractions. All cost around £10/€14/US$22 from ISIC (ⓦwww.isiccard.com) or ISTC (ⓦwww.isic.org). Several other travel organizations and accommodation groups (including the youth hostel organization, IYHF) have their own cards providing various discounts. Specialist travel agencies in your home country (including STA worldwide) can provide more information and application forms.

Non-UK residents can buy a **Great British Heritage Pass** (4 days £28/US$54/€42; 7 days £39/US$75/€58; 15 days £52/US$99/€76; 30 days £70/US$133/€102), which gives free entry into 600 cultural and historic properties, including those operated by the National Trust and English Heritage. You can buy it (at equivalent local rates) from travel agents in your own country before you come, or at major tourist offices in the UK on arrival – see ⓦwww.visitbritain.com or ⓦwww.britishheritagepass.com for more details.

Crime and personal safety

Terrorist attacks on London may have changed the general perception of how safe England feels, with heightened **security** at airports, major train stations and other transport termini; however, it's still highly unlikely that you'll be at any risk as you travel around the country.

While England is far from crime-free, the vast majority of tourists experience few, if any, problems, at least in part because they are unlikely to visit the inner-city estates where crime flourishes. You can walk around

Emergencies

For Police, Fire Brigade, Ambulance, Mountain Rescue and Coastguard, dial ☎999 or 112.

most areas of London and the larger cities without fear of harassment or assault, though all the big conurbations have their edgy districts and it's always better to err on the side of caution late at night, when – for instance – badly lit streets and drunken groups should be avoided. If possible, always leave your passport and valuables in a hotel or hostel safe (carrying **ID** is not yet compulsory in the UK), and exercise the usual caution on the tube, trains and buses. After public transport shuts down for the night, take a licensed taxi to your destination. If you are robbed, you need to report it to the police, not least because your insurance company will require a **crime report number** – make sure you get one.

Other than asking for directions, most visitors rarely come into close contact with the British **police**, who as a rule are approachable and helpful – though they can get tetchy at football matches, demonstrations and in the evenings when pubs close and clubs open. Most wear chest guards and carry batons, though street officers do not normally carry guns.

Being caught in possession of a small quantity of "soft" **drugs** – mainly marijuana and cannabis – will probably result in a police caution. If, on the other hand, the police suspect you are dealing, you can expect to be held in custody and ultimately prosecuted. Finally, making "jokes" about bombs or **suspicious packages** in check-in lines or at security barriers is not advised, and can result in serious trouble, heavy delays and possibly prosecution.

Customs

Travellers coming into Britain directly **from most other EU countries** can bring almost as many cigarettes and as much wine or beer into the country as they can carry. The guidance levels are 10 litres of spirits, 90 litres of wine and 110 litres of beer – any more than this and you'll have to provide proof that it's for personal use only. The general guidelines for tobacco are 3200 cigarettes, 400 cigarillos, 200 cigars or 3kg of loose tobacco – note that the limits from some new EU member countries are lower than this.

If you're travelling to or from a non-EU country, you can still buy a limited amount of **duty-free goods**, but within the EU, this perk no longer exists. If you need any clarification on British import regulations, contact **HM Revenue and Customs** (☎0845/010 9000 or +44 292/050 1261 for international callers; ⓦcustoms.hmrc.gov.uk).

Electricity

In England the current is 240V AC. North American appliances will need a transformer and adaptor; those from Europe, Australia and New Zealand only need an adaptor.

Entry requirements

EU citizens have the right of free movement and residence throughout the UK, with just a passport or identity card. US, Canadian, South African, Australian and New Zealand citizens can stay in the country for up to six months without a visa, provided they have a valid passport. Most other nationalities require a **visa**, obtainable from the British consular office in the country of application. Incidentally, the Channel Islands and the Isle of Man have their own immigration laws and policies, but UK visa offices can issue visas for these islands. For current details about entry and visa requirements, consult the UK's Foreign and Commonwealth Office's visa website ⓦwww.ukvisas.gov.uk.

Citizens of EU countries who want to stay in the UK other than as a short-term visitor or tourist can apply for a residence permit. Non-EU citizens can apply to extend their visas, though this must be done before the current visa expires. In both cases, you should first contact the **Border and Immigration Agency**, (☎0870/606 7766, ⓦwww.ind.homeoffice.gov.uk); there are other offices in Liverpool and Birmingham. US, Canadian, South African, Australian and New Zealand citizens who want to stay longer than six months will need an **entry clearance certificate**, available from

British embassies and high commissions abroad

Australia British High Commission, Commonwealth Ave, Yarralumla, Canberra, ACT 2600 ☎02/6270 6666, ⊛www.britaus.net.

Canada British High Commission, 80 Elgin St, Ottawa, ON K1P 5K7 ☎613/237-1530, ⊛www.britaincanada.org.

Ireland British Embassy, 29 Merrion Rd, Ballsbridge, Dublin 4 ☎01/205 3700, ⊛www.britishembassy.ie.

New Zealand British High Commission, 44 Hill St, Thorndon, Wellington 6011 ☎04/924 2888, ⊛www.britain.org.nz.

South Africa British High Commission, 255 Hill St, Arcadia 0002, Pretoria ☎202/421-7500, ⊛www.britain.org.za.

USA British Embassy, 3100 Massachusetts Ave, Washington DC 20008 ☎202/588-7800, ⊛www.britainusa.com.

the British consular office at the embassy/high commission in their own country.

Gay and lesbian travellers

England offers one of the most diverse and accessible lesbian and gay scenes anywhere in Europe. Nearly every town of any size has some kind of organized gay life – from bars and clubs to community groups – with the major scenes found in London, Manchester and Brighton. Many gay and lesbian venues are listed in this book, and virtually every town will have a free local listings sheet. Other listings and news can be found in the fortnightly *Pink Paper* (⊛www.pinkpaper.com) and the glossy monthly *Gay Times* (⊛www.gaytimes.co.uk), available from many newsagents and alternative bookstores. The Gay Britain Network (⊛www.gaybritain.co.uk) has comprehensive information and links for events, restaurants, bars, clubs, and services across the UK, while ⊛www.gaytravel.co.uk lists over 400 gay and lesbian hotels and travel establishments from Brighton to Blackpool. The homosexual age of consent in England is 16.

Health

No vaccinations are required for entry into Britain. Citizens of all EU and EEA countries are entitled to free medical treatment within the UK's National Health Service (NHS), which includes the vast majority of hospitals

and doctors, on production of their **European Health Insurance Card** (EHIC) or, in extremis, their passport or national identity card. The same applies to those Commonwealth countries which have reciprocal healthcare arrangements with the UK – for example Australia and New Zealand. If you don't fall into either of these categories, you will be charged for all medical services, so health insurance is strongly advised.

Pharmacies and medical treatment

Pharmacists (known as **chemists** in England) can dispense only a limited range of drugs without a doctor's prescription. Most chemists are open standard shop hours, though in large towns some stay open until 10pm – local newspapers carry lists of late-opening "duty" pharmacies, and the information will also be posted on pharmacy doors. For generic, off-the-shelf pain-relief tablets, cold cures and the like, the local supermarket is usually the cheapest option.

Minor complaints and injuries can be dealt with at a **doctor's (GP's) surgery** – any tourist office or hotel should be able to point you in the right direction. For complaints that require immediate attention, you can turn up at the 24-hour casualty (A&E) department of the local **hospital** (detailed in our main city and town accounts). In an **emergency**, call an ambulance on ☎999 or 112.

NHS Direct (☎0845/4647, ⊛www.nhsdirect.nhs.uk) provides 24-hour medical advice by phone, and also runs an increasing number of walk-in centres (usually daily 7.30am–9pm) in the bigger towns and cities.

Insurance

Visitors are advised to take out an **insurance policy** before travelling to cover against theft, loss and illness or injury. A typical policy will provide cover for loss of baggage, tickets and – up to a certain limit – cash or travellers' cheques, as well as cancellation or curtailment of your journey. Most exclude so-called dangerous sports unless an extra premium is paid: in England this can mean most water sports, rock climbing and mountaineering, though hiking, kayaking and jeep safaris would probably be covered.

Medical coverage is strongly advised, though beforehand you should always ascertain whether benefits will be paid as treatment proceeds or only after you return home, and whether there is a 24-hour medical emergency number. When securing **baggage cover**, make sure that the per-article limit will cover your most valuable possession. If you need to make a claim, you should keep receipts for medicines and medical treatment, and in the event you have anything stolen you must obtain an official statement from the police – we've noted the contact details for police stations in all major towns and cities.

Internet access

There are **Internet cafés** in virtually every town and resort in England, mainly open daytime only, though you can find late-night and 24-hour access in London and other major centres. Charges vary wildly, but average around £2–3 an hour. An increasing number of hotels, guesthouses, hostels, cafés and tourist offices have Internet terminals for public use, and many have a **Wi-Fi** facility (branches of McDonald's and Starbucks, for example, are Wi-Fi enabled). Almost every **public library** in the country also offers Internet access, usually for free (though you may be limited to 30 minutes or so) – where there is a charge it's always almost cheaper than the alternative. You may have to wait for a free terminal, though slots can usually be booked.

Laundry

Coin-operated laundries (launderettes) are commonplace in every large city and town. Most operate extended opening hours – usually about twelve hours a day – and many offer "service washes", with your laundry washed and dried for you in just a few hours; this costs around £6 for a bagful of clothes. Using a hotel laundry service is always far more expensive.

Living in England

Provided you have fulfilled the visa requirements (see Entry requirements, p.59), there are numerous opportunities to extend your stay in England. **Student exchange** programmes, **work exchange** schemes and **volunteer programmes** organized in advance allow you to set up home in different parts of the country, usually with a back-up apparatus in place to provide accommodation and assist with the bureaucracy. Without this kind of support, finding a home and a job are the main challenges for those intending to stay on. For **accommodation**, seek out estate agencies

and rental agencies, and scour the small ads section of local newspapers as well as cards advertising rooms displayed in some newsagents and food shops. In towns and cities, job centres will try to match you up with suitable **employment**. Again, ads in newspapers and shop windows are best for casual work. Temporary jobs are most commonly available in hotels, pubs, bars and restaurants, especially in holiday destinations – though this kind of work is usually seasonal. Obviously, a good knowledge of English is a big advantage.

Study and work programmes

AFS Intercultural Programs US℡1-800/AFS-INFO, Canada ℡1-800/361-7248 or 514-288-3282, UK ℡0113/242 6136, Australia ℡1300/131 736 or ℡02/9215 0077, New Zealand ℡0800/600 300 or 04/494 6020, South Africa ℡11/447 2673, international enquiries ℡1-212-807-8686; Ⓦwww.afs.org. Study and volunteer programs in England, mainly for under-30s.
American Institute for Foreign Study US ℡1-866/906-2437, Ⓦwww.aifs.com. Intercultural exchange organization which arranges arts and business courses in London for a semester, summer or a whole year.
BTCV (British Trust for Conservation Volunteers) ℡01302/388 888, Ⓦwww.btcv.org.uk. One of the largest environmental charities in Britain, with a programme of working holidays (as a paying volunteer) in all English regions.
BUNAC US ℡1-800/GO-BUNAC, UK ℡020/7251 3472, Republic of Ireland ℡01/477 3027; Ⓦwww.bunac.org. Organizes working holidays for students in a range of destinations, including London, York and Manchester.
Council on International Educational Exchange (CIEE) US ℡1-800/40-STUDY or ℡1-207/533-7600, UK ℡020/8939 9057; Ⓦwww.ciee.org. Leading NGO offering study programmes in London.
Earthwatch Institute US ℡1-800/776-0188 or 978-461/0081, UK ℡01865/318 838, Australia ℡03/9682 6828; Ⓦwww.earthwatch.org. Scientific expedition project that includes environmental and archeological ventures in England, such as 15 days' excavating in the Yorkshire Dales.

Mail

The national **postal system** is operated by **Royal Mail** (℡0845/774 0740, Ⓦwww .royalmail.com), whose customer service line

and website details postal services and current postage costs, and can help you find individual post offices. Virtually all **post offices** are open Monday to Friday from 9am to 5.30pm, and on Saturdays from 9am to 12.30 or 1pm, with smaller branches closing on Wednesday afternoons too. In London and other major cities main offices stay open all day Saturday. In small and rural communities you'll find sub-post offices operating out of general stores, though post office facilities are only available during the hours above even if the shop itself is open for longer.

Stamps are on sale at post offices, though if you know which ones you want, you can avoid queues by buying them instead at newsagents and other stores advertising them. Postage rates depend on the size and weight of the envelope or package, and when you want it to arrive. For UK destinations, postcards and letters up to 100g in weight and of a size no greater than 240mm length, 165mm width and 5mm thickness can be sent either first-class (theoretically for next-day delivery), costing 34p, or second-class (for delivery within three working days), costing 24p. A post office will have a full list of prices for letters exceeding these dimensions. For non-UK destinations, postcards and letters up to 20g cost 48p to Europe, those sent outside Europe cost 54p up to 10g, or 78p 10–20g. Above 20g, rates rise incrementally. Airmail to European destinations should arrive within three working days, and outside Europe countries within five. Slower "surface mail" and express delivery services are also available.

Maps

For an overview of the whole of England on one (double-sided) map, Collins' 1:550,000 and Ordnance Survey's 1:625,000 maps are probably the best; both include some city plans. Ordnance Survey (OS; Ⓦwww .ordnancesurvey.co.uk) and Michelin also produce useful regional maps at a scale of 1:250,000 and 1:400,000 respectively, while Philips, in conjunction with OS, produce detailed county maps at a scale of 1:18,000. Otherwise, for general route-finding the most useful resources are the road atlases produced by AA, RAC, Geographers' A–Z and Collins, among others, at a scale of around 1:250,000.

The **National Cycle Network** of cross-country routes along country lanes and traffic-free paths is covered by a series of excellent waterproof maps (1:100,000) published by Sustrans (@www.sustrans.org .uk). For **hikers**, the large-scale topographic maps produced by OS are renowned for their accuracy and clarity, covering England on just over 100 sheets in their Landranger series at 1:50,000, or just under 200 in the more detailed Explorer series at 1:25,000.

Finally, **Rough Guides' London map** (1:5000/25,000), on waterproof, tearproof paper, and with full city listings, is invaluable for exploring the capital.

Most of these maps are available from large bookshops or **specialist map and travel stores** in your own country. Alternatively, try a general online bookstore or a world map specialist like @www.randmcnally.com. **In the UK** main bookshops and tourist offices usually stock a good range of local/regional maps, while visitors to London, Bristol or Manchester should call in at **Stanfords** (@www.stanfords.co.uk), England's premier map and travel specialist.

Online maps include @www.multimap .com, which has town plans and area maps with scales up to 1:3600, plus address search, traffic info and more, and @www .visitmap.com, with clickable A–Z maps covering cities and large and small towns.

Money

England's currency is the **pound sterling** (£), divided into 100 pence (p). Coins come in denominations of 1p, 2p, 5p, 10p, 20p, 50p and £1 and £2. Notes are in denominations of £5, £10, £20 and £50. Very occasionally you may receive Scottish or Northern Irish banknotes: they're legal tender throughout Britain, though some traders may be unwilling to accept them.

Every sizeable town and village has a branch of at least one of the main high-street **banks**: Barclays, Halifax, HSBC, Lloyds-TSB and NatWest. The easiest way to get hold of cash is to use your **debit card** in an **ATM**; there's usually a daily withdrawal limit of £250. You'll find **ATMs** outside banks, at all major points of arrival and motorway service areas, at most large supermarkets, some petrol stations and even in some pubs, rural

post offices and village shops (though a charge may be levied on cash withdrawals at small, stand-alone ATMs). Depending on your bank and your debit card, you may also be able to ask for "cash back" when you shop at supermarkets.

Some overseas travellers still prefer sterling **traveller's cheques**, at least as a back-up. The most commonly accepted are issued by American Express, followed by Visa. American Express will not charge commission if you exchange cheques at their own offices, nor will some banks (such as Natwest) – otherwise you will be charged 2–3 percent commission. Note that in the UK you are unlikely to be able to use your traveller's cheques as cash – you'll always have to cash them first, making them an unreliable source of funds in more remote areas.

Outside banking hours, you can change cheques or cash at **post offices** (locations are detailed in the Guide) and **bureaux de change** – the latter tend to be open longer hours and are found in most city centres, and at major airports and train stations. Avoid changing cash or cheques in hotels, where the rates are normally poor.

Finally, **credit cards** can be used widely either in ATMs or over the counter. MasterCard and Visa are accepted in most hotels, shops and restaurants in England, American Express and Diners Club less so. Plastic is less useful in rural areas, and smaller establishments all over the country, such as B&Bs, will often accept cash only. Remember that cash advances from ATMs using your credit card are treated as loans, with interest accruing daily from the date of withdrawal. You can avoid interest fees by depositing money into your credit card account before leaving (though some companies will not allow this).

At the time of writing, £1 was equivalent to €1.40 and US$2.05; €1 was 72p, and US$1 was 49p.

Opening hours and public holidays

General **business hours** for most businesses, shops and offices are Monday to Saturday 9am to 5.30 or 6pm, although the **supermarket** chains tend to stay open until 8 or 9pm from Monday to Saturday, with

Public holidays

England's public holidays are:
January 1
Good Friday
Easter Monday
First Monday in May
Last Monday in May
Last Monday in August
December 25
December 26
Note that if January 1, December 25 or December 26 falls on a Saturday or Sunday, the next weekday becomes a public holiday.

larger ones staying open round the clock. Many major stores and supermarkets now **open on Sundays**, too, usually from 11am or noon to 4pm, though some provincial towns still retain an **early-closing day** (usually Wednesday) when most shops close at 1pm. **Banks** are usually open Monday to Friday 9am–4pm, with some branches also open Saturday mornings. You can usually get fuel any time of the day or night in larger towns and cities (though note that not all motorway **service stations** open for 24 hours). Full opening hours for specific museums, galleries and other tourist attractions are given in the Guide – where these are seasonal (summer hours are usually Easter–Oct, winter Nov–Easter), they are shown in the format 9/10am–5/6pm. For the usual opening hours of cafés, restaurants and pubs, see pp.43, 44 and 45.

Banks, businesses and most shops close on **public holidays**, though large supermarkets, small corner shops and many tourist attractions don't. However, nearly all museums, galleries and other attractions are closed on Christmas Day and New Year's Day, with many also closed on Boxing Day (Dec 26). Confusingly, several of England's public holidays are usually referred to as **bank holidays** (though it's not just the banks who have a day off).

Phones

Public **pay phones** are plentiful and take coins (with a minimum charge of 40p), while most also accept phone and credit cards.

You can make direct-dial **international phone calls** from any telephone box, though it's usually cheaper to buy an **international phonecard**, available from many newsagents in denominations of £5, £10 and upwards. You dial the company's local access number, key in the pin number on the card and then dial your number. Your phone company back home may also provide a **telephone charge card**, with which calls can be charged to your own telephone account. Bear in mind, however, that rates aren't necessarily cheaper than making an ordinary call.

Every English phone number has a prefix which, if beginning ☎01 or 02 represents an **area code**, and can (but does not have to) be omitted when you are dialling a local number. However, some prefixes relate to the cost of calls rather than the location of the subscriber, including: ☎0800 and ☎0808 prefixes, which are free of charge to the caller; ☎0845 numbers, which are charged at local rates; and ☎0870 numbers, where callers are charged at national rates irrespective of where they call from. Beware of **premium-rate numbers**, which are common for pre-recorded information services (including some tourist authorities), and usually have the prefix ☎0906 or 0909; these are charged at anything up to £1.50 a minute.

For domestic and international **directory enquiries**, there are numerous competing information lines, all of them expensive. BT's domestic service, on ☎118 500, is as good as any (and it's free online at ⌨www.bt.com); its international directory assistance number is ☎118 505. Or you can look business and service numbers up for free in public libraries or on the very useful ⌨www.yell.com.

In England, **mobile phone** access is routine in all the major cities and in most of the countryside. There are occasional blind spots, and coverage can be patchy in rural and hill areas, but generally you should have few problems.

If you want to use your own mobile phone in England, check with your phone provider before you set out – some networks need to have international roaming activated, others do it automatically. Phones bought for use in the US, however, rarely work outside the States. If you do bring your own phone,

Calling home from abroad

Note that the initial zero is omitted from the area code when dialling the countries listed here from abroad.

Australia international access code + 61 + city code.
New Zealand international access code + 64 + city code.
US and Canada international access code + 1 + area code.
Republic of Ireland international access code + 353 + city code.
South Africa international access code + 27 + city code.

note that you are likely to be charged extra for incoming calls when abroad as the people calling you will be paying the usual domestic rate. It might be simplest, certainly if you're staying in England for any length of time, to **buy a mobile** in the UK – basic non-contract "pay as you go" models start at around £50, usually including a few pounds' worth of free calls.

In the UK, dial ☎100 for the **operator**, ☎155 for the international operator. To call **England from abroad**, dial your international access code + ☎44 + area code minus initial zero + number.

Time

Greenwich Mean Time (GMT) is used from late October to late March, when the clocks go forward an hour for British Summer Time (BST). GMT is five hours ahead of the US Eastern Standard Time and ten hours behind Australian Eastern Standard Time.

Tourist information

VisitBritain – the UK tourism agency – has offices worldwide, while regional tourism boards within England concentrate on particular areas. The official national websites, ⓦwww.visitbritain.com and ⓦwww.enjoyengland.com, are very useful, covering everything from local accommodation to festival dates, and regional and other specialist websites dedicated to England are also worth consulting.

Tourist offices (also called Tourist Information Centres, or "TICs" for short) exist in virtually every English town. They tend to follow standard shop hours (Mon–Sat 9am–5.30pm), though sometimes also open on Sundays, with hours curtailed during the winter season (Nov–Easter).

Staff at tourist offices will nearly always be able to book accommodation, reserve space on guided tours, and sell guidebooks, maps and walk leaflets. They can also provide lists of local cafés, restaurants and pubs, and though they aren't supposed to recommend particular places you'll often be able to get a feel for the best local places to eat. An increasing number of offices have Internet access for visitors, but rarely have the space to look after baggage while you scoot around town.

Areas designated as **national parks** usually have their own dedicated information centres, which offer similar services to TICs but can also provide expert guidance on local walks and outdoor pursuits.

Regional tourism organizations

East of England Tourism ☎01284/727470, ⓦwww.visiteastofengland.com. Bedfordshire, Cambridgeshire, Hertfordshire, Essex, Norfolk and Suffolk.

East Midlands Tourism ⓦwww.enjoyeastmidlands.com. Derbyshire, Lincolnshire, Nottinghamshire, Leicestershire, Rutland and Northamptonshire.

England's Northwest ⓦwww.visitenglandsnorthwest.com. Cumbria and the Lake District, Cheshire, Lancashire, Manchester, Liverpool and Merseyside.

Heart of England Tourism ⓦwww.visittheheart.co.uk. Birmingham, Worcestershire, Herefordshire, Shropshire, Staffordshire and Warwickshire.

North East England Tourism ⓦwww.visitnortheastengland.com. County Durham, Northumberland, Tees Valley, and Tyne and Wear.

South West Tourism ☎0870/442 0880, ⓦwww.visitsouthwest.co.uk. Bath, Bristol, Devon, Cornwall, Dorset, Gloucestershire and the Cotswolds, Somerset and Wiltshire.

Tourism South East ⓦwww
.visitsoutheastengland.com. Sussex, Kent, Surrey,
Berkshire, Hampshire, Oxfordshire, Buckinghamshire
and the Isle of Wight.
Visit London ⓦwww.visitlondon.com.
Yorkshire Tourist Board ⓦwww.yorkshire.com.

Travellers with disabilities

In many ways, the UK is ahead of the field in
terms of facilities for travellers with disabilities. All new public buildings – including
museums, galleries and cinemas – are
obliged to provide wheelchair access, train
stations and airports are generally fully
accessible, many buses have easy-access
boarding ramps, while dropped kerbs and
signalled crossings are the rule in every city
and town. The number of accessible hotels
and restaurants is also growing, and
reserved parking bays are available almost
everywhere, from shopping malls to
museums.

If you have specific requirements, it's
always best to talk first to your travel agent,
chosen hotel or tour operator.

Useful organizations

abletogo ⓦwww.abletogo.com. Accommodation in
England for disabled and elderly travellers, rated for
accessibility.
Access-Able ⓦwww.access-able.com. US-based
resource for travellers with disabilities, with links to UK
operators and organizations.
All Go Here ⓦwww.allgohere.com. Information on
airline services, accommodation and other
hospitality-related matters for disabled travellers
throughout the UK.

Door-to-Door ⓦwww.dptac.gov.uk/door-to-door.
Transport and travel website offering information
and advice on UK transport for those with a mobility
problem.
Holiday Care ⓣ0845/124 9971, ⓦwww
.holidaycare.org.uk. Holiday and travel information
service for disabled and older travellers, offering
advice on accessible accommodation, attractions and
activity holidays in the UK.
**RADAR (Royal Association for Disability and
Rehabilitation)** ⓦwww.radar.org.uk. National
network of disability organizations whose website has
links to holiday and travel services in the UK. Also
publish the excellent *Holidays in Britain and Ireland*.

Travelling with children

On the whole, facilities in England for travellers
with children are no worse than in most other
European countries. **Baby-changing**
apparatus is usually available in shopping
centres and train stations, while pharmacies
and supermarkets stock every conceivable
product (shops in rural areas will have less
choice). Children aren't allowed in certain
licensed (alcohol-serving) premises, though
this doesn't apply to restaurants, and many
pubs and inns have family rooms or beer
gardens where children are welcome. Some
B&Bs and hotels won't accept children under
a certain age (usually 12) – we've pointed out
places in the Guide where this applies. Under-
5s generally travel free on public transport and
get in free to attractions; 5–16-year-olds are
usually entitled to concessionary rates of up to
half the adult rate/fare.

The **websites** ⓦwww.travellingwithchildren
.co.uk and ⓦwww.babygoes2.com offer
advice and services.

Guide

Guide

London

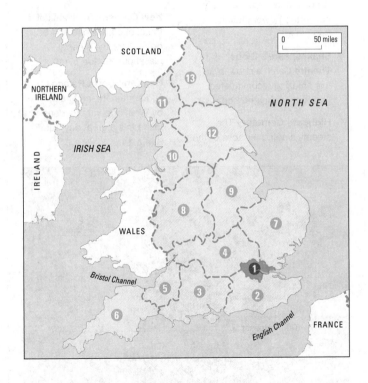

CHAPTER 1 # Highlights

* **British Museum** Quite simply one of the world's greatest museums. See p.104

* **London Eye** The universally loved observation wheel is now a key London landmark. See p.120

* **Tate Modern** The city's superb modern-art museum is housed in a spectacularly converted power station. See p.121

* **Shakespeare's Globe Theatre** Catch a show in this amazing reconstructed Elizabethan theatre. See p.122

* **Highgate Cemetery** The steeply sloping terraces of the West Cemetery's overgrown graves are the last word in Victorian Gothic gloom. See p.133

* **Greenwich** Picturesque riverside spot, boasting a weekend market, the National Maritime Museum and old Royal Observatory. See p.135

* **Kew Gardens** Stroll amidst the exotic trees and shrubs, or head for the steamy glasshouses. See p.140

* **Hampton Court Palace** Tudor interiors, architecture by Wren and vast gardens make this a great day out. See p.141

▲ British Museum

London

What strikes visitors more than anything about **LONDON** is the sheer size of the place. Stretching for more than thirty miles east to west, on either side of the River Thames, and with an ethnically diverse population of over seven million, it's one of the largest cities in Europe. Londoners tend to cope with all this by compartmentalizing the city, identifying with the neighbourhoods in which they work or live, and just making occasional forays into the "centre of town" or "up West", to the West End, London's shopping and entertainment heartland.

Despite Scottish, Welsh and Northern Irish devolution, London still dominates the national horizon, too: this is where the country's news and money are made, it's where the central government resides and, as far as its inhabitants are concerned, provincial life begins beyond the circuit of the city's orbital motorway. Londoners' sense of superiority causes enormous resentment in the regions, yet it's undeniable that the capital has a unique aura of excitement and success – in most walks of British life, if you want to get on, you've got to do it in London.

And it's looking better than it has done for some time, thanks to the Lottery- and millennium-driven investment that has seen virtually all London's world-class **museums, galleries** and **institutions** reinvented, from the Royal Opera House to the British Museum. The city now boasts the world's largest modern art gallery in Tate Modern, the tallest observation wheel in the London Eye, and two fantastic pedestrian bridges that have helped transform the south bank of the Thames into a magnet for visitors and Londoners alike. London's running more smoothly too, thanks to the efforts of Ken Livingstone, mayor since 2000, who's determined to try and solve one of the city's biggest problems – transport. He was also instrumental in helping London win the right to stage the Olympics in 2012, something that will see a large slice of the city's East End transformed over the next few years.

In the meantime, London's **traditional sights** – Big Ben, Westminster Abbey, Buckingham Palace, St Paul's Cathedral and the Tower of London – continue to draw in millions of tourists every year. Monuments from the capital's more glorious past are everywhere to be seen, from medieval banqueting halls and the great churches of Christopher Wren to the eclectic Victorian architecture of the triumphalist British Empire. There is also much enjoyment to be had from the city's quiet Georgian squares, the narrow alleyways of the City of London, the riverside walks, and the quirks of what is still identifiably a collection of villages. Even London's heavy traffic is offset by surprisingly large **expanses of greenery**: Hyde Park, Green Park

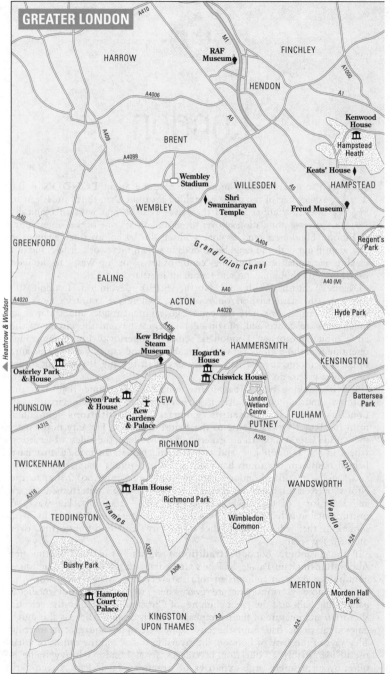

GREATER LONDON

Luton

A410

A4006

HARROW

RAF
Museum

FINCHLEY

HENDON

A1000

A1

M1

A5

BRENT

A4088

Kenwood
House

Hampstead
Heath

Keats' House

HAMPSTEAD

Wembley
Stadium

WILLESDEN

A5

WEMBLEY

Shri
Swaminarayan
Temple

Freud Museum

A409

A40

GREENFORD

Grand Union Canal

A404

Regent's
Park

EALING

A40

A40 (M)

ACTON

A4020

Hyde Park

A4020

Heathrow & Windsor

A4020

M4

Kew Bridge
Steam
Museum

A406

Hogarth's
House

HAMMERSMITH

KENSINGTON

Osterley Park
& House

Chiswick House

London
Wetland
Centre

Battersea
Park

Syon Park
& House

KEW

HOUNSLOW

A315

Kew
Gardens
& Palace

FULHAM

PUTNEY

A205

A214

RICHMOND

TWICKENHAM

Ham House

Richmond Park

WANDSWORTH

Wandle

Thames

A316

Wimbledon
Common

TEDDINGTON

A307

A24

Bushy Park

A308

MERTON

Morden Hall
Park

Hampton
Court
Palace

KINGSTON
UPON THAMES

A3

A24

74

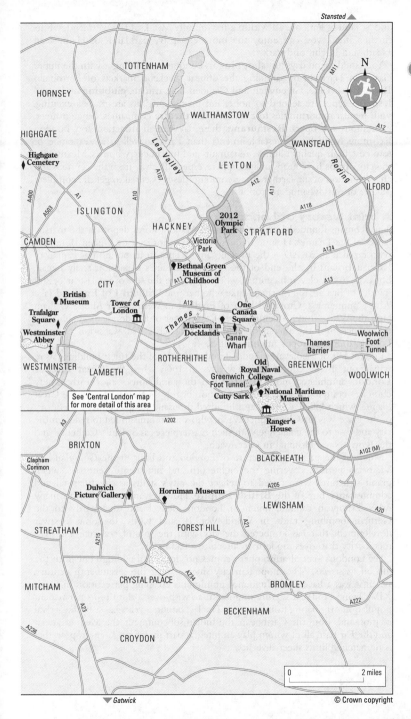

Stansted ▲

N

Gatwick ▼

© Crown copyright

0   2 miles

See 'Central London' map for more detail of this area

and St James's Park are all within a few minutes' walk of the West End, while, further afield, you can enjoy the more expansive parklands of Hampstead Heath and Richmond Park.

You could spend days just **shopping** in London too, mixing it with the upper classes in Harrods, or sampling the offbeat weekend markets of Portobello Road, Brick Lane, Greenwich and Camden. The **music**, **clubbing** and **gay/lesbian** scenes are second to none, and mainstream arts are no less exciting, with regular opportunities to catch brilliant **theatre** companies, dance troupes, exhibitions and opera. **Restaurants** these days are an attraction, too. London has more Michelin-star establishments than Paris as well as a vast range of low-cost, high-quality Chinese restaurants and Indian curry houses. Meanwhile, the city's **pubs** have heaps of atmosphere, especially away from the centre – and an exploration of the farther-flung communities is essential to get the complete picture of this dynamic metropolis.

A brief history of London

The Romans founded **Londinium** in 43 AD as a stores depot on the marshy banks of the Thames. Despite frequent attacks – not least by Queen Boudicca, who razed it in 61 AD – the port became secure in its position as capital of Roman Britain by the end of the century. London's expansion really began, however, in the eleventh century, when it became the seat of the last successful invader of Britain, the Norman duke who became **William I of England** (aka "the Conqueror"). Crowned king of England in Westminster Abbey, William built the White Tower – centrepiece of the Tower of London – to establish his dominance over the merchant population, the class that was soon to make London one of Europe's mightiest cities.

Little is left of medieval or Tudor London. Many of the finest buildings were wiped out in the course of a few days in 1666 when the **Great Fire of London** annihilated more than thirteen thousand houses and nearly ninety churches, completing a cycle of destruction begun the year before by the Great Plague, which killed as many as a hundred thousand people. Chief beneficiary of the blaze was Sir Christopher Wren, who was commissioned to redesign the city and rose to the challenge with such masterpieces as St Paul's Cathedral and the Royal Naval Hospital in Greenwich.

Much of the public architecture of London was built in the Georgian and Victorian periods covering the eighteenth and nineteenth centuries, when grand structures were raised to reflect the city's status as the financial and administrative hub of the **British Empire**. However, in comparison to many other European capitals, much of London looks bland, due partly to the German bombing raids in World War II, and partly to some postwar development that has lumbered the city with the sort of concrete-and-glass mediocrity that gives modern architecture a bad name.

Yet London's special atmosphere comes not from its buildings, but from the life on its streets. A cosmopolitan city since at least the seventeenth century, when it was a haven for Huguenot immigrants escaping persecution in Louis XIV's France, today it is truly multicultural, with over a third of its permanent population originating from overseas. The last hundred years has seen the arrival of thousands from the Caribbean, the Indian subcontinent, the Mediterranean and the Far East, all of whom play an integral part in defining a metropolis that is unmatched in its sheer diversity.

Orientation, arrival and information

Stretching for more than thirty miles at its broadest point, **London** is a big place. The majority of its sights are situated to the north of the **River Thames**, which loops through the city from west to east. However, there is no single predominant focus of interest, since the city has grown not through centralized planning but by a process of agglomeration – villages and urban developments that once surrounded the core are now lost within the amorphous mass of Greater London.

One of the few areas that is manageable on foot is **Westminster** and **Whitehall**, the city's royal, political and ecclesiastical power base for centuries, where you'll find some of London's most famous landmarks: Downing Street, Big Ben, the Houses of Parliament, Westminster Abbey and, across St James's Park, Buckingham Palace. The grand streets and squares of **St James's**, **Mayfair** and **Marylebone**, to the north of Westminster, have been the playground of the rich since the Restoration, and now contain the city's busiest shopping zones.

East of Piccadilly Circus, **Soho** and **Covent Garden** are also easy to walk around and form the heart of the West End entertainment district, containing the largest concentration of theatres, cinemas, clubs, flashy shops, cafés and restaurants. To the north lie the university quarter of **Bloomsbury**, home to the ever-popular British Museum, and the secluded quadrangles of **Holborn's** Inns of Court, London's legal heartland.

The City – the City of London, to give it its full title – is both the most ancient and the most modern part of London. Settled since Roman times, it's now one of the world's great financial centres, yet retains its share of historic sights, notably the **Tower of London** and a fine cache of Wren churches that includes **St Paul's Cathedral**. Despite creeping gentrification, the **East End**, to the east of the City, is not conventional tourist territory, but to ignore it entirely is to miss out a crucial element of contemporary London. **Docklands** is a mixture of abandoned warehouses now converted into swanky flats and brand new apartment blocks of dubious architectural merit – at its centre is the **Canary Wharf** tower, the country's tallest building, epitomizing the pretensions of the Docklands dream.

A small slice of central London south of the Thames is definitely worth exploring. First off, there's the **South Bank Centre**, London's little-loved concrete culture bunker, which is enjoying a new lease of life thanks to inspired artistic direction and its proximity to the **London Eye**, the world's biggest observation wheel. Further east along the river in Bankside is **Tate Modern**, one of the world's greatest modern art museums, linked to the City by the funky pedestrian-only Millennium Bridge.

The largest segment of greenery in central London is Hyde Park, which separates wealthy **Kensington and Chelsea** from the West End. The **museums** of South Kensington – the Victoria and Albert Museum, the Science Museum and the Natural History Museum – are a must; and if you have designer label shopping on your agenda, you'll want to check out the hive of plush stores in the vicinity of Harrods.

The capital's most hectic weekend market takes place around **Camden Lock** in North London. Further out, in the literary suburbs of Hampstead and Highgate, there are unbeatable views across the city from half-wild **Hampstead Heath**, the favourite parkland of thousands of Londoners. The glory of South London is **Greenwich**, with its nautical associations, royal park and observatory. Finally, there are plenty of rewarding day-trips along the Thames from **Chiswick** to **Windsor**, most notably to Hampton Court Palace and Windsor Castle.

Arrival

Flying into London, you'll arrive at one of the capital's five **international airports**: Heathrow, Gatwick, Stansted, Luton or City Airport, all of which are less than an hour from the city centre.

Heathrow (℡0870/000 0123, ⓦwww.baa.co.uk), fifteen miles west of the centre, has five terminals and three train/tube stations: one for terminals 1, 2 and 3, and separate ones for terminals 4 and 5. The high-speed **Heathrow Express** (ⓦwww.heathrowexpress.com) trains travel non-stop to Paddington Station (every 15min; 15–20min) for £28 return (£1 less if you book online, £2 more if you buy your ticket on board). A much cheaper alternative is to take the **Piccadilly Underground line** into central London (every 5–9min; 50min) for £4 one-way. If you plan to make several sightseeing journeys on your arrival day, buy a Travelcard at the station (see opposite). National Express run **bus services** (ⓦwww.nationalexpress.com) from Heathrow direct to Victoria Coach Station (daily every 20–30min 5am–9.30pm; 40min–1hr), which cost £4 single, £8 return. After midnight, you can take **night bus** #N9 (every 30min; 1hr) from Heathrow to Trafalgar Square for a bargain fare of £2.

Gatwick (℡0870/000 2468, ⓦwww.baa.co.uk) is around thirty miles south of London: the non-stop **Gatwick Express** (ⓦwww.gatwickexpress.com) trains run between the airport's South Terminal and Victoria Station (every 15min; 30min) for £27 return. Other train options include the **Southern** services to Victoria (every 15–20min; 40min) for £9 one-way, or **Thameslink** to King's Cross (every 15–30min; 50min) for around £10 one-way.

Stansted (℡0870/000 0303, ⓦwww.baa.co.uk) lies roughly 35 miles northeast of the capital, and is served by the **Stansted Express** (ⓦwww.stanstedexpress .co.uk) to Liverpool Street (every 15–30min; 45min), which costs £25.50 return. National Express **Airbus** #6 runs 24 hours a day to Victoria Coach Station (every 30min; 1hr 30min), and costs £10 single, £15 return. **Terravision** (ⓦwww .lowcostcoach.com) also run coaches to Victoria and to Liverpool St, with services every thirty minutes from 7am to 1am (£8 single, £14 return).

Luton Airport (℡01582/405100, ⓦwww.london-luton.com) is roughly thirty miles north of the city centre, and mostly handles charter flights. A **free shuttle bus** takes five minutes to transport passengers to Luton Airport Parkway station, connected by train (every 15min; 30–40min) to St Pancras, King's Cross and other stations in central London; tickets cost £10 single. Alternatively, **Green Line** bus #757 and **Terravision** run from Luton to Victoria Station (every 30min; 1hr 15min), costing around £10 single. From late spring to early autumn, **Easybus** (ⓦwww.easybus.co.uk) also runs coach services every 45 minutes to near Baker Street tube for a bargain fare of just £8 one-way, or as little as £2 if you book in advance online.

City Airport (℡020/7646 0000, ⓦwww.londoncityairport.com), London's smallest, is used primarily by business folk and is situated in Docklands, eight miles east of central London. The **Docklands Light Railway** (DLR) will take you straight to Bank in the City (20min), where you can change to the tube; tickets cost around £4.

Eurostar trains arrive at **St Pancras International** (ⓦwww.stpancras.com), north of the centre. Arriving by train (℡08457/484950, ⓦwww.nationalrail .co.uk) from elsewhere in Britain, you'll come into one of London's numerous main-line stations, all of which have adjacent Underground stations linking into the city centre's tube network. Coming into London **by coach** (℡0870/580 8080, ⓦwww.nationalexpress.com), you're most likely to arrive at **Victoria Coach Station**, a couple of hundred yards south down Buckingham Palace Road from the train and Underground stations of the same name.

Information

The main tourist office in London is the **London Visitor Centre**, near Piccadilly Circus at 1 Regent St (Mon 9.30am–6.30pm, Tues–Fri 9am–6.30pm, Sat & Sun 10am–4pm; June–Sept same times except Sat 9am–5pm; ⓦwww .visitbritain.com); there's also a tiny information window in the tickets kiosk on Leicester Square (Mon–Fri 8am–11pm, Sat & Sun 11am–6pm; ⓦwww .visitlondon.com). Individual boroughs also run tourist offices, the most central one being on the south side of St Paul's Cathedral (May–Sept daily 9.30am–5pm; Oct–April Mon–Fri 9.30am–5pm; ☏020/7332 1456, ⓦwww.cityoflondon.gov.uk).

London: The Rough Guide Map is a comprehensive full-colour, waterproof and non-tearable **map** detailing restaurants, bars, shops and visitor attractions. If you want to find your way around every nook and cranny of the city you'll need to invest in either an *A–Z Atlas* or a *Nicholson Streetfinder*, both of which have a street index covering every street in the capital. You can get them at most bookshops and newsagents for less than £5.

The only comprehensive and critical weekly **listings** magazine is *Time Out*, which comes out every Tuesday afternoon. In it you'll find details of all the latest exhibitions, shows, films, music, sport, guided walks and events in and around the capital.

City transport

London's transport network is among the most complex and expensive in the world. **Transport for London** (TfL) provides excellent free maps and details of bus and tube services from its **travel information** offices: the main one is at Piccadilly Circus tube station (Mon–Sat 7.15am–9pm, Sun 8.15am–8pm), and there are other desks at Heathrow and various tube and train stations. There's also a 24-hour phone line for information on all bus and tube services ☏020/7222 1234 and a website ⓦwww.tfl.gov.uk. One word of warning – avoid travelling during the **rush hour** (Mon–Fri 8–9.30am & 5–7pm), when tubes become unbearably crowded (and the lack of air conditioning doesn't help), and some buses get so full they literally won't let you on.

Except for very short journeys, the fastest way of moving around the city is by **Underground** or tube, as it's known to all Londoners. The twelve different

Travelcards

To get the best value out of the transport system, buy a **Travelcard**. Available from machines and booths at all tube and train stations, and at some newsagents (look for the sign), these are valid for the bus, tube, Docklands Light Railway, south London's Tramlink and suburban rail networks. **Day Travelcards** come in two varieties – Off-Peak, which are valid after 9.30am on weekdays and all day during the weekend, and Peak. A Day Travelcard (Off-Peak), costs £5.10 for the central zones 1 and 2, rising to £6.70 for zones 1–6 (including Heathrow); the Day Travelcard (Peak) starts at £6.60 for zones 1 and 2. A **3-Day Travelcard** costs £16.40 for zones 1 and 2, but is obviously only worth it if you need to travel during peak hours; **Weekly Travelcards** are much more economical, beginning at £23.20 for zones 1 and 2. **Children** under 5 travel free at all times, while under 11s travel free on all forms of transport off-peak; under 14s get free travel on buses. All-zone Off-Peak Day Travelcards for under 16s costs £2, or if they're travelling with an adult, just £1.

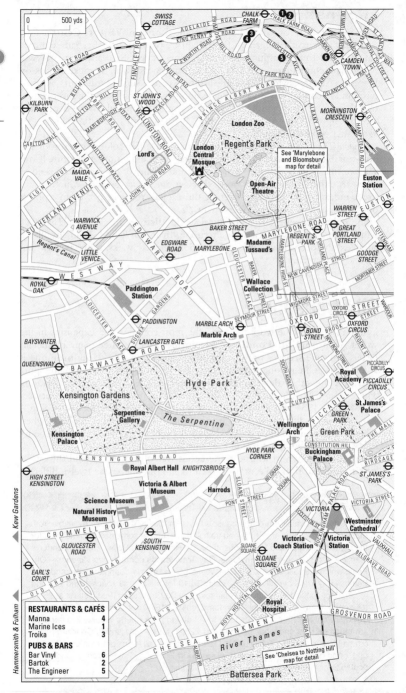

RESTAURANTS & CAFÉS	
Manna	4
Marine Ices	1
Troika	3
PUBS & BARS	
Bar Vinyl	6
Bartok	2
The Engineer	5

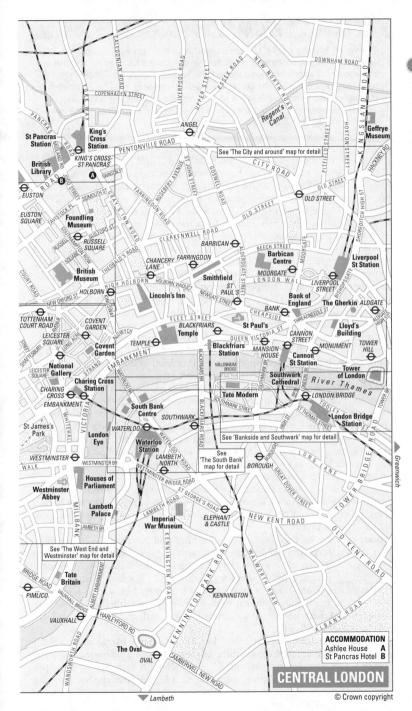

ACCOMMODATION
Ashlee House   **A**
St Pancras Hotel   **B**

CENTRAL LONDON

© Crown copyright

▼ Lambeth

Congestion charge

All vehicles entering central London on weekdays between 7am and 6.30pm are liable to a **congestion charge** of £8 per vehicle. Drivers can pay for the charge online, over the phone or at garages and shops, and must do so before 10pm the same day or incur a surcharge. The congestion-charging zone is bounded by Marylebone and Euston roads in the north, Commercial Street and Tower Bridge in the east, Kennington Lane and the river in the south, and Earl's Court Road in the west. For the latest visit ⊛www.cclondon.com.

tube lines cross much of the metropolis, although London south of the river is not very well covered. Each line has its own colour and name – all you need to know is which direction you're travelling in: northbound, eastbound, southbound or westbound. Services operate from around 5.30am until 12.30am Monday to Saturday, and from 7.30am until 11.30pm on Sundays; you rarely have to wait more than five minutes for a train from central stations. **Tickets** must be bought in advance; if you're caught without a valid ticket, you'll be charged an on-the-spot Penalty Fare of £20. A one-way journey in the central zone costs an unbelievable £4, so if you're intending to travel about a bit, a Travelcard is a much better bet (see box, p.79). Since the introduction of the **Oyster card**, London's transport smartcard, most Londoners don't bother with paper tickets any more. However, they are only really worth it if you are staying in London longer than a week; for more details see the TfL website.

London's famous red **double-decker buses** are fun to ride on, but tend to get stuck in traffic jams, which prevent them running to a regular timetable. In central London, and on all the extra-long "bendy buses", you must **have a valid ticket before boarding**, whether a Travelcard or one from the machines at the bus stop. Tickets for all bus journeys cost a flat fare of £2. Another option is a **One-Day Bus Pass**, which costs £3.50 for adults and can be used on all buses anytime anywhere in London. Some buses run a 24-hour service, but most run between about 5am and midnight, with a network of **night buses** (prefixed with the letter "N") operating outside this period. Night bus routes radiate out from Trafalgar Square at approximately twenty to thirty-minute intervals, more frequently on some routes and on Friday and Saturday nights. All stops are treated as request stops, so you must signal to get the bus to stop, and press the bell in order to get off.

Large areas of London's suburbs are best reached by the **suburban train** network (Travelcards valid). Wherever a sight can only be reached by overground train, we've indicated the nearest train station and the central terminus from which you can depart.

Boat services on the Thames are much improved, but they still do not form part of an integrated public transport system. As a result fares are quite expensive, with Travelcards currently only giving the holders a 33 percent discount on tickets. Typical **fares** are £6 one-way, £7 return Westminster to the Tower or £7 one-way, £9 return from Westminster to Greenwich – £9.50 will buy you an unlimited hop-on, hop-off ticket. **Timetables** and services are complex, and there are numerous companies and small charter operators – for a full list check with TfL.

Compared to many capital cities, London's metered **black cabs** are an expensive option unless there are three or more of you – a ride from Euston to Victoria, for example, costs around £12–15 (Mon–Fri 6am–8pm). After 8pm on weekdays and all day during the weekend, a higher tariff applies, and after

10pm, a much higher one. A yellow light over the windscreen tells you if the cab is available – just stick your arm out to hail it. To order a black cab in advance, phone ☎0871/871 8710, and be prepared to pay an extra £2.

Minicabs look just like regular cars and are considerably cheaper than black cabs, but the best way to pick a company is to take the advice of the place you're at. If you want to be certain of a woman driver, call Ladycabs (☎020/7272 3300), or if you want a gay/lesbian-friendly driver, call Liberty Cars (☎020/7734 1313).

Last, and definitely least, there are usually plenty of **bicycle taxis** available for hire in the West End. The oldest and biggest of the bunch are Bugbugs (☎020/7620 0500, ⓦwww.bugbugs.com), who have over fifty rickshaws operating Monday to Saturday from 7pm until the early hours of the morning. The rickshaws take up to three passengers and fares are negotiable, though they should work out at around £5 per person per mile.

Accommodation

There's no getting away from the fact that **accommodation** in London is expensive. Compared with most European cities, you pay over the odds in every category. The city's hostels are among the most costly in the world, while venerable institutions such as the *Ritz*, the *Dorchester* and the *Savoy* (closed until mid-2009) charge guests the very top international prices – from £300 per luxurious night. For a decent **hotel** room, you shouldn't expect much change out of £100 a night. Even the most basic **B&Bs** struggle to bring their tariffs down to less than £45 for a double with shared facilities, and you're more likely to find yourself paying £60 or more. A dorm bed in an official YHA **hostel** will cost you £20 or more, while an independent hostel will cost you around £12. The cheapest places to stay are the city's **campsites**, some of which also have dormitories, charging as little as £6 a night.

All London tourist offices (see p.79) operate a **room-booking service**, for which a small fee is levied (they also take the first night's fee in advance). The **British Hotel Reservation Centre** (BHRC; ⓦwww.bhrc.co.uk) desks at Heathrow, Gatwick and Victoria train and coach stations don't charge a fee for booking rooms, and most of their offices are open daily from 6am till midnight. You can also book for free **online** at ⓦwww.londontown.com; payment is made directly to the hotel on checking out and they can offer discounts of up to fifty percent.

Hotels and B&Bs

With **hotels** you get less for your money in London than elsewhere in the country – generally breakfasts are more meagre and rooms more spartan than in similarly priced places in the provinces. Whatever the time of year, you should phone as far in advance as you can if you want to stay within a couple of tube stops of the West End. When choosing your **area**, bear in mind that the West End – Soho, Covent Garden, St James's, Mayfair and Marylebone – and the western districts of Knightsbridge and Kensington are dominated by expensive, upmarket hotels, whereas Bloomsbury is both inexpensive and very central. For cheaper rooms, the widest choice is close to the main train termini of Victoria and Paddington, and amongst the budget B&Bs of Earl's Court. Where possible, we've marked the following on the maps in this chapter.

St James's, Mayfair and Marylebone

Edward Lear 28–30 Seymour St, W1 ⊕020/7402 5401, ⊛www.edlear.com; Marble Arch tube. See map, pp.126–127. Lear's former home enjoys a great location close to Oxford Street and Hyde Park, with lovely flower boxes and a plush foyer. Rooms themselves need a bit of a makeover, but the low prices reflect both this and the fact that most only have shared facilities. ④

Lincoln House 33 Gloucester Place, W1 ⊕020/7486 7630, ⊛www.lincoln-house-hotel .co.uk; Marble Arch or Baker Street tube. See map, pp.126–127. Dark wood panelling gives this Georgian B&B in Marylebone a ship's-cabin feel, while all the rooms are en suite and well equipped. Rates vary according to the size of the bed and length of stay. ⑤

Wigmore Court 23 Gloucester Place, W1 ⊕020/7935 0928, ⊛www.wigmore-court-hotel .co.uk; Marble Arch or Baker Street tube. See map, pp.126–127. The decor may not be to everyone's taste, but this Georgian town house is a better-than-average B&B, boasting a high tally of returning clients. Comfortable rooms with en-suite facilities, plus two cheaper doubles with shared facilities. Also a laundry and basic kitchen for guests' use. ⑦

Soho, Covent Garden and Holborn

The Fielding 4 Broad Court, Bow Street, WC2 ⊕020/7836 8305, ⊛www.the -fielding-hotel.co.uk; Covent Garden tube. See map, pp.90–91. Quietly and perfectly situated on a traffic-free and gas-lit court, this excellent hotel is one of Covent Garden's hidden gems. Its en-suite rooms are a firm favourite with visiting performers, since it's just a few yards from the Royal Opera House. Breakfast is extra. ⑥

Hazlitt's 6 Frith St, W1 ⊕020/7434 1771, ⊛www .hazlittshotel.com; Tottenham Court Road tube. See map, pp.90–91. Located off the south side of Soho Square, this early eighteenth-century building is a hotel of real character and charm, offering en-suite rooms decorated and furnished as close to period style as convenience and comfort allow. There's a small sitting room, but no dining room; continental breakfast (served in the rooms) is extra. ⑨

St Martin's Lane 45 St Martin's Lane, WC2 ⊕020/7300 5500, ⊛www.morganshotelgroup .com; Leicester Square tube. See map, pp.90–91. This self-consciously chic boutique hotel, with a bafflingly anonymous glassed facade, is a big hit with the media crowd. The *Light Bar* is the most startling of the hotel's eating and drinking outlets. Rooms currently start at around £250 a double, but rates come down at the weekend. ⑨

Seven Dials 7 Monmouth St, WC2 ⊕020/7681 0791, ⊛www.smoothhound.co.uk/hotels /sevendials; Covent Garden tube. See map, pp.90–91. Pleasant family-run hotel in the heart of theatreland. All rooms are en suite and have TV, tea/coffee-making facilities and direct-dial phones. ④

Travelodge High Holborn 166 High Holborn, WC2 ⊕020/7836 0877, ⊛www.travelodge.co.uk; Covent Garden tube. See map, pp.90–91. A functional but decent modern hotel, in a dream location between Covent Garden and Bloomsbury. Family rooms available. ⑥

Bloomsbury

Cavendish 75 Gower St, WC1 ⊕020/7636 9079, ⊛www.hotelcavendish.com; Goodge Street tube. See map, p.105. A real bargain, with lovely owners and a walled garden. All rooms have shared facilities, and there are some good-value family rooms, too. ②

Crescent 49–50 Cartwright Gardens, WC1 ⊕020/7387 1515, ⊛www.crescenthoteloflondon .com; Euston, King's Cross or Russell Square tube. See map, p.105. Comfortable and clean B&B, with pink furnishings. All doubles are en suite, but there are a few bargain singles with shared facilities. ⑤

Ridgemount 65–67 Gower St, WC1 ⊕020/7636 1141, ⊛www.ridgemounthotel.co.uk; Goodge Street tube. See map, p.105. Old fashioned, very friendly, family-run place, with small rooms, half with shared facilities, a garden, free hot-drinks machine and a laundry service. A reliable, basic bargain. ❸

Thanet 8 Bedford Place, WC1 ☏ 020/7636 2869, ⓦ www.thanethotel.co.uk; Russell Square tube. See map, p.105. Small, friendly, family-run B&B close to the British Museum. Rooms are clean, bright and freshly decorated, all with en-suite showers and tea- and coffee-making facilities. ❻

Clerkwenwell and the City

City 12 Osborn St, E1 ☏ 020/7247 3313, ⓦ www.cityhotellondon.co.uk; Aldgate East tube. See map, pp.108–109. Spacious modern hotel on the eastern edge of the City, in the heart of the Bengali East End at the bottom of Brick Lane. The plainly decorated rooms are all en suite, and many have kitchens, too; four-person rooms are a bargain for families or small groups. ❺

🏃 **The King's Wardrobe** 6 Wardrobe Place, Carter Lane EC4 ☏ 020/7792 2222, ⓦ www.bridgestreet.com; St Paul's tube. See map, pp.108–109. In a quiet courtyard just behind St Paul's Cathedral, this place is part of an international chain that caters largely for a business clientele. The apartments (1- to 3-bed) offer fully equipped kitchens and workstations, a concierge service and housekeeping. Though housed in a fourteenth-century building that once contained Edward III's royal regalia, the interior is unrelentingly modern. £130–160 per night per apartment. ❼

🏃 **The Rookery** 12 Peter's Lane, Cowcross Street, EC1 ☏ 020/7336 0931, ⓦ www.rookeryhotel.com; Farringdon tube. See map, pp.108–109. Rambling Georgian town house on the edge of the City in trendy Clerkenwell that makes a fantastically discreet little hideaway. The rooms start at £245 a double; each one has been individually designed in a deliciously camp, modern take on the Baroque period, and all have super bathrooms with lots of character. ❾

Travelodge Farringdon 10–42 King's Cross Rd, WC1 ☏ 0870/191 1774, ⓦ www.travelodge.co.uk; King's Cross/Farringdon tube. See map, pp.108–109. A bunker-like building and rather dated 1970s-style decor, though the swirly plaster and chunky pine in the rooms makes them more characterful than those of most chain hotels. Full English breakfast £7.50. ❹

Zetter 86–88 Clerkenwell Rd, EC1 ☏ 020/7324 4444, ⓦ www.thezetter.com; Farringdon tube. See map, pp.108–109. A warehouse converted with real style and a dash of 1960s glamour. Rooms are simple and minimalist, with fun touches such as lights which change colour and decorative floral panels; ask for a room at the back, overlooking

quiet, cobbled St John's Square. The attached restaurant serves good modern Italian food, and water for guests is supplied from the Zetter's own well, beneath the building. ❼

South Bank and Southwark

London County Hall Travel Inn Belvedere Rd, SE1 ☏ 020/7902 1619, ⓦ www.premiertravelinn.com; Waterloo or Westminster tube. See map, p.120. Don't expect river views at these prices, but the location in County Hall itself is pretty good if you're up for a bit of sightseeing. Decor and ambience are functional, but for those with kids, the flat-rate rooms are a bargain. ❻

Premier Travel Inn 34 Park Street SE1 ☏ 0870/990 6402, ⓦ www.premiertravelinn.com; London Bridge tube. See map, pp.122–123. Pleasant decent-sized rooms and friendly multilingual staff – this is a no-frills place, but the location near the Tate Modern and low rates make it a real winner. ❺

🏃 **Southwark Rose** 43–47 Southwark Bridge Rd, SE1 ☏ 020/7015 1490, ⓦ www.southwarkrosehotel.co.uk; London Bridge tube. See map, pp.122–123. The *Southwark Rose* markets itself as a budget hotel with boutique style, and nice design touches raise the rooms several notches above the bland chain hotels in the area. Giant aluminium lamps hover over the lobby, which is lined with funky photographs, while the penthouse restaurant offers breakfast with a rooftop view and free Internet access. ❼

Victoria

🏃 **B&B Belgravia** 64–66 Ebury St, SW1 ☏ 020/7823 4928, ⓦ www.bb-belgravia.com; Victoria tube. See map, pp.90–91. A real rarity in this neck of the woods – a B&B with flair, very close to the train and coach station. The 17 rooms are of boutique-hotel quality, with original cornicing and large sash windows and have stylish modern touches – all have flatscreen TVs and funky bathrooms with mosaic tiling. Staff are welcoming and enthusiastic. Free in-room Internet access. ❻

Morgan House 107 & 120 Ebury St, SW1 ☏ 020/7730 2384, ⓦ www.morganhouse.co.uk. See map, pp.90–91; Victoria tube. An above-average B&B, split between two locations, on opposite sides of the street. It's run by a vivacious couple, and there are great breakfasts, a patio garden, and a fridge for guests to use. Most rooms are en suite. ❺

Sanctuary House 33 Tothill St, SW1 ☏ 020/7799 4044, ⓦ www.fullershotels.co.uk; St James's Park tube. See map, pp.90–91. Run by Fuller's Brewery, situated above a Fuller's pub, and decked out like one too, in gaudy pseudo-Victoriana. Breakfast is extra, and is served in the pub, but the location right by St James's Park is terrific. Ask about the weekend deals. ⑦

Paddington, Bayswater and Notting Hill

Columbia 95–99 Lancaster Gate, W2 ☏ 020/7402 0021, ⓦ www.columbiahotel.co.uk; Lancaster Gate tube. See map, pp.126–127. This large hotel, once five Victorian houses, offers simply decorated rooms, some with views over Hyde Park, as well as a spacious public lounge with a vaguely Art Deco feel and a cocktail bar. Rooms are en suite. ⑤

The Pavilion 34–36 Sussex Gardens, W2 ☏ 020/7262 0905, ⓦ www.pavilionhoteluk.com; Paddington tube. See map, pp.126–127. A decadent rock star's home from home, with outrageously over-the-top decor and every room individually themed, from "honky tonk Afro" to "Highland Fling". ⑥

🏃 **Portobello Gold** 95–97 Portobello Rd, W11 ☏ 020/7460 4900, ⓦ www .portobellogold.com; Notting Hill Gate or Holland Park tube. See map, pp.126–127. A fun and friendly option – six rooms and an apartment above a cheery modern pub. Rooms are plain and some are tiny, with miniature en-suite bathrooms, but all are fairly priced. The apartment is a brilliant option for a group – it sleeps 6 (at a bit of a pinch) and costs £170 a night. ④

St David's Hotels 14–20 Norfolk Square, W2 ☏ 020/7723 3856 or 4963, ⓦ www.stdavidshotels .com; Paddington tube. See map, pp.126–127. A friendly welcome is assured at this inexpensive B&B, famed for its substantial English breakfast. Most rooms are en suite. The large rooms make it a good option for families on a budget. Basic singles start at £35, family rooms at £130. ③

Vancouver Studios 30 Prince's Square, W2 ☏ 020/7243 1270, ⓦ www.vancouverstudios.co. uk; Bayswater tube. See map, pp.126–127. Part of a growing trend away from standard hotel accommodation, *Vancouver Studios* offers self-contained apartments in a grand Victorian town house, with fully equipped kitchens and hotel-style porterage and maid service. Decor is to a high standard and mixes modern trends with traditional period touches. ⑥

Knightsbridge, Kensington and Chelsea

Abbey House 11 Vicarage Gate, W8 ☏ 020/7727 2594, ⓦ www.abbeyhousekensington.com; High Street Kensington tube. See map, pp.126–127.

Inexpensive Victorian B&B in a quiet street just north of Kensington High Street, maintained to a very high standard by its attentive owners. Rooms are large and bright – prices are kept down by sharing facilities. Full English breakfast, with free tea and coffee available all day. Cash only. ⑤

🏃 **Aster House** 3 Sumner Place, SW7 ☏ 020/7581 5888, ⓦ www.asterhouse.com; South Kensington tube. See map, pp.126–127. Pleasant award-winning B&B in a luxurious South Ken white-stuccoed street; there's a lovely garden at the back and a large conservatory, where breakfast is served. Singles with shared facilities start at around £120 a night. ⑧

The Gore 189 Queen's Gate, SW7 ☏ 020/7584 6601, ⓦ www.gorehotel.com; South Kensington, Gloucester Road or High Street Kensington tube. See map, pp.126–127. Popular, privately owned century-old hotel, a step away from Hyde Park and awash with oriental rugs, rich mahogany, walnut panelling and other Victoriana. Rooms, some with four-poster beds, from £190. ⑧

Hotel 167 167 Old Brompton Rd, SW5 ☏ 020/7373 3221, ⓦ www.hotel167.com; Gloucester Road tube. See map, pp.126–127. Small, stylishly furnished B&B with en-suite facilities, double glazing and a fridge in all rooms. Continental buffet-style breakfast is served in the attractive morning room/reception. ⑥

Vicarage 10 Vicarage Gate, W8 ☏ 020/7229 4030, ⓦ www.londonvicaragehotel.com; Notting Hill Gate or Kensington High Street tube. See map, pp.126–127. Ideally located B&B a step away from Hyde Park. Clean and smart floral rooms with shared facilities, and a full English breakfast included in the rates. Cash or travellers' cheques only. ⑤

Earl's Court

🏃 **Mayflower** 26–28 Trebovir Rd, SW5 ☏ 020/7370 0991, ⓦ www.mayflower -group.co.uk. See map, pp.126–127. In a street of bog-standard B&Bs, this is a real winner, decked out in bold warm colours, strewn with Indian antiques, and featuring parrots in the lounge. Rooms are en suite, comfortable and appealing. Singles from £75, and there are also apartments from £109, which are economical if you're in a group. ⑦

Merlyn Court 2 Barkston Gardens, SW5 ☏ 020/7370 1640, ⓦ www.merlyncourthotel.com. See map, pp.126–127. Well-appointed and popular B&B in a quiet leafy street close to the tube. Some rooms with en-suite facilities; English breakfast is included. ③

Hampstead

🏃 **Hampstead Village Guesthouse** 2 Kemplay Rd, NW3 ☏ 020/7435 8679,

@www.hampsteadguesthouse.com; Hampstead tube. Lovely B&B in a freestanding Victorian house on a quiet backstreet between Hampstead village and the Heath. Rooms (most en suite) are wonderfully characterful, crammed with books, pictures and handmade and antique furniture. Cute cabin-like single for £48, and a self-contained studio for £90. Meals to order. ⑤

La Gaffe 107–111 Heath St, NW3 ☏ 020/7435 8965, @www.lagaffe.co.uk; Hampstead tube. Small hotel situated above a long-established Italian restaurant and bar in the heart of Hampstead village. All rooms are en suite and there's a roof terrace for use in fine weather. ⑥

Hostels and campsites

London's official **Youth Hostel Association (YHA) hostels** (@www.yha .org.uk) are generally the cleanest, most efficiently run hostels in the capital. However, they charge around fifty percent or more above the rates of private hostels, and tend to get booked up several months in advance. **Independent hostels** are cheaper and more relaxed, but can be less reliable in terms of facilities. A good **website** for booking independent places online is @www .hostellondon.com. London's **campsites** are all on the perimeter of the city, though they are without doubt the cheapest accommodation available.

Where possible we've marked the location of hostels on one of the maps in this chapter.

YHA hostels

London Earl's Court 38 Bolton Gardens, SW5 ☏ 0870/770 5804, @earlscourt@yha.org.uk; Earl's Court tube. See map, pp.126–127. Better than a lot of accommodation in Earl's Court, offering dorms of mostly four or six beds, plus ten twins. Kitchen, café and patio garden. No groups. £24.50 per person. ②

London Holland Park Holland Walk, W8 ☏ 0870/770 5866, @hollandpark@yha.org.uk; Holland Park or High Street Kensington tube. See map, pp.126–127. Idyllically situated in the wooded expanse of Holland Park and fairly convenient for the centre, this extensive hostel offers a decent kitchen and an inexpensive café, but tends to be popular with school groups. Dorms only (most with over ten beds) at £22 per person.

London Oxford Street 14 Noel St, W1 ☏ 0870/770 5984, @oxfordst@yha.org.uk; Oxford Circus or Tottenham Court Road tube. See map, pp.90–91. The West End location and modest size (75 beds in rooms of 2, 3 and 4 beds) mean that this hostel tends to be full year round. No children under 6, no groups, no café, but a large kitchen. From £23.50 per person. ②

London St Pancras 79–81 Euston Rd, NW1 ☏ 0870/770 6044, @stpancras@yha.org.uk; King's Cross or Euston tube. See map, pp.80–81. Housed on six floors of a former police station, directly opposite the British Library, on the busy Euston Road. Beds cost £25 per person, and rooms are very clean, bright, triple-glazed and air-conditioned – some even have en-suite facilities. All doubles

are en suite and family rooms are available, all with TVs, from £50. No groups. ③

London St Pauls 36 Carter Lane, EC4 ☏ 0870/770 5764, @stpauls@yha.org.uk; St Paul's tube. See map, pp.108–109. Large 200-bed hostel in a superb location opposite St Paul's Cathedral. Some twins at £50 a room, but mostly four- to eight-bed dorms for £25 per person. There's no kitchen, but it has a café for dinner. No groups. Breakfast included. ②

London Thameside 20 Salter Rd, SE16 ☏ 0870 770 6010, @rotherhithe@yha.org.uk; Rotherhithe or Canada Water tube. London's largest purpose-built hostel can feel a little out of things, but is well connected to central London. Often has space when more central places are full. Breakfast, packed lunch and evening meals available. Rooms have 2, 4, 6 or 10 beds and cost from £24 per person. ②.

Private hostels

Ashlee House 261–265 Gray's Inn Rd, WC1 ☏ 020/7833 9400, @www.ashleehouse.co.uk; King's Cross tube. See map, pp.80–81. Clean and friendly hostel in a converted office block near King's Cross Station. Internet access, laundry and kitchen facilities are provided. Dorms, which vary in size from four to sixteen beds, start at £9 if you book online; there are also a few private singles and twins, starting at £25 per person. Breakfast is included. ②

Generator Compton Place, off Tavistock Place, WC1 ☏ 020/7388 7666, @www.the-generator.co.uk;

Russell Square or Euston tube. See map, p.105. A huge, funky 800-bed hostel, with post-industrial decor and prices starting at just £12.50 a night for a dorm bed and breakfast. Continental breakfast (included in the room rate) and evening meals from just £3.50. Room prices range from £35 for a single, £46 for a twin and £60 for a triple. **②**

Leinster Inn 7–12 Leinster Square, W2 ☎020/7229 9641, ⓦwww.astorhostels.com; Queensway or Notting Hill Gate tube. See map, pp.126–127. With 360 beds, this is the biggest and liveliest of the *Astor* chain, with a party atmosphere, and two bars open until the small hours. Some rooms in all categories have their own shower. Dorm beds (4–8 per room) £12–18 per person, singles £26.50, doubles from £41. **②**

Museum Inn 27 Montague St, W1 ☎020/7580 5360, ⓦwww.astorhostels.com; Holborn tube. See map, p.105. In a lovely Georgian house by the British Museum, this is the quietest of the *Astor* hostels. There's no bar, though it's still a sociable, laid-back place, and well situated. There are 75 beds in dorms of four to ten for £16–19, plus some twins at £50, including breakfast. Decent-sized kitchen and TV lounge, plus laundry and Internet access. **②**

St Christopher's Village 161–165 Borough High St, SE1 ☎020/7407 1856, ⓦwww.st-christophers .co.uk; Borough tube. See map, pp.122–123. Flagship of a chain of independent hostels, with branches on Borough High Street, in Camden, Greenwich and Shepherd's Bush. The decor is upbeat and cheerful, the place is efficiently run and there's a party-animal ambience, fuelled by the neighbouring bar and the rooftop hot tub and sauna. Beds in dorms of four to fourteen £14–22, twins £44. **②**

Campsites

Crystal Palace Crystal Palace Parade, SE19 ☎020/8778 7155; Crystal Palace train station from Victoria or London Bridge. All-year Caravan Club site; some traffic noise.

Lea Valley Leisure Centre Caravan Park Meridian Way, N9 ☎020/8803 6900; Ponders End train station from Liverpool Street. Well-equipped site, situated behind the leisure centre at Pickett's Lock, backing onto a vast reservoir.

Westminster and Whitehall

Political, religious and regal power has emanated from **Westminster** and **Whitehall** for almost a millennium. It was Edward the Confessor (1042–66) who first established Westminster as London's royal and ecclesiastical power base, some three miles west of the City of London. The embryonic English parliament used to meet in the abbey and eventually took over the old royal palace of Westminster. In the nineteenth century, Whitehall became the "heart of the Empire", its ministries ruling over a quarter of the world's population. Even now, though the UK's world status has diminished, the institutions that run the country inhabit roughly the same geographical area: Westminster for the politicians, Whitehall for the civil servants.

The monuments and buildings in and around Whitehall and Westminster also span the millennium, and include some of London's most famous landmarks – **Nelson's Column**, **Big Ben** and the **Houses of Parliament**, **Westminster Abbey**, plus two of the city's finest permanent art collections, the **National Gallery** and **Tate Britain**. This is a well-trodden tourist circuit since it's also one of the easiest parts of London to walk round, with all the major sights within a mere half-mile of each other and linked by one of London's most majestic streets, **Whitehall**.

Trafalgar Square

Despite the persistent noise of traffic, **Trafalgar Square** is still one of London's grandest architectural set-pieces. John Nash designed the basic layout in the 1820s, but died long before the square took its present form. The Neoclassical National Gallery filled up the northern side of the square in 1838, followed five years later by the central focal point, **Nelson's Column**,

Blue Plaques

Blue plaques on buildings across England – but especially in London, where there are around 800 – celebrate **historical figures** and the buildings they inhabited. Follow the links at ⓦ www.english-heritage.org.uk to track down the former homes of the famous, from Matthew Arnold to Emile Zola.

topped by the famous admiral; the very large bronze lions didn't arrive until 1868, and the fountains – a real rarity in a London square – didn't take their present shape until the late 1930s.

As one of the few large public squares in London, Trafalgar Square has been both a tourist attraction and a focus for **political demonstrations** since the Chartists assembled here in 1848 before marching to Kennington Common. Since then countless demos and rallies have taken place here, and nowadays various free events, commemorations and celebrations are staged here throughout the year.

Stranded on a traffic island to the south of the column, and predating the entire square, is an **equestrian statue of Charles I**, erected shortly after the Restoration on the very spot where eight of those who had signed the king's death warrant were disembowelled. Charles's statue also marks the original site of the thirteenth-century **Charing Cross**, from where all distances from the capital are measured – a Victorian imitation now stands outside Charing Cross train station.

The northeastern corner of the square is occupied by James Gibbs's church of **St Martin-in-the-Fields** (Mon–Sat 10am–8pm, Sun noon–8pm; free; ⓦ www.stmartin-in-the-fields.org), fronted by a magnificent Corinthian portico. Completed in 1726, the interior is purposefully simple, though the Italian plasterwork on the barrel vaulting is exceptionally rich; it's best appreciated while listening to one of the church's free lunchtime concerts (Mon, Tues & Fri). There's a licensed café in the roomy **crypt**, not to mention a shop, gallery and brass-rubbing centre (open till 6pm).

The National Gallery

Unlike the Louvre or the Hermitage, the **National Gallery**, on the north side of Trafalgar Square (daily 10am–6pm, Wed until 8pm; free; ⓦ www .nationalgallery.org.uk), is not based on a royal collection; in fact it was the British government that started procuring works as late as 1824. The gallery's subsequent canny acquisition policy has resulted in more than 2300 paintings, but the collection's virtue is not so much its size, but the range, depth and sheer quality of its contents.

To view the collection chronologically, begin with the **Sainsbury Wing**, the softly-softly, postmodern 1980s adjunct that playfully imitates elements of the original gallery's Neoclassicism. However, with more than a thousand paintings on permanent display in the main galleries, you'll need real stamina to see everything in one day, so if time is tight your best bet is to home in on your areas of special interest, having picked up a gallery plan at one of the information desks. **Audioguides**, with a brief audio commentary on each of the paintings on display, are available for a "voluntary contribution", but much better are the gallery's **free guided tours** (daily 11.30am & 2.30pm, plus Wed 6 & 6.30pm, Sat also 12.30 & 3.30pm), which set off from the Sainsbury Wing foyer.

Among the National's **Italian** masterpieces are Leonardo's melancholic *Virgin of the Rocks*, Uccello's *Battle of San Romano*, Botticelli's *Venus and Mars*

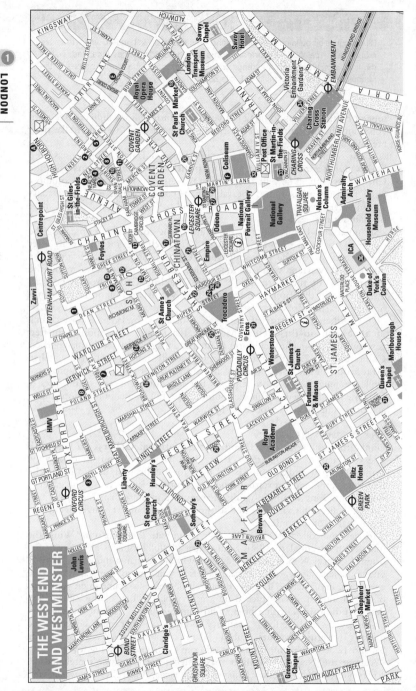

THE WEST END
AND WESTMINSTER

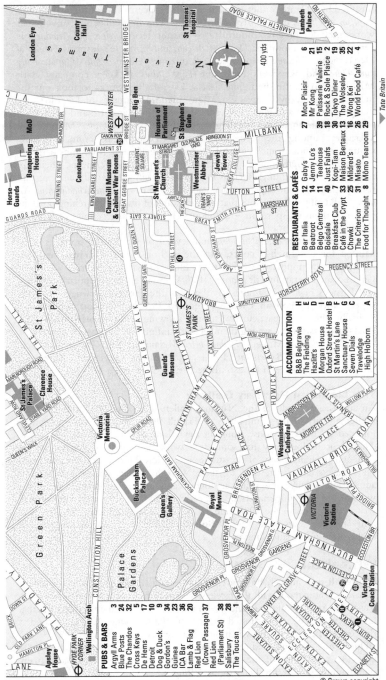

(inspired by a Dante sonnet) and Piero della Francesca's beautifully composed *Baptism of Christ*, one of his earliest works. The fine collection of Venetian works includes Titian's colourful early masterpiece *Bacchus and Ariadne*, his very late, much gloomier *Death of Acteon*, and Veronese's lustrous *Family of Darius before Alexander*. Elsewhere, Bronzino's erotic *Venus, Cupid, Folly and Time* and Raphael's trenchant *Pope Julius II* keep company with Michelangelo's unfinished *Entombment*. Later Italian works to look out for include a couple by Caravaggio, a few splendid examples of Tiepolo's airy draughtsmanship and glittering vistas of Venice by Canaletto and Guardi.

From **Spain** there are dazzling pieces by El Greco, Goya, Murillo and Velázquez, among them the provocative *Rokeby Venus*. From the **Low Countries**, standouts include van Eyck's *Arnolfini Marriage*, Memlinc's perfectly poised *Donne Triptych*, and a couple of typically serene Vermeers. There are numerous genre paintings, such as Frans Hals' *Family Group in a Landscape*, and some superlative landscapes, most notably Hobbema's *Avenue, Middleharnis*. An array of Rembrandt paintings that features some of his most searching portraits – two of them self-portraits – is followed by abundant examples of Rubens' expansive, fleshy canvases.

Holbein's masterful *Ambassadors* and several of van Dyck's portraits were painted for the English court, and there's home-grown **British** art, too, represented by important works such as Hogarth's satirical *Marriage à la Mode*, Gainsborough's translucent *Morning Walk*, Constable's ever-popular *Hay Wain*, and Turner's *Fighting Téméraire*. Highlights of the **French** contingent include superb works by Poussin, Claude, Fragonard, Boucher, Watteau, and David.

Finally, there's a particularly strong showing of **Impressionists** and **Post-Impressionists**, among them Manet's unfinished *Execution of Maximilian*, Renoir's *Umbrellas*, Monet's *Thames below Westminster*, Van Gogh's *Sunflowers*, Seurat's pointillist *Bathers at Asnières*, a Rousseau junglescape, Cézanne's proto-Cubist *Bathers* and Picasso's Blue Period *Child with a Dove*.

The National Portrait Gallery

Around the east side of the National Gallery lurks the **National Portrait Gallery** (daily 10am–6pm, Thurs & Fri till 9pm; free; Ⓦ www.npg.org.uk), founded in 1856 to house uplifting depictions of the good and the great. Though it undoubtedly has some fine works among its collection of ten thousand portraits, many of the studies are of less interest than their subjects. Nevertheless, it's interesting to trace who has been deemed worthy of admiration at any one time: aristocrats and artists in previous centuries, warmongers and imperialists in the early decades of the twentieth century, writers and poets in the 1930s and 1940s, and, latterly, retired footballers, and film and pop stars. The NPG's **Sound Guide** gives useful biographical background information and costs £2.

Whitehall

Whitehall, the unusually broad avenue connecting Trafalgar Square to Parliament Square, is synonymous with the faceless, pinstriped bureaucracy charged with the day-to-day running of the country, who inhabit the governmental ministries that line the street. The statues dotted about recall the days when Whitehall stood at the centre of an empire on which the sun never set.

During the sixteenth and seventeenth centuries, however, Whitehall was the permanent residence of the kings and queens of England, and was actually synonymous with royalty. The original Whitehall Palace was the London seat of

The Changing of the Guard

The Queen is colonel-in-chief of the seven **Household Regiments**: the Life Guards (who dress in red and white) and the Blues and Royals (who dress in blue and white) are the two Household Cavalry regiments; while the Grenadier, Coldstream, Scots, Irish and Welsh Guards make up the Foot Guards.

All these regiments still form part of the modern army as well as performing ceremonial functions such as the Changing of the Guard. If you're keen to find out more about the Foot Guards, pay a visit to the **Guards' Museum** (daily 10am–4pm; £2), in the Wellington Barracks on the south side of St James's Park. To find out more about the Household Cavalry, head for the new **Household Cavalry Museum** (daily 10am–6pm; £6), on the north side of the parade ground at the back of Horse Guards.

The **Changing of the Guard** takes place at two separate locations in London: the two Household Cavalry regiments take it in turns to stand guard at Horse Guards on Whitehall (Mon–Sat 11am, Sun 10am, with inspection daily at 4pm), while the Foot Guards take care of Buckingham Palace (see p.97). A ceremony also takes place regularly at Windsor Castle (see p.141).

the Archbishop of York, confiscated and greatly extended by Henry VIII after a fire at Westminster forced him to find alternative accommodation. The chief section of the old palace to survive the fire of 1698 was the **Banqueting House** (Mon–Sat 10am–5pm; £4.50; ⓦ www.hrp.org.uk), begun by Inigo Jones in 1619 and the first Palladian building to be built in England. The one room open to the public has no original furnishings, but is well worth seeing for the superlative Rubens ceiling paintings glorifying the Stuart dynasty, commissioned by Charles I in the 1630s. Charles himself walked through the room for the last time in 1649 when he stepped onto the executioner's scaffold from one of its windows.

Across the road, two mounted sentries of the Queen's Household Cavalry and two horseless colleagues, all in ceremonial uniform, are posted daily from 10am to 4pm. Ostensibly they are protecting the **Horse Guards** building, originally the main gateway to St James's Park and Buckingham Palace. The mounted guards are changed hourly, and those standing every two hours. Try to coincide your visit with the Changing of the Guard (see box above).

Further down this west side of Whitehall is London's most famous address, **Number 10 Downing Street** (ⓦ www.number-10.gov.uk), the seventeenth-century terraced house that has been the residence of the prime minister since it was presented to Sir Robert Walpole, Britain's first PM, by George II in 1732. Facing Downing Street's locked gates, in the middle of the road, stands Edwin Lutyens' **Cenotaph**, eschewing any kind of Christian imagery, and inscribed simply with the words "The Glorious Dead". The memorial remains the focus of the Remembrance Sunday ceremony in November.

In 1938, in anticipation of Nazi air raids, the basements of the civil service buildings on the south side of King Charles Street, south of Downing Street, were converted into the **Cabinet War Rooms** (daily 9.30am–6pm; £11; ⓦ cwr.iwm.org.uk). It was here that Winston Churchill directed operations and held Cabinet meetings for the duration of World War II, and the rooms have been left pretty much as they were when they were finally abandoned on VJ Day 1945, making for an atmospheric underground trot through wartime London. Also in the basement is the excellent **Churchill Museum**, where you can hear snippets of Churchill's most famous speeches and check out his trademark bowler, spotted bow tie and half-chewed Havana, not to mention his wonderful burgundy zip-up "romper suit".

The Houses of Parliament

Clearly visible at the south end of Whitehall is one of London's best-known monuments, the Palace of Westminster, better known as the **Houses of Parliament** (ⓦwww.parliament.uk). The city's finest Gothic Revival building and symbol of a nation once confident of its place at the centre of the world, it's distinguished above all by the ornate, gilded clocktower popularly known as **Big Ben**, after the thirteen-ton main bell that strikes the hour (and is broadcast across the world by the BBC).

The original medieval palace burned down in 1834, and everything you see now – save for **Westminster Hall**, the westernmost building – dates from Victorian times. You get a glimpse of the hall en route to the public galleries; its huge oak hammerbeam roof makes it one of the most magnificent secular medieval halls in Europe. The **Jewel Tower** (daily: 10am–4/6pm; £2.70; EH), across the road from parliament, is another remnant of the medieval palace, now housing an excellent exhibition on the history of parliament – worth visiting before you queue up to get into the Houses of Parliament.

To watch the proceedings in either the House of Commons or the Lords, simply join the queue for the **public galleries** outside St Stephen's Gate. The public are let in slowly from about 4pm onwards on Mondays and Tuesdays, from around 1pm on Wednesdays and Thursdays, and from 10am on Fridays. If you want to avoid the queues, turn up an hour or more later, when the crowds have usually thinned. Recesses (holiday closures) of both Houses occur at Christmas, Easter, and from August to the middle of October; phone ⓣ020/7219 4272 for more information or visit the website.

Question Time – when the House is at its most raucous and entertaining – takes place at 2.30pm (Mon & Tues), 11.30am (Wed) and 10.30am (Thurs); **Prime Minister's Question Time** is on Wednesday from noon until 12.30pm. UK citizens can attend either session by booking a **ticket** (several weeks in advance) from their local MP; they can also organize a free guided tour of the building and Big Ben (no under 11s) via their MP. For part of

▲ Houses of Parliament from the South Bank

the summer recess, there are **guided tours** (Aug & Sept Mon–Sat; £7) for foreign and domestic tourists, lasting an hour and fifteen minutes; visitors can book in advance by phoning ☏0870/906 3773, or simply head for the ticket office on Abingdon Green, opposite Victoria Tower at the southern end of the palace.

Westminster Abbey

The Houses of Parliament dwarf their much older neighbour, **Westminster Abbey** (Mon–Fri 9.30am–3.45pm, Wed until 6pm, Sat 9.30am–1.45pm; £10; Ⓦ www.westminster-abbey.org), yet this single building embodies much of the history of England: it has been the venue for all coronations since the time of William the Conqueror, and the site of more or less every royal burial for some five hundred years between the reigns of Henry III and George II. Scores of the nation's most famous citizens are honoured here, too (though many of the stones commemorate people buried elsewhere), and the interior is crammed with hundreds of monuments and statues.

Entry is via the north transept, cluttered with monuments to politicians and traditionally known as **Statesmen's Aisle**, shortly after which you come to the abbey's most dazzling architectural set-piece, the **Lady Chapel**, added by Henry VII in 1503 as his future resting place. With its intricately carved vaulting and fan-shaped gilded pendants, the chapel represents the final spectacular gasp of the English Perpendicular style. The public are no longer admitted to the **Shrine of Edward the Confessor**, the sacred heart of the building (except on a guided verger tour; £4) though you do get to inspect Edward I's **Coronation Chair**, a decrepit oak throne dating from around 1300 and still used for coronations.

Nowadays, the abbey's royal tombs are upstaged by **Poets' Corner**, in the south transept, though the first occupant, Geoffrey Chaucer, was in fact buried here not because he was a poet, but because he lived nearby. By the eighteenth century this zone had become an artistic pantheon, and since then, the transept has been filled with tributes to all shades of talent. From the south transept, you can view the central sanctuary, site of the coronations, and the wonderful **Cosmati floor mosaic**, constructed in the thirteenth century by Italian craftsmen, and often covered by a carpet for protection.

Doors in the south choir aisle (plus a separate entrance from Dean's Yard) lead to the **Great Cloisters** (daily 8am–6pm; free), rebuilt after a fire in 1298. At the eastern end of the cloisters lies the octagonal **Chapter House** (daily 10.30am–4pm; free), where the House of Commons met until 1395. The thirteenth-century decorative paving tiles and apocalyptic wall-paintings have survived intact. Also worth a look is the **Abbey Museum** (daily 10.30am–4pm; free), filled with generations of lifelike (but bald) royal funereal effigies.

It's only after exploring the cloisters that you get to see the **nave** itself: narrow, light and, at over a hundred feet in height, by far the tallest in the country. The most famous monument in this section is the **Tomb of the Unknown Soldier**, by the west door, which now serves as the main exit.

Tate Britain

A purpose-built gallery half a mile south of parliament, founded in 1897 with money from Henry Tate, inventor of the sugar cube, **Tate Britain** (daily 10am–5.50pm, first Fri of month until 10pm; free; Ⓦ www.tate.org.uk) is devoted exclusively to British art. As well as the collection covering from 1500 to the present, the gallery also puts on large-scale temporary exhibitions (for which there is a charge) that showcase British artists and continues to sponsor the Turner Prize, the country's most prestigious modern-art prize.

The pictures are rehung more or less annually, but always include a fair selection of works by British artists such as Hogarth, Constable, Gainsborough, Reynolds and Blake, plus foreign artists like van Dyck who spent much of their career over here. The ever-popular **Pre-Raphaelites** are always well represented, as are established twentieth-century greats such as Stanley Spencer and Francis Bacon alongside living artists such as David Hockney and Lucien Freud. Lastly, don't miss the Tate's outstanding **Turner collection**, displayed in the Clore Gallery.

Westminster Cathedral

Halfway down Victoria Street, which runs southwest from Westminster Abbey, you'll find one of London's most surprising churches, the stripey neo-Byzantine concoction of the Roman Catholic **Westminster Cathedral** (Mon–Fri 7am–7pm, Sat 8am–7pm, Sun 8am–8pm; free; Ⓦ www .westminstercathedral.org.uk). Begun in 1895, and thus one of the last monuments to the Victorian era, it's constructed from more than twelve million terracotta-coloured bricks, decorated with hoops of Portland stone, and culminating in a magnificent tapered campanile which rises to 274 feet, served by a lift (daily 9.30am–12.30pm & 1–5pm; £3). The **interior** is only half finished, so to get an idea of what the place will look like when it's finally completed, explore the series of **side chapels** whose rich, multicoloured decor makes use of over one hundred different marbles from around the world.

St James's

St James's, the exclusive little enclave sandwiched between St James's Park and Piccadilly, was laid out in the 1670s close to St James's Palace. Regal and aristocratic residences overlook Green Park, gentlemen's clubs cluster along Pall Mall and St James's Street, while jacket-and-tie restaurants and expense-account gentlemen's outfitters line Jermyn Street. Hardly surprising then that most Londoners rarely stray into this area. Plenty of folk, however, frequent **St James's Park**, with large numbers heading for the Queen's chief residence, **Buckingham Palace**, and the adjacent Queen's Gallery and Royal Mews.

The Mall and St James's Park

The tree-lined sweep of **The Mall** is at its best on Sundays, when it's closed to traffic. It was laid out in the first decade of the twentieth century as a memorial to Queen Victoria, and runs from Trafalgar Square to Buckingham Palace. The bombastic **Admiralty Arch** was erected to mark the entrance at the Trafalgar Square end of The Mall, while at the other end stands the ludicrous **Victoria Memorial**, Edward VII's overblown 2300-ton marble tribute to his mother, which is topped by a gilded statue of Victory, while the six outlying allegorical groups in bronze confidently proclaim the great achievements of his reign.

Flanking nearly the whole length of The Mall, **St James's Park** is the oldest of the royal parks, having been drained and enclosed for hunting purposes by Henry VIII. It was landscaped by Nash in the 1820s, and today its lake is a favourite picnic spot for the civil servants of Whitehall. Pelicans can still be seen at the eastern end of the lake, and there are exotic ducks, swans and geese aplenty.

Buckingham Palace

The graceless colossus of **Buckingham Palace** (Aug & Sept daily 9.30am–3.45pm; £15; ⓦwww.royal.gov.uk), popularly known as "Buck House", has served as the monarch's permanent London residence only since the accession of Victoria. Bought by George III in 1762, the building was overhauled in the late 1820s by Nash and again in 1913, producing a palace that's as bland as it's possible to be.

For two months of the year, the hallowed portals are grudgingly nudged open; timed tickets are sold from the box office on the south side of the palace – to avoid queuing, you must book in advance (for an extra £1.25 per ticket) on ⓣ020/7766 7300 or online. The interior, however, is a bit of an anticlimax: of the palace's 660 rooms you're permitted to see only twenty or so, and there's little sign of life, as the Queen decamps to Scotland every summer. For the other ten months of the year there's little to do here – not that this deters the crowds who mill around the railings, and gather in some force to watch the **Changing of the Guard** (April–Aug daily 11.30am; Sept–March alternate days), in which a detachment of the Queen's Foot Guards marches to appropriate martial music from St James's Palace (unless it rains, that is).

The public can also pay through the nose to view a small portion of the Royal Collection at the rebuilt **Queen's Gallery** (daily 10am–5.30pm; £7.50), on the south side of the palace. Exhibitions change regularly, drawn from a collection which is three times larger than the National Gallery, and includes masterpieces by Michelangelo, Reynolds, Gainsborough, Vermeer, van Dyck, Rubens, Rembrandt and Canaletto, as well as the odd Fabergé egg and heaps of Sèvres china.

There's more pageantry on show at the Nash-built **Royal Mews** (March–July & Oct daily except Fri 11am–4pm; Aug & Sept daily 10am–5pm; £7), further along Buckingham Palace Road. The royal carriages, lined up under a glass canopy in the courtyard, are the main attraction, in particular the Gold Carriage which was made for George III in 1762 and is smothered in 22-carat gilding weighing four tons, its axles supporting four life-size figures.

Waterloo Place to St James's Palace

Away from Buckingham Palace, St James's does contain some interesting architectural set pieces, such as **Waterloo Place**, at the centre of which stands the Guards' Crimean Memorial, fashioned from captured Russian cannon and featuring a statue of Florence Nightingale. Clearly visible, beyond, is the "Grand Old" **Duke of York's Column**, erected in 1833, ten years before Nelson's more famous one in Trafalgar Square.

Cutting across Waterloo Place, Pall Mall leads west to **St James's Palace**, whose main red-brick gate-tower is pretty much all that remains of the Tudor palace erected here by Henry VIII. When Whitehall Palace burned down in 1698, St James's became the principal royal residence and, in keeping with tradition, an ambassador to the UK is still accredited to the "Court of St James's", even though the court has since moved down the road to Buckingham Palace. The modest, rambling, crenellated complex is off limits to the public, with the exception of the **Chapel Royal** (Oct to Good Friday: Sun 8.30am & sometimes 11.15am), situated within the palace, and the

Queen's Chapel (Easter–July Sun 8.30am & sometimes 11.15am), on the other side of Marlborough Road; both are open for services only. **Clarence House** (Aug & Sept daily 10am–5.30pm; £7.50; ⓦwww.royal.gov.uk), connected to the palace's southwest wing, was home to the Queen Mother, and now serves as the official London home of Prince Charles and his second wife Camilla; the public are allowed to view a handful of unremarkable rooms on the ground floor by guided tour only; tours are popular so you'll need to book ahead.

Mayfair and Marylebone

Mayfair and **Marylebone** emerged in the late seventeenth century as London's first real suburbs, characterized by grid-plan streets feeding into grand, formal squares. This expansion set the westward trend for middle-class migration, and as London's wealthier consumers moved west, so too did the city's more upmarket shops and luxury hotels, which are still a feature of the area.

Piccadilly, which forms the southern border of **Mayfair**, is no longer the fashionable promenade it once was, but a whiff of exclusivity still pervades **Bond Street** and its tributaries. **Regent Street** was created as a new "Royal Mile", but, along with **Oxford Street**, it has since become London's busiest shopping district – it's here that Londoners mean when they talk of "going shopping up the West End".

Marylebone, which lies to the north of Oxford Street, is another grid-plan Georgian development, a couple of social and real-estate leagues below Mayfair, but a wealthy area nevertheless. It boasts a very fine art gallery, the **Wallace Collection**, and, in its northern fringes, one of London's biggest tourist attractions, **Madame Tussaud's**, the oldest and largest wax museum in the world.

Piccadilly Circus and Regent Street

Anonymous and congested it may be, but **Piccadilly Circus** is, for many Londoners, the nearest their city comes to having a centre. A much-altered product of Nash's grand 1812 Regent Street plan and now a major traffic interchange, it may not be a picturesque place, but thanks to its celebrated aluminium statue, popularly known as **Eros**, it's prime tourist territory. The fountain's archer is one of the city's top attractions, a status that baffles all who live here. Despite the bow and arrow, it's not the god of love at all but the *Angel of Christian Charity*, erected to commemorate the Earl of Shaftesbury, a bible-thumping social reformer who campaigned against child labour.

Regent Street, leading north off Piccadilly Circus, is reminiscent of one of Haussmann's Parisian boulevards, without the trees. Drawn up by John Nash in 1812 as both a luxury shopping street and a triumphal way between George IV's Carlton House and Regent's Park, it was the city's earliest attempt at dealing with traffic congestion, slum clearance and planned social segregation, which would later be perfected by the Victorians.

Despite the subsequent destruction of much of Nash's work in the 1920s, it's still possible to admire the stately intentions of his original Regent Street plan. The increase in the purchasing power of the city's middle classes in the last century brought the tone of the street "down" and heavyweight stores catering for the masses now predominate. Among the best known are **Hamley's**, reputedly the world's largest toyshop, and **Liberty**, the department store that popularized Arts and Crafts designs in the early 1900s.

Piccadilly

Piccadilly apparently got its name from the ruffs or "pickadills" worn by the dandies who used to promenade here in the late seventeenth century. Despite its fashionable pedigree, it's no place for promenading in its current state, with traffic careering down it nose to tail most of the day and night. Infinitely more pleasant places to window-shop are the various nineteenth-century **arcades** on Piccadilly, originally built to protect shoppers from the mud and horse-dung on the streets, but now equally useful for escaping exhaust fumes.

Piccadilly may not be the shopping heaven it once was, but it does still have the **Ritz Hotel** (Ⓦwww.theritzhotel.co.uk), a byword for decadence since it first wowed Edwardian society in 1906. The hotel's design, with its two-storey French-style mansard roof and long arcade, was based on the buildings of Paris's Rue de Rivoli. For a prolonged look inside, you'll need to be in good appetite and dress appropriately, and book in advance for the famous afternoon tea (see box, p.145).

The **Royal Academy of Arts** (daily 10am–6pm, Fri until 10pm; £7–10; Ⓦwww.royalacademy.org.uk) occupies one of the few surviving aristocratic mansions that once lined the north side of Piccadilly. The country's first-ever formal art school, the RA was founded in 1768 by a group of English painters that included Thomas Gainsborough and Joshua Reynolds. It hosts a wide range of art exhibitions, and an annual **Summer Exhibition** that remains a stop on the social calendar of upper middle-class England. Anyone can enter paintings in any style, and the lucky winners get hung, in rather close proximity, and sold. RA "Academicians" are allowed to display six of their own works – no matter how awful. The result is a bewildering display, which gets panned annually by highbrow critics.

Bond Street

While Oxford Street, Regent Street and Piccadilly have all gone downmarket, **Bond Street**, which runs parallel with Regent Street, has carefully maintained its exclusivity. It is, in fact, two streets rolled into one: the southern half, laid out in the 1680s, is known as Old Bond Street; its northern extension, which followed less than fifty years later, is known as New Bond Street. They are both pretty unassuming streets architecturally, yet the shops that line them are among the flashiest in London, dominated by perfumeries, **jewellers** and designer clothing stores. In addition to fashion, Bond Street is also renowned for its fine art galleries and its auction houses, the oldest of which is **Sotheby's**, 34–35 New Bond St (Ⓦwww.sothebys .com), whose viewing galleries are open free of charge.

Oxford Street and around

As wealthy Londoners began to move out of the City in the eighteenth century in favour of the newly developed West End, so **Oxford Street** (Ⓦwww.oxfordstreet.co.uk) – the old Roman road to Oxford – gradually became London's main shopping thoroughfare. Today, despite sky-high rents, this two-mile hotchpotch of shops is still probably England's busiest street, and is home to (often several) flagship branches of Britain's major retailers (see p.159). The street's only real landmark store is **Selfridges**, opened in 1909 with a facade featuring the Queen of Time riding the ship of commerce and supporting an Art Deco clock.

The Wallace Collection

Immediately north of Oxford Street, on Manchester Square, stands Hertford House, a miniature eighteenth-century French chateau which holds the splendid **Wallace Collection** (daily 10am–5pm; free; Ⓦ www .wallacecollection.org), a museum-gallery best known for its eighteenth-century French paintings, Franz Hals' *Laughing Cavalier*, Titian's *Perseus and Andromeda*, Velázquez's *Lady with a Fan* and Rembrandt's affectionate portrait of his teenage son, Titus. There's a modern café in the newly glassed-over courtyard, but at heart, the Wallace Collection remains an old-fashioned place, with exhibits piled high in glass cabinets, and paintings covering every inch of wall space. The fact that these exhibits are set amidst period fittings – and a vast armoury – makes the place even more remarkable.

Madame Tussaud's

Madame Tussaud's (Mon–Fri 9.30am–5.30pm, Sat & Sun 9am–6pm; £23; ℡0870/400 3000, Ⓦ www.madame-tussauds.co.uk), on Marylebone Road, has been pulling in the crowds ever since the good lady arrived in London from Paris in 1802 bearing the sculpted heads of guillotined aristocrats. The entrance fee might be extortionate, the waxwork likenesses of the famous occasionally dubious and the attempts to relieve you of yet more cash relentless, but you can still rely on finding London's biggest queues here. The only way to avoid joining the line is to book a timed entry ticket in advance over the phone or on the Internet. Visitors can choose to opt out of Chamber of Horrors Live which features live actors trained to frighten the living daylights out of tourists.

Soho

Bounded by Regent Street to the west, Oxford Street to the north and Charing Cross Road to the east, **Soho** gives you the best and worst of London. The porn joints that proliferated from the mid-1960s onwards still have a strong presence, but the area also boasts a lively fruit and vegetable market (on Berwick Street) and a nightlife that has attracted writers and ravers of every sexual persuasion since the eighteenth century. The area's most recent transformation has seen it become Europe's leading gay centre, with bars and cafés bursting out from the Old Compton Street area. Despite regeneration, it has retained a diverse and slightly raffish air, born of an immigrant history as rich as that of the East End (see p.117).

Conventional sights are few and far between, yet it's a great area to wander through, with probably more streetlife than anywhere else in London – whatever the hour there's always something going on. Most folk head here to visit one of the big movie houses on **Leicester Square**, to drink in the latest designer bar or to grab a bite to eat at the innumerable cafés and restaurants, ranging from the inexpensive Chinese places that pepper the tiny enclave of **Chinatown**, to exclusive, Michelin-starred establishments in the backstreets of central Soho, or its adjunct, **Fitzrovia**, to the north of Oxford Street.

Leicester Square and Chinatown

By night, when the big cinemas and discos are doing good business, and the buskers are entertaining the crowds, **Leicester Square** is one of the most crowded places in London, particularly on a Friday or Saturday when huge numbers of tourists and half the youth of the suburbs seem to congregate here. It wasn't until the mid-nineteenth century that the square actually began to emerge as an entertainment zone; cinema moved in during the 1930s, a golden age evoked by the sleek black lines of the Odeon on the east side, and maintains its grip on the area. The Empire, on the north side, is the favourite for the big royal premieres.

Chinatown, hemmed in between Leicester Square and Shaftesbury Avenue, is a self-contained jumble of shops, cafés and restaurants that makes up one of London's most distinct and popular ethnic enclaves. **Gerrard Street**, Chinatown's main drag, has been endowed with ersatz touches – telephone kiosks rigged out as pagodas and fake oriental gates or *paifang* – though few of London's 80,000 or so Chinese actually live in the three small blocks of Chinatown. Nonetheless, it remains a focus for the community, a place to do business or the weekly shopping, celebrate a wedding, or just meet up for meals, particularly on Sundays, when the restaurants overflow with Chinese families tucking into *dim sum*.

Old Compton Street

If Soho has a main drag, it has to be **Old Compton Street**, which runs parallel with Shaftesbury Avenue. The corner shops, peep shows, boutiques and trendy cafés here are typical of the area and a good barometer of the latest fads. Soho has been a permanent fixture on the **gay scene** for the better part of a century, but the approach is much more upfront nowadays, with gay bars, clubs and cafés jostling for position on Old Compton Street and round the corner in Wardour Street.

The streets round here are lined with Soho institutions past and present. One of the best known is London's longest-running jazz club, *Ronnie Scott's*, on Frith Street, founded in 1958 and still capable of pulling in the big names. Opposite is *Bar Italia*, an Italian café with late-night hours popular with Soho's clubbers. It was in this building, appropriately enough for such a media-saturated area, that John Logie Baird made the world's first public television transmission in 1926.

Covent Garden and the Strand

Covent Garden's transformation from a workaday fruit and vegetable market into a fashionable *quartier* is one of the most miraculous and enduring developments of the 1980s. More sanitized and brazenly commercial than neighbouring Soho, it's a far cry from the district's heyday when the piazza was the great playground (and red-light district) of eighteenth-century London. The buskers in front of St Paul's Church, the theatres round about, and the **Royal Opera House** on Bow Street are survivors of this tradition, and on a balmy summer evening, **Covent Garden Piazza** is still an undeniably lively place to be. Another positive side-effect of the market development has been the renovation of the run-down warehouses to the north of the piazza, especially around the Neal Street area, which now boasts some of the West End's trendier shops, selling everything from shoes to skateboards.

As its name suggests, the **Strand**, just to the south of Covent Garden, once lay along the riverbank: it achieved its present-day form when the Victorians shored up the banks of the Thames to create the Embankment. The Strand's most intriguing sight is **Somerset House**, sole survivor of the street's grandiose river palaces, now housing several museums and galleries as well as a lovely fountain courtyard.

Covent Garden

London's oldest planned square, laid out in the 1630s by Inigo Jones, **Covent Garden Piazza** was initially a great success, its novelty value alone attracting a rich and aristocratic clientele, but over the next century the tone of the place fell as the fruit and vegetable market expanded, and theatres and coffee houses began to take over the peripheral buildings. When the market closed in 1974, the piazza narrowly survived being turned into an office development. Instead, the elegant Victorian market hall and its environs were restored to house shops, restaurants and arts-and-crafts stalls. Of Jones's original piazza, the only remaining parts are the two rebuilt sections of north-side arcading, and **St Paul's Church**, facing the west side of the market building.

London Transport Museum

A former flower-market shed on the piazza's east side is now home to the **London Transport Museum** (daily 10am–6pm, Fri 11am–9pm; £8; Ⓦ www.ltmuseum.co.uk), a glorious celebration of the city's transport system over the last two centuries. The reconstructed 1829 Shillibeer's Horse Omnibus, which provided the city's first regular horse-bus service, is dwarfed by several wonderful double-decker electric trams, which, in the 1930s, formed part of the world's largest electric tram system. By 1952 the whole network had been dismantled, to be superseded by trolleybuses, of which the museum has several examples – these, in turn, bit the dust in the following decade. Look out, too, for the first "tube train", whose lack of windows earned it the nickname "the padded cell". The artistically inclined can buy reproductions of London Transport's stylish maps and posters, many commissioned from well-known artists, at the shop on the way out.

The Royal Opera House

The arcading on the northeast side of the piazza was rebuilt as part of the recent redevelopment of the **Royal Opera House** (Ⓦ www .royaloperahouse.org), whose main Neoclassical facade dates from 1811 and opens onto Bow Street. Now, however, you can reach the opera house from a passageway in the corner of the arcading. The spectacular wrought-iron **Floral Hall** (daily 10am–3pm) serves as the opera house's main foyer, and is open to the public, as is the *Amphitheatre* bar/restaurant (from one and a half hours before performance to the end of the last interval), which has a glorious terrace overlooking the piazza. For backstage tours of the opera house, it's best to book in advance (Mon–Fri 10.30am, 12.30 & 2.30pm, Sat 10.30am, 11.30am, 12.30 & 1.30pm; £9; ☏020/7304 4000).

Strand

Once famous for its riverside mansions, and later its music halls, the **Strand** – the main road connecting Westminster to the City – is a shadow of its former self. One of the few vestiges of glamour is **The Savoy**, London's grandest hotel, built in 1889 on the site of the medieval Savoy Palace on the south side of the street. César Ritz was the original manager, Guccio Gucci started out as a dishwasher here, and the list of illustrious guests is endless: Monet painted the Thames from one of the south-facing rooms, Sarah Bernhardt nearly died here, and Strauss the Younger arrived with his own orchestra.

▲ Covent Garden market hall

Somerset House

Further east along the Strand, **Somerset House** (Ⓦwww.somerset-house.org
.uk) is the sole survivor of the grand edifices which once lined the riverfront,
its four wings enclosing a large **courtyard** (daily 7.30am–11pm; free) featuring

a wonderful 55-jet fountain that spouts straight from the cobbles; in winter, an ice rink is set up in its place. The present building was begun in 1776 by William Chambers as a purpose-built governmental office development, but now also houses a series of museums and galleries.

The south wing, overlooking the Thames, is home to the **Hermitage Rooms** (daily 10am–6pm; £5; Ⓦwww.hermitagerooms.com), featuring changing displays drawn from St Petersburg's Hermitage Museum, and the **Gilbert Collection** (daily 10am–6pm; £5; Ⓦwww.gilbert-collection.org.uk), a museum of decorative arts displaying gaudy European silver and gold nick-nacks, micro-mosaics, clocks, portrait miniatures and snuffboxes. Alternatively, save yourself some money and go and admire the Royal Naval Commissioners' gilded eighteenth-century barge in the **King's Barge House**, at ground level in the south wing.

In the north wing are the **Courtauld Institute galleries** (daily 10am–6pm; £5; free Mon 10am–2pm; Ⓦwww.courtauld.ac.uk), chiefly known for their dazzling collection of Impressionist and Post-Impressionist paintings. Among the most celebrated works is a small-scale version of Manet's *Déjeuner sur l'herbe*, Renoir's *La Loge*, and Degas's *Two Dancers*, plus a whole heap of Cézanne's canvases, including one of his series of *Card Players*. The Courtauld also boasts a fine selection of works by the likes of Rubens, van Dyck, Tiepolo and Cranach the Elder. The collection has recently been augmented by the long-term loan of a hundred top-notch twentieth-century paintings and sculptures by, among others, Kandinksy, Matisse, Dufy, Derain, Rodin and Henry Moore.

Bloomsbury

Bloomsbury was built over in grid-plan style from the 1660s onwards, and the formal bourgeois Georgian squares laid out then remain the area's main distinguishing feature. In the twentieth century, Bloomsbury acquired a reputation as the city's most learned quarter, dominated by the dual institutions of the **British Museum** and **London University**, and home to many of London's chief book publishers, but perhaps best known for its literary inhabitants, among them T.S. Eliot and Virginia Woolf. Today, the British Museum is clearly the star attraction, but there are other minor sights, such as the **Foundling Museum** and the **Dickens House Museum**. Only in its northern fringes does the character of the area change dramatically, becoming steadily seedier as you near the main line train stations of Euston, St Pancras and King's Cross.

The British Museum

The **British Museum** (daily 10am–5.30pm, Thurs & Fri until 8.30pm; free; Ⓦwww.britishmuseum.ac.uk) is one of the great museums of the world. With seventy thousand exhibits ranged over two and a half miles of galleries, the museum boasts one of the largest and most comprehensive collections of antiquities, prints and drawings to be housed under one roof – over thirteen million at the last count (a number increasing daily with the stream of new acquisitions, discoveries and bequests). Its assortment of Roman and Greek art is unparalleled, its Egyptian collection is the most significant outside Egypt and, in addition, there are fabulous treasures from Anglo-Saxon and Roman Britain, from China, Japan, India and Mesopotamia – not to mention an enormous collection of prints and drawings, only a fraction of which can be displayed at any one time.

MARYLEBONE AND BLOOMSBURY

RESTAURANTS & CAFÉS

Eat & Two Veg	3
Fairuz	10
Ikkyu	4
Indian YMCA	2
Patisserie Valerie at Sagne	6
The Providores & Tapa Room	5
Rasa Samudra	8
Wagamama	9

ACCOMMODATION

Cavendish	C
Crescent	A
Generator	B
Museum Inn	F
Ridgemount	D
Thanet	E

PUBS & BARS

Lamb	1
Museum Tavern	7
O'Conor Don	12
Princess Louise	11
The Social	13

© Crown copyright

The building itself, begun in 1823, is the grandest of London's Greek Revival edifices, dominated by the giant Ionic colonnade and portico that forms the main entrance. At the heart of the museum is the **Great Court** (daily 9am–6pm, Thurs–Sat until 11pm), with its remarkable, curving glass-and-steel roof, designed by Norman Foster. At the centre stands the copper-domed former **Round Reading Room**, built in the 1850s to house the British Library. It was here, reputedly at desk O7 that Karl Marx penned *Das Kapital*. The building is now a public study area, and features a multimedia guide to the museum's displays.

You'll never manage to see everything in one visit, so the best advice is to concentrate on one or two areas of interest, or else sign up with one of the museum's **guided tours**. One place you could start is the BM's collection of **Roman and Greek antiquities**, perhaps most famous for the Parthenon sculptures, better known as the **Elgin Marbles**, after the British aristocrat who walked off with the reliefs in 1801.

The **Egyptian collection** ranges from monumental sculptures, such as the colossal granite head of Amenophis III, to the ever-popular **mummies** and their ornate outer caskets. Also on display is the **Rosetta Stone**, which finally unlocked the secret of Egyptian hieroglyphs. There's a splendid series of **Assyrian reliefs** from Nineveh, depicting events such as the royal lion hunts of Ashurbanipal, in which the king slaughters one of the cats with his bare hands.

The leathery half-corpse of the 2000-year-old **Lindow Man**, discovered in a Cheshire bog, and the Anglo-Saxon treasure from the **Sutton Hoo** ship burial, are among the highlights of the prehistoric and Romano-British section. The medieval and modern collections, meanwhile, range from the twelfth-century **Lewis chessmen**, carved from walrus ivory, to twentieth-century exhibits such as a copper vase by Frank Lloyd Wright.

The dramatically lit Mexican and North American galleries, plus the African galleries in the basement, represent just a small fraction of the museum's **ethnographic collection**, while select works from the BM's enormous collection of **prints and drawings** can be seen in special exhibitions. In addition, there are fabulous **Oriental treasures** in the north wing, closest to the back entrance on Montague Place. The displays include ancient Chinese porcelain, ornate snuffboxes, miniature landscapes, and a bewildering array of Buddhist and Hindu gods.

Foundling Museum

To the east of Russell Square tube is the site of the Foundling Hospital, founded in 1756 by Thomas Coram, a retired sea captain. All that remains of the original eighteenth-century buildings is the alcove where the foundlings used to be abandoned and the whitewashed loggia which now forms the border to **Coram's Fields**, an inner-city haven for children, with a whole host of hens, horses, sheep, goats and ducks. Adults are not allowed into the grounds unless accompanied by a child. At the **Foundling Museum** (Tues–Sat 10am–6pm, Sun noon–6pm; £5; ☎020/7841 3600, ⊛www.foundlingmuseum.org.uk), just to the north of Coram's Fields, at 40 Brunswick Square, you can learn more about the fascinating story of the hospital. One of the hospital's founding governors – who even fostered two of the children – was the artist **William Hogarth**, and as a result the museum boasts an impressive art collection including works by artists such as Gainsborough and Reynolds, now hung in the eighteenth-century interiors carefully preserved in their entirety from the original hospital.

Dickens House

Despite the plethora of blue plaques marking the residences of local luminaries, **Dickens House** (Mon–Sat 10am–5pm, Sun 11am–5pm; £5; Ⓦwww .dickensmuseum.com), at 48 Doughty St, in Bloomsbury's eastern fringes, is the area's only literary museum. Dickens moved here in 1837 shortly after his marriage to Catherine Hogarth, and they lived here for two years, during which time he wrote *Nicholas Nickleby* and *Oliver Twist*. Although Dickens painted a gloomy Victorian world in his books, the drawing room here, in which Dickens entertained his literary friends, was decorated in a rather upbeat Regency style. Letters, manuscripts and first editions, the earliest known portrait (a miniature painted by his aunt in 1830) and the reading copies he used during extensive lecture tours in Britain and the States are the rewards for those with more than a passing interest in the novelist. There's also a half-hour film of his life.

The British Library

The **British Library** (Mon & Wed–Fri 9.30am–6pm, Tues 9.30am–8pm, Sat 9.30am–5pm, Sun 11am–5pm; free; Ⓦwww.bl.uk), located on the busy Euston Road on the northern fringes of Bloomsbury, opened to the public in 1998. As the country's most expensive public building it was hardly surprising that the place drew fierce criticism from all sides. Yet while it's true that the building's red-brick brutalism is horribly out of fashion, and compares unfavourably with its cathedralesque Victorian neighbour, the former *Midland Grand Hotel*, the interior of the library has met with general approval, and the high-tech exhibition galleries are superb.

With the exception of the reading rooms, the library is open to the general public. The three exhibition galleries are to the left as you enter; straight ahead is the spiritual heart of the BL, a multistorey glass-walled tower housing the vast **King's Library**, collected by George III, and donated to the museum by George IV in 1823; to the side of the King's Library are the pull-out draws of the **philatelic collection**. If you want to explore the parts of the building not normally open to the public, you must sign up for a **guided tour** (Mon, Wed & Fri 3pm, Sat 10.30am & 3pm; £6; or Sun 11.30am & 3pm if you want to see the reading rooms; £7).

The first of the three exhibition galleries to head for is the dimly lit **John Ritblat Gallery**, where a superlative selection of the BL's ancient manuscripts, maps, documents and precious books, including the richly illustrated Lindisfarne Gospels, is displayed. One of the most appealing innovations is that you can turn the pages of various texts – from the Mercator's 1570s atlas of Europe to Leonardo da Vinci's notebook – "virtually" on the touch-screen computers, thus allowing you to see much more than the double page displayed in the glass cabinets. The **Pearson Gallery of Living Words** puts on excellent temporary exhibitions, for which there is sometimes an admission charge.

Holborn to Hoxton

Holborn (pronounced "Ho-bun"), on the periphery of the financial district of the City, has long been associated with the law, and its **Inns of Court** make for an interesting stroll, their archaic, cobbled precincts exuding the rarefied atmosphere of an Oxbridge college, and sheltering one of the city's oldest churches, the twelfth-century **Temple Church**. Close by the Inns,

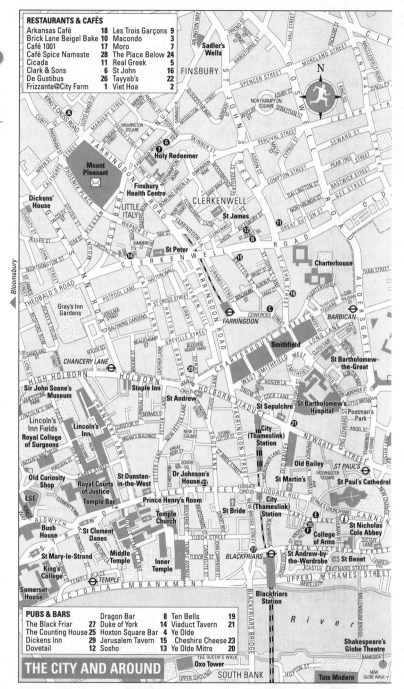

RESTAURANTS & CAFÉS

Arkansas Café	18
Brick Lane Beigel Bake	10
Café 1001	17
Café Spice Namaste	28
Cicada	11
Clark & Sons	6
De Gustibus	26
Frizzante@City Farm	1
Les Trois Garçons	9
Macondo	3
Moro	7
The Place Below	24
Real Greek	5
St John	16
Tayyab's	22
Viet Hoa	2

PUBS & BARS

The Black Friar	27	Dragon Bar	8
The Counting House	25	Duke of York	14
Dickens Inn	29	Hoxton Square Bar	4
Dovetail	12	Jerusalem Tavern	15
		Sosho	13
Ten Bells	19		
Viaduct Tavern	21		
Ye Olde Cheshire Cheese	23		
Ye Olde Mitre	20		

THE CITY AND AROUND

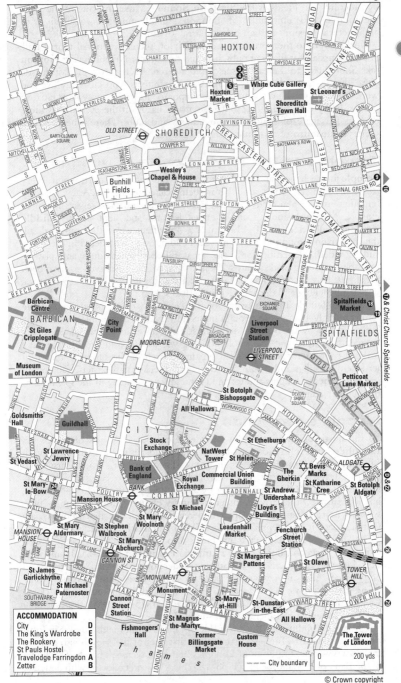

White Cube Gallery

HOXTON

Hoxton Market

St Leonard's

Shoreditch Town Hall

OLD STREET

SHOREDITCH

Wesley's Chapel & House

Bunhill Fields

Barbican Centre

BARBICAN

St Giles Cripplegate

City Point

Spitalfields Market

SPITALFIELDS

MOORGATE

Museum of London

LONDON WALL

Liverpool Street Station

LIVERPOOL STREET

Petticoat Lane Market

Goldsmiths' Hall

Guildhall

C I T Y

St Botolph Bishopsgate

All Hallows

St Lawrence Jewry

St Vedast

Stock Exchange

NatWest Tower

St Ethelburga

St Helen

The Gherkin

Bevis Marks

Bank of England

Royal Exchange

Commercial Union Building

St Katharine Cree

St Botolph Aldgate

St Mary-le-Bow

Mansion House

BANK

CORNHILL

St Andrew Undershaft

St Michael

Lloyd's Building

St Mary Woolnoth

St Stephen Walbrook

Leadenhall Market

Fenchurch Street Station

St Mary Aldermary

CANNON ST

St Mary Abchurch

St Margaret Pattens

St Olave

St James Garlickhythe

St Michael Paternoster

MONUMENT

Monument

St-Mary-at-Hill

St-Dunstan-in-the-East

TOWER HILL

Cannon Street Station

Fishmongers' Hall

St Magnus-the-Martyr

Former Billingsgate Market

Custom House

All Hallows

The Tower of London

T h a m e s

ACCOMMODATION

City	D
The King's Wardrobe	E
The Rookery	C
St Pauls Hostel	F
Travelodge Farringdon	A
Zetter	B

0   200 yds

City boundary

© Crown copyright

by Lincoln's Inn Fields, is the **Sir John Soane's Museum**, one of the most memorable and enjoyable of London's small museums, packed with architectural illusions and an eclectic array of curios.

Clerkenwell, to the northeast, is definitely off the conventional tourist trail, but harbours a host of good pubs, bars and restaurants. Neighbouring **Hoxton** (aka Shoreditch) to the east, has acquired a certain cachet over the last decade or so, due to the high density of artists and architects who currently live and work here, and several of London's contemporary art dealers now have Hoxton outlets. Badly damaged in the Blitz, it remains harsh on the eye but has more than its fair share of trendy bars, restaurants and clubs. There's the excellent **Geffrye Museum** of furniture design to aim for too.

Temple and the Royal Courts of Justice

Temple is the largest and most complex of the Inns of Court, where every barrister in England must study before being called to the Bar. A few very old buildings survive here and the maze of courtyards and passageways is fun to explore. Medieval students ate, attended lectures and slept in the **Middle Temple Hall** (Mon–Fri 10–11.30am & 3–4pm; free), across the courtyard, still the Inn's main dining room. The present building was constructed in the 1560s and provided the setting for many great Elizabethan masques and plays – probably including Shakespeare's *Twelfth Night*, which is believed to have been premiered here in 1602. The hall is worth a visit for its fine hammerbeam roof, wooden panelling and decorative Elizabethan screen.

The two Temple Inns share use of the complex's oldest building, **Temple Church** (daily 11am–4pm, though hours do vary; ⓦ www.templechurch.com), built in 1185 by the Knights Templar. An oblong chancel was added in the thirteenth century, and the whole building was damaged in the Blitz, but the original round church – modelled on the Church of the Holy Sepulchre in Jerusalem – still stands, with its striking Purbeck marble piers, recumbent marble effigies of knights and tortured grotesques grimacing in the spandrels of the blind arcading.

Lincoln's Inn Fields

To the north of Temple, on the far side of the Royal Courts of Justice lies **Lincoln's Inn Fields**, London's largest square, laid out in the early 1640s with **Lincoln's Inn** (Mon–Fri 9am–6pm; ⓦ www.lincolnsinn.org.uk), the first – and in many ways the prettiest – of the Inns of Court on its east side. The Inn's fifteenth-century **Old Hall** is open by appointment only (ⓣ 020/7405 1393), but you can view the early seventeenth-century **chapel** (Mon–Fri noon–2pm), with its unusual fan-vaulted open undercroft and, on the first floor, its late Gothic nave, hit by a zeppelin in World War I and much restored since.

The south side of Lincoln's Inn Fields is occupied by the gigantic Royal College of Surgeons, home to the **Hunterian Museum** (Tues–Sat 10am–5pm; free; ⓦ www.rcseng.ac.uk), a fascinating collection of pickled skeletons and body pieces. Also on view are the skeleton of the "Irish giant", Charles Byrne (1761–83), who was seven feet ten inches tall, and, in the adjacent McCrae Gallery, the Sicilian midget Caroline Crachami (1815–24), who stood at only one foot ten and a half inches when she died at the age of nine.

A group of buildings on the north side of Lincoln's Inn Fields house **Sir John Soane's Museum** (Tues–Sat 10am–5pm; first Tues of the month also 6–9pm; free; ⓦ www.soane.org), one of London's best-kept secrets. The chief architect of the Bank of England, Soane (1753–1837) was an avid collector who designed this house not only as a home and office, but also as a place to stash his large collection of art and antiquities. Arranged much as it was in his lifetime, the ingeniously planned house has an informal, treasure-hunt atmosphere, with surprises in every alcove; the museum has also begun to exhibit contemporary art. At 2.30pm every Saturday, a fascinating, hour-long **guided tour** (£3) takes you round the museum and the enormous research library, next door, containing architectural drawings, books and exquisitely detailed cork and wood models.

Hoxton

Until recently, **Hoxton** was an unpleasant amalgam of wholesale clothes and shoe shops, striptease pubs and roaring traffic. Over the last decade, however, it has been colonized by artists, designers and architects and transformed itself into the city's most vibrant artistic enclave, peppered with contemporary art galleries and a whole host of very cool bars and clubs.

On City Road stands one of Hoxton's few formal sights, the Georgian ensemble of **Wesley's Chapel and House** (Mon–Sat 10am–4pm, Sun 12.30–2pm; free; ⓦ www.wesleyschapel.org.uk). A place of pilgrimage for Methodists, the uncharacteristically ornate chapel, built in 1777, heralded the coming of age of Wesley's sect. The **Museum of Methodism** (same hours) in the basement tells the story of Wesley and Methodism, and there's even a brief mention of Mrs Mary Vazeille, the 41-year-old, insanely jealous, wealthy widow he married, and who eventually left him. Wesley himself lived his last two years in the Georgian **house** to the right of the main gates, and inside you can see bits of his furniture and his deathbed, plus an early shock-therapy machine with which he used to treat members of his congregation. Wesley's **grave** is round the back of the chapel, in the shadow of a modern office block.

The geographical focus of the area's current transformation is **Hoxton Square**, situated northeast of Old Street tube, a strange and not altogether happy mixture of light industrial units and artists' studios arranged around a leafy, formal square. Despite the lack of aesthetic charm, the area has become an increasingly fashionable place to live and work and several leading West End **art galleries** have opened up premises here, among them Jay Jopling's **White Cube** at the south end of the square itself. Other than cruising the bars, clubs (listed on pp.149 &152) and art galleries, there are no real sights as such.

Hoxton's one other conventional tourist sight is the **Geffrye Museum** (Tues–Sat 10am–5pm, Sun noon–5pm; free; ⓦ www.geffrye-museum.org.uk), a museum of furniture design, set back from Kingsland Road in a peaceful little enclave of eighteenth-century ironmongers' almshouses. A series of period living rooms, ranging from the oak-panelled seventeenth century through refined Georgian and cluttered Victorian, leads to the excellent twentieth-century section and a pleasant café/restaurant. To get to the museum, take bus #149 or #242 from Liverpool Street tube.

The City

The City is where London began. Long established as the financial district, it stretches from Temple Bar in the west to the Tower of London in the east – administrative boundaries that are only slightly larger than those marked by the Roman walls and their medieval successors. However, in this Square Mile (as the City is sometimes referred to), you'll find few leftovers of London's early days, since four-fifths of the area burnt down in the Great Fire of 1666. Rebuilt in brick and stone, the City gradually lost its centrality as London swelled westwards, though it has maintained its position as Britain's financial heartland. What you see on the ground is mostly the product of three fairly recent building phases: the Victorian construction boom of the latter half of the nineteenth century; the overzealous postwar reconstruction following the Blitz; and the building frenzy that began in the 1980s, and which has seen fifty percent of the City's office space rebuilt.

When you consider what has happened here, it's amazing that so much has survived to pay witness to the City's two-thousand-year history. Wren's spires still punctuate the skyline here and there and his masterpiece, **St Paul's Cathedral**, remains one of London's geographical pivots. At the eastern edge of the City, the **Tower of London** still stands protected by some of the best-preserved medieval fortifications in Europe. Other relics, such as the City's few surviving medieval alleyways, Wren's **Monument** to the Great Fire and London's oldest synagogue and church, are less conspicuous, and even locals have problems finding the more modern attractions of the **Museum of London** and the **Barbican** arts complex.

Fleet Street

In 1500, a certain Wynkyn de Worde, a pupil of William Caxton, moved the Caxton presses from Westminster to **Fleet Street**, to be close to the lawyers of the Inns of Court and to the clergy of St Paul's. However, the street really begun to boom two hundred years later when, in 1702, the now-defunct *Daily Courant*, Britain's first daily newspaper, was published here. By the nineteenth century all the major national and provincial dailies had their offices and printing presses in the Fleet Street district, a situation that prevailed until the 1980s, when the press barons relocated their operations elsewhere. The best source of information about the old-style Fleet Street is the so-called

---

The City's churches

The City of London boasts over forty churches (Ⓦ www.london-city-churches.org), the majority of them built or rebuilt by Wren after the Great Fire. As a general rule, weekday lunchtimes are the best time to visit these churches, as many put on free lunchtime concerts for the local wage slaves. Below is a list of six of the most varied and interesting churches within the Square Mile:

St Bartholomew-the-Great Cloth Fair. The oldest surviving church in the City and by far the most atmospheric; a fascinating building. St Paul's aside, if you visit just one church in the City, it should be this one.

St Mary Abchurch Abchurch Lane, Cannon Street. Uniquely for Wren's City churches, the interior features a huge painted domed ceiling, plus the only authenticated Gibbons reredos.

St Mary Aldermary Queen Victoria Street. Wren's most successful stab at Gothic, with fan vaulting in the aisles and a panelled ceiling in the nave.

St Mary Woolnoth Lombard Street. Hawksmoor's only City church, sporting an unusually broad, bulky tower and a Baroque clerestory that floods the church with light from its semicircular windows.

St Olave Hart Street. Built in the fifteenth century, and one of the few pre-Fire Gothic churches in the City.

St Stephen Walbrook Walbrook. Wren's dress rehearsal for St Paul's, with a wonderful central dome and plenty of original woodcarving.

"journalists' and printers' cathedral", the church of **St Bride's** (Mon–Fri 9am–5pm, Sat 11am–3pm; ⓦ www.stbrides.com), which boasts Wren's tallest and most exquisite spire (said to be the inspiration for the tiered wedding cake), and whose crypt contains a little museum of Fleet Street history.

The western section of Fleet Street was spared the Great Fire, which stopped just short of **Prince Henry's Room** (Mon–Fri 11am–2pm; free; ⓦ www .cityoflondon.gov.uk/phr), a fine Jacobean house with timber-framed bay windows. The first-floor room now contains material relating to the diarist **Samuel Pepys**, who was born nearby in Salisbury Court in 1633 and baptized in St Bride's. Even if you've no interest in Pepys, the wooden-panelled room is worth a look – it contains one of the finest Jacobean plasterwork ceilings in London, and a lot of original stained glass.

Numerous narrow alleyways lead off the north side of Fleet Street, two of which – Bolt Court and Hind Court – eventually open out into Gough Square, on which stands **Dr Johnson's House** (Mon–Sat 11am–5/5.30pm; £4.50; ⓦ www.drjohnsonshouse.org). The great savant, writer and lexicographer lived here from 1747 to 1759, whilst compiling the 41,000 entries for the first dictionary of the English language, two first editions of which can be seen in the grey-panelled rooms of the house. You can also view the open-plan attic, in which Johnson and his six helpers put together the dictionary.

St Paul's Cathedral

Designed by Christopher Wren and completed in 1711, **St Paul's Cathedral** (Mon–Sat 8.30am–4pm; £9.50; ⓦ www.stpauls.co.uk) remains a dominating presence in the City, despite the encroaching tower blocks. Topped by an enormous lead-covered dome, its showpiece west facade is particularly magnificent. Westminster Abbey has the edge, however, when it comes to celebrity corpses, pre-Reformation sculpture, royal connections and sheer atmosphere. St Paul's, by contrast, is a soulless but perfectly calculated architectural set-piece, a burial place for captains rather than kings, though it does contain more artists than Westminster Abbey.

The best place from which to appreciate the glory of St Paul's is beneath the **dome**, decorated (against Wren's wishes) with Thornhill's trompe l'oeil frescoes. The most richly decorated section of the cathedral, however, is the Quire or **chancel**, where the mosaics of birds, fish, animals and greenery, only dating from the 1890s, are particularly spectacular. The intricately carved oak and limewood **choir stalls**, and the imposing organ case, are the work of Wren's master carver, Grinling Gibbons.

A series of stairs, beginning in the south aisle, lead to the dome's three **galleries**, the first of which is the internal **Whispering Gallery**, so called because of its acoustic properties – words whispered to the wall on one side are distinctly audible over one hundred feet away on the other, though the place is often so busy you can't hear much above the hubbub. The other two galleries are exterior: the wide **Stone Gallery**, around the balustrade at the base of the dome, and ultimately the tiny **Golden Gallery**, below the golden ball and cross which top the cathedral.

Although the nave is crammed full of overblown monuments to military types, burials in St Paul's are confined to the whitewashed **crypt**, reputedly the largest in Europe. Immediately to your right is Artists' Corner, which boasts as many painters and architects as Westminster Abbey has poets, including Christopher Wren himself, who was commissioned to build the cathedral after its Gothic predecessor, Old St Paul's, was destroyed in the Great Fire. The crypt's two other star tombs are those of **Nelson** and **Wellington**, both occupying centre stage and both with more fanciful monuments upstairs.

Museum of London and the Barbican

Despite London's long pedigree, very few of its ancient structures are now standing. However, numerous Roman, Saxon and Elizabethan remains have been discovered during the City's various rebuildings, and many of these finds are now displayed at the **Museum of London** (Mon–Sat 10am–5.50pm, Sun noon–5.50pm; free; @www.museumoflondon.org.uk), hidden above the western end of London Wall, in the southwestern corner of the Barbican complex. The museum's permanent exhibition is basically an educational trot through London's past from prehistory to the present day; hence the large number of school groups who pass through. The new displays are imaginatively set out, but half the museum (from Tudor times onwards) is undergoing refurbishment until 2009. In the meantime, excellent temporary exhibitions, lectures, walks and films still take place throughout the year.

The City's only large residential complex is the **Barbican**, a phenomenally ugly concrete ghetto built on the heavily bombed Cripplegate area. The zone's solitary pre-war building is the heavily restored sixteenth-century church of **St Giles Cripplegate** (Mon–Fri 11am–4pm), situated across from the infamously user-repellent **Barbican Arts Centre** (@www.barbican.org.uk), London's answer to Paris's Pompidou Centre, which was formally opened in 1982. The complex, which is at least traffic-free, serves as home to the London Symphony Orchestra and holds free gigs in the foyer area.

Guildhall

Situated at the geographical centre of the City, **Guildhall** (May–Sept daily 10am–5pm; Oct–April Mon–Sat 10am–5pm; free; @www.cityoflondon.gov .uk) has been the ancient seat of the City administration for over eight hundred years. It remains the headquarters of the Corporation of London, the City's version of local government, and is still used for many of the City's formal civic occasions. Architecturally, however, it is not quite the beauty it once was, having been badly damaged in both the Great Fire and the Blitz, and scarred by the addition of a 1970s concrete cloister and wing.

Nonetheless, the **Great Hall**, basically a postwar reconstruction of the fifteenth-century original, is worth a brief look, as is the **Clockmakers' Museum** (Mon–Sat 9.30am–4.30pm; free; @www.clockmakers.org), a collection of over six hundred timepieces, including one of the clocks that won John Harrison the Longitude prize (see p.137). Also worth a visit is the purpose-built **Guildhall Art Gallery** (Mon–Sat 10am–5pm, Sun noon–4pm; £2.50, free Fri and daily after 3.30pm), which contains one or two exceptional works, such as Rossetti's *La Ghirlandata*, and Holman Hunt's *The Eve of St Agnes*, plus a massive painting depicting the 1782 Siege of Gibraltar, commissioned by the Corporation, and a marble statue of Margaret Thatcher. In the basement, you can view the remains of a **Roman amphitheatre**, dating from around 120 AD, which was discovered during the gallery's construction.

The financial centre

Bank is the finest architectural arena in the City. Heart of the finance sector and the busy meeting point of eight streets, it's overlooked by a handsome collection of Neoclassical buildings – among them, the Bank of England, the Royal

Exchange and Mansion House (the Lord Mayor's official residence) – each one faced in Portland Stone.

Sadly, only the **Bank of England** (🌐www.bankofengland.co.uk), which stores the nation's vast gold reserves in its vaults, actually encourages visitors. Established in 1694 by William III to raise funds for the war against France, the bank wasn't erected on its present site until 1734. All that remains of the building on which Sir John Soane spent the best part of his career from 1788 onwards is the windowless, outer curtain wall, which wraps itself round the three-and-a-half-acre island site. However, you can view a reconstruction of Soane's Bank Stock Office, with its characteristic domed skylight, in the **museum** (Mon–Fri 10am–5pm; free), which has its entrance on Bartholomew Lane.

East of Bank, beyond Bishopsgate, stands Richard Rogers' glitzy **Lloyd's Building**, completed in 1984. A startling array of glass and blue steel pipes – a vertical version of Rogers' own Pompidou Centre – the building is now overshadowed by Norman Foster's giant **Gherkin**, built on the site of the old Baltic Exchange which was blown up by the IRA in the early 1990s, and officially known as 30 St Mary Axe (🌐www.30stmaryaxe.com).

Hidden away behind a modern red-brick office block in a little courtyard off Bevis Marks, north up St Mary Axe from the Lloyd's building, the **Bevis Marks Synagogue** (guided tours Wed & Fri noon, Sun 11.15am; £2; 🌐www.sandp .org) was built in 1701 by Sephardic Jews who had fled the Inquisition in Spain and Portugal. This is the country's oldest surviving synagogue, and its roomy, rich interior gives an idea of just how wealthy the congregation was at the time. Nowadays, the Sephardic community has dispersed across London and the congregation has dwindled, though the magnificent array of chandeliers makes it popular for candle-lit Jewish weddings.

Just south of the Lloyd's building you'll find the picturesque **Leadenhall Market**, whose richly painted, graceful Victorian cast-ironwork dates from 1881. Inside, the traders cater mostly for the lunchtime City crowd, their barrows laden with exotic seafood and game, fine wines, champagne and caviar.

London Bridge and Monument

Until 1750, **London Bridge** was the only bridge across the Thames. The Romans were the first to build a permanent crossing here, but it was the medieval bridge that achieved world fame: built of stone and crowded with timber-framed houses, it became one of the great attractions of London – there's a model in the nearby church of St Magnus-the-Martyr (Tues–Fri 9.30am–4pm, Sun 10am–1pm). The houses were finally removed in the mid-eighteenth century, and a new stone bridge erected in 1831; that one now stands in the middle of the Arizona desert, having been bought for US$2.4 million in the late 1960s by a gentleman who, so the story goes, was under the impression he had purchased Tower Bridge. The present concrete structure, without doubt the ugliest yet, dates from 1972.

The only reason to go anywhere near London Bridge is to see the **Monument** (daily 9.30am–5.30pm; £2), which was designed by Wren to commemorate the Great Fire of 1666. Crowned with spiky gilded flames, this plain Doric column stands 202 feet high, making it the tallest isolated stone column in the world; if it were laid out flat it would touch the bakery where the Fire started, east of Monument. The bas-relief on the base, now in very bad shape, depicts Charles II and the Duke of York in Roman garb conducting the emergency relief operation. The 311 steps to the viewing gallery once guaranteed an incredible view; nowadays it is somewhat dwarfed by the buildings around it.

The Tower of London

One of Britain's main tourist attractions, the **Tower of London** (March–Oct Mon & Sun 10am–6pm, Tues–Sat 9am–6pm; Nov–Feb closes 5pm; £16; ⓦ www.hrp.org.uk), overlooks the river at the eastern boundary of the old city walls. Despite all the hype and heritage claptrap, it remains one of London's most remarkable buildings, site of some of the goriest events in the nation's history, and somewhere all visitors and Londoners should explore at least once. Chiefly famous as a place of imprisonment and death, it has variously been used as a royal residence, armoury, mint, menagerie, observatory and – a function it still serves – a safe-deposit box for the Crown Jewels.

Before you set off to explore the Tower complex, it's a good idea to get your bearings by taking one of the free **guided tours**, given every thirty minutes or so by one of the Tower's **Beefeaters** (officially known as Yeoman Warders). Visitors today enter the Tower along Water Lane, but in times gone by most prisoners were delivered through **Traitors' Gate**, on the waterfront. The nearby **Bloody Tower**, which forms the main entrance to the Inner Ward, is where the 12-year-old Edward V and his 10-year-old brother were accommodated "for their own safety" in 1483 by their uncle, the future Richard III, and later murdered. It's also where **Walter Raleigh** was imprisoned on three separate occasions, including a thirteen-year stretch.

The **White Tower**, at the centre of the Inner Ward, is the original "Tower", begun in 1076, and now home to displays from the **Royal Armouries**. Even if you've no interest in military paraphernalia, you should at least pay a visit to the **Chapel of St John**, a beautiful Norman structure on the second floor that was completed in 1080 – making it the oldest intact church building in London. To the west of the White Tower is the execution spot on **Tower Green** where seven highly placed but unlucky individuals were beheaded, among them Anne Boleyn and her cousin Catherine Howard (Henry VIII's second and fifth wives).

The Waterloo Barracks, to the north of the White Tower, hold the **Crown Jewels**, perhaps the major reason so many people flock to the Tower; however, the moving walkways are disappointingly swift, allowing you just 28 seconds' viewing during peak periods. The oldest piece of regalia is the twelfth-century **Anointing Spoon**, but the vast majority of exhibits postdate the Common-wealth (1649–60), when many of the royal riches were melted down for coinage or sold off. Among the jewels are the three largest cut diamonds in the world, including the legendary **Koh-i-Noor**, set into the Queen Mother's Crown in 1937.

Tower Bridge

Tower Bridge ranks with Big Ben as the most famous of all London landmarks. Completed in 1894, its neo-Gothic towers are clad in Cornish granite and Portland stone, but conceal a steel frame, which, at the time, represented a considerable engineering achievement, allowing a road crossing that could be raised to give tall ships access to the upper reaches of the Thames. The raising of the bascules (from the French for "see-saw") remains an impressive sight – phone ahead to find out when the bridge is opening (☎020/7940 3984). If you buy a ticket (daily: April–Sept 10am–6.30pm; Oct–March 9.30am–6pm; £5.50; ⓦ www.towerbridge.org.uk), you get to walk across the elevated walkways linking the summits of the towers and visit the Tower's Engine Room, on the south side of the bridge, where you can see the now defunct giant coal-fired boilers which drove the hydraulic system until 1976, and play some interactive engineering games.

The East End and Docklands

Few places in London have engendered so many myths as the **East End** (a catch-all title which covers just about everywhere east of the City, but has its heart closest to the latter). Its name is synonymous with slums, sweatshops and crime, as epitomized by antiheroes such as Jack the Ripper and the Kray Twins, but also with the rags-to-riches careers of the likes of Harold Pinter and Vidal Sassoon, and whole generations of Jews who were born in the most notorious of London's cholera-ridden quarters and then moved to wealthier pastures.

The area's first immigrants were French Protestant Huguenots, fleeing religious persecution in the late seventeenth century. Within three generations the Huguenots were entirely assimilated, and the Irish became the new immigrant population, but it was the influx of Jews escaping pogroms in eastern Europe and Russia that defined the character of the East End in the late nineteenth century. The East End remains at the bottom of the pile; even the millions poured into the neighbouring **Docklands** development have failed to make much impression on local unemployment and housing problems. Racism is still a problem, and is directed, for the most part, against the large Bengali community, who came here from the poor rural area of Sylhet in Bangladesh in the 1960s and 1970s.

As the area is not an obvious place for sightseeing, and certainly no beauty spot – Victorian slum clearances, Hitler's bombs and postwar tower blocks have all left their mark – most visitors to the East End come for its famous **Sunday markets** (Ⓦ www.eastlondonmarkets.com). As for Docklands, most of it can be gawped at from the overhead light railway, including the vast **Canary Wharf** redevelopment, which has to be seen to be believed.

Spitalfields

Spitalfields, within sight of the sleek tower blocks of the financial sector, lies at the old heart of the East End, where the French Huguenots settled in the seventeenth century, where the Jewish community was at its strongest in the late nineteenth century, and where today's Bengali community eats, sleeps, works and prays. If you visit just one area in the East End, it should be this zone, which preserves mementos from each wave of immigration.

East End Sunday markets

Approaching from Liverpool Street, the first market you come to, on the east side of Bishopsgate, is **Petticoat Lane** (Sun 9am–2pm), not one of London's prettiest streets, but one of its longest-running Sunday markets, specializing in cheap (and often pretty tacky) clothing. Two blocks north of Middlesex Street, down Brushfield Street, lies **Old Spitalfields Market** (organic market Fri & Sun 10am–5pm; general market Mon–Fri 11am–3pm & Sun 10am–5pm), once the capital's premier wholesale fruit and vegetable market, now specializing in organic food, plus clothes, crafts and jewellery. Further east lies **Brick Lane** (Sun 8am–1pm), heart of the Bengali community, famous for its bric-à-brac Sunday market, wonderful curry houses and non-stop bagel bakery, and now also something of a magnet for young designers. From Brick Lane's northernmost end, it's a short walk to **Columbia Road** (Sun 8am–1pm), the city's best market for flowers and plants, though you'll need to ask the way, or head in the direction of the folk bearing plants.

The easiest approach is from Liverpool Street Station, a short stroll west of **Spitalfields Market**, the red-brick and green-gabled market hall built in 1893, half of which was demolished in order to make way for yet more City offices. The dominant architectural presence in Spitalfields, however, is **Christ Church** (Tues 11am–4pm, Sun 1–4pm), built in 1714–29 to a characteristically bold design by Nicholas Hawksmoor, and now facing the market hall. Best viewed from Brushfield Street, the church's main features are its huge 225-foot-high spire and a giant Tuscan portico, raised on steps and shaped like a Venetian window (a central arched opening flanked by two smaller rectangles), a motif repeated in the tower and doors.

The East End's most popular museum is the **V&A Museum of Childhood** (daily 10am–5.50pm; free; ⓦwww.vam.ac.uk/moc), situated opposite Bethnal Green tube station. The open-plan, wrought-iron hall, originally part of the V&A (see p.129), was transported here in the 1860s to bring art to the East End. On the ground floor there are clockwork **toys**, everything from classic robots to a fully functioning model railway, marionettes and puppets, teddies and Smurfs and even Inuit dolls. The most famous exhibits are the remarkable antique **dolls' houses**, dating back to 1673, which are now displayed upstairs, where you'll also find a play area for very small kids and the museum's space for temporary exhibitions.

Docklands

Built in the nineteenth century to cope with the huge volume of goods shipped along the Thames from all over the Empire, **Docklands** was once the largest enclosed cargo-dock system in the world. No one thought the area could be rejuvenated when the docks closed in the 1960s, but over the last 25 years warehouses have been converted into luxury flats, waterside penthouse apartments have been built and a huge high-rise office development has sprung up around Canary Wharf. Although Canary Wharf is on the Jubilee line, the best way to view Docklands is either from one of the boats that course up and down the Thames (see p.139), or from the driverless, overhead **Docklands Light Railway** or DLR (ⓦwww.tfl.gov.uk/dlr), which sets off from Bank, or from Tower Gateway, close to Tower Hill tube.

The only really busy bit of the new Docklands, **Canary Wharf** is best known as the home of Britain's tallest building, Cesar Pelli's landmark tower, officially known as One Canada Square. The world's first skyscraper to be clad in stainless steel, it's an undeniably impressive sight, both from a distance (its flashing pinnacle is a feature of the horizon at numerous points in London) and close up. However, it no longer stands alone, having been joined by several other skyscrapers that stop just short of Pelli's stumpy pinnacle.

One of the few original warehouses left to the north of Canary Wharf has been converted into the **Museum in Docklands** (daily 10am–6pm; £5; ⓦwww.museumindocklands.org.uk), an excellent stab at charting the history of the area from Roman times to the present day. Highlights include a great model of old London Bridge, an eight-foot-long watercolour and a soft play area for kids. Unless you're keen to visit the museum, though, there's little point in getting off the DLR at Canary Wharf. Instead, stay on the train as it cuts right through the middle of the office buildings under a parabolic steel-and-glass canopy and keep going until you reach Greenwich (see p.135).

The South Bank

The **South Bank** – the area immediately opposite Victoria Embankment – is best known for the **London Eye**, one of the capital's most popular millennium projects. The arrival of the Eye helped kick-start the renovation of the **South Bank Centre**, London's much unloved concrete culture bunker of theatres and galleries, built, for the most part, in the 1960s. After decades in the doldrums, the centre is currently under inspired artistic direction and the whole area is enjoying something of a renaissance.

The wheel's success has rubbed off on the rest of the area too, prompting a major refurbishment programme beginning with the transformation of **Hungerford Bridge**, connecting the South Bank to Embankment, into a gleaming double suspension footbridge. What's more, you can now happily explore the whole area on foot, free from the traffic noise and fumes that blight so much of central London, thanks to the well-marked **Thames Path** which runs along the riverside.

It's also worth visiting the **Imperial War Museum**, a short walk inland from the river, which contains the most detailed exhibition on the Holocaust in Britain.

The South Bank Centre

The modern development of the South Bank dates back to the 1951 **Festival of Britain**, when the South Bank Exhibition was held on derelict land south of the Thames. The festival was an attempt to revive postwar morale by celebrating the centenary of the Great Exhibition (when Britain really did rule over half the world). The most striking features of the site were the Royal Festival Hall, the ferris wheel (inspiration for the current London Eye), the saucer-shaped Dome of Discovery (disastrously revisited in the guise of the Millennium Dome, now the O_2), and the cigar-shaped Skylon tower.

▲ The London Eye

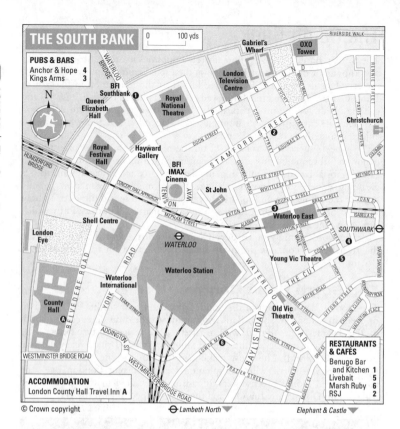

The Festival of Britain's success provided the impetus for the eventual creation of the **South Bank Centre** (Ⓦwww.southbankcentre.co.uk), now home to artistic institutions such as the Royal Festival Hall, the Hayward Gallery, the arts cinema BFI Southbank (formerly the NFT), London IMAX Cinema, and lastly Denys Lasdun's National Theatre (Ⓦwww.nationaltheatre.org.uk). Its unprepossessing appearance is softened, too, by its riverside location, its avenue of trees, its fluttering banners, its occasional buskers and skateboarders and the secondhand bookstalls outside the BFI Southbank.

The London Eye and around

South of the South Bank Centre proper is the **London Eye** (daily: June–Sept 10am–9pm; Oct–May 10am–8pm; £14.50; ℡0870/500 0600, Ⓦwww.ba -londoneye.com), the magnificently graceful Millennium Wheel which spins slowly and silently over the Thames. Standing 443ft high, the wheel is constantly in slow motion – a full-circle "flight" in one of its 32 pods takes around thirty minutes, and lifts you high above the city. It's one of the few places (apart from a plane window) from which London looks a manageable size, as you can see right out to where the suburbs slip into the countryside. Ticket prices are outrageously high, and queues can be very bad at the weekend, so book in advance over the phone or online.

Next to the London Eye is the only truly monumental building on the South Bank, **County Hall** (Ⓦwww.londoncountyhall.com) with its colonnaded crescent. Completed in 1933, it housed the LCC (London County Council), and later the GLC (Greater London Council), until 1986, and is now home to, among other things, two hotels, several restaurants, a giant aquarium, a glorified amusement arcade called Namco Station and an art gallery.

County Hall's most popular attraction is the **London Aquarium** (daily 10am–6pm; mid-July to Aug closes 7pm; £13.25; Ⓦwww.londonaquarium.co.uk), laid out across three floors of the basement. With some super-large tanks, and everything from dog-face puffers and piranhas to robot fish (seriously), this is an attraction that's pretty much guaranteed to please younger kids. The Touch Pool, where children can actually stroke the (non-sting) rays, is particularly popular.

Imperial War Museum

The domed building at the east end of Lambeth Road, formerly the infamous lunatic asylum "Bedlam" is now the **Imperial War Museum** (daily 10am–6pm; free; Ⓦwww.iwm.org.uk), by far the best military museum in the capital. The treatment of the subject is impressively wide-ranging and fairly sober, with the main hall's militaristic display offset by the lower-ground-floor array of documents and images attesting to the human damage of war. The museum also has a harrowing **Holocaust Exhibition** (not recommended for children under 14), which you enter from the third floor. The exhibition pulls few punches, and has made a valiant attempt to avoid depicting the victims of the Holocaust as nameless masses by focusing on individual cases, and interspersing the archive footage with eyewitness accounts from contemporary survivors.

Southwark

Until well into the seventeenth century, the only reason for north-bank residents to cross the Thames, to what is now **Southwark**, was to visit the infamous Bankside entertainment district around the south end of London Bridge, which lay outside the jurisdiction of the City. What started out as a red-light district under the Romans, reached its peak as the pleasure quarter of Tudor and Stuart London, where disreputable institutions banned in the City – most notably theatres – continued to flourish until the Puritan purges of the 1640s.

Thanks to wholesale regeneration in the last decade, Southwark's riverfront is once more somewhere to head for. The area is linked to St Paul's and the City by the fabulous Norman Foster-designed **Millennium Bridge**, London's first pedestrian-only bridge. Close by, a whole cluster of sights vie for attention, most notably the **Tate Modern** art gallery, housed in a converted power station, and next to it, a reconstruction of Shakespeare's **Globe Theatre**. The **Thames Path** connects the district with the South Bank to the west, and allows you to walk east along Clink Street and Tooley Street, home to a further rash of popular sights such as the **London Dungeon**. Further east still, Butler's Wharf is a thriving little warehouse development centred on the excellent **Design Museum**.

Tate Modern

The masterly conversion of the austere Bankside power station into the **Tate Modern** (daily 10am–6pm; Fri & Sat until 10pm; free; Ⓦwww.tate.org.uk) has

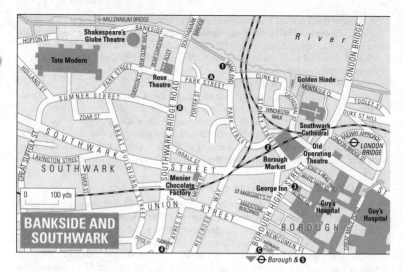

left plenty of the original, industrial feel, while providing wonderfully light and spacious galleries in which to show off the Tate's vast international twentieth-century art collection. The best way to enter is down the ramp from the west, so you get the full effect of the stupendously large turbine hall. It's easy enough to find your way around the galleries, with levels 3 and 5 displaying the permanent collection, level 4 used for fee-paying temporary exhibitions, and level 7 home to a café with a great view over the Thames.

Given that Tate Modern is the largest modern art gallery in the world, you need to spend the best part of a day here to do justice to the place, or be very selective. Start by picking up a plan (and, for an extra £2, a multimedia guide), and taking the escalator to level 3. The curators have eschewed the usual chronological approach through the "isms", preferring to group works together thematically. On the whole this works very well, though the early twentieth-century canvases, in their gilded frames do struggle when made to compete with contemporary installations.

The displays change every six months or so but you're still pretty much guaranteed to see at least some works by **Monet** and Bonnard, Cubist pioneers **Picasso** and Braque, Surrealists such as **Dalí**, abstract artists like **Mondrian**, Bridget Riley and Pollock, and Pop supremos **Warhol** and Lichtenstein. There are seminal works such as a replica of **Duchamp**'s urinal, entitled *Fountain* and signed "R. Mutt" and Yves Klein's totally blue paintings. And such is the space here that several artists get whole rooms to themselves, among them Joseph Beuys and his shamanistic wax and furs, and **Mark Rothko**, whose abstract "Seagram Murals", originally destined for a posh restaurant in New York, have their own shrine-like room in the heart of the collection.

From the Globe to the Cathedral

Seriously dwarfed by the Tate Modern but equally spectacular is **Shakespeare's Globe Theatre** (Ⓦ www.shakespeares-globe.org), a reconstruction of the polygonal playhouse where most of the Bard's later works were first performed, and which was originally erected on nearby Park Street in 1598. To find out

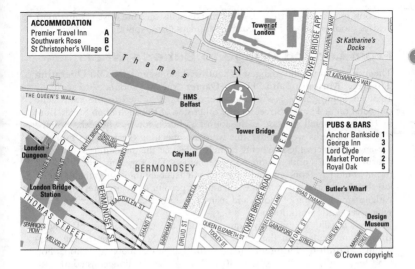

ACCOMMODATION
Premier Travel Inn	A
Southwark Rose	B
St Christopher's Village	C

PUBS & BARS
Anchor Bankside	1
George Inn	3
Lord Clyde	4
Market Porter	2
Royal Oak	5

© Crown copyright

more about Shakespeare and the history of Bankside, the Globe's stylish **exhibition** (daily: May–Sept 9am–noon & 12.30–5pm; Oct–April 10am–5pm; £9) is well worth a visit. It begins by detailing the long campaign by American actor Sam Wanamaker to have the Globe rebuilt, but it's the imaginative hands-on exhibits that really hit the spot. You can have a virtual play on medieval instruments such as the crumhorn or sackbut, prepare your own edition of Shakespeare, and feel the thatch, hazelnut-shell and daub used to build the theatre. Visitors also get taken on an informative **guided tour** round the theatre itself; during the summer season, you get to visit the exhibition and the remains of the nearby Rose Theatre instead.

An exact replica of the **Golden Hinde** (daily 10am–5.30pm, but phone ahead; £5.50; ☏0870/011 8700, ⓦwww.goldenhinde.org), the galleon in which Francis Drake sailed around the world from 1577 to 1580, nestles in St Mary Overie Dock, at the eastern end of Clink Street. The ship is surprisingly small, and its original crew of eighty-plus must have been cramped to say the least. There's a lack of interpretive panels, so it's worth paying the little bit extra and getting a guided tour from one of the folk in period garb – ring ahead to check a group hasn't booked it up.

Close by the *Golden Hinde* stands **Southwark Cathedral** (Mon–Fri 7.30am–6pm, Sat & Sun 8.30am–6pm; free; ⓦwww.southwark.anglican .org/cathedral), built as the medieval Augustinian priory church of St Mary Overie, and given cathedral status only in 1905. Of the original thirteenth-century church, only the choir and retrochoir now remain, separated by a tall and beautiful stone Tudor screen, making them probably the oldest Gothic structures left in London. The nave was entirely rebuilt in the nineteenth century, but the cathedral contains numerous interesting monuments, from a thirteenth-century oak effigy of a knight to an early twentieth-century memorial to Shakespeare.

Borough Market (ⓦwww.boroughmarket.org.uk), squeezed underneath the railway arches by the cathedral, is one of the few wholesale fruit and vegetable markets still trading under its original Victorian wrought-iron shed. In recent years it's undergone a transformation from scruffy obscurity to a small foodie haven, with permanent outlets such as Neal's Yard Dairy and Konditor

& Cook joined by gourmet daytime market stalls on Thursdays (11am–5pm), Fridays (noon–6pm) and, particularly, Saturdays (9am–4pm).

From London Bridge to Butler's Wharf

The most educative and strangest of Southwark's museums, the **Old Operating Theatre, Museum and Herb Garret** on St Thomas Street (daily 10.30am–5pm; £5.25; ⓦ www.thegarret.org.uk) is located to the east of the cathedral on St Thomas Street, on the other side of Borough High Street. Built in 1821 up a spiral staircase at the top of a church tower, where the hospital apothecary's herbs were stored, this women's operating theatre dates from the pre-anaesthetic era. Despite being entirely gore-free, the museum is as stomach-churning as the London Dungeon (see below). The surgeons who used this room would have concentrated on speed and accuracy (most amputations took less than a minute), but there was still a thirty percent mortality rate, with many patients simply dying of shock, and many more from bacterial infection, about which very little was known.

There's usually an impressive queue beside the railway arches of London Bridge train station, on the south side of Tooley Street, home to the ever-popular **London Dungeon** (daily: 10/10.30am–5/5.30pm; school hols 9.30am–6.30/7pm; £17; ⓣ020/7403 7221, ⓦ www.thedungeons.com) – to avoid the inevitable queue, buy your ticket online. Young teenagers and the credulous probably get the most out of the life-sized waxwork tableaux of folk being hanged, drawn, quartered and tortured, the general hysteria being boosted by actors dressed as top-hatted Victorian vampires, executioners and monks pouncing out of the darkness. Visitors are led into the labyrinth, an old-fashioned mirror maze, before being herded through a series of live action scenarios, passing through the exploitative "Jack the Ripper Experience", and ending with a walk through a revolving tunnel of flames.

HMS Belfast (daily: March–Oct 10am–6pm; Nov–Feb 10am–5pm; £10; ⓦ www.iwm.org.uk), a World War II cruiser, is permanently moored between London Bridge and Tower Bridge. Armed with six torpedoes, and six-inch guns with a range of over fourteen miles, the *Belfast* spent over two years of the war in the Royal Naval shipyards after being hit by a mine in the Firth of Forth at the beginning of hostilities. It later saw action in the Barents Sea and during the Korean War, before being decommissioned. The maze of cabins is fun to explore but if you want to find out more about the *Belfast*, head for the exhibition rooms in zone 5.

A short stroll east of the *Belfast* is Norman Foster's startling glass-encased **City Hall** (Mon–Fri 8am–8pm; ⓦ www.london.gov.uk), the new Greater London Authority headquarters that looks like a giant car headlight. Visitors are welcome to stroll around the building and watch the London Assembly proceedings from the second floor.

In contrast to the brash offices on Tooley Street, **Butler's Wharf**, east of Tower Bridge, has retained its historical character. **Shad Thames**, the narrow street at the back of Butler's Wharf, has kept the wrought-iron overhead gangways by which the porters used to transport goods from the wharves to the warehouses further back from the river, and is one of the most atmospheric alleyways in the whole of Bermondsey. The chief attraction of Butler's Wharf is the superb riverside **Design Museum** (daily 10am–5.45pm; £7; ⓦ www.designmuseum .org), a stylish, Bauhaus-like conversion of a 1950s warehouse at the eastern end of Shad Thames. The museum has no permanent display, but instead hosts a series of temporary exhibitions (up to four at any one time) on important designers, movements or single products. The small coffee bar in the foyer is a great place to relax, and there's a pricier restaurant on the top floor.

Hyde Park, Kensington and Chelsea

Hyde Park, together with its westerly extension, Kensington Gardens, covers a distance of two miles from Oxford Street in the northeast to Kensington Palace in the southwest. At the end of your journey, you've made it to one of London's most exclusive districts, the Royal Borough of **Kensington** and **Chelsea**. Other districts go in and out of fashion, but this area has been in vogue ever since royalty moved into **Kensington Palace** in the late seventeenth century.

Aside from the shops around Harrods in **Knightsbridge**, however, the popular tourist attractions lie in **South Kensington**, where three of London's top (and currently free) **museums** – the Victoria and Albert, Natural History and Science museums – stand on land bought with the proceeds of the Great Exhibition of 1851. Chelsea, to the south, has a slightly more bohemian pedigree. In the 1960s, the **King's Road** carved out its reputation as London's catwalk, while in the late 1970s it was the epicentre of the punk explosion. Nothing so rebellious goes on in Chelsea now, though its residents like to think of themselves as rather more artistic and intellectual than the purely moneyed types of Kensington. North of Kensington is Notting Hill, home of the longest-running, best-known and biggest street party in Europe, the **Notting Hill Carnival**. For more, the see the *Festivals and events* colour section.

Hyde Park and Kensington Gardens

Hangings, muggings, duels and the Great Exhibition of 1851 are just some of the public events that have taken place in **Hyde Park** (Ⓦ www.royalparks.gov.uk) which remains a popular spot for political demonstrations. For most of the time, however, the park is simply a lazy leisure ground – a wonderful open space that allows you to lose all sight of the city beyond a few persistent tower blocks.

At the treeless northeastern corner is **Marble Arch**, erected in 1828 as a triumphal entry to Buckingham Palace, but now stranded on a busy traffic island at the west end of Oxford Street. This is a historically charged piece of land, as it marks the site of **Tyburn gallows**, the city's main public execution spot until 1783. It's also the location of **Speakers' Corner**, a peculiarly English Sunday morning tradition, featuring an assembly of ranters and hecklers.

A more immediately appealing approach is to enter from the southeast around **Hyde Park Corner**, where the **Wellington Arch** (Wed–Sun 10am–4/5pm; EH; £3.10) stands in the midst of another of London's busiest traffic interchanges. Erected in 1828, the arch was originally topped by an equestrian statue of the Duke himself, later replaced by Peace driving a four-horse chariot. Inside, you can view an exhibition on London's outdoor sculpture and take a lift to the top of the monument where the exterior balconies offer a bird's-eye view of the swirling traffic.

Close by stands **Apsley House** (Tues–Sun 10am–4/5pm; EH; £5.10), Wellington's London residence and now a museum to the "Iron Duke". Unless you're a keen fan of the Duke, the highlight of the museum is the **art collection**, much of which used to belong to the King of Spain. Among the best pieces, displayed in the Waterloo Gallery on the first floor, are works by de Hooch, van Dyck, Velázquez, Goya, Rubens and Murillo. The famous, more

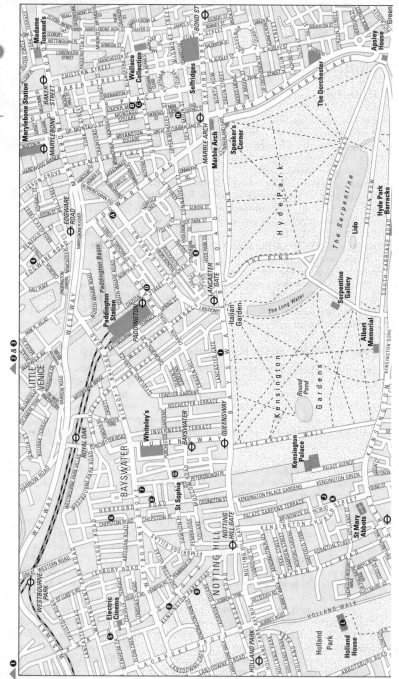

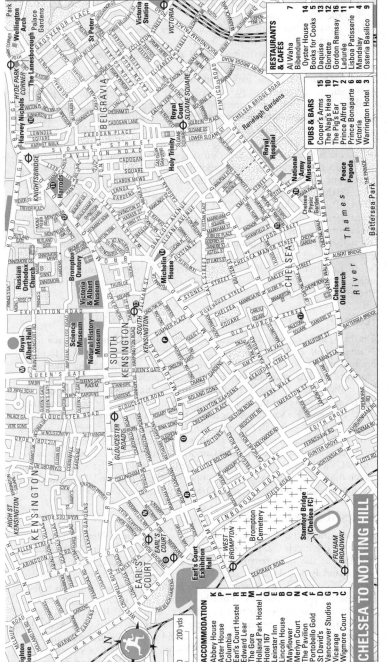

CHELSEA TO NOTTING HILL

RESTAURANTS & CAFÉS

Al Waha	7
Bibendum	14
Oyster House	5
Books for Cooks	13
Daquise	15
Gloriette	12
Gordon Ramsay	16
Ladurée	11
Lisboa Patisserie	1
Mandalay	4
Osteria Basilico	9

PUBS & BARS

Cooper's Arms	15
The Nag's Head	10
The Pig's Ear	17
Prince Alfred	2
Prince Bonaparte	6
Victoria	8
Warrington Hotel	3

ACCOMMODATION

Abbey House	K
Aster House	P
Columbia	I
Earl's Court Hostel	R
Edward Lear	H
The Gore	M
Holland Park Hostel	L
Hotel 167	Q
Leinster Inn	E
Lincoln House	B
Mayflower	O
Merlyn Court	N
The Pavilion	A
Portobello Gold	F
St David's	D
Vancouver Studios	G
Vicarage	J
Wigmore Court	C

0   200 yds

than twice life-size, nude statue of Napoleon by Antonio Canova stands at the foot of the main staircase.

Back outside, Hyde Park is divided in two by **The Serpentine**, which has a popular **Lido** (mid-June to mid-Sept daily 10am–6pm; £3.75) on its south bank and a pretty upper section known as the **Long Water**, which narrows until it reaches a group of four fountains.

The western half of the park is officially known as **Kensington Gardens** (daily 6am to dusk), and its two most popular attractions are the **Serpentine Gallery** (daily 10am–6pm; free; Ⓦwww.serpentinegallery.org), which hosts contemporary art exhibitions, and the richly decorated, High Gothic **Albert Memorial** (guided tours Sun 2 & 3pm; £4.50), clearly visible to the west. Erected in 1876, the memorial is as much a hymn to the glorious achievements of Britain as to its subject, Queen Victoria's husband (who died of typhoid in 1861). Albert occupies the central canopy, gilded from head to toe and clutching a catalogue for the 1851 Great Exhibition that he helped to organize.

The Exhibition's most famous feature, the gargantuan glasshouse of the Crystal Palace, no longer exists, but the profits were used to buy a large tract of land south of the park, now home to South Kensington's remarkable cluster of museums and colleges, plus the vast **Royal Albert Hall** (Ⓦwww .royalalberthall.com), a splendid iron-and-glass-domed concert hall, with an exterior of red brick, terracotta and marble that became the hallmark of South Ken architecture. The hall is the venue for Europe's most democratic music festival, the Henry Wood Promenade Concerts, better known as the **Proms** (see p.158).

Kensington Palace

On the western edge of Kensington Gardens stands **Kensington Palace** (daily 10am–5/6pm; £12; Ⓦwww.hrp.org.uk), a modestly proportioned Jacobean brick mansion bought by William and Mary in 1689, and the chief royal residence for fifty years afterwards. KP, as it's fondly known in royal circles, is best known today as the place where **Princess Diana** lived until her death in 1997. Visitors don't get to see Diana's apartments, which were on the west side of the palace, where various minor royals still live. Instead, they get to view some of Diana's frocks – and also several worn by the Queen – and then the sparsely furnished state apartments. The highlights are the trompe l'oeil ceiling paintings by William Kent, in particular the Cupola Room, and the oil paintings in the King's Gallery. En route, you also get to see the tastelessly decorated rooms in which the future Queen Victoria spent her unhappy childhood. To recover from the above, take tea in the exquisite **Orangery** (times as for palace).

Leighton House

A number of wealthy Victorian artists rather self-consciously founded an artists' colony in the streets that lay to the west of Kensington Gardens. It's possible to visit one of the most remarkable of these artist pads, **Leighton House**, at 12 Holland Park Rd (daily except Tues; 11am–5.30pm; guided tours Wed & Thurs 2.30pm; £3; Ⓦwww.rbkc.gov.uk/leightonhousemuseum). "It will be opulence, it will be sincerity," Lord Leighton opined before starting work on the house in the 1860s – he later became President of the Royal Academy and was ennobled on his deathbed. The big attraction is the domed Arab Hall, decorated with Saracen tiles, gilded mosaics and woodwork drawn from all over the Islamic world. The other rooms are less spectacular but, in compensation, are hung with paintings by Lord Leighton and his Pre-Raphaelite chums.

Knightsbridge and Harrods

South of Hyde Park lies the irredeemably snobbish **Knightsbridge**, revelling in its reputation as the swankiest shopping area in London, a status epitomized by **Harrods** (Mon–Sat 10am–8pm, Sun noon–6pm; Ⓦ www.harrods.com) on Brompton Road. London's most famous department store started out as a family-run grocery store in 1849, with a staff of two. The current 1905 terracotta building is owned by the Egyptian Mohammed Al Fayed and employs in excess of 3000 staff. The store even has a few sections that are architectural sights in their own right: the Food Hall, with its exquisite Arts and Crafts tiling; the Egyptian Hall, with its pseudo-hieroglyphs and sphinxes; and the fountain at the foot of the Egyptian Escalators dedicated to Di and Dodi. Note that the store has a draconian **dress code**: no ripped jeans, no flip-flops or thong sandals, no shorts, no vest T-shirts, and backpacks either have to be carried in the hand or placed in the store's left luggage (£2.50).

Victoria and Albert Museum (V&A)

In terms of sheer variety and scale, the **Victoria and Albert Museum**, on Cromwell Road (daily 10am–5.45pm, Fri until 10pm; free; Ⓦ www.vam.ac.uk), popularly known as the V&A, is the greatest museum of applied arts in the world. The range of exhibits on display here means that, whatever your taste, there's bound to be something to grab your attention. If you're flagging, there's an edifying café in the museum's period-piece **Morris**, **Gamble** and **Poynter Rooms**.

The most celebrated of the V&A's numerous exhibits are the **Raphael Cartoons**, seven vast biblical paintings that served as designs for a set of tapestries destined for the Sistine Chapel. Close by, you can view highlights from the country's largest dress collection, and the world's largest collection of Indian art outside India. In addition, there are galleries devoted to British, Chinese, Islamic, Japanese and Korean art, as well as costume jewellery, glassware, metalwork and photography. Wading through the huge collection of European sculpture, you come to the surreal **Cast Courts**, filled with copies of European art's greatest hits, from Michelangelo's *David* to Trajan's Column (sawn in half to make it fit).

If you've energy left after your visit, stop by London's most flamboyant Roman Catholic church, the **Brompton Oratory**, built in neo-Baroque style in the 1880s, which lies just next door to the museum on Brompton Road.

Science Museum

Established as a technological counterpart to the V&A, the **Science Museum**, on Exhibition Road (daily 10am–6pm; free; Ⓦ www.sciencemuseum.org.uk), is undeniably impressive, filling seven floors with items drawn from every conceivable area of science, including space travel, digital technology, steam engines and carbon emissions. Keen to dispel the enduring image of museums devoted to its subject as boring and full of dusty glass cabinets, the Science Museum has updated its galleries with interactive displays, and puts on daily demonstrations to show that not all science teaching has to be deathly dry.

First stop inside should be the **information desk**, where you can pick up a museum plan and find out what events and demonstrations are taking place; you can also sign up for a free **guided tour** on a specific subject. Most people will want to head for the **Wellcome Wing**, full of state-of-the-art interactive computers and an IMAX cinema, and geared to appeal to even the most museum-phobic teenager. To get there, you must first pass by the world's first steam engines in the Energy Hall, through the Space gallery, to the far side of the Making of the Modern World, a display of iconic inventions from Robert Stephenson's *Rocket* train of 1829 to the Ford Model T, the world's first mass-produced car.

The **Launch Pad**, one of the first hands-on displays aimed at kids, has been redesigned and relocated to Level 3 and remains as popular and enjoyable as ever. The **Materials** gallery, on Level 1, is aimed more at adults, and is an extremely stylish exhibition covering the use of materials ranging from aluminium to zerodur (used for making laser gyroscopes), while **Energy**, on the second floor, has a great "do not touch" electric shock machine that absolutely fascinates kids.

Natural History Museum

Alfred Waterhouse's purpose-built mock-Romanesque colossus ensures the **Natural History Museum** (daily 10am–5.50pm, last Fri of month closes 9.30pm; free; Ⓦ www.nhm.ac.uk) its status as London's most handsome museum. The museum has been massively redeveloped over the last decade or so, and is now, by and large, imaginatively designed, though there are still one or two sections that remain little changed since the original opening in 1881. The museum's dinosaur collection is a real hit with the kids, but its collections are also an important resource for serious zoologists.

The main entrance leads to what are now known as the **Life Galleries**, which include the ever-popular Dinosaur gallery, with its grisly life-sized animatronic dinosaur tableau, currently a roaring Tyrannosaurus rex. Other popular sections include the Creepy-Crawlies, the Mammals gallery with its life-size model of a blue whale, and the excellent **Investigate** gallery (Mon–Fri 2.30–5pm, Sat & Sun 11am–5pm; during school hols daily 11am–5pm), where children aged 7 to 14 get to play at being scientists (you need to obtain a timed ticket).

Visitors can view more of the museum's millions of zoological specimens in the **Darwin Centre**. To see the rest of the building, however, you need to sign up for an **Explore tour** (book on the day at the information desk or by phoning ☏ 020/7942 6128; free). The tours last about 45 minutes, allowing visitors to get a closer look at the specimens. You also get to see behind the scenes at the labs, and even talk to one of the museum's scientists about their work.

If the queues for the museum are long (as they can be at weekends and during school holidays), you might be better off heading for the side entrance on Exhibition Road, which leads into the former Geology Museum, now known as the **Red Zone**, a visually exciting romp through the earth's evolution. The most popular sections are the slightly tasteless Kobe earthquake simulator, and the spectacular display of gems and crystals in the Earth's Treasury.

Chelsea

From the Swinging Sixties and even up to the Punk era, **Chelsea** had a slightly bohemian pedigree; these days, it's just another wealthy west London suburb. Among the most nattily attired of all those parading down the King's Road nowadays are the scarlet or navy-blue clad Chelsea Pensioners, army veterans from the nearby **Royal Hospital** (Mon–Sat 10am–noon & 2–4pm; April–Sept also Sun 2–4pm; free; Ⓦ www.chelsea-pensioners.co.uk), founded by Charles II in 1681. The hospital's majestic red-brick wings and grassy courtyards became a blueprint for institutional and collegiate architecture all over the English-speaking world. The public are allowed to view the austere hospital chapel, and the equally grand, wood-panelled dining hall, opposite, which has a vast allegorical mural of Charles II.

The concrete bunker next door to the Royal Hospital, on Royal Hospital Road, houses the **National Army Museum** (daily 10am–5.30pm; free; Ⓦ www.national-army-museum.ac.uk). The militarily obsessed are unlikely to be disappointed by the succession of uniforms and medals, and the temporary exhibitions staged on the ground floor can be very good, but there's little here for non-enthusiasts.

North London

Almost all of **North London**'s suburbs are easily accessible by tube from the centre – indeed it was the expansion of the tube which encouraged the forward march of bricks and mortar into many of these areas – though just a handful of these satellite villages, now subsumed into the general mass of the city, are worth bothering with.

First off, is one of London's finest parks, **Regent's Park**, framed by Nash-designed architecture and home of London Zoo. Close by is **Camden Town**, where the weekend market is one of the city's big attractions – a warren of stalls selling street fashion, books, records and ethnic goods. The real highlights of north London, though, for visitors and residents alike, are the village-like suburbs of **Hampstead** and **Highgate**, which have the added advantage of proximity to one of London's wildest patches of greenery, **Hampstead Heath**.

Regent's Park

According to John Nash's masterplan, devised in 1811 for the Prince Regent (later George IV), **Regent's Park** (daily 5am–dusk; Ⓦ www.royalparks.org .uk) was to be girded by a continuous belt of terraces, and sprinkled with a total of 56 villas, including a magnificent pleasure palace for the Prince himself. The plan was never fully realized, due to lack of funds, but enough was built to create something of the idealized garden city that Nash and the Prince Regent envisaged.

Prominent on the park's skyline is the shiny copper dome of **London Central Mosque** at 146 Park Rd (Ⓦ www.iccuk.org), an entirely appropriate addition given the Prince Regent's taste for the Orient. Within the Inner Circle is the **Open Air Theatre** (Ⓦ www.openairtheatre.org), which puts on summer performances of Shakespeare, opera and ballet, and **Queen Mary's Gardens**, by far the prettiest section of the park.

Regent's canal by boat

Three companies run **boat services** (roughly speaking April–Oct daily, Nov–March Sat & Sun only, weather permitting) on the Regent's Canal between Camden and Little Venice, passing through the Maida Hill tunnel and stopping off at London Zoo on the way. The narrowboat *Jenny Wren* (☎020/7485 4433, Ⓦwww.walkersquay .com) starts off at Camden, goes through a canal lock (the only company to do so) and heads for Little Venice, while Jason's narrowboats (☎020/7286 3428, Ⓦwww .jasons.co.uk) start off at Little Venice; the London Waterbus Company (☎020/7482 2660, Ⓦwww.londonwaterbus.com) sets off from both places. Whichever you choose, you can board at either end; **tickets** cost around £6–7 one-way (and only a little more return) and journey time is 50 minutes one-way.

The northeastern corner of the park is occupied by **London Zoo** (daily 10am–4/5.30pm; £12; @ www.zsl.org/london-zoo). Founded in 1826 with the remnants of the royal menagerie, the zoo has had to change with the times, and now bills itself as an eco-conscious place whose prime purpose is to save species under threat of extinction. It's still not the most uplifting spot for animal-lovers, though the enclosures are as humane as any inner-city zoo could make them, and kids usually love the place. Most are particularly taken by the children's enclosure, where they can actually handle the animals, and the regular "Animals in Action" live shows. The invertebrate house, now known as BUGS, the new Gorilla Kingdom and the walk-through rainforest and monkey forest, called the Clore Rainforest Lookout, are all guaranteed winners.

Camden Town

For all its tourist popularity, **Camden Market** remains a genuinely offbeat place. More than 100,000 shoppers turn up here each weekend, and parts of the market now stay open week-long, alongside a similarly-oriented crop of shops, cafés and bistros. The sheer variety of what's on offer: from bootleg tapes to furniture, along with a mass of street fashion and clubwear, and plenty of foodstalls, is what makes Camden so special. To avoid the crowds, which can be overpowering on a summer Sunday afternoon, you'll need to get here by 10am.

Despite having no significant Jewish associations, Camden is home to London's **Jewish Museum** (Mon–Thurs 10am–4pm, Sun 10am–5pm; £3.50; @ www .jewishmuseum.org.uk), at 129 Albert St, just off Parkway. The purpose-built premises are smartly designed, and the collection of Judaica includes treasures from London's Great Synagogue, burnt down by Nazi bombers in 1941, and a sixteenth-century Venetian Ark of the Covenant. More compelling are the temporary exhibitions, discussions and occasional concerts put on by the museum.

Hampstead and Highgate

The high points of North London, both geographically and aesthetically, the elegant, largely eighteenth-century developments of **Hampstead** and **Highgate** have managed to cling onto their village origins. Of the two, Highgate is slightly sleepier and more aloof, with fewer conventional sights, while Hampstead is busier and buzzier, with high-profile intelligentsia and discerning pop stars among its residents. Both benefit from direct access to **Hampstead Heath**, where you can enjoy stupendous views over London, kite flying and nude bathing, as well as outdoor concerts and high art in and around the Neoclassical country mansion of Kenwood House.

Keats' House and the Freud Museum

Hampstead's most lustrous figure is celebrated at **Keats' House** (Tues–Sun 1–5pm; £3.50), an elegant, whitewashed Regency double villa on Keats Grove, off Downshire Hill at the bottom of the High Street. Inspired by the peaceful-ness of Hampstead and by his passion for girl-next-door Fanny Brawne (whose house is also part of the museum), Keats wrote some of his most famous works here before leaving for Rome, where he died of consumption in 1821. The neat, rather staid interior contains books and letters, Fanny's engagement ring and the four-poster bed in which the poet first coughed up blood, confiding to his companion, Charles Brown, "that drop of blood is my death warrant".

One of the most poignant of London's house museums is the **Freud Museum** (Wed–Sun noon–5pm; £5; @ www.freud.org.uk), hidden away in the leafy streets of south Hampstead at 20 Maresfield Gardens. Having lived in Vienna for his entire adult life, Freud, by now semi-disabled with only a year to live, was forced to flee the Nazis, arriving in London in the summer of 1938. The ground-floor study and library look exactly as they did when Freud lived here; the collection of erotic antiquities and the famous couch, sumptuously draped in Persian carpets, were all brought here from Vienna. Upstairs, home movies of family life in Vienna are shown continually, and a small room is dedicated to his daughter, Anna, herself an influential child analyst, who lived in the house until her death in 1982.

Hampstead Heath and Kenwood

North London's "green lung", **Hampstead Heath** is the city's most enjoyable public park. It may not have much of its original heathland left, but it packs a wonderful variety of bucolic scenery into its 800 acres. At its southern end are the rolling green pastures of **Parliament Hill**, north London's premier spot for kite flying. On either side are numerous ponds, three of which – one for men, one for women and one mixed – you can swim in for free. The thickest woodland is to be found in the **West Heath**, beyond Whitestone Pond, also the site of the most formal section, **Hill Garden**, a secretive and romantic little gem with eccentric balustraded terraces and a ruined pergola. Beyond lies **Golders Hill Park**, where you can gaze at pygmy goats and fallow deer, and inspect the impeccably maintained aviaries, home to flamingoes, cranes and other exotic birds.

Finally, don't miss the landscaped grounds of Kenwood, in the north of the Heath, which are focused on the whitewashed Neoclassical mansion of **Kenwood House** (daily 11am–4/5pm; EH; free). The house is now home to a collection of seventeenth- and eighteenth-century art, including a handful of real masterpieces by the likes of Vermeer, Rembrandt, Boucher, Gainsborough and Reynolds. Of the house's period interiors, the most spectacular is Robert Adam's sky-blue and gold library, its book-filled apses separated from the central entertaining area by paired columns.

Highgate Cemetery

Receiving far more visitors than Highgate itself, **Highgate Cemetery** (Ⓦhighgate-cemetery.org), ranged on both sides of Swain's Lane, is London's best-known graveyard. The most illustrious incumbent of the **East Cemetery** (Mon–Fri 10am–4/5pm, Sat & Sun 11am–4/5pm; £2) is **Karl Marx**. Marx himself asked for a simple grave topped by a headstone, but by 1954 the Communist movement decided to move his grave to a more prominent position and erect the vulgar bronze bust that now surmounts a granite plinth. Close by lies the much simpler grave of the author George Eliot.

What the East Cemetery lacks in atmosphere is in part compensated for by the fact that you can wander at will through its maze of circuitous paths, whereas to visit the more atmospheric and overgrown **West Cemetery**, with its spooky Egyptian Avenue and sunken catacombs, you must go round with a guided tour (March–Nov Mon–Fri 2pm, Sat & Sun hourly 11am–4pm; Dec–Feb Sat & Sun hourly 11am–3pm; £3; no under 8s). Among the prominent graves usually visited are those of artist Dante Gabriel Rossetti, and lesbian novelist Radclyffe Hall.

Hendon: The RAF Museum

A world-class assembly of historic military aircraft can be seen at the **RAF Museum** (daily 10am–6pm; free; Ⓦwww.rafmuseum.org.uk; Colindale tube), located in a godforsaken part of north London beside the M1 motorway.

▲ Highgate Cemetery

Enthusiasts won't be disappointed, but those looking for a balanced account of modern aerial warfare will – the overall tone is unashamedly militaristic, not to say jingoistic. Those with children should head for the hands-on Aeronauts gallery; those without might prefer to explore the often overlooked display galleries, ranged around the edge of the Main Aircraft Hall, which contain an art gallery and an exhibition on the history of flight, accompanied by replicas of some of the death-traps of early aviation.

Neasden: the Shri Swaminarayan Temple

Perhaps the most remarkable building in the whole of London lies just off the North Circular Road, in the glum suburb of **Neasden**. Here, rising majestically above the surrounding semi-detached houses like a mirage, is the **Shri Swaminarayan Mandir** (daily 9am–6pm; free; ⓦwww.mandir.org; Neasden tube), a traditional Hindu temple topped with domes and shikharas, erected in 1995 in a style and scale unseen outside of India for more than a millennium. To reach the temple, you must enter through the adjacent Haveli, or cultural complex, with its carved wooden portico and balcony. After taking off your shoes, you can proceed to the Mandir (temple) itself, carved entirely out of Carrara marble, with every possible surface transformed into a honeycomb of arabesques, flowers and seated gods. Beneath the Mandir, an **exhibition** (£2) explains the basic tenets of Hinduism and details the life of Lord Swaminarayan, and includes a video about the history of the building.

South London

Now largely built up into a patchwork of Victorian terraces, **South London** nevertheless boasts one outstanding area for sightseeing, and that is **Greenwich**, with its impressive ensemble of the Royal Naval College and the Queen's House, courtesy of Christopher Wren and Inigo Jones respectively. Most visitors, it has to be said, come to see the National Maritime Museum, the Royal Observatory, and the beautifully landscaped royal park, though Greenwich also pulls in an ever-increasing volume of Londoners in search of bargains at its Sunday **market**.

The only other suburban sights that stand out are the **Dulwich Picture Gallery**, a public art gallery even older than the National Gallery, and the eclectic **Horniman Museum**, in neighbouring Forest Hill.

Greenwich

Greenwich is one of London's most beguiling spots, but Greenwich town centre, laid out in the 1820s with Nash-style terraces, is nowadays plagued with heavy traffic. In addition to the sights below, one of Greenwich's major draws has been the **Cutty Sark** (ⓦwww.cuttysark.org.uk), the world's last surviving tea clipper, which was built in 1869 and is wedged in a dry dock by the riverside. After a devastating fire in 2007, it is currently being restored, though a visitor centre remains open. To reach Greenwich, you can take a **train** from London Bridge (every 30min), a **boat** from one of the piers in central London, or the **DLR** to Cutty Sark station.

The Old Royal Naval College

To escape Greenwich's busy streets, head for the **Old Royal Naval College** (daily 10am–5pm; free; ⓦwww.oldroyalnavalcollege.org), Wren's beautifully symmetrical Baroque ensemble which makes the most of its riverbank location. Initially built as a royal palace, but eventually converted into a hospital for disabled seamen, the complex was home to the Royal Naval College from 1873 until 1998, but now houses the University of Greenwich and the Trinity College of Music. The two grandest rooms, situated underneath Wren's twin domes, are open to the public and well worth visiting. The **Chapel**, in the east wing, has exquisite pastel-shaded plasterwork and spectacular, decorative detailing on the ceiling, all designed by James "Athenian" Stuart after a fire in 1799 destroyed the original interior. Opposite the chapel is the magnificent **Painted Hall** in the west wing, which is dominated by James Thornhill's gargantuan allegorical ceiling painting, and his trompe l'oeil fluted pilasters.

National Maritime Museum

The main entrance to the excellent **National Maritime Museum** (daily 10am–5pm; July & Aug closes 6pm; free; ⓦ www.nmm.ac.uk), which occupies the old Naval Asylum, is on Romney Road. From here, you enter the spectac-ular glass-roofed central courtyard, which houses the museum's largest artifacts. Among them the splendid 63-foot-long gilded **Royal Barge**, designed in Rococo style by William Kent for Prince Frederick, the much unloved eldest son of George II.

The various themed galleries are superbly designed to appeal to visitors of all ages. In **Explorers**, on Level 1, you get to view some *Titanic* relics; **Passengers** re-lives the glory days of transatlantic shipping, which officially came to an end in 1957 when more people went by air than by sea; **Oceans of Discovery**, on Level 3, boasts Captain Cook's sextant and K1 marine clock, Shackleton's compass, and Captain Scott's overshoes, watch and funky sledging goggles.

Level 3 also boasts two hands-on galleries: **The Bridge**, where you can attempt to navigate a catamaran, a paddle steamer and a rowing boat to shore; and **All Hands**, where children can have a go at radio transmission, loading miniature cargo, firing a cannon and so forth. **Nelson's Navy** boasts lots of nineteenth-century Nelson kitsch, a video replay of the Battle of Trafalgar, and the great man's diminutive "undress coat", worn during the battle, with a tiny bullet hole made by the musket shot that killed him.

Inigo Jones's **Queen's House**, originally built amidst a rambling Tudor royal palace, is now the focal point of the Greenwich ensemble, and is an integral part of the Maritime Museum. As royal residences go, it's fairly unassuming, but as the first Neoclassical building in the country it has enormous architectural significance. Very few features survive from Stuart times, and the interior is currently used for temporary exhibitions. Off the Great Hall, a perfect cube, lies the beautiful Tulip Staircase, Britain's earliest cantilevered spiral staircase – its name derives from the floral patterning in the wrought-iron balustrade.

Royal Observatory

Perched on the crest of Greenwich Park's highest hill, the **Royal Observatory** (daily 10am–5pm; July & Aug closes 6pm; free; ⓦ www.nmm.ac.uk) is housed in a rather dinky Wren-built red-brick building, whose northeastern turret sports a bright-red time-ball that climbs the mast at 12.58pm and drops at 1pm GMT precisely; it was added in 1833 to allow ships to set their clocks.

Greenwich's greatest claim to fame, of course, is as the home of Greenwich Mean Time (GMT) and the Prime Meridian. Since 1884, Greenwich has occupied zero longitude – hence the world sets its clocks by GMT. The observatory itself was established in 1675 by Charles II to house the first Astronomer Royal, John Flamsteed, whose chief task was to study the night sky in order to discover an astronomical method of finding the longitude of a ship at sea. Astronomers continued to work here at Greenwich until the postwar smog forced them to decamp; the old observatory, meanwhile, is now a very popular museum.

The oldest part of the observatory is the aforementioned Wren-built **Flamsteed House**, containing the Octagon Room, where the king used to show off to his guests. The Time galleries, beyond, focus on the search for the precise measurement of longitude, and display four of the clocks designed by **John Harrison**, including "H4", which helped win the Longitude Prize in 1763.

The observatory has also recently updated its **Astronomy** galleries and built a state-of-the-art **Planetarium** in the South Building, with regular shows presented by a Royal Observatory astronomer (Mon–Fri 1, 2, 3 & 4pm, Sat & Sun noon, 1, 3 & 4pm; £6).

The Ranger's House and the Fan Museum

Southwest of the observatory, and backing onto Greenwich Park's rose garden, is the **Ranger's House** (April–Sept Mon–Wed & Sun 10am–5pm; EH; £5.50), a red-brick Georgian villa that houses an art collection amassed by Julius Wernher, the German-born millionaire who made his money by exploiting the diamond deposits of South Africa. His taste in art is eclectic, ranging from medieval ivory miniatures to Iznik pottery, though he was definitely a man who placed technical virtuosity above artistic merit. The high points of the collection are Memlinc's *Virgin and Child* and the pair of sixteenth-century majolica dishes decorated with mythological scenes for Isabella d'Este (all located upstairs), and the Reynolds portraits and de Hooch interior (located downstairs).

Croom's Hill, running down the west side of the park, boasts some of Greenwich's finest Georgian buildings, one of which houses the **Fan Museum** at no. 12 (Tues–Sat 11am–5pm, Sun noon–5pm; £3.50; ⓦ www.fan-museum .org). It's a fascinating little place (and an extremely beautiful house), revealing the importance of the fan as a social and political object. The permanent exhibition on the ground floor traces the history of the materials employed, from peacock feathers to straw, while temporary exhibitions on the first floor explore such subjects as techniques of production and changing fashion.

Dulwich Picture Gallery and the Horniman Museum

Dulwich Picture Gallery (Tues–Fri 10am–5pm, Sat & Sun 11am–5pm; £4; ⓦ www.dulwichpicturegallery.org.uk; West Dulwich train station from Victoria), on College Road, is the nation's oldest public art gallery, designed by John Soane and opened in 1817. Soane created a beautifully spacious building, awash with natural light and crammed with superb paintings – elegiac landscapes by Cuyp, one of the world's finest Poussin series, and splendid works by Hogarth, Gainsborough, van Dyck, Canaletto and Rubens, plus **Rembrandt's** tiny *Portrait of a Young Man*, a top-class portrait of poet, playwright and Royalist, the future Earl of Bristol. At the centre of the museum is a tiny mausoleum designed by Soane for the sarcophagi of the gallery's founders.

To the southeast of Dulwich Park, on the busy South Circular Road, is the wacky **Horniman Museum** (daily 10.30am–5.30pm; free; ⓦ www .horniman.ac.uk; Forest Hill train station from Victoria or London Bridge), purpose-built in 1901 by Frederick Horniman, a tea trader with a passion for collecting. In addition to the museum's natural history collection of stuffed birds and animals, there's an amazingly eclectic ethnographic collection, and a musical department with more than 1500 instruments from Chinese gongs to electric guitars. Don't miss the museum's new **aquarium** in the basement, and look out for the special sessions at the **Hands on Base**, which allow you to handle and learn more about a whole range of the museum's artefacts.

Out west: Chiswick to Windsor

Most visitors experience **west London** en route to or from Heathrow Airport, either from the confines of the train or tube (which runs overground at this point), or the motorway. The city and its satellites seem to continue unabated, with only fleeting glimpses of the countryside. However, in the five-mile stretch from Chiswick to Osterley there are several former country retreats, now surrounded by suburbia, which are definitely worth digging out. The Palladian villa of **Chiswick House** is perhaps the best known of these attractions. However, it draws nothing like as many visitors as **Syon House**, most of whom come for the gardening centre rather than for the house itself, a showcase for the talents of Robert Adam, who also worked at **Osterley House**, another Elizabethan conversion.

Running through the area is the **River Thames**, once known as the "Great Highway of London" and still the most pleasant way to travel in these parts during the summer. Boats plough up the Thames all the way from central London via the **Royal Botanic Gardens** at **Kew** and the picturesque riverside at **Richmond**, as far as **Hampton Court**, home of the country's largest royal residence and the famous maze. To reach the heavily touristed royal outpost of **Windsor Castle**, however, you need to take the train.

Chiswick

Chiswick House (April–Oct Wed–Fri & Sun 10am–5pm, Sat 10am–2pm; EH; £4.20; Chiswick train station from Waterloo) is a perfect little Neoclassical villa, designed in the 1720s by the Earl of Burlington, and set in one of the most beautifully landscaped gardens in London. Like its prototype, Palladio's Villa Rotonda near Vicenza, the house was purpose-built as a "temple to the arts" where, amid his fine-art collection, Burlington could entertain artistic friends such as Swift, Handel and Pope. Entertaining took place on the **upper floor**, a series of cleverly interconnecting rooms, each enjoying a wonderful view out onto the gardens – all, that is, except the **Tribunal**, the domed octagonal hall at the centre of the villa, where the earl's finest paintings and sculptures would have been displayed.

If you leave Chiswick House gardens by the northernmost exit, beyond the Italian garden, it's just a short walk along the thunderous A4 road to **Hogarth's House** (Tues–Fri 1–4/5pm, Sat & Sun 1–5/6pm; closed Jan; free), where the artist spent each summer with his wife, sister and mother-in-law from 1749 until his death in 1764. Nowadays it's difficult to believe Hogarth came here for "peace and quiet", but in the eighteenth century the house was almost entirely surrounded by countryside. In addition to scores of Hogarth's engravings, you can see copies of his satirical series *An Election*, *Marriage à la Mode* and *A Harlot's Progress*, and compare the modern view from the parlour with the more idyllic scene in *Mr Ranby's House*.

Around Kew Bridge

Difficult to miss thanks to its stylish Italianate standpipe tower, **Kew Bridge Steam Museum** (daily 11am–5pm; Mon–Fri £4.25, Sat & Sun £5.75; ⓦ www.kbsm.org; Kew Bridge train station from Waterloo; or bus #237 or #267 from Gunnersbury tube) occupies a former pumping station, on the corner of Kew Bridge Road and Green Dragon Lane, 100m west of the bridge itself. At the heart of the museum is the Steam Hall, which contains a triple expansion steam engine and four gigantic nineteenth-century Cornish beam

River transport

Westminster Passenger Services (☎020/7930 2062, ⓦwww.wpsa.co.uk) runs four boats from Westminster Pier to Kew, and two boats to Richmond and Hampton Court daily from April to September. The full trip takes 3hr one way, and costs £13.50 one way, £19.50 return. In addition, Turks (☎020/8546 2434, ⓦwww.turks.co.uk) run a regular service from Richmond to Hampton Court (April to mid-Sept, Tues–Sun) which costs £5.50 one-way or £7 return.

engines. The museum also has a hands-on **Water for Life** gallery in the basement, devoted to the history of the capital's water supply. The best time to visit is at weekends, when each of the museum's industrial dinosaurs is put through its paces, and the small **narrow-gauge steam railway** runs back and forth round the yard (March–Nov Sun).

Syon House

Across the water from Kew stands **Syon Park** (ⓦwww.syonpark.co.uk), seat of the Duke of Northumberland since Elizabethan times. It's now as much a working commercial concern as a family home, embracing a garden centre, a wholefood shop, an aquatic centre stocked with tropical fish, a mini-zoo and a butterfly house, as well as the old aristocratic mansion and its gardens.

From its rather plain castellated exterior, you'd never guess that **Syon House** (April–Oct Wed, Thurs & Sun 11am–5pm; £8; bus #237 or #267 from Gunnersbury tube or Kew Bridge train station) contains the most opulent eighteenth-century interiors in the whole of London. The splendour of Robert Adam's refurbishment is immediately revealed, however, in the pristine **Great Hall**, an apsed double cube with a screen of Doric columns at one end and classical statuary dotted around the edges. There are several more Adam-designed rooms to admire in the house, plus a smattering of works by van Dyck, Lely, Gainsborough and Reynolds.

While Adam beautified Syon House, Capability Brown laid out its **gardens** (daily: March–Oct 10.30am–5pm or dusk; Nov–Feb Sat & Sun 10.30am–4pm; £4) around an artificial lake, surrounding it with oaks, beeches, limes and cedars. The gardens' chief focus now, however, is the crescent-shaped **Great Conservatory**, an early-nineteenth-century addition which is said to have inspired Joseph Paxton, architect of the Crystal Palace.

Osterley Park and House

Robert Adam redesigned another colossal Elizabethan mansion three miles northwest of Syon at **Osterley Park** (daily 9am–7.30pm or dusk; free), which maintains the impression of being in the middle of the countryside, despite the presence of the M4 to the north of the house. The park itself is well worth exploring, and there's a great café in the Tudor stables, but anyone with a passing interest in Adam's work should pay a visit to **Osterley House** (mid-March to Oct Wed–Sun 1–4.30pm; Dec Sat & Sun 12.30–3.30pm; NT; £7.50; Osterley tube). From the outside, Osterley bears some similarity to Syon, the big difference being Adam's grand entrance portico, with its tall, Ionic colonnade. From here, you enter a characteristically cool **Entrance Hall**, followed by the so-called State Rooms of the south wing. Highlights include the **Drawing Room**, with Reynolds portraits on the damask walls and a coffered ceiling centred on a giant marigold, and the **Etruscan Dressing Room**, in which every surface is covered in delicate painted trelliswork, sphinxes and urns, a style that Adam (and Wedgwood) dubbed "Etruscan", though it is in fact derived from Greek vases found at Pompeii.

Kew Gardens

Established in 1759, the **Royal Botanic Gardens** (daily 9.30am–7.30pm or dusk; £12.25; ⓦ www.kew.org; Kew Gardens tube) have grown from their original eight acres into a three-hundred-acre site in which more than 33,000 species are grown in plantations and glasshouses. It's a display that attracts over a million visitors every year, most of them with no specialist interest at all. There's always something to see, whatever the season, but to get the most out of the place, come sometime between spring and autumn, bring a picnic and stay for the day.

Of all the glasshouses, by far the most celebrated is the **Palm House**, a curvaceous mound of glass and wrought iron, designed by Decimus Burton in the 1840s. Its drippingly humid atmosphere nurtures most of the known palm species, while in the basement there's a small but excellent tropical aquarium. Kew's origins as an eighteenth-century royal pleasure garden are evident in the numerous follies dotted about Kew, the most conspicuous of which is the ten-storey, 163-foot-high **pagoda**.

The three-storey red-brick mansion of **Kew Palace** (Easter–Oct Tues–Sun 10am–5pm; £5), to the northwest of the Palm House, was bought by George II as a nursery and schoolhouse for his umpteen children. Later, George III was confined to the palace and subjected to the dubious attentions of doctors who attempted to find a cure for his "madness". There are one or two bits and bobs belonging to the royals, like the much-loved dolls' house, on the ground floor, which belonged to George III's daughters. Upstairs, you can view the chair in which Queen Charlotte passed away in 1818, while the top floor has been left pretty much untouched since those days.

Richmond Park and Ham House

Richmond, upriver from Kew, basked for centuries in the glow of royal patronage, with Plantagenet kings and Tudor monarchs frequenting the riverside palace. Although most of the courtiers and aristocrats have gone, Richmond is still a wealthy district, with two theatres and highbrow pretensions. Richmond's greatest attraction though, is the enormous **Richmond Park** (daily: March–Sept 7am–dusk; Oct–Feb 7.30am–dusk; free; ⓦ www.royalparks.gov.uk), at the top of Richmond Hill – 2500 acres of undulating grassland and bracken, dotted with coppiced woodland and as wild as anything in London. Eight miles across at its widest point, this is Europe's largest city park, famed for its red and fallow deer, which roam freely, and for its ancient oaks. For the most part untamed, the park does have a couple of deliberately landscaped plantations that feature splendid springtime azaleas and rhododendrons, in particular the Isabella Plantation.

Back down the hill, if you continue along the towpath beyond Richmond Bridge, after a mile or so, you leave the rest of London far behind and arrive at **Ham House** (April–Oct Mon–Wed, Sat & Sun 1–5pm; £9; NT; Richmond tube), home to the earls of Dysart for nearly three hundred years. Expensively furnished in the seventeenth century, but little altered since then, the house boasts one of the finest Stuart interiors in the country, from the stupendously ornate Great Staircase to the Long Gallery, featuring six "Court Beauties" by Peter Lely. Elsewhere, there are several fine Verrio ceiling paintings, some exquisite parquet flooring and works by Van Dyck and Reynolds. Another bonus is the formal seventeenth-century **gardens** (Mon–Wed, Sat & Sun 11am–6pm; £3, free with ticket for house), especially the Cherry Garden, laid out with a pungent lavender parterre, surrounded by yew hedges and pleached hornbeam arbours. The Orangery, overlooking the original kitchen garden, currently serves as a tearoom.

Hampton Court

Hampton Court Palace (daily 10am–4.30/6pm; £13; ⓦ www.hrp.org.uk; Hampton Court train station from Waterloo), a sprawling red-brick ensemble on the banks of the Thames, thirteen miles southwest of London, is the finest of England's royal abodes. Built in 1516 by the upwardly mobile **Cardinal Wolsey**, Henry VIII's Lord Chancellor, it was purloined by Henry himself after Wolsey fell from favour. In the second half of the seventeenth century, Charles II laid out the gardens, inspired by what he had seen at Versailles, while William and Mary had large sections of the palace remodelled by Wren a few years later.

The **Royal Apartments** are divided into six thematic walking tours. There's not a lot of information in any of the rooms, but guided tours, each lasting 45 minutes, are available at no extra charge and led by period-costumed historians, who do a fine job of bringing the place to life. If your energy is lacking – and Hampton Court is huge – the most rewarding sections are: **Henry VIII's State Apartments**, which feature the glorious double hammerbeamed Great Hall; the **King's Apartments** (remodelled by William III); and the vast **Tudor Kitchens**. The last two are also served by audioguides. Part of the Royal Collection is housed in the **Renaissance Picture Gallery** and is chock-full of treasures, among them paintings by Tintoretto, Lotto, Titian, Cranach, Bruegel and Holbein.

Tickets to the Royal Apartments cover entry to the rest of the sights in the grounds. Those who don't wish to visit the apartments are free to wander around the gardens, visit the curious **Royal Tennis Courts** (April–Oct), but have to pay extra to try out the palace's famously tricky yew-hedge **Maze** (£3.50), and visit the **Privy Garden** (£4.50), where you can view Andrea Mantegna's colourful, heroic canvases, *The Triumphs of Caesar*, housed in the Lower Orangery, and the celebrated **Great Vine**, whose grapes are sold at the palace each year in September.

Windsor and Eton

Every weekend trains from Waterloo and Paddington are packed with people heading for **WINDSOR**, the royal enclave 21 miles west of London, where they join the human conveyor belt round **Windsor Castle** (daily 9.45am–4.15/5.15pm; £14.20; ⓦ www.royal.gov.uk; Paddington to Windsor & Eton Central via Slough, or Waterloo to Windsor & Eton Riverside – note that you must arrive and depart from the same station, as tickets are not interchangeable). Towering above the town on a steep chalk bluff, the castle is an undeniably awesome sight, its chilly grey walls, punctuated by mighty medieval bastions, continuing as far as the eye can see. Inside, most visitors just gape in awe at the monotonous, gilded grandeur of the **State Apartments**, while the real highlights – the paintings from the Royal Collection that line the walls – are rarely given a second glance. More impressive is **St George's Chapel** (Mon–Sat 10am–4pm), a glorious Perpendicular structure ranking with Henry VII's chapel in Westminster Abbey (see p.95), and the second most important resting place for royal corpses after the Abbey. On a fine day, it pays to put aside some time for exploring Windsor Great Park, which stretches for several miles to the south of the castle.

Crossing the bridge at the end of Thames Avenue in Windsor town brings you to **ETON**, a one-street village lined with bookshops and antique dealers, but famous all over the world for **Eton College** (Easter, July & Aug daily 10.30am–4.30pm; after Easter to June & Sept daily 2–4.30pm; £4; ⓦwww .etoncollege.com), a ten-minute walk from the river. When the school was founded in 1440, its aim was to give free education to seventy poor scholars and choristers – how times have changed. The original fifteenth-century **schoolroom**, gnarled with centuries of graffiti, survives, but the real highlight is the **College Chapel**, completed in 1482, a wonderful example of English Perpendicular architecture. The self-congratulatory **Museum of Eton Life**, where you're deposited at the end of the tour, is well worth missing unless you have a fascination with flogging, fagging and bragging about the school's facilities and alumni – Percy Bysshe Shelley is a rare rebellious figure in the roll call of Establishment greats.

Eating

London is an exciting (though often expensive) place in which to eat out. It's home to people from all over the globe, and you can pretty much sample any kind of cuisine here, from Georgian to Peruvian. Indeed, London is now home to some of the best **Cantonese** restaurants in the whole of Europe, is a noted centre for **Indian** and **Bangladeshi** food, and has numerous French, Greek, Italian, Japanese, Spanish and Thai restaurants; and within all these cuisines, you can choose anything from simple meals to gourmet spreads. **Traditional and Modern British** food is available all over town, and some of the best venues are reviewed below.

Cafés and snacks

There are plenty of **cafés** and small, basic restaurants all over London that can fill you up for under £10, including tea or coffee. Several of the places listed are also open in the evening, but the turnover is fast, so don't expect to linger; they're best seen as fuel stops before – or in a few cases, after – a night out. It's worth bearing in mind that most **pubs** (which are covered in the following section) serve meals, and many take their food quite seriously. We've marked places on the maps in this chapter wherever possible.

Whitehall, Westminster and Victoria

Café in the Crypt St Martin-in-the-Fields, Duncannon Street, WC2; see map, pp.90–91. The self-service buffet food is nothing special, but there are regular veggie dishes, and the handy (and atmospheric) location makes this an ideal spot.

Jenny Lo's Teahouse 14 Ecclestone St, SW1; see map, pp.90–91. Bright, bare and utilitarian yet somehow stylish and fashionable too, *Jenny Lo's* serves good Chinese food at low prices. Be sure to check out the therapeutic teas. Closed Sun.

St James's, Mayfair and Marylebone

Eat & Two Veg 50 Marylebone High St, W1; see map, p.105. A lively and modern veggie restaurant, with some vegan and soya protein choices. The menu is eclectic, with Thai, Greek and Italian dishes.

Mômo Tearoom 25 Heddon St, W1; see map, pp.90–91. The ultimate Arabic pastiche, and a successful one at that. The adjacent restaurant is pricey, but the tearoom serves delicious snacks and is a great place to hang out, with tables and hookahs spilling out onto the pavement of this little Mayfair alleyway behind Regent Street.

Patisserie Valerie at Sagne 105 Marylebone High St, W1; see map, p.105. Founded as Swiss-run *Maison Sagne* in the 1920s, and preserving its wonderful decor from those days, the café is now run by Soho's fab patisserie makers, and is without doubt Marylebone's finest.

🏃 The Wolseley 160 Piccadilly, W1; see map, pp.90–91. The lofty and stylish 1920s interior of this brasserie/restaurant (built as the showroom for Wolseley cars) is a big draw, and service is attentive and non-snooty. Given the glamour levels it's surprisingly affordable and the Viennese-inspired food delivers too. A great place for breakfast or a cream tea (£7.75).

Soho, Chinatown and Fitzrovia

Bar Italia 22 Frith St, W1; see map, pp.90–91. A tiny café that's a Soho institution, serving coffee, croissants and sandwiches more or less around the clock, as it has done since 1949.

Beatroot 92 Berwick St, W1; see map, pp.90–91. Great little veggie café by the market, doling out hot savoury bakes, stews and salads (plus delicious cakes) in boxes of varying sizes – all under £5.

🏃 Breakfast Club 33 D'Arblay St, W1; see map, pp.90–91. Small, laidback Aussie-style place, with substantial toasted sarnies, fresh juice and great coffee, plus free Wi-Fi and two computer terminals. Closed Sun.

Gaby's 30 Charing Cross Rd, WC2; see map, pp.90–91. Busy café and takeaway joint that stays open till late serving a wide range of home-cooked veggie and Middle Eastern specialities. Hard to beat for value or choice and it's licensed, too. Closed Sun.

Indian YMCA 41 Fitzroy Square, W1; see map, p.105. Don't take any notice of the signs saying the canteen is only for students – this place is open to all; just press the bell and pile in. The entire menu is portioned up into pretty little bowls; go and collect what you want and pay at the till. The food is great and the prices unbelievably low.

Kopi-Tiam 9 Wardour St, W1; see map, pp.90–91. Bright, cheap Malaysian café serving up curries, coconut rice, juices and "herbal soups" to local Malays, all for around a fiver.

🏃 Maison Bertaux 28 Greek St, W1; see map, pp.90–91. Long-standing, old-fashioned and terribly French patisserie, with tables on two floors (and one or two outside) and a loyal clientele that keeps things busy.

Misato 11 Wardour St, W1; see map, pp.90–91. Modern, canteen-style Japanese café serving stomach-filling rice and noodle dishes for around a fiver, plus miso soup, sushi and bento boxes.

Patisserie Valerie 44 Old Compton St, W1; see map, pp.90–91. Popular coffee, croissant and cake emporium dating from the 1950s and attracting a loud-talking, arty Soho crowd.

Tokyo Diner 2 Newport Place, WC2; see map, pp.90–91. Friendly place on the edge of Chinatown that shuns elaboration for fast food, Tokyo-style. Minimalist decor lets the sushi do the talking.

Covent Garden

🏃 Food for Thought 31 Neal St, WC2; see map, pp.90–91. Long-established but minuscule bargain veggie restaurant and takeaway counter – the food is good, with the menu changing twice daily. Expect to queue and don't expect to linger at peak times.

Just Falafs 27b Covent Garden Piazza, WC2; see map, pp.90–91. Mainly takeaway joint at the southeast corner of the piazza – wholesome falafels, mainly organic salad, yoghurt and seasonal beans rolled in a flatbread.

Rock & Sole Plaice 47 Endell St, WC2; see map, pp.90–91. A rare survivor: a no-nonsense (though not cheap) traditional fish and chip shop in central London. Takeaway, eat in or out at one of the pavement tables.

Wagamama 4 Streatham St, WC1; see map, pp.90–91. Much copied since, *Wagamama* was the pioneer when it comes to austere, minimalist, canteen-style noodle bars. Branches around central London.

World Food Café 14 Neal's Yard, WC2; see map, pp.90–91. First-floor veggie café that comes into its own in summer, when the windows are flung open and you can gaze down upon trendy humanity as you tuck into pricey but tasty dishes from all corners of the globe. Closed Sun.

Clerkenwell and Hoxton

Clark & Sons 46 Exmouth Market, EC1; see map, pp.108–109. With Exmouth Market having undergone something of a transformation, it's all the more surprising to find this genuine eel and pie shop still going strong. Closed Sun.

🏃 Macondo 8–9 Hoxton Square, N1; see map, pp.108–109. Really relaxing Spanish café where you can hang out for hours, fuelling yourself with great tortilla and huge and delicious home-made cakes.

The City and the East End

Arkansas Café Unit 12, Old Spitalfields Market, E1; see map, pp.108–109. American barbecue fuel stop, using only the very best free-range ingredients. Closed Sat.

Brick Lane Beigel Bake 159 Brick Lane, E1; see map, pp.108–109. Classic 24hr bagel takeaway shop in the heart of the East End – unbelievably cheap, even for your top-end filling, such as smoked salmon and cream cheese.

Café 1001 1 Dray's Lane, E1; see map, pp.108–109. Off Brick Lane, tucked in by the Truman Brewery, this café has a beaten-up studenty look, with lots of sofas to crash in, and dishes out simple sandwiches and delicious cakes.

De Gustibus 53–55 Carter Lane, EC2; see map, pp.108–109. Award-winning bakery that creates a wide variety of sandwiches, bruschetta, *croque-monsieurs* and quiches to eat in or take away. Closed Sat & Sun.

Frizzante@City Farm 1a Goldsmith's Row, E2; see map, pp.108–109. Hackney City Farm's café serves up home-made family-friendly generous all-day "Big Farm" or veggie breakfasts, risottos and delicious pizza-like *piadinas*, all for around a fiver.

The Place Below St Mary-le-Bow, Cheapside, EC2; see map, pp.108–109. City café serving imaginative vegetarian dishes and delicious breakfast pastries, in a wonderful Norman crypt. Closed Sat & Sun.

The South Bank and Southwark

Benugo Bar & Kitchen BFI Southbank, SE1; see map, p.120. Former NFT bar is now welcoming and glamorous option, with cosy armchairs in vibrant colours and free Wi-Fi. Pricey but delicious sarnies and a range of bar snacks, from chunky chips to a pint of sausage rolls.

Marsh Ruby 30 Lower Marsh, SE1; see map, p.120. Terrific filling lunchtime curries for under a fiver: the food is organic/free range and there's a basic but cheery communal dining area at the back. Closed Sat & Sun.

Kensington, Chelsea and Notting Hill

Books for Cooks 4 Blenheim Crescent, W11; see map, pp.126–127. Tiny café/restaurant within London's top cookery bookshop – just wander in and have a coffee while browsing, or get there in time to grab a table for the set menu lunch. Closed Mon, Sun & three weeks in Aug.

Daquise 20 Thurloe St, SW7; see map, pp.126–127. This old-fashioned Polish café right by the tube is something of a South Ken institution, serving Polish home cooking or simple coffee, tea and cakes depending on the time of day.

Gloriette 128 Brompton Rd, SW7; see map, pp.126–127. Long-established Viennese café that makes a perfect post-museum halt for coffee and outrageous cakes; also serves sandwiches, Wiener schnitzel, pasta dishes, goulash and fish and chips.

Ladurée Harrods, 87–135 Brompton Rd, SW1; see map, pp.126–127. This pretty white marble corner of Harrods has been taken over by Parisian tearoom *Ladurée*, with pyramids of coloured macaroons, sumptuous cakes, scented teas and a mirrored champagne bar.

Lisboa Patisserie 57 Golborne Rd, W10; see map, pp.126–127. Authentic and friendly Portuguese *pastelaria*, with coffee and cakes, including the best custard tarts this side of Lisbon. The *O'porto*, at 62a Golborne Rd, is a good fallback if this place is full.

Camden and Hampstead

Brew House Kenwood, Hampstead Lane, NW3; bus #210 from Archway tube or a walk across the Heath from Hampstead tube. Everything from full English breakfast to lunches, cakes and teas, served in the old laundry at Kenwood, or enjoyed on the terrace overlooking the lake.

Café Mozart 17 Swains Lane, N6; Gospel Oak train station. Conveniently located on the southeast side of Hampstead Heath, the best thing about this café is the Viennese cake selection and soothing classical music.

Louis Patisserie 32 Heath St, NW3; Hampstead tube. Popular Hungarian tearoom serving sticky cakes to a mix of Heath-bound hordes and elderly locals.

Marine Ices 8 Haverstock Hill, NW3; see map, pp.80–81. Situated halfway between Camden and Hampstead, this is a splendid and justly famous old-fashioned Italian ice-cream parlour; pizza and pasta are served in a kiddie-friendly restaurant.

Greenwich

Goddard's 45 Greenwich Church St, SE10; Cutty Sark DLR. Established in 1890, *Goddard's* serves traditional pies (including veggie ones), eels and mash in an emerald green-tiled interior, with crumble and custard for afters.

Tai Won Mein 39 Greenwich Church St, SE10; Cutty Sark DLR or Greenwich DLR/train station. Good quality fast-food noodle bar that gets very busy at weekends. Decor is functional and minimalist; choose between rice, soup or various fried noodles, all for under a fiver.

Afternoon tea

The classic English **afternoon tea** – assorted sandwiches, scones and cream, cakes and tarts, and, of course, lashings of tea – is available all over London. The best venues are the capital's top hotels and most fashionable department stores; a selection of the best is given below. To avoid disappointment it's essential to book ahead. Expect to spend £15–30 a head, and leave your jeans and trainers at home – most hotels will expect "smart casual attire", though only The Ritz insists on jacket and tie.

Brown's 33–34 Albemarle St, W1 T020/7493 6020, ⓦwww.brownshotel.com; Green Park tube. Daily 2–6pm.

Claridge's Brook St, W1 ⓣ020/7629 8860, ⓦwww.savoy-group.co.uk; Bond Street tube. Daily 3–5.30pm.

The Dorchester 54 Park Lane, W1 ⓣ020/7629 8888, ⓦwww.dorchesterhotel.com; Hyde Park Corner tube. Daily 3–6pm.

Fortnum & Mason 181 Piccadilly, W1 ⓣ020/7734 8040, ⓦwww.fortnumandmason .com; Green Park or Piccadilly Circus tube. Daily 3–5.30pm.

Lanesborough Hyde Park Corner, SW1 ⓣ020/7259 5599, ⓦwww.lanesborough .com; Green Park tube. Mon–Sat 3.30–6pm, Sun 4–6pm.

The Ritz Piccadilly, W1 ⓣ020/7493 8181, ⓦwww.theritzhotel.co.uk; Green Park tube. Daily 11.30am, 1.30, 3.30 & 5.30pm – check website for details.

The Savoy Strand, WC2 ⓣ020/7836 4343, ⓦwww.savoy-group.co.uk; Charing Cross tube. Closed until mid-2009 – check website for details.

The Wolseley 160 Piccadilly, W1 ⓣ020/7499 699, ⓦwww.thewolseley.com; Green Park tube. Mon–Fri 3–5.30pm, Sat & Sun 3.30–6pm.

Restaurants

Many of the restaurants we've listed will be busy on most nights of the week, particularly on Thursday, Friday and Saturday, and it's best to **reserve a table**. As for **prices**, you can pay an awful lot for a meal in London, and if you're used to North American portions, you're not going to be particularly impressed by the volume in most places. For cheaper eats, see the Cafés and snacks section above. Where possible we've marked the following options on the maps in this chapter.

Westminster and Whitehall

Boisdale 15 Eccleston St, SW1 ⓣ020/7730 6922; see map, pp.90–91. Owned by Ranald MacDonald, son of the Chief of Clanranald, this is a very Scottish place, strong on hospitality, and fresh Scottish produce. Live jazz every evening. Closed Sun. Expensive.

St James's, Mayfair and Marylebone

The Criterion 224 Piccadilly, W1 ⓣ020/7930 0488; see map, pp.90–91. The predominately French food doesn't come cheap at this Marco Pierre White restaurant (though lunch is more of a bargain), but it is one of the city's most beautiful eating places, with a sparkling gold mosaic ceiling. Closed Sun. Very expensive.

Fairuz 3 Blandford St, W1 ⓣ020/7486 8108; see map, p.105. One of London's more accessible Middle Eastern restaurants, with an epic list of mezze, a selection of charcoal grills and one or two oven-baked dishes. Moderate.

Mandalay 444 Edgware Rd, W2 ⓣ020/7258 3696; see map, pp.126–127. Pure and unexpurgated Burmese cuisine – a melange of Thai, Malaysian and a lot of Indian. The portions are huge, the service friendly and the prices relatively low. Closed Sun. Moderate.

The Providores & Tapa Room 109 Marylebone High St, W1 ⓣ020/7935 6175; see map, p.105. Outstanding fusion restaurant run by an amiable New Zealander and split into two: snacky *Tapa Room* downstairs and an elegant restaurant upstairs. The food at both is original and wholly satisfying. *Tapa Room*: inexpensive; *Providores*: very expensive.

Soho, Chinatown and Fitzrovia

Chowki 2–3 Denman St, W1 ☎020/7439 1330; see map, pp.90–91. Large, cheap Indian restaurant serving authentic food in stylish surroundings. The menu changes every month in order to feature three different regions of India – the regional feast for around £12.95 is great value. Inexpensive.

Ikkyu 67a Tottenham Court Rd, W1 ☎020/7636 9280; see map, p.105. Busy basement Japanese restaurant, good for a quick lunch or a more elaborate dinner. Either way, prices are infinitely more reasonable than elsewhere in the capital, and the food is tasty and authentic. Closed all Sat & Sun lunch. Moderate.

Mildred's 45 Lexington St, W1 ☎020/7494 1634; see map, pp.90–91. This has a fresher and more stylish feel than many veggie restaurants, and the stir-fries, pasta dishes and burgers are wholesome, delicious and inexpensive. No bookings or credit cards. Moderate.

Mr Kong 21 Lisle St, WC2 ☎020/7437 7923; see map, pp.90–91. One of Chinatown's finest. To sample the restaurant's more unusual dishes order from the "Today's" and "Chef's Specials" menu, and don't miss the mussels in black-bean sauce or the fresh razor clam with garlic. Inexpensive.

Patara 15 Greek St, W1 ☎020/7437 1071. A low-lit and glamorous place, with orchids on the tables, serving fine Thai cooking with wonderful fresh ingredients. Set lunch is around £12. Moderate.

Rasa Samudra 5 Charlotte St, W1 ☎020/7637 0222; see map, p.105. The food served at *Rasa Samudra* would be more at home in Mumbai than in London, consisting as it does of sophisticated South Indian fish dishes – a million miles from curry-house staples. Moderate.

Wong Kei 41–43 Wardour St, W1 ☎020/7437 8408; see map, pp.90–91. A restaurant renowned for rudeness may not seem like much of a recommendation, but if you want quick, cheap Chinese then this is the place. Communal seating; have a look at the Art Noveau exterior on the way in. Inexpensive.

Covent Garden

Belgo Centraal 50 Earlham St, WC2 ☎020/7813 2233; see map, pp.90–91. Massive metal-minimalist cavern off Neal Street, serving excellent kilo buckets of *moules marinière* with frites and mayonnaise, a bewildering array of Belgian beers to choose from, and waffles for dessert. The £6.50

lunchtime specials are a bargain for central London. Moderate.

Mon Plaisir 21 Monmouth St, WC2 ☎020/7836 7243; see map, pp.90–91. An atmospheric and sometimes formidably French restaurant with an intimate vintage feel, serving classic and reliably excellent French meat and fish dishes. The pre- and post-theatre menu is a bargain at £12.50 for two courses, £14.50 for three. Closed Sat eve & Sun. Moderate.

Clerkenwell and Hoxton

Cicada 132 St John St, EC1 ☎020/7608 1550; see map, pp.108–109. Bar-restaurant set back from the street with alfresco eating and an unusual pan-Asian menu. Closed Sat lunch & Sun. Expensive.

Moro 34–36 Exmouth Market, EC1 ☎020/7833 8336; see map, pp.108–109. Modern, spartan restaurant that's a place of pilgrimage for disciples of the wood-fired oven and those who love food that is both Moorish and more-ish. Expensive.

Real Greek 15 Hoxton Market, N1 ☎020/7739 8212; see map, pp.108–109. Modern and attractive with excellent service and a menu that showcases authentic Greek cuisine. Set lunch and early-doors dinner are a bargain. Neighbouring *Mezedopolio*, in a sympathetically converted mission building, serves *mezedes* and has a glamorous marble bar. Closed Sun. Moderate.

St John 26 St John St, EC1 ☎020/7251 0848; see map. pp.108–109. Pricey genuinely English restaurant, specializing in all those strange and unfashionable cuts of meat that were once commonplace in rural England – brains, bone marrow. Closed Sat lunch & Sun. Expensive.

Viet Hoa Café 72 Kingsland Rd, E2 ☎020/7729 8293; see map, pp.108–109. Light and airy Vietnamese café not far from the Geffrye Museum, serving splendid "meals in a bowl" – soups and noodle dishes with everything from spring rolls to tofu. Inexpensive.

The East End

Café Spice Namaste 16 Prescot St, E1 ☎020/7488 9242; see map, pp.108–109. Very popular Indian on the fringe of the City that is definitely not your average curry house. Goan and Kashmiri dishes are often included, and the tandoori specials, in particular, are awesome. Closed Sat lunch & Sun. Expensive.

Les Trois Garcons 1 Club Row, E1 ☎020/7613 1924; see map, pp.108–109. Wildly camp decor, with a bejewelled stuffed tiger to greet you at the door, handbags hanging from the ceilings, ornate tiles and glittering engraved mirrors. The opulence is reflected in the prices and the dishes, with scallops, foie gras and oysters a regular feature. Expensive.

Tayyab's 83–89 Fieldgate St, E1 ☎020/7247 9543; see map, pp.108–109. Smart, designer restaurant serving straightforward Pakistani fare: good, freshly cooked and served without pretension. Booking is essential and service is speedy and slick. Inexpensive.

South Bank and Southwark

Livebait The Cut, SE1 ☎020/7928 7211; see map, p.120. This bustling green- and white-tiled restaurant dishes up seafood galore, from classic fish and chips to platters heaped with lobster, crab and prawns. Expensive.

RSJ 13a Coin St, SE1 ☎020/7928 4554; see map, p.120. Regularly high standards of Anglo-French cooking make this a good spot for a meal after or before an evening at a South Bank theatre or concert hall. The set meals for around £17 are particularly popular. Closed Sat lunch & Sun. Moderate.

Kensington and Chelsea

Bibendum Oyster House Michelin House, 81 Fulham Rd, SW3 ☎020/7589 1480; see map, pp.126–127. A glorious tiled affair built in 1911, this former garage is one of the prettiest places to eat shellfish in London – if you're really hungry, go for the "Plateau de Fruits de Mer". Expensive.

Gordon Ramsay 68–69 Royal Hospital Rd, SW3 ☎020/7352 4441; see map, pp.126–127. To order successfully here, just pick a dish or even an ingredient you like and see how it arrives; you won't be disappointed. Gordon Ramsay's Chelsea restaurant is a class act through and through, though you have to book well ahead. Closed Sat & Sun. Very expensive.

Bayswater and Notting Hill

Al Waha 75 Westbourne Grove, W2 ☎020/7229 0806; see map, pp.126–127. Arguably London's best Lebanese restaurant; *mezze*-obsessed, but also painstaking in its preparation of the main-

course dishes, where spanking fresh and accurately cooked grills predominate. Moderate.

Osteria Basilico 29 Kensington Park Rd, W11 ☎020/7727 9372; see map, pp.126–127. A pretty, traditional Italian restaurant on a picturesque street just off Portobello Road. It's a good place for the full Italian monty – antipasto, home-made pasta and then a fish or meat dish – or just for a pizza. Moderate.

Camden and Hampstead

Jin Kichi 73 Heath St, NW3 ☎020/7794 6158; Hampstead tube. Eschewing the slick minimalism and sushi-led cuisine of most Japanese restaurants, *Jin Kichi* is cramped, homely and very busy (so book ahead) and specializes in grilled skewers of meat. Closed Mon. Moderate.

Manna 4 Erskine Rd, NW3 ☎020/7722 8028; see map, pp.80–81. Old-fashioned, casual vegetarian restaurant with 1970s decor, serving large portions of very good food. Closed Mon–Sat lunch. Moderate.

Troika 101 Regent's Park Rd, NW1 ☎020/7483 3765; see map, pp.80–81. A pleasant neighbourhood restaurant with filling and tasty Russian and Eastern European food. The menu has a whole section on blinis and caviar, plus there are sturdy standbys such as stroganoff, and grills served with Trojka's own tartare sauce. Moderate.

Chiswick to Richmond

Chez Lindsay 11 Hill Rise, Richmond ☎020/8948 7473; Richmond tube. Small, bright, authentic Breton creperie, with a "Cider with Lindsay" fixed menu (£15.75) offering three courses plus a cup of Breton cider. Choose between galettes, crepes or more formal French main courses, including lots of fresh fish and shellfish. Moderate.

The Gate 51 Queen Caroline St, W6 ☎020/8748 6932; Hammersmith tube. Tucked away behind the Hammersmith Apollo, this is a vegetarian restaurant that eschews healthy, wholefood eating. It's as rich, colourful, calorific and naughty as anywhere in town, just without meat. Closed Sat lunch & Sun. Expensive.

Drinking

London's **drinking** establishments run the whole gamut from grand Victorian gin palaces to funky modern bars with resident DJs catering to a pre-club crowd. The emergence of **gastropubs**, where the food is as important as the drink, has had a huge impact on the rest of the pub trade. Where possible, we've marked the places below on the maps in this chapter.

Whitehall and Westminster

The Chandos 29 St Martin's Lane, WC2; see map, pp.90–91. If you can get one of the booths downstairs, or the leather sofas upstairs in the more relaxed Opera Room Bar, then you'll find it difficult to leave, especially given the cheap Sam Smith's beer.

Red Lion 48 Parliament St, SW1; see map, pp.90–91. Good old pub, convenient for Westminster Abbey and Parliament. Popular with MPs, who are called to votes by a division bell in the bar.

St James's, Mayfair and Marylebone

Guinea 30 Bruton Place, W1; see map, pp.90–91. Pretty, old-fashioned, flower-strewn mews pub, serving good Young's bitter and excellent steak-and-kidney pies. Invariably packed to its tiny rafters. Closed Sun.

ICA Bar 94 The Mall, SW1; see map, pp.90–91. You have to be a member to drink at the *ICA Bar* – but anyone can join on the door (Mon–Fri £2, Sat & Sun £3). It's a cool drinking venue, with a noir dress code observed by the arty crowd and staff. Occasional club nights.

O'Conor Don 88 Marylebone Lane, W1; see map, p.105. A stripped bare pub that's a cut above the average, with excellent Guinness, a pleasantly measured pace and Irish food on offer. Closed Sat & Sun.

Red Lion 23 Crown Passage, SW1; see map, pp.90–91. Hidden away in a narrow passageway off Pall Mall, this is a genuinely warm and cosy local, with a distinctive country-inn feel and super friendly bar staff. Closed Sun.

Soho and Fitzrovia

Argyll Arms 18 Argyll St, W1. see map, pp.90–91. A stone's throw from Oxford Circus, this is a great Victorian pub, which has preserved many of its original features and serves good real ales.

Blue Posts 28 Rupert St, W1; see map, pp.90–91. Colourful, welcoming local with a relaxed vibe, frequented by a cheerful, hardy array of punters. The upstairs bar is frequently used for art exhibitions.

De Hems 11 Macclesfield St, W1; see map, pp.90–91. Probably your best bet in Chinatown, this is London's official Dutch pub, and has been since the 1890s; a simple wood-panelled affair with Oranjeboom on tap and Belgian beers in bottles.

Dog & Duck 18 Bateman St, W1; see map, pp.90–91. Tiny Soho pub that retains much of its old character, beautiful Victorian tiling and mosaics, and a loyal clientele.

The Social 5 Little Portland St, W1; see map, p.105. Industrial club-bar with great DJs playing everything from rock to rap, a truly hedonistic-cum-alcoholic crowd and the ultimate snacks – beans on toast and fish-finger sarnies – for when you get an attack of the munchies.

The Toucan 19 Carlisle St; see map, pp.90–91. Small bar serving excellent Guinness and a wide range of Irish whiskeys, plus cheap, wholesome and filling food. So popular it can get mobbed. Closed Sun lunch.

Covent Garden and Strand

Cross Keys 31 Endell St, WC2; see map, pp.90–91. Stuffed with copper pots, brass instruments, paintings and other curios, this welcoming West End pub attracts an appealing blend of local residents, young workers and tourists – you'll do well to find a seat.

Detroit 35 Earlham St, WC2; see map, pp.90–91. Cavernous underground venue with an open-plan bar area, secluded Gaudíesque booths and a huge range of spirits. DJs take over at the weekends. Closed Sun.

Gordon's 47 Villiers St, WC2; see map, pp.90–91. Cavernous, shabby, atmospheric wine bar specializing in ports, right next door to Charing Cross Station. The excellent and varied wine list, decent buffet food and genial atmosphere make this a favourite with local office workers, who spill outdoors in the summer.

Lamb & Flag 33 Rose St, WC2; see map, pp.90–91. Undeniably showing its age (more than 350 years old), this agreeably tatty yet much revered pub is tucked away down an alley between Garrick Street and Floral Street.

Salisbury 90 St Martin's Lane, WC2; see map, pp.90–91. Easily one of the most beautifully preserved Victorian pubs in the capital – and certainly the most central – with cut, etched and engraved windows, bronze figures, red velvet seating and a fine lincrusta ceiling.

Bloomsbury and Holborn

Lamb 94 Lamb's Conduit St, WC1; see map, p.105. Fine Young's pub with a marvellously well-preserved Victorian interior of mirrors, polished wood and etched glass "snob" screens gracing the bar.

Museum Tavern 49 Great Russell St, WC1. see map, p.105. Large and characterful old pub, right opposite the British Museum, that was the erstwhile drinking hole of Karl Marx.

Princess Louise 208 High Holborn, WC1; see map, p.105. Architecturally, this is one of London's most impressive pubs, featuring gold trimmed mirrors, gorgeous mosaics and a fine moulded ceiling. The Sam Smith's beer is very reasonably priced and there's always a lively crowd.

Ye Olde Mitre 1 Ely Court, off Ely Place, EC1; see map, pp.108–109. Hidden down a tiny alleyway off Ely Place, this wonderfully atmospheric pub dates back to 1546, although it was actually rebuilt in the eighteenth century. Closed Sat & Sun.

Clerkenwell

Dovetail 9 Jerusalem Passage, EC1; see map, pp.108–109. Marvellous, understated Belgian bar offering dozens of beers. The curious decor comprises pew-style seating, green-tiled tables and kitchen-style wall tiling. First rate Belgian food, too. Closed Sun.

Duke of York 156 Clerkenwell Rd, EC1; see map, pp.108–109. Just the basics you need for a good pub – clear glass windows, bare boards, bold red and blue paintwork, table football, pool, TV sport, mixed clientele and groovy tunes – and a lot less posey than most of Clerkenwell. Thai food available (except Sun).

Jerusalem Tavern 55 Britton St, EC1; see map, pp.108–109. Converted Georgian coffee house that has retained much of its original character. Better still is the range of draught beers from the St Peter's Brewery in Suffolk. Closed Sat & Sun.

Hoxton

Dragon Bar 5 Leonard St, EC2; see map, pp.108–109. Discreetly signed clubby pub with bare-brick walls and crumbling leather sofas, that attracts a mixed crowd happy to listen to whatever takes the resident DJ's fancy.

Hoxton Square Bar and Kitchen 2–4 Hoxton Square, N1; see map, pp.108–109. This *Blade Runner*-esque concrete bar attracts trendy types with its mix of modern European food, kitsch-to-club soundtracks, worn leather sofas, and temporary painting and photography exhibitions.

Sosho 2 Tabernacle St, EC2; see map, pp.108–109. Trendy club-bar with good cocktails and decent food. The ambience is chilled until the very popular DJs kick in (Wed–Sun), playing house, disco and electronica; there's a charge at the weekend. Closed Mon.

The City

The Black Friar 174 Queen Victoria St, EC4; see map, pp.108–109. A gorgeous, utterly original pub, with Art Nouveau marble friezes of boozy monks and a wonderful highly decorated alcove, all dating from 1905.

The Counting House 50 Cornhill, EC2; see map, pp.108–109. Converted from a bank, with a magnificent interior featuring high ceilings, marble walls and mosaic flooring. The large, oval island bar – above which is an enormous glass dome – offers the full range of Fuller's ales. Closed Sat & Sun.

Viaduct Tavern 126 Newgate St, EC1; see map, pp.108–109. Glorious gin palace built in 1869 opposite what was then Newgate Prison and is now the Old Bailey: ask to see the old cells, now used for storing beer. The walls are adorned with oils of faded ladies representing Commerce, Agriculture and the Arts. Closed Sat & Sun.

Ye Old Cheshire Cheese Wine Office Court, 145 Fleet St, EC4; see map, pp.108–109. A famous seventeenth-century watering hole, with several snug, dark panelled bars and real fires. Popular with tourists, but by no means exclusively so. Closed Sun eve.

▲ Ye Old Cheshire Cheese

East End and Docklands

Dickens Inn St Katharine's Way, E1; see map, pp.108–109. Eighteenth-century timber-framed warehouse transported on wheels from its original site, with a great view over the docks, but very firmly on the tourist trail.

The Gun 27 Cold Harbour, E14; South Quay or Blackwall DLR, or Canary Wharf tube. Refurbished old dockers' pub with a classy restaurant, a cosy back bar with a couple of snugs, and an outside deck offering an unrivalled view of the Dome.

Prospect of Whitby 57 Wapping Wall, E1; Wapping tube. London's most famous riverside pub, with a pewter bar, flagstone floor, ancient timber beams and stacks of maritime memorabilia. Terrific views out across the Thames.

Ten Bells 84 Commercial St, E1; see map, pp.108–109. This pleasantly ramshackle pub has Jack the Ripper associations, but the interior has some great Victorian tiling and the crowd these days is a trendy, relaxed bunch. DJs play Fri–Sun.

Town of Ramsgate 62 Wapping High St, E1; Wapping tube. Dark, narrow medieval pub where Captain Blood was discovered with the crown jewels under his cloak, and Admiral Bligh and Fletcher Christian were regular drinking partners in pre-Mutiny days.

South Bank and Southwark

Anchor & Hope 36 The Cut, SE1; see map, p.120. The *Anchor* is a welcoming and unfussy gastropub, dishing up truly excellent grub: soups, salads and mains such as slow-cooked pork with choucroute, as well as mouth-watering puds. Closed Sun.

Anchor Bankside 34 Park St, SE1; see map, pp.122–123. While the rest of Bankside has changed almost beyond all recognition, this pub still looks much as it did when first built in 1770 (on the inside, at least). Good for alfresco drinking by the river.

George Inn 77 Borough High St, SE1; see map, pp.122–123. London's only surviving coaching inn – dating from the seventeenth century and now owned by the National Trust – serving a good range of real ales.

Kings Arms 25 Roupell St, SE1; see map, p.120. Terrific hideaway divided into two; the front part is a traditional drinking area, while the rear, where Thai food is served, is a tastefully cluttered, glass and wood conservatory-style space featuring a large open fire and long wooden table.

Lord Clyde 27 Clenham St, SE1; see map, pp.122–123. A genuinely hospitable, family-run boozer, with a good choice of ales and obliging staff. Before entering, take a look at the superb frontage, with its cream-and-green glazed earthenware dating from 1913.

Market Porter 9 Stoney St, SE1; see map, pp.122–123. Handsome pub with early opening hours for workers at the Borough Market, and a seriously huge range of real ales.

Royal Oak 44 Tabard St, SE1; see map, pp.122–123. Beautiful, lovingly restored Victorian pub that eschews jukeboxes and one-armed bandits and opts simply for serving real ales from Lewes in Sussex. Closed Sat lunch & Sun eve.

Kensington and Chelsea

Cooper's Arms 87 Flood St, SW3; see map, pp.126–127. An attractively understated interior with quirky decor (vintage travel posters, grandfather clocks), first rate beer and food, and an easy-going atmosphere all contrive to give this very fine neighbourhood pub its deservedly popular reputation.

The Nag's Head 53 Kinnerton St, SW1; see map, pp.126–127. A convivial, quirky and down-to-earth little pub tucked down a posh cobbled mews, with dark wood-panelling and nineteenth-century china handpumps. The unusual sunken backroom has a flagstone floor and fires in winter.

The Pig's Ear 35 Old Church St SW1; see map, pp.126–127. Deep in Chelsea village, *The Pig's Ear* is a sympathetically converted and stylish place. Enjoy a leisurely boardgame and a pint of the house brew in the panelled downstairs bar, where classy pub grub is served, or head upstairs to the posh dining room.

Paddington and Notting Hill

Prince Bonaparte 80 Chepstow Rd, W2; see map, pp.126–127. Pared-down, minimalist pub, with acres of space for sitting and supping or enjoying the excellent Brit or Med food.

Victoria 10a Strathearn Place, W2; see map, pp.126–127. Fabulously ornate corner pub, with two open fires, much Victorian brass and tilework, and gold trimmed mirrors.

Maida Vale

Prince Alfred 9 Formosa St, W9; see map, pp.126–127. A fantastic period-piece Victorian pub with all its original 1862 fittings intact, right down to the glazed snob screens that divide the bar into a series of snugs, and a surprisingly young and funky clientele.

Warrington Hotel 93 Warrington Crescent, W9; see map, pp.126–127. Yet another architectural gem – this time flamboyant Art Nouveau – in an area replete with them. The interior is rich and satisfying, as are the draught beers and the Thai restaurant upstairs.

Camden Town

Bar Vinyl 6 Inverness St, NW1; see map, pp.80–81. Small, funky glass-bricked place with a record shop downstairs (open noon–8pm) and nightly DJs providing a breakbeat, funky house or electro vibe.

Bartok 78–79 Chalk Farm Rd, NW1; see map, pp.80–81. Stylish bar where punters can sink into a sofa and listen to a varied programme of classical music. Eve only.

The Engineer 65 Gloucester Ave, NW1; see map, pp.80–81. Smart Victorian pub and restaurant for the Primrose Hill posse. The food is excellent though pricey, and it's popular, so get here early to eat in the pub, or book a table in the restaurant or lovely garden out back.

Hampstead and Highgate

The Flask 14 Flask Walk, NW3; Hampstead tube. Tucked down one of Hampstead's more atmospheric lanes, a convivial Hampstead local that retains much of its original Victorian interior.

The Flask 77 Highgate West Hill, N6; Highgate tube. Ideally situated at the heart of Highgate village green – with a rambling, low-ceilinged interior and a summer terrace – and as a result, very popular.

Holly Bush 22 Holly Mount, NW3; Hampstead tube. A lovely old pub, with a real fire in winter, tucked away in the steep backstreets of Hampstead village, which can get a bit too mobbed at weekends. Good food too.

Dulwich and Greenwich

Crown & Greyhound 73 Dulwich Village, SE21; West Dulwich train station from Victoria. Grandiose Victorian pub, convenient for the Picture Gallery, with an ornate plasterwork ceiling and a nice summer beer garden.

Cutty Sark Ballast Quay, off Lassell St, SE10; Cutty Sark DLR or Maze Hill train station. This Georgian pub is the nicest place for a riverside pint in Greenwich, and much less touristy than the *Trafalgar Tavern* (it's a couple of minutes' walk further east, following the river).

Chiswick to Richmond

Dove 19 Upper Mall, W6; Ravenscourt Park tube. Wonderful low-beamed old riverside pub with literary associations, the smallest bar in the UK (4ft by 7ft), and very popular Sunday roast dinners.

White Cross Hotel Water Lane, Richmond; Richmond tube. With a longer pedigree and more character than its rivals, the *White Cross* has a very popular, large garden.

Nightlife

On any night of the week London offers a bewildering range of things to do after dark, ranging from top-flight opera and theatre to clubs with a life span of a couple of nights. The **listings magazine** *Time Out*, which comes out every Tuesday afternoon, is essential if you want to get the most out of this city, giving full details of prices and access, plus previews and reviews.

Live music venues

Over the past ten years London has established itself as the music capital of not just Europe, but the world. Rio may be sunnier, Paris prettier and Madrid madder but for sheer range and diversity there's nowhere to beat London. The **live music** scene remains extremely diverse, encompassing all variations of rock, blues, roots and world music; and although London's jazz clubs aren't on a par with those in the big American cities, there's a highly individual scene of home-based artists, supplemented by top-name visiting players.

General venues

100 Club 100 Oxford St, W1 ☎020/7636 0933, ⓦwww.the100club.co.uk; Tottenham Court Road tube. An unpretentious, inexpensive and fun venue with an incredible vintage – expect anything from jazz to indie.

Cargo 83 Rivington St, EC2 ☎020/7739 3440, ⓦwww.cargo-london.com; Old St tube. Small but upmarket club/venue that hosts a wide variety of interesting live acts, including jazz, Latin, hip-hop, indie and folk, which are often part of their excellent line-up of club nights.

Brixton Academy 211 Stockwell Rd, SW9 ☎020/7771 3000, ⓦwww.brixton-academy.co.uk; Brixton tube. This refurbished Victorian hall, complete with Neoclassical decorations, can hold four thousand but still manages to seem small and friendly.

Forum 9–17 Highgate Rd, NW5 ☎0844/847 2405, ⓦwww.kentishtownforum.com Kentish

Town tube. This is one of the capital's best medium-sized venues: it's large enough to attract established bands, but also promotes less well-known ones.

Hammersmith Apollo Queen Caroline St, W6 ℡0844/844 4748, 🌐www.hammersmithapollo.net; Hammersmith tube. The former Hammersmith Odeon is a cavernous, theatre-style venue which, for the most part, tends to host safe, middle-of-the-road bands. If you don't like sitting, there's a large and atmospheric standing area at the front.

Roundhouse Chalk Farm Rd, NW1 ℡020/7424 9998, 🌐www.roundhouse.org.uk; Chalk Farm tube. This magnificently restored Victorian engine house is now one of London's premier performing arts centres; its wide-ranging programme includes regular appearances by both mainstream and world music stars.

Shepherd's Bush Empire Shepherds Bush Green, W12 ℡020/8354 3300, 🌐www.shepherds-bush-empire.co.uk; Shepherd's Bush tube. Grand old West London theatre that regularly draws the finest cross-section of mid-league UK and US bands.

Union Chapel Compton Terrace, N1 ℡020/7226 1686, 🌐www.unionchapel.org.uk; Highbury & Islington tube. Wonderful, intimate venue that doubles as a church, hence the pew-style seating arrangements; the eclectic array of artists ranges from international contemporary stars to world music legends.

Rock, blues and indie

12 Bar Club Denmark Street, WC2 ℡020/7240 2120, 🌐www.12barclub.com; Tottenham Court Road tube. Tiny, atmospheric bar, café and venue offering blues, contemporary country and acoustically driven pop and folk.

Borderline Orange Yard, off Manette St, W1 🌐www.meanfiddler.com; Tottenham Court Road tube. Small basement joint with a diverse musical policy, though it's particularly strong on Americana and alt-country acts.

Metro 19–23 Oxford St, W1 🌐www.blowupmetro.com; Tottenham Court Road tube. An intimate

venue with a forward-thinking booking policy that makes it a good place to head to for new bands just before they get big. Also has club nights Mon–Sat till late.

Neighbourhood 12 Acklam Rd, W10 ℡0871/971 3995; Ladbroke Grove tube. Run by Ben Watt of Everything But the Girl, this is a live-music/club crossover venue in an arch under a flyover, where the crowd is as trendy as the house-oriented music.

Underworld 174 Camden High St, NW1 🌐www.theunderworldcamden.co.uk; Camden Town tube. Popular grungy venue under the *World's End* pub, that's a great place to check out metal, hard core, ska punk and heavy rock bands.

Jazz, world music and roots

606 Club 90 Lots Rd, SW10 ℡020/7352 5953, 🌐www.606club.co.uk; Fulham Broadway tube. A rare all-jazz venue, off the end of the King's Road. You can book a table, and if you're a non-member you must eat if you want to drink.

Jazz Café 5 Parkway, NW1 ℡020/7916 6060, 🌐www.meanfiddler.com; Camden Town tube. Excellent, chilled-out venue with an adventurous booking policy exploring Latin, rap, funk, hip-hop and musical fusions. There's a restaurant upstairs with a few prime tables overlooking the stage (book ahead if you want one).

Pizza Express 10 Dean St, W1 🌐www.pizzaexpresslive.com; Tottenham Court Road tube. Also known as Jazz Club Soho, this restaurant hosts the best in both established and new jazz artists, and serves a good pizza, too.

Ronnie Scott's 47 Frith St, W1 ℡020/7439 0747, 🌐www.ronniescotts.co.uk. Leicester Square tube. The most famous jazz club in London, great for top-line names, who play two sets – one at around 10pm, the other after midnight, except on Sundays when the club shuts at midnight. Book a table or you'll have to stand.

Clubs

London remains *the* place to come if you want to party after dark. The sheer diversity of dance music has enabled the city to maintain its status as the **world's dance capital** – and it's still a port of call for DJs from around the globe. The relaxation of late-night licensing laws has encouraged many of the city's dance **clubs** to keep serving until 6am or even later. Some are open six or seven nights a week, some keep irregular days, others just open at the weekend – and very often a venue will host a different club on each night of the week; for up-to-the-minute listings, pop into one of Soho's many record shops to pick up flyers or check *Time Out*.

Admission charges vary enormously, with small midweek nights starting at around £3–5 and large weekend events charging as much as £25; around £10–15 is the average, but bear in mind that profit margins at the bar are even more outrageous than at live-music venues.

93 Feet East 150 Brick Lane, E2 ☏ 020/7247 3293, ⓦ www.93feeteast.co.uk; Old St tube. An old East End brewery with four rooms across two levels, as well as an excellent rooftop balcony and outdoor space that's well worth a visit in the summer.

333 333 Old St, EC1 ⓦ www.333mother.com; Old Street tube. One of London's best clubs for new dance music: three floors of drum'n'bass, twisted disco and breakbeat madness.

Bar Rumba 36 Shaftesbury Ave, W1 ☏ 020/7287 6933, ⓦ www.barrumba.co.uk; Piccadilly Circus tube. Fun, smallish West End venue with an adventurous mix of nights ranging from salsa, R&B and dance to popular drum'n'bass.

Cuba 11–13 Kensington High St, W8 ☏ 020/7938 4137 ⓦ www.fiestahavana.com; Kensington High Street tube. Grab a cocktail upstairs in the sociable bar before heading below for club nights that focus around Latin, salsa and Brazilian bossa nova.

The End 18 West Central St, WC1 ☏ 020/7419 9199, ⓦ www.endclub.com; Tottenham Court Road or Holborn tube. Designed for clubbers by clubbers, *The End* is large and spacious, with chrome minimalist decor and a devastating sound system.

Fabric 77a Charterhouse St, EC1 ☏ 020/7336 8898, ⓦ www.fabriclondon .com; Farringdon tube. If you're a serious dance music fan then there really isn't a better weekend venue than *Fabric*, a cavernous, underground brewery-like space with three rooms. Get there early to avoid a night of queuing.

Fridge Town Hall Parade, Brixton Hill, SW2 ☏ 0871/223 2845 ⓦ www.fridgerocks.com; Brixton tube. Weekends alternate between pumping mixed/gay nights and trance favourites with a psychedelic vibe.

Herbal 12–14 Kingsland Rd, E2 ⓦ www.herbaluk .com; Old Street tube. An intimate two-floor venue comprising a cool loft and sweaty ground-floor club

– a great place to check out drum'n'bass and breaks.

Ministry of Sound 103 Gaunt St, SE1 ⓦ www .ministryofsound.com; Elephant & Castle tube. Vast, state-of-the-art club, with an exceptional sound system. Corporate clubbing and full of tourists, but it still draws the top talent.

Notting Hill Arts Club 21 Notting Hill Gate, W11 ☏ 020/7460 4459, ⓦ www .nottinghillartsclub.com; Notting Hill Gate tube. Basement club that's popular for everything from Latin-inspired funk, jazz and disco through to soul, house and garage, and famed for its Sunday afternoon/evening deep-house session and "concept visuals".

Plastic People 147–149 Curtain Rd, EC2 ☏ 020/739 6471, ⓦ www.plasticpeople.co.uk; Old Street tube. A state-of-the-art sound system and an interesting mix of nights, ranging from punk, funk and rock'n'roll to Latin, Afro-jazz and hip-hop.

Rhythm Factory 16–18 Whitechapel Rd ☏ 020/7375 3774, ⓦ www.rhythmfactory.co.uk; Aldgate East or Whitechapel tube. This former textile factory turned club houses a bar area serving Thai food and two medium-sized rooms which usually see a range of excellent monthly shenanigans at the weekends.

Scala 278 Pentonville Rd, N1 ☏ 020/7833 2022, ⓦ www.scala-london.co.uk; King's Cross tube. Sprawling club that holds some unusual one-off nights as well as live bands and the long-running gay/mixed Popstarz.

Turnmills 63 Clerkenwell Rd, EC1 ⓦ www .turnmills.co.uk; Farringdon tube. The place to come if you want to sweat to trance and house from dusk till dawn, with an alien-invasion-style bar and funky split-level dancefloor in the main room.

Gay and lesbian London

London's **lesbian and gay scene** is so huge, diverse and well established that it's easy to forget just how much – and how fast – it has grown over the last couple of decades. **Soho** is the obvious place to start exploring, with a mix of traditional gay pubs, designer café-bars and a range of gay-run services. Details of most events appear in *Time Out*, while another excellent source of information is the London **Lesbian and Gay Switchboard** (☏ 020/7837 7324, ⓦ www.queery.org.uk), which operates around the clock. The **outdoor event** of the year is **Pride London** (ⓦ www.pridelondon.org) in July, a colourful, whistleblowing march through the city streets followed at the end of the month by a huge, ticketed party in a central London park.

Many of London's gay **cafés**, **bars and pubs** have been around for years, but such is the fickle nature of the scene that some pop up and disappear within months. Our list is by no means exhaustive as every corner of the city has its own gay local. Many cafés and bars transform themselves into **drinking dens** at night and, as some open beyond licensing hours, they can be a cheap alternative to some **clubs**, which open up and shut down with surreal frequency – it's a good idea to check the gay press and listings mags before you set out. Bear in mind that although more and more lesbian bars admit gay men, mixed, as ever, tends to mean mostly men.

Mixed bars

The Black Cap 171 Camden High St, NW1; Camden Town tube. Venerable North London institution offering cabaret of wildly varying quality almost every night. Laugh, sing and lip-synch along, and then dance to 1980s tunes until the early hours.

The Box 32–34 Monmouth St, WC2; Covent Garden or Leicester Square tube. Popular, bright café/bar serving good food for a mixed gay/straight crowd during the day, and becoming queerer as the night draws in.

The Edge 11 Soho Square, W1; Tottenham Court Rd tube. Busy, style-conscious and pricey Soho café/bar spread over several floors, and (in summer) onto the pavement. Food daily, DJs most nights.

First Out 52 St Giles High St, WC2; Tottenham Court Rd tube. The West End's original gay café-bar, and still permanently packed, serving good veggie food at reasonable prices. Girl Friday (Fri) is a busy pre-club session for grrrls; gay men are welcome as guests.

Freedom 60–66 Wardour St, W1; Piccadilly Circus tube. Hip, busy, late-opening place, popular with a straight/gay Soho crowd. The basement transforms itself at night into a funky, intimate basement club, complete with pink banquettes and masses of glitter balls.

Retro Bar 2 George Court (off Strand), WC2; Charing Cross tube. Friendly, indie/retro bar playing 1970s, 80s, rock, pop, goth and alternative sounds, and featuring regular DIY DJ nights.

The Yard 57 Rupert St, W1; Piccadilly Circus tube. Attractive bar with courtyard, loft areas and a laid-back, sociable atmosphere – one of the best in Soho for al fresco drinking.

Lesbian bars

Candy Bar 4 Carlisle St, WC2. Tottenham Court Road tube; Now re-established at its original venue but still with the same crucial, cruisey vibe that made it the hottest girl bar in central London.

The Glass Bar West Lodge, Euston Square Gardens, 190 Euston Rd, NW1; Euston tube. Difficult to find (and hard to forget), you knock on the door and become a member to enter this friendly and intimate late-opening women-only bar. Closed Sat & Sun.

Star at Night 22 Great Chapel St, W1; Tottenham Court Road tube. Comfortable new venue open from 6pm Tues–Sat, popular with a slightly older crowd who want somewhere to sit, a superior glass of wine and good conversation.

Gay men's bars

79CXR 79 Charing Cross Rd, WC2; Leicester Square tube. Busy, cruisey men's den on two floors, with industrial decor, late licence and a no-messing atmosphere.

Central Station 37 Wharfdale Rd, N1; King's Cross tube. Award-winning, late-opening community pub on three floors, offering cabaret, cruisey club nights, and the UK's only gay sports bar. Not strictly men-only, but mostly so.

Compton's of Soho 53 Old Compton St, W1; Leicester Square or Piccadilly tube. This large, traditional-style pub is a Soho institution, always busy with a butch crowd, but still a relaxed place to cruise or just hang out. The upstairs Club Lounge is more chilled and attracts a younger crowd.

Kings Arms 23 Poland St, W1; Oxford Circus tube. London's best-known bear bar, perennially popular, with a traditional London pub atmosphere, DJ on Sat and karaoke night Sun.

Clubs

Area 67–68 Albert Embankment, SE1 @www.areaclub.Info; Vauxhall tube. Stylish club with two dancefloors, several bars and chic decor. It hosts the long-running Coco Latte, as well as offering a London venue for big-na me international DJs. Second Sat of the month is Bootylicious, devoted to urban dance music.

Crash 66 Goding St, SE11 @www.crashlondon .com; Vauxhall tube. Four bars, two dancefloors, chill-out areas and hard bodies make this weekly Saturday-nighter busy, buzzy and sexy.

Duckie *Royal Vauxhall Tavern*, 372 Kennington Lane, SE11 Ⓦ www.duckie.co.uk. Vauxhall tube. Modern, rock-based hurdy-gurdy provides a creative and cheerfully ridiculous antidote to the dreary forces of gay house domination.

Exilio Latino UCL, Houghton Street, WC2 Ⓦ www .exilio.co.uk; Holborn tube. Every Sat night, Exilio erupts in a lesbian and gay Latin frenzy, spinning salsa, cumbias and merengue, and also features live acts.

G.A.Y. The Astoria, 157 Charing Cross Rd, WC2 Ⓦ www.g-a-y.co.uk; Tottenham Court Road tube. Widely considered as the launch venue for new (and ailing) boy and girl bands, this huge, unpretentious and fun-loving dance night is where the young crowd gathers.

Heaven The Arches Villiers St, WC2 Ⓦ www .heaven-london.com; Charing Cross or Embankment tube. Widely regarded as the UK's most popular gay club, this legendary, 2000-capacity venue continues to reign supreme. More Muscle Mary than Diesel Doris.

Popstarz Scala, 27 Pentonville Rd, N1 Ⓦ www .popstarz.org; King's Cross tube. Groundbreaking Friday-night indie club *Popstarz* has had to enforce a gay and lesbian majority door policy as its still-winning formula of alternative toons, 70s and 80s trash, cheap beer and no attitude attracts a growing straight, studenty crowd.

Theatre

The **West End** is the heart of London's "Theatreland", with Shaftesbury Avenue its most congested drag, but the term is more of a conceptual pigeon-hole than a geographical term. West End theatres tend to be dominated by tourist-magnet musicals, but some offer more intriguing productions. The **Royal Shakespeare Company** and the **National Theatre** often put on extremely original productions of mainstream masterpieces, while some of the most exciting work is performed in what have become known as the **Off-West End** theatres. Further down the financial ladder still are the **Fringe** theatres, more often than not pub venues, where ticket prices are lower, and quality more variable. To find out what's on, in addition to *Time Out*, check Ⓦ www.londontheatre.co.uk.

Tickets for £10 are restricted to the Fringe; the box-office average is closer to £20–25, with £30–50 the usual top whack. Ticket agencies such as Ticketmaster (☎ 0161/385 3211, Ⓦ www.ticketmaster.co.uk) or First Call (☎ 0870/840 1111, Ⓦ www.firstcalltickets.com) can get seats for most West End shows, but add up to twenty percent on the ticket price. The cheapest way to buy your ticket is to go to the theatre box office in person; if you book over the phone or online, you're likely to be charged a booking fee. Students, senior citizens and the unemployed can get **concessionary rates** on tickets for many shows, and several theatres offer reductions on standby tickets to these groups. Whatever you do, avoid the touts and the ticket agencies that abound in the West End.

The Society of London Theatre (Ⓦ www.officiallondontheatre.co.uk) runs the **Half Price Ticket Booth** in Leicester Square, now known as **tkts** (Mon–Sat 10am–7pm, Sun noon–3pm), which sells on-the-day tickets for all the West End shows at discounts of up to fifty percent, though they tend to be in the top end of the price range, are limited to four per person, and carry a service charge of £2.50 per ticket.

Venues

What follows is a list of those West End theatres that offer a changing roster of good plays, along with the most consistent of the Off-West End and Fringe venues. This by no means represents the full tally of London's stages, as there are scores of fringe places that present work on an intermittent basis – the weekly listings mag *Time Out* provides the most comprehensive and detailed up-to-the-minute survey.

Almeida Almeida St, N1 ☎020/7359 4404, ⓦwww
.almeida.co.uk; Angel or Highbury & Islington tube.
Deservedly popular Off-West End venue in Islington
that continues to premiere excellent new plays and
excitingly reworked classics, and has attracted some
big Hollywood names.

Barbican Centre Silk St, EC2 ☎020/7638 8891,
ⓦwww.barbican.org.uk; Barbican or Moorgate
tube. The Barbican's two venues – the excellently
designed Barbican Theatre and the much smaller
Pit – put on a wide variety of theatrical spectacles
from puppetry and musicals to new drama works,
as well as Shakespeare, courtesy of the Royal
Shakespeare Company who perform here (and
elsewhere in London) on and off from autumn to
spring each year.

Battersea Arts Centre 176 Lavender Hill, SW11
☎020/7223 2223, ⓦwww.bac.org.uk; Clapham
Junction train station from Victoria or Waterloo. The
BAC is a triple-stage building, housed in an old
town hall in south London, and has acquired a
reputation for excellent fringe productions, from
straight theatre to comedy and cabaret.

Bush Shepherd's Bush Green, W12 ☎020/7610
4224, ⓦwww.bushtheatre.co.uk; Goldhawk Road
or Shepherd's Bush tube. This minuscule above-
pub theatre is London's most reliable venue for
new writing after the Royal Court, and it has turned
out some great stuff.

Donmar Warehouse Thomas Neal's, Earlham St,
WC2 ☎020/7369 1732, ⓦwww.donmarwarehouse
.com; Covent Garden tube. An intimate central
performance space that's noted for new plays and
top-quality reappraisals of the classics.

Drill Hall 16 Chenies St, WC1 ☎020/7307 5060,
ⓦwww.drillhall.co.uk; Goodge Street tube. This
studio-style venue specializes in gay, lesbian,
feminist and all-round politically correct new work.

ICA Nash House, The Mall, SW1 ☎020/7930 3647,
ⓦwww.ica.org.uk; Piccadilly Circus or Charing Cross
tube. The Institute of Contemporary Arts attracts
the most innovative practitioners in all areas of
performance. It also attracts a fair quantity of modish
junk, but the hits generally outweigh the misses.

Menier Chocolate Factory 51–53 Southwark
St, SE1 ☎020/7907 7060, ⓦwww
.menierchocolatefactory.com; London Bridge
tube. Great fringe venue in an old Victorian
factory; consistently good shows and has a good
bar and restaurant attached.

National Theatre South Bank Centre, South Bank,
SE1 ☎020/7452 3000, ⓦwww.nationaltheatre
.org.uk; Waterloo tube. The Royal National Theatre,
as it's now officially known, consists of three
separate theatres. The country's top actors and
directors perform here in a programme ranging
from Greek tragedies to Broadway musicals.
Twenty to thirty cheap tickets go on sale on the
morning of each performance – get there by 8am
for the popular shows.

Open Air Theatre Regent's Park, Inner Circle, NW1
☎020/7486 2431, ⓦwww.openairtheatre.org;
Baker Street tube. If the weather's good, there's
nothing quite like a dose of alfresco drama. This
beautiful space in Regent's Park hosts a tourist-
friendly summer programme of Shakespeare,
musicals, plays and concerts.

Royal Court Sloane Square, SW1 ☎020/7565
5000, ⓦwww.royalcourttheatre.com; Sloane
Square tube. The Royal Court is one of the best
places in London to catch radical new writing,
either in the proscenium arch Theatre
Downstairs, or the smaller-scale Theatre
Upstairs studio space.

Shakespeare's Globe New Globe Walk, SE1
☎020/7401 9919, ⓦwww.shakespeares-globe
.org; London Bridge, Blackfriars or Southwark tube.
This thatch-roofed replica Elizabethan theatre uses
only natural light and the minimum of scenery, and
puts on solid, fun Shakespearean shows from mid-
May to mid-Sept, with "groundling" tickets
(standing-room only) for around a fiver.

Tricycle Theatre 269 Kilburn High Rd, NW6
☎020/7328 1000, ⓦwww.tricycle.co.uk; Kilburn
tube. One of London's most dynamic fringe venues,
showcasing a mixed bag of new plays, often aimed
at the theatre's multicultural neighbourhood, and
often with a sharp political focus.

Comedy

The **comedy scene** continues to thrive in London, with the leading funny-
persons catapulted to unlikely stardom on both stage and screen. The Comedy
Store is the best known and most central venue on the circuit, but just about
every London suburb has a pub stage giving a platform to young hopefuls (full
listings appear on ⓦwww.chortle.co.uk and in *Time Out*). Note that many
venues operate only on Friday and Saturday nights, and that August is a lean
month, as much of London's talent heads north for the Edinburgh Festival.
Tickets at smaller venues can be had for £5–7, but in the more established
places, you're looking at £10 or more.

Backyard Comedy Club 231 Cambridge Heath Rd, E2 ☎ 020/7739 3122, ⓦ www.leehurst.com; Bethnal Green tube. Purpose-built club in Bethnal Green established by comedian Lee Hurst, who has successfully managed to attract a consistently strong line-up. Thurs–Sat.

Canal Café Theatre Delamere Terrace, W2 ☎ 020/7289 6054, ⓦ www.canalcafetheatre.com; Warwick Avenue tube. Perched on the water's edge in Little Venice, this venue is good for improvisation acts and is home to the *Newsrevue* team of topical gagsters; there's usually something going on Thurs–Sun.

Comedy Café 66 Rivington St, EC2 ☎ 020/7739 5706, ⓦ www.comedycafe.co.uk; Old Street tube. Long-established, purpose-built club in Shoreditch/ Hoxton, often with impressive line-ups; free admission for the new-acts slot on Wed nights. Wed–Sat.

Comedy Store Haymarket House, 1a Oxendon St, SW1 ☎ 020/7344 0234, ⓦ www .thecomedystore.co.uk; Piccadilly Circus tube. Widely regarded as the birthplace of alternative comedy, the Comedy Store has catapulted many a stand-up onto primetime TV. Improvisation by in-house comics on Wed and Sun, in addition to a stand-up bill; Fri and Sat are the busiest nights, with two shows, at 8pm and midnight – book ahead.

Jongleurs Camden Lock, Dingwalls Building, 36 Camden Lock Place, Chalk Farm Road, NW1 ☎ 0870/787 0707, ⓦ www.jongleurs.com for branches; Camden tube. Jongleurs is the chain store of comedy, doling out high quality stand-up and post-revelry disco-dancing nightly on Fri. Book well in advance.

Cinema

There are an awful lot of **cinemas** in the West End, but very few places committed to independent films, and even fewer repertory cinemas programming serious films from the back catalogue. November's **London Film Festival** (ⓦ www.lff.org.uk), which occupies half a dozen West End cinemas, is now a huge event, and so popular that many of the films sell out soon after publication of the festival's programme. Below is a selection of the cinemas that put on the most interesting programmes.

BFI Imax South Bank, SE1 ☎ 0870/787 2525, ⓦ www.bfi.org.uk; Waterloo tube. The BFI's remarkable glazed drum houses Europe's largest screen. It's stunning, state-of-the-art stuff all right, showing 2D and 3D films on a massive screen, but like all IMAX cinemas, it suffers from the paucity of good material that's been shot in the format.

BFI Southbank Belvedere Rd, South Bank, SE1 ☎ 020/7928 3232, ⓦ www.bfi.org.uk; Waterloo tube. Known for its attentive audiences and an exhaustive, eclectic programme that includes directors' seasons and thematic series. Around six films daily are shown in each of the three theatres – the vast NFT1 and the smaller NFT2 and NFT3.

Electric 191 Portobello Rd, W11 ☎ 020/7908 9696, ⓦ www.the-electric.co.uk; Notting Hill Gate or Ladbroke Grove tube. One of the oldest cinemas in the country (opened 1910), the Electric has been filled out with luxury leather

armchairs, footstools and sofas. Most seats cost £12.50.

Everyman Hollybush Vale, NW3 ☎ 0870/066 4777, ⓦ www.everymancinema.com; Hampstead tube. The city's oldest rep cinema, and still one of its best, with strong programmes of classics, cultish crowd-magnets and directors' seasons. Two screens and some very plush seating.

ICA Cinema Nash House, The Mall, SW1 ☎ 020/7930 3647, ⓦ www.ica.org.uk; Piccadilly Circus or Charing Cross tube. Vintage and underground movies shown on one of two tiny screens in the avant-garde HQ of the Institute of Contemporary Arts.

Prince Charles 2–7 Leicester Place, WC2 ☎ 020/7494 3654, ⓦ www.princecharlescinema .com; Leicester Square or Piccadilly Circus tube. The bargain basement of London's cinemas (entry for most shows is just £4.50), with a programme of new movies, classics and cult favourites, plus participatory "singalong" romps.

Classical music, opera and dance

London is spoilt for choice when it comes to **orchestras**. On most days you'll be able to catch a concert by the London Symphony Orchestra, the London

Philharmonic, the Royal Philharmonic, the Philharmonia or the BBC Symphony Orchestra, or a smaller-scale performance from the English Chamber Orchestra or the Academy of St Martin-in-the-Fields. During the week, there are also **free lunchtime concerts** by students or professionals in numerous London churches, particularly in the City; performances in the Royal College of Music and Royal Academy of Music are of an amazingly high standard, and the choice of work is often a lot riskier than at commercial venues.

The principal **large-scale venue** is the **South Bank Centre** (☎0871/663 2500, ⓦwww.southbankcentre.org.uk), where the biggest names appear at the Royal Festival Hall, with more specialized programmes staged in the Queen Elizabeth Hall and Purcell Room. With the outstanding London Symphony Orchestra as its resident orchestra, and with top foreign orchestras and big-name soloists in regular attendance, the **Barbican** (☎020/7638 8891, ⓦwww.barbican.org.uk) is one of the capital's best arenas for classical music. Programming is much more adventurous than it used to be, and free music in the foyer is often very good. For **chamber music**, the intimate and elegant Wigmore Hall, 36 Wigmore St, W1 (☎020/7935 2141, ⓦwww.wigmore-hall .org.uk), is many a Londoner's favourite.

From July to September each year, **the Proms** at the **Royal Albert Hall** (ⓦwww.bbc.co.uk/proms) feature at least one concert daily, with hundreds of standing tickets sold for just £4 on the night. The acoustics aren't the world's best, but the calibre of the performers is unbeatable and the programme is a fascinating mix of standards and new or obscure works. The hall is so vast that if you turn up half an hour before the show starts there should be little risk of being turned away.

London is extremely well served for **opera**, with two opera houses, both of which have recently been refurbished. The **Royal Opera House** (☎020/7304 4000, ⓦwww.royaloperahouse.org), in Covent Garden, is the pricier and more conservative of the two, with a fairly standard repertoire performed in the original language (with surtitles), while **English National Opera** at the Coliseum on St Martin's Lane (☎0870/145 0200, ⓦwww.eno.org) puts on lively, radical productions, sung in English.

From the time-honoured showpieces of the **Royal Ballet** (☎020/7304 4000, ⓦwww.royaloperahouse.org) to the diverse and exciting range of British and international dance that goes on at Sadler's Wells (☎0844/412 4300, ⓦwww.sadlers-wells.com), on Rosebery Avenue in Clerkenwell, and at the much smaller venue, The Place (☎020/7121 1000, ⓦwww.theplace .org.uk), 17 Duke's Rd, near King's Cross, there's always a **dance performance** of some kind afoot in London. The city also has a good reputation for international dance festivals showcasing the work of a spread of ensembles, the biggest of which is the annual **Dance Umbrella** (☎020/8741 4040, ⓦwww.danceumbrella.co.uk), a six-week season (Sept–Nov) of new work from bright young choreographers and performance artists at venues across the city.

Shopping

Whether you've got time to kill or money to burn, London is one big **shopper's playground**. Although chains and superstores predominate along the high streets, you're never too far from the kind of oddball, one-off establishment that makes shopping an adventure rather than a routine. From the *folie de* *grandeur* that is Harrods to the frenetic street markets of the East End, there's probably nothing you can't find in some corner of the capital.

In the centre of town, **Oxford Street** is the city's hectic chain-store mecca, and, together with **Regent Street**, offers pretty much every mainstream clothing label you could wish for. Just off Oxford Street you can find expensive designer outlets in St Christopher's Place and South Molton Street, and even pricier designers and jewellers on the very chic **Bond Street**.

Tottenham Court Road is the place to go for stereos, computers, electrical goods and, in its northern section, furniture and design shops. **Charing Cross Road** is the centre of London's book trade, both new and secondhand. At its north end, and particularly on Denmark Street, you can find music shops selling everything from instruments to sound equipment and sheet music. **Soho** offers an offbeat mix of sex boutiques, specialist record shops and fabric stores, while the streets surrounding **Covent Garden** yield art and design shops, mainstream fashion chains, designer wear and camping gear; Neal Street is the place to go to indulge a shoe-shopping habit.

Just off Piccadilly, **St James's** is the natural habitat of the quintessential English gentleman, with **Jermyn Street** in particular harbouring shops dedicated to his grooming. **Knightsbridge**, further west, is home to Harrods, and the big-name fashion stores of **Sloane Street** and **Brompton Road**.

Books

The biggest bookstore in the capital is Waterstones' Piccadilly branch (Piccadilly Circus tube), but the largest choice of bookshops is still on **Charing Cross Road**. Here you'll find not only find most of the **chain stores** but also the long-established and idiosyncratic Foyles at no. 113–119, as well as other smaller **independent shops** such as art specialists Zwemmer at no. 80 and **secondhand stores**, including Any Amount of Books at no. 62. For travel books and maps, head to Stanfords, 12–14 Long Acre (℡020/7836 1321, Ⓦwww.stanfords.co.uk).

Department stores

Fortnum & Mason, 181 Piccadilly (Green Park or Piccadilly Circus tube), is the place to go for fabulous, gorgeously presented and pricey food, plus upmarket clothes, furniture and stationery. **Harrods**, Knightsbridge (Knightsbridge tube), is famous for its fantastic Art Nouveau tiled food hall, obscenely huge toy department and supremely tasteless memorial to Di and Dodi; beware the draconian dress code (see p.129). Nearby, **Harvey Nichols**, 109–125 Knightsbridge, offers all the latest designer collections and famously frivolous and pricey luxury foods. Over at Oxford Circus, several major stores are close at hand, among them: **John Lewis**, 278–306 Oxford St (Oxford Circus tube), which offers everything from buttons to stockings to furniture and household goods; **Liberty**, 210–220 Regent St (Oxford Circus tube), founded as a retail outlet for the Victorian Arts and Crafts Movement, and still the place to go for regal fabrics and decorative household goods; and **Selfridge's**, 400 Oxford St (Bond Street tube), London's first great department store, which has a wide range of clothing, food and furnishings.

Markets

Camden, running from Camden High Street to Chalk Farm Road (daily; Camden Town tube), is top of the list for market shopping on most tourist itineraries; the atmosphere is a studenty mix of clubby and grungy and the stuff on sale is mainly cheap clothes and jewellery, though the stalls around

Camden Lock are generally more interesting; weekends are the best – and busiest – times to visit. For a real foody experience, head for **Borough Market** (see p.123). **Spitalfields**, Commercial Street (Sun; Liverpool Street tube), also offers fabulous food, but is otherwise more of an arty-crafty market similar to Camden. Nearby, **Brick Lane** (Sun; Aldgate East, Shoreditch or Liverpool Street tube) has everything from sofas and antiques to cheap junk. **Bermondsey** (New Caledonian) Market, Bermondsey Square (Fri; Borough, London Bridge or Bermondsey tube), is a huge, unglamorous but highly regarded antique market that kicks off at 5am; while **Portobello**, Portobello Rd (Fri–Sun; Notting Hill or Ladbroke Grove tube), is mostly boho-chic clothes and (Sat only) portable antiques. South of the river, **Greenwich**, Market Square (Sat & Sun; Cutty Sark DLR or Greenwich train station), is another small arty-crafty market, with second-hand clothing and antiques on sale, too.

Music

The **megastores** are: HMV, 150 Oxford St (Oxford Circus tube); Tower Records, 1 Piccadilly Circus (Piccadilly Circus tube); and Zarri, 14–16 Oxford St (Tottenham Court Road tube). For **jazz**, try Ray's on the first floor of Foyles (see p.159). For **indie music**, there's Sister Ray, 94 Berwick St (Oxford Circus or Piccadilly Circus tube). For **African and world music**, head to Stern's, 293 Euston Rd, NW1 (Euston Square tube). **Hip-hop** is available at Mr Bongo, 44 Poland St (Oxford Circus tube), while for **house**, **techno** and **trance** try Eukatech, 49 Endell St (Covent Garden tube).

Listings

Bike rental London Bicycle Tour Company, 1a Gabriel's Wharf SE1 ☎020/7928 6838, ⓦwww .londonbicycle.com; Waterloo or Southwark tube. On Your Bike, 52–54 Tooley St, SE1 ☎020/7378 6669, ⓦwww.onyourbike.com; London Bridge tube.

Car rental For the most competitive rates, ring round a few local firms from the Yellow Pages (ⓦwww.yell.com) before you try your luck with the usual suspects.

Consulates and embassies Australia, Australia House, Strand, WC2 ☎020/7379 4334, ⓦwww.australia.org.uk; Canadian High Commission 1 Grosvenor Square, W1 ☎020/7528 6600, ⓦwww.canada.org.uk; Ireland, 17 Grosvenor Place, SW1 ☎020/7235 2171, ⓦwww.irlgov.ie; New Zealand, New Zealand House, 80 Haymarket, SW1 ☎020/7930 8422, ⓦwww.nzembassy.com; South Africa, South Africa House, Trafalgar Square, WC2 ☎020/7451 7299, ⓦwww.southafricahouse.com; USA, 24 Grosvenor Square, W1 ☎020/7499 9000, ⓦwww.usembassy.org.uk.

Cricket Three Test matches are played in London each summer: two at Lord's (☎020/7432 1000, ⓦwww.lords.org; St John's Wood tube), the home of English cricket; the other at The Oval (☎020/7582 6660, ⓦwww.surreycricket.com; Oval tube) in south London. In tandem with the full-blown five-day Tests, there are also two series of one-day internationals and the wham-bam Twenty20 Internationals.

Football Despite the recent successes of Chelsea (☎020/7386 9373, ⓦwww.chelseafc .com; Fulham Broadway tube), for the last decade or so Arsenal (☎020/7704 4040, ⓦwww.arsenal.com; Arsenal tube) have been London's most successful club; their closest rivals (geographically) are Tottenham Hotspur (☎0870/420 5000, ⓦwww.tottenhamhotspur .com; White Hart Lane train station from Liverpool St). Tickets for most Premiership games start at £30–35 and are virtually impossible to get hold of on a casual basis; you're more likely to have success if you try one of the smaller London sides, such as Fulham (☎0870/442 1234, ⓦwww.fulhamfc.com; Putney Bridge tube), West Ham (☎0870/112 2700, ⓦwww.whufc.co.uk; Upton Park tube) or Charlton Athletic (☎0871/226 1905, ⓦwww.cafc.co.uk; Charlton train station from Charing Cross).

Hospitals For 24hr accident and emergency: St Mary's Hospital, Praed Street, W2 ☎020/7886 6666; University College London Hospital, Grafton Way, WC1 ☎020/7387 9300.

Internet cafés easyInternetcafe (⊛www .easyeverything.com) has branches at 456 Strand, off Trafalgar Square (8am–11pm; Charing Cross tube), 9–16 Tottenham Court Rd (Mon–Wed & Sun 8am–midnight, Thurs–Sat 8am–2am; Tottenham Court Road tube). Alternatively, there's the more congenial *Be the Reds!* (☎020/7209 0984; Mon–Sat 10.30am–2am) at 39 Whitfield St, just off Tottenham Court Road (Goodge Street tube) – a Korean-run place serving *kimbab* and coffee, with billiards in the basement.

Laundry Regent Dry Cleaners, 18 Embankment Place WC2 ☎020/7839 6775; Embankment or Charing Cross tube.

Left luggage Left luggage is available at all airports and major train terminals.

Motorbike rental Raceways, 201–203 Lower Rd, SE16 ☎020/7237 6494 (Surrey Quays tube) and 17 The Vale, Uxbridge Road, W3 ☎020/8749 8181 (Shepherd's Bush tube), ⊛www.raceways.net.

Police Metropolitan Police (⊛www.met.police.uk) stations include: Charing Cross, Agar St, WC2 ☎020/7240 1212; Holborn, 10 Lambs Conduit St, WC1 ☎020/7704 1212; Marylebone, 1–9 Seymour St, W1 ☎020/7486 1212; West End Central, 27 Savile Row, W1 ☎020/7437 1212; City of London Police (⊛www.cityoflondon.uk): Bishopsgate, EC2 ☎020/7601 2222.

Post offices The only (vaguely) late-opening post office is the Trafalgar Square branch at 24–28 William IV St, WC2 (Mon 8.30am–6.30pm, Tues 9.15am–6.30pm, Wed–Fri 8.30am–6.30pm, Sat 9am–5pm); it's also the city's poste restante collection point. For general postal enquiries phone ☎0845/774 0740 (Mon–Fri 8am–7.30pm, Sat 8am–2.30pm), or visit the website ⊛www.royalmail.com.

Tennis Tennis in England is synonymous with Wimbledon (☎020/8971 2473, ⊛www .wimbledon.com), the only Grand Slam tournament in the world to be played on grass, and for many players the ultimate goal of their careers. To buy tickets on the day, you must arrive by around 7am for tickets on Centre, No. 1 & No. 2 courts, or by around 9am for the outside courts (and avoid the middle Sat of the tournament); alternatively, if you start queuing around 2pm, you should get in to see some play in the evening.

Train stations and information As a rough guide, Charing Cross handles services to Kent; Euston to the Midlands, northwest England and Glasgow; Fenchurch Street south Essex; King's Cross northeast England and Edinburgh; Liverpool Street East Anglia; Marylebone the Midlands; Paddington southwest England; St Pancras Eurostar, East Midlands and South Yorkshire; Victoria and Waterloo southeast England and the south coast. For information, contact national rail enquiries ☎08457/484950, ⊛www.rail.co.uk.

Travel details

Buses

For information on all local and national bus services, contact Traveline ☎0871/200 2233, ⊛www.traveline .org.uk.

London Victoria Coach Station to: Bath (every 1–2hr; 3hr 30min); Birmingham (hourly; 2hr 40min); Brighton (hourly; 2hr 10min); Bristol (hourly; 2hr 30min); Cambridge (hourly; 2hr); Canterbury (hourly; 2hr); Dover (hourly; 2hr 30min–3hr); Exeter (every 2hr; 4hr 15min); Gloucester (hourly; 3hr 20min); Liverpool (6 daily; 4hr 50min–5hr 30min); Manchester (9 daily; 4hr 15min–5hr 20min); Newcastle (5 daily; 6hr 25min–7hr 45min); Oxford (every 15min; 1hr 50min); Plymouth (6 daily; 5hr 20min); Stratford (4 daily; 3hr).

Trains

For information on all local and national rail services, contact National Rail Enquiries ☎08457/484950, ⊛www.nationalrail.co.uk.

London Charing Cross to: Canterbury West (hourly; 1hr 40min); Dover Priory (Mon–Sat every 30min; 1hr 40min–1hr 50min).

London Euston to: Birmingham New St (every 30min; 1hr 30min–2hr 10min); Carlisle (hourly; 3hr 30min–4hr); Lancaster (hourly; 2hr 50min); Liverpool Lime St (hourly; 2hr 30min); Manchester Piccadilly (hourly; 2hr 20min).

London King's Cross to: Brighton (Thameslink; every 15–30min; 1hr 15min); Cambridge (every 30min; 50min); Durham (hourly; 2hr 40min–3hr); Leeds (hourly; 2hr 25min); Newcastle (every

30min; 3hr); Peterborough (every 30min; 45min); York (every 30min; 2hr).

London Liverpool Street to: Cambridge (every 30min; 1hr 20min); Norwich (every 30min; 1hr 55min).

London Paddington to: Bath (every 30min–hourly; 1hr 30min); Bristol (every 30–45min; 1hr 40min); Cheltenham (every 2hr; 2hr 15min); Exeter (hourly; 2hr 15min); Gloucester (every 2hr; 2hr); Oxford (every 30min–hourly; 55min); Penzance (every 1–2hr; 5hr 30min); Plymouth (hourly; 3hr 15min–3hr 40min); Windsor (change at Slough; Mon–Fri every 20min; Sat & Sun every 30min; 30–40min); Worcester (hourly; 2hr 20min).

London St Pancras to: Leicester (every 30min; 1hr 10min); Nottingham (every 30min; 1hr 40min–2hr); Sheffield (hourly; 2hr 20min).

London Victoria to: Brighton (every 30min; 50min); Canterbury East (every 30min–hourly; 1hr 25min); Dover Priory (Mon–Sat every 30min; 1hr 40min–1hr 55min).

London Waterloo to: Portsmouth Harbour (every 30min; 1hr 35min); Southampton Central (every 30min; 1hr 15min); Winchester (every 30min; 1hr); Windsor (Mon–Sat every 30min, Sun hourly; 50min).

Surrey, Kent and Sussex

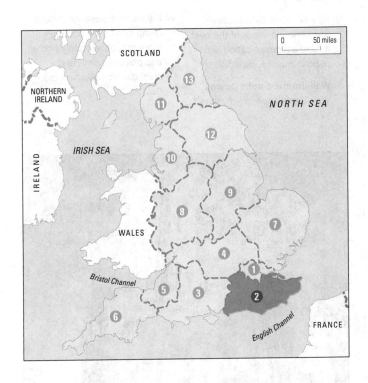

CHAPTER 2 # Highlights

* **Canterbury Cathedral** An essential tourist stop stuffed with historical interest – for once transcending the hype. See p.179

* **The White Cliffs of Dover** Best seen from a boat, the famed chalky cliffs also offer walks and vistas over the Channel. See p.188

* **Rye** Wonderfully set hilltop town offering some of the best meals, accommodation and pubs in Sussex. See p.201

* **Walking the South Downs Way** Experience great vistas, pubs, wildlife and the best walking in the southeast on this national trail. See p.204

* **Brighton's Lanes** Diversity and quirky originality mark out the shops and cafés crammed into Brighton's tight-knit Lanes area, ideal for a leisurely wander. See p.213

* **Petworth House** As well as being one of the country's most attractive stately homes, this place is home to a splendid art collection too. See p.221

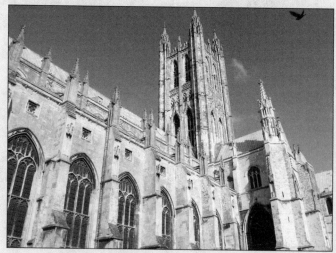

▲ Canterbury Cathedral

2

Surrey, Kent and Sussex

The southeast corner of England was traditionally where London went on holiday. In the past, trainloads of Eastenders were shuttled to the hop fields and orchards of **Kent** for a working break from the city; boats ferried people down the Thames to the beach at Margate; and everyone from royalty to illicit couples enjoyed the seaside at Brighton, a blot of decadence in the otherwise sedate county of **Sussex**. **Surrey** is the least pastoral and historically significant of the three counties – the home of wealthy metropolitan professionals prepared to commute from what has become known as the "stockbroker belt".

In recent years, many of the old seaside resorts have struggled to keep their tourist custom in the face of ever more accessible foreign destinations combined with the vagaries of the English weather. To make matters worse, **Brighton**, long known as "London beside the sea", now matches the capital with one of the highest proportions of homeless people in the country. On the positive side, there has been something of a renaissance in recent years, with various celebrities and other big-city refugees choosing to settle in more congenial surroundings away from the metropolitan hubbub, while the whole region has maintained consistently high standards of both accommodation and gourmet dining. Narrow country lanes and verdant meadows preserve their picturesque charm, and there are even pockets of comparative wilderness, not to mention the miles of bleak and cliffy coastline.

The proximity of Kent and Sussex to the Continent has dictated the history of this region, which has served as a gateway for an array of invaders, both rapacious and benign. **Roman** remains dot the coastal area – most spectacularly at **Bignor** in Sussex and **Lullingstone** in Kent – and many roads, including the main A2 London to Dover road, follow the arrow-straight tracks laid by the legionaries. When **Christianity** spread through Europe, it arrived in Britain on the **Isle of Thanet** – the northeast tip of Kent, since rejoined to the mainland by silting and subsiding sea levels. In 597 AD Augustine moved inland and established a monastery at **Canterbury**, still the home of the Church of England and the county's prime historic attraction. (Surprisingly, Sussex was among the last counties to accept the Cross – due more to the region's then impenetrable forest than to its innate ungodliness.)

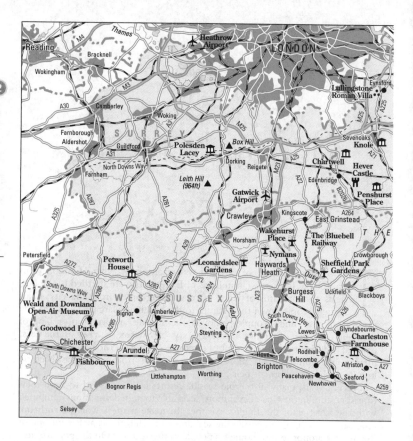

The last successful invasion of England took place in 1066, when the **Normans** overran King Harold's army near **Hastings**, on a site now marked by **Battle Abbey**. The Normans left their mark all over this corner of the kingdom, and Kent remains unmatched in its profusion of medieval castles, among them **Dover**'s sprawling cliff-top fortress guarding against continental invasion and **Rochester**'s huge, box-like citadel, close to the old dockyards of **Chatham**, power-base of the formerly invincible British navy.

Away from the great historic sites, you can spend unhurried days in elegant old towns such as **Royal Tunbridge Wells**, **Rye** and **Lewes**, or enjoy the less-elevated charms of the traditional resorts, of which **Brighton** is far and away the best, combining the buzz of a university town with a blowsy good-time atmosphere and an excellent range of eating options. Dramatic scenery may be in short supply, but in places the **South Downs Way** offers an expanse of rolling chalk uplands that, as much as anywhere in the crowded southeast, gets you away from it all. And of course Kent, Sussex and Surrey harbour some of the country's finest **gardens**, ranging from Kew Gardens' country home at **Wakehurst Place** to the lush flowerbeds of **Sissinghurst** and the great landscaped estates of **Petworth** and **Sheffield Park**.

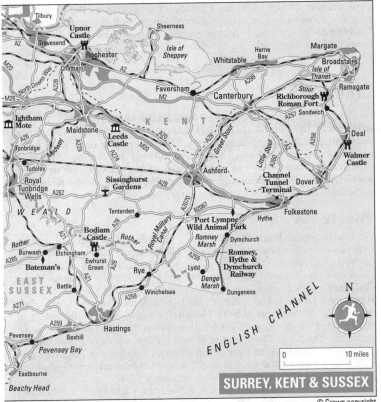

© Crown copyright

The commuter traffic in this corner of England is the heaviest in Europe, so almost everywhere of interest is close to a **train** station. National Express services from London and other parts of England to the region are pretty good, but local **bus** services are much less impressive.

Surrey

Effectively a rural suburb of southern London for those who can afford it, **Surrey** is bisected laterally by the chalk escarpment of the **North Downs** which rise west of Guildford, peak around **Box Hill** near **Dorking**, and continue east into Kent. The portion of Surrey within and around the M25 orbital motorway has little natural and virtually no historical appeal, being a collection of satellite towns and light industrial installations. But beyond the ring, the county takes on a more pastoral aspect, with the county town of **Guildford**, the open heath land of Surrey's western borders and **Farnham**, home to the county's only intact castle.

Guildford

Nestling in a gap carved through the North Downs by the River Wey, 35 miles southwest of London, **GUILDFORD** is largely blighted by one-way systems and a surfeit of shopping precincts, yet its town centre does retain some traces of its past. During the thirteenth century Guildford was the site of the only royal castle in Surrey – parts of which survive – while the Guildhall recalls the town's importance as a major staging post between London and the flourishing Portsmouth docks in the seventeenth century.

The Town

Guildford's sloping **High Street** retains a great deal of architectural interest, with picturesque narrow lanes and courtyards leading off it. As you look up the cobbled street you can't fail to spot the wonderful gilded clock that has marked the town's time for more than three hundred years. The clock belongs to the **Guildhall** (guided tours Tues & Thurs 2pm & 3pm; free), whose elaborate Restoration facade disguises Tudor foundations. A little further up the High Street is the **Archbishop Abbot's Hospital**, a hospice built for the elderly in 1619 fronted by a palatial red-brick Tudor gateway. You can take a peek at the pretty courtyard, but if you want to inspect the Flemish stained glass and oak beams that characterize the interior you must join a guided tour (Sat 11am; £3). Back down towards the river at no. 72 is the **Undercroft**, a well-preserved thirteenth-century basement of vaulted arches.

Surrounded by flower-filled gardens behind the High Street, the Norman keep is all that remains of **Guildford Castle** (March & Oct Sat & Sun 11am–5pm; April–Sept daily 11am–5pm; £2.40), which was frequently used as a palace by King John – he is thought to have departed from here to Runnymede to sign the Magna Carta in 1215. Various exhibits are displayed in the renovated first-floor reception chamber, and there are memorable views from the top of the keep. Beneath the castle on Quarry Street, **Guildford Museum** in Castle Arch (Mon–Sat 11am–5pm; free) gives an account of the region's pre-Christian culture and displays cases of ceramic relics as well as some exquisite Saxon jewellery. Upstairs are mementoes of Lewis Carroll (aka the Reverend Charles Dodgson), author of *Alice's Adventures in Wonderland* and *Alice Through the Looking Glass*. An imaginative sculpture of Alice passing through the looking glass can be seen in the Castle Gardens, and Dodgson's grave can be visited in the cemetery off the Mount, on the other side of the river.

At the bottom of the High Street, the **River Wey** is a rather neglected feature of the town, although the once crucial River Wey and Godalming Navigation Canal has been restored into a picturesque waterway. Canoes and rowing boats are available for hire, and in summer **pleasure cruises** can be taken up the river.

Practicalities

Guildford's **train station** lies just over the river to the west of the town centre; the **bus station** is nearby at the western end of North Street. The **tourist** office is at 14 Tunsgate (Mon–Sat 9/9.30am–5/5.30pm, May–Sept also Sun 10am–4.30pm; ☎01483/444333, ⒲www.guildford.gov.uk), just off the High Street near the Guildhall. Free guided **tours** of the town (May–Sept Mon 11am, Wed & Sun 2.30pm, May–Aug also Thurs 7pm) leave from Tunsgate Arch, just below the tourist office.

Guildford's less expensive **accommodation** options are in Stoke Road, a ten-minute walk up the A320 Woking road from the town centre: try *Stoke House*, at no.113 (☎01483/453025, ⒲www.stokehouse.net; ②–③), which has smallish, modern rooms, some en suite. Alternatively, head three miles northwest of town, on the Aldershot road, to *Littlefield Manor*, Littlefield Common (☎01483/233068, ⒲www.littlefieldmanor.co.uk; ④), a gorgeous Tudor and Jacobean farmhouse offering three spacious rooms. For a **meal**, head south off the High Street to find *Café de Paris* at 35 Castle St (☎01483/534896; closed Sun eve), a busy French-style brasserie in a listed building, offering reasonable set-price menus and a terrace for open-air dining, while *Olivo*, housed in the town's sixteenth-century dispensary at 53 Quarry St (☎01483/303535), specializes in delicious regional Italian dishes and has a roof-terrace. For a drink, try the *Weyside* on Millbrook, a pleasant riverside **pub** with gardens. Also on Millbrook, the well-reputed Yvonne Arnaud **theatre** (☎01483/440000, ⒲www.yvonne-arnaud.co.uk) often stages plays before they reach London's West End. The nearby Electric Theatre (☎01483/444789, ⒲www.electrictheatre.co.uk), based in the former electric works on Onslow Street, is an innovative riverside venue for both music and theatre and houses an excellent café.

Farnham and around

Tucked into Surrey's southwestern corner, ten miles west of Guildford along the exposed ridge-top of the Hog's Back, lies **FARNHAM**. Smaller and more charming than Guildford, the town moves at a slower pace – though, despite its bypass, the centre is often clogged by traffic. Notwithstanding its thousand-year history, the majority of Farnham's architecture dates from the eighteenth century, when it enjoyed a boom period based on hop farming.

Farnham is home to Surrey's only intact **castle**, built around 1138 by Henry de Blois, Bishop of Winchester, as a convenient residence halfway between his diocese and London. The castle was continuously occupied until 1927, but now houses a conference venue. The **keep** (Easter, July & Aug Fri–Sun 1–5pm; £3; EH), from where there are good views over the rooftops to the downs beyond, is the only part that is open to the public.

Farnham's refined Georgian dwellings are at their best along the broad **Castle Street**, linking the town centre with the castle. To see inside one, however, head to 38 West St, where the **Museum of Farnham** (Tues–Sat 10am–5pm; free) is housed inside the former home of a wealthy hop merchant. The museum contains a succinct rundown of the town's history, its local hero, the late eighteenth-century journalist and social reformer William Cobbett, and the highly regarded local art school. On the same street, the town's library is located in **Vernon House**, where Charles I spent the night in 1648 en route to his trial and eventual execution in London.

Farnham **train station** is five minutes from the centre, over the river on the southern edge of town. The **tourist office** is in the council offices on South Street, midway between the station and the centre (Mon–Fri 9am–4.30/5pm;

①01252/712667, ⓦwww.farnham.gov.uk). There's comfortable town-house **accommodation** at *Meads Guest House*, 48 West St (①01252/715298; no credit cards; ❸), or try the excellent *Stafford House Hotel*, 22 Firgrove Hill (①01252/724336; ❸), close to the station. The friendly *Caffe Piccolo*, 84 West St (①01252/723277), serves inexpensive **meals**, while the more upmarket *Vienna Stuberl* at 112 West St (①01252/722978; closed Sun) is good for seafood. Among the local **pubs**, the oak-beamed *Nelson Arms* on Castle Street serves reasonable bar food.

Dorking and Box Hill

Set at the mouth of a gap carved by the River Mole through the North Downs, **DORKING**, 25 miles from London (frequent trains from London Victoria), lies at the intersection of the former Roman Stane Street and the medieval byway known as the Pilgrim's Way. There's little to see in Dorking itself, but it makes a convenient base for exploring the surrounding countryside. If you want to **stay**, try *The White Horse Hotel* (①01306/881138, ⓦwww.whitehorsedorking .co.uk; ❻) on the High Street, an oak-beamed former coaching inn dating from the seventeenth century that is also the town's best **food** option.

Box Hill, on the northern edge of town, is a popular draw for suburban weekenders and a staple of school trips during the week, when the intricacies of the River Mole's contrary flow through the chalk downs are explained. It's a three-hour climb to the top, but the snack-bar (daily 9am–5pm), the view south over the town and the Weald's sandstone ridges reward the effort. You'll also find the grave of the eccentric local resident Major Peter Labilliere here; the major was famously buried head first, so that, in a topsy-turvy world, he would be the only one to "face his Maker the right way up". Box Hill sits on the most interesting part of the 151-mile **North Downs Way**, a tame long-distance footpath that stretches from Farnham to Dover. Though walkable from Dorking (around 45min), the nearest **train station** to Box Hill is at Westhumble, on the Dorking–London line.

Kent

Not so long ago Kent's tourist industry was focused chiefly on the resorts of its northern coast and the **Isle of Thanet**, the northeastern tip of the county. Certainly the area had a great appeal for **Charles Dickens**, who spent many years at various spots along this coast. Nowadays these seaside towns have lost much of their gloss, but the county still boasts one of the most popular destinations in the entire country – the county town of **Canterbury**, site of one of the great English cathedrals. Furthermore, Kent can also boast its fair share of alluring castles and gardens, the best known of which are the estate of **Knole**, on the edge of Sevenoaks, **Leeds Castle**, to the east of Maidstone, and **Sissinghurst Gardens**, in the heart of the Weald and an inspiration to thousands of amateur horticulturalists. Exploration of the county's other scattered attractions – such as Winston Churchill's home at **Chartwell**, **Penshurst Place**, **Hever Castle** or the remnants of the Roman villa at **Lullingstone** – could fill a long and pleasurable weekend.

   Transport links from London are good: the A2, M2 and M20 link the Channel ports of Ramsgate and Dover with London and rail connections to the county's key towns from London are reliable. Sevenoaks, Tunbridge Wells and Canterbury are well served by daily National Express bus services too, but local rail and bus links are slow.

The North Kent coast

Though most visitors only glimpse the northern part of Kent as they race to or from the Channel ports, the region merits a more prolonged exploration, with all its varied attractions easily accessible from London. There is a knot of historic sites at **Rochester** and **Chatham**, two of the five "Medway towns" – so-called because they are grouped around the River Medway (the others are Strood, Gillingham and Rainham) – while the seaside resorts of **Whitstable**, **Margate** and **Broadstairs**, ranging from genteel to seedy, have a growing cachet among weekenders from the capital.

Rochester and around

ROCHESTER, the most pleasant of the Medway towns, was first settled by the Romans, who built a fortress on the site of the present **castle** (daily 10am–4/6pm; £4; Ⓦwww.medway.gov.uk), at the northwest end of the High Street; some kind of fortification has remained here ever since. In 1077, William I gave Gundulf – architect of the White Tower at the Tower of London – the See of Rochester and the job of improving the defences on the River Medway's northernmost bridge on Watling Street. The resulting castle remains one of the best-preserved examples of a Norman fortress in England, with the stark hundred-foot-high keep glowering over the town, while the interior is all the better for having lost its floors, allowing clear views up and down the dank interior.

   The foundations of the adjacent **cathedral** (daily 8.30am–6pm; suggested donation £3) were also Gundulf's work, but the building has been much modified over the past nine hundred years. Plenty of Norman touches have endured, however, particularly in the cathedral's west front, with its pencil-shaped towers, blind arcading and richly carved portal and tympanum above the doorway. Norman round arches, decorated with zigzags and made from lovely honey-coloured Caen stone, also line the nave. Some fine paintings survived the Dissolution, most notably the thirteenth-century depiction of the Wheel of Fortune on the walls of the choir (only half of which survives); shown as a treadmill, it's a trenchant image of medieval life's relentless slog.

   Rochester's long, semi-pedestrianized **High Street** is a handsome affair, lined with antique shops, cafés and pubs, many of which are housed within appealingly old half-timbered and weatherboarded buildings. The town's most famous son **Charles Dickens** spent his youth here, but would seem to have been less than impressed by the place – it appears as "Mudfog" in *The Mudfog Papers*, and "Dullborough" in *The Uncommercial Traveller*. Many of the buildings feature in his novels: the *Royal Victoria and Bull Hotel*, at the top of the High Street, became the *Bull* in *Pickwick Papers* and the *Blue Boar* in *Great Expectations*, while most of his last book, the unfinished *Mystery of Edwin Drood*, was set in the town.

At the northwest end of the High Street, a splendid building dating from 1687 houses the excellent **Guildhall Museum** (daily 10am–4.30pm; free), home to a vivid model of the siege of Rochester Castle in 1215 by King John, and a chilling exhibition on the prison ships or hulks used to house convicts in the late eighteenth century before the establishment of Botany Bay.

Practicalities

Rochester **train station** is at the southeastern end of the High Street, where you'll also find the **tourist office** at no. 95, opposite the cathedral (Mon–Fri 9am–5pm, Sat 10am–5pm, Sun 10.30am–5pm; ☎01634/843666, Ⓦwww .medway.gov.uk). From here you can join a free **guided tour** of the town (Easter–Sept Wed, Sat, Sun & public holidays at 2.15pm).

As for **accommodation**, you can spend the night with some Dickensian ghosts at the ancient *Royal Victoria and Bull Hotel*, 16–18 High St (☎01634/846266, Ⓦwww.rvandb.co.uk; ❺). Decent B&Bs include the *Grayling House*, 54 St Margaret's St (☎01634/826593, Ⓔgraylinghouse@aol .com; no credit cards; ❷), further up the hill behind the castle. The nearest **youth hostel** (☎0870/770 5964, Ⓔmedway@yha.org.uk; dorm beds £14, rooms ❶) is at Capstone Farm, Gillingham, two miles southeast of Chatham; to get there by bus, take the #114 from Chatham bus station and get off at Luton Recreation Ground.

Rochester has a varied, if unremarkable selection of cafés and **restaurants**. *Don Vincenzo*, 108 High St (☎01634/408373), is the best of the Italian places, while the *Cumin Club* at no.188 (☎01634/400880) serves contemporary Indian cuisine in modern surroundings. As for **pubs**, the *Coopers Arms* on St Margaret's Street, between the castle and cathedral, serves good lunches in its small beer garden, while the trendier *City Wall Bar*, 122 High St, has a decent lunchtime menu.

Chatham

CHATHAM, less than two miles east of Rochester, has none of the charms of its neighbour and is, in truth, rather a grim place. Its chief attraction is its dockyards, originally founded by Henry VIII and once the major base of the Royal Navy, many of whose vessels were built, stationed and victualled here and which commanded worldwide supremacy until the end of the Victorian age. The shipbuilding era ended for good when the dockyards were closed in 1984, reopening soon afterwards as a tourist attraction.

The **Historic Dockyard** (mid-Feb to Oct daily 10am–6pm or dusk; Nov Sat & Sun 10am–4pm, last entry 2hr before closing; £12.50; Ⓦwww.chdt.org.uk) occupies a vast eighty-acre site about one mile north of the town centre along the Dock Road; it's a fifteen-minute walk from Chatham town centre, or a short bus ride (either from bus stop B at Chatham Station, or take the Dockside Shuttle Bus from the bus station). Once there, take advantage of the free vintage-bus service to take you around. Behind the stern brick wall you'll find an array of historically and architecturally fascinating buildings dating back to the early eighteenth century. Here too lie the *Ocelot* submarine, the last warship built at Chatham, whose crew endured unbelievably cramped conditions – a major deterrent to visiting claustrophobes – and a restored Victorian sloop, the *Gannet*. The main part of the exhibition, however, consists of the Ropery complex including the former rope-making room – at a quarter of a mile long, it's the longest room in the country.

From the Historic Dockyard, **boat trips** (summer only; £9) run along the River Medway on Britain's last working coal-fired paddle steamer, the *Kingswear Castle*, built in 1924 (☎01634/827648). The cruise takes you past **Upnor**

Castle (Easter–Oct daily 10am–4/6pm; £4.50; EH), an atmospheric sixteenth-century gun fort built on the river to protect Elizabeth I's fleet.

Following Dock Road further up to Leviathan Way, you'll come to **Dickens World** (daily 10am–5.30pm, closes 7pm during school hols; last admission 90min before closing; £12.50, or £9.75 after 3pm), devoted to recreating Dickensian London. Here, you can spend a couple of hours exploring lanes packed with references to scenes from Dickens and peopled by over-enthusiastic cockney staff in period garb. Highlights include a four-dimensional film of Dickens' life and a boat ride through the "sewers". Dickens enthusiasts may quail at some of this – primarily a family attraction, it's aimed more at entertaining kids than informing adults.

Whitstable

Peculiarities of silt and salinity have made **WHITSTABLE** an oyster-friendly environment since classical times, when the Romans feasted on the region's marine delicacies. Indeed, production grew to such levels during the Middle Ages that **oysters** were exported all over Europe, and they were so cheap and plentiful that they became regarded as poor people's food – as Dickens observed, "where there are oysters, there's poverty". However, the whole industry collapsed during the twentieth century, the result of pollution and, in particular, a destructive storm in the 1950s which wrecked all the farms. Though oysters are once more farmed in the area – mostly the faster-growing Pacific oysters, which have displaced the original native oysters – Whitstable is now more dependent on its commercial port, fishing and seaside tourism, while small-scale boat-building and a mildly bohemian ambience make this one of the few pleasant spots along the north Kent coast and a popular day-trip destination for Londoners.

Walking along Whitstable's busy High Street, you'd never guess that you're just a stone's throw from the sea. Follow the signs at the top of the street to reach the seafront, a very pleasant, quiet shingle beach, backed by some pretty

▲ Oysters, Whitstable

weatherboard cottages. For local maritime history, head for the **Whitstable Museum and Gallery** (Mon–Sat 10am–4pm, plus Sun 1–4pm in July & Aug; free), heralded by its eye-catching entrance on Oxford Street, with displays on diving and some good photographs and old film footage of the town's heyday.

Whitstable's **train station** is five minutes' walk along Cromwell Road, east of Oxford Street, the southern continuation of the High Street, while the **tourist office** is next to the museum at 7 Oxford St (Mon–Sat 10am–4/5pm; ℡01227/275482, ⓦwww.canterbury.co.uk). For **accommodation** along the seafront, try *Copeland House*, 4 Island Wall (℡01227/266207, ⓦwww .copelandhouse.co.uk; no credit cards; ❺), west of the High Street, with a garden that backs onto the beach, or the Art Deco *Hotel Continental*, 29 Beach Walk (℡01227/280280, ⓦwww.hotelcontinental.co.uk; ❺), off the northern tip of Harbour Street, which also has accommodation in wooden fishermen's huts close to the beach. For **campsites**, head to *Seaview Caravan Park* (℡01227/792246; closed Nov–March), which backs onto the beach towards Herne Bay, though it can get very busy.

Whitstable's fishing background is reflected in its **eating** places, from any number of fish-and-chip outlets along the High Street and Harbour Street to the very popular *Whitstable Oyster Fishery Restaurant*, The Horsebridge (℡01227/276856; closed Mon), one of the town's best, with fish mains starting at £16; half a dozen local oysters cost £15.50. On the way into town, *Giovanni's*, 49–55 Canterbury Rd (℡01227/273034: closed Mon), is deservedly reckoned to be one of the best Italian restaurants in the county – and probably the largest, consisting of five converted houses. For a **drink** and excellent atmosphere check out the *Old Neptune* pub, standing alone in its white weatherboards on the shore. Whitstable is at its most lively during the annual **Oyster Festival** (last two weeks of July), featuring lots of crustacean-crunching, jazz and parades.

The Thanet resorts

The **Isle of Thanet**, a featureless plain fringed by low chalk cliffs and the odd sandy bay, became part of the mainland when the navigable Wantsum Channel began silting up around the time of the first Roman invasion. The evangelist Augustine arrived here in 597 on a divine mission to end Anglo-Saxon paganism, and is supposed to have preached his first sermon at a spot three miles west of Ramsgate – a cross marks the location at Ebbsfleet, next to St Augustine's Golf Club. Over the next thousand years or so, civilization advanced to the point at which, in 1751, one Mr Benjamin Beale (a resident of Margate) invented the bathing machine, a wheeled cubicle that enabled people to slip into the sea without undue exhibitionism. It heralded the birth of sea bathing as a recreational and recuperative activity, and led to the growth of **seaside resorts**. By the mid-twentieth century the Isle's intermittent expanses of sand had become fully colonized as the "bucket and spade" resorts of the capital's leisure-seeking proletariat. That heyday has long passed, but these earliest of resorts still cling to their traditional attractions to varying degrees.

Getting to the Thanet resorts is straightforward: **trains** and **buses** make the two-hour journey from London Victoria to Margate, Ramsgate and Broadstairs several times a day, and there are local rail and bus services from Canterbury and Dover.

Margate

MARGATE – memorably summarized by Oscar Wilde as "the nom–de–plume of Ramsgate" – is a ragged assortment of cafés, shops and amusement arcades wrapped around a broad bay. More than two centuries of tourism are embodied here: at the resort's peak thousands of Londoners were ferried down the Thames every summer's day, to be disgorged at the pier – the functional precursor of all such seaside structures – and still today, on a fine summer weekend, the place is heaving with day-trippers enjoying the traditional fish and chips, candyfloss and donkey rides.

Other than the small but agreeable sandy beach, and the amusement arcades on the tacky seafront, Margate's main attraction is the intricately decorated **Shell Grotto** on Grotto Hill, off Northdown Road (Easter–Oct daily 10am–5pm; Nov–Easter Sat & Sun 10am–4pm; £2.50), which has been open to the public since its discovery by schoolchildren in 1835. The town's profile will be much greater, however, with the opening of a new art gallery on the pier, Turner Contemporary, scheduled for completion in 2010, and already hailed as the hopeful symbol of Margate's renaissance.

Practicalities

Margate's **train station** is right by the seafront on Station Road, while all buses pull into Cecil Square, a few minutes away. The **tourist office** is nearby at 12–13 The Parade (Mon–Sat 9am–4/5pm; ☎0870/264 6111, ⓦwww .visitthanet.co.uk). The town is packed with mainly mediocre **B&Bs**, but its most interesting accommodation is the grand 1920s *Walpole Bay Hotel* on Fifth Avenue in Cliftonville, a few minutes' walk east of the centre (☎01843/221703, ⓦwww.walpolebayhotel.co.uk; ⑤), styled as a "living museum", whose motley exhibits – from urinals to fossils – you can browse around for free. There's a YHA **hostel** at 3–4 Royal Esplanade, by Westbrook Bay to the west of the train station (☎0870/770 5956, ⓔmargate@yha.org.uk; dorm bed £14; rooms ①).

For a full **meal**, try *Stone's Bistro* (☎01843/224347; closed Sun & Mon) at 4 Hawley Square, near the Regency Theatre, which offers a traditional French/ English menu. The *Walpole Bay Hotel* is the place for afternoon tea or Sunday lunch with piano accompaniment (book for lunch). Most of Margate's **pubs** are a bit rough round the edges, and it's worth steering away from the seafront: try the tiny Victorian *Rose in June* on Trinity Square, or for real ales (and pizzas), the *Spread Eagle*, at the top of Victoria Road.

Broadstairs

Said to have been established on the profits of shipbuilding and smuggling, **BROADSTAIRS** is the smallest, quietest and, undoubtedly, the most pleasant of Thanet's resort towns. From its cliff-top setting, it overlooks the pretty little Viking Bay, one of several **sandy coves** punctuating Thanet's eastern shore; between Broadstairs and Margate you'll find Stone, Joss, Kingsgate and Botany bays with Louisa Bay to the south – all quiet and undeveloped gems that make a good antidote to the busier resort areas.

Broadstairs' main claim to fame, however, is as Dickens' holiday retreat – he described it as "one of the freest and freshest little places in the world". Throughout his most productive years he stayed in various hostelries here, and eventually rented an "airy nest" overlooking Viking Bay from Fort Road, since renamed Bleak House, where he planned the eponymous novel as well as finishing *David Copperfield*. The **Dickens House Museum**, 2 Victoria Parade (daily: Easter–June & Oct 2–5pm; July–Sept 10am–5pm; £2.50), is in the house Dickens used as a model for Betsey Trotwood's House, while the annual **Dickens Festival** (third week in June), has been held since 1937, featuring lectures, dramatizations of the author's works and a nightly Victorian music hall.

Practicalities

It's a ten-minute walk along the High Street from the **train station** to Broadstairs' seafront. The **tourist office** is currently at the Dickens House Museum (see p.175; April–Sept daily 9am–5pm; Oct–March Mon–Sat 9am–4.30pm; ℡0870/264 6111, ⓦwww.visitthanet.co.uk) – though plans are afoot for a move to a separate building in 2008, with the same telephone number. Many of the local **hotels** cash in on the Dickens angle, for example the comfortable, family-run *Royal Albion Hotel*, 6–12 Albion St (℡01843/868071, ⓦwww.albionbroadstairs.co.uk; ❻), where he wrote part of *Nicholas Nickleby*. More modestly, there's the *East Horndon Hotel* (℡01843/868306, ⓦwww .easthorndonhotel.com; ❶) and the *Devonhurst Hotel* (℡01843/863010, ⓦwww.devonhurst.co.uk; ❶), both on the Eastern Esplanade.

As for **restaurants**, the *Osteria Pizzeria Posillipo* on Albion Street (℡01843/601133) serves excellent pizza, pasta and other Italian standards, with a balcony overlooking the bay, while *Harpers Wine Bar*, 8 Harbour St (℡01843/602494; eve only), dishes up moderately priced fish and seafood in a congenial setting. At the top of Harbour Street, the popular and friendly *Neptune's Hall* **pub** serves great beer, while the *Tartar Frigate*, also on Harbour Street, is a solid, sociable English tavern with its own seafood restaurant upstairs.

The annual Broadstairs **Folk Week** (middle of Aug; ⓦwww .broadstairsfolkweek.org.uk) is one of England's longest-standing folk music events and features singers, bands and dancing in locations around the town, both indoor and alfresco.

Ramsgate

If Thanet had a capital, it would be **RAMSGATE**, a handsome Victorian red-brick resort, most of it set high on a cliff linked to the seafront and harbour by broad, sweeping ramps. Housed in the nineteenth-century Clock House on the quayside, the **Ramsgate Maritime Museum** (Easter–Sept Tues–Sun 10am–5pm; Oct–Easter Thurs–Sun 11am–4.30pm; £1.50) chronicles municipal life from Roman times onwards: its most interesting display is the section on the Goodwin Sands sandbanks, six miles southeast of Ramsgate – the occasional playing arena of the eccentric Goodwin Sands Cricket Club.

Ramsgate is connected to Broadstairs by frequent **buses**, and its **train station** is about a mile northwest of the centre, at the end of Wilfred Road, at the top of the High Street. The **tourist office** is at 17 Albert Court, York Street (Tues–Sat 10am–4/6pm; ℡0870/264 6111, ⓦwww.visitthanet.co.uk). For an overnight **stay**, book into the attractive seafront *Crescent*, 19 Wellington Crescent (℡01843/591419, ⓦwww.ramsgate-uk.com; ❷). Amongst the town's **restaurants**, the award-winning *Surin Thai*, 30 Harbour St (℡01843/592001; closed Sun), scores highly for its reasonably priced, quality Cambodian, Lao and Thai food, while the gaudy *Peter's Fish Factory* at 96 Harbour Parade is the best for fish and chips. For traditional **pubs**, try the ornately tiled *Queen's Head* on Harbour Parade, and for harbour views, real ales and live music, head for the *Churchill Tavern* on The Paragon.

Canterbury

One of England's most venerable cities, **CANTERBURY** offers a rich slice through two thousand years of history, with Roman and early Christian ruins, a Norman castle and a famous cathedral that dominates a medieval warren of time-skewed Tudor dwellings. The city began as a Belgic settlement that was overrun by the Romans and renamed **Durovernum**, which they established as a garrison and supply base and from where they went on to build a system of roads that was to reach as far as the Scottish borders. With the empire's collapse came the Saxons, who renamed the town **Cantwarabyrig**; it was a Saxon king, Ethelbert, who in 597 welcomed Augustine, despatched by the pope to convert the British Isles to Christianity. By the time of his death, Augustine had founded two Benedictine monasteries, one of which – Christ Church, raised on the site of the Roman basilica – was to become the first cathedral in England.

At the end of the first millennium Canterbury suffered repeated sackings by the Danes until Canute, a recent Christian convert, restored the ruined Christ Church, only for it to be destroyed by fire a year before the Norman invasion. As Christianity became a tool of control, a struggle for power developed between the archbishops, the abbots from the nearby Benedictine abbey and King Henry II, culminating in the assassination of Archbishop Thomas à Becket in 1170, a martyrdom that effectively established the autonomy of the archbishops and made this one of Christendom's greatest shrines. Geoffrey Chaucer's *Canterbury Tales*, written towards the end of the fourteenth century, portrays the unexpectedly festive nature of pilgrimages to Becket's tomb, which was later plundered and destroyed on the orders of Henry VIII.

In 1830 a pioneering passenger railway service linked Canterbury to the sea and prosperity grew until the city suffered extensive German bombing on June 1, 1942, in one of the notorious **Baedeker Raids** – the Nazi plan to destroy Britain's most treasured historic sites as described in the eponymous German travel guides. Today the cathedral and compact town centre, enclosed on three sides by medieval walls, remain the focus for leisure-motivated pilgrims from across the globe.

Arrival, information and tours

Canterbury has two **train stations**, Canterbury East for services from London Victoria and Dover Priory, and Canterbury West for services from London Charing Cross and the Isle of Thanet – each a ten-minute walk from the cathedral. National Express services and local **buses** use the bus station on St George's Lane. **Parking** can be problematic and drivers are best advised to use the signposted park-and-ride services available on Wincheap, Sturry Road and New Dover Road. The busy **tourist office** is in the Butter Market at 12–13 Sun St (Easter–June Mon–Sat 9.30am–5pm, Sun 10am–4pm; July & Aug Mon–Sat 9.30am–6pm, Sun 10am–4pm; Sept–Easter Mon–Sat 10am–4pm; ☎01227/378100, ⓦwww.canterbury.co.uk), opposite the main entrance to the cathedral. For **Internet** access, go to Dot Café, 21 St Dunstans St (daily 9am–9pm).

Canterbury is compact enough to find your own way around, but there are various **tours** available. The Guild of Guides runs informative walking tours of the city, leaving from the tourist office (April–June, Sept & Oct daily 2pm; July & Aug Mon–Sat 11.30am & 2pm; 1hr 30min; £4.50), while the Ghostly Tour of Old Canterbury (Fri & Sat 8pm; 1hr 15min; £5) is a spicy mix of the supernatural and local folklore, leaving from Canterbury East station. Alternatively, you can take a **boat trip** along the Stour on a Historic River Tour (April–Sept daily 10am–5pm; ☎07790/534744; £6), or rent a **bike** from Downland Cycles on Malthouse Road, off St Stephens Road (☎01227/479643; from £12 per day).

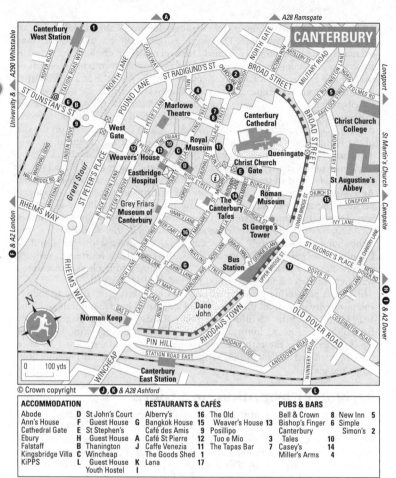

CANTERBURY

Map labels

Canterbury West Station ❶
A28 Ramsgate
NORTH GATE
ST RADIGUND'S ST
BROAD STREET
THE BOROUGH
Marlowe Theatre
Canterbury Cathedral
Christ Church College
West Gate
Royal Museum
Weavers' House
Christ Church Gate
Queningate
St Augustine's Abbey
Eastbridge Hospital
Roman Museum
The Canterbury Tales
Grey Friars Museum of Canterbury
St George's Tower
Bus Station
Norman Keep
Dane John
RHODAUS TOWN
PIN HILL
Canterbury East Station
© Crown copyright

Accommodation

In the city centre, some old **hotels** offer all the creaking, authentic antiquity you could ask for, while there's a host of cheaper **B&Bs** to be found just outside the city walls. Accommodation can be difficult to secure in July and August; the tourist office can help, though they charge £2.50 for the service.

Hotels and B&Bs

Abode 30 High Street ☎01227/766266, ⓦwww.abodehotels.co.uk/canterbury. Luxurious and stylish, this state-of-the-art hotel has spacious rooms with contemporary designs, the more expensive rooms with balconies overlooking the cathedral. There's also a top-notch restaurant. ❼

Ann's House 63 London Rd ☎01227/768767, ⓦwww.annshousecanterbury.co.uk. Traditional Victorian villa offering comfortable rooms, most of which are en suite, a ten-minute walk from the centre. ❷

Cathedral Gate 36 Burgate ☎01227/464381, ⓦwww.cathgate.co.uk. Built in 1438 and set in the city's medieval heart, this venerable pilgrims' hostelry features crooked floors and exposed timber beams alongside more modern amenities and fantastic views of the cathedral. ④

Ebury 65–67 New Dover Rd ℡ 01227/768433, ⓦ www.eburyhotel.co.uk. Very comfortable and spacious family-owned Victorian hotel, fifteen minutes' walk from the centre, with an indoor pool and well-appointed rooms. ⑤

Falstaff 8–10 St Dunstan's St ℡ 01227/462138, ⓦ www.foliohotels.com. Popular fifteenth-century coaching inn by the West Gate, with four-poster beds and an award-winning restaurant. ⑥

Kingsbridge Villa 15 Best Lane ℡ 01227/766415, ⓦ www.canterburyguesthouse.com. Rooms 2 and 4 of this very central and well-furnished Victorian house have views of the cathedral. Vegan and vegetarian breakfasts on offer too. ②

St John's Court Guest House St John's Lane ℡ 01227/456425, ⓦ www.s-h-systems.co.uk. Obliging and good-value B&B in a quiet but central location, just south of the old town. Vegan breakfasts available. No credit cards. ①

St Stephen's Guest House 100 St Stephen's Rd ℡ 01227/767644, ⓦ www.st-stephens.fsnet.co .uk. A mock-Tudor house on the northern side of the city, ten minutes' walk along the Stour and handily placed for the university, offering excellent-value en-suite accommodation. No credit cards. ③

Thanington 140 Wincheap ℡ 01227/453227, ⓦ www.thanington-hotel.co.uk. Comfortably converted Georgian building, ten minutes' walk from the centre, with an indoor pool, games room and friendly, attentive service. ⑤

Wincheap Guest House 94 Wincheap ℡ 01227/762309, ⓦ www.wincheapguesthouse .com. Good-value Victorian B&B close to Canterbury East Station, with en-suite rooms. ③

Hostels and campsite

The Caravan and Camping Club Site Bekesbourne Lane ℡ 01227/463216. Large year-round caravan park, one and a half miles east of the city off the A257 road to Sandwich.

KiPPS 40 Nunnery Fields ℡ 01227/786121, ⓦ www.kipps-hostel.com. Self-catering hostel a few minutes' walk from Canterbury East Station, offering single and double rooms (①) as well as dorm accommodation (from £15). Internet access available.

Youth Hostel 54 New Dover Rd ℡ 0870/770 5744, ⓔ canterbury@yha.org.uk. Half a mile out of town, and 15min on foot from Canterbury East Station, this friendly hostel is set in a Victorian villa. Dorm beds £17.50, rooms ①

The City

Though surprisingly small, with a population of just 40,000, Canterbury ranks as England's second most visited city, with some two and a half million tourists arriving each year. Its centre, partly ringed by ancient **walls**, is virtually car free, but this doesn't stop the High Street seizing up all too frequently with the milling crowds. Don't let this put you off – the city's popularity is well founded, with a dense concentration of historical sites and a lively atmosphere, making it a highly rewarding stop on any tour of southeast England.

The Cathedral

Mother Church of the Church of England and seat of the Primate of All England, **Canterbury Cathedral** (Mon–Sat 9am–5/6.30pm, Sun 12.30–2.30pm & 4.30–5.30pm; closed on some days in mid-July for university graduation ceremonies; £6.50; ⓦ www.canterbury-cathedral.org) fills the northeast quadrant of the old city with a befitting sense of authority. A cathedral has stood here since 602, but in 1070 the first Norman archbishop, Lanfranc, levelled the original Saxon structure to build a new cathedral. Over successive centuries the masterpiece was heavily modified, with the puritanical lines of the Perpendicular style gaining ascendancy in late medieval times. Though architecturally it's perhaps not among the country's most impressive, the cathedral derives its distinctiveness from the thrust of the 235-foot-high Bell Harry Tower, completed in 1505. The precincts (daily 9am–5.30pm) are entered through the superbly ornate early-sixteenth-century **Christ Church Gate**, where Burgate and St Margaret's Street meet. This junction, the city's

Thomas à Becket and the Canterbury Tales

Appointed Archbishop of Canterbury in 1162 by his good friend and drinking partner Henry II, **Thomas à Becket** fell out with the king when the latter attempted to impose his jurisdiction over that of the Church. After a six-year spell in France, Becket was reconciled with Henry and returned home in 1170 – only to incur the king's wrath once more by refusing to absolve two bishops whom he had previously excommunicated, provoking Henry to utter the well-known words, "Will no one rid me of this turbulent priest?" Four knights took it upon themselves to seek out Becket and, finding him at prayer in the cathedral, murdered him on the spot. Almost immediately miracles were said to occur at his tomb, and Becket was canonized in 1173, by which time a steady stream of pilgrims had already begun to arrive at the shrine.

One such pilgrimage provided the setting for Geoffrey Chaucer's **Canterbury Tales**. Written between 1387 and 1400, the *Tales* are a collection of stories within a story, in which a group of thirty pilgrims exchange a series of fantastic yarns to while away the time as they journey. The group is a colourful cross-section of medieval society, including a knight, a monk, a miller, a squire and the oft-widowed Wife of Bath. Chaucer chose to write their earthy and often raunchy stories in English – at a time when French was very much the language of literature – and this, combined with their universal themes, has ensured their continuing popularity today, as witnessed by the regular film and television treatments. The narrator of the best tale was promised a free meal at Canterbury's *Tabard Inn* – though as Chaucer died before he could complete his work, the winner was never announced.

medieval core, is known as the Butter Market; here, religious relics were once sold to pilgrims hoping to prevent an eternity in damnation. Having paid your entrance fee, you pass through the gatehouse and get one of the finest views of the cathedral, foreshortened and crowned with soaring towers and pinnacles.

Once in the magnificent **interior**, look for the tomb of Henry IV and his wife, Joan of Navarre, and for the gilded effigy of Edward III's son, the Black Prince, all of them to be found in the Trinity Chapel, behind the main altar. Also here, until demolished by Henry VIII's act of ecclesiastical vandalism in 1538, was the shrine of Thomas à Becket; the actual spot where he died, known as "The Martyrdom", is marked by the **Altar of the Sword's Point** in the northwest transept, where a jagged sculpture of the assassins' weapons is suspended on the wall. Steps from here descend to the low, Romanesque arches of the **crypt**, one of the few remaining relics of the Norman cathedral and considered the finest such structure in the country, with some amazingly well-preserved carvings on the capitals of the columns. Particularly vivid is the medieval **stained glass**, much of which dates back to the twelfth and thirteenth centuries, notably in the Trinity Chapel, where the life and miraculous works of Thomas à Becket are depicted. Look out too for Adam, dressed in an animal skin, in the west window and Jonah and the whale in the Corona (the eastern end of the cathedral, beyond the Trinity Chapel). Contemporary with the windows (1220) is the white marble **St Augustine's Chair** on which all archbishops of Canterbury are enthroned; it's located in the choir at the top of the steps beyond the high altar.

On the cathedral's north flank are the fan-vaulted colonnades of the **Great Cloister**, from where you enter the **Chapter House**, with its intricate web of fourteenth-century tracery supporting the roof and a wall of stained glass. In 1935 it was a fitting venue for the inaugural performance of T.S. Eliot's *Murder in the Cathedral*.

St Augustine's Abbey and St Martin's Church

Passing through the cathedral grounds and out through the city walls at the (exit-only) Queningate, you come to the vestigial remains of **St Augustine's Abbey** (April–June Wed–Sun 10am–5pm; July & Aug daily 10am–6pm; Sept–March Sat & Sun 11am–5pm; £4.20; EH), occupying the site of the church founded by Augustine in 598. It was built outside the city because of a Christian tradition that forbade burials within the walls, and became the final resting place of Augustine, Ethelbert and successive archbishops and kings of Kent, although no trace remains either of them or of the original Saxon church. Shortly after the Normans arrived, the church was demolished in the same building frenzy that saw the creation of the cathedral. It was replaced by a much larger abbey, most of which was destroyed in the Dissolution so that today only the ruins and foundations remain. To help bring the site to life, pick up an audioguide from the abbey's excellent interpretive centre.

Nearby, on the corner of North Holmes Road and St Martin's Lane is **St Martin's Church** (Easter–Sept Tues, Thurs & Sat 10am–4pm; free), one of England's oldest churches, built on the site of a Roman villa or temple and used by the earliest Christians. Although medieval additions obscure the original Saxon structure, this is perhaps the earliest Christian site in Canterbury – it was here that Queen Bertha welcomed St Augustine in 597, and her husband King Ethelbert was baptized.

Along the High Street

For the most part, the **High Street** is lined with picturesque and ancient buildings – the view up Mercery Lane towards Christ Church Gate is one of the most photographed scenes in the city: a narrow, medieval street of crooked, overhanging houses behind which loom the turreted gatehouse and the cathedral's towers.

Just before High Street becomes St Peter's Street, you come to the **Royal Museum and Art Gallery** (Mon–Sat 10am–5pm; free), housed on the first floor of an awesome mock-Tudor building, with big wooden gables and a mosaic infilling between its timbers. There's lots of military memorabilia in the Buffs regimental gallery, which traces the history of the local regiment raised in Tudor times and merged in 1967. The art gallery has the odd Henry Moore and Gainsborough hidden among the local artists; note though that it will be closing for a three-year refurbishment at the end of 2008.

Where the street passes over a branch of the River Stour stands **Eastbridge Hospital** (Mon–Sat 10am–5pm; £1), founded in the twelfth century to provide poor pilgrims with shelter. Inside you can visit a refectory, a gallery showing the history of the hospital and sleeping quarters restored to their original medieval state. Over the road is the wonky, half-timbered **Weavers' House** – built around 1500 and now a café – that was once inhabited by Huguenot textile workers who had been offered religious asylum in post-Reformation England.

St Peter's Street terminates at the two massive crenellated towers of the medieval **West Gate**, between which local buses just manage to squeeze. The only one of the town's seven city gates to have survived intact, its prison cells and guard chambers house a small **museum** (Mon–Sat 11am–12.30pm & 1.30–3.30pm; £1.25), which displays contemporary armaments and weaponry used by the medieval city guard, as well as giving access to the battlements. From the nearby bridge, **chauffeured punts** (☎07816/760869; from £7 per person) leave for a 30-, 45- or 60-minute trip along the gentle River Stour.

2

Museum passport

The **museum passport** (£6.20) gives entry to the Museum of Canterbury, the Roman Museum and the West Gate Museum and is available from the ticket offices of each.

The Roman Museum, The Canterbury Tales and the Museum of Canterbury

Redevelopment of the Longmarket area (situated between Burgate and the High Street) in the early 1990s exposed Roman foundations and mosaics that are now part of the **Roman Museum** (Mon–Sat 10am–5pm; also open Sun 1.30–5pm June–Oct; £3.10). The remnants of the larger building are pretty dull, and better mosaics can be seen at Lullingstone (see p.196), but the display of recovered artefacts and general design of the museum are tasteful, with Roman domestic scenes recreated, as well as a computer-generated view of Durovernum.

Turning in the other direction down St Margaret's Street leads to the former church that's now **The Canterbury Tales** (daily 9.30/10am–4.30/5pm; £7.50), a quasi-educational show based on Geoffrey Chaucer's book, which lays claim to being the first original work of English literature ever to be printed. Equipped with an audioguide, visitors set off on a wander through mildly odour-enhanced galleries in which mannequins occupy idealized fourteenth-century tableaux and recount five of Chaucer's tales.

Genuinely educational and better value is the **Museum of Canterbury**, round the corner in Stour Street (Mon–Sat 10.30am–5pm, also June–Oct Sun 1.30–5pm; £3.40), an interactive exhibition spanning local history from the splendour of Durovernum through to the more recent literary figures of Joseph Conrad (buried in the cemetery on London Road) and Oliver Postgate, originator of *Bagpuss* and *The Clangers*. The check-trousered philanthropist Rupert Bear, created by local-born Mary Tourtel, merits a museum of his own within the main museum. An excellent thirty-minute video on the Becket story details the intriguing personalities and events that led up to his assassination, presenting Becket as an overbearing and unpopular figure whose genuine piety was only recognized after his death.

Eating and drinking

The combination of a large student population and the tourist trade means Canterbury has a good selection of places to eat and drink, with many **restaurants** and **pubs** in genuinely old settings. However, the Church, which owns much of the city within the walls, keeps a tight rein on any wanton revelry and, bar the occasional yelp of an over-intoxicated student, at night all is as quiet as Becket's tomb.

Restaurants and cafés

Alberry's 38 St Margaret's St ☎ 01227/452378. This lively wine bar has good snacks and a range of more substantial meals, including various pasta, fish and meat dishes. Moderate.

Bangkok House 13 Church St ☎ 01227/471141. Excellent, well-presented Thai fare with spices adjusted to suit every palate in this small restaurant near St Augustine's Abbey. Good selection of cocktails and rum too. Closed Mon. Moderate.

Café des Amis 93–95 St Dunstan's St ☎ 01227/464390. Very popular, authentic Mexican place close to Westgate; try the sizzling chicken *fajitas* or the delicious paella followed by a bubbling chocolate *fondido*. "Phenomenally hot" habanero chilis are only for the brave. Moderate.

Café St Pierre 41 St Peter's St. Excellent French patisserie and bakery with tables on the pavement and in the garden when the weather's fine.

Caffè Venezia 60–61 Palace St. Spacious self-service Italian café with decent sandwiches, pasta dishes, pizza slices and good coffee.

The Goods Shed Station Road West ☏01227/459153. Everything from a bowl of soup or sandwich to a first-class full meal, guaranteed super-fresh as it comes from the adjacent farmers' market. Closed Sun eve & all day Mon. Inexpensive to moderate.

Lana 2 Dover St ☏01227/462876. The refined delights of Thai cuisine at a reasonable price – the *Nua pud naman hoy*, beef marinated in oyster sauce and served sizzling with mushrooms and baby corn, is delicious. Closed Mon. Inexpensive.

The Old Weaver's House 1 St Peter's St ☏01227/464660. With cosy, old-fashioned decor and an outdoor terrace overlooking the River Stour, this place dishes up everything from traditional British food to slap-up curries. Inexpensive.

Posillipo Tuo e Mio 16 The Borough ☏01227/761471. Long-established restaurant serving classy Italian dishes, a range of pizzas and some delicious, home-made desserts. Closed Mon & Tues lunch. Moderate.

The Tapas Bar 13 Palace St ☏01227/762637. Tasty Spanish tapas from £4 to £8 a dish, accompanied by occasional live music. Inexpensive.

Pubs and bars

Bell & Crown 10 Palace St. Authentic and cramped medieval hostelry.

Bishop's Finger 13 St Dunstan's St. Popular wood-panelled bar just through the West Gate with a fine range of ales and a patio suntrap.

Canterbury Tales 12 The Friars. Marble-top bar and lots of polished wood in this tidy little pub opposite the Marlowe Theatre. Nachos and BLTs on the bar menu.

Casey's 5 Butchery Lane. Cosy, low-ceilinged Irish pub serving soda bread, pies and other pub grub, with occasional live folk music.

Miller's Arms 1–2 Mill Lane. A pleasant weir-side spot for a summertime pint, whose splendid bar snacks and meals ensure its continued popularity.

New Inn 19 Havelock St. One of Canterbury's tiniest pubs, this converted terrace house is popular with students and locals and offers a decent selection of real ale.

Simple Simon's Radigund's Hall, 1–9 Church Lane. Old hostelry that's popular with the university and King's School crowd; live music Tues–Sat.

Nightlife and entertainment

Nightlife in Canterbury keeps a low profile – check out what there is going on in the free *What, Where and When* **listings magazine** available at the tourist office. Opposite Canterbury East Station at 15 Station Rd East there are three **nightclubs** in the same building: *BaaBars*, also open during the day, the *Works*, good for party pop and R&B, and the more civilized *Bizz* (for all three ☏01227/462520). On the other side of town, the university puts on the best **gigs**, though check out too the Penny Theatre on Northgate, which presents local and global live music.

The university also houses the **Gulbenkian Theatre** (☏01227/769075, Ⓦwww.kent.ac.uk/gulbenkian), which hosts various cultural events, as does the **Marlowe Theatre** (☏01227/787787, Ⓦwww.marlowetheatre.com) – named after the sixteenth-century Canterbury-born playwright – in The Friars. A good range of art **films** is shown at the university's Gulbenkian Cinema (same website as theatre), while there are more commercial celluloid offerings at the Odeon on St George's Place by the ring road. Finally, the **Canterbury Festival** (☏01227/452853, Ⓦwww.canterburyfestival.co.uk), an international potpourri of music, theatre and arts, takes place annually during the last two weeks of October.

The Channel Ports: Sandwich to Dover

Dover, just 21 miles from mainland Europe (Calais' low cliffs are visible on a clear day), is Britain's principal cross-Channel port. As a town it is not

The Cinque Ports

In 1278 Dover, Hythe, Sandwich, New Romney and Hastings – already part of a long-established but unofficial confederation of defensive coastal settlements – were formalized under Edward I's charter as the **Cinque Ports** (pronounced "sink", despite its French origin). In return for providing England with maritime support when necessary, chiefly in the transportation of troops and supplies to the Continent during times of war, the five ports were given trading privileges and other liberties, which enabled them to prosper while neighbouring ports struggled to survive. Some took advantage of this during peacetime, boosting their wealth by various nefarious activities such as piracy and the smuggling of tax-free contraband.

Later, Rye and Winchelsea were added to the confederation along with several other "limb" ports on the southeast coast which joined up at various times. The confederation continued until 1685, when the ports' privileges were revoked. Their maritime services had become increasingly unnecessary after Henry VIII had founded a professional navy and, due to a shifting coastline, several of the ports' harbours had silted up anyway, leaving some of them several miles inland. Nowadays, only Dover is still a major working port, though the post of Lord Warden of the Cinque Ports still exists as an honorary title, bestowed by the presiding monarch.

---

immensely appealing, even though its key position has left it with a clutch of historic attractions. To the north lie **Sandwich**, once the most important of the Cinque Ports but now no longer even on the coast, and the pleasant resort towns of **Deal** and **Walmer**, each with its own set of distinctive fortifications as well as a smattering of traditional seaside B&Bs.

There are frequent **train** – from both Victoria and Charing Cross – and **bus** connections to Dover from the capital. A useful branch-line offers train connections from Dover up the coast to Walmer, Deal and Sandwich and on to Ramsgate. For late ferry arrivals at Dover, the last train service leaves for London at 11pm, though the last, much faster direct service departs an hour earlier.

Sandwich and around

SANDWICH, situated on the River Stour four miles north of Deal, is best known nowadays for giving rise to England's favourite culinary contribution when, in 1762, the Fourth Earl of Sandwich, passionately absorbed in a game of cards, ate his meat between two bits of bread for a quick snack. Aside from this incident, the town's main interest lies in its maritime connections – it was chief among the Cinque Ports (see box above) until the Stour silted up. Unlike at other former harbour inlets, however, the river hasn't silted up completely and still flows through town, its grassy willow-lined banks adding to the once great medieval port's charm today.

By the bridge over the Stour stands Sandwich's best-known feature, the sixteenth-century **Barbican**, a stone gateway decorated with chequerwork, where tolls were once collected. Running parallel to the river is **Strand Street**, whose crooked half-timbered facades front antique shops and private homes while, back in the town centre, another fine sixteenth-century edifice, the **Guildhall**, houses both the tourist office (see opposite) and a small **museum** recounting the town's history (April–Nov Tues, Wed, Fri & Sat 10.30am–12.30pm & 2–4pm, Thurs & Sun 2–4pm; £1). The genteel town is separated from the sandy beaches of Sandwich Bay by the **Royal St George Golf Course** – frequent venue of the British Open tournament – and a mile of nature reserves. Most ornithologists head three miles north of town to the **Gazen Salts Nature Reserve**, renowned for its diversity of seabirds.

Overlooking the doleful expanse of Pegwell Bay, two miles northwest of Sandwich, is **Richborough Roman Fort** (Easter–Sept daily 10am–6pm; £4.20; EH), one of the earliest coastal strongholds built by the Romans along what later became known as the Saxon Shore on account of the frequent raids by the Germanic tribe. Rumour has it that Emperor Claudius, on his way to London, once rode on an elephant through a triumphal arch erected inside the castle, but all that remains within the well-preserved Roman walls are the relics of an early Saxon church. Richborough's historical significance far outshines its present appearance, especially as Pegwell Bay is now blighted by an ugly chemical works. The nicest way of reaching the fort is to take the **river bus** up the Stour from Sandwich Quay (☎07958/376183; £12).

Practicalities

Finding **accommodation** in Sandwich shouldn't be much of a problem – the local **tourist office**, housed in the Guildhall (April–Oct daily 10am–4pm; ☎01304/613565, ⓦwww.whitecliffscountry.org.uk), will provide you with a list of local **hotels** and **guest houses**. Try the central *Fleur de Lis*, an old coaching inn near the Guildhall at 6–8 Delf St (☎01304/611131, ⓦwww.thefleur-sandwich.co.uk; ❻), with fully-equipped en-suite rooms, or the more affordable *Le Trayas* bungalow, 10 Poulders Rd (☎01304/611056, ⓦwww.letrayas.co.uk; no credit cards; ❸), a ten-minute walk from The Quay. A couple of miles southeast of Sandwich in the village of Worth, the *St Crispin Inn* (☎01304/612081, ⓦwww.stcrispininn.com; ❸) is an attractive fifteenth-century pub with accommodation as well as good bar **food**. Back in Sandwich, your best choice for excellent, though pricey, seafood, as well as burgers and huge deli sandwiches, is *Fishermans Wharf* on the quayside (☎01304/613636). Alternatively, the **pubs** by the Barbican or *The Haven*, 20a King St, serve good coffee, snacks and light meals. For the definitive Sandwich sandwich, head for the twee *Little Cottage Tearooms*, on The Quay.

Deal and around

One of the most unusual of Henry VIII's forts is the diminutive castle at **DEAL**, six miles southeast of Sandwich and site of Julius Caesar's first successful landfall in Britain in 55 BC. Situated off the Strand at the south end of town, the **castle** (Easter–Sept Mon–Fri & Sun 10am–6pm, Sat 10am–5pm; £4.20; EH) is shaped like a Tudor rose when viewed from the air: the premise for its unusual form was that the rounded walls would be better at deflecting missiles. Inside the castle, you can see a comprehensive display on other similar forts built during Henry VIII's reign.

Another aspect of Deal's history is explored in the **Maritime Museum** (April–Sept Mon–Sat 2–5pm; £2) in St George's Road, just around the corner from the tourist office. A mildly interesting look at the town's seafaring past, the museum contains both real and model boats, relics from ships and tales of the destructive powers of the Goodwin Sands. Out on the seafront, at the corner with Sondes Road, stands a real oddity, the **Timeball Tower** (Easter–Sept Sat 11am–4pm, Sun & public hols noon–4pm; £2; ⓦdealtimeball.tripod.com), a four-storey pink-faced building that began life as a shutter telegraph during the Napoleonic Wars. After the wars, in 1815, it was used as a semaphore tower for catching smugglers. A further conversion took place in 1853, when a giant timeball was built surmounted by a cross, large enough to be visible from ships at sea. The ball dropped from the roof at exactly 1pm in summer, so providing an accurate time check in the days before radio. It still drops regularly and the building also houses a small museum of horology and telegraphy.

Deal's **tourist office** is situated in the Landmark Centre on the High Street (Mon–Fri 10am–4pm, Sat 10am–noon; ☎01304/369576, ⓦwww .whitecliffscountry.org.uk). There's a whole host of places offering **accommodation** on Beach Street: try the winsome *King's Head* pub at no. 9 (☎01304/368194, ⓦwww.kingsheaddeal.co.uk; ❸), or the nearby town house, *Channel View*, at no. 17 (☎01304/368194; ❸), run by the same proprietor. Next door at no. 19, *Dunkerley's* (☎01304/375016) has Deal's finest (and priciest) **restaurant**, where seafood is the speciality.

Walmer Castle

A mile south of Deal, **Walmer Castle** (March & Oct Wed–Sun 10am–4pm; April–Sept Mon–Fri & Sun 10am–6pm, Sat 10am–4pm; £6.50; EH) is another rotund Tudor-rose-shaped affair, commissioned when the castle became the official residence of the Lord Warden of the Cinque Ports in 1730. Now it more resembles a heavily fortified stately home than a military stronghold. The best-known resident was the Duke of Wellington, who died here in 1842, and not surprisingly, the house is devoted primarily to his life and times. Busts and portraits of the Iron Duke crowd the rooms and corridors, where you'll also find the armchair in which he expired and the original Wellington boots in which he triumphed at Waterloo. The castle's terraced gardens, overlooking the Channel, are a good spot for a picnic, or you can have afternoon tea in *The Lord Warden's Tearooms* (April–Oct daily). To get to Walmer Castle from Deal, you can either catch one of the hourly buses or, if the weather's good, make the pleasant walk along the seafront (30min).

Dover

Badly bombed during the World War II, **DOVER**'s town centre and seafront just don't have what it takes to induce many travellers to linger. That said, the local authorities have put a lot of effort and money into sprucing the place up, particularly the early Victorian New Bridge development along the Esplanade. Despite such valiant attempts, **Dover Castle** is still by far the most interesting attraction, closely followed by a walk along Dover's legendary **White Cliffs**, which dominate the town and have long been a source of inspiration for travellers, lovers and soldiers sailing off to war.

Arrival, information and accommodation

There are frequent train services from both Charing Cross and Victoria stations in London to Dover Priory **train station**, situated off Folkestone Road, a ten-minute walk west of the centre; regular shuttle buses run to and from the Eastern and Western Docks. Buses from London (hourly; 2hr 30min) run to the Eastern Docks and the town-centre **bus station** on Pencester Road.

The **tourist office**, situated in the Old Town Gaol in Biggin Street (June–Aug daily 9am–5.30pm; Sept–May Mon–Fri 9am–5.30pm, Sat & Sun 10am–4pm; Oct–March closed Sun; ☎01304/205108, ⓦwww.whitecliffscountry.org.uk), has a free *White Cliffs Trails* pamphlet that outlines many good walks near Dover, both coastal and inland. The estate agents *Miles and Barr* on Cannon Street, off Market Square, provide **Internet** access (Mon–Sat 9am–5.30pm).

Accommodation in Dover – mainly small hotels and B&Bs – is plentiful. The biggest concentration is to be found on the Folkestone Road, close to the

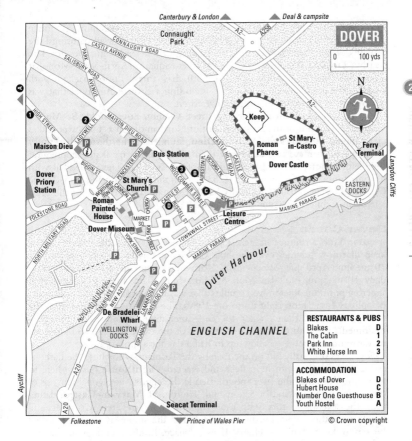

train station, but those around the base of Castle Hill Road on the other side of town are generally nicer. There's a busy **youth hostel** in a listed Georgian house at 306 London Rd (☎0870/770 5798, ✉dover@yha.org.uk; dorm beds £17.50, rooms ❶), a mile up the High Street from the train station. The most convenient **campsite** is *Hawthorn Farm* (☎01304/852658; closed Nov–Feb) close to Martin Mill train station, one stop up the line towards Ramsgate.

B&Bs and guest houses

Blakes of Dover 52 Castle St ☎01304/202194, ⓦwww.blakesofdover.com. Small, comfortable en-suite rooms are available in this real-ale pub and restaurant, which has a very genial owner. ❷
Hubert House 9 Castle Hill Rd ☎01304/202253, ⓦwww.huberthouse.co.uk. Friendly Georgian-era B&B convenient for the Eastern Dock, with cakes

and croissants home-cooked daily, and special diets catered for. Wi-Fi Internet access. ❷
Number One Guesthouse 1 Castle St ☎01304/202007, ⓦwww .number1guesthouse.co.uk. Great-value B&B with Victorian furnishings and a walled garden with views of the castle. Optional breakfast is served in your room. ❷

The Town

Postwar rebuilding has made Dover town centre rather unprepossessing, but it does hold a handful of low-key attractions. The **Roman Painted House** on New Street (April–Sept Tues–Sat 10am–5pm, Sun 1-4.30pm; £2), once a hotel for official guests, boasts some reasonable Roman wall paintings, the remains of an underground Roman heating system and some mosaics. The nearby **Dover Museum** on the Market Square (April–Sept Mon–Sat 10am–5.30pm, Sun noon–5pm; £2.50) has three floors packed with informative displays on Dover's past, including a Bronze-Age boat that was discovered in the town in 1992 and restored.

The pedestrianized main shopping street, Cannon Street, holds **St Mary's Church**, Victorian for the most part, but of Norman origin as the tower makes clear. Biggin Street has the **Maison Dieu**, founded in the thirteenth century for pilgrims en route to Canterbury, then turned into a naval storehouse after the Reformation and later becoming part of the town hall. The Stone Hall, with its fine timber roof, dates from 1253, while the neighbouring neo-Gothic Connaught Hall and the Council Chamber upstairs are the work of the great Victorian architects Poynter and Burges.

Dover Castle

It was in 1168, a century after the Conquest, that the Normans constructed the keep that now presides over the bulk of **Dover Castle** (Feb & March daily 10am–4pm; April–July & Sept daily 10am–6pm; Aug daily 9.30am–6pm; Oct daily 10am–5pm; Nov–Jan Mon & Thurs–Sun 10am–4pm; £10.30; EH), a superbly positioned defensive complex that was in continuous use as some sort of military installation right up to the 1980s. The castle's a stiff climb from the town centre, and there's a lot to see – including a Roman lighthouse, a multimedia re-creation of the French siege of the castle in 1216 and a tour of its warren of tunnels – so allow up to half a day for a thorough visit.

Dover was originally put on the map by the Romans, who chose the harbour as the base for their northern fleet, and erected a **lighthouse** (*pharos*) here to guide the ships into the river mouth. Beside the chunky hexagonal remains of the Roman *pharos* stands a Saxon-built church, **St Mary-in-Castro**, dating from the seventh century, with motifs graffitied by irreverent Crusaders still visible near the pulpit. Further up the hill is the impressive, well-preserved **Norman keep**, built by Henry II as a palace. Inside, there's an interactive exhibition on spying, and you can also climb the spiral stairs to lofty battlements for views over the sea to France.

The castle's other main attraction is its network of **Secret Wartime Tunnels** dug during the Napoleonic war and extended during World War II. You can tour "Hellfire Corner" – the tunnels' wartime nickname – on a fifty-minute guided tour (leaving every 20min). During World War II, the tunnels were used as a headquarters to plan the Dunkirk evacuation, which successfully brought back 330,000 stranded British and French troops from the Continent in a flotilla of local fishing and pleasure boats. The tour is spiced up with a little gore, and reveals the quaintly low-tech communications systems of the navy's command post.

Dover's cliffs

As the first and last sight of England for travellers throughout the centuries, the **White Cliffs of Dover** hold a complex role in the English psyche. Matthew Arnold invoked their massive grandeur in his famous elegy for lost belief, *Dover Beach*, written in the 1860s. Today, the beach has little of the romance invested in the spot by Arnold, but the cliffs flanking the town retain their majesty, even if pollution has taken some of the edge off their whiteness. The best views, of course, are to be had from several miles out to sea and **boats** leave hourly from

▲ White Cliffs of Dover

De Bradelei Wharf in Dover Marina (hourly; £6), but an alternative vantage point on land is the Prince of Wales Pier in the harbour.

There are some great **walks** to be had along the cliffs themselves. To reach **Shakespeare Cliff**, catch bus #D2A from Worthington Street towards Aycliff. Alternatively, there's a steep two-and-a-half-mile climb to Shakespeare Cliff from North Military Road, off York Street, taking you by the **Western Heights**, a series of defensive battlements built into the cliff in the nineteenth century. From here there's a sweeping panorama of the Straits of Dover – the world's busiest shipping lanes – and a bird's-eye view of the harbour and the surrounding cliffs. It's even possible to catch a glimpse of France on a clear day.

At Langdon Cliffs, a couple of miles east of town, the **Gateway to the White Cliffs** (daily: 10/11am–4/5pm; free; NT) has excellent displays explaining the ecology and history of the local coast and countryside. There's a coffee shop here, too, and regular countryside events and guided walks (℡01304/202756).

Eating and drinking

Despite Dover's uninspiring air, its **pubs** are surprisingly characterful, although some have a rather rough reputation from the shift-workers servicing the docks and ferries. Near the town hall, the big, Victorian *Park Inn*, at 1–2 Park Place, Ladywell, has plenty of real ales and tasty bar snacks, while the *White Horse Inn* on St James Street is a nice old eighteenth-century pub at the foot of the castle. Dover's **restaurant** scene is generally poor, though *The Cabin*, 91 High St (℡01304/206118; closed Mon–Wed & some lunchtimes), serves Modern British dishes with good-value set menus (£12.50 and £14.50), while *Blakes* (see p.187) has a lovely wood-panelled cellar bar and restaurant and is good for fresh fish and malt whiskies.

Hythe and Dungeness

In Roman times, what is now the southernmost part of Kent was submerged beneath the English Channel, but the lowering of sea levels in the Middle Ages and later reclamation created a forty-square-mile area of shingle and marshland now known as the **Romney and Denge marshes.** The forlorn, sheep-speckled expanse has an eerie appearance today, which you can take in on foot or aboard a steam locomotive that runs between the ancient town of **Hythe,** on the eastern edge of the reclaimed marshes, and the headland of **Dungeness**.

Hythe

Separated from the nearby port of Folkestone by the massive earthworks of the Channel Tunnel, **HYTHE** is a sedate seaside resort bisected by the disused waterway of the Royal Military Canal, which was built as a defensive obstacle during the perceived threat of Napoleonic invasion. Hythe's receding shoreline reduced its usefulness as a port and the nearby coast is now just a sweep of beach punctuated by **Martello towers**, part of a chain of 74 such towers built along the south and east coasts in the early nineteenth century as a defence against the French.

The nicest part of Hythe is not the seafront, but the old town, and in particular the quiet back alleys to the north of the High Street: follow signs to the crypt (May–Sept Mon–Sat 10.30am–noon & 2.30–4pm, Sun noon–4.30pm; 50p) of the eleventh-century **St Leonard's Church**, with its macabre collection of ancient bones and skulls. Hythe is also home to the **Romney, Hythe and Dymchurch Railway**, a fifteen-inch-gauge line which runs fourteen miles south down the coast to Dungeness (April–Sept daily; March & Oct Sat & Sun, plus school hols throughout the year; £11.20 return; ℡01797/362353, www .rhdr.org.uk). Built in the 1920s as a tourist attraction, its fleet of steam locomotives are mainly one-third scale models from the Twenties and Thirties

– making for a cramped ride for most adults. The station is to the west of the town centre, on the south bank of the canal by Station Bridge.

Five miles west of Hythe, the **Port Lympne Wild Animal Park** (daily 10am–5/6pm; last admission 90min before closing; £14.45) is home to more than 650 beasts, including gorillas, African elephants, Barbary lions, Siberian and Indian tigers and the largest breeding herd of black rhinos outside Africa.

Practicalities

Hythe is easily accessible by hourly **buses** from Dover. The **tourist office** is, bizarrely, situated in the old public toilets in Red Lion Square (Mon–Fri daily 9am–5pm; ☎01303/267799, ⊛www.shepway.gov.uk). For **accommodation**, the Tudor-style *Seabrook House*, 81 Seabrook Rd (☎01303/269282, ⊛www .seabrook-house.co.uk; ❸), has pleasing light and airy rooms, while the tasteful, friendly *Swan Hotel*, on the High Street (☎01303/266236, ⊛www .theswanhotelhythe.co.uk; ❷), has a Nepalese **restaurant** attached. Also on the High Street, *Torbay of Hythe*, at no. 81, serves high-class fish and chips (closed Sun & Mon), while the *King's Head*, no. 117 (☎01303/266283), dishes up sensibly priced home-cooked meals.

Dungeness

The spooky, shingle-swathed expanse of **DUNGENESS**, fourteen miles south of Hythe, was until the nineteenth century affected by malaria, and since the 1960s has been the appropriate setting for a nuclear power station. A more benign local landmark is the pair of lighthouses located close to the RHDR station – five in all have been constructed here since 1615. Decommissioned since the erection of its successor in 1961, the **Old Lighthouse** (Jan–June Thurs–Sun 10am–4.30pm; July–Sept & school hols daily 10am–4.30pm; Oct Sat & Sun 10am–4.30pm; £3), built in 1904, affords sweeping views and displays navigational equipment and information panels on its six floors.

The haunted landscape of Dungeness has become the abode of eccentric and reclusive characters living in basic fishermen's cabins or disused railway carriages, apparently relishing the area's bleak austerity and carcinogenic threat. The barren marshy environment also attracts huge colonies of gulls and terns, as well as smews and gadwalls – the **RSPB visitor centre** (daily 10am–4pm/5pm; £3) off the Lydd road, three miles from Dungeness, can provide further information. The local floral ecology is also unique and all around you'll see tiny communities of wildflowers struggling against the unrelenting breeze.

Back in Dungeness, between the two lighthouses, you can refuel at the unprepossessing but welcoming *Britannia* **pub.**

The Kent Weald

The Weald is usually taken to refer to the region around the spa town of **Royal Tunbridge Wells**, but in fact it stretches across a much larger area between the North and South Downs and includes parts of both Kent and Sussex, though the majority of its attractions are just inside Kent. We've taken the wider definition to include the medieval manor at **Penshurst** and nearby **Hever Castle**, just northwest of Tunbridge Wells, as well as the town of **Sevenoaks**, on the edge of the North Downs.

During Saxon times, much of the Weald was covered in thick forest – the word itself derives from the Germanic word *Wald*, meaning forest, and the suffixes -hurst (meaning wood) and -den (meaning clearing) are commonly found in Wealden village names. Now, however, the region is epitomized by gentle hills, sunken country lanes and somnolent villages as well as some of England's most beautiful gardens – **Sissinghurst**, fifteen miles east of Tunbridge Wells, being the best known.

Public transport to the area is good, but in order to explore the Wealden countryside in any depth, you'll need your own vehicle. If you are driving or on a bicycle, you may want to follow the signs indicating the **High Weald Country Tour**, a seventy-mile back-country loop stretching through the best of the Kentish Weald, from Penshurst in the west to Tenterden in the east. Ask for the leaflet and map at tourist offices in the area.

Royal Tunbridge Wells and around

ROYAL TUNBRIDGE WELLS – not to be confused with the more mundane Tonbridge, a few miles to the north – is the home of the mythical whingeing reactionary letter-writer known as "Disgusted of Tunbridge Wells". Most British people, therefore, view it with derision, but don't be misled – this prosperous spa town, surrounded by gorgeous countryside, is an elegant and diverting place, meriting a few hours' visit.

In 1606 Lord North discovered a bubbling spring while riding through the Waterdown Forest, which covered the area at that time. From the claim that this spring had curative properties a spa resort evolved, reaching its height of popularity during the Regency period when such restorative cures were in vogue. The distinctively well-mannered architecture of that period, generously surrounded by parklands in which the rejuvenated gentry exercised, gives the southern and western part of town its special character. In late July, the five-day **Georgian Festivities** celebrate this era, with many of the townsfolk taking to the streets in eighteenth-century garb.

Tunbridge Wells also makes a good base for several local attractions, including ancient **Leeds Castle**, two country piles with strong Tudor associations, **Penshurst Place** and **Hever Castle**, and another, **Sissinghurst**, from the same period, but more famous for its twentieth-century gardens.

The spa and the town

The icon of those genteel times, and the best place to start your wanderings, is the **Pantiles**, an elegant colonnaded parade of shops, ten minutes' walk south of the train station, where the fashionable once gathered to promenade and take the waters. Hub of the Pantiles is the original **Chalybeate Spring** (pronounced with the emphasis on the "be") in the Bath House (Easter–Sept daily 10am–5pm), where a "Dipper" has been employed since the late eighteenth century to serve the ferrous waters. A period-dressed incumbent will fetch you a glass from the cool spring for 40p – or, if you bring your own cup, you can help yourself for free from the adjacent source.

A fifteen-minute walk up the High Street from the Pantiles, on Mount Pleasant Road, the **Museum and Art Gallery** (Mon–Sat 9.30am–5pm; Sun 10am–4pm; free) is worth a look for its exquisite collection of locally made wooden boxes, known as "Tunbridge Ware". Dating from the 1830s, their mosaic-style, inlaid lids are decorated with rural scenes and ornamental borders.

On the east side of the High Street, the Grove and, to the north, Calverley Grounds are havens of urban tranquillity, while **The Common**, spreading out on the west side of town, is laced with pathways carved by the original visitors to the spa. You can trace the course of the old horseracing track, or simply sit among the strange sandstone formations of Wellington Rocks.

Practicalities

The **train station**, on the London Charing Cross to Hastings line, is centrally located, close to the point where the High Street becomes Mount Pleasant Road. The **bus station** is north of the centre on St John's Road, but most buses stop on Mount Pleasant and at the train station. The Tunbridge Wells **tourist office**, housed in the Old Fish Market in the Pantiles (Mon–Sat 9am–5pm, Sun 10am–4/5pm; ☎01892/515675, ⓦwww.visittunbridgewells.com), can supply a town map.

Tunbridge Wells has a number of very plush **hotels**, such as the chic ♣ *Hotel du Vin* in Crescent Road (☎01892/526455, ⓦwww.hotelduvin.com; ❻), a blend of sleek boutique hotel and gentleman's club, with a superb bistro. There's also an attractive Regency-style **B&B** at 40 York Rd (☎01892/531342, ⓦwww.yorkroad.co.uk; ❸).

The town has an excellent range of **restaurants**, one of the best being *Thackeray's House*, one-time home of the writer, at 85 London Rd (☎01892/511921; closed Sun eve & Mon); it's expensive, but there's a bargain three-course lunch for £14. For top-notch seafood at moderate prices try *Sankey's* at 39 Mount Ephraim (☎01892/511422; main restaurant closed Sun), with a secluded decked garden and a great selection of specialist beers in its cosy cellar wine bar. There are excellent veggie options at the *Trinity Arts Centre Café* in a converted church on Church Road (lunch & pre-theatre deals only; closed Sun).

One **pub** you're unlikely to miss is the popular ♣ *Opera House*, converted from a 1902 theatre on Mount Pleasant Road – you can sit in the foyer, the stalls or even on stage and gaze up at the balconies. *Chaplins*, in the Pantiles, is much smaller and snug.

Penshurst Place and Hever Castle

Tudor timber-framed houses and shops line the high street of the attractive village of **PENSHURST**, five miles northwest of Tunbridge Wells (bus #231 or #233; not Sun). The main reason for coming here is to visit **Penshurst Place** (daily noon–4pm, grounds 10.30am–6pm; £7.50, grounds only £6), home to the Sidney family since 1552 and birthplace of the Elizabethan soldier and poet, Sir Philip Sidney. The fourteenth-century Barons Hall, built for Sir John de Pulteney, four times Lord Mayor of London, is the chief glory of the interior, with its sixty-foot-high chestnut roof still in place. The ten acres of grounds include a formal Italian garden with clipped box hedges, and double herbaceous borders mixed with an abundance of yew hedges.

Three miles further west, the moated and much-altered **Hever Castle** (March–Easter Wed–Sun 10.45am–4pm; Easter–Oct daily 10.45am–6pm; Nov & Dec Thurs–Sun 10.45am–4pm; last entry 1hr before closing; £11.50, gardens only £9.30), was the childhood home of Anne Boleyn, second wife of Henry VIII, and where Anne of Cleves, Henry's fourth wife, lived after their divorce. In 1903, having fallen into disrepair, the castle was bought by William Waldorf-Astor, American millionaire owner of *The Times*, who had the house assiduously restored, panelling the rooms with worthy reproductions of Tudor woodcarvings. In the Inner Hall hangs a fine portrait of Henry VIII by Holbein; a further Holbein painting of Elizabeth I is on display on the middle floor. Upstairs, in Anne Boleyn's room, you can see her book of prayers which she carried with her to the executioner's block, but more impressive is the Anne of Cleves room, which houses an unusually well-preserved tapestry, illustrating the marriage of Henry's sister to King Louis XII of France, with Anne Boleyn as one of the ladies-in-waiting.

Outside in the grounds, the absorbing **Guthrie Miniature Model Houses Collection** shows the development of aristocratic seats from feudal times on. However, the best feature of the grounds is Waldorf-Astor's beautiful **Italian Garden**, built on reclaimed marshland and decorated with Roman statuary. Also in the grounds is a traditional **yew hedge maze**, an adventure playground and a **water maze**, as well as a twenty-bedroom mock-Tudor annexe, built by Waldorf-Astor, who decided that the castle didn't have enough rooms to accommodate the guests of a thrusting newspaper magnate in style; it's now used solely as a conference venue.

No bus routes serve Hever Castle, but there are **train stations** at Hever, a mile west of the castle, and Edenbridge, three miles northwest, from which taxis are usually available.

Sissinghurst

Sissinghurst, fourteen miles east of Tunbridge Wells (late March to Oct Mon, Tues & Fri–Sun 11am–6.30pm or dusk; £8.60; NT), was described by Vita Sackville-West (see p.196) as "a garden crying out for rescue" when she and her husband took it over in the 1920s. Over the following years they transformed the five-acre plot into one of England's greatest and most popular modern gardens.

Spread over the site of a medieval moated manor (which was rebuilt into an Elizabethan mansion, of which only one wing remains today), the gardens were designed around the linear pattern of the former buildings' walls. A major part of Sissinghurst's appeal derives from the way that the flowers are allowed to spill over onto the narrow walkways, defying the classical formality of the great gardens that preceded it. The brick tower that Vita had restored and used as her study acts as a focal point and offers the best views of the walled gardens. Most impressive are the **White Garden**, composed solely of white flowers and silvery-grey foliage, and the **Cottage Garden**, featuring flora in shades of orange, yellow and red.

The reputation of Sissinghurst, as well as its limited capacity for visitors, is such that the gardens get extremely busy in summer when timed tickets for half-hourly visits are issued. Food options are limited and overpriced – your best bet is to bring a picnic. **Bus** #297 from Royal Tunbridge Wells takes you within two miles of the gardens, and bus #5, between Maidstone and Hastings, stops in Sissinghurst village en route.

Leeds Castle

Named after the local village, **Leeds Castle**, eighteen miles northeast of Tunbridge Wells and five miles east of Maidstone, off the A20 (daily 10am–5/7pm; last admission 2hr before closing; castle, park & gardens £14 for an annual pass), more closely resembles a fairytale palace than a defensively efficient fortress. Set half on an island in the middle of a lake and half on the mainland surrounded by landscaped parkland, the castle began life around 1120. Following centuries of regal and noble ownership (and, less glamorously, service as a prison) it is now run as a commercial concern, hosting conferences and sporting and cultural events. Its interior fails to match the castle's stunning, much-photographed external appearance and, in places, twentieth-century renovations have quashed any of its historical charm; possibly the most unusual feature inside is the dog collar museum in the gatehouse. In the grounds, there's a fine aviary with some superb and colourful exotic specimens, as well as manicured gardens and a mildly challenging maze.

▲ Leeds Castle

The easiest way to get to Leeds Castle by public transport is to buy an all-inclusive ticket; you can travel either by rail to Bearsted Station from London Victoria via Maidstone East, or by coach from Victoria Coach Station, with a shuttle service and entry to the castle included.

Sevenoaks and around

Set among the green sand ridges of west Kent, 25 miles from London, **SEVENOAKS** is a very popular commuter town, with trains reaching London in under an hour. Sadly, the place lost all but one of the ageing oaks from which it derives its name in a storm that struck southern England in October 1987. With mere saplings having taken their place, the only real reason to come to the town is to visit the immense baronial estate of **Knole**, or to use it as a base for seeing the mosaics at **Lullingstone Roman Villa**, memorabilia relating to Winston Churchill at his home of **Chartwell**, and **Ightham Mote**, a winning blend of architectural styles in a lovely rural setting.

Knole

Knole (mid-March to Oct Wed–Sun noon–4pm; garden late March to Oct Wed 11am–4pm; £8.50, garden £2; NT) is entered from the south end of Sevenoaks High Street, making it very nearly half an hour's walk from the train station, fifteen minutes from the bus station. The house was created in 1456 by Archbishop Thomas Bourchier, who transformed the existing dwelling into a palace for himself and succeeding archbishops of Canterbury. The palace, numerically designed to match the calendar with 365 rooms, 7 courtyards and 52 staircases, was appropriated by Henry VIII, who lavished further expense on it and hunted in the thousand acres of **parkland** (free access throughout the year), still home to several hundred deer. Elizabeth I passed the estate on to her cousin, Thomas Sackville, who remodelled the house in 1605; it has remained in the family's hands ever since, with its Jacobean exterior preserved.

Vita Sackville-West, who in 1923 penned a definitive history of her family entitled *Knole and the Sackvilles*, was brought up here, and her one-time lover Virginia Woolf derived inspiration for her novel *Orlando* from her frequent visits to the house. Only thirteen rooms are open to the public, featuring an array of fine, if well-worn, furnishings and tapestries. Paintings by Gainsborough and Van Dyck are on display, as are Reynolds's depictions of George III and of Queen Charlotte – between them hangs a painting of their strutting, dandified progeny, George IV, one of the fifteen children she bore the king.

Practicalities

Sevenoaks' **tourist office** is in the library (Mon–Sat 9.30am–4.30/5pm; ☎01732/450305, ⓦwww.visitheartofkent.com), just beyond the **bus station** in Buckhurst Lane; the **train station** is fifteen minutes' walk north of the town centre on London Road. The town's smartest **accommodation** is at the excellent *Royal Oak Hotel*, a seventeenth-century coaching inn at the south end of the High Street (☎01732/451109, ⓦwww.brook-hotels.co.uk/royaloak; ⑥), beyond the entrance to Knole. Alternatively, you could have a timber-clad cottage to yourself at *4 Old Timber Top Cottages*, Bethel Road (☎01732/460506, ⓦwww.timbertopcottage.co.uk; ④); breakfast is included in the nightly rate, though the cottage also has basic self-catering facilities.

For a **snack** (and really good coffee), pop into *Coffee Call* on Dorset Street. The menu at the nearby *Dorset Arms* **pub** is better than average, as is *The Black Boy* on Bank Street. For top-class, but expensive, food, the *Royal Oak's* restaurant, *No. 5* (☎01732/455555), is the place to go, while the hotel's bar also serves good food at half the price.

Lullingstone Roman Villa

Lullingstone Roman Villa, seven miles north of Sevenoaks and three-quarters of a mile along the river west of the village of Eynsford (April–Sept daily 10am–6pm; Oct, Nov, Feb & March daily 10am–4pm; Dec & Jan Wed–Sun 10am–4pm; £5.50; EH), has some of the best-preserved Roman mosaics in southeast England, in a pleasant location alongside the trickle of the River Darent. Believed to have been the first-century residence of a farmer, the site has yielded some fine marble busts (now on display in London's British Museum) and a superb floor depicting the killing of the Chimera, a mythical fire-breathing beast with a lion's head, goat's body and a serpent's tail. Excavation in a nearby chamber has revealed early Christian iconography, which suggests that the villa may have become a Romano-Christian chapel in the third century, pre-empting the official arrival of that religion by three hundred years and making Lullingstone one of the earliest sites of clandestine Christian worship in England. From Sevenoaks there are hourly trains to Eynsford, from where it's a fifteen-minute walk.

Chartwell

The residence of Winston Churchill from 1924 until his death in 1965, **Chartwell**, six miles west of Sevenoaks (mid-March to Oct Wed–Sun 11am–5pm; July & Aug also Tues; £9.80; NT), is one of the most visited of the National Trust's properties. It's an unremarkable, heavily restored Tudor building whose main appeal is the wartime premier's memorabilia, including his paintings, which show an unexpectedly contemplative side to the famously gruff statesman. Entry to the house is by timed ticket at peak times – expect long queues. A direct bus service runs to Chartwell from Sevenoaks bus station four times daily on Sundays and public holidays.

Ightham Mote

The secluded, moated manor house of picturesque **Ightham Mote** (pronounced "I-tam"), six miles southeast of Sevenoaks just off the A227 (March–Oct Mon, Wed–Fri, Sun & public hols 10.30am–5.30pm; £8.60; NT) originates from the fourteenth century, though the original defensive appearance of this half-timbered ragstone building has been muted by Tudor alterations. A tour of the interior reveals a mixture of architectural styles ranging from the fourteenth-century Old Chapel and crypt, through a barrel-vaulted Tudor chapel with a painted ceiling to an eighteenth-century Palladian window. Ightham is tricky to get to by bus, with only the infrequent #404 from Sevenoaks (not Sun) making the trip.

Sussex

Although now separated into two counties, East and West, **Sussex** (deriving from "land of the south Saxons") retains a unified identity. Most of the region was covered in dense forest until the Tudor era, when the huge demand for timber and charcoal began its deforestation. However, large areas of woodland still exist in inland parts of the counties and contribute to Sussex's bucolic character. Nowhere is this rural atmosphere more evident than on the southeast's main long-distance footpath, the **South Downs Way**, which runs along the grassy ridge of the South Downs, giving dramatic views over some fine countryside as well as over the coast, where the Downs meet the sea at the chalk cliffs of **Beachy Head** and **Seven Sisters**.

However, Sussex also has its fair share of urban centres, many of which are populated by London commuters. The best known is the traditional seaside resort of **Brighton**, the counties' biggest and brashest city, while a few miles inland more sedate **Lewes**, the county town of East Sussex, is famed for its bonfire night celebrations. **Hastings**, farther east, is best known for its historical connections, although the eponymous fight actually took place six miles away at **Battle**. Farther east still, on the edge of the Romney Marshes, the former Cinque Port of **Rye** has cobbled streets and a well-preserved cluster of fifteenth-to-eighteenth-century buildings. In West Sussex, the main centres of interest are the attractive hilltop town of **Arundel**, surrounded by unspoilt countryside, and the county town of **Chichester**.

Hastings and around

During the twelfth and thirteenth centuries, **Hastings** flourished as an influential Cinque Port (see box on p.184). In 1287 its harbour creek was silted up by the same storm that washed away nearby **Winchelsea**, forcing the settlement to be temporarily abandoned. These days, the town is a curious mixture of unpretentious fishing port, traditional seaside resort and arty retreat popular with painters (there's even a street and quarter named Bohemia).

In 1066, William, Duke of Normandy, landed at Pevensey Bay, a few miles west of town, and made Hastings his base, but his forces met Harold's army – exhausted after quelling a Nordic invasion near York – at **Battle**, six miles northwest of Hastings. Battle today boasts a magnificent abbey built by William in thanks for his victory, which makes a good afternoon's excursion from Hastings. Farther north, **Bateman's**, once the home of Rudyard Kipling, and the classic **Bodiam Castle** are both easily reached from Hastings in a day-trip, as is the atmospheric little town of **Rye**.

Arrival, information and accommodation

Hastings' **train station**, served by regular trains from London Victoria, is a ten-minute walk from the seafront along Havelock Road, while National Express **bus** services operate from the station at the junction of Havelock and Queen's roads. The **tourist office** is located within the town hall on Queen's Road (Mon–Fri 8.30am–6.15pm, Sat 9am–5pm, Sun 10.30am–4.30pm; ☎0845/274 1001, ⓦwww.visit1066country.com); there's also a smaller seafront office (Easter–Oct daily 10am–6pm, Nov–Easter Sat & Sun only 10am–4.30pm; ☎01424/781120) near the Boating Lake on East Parade by the old town. You'll find **Internet** access at Revolver Lounge, 26 George St (☎01424/439899), and **bikes** can be rented from Hastings Cycles (☎01424/444013) in St Andrews Market off Queens Road.

Hastings has a preponderance of drab **hotels** and chintzy **B&Bs**, but you can still find some more upbeat places, especially in the old town. The nearest **campsite**, *Shear Barn Holiday Park*, Barley Lane (☎01424/423583, ⓦwww .shearbarn.co.uk), is next to the seafront Hastings Country Park, a mile east of the town centre off All Saints Street.

Accommodation

Argyle Guest House 32 Cambridge Gardens ☎01424/421294. Good-value rooms with or without private bathrooms, in a friendly B&B near the station. Continental breakfast on request. ❶
Lavender and Lace 106 All Saints St ☎01424/716290, ⓦwww.lavenderlace1066.co.uk. Popular, cosy, timber-framed guesthouse right in the middle of the old town. Closed Jan & Feb. No credit cards. ❹
Swan House 1 Hill St ☎01424/430014, ⓦwww .swanhousehastings.co.uk. Centrally located, this stylishly renovated Tudor guesthouse has inglenook fireplaces, wood panelling and beams but modern facilities, including Wi-Fi. ❻

The Town

Hastings **old town**, east of the pier, holds most of the appeal of this part tacky, part pretty seaside resort. Other than the oddly neglected Regency architecture of **Pelham Crescent**, directly beneath the castle ruins, **All Saints Street** is by far the most evocative thoroughfare, punctuated with the odd, rickety, timber-framed dwelling from the fifteenth century. The thirteenth-century **St Clement's Church** stands in the High Street, which runs parallel to All Saints Street, on the other side of The Bourne. By a louvred window at the top of the church's tower rests a cannonball that was lodged there by a Dutch galleon in the 1600s – its poignancy rather dispelled by a companion fitted in the eighteenth century for the sake of symmetry. On the right as you walk up the High Street, you'll see **Starr's Cottages**, one of which is wedge-shaped and painted to resemble a piece of cheese, while the tiny working **Flower-makers Museum** at 58a High St (Mon–Fri 9.30am–4pm, Sat 11am–4pm; £1) creates petals and leaves for weddings, television, theatre and film sets (it was responsible for 100,000 rose petals for *Gladiator*), using the original Victorian tools and moulds.

Down by the seafront, the area known as **The Stade** is characterized by its tall, black weatherboard **net shops**, most dating from the mid-nineteenth century (and still in use), but which first appeared here in Tudor times. To raise Hastings' tone, the town council attempted to shift the fishermen and their malodorously drying nets from the beach by increasing rents per square foot, and these sinister-looking towers were their response. Somewhat remarkably, Hastings still boasts a working fishing fleet, and you can buy fresh fish from several of the net shops.

There's a trio of nautical attractions on nearby Rock-a-Nore Road. The **Fishermen's Museum** (daily: 10/11am–4/5pm; free), a converted seaman's chapel, offers an account of the port's commercial activities and displays one of Hastings' last clinker-built luggers – exceptionally stout trawlers able to withstand being winched up and down the shingle beach. The neighbouring **Shipwreck Heritage Centre** (daily: 10.30/11am–4/5pm; free) details the dramas of unfortunate mariners, focusing on the wreck of the *Amsterdam*, beached in 1749 and now embedded in the sand three miles west of town awaiting excavation. Opposite is **Underwater World** (daily: 10/11am–4/5pm; £6.60), a series of aquariums with walk-through tunnels, magnified tanks housing marine creatures and showing an excellent, sympathetic film on sharks.

Castle Hill, separating the old town from the visually less interesting modern quarter, can be ascended by the **West Hill Cliff Railway** from George Street, off Marine Parade, one of two Victorian funicular railways in Hastings (daily 10/11am–4/5.30pm; £1.60), the other being the **East Cliff Railway**, on Rock-a-Nore Road (same times and price). Castle Hill is where William the Conqueror erected his first **Castle** in 1066, one of several prefabricated wooden structures brought over from Normandy in sections. Built on the site of an existing fort, probably of Saxon origins, it was soon replaced by a more permanent stone structure, but in the thirteenth century storms caused the cliffs to subside, tipping most of the castle into the sea; the surviving ruins, however, offer an excellent prospect of the town. The castle is home to **The 1066 Story** (daily 10/11am–3/5pm; £3.75), in which the events of the last successful invasion of the British mainland are described inside a mock-up of a siege tent. The twenty-minute audiovisual details the history of the castle and corrects a few myths about the famous battle.

Eating

Hastings has a good range of affordable places to eat, most very central.

Gannets Bistro 45 High St. Friendly place offering a wide daytime range of food and good afternoon teas. Closed Mon. Inexpensive.

Harris 58 High St ☎01424/437221. Wood-panelled walls and potted plants enhance the ambience of this tapas bar, which serves set-price fish and vegetarian dinners. Closed Sun eve and Mon. Moderate.

Mermaid 2 Rock-a-Nore ☎01424/438100. The best fish and chips in town are at this eat-in restaurant, right by the beach; jellied eels can be sampled from the adjacent net shop. Inexpensive.

Pissarro's 10 South Terrace ☎01424/421363, ⓦwww.pissarros.co.uk. Good variety of bistro food; you can graze or have a full meal while listening to live jazz and blues. Moderate.

Drinking and nightlife

There are more than thirty **pubs** to choose from in Hastings: the local fishermen's favourite is the *Lord Nelson* right by the front on The Bourne; others to check out are the ever-popular *First In Last Out,* 15 High St in the old town, the creaky-beamed hostelry *Ye Olde Pump House*, 64 George St, or the trendy clubby bar, *The Street*, 53 Robertson St, accessed via a tiny entrance on Cambridge Road in the centre of the new town.

For **entertainment**, *The Hastings Arms* at 2 George St has a blues night every Monday, and there's jazz at *Pissarro's* (see p.199) and at *The Anchor* further up George Street on Tuesdays. *The Stag Inn*, 14 All Saints St, has a folk session on Wednesdays and bluegrass on Thursdays. For comprehensive **listings** of what's on, get the free *Ultimate Alternative*, available in pubs, clubs and record shops and at ⓦwww.ua1066.co.uk.

Battle

The town of **BATTLE** – a ten-minute train ride inland from Hastings – occupies the site of the most famous land battle in British history. Here, on October 14, 1066, the invading Normans swarmed up the hillside from Senlac Moor and overcame the Anglo-Saxon army of King Harold, who is thought to have been killed not by an arrow through the eye – a myth resulting from the misinterpretation of the Bayeux Tapestry – but by a workaday clubbing about the head. Before the battle took place, William vowed that, should he win the engagement, he would build a religious foundation on the very spot of Harold's slaying to atone for the bloodshed, and, true to his word, **Battle Abbey** (daily 10am–4/6pm; £6.50; EH) was built four years later and subsequently occupied by a fraternity of Benedictines. The magnificent structure, though partially destroyed in the Dissolution and much rebuilt and revised over the centuries, still dominates the town. You can wander through the ruins of the abbey to the spot where Harold was killed – the site of the high altar of William's abbey, now marked by a memorial stone – while a visitor centre holds an interactive exhibition and an auditorium where you can view a dramatic re-enactment of the battle using film and computer simulations.

Though nothing can match the resonance of the abbey, the rest of the town is worth a stroll. **St Mary's Church**, on High Street, has a fine Norman font and nave and the churchyard contains the grave of one Isaac Ingall who, according to the inscription on his tomb, was 120 years old when he died in 1798. At the far end of High Street is the fourteenth-century **almonry** – the present town hall – at the back of which is a **museum** (April–Oct Mon–Sat 10am–4.30pm, Sun noon–3pm; £1), which contains the only battle-axe discovered at Battle and the oldest Guy Fawkes in the country. Every year, on the Saturday nearest to November 5, this 300-year-old effigy is paraded along High Street at the head of a torch-lit procession culminating at a huge bonfire in front of the abbey gates – similar celebrations occur in Lewes (see p.206).

Wealden Hall House, just past the tourist office, houses a more modern diversion, though one still firmly rooted in the past. **Buckleys Yesterday's World** (daily 9.30am–6pm, closes 5.30pm in winter, last entry 1hr 15min before closing; £8) is a must for nostalgia buffs, consisting of thirty re-created rooms and shop settings stocked with original materials and goods. Highlights include a Bakelite-crammed 1930s wireless shop, a Victorian kitchen replete with authentic accessories and a re-created Victorian street scene. The grounds include a country garage and railway station, a café and play areas for children and toddlers.

Practicalities

The **tourist office** is in the Gatehouse at Battle Abbey (daily 9/10am– 4/5.30pm;ⓣ01424/773721,ⓦwww.visitsussex.org).Battle's **accommodation** tends to be pricey, but there are a few more affordable B&Bs, including the central and cosy *White Lodge*, 42 Hastings Rd (℡01424/772122, Ⓦwww .bedandbreakfastbattle.co.uk; ❹), with a heated outdoor pool in the summer, and the en-suite rooms above *Jempson's Café*, 78 High St (℡01424/772856; ❷). You can eat well at the excellent *Pilgrims* **restaurant**, 1 High St (℡01424/772314; closed Sun eve), a fifteenth-century hall next to the abbey which offers good-value set-price meals (not weekends); it's also an ideal spot for afternoon tea. Town-centre **pubs** serving decent meals include the fifteenth-century *Old King's Head* on Mount Street and the *Chequers Inn* at Lower Lake, on High Street.

Rye and Winchelsea

Perched on a hill overlooking the Romney Marshes, ten miles east of Hastings, sits the ancient town of **RYE**. Added as a "limb" to the original Cinque Ports (see box, p.184), the town then became marooned two miles inland with the retreat of the sea and the silting-up of the River Rother. It is now one of the most popular places in East Sussex – half-timbered, skew-roofed and quintessentially English, but also very commercialized.

From Strand Quay, head up The Deals to Rye's most picturesque lane, the sloping cobbled **Mermaid Street**, which brings you eventually to the peaceful oasis of Church Square. Henry James, who strangely suggested that "Rye would … remind you of Granada", lived from 1898 until his death in 1916 in **Lamb House** at the east end of Mermaid Street (March–Oct Thurs & Sat 2–6pm; £3.30; NT). The house's three rooms and garden are of interest chiefly to fans of James's novels, or to admirers of E.F. Benson, who lived here after James. A blue plaque in High Street testifies that Radclyffe Hall, author of the seminal lesbian novel, *The Well of Loneliness*, was also once a resident of the town. At the centre of Church Square stands **St Mary's Church**, home of England's oldest functioning pendulum clock; the ascent of the church tower – whose bells were looted by French raiders in 1377 and then retrieved with similar audacity – offers fine views over the clay-tiled roofs and grid of narrow lanes. In the far corner of the square stands the **Ypres Tower** (April–Oct Mon & Thurs–Sun 10.30am–5pm; £2.95), formerly used to keep watch for cross-Channel invaders, and now a part of the **Rye Castle Museum** on nearby East Street (Mon, Thurs & Fri 2–5pm, Sat & Sun 10.30am–5pm; £2.50, or £5 for both sites), which houses a number of relics from Rye's past, including an eighteenth-century fire engine. Also worth seeking out is the **Rye Art Gallery**, spread across two lovely houses: the Easton Rooms, 107 High St (daily except Tues 10.30am–1pm & 2–5pm; free), which stages exhibitions by local contemporary artists; and the Stormont Studio, around the corner in Ockman Lane, off East Street (Thurs–Sun 10.30am–1pm & 2–5pm), which has a small permanent collection, including works by artists associated with Rye, such as Burra and Nash. Rye's acclaimed **literary festival** (℡01797/224442, Ⓦwww.ryefestival .co.uk) takes place over the first two weeks in September and also features a wide range of musical and visual arts events.

WINCHELSEA, perched on a hill two miles southwest of Rye and easily reached by train, bus, foot or bike, shares Rye's indignity of having become detached from the sea, but has a very different character. Rye gets all the visitors, whereas Winchelsea feels positively deserted, an impression augmented as you pass through the medieval Strand Gate and see the ghostly ruined **Church of St Thomas à Becket**. The original settlement was washed away in the great storm in 1287, after which Edward I planned a new port with a chequerboard pattern of streets. Even at the height of Winchelsea's economic activity, however, not all the plots on the grid were used. The town also suffered from incursions by the French in the fourteenth and fifteenth centuries, at which time the church was pillaged; the remains of the church constitute Sussex's finest example of the Decorated style. Head south for a mile and a half and you get to **Winchelsea beach**, a long expanse of pebbly sand. Three miles further east, **Camber Sands** is a two-mile stretch of sandy beach that has become a renowned centre of wind and water sports.

Practicalities

Hourly **trains** run to Rye and Winchelsea from Hastings; Rye's station is at the bottom of Station Approach, off Cinque Ports Street, while Winchelsea's is a mile north of the town. **Bus** #711 runs into the centre of both towns from Hastings. Rye's **tourist office** is in the Heritage Centre on Strand Quay (daily 10am–4/5pm; ☎01797/226696, ⓦwww.visitrye.co.uk), which has masses of information on local attractions, a scaled-down model of the town on display, and audioguides to rent (£2.50).

The town's popularity with weekending Londoners gives it an excellent choice of **accommodation**, much of it on the expensive side. There's also a good selection of quality **restaurants**, equally pricey, though you can sup more economically in one of Rye's agreeable old **pubs**, many of which serve real ales.

Hotels

Durrant House 2 Market St, Rye ☎01797/223182, ⓦwww.durranthouse.com. Friendly and attractive Georgian hotel with a garden looking out towards Dungeness and the marshes. ⑤

Mermaid Inn Mermaid Street, Rye ☎01797/223065, ⓦwww.mermaidinn.com. The most luxurious option locally, this fifteenth-century, half-timber inn pulls no punches, with wood-panelled rooms and four-posters. ⑧

Strand House Tanyards Lane, Winchelsea ☎01797/226276, ⓦwww.thestrandhouse.co.uk. At the foot of the cliff below Strand Gate, this Tudor hotel is Winchelsea's best accommodation option, with inglenook fireplaces and a grassy garden. Meals available, and special diets catered for. ③

Restaurants and pubs

Flushing Inn 4 Market St ☎01797/223292. Excellent fish dishes, both freshwater and sea, are the speciality here, with options ranging from fish soup to crab and lobster. Closed Mon eve & all Tues. Expensive.

Landgate Bistro 5–6 Landgate ☎01797/222829. Good game and lamb are on the menu at this formal bistro, worth the steep prices. Open Tues–Thurs eve only. Expensive.

The Mermaid With heavy exposed timbers throughout, *The Mermaid* overflows with medieval atmosphere, though it does get very busy. You can eat formally (and expensively) or in the bar – or just have a drink. Patio seating. Moderate–expensive.

Peacock Tearooms 8 Lion St. Everything from snacks to moderately priced fresh Rye Bay plaice are served up in this suitably ancient setting – it's also good for delicious cream teas. Closed eves. Inexpensive.

Ypres Castle Gun Gardens, down the steps behind the Ypres Tower. An unspoiled spot often used for film locations, with real ales, a boules pitch and regular live music.

Bodiam Castle

Ask a child to draw a castle and the outline of **Bodiam Castle**, nine miles north of Hastings (Feb–Oct daily 10am–6pm or dusk; Nov–Jan Sat & Sun 10.30am–4pm or dusk; £4.50; NT), would be the result: a classically stout square block with rounded corner turrets, battlements and a wide moat. When it was built in 1385 to guard what were the lower reaches of the River Rother, Bodiam was state-of-the-art military architecture, but during the

Civil War a company of Roundheads breached the fortress and removed its roof to reduce its effectiveness as a possible stronghold for the king. Over the next 250 years Bodiam fell into neglect until restoration in the last century by Lord Curzon. The original portcullis is still in place, while the extremely steep spiral staircases, leading to the crenellated battlements, will test all but the strongest of thighs. An absorbing fifteen-minute audiovisual film portrays medieval life in a castle.

You can get here from Hastings by regular bus #349, or, from May to September, from Tenterden, ten miles northeast, on a full-scale steam train run by the **Kent and East Sussex Railway** (℡01580/765155; £11 all day; Ⓦwww.kesr.org.uk). The best local option for **accommodation** and **food** is the *White Dog Inn* (℡01580/830264, Ⓦwww.the-white-dog-inn.co.uk; ➒), a quaint country pub a mile or so southeast of Bodiam, in the lovely village of Ewhurst Green.

Burwash and Bateman's

Fifteen miles northwest of Hastings on the A265, halfway to Tunbridge Wells, **BURWASH**, with its red-brick and weather-boarded cottages and Norman church tower, exemplifies the pastoral idyll of inland Sussex. Half a mile south of the village lies the main attraction, **Bateman's** (house: mid-March to Oct Mon–Wed, Sat & Sun 11am–5pm; £6.20; garden: early March Sat & Sun 11am–4pm, mid-March to Oct Mon–Wed, Sat & Sun 11am–5.30pm; Nov & Dec Wed–Sun 11am–4pm; garden free in Nov & Dec; NT), home of the Nobel Prize-winning writer and journalist **Rudyard Kipling** from 1902 until his death in 1936. Built by a local ironmaster in the seventeenth century and set amid attractive gardens, the house features a working watermill converted by Kipling to generate electricity, and which now grinds corn most Wednesdays and Saturdays at 2pm. Inside, the house is laid out as Kipling left it, with letters, early editions of his work and mementoes from his travels on display. Next to it, a garage houses the last of Kipling's Rolls-Royces, one of many that he owned during his lifetime, although he never actually drove them himself, preferring the services of a chauffeur. Getting here without your own transport involves a three-mile walk from Etchingham Station, which is served by regular trains from London and Hastings.

Eastbourne and around

Like so many of the southeast's seaside resorts, **EASTBOURNE** was kick-started into life in the 1840s, when the Brighton, Lewes and Hastings Rail Company built a branch line from Lewes to the sea, after which it was swiftly developed by the Seventh Duke of Devonshire, William Cavendish. Past holiday-makers include George Orwell, the composer Claude Debussy, who finished writing *La Mer* here, as well as Marx and Engels. Nowadays Eastbourne has a solid reputation as a retirement town, and its greatest draw is the nearby South Downs, which the sea has ground into a series of dramatic chalk cliffs around **Beachy Head**, just southwest of town (see box, p.204).

Conforming to tradition, the **pier** is the focal point of the elegant Grand Parade: opened in 1872, it was intended to match the best on the south coast, which it certainly does. To the west, on the promenade, the **Wish Tower** – whose name derives from an old Sussex word meaning "marsh" – is the first of the prom's two prominent red-brick Martello towers. The **Redoubt Fortress**,

The South Downs Way

Following the undulating crest of the South Downs, between the city of Winchester and the spectacular cliffs at Beachy Head, the **South Downs Way** rises and dips over eighty miles along the chalk uplands, offering the southeast's finest walks. If undertaken in its entirety, the bridle-path is best traversed from west to east, taking advantage of the prevailing wind, Eastbourne's better transport services and accommodation, and the psychological appeal of ending at the sea. **Steyning**, the halfway-point, marks a transition between predominantly wooded sections and more exposed chalk uplands – to the east of here you'll pass the modern **youth hostel** at Truleigh Hill (☎0870/770 6078, ✉truleigh@yha.org.uk; dorms £14; ●). Other hostels along the way are at Telscombe (see p.207) and at Alfriston (see p.205), where you can take a southern loop to Eastbourne along the cliffs of the Seven Sisters, and there's a bunkhouse at an old bothy (a small, stone-built outhouse) at Gumber Farm (☎01243/814484; closed Nov–Easter; £9), near Bignor Hill.

The OS Landranger **maps** #198 and #199 cover the eastern end of the route; you'll need #185 and #197 as well to cover the lot. Half a dozen guides are available, the best being by Kev Reynolds (written for following the route in either direction; published by Cicerone Press), or the more detailed guides by Paul Millmore (east–west; Aurum Press) and Jim Manthorpe (west–east; Trailblazer) – each is titled simply *South Downs Way*. You can also check the website ⓦwww.nationaltrail.co.uk/southdowns.

---

half a mile east of the pier, now houses a military museum (April to early Nov Tues–Sun 10am–5pm; £4).

A ten-minute walk northwest of the train station on High Street, Old Town, the **Towner Art Gallery and Museum** (Tues–Sat noon–5pm, Sun 2–5pm; free) displays a refreshingly contemporary range of work. In contrast, the **"How We Lived Then" Museum of Shops** at 20 Cornfield Terrace (daily 10am–5.30pm; £4), just down from the tourist office, contains a staggering amount of artefacts – old packages, coronation cups, toys – from the last hundred years of consumerism, all crammed into mock-up shops spread over several floors. A more serious attempt to tackle the history of the town is made at the **Eastbourne Heritage Centre** (April–Oct daily 2–5pm; £2), in a distinctive corner house opposite the Winter Gardens.

Practicalities

Eastbourne's **train station**, a splendid Italianate terminus, is ten minutes' walk from the seafront up Terminus Road, while the **bus station** is on Cavendish Place right by the pier. The **tourist office** is at 3 Cornfield Rd, just off Terminus Road (July to early Sept Mon–Fri 9.30am–5.30pm, Sat 9.30am–4.30pm, Sun 10am–1pm; mid-Sept to June closed Sun; ☎0871/663 0031, ⓦwww .visiteastbourne.com). The town's trackless **Dotto trains** ply up and down the sea front and into the centre (Easter to Oct daily 10.30am–5.30pm); a day ticket (£5.50) allows visitors to hop on or off at a series of designated stops.

There are hundreds of places to **stay**, including the cheap and cheerful *Sea Breeze Guest House*, 6 Marine Rd (☎01323/725440, ⓦwww .seabreezeguesthouse.co.uk; no credit cards; ●), a hundred yards from the sea, and *Sea Beach House Hotel*, 39–40 Marine Parade (☎01323/410458, ⓦwww .seabeachhouse.co.uk; ●), on the seafront. You can camp right by a sandy beach at the secluded *Bay View* **campsite** (☎01323/768688, ⓦwww.bay-view.co.uk; closed late Oct to March), off the A259 east to Pevensey.

The best **restaurant** is the *Café Belge* on the seafront at 11–23 Grand Parade, serving decent *moules et frites* and snack lunches. Otherwise, there's a concentration of moderately priced places in the Terminus Road area, between the train station and the sea, including the Italian *Mediterraneo* at no. 72 (℡01323/736994; closed Sun eve). For huge ice-cream sundaes, go to *Fusciardi's* on Marine Parade.

The best **pubs** are some distance from the seafront: the *Hurst Arms* at 76 Willingdon Rd, a ten-minute walk inland from the station up Upperton Road, has Harvey's locally brewed beers on tap, as does the *Lamb*, a slightly over-enthusiastic but very pleasant traditional English inn situated in the nearby High Street.

Beachy Head, Seven Sisters and the Cuckmere

A short walk west from Eastbourne takes you out along the most dramatic stretch of coastline in Sussex, where the chalk uplands of the Sussex Downs are cut by the sea into a sequence of splendid cliffs. The most spectacular of all, **Beachy Head**, is 575ft high, with a diminutive-looking lighthouse, but no beach – the headland's name derives from the French *beau chef* meaning "beautiful head". The beauty certainly went to Friedrich Engels' head; he insisted his ashes be scattered here, and depressed individuals regularly try to join him by leaping to their doom from this well-known suicide spot. An open-top bus runs every thirty minutes (late April to Oct; £7; ⓦwww.city-sightseeing.co.uk) from Eastbourne Pier to the top of Beachy Head.

West of the headland the scenery softens into a diminishing series of cliffs, a landmark known as the **Seven Sisters**. The eponymous country park provides some of the most impressive walks in the county, taking in the cliff-top path and the lower valley of the meandering River Cuckmere, into which the Seven Sisters subside. On the opposite bank of the river in **ALFRISTON** is the fourteenth-century timber-framed and thatched **Clergy House** (early March Sat & Sun 11am–4pm; mid-March to late Dec Mon, Wed, Thurs, Sat & Sun 10am/11am–4/5pm; £3.60; NT), the first property to be acquired by the National Trust in 1896. Less edifying, but potentially more fun, a mile or so up the valley, is **Drusillas Park** (daily 10am–4/5pm; £12.95), where visitors can view penguins and meerkats, milk a cow, touch snakes, and lark about on the adventure playground and miniature railway.

Local **accommodation** includes the *Birling Gap Hotel* (℡01323/423197; ⓦwww.birlinggaphotel.co.uk; ❹), a Victorian villa overlooking the dramatic cliffs between Seven Sisters and Beachy Head, and the Frog Firle **youth hostel** (℡0870/770 5666, ⓔalfriston@yha.org.uk; dorm bed £13.75), in a traditional Sussex flint building a couple of miles south of Alfriston, wonderfully set in the Cuckmere Valley.

Lewes and around

East Sussex's county town, **LEWES** straddles the River Ouse as it carves a gap through the South Downs on its final stretch to the sea. Though there's been some rebuilding in the riverside Cliffe area (the place where Lewes started), and new housing estates are spreading from the town's fringes, the core of Lewes remains remarkably good-looking: Georgian and crooked older dwellings still line the High Street, with narrow lanes – or "Twittens" – leading off it and its continuations, with views onto the Downs. With some of England's most appealing chalkland right on its doorstep, numerous traces of a history that stretches back to the Saxons, and one of the houses most closely associated with the Bloomsbury group – **Charleston** – close by, Lewes is a worthwhile stopover on any tour of the southeast – and an easy one, with good rail connections with London and along the coast.

The Town

The best way to begin a tour of the town from the train station is to walk up Station Road, then left down the High Street. Lewes's **castle** (Tues–Sat 10am–5.30pm, Mon & Sun 11am–5.30pm; closed Mon in Jan; winter closes at dusk; £4.70) is hidden from view behind the houses on your right. Inside the castle complex – unusual for being built on two mottes, or mounds – the shell of the eleventh-century keep remains, and both the towers can be climbed for excellent views over the town to the surrounding Downs. Tickets for the castle include admission to the **museum** (same hours as castle), by the castle entrance, holding a collection of archeological artefacts and a town model, among other items.

A few minutes' walk further west along the High Street, past St Michael's Church with its unusual twin towers, one wooden and the other flint, brings you to the steep cobbled and much photographed **Keere Street**, down which the reckless Prince Regent is alleged to have driven his carriage. Keere Street leads to **Southover Grange** (daily dawn–dusk; free), with its lovely gardens. Built in 1572 from the priory's remains, the Grange was also the childhood home of the diarist John Evelyn and now houses the local Registry Office. Past the gardens, a right turn down Southover High Street leads to the Tudor-built **Anne of Cleves House** (Tues–Sat 10am–5pm; also March–Oct Mon & Sun 11am–5pm; £3.50, combined ticket with the castle £7), given to her in

---

The bonfire societies

Each November 5, while the rest of Britain lights small domestic bonfires or attends municipal firework displays to commemorate the 1605 foiled Catholic plot to blow up the Houses of Parliament (see p.94), Lewes puts on a more dramatic show, whose origins lie in the deaths of the town's Protestant martyrs in 1556. By the end of the eighteenth century, Lewes' **Bonfire Boys** had become notorious for the boisterousness of their anti-Catholic demonstrations, in which they set off fireworks indiscriminately and dragged rolling tar barrels through the streets – a tradition still practised today, although with a little more caution. In 1845 events came to a head when the incorrigible pyromaniacs of Lewes had to be read the Riot Act, instigating a night of violence between the police and Bonfire Boys. Lewes' first **bonfire societies** were established soon afterwards, to try to get a bit more discipline into the proceedings, and in the early part of the last century they were persuaded to move their street fires to the town's perimeters.

Today's tightly-knit bonfire societies, each with its quasi-militaristic motto ("Death or Glory", "True to Each Other", etc), spend much of the year organizing the Bonfire Night shenanigans, when their members dress up in traditional costumes and parade through the town carrying flaming torches, before marching off onto the Downs for their society's big fire. At each of the fires, effigies of Guy Fawkes and the pope are burned alongside contemporary, but equally reviled, figures – politicians are popular choices.

settlement after her divorce from Henry VIII – though she never actually lived here. The magnificent oak-beamed Tudor bedroom is impressive, with a 400-year-old Flemish four-poster and a cumbersome "bed wagon", a bed-warming brazier which would fail the slackest of fire regulations.

Heading east down the High Street, off Fisher Street, the **Star Gallery** (Mon–Sat 11am–5.30pm; free) displays the creative talents of a collective of artists, bookbinders, carpenters and other artisans. At the east end of the High Street, School Hill descends towards **Cliffe Bridge**, built in 1727 and the entrance to the commercial centre of the medieval settlement. For the energetic, a path leads up onto the Downs from the end of Cliffe High Street, passing close to an obelisk that commemorates the Lewes Martyrs, seventeen Protestants who were burned here in 1556 at the height of Mary Tudor's militant revival of Catholicism.

Practicalities

The **train station** is south of High Street down Station Road, while the **bus station** is on Eastgate Street, near the foot of School Hill. At the junction of the High Street and Fisher Street, the **tourist office** (Mon–Fri 9am–5pm, Sat 10am–2/5pm, Sun 10am–2pm; Oct–March Mon–Fri 9am–5pm, Sat 10am–2pm; closed Sun; ℡01273/483448, Ⓦwww.lewes.gov.uk) provides free copies of the monthly **listings magazine**, *Lewes News*

For **accommodation**, *Castle Banks Cottage*, 4 Castle Banks (℡01273/476291, Ⓦwww.castlebankscottage.co.uk; no credit cards; ❸), is a beamed period house with great views and a small breakfast garden, tucked away off West Street, or try the *Crown Inn*, 191 High St, close to the tourist office (℡01273/480670, Ⓦwww.crowninn-lewes.co.uk; ❶). The nearest **youth hostel** is in the village of Telscombe, six miles south of Lewes (℡0870/770 6062; dorm bed £11; bus #123 from Lewes), with simple accommodation in two-hundred-year-old cottages; there's another hostel, a rustic wooden cabin with basic facilities, eleven miles northeast of town at Blackboys, near Uckfield (℡0870/770 6062; dorm bed £12; ❶).

Lewes is the home of the excellent Harvey's brewery and most of the **pubs** serve its beer – try the *Brewers' Arms*, opposite St John the Baptist church, or the *Lewes Arms* tucked behind the Star Gallery. The lively *Snowdrop Inn* on the outskirts of town at 119 South St also serves excellent **food** including vegetarian and vegan dishes. Other inexpensive alternatives include the Indian *Dilraj*, 12 Fisher St (℡01273/479279). Pricier, upmarket and eclectic contemporary food can be found at ⚘ *Circa*, a stylish brasserie on St Andrews Lane, off the High Street (℡01273/471333).

The annual **Glyndebourne** opera season (see the *Festivals and events* colour section) runs from mid-May until the end of August, with performances held at the opera house at Glynde, three miles east of town. It's expensive and exclusive, though there are tickets available at reduced prices for dress rehearsals or for standing-room-only; call ℡01273/813813 for details or check the website at Ⓦwww.glyndebourne.com.

Charleston Farmhouse

Six miles east of Lewes, off the A27, **Charleston Farmhouse** (March–Oct Thurs, Fri, Sun & public hols 2–6pm, Wed & Sat 11.30am–6pm; July & Aug also Thurs & Fri opens 11.30am; £6.50; guided tours Wed–Sat; last entry 5pm) was home to Virginia Woolf's sister Vanessa Bell, Vanessa's husband, Clive Bell, and her lover, Duncan Grant. As conscientious objectors, the trio moved here during World War I so that the men could work on local farms (farm labourers were exempted from military service). The farmhouse became a gathering point for other members of the Bloomsbury Group, including the biographer Lytton Strachey, the economist John Maynard Keynes and the novelist E.M. Forster. Duncan Grant continued to live in the house until his death in 1978.

Unless it's a Sunday, you have to join a fifty-minute guided tour in order to view the interior of the farmhouse, where almost every surface is decorated and the walls are hung with paintings by Picasso, Renoir and Augustus John, alongside the work of the markedly less talented residents. Many of the fabrics, lampshades and other artefacts bear the unmistakable mark of the Omega Workshop, the Bloomsbury equivalent of William Morris's artistic movement.

Brighton

Recorded as the tiny fishing village of Brithelmeston in the Domesday Book, **BRIGHTON** seems to have slipped unnoticed through history until the mid-eighteenth-century sea-bathing trend established it as a resort; it hasn't looked back since. The fad received royal approval in the 1780s when the decadent Prince of Wales (the future George IV) began patronizing the town in the company of his mistress, thus setting a precedent for the "dirty weekend", Brighton's major contribution to the English collective consciousness. Trying to shake off this blowsy reputation, Brighton now highlights its Georgian charm, its upmarket shops and classy restaurants, and a thriving conference industry. Yet, however much it tries to present itself as a comfortable middle-class town (granted city status in 2000), the essence of Brighton's appeal is its faintly bohemian vitality, a buzz that comes from a mix of English holiday-makers, thousands of young foreign students from the town's innumerable language schools, a thriving gay community and an energetic local student population from the art college and two universities.

Arrival and information

Brighton **train station** is at the head of Queen's Road, which descends to the Clock Tower, where it becomes West Street before continuing to the seafront – a distance of about half a mile. National Express and Southdown **bus services** arrive at Pool Valley **bus station**, tucked just in from the seafront on the south side of the Old Steine. Open-top **bus tours** (April–Oct; £6.50) operate on a circular route around the town and up and down the sea front, passing both the train station and tourist office – tickets are valid all day. If you're coming by car, make use of the car parks; vouchers, available from the tourist office and newsagents, are required for on-street parking in the centre.

The **tourist office** is opposite the Royal Pavilion at 4–5 Pavilion Buildings (daily 9.30am–5pm; ☎0906/711 2255, ⓦwww.visitbrighton.com).

Accommodation

You'll find most budget **accommodation** clustered around the **Kemp Town** district, to the east of the Palace Pier, with the more elegant and expensive hotels west of the town centre around Regency Square, opposite the West Pier. Many places offer reductions for stays of two nights or more and at weekends there's often a two-night stay minimum required. Brighton's official **campsite** is the *Sheepcote Valley* site (℡01273/626546), just north of Brighton Marina; take bus #1 or #1a to Wilsons Avenue, or take the Volks railway (see p.213) and walk up Arundel Road to Wilsons Avenue; book early as it's popular.

Hotels, B&Bs and guest houses

Adelaide 51 Regency Square ℡01273/205286, Ⓦwww.adelaidehotel.co.uk. Top-notch guest house on five floors (no lift) in the fancier part of town. Some rooms have sea views. Veggies and vegans catered for. ④

Ainsley House 28 New Steine ℡01273/605310, Ⓦwww.ainsleyhotel.com. Friendly, rather old-fashioned place in an attractive Regency terrace. ⑤

Cavalaire House 34 Upper Rock Gardens ℡01273/696899, Ⓦwww.cavalaire.co.uk. Victorian building, just off Marine Parade, with contemporary fittings, including iron beds. Triples and quads available. Room 9 has a sea view. ⑤

Hotel du Vin Ship St ℡01273/718588, Ⓦwww.hotelduvin.com. A Gothic Revival building in a contemporary style, luxuriously furnished in subtle seaside colours, with an excellent bar and bistro. ⑦

Legends 31–34 Marine Parade ℡01273/624462, Ⓦwww.legendsbrighton.com. Large, buzzing, gay hotel on the seafront, with late bar for residents and their guests and regular cabaret nights. ④

Lichfield House 30 Waterloo St ℡01273/777740, Ⓦwww.fieldhousehotels.co.uk. Stylish and colour-fully furnished town house with Wi-Fi-enabled rooms, with or without private bathrooms. ④

Pelirocco 10 Regency Square ℡01273/327055, Ⓦwww.hotelpelirocco.co.uk. Self-styled rock'n'roll hangout with extravagantly themed rooms, a bohemian atmosphere and a late-opening bar. ⑤

Sea Spray 25 New Steine ℡01273/680332, Ⓦwww.seaspraybrighton.co.uk. Boutique hotel with themed rooms, from Warhol to boudoir, at varying prices. Breakfast in bed is provided, with veggie and vegan options. ⑤

The Twenty One 21 Charlotte St, off Marine Parade ℡01273/686450, Ⓦwww.thetwentyone .co.uk. Classy Kemp Town B&B in an ornate, early Victorian house where the comfortable rooms have fridges. ⑤

Urban House 20–21 New Steine ℡01273/688085, Ⓦwww.urbanhouse.uk .com. Plusher than average choice in New Steine, with sleek, modern rooms fitted with flat screen TVs and Wi-Fi. A relaxation centre complete with sauna and steam room is available to guests. ⑥

Westbourne 46 Upper Rock Gardens ℡01273/686920, Ⓦwww.westbournehotel.co.uk. Well-appointed, traditional B&B close to the seafront and all amenities. Limited parking. ⑤

Hostels

Baggies Backpackers 33 Oriental Place ℡01273/733740. Spacious house a little west of the West Pier with private rooms and large bright dorms (starting at £13 a night), decent showers and plenty of room to spread out. No credit cards. ①

The Grapevine 29–30 North Rd ℡01273/703985, Ⓦwww.grapevinewebsite.co.uk. Friendly, modern hostel in the heart of the North Laine area, with Internet access and free bike and luggage storage. There's another *Grapevine* on the seafront, geared towards stag and hen parties. No credit cards. Dorm beds from £15. ①

The City

Any visit to Brighton inevitably begins with a visit to its two most famous landmarks – the exuberant **Royal Pavilion** and the wonderfully tacky **Palace Pier**, a few minutes away – followed by a stroll along the seafront promenade or the pebbly beach. Just as interesting, though, is an exploration of Brighton's pedestrianized **Lanes**, where some of the town's diverse restaurants, bars and tiny bric-à-brac, jewellery and antique shops can be found, or an idle meander through the quaint, but more bohemian streets of **North Laine**.

The Royal Pavilion and the Brighton Museum

In any survey to find England's most loved building, there's always a bucketful of votes for Brighton's exotic extravaganza, the **Royal Pavilion** (daily 9.30/10am–5.15/5.45pm; last entry 45min before closing; £7.70), which flaunts itself in the middle of the Old Steine, the main thoroughfare along

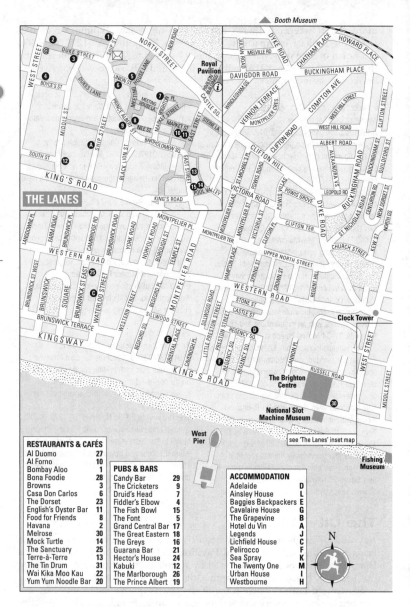

RESTAURANTS & CAFÉS

Al Duomo	27
Al Forno	10
Bombay Aloo	1
Bona Foodie	28
Browns	3
Casa Don Carlos	6
The Dorset	23
English's Oyster Bar	11
Food for Friends	8
Havana	2
Melrose	30
Mock Turtle	14
The Sanctuary	25
Terre-à-Terre	13
The Tin Drum	31
Wai Kika Moo Kau	22
Yum Yum Noodle Bar	20

PUBS & BARS

Candy Bar	29
The Cricketers	9
Druid's Head	7
Fiddler's Elbow	4
The Fish Bowl	15
The Font	5
Grand Central Bar	17
The Great Eastern	18
The Greys	16
Guarana Bar	21
Hector's House	24
Kabuki	12
The Marlborough	26
The Prince Albert	19

ACCOMMODATION

Adelaide	D
Ainsley House	L
Baggies Backpackers	E
Cavalaire House	G
The Grapevine	B
Hotel du Vin	A
Legends	J
Lichfield House	C
Pelirocco	F
Sea Spray	K
The Twenty One	M
Urban House	I
Westbourne	H

which most of the seafront-bound road traffic gets funnelled. Until 1787, the building that stood here was a well-appointed but conventional farmhouse, which was first rented by the fun-loving Prince of Wales in the previous year. He then commissioned its conversion into something more regal, and for a couple of decades the prince's south-coast pied-à-terre was a Palladian villa, with mildly Oriental embellishments.

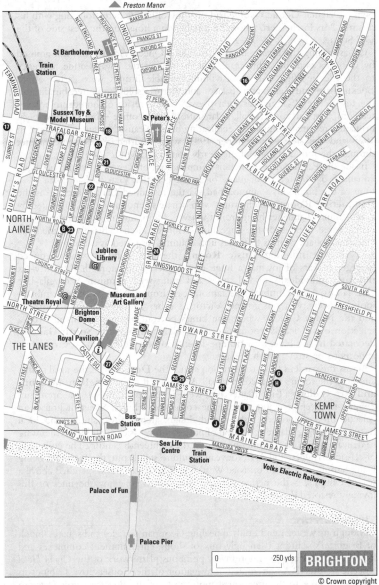

© Crown copyright

Upon becoming Prince Regent, however, George was fully able to indulge his taste for excess, and in 1815 his patronage fell upon John Nash, architect of London's Regent Street. What Nash came up with was an extraordinary confection of slender minarets, twirling domes, pagodas, balconies and miscellaneous motifs imported from India and China, all supported on an innovative cast-iron frame, creating an exterior profile that defines a genre of its own – Oriental-Gothic. George had the time of his life here, frolicking with his mistress, Mrs Fitzherbert, whom he installed in a house on the west side of the Old Steine.

On ascending the throne in 1837 the dour Queen Victoria was not amused by George's taste in architecture, and she shifted the royal seaside residence to the Isle of Wight. All the Pavilion's valuable fittings were carted off to Buckingham and Kensington palaces and Victoria sold the gutted building to the town. The Pavilion was then pressed into a series of humdrum roles – tearoom, hospital, concert hall, radar station, ration office – but has now been brilliantly restored, completely eradicating damage caused by an arson attack in 1975 and the storm in October 1987, which hurled a dislodged minaret through the roof and floor of the nearly completed Music Room.

Inside the Pavilion the exuberant compendium of Regency exotica has been enhanced by the return of many of the objects that Victoria had taken away. One of the highlights – approached via the restrained Long Gallery – is the **Banqueting Room**, which erupts with ornate splendour and is dominated by a one-tonne chandelier hung from the jaws of a massive dragon cowering in a plantain tree. Next door, the huge, high-ceilinged kitchen, fitted with the most modern appliances of its time, has iron columns disguised as palm trees.

Nearby, the stunning **Music Room**, the first sight of which reduced George to tears of joy, has a huge dome lined with more than twenty-six thousand individually gilded scales and hung with exquisite umbrella-like glass lamps. After climbing the famous cast-iron staircase with its bamboo-look banisters, you can go into Victoria's sober and seldom-used bedroom and the North Gallery where the king's portrait hangs, accompanied by a selection of satirical cartoons. More notable, though, is the **South Gallery**, decorated in sky blue with trompe-l'oeil bamboo trellises and a carpet that appears to be strewn with flowers.

Across the gardens from the Pavilion stands the **Dome**, once the royal stables and now the town's main concert hall. Adjoining it is the **Brighton Museum and Art Gallery** (Tues 10am–7pm, Wed–Sat & public hols 10am–5pm, Sun 2–5pm; free), entered just around the corner on Church Street. It houses an eclectic mix of modern fashion and design, archeology, painting and local history, including a large collection of pottery from basic Neolithic earthenware to delicate porcelain figurines popular in the eighteenth century. The collection of classic Art Deco and Art Nouveau furniture stands out, the highlight being Dalí's famous sofa based on Mae West's lips. The *Balcony Café*, perched above a sea of exhibits, is the perfect setting from which to enjoy the lines of this lovingly restored Victorian building.

The seafront

Although its western end holds appealing Georgian terraces and squares, much of Brighton's seafront is an ugly mix of shops, entertainment complexes and hotels, ranging from the impressively pompous plasterwork of the *Grand Hotel* – scene of the IRA's attempted assassination of the Conservative Cabinet in October 1984 – to the green-glass monstrosity of the *Brighton Thistle Hotel*. To appreciate fully the tackier side of Brighton, take a stroll along the **Palace Pier**. Completed in 1899, its every inch is devoted to fun and money-making, from the cacophonous Palace of Fun and the Pleasure Dome to the state-of-the-art video games and the fairground rides and karaoke sessions at the end of the pier. Brighton's architecturally superior **West Pier**, built in 1866 half a mile west along the seafront, was damaged in World War II and then fell into disrepair, suffering partial collapse in 2002 and two separate fires in 2003, followed by further collapse. Heroically dedicated to restoring the ruin to its former glory, the West Pier Trust has announced plans to fund what amounts to a total reconstruction by erecting a "vertical pier", or viewing mast, 183m tall, known as the i360 and scheduled to open in 2009 – though this may end up by replacing the pier altogether.

Underneath the arches between the Palace and West piers, there are two small museums: the **National Museum of Penny Slot Machines** (Easter–Oct Sat, Sun & school hols 11am–6pm; free) houses decrepit antique slot machines which struggle to function; while the **Brighton Fishing Museum** (daily 9am–5pm; free), displays old photos and video footage of the golden days of the local fishing industry and houses a large Sussex clinker, once a common boat on Brighton beach.

Across the road from the Palace Pier, on Marine Parade, the **Sea Life Centre** (daily 10am–5pm; last entry 4pm; £12.95) is one of the best marine life displays of its kind, with a transparent tunnel passing through a huge aquarium – a walk along the bottom of the sea with sharks and rays gliding overhead. Nearby, the antiquated locomotives of **Volk's Electric Railway** (Easter to mid-Sept Mon–Fri 10am–5pm, Sat & Sun 10am–6pm; £2.50 return) – the first electric train in the country – run eastward towards the Marina and the nudist beach, usually the preserve of just a few thick-skinned souls.

The Lanes and North Laine

Tucked between the Pavilion and the seafront is a warren of narrow, pedestrianized thoroughfares known as **the Lanes** – the core of the old fishing village from which Brighton evolved. Long-established antiques shops, designer outlets and several bars, pubs and restaurants generate a lively and intimate atmosphere in this part of town. **North Laine** – "laine" was the local term for a strip of land – which spreads north of North Street along Kensington, Sydney, Gardner and Bond streets, is more bohemian with its hub along pedestrianized Kensington Gardens. Here the shops are more eclectic, selling secondhand records, clothes, bric-à-brac and New Age objects, and mingle with earthy coffee shops and downbeat cafés. Slightly to the north of here is the **Sussex Toy and Model Museum** (Tues–Fri 10am–5pm, Sat 11am–5pm; last entry 1hr before closing; £3.50), housed in an old stables beneath the train station. The collection is impressive, ranging from an entire cabinet of Smurfs to a set of Pelham puppets, but it's the working model railways that attract most children's attention.

Jubilee Library

Off North Road on Jubilee Street, the **Jubilee Library** (℡01273/290800; Mon & Tues 10am–7pm; Wed & Fri 10am–2pm; Thurs 10am–8pm; Sat 10am–4pm), opened in 2005, has become an icon of Brighton's new metropolitan image. With its generous glass front and a lofty interior adorned with modern sculptures and state-of-the-art technology, the building claims to be one of the most energy-efficient in the country, pleasing eco- and architecture enthusiasts alike. The library includes a collection of rare books spanning six centuries, and there's unlimited free **Internet** access.

St Bartholomew's, Booth Museum and Preston Manor

Towering above Anne Street, just east of the train station, **St Bartholomew's** (daily 10am–4.30pm), one of the biggest brick churches in Europe, deserves a brief inspection. Known locally as the Ark, it was completed in 1894; undivided

▲ The Lanes, Brighton

by side aisles or chancel, the soaring nave contains a 45-foot-high marble baldacchino, dazzling figurative mosaics and intricate Art Nouveau metalwork.

A pair of sights in Brighton's northern suburbs also merit a detour. The big municipal museum, the **Booth Museum of Natural History** (Mon–Sat 10am–5pm, Sun 2–5pm; free), lies a mile up Dyke Road from the centre of town (bus #27, #27A or #27B). Purpose-built to house Mr E.T. Booth's prodigious collection of stuffed birds, this is a wonderfully fusty old Victorian museum with beetles, butterflies and animal skeletons galore, but which also displays very imaginative temporary shows.

Two miles north of Brighton on the A23 – but only a short walk from Preston Park train station – the delightful **Preston Manor** (April–Oct Tues–Sat 10am–5pm, Sun 2–5pm; £3.30) was originally built in 1250, though the present building dates from 1738 and 1905. Its series of period interiors engagingly evokes the life of the Edwardian gentry, from the servants' quarters downstairs to the luxury nursery upstairs.

Eating, drinking and nightlife

Brighton has the greatest concentration of **restaurants** anywhere in the southeast, outside London. Around North Laine are some wonderful, inexpensive **cafés**, while for classier establishments head to the Lanes and out towards neighbouring Hove. Many of the cheaper places fight hard to attract the large student market with discounted deals of around ten percent, so if you have student ID, use it.

Nightlife is hectic and compulsively pursued throughout the year, making Brighton unique in the sedate southeast. As well as the mainstream **theatre** and **concert** venues, there are myriad **clubs**, lots of **live music** and plenty of cinemas. Midweek entry into the clubs can cost less than a fiver, and cinema seats are similarly priced before 6pm. Many pubs are open until at least midnight, while clubs are open until around 4am (often all night at weekends).

Every May the three-week-long **Brighton Festival** (℡01273/709709, Ⓦwww.brightonfestival.org) takes over various venues around town. This arty celebration includes funfairs, exhibitions, street theatre and concerts from classical to jazz. Running at the same time is the **Brighton and Hove Fringe Festival** (℡01273/709709, Ⓦwww.brightonfestivalfringe.org.uk), which also stages live music and drama, literature readings and tons of club nights.

Brighton has one of the longest established and most thriving **gay communities** in Britain, with a variety of lively clubs and bars drawing people from all over the southeast. It also hosts a number of gay events including the annual **Gay Pride Festival**, held over two weeks at the beginning of July. It's a great excuse for a party with loads going on from performing arts to exhibitions, not to mention the **Brighton Parade**, a day-and-night-long jamboree. For details check out Ⓦwww.gay.brighton.co.uk.

For up-to-date information, pick up the free monthly **listings** magazine *Insight* (Ⓦwww.theinsight.co.uk) from the tourist office. Other similar magazines such as *What's On, Source, This is Brighton* and *3Sixty*, which covers gay events, can be found in various cafés and bars around the city. Also check out the **websites** Ⓦwww.brighton.co.uk, Ⓦwhatson.brighton.co.uk and Ⓦmagazine.brighton.co.uk.

Cafés

Bona Foodie 21 St James's St, Kemp Town. Delicatessen with colourful, cosy café at the back, serving excellent baguettes; choose from the speciality pâtés and cheeses. Come early for lunch.

The Dorset corner of Gardner St and North Rd. Bar, café and restaurant rolled into one, with delicious French vegetarian dishes. They also do real-cream teas.

Mock Turtle 4 Pool Valley. Old-fashioned teashop crammed with bric-à-brac and inexpensive home-made cakes. Closed Mon.

The Sanctuary 51–55 Brunswick St East, Hove ℡01273/770002. Arty vegetarian café with a cosy, relaxed ambience, and there's a cellar performance venue. Deservedly popular, despite its not-very-central location. Open till 11pm.

Restaurants

Al Duomo 7 Pavilion Buildings ℡01273/326741. Brilliant pizzeria, with a genuine wood-burning oven. There's a more intimate sister restaurant, *Al Forno*, at 36 East St (℡01273/324905). Inexpensive.

Bombay Aloo 39 Ship St ☎01273/776038. No flock wallpaper and an all-you-can-eat veggie buffet for a fiver – what more could you ask? Inexpensive.

Browns 3–4 Duke St ☎01273/323501. A mixture of meat, seafood and pasta dishes as well as traditional favourites like Guinness-marinated steak-and-mushroom pie, served in a sophisticated Continental setting. Moderate.

Casa Don Carlos 5 Union St ☎01273/327177. Small, long-established tapas bar in the Lanes with outdoor seating and daily specials. Also serves more substantial Spanish dishes and drinks. Inexpensive.

English's Oyster Bar 29–31 East St ☎01273/327980. Three fishermen's cottages knocked together to house a marble and brass oyster bar and a red velvet dining room. Seafood's the speciality with a mouth-watering menu and better value than you might expect, especially the set menus. Expensive.

Food for Friends 18 Prince Albert St ☎01273/202310. Brighton's ever-popular wholefood veggie eatery is imaginative enough to please die-hard meat-eaters too. It's usually busy, but well worth the squeeze. Moderate.

Havana 32 Duke St ☎01273/773388. Very stylish Continental brasserie with just a hint of colonial ambience – palms and rattan chairs – to evoke tropical luxury and a feeling of being pampered. The menu is French influenced – the lunchtime deal is particularly good value. Expensive.

Melrose 132 King's Rd ☎01273/326520. Traditional seafront establishment that has been serving seafood, roasts and custard-covered puddings for over forty years. The next door *Regency Restaurant* is smaller and similar. Inexpensive.

Terre-à-Terre 71 East St ☎01273/729051. Original, if sometimes over-imaginative global veggie cuisine in a modern arty setting. Closed Mon lunch. Moderate–expensive.

The Tin Drum 43 St James's St ☎01273/777575. Buzzing Continental-style café-bar and restaurant with a taste for Baltic-rim cooking and a blend of Eastern European influences; fresh seasonal ingredients and speciality vodkas. One of four around the city, similarly styled. Moderate.

Wai Kika Moo Kau 11 Kensington Gardens ☎01273/671117. Global veggie café/ restaurant, very popular, with award-winning veggie burgers among more eclectic choices – all for around £5. Inexpensive.

Yum Yum Noodle Bar 22–23 Sydney St ☎01273/606777. Lunch-only place serving anything Southeast Asian – Chinese, Thai, Indonesian and Malaysian – at good-value prices. Located above a Chinese supermarket. Inexpensive.

Pubs and bars

Candy Bar 129 St James's St. Stylish lesbian hangout on two floors. Gay or straight men are welcomed as guests.

The Cricketers 15 Black Lion St. Just west of the Lanes, this is Brighton's oldest pub and it looks it too; very popular with good daytime grub served in the pleasant setting of its courtyard bar.

Druid's Head 9 Brighton Place. Great old pub in the heart of the Lanes with a flagstone floor and local art on the walls.

Fiddler's Elbow 11 Boyce's St ☎01273/325850. Irish pub with traditional music on Wed & Thurs nights.

The Fish Bowl 74 East St ☎01273/777505. A popular pre-club choice for its range of music (DJs four nights a weeks plus a live acoustic night), which is sometimes better than at the clubs themselves. Also a relaxing spot during the day, when there's a good, inexpensive menu.

The Font Union St ☎01273/747727. Spacious converted chapel with a bar in place of the altar and occasional live music.

Grand Central Bar 29–30 Surrey St ☎01273/329086. Cool, light and comfy bar opposite the station. Exemplary, well-priced breakfasts and snacks; live jazz and funk at weekends and a theatre upstairs.

The Great Eastern 103 Trafalgar St. Small and mellow pub with bare boards and bookshelves, lots of real ales and malt whiskies, and no fruit machines or TV.

The Greys 105 Southover St ☎01273/680734, ⓦwww.greyspub.com. Old-fashioned pub with an open fire, stone floors and wooden benches, plus good menu and Belgian beers. Frequent live bands.

Guarana Bar 36 Sydney St. Brazilian-style daytime bar in the North Laine quarter serving herbal cocktails and shakes made with guarana (extract of Amazonian vine).

Hector's House 52 Grand Parade ☎01273/681228. Big bare-boards-and-sofa student pub that has nightly pre-club music (except Mon) with in-house DJs and occasional live bands.

Kabuki 8–12 Middle St. Designer-cool Pacific-rim bar with DJs spinning R&B and hip-hop.

The Marlborough 4 Princes St ☎01273/570028. Friendly pub with good food, just off Old Steine, popular with a lesbian and student crowd. The small theatre upstairs hosts readings and other performances.

The Prince Albert 48 Trafalgar St ☎01273/730499. A listed building, right by the

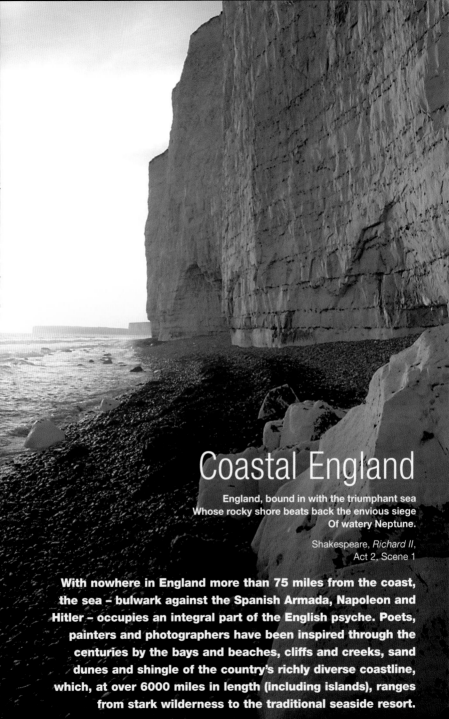

Coastal England

England, bound in with the triumphant sea
Whose rocky shore beats back the envious siege
Of watery Neptune.

Shakespeare, *Richard II*,
Act 2, Scene 1

With nowhere in England more than 75 miles from the coast,
the sea – bulwark against the Spanish Armada, Napoleon and
Hitler – occupies an integral part of the English psyche. Poets,
painters and photographers have been inspired through the
centuries by the bays and beaches, cliffs and creeks, sand
dunes and shingle of the country's richly diverse coastline,
which, at over 6000 miles in length (including islands), ranges
from stark wilderness to the traditional seaside resort.

Par Beach ▲
Holkham Bay ▼

Blackpool ▼

Beaches

Although rarely mentioned in the same breath as the sun-baked sands of the Mediterranean or Caribbean seas, England's beaches can compare with the best of them in terms of sheer natural beauty. For a combination of decent climate and good sand, the **southwest** of the country is hard to beat, especially the coasts of Cornwall and Devon. The beaches of England's **southern coast** are less appealing for lounging, becoming more pebbly as you approach the southeastern corner of the country, while the low cliffs and gravel beaches of **East Anglia**'s shoreline give way to a string of wide sandy beaches between Cromer and Hunstanton. There are spectacular swathes of wild strands in the **northeast**, notably around Scarborough in Yorkshire and in Northumberland, though here the stiff North Sea breezes may require a degree of stoicism.

England's beaches have seen a great improvement in recent years and are generally as **clean** as any in Europe, with

Top five beaches

▸▸ **Par Beach**, St Martin's, Isles of Scilly. Hugely scenic and usually empty, despite the perfect sands. See p.447

▸▸ **Bamburgh**, Northumberland. Sky, sea, dunes and acres of sand, with a dramatic castle backdrop. See p.913

▸▸ **Porthcurno**, West Cornwall. Surrounded by cliffs, with an open-air theatre nearby. See p.445

▸▸ **Holkham**, Norfolk. Beyond the pines and dunes lie three miles of pancake-flat sands. See p.509

▸▸ **Blackpool**, Lancashire. England's biggest resort has seven miles of clean beach, plus donkeys, trams and amusements. See p.698

the best being awarded the prestigious Blue Flag award (the Seaside Award is slightly less demanding). For annually updated, detailed information on the condition of England's beaches, the definitive source is the *Good Beach Guide*, compiled by the Marine Conservation Society (Wwww.goodbeachguide.co.uk).

Coastal paths

The cliffs and gently undulating slopes of England's coastline invite anything from a brief leisurely stroll to a vigorous long-distance hike. In the southeast, invigorating excursions can be made over the lovely **Seven Sisters** cliffs around Eastbourne, and over the iconic **white cliffs of Dover**. But almost every stretch of English coast is walkable, and mostly waymarked – check out the **Norfolk Coast Path** or the **Cleveland Way** along the Yorkshire coast (for both see Wwww.nationaltrail.co.uk), or the 630-mile **South West Coast Path** (Wwww.southwestcoastpath.com), Britain's longest National Trail, which extends from Minehead in Somerset around the peninsula to Poole in Dorset, taking in some of the country's wildest and most picturesque scenery along the way.

Seaside resorts

At the height of summer England's seaside resorts can be an assault on the senses, with the piercing screech of gulls, the ubiquitous smell of takeaway fish and chips, and rows of saucy postcards and lobster-red flesh at every turn. Out of season, however, they often relapse into a sleepy inertia, though some, like **Brighton** in the southeast, have a strong independent identity and are always busy. In the northwest, **Blackpool** is the brilliant apotheosis of the genre

▲ Beachy Head
▼ South West Coast Path

Brighton beach ▲
Blakeney Point ▼

– riotously full-on, glamorous and tawdry all at once. Both of these towns have that quintessential characteristic of English seaside resorts – a pier overloaded with gaudy amusements. Other resorts have various mixes of the same basic ingredients, usually blended with varying degrees of old-fashioned gentility: **Scarborough** (Yorkshire), said to be the country's oldest resort; **Margate** (Kent), tacky but fun; Suffolk's **Aldeburgh** and **Southwold**, where elegance is the keynote; and, on the south coast, **Bournemouth** (Dorset) and **Torquay** (Devon), both genteel and sedate by day, but with an energetic clubbing scene pulling in the punters by night. Aside from the sticks of rock to suck, the requisite ingredients of the best English resorts are rollicking fairgrounds, donkey rides, Punch and Judy puppet shows, and strips of sand with space for paddling in rockpools and building sandcastles. Pull up a deckchair, roll up your trousers, and soak up the spectacle.

Top five coastal beauty spots

▸▸ **Calf of Man**, Isle of Man. Take the boat across to this remote bird sanctuary for its high cliffs and grassy meadows. See p.719

▸▸ **Lizard Point**, Cornwall. Raging seas surround this rocky promontory. See p.442

▸▸ **Holy Island**, Northumberland. A castle, priory ruins and abandoned hulks of boats add to the brooding character of this ancient spot. See p.914

▸▸ **The Needles**, Isle of Wight. Spectacular pinnacles of rock thrust up from the sea. See p.245

▸▸ **Blakeney**, Norfolk. Picturesque retreat, with creeks, channels and sand banks to explore. See p.506

train station, often crowded with students. Live rock upstairs, real ale downstairs, regular theme nights, and big-screen football.

Clubs and live music venues

Audio 10 Marine Parade ☎01273/606906, ⒲www.audiobrighton.com. Brighton's trendiest nightclub packs them in night after night, specializing in funk and house, great cocktails and tasty nibbles.

The Beach King's Rd Arches ☎01273/722272, ⒲www.thebeachbrighton.co.uk. House, anthems, commercial dance and 1970s funk.

Casablanca Jazz Club 2 Middle St ☎01273/321817, ⒲www.casablancajazzclub.com. Basement venue featuring live bands and all types of funk, including Latin and jazz.

Charles Street 8–9 Marine Parade ☎01273/624091, ⒲www.charles-street.com. Small, smart gay club and bar that hosts special nights and cabaret. Women's night on first Sat of month. Cheap food available in the street-level bar.

Concorde 2 Madeira Shelter, Madeira Drive ☎01273/673311, ⒲www.concorde2.co.uk. Live music venue, with an admirable booking policy that has featured everyone from Bert Jansch to Toots & The Maytals; also has club nights at the weekend and regular early shows for young teenagers.

Digital 180–192 King's Rd Arches ☎01273/202407. Formerly *The Zap*, this is a New-Age, big-name venue where DJs spin a range of sounds from breaks to rock/indie, and there are regular live bands. Expect laser shows and a great sound system.

Funky Buddha Lounge 169 King's Rd Arches ☎01273/725541, ⒲www.funkybuddhabrighton .co.uk. Tiny venue renowned for progressive house, breakbeats and soul.

Honey Club 214 King's Rd Arches ☎07000/446639, ⒲www.thehoneyclub.co.uk. Garage, trance, house, hip-hop, you name it, this club has a night for it – as well as big name DJs.

Revenge 32 Old Steine ☎01273/606064, ⒲www .revenge.co.uk. The south's largest gay club with Mon night cabarets plus upfront dance and retro boogie on two floors; also has great sea views.

Volks Tavern 3 The Colonnade, Madeira Drive ☎01273/682828, ⒲www.volksclub.co.uk. Under the arches on Marine Parade you'll find a groovy crowd with live bands, reggae revival nights, hip-hop and breakbeats.

Arts centres, theatres and comedy clubs

Brighton Dome 29 New Rd ☎01273/709709, ⒲www.brighton-dome.org.uk. Three venues under one roof – Pavilion Theatre, Dome Auditorium and Corn Exchange – offering mainstream theatre, concerts, ballet and even Viennese tea dances.

Komedia Gardner Street, North Laine ☎01273/647100, ⒲www.komedia.co.uk. Lively alternative theatre-café notable for its regular roll call of stand-up comedy and live music. Late bar.

Theatre Royal New Rd ☎01273/328488, ⒲www .theambassadors.com/theatreroyal. Mixture of mainstream and progressive plays, opera, musicals and one-man shows.

Listings

Bike rental Planet Cycles, West Pier, King's Rd Arches ☎01273/748881.

Car rental Lee Hire, 7 Church Place ☎01273/683344; Thrifty, 47 Trafalgar St ☎01273/738227.

Hospital Royal Sussex County, Eastern Rd ☎01273/696955.

Internet Eazinet, 47 West St (daily 9.30am–midnight); Y2M, 38 Bond St (Mon–Sat 8am–7.30pm, Sun 1–8pm). You can also log on for free at Jubilee Library (see p.213).

Laundry Elm Grove Launderette, 10–12 Elm Grove.

Lesbian and Gay Switchboard ☎01273/204050 (daily 5–11pm).

Pharmacies Ashtons, 98 Dyke Rd ☎01273/325020 (daily till 10pm).

Police John St, off Edward St, near the Pavilion ☎0845/607 0999.

Post office 51 Ship St.

Taxis ☎01273/205205, 204060 or 747474.

Mid-Sussex

North of Brighton, the principal attraction of **Mid-Sussex** is its wealth of fine gardens, ranging from the majestic **Sheffield Park** and the tree plantations of **Wakehurst Place** to the luscious flowerbeds of **Nymans** and the landscaped lakes of **Leonardslee**. Exploring this region by public transport isn't really feasible unless you take your bike on the train; tourist information is thin on the ground too – it's best to get clued up at Brighton's tourist office beforehand, if you're interested in doing a thorough tour.

Sheffield Park and the Bluebell Railway

Around twenty miles northeast of Brighton lies the country estate of **Sheffield Park**, its centrepiece a Gothic mansion built for Lord Sheffield by James Wyatt. The house is closed to the public, but you can roam around the hundred-acre **gardens** (Jan & Feb Sat & Sun 10.30am–4pm; March, April & June–Sept Tues–Sun 10.30am–5.30pm; May & Oct daily 10.30am–5.30pm; Nov & Dec Tues–Sun 10.30am–4pm; £6.30; combined ticket with Bluebell Railway £15.50; NT), which were laid out by Capability Brown.

A mile southwest of the gardens lies the southern terminus of the **Bluebell Railway** (May–Sept daily; Oct–April Sat, Sun & school hols; day ticket £9.80; ℡01825/722370 24hr information line, ⓦwww.bluebellrailway.co.uk), whose vintage steam locomotives chuff nine miles north via Horsted Keynes to Kingscote. Although the service gets extremely crowded at weekends – especially in May, when the bluebells blossom in the woods through which the line passes – it's an entertaining and nostalgic way of travelling through the Sussex countryside and your day ticket lets you go to and fro as often as you like. A vintage bus service connects the northern terminus of Kingscote (no car access) with East Grinstead train station (hourly trains from London Victoria), though this will be unnecessary when the remaining two miles of track have been restored and link the Bluebell directly with East Grinstead – scheduled to be completed in 2008.

Wakehurst Place and Nymans

Wakehurst Place, a Jacobean mansion eighteen miles north of Brighton (daily 10am–4.30/6pm; £9; NT), is the country home of Kew Royal Botanic Gardens. Guided tours take place at 11.30am and 2pm throughout the year. The 180-acre site is given over mainly to trees and shrubs in a variety of horticultural environments, spreading down from the house to beyond Westwood Lake, from where paths then lead back to the house. Wakehurst is also home to the Millennium Seed Bank, whose aim is to safeguard some 24,000 plant species by cleaning and then freezing the seeds in underground vaults. The nearest station is Haywards Heath, on the London–Brighton line, from where you can catch daily buses #81 or #82.

For one of the southeast's greatest gardens, head five miles southwest of Wakehurst Place to **Nymans** (Jan to mid-Feb Sat & Sun 11am–4pm; mid-Feb to Dec Wed–Sun 11am–6pm; £7; NT), near the village of Handcross; bus #273 from Brighton to Crawley can drop you off on the A23 beside the village. Created by Ludwig Messel, a banker and inspired plantsman, the gardens are centred on the picturesque ruins of a mock-Tudor manor house and are linked by gently sloping paths. The valuable collection of exotic trees and shrubs is interspersed with more everyday plants, of which the colourful rhododendrons, azaleas and roses are particularly prolific. The highlight of the various enclosures is the large, romantic walled garden, almost hidden from sight by an abundance of climbing plants and housing a collection of rare Himalayan magnolia trees.

Leonardslee Gardens

Arguably the most picturesque of all the mid-Sussex gardens is at **Leonardslee** (April–Oct daily 9.30am–6pm, last admission 4.30pm; £6, £8/£9 in May), four miles southwest of Nymans, near the village of Crabtree; bus #17 from Brighton to Horsham passes by the garden gates. Set in a wooded valley, the seventy-acre grounds are crisscrossed by steep paths, which link six lakes created – like those at Sheffield Park – in the sixteenth century to power waterwheels for iron foundries. The range of flora is especially impressive here, featuring many hybrid species of rhododendron that were created specifically for this garden and are at their best in May. Wallabies, sika and fallow deer roam freely, adding to the Edenic atmosphere.

Arundel and around

The hilltop town of **ARUNDEL**, eighteen miles west of Brighton, has for seven centuries been the seat of the dukes of Norfolk, whose fine castle looks over the valley of the River Arun. The medieval town's well-preserved appearance and picturesque setting draws in the crowds on summer weekends, but at any other time a visit reveals one of West Sussex's least spoilt old towns. Arundel also has a unique place in English cricket: traditionally, the first match of every touring side is played against the Duke of Norfolk's XI on the ground beneath the castle and other matches are played regularly throughout the summer. North of here lie two contrasting sites: **Bignor Roman Villa**, containing some of the best Roman mosaics in the country, and the grand seventeenth-century **Petworth House**, replete with an impressive collection of paintings.

The Town

Towering over the High Street, **Arundel Castle** (April–Oct Tues–Sun noon–5pm; castle, keep, grounds & chapel £12; keep, grounds & chapel only £6.50) has an imposing medieval appearance, though most of what you see is little more than a century old. The structure dates from Norman times, but was ruined during the Civil War, then lavishly reconstructed from 1718 onwards by the eighth, eleventh and fifteenth dukes. From the top of the keep, you can see the current duke's spacious residence and the pristine castle grounds. Inside the castle, the renovated quarters include the impressive **Barons Hall** and the **library**, which boasts paintings by Gainsborough, Holbein and Van Dyck. On the edge of the castle grounds, the fourteenth-century **Fitzalan Chapel** houses tombs of past dukes of Norfolk including twin effigies of the seventh duke – one as he looked when he died and, underneath, one of his emaciated corpse. The Catholic chapel belongs to the Norfolk estate, but is actually physically joined to the **Church of St Nicholas**, the parish church, whose entrance is in London Road. It is separated from the altar of the main Anglican church by an iron grille and a glass screen. Although traditionally Catholics, the dukes of Norfolk have shrewdly played down their papal allegiance in sensitive times – such as during the Tudor era when two of the third duke's nieces, Anne Boleyn and Catherine Howard, became Henry VIII's wives.

West of the parish church, further along London Road, is Arundel's other major landmark, the towering Gothic bulk of **Arundel Cathedral** (daily 9am–6pm or dusk). Constructed in the 1870s by the fifteenth duke of Norfolk on the site of the town's former Catholic church, the cathedral's spire was designed by John Hansom, inventor of the hansom cab, the earliest taxi. Inside are the enshrined remains of St Philip Howard, the fourth duke's son, exhumed from the Fitzalan Chapel after his canonization in 1970. Following his wayward youth, Howard returned to the Catholic fold at a time when the Armada's defeat saw anti-Catholic feelings soar. Caught fleeing overseas and sentenced to death for praying for Spanish victory, he spent the next decade in the Tower of London, where he died. The cathedral's impressive outline is more appealing than the interior, but it fits in well with the townscape of the medieval seaport.

The rest of Arundel is pleasant to wander round, with the antique-shop-lined Maltravers and Arun streets being the most attractive thoroughfares.

Practicalities

Arundel's **train station** is half a mile south of the town centre over the river on the A27, with **buses** arriving either on High Street or River Road. The **tourist office** is at 1–3 River Rd (Easter–Sept Mon–Sat 10am–6pm, Sun 10am–4pm; Oct–Easter daily 10am–3pm; ℡01903/882268, ℗www.sussexbythesea.com). **Boat rental** (motor boats £25/hour) and hourly riverboat **cruises** upstream to Arundel Castle (£6) are available from River Arun Cruises (℡01903/882609).

Arundel's **festival** takes place throughout the last week in August in a variety of locations around the town, and features everything from open-air theatre to pop and opera. For details see ℗www.arundelfestival.co.uk.

Accommodation

The town has a range of accommodation to suit all pockets. You'll find a **campsite**, *Maynards* (℡01903/882075) at the top of the hill on the A27 two miles southeast of town, or you can pitch a tent at the youth hostel (see below).

Amberley Castle Amberley, four miles north of Arundel ℡01798/831992, ℗www.amberleycastle .co.uk. For a real splurge, head to this luxurious 600-year-old lodging, complete with gatehouse and portcullis. Several of the antique-studded rooms have four-posters ⑧

Arundel YHA Warningcamp ℡0870/770 5676, ℮arundel@yha.org.uk. This Georgian villa feels like a luxury B&B, a mile and a half northeast of town and connected by a riverside walk. Dorm beds from £20 (including breakfast), and you can camp here too.

Byass House 59 Maltravers St ℡01903/882129, ℗www.byasshouse.com. Elegant

eighteenth-century building with log fire, period furnishings and breakfast served in the conservatory or garden. No credit cards. ⑤

Town House 65 High St ℡01903/883847, ℗www.thetownhouse.co.uk. In the centre of Arundel, and with views to the castle, this genial Regency place offers four ornate rooms, two with four-posters. ⑤

Woodpeckers 15 Dalloway Rd ℡01903/883948. Modern house on the outskirts of town with a garden and valley views. There's normally a two-night minimum stay. No children. No credit cards. ④

Eating and drinking

Restaurants can be pricey, but a good range of snack bars and **pubs** ensures that sustenance is never hard to find.

Black Rabbit Mill Road, Offham. A pleasant half-hour's walk around the castle will bring you to this spot, overlooking the river, castle and surrounding wetlands, with decent pub grub. Moderate.

King's Arms 36 Tarrant St. The best real-ale pub in town, though can be cramped. No food.

Town House See above. You can dine on quality Modern British dishes here under a spectacular

Italian gilded ceiling. Set-price menus cost £12.50 or £16 for lunch, £22 or £27 for supper. Closed Mon. Expensive.

White Hart 3 Queen St ☎01903/882374. Pub just east of the river with a courtyard and good restaurant. Inexpensive.

Bignor and Petworth

Six miles north of Arundel, the excavated second-century ruins of the **Bignor Roman Villa** (March & April Tues–Sun 10am–5pm; May–Oct daily 10am–5/6pm; £4.50) reveal some well-preserved mosaics, of which the Ganymede is the most outstanding. The site, first excavated between 1811 and 1819, is superbly situated at the base of the South Downs and features the longest extant section of mosaic in England, as well as the remains of a hypocaust, the underfloor heating system developed by the Romans. There are no public transport links to the site, so without your own transport you need to take a taxi from Arundel or Pulborough (about £14).

Adjoining the pretty little town of **PETWORTH**, replete with antiques shops, eleven miles north of Arundel, is **Petworth House** (mid-March to Oct 11am–4/5pm; park daily 8am–dusk; £8.10, park free; NT), one of the southeast's most impressive stately homes. Built in the late seventeenth century, the house contains an outstanding art collection, with paintings by Van Dyck, Titian, Gainsborough, Bosch, Reynolds, Blake and Turner – the last a frequent guest here. Highlights of the interior decor are Louis Laguerre's murals around the **Grand Staircase** and the **Carved Room**, where work by Grinling Gibbons and Holbein's full-length portrait of Henry VIII can be seen. The seven-hundred-acre grounds were landscaped by Capability Brown and are considered one of his finest achievements. The extensive **Servants' Quarters**, connected by a tunnel to the main house, contain an impressive series of kitchens bearing the latest technological kitchenware of the 1870s. For an alternative and intriguing view of the life of one of the house's former employees, **Petworth Cottage Museum**, 346 High St (April–Oct Wed–Sun 2–4.30pm; Nov & Dec Sat & Sun roughly 4–6pm; £2.50), is well worth a visit. Seamstress Mary Cummings lived in this gas-lit abode, which has been restored using her own possessions to how it must have looked in 1910. The property is open on winter weekends to allow visitors to experience nightfall unilluminated by electric lighting.

To get to Petworth from Arundel involves a **train** journey to Pulborough Station from where you can pick up the regular Stagecoach Coastline #1 **bus**. Petworth's **tourist office** is on Golden Square (April–Sept Mon–Fri 9.30am–4.30pm, Sat 9.30am–5pm; Oct–March Mon–Fri 9.30am–4.30pm, Sun 11am-3.30pm; ☎01798/343523, ⊛www.chichester.gov.uk). For a memorable night's **stay**, book in at the converted *Old Railway Station* (☎01798/342346, ⊛www.old-station.co.uk; ❺), two miles south of Petworth on the A285 Chichester road.

Chichester and around

The county town of West Sussex and its only city, **CHICHESTER** is an attractive, if stuffy, market town, which began life as a Roman settlement – the Roman cruciform street plan is still evident in the four-quadrant symmetry of the town centre, spread around the Market Cross. Chichester's chief attraction is its Gothic cathedral, while there are a handful of major draws in the surrounding area. Chief among these are the restored Roman ruins at

Fishbourne, one of the most visited ancient sites in the county, two miles west of town, while north of Chichester, one of England's most fashionable racing events takes place at **Goodwood Park**. A couple of miles further north, the **Weald and Downland Open-Air Museum** contains around fifty reconstructed historic buildings in a beautiful rural setting.

The City

The main streets lead off to the compass's cardinal points from the Gothic **Market Cross**, a bulky octagonal rotunda topped by ornate finials and a crown lantern spire. It was built in 1501 to provide shelter for the market traders, although it appears far too small for its function.

A short stroll down West Street brings you to the neat form of the **Cathedral** (daily 7.15am–6/7pm), whose slender spire – a nineteenth-century addition – is visible out at sea. Building began in the 1070s, but the church was extensively rebuilt following a fire a century later and has been only minimally modified since about 1300, except for the spire and the unique, freestanding fifteenth-century bell tower. The **interior** is renowned for its contemporary devotional art, which includes a stained-glass window by Marc Chagall and an enormous altar-screen tapestry by John Piper. Other points of interest are the sixteenth-century painting in the north transept of the past bishops of Chichester, and the fourteenth-century Fitzalan tomb which inspired a poem by Philip Larkin, *An Arundel Tomb*. However, the highlight is a pair of reliefs in the south aisle, close to the tapestry – created around 1140, they show the raising of Lazarus and Christ at the gate of Bethany. Originally highly coloured, the reliefs once featured semi-precious stones set in the figures' eyes and are among the finest Romanesque stone carvings in England.

There are several fine buildings up North Street, including a dinky little **Market House**, built by Nash in 1807 and fronted by a Doric colonnade and a tiny flint **Saxon church** – now an ecclesiastical bookshop – with a diminutive wooden shingled spire. Finally, you come to the appealingly dumpy red-brick **Council House**, built in 1731, with Ionic columns and delightful intersecting tracery on its street facade, and crowned by a wonderful stone lion. East off South Street, in the well-preserved Georgian quadrant of the city known as the Pallants, you'll find **Pallant House Gallery**, 9 North Pallant (Tues, Wed, Fri & Sat 10am–5pm, Thurs 10am–8pm, Sun 12.30–5pm; £6.50). Stone dodos stand guard over the gates of this fine mansion, which houses artefacts and furniture from the early eighteenth century. Modern works of art are also included, among them pieces by Henry Moore and Barbara Hepworth and Graham Sutherland's portrait of Walter Hussey, the former Dean of Chichester, who commissioned much of the cathedral's contemporary art. A recent refurbishment has allowed space for regular modern art exhibitions as well as a venue for concerts and lectures.

Continuing in an anticlockwise direction around the town and crossing East Street to head north up Little London brings you to the **Chichester District Museum** (Tues–Sat 10am–5.30pm; free), housed in an old white weatherboarded corn store. Inside, the modest but entertaining display on local life includes a portable oven carried by Joe Faro, the city pieman, as well as the portable stocks used for the ritual humiliation of petty criminals. The **Guildhall** (June to mid-Sept Sat noon–4pm; free), a branch museum within a thirteenth-century Franciscan church in the middle of Priory Park, at the north end of Little London, has some well-preserved medieval frescoes. It was formerly a town hall and court of law, and the poet, painter and visionary William Blake was tried here for sedition in 1804.

Practicalities

Chichester's **train station** is on Stockbridge Road, with the **bus station** across the road at South Street. From either station it's a ten-minute walk north to the Market Cross, passing the **tourist office** at 29a South St (April–Sept Mon 10.15am–5.15pm, Tues–Sat 9.15am–5.15pm, Sun 11am–3.30pm; Oct–March closed Sun; ☎01243/775888, ☮www.chichester.gov.uk). There's **Internet** access at the *Internet Junction* café, 2 Southdown Buildings, next to the bus station.

Seemingly every other house on the main roads out of Chichester offers **accommodation**, so there's no problem finding a place to stay other than during the festival. If you want to splash out, try *The Ship Hotel*, North Street (☎01243/778000, ☮www.shiphotel.com; ●), a comfortable and characterful inn in the centre of town. Less expensive central B&B options include *Litten House,* with an attractive walled garden at 148 St Pancras, off East Street (☎01243/774503; ●), and the two-hundred-year-old *Friary Close*, Friary Lane (☎01243/527294, ☮www.friaryclose.co.uk; ●), just inside the city wall. You can **camp** at the *Red House Farm*, Brookers Lane, Earnley (☎01243/512959; closed Nov–Easter), six miles southwest of town, a mile or so from the beach.

As well as offering excellent accommodation, *The Ship* is a good place for a **drink**, as is *The Park Tavern*, a convivial pub serving excellent Gale's ales at 11 Priory Rd, overlooking Priory Park, and *The Fountain*, a fourteenth-century pub at the top of Southgate. For something to **eat**, *Sadlers Wine Bar and Restaurant* at 42 East St (☎01243/778261) serves innovative Modern English cooking, while *Purchase's Wine* Bar, 31 North St (☎01243/537532; closed Sun), dishes up a good selection of Danish open sandwiches, pâtés and salads.

Chichester is one of southern England's major cultural centres, well known for its **Festival Theatre** in Oaklands Park (☎01243/784437, ☮www.cft.org.uk), with a season running roughly between Easter and October. In addition, **Chichester Festivities** (☎01243/785718, ☮www.chifest.org.uk), taking place over two weeks in late June and early July, features music from blues to classical, plus talks and other events; the main venue is the cathedral, but the theatre and Goodwood Park (see p.224) are also used.

Fishbourne Roman Palace

Fishbourne, two miles west of Chichester (March–July, Sept & Oct daily 10am–5pm; Aug daily 10am–6pm; Nov to mid-Dec & mid-Jan to Feb daily 10am–4pm; mid-Dec to mid-Jan Sat & Sun 10am–4pm; £6.80), is the largest and best-preserved Roman palace in the country. Roman relics have long been turning up in Fishbourne and in 1960 a workman unearthed their source – the site of a depot used by the invading Romans in 43 AD which is thought later to have become the vast, hundred-room palace of the Romanized Celtic aristocrat, Cogidubnus. A pavilion has been built over the north wing of the excavated remains, where floor mosaics depict Fishbourne's famous dolphin-riding cupid as well as the more usual geometric patterns.

Like the more evocative remains at Bignor (see p.221), only the residential wing of the former quadrangle has been excavated – other parts of the dwelling fulfilled mundane service roles and probably lacked the mosaics that give both sites their singular appeal. The underfloor heating system has also been well restored and an audio-visual programme gives a fuller picture of the palace as it would have been in Roman times. The extensive gardens attempt to re-create the appearance of the palace grounds.

To get to Fishbourne take the train from Chichester to Fishbourne Station, turn right as you leave the station and the palace is a few minutes' walk away.

Goodwood

Three miles north of Chichester lies **Goodwood House** (April–July, Sept & Oct Sun & Mon 1–5pm; Aug Mon–Thurs & Sun 1–5pm; closed on race days; £8), an imposing Regency mansion set in the heart of a 12,000-acre estate and home to the dukes of Richmond for three hundred years. In addition to collections of furniture and porcelain, the house's highlights include Canaletto's views from the family's London home and paintings of their horses by Stubbs.

Just to the east of Goodwood House, **Sculpture at Goodwood** (March–Nov Tues–Sun 10.30am–4.30pm; £10) is an absolute must for anyone interested in contemporary art – the entry fee appears deliberately designed to put off casual punters. Since 1994 Wilfred and Jeanette Cass, long-time collectors of sculpture, have created a unique woodland environment for more than forty large-scale works, some of which have been specially commissioned and each of which is sited to allow you to appreciate it in isolation. The selection of pieces on display changes from year to year, and has included Turner Prize winners.

Goodwood Park (☎01243/774107, ⓦwww.goodwood.co.uk), four miles north of Chichester train station (and connected to it by bus on race days), hosts "Glorious Goodwood" in late July, one of the social events of the racing year. If you miss the main event, there are plenty of other meetings from May to October, and even without the racing, it's a wonderful location, on a lush green hill overlooking Chichester with the South Downs as a backdrop.

Weald and Downland Open-Air Museum

Five miles north of Chichester, the **Weald and Downland Open-Air Museum** (Jan & Feb Wed, Sat & Sun 10.30am–4pm; March, Nov, Dec & school hols daily 10.30am–4pm; April–Oct daily 10.30am–6pm; £8.25; ☎01243/811363), just outside the village of Singleton, is one of the best rural museums in the southeast. More than forty old buildings – from a Tudor market hall to a medieval farmstead – have been saved from destruction and reconstructed at the fifty-acre museum site. There's a daily guided tour at 1.30pm of the latest building, the innovative timber Downland Gridshell, the museum's workshop and store. Besides a whole range of livestock there are also numerous special events and activities, particularly in July and August, so it's worth calling ahead for details. There's a bus a every thirty miutes from Chichester (#60), which will drop you off in Singleton; a Weald and Downland ticket (£9) combines a day's unlimited travel on Stagecoach Coastline buses and museum entry.

Travel details

Buses

For information on all local and national bus services, contact Traveline ☎0871/200 2233, ⓦwww.traveline .org.uk.

Arundel to: Brighton (Mon–Sat every 30min, Sun 1; 50min–2hr 10min); Chichester (Mon–Sat hourly, Sun 1; 35min).

Battle to: Hastings (Mon–Sat hourly, Sun 1; 15–30min).

Brighton to: Chichester (Mon–Sat every 30min, Sun hourly; 2hr 30min); Eastbourne (every 20min; 1hr 10min); Lewes (Mon–Sat every 15min, Sun hourly; 25–30min); London Victoria (1–2 hourly; 2hr 20min); Portsmouth (Mon–Sat every 30min, Sun hourly; 3hr 30min); Tunbridge Wells (Mon–Sat every 30min, Sun hourly; 1hr 35min).

Broadstairs to: Margate (every 5–15 min; 25min); Ramsgate (every 10min; 15min).

Canterbury to: Deal (Mon–Fri 1–3 hourly, Sat hourly, Sun 5; 1hr 5min); Dover (Mon–Sat 1–2 hourly, Sun 6; 35min); London Victoria (hourly; 2hr); Margate (Mon–Sat every 20 min, Sun every 30min; 50min); Ramsgate (Mon–Sat hourly; 45min); Sandwich (Mon–Sat 1–3 hourly, Sun 5; 40min); Whitstable (Mon–Sat every 5–15min, Sun every 30min; 30min).

Chatham to: Rochester (every 5min; 5min).

Chichester to: Arundel (Mon–Sat 4–6 daily, Sun 1; 20–35min), Brighton (Mon–Sat every 30min, Sun hourly; 2hr 30min); Portsmouth (Mon–Sat every 30min, Sun hourly; 55min).

Deal to: Canterbury (hourly; 1hr 10min); Dover (Mon–Sat hourly, Sun every 2hr; 40min); Sandwich (Mon–Sat 2 hourly, Sun every 2hr; 30min).

Dorking to: Guildford (Mon–Sat 1–2 hourly; 45min).

Dover to: Canterbury (Mon–Sat hourly, Sun every 2hr; 35min); Deal (Mon–Sat 1–2 hourly, Sun every 2hr; 30min); Hastings (Mon–Sat hourly, Sun every 2hr; 2hr 40min); Hythe (Mon–Sat every 30min, Sun hourly; 50min); London Victoria (hourly; 2hr 30min–3hr); Sandwich (Mon–Sat 8 daily; 55min).

Eastbourne to: Brighton (2–3 hourly; 1hr 15min); Hastings (Mon–Sat every 20min, Sun hourly; 1hr 10min); London (2 daily; 3–4hr).

Farnham to: Guildford (Mon–Sat hourly; 30min).

Guildford to: Farnham (Mon–Sat 1–2 hourly; 25min or 1hr); London Victoria (8 daily; 1hr 30min).

Hastings to: Eastbourne (Mon–Sat every 20–30min, Sun hourly; 1hr 15min); Dover (Mon–Sat hourly, Sun 6; 2hr 50min); London Victoria (2 daily; 2hr 50min–3hr 50min); Rye (Mon–Sat 2 hourly, Sun 6; 40min).

Hythe to: Dover (Mon–Sat every 30min, Sun hourly; 55min); Rye (Mon–Sat 2 hourly, Sun 6; 1hr–1hr 15min).

Lewes to: Brighton (Mon–Sat every 15min, Sun hourly; 30min); Tunbridge Wells (Mon–Sat every 30min, Sun hourly; 1hr 10min).

Maidstone to London Victoria (3 daily; 1hr 25min); Tunbridge Wells (Mon–Sat every 20min, Sun 5 daily; 1hr 15min)

Margate to: Broadstairs (Mon–Sat every 5min, Sun 5 hourly; 25min); Canterbury (Mon–Sat every 20min, Sun every 30min; 50min); London Victoria (5 daily; 2hr 30min); Ramsgate (every 5–10min; 35–40min).

Ramsgate to: Broadstairs (every 10–20min; 10min); Canterbury (Mon–Sat hourly; 45min); London Victoria (4 daily; 3hr); Margate (every 10min; 30min).

Rochester to: Chatham (every 5min; 5min).

Rye to: Hastings (Mon–Sat 1–2 hourly, Sun 6;

30–45min); Hythe (Mon–Sat hourly, Sun 6; 1hr 10min).

Sandwich to: Canterbury (Mon–Sat every 30min, Sun 6; 45min); Deal (Mon–Sat 1–2 hourly, Sun 5; 25min); Dover (Mon–Sat hourly, Sun every 2hr; 55min).

Sevenoaks to: Tunbridge Wells (Mon–Sat 2 hourly, Sun every 2hr; 40–55min).

Tunbridge Wells to: Brighton (Mon–Sat every 30min, Sun 9; 1hr 40min); Lewes (Mon–Sat every 30min, Sun 9; 1hr 10min); London (1 daily; 1hr 30min); Sevenoaks (Mon–Sat 2 hourly, Sun every 2hr; 40–50min).

Whitstable to: Canterbury (every 15–30min; 30min);

Trains

For information on all local and national rail services, contact National Rail Enquiries: ☎08457/484950, Ⓦ www.nationalrail.co.uk.

Arundel to: Chichester (Mon–Sat 2 hourly, Sun hourly; 20min); London Victoria (Mon–Sat every 30min, Sun hourly; 1hr 30min); Portsmouth (hourly; 55min); Pulborough (Mon–Sat 2 hourly, Sun hourly; 10min).

Battle to: Hastings (2 hourly; 15–30min); London Charing Cross (2 hourly; 1hr 30min); Tunbridge Wells (2–3 hourly; 30min).

Brighton to: Chichester (Mon–Sat every 30min, Sun hourly; 50min); Eastbourne (2 hourly; 35min); Hastings (Mon–Sat 2 hourly, Sun hourly; 1hr–1hr 20min); Haywards Heath (3–6 hourly; 20–45min); Lewes (every 10–20min; 15min); London Bridge (Mon–Sat 4 hourly; 1hr); London King's Cross (Mon–Sat 2–4 hourly; 1hr 15min); London Victoria (1–2 hourly; 55min–1hr 20min); Portsmouth Harbour (Mon–Sat hourly; 1hr 30min).

Broadstairs to: London Victoria (Mon–Sat every 30min, Sun hourly; 1hr 50min).

Canterbury East to: Dover Priory (Mon–Sat every 30min, Sun hourly; 30min); London Victoria (Mon–Sat every 30min; 1hr 35min).

Canterbury West to: London Charing Cross (Mon–Sat every 30min, Sun hourly; 1hr 45min).

Chatham to: Dover Priory (Mon–Sat every 30min, Sun hourly; 1hr 10min); London Victoria (every 15min; 45min–1hr).

Chichester to: Arundel (Mon–Sat 2 hourly, Sun hourly; 20min); London Victoria (Mon–Sat 3 hourly, Sun hourly; 2hr–2hr 20min); Portsmouth Harbour (Mon–Sat every 30min, Sun hourly; 40min).

Dorking to: London Victoria (Mon–Sat every 30min; 50min); London Waterloo (Mon–Sat every 30min; 50min).

Dover Priory to: London Charing Cross (Mon–Sat 2 hourly; 1hr 40min); London Victoria (Mon–Sat 2 hourly, Sun hourly; 1hr 50min).

Eastbourne to: Brighton (2 hourly; 35min); Hastings (every 20–30min; 30min); Lewes (every 20–30min; 20–30min); London Victoria (Mon–Sat every 30min, Sun hourly; 1hr 35min).

East Grinstead to: London Victoria (Mon–Sat 2 hourly, Sun hourly; 1hr).

Farnham to: London Waterloo (every 30min; 1hr).

Guildford to: London Waterloo (every 15–30min; 45min).

Hastings to: London Victoria (hourly; 2hr–2hr 15min); Rye (hourly; 20min).

Haywards Heath to: Brighton (3–6 hourly; 20–45min); London Bridge (Mon–Sat 3–5 hourly; 45min); London Victoria (Mon–Sat; 45min).

Lewes to: Brighton (every 15–20min; 15min); Eastbourne (every 20–30min; 20–30min); London Victoria (Mon–Sat every 30min, Sun hourly; 1hr 10min).

Maidstone East to: London Victoria (Mon–Sat every 30min, Sun hourly; 1hr 10min).

Margate to: Canterbury West (Mon–Sat hourly, Sun 3; 30min); London Victoria (Mon–Sat 2 hourly, Sun hourly; 1hr 45min).

Ramsgate to: London Victoria (Mon–Sat hourly; 1hr 45min).

Rochester to: Dover Priory (Mon–Sat every 30min, Sun hourly; 1hr–1hr 15min); London Charing Cross (every 30min; 1hr 10min); London Victoria (every 30min; 45min).

Rye to: Hastings (hourly; 20min).

Sandwich to: Dover Priory (hourly; 25min).

Sevenoaks to: London Charing Cross (3–5 hourly; 35min); London Blackfriars (Mon–Sat every 30min; 1hr); London Victoria (Sun hourly; 1hr); Tunbridge Wells (2 hourly; 20min).

Tunbridge Wells to: London Charing Cross (2 hourly; 55min).

Whitstable to: London Victoria (Mon–Sat every 30min; 1hr 20min).

3

Hampshire, Dorset and Wiltshire

CHAPTER 3 Highlights

* **Cowes Week, Isle of Wight** This yachting jamboree draws thousands, with sailing fever infecting even the staunchest landlubbers. See p.245

* **Wykeham Arms, Winchester** Ancient tavern serving gourmet-standard food alongside the real ales. See p.249 & p.251

* **The New Forest** William the Conqueror's old hunting ground, and home to wild ponies and deer, the New Forest is ideal for walking, biking and riding. See p.252

* **Corfe Castle** Picturesque ruins with a weathered, romantic charm. See p.263

* **Durdle Door** This crumbling natural arch stands at the end of a splendid beach – a great place for walkers and swimmers alike. See p.265

* **Avebury** This crude stone circle has a more powerful appeal than nearby Stonehenge, not least for its great size and easy accessibility, in a peaceful village setting. See p.286

▲ Cowes Week

3

Hampshire, Dorset and Wiltshire

The distant past is perhaps more tangible in **Hampshire** (often abbreviated to "Hants"), **Dorset** and **Wiltshire** than in any other part of England. Predominantly rural, these three counties overlap substantially with the ancient kingdom of **Wessex**, whose most famous ruler, Alfred, repulsed the Danes in the ninth century and came close to establishing the first unified state in England. Before Wessex came into being, however, many earlier civilizations had left their stamp on the region. The chalky uplands of Wiltshire boast several of Europe's greatest Neolithic sites, including **Stonehenge** and **Avebury**, while in Dorset you'll find **Maiden Castle**, the most striking Iron Age hill fort in the country, and the **Cerne Abbas giant**, source of many a legend. The Romans tramped all over these southern counties, leaving the most conspicuous signs of their occupation at the amphitheatre of **Dorchester** – though that town is more closely associated with the novels of Thomas Hardy and his distinctively gloomy vision of Wessex.

None of the landscapes of this region could be described as grand or wild, but the countryside is consistently seductive, its appeal exemplified by the crumbling fossil-bearing cliffs around **Lyme Regis**, the managed woodlands of the **New Forest** and the gentle, open curves of **Salisbury Plain**. Its towns are also generally modest and slow-paced, with the notable exceptions of the two great maritime cities of **Portsmouth** and, to a lesser extent, **Southampton**, a fair proportion of whose visitors are simply passing through on their way to the more genteel pleasures of the **Isle of Wight**. This is something of an injustice, though neither place can compete with the two most interesting cities in this part of England – **Salisbury** and **Winchester**, each of which possesses a stupendous cathedral amid an array of other historic sights. Of the region's great houses, **Wilton**, **Stourhead**, **Longleat** and **Kingston Lacy** are the ones that attract the crowds, but every cranny has its medieval church, manor house or unspoilt country inn – there are few parts of England in which an aimless meander can be so rewarding. If it's straightforward seaside fun you're after, **Bournemouth** leads the way, with Weymouth and Lyme Regis heading the ranks of the minor resorts, along with the yachtie havens on the Isle of Wight.

The **roads** in this area get choked in summer, the bulk of the traffic heading either for the West Country, the Bournemouth beaches, or for the ferry ports of Poole, Portsmouth and Southampton. If you're heading for one particular

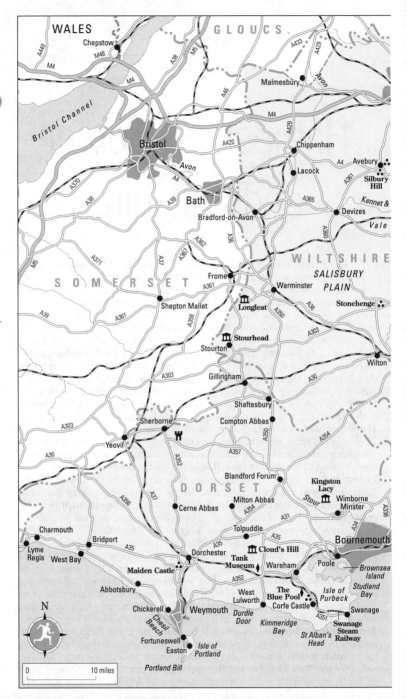

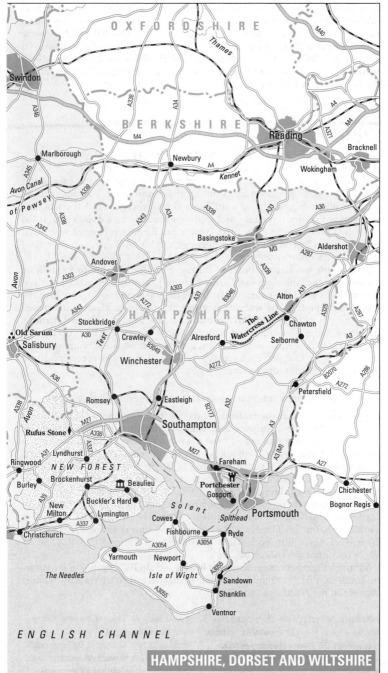

HAMPSHIRE, DORSET AND WILTSHIRE

© Crown copyright

spot, it's often easier to reach it by **rail**, on the fast direct services from London's Waterloo Station. For many inland areas, though, **buses** are more convenient; most services in the region are run by First (℡0870/010 6022, ⓦwww .firstgroup.com), Stagecoach (℡0845/121 0170, ⓦwww.stagecoachbus.com /south) and Wilts & Dorset (℡01202/673555, ⓦwww.wdbus.co.uk). Keen **walkers** can avoid the hordes by taking to the New Forest's quieter spots or to the Dorset Coast Path, which runs from Lyme Regis to Poole.

Portsmouth

Britain's foremost naval station, **PORTSMOUTH** occupies the bulbous peninsula of Portsea Island, on the eastern flank of a huge, easily defended harbour. The ancient Romans raised a fortress on the northernmost edge of this inlet, and a small port developed during the Norman era, but this strategic location wasn't fully exploited until Tudor times, when Henry VII established the world's first dry dock here and made Portsmouth a royal dockyard. It has flourished ever since and nowadays Portsmouth harbour is clogged with naval frigates, ferries bound for the Continent or the Isle of Wight, and swarms of dredgers, tugs and pleasure craft.

Portsmouth was heavily bombed during World War II due to its military importance and, although the Victorian slums got what they deserved, bland tower blocks from the nadir of British architectural endeavour now give the city an ugly profile. The seafront, however, has been considerably smartened in recent years, while **Old Portsmouth**, based around the original harbour, preserves some Georgian and a little Tudor character. East of here is **Southsea**, a residential suburb with a rash of stoic military monuments overlooking its shingle beach, as well as most of the city's accommodation and a good selection of restaurants.

Arrival, information and accommodation

Portsmouth's main **train station**, Portsmouth and Southsea, is in the city centre, but the line continues to **Harbour Station**, the most convenient stop for the main sights and old town. Long-distance and most local buses stop at The Hard, by the Harbour Station and the entrance to the dockyards. Passenger **ferries** for Ryde, on the Isle of Wight (see p.240), and Gosport, on the other side of Portsmouth Harbour, leave from the jetty at Harbour Station, while Wightlink car ferries for Fishbourne, Isle of Wight (see p.240), depart from the ferry port off Gunwharf Road. Hovertravel hovercraft to Ryde go from Clarence Pier, Southsea. There are two **tourist offices** in Portsmouth, one on The Hard, the other on Southsea's seafront, next to the Blue Reef Aquarium (both daily 9.30am–5.15/5.45pm; ℡023/9282 6722, ⓦwww.visitportsmouth.co.uk).

Although the main concentration of **hotels** and **B&Bs** lies south of the centre in Southsea, Old Portsmouth has more character and is within easy walking distance of the Naval Base.

Hotels and guest houses

Albatross Guest House 51 Waverley Rd, Southsea ℡023/9282 8325, ⓦwww.albatrossguesthouse .co.uk. One of many good-value B&Bs in this part of Southsea, this one has nautically themed rooms (most en suite), Wi-Fi Internet and some parking space. No credit cards. ❸

Fortitude Cottage 51 Broad St, Old Portsmouth ℡023/9282 3748, ⓦwww.fortitudecottage.co.uk. Comfortable cottage overlooking the quayside

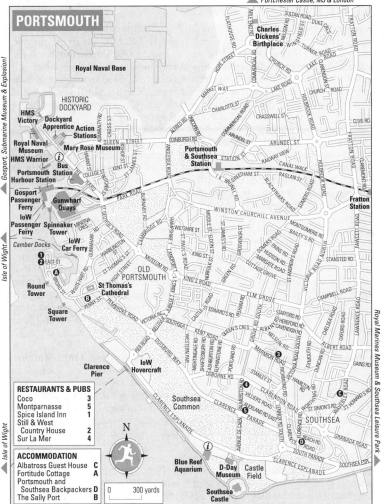

PORTSMOUTH

Portchester Castle, M3 & London

Royal Naval Base

HISTORIC DOCKYARD

HMS Victory
Dockyard Apprentice Action Stations
Royal Naval Museum
HMS Warrior
Bus
Portsmouth Station
Portsmouth Harbour Station
Mary Rose Museum

Charles Dickens Birthplace

Portsmouth & Southsea Station

Gosport, Submarine Museum & Explosion!

Gosport Passenger Ferry
IoW Passenger Ferry
Gunwharf Quays
Spinnaker Tower
IoW Car Ferry

Isle of Wight

Camber Docks

Round Tower
Square Tower

Clarence Pier

Isle of Wight

Fratton Station

Winston Churchill Avenue

OLD PORTSMOUTH

St Thomas's Cathedral

IoW Hovercraft

Southsea Common

Southsea Esplanade

Clarence Esplanade

SOUTHSEA

Blue Reef Aquarium
D-Day Museum
Castle Field

Southsea Castle

RESTAURANTS & PUBS

Coco	3
Montparnasse	5
Spice Island Inn	1
Still & West	
Country House	2
Sur La Mer	4

ACCOMMODATION

Albatross Guest House	C
Fortitude Cottage	A
Portsmouth and	
Southsea Backpackers	D
The Sally Port	B

N

0   300 yards

---

offering five rooms with private bathrooms, and a beamed breakfast room with views of the boats. Free parking. ④

The Sally Port 57–58 High St, Old Portsmouth ☏023/9282 1860. Opposite the cathedral, this historic inn has sloping floors and extremely comfortable bedrooms, some with en-suite showers. ⑤

Hostels and campsites

Portsmouth and Southsea Backpackers 4 Florence Rd, Southsea ☏023/9283 2495, ⓦwww .portsmouthbackpackers.co.uk. 54-bed hostel with full facilities, including a large kitchen, at the east end of Clarence Esplanade. CCTV cameras and strict rules are off-putting. Dorm beds go for £13, and there are doubles with shared or private (both ①) bathrooms. A thirty-minute walk from the city centre, or catch any bus to Southsea and get off at the Strand.

Southsea Leisure Park Melville Rd, Southsea ☏023/9273 5070, ⓦwww.southsealeisurepark .com. Useful campsite right at the east end of Southsea Esplanade (bus #15 or #16A from the Harbour station), but it's dominated by caravans and ridiculously overpriced.

The City

You are unlikely to spend any time in Portsmouth's modern **city centre**, a functional area of shops, offices and heavy traffic. Most items of interest, including the Historic Dockyard, lie west of here, in **Old Portsmouth** and the adjacent **waterfront district**. Across Portsmouth Harbour from here, and reachable by regular ferries, **Gosport** has a couple of naval museums, but little else worth lingering over. East of the old centre stretches **Southsea**, bounded to the south by Southsea Esplanade and the gravelly seafront, and holding a scattering of attractions as well as hotels and restaurants.

The Royal Naval Base

For most visitors, a trip to Portsmouth begins and ends at the **Historic Dockyard** (ⓦ www.historicdockyard.co.uk), in the **Royal Naval Base** at the end of Queen Street (daily 10am–5.30/6pm; last entry 90min before closing). The complex comprises three ships and as many museums, with each ship visitable separately. Most people, however, opt for an all-inclusive ticket (£16.50), which is valid for a year, though you can only visit each attraction once. The main highlights are HMS *Victory*, HMS *Warrior* (including the Royal Naval Museum), Action Stations (an interactive simulation of life aboard a modern naval frigate), the Mary Rose Museum, and a harbour tour. Note that visits to the *Victory* are guided, with limited numbers at set times, so it's worth booking early to ensure a place, and even then you may have to wait up to two hours for your turn. Also, visitors with disabilities will have a hard time moving between decks on the two complete ships; a virtual tour by video is a good alternative, currently at noon and 3pm aboard the *Victory* (worth booking ahead at the ticket desk or on ☎023/9272 2562 in busy periods).

Nearest the entrance to the complex is the youngest ship, **HMS Warrior** (£12), dating from 1860. It was Britain's first armoured, or "iron-clad" battleship, complete with sails and steam engines, and was the pride of the fleet in its day. Longer and faster than any previous naval vessel, and the first to be fitted with washing machines, the *Warrior* was described by Napoleon III as a "black snake amongst the rabbits". You can wander around its main deck and see where eighteen seamen ate, slept and relaxed in the tiny spaces between each of the ship's 36 cannons.

HMS Victory (£12) was already forty years old when she set sail from Portsmouth for Trafalgar on September 14, 1805, returning in triumph three months later, but bearing the corpse of Admiral Nelson. Shot by a sniper from a French ship at the height of the battle, Nelson expired below decks three hours later, having been assured that victory was in sight. Although badly damaged during the battle, the *Victory* continued in service for a further twenty years, before being retired to the dry dock where she rests today.

Opposite the *Victory*, various buildings house the exhaustive **Royal Naval Museum** (same ticket as *Victory*, or £4.50 just for museum), which traces naval history from Alfred the Great's fleet to the present day. A shed behind the *Victory* displays the remains of the **Mary Rose** (£12), Henry VIII's flagship, which capsized before his eyes off Spithead in 1545 while engaging French intruders. Whether she was top-heavy (she was certainly overloaded at the time) or took in water through her lower gunports having reeled from a broadside is uncertain, but the *Mary Rose* sank swiftly with almost all her 700-strong crew. In 1982 a massive conservation project successfully raised the remains of the hull, which silt had preserved beneath the seabed, and it was moved to its present position. Many of the thousands of objects that were found near the

▲ HMS Victory, Portsmouth

wreck are now displayed in an absorbing exhibition close to the *Warrior*, where you can see videos of the recovery operation, as well as depictions of life aboard a sixteenth-century warship. Lastly, **Action Stations** (£12) has interactive games, videos and graphics to simulate life aboard ship, and the Dockyard Apprentice (free) illustrates the various skills involved in equipping and repairing ships in 1911.

Gosport

The naval theme is continued at the **Submarine Museum** on Haslar Jetty in Gosport (daily 10am–4.30/5pm; last tour 1hr before closing; £7.50), reached by taking the passenger ferry from Harbour train station jetty (daily 5.30am–midnight; £2.10 return), just south of the entrance to the Royal Naval Base. Allow a couple of hours to explore these slightly creepy vessels – a guided tour inside HMS *Alliance* gives you an insight into life on board and the museum elaborates evocatively on the long history of submersible craft. Nearby, housed in the old armaments depot at Priddy's Hard, **Explosion! The Museum of Naval Firepower** (Sat & Sun 10am–4pm; last entry at 3pm; £4) tells the story of naval warfare from the days of gunpowder to the present, much helped by computer animations.

The waterfront and Old Portsmouth

Back at the Harbour train station in Portsmouth, it's a short walk to the soaring **Spinnaker Tower** (Mon–Fri & Sun 10am–5/6pm; Sat 10am–10pm; Aug daily 10am–10pm; £6.20), Portsmouth's newest and most conspicuous attraction. Opened in 2005, the elegant, sail-like structure dominates the historic harbour, rising to 170m above the city and offering stunning vistas for up to twenty miles over land and sea. The two viewing decks can be reached by either a high-speed lift or a slower "panoramic" glass lift (£2 extra).

   Below the tower, the sleek **Gunwharf Quays** development stretches along the waterfront, hosting cafés, restaurants and nightspots alongside the retail outlets. From here, it's a well-signposted fifteen-minute walk south to what remains of **Old Portsmouth**. Along the way, you pass the simple but elegant **Cathedral of St Thomas** on the High Street, whose original twelfth-century features have been obscured by rebuilding, first after the Civil War and again in the twentieth century. The High Street ends at a maze of cobbled Georgian streets huddling behind a fifteenth-century wall protecting the **Camber**, or old port, where Walter Raleigh landed the first potatoes and tobacco from the New World. Nearby, the Round and Square Towers, which punctuate the Tudor fortifications, are popular vantage points for observing nautical activities.

Southsea

South of Old Portsmouth, **Southsea** is worth exploring above all for the **D-Day Museum** on Clarence Esplanade (daily: 10am–5/5.30pm; last entry 1hr before closing; £6), which relates how Portsmouth avenged its wartime bombing by being the main assembly point for the D-Day invasion, code-named "Operation Overlord". The museum's most striking exhibit is the 272-foot-long Overlord Embroidery, which tells the tale of the Normandy landings. Next door to the museum, the squat profile of **Southsea Castle** (April–Sept daily 10am–5.30pm; £3.50) may have been the spot from where Henry VIII watched the *Mary Rose* sink in 1545. A mile further along the shoreside South Parade, just past South Parade pier, the **Royal Marines Museum** (daily 10am–5pm; last entry 4pm; £5.25) describes the origins and greatest campaigns of the navy's elite fighting force.

Charles Dickens' Birthplace and Portchester Castle

The only other point of interest in Portsmouth itself is **Charles Dickens' Birthplace** at 393 Old Commercial Rd (mid-April to Sept daily 10am–5.30pm; £3.50), half a mile north of the town centre, where the writer was born in 1812. A couple of rooms have been fitted out as they were during his lifetime, though dedicated fans will find more of interest in

Rochester (see p.171) and Broadstairs (see p.175), where Dickens wrote many of his greatest books.

More compelling is **Portchester Castle** (daily 10am–4/6pm; £4.20; EH), six miles out of the centre, just past the marina development at Port Solent. Built by the Romans in the third century, this fortification boasts the finest surviving Roman walls in northern Europe – still over twenty feet high and incorporating some twenty bastions. The Normans felt no need to make any substantial alterations when they moved in, but a castle was later built within Portchester's precincts by Henry II, which Richard II extended and Henry V used as his garrison when assembling the army that was to fight the Battle of Agincourt. Today its grassy enclosure makes a sheltered spot for a congenial game of cricket or a kickabout with a football.

Eating and drinking

Portsmouth has a small and fairly unremarkable range of **restaurants**, though you'll find more choice in Southsea. In Old Portsmouth, your best bet is one of the old seafaring **pubs** on Bath Square, the *Spice Island Inn* and the *Still & West Country House*, two handsome hostelries of a similar age, with good ales, snacks and full meals available and seats outside to view the comings and goings on the Solent.

Restaurants

Coco 59 Marmion Rd, Southsea ☏ 023/9281 9647. This patisserie (with delicious home-made chocolates) is also a great spot for breakfast, a snack or full evening meal (£24.50 for three courses; Fri & Sat only) in the upstairs restaurant. Closed Sun.
Montparnasse 103 Palmerston Rd, Southsea ☏ 023/9281 6754. Elegant bistro offering good-quality French and seafood dishes. Set menus are £26.50 and £31.50. Closed Sun & Mon.
Sur La Mer 69 Palmerston Rd, Southsea ☏ 023/9287 6678. Good-value and informal French and seafood restaurant with set-price three-course meals for around £8 and £16. Closed Sun.

Southampton

A glance at the map gives some idea of the strategic maritime importance of **SOUTHAMPTON**, which stands on a triangular peninsula formed at the place where the rivers Itchen and Test flow into Southampton Water, an eight-mile inlet from the Solent. Sure enough, Southampton has figured in numerous stirring events: it witnessed the exodus of Henry V's Agincourt-bound army, the Pilgrim Fathers' departure in the *Mayflower* in 1620 and the maiden voyages of such ships as the *Queen Mary* and the *Titanic*. Unfortunately, since its pummelling by the Luftwaffe and some disastrous postwar planning, the thousand-year-old city is now a sprawling conurbation easily bypassed by motorways. It'll be pretty low on your list of places to visit in southern England, but has enough of interest to occupy a couple of hours while you wait for the ferry to the Isle of Wight.

Core of the modern town is the **Civic Centre**, a short walk east of the train station. Its clocktower is the most distinctive feature of the skyline, and it houses an excellent **art gallery** that's particularly strong on twentieth-century British artists such as Sutherland, Piper and Spencer (Tues–Sat 10am–5pm, Sun 1–4pm; free). The **Western Esplanade**, curving southward from the station, runs alongside the best remaining bits of the old city **walls**. Rebuilt after a French attack in 1338, they feature towers with evocatively chilly names – Windwhistle,

Catchcold and God's House – the last of these, at the southern end of the old town in Winkle Street, houses a **Museum of Archeology** (Tues–Fri 10am–4pm, Sat 10am–1pm & 2–4pm, Sun 1–4pm; free). Best preserved of the city's seven gates is **Bargate**, at the opposite end of the old town at the head of the High Street; an elaborate structure, cluttered with lions, classical figures and defensive devices, it was formerly the guildhall and court house.

Other ancient buildings survive amid the piecemeal redevelopment of the High Street area. The oldest church is **St Michael's**, to the west of the High Street, with a twelfth-century font of black Tournai marble. The nearby **Tudor House Museum**, in Bugle Street (currently closed for refurbishment: contact tourist office for information), is an impressive fifteenth-century timber-framed building, its grand banqueting hall and reconstructed Tudor garden outshining the sundry exhibits of Georgian, Victorian and early twentieth-century social history. Down at the southwest corner of the old town, by the seafront, the **Wool House** is a fine fourteenth-century stone warehouse, formerly used as a jail for Napoleonic prisoners and now home to a **Maritime Museum** (same hours as Museum of Archeology; £2), focusing on the heyday of ocean liners, and including a huge model of the *Queen Mary* as well as various mementoes from the *Titanic*.

Practicalities

Services from London Waterloo arrive at the central **train station** in Blechynden Terrace, west of the Civic Centre; the **bus** and **coach stations** are immediately south and north of the Civic Centre. The **tourist office** is at 9 Civic Centre Rd (Mon–Sat 9.30am–5pm, Sun 10am–3.30pm; ☎023/8083 3333, ⓦwww.visit-southampton.co.uk).

Southampton isn't a wildly attractive **place to stay**, though there are plenty of business hotels and commercial guest houses in the centre, and a pair of historic hostelries halfway down the High Street: the four-hundred-year-old *Star* (☎023/8033 9939, ⓦwww.thestarhotel.com; ⑤), with all the antique trimmings, and the *Dolphin* (☎023/8033 9955, ⓦwww.thedolphin.co.uk; ⑦), equally ancient but with contemporary art in the rooms. For something a bit simpler and cheaper, try *Alcantara House,* 20 Howard Rd (☎023/8033 2966, ⓦwww.alcantaraguesthouse.co.uk; ④), a B&B a mile north of the train station off Shirley Road, with bright, en-suite rooms.

There's a cluster of lively **eating** places on and around Oxford Street (off Bernard Street from the High Street), among them *The Olive Tree*, 29 Oxford St (☎023/8034 3333), serving Mediterranean dishes in an airy setting with pavement seating; you can have a good-value lunch for under £8, and main courses in the evening cost £10–14 – brunches at weekends until 3pm and live music on Sundays are further enticements. Elsewhere, in a stylishly converted church at 61 Commercial Rd, *Joe Daflo's* (☎023/8023 1101) provides drinks, bar snacks and full meals, with some outdoor seating. As for **pubs**, the tiny old *Platform Tavern* in Winkle Street, at the south end of the High Street, and the twelfth-century *Red Lion*, complete with minstrels' gallery, at 55 High St, are more charismatic alternatives to the bars at the *Star* and *Dolphin* hotels.

The Isle of Wight

In recent years the **ISLE OF WIGHT** has begun to shake off its image as a comfortable, tidy and unadventurous adjunct of rural southern England, and has

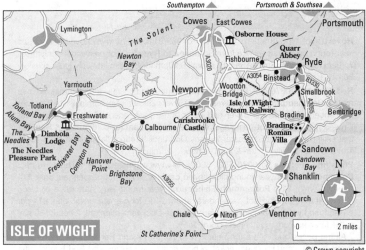

ISLE OF WIGHT

© Crown copyright

started to attract a younger, more lively crowd, with a couple of major annual music festivals and a scattering of fashionable hotels. Measuring over 20 miles at its widest point and divided fairly neatly by a chalk spine that runs east to west across its centre, the island packs a surprising variety of landscapes and coastal scenery. North of the ridge is a terrain of low-lying woodland and pasture, deeply cut by meandering rivers; southwards lies open chalky downland fringed by high cliffs. Two **Heritage Coast** paths follow the best of the shoreline, one running from Totland to St Lawrence on the south coast, the other from east of Yarmouth to west of Cowes along the north coast. Blending into this background is a splendid array of well-preserved Victoriana, often grandiose but also charming and elegant too. The Victorian character of the Isle of Wight is scarcely surprising, for the founding Victorian herself felt most at home here – **Osborne House**, in the north of the island, was originally designed as a summer retreat for the royal family but became Queen Victoria's permanent home after Albert died. Several other eminent Victorians also frequented the island, and you can't go far without coming across traces of Tennyson, Dickens, Swinburne and the photographer Julia Margaret Cameron, among others. Older remains include the castles at **Yarmouth** and **Carisbrooke**.

Information and getting around

There are **tourist offices** in Ryde, Sandown, Shanklin, Yarmouth, Cowes and Newport, all open more or less the same hours (Mon–Sat 9.30/10am–4.30/5pm, Sun 10am–3.30pm; offices may close an hour earlier and all day Sun in winter). All share the same telephone number (☎01983/813813), and website (🌐www.islandbreaks.co.uk).

Local **buses** are operated by Southern Vectis (☎0871/200 2233, 🌐www.islandbuses.info) – pick up a route map and timetable from any tourist office, ferry office or bus station. A Rover Ticket gives unlimited travel on the whole network, costing £10 for one day or £15 for two days; there's also a good-value seven-day Freedom Pass for £20. All tickets are available on board any bus or from a bus station or travel shop. You might also make use of the useful east-coast **train** line linking Ryde, Brading, Sandown and Shanklin.

Sea routes to the Isle of Wight

Hovertravel ☏023/9281 1000 or 01983/811000, ⓦwww.hovertravel.co.uk. Year-round hovercraft service from **Southsea to Ryde** for foot passengers only: from 7.10am (or 8.45am Sat, 9.15am Sun) until 8.10pm (or 8.45pm late July to Aug); every 30min; 10min; £14.40.

Red Funnel ☏0870/444 8898, ⓦwww.redfunnel.co.uk. Year-round ferries on two routes: **Southampton–East Cowes** hourly (every 2hr at night); 55min; £12.40 for foot passengers; £54 for car, driver and up to three passengers; **Southampton–West Cowes** high-speed foot-passenger service from 5.45am (or 6.45am Sat & Sun, but first sailing at 6.15am Sat Easter to early Oct) until 10.45pm (last sailing at 11.45pm Thurs–Sat and daily Easter–Aug); 1–2 hourly; 25min; £17.90.

Wightlink Ferries ☏0870/582 0202, ⓦwww.wightlink.co.uk. Three routes: **Portsmouth–Ryde** year-round high-speed catamaran for foot passengers only; 1–2 hourly; 20min; £17; **Portsmouth–Fishbourne** year-round ferry runs once or twice hourly; 40min; £14 for foot passengers; about £130 for car and driver, plus £14 per passenger; **Lymington–Yarmouth** ferry (Easter–Dec) 4am–midnight; 2 hourly; 30min; same fares as Portsmouth–Fishbourne ferry.

All the prices quoted are for a ninety-day (Wightlink and Red Funnel) or one-year (Hovertravel) standard return ticket in high season. Wightlink and Red Funnel offer day returns as well as a range of discounted short-break deals for vehicles. Online booking and off-peak sailings are also cheaper.

Cycling is a popular way of getting around the Isle of Wight, especially as bikes are carried free on all ferry services, though in summer the island's narrow lanes can get very busy. For bike **rental**, contact Wight Offroad (☏01983/408587 or 07976/740736, ⓦwww.wightoffroad.co.uk), which, with a day's notice, can deliver and collect mountain bikes anywhere on the island (£10 per half-day, or £16 per day; discounts for longer rents), and also organizes guided rides.

Ryde and around

As a major ferry terminal, **RYDE** is the first landfall many visitors make on the island, but does not invite much lingering. A working town that came to prominence as a resort in the Victorian era, it offers some grand nineteenth-century architecture and decent beach amusements, however. Reaching out over the shallows of Ryde Sands, the functional half-mile-long **pier** is where the ferries dock and former London Underground rolling stock carries the seasonal throngs inland. Backed by sandy beaches, the **Esplanade** extends eastwards from the pier, with the small Gothic Revival folly of Appley Tower at its far end, celebrating the sailing of the First Fleet to Botany Bay from Mother Bank, off Ryde, in 1787.

Just outside the village of Binstead, two miles west of Ryde's centre, lies one of the island's earliest Christian relics. In 1132 **Quarr Abbey** was founded by Richard de Redvers as one of the first Cistercian monasteries in Britain. Its name was derived from the quarries nearby, where stone was extracted for use in the construction of Winchester and Chichester cathedrals. Only stunted ruins survived the Dissolution and ensuing plunder of ready-cut stone, although an ivy-clad archway still hangs picturesquely over a farm track. In 1907 a new Benedictine abbey was founded just west of the ruins – a striking rose-brick building with Byzantine overtones that is open to the public (daily 9am–9pm; vespers 5pm, or 6pm Thurs in summer).

Practicalities

Ryde's **tourist office**, **bus station**, **hovercraft terminal** and **Esplanade train station** (the northern terminus of the Island Line train line) are all located near the base of the pier; there's also a **taxi** rank close by.

The central *Yelf's Hotel* on Union Street (℡01983/564062, Ⓦwww.yelfshotel .com; Ⓢ) is one of Ryde's oldest **hotels**, while the more contemporary Kasbah at 76 Union St (℡01983/810088, Ⓦwww.kas-bah.co.uk; Ⓢ) has exotic, Moroccan-themed rooms. Less expensive **B&B** accommodation is available just south of the Esplanade at *Trentham Guest House*, 38 The Strand (℡01983/563418, Ⓦwww.trentham-guesthouse.co.uk; no credit cards; ❶).

Union Street has the best **eating** opportunities, with Kasbah offering bags of character with its tapas and daily specials, and Room 4, at no. 30, good for baguettes, wraps and jacket potatoes. Dillangreli's, on parallel George Street, offers great-value breakfasts and snacks.

Brading and around

Due south of Ryde on the busy Sandown road (A3055; bus #2 or #3), the village of **BRADING** boasts a disparate collection of ancient sites. Just south of the village are the remains of **Brading Roman Villa** on Morton Old Road (daily 9.30am–5pm; £4.25), one of two such villas on the island (the other is in Newport), both of which were probably sites of bacchanalian worship. The Brading site is notable for its superbly preserved mosaics, including intact images of Medusa and depictions of Orpheus – associated with the cult of Bacchus – as well as a mysterious and unique man with a cockerel's head.

In the centre of Brading, what is believed to be the island's oldest intact dwelling – dating from 1228 – is now part of **Brading: the Experience**, which includes a waxworks museum, chamber of horrors, museum of cars and bikes, and stuffed animals (Easter–Oct daily 10am–5pm, last entry 3.30pm; Nov–Easter call ℡01983/407286 for times; £6.75). Next door is the **Old Town Hall**, which still has the original stocks and whipping post once used to immobilize miscreants. At 56 High St, the *Bugle Inn*, formerly a smugglers' rendezvous, offers refreshments. From behind the pub, a path leads to Brading Haven, formerly an inlet connected to the sea, where the smugglers used to land their contraband.

Brading is also a stop on the main Ryde–Shanklin train line, that connects at Smallbrook (one stop up from Brading) with the **Isle of Wight Steam Railway** (June–Sept, plus some dates in April, May, Oct & Dec, roughly 11am–4.20pm; £8.50, valid all day; ℡01983/882204, Ⓦwww.iwsteamrailway .co.uk). Its impeccably restored carriages in traditional green livery make the delightful ten-mile return trip to Wootton Bridge, between Ryde and Newport, through lovely unspoilt countryside.

Sandown and Shanklin

The two eastern resorts of Sandown and Shanklin merge into each other across the sandy reach of Sandown Bay, representing the island's holiday-making epicentre. Frequently recorded as among Britain's sunniest spots, Sandown is a traditional bucket-and-spade resort – though rather desolate out of season – while Shanklin, with its auburn cliffs, Old Village and scenic chine, has a marginally more sophisticated aura.

Appropriately, **SANDOWN** possesses the island's only surviving pleasure **pier**, bedecked with amusement arcades, cafés, dodgems and a theatre. The main distractions lie next to each other at the northern end of the Esplanade, chief among them the **Isle of Wight Zoo** (daily: mid-Feb to March & Oct 10am–4pm; April–Sept 10am–6pm; Nov Sat & Sun 10am–4pm, weather permitting; T01983/403883; £5.95), containing several species of tigers, panthers and other big cats, as well as some frisky lemurs and monkeys and an exhaustive selection of spiders and snakes.

Being separated from the shore by hundred-foot cliffs has preserved **SHANKLIN** from the tawdry excesses of its northern neighbour – though it hasn't stopped the promotion of the **Old Village**'s rose-clad, thatched charm with the same zeal as Sandown's pier. More authentic examples can be found in any number of inland villages, but with the adjacent **Shanklin Chine** (daily: April to late May & mid-Sept to Oct 10am–5pm; late May to mid-Sept 10am–10pm; £3.75), a twisting pathway descending a mossy ravine and decorated on summer nights with fairy lights, it all adds up to a picturesque spot.

Practicalities

Sandown's **tourist office** is located at 8 High St, and Shanklin's at 67 High St. Both towns have Island Line train stations about half a mile inland from their beachfront centres.

Accommodation

Perennially popular, Sandown and Shanklin have numerous accommodation options, mostly open year-round, though availability often dwindles to nothing in summer. There's an inexpensive and well-equipped **campsite**, a ten-minute walk north of the Shanklin station: *Landguard Camping Park*, Landguard Manor Rd, Shanklin (T01983/867028, Wwww.landguard-camping.co.uk; closed Oct–March).

Holliers 3 Church Rd, Shanklin Old Village
T01983/862764, Wwww.holliershotel.co.uk.
Seventeenth-century hotel where Longfellow once stayed. Equipped with sauna and indoor and outdoor swimming pools as well as a carvery restaurant and two bars. 5

The Montpelier Pier Street, Sandown
T01983/403964, Wwww.themontpelier.co.uk.
Central B&B with a range of en-suite rooms, all with fridges and some overlooking the beach and pier. Breakfast optional. 3

Pink Beach 20 Esplanade, Shanklin
T01983/862501, Wwww.pink-beach-hotel.co.uk.
Victorian hotel fronted by lawns, a stone's throw from the beach. Rooms with sea views cost extra. Closed Nov–Jan. 4

Ryedale Private Hotel 3 Atherley Rd, Shanklin
T01983/862375, Wwww.ryedale-hotel.co.uk.
Agreeably cluttered, family-run guest house just steps from Shanklin train station; it's a short downhill walk to the beach. Closed Nov–Feb. 3

Eating and drinking

Don't expect much in the way of gourmet **cuisine** in Shanklin or Sandown, though there's no shortage of straightforward seaside grub at low prices, with generally friendly service.

Fat Harry's 53 High St, Sandown. Superior fish-and-chip joint which also offers chicken, pies, burgers and vegetarian dishes, all freshly cooked. Inexpensive.

Fisherman's Cottage Free House Esplanade, Shanklin. Atmospheric seafaring pub at the southern end of the Esplanade, on Appley Beach, serving wholesome food. Closed Nov–Feb. No credit cards. Moderate.

Morgans 36 High St, Shanklin T01983/864900.
Contemporary restaurant offering sophisticated, nouvelle-type dishes, including a good selection of seafood at £10–18. Expensive.

Saffrons 29 North Rd, Shanklin T01983/861589.
Relaxed bistro offering an eclectic range of dishes with musical accompaniment. Closed Sun Sept–June. Moderate.

3

Ventnor and Bonchurch

The seaside resort of **VENTNOR** sits at the foot of St Boniface Down, the island's highest point at 787ft. The down periodically disintegrates into landslides, creating the jumbled terraces known locally as the **Undercliff**, whose sheltered, south-facing aspect, mild winter temperatures and thick carpet of undergrowth have contributed to the former fishing village becoming a fashionable health spa. Thanks to these unique factors, the town possesses rather more character than the island's other resorts, its Gothic Revival buildings clinging dizzily to zigzagging bends.

The floral terraces of the **Cascade** curve down to the slender Esplanade and narrow beach, where former boat builders' cottages now provide more recreational services. From the shoreside *Spyglass Inn* (see below) on the Esplanade, it's a pleasant mile-long stroll to Ventnor's famous **Botanical Gardens**, where 22 landscaped acres of subtropical vegetation flourish. Displays are divided thematically, ranging from the South African and Australian banks to the Culinary Herb and the Medicinal Gardens.

To the east of Ventnor, the ancient village of **BONCHURCH** exudes an alluring rustic charm with its duck pond and rows of quaint cottages set on the Undercliff's wooded slopes. Behind high stone walls loom grand Victorian country houses where writers such as Dickens, Thackeray and Swinburne once stayed. At Bonchurch's east end is the spartan, towerless edifice of the eleventh-century **Old Church of St Boniface** with its wreath of skewed gravestones and mature trees further enhancing the scene. Above the village the **Landslip Footpath** descends the Undercliff. It's occasionally closed due to subsidence, so check first with any island tourist office before setting off on an exploration.

Practicalities

The best of the area's **accommodation** lies in Bonchurch. Among the options listed here, you can **eat** well at *Horseshoebay House*, where there's a café with outdoor tables (closed Nov–Easter), and at the *Spyglass Inn* for pub meals. Alternatively, try the *Pond Café*, Bonchurch Village Road (℡01983/855666; closed Mon), a stylish restaurant in a picturesque spot, serving main courses for around £14.

Hotels and guest houses

Horseshoebay House Horseshoe Bay, Bonchurch ℡01983/856800, ℡www.horseshoebayhouse.co.uk. B&B right on the beach, with sea views from all rooms. ❹

Lisle Combe Undercliff Drive ℡01983/852582, ℡www.lislecombe.co.uk. On the main A3055, this place offers B&B in a beautifully preserved early Victorian villa that was once the home of poet Alfred Noyes. No credit cards. Closed Dec–Feb. ❺

Spyglass Inn Esplanade, Ventnor ℡01983/855338. Small, self-contained flats with kitchenettes and balconies next to the pub and right by the sea. ❹

Winterbourne House off Shore Road ℡01983/852535, ℡www.winterbournehouse.co.uk. Charles Dickens wrote much of *David Copperfield* here, now a classy hotel where most rooms have sea views. It's right by St Boniface Church. ❻

St Catherine's Point and the southwest coast

The western Undercliff begins to recede at the village of Niton, where a footpath continues to the most southerly tip of the island, **St Catherine's Point**, marked by a modern lighthouse. A prominent landmark on the downs behind is **St Catherine's Oratory**, known locally as the "Pepper Pot". In fact it's a medieval lighthouse, reputedly built in 1325 as an act of expiation by a local landowner, Walter de Goditon who had attempted to pilfer a cargo of wine owned by a monastic community.

From Chale, a couple of miles north, Military Road continues along the coast, a flat windswept drive with occasional turn-offs to small bays – though swimming is too dangerous on this stretch – and chines, of which **Hanover Point** is the most impressive. Several old buildings in the area – including the *Wight Mouse Inn* (see below) – were once extended using timber salvaged from wrecks which foundered here.

At the village of Brook, where the impressive Brook House overlooks the valley, Military Road ascends the flank of Compton Down before descending into Freshwater Bay. If you're walking this way, you might stop off at the National Trust-owned **Compton Bay,** a splendid spot for a swim or a picnic, frequented by local surfers and accessed by a steep path leading down from the dark red cliffs.

Accommodation on the southwestern coast includes the welcoming *Wight Mouse Inn*, Newport Road, Chale (℡01983/730431, ⓦwww.innforanight .co.uk; ❺), where meals are also available. Local **campsites** include *Grange Farm*, Brighstone Bay (℡01983/740296, ⓦwww.brighstonebay.fsnet.co.uk; closed Nov–Feb) and the much smaller *Compton Farm*, Brook (℡01983/740215, ⓦwww .comptonfarm.co.uk; closed Oct–April) – both working farms with free-range hens, ducks and milking cows (*Grange Farm* even has llamas and water buffalos).

Dimbola Lodge and Freshwater

The western tip of the Isle of Wight holds sundry traces of some of the venerable Victorians who were drawn to the area. On the coastal road at Freshwater Bay, on the corner with Terrace Lane, **Dimbola Lodge** (Tues–Sun: Feb–Oct 10am–5pm, also Mon during school summer hols; Nov–Jan 10am–4pm; £4) was the home of pioneer photographer **Julia Margaret Cameron**. After visiting local resident Tennyson in 1860, Cameron immediately bought adjacent land on the nearby coast, joining two cottages to make a substantial home for herself and her family, where she practised her art until moving to Ceylon in 1875. The building now houses a gallery of her work, including an impressive range of portraits of some of the foremost society figures of her day, and also features changing exhibitions. There's a bookshop and good tearoom/restaurant on the premises too.

If you're prepared to splash out for **accommodation**, book into *Farringford Hotel*, on Bedbury Lane (℡01983/752500, ⓦwww.farringford.co.uk; ❼), Tennyson's former home, whose facilities now include an outdoor pool, putting green and tennis courts as well as several cottage suites. On the way, you'll pass Freshwater's unusual ninety-year-old thatched **Church of St Agnes**, containing memorials to Tennyson and Thackeray's daughter, Lady Ritchie; Tennyson's wife is buried in the churchyard.

Between Freshwater Bay and the Needles, the breezy four-mile ridge of **Tennyson Down** is one of the island's most satisfying walks, with another monument to the poet at its 485-foot summit and vistas onto rolling downs and vales.

Alum Bay and The Needles

One of the two major focal points of the Isle's western tip are the multichrome cliffs of **Alum Bay**. To get here during the summer months, you can make use of an open-top bus that circulates every thirty minutes between Yarmouth, Freshwater Bay and **The Needles Pleasure Park** (daily 10am–4/5pm; free), a collection of fairground amusements and a glass studio, where you can watch the manufacture of glass objects. A chair lift (£4 return) runs down to the foot of the cliffs of Alum Bay whose ochre-hued sands, used as pigments for painting local landscapes in the Victorian era, contrast brightly with the chalk face of the Needles headland.

From the Pleasure Park, it's a twenty-minute walk to the lookout on top of the three tall chalk stacks known as **The Needles**, where Tennyson Down slips into the Channel. The Needles are best appreciated from the sea, whether on a pleasure boat (every 15–30min; 25min; £4) or RIB (inflatable boat; 15min; £8), both of which are operated by Needles Pleasure Cruises at Alum Bay (℡01983/761587) between April and October. Alternatively, you'll get a fine view from the end of the tunnel that burrows through the cliffs at the **Old Battery**, a gun emplacement built 250ft above the sea in 1863 (late March to June, Sept & Oct Mon–Thurs, Sat & Sun 10.30am–5pm; July & Aug daily 10.30am–5pm; £4.20; NT). The fort may be closed in bad weather; call to check on ℡01983/754772.

There's a **youth hostel** a short walk northeast from The Needles, at Totland Bay (℡0870/770 6070, ⓔtotland@yha.org.uk; dorms from £16.50; closed Nov–Jan); by bus, alight at Totland War Memorial, and walk a quarter-mile up Weston Road and Hurst Hill.

Yarmouth

Situated at the mouth of the River Yar, the relaxed town of **YARMOUTH** stretches east along the seashore from its pocket-sized harbour. The island's first purpose-built port, it was razed by the French in 1377 on their way to Carisbrooke (see p.247), but regained prosperity in the sixteenth century, after Henry VIII ordered the construction of **Yarmouth Castle** (Easter–Sept Mon–Thurs & Sun 11am–4pm; £3.50; EH). Amid a warren of chambers and corridors, the castle has exhibitions on local history and the development of Henry's fortress, while stairs lead up to a small green from where there are splendid views across to the mainland.

Yarmouth's **tourist office** is just back from the harbour. The best place in town to **stay** is *The George*, on Quay Street (℡01983/760 331, Ⓦwww .thegeorge.co.uk; ❽), a seventeenth-century hotel right by the ferry dock, with elegantly furnished rooms – Charles II stayed here when he visited the island. More affordable accommodation can be found on The Square at *Harvey's* (℡01983/760738, Ⓦwww.harveysbandb.co.uk; ❷), offering more contemporary rooms and breakfasts for every diet. **Bike hire** is also available from here (£12 a day). *The George* has a superb seafood **restaurant** (expensive) with tables in the garden overlooking the sea, as well as a pleasant panelled bar.

Cowes and around

COWES, at the island's northern tip, is inextricably associated with sailing and boat building: Henry VIII built a castle here to defend the Solent's expanding naval dockyards from the French and Spanish, and in the 1950s the world's first hovercraft made its test runs here. In 1820 the Prince Regent's patronage of the yacht club gave the port its cachet with the Royal Yacht Squadron, now one of the world's most exclusive sailing clubs. The first week of August sees the international yachting festival known as **Cowes Week** (Ⓦwww.skandiacowesweek .co.uk), which visiting royalty turns into a high-society gala, although the presence of serious sailors helps to lift the event above the merely ceremonial. In fact, it's a great opportunity to view some extraordinary craft and immerse yourself in yachting lore among the cognoscenti, while the glitzy element invests the proceedings with a bit of glamour and frivolity. There are dozens of organized events, including a spectacular fireworks display on the Friday night, and a great party atmosphere. You don't need to be in Cowes during Cowes Week to sample the nautical vibe, however, as most summer weekends there's some form of yachting or powerboat racing.

The town is bisected by the River Medina, with West Cowes being the older and more interesting half, its High Street meandering up from the waterfront Parade. Along the High Street you'll find shops reflecting the town's gentrified heritage, interspersed with boatyards and chandlers. The more industrial East Cowes, where you'll find Osborne House, is connected to West Cowes by a "floating bridge", or chain ferry (Mon–Sat 5am–12.10am, Sun 6.35am–12.10am; pedestrians free, cars £1.40).

Practicalities

Cowes' **tourist office** is at the Arcade, Fountain Quay, West Cowes, with extended opening hours during Cowes Week. **Boat trips** upriver and around the harbour and the Solent leave from Thetis Wharf, near the Parade; for details contact Solent & Wight Line Cruises (℡01983/564602, ⓦwww.solentcruises.co.uk).

Accommodation options in West Cowes include the *Union Inn* in Watch House Lane, off High Street (℡01983/293163; ❺), and *Halcyone Villa*, Grove Road, up Mill Hill Road from the east end of the High Street (℡01983/291334, ⓔsandraonwight@btinternet.com; no credit cards; ❸). In East Cowes, try the *Crossways House Hotel* (℡01983/298282, ⓦwww.bedbreakfast-cowes.co.uk; ❹), opposite Osborne House on Crossways Road, with four-poster beds and a garden. Prices rise steeply during Cowes Week, when most places are booked up well in advance.

The town has a narrow selection of **places to eat**, though for a quick snack you can't beat the ⚄ *Octopus's Garden*, 63 High St, a café/bistro filled with Beatles memorabilia and serving all-day breakfasts, pastas and curries as well as baguettes, open daytime only. Traditional **pub** meals are served at the *Union Inn* as well as the *Anchor* on the High Street, which has a garden and live music on Wednesdays, Fridays and Saturdays.

Osborne House

East Cowes' only place of interest is Queen Victoria's family home, **Osborne House** (Easter–Sept daily 10am–6pm; Oct daily 10am–4pm; Nov–Easter Wed–Sun 10am–4pm; pre-booked tours only ℡01983/200022; house and grounds £10, grounds only £6; EH), signposted one mile southeast of town (take bus #4 from Ryde or #5 from Newport, or either from East Cowes). The house was built in the late 1840s by Prince Albert and Thomas Cubitt, with extensions such as the Household Wing and the exotic, Indian-style Durbar Room added over the next half-century. Albert designed the private family home as an Italianate villa, with balconies and large terraces overlooking the landscaped gardens towards the Solent. The state rooms, used for entertaining visiting dignitaries, exude formality, while the private apartments feel more homely, like the affluent family holiday residence that Osborne was – far removed from the pomp and ceremony of state affairs in London. Following Albert's death, the desolate Victoria spent much of her time here, and it's where she eventually died in 1901. Since then, according to her wishes, the house has remained virtually unaltered, allowing an unexpectedly intimate glimpse into Victoria's family life. Included in the entry ticket is a minibus to the Swiss Cottage, built in the grounds for Victoria's children to play and study.

Newport and Carisbrooke Castle

NEWPORT, the capital of the Isle of Wight, sits at the centre of the island at a point where the River Medina's commercial navigability ends. Apart from a few pleasant old quays dating from its days as an inland port, the town isn't particularly engaging, though it merits a visit for the hilltop fortress of **Carisbrooke Castle** (daily 10am–4/5pm; £6.50; EH), on the southwest outskirts (buses #6, #7 or #11 from Newport). The austere Norman keep was greatly extended over the years, first in the thirteenth century by the imperious Countess Isabella who inherited much of the island and ruled it as a petty kingdom. Having tolerated her excesses, the Crown bought her estates as she lay dying in 1293 and appointed governors to defend the island, rather than risking its security to the vagaries of birthright.

Carisbrooke's most famous visitor was Charles I, detained here (and caught one night ignominiously jammed between his room's bars while attempting escape) prior to his execution in London. The **museum** in the centre of the castle features many relics from his incarceration, as well as those of the last royal resident, Princess Beatrice, Queen Victoria's youngest daughter. The castle's other notable curiosity is the sixteenth-century well-house, where donkeys still trudge inside a huge treadmill to raise a barrel 160ft up the well shaft. A stroll around the battlements provides several lofty perspectives of the castle's interior as well as sweeping views across the centre of the island.

Newport's **tourist office** is in the centre of town at the Guildhall, High Street. Your best options for a meal or a drink are both on Carisbrooke High Street, near the castle, at the top of the hill: the *Eight Bells* **pub** serves food all day, or try the ever-popular, moderately priced *Valentino's* Italian restaurant (☎01983/522458; closed daytime & Sun).

Winchester and around

Nowadays a tranquil, handsome market town, set amid docile hay-meadows and watercress beds, **WINCHESTER** was once one of the mightiest settlements in England. Under the Romans it was Venta Belgarum, the fifth largest town in Britain, but it was **Alfred the Great** who really put Winchester on the map when he made it the capital of his Wessex kingdom in the ninth century. For the next couple of centuries Winchester ranked alongside London, its status affirmed by William the Conqueror's coronation in both cities and by his commissioning of the local monks to prepare the **Domesday Book**. As the shrine of St Swithun, King Alfred's tutor, Winchester attracted innumerable pilgrims, and throughout the medieval era the city continued to command enormous ecclesiastical and political influence – Bishop **William of Wykeham**, founder of Winchester College and Oxford's New College, was twice chancellor of England. It wasn't until after the Battle of Naseby in 1645, when Cromwell took the city, that Winchester began to decline into provinciality.

Hampshire's county town now has a scholarly and slightly anachronistic air, embodied by the ancient almshouses that still provide shelter for senior citizens of "noble poverty" – the pensioners can be seen wandering round the town in medieval black or mulberry-coloured gowns with silver badges. A trip to this secluded old city is a must – not only for the magnificent **cathedral**, chief relic

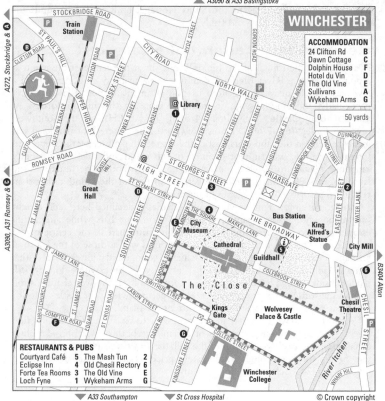

Map labels:

A3090 & A33 Basingstoke

A272, Stockbridge & A

A3090, A31 Romsey & C

WINCHESTER

ACCOMMODATION
24 Clifton Rd	B
Dawn Cottage	C
Dolphin House	F
Hotel du Vin	D
The Old Vine	E
Sullivans	A
Wykeham Arms	G

0   50 yards

STOCKBRIDGE ROAD
Train Station
ST PAUL'S HILL
CLIFTON ROAD
N
CLIFTON TERRACE
CLIFTON HILL
ROMSEY ROAD
ST JAMES TERRACE
ST JAMES LANE
CHRISTCHURCH ROAD
COMPTON ROAD
ST JAMES VILLAS
UPPER HIGH ST
SUSSEX STREET
STATION ROAD
TOWER STREET
STAPLE GARDENS
CASTLE HILL
Great Hall
SOUTHGATE STREET
ST THOMAS STREET
ST SYMONDS STREET
ST SWITHUN STREET
CANON STREET
EDGAR ROAD
ST CROSS ROAD
CROSS ROAD
CULVER RD
KINGSGATE STREET
CITY ROAD
HYDE STREET
JEWRY STREET
Library
@
HIGH STREET
ST GEORGE'S STREET
ST CLEMENT STREET
GREAT MINSTER ST
THE SQUARE
City Museum
Cathedral
The Close
Kings Gate
COLLEGE STREET
Winchester College
NORTH WALLS
ST PETER'S STREET
PARCHMENT STREET
UPPER BROOK STREET
MIDDLE BROOK ST
GORDON ROAD
PARK AVENUE
DURNGATE
UNION STREET
FRIARSGATE
LOWER BROOK STREET
EASTGATE STREET
WATER LANE
THE BROADWAY
MARKET LANE
Bus Station
King Alfred's Statue
City Mill
Guildhall
COLEBROOK STREET
Wolvesey Palace & Castle
Chesil Theatre
CHESIL STREET
River Itchen
WHARF HILL
B3404 Alton

RESTAURANTS & PUBS
Courtyard Café	5	The Mash Tun	2
Eclipse Inn	4	Old Chesil Rectory	6
Forte Tea Rooms	3	The Old Vine	E
Loch Fyne	1	Wykeham Arms	G

A33 Southampton   St Cross Hospital   © Crown copyright

of Winchester's medieval glory, but for the all-round, well-preserved ambience of England's one-time capital. The city also makes a good base from which to explore a trio of villages to the east, **Alton**, **Chawton**, home of Jane Austen, and **Selbourne**.

Arrival, information and accommodation

Winchester **train station** is about a mile northwest of the cathedral on Stockbridge Road. If you arrive by **bus**, you'll find yourself on the Broadway, opposite the **tourist office** in the imposing Guildhall (May–Sept Mon–Sat 9.30am–5.30pm, Sun 11am–4pm; Oct–April Mon–Sat 10am–5pm; ☎01962/840500, ⓦ www.visitwinchester.co.uk), which has plenty of information about the city and its environs, and distributes excellent visitors' guides, walks leaflets (£1) and literature on the eighty-mile South Downs Way (see p.204). Ask here too about daily **guided walks** of the city (1hr 30min; £4). You can access the **Internet** at Mailboxes Etc at 80 High St (Mon–Fri 8.30am–6pm, Sat 10am–4pm), or for free at the public library on Jewry Street (Mon–Sat 9.30am–5/7pm; book on ☎01962/862748).

Winchester has a range of attractive **accommodation**, though you'll pay fairly high rates to stay right in the centre. There's **camping** with full facilities at *Folly Farm Touring Caravan Park* in Crawley (☎01962/776486;

closed Nov–Feb), a working farm four miles west of town towards Stockbridge off the B3049: take any bus towards Salisbury (#68 is the most frequent), and there's a stop right outside the back gate.

Hotels and B&Bs

24 Clifton Rd ☎01962/851620, ✉a.williams1997@btinternet.com. Convenient for the train station, this clean Victorian house in a quiet street has one room with a private bathroom, and there's a guests' lounge. No credit cards. ②

Dawn Cottage 99 Romsey Rd ☎01962/869956, ✉dawncottage@hotmail.com. Classy B&B about a mile west of the centre and connected by frequent bus services. The three comfortable rooms with en-suite bathrooms have great views over the Itchen Valley. ④

Dolphin House 3 Compton Rd ☎01962/853284, ⓦwww.dolphinhousestudios.co.uk. The two large en-suite rooms here have separate entrances from the large garden. Self-catering and washing facilities are also available. Wi-Fi enabled. No credit cards. ④

Hotel du Vin Southgate Street ☎01962/841414, ⓦwww.hotelduvin.com. This was the first in this small chain of stylish designer hotels: the Georgian town house has a champagne bar, bistro, walled garden and bags of charm. Wi-Fi enabled. ⑦

The Old Vine 8 Great Minster St ☎01962/854616, ⓦwww .oldvinewinchester.com. The spacious, comfortable and sumptuously furnished rooms above this old tavern include three at the front and a top-floor suite, which all have cathedral views (costing extra). Breakfast served in room. ⑦

Sullivans 29 Stockbridge Rd ☎01962/862027, ✉sullivans_bandb@hotmail.com. Victorian cottage a few minutes' walk from the train station, with shared bathrooms, low rates and multilingual owners. No credit cards. ②

Wykeham Arms 75 Kingsgate St ☎01962/853834, ✉wykehamarms@fullers .co.uk. Fine old hostelry where the art of classy inn-keeping has not yet vanished. Fourteen beamed and quirkily shaped rooms are adorned with assorted antiques and curios. ⑥

The City

Winchester is a compact city, easily toured on foot – indeed, a car is a liability here, and should be parked up at the first opportunity. Once away from the streams of traffic threading through the centre, you can relax – the lanes are peppered with refreshment stops, and the Cathedral Close makes a pleasant spot for a quiet sit-down.

The Cathedral

The first minster to be built in Winchester was raised by Cenwalh, the Saxon king of Wessex in the mid-seventh century and traces of this building have been unearthed near the present **Cathedral** (Mon–Sat 8.30am–6pm, Sun 8.30am–5.30pm; £5 donation requested; ⓦwww.winchester-cathedral .org.uk), which was begun in 1079 and completed some three hundred years later, producing a church whose elements range from early Norman to Perpendicular styles.

The exterior is not the cathedral's best feature – squat and massive, the cathedral crouches stumpily over the tidy lawns of the Cathedral Close. The interior is rich and complex, however, and its 556-foot **nave** makes this Europe's longest medieval church. Outstanding features include its carved Norman font of black Tournai marble, the fourteenth-century misericords (the choir stalls are the oldest complete set in the country) and some amazing monuments – **William of Wykeham's Chantry**, halfway down the nave on the right, is one of the best. Jane Austen, who died in Winchester, is commemorated close to the font by a memorial brass and slab beneath which she's interred, though she's recorded simply as the daughter of a local clergyman. Above the high altar lie the mortuary chests of pre-Conquest kings, including Knut, or Canute (though the bones were mixed up after Cromwell's

Roundheads broke up the chests in 1645); William Rufus (see p.254), killed while hunting in the New Forest in 1100, lies in the presbytery. The statuary on the impressive screen at the end of the presbytery, showing Queen Victoria and Alfred the Great among many others, was added in the Victorian era to replace the original images destroyed during the Reformation. Beyond the screen, near Cardinal Beaufort's Chantry Chapel, look out too for the memorial shrine to St Swithun. Originally buried outside in the churchyard, his remains were later interred inside the cathedral where the "rain of heaven" could no longer fall on him, whereupon he took revenge and the heavens opened for forty days – hence the legend that if it rains on St Swithun's Day (July 15) it will continue for another forty. His exact burial place is unknown.

Accessible from the north transept, the Norman **crypt** is only rarely open, since it's flooded for much of the time – the cathedral's original foundations were dug in marshy ground, and at the beginning of last century a steadfast diver, William Walker, spent five years replacing the rotten timber foundations with concrete (Deep Sea Adventure in Weymouth gives you the full story; see p.267). If you catch it open, though, have a look inside at the two fourteenth-century statues of William of Wykeham as well as Antony Gormley's standing figure, "Sound II", one of the country's most adventurous ecclesiastical commissions in recent years.

To appreciate the cathedral at its most atmospheric, try to be here for **evensong**, currently 5.30pm most days (Sun at 3.30pm). Free **guided tours** take place all year Monday–Saturday 10am–3pm on the hour, less frequently in winter. Crypt and tower tours are also available.

The City Museum and the Great Hall

Outside the cathedral, the **City Museum**, a basic local history display, sits on The Square (April–Oct Mon–Sat 10am–5pm, Sun noon–5pm; Nov–March Tues–Sat 10am–4pm, Sun noon–4pm; free). The nearby High Street is a standard municipal mishmash of ancient and modern facades. Walk west along here and you'll eventually arrive at the **Great Hall** on Castle Avenue (daily 10am–4/5pm; free), the vestigial remains of a thirteenth-century castle destroyed by Cromwell. Sir Walter Raleigh heard his death sentence here in 1603, though he wasn't finally dispatched until 1618, and Judge Jeffreys held one of his Bloody Assizes in the castle after Monmouth's rebellion in 1685. The main interest now, however, is a large, brightly painted disc slung on one wall like some curious antique dartboard. This is alleged to be King Arthur's Round Table, but the woodwork is probably fourteenth-century, later repainted as a PR exercise for the Tudor dynasty – the portrait of Arthur at the top of the table bears an uncanny resemblance to Henry VIII. Below the table, the floor of the Great Hall is dominated by a huge and gaudy sculpture of Queen Victoria, carved by Sir Alfred Gilbert (responsible for *Eros* in London's Piccadilly Circus) to mark her Golden Jubilee in 1887, and deposited here for lack of anywhere else in town large enough to hold it. Adjoining the Great Hall, an illuminating exhibition relates the history of the Norman castle and Great Hall, and you can also take a brief wander in Queen Eleanor's Medieval Garden – a recreation of a noblewoman's shady retreat.

East and south of the Cathedral

Head east along the High Street, past the striking, Neo-Gothic Guildhall and the august bronze statue of King Alfred on the Broadway, to reach the River Itchen and the **City Mill** (March, mid-April to June & mid-Sept to late Oct Wed–Sun 11am–5pm; early April, July to early Sept & late Oct daily

11am–5pm; Nov Wed–Sun 11am–4.30pm; Dec daily 11am–4.30pm; £3.40; NT), where you can see restored mill machinery. Turning right before the bridge you pass what remains of the Saxon walls, which bracket the ruins of the twelfth-century **Wolvesey Castle** (early April to Sept daily 10am–5pm; free; EH) and the Bishop's Palace, built by Christopher Wren. Immediately to the west up College Street stand the buildings of **Winchester College**, the oldest public school in England – established in 1382 by William of Wykeham for "poor scholars", it now educates the wealthy and privileged. The cloisters and chantry are open during term time and the chapel is open all year. Beyond the college at 8 College Street, you'll pass the house where Jane Austen died, having moved here from Chawton in 1817 (see p.252), when already ill with Addison's Disease. At the top of College Street, the thirteenth-century **Kings Gate** is one of the city's original medieval gateways, housing the tiny St Swithun's Church.

About a mile south of College Walk, reached by a pleasant stroll across the watermeadows of the Itchen, lies **St Cross Hospital** (April–Oct Mon–Sat 9.30am–5pm, Sun 1–5pm; Nov–March Mon–Sat 10.30am–3.30pm; £2.50). Founded in 1136 as a hostel for poor brethren, it boasts a fine church, begun in that year and completed a century or so later, where you can see a triptych by the Flemish painter Mabuse. Needy wayfarers may still apply for the "dole" at the Porter's Lodge – a tiny portion of bread and beer.

Eating and drinking

Winchester's **restaurants** and **pubs** offer fairly traditional meals on the whole, with a handful of places worth going out of your way for. For takeaway food, the town has one of the country's biggest farmers' markets, taking place on the second and last Sunday of each month (until around 2pm).

Courtyard Café The Guildhall, Broadway. Excellent lunches and teas are served at this relaxed café with gallery attached. Some outdoor tables. Closed evenings. Inexpensive.

Eclipse Inn 25 The Square. Picturesque sixteenth-century inn with some pavement seating, occupying the former rectory of St Lawrence's Church. Specializes in pies and casseroles. Inexpensive.

Forte Tea Rooms 78 Parchment St. Animated spot in the heart of the shopping area. Buffalo burgers, vegetable tagine and red chicken curry are on the menu, as well as a range of snacks, including renowned scones. Closed Mon–Wed eves & Sun all day. Inexpensive to moderate.

Loch Fyne 18 Jewry St ☎01962/872930. Dating from 1509, this converted jailhouse specializes in fish flown in direct from Scotland, but also serves up superb meat and vegetarian dishes. You can have lunch for £11, and great breakfasts too (£6–7). Moderate.

The Mash Tun 60 Eastgate St. Riverside alehouse popular with students, with a secluded terrace. There are DJs and live music nightly, plus discounts for students.

Old Chesil Rectory 1 Chesil St ☎01962/851555, Ⓦwww.thechesilrectory.co.uk. Push the boat out at this fifteenth-century oak-beamed restaurant serving gourmet English cuisine. A three-course menu is currently £23 for lunch, £49 for supper. Closed Sun, Mon & daytime Tues.

The Old Vine 8 Great Minster St ☎01962/854616. Close to the cathedral, this inn has oak beams, a log fire in winter, patio in summer, and real ales on tap. Toothsome evening meals are worth booking. Moderate.

Wykeham Arms 75 Kingsgate St ☎01962/853834. Winchester's most famous pub is somewhat unprepossessing from the outside, but inside it's a maze of characterful, intimate spaces where top-class food is served daily (not Sun eve) at school desks. Main courses are £12–19. Booking advised.

Alton, Chawton and Selborne

Fifteen miles northeast of Winchester, **ALTON** is an attractive town, whose major point of interest is the fifteenth-century **Church of St Lawrence**

(Mon–Sat 7.30am–4.30pm, Sun 8am–6.30pm), notable for its austere Perpendicular style. Its west doors still bear the marks of the shot that killed Royalist commander Colonel Boles, who had been chased by Roundheads through the streets of Alton and into the church during the Civil War. Buried in the church's cemetery is Fanny Adams, a little girl brutally hacked to death in 1867, whose name gave rise to the expression "sweet Fanny Adams" – meaning something negligible or without value; sailors at that time used the murder victim's name to describe the recent issue of tinned mutton, whose nutritional value they doubted.

Alton is also the terminus for the **Mid-Hants Watercress Line** (March, April, Oct & Dec Sat & Sun; May–Sept & school hols daily; ☏01962/733810, Ⓦwww.watercressline.co.uk; £10), a jolly, steam-powered train, so named because it passes through the former watercress beds that once flourished here. The train chuffs ten miles to Alresford, east of Winchester, with gourmet dinners served on board on Saturday evenings, traditional Sunday lunches and real ale evenings, too.

A mile southwest of Alton lies the village of **CHAWTON**, where Jane Austen lived from 1809 to 1817, during the last and most prolific years of her life, and where she wrote or revised almost all her six books, including *Sense and Sensibility* and *Pride and Prejudice*. **Jane Austen's House** (daily 10.30am–4.30/5pm; Jan & Feb Sat & Sun only; £5), in the centre of the village, is a plain red-brick building, containing first editions of some of her greatest works.

Four miles south of Chawton, the little village of **SELBORNE** is where the eighteenth-century naturalist Gilbert White wrote his ecological treatise, *The Natural History and Antiquities of Selborne*. In the High Street his house, **The Wakes** (June–Aug daily 11am–5pm; Sept–May Tues–Sun 11am–5pm; £6.50), is preserved as a memorial to his work and contains the original manuscript. White constructed the Zig Zag Path with his brother and made many of his observations on Selborne Hill, just southwest of the village, which is a pleasant hour's walk up to the top from The Wakes. The house also contains a **museum** commemorating Captain Oates, a member of Scott's ill-fated Antarctic expedition in 1912 – though Oates had no connection with the house or even the locality.

The New Forest

Covering about 220 square miles, the **New Forest** is one of southern England's main rural playgrounds, attracting some 13.5 million day-visits annually. The name itself is misleading, for much of this region's woodland was cleared for agriculture and settlement long before the Normans arrived, and its poor sandy soils support only a meagre covering of heather and gorse in many areas. The forest was requisitioned by William the Conqueror in 1079 as a game reserve, and the rights of its inhabitants soon became subservient to those of his precious deer. Fences to impede their progress were forbidden and terrible punishments were meted out to those who disturbed the animals – hands were lopped off, eyes put out. Later monarchs less passionate about hunting than the Normans gradually restored the forest-dwellers' rights, and today the New Forest enjoys a unique patchwork of ancient laws and privileges, alongside the regulations applying to its National Park status.

The **trees** of the forest are now much more varied than they were in pre-Norman times, with birch, holly, yew, Scots pine and other conifers interspersed with the ancient oaks and beeches. One of the most venerable is the much-visited **Knightwood Oak**, just a few hundred yards north of the A35 three miles southwest of Lyndhurst, which measures about 22ft in circumference at shoulder height. The most conspicuous species of New Forest **fauna** are the New Forest **ponies** (reputedly descendants of the survivors of the small Spanish horses of the Armada), now thoroughly domesticated – you'll see them grazing nonchalantly by the roadsides and ambling through villages. The local deer are less likely to be seen now that some of the faster roads are fenced, although several species still roam the woods, including the tiny **sika deer**, descendants of a pair that escaped from nearby Beaulieu in 1904.

The main wooded areas are around **Lyndhurst**, the "capital" of the New Forest, though **Brockenhurst** makes a more pleasant stopover. On the edge of the region lies the stately home and motor vehicle museum of **Beaulieu**, while on the coast, **Lymington** is a charming yachting town, popular with weekending city types.

Practicalities

Trains from London Waterloo serve Brockenhurst twice hourly; for Lyndhurst you have to alight at Lyndhurst Road Station, a couple of miles east of the town proper. There are bus routes from Lyndhurst and Brockenhurst to most parts of the forest, and between June and September you can take advantage of the New Forest tour bus (Ⓦwww.thenewforesttour.info), an open-top double-decker with a bike trailer that circulates between Lyndhurst, Brockenhurst, Lymington and Beaulieu eight times a day; you can get on or off anywhere along the route (all-day tickets £9).

To get the best from the region, however, you need to **walk** or **ride** through it, avoiding the roads. There are 150 miles of car-free gravel roads in the forest, making cycling an appealing prospect – pick up a book of route maps from tourist offices or bike rental shops (£2). The Ordnance Survey OS Explorer Map 22 of the New Forest is worth getting if you want to explore in any detail, and tourist offices sell numerous walking itineraries (from £1.25), specialist walking books and natural history guides.

Both Lyndhurst and Brockenhurst have plenty of reasonably priced accommodation, though there are also several expensive country house hotels and restaurants scattered in isolated settings. The forest has nine **campsites** run by the Forestry Commission, all but one closed between October and Easter – for more details, see Ⓦwww.forest-holidays.com or call ☎0845/130 8224. There's an excellently situated **youth hostel** in Cottesmore House, Cott Lane, Burley, in the west of the Forest (☎0870/770 5734, Ⓔburley@yha.org.uk; closed Nov–March; from £18), which also rents tents (sleeping 4; £40–50) and tipis (sleeping 6; £70), as well as having a few pitches for your own tent. The hostel's not directly accessible on public transport; it's a quarter-mile walk from Durmast Corner (buses #X34/35 from Bournemouth, Lyndhurst and Southampton), and half a mile from Burley (bus #176 from Christchurch and Ringwood). Note that the path leading through the forest is unlit. Drinks and meals are available next door at the *White Buck Inn*, which has a spacious garden.

Lyndhurst and around

LYNDHURST, its town centre skewered by an agonizing one-way system, isn't a particularly interesting place, but it has a concentration of useful services. At the **New Forest Visitor Centre**, in the central car park off the High Street (daily 10am–5pm; ☎023/8028 2269, Ⓦwww.thenewforest.co.uk), you can buy a very rough map of cycling routes, and pick up a list of riding outlets. The adjoining **New Forest Museum** (same times, last entry at 4pm; £3) has child-friendly displays focusing on the forest, its history, wildlife and industries. Otherwise, Lyndhurst is mainly interesting for its brick **parish church**, which boasts William Morris glass, a fresco by Lord Leighton and the grave of one Mrs Reginald Hargreaves, better known as Alice Liddell, Lewis Carroll's model for Alice.

Near the visitor centre in Gosport Lane, AA Bike Hire (☎023/8028 3349) rents **bikes** (£10 a day). For **accommodation** try: *Forest Cottage*, at the west end of the High Street (☎023/8028 3461, ⓦwww.forestcottage.co.uk; no credit cards; ❸), with a flowery garden and well-stocked library; *Burwood Lodge*, 27 Romsey Rd (☎023/8028 2445, ⓦwww.burwoodlodge.co.uk; no credit cards; ❹), a large Victorian house a few minutes from the High Street; or *The Stag*, one of the large inns lining the High Street (☎023/8028 2999, ⓦwww.stag-hotel.co.uk; ❺), with modern, airy rooms. The *Parisien* **café** at 64 High St sells baguettes and other snacks that you can eat in its small garden in summer; for larger meals, head for the Italian **restaurant** at *The Stag*, or the bar or restaurant at the *Crown Hotel*, also on the High Street.

The forest's most visited site, the **Rufus Stone** stands a few hundred yards from the M27 motorway, three miles northwest of Lyndhurst. Erected in 1745, the monument marks the putative spot where the Conqueror's ghastly son and heir, **William II** – aka William Rufus after his ruddy complexion – was killed in 1100. The official version is that a crossbow bolt fired by a member of the royal hunting party glanced off a stag and struck the king in the heart, though it's quite likely that this was a political assassination. The stone is remarkably unimpressive for such a landmark: the Victorians encased it in a protective layer of metal to deter vandals, and now it can't be seen at all clearly.

Three miles southwest of Lyndhurst, the popular **Ornamental Drives** of Bolderwood and Rhinefield are Victorian plantations of exotic trees, which are suggestive of overgrown ancient woodland. The Forestry Commission runs ranger-led hikes in the area: for details, ask at any New Forest visitor centre or call ☎023/8028 3141.

Brockenhurst

BROCKENHURST, four miles south of Lyndhurst, is a useful centre for visitors without their own transport; it's also attractive, with a village green, wide ford and surrounding woods. There's a train station right in town and **bikes for rent** at Cycle Experience (☎01590/624204, ⓦwww.cyclex.co.uk) by the level-crossing; they can also deliver bikes. The town has some decent places to **stay**: try the *Cottage Hotel* on Sway Road (☎01590/622296, ⓦwww.cottagehotel.org; ❺), which offers significant discounts on weekdays, or, just north of here on Grigg Lane, the quiet *Seraya* (☎01590/622426, ⓦwww.serayanewforest.co.uk; no credit cards; ❺), where two of the three neat, cottagey rooms share a bathroom. Brockenhurst offers fine dining at ⚜ *Simply Poussin*, The Courtyard, Brookley Road (☎01590/623063; closed Sun & Mon), with set-price menus to offset the expensive prices; the brasserie-type selection features adventurous local meat dishes, and you can eat alfresco in the courtyard. The *Snakecatcher* **pub** on Lyndhurst Road serves decent bar meals and has a garden.

Beaulieu and Buckler's Hard

The village of **BEAULIEU** (whose name originates from the French meaning "Beautiful Place", but is pronounced "Bewley"), in the southeast corner of the New Forest, was the site of one of England's most influential monasteries, a Cistercian house founded in 1204 by King John – in remorse, it is said, for ordering a group of supplicating Cistercian monks to be trampled to death. Built using stone ferried from Caen in northern France and Quarr on the Isle of Wight, the **abbey** managed a self-sufficient estate of ten thousand acres and became a famous sanctuary, offering shelter to Queen Margaret of Anjou among many others. It was dismantled soon after the Dissolution, and its refectory now forms the parish church, which, like everything else in Beaulieu, has been subsumed by the Montagu family, who have owned a large chunk of the New Forest since one of Charles II's illegitimate progeny was created duke of the estate.

The estate has been transformed with a prodigious commercial vigour into **Beaulieu** (daily: late May to Sept 10am–6pm; Oct to late May 10am–5pm; £15.25, or £8.40 excluding Motor Museum; ⓦ www.beaulieu.co.uk), a tourist complex comprising **Palace House**, the attractive if unexceptional family home, the remains of Beaulieu Abbey, and the main attraction, Lord Montagu's **National Motor Museum**. An undersized monorail and an old London bus ease the ten-minute walk between the entry point and Palace House. The home, formerly the abbey's gatehouse, contains masses of Montagu-related memorabilia while the undercroft of the adjacent abbey houses an exhibition depicting medieval monastic life. Inside the celebrated Motor Museum, a collection of 250 cars and motorcycles includes a £650,000 McLaren F1, James Bond-related vehicles, star-owned cars, spindly antiques and recent classics, as well as a quartet of svelte land-speed racers.

If Beaulieu amply deserves its name, **Buckler's Hard**, a couple of miles downstream on the Beaulieu River (daily: March–June, Sept & Oct 10am–5pm; July & Aug 10am–5.30pm; Nov–Feb 10am–4.30pm; £5.90), has an even more wonderful setting. It doesn't look much like a shipyard now, but from Elizabethan times onwards dozens of men o' war were assembled here from giant New Forest oaks. Several of Nelson's ships, including HMS *Agamemnon*, were launched here, to be towed carefully by rowing boats past the sandbanks and across the Solent to Portsmouth. The largest house in this hamlet of shipwrights' cottages, which forms part of the Montagu estate, belonged to Henry Adams, the master builder responsible for most of the Trafalgar fleet; it's now an upmarket **hotel** and **restaurant**, the *Master Builder's House Hotel* (☎01590/616253, ⓦ www.themasterbuilders.co.uk; ❸). At the top of the village, the **Maritime Museum** traces the history of the great ships and incorporates a labourer's cottage as it was in the 1790s, as well as the *New Inn*, shipwright's cottage and chapel – all preserved in their eighteenth-century form.

Lymington and around

The most pleasant point of access for the Isle of Wight (for ferry detail, see p.240) is **LYMINGTON**, a sheltered haven that's linked by ferry to Yarmouth and has become one of the busiest leisure harbours on the south coast. Rising from the quay area, the old town is full of cobbled streets and Georgian houses with one unusual building – the thirteenth-century church of **St Thomas the Apostle**, whose cupola-topped tower was added in 1670.

Information is available in summer from the local **visitor centre** in New Street, off the High Street (Mon–Sat 10am–4pm; ☎01590/689000). Places to **stay** in town include *Durlston House*, Gosport Street (☎01590/677364, ⓦ www .durlstonhouse.co.uk; ❹), a smart and clean townhouse with six en-suite rooms, and *The Angel Inn*, 108 High St (℡01590/672050, ⓦwww.roomattheinn .info; ⑤), an old coaching stop with functional rooms. As well as *The Angel*, Lymington has a good selection of **pubs** for food and drink, including the *Chequers* on Ridgeway Lane, on the west side of town, the *Bosun's Chair*, on Station Road, and the harbourfront *Ship Inn*, on the quayside, with seats outside looking over the water.

Signposted two miles west of Lymington, the **Sammy Miller Museum**, outside New Milton (daily 10am–4.30pm; £4.90), gives classic motorcycles the "Beaulieu" treatment. Many of the once-eminent British marques, from Ariel to Vincent, are displayed, as well as exotica from MV, NSU and several acclaimed trials bikes ridden by Sammy Miller himself, one of Britain's most successful trials riders.

Bournemouth and around

Renowned for its clean sandy beaches, the resort of **Bournemouth** is the nucleus of a vast and mainly monotonous conurbation stretching between Lymington and Poole harbour. The resort has a single-minded holiday-making atmosphere, though neighbouring **Poole** and **Christchurch** are more interesting historically. North of this coastal sprawl, the pleasant old market town of **Wimborne Minster** has one of the area's most striking churches, while the stately home of **Kingston Lacy** contains an outstanding collection of old masters and other paintings.

Bournemouth

BOURNEMOUTH dates only from 1811, when a local squire, Louis Tregonwell, built a summerhouse on the wild, unpopulated heathland that once occupied this stretch of coast, and planted the first of the pine trees that now characterize the area. By the end of the century Bournemouth's mild climate, sheltered site and glorious sandy beach had attracted nearly sixty thousand inhabitants. Today the resort has twice that number of residents, and an unshakably genteel, elderly image, though its geriatric nursing homes are counterbalanced by burgeoning numbers of language schools, a nightclub scene fuelled by a transient youthful population, and the construction of an artificial surf reef planned for 2008.

Arrival, information and accommodation
Trains from London Waterloo stop just under a mile east of Bournemouth town centre; from the **bus station** opposite, frequent buses run into town. The **tourist office**, right in the centre of town on Westover Road (mid-July to mid-Sept daily 9.30am–6pm; mid-Sept to mid-July Mon–Sat 10am–5/5.30pm; ℡0845/051 1701, ⓦwww.bournemouth.co.uk), books National Express tickets, bus tours and boat trips.

There's no shortage of **accommodation** in the Bournemouth area – the town has more than four hundred hotels and guest houses covering every budget – but most are pretty charmless. **Campers** should head out to *Mount Pleasant Touring Park*, Matchams Lane, Hurn (℡01202/475474, ⓦwww .mount-pleasant-cc.co.uk; closed Nov–Feb), five miles northeast of town on the A338 to Ringwood – though, located between the dual carriageway and Bournemouth Airport, the site can be noisy.

▲ Bournemouth beach

Hotels, B&Bs and hostels

Bournemouth Backpackers 3 Frances Rd
℡01202/299491, www
.bournemouthbackpackers.co.uk. Small, friendly
hostel, three minutes from train and bus stations,
for non-UK nationals only. Dorm beds cost up to
£16 on a Saturday in peak season, considerably
lower at other times, and one double also
available (●). Two-night minimum stay (single

nights are sometimes available but cannot be
booked, and cost £3 extra), with check-in only
possible 5–6pm (and not at all Sat). ●
Earlham Lodge 91 Alumhurst Rd, Alum Chine
℡01202/761943, www.earlhamlodge.com.
Behind the bland exterior of this guest house near
the beach are a variety of richly decorated en-suite
rooms (named after dolls), one with a four-poster.
Parking available. ●

Langtry Manor 26 Derby Rd, East Cliff
☎01202/553887, ⊛www.langtrymanor.com.
Former hideaway of Edward VII and his mistress,
Lillie Langtry, this luxury hotel has Edwardian
furnishings and hosts period-style banquets on Sat
evenings. Discounted online rates. ❻

Tudor Grange 31 Gervis Rd, East Cliff
☎01202/291472, ⊛www.tudorgrangehotel
.co.uk. Tudor-style hotel whose gardens and
oak-panelled interior give it more character than
most places hereabouts. Live acoustic music on
Wed. ❺

The Town

The blandly modern town that you see today has little to remind you of
Bournemouth's Victorian heyday, though the River Bourne still runs down
through a park to the town's centre, which consists of a network of one-way
streets running around The Square and down to **Bournemouth Pier**. Other
than sunbathing along the pristine sandy beach – one of southern England's
cleanest – the town's greatest attraction is its unusually high proportion of green
space, set aside during the boom years at the end of the nineteenth century. As
well as having more than three million pine trees, a sixth of the town – around
two thousand acres – is given over to horticultural displays, and exploring
Bournemouth's **public gardens** can easily fill a day.

The most enthralling experience in Bournemouth, however, is one of the
region's best collections of Victoriana, the excellent **Russell–Cotes Art
Gallery and Museum** on East Cliff Promenade (Tues–Sun 10am–5pm; free)
which houses a motley assortment of artworks and oriental souvenirs gathered
from around the world by the Russell-Cotes family, hoteliers who grew wealthy
during Bournemouth's late-Victorian tourist boom. The benefactors' lavishly
decorated former home, featuring unusual stained glass and ornate painted
ceilings, is jam-packed with their eclectic collections, of which the Japanese
artefacts are especially interesting. There are some good examples of
Pre-Raphaelite and other British art downstairs, with period decor throughout
and a cliff-top landscaped garden.

In the centre of town, just east of The Square, the graveyard of **St Peter's
Church** houses the body of Mary Shelley, author of the Gothic horror tale
Frankenstein, together with the heart belonging to her husband, the poet Percy
Bysshe Shelley, former resident of Boscombe, a suburb of the town. The tombs
of Mary's parents – radical thinker William Godwin and early feminist Mary
Wollstonecraft – are also here.

Eating and drinking

With ubiquitous fast-food joints, Bournemouth has few noteworthy places for
a **meal**, though it is possible to unearth a decent seafood dish in congenial
surroundings. Likewise, the town is awash with big booze halls, but you'll need
to venture off the beaten track to find a decent pub with both ale and
atmosphere.

Bistro on the Beach Esplanade, South-
bourne end ☎01202/431473. Situated
right on the beach, this informal place is a café by
day, good for coffees and snacks, and has bistro
meals including steaks and seafood in the evening
(worth booking). Closed Mon & Tues in winter.
Inexpensive to moderate.

Goat and Tricycle 27 West Hill Rd. This quiet and
unpretentious pub is worth a trek up the hill for the
real ales and good food. Inexpensive to moderate.

Salathai 1066 Christchurch Rd, Boscombe
☎01202/420772. The huge menu has authentic
spicy Thai dishes, including chilli-laced chicken and
fried noodles. Abundant set-price menus cost
£18–21. Closed Mon lunch.

West Beach Pier Approach ☎01202/587785.
Lively, modern seafood restaurant with an attached
takeaway (in summer) and a great outdoor terrace
on the Promenade by the pier. Live jazz every Thurs
evening. Expensive.

The university and foreign-language students and young holiday-makers help keep Bournemouth's **nightlife** lively; the free monthly listings magazine *Live Wire* has news of gigs in the town. Of the **nightclubs**, the biggest and best known is *Elements*, in the centre of town on Firvale Road (℡01202/311178, Ⓦwww.elements-nightclub.com; closed Mon), playing mainstream dance, retro and R'n'B on three levels. Boscombe has the flamboyant *Opera House*, 570 Christchurch Rd (℡0870/198 9897, Ⓦwww.operahouse.co.uk), featuring mainstream, funk and drum and bass, plus regular **bands**.

The **Bournemouth Live** music festival (Ⓦwww.bournemouthlive.info), taking place over a week in late June, draws a range of performers of every genre; as well as indoor venues all over town there are four free outdoor stages.

Christchurch

CHRISTCHURCH, five miles east of Bournemouth, is best known for its colossal parish church, **Christchurch Priory** (Mon–Sat 9.30am–5pm, Sun 2.15–5.30pm; £2 donation requested), which is bigger than most cathedrals. Built on the site of a Saxon minster dating from 650 AD, but exhibiting chiefly Norman and Perpendicular features, the church is the longest in England, at 311ft, and its fan-vaulted North Porch is the country's biggest. Legend tells of how the building materials were moved overnight to the present location and of the hand of a mysterious carpenter who assisted in the work, hence the priory's name. The choir, beautifully lit by huge, clear-glass windows and separated from the nave by a finely carved Jesse Screen, contains what is probably the oldest misericord in England, dating from 1210, and complemented by a 1960s mural by Hans Feibush above the stone reredos. Fine views can be gained from the top of the 120-foot tower (£2).

The area around the old town quay has a carefully preserved charm, with the **Red House Museum and Gardens** on Quay Road (Tues–Sat 10am–5pm, Sun 2–5pm; free) containing an affectionate collection of local memorabilia, and hosting varied temporary exhibitions. **Boat trips** (Easter–Oct daily; ℡01202/429119) leave from the grassy banks of the riverside quay east to Mudeford (30min; £5.50 return) or upriver to the *Tuckton Tea Rooms* (15min; £2.50 return). Rowing boats (£15 per hour) and self-drive motor-boats (£20 per hour) are also available.

The **tourist office**, 23 High St (Mon–Fri 9.30am–5/5.30pm, Sat 9.30am–4.30/5pm; ℡01202/471780, Ⓦwww.visitchristchurch.info), can supply you with a town map and a visitor's guide. There's no shortage of accommodation in town, with Barrack and Stour roads, a few minutes northwest of the centre, lined with unexciting but reliable guest houses. Alternatively, head out to the Highcliffe area, three miles east of town on the A337, where the airy, Art Deco *Beechcroft Place*, 106 Lymington Rd (℡01425/277171, Ⓦwww .beachmeetsforest.co.uk; ❹), offers more stylish B&B, with organic breakfasts served in private lounges.

For **food**, *La Mamma*, 51 Bridge St (℡01202/471608; closed Sun lunch & Mon), serves cheap and cheerful Italian classics (including pizzas), with alfresco eating in summer, while *The Boathouse* on the Quay offers breakfasts, snack lunches and full evening meals, and has great views (℡01202/480033; closed eves Sun, Mon & Tues in winter). Christchurch's oldest pub, *Ye Olde George Inn*, 2a Castle St, has an attractive courtyard and a good menu.

Poole and around

Five miles west of Bournemouth's centre – though effectively joined to the town – **POOLE** is an ancient seaport on a huge, almost landlocked harbour. The port developed in the thirteenth century and was successively colonized by pirates, fishermen and timber traders, more recently replaced by companies prospecting for oil in the shallow waters – the harbour's environmental significance ensures that the extraction process is carefully disguised. The old quarter by the quayside is worth exploring: the old Custom House, Scaplen's Court and Guildhall are the most striking of over a hundred historic buildings within a fifteen-acre site.

At the bottom of Old High Street, near the Poole Pottery showroom and crafts centre, **Scaplen's Court** (Aug Mon–Sat 10am–5pm, Sun noon–5pm; free) is a late medieval building where Cromwell's troops were once billeted (you can see their graffiti around the fireplace). It has now been restored as an educational centre, with reconstructions of a Victorian kitchen, pharmacy and schoolroom and displays of old-time toys and games. Over the road, the well-presented **Poole Museum** (Easter–Oct Mon–Sat 10am–5pm, Sun noon–5pm; Nov–Easter Tues–Sat 10am–4pm, Sun noon–4pm; free) traces the town's development over the centuries and features local ceramics and tiles and a rare Iron Age log boat, in addition to changing exhibitions.

From Poole Quay, **boat trips** run to Brownsea Island (see box below) and between Easter and October to Swanage (£8 return), the Isle of Wight (£20 return), and upriver to Wareham (£8.50 return), depending on the tides (check Ⓦwww.poolequay.com for details).

One of the area's most famous gardens lies on the outskirts of Poole, **Compton Acres** (daily 9am–4/6pm; last entry 1hr before closing; £6.95; Ⓦwww.comptonacres.co.uk), signposted off the A35 Poole Road, towards Bournemouth. Here you'll find seven gardens, each with a different international theme, the best of which, the elegantly understated Japanese Garden, contrasts with the more familiar classical symmetry of the Italian Garden. Buses #150 (Bournemouth–Swanage) and #151 (Bournemouth–Poole) stop here.

Practicalities

Poole's train station is on Serpentine Lane, by the Dolphin Shopping Centre, a fifteen-minute walk from the waterfront down the High Street. The bus station, also close to the shopping centre, is on Kingland Road. The **tourist office** is on Poole Quay (April–June, Sept & Oct daily 10am–5pm; July & Aug daily 9.15am–6pm; Nov–March Mon–Fri 10am–5pm, Sat 10am–4pm;

Brownsea Island

In the middle of Poole harbour, the five-hundred-acre **Brownsea Island** (Easter to late July & Sept daily 10am–5pm; late July to Aug daily 10am–6pm; Oct daily 10am–4pm; £4.70; NT) is famed for its red squirrels, wading birds and other wildlife, which you can spot along themed trails. The surprisingly diverse landscape – including heath, woodland and fine beaches – affords striking views. The most regular visitors here are scouts and guides: the Boy Scout movement was formed in the wake of a camping expedition to the island led by Lord Baden-Powell in 1907, and scouts are the only people allowed to camp here. The island is now managed by the National Trust.

Brownsea Island is linked by regular **ferries** with Poole's quayside (20min; £7.50 return; ☎01929/462383); there are also departures from the Sandbanks peninsula (west of Poole), Swanage (see p.265) and Bournemouth (see p.256).

①01202/253253, Ⓦwww.pooletourism.com). Quality **accommodation** in town includes the *Antelope Hotel* at 8 High St (①01202/672029, Ⓦwww .antelopeinn.com; ❻), a handsome old hostelry in the old town centre, and, further north, but close to the station, the Victorian B&B *Cranborne House*, 45 Shaftesbury Rd (①01202/685200, Ⓦwww.cranborne-house.co.uk; ❺), a few minutes' walk from the bus and train stations. Alternatively, at the bottom of the High Street on the Quay, the café-restaurant *Corkers* (①01202/681393, Ⓦwww.corkers.co.uk; ❹) has five en-suite rooms upstairs, two with panoramic roof balconies.

There's a collection of good **restaurants** on the High Street, among them *Storm*, a moderate-to-expensive seafood restaurant at no. 16 (①01202/674970; closed Sun lunch), and, at the top end of the street, *Alcatraz* (①01202/660244), a relaxed Italian brasserie with outdoor tables. *Corkers* (see above) has a café and bar downstairs and a restaurant above, serving tasty meat and seafood dishes for around £15. Among Poole's **pubs**, try the medieval hall in the *King Charles* on Thames Street, with its leather armchairs and big screen, or, on the Quay, the green tile-fronted *Poole Arms*, which serves seafood and pub grub at reasonable prices.

Wimborne Minster and Kingston Lacy

An ancient town on the banks of the Stour, just a few minutes' drive north from the suburbs of Bournemouth, **WIMBORNE MINSTER**, as the name suggests, is mainly of interest for its great church, the **Minster of St Cuthberga** (Mon–Sat 9.30am–5.30pm, Sun 2.30–5.30pm). Built on the site of an eighth-century monastery, its massive twin towers of mottled grey and tawny stone dwarf the rest of the town; at one time the church was even more imposing – its spire crashed down during morning service in 1602, though amazingly no one was injured, and since then Wimborne has not risked heavenly ire by replacing it. What remains today is basically Norman with later features added such as the Perpendicular west tower, which bears a figure dressed as a grenadier of the Napoleonic era, who strikes every quarter-hour with a hammer. Inside, the church is crowded with memorials and eye-catching details – look out for the orrery clock inside the west tower, with the sun marking the hours and the moon marking the days of the month, and for the organ with trumpets pointing out towards the congregation instead of pipes. The **Chained Library** above the choir vestry (Easter–Oct Mon–Fri 10.30am–12.30pm & 2–4pm, Sat 10.30am–12.30pm, Nov–Easter Sat 10.30am–12.30pm), dating from 1686, is Wimborne's most prized possession and one of the oldest public libraries in the country.

Wimborne's older buildings stand around the main square near the minster, and are mostly from the late eighteenth or early nineteenth century. The **Priest's House** on the High Street started life as lodgings for the clergy, then became a stationer's shop. Now it is an award-winning **museum** (Easter–Oct 10am–4.30pm; also open two weeks after Christmas; £3), each room furnished in the style of a different period. A working Victorian kitchen, a Georgian parlour and an ironmonger's shop are among its exhibits, and there's a display of items relating to local archeology and history; a walled garden at the rear provides an excellent place for summer teas.

One of the country's finest seventeenth-century country houses, **Kingston Lacy** (house: Easter to Oct Wed–Sun 11am–4pm; grounds: Feb to mid-March Sat & Sun 10.30am–4pm; Easter–Oct daily 10.30am–6pm or dusk; Nov to mid-Dec Fri–Sun 10.30am–4pm; house & grounds £10, grounds only £5; NT), lies two miles northwest of Wimborne Minster, in 250 acres of parkland grazed by a herd of Red Devon cattle. Designed for the Bankes family, who were exiled from Corfe Castle (see opposite) after the Roundheads reduced it to rubble, the brick building was clad in grey stone during the nineteenth century by Charles Barry, co-architect of the Houses of Parliament. William Bankes, then owner of the house, was a great traveller and collector, and the **Spanish Room** is a superb scrapbook of his Grand Tour souvenirs, lined with gilded leather and surmounted by a Venetian ceiling. Kingston Lacy's **picture collection** is also outstanding, featuring Titian, Rubens, Velázquez and many other old masters. The place can get swamped with visitors, so entry is by timed tickets on busy weekends.

Wimborne's **tourist office** is at 29 High St (Mon–Sat 9.30am–4.30/5.30pm; ℡01202/886116, ⓦwww.ruraldorset.com). For bistro **lunches** or suppers, try *Primizia* on West Borough (℡01202/883518; closed Sat lunch, Sun & Mon), with low ceiling and vibrant decor, or the plainer *Cloisters* at 40 East St, which also serves teas, coffees and snacks (closed eve & Sun afternoon).

The Isle of Purbeck

Though not actually an island, the **Isle of Purbeck** – a promontory of low hills and heathland jutting out beyond Poole Harbour – does have an insular and distinctive feel. Reached from the east by the **ferry from Sandbanks** (see p.264), at the narrow mouth of Poole harbour, or by a long and congested landward journey via the bottleneck of **Wareham**, Purbeck's villages are immensely pretty, none more so than **Corfe Castle**, with its majestic ruins. **Swanage**, a low-key seaside resort, is flanked by more exciting coastlines, all accessible on the Dorset Coast Path: to one side the chalk stacks and soft dunes of Studland Bay, to the other the cliffs of Durlston Head and Dancing Ledge, leading to the oily shales of **Kimmeridge Bay**, the spectacular cove at **Lulworth** and the much-photographed natural arch of **Durdle Door**. Like Portland, further west, the area is pockmarked with stone quarries – Purbeck marble is the finest grade of the local oolitic limestone. The villages and landscape hereabouts were the backdrop for Enid Blyton's Famous Five tales.

Wareham and around

The grid pattern of its streets indicates the Saxon origins of **WAREHAM**, and the town is surrounded by even older earth ramparts known as the Walls. A riverside setting adds greatly to its charms, though there can be horrible traffic queues in summer, and the scenic stretch along the Quay also gets fairly overrun. Nearby lies an oasis of quaint houses around **Lady St Mary's Church**, which contains the marble coffin of Edward the Martyr, murdered at Corfe Castle in 978 by his stepmother, to make way for her unready son Ethelred.

St Martin's Church, at the north end of town, dates from Saxon times and the chancel contains a faded twelfth-century mural of St Martin offering his cloak to a beggar, but the church's most striking feature is a romantic effigy of T.E. Lawrence in Arab dress, which was originally destined for Salisbury Cathedral, but was rejected by the dean there who disapproved of Lawrence's sexual proclivities. Lawrence was killed in 1935 in a motorbike accident on the road from Bovington (six miles west), after returning to Dorset from his Middle Eastern adventures. Some of Lawrence's memorabilia is displayed in the small **museum** next to the town hall in East Street (Easter–Oct Mon–Sat 10am–4pm; free)

Lawrence's simply furnished cottage is at **Clouds Hill** (mid-March to Oct Thurs–Sun noon–5pm or dusk; £4; NT), seven miles northwest of Wareham, while further Lawrence effects are on show at the absorbing but overpriced **Tank Museum** in Bovington Camp, five miles west of town (daily 10am–5pm; £10; ⊛ www.tankmuseum.co.uk). The 150 vehicles here include tanks from many of the conflicts from World War I onwards, including British Challenger I and Challenger II tanks and captured Iraqi tanks from both Gulf Wars. You can also walk through a replica trench of the Somme, and watch a mock tank battle complete with pyrotechnics (usually Thurs: call ☎01929/405096 for info).

Some three miles south of Wareham, near Furzebrook, the **Blue Pool**, centred on an intensely coloured clay-pit lake, has a small museum (mid-March to Oct daily 10am–5/6pm; £4.80) that gives the background to the local clay industry, and there are cream teas and nature trails.

Practicalities

Arriving at the train station north of town, you can either pick up a connecting bus service or walk into the centre (about 15min). Holy Trinity Church, on South Street, contains Wareham's **tourist office** (Mon–Sat 9.30am–4/5pm, also Sun in summer school holidays 9.30am–5pm; ☎01929/552740, ⊛ www .purbeck.gov.uk). From the nearby Quay, row- and motorboats are available to rent (£16 and £24 an hour).

The best central **accommodation** option is *Anglebury House*, 15 North St (☎01929/552988, ⊛ www.angleburyhouse.co.uk; ❸), an old-fashioned hotel whose previous guests have included Thomas Hardy and T.E. Lawrence. The *Old Granary* **restaurant** on the Quay (☎01929/552010) has views over the river and the meadows beyond, while *Harry's*, 21 South St (closed Sun), offers filling snacks and free **Internet** access.

Corfe Castle

The romantic ruins crowning the hill behind the village of **CORFE CASTLE** (daily 10am–4/6pm; £5.30; NT) are perhaps the most evocative in England. The family seat of Sir John Bankes, Attorney General to Charles I, this Royalist stronghold withstood a Cromwellian siege for six weeks, gallantly defended by Lady Bankes. One of her own men, Colonel Pitman, eventually betrayed the castle to the Roundheads, after which it was reduced to its present gap-toothed state by gunpowder. Apparently the victorious Roundheads were so impressed by Lady Bankes's courage that they allowed her to take the keys to the castle with her – they can still be seen in the library at the Bankes's subsequent home, Kingston Lacy (see p.261).

The village is well stocked with tearooms and gift shops and has a couple of good **pubs** too: the *Fox* on West Street, where you can drink or have lunch in a large garden with views to the castle, and, below the castle ramparts, the *Greyhound*. The *Bankes Arms Hotel*, an old inn outside the castle entrance, also serves pub lunches in its beer garden and provides reasonable **accommodation** (☎01929/480206, ⊛ www.dorset-hotel.co.uk; ❺), though some of the rooms are shabby. Cheaper and cleaner lodging can be found at *Westaway*, 88 West St (☎01929/480188, ⊛ www.westaway-corfecastle.co.uk; no credit cards; ❸), a B&B five minutes from the castle, with a garden and views of the Purbeck Hills.

▲ Corfe Castle

Shell Bay to St Alban's Head

Purbeck's most northerly coastal stretch, **Shell Bay**, is a magnificent beach of icing-sugar sand backed by a remarkable heathland ecosystem that's home to all six British species of reptile – adders are quite common, so be careful. At the top end of the beach, a chain **ferry** (7am–11pm every 20min; pedestrians 90p, bikes 80p, cars £3) crosses the mouth of Poole harbour connecting the Isle of Purbeck with the ostentatious Sandbanks peninsula in Poole. To the south the broad and sheltered sweep of **Studland Bay** holds one of the loveliest beaches on this coast – all white sands and dramatic white chalk stacks at its southernmost end, with one section designated for naturists.

Beyond Studland Bay lies **SWANAGE**, a traditional seaside resort with a pleasant sandy beach and an ornate town hall, the facade of which once adorned the Mercers' Hall in the City of London and was brought back here as ballast on a cargo ship. The town's station is the southern terminus of the **Swanage Steam Railway** (April–Oct daily; Nov, Dec & mid-Feb to March Sat & Sun; £7.50 all day; ☏01929/425800, ⓦwww.swanagerailway.co.uk), which runs for six miles to Norden (on the A351). Swanage's **tourist office** is by the beach on Shore Road (Easter–Oct daily 10am–5pm; Nov–Easter Mon–Sat 10am–5pm; ☏01929/422885, ⓦwww.swanage.gov.uk), and there's a **youth hostel**, with good views across the bay, on Cluny Crescent (☏0870/770 6058, ⓔswanage@yha.org.uk; open mainly during school hols, closed Dec & Jan), costing from £22 for a dorm bed plus breakfast, with private rooms also available (❶). There are scores of **B&Bs** in Swanage, including a cluster just off the High Street, along Park Road – try the spacious Victorian 🏠 *Clare House*, at no. 1 (☏01929/422855, ⓦwww.clare-house.com; ❺), 200m from the beach and offering pancakes for breakfast – and there's a handy trio on King's Road near the train station. Among Swanage's wide variety of **places to eat**, try the cosy, family-run *Trattoria*, 12 High St (☏01929/423784), a good bet for moderately priced Italian meals, while cappuccinos and baguettes are served next door at *Forte's Caffè Tratt*. If you're interested in exploring the Purbeck Cycleway (map available from the tourist office), **rent bikes** from Bikeabout, 71 High St (☏01929/425050; closed Sun except during Easter and summer school hols), opposite the town hall.

Highlights of the coast beyond Swanage are the cliffs of **Durlston Head**, topped by a lighthouse. Nearby stands a vast stone globe weighing forty tonnes, installed by George Burt, an eccentric Victorian building contractor from Swanage, who also erected the local folly castle, now housing a good café. The cliffs continue to **St Alban's Head**, their ledges crowded with seabirds and rare wildflowers in spring. Paths lead inland to the attractive villages of **Langton Matravers**, where a **museum** behind the church interprets the local stone-quarrying industry (April–Sept Mon–Sat 10am–noon & 2–4pm; £1.50), and **Worth Matravers**, with a fine Norman church and a great **pub**, the *Square & Compass,* full of nooks and crannies, and with outdoor seating to enjoy the views; home-made pies are available.

Kimmeridge Bay to Durdle Door

Beyond St Alban's Head the coastal geology suddenly changes as the grey-white chalk and limestone give way to darker beds of shale. **Kimmeridge Bay** may not have a sandy beach but it does have a remarkable marine wildlife reserve much appreciated by divers – there's a Dorset Wildlife Trust **information centre** by the slipway (Easter–Sept daily 10am–5pm; Oct–Easter Sat & Sun 11.30am–4.30pm; ☏01929/481044, ⓦdorsetwildlife.co.uk). The amazing range of species is all the more surprising because the bay has been the site of small-scale industry for centuries. The Saxons crafted amulets from the shale and the extraction of alum (for glassmaking) and coal followed. Today a low-tech "nodding donkey" oil well fits unobtrusively into the landscape.

The Lulworth artillery ranges west of Kimmeridge are inaccessible during weekdays but generally open at weekends and in school holidays – watch out for the red warning flags and notices and always stick to the path. Roads in this area have similar restrictions, but generally open before 9am and after 5pm to allow commuters through; call ☎01929/404819 or 01929/404712 for current details. The coastal path passes close to the deserted village of **Tyneham**, whose residents were summarily evicted by the army in 1943; the abandoned stone cottages have an eerie fascination, and an exhibition in the church explains the history of the village. The army's presence has helped to preserve the local habitat, which hosts many species of flora and fauna long since vanished from farmed or otherwise developed areas.

The quaint thatch-and-stone villages of East and West Lulworth form a prelude to **Lulworth Cove**, a perfect shell-shaped bite formed when the sea broke through a weakness in the cliffs and then gnawed away at them from behind, forming a circular cave which eventually collapsed to leave a bay enclosed by sandstone cliffs. Lulworth's scenic charms are well known, and as you descend the hill through West Lulworth in summer the sun glints off the metal of a thousand car roofs in the car park behind the cove. At the **Lulworth Heritage Centre** the mysteries of the local geology are explained (daily 10am–4/6pm; free).

Immediately west of the cove you come to **Stair Hole**, a roofless sea cave riddled with arches that will eventually collapse to form another Lulworth, and a couple of miles west is **Durdle Door**, a famous limestone arch that appeals to serious geologist and casual sightseer alike. Most people take the uphill route to the arch which starts from the car park at Lulworth Cove, but there's also an alternative, if tide-dependent, route up the private drive from the Heritage Centre and down into the secluded St Oswald's Bay which separates Lulworth from Durdle Door. If you've timed it right you can slip round the headland and climb up to the arch although you may prefer to stay on the more agreeable St Oswald's Beach.

WEST LULWORTH is the obvious place to stay or eat on this section of coast. The *Castle Inn* (☎01929/400311, ⓦwww.thecastleinn-lulworthcove .co.uk; ⑤), *Cromwell House Hotel* (☎01929/400253, ⓦwww.lulworthcove .co.uk; ⑥), right on the coast path with a heated pool (ask about cheaper rooms in the next-door *Rose Cottage*, under the same management), and the seventeenth-century *Ivy Cottage* (☎01929/400509, ⓦwww.ivycottage.biz; no credit cards; ③), with an inglenook fireplace, all make good stop-offs. There's a **youth hostel** at the end of School Lane (☎0870/770 5940, Ⓔlulworth@yha.org.uk; closed Dec–Feb, also Sun & Mon in low season; dorm beds from £16); a plain chalet with small rooms, it's a stone's throw from the Dorset Coast Path. **Campers** can find a pitch at the *Durdle Door Holiday Park*, a mile from West Lulworth, towards East Chaldon (☎01929/400200, ⓦwww.lulworth.com; closed Nov–Feb).

The *Castle* in West Lulworth and the similarly thatched *Weld Arms* in East Lulworth offer refreshments and meals, while in East Chaldon, four miles northwest of Lulworth Cove, the *Sailor's Return* serves great beer and a range of **pub food**.

Weymouth to West Bay

Whether George III's passion for sea bathing was a symptom of his eventual madness is uncertain, but it was at the bay of **Weymouth** that in 1789 he became the first reigning monarch to follow the craze. Sycophantic gentry rushed into the waves behind him, and soon the town, formerly a workaday harbour, took on the elegant Georgian stamp which it bears today. A likeness of the monarch on horseback is even carved into the chalk downs northwest of the town, like some guardian spirit. Weymouth nowadays plays second fiddle to the vast resort of Bournemouth to the east, but it's still a lively family holiday destination, alternately seedy and sedate.

Just south of the town stretch the giant arms of Portland Harbour, and a long causeway links Weymouth to the strange five-mile-long excrescence of the **Isle of Portland**. West of the causeway, the bank of pebbles known as **Chesil Beach** runs eighteen miles northwest in the direction of **West Bay**.

Weymouth

WEYMOUTH had long been a port before the Georgians popularized it as a resort. It's possible that a ship unloading a cargo here in 1348 first brought the Black Death to English shores, and it was from Weymouth that John Endicott sailed in 1628 to found Salem in Massachusetts. A few buildings survive from these pre-Georgian times: the restored **Tudor House** on Trinity Street (Feb–May & Oct–Dec first Sun of month 2–4pm; June–Sept Tues–Fri 1–4pm; £3) and the ruins of **Sandsfoot Castle** (free access), built by Henry VIII, overlooking Portland Harbour. But Weymouth's most imposing architectural heritage stands along the Esplanade, a dignified range of bow-fronted and porticoed buildings gazing out across the graceful bay, an ensemble rather disrupted by the garish **clocktower** commemorating Victoria's jubilee. The more intimate quayside of the Old Harbour, linked to the Esplanade by the main pedestrianized thoroughfare St Mary's Street, is lined with waterfront pubs from where you can view the passing yachts, trawlers and ferries.

Weymouth boasts a number of "all-weather" attractions, notably: **Sea Life Park** in Lodmoor Country Park, east of the Esplanade (daily 10am–6pm; winter closes at 4 or 5pm, last admission 1hr before closing; £12.95, or £9 from tourist office), where you can get close to sharks and rays; **Deep Sea Adventure** at the Old Harbour (daily 9.30am–5.30pm, closes later in summer; last entry 90min before closing; £3.95), which describes the origins of modern diving and the *Titanic* disaster; and, over the river on Hope Square, **Timewalk** (March–Oct daily 10am–4pm; summer school hols open until 9pm; last entry 1hr before closing; £4.75, or £4 from tourist office), holding an entertaining and educational walk-through exhibition of Weymouth's maritime and brewing past.

A fifteen-minute walk southwards leads to **Nothe Fort** (May–Sept daily 10.30am–5.30pm; Oct–April Sun 11am–4pm; £5), built in 1860–72 to defend Portland Harbour. Inside, there are displays on military themes and a museum describing garrison life and the castle's role in coastal defence. For further exploration of the bay, the glass-bottomed *Fleet Observer* sails from the *Ferrybridge* pub, on the A354 Portland Road (Easter–Oct 6–7 daily; 1hr; £6; ☎01305/759692).

Practicalities

Weymouth's **train station** and **bus station** are next to each other off King Street, just steps away from the **tourist office** at King's Statue, the Esplanade (daily 9.30/10am–4/5pm; ☎01305/785747, ⓦwww.visitweymouth.co.uk). Condor Ferries (☎0870/240 8003, ⓦwww.condorferries.com) operates a **catamaran** from Weymouth's harbour to the Channel Islands (April–Oct daily; Nov–March 2–4 weekly).

Accommodation

Weymouth has a plethora of accommodation, much of it fairly tacky, though a cluster of more attractive options lies at the south end of the Esplanade, between the bay and harbour and close to the Condor ferry terminal. There are ten campsites in the area – *Bagwell Farm Touring Park*, a couple of miles west of town at Chickerell (℡01305/782575), is the only one that's open all year.

Cavendish House 6 The Esplanade ℡01305/782039, ⊛www.cavendishhousehotel .co.uk. Well-positioned B&B in a detached Georgian terrace overlooking the bay, with harbour views at the back. No credit cards. ❸

The Chatsworth 14 The Esplanade ℡01305/785012, ⊛www.thechatsworth.co.uk. Harbourside hotel with great views from the rooms (one with a balcony), and there's a nice terrace for eating out. ❻

The Pebbles 18 Kirtleton Avenue ℡01305/784331, ⊛www.thepebbles.co.uk. In a quiet location 10 minutes' walk from the centre, this Victorian B&B has smallish but clean and good-value rooms with and without bathrooms. ❷

Wilton Guest House 5 Gloucester St ℡01305/782820, ⊛www.thewiltonguesthouse .co.uk. Just a few steps from the seafront and 400m from the train station, this agreeable B&B has bright, good-size rooms, all en suite, with crisp bed linen. There's also a small terrace. ❹

Eating and drinking

The town is also well equipped with places to eat, and you'll usually find seafood on the menu. Many **pubs** also offer inexpensive meals.

Lazy Lizard 52–53 The Esplanade. Seafront lounge bar good for a snack or a late drink. Indie bands play Fri & Sat.

Nothe Tavern Nothe Gardens (south of the harbour on Barrack Road). Tasty bar meals and real ales are offered here, enhanced by excellent harbour views from the garden. Moderate.

Perry's 4 Trinity Rd ℡01305/785799. For seafood, you can't do better than this classy restaurant overlooking the quay. There's a two-course lunchtime menu for £15. Closed Sat lunch & Mon. Expensive.

Rendezvous Town Bridge. This busy place includes a bar, restaurant and nightclub, so it can get rowdy at weekends.

Sailors Return Corner of St Nicholas St and Commercial Rd. Harbourside tavern decorated with angling paraphernalia, offering Wadworths and Fullers among other ales (but no food).

Seagull Café 10 Trinity St. Family-run chippie with fresh fish and lashings of chips. Closed Mon & mid-Dec to Feb. Inexpensive.

Portland

Stark, wind-battered and treeless, the **Isle of Portland** is famed above all for its hard white limestone, which has been quarried here for centuries – Wren used it for St Paul's Cathedral, and it clads the UN headquarters in New York. It was also used for the six-thousand-foot breakwater that protects Portland Harbour – the largest artificial harbour in Britain, which was built by convicts in the mid-nineteenth century. The quarries are prominent and unlovely features of the island today.

By public transport, you can reach the Isle of Portland from Weymouth on the frequent #1 and (in summer) #501 buses. The causeway road by which the Isle is approached stands on the easternmost section of the Chesil shingle. The first settlement you come to, **FORTUNESWELL**, overlooks the huge harbour and is itself surveyed by a 460-year-old Tudor fortress, **Portland Castle** (Easter–June & Sept daily 10am–5pm; July & Aug daily 10am–6pm; Oct daily 10am–4pm; £4; EH), commissioned by Henry VIII. The craggy limestone of the isle rises to 496 feet at Verne Hill, southeast of here. South of **EASTON**, the main village on the island, Wakeham Road holds **Pennsylvania**

Castle (now a private house), built in 1800 for John Penn, governor of the island and a grandson of the founder of Pennsylvania. A couple of hundred yards beyond the house, the seventeenth-century **Avice's Cottage**, a gift of Marie Stopes, the pioneer of birth control, is now part of the small Portland **Museum** (Easter–Oct Mon, Tues & Fri–Sun 11am–1pm & 1.30–5pm; £2.20), with exhibitions on local shipwrecks, smuggling and quarrying. The cottage owes its name to Thomas Hardy, who described it in his novel, *The Well-Beloved*. Nearby, in **Church Ope Cove**, you can see the ruins of St Andrew's Church and those of Rufus Castle, associated with William II (William Rufus, son of William the Conqueror), though there is evidence of an older Saxon fortification here, while the visible remains probably belong to a reconstruction after the Norman castle was destroyed in 1142.

At **Portland Bill**, the southern tip of the island, a lighthouse has guarded the promontory since the eighteenth century. You can climb the 153 steps of the present one, dating from 1906, for the views (April–June Mon–Thurs & Sun 11am–5pm; July & Sept daily except Sat 11am–5pm; £2.50), and it also houses Portland's **tourist office** (Easter–Sept daily 11am–5pm; Oct–Easter Sat & Sun 11am–4pm; ☎01305/861233), which can supply leaflets on the area's special features, including geology and wildlife. **Accommodation** options in the area include *Brackenbury House* (☎01305/826509, ⓦwww.brackenburyhouse.co.uk; no credit cards; ❷; closed Dec & Jan), a converted vicarage in Fortuneswell, and a **youth hostel** just south of Portland Castle, on Castle Road (☎0870/770 6000, ⓔportland@yha.org.uk; closed Nov–Easter, also Sun & Mon in low season; dorm beds £20 including breakfast); it's left off Victory Square onto Victory Road, then left again.

Chesil Beach to West Bay

Chesil Beach is the strangest feature of the Dorset coast, a two-hundred-yard-wide, fifty-foot-high bank of pebbles that extends for eighteen miles, its component stones gradually decreasing in size from fist-like pebbles at Portland to "pea gravel" at Burton Bradstock in the west. This sorting is an effect of the powerful coastal currents, which make it one of the most dangerous beaches in Europe – churchyards in the local villages display plenty of evidence of wrecks and drownings. Though not a swimming beach, Chesil is popular with sea anglers, and its wild, uncommercialized atmosphere makes an appealing antidote to the south coast resorts. To explore it, you need your own transport or plenty of time – infrequent bus services connect the main villages, and the Dorset Coast Path runs close to the shore for most of the way.

Chesil Beach encloses a brackish lagoon called **The Fleet** for much of its length – it was the setting for J. Meade Faulkner's classic smuggling tale, *Moonfleet*. At the point where the shingle beach attaches itself to the shore is the pretty village of **ABBOTSBURY**, all tawny ironstone and thatch. The three main attractions here draw people from far and wide (all open daily: mid-March to Sept 10am–6pm; Oct 10am–5pm; last admission 1hr before closing), and can be visited separately or on a passport ticket for £15. The most absorbing is the village **Swannery** (£8.50), a wetland reserve for mute swans dating back to medieval times, when presumably it formed part of the abbot's larder. The eel-grass reeds through which the swans paddle were once harvested to thatch roofs throughout the region. One example can be seen on the fifteenth-century Tithe Barn, the last remnant of the village's Benedictine abbey; today it houses the **Children's Farm** (£7), whose highlights include goat-racing and pony rides. Lastly, in the **Subtropical Gardens** (£8.50), delicate species thrive in the microclimate created by Chesil's stones, which act as a giant radiator to keep out all but the worst frosts. Other local attractions are the hilltop, fifteenth-century **Chapel of St Catherine**, and, up on the downs a couple of miles inland from Abbotsbury, a monument to Thomas Hardy – not the usual one associated with Dorset, but the flag captain in whose arms Admiral Nelson expired. In the village centre, the handsome *Ilchester Arms* offers fine food as well as comfortable accommodation (℡01305/871243, @www.ilchester-arms.co.uk; ⑤).

Ten miles west of Abbotsbury, west of Bridport, majestic red cliffs rear up above the peaceful fishing resort of **West Bay**. Here you'll find the area's best **place to eat**, the *Riverside Restaurant*, a renowned but informal fish place with good views over the river, worth booking ahead (℡01308/422011, @www .thefishrestaurant-westbay.co.uk; closed Sun eve, Mon, Thurs eve in winter & Dec to mid-Feb). Seafood dishes are £16–22, and there are fixed-price lunches for £16.50 and £21. Alternatively, you can eat and drink well for considerably less just across the road at *The George*, where there's a separate restaurant and comfortable en-suite rooms are available (℡01308/423191; ④).

Lyme Regis and around

From the end of Chesil Beach an ever more dramatic sequence of cliffs runs westward, followed as closely as possible by the **Dorset Coast Path**, which has to deviate inland in a few places to avoid areas of landslip. This is a particularly fossil-rich section of the so-called **Jurassic Coast** (@www.jurassiccoast.com), a World Heritage Site stretching from Purbeck to Exmouth in Devon. The hilly coast is characterized by such features as **Golden Cap**, an outcrop of sandstone close to west Dorset's main resort, **Lyme Regis**. On summer days it can seem that tourism is threatening to choke the life out of Lyme – but you can take refuge inland, where you'll find picturesque Dorset villages of golden stone and thatched cottages, or else along the coast path.

Lyme Regis

LYME REGIS, Dorset's most westerly town, shelters snugly between steep hills, its intimate size and photogenic appeal making it a tourist honey-pot in high summer. For all that, the town lives up to the classy impression created by its regal name, which it owes to a royal charter granted by Edward I in 1284. It has some upmarket literary associations to further bolster its self-esteem – Jane Austen summered in a seafront cottage and set part of *Persuasion* here (and the town appears in the 1995 film adaptation), while novelist John Fowles lived here until his death in 2005. It was the film adaptation of Fowles' book, *The French Lieutenant's Woman*, shot on location here, that did more than any tourist industry promotion to place the resort firmly on the map.

Though Lyme Regis now relies mostly on holiday-makers for its keep, it was for centuries a port for the wool traders of Somerset, and shipbuilding thrived here until Victorian times. Colourwashed cottages and elegant Regency and Victorian villas line its seafront and flanking streets, but Lyme's best-known feature is a briskly practical reminder of its commercial origins: **The Cobb**, the curving harbour wall, was first constructed in the thirteenth century but has undergone many alterations since, most notably in the nineteenth century, when its massive boulders were clad in neater blocks of Portland stone.

As you walk along the seafront and out towards The Cobb, look for the outlines of ammonites in the walls and paving stones. The cliffs around

Lyme are made up of a complex layer of limestone, greensand and unstable clay, a perfect medium for preserving fossils, which are exposed by landslips of the waterlogged clays. In 1811, after a fierce storm caused parts of the cliffs to collapse, 12-year-old Mary Anning, a keen fossil-hunter, discovered an almost complete dinosaur skeleton, a thirty-foot ichthyosaurus now displayed in London's Natural History Museum (see p.130). Landslips are a continual occurrence on his coast. A few years later, in 1839, a large block of land, complete with a crop of turnips, was severed from its neighbouring fields by a chasm so dramatic that Queen Victoria came to inspect the scene from her yacht.

Hammering fossils out of the cliffs is frowned on by today's conservationists, and in any case is rather hazardous. Hands-off inspection of the area's complex geology can be enjoyed on both sides of town: to the west lies the **Undercliff**, a fascinating jumble of overgrown landslips, now a nature reserve. East of Lyme, the Dorset Coast Path is closed as far as **Charmouth** (Jane Austen's favourite resort), but at low tide you can walk for two miles along the beach, then, just past Charmouth, rejoin the coastal path to the headland of **Golden Cap**, whose brilliant outcrop of auburn sandstone is crowned with gorse. A good way of exploring the area is on a two- to three-hour **guided walk** (£7–8) focusing on the area's fossil heritage: for details, call the guide directly (☎01297/443370), or contact either the tourist office or the excellent **Lyme Regis Museum** on Bridge Street (Easter–Oct Mon–Sat 10am–5pm, Sun 11am–5pm; Nov–Easter Wed–Sun, daily in school holidays, 11am–4pm; £3; ☎01297/443370), which provides a crash course in local history and geology. Further fossil information can be gleaned from **Dinosaurland** on Coombe Street (Jan & Feb Sat & Sun 10am–4.30pm; March–Oct daily 10am–5pm, Aug until 6pm; Nov & Dec daily 10am–4.30pm; £4.50), which fills out the story on ammonites and other local finds.

Also worth seeing are the small **Marine Aquarium** on The Cobb (March–Oct 10am–5pm, with later closing in July & Aug; call for winter opening ☎01297/444230; £4), where local fishermen bring unusual catches, and the fifteenth-century **parish church** of St Michael the Archangel, up Church Street, which contains a seventeenth-century pulpit and a massive chained Bible.

Practicalities

Lyme's nearest **train station** is in Axminster, five miles north; the hourly #31 **bus** (6 on Sun) runs from here to Lyme Regis. The **tourist office** is on Church Street (May–Oct Mon–Sat 10am–5am, Sun 10am–4pm; Nov–April Mon–Sat 10am–3pm; ☎01297/442138, ⓦwww.lymeregistourism.co.uk). With its year-round tourism, the town offers a range of decent accommodation options as well as restaurants and cafés. The best **pubs** are the *Royal Standard* at the western end of Marine Parade, and the *Pilot Boat* on Bridge Street, which also does tasty seafood and vegetarian meals.

Accommodation

Cobb Arms Marine Parade ☎01297/443242. A good choice if you want to stay right next to the sea, though rooms are fairly basic. ❺

Coombe House 41 Coombe St ☎01297/443849, ⓦwww.coombe-house.co.uk. Friendly B&B with large rooms, which also offers self-catering apartments. No credit cards. ❸

New Haven Hotel 1 Pound St ☎01297/442499, ⓦwww.lymeregishotels.co.uk. Tastefully furnished eighteenth-century town house 200m from the Cobb, with most rooms en suite. Vegetarian and vegan breakfasts available. ❸

Old Monmouth Hotel 12 Church St ☎01297/442456, ⓦwww.lyme-regis-hotel.co.uk. Seventeenth-century coaching inn where Oscar Wilde once stayed, a short walk from the sea. ④

Restaurants, cafés and pubs

Bell Cliff Restaurant 5–6 Broad St. For a crowded but cheerful atmosphere, head for this central spot, which lists excellent salmon fishcakes on its wide-ranging menu. It's open until 9pm between Easter and Sept, otherwise daytime only, and you can sit outside in summer. Inexpensive.

Lyme Bay Kitchen 44 Coombe St ☎01297/445371. Congenial café and snack bar by day, and informal bistro serving pasta, pizza (both

around £8) and fish in the evening. Closed Tues. Inexpensive.

Pilot Boat Bridge St. Central pub-cum-café/ restaurant with tasty seafood and vegetarian meals.

Royal Standard 25 Marine Parade. Near *The Cobb Arms*, you can tipple on real ales and dine on a pint of prawns with crusty bread at this great pub with a courtyard.

Town Mill Bakery Mill Lane, off Coombe St. Apart from selling first-class organic breads, this friendly place with wooden plates and big wooden tables dishes out vegetable soup, Welsh rarebit and spinach pancakes. Daytime only, but stays open Fri & Sat eves for pizzas. Inexpensive.

Dorchester and around

The county town of Dorset, **DORCHESTER** still functions as the main agricultural centre for the region, and if you catch it on a Wednesday when the market is in full swing you'll find it at its liveliest. For the literature lover, however, this is essentially **Thomas Hardy**'s town: he was born at Higher Bockhampton, three miles east of here; his heart is buried in Stinsford, a couple of miles northeast (the rest of him is in Westminster Abbey); and he spent much of his life in Dorchester itself, where his statue now stands on High West Street. Even without the Hardy connection, Dorchester makes an attractive stop, with its pleasant central core of mostly seventeenth-century and Georgian buildings, and the prehistoric Maumbury Rings on the outskirts. To the southwest of town looms the massive hill fort of **Maiden Castle**, the most impressive of Dorset's many pre-Roman antiquities.

Arrival, information and accommodation

Dorchester has two **train stations**, both of them to the south of the centre: trains from Weymouth and London arrive at Dorchester South, while Bath and Bristol trains use the Dorchester West station. Most regional and local **buses** stop on Trinity Street, off the High Street. The **tourist office** is on the corner of Trinity Street and Antelope Walk (Mon–Sat 9am–4/5pm; ☎01305/267992, ⓦwww.westdorset.com). **Bikes for rent** are available at Dorchester Cycles, 31 Great Western Rd (☎01305/268787; £12 a day; deposit required).

Dorchester has a good selection of **accommodation**, though early booking is recommended. The closest **campsite** is the *Giant's Head Caravan and Camping Park*, Old Sherborne Road (☎01300/341242, ⓦwww.giants head.co.uk), about five miles north of town, above the Cerne Abbas giant (see p.275).

Hotels, B&Bs and hostels

Aquila Heights 44 Maiden Castle Rd ☎01305/267145, ⓦwww.aquilaheights.co.uk. A few minutes' walk from the centre, near Maumbury Rings and with views to Maiden Castle from some rooms, this B&B has a range

of functional accommodation including a garden room and two singles. ④

Casterbridge Hotel 49 High East St ☎01305/264043, ⓦwww.casterbridgehotel.co.uk. Top-notch Georgian lodging in the centre of town; one room has French windows opening onto a tiny private garden. ⑥

King's Arms High East St ☎01305/265353, ⓦwww.kingsarmsdorchester.com. Historic landmark hotel with plenty of period trappings. Some rooms are smallish but all are well equipped, with broadband access. ❺

Old Rectory Winterbourne Steepleton ☎01305/889468, ⓦwww.theoldrectorybandb .co.uk. Tranquil retreat three miles west of town, surrounded by lawns. No credit cards. ❺

Westwood House 29 High West St ☎01305/268018, ⓦwww.westwoodhouse.co.uk.

Clean and tidy, this central place has mostly en-suite rooms – two with spa baths – and fresh fruit for breakfast in the conservatory. ❹

Youth hostel Litton Cheney ☎0870/770 5922, ⓦwww.yha.org.uk. Halfway between Dorchester and Bridport, this tiny, basic youth hostel has dorm beds for £14. Take bus #31 to Whiteway, then follow directions for a mile and a half. Closed Nov–Easter.

The Town

Dorchester was Durnovaria to the Romans, who founded the town in about 70 AD. The original Roman walls were replaced in the eighteenth century by tree-lined avenues called "Walks" (Bowling Alley Walk, West Walk and Colliton Walk), but some traces of the Roman period have survived. South of the centre of town (off Maumbury Road), **Maumbury Rings** is where the Romans held gladiatorial combats in an amphitheatre adapted from a Stone Age site; the gruesome traditions continued into the Middle Ages, when gladiators were replaced by bear-baiting and public executions or "hanging fairs".

Continuing the gory theme, after the ill-fated rebellion of the Duke of Monmouth (another of Charles II's illegitimate offspring) against James II, Judge Jeffreys was appointed to punish the rebels. His "Bloody Assizes" of 1685, held in the Oak Room of the **Antelope Hotel** on Cornhill, sentenced 292 men to death. In the event, 74 were hanged, drawn and quartered, and their heads stuck on pikes throughout Dorset and Somerset; the luckier suspects were merely flogged and transported to the West Indies. Judge Jeffreys lodged just round the corner from the *Antelope* in High West Street, in what is now a half-timbered Italian restaurant.

In 1834 the **Shire Hall**, further down High West Street, witnessed another cause célèbre, when six men from the nearby village of Tolpuddle were sentenced to transportation for banding together to form the Friendly Society of Agricultural Labourers, in order to present a request for a small wage increase on the grounds that their families were starving. After a public outcry the men were pardoned, and the **Tolpuddle Martyrs** passed into history as founders of the trade union movement. The room in which they were tried is preserved as a memorial to the martyrs, and you can find out more about them in Tolpuddle itself, eight miles east on the A35, where there's a fine little **museum** (April–Oct Tues–Sat 10am–5pm, Sun 11am–5pm; Nov–March Thurs–Sat 10am–4pm, Sun 11am–4pm; free).

The best place to find out about Dorchester's history is the engrossing **Dorset County Museum** on High West Street (July–Sept daily 10am–5pm; Oct–June Mon–Sat 10am–5pm; £6), where archeological and geological displays trace Celtic and Roman history, including a section on Maiden Castle. Pride of place goes to the recreation of Thomas Hardy's study, where his pens are inscribed with the names of the books he wrote with them.

Dorchester has a weirdly eclectic range of other museums to visit, including a small **Dinosaur Museum** off High East Street on Icen Way (daily 9.30/10am–4.30/5.30pm; £6.75), chiefly aimed at children, and the formidably turreted **Keep Military Museum** (April–Sept Mon–Sat 9.30am–5pm; Oct–March Tues–Sat 9.30am–5pm; last entry 4pm; £5), at the top of High West Street, which traces the fortunes of the Dorset and Devonshire regiments over three hundred years and offers sweeping views over the town. Best of all is **Tutankhamun: The Exhibition** on the High Street (Easter–Oct daily

Hardy's Wessex

Thomas Hardy (1840–1928) resurrected the old name of **Wessex** to describe the region in which he set most of his fiction. In his books, the area stretched from Devon and Somerset ("Lower Wessex" and "Outer Wessex") to Berkshire and Oxfordshire ("North Wessex"), though its central core was Dorset ("South Wessex"), the county where Hardy spent most of his life. His books richly depict the life and appearance of the towns and countryside of the area, often thinly disguised under fictional names. Thus Salisbury makes an appearance as "Melchester", Weymouth (where he briefly lived) as "Budmouth Regis", and Bournemouth as "Sandbourne" – described as "a fairy palace suddenly created by the stroke of a wand, and allowed to get a little dusty" in *Tess of the d'Urbervilles*. But it is **Dorchester**, the "Casterbridge" of his novels, that is portrayed in most detail, to the extent that many of the town's buildings and landmarks that still remain can be identified in the books (especially *The Mayor of Casterbridge* and *Far From the Madding Crowd*).

Hardy knew the town well; he was born and lived (1840–62 and 1867–70) in Higher Bockhampton, three miles northeast of town, in what is now **Hardy's Cottage** (April–Oct Mon–Thurs & Sun 11am–5pm or dusk; £3.50; NT), where a few bits of period furniture and some original manuscripts are displayed. Buses #184, #311 and #387 pass within half a mile – otherwise you can walk (on the A35 and Bockhampton Road) or take a taxi. Having worked as an architect in Cornwall and London, Hardy returned to Dorchester in 1885, spending the rest of his life in a house built to his own designs at Max Gate, on the A352 Wareham Road, a twenty-minute walk east from Dorchester's centre (April–Sept Mon, Wed & Sun 2–5pm; £3; NT). Here, the writer completed *Tess of the D'Urbervilles*, *Jude the Obscure* and much of his poetry, though only the garden and dining and drawing rooms are open to the public.

The **Thomas Hardy Society** (Ⓦ www.hardysociety.org) organizes walks and tours, including a fifteen-mile hike which follows in the steps of Tess on her Sunday mission to visit her father-in-law, Parson Clare of Beaminster, in order to rescue her failed marriage. If this sounds ambitious, content yourself with the walking itinerary outlined in the leaflet available free from the tourist office.

Alternatively, you could read the books: *Under the Greenwood Tree* (1872) evokes Hardy's childhood in and around Higher Bockhampton; *Tess of the d'Urbervilles* (1891) gives elegiac descriptions of the Frome Valley; *The Return of the Native* (1878) describes wild Egdon Heath and the eerie yew forest of Cranborne Chase; and *The Mayor of Casterbridge* (1886) is set around Dorchester and Maumbury Rings.

9.30am–5.30pm; Nov–Easter Mon–Fri 9.30am–5.30pm, Sat 10am–5pm, Sun 10am–4.30pm; £6.75), a fascinating exploration of the young pharaoh's life and afterlife through to the eventual discovery of his tomb in 1922. There's an absorbing appendage to this museum a few doors down on Alington Street, the **Mummies Exhibition**, focusing on the technique of mummification (same hours; £3.90, or £1.90 with a Tutankhamun ticket) – worth the extra cost. Lastly, at the bottom of High East Street lies the equally incongruous **Terracotta Warriors Museum** (daily 10.30am–5/4.30pm; £5.50), which displays copies of the famous clay models unearthed in China in 1974. You can find out all about the discovery, excavation and recreation of these life-size figures originally intended to guard the tomb of China's first emperor some 2,200 years ago, with panels, soundtracks, and a 40-minute film.

Eating and drinking

Dorchester is not overwhelmed by eating outlets, though the **restaurants and cafés** listed below should satisfy most appetites. On High West Street, there are two highly recommended **pubs** – the *Royal Oak*, for good-value meals and with a beer garden, and the *Old Ship Inn*.

Restaurants and cafés

🕴 Café Jagos 8 High West St
☎01305/266056. With a minimalist interior and a courtyard garden, this easy-going café/ restaurant near the tourist office offers panini and ciabattas, plus a range of mainly Mediterranean hot dishes (£7–11) and tasty desserts.

Old Tea House 44 High West St. Rather twee place, in a seventeenth-century building, good for traditional teas and snacks. Closed Mon, also Tues Nov–May.

Potter's 19 Durngate St (off pedestrianized South Street) ☎01305/260312. Good choice for coffees and wholesome lunches by day (when you can sit in the garden), and casseroles, seafood and vegetarian dishes in the evenings. Set-price menus come to around £16 and £20. Closed Sun & eves Mon–Thurs.

Sienna 36 High West St ☎01305/250022. Tiny place renowned for its quality Modern British and Mediterranean cuisine. Two- and three-course set price menus cost £18.50 and £21.50 for lunch, £27.50 and £33.50 for dinner. Closed Sun & Mon.

Maiden Castle

One of southern England's finest prehistoric sites, **Maiden Castle** (free access) stands on a hill two miles or so southwest of Dorchester. Covering about 115 acres, it was first developed around 3000 BC by a Stone Age farming community and then used during the Bronze Age as a funeral mound. Iron Age dwellers expanded it into a populous settlement and fortified it with a daunting series of ramparts and ditches, just in time for the arrival of Vespasian's Second Legion. The ancient Britons' slingstones were no match for the more sophisticated weapons of the Roman invaders, and Maiden Castle was stormed in a bloody massacre in 43 AD.

What you see today is a massive series of grassy concentric ridges about sixty feet high, creasing the surface of the hill. The site is best visited early or late in the day, when the low-angled sun casts the earthworks in shadow, showing them up more clearly. The main finds from the site are displayed in the Dorset County Museum (see p.273).

Inland Dorset and southern Wiltshire

Heading north from Dorchester, the main pleasures of inland Dorset come from unscheduled meandering through its ancient landscapes and tiny rural settlements, many of which boast preposterously winsome names such as Ryme Intrinseca, Piddletrenthide, Up Sydling and Plush. Two of the most interesting of these villages are **Cerne Abbas** and **Milton Abbas**, the former distinguished by its rumbustious chalk-carved giant, the latter by its curious artificiality. The major tourist spots, however, are the towns of **Sherborne** and **Shaftesbury**, the landscaped garden at **Stourhead** across the county boundary in Wiltshire, and the brasher stately home at **Longleat**, an unlikely hybrid of safari park and historic monument.

Cerne Abbas and Milton Abbas

Eight miles north of Dorchester, just off the A352, the village of **CERNE ABBAS** has bags of charm in its own right, with gorgeous Tudor cottages and abbey ruins, not to mention a clutch of decent pubs. The main draw hereabouts, however, is the enormously priapic **giant** carved in the chalk hillside, standing

180ft high and flourishing a club over his disproportionately small head. The age of the monument is disputed, some authorities believing it to be pre-Roman, others thinking it might be a Romano-British figure of Hercules, but in view of his prominent feature it's probable that the giant originated as some primeval fertility symbol. Folklore has it that lying on the outsize member will induce conception, but the National Trust, which now owns the site, does its best to stop people wandering over it and eroding the two-foot trenches that form the outlines. You can reach the giant on the bookable #D12 bus service from Dorchester or Sherborne (call ☎0845/602 4547).

The village of **MILTON ABBAS**, ten miles east of Cerne Abbas and eleven miles northeast of Dorchester (reachable on bus #311 from Dorchester), is an unusual English rural idyll. It owes its model-like neatness to the First Earl of Dorchester who, in the eighteenth century, found the medieval squalor of former "Middleton" a blot on the landscape of his estate. Although some see the earl as an enlightened advocate of modern town planning, the more likely truth is that he simply wanted to beautify his land, so he had the village razed and rebuilt in its present location as thirty semi-detached, whitewashed and thatched cottages on wide grassy verges. No trace remains of the old village which once surrounded the fourteenth-century **abbey church** (dawn–dusk; small charge during school hols), a mile's walk away near the lake at the bottom of the village. Delayed by the Black Death and cut short by the Dissolution, the abbey church lacks much internal decoration, and instead retains a spacious, uncluttered feel.

The best bet for a drink and a good **meal** in the village is the *Hambro Arms*, at the top of the hill, which serves bar food and (Wed–Sat only) more substantial dinners. The pub also provides a couple of comfortable, en-suite rooms (☎01258/880233, ⓦwww.hambroarms.com; ⑤).

Sherborne

Tucked away in the northwest corner of Dorset, the pretty town of **SHERBORNE** was once the capital of Wessex, its church having cathedral status until Old Sarum (see p.283) usurped the bishopric in 1075. This former glory is embodied by the magnificent **Abbey Church** (daily 8am–4/6pm), which was founded in 705, later becoming a Benedictine abbey. Most of its extant parts date from a rebuilding in the fifteenth century, and it is one of the best examples of Perpendicular architecture in Britain, particularly noted for its outstanding **fan vaulting**. The church also has a famously weighty peal of bells, led by "Great Tom", a tenor bell presented to the abbey by Cardinal Wolsey. Among the church's many tombs are those of Alfred the Great's two brothers, Ethelred and Ethelbert, and the Elizabethan poet Thomas Wyatt, all located in the northeast corner. The **almshouse** on the opposite side of the Abbey Close was built in 1437 and is a rare example of a medieval hospital; another wing provides accommodation for Sherborne's well-known public school.

The town also has two "castles", both associated with Sir Walter Raleigh. Queen Elizabeth I first leased, then gave, Raleigh the twelfth-century **Old Castle** (Easter–June & Sept daily 10am–5pm; July & Aug daily 10am–6pm; Oct daily 10am–4pm; £2.50; EH), but it seems that he despaired of feudal accommodation and built himself a more comfortably domesticated house, **Sherborne Castle**, in adjacent parkland (Easter–Oct Wed–Fri & Sun 11am–5pm, Sat 2–5pm; castle & gardens £8.50, gardens only £4). When Sir Walter fell from the queen's favour by seducing her maid of honour, the Digby family acquired the house and have lived here ever since; portraits, furniture and books are displayed in a whimsically Gothic interior, remodelled in the nineteenth century. The Old Castle fared less happily, and was pulverized by Cromwellian cannonfire for the obstinately Royalist leanings of its occupants. The **museum** near the abbey on Church Lane (April–Oct Tues–Sat 10.30am–4.30pm, some Sun 2.30–4.30pm; £2, free on Wed) includes a model of the Old Castle and photographs of parts of the fifteenth-century Sherborne Missal, a richly illuminated tome weighing nearly fifty pounds, now housed in the British Library.

Bus service #D12 connects Sherborne with Dorchester, while #58 and #58A run between Shaftesbury and Sherborne (all Mon–Sat). The **tourist office** is on Digby Road (Mon–Sat: 9/10am–3/5pm; ☎01935/815341, ⓦwww.westdorset.com). For an **overnight stay**, try the *Half Moon*, Half Moon Street (☎01935/812017; ⑤). *Oliver's*, 19 Cheap St, is good for teas and light lunches, or try the *Cross Keys Hotel*, 88 Cheap St, a cosy **pub** which has a few tables out front.

Shaftesbury

Fifteen miles north of Milton Abbas, on the scenic A350, **SHAFTESBURY** perches on a spur of lumpy green-gold hills, with severe gradients on three sides of the town. On a clear day, views from the town are terrific – one of the best vantage points is **Gold Hill**, quaint, cobbled and very steep. The local history **museum** at the top of Gold Hill (April–Oct daily 10.30am–4.30pm; £2.50, or £4 with Abbey) displays items ranging from a collection of locally made buttons, for which the area was once renowned, to a mummified cat.

Pilgrims used to flock to Shaftesbury to pay homage to the bones of Edward the Martyr, which were brought to the **Abbey** in 978, though now only the footings of the abbey church survive, just off the main street (April–Oct daily 10am–5pm; £2.50, or £4 with museum). **St Peter's Church** on the market place is one of the few reminders of Shaftesbury's medieval grandeur, when it boasted a castle, twelve churches and four market crosses.

You can reach Shaftesbury on **buses** #83 from Blandford Forum (for which take the #184 or #311 from Dorchester) and #26, #27 or #29 from Salisbury. The helpful **tourist office** on Bell Street (Mon–Sat 10am–3/5pm; Oct–March 10am–3pm, ☎01747/853514, ⓦwww.ruraldorset.com) can provide a full list of available **accommodation**. *The Chalet* on Christy's Lane has three modern, Wi-Fi-enabled rooms in an eco-friendly house (☎01747/853945, ⓦwww.thechalet.biz; no children under 12; no credit cards; ④). Three miles south of town in the village of Compton Abbas, on the A350 to Blandford Forum, the *Old Forge* B&B on Chapel Hill (☎01747/811881, ⓦwww.theoldforgedorset.co.uk; no children under 8; no credit cards; ④) is a beautifully restored eighteenth-century thatched cottage with log fires and hearty farmhouse breakfasts; a gypsy caravan and self-catering cottages are also offered. Shaftesbury's *Salt Cellar* café at the top of Gold Hill is a panoramic spot for a **snack** or lunch.

Stourhead

Landscape gardening – the creation of an artificially improved version of nature – was a favoured mode of display among the grandest eighteenth-century landowners, and **Stourhead**, ten miles northwest of Shaftesbury, is one of the most accomplished survivors of the genre (house: Easter–Oct Mon, Tues & Fri–Sun 11.30am–4.30pm or dusk; garden: daily 9am–7pm or dusk; house & garden £11.60, house £7, garden £7; NT). The Stourton estate was bought in

1717 by Henry Hoare, who commissioned Colen Campbell to build a new villa in the Palladian style. Hoare's heir, another Henry, returned from his Grand Tour in 1741 with his head full of the paintings of Claude and Poussin, and determined to translate their images of well-ordered, wistful classicism into real life. He dammed the Stour to create a lake, then planted the terrain with blocks of trees, domed temples, stone bridges, grottoes and statues, all mirrored vividly in the water. In 1772 the folly of **King Alfred's Tower** (Easter–Oct daily 11.30am–4.30pm or dusk; £2.40) was added and today affords fine views across the estate and into neighbouring counties. The rhododendrons and azaleas that now make such a splash in early summer are a later addition to this dream landscape. The house, in contrast, is fairly run-of-the-mill, though it has some good Chippendale furniture.

A mile to the southeast, in the showpiece village of **STOURTON**, also now owned by the National Trust, the *Spread Eagle Inn* has five spacious, en-suite **rooms** available (℡01747/840587, Ⓦwww.spreadeagleinn.com; Ⓞ) – it's also a good place to have **lunch**, serving everything from pasties to slow-cooked stews. However, Stourton is difficult to reach without your own transport – the nearest train station is at Gillingham, over six miles away.

Longleat

If Stourhead is an unexpected outcrop of Italy in Wiltshire, the African savannah intrudes even more bizarrely at **Longleat** (house Easter–Oct Mon–Fri 10am–5pm, Sat & Sun 10am–5.30pm; Oct–March guided tours once or twice hourly 11am–3pm; safari park Easter–Oct Mon–Fri 10am–4pm, Sat, Sun & school holidays 10am–5pm; house £10; safari park £11, plus £4 for the safari bus; all attractions £20; Ⓦwww.longleat.co.uk), two and a half miles south of the road from Warminster to Frome. In 1946 the sixth marquess of Bath raised eyebrows among his peers as the first stately-home owner to open his house to the paying

▲ Longleat

public on a regular basis to help make ends meet. In 1966 he caused even more amazement when Longleat's Capability Brown landscapes were turned into a drive-through **safari park** – the first in the country – which today features lions, tigers, giraffes, rhinos, elephants, zebras and hippos, amongst other animals. Once committed to such commercial enterprise, the bosses of Longleat knew no limits: other attractions now include the world's largest hedge maze, a Doctor Who exhibition, a high-tech simulation of the world's most dangerous modes of travel and the seventh marquess's steamy murals encapsulating his interpretation of life and the universe (children may not be admitted). Beyond the brazen razzmatazz, though, there's an exquisitely furnished Elizabethan **house**, built for Sir John Thynne, Elizabeth's High Treasurer, with the largest private library in Britain and a fine collection of pictures, including Titian's *Holy Family*.

Longleat is about four miles from the train stations of Frome and Warminster; the #53 bus (Mon–Sat) shuttles roughly every hour between Warminster and Frome train stations – though you'll have to walk the two and a half miles from the entrance of the house to its grounds.

Salisbury and around

SALISBURY, huddled below Wiltshire's chalky plain in the converging valleys of the Avon and Nadder, looks from a distance very much as it did when Constable painted his celebrated view of it from across the water meadows, even though traffic may clog its centre and military jets scream overhead from local air bases. Prosperous and well kept, Wiltshire's only city is designed on a pleasantly human scale, with no sprawling suburbs or high-rise buildings to challenge the supremacy of the cathedral's immense spire – unusually, the local planners have imposed a height limit on new construction.

The town sprang into existence in the early thirteenth century, when the bishopric was moved from **Old Sarum**, an ancient Iron Age hillfort settled by the Romans and their successors. The deserted remnant of Salisbury's precursor now stands on the northern fringe of the town, just a bit closer in than **Wilton House** to the west, one of Wiltshire's great houses.

Arrival, information and accommodation

Trains arrive half a mile west of the centre, on South Western Road; the **bus station** is a short way north of the Market Square on Endless Street, with an adjacent office (Mon–Fri 8.15am–5.30pm, Sat 8am–5pm; ☎01722/336855, ⓦwww.wdbus.co.uk) providing details of services throughout the region, including tours to Stonehenge and around. For a **taxi**, call ☎07885/102114.

The main **tourist office** is on Fish Row, just off Market Square (May–Sept Mon–Sat 9.30am–5/6pm, Sun 10.30am–4.30pm; Oct–April Mon–Sat 9.30am–5pm; ☎01722/334956, ⓦwww.visitsalisbury.com), and there's a seasonal office at the train station (April–Sept Mon–Sat 9.30am–4.30pm). The city office is the starting point for informative **guided walks** of the city (daily 11am; 1hr 30min; £3.50); in summer there are also themed walks (£4), including a Ghost Walk (call ☎01722/320349 for details). **Bike rental** is available from Hayball's Cycle Shop, 30 Winchester St (☎01722/411378) for £10 a day (with £25 cash deposit). There's one terminal for free **Internet** access at the main tourist office, or you can log on at the Public Library at the bottom of Castle Street (Mon 10am–7pm, Tues, Wed & Fri 9am–7pm, Thurs & Sat 9am–5pm).

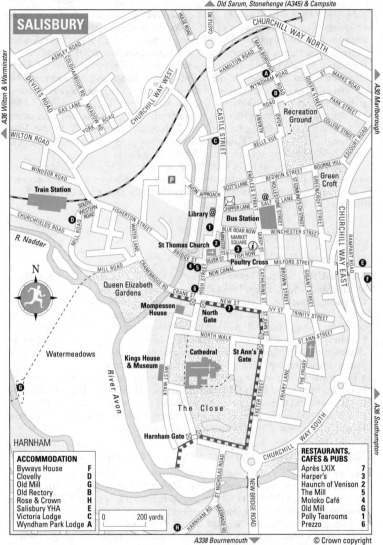

SALISBURY

Old Sarum, Stonehenge (A345) & Campsite

A36 Wilton & Warminster

A30 Marlborough

A36 Southampton

Recreation Ground

Green Croft

Train Station

R. Nadder

Library

Bus Station

St Thomas Church

Poultry Cross

Queen Elizabeth Gardens

Mompesson House

North Gate

Watermeadows

Kings House & Museum

Cathedral

St Ann's Gate

River Avon

The Close

HARNHAM

Harnham Gate

A338 Bournemouth

© Crown copyright

ACCOMMODATION

Byways House	F
Clovelly	D
Old Mill	G
Old Rectory	B
Rose & Crown	H
Salisbury YHA	E
Victoria Lodge	C
Wyndham Park Lodge	A

0   200 yards

RESTAURANTS, CAFÉS & PUBS

Après LXIX	7
Harper's	3
Haunch of Venison	2
The Mill	5
Moloko Café	4
Old Mill	G
Polly Tearooms	1
Prezzo	6

Bus **tours** to Stonehenge (City Sightseeing ☎01789/294466, ⓦwww .city-sightseeing.com; £16.50) leave three times a day from the train station, with a stop on Blue Boar Row (Easter to mid-May & Oct Sat & Sun only; mid-May to Sept daily); tickets for the two-hour tours include access to the monument.

Accommodation

With its year-round stream of visitors, Salisbury offers numerous accommodation possibilities, mostly in or within a short walk of the centre, though booking ahead is always advised. There's a well-appointed **campsite** with clean facilities a mile and a half north of Salisbury, close to Old Sarum: *Salisbury Camping and Caravanning Club Site*, Hudson's Field (℡01722/320713, ⓦwww.campingandcaravanningclub.co.uk; call for details of winter opening.

Byways House 31 Fowlers Rd ℡01722/328364, ⓦwww.bed-breakfast-stonehenge.co.uk. Plush Victorian house in a quiet location, offering rooms with or without bath. Two rooms have a view of the cathedral. ❸

Clovelly 17 Mill Rd ℡01722/322055, ⓦwww .clovellyhotel.co.uk. Useful choice close to the train station, with traditionally furnished rooms and fruit and home-made yoghurt for breakfast. ❺

Old Mill Town Path, Harnham ℡01722/327517, ⓦwww.signature-hospitality.com. Great views across the meadows to the cathedral from the fully equipped rooms of this riverside pub about a mile from the centre. Real ales are on tap in the bar, and there's an adjoining 800-year-old restaurant. ❻

Old Rectory 75 Belle Vue Rd ℡01722/502702, ⓦwww .theoldrectory-bb.co.uk. Light and modern conversion of a 1920s building, with breakfast in the conservatory overlooking the garden. The three rooms have private or en-suite bathrooms. No credit cards. ❹

Rose & Crown Harnham Road ℡0870/832 9946, ⓦwww.legacy-hotels.co.uk. Riverside hostelry dating from the thirteenth century, with traditional oak beams, grand four-poster beds and a huge pavilion restaurant. ❼

Salisbury YHA Milford Hill ℡0870/770 6018, ⓔsalisbury@yha.org.uk. A 220-year-old building in its own spacious grounds, ten minutes' walk east of the cathedral. Dorm bed and breakfast costs £17.50. Camping pitches available in summer. ❷

Victoria Lodge 61 Castle Rd ℡01722/320586, ⓦwww.viclodge.co.uk. One of several good-value B&Bs along this main road to Stonehenge, with all rooms en suite and family rooms available. ❹

Wyndham Park Lodge 51 Wyndham Rd ℡01722/416517, ⓦwww .wyndhamparklodge.co.uk. Victorian B&B in a quiet part of town (off Castle Street), full of period furniture, wallpaper and hangings. One room has its own patio. ❸

The City

Begun in 1220, **Salisbury Cathedral** (daily 7.15am–6.15pm, mid-June to late Aug Mon–Sat closes 7.15pm; £5 suggested donation; ⓦwww .salisburycathedral.org.uk) was mostly completed within forty years and is thus unusually consistent in its style, with one extremely prominent exception – the **spire**, which was added a century later and at 404ft is the highest in England. Its survival is something of a miracle, for the foundations penetrate only about six feet into marshy ground, and when Christopher Wren surveyed it he found the spire to be leaning almost two and a half feet out of true. He added further tie-rods, which finally arrested the movement.

The interior is over-austere after James Wyatt's brisk eighteenth-century tidying, but there's an amazing sense of space and light in its high nave, despite the sombre pillars of grey Purbeck marble, which are visibly bowing beneath the weight they bear. Monuments and carved tombs line the walls, where they were neatly placed by Wyatt, and in the north aisle there's a fascinating clock dating from 1386, one of the oldest functioning clock mechanisms in Europe. Other features not to miss are the vaulted colonnades of the **cloisters**, and the octagonal **chapter house** (Mon–Sat 9.30/10am–4.30/6.45pm, Sun noon/12.45pm–4.30/5.30pm), which displays a rare original copy of the Magna Carta, and whose walls are decorated with a frieze of scenes from the Old Testament. On most days, you can join a free 45-minute tour of the church leaving two or more times a day, and there are also 90-minute tours to the roof and tower, involving a climb of more than 300 steps (Mon–Sat 1–4 times daily, Sun 1 daily May–Sept; call ℡01722/555156 for times and booking; £5.50).

Surrounding the cathedral is the peaceful precinct of lawns and mellow old buildings that makes up **The Close**, the largest and most impressive in the country. Most of the houses have seemly Georgian facades, though some, like the Bishop's Palace and the deanery, date from the thirteenth century. **Mompesson House** (Easter–Oct Mon–Wed, Sat & Sun 11am–5pm; £4.70, garden only £1; NT), built by a wealthy merchant in 1701, contains some beautifully furnished eighteenth-century rooms and a superbly carved staircase, as displayed to great effect in the film *Sense and Sensibility*. The other building to head for in The Close is the **Kings House**, home of the **Salisbury and South Wiltshire Museum** (Mon–Sat 10am–5pm; £5) – an absorbing account of local history. It includes a good section on Stonehenge and also focuses on the life and times of General Pitt-Rivers, the father of modern archeology, who excavated many of Wiltshire's prehistoric sites, including Avebury (see p.286).

The Close's **North Gate** opens onto the centre's older streets, where narrow pedestrianized alleyways bear names like Fish Row and Salt Lane, indicative of their trading origin. Many half-timbered houses and inns have survived all over the centre, and the last of four market crosses, **Poultry Cross**, stands on stilts in Silver Street, near the Market Square. The market, held on Tuesdays and Saturdays, still serves a large agricultural area, as it did in earlier times when the city grew wealthy on wool. Nearby, the church of **St Thomas** – named after Thomas à Becket – is worth a look inside for its carved timber roof and "Doom painting" over the chancel arch, depicting Christ presiding over the Last Judgment. Dating from 1475, it's the largest of its kind in England.

Lastly, to best appreciate the city's inspiring silhouette – the view made famous by Constable – take a twenty-minute walk through the water meadows southwest of the centre to **Harnham**; the *Old Mill* here serves drinks and modestly priced meals.

Eating and drinking

You don't need to search far for food in Salisbury, with its good mix of traditional and contemporary outlets. The centre also has a good sprinkling of pubs, many of which serve meals.

Après LXIX 69 New St ☎01722/340000. Very close to the cathedral, this modern wine bar and bistro serves upmarket cooking using local ingredients. Set lunches are especially good value, while mains in the evening cost £8–12. Closed Sun. Moderate.

Harper's Market Square ☎01722/333118. Endearingly old-fashioned place serving traditional English fare, with modestly priced set lunches and early evening meals. Closed Sun lunch, plus all day Sun Oct–May. Inexpensive to moderate.

Haunch of Venison Minster Street. One of the city's most atmospheric pubs, which also serves good food at the bar or in the upstairs restaurant. Look out for the mummified hand of a nineteenth-century card player still clutching his cards. Inexpensive to moderate.

The Mill Bridge Street. Popular pub with riverside seating, right in the city centre. Real ales are available, and food, tea and coffee served until 9pm. Inexpensive.

Moloko Café 5 Bridge St. Cool café and vodka bar, open till late.

Polly Tearooms 8 St Thomas's Square. Established and popular patisserie right outside St Thomas' church, with outdoor tables. Open until 5pm (4pm Sun).

Prezzo 52–54 High St ☎01722/341333. Steps from the cathedral, and housed in one of Salisbury's wonkiest buildings – all sagging timbers – with a good selection of antipasti (£4–5), pastas and pizzas (£7–9), plus daily specials. Moderate.

Old Sarum and Wilton

The ruins of **Old Sarum** (daily: March & Oct 10am–4pm; April–June & Sept 10am–5pm; July & Aug 9am–6pm; Nov–Feb 11am–3pm; £3; EH) occupy a bleak hilltop site two miles north of the city centre – it's an easy walk, but buses #4, #5, #6 and #8 run every fifteen minutes or so (only #6 and #8 on Sun, less frequently), and a taxi costs around £7. Possibly occupied up to five thousand years ago, then developed as an Iron Age fort whose double protective ditches remain, it was settled by Romans and Saxons before the Norman bishopric of Sherborne was moved here in the 1070s. Within a couple of decades a new cathedral had been consecrated at Old Sarum, and a large religious community was living alongside the soldiers in the central castle. Old Sarum was an uncomfortable place, parched and windswept, and in 1220 the dissatisfied clergy – additionally at loggerheads with the castle's occupants – appealed to the pope for permission to decamp to Salisbury (still known officially as New Sarum). When permission was granted, the stone from the cathedral was commandeered for Salisbury's gateways, and once the church had gone the population waned. By the nineteenth century Old Sarum was deserted, but it continued to exist as a political constituency – William Pitt was one of its representatives. The most notorious of the "rotten boroughs", it returned two MPs at a time to Westminster up until the 1832 Reform Act put a stop to it. Huge earthworks, banks and ditches are the dominant features of the site today, with a broad trench encircling the promontory, on which lie the rudimentary remains of the Norman palace, castle and cathedral.

WILTON, five miles west of Salisbury, is renowned for its carpet industry and the splendid **Wilton House** (11am–5.30pm: April–Aug Mon–Thurs, Sun & occasional Sat Sept Tues–Thurs only; last entry 4.30pm; £12, grounds only £5; ⓦwww.wiltonhouse.com), of which Daniel Defoe wrote: "One cannot be said to have seen any thing that a man of curiosity would think worth seeing in this county, and not have been at Wilton House." The Tudor house, built for the First Earl of Pembroke on the site of a dissolved Benedictine abbey, was ruined by fire in 1647 and rebuilt by Inigo Jones, whose classic hallmarks can be seen in the sumptuous Single Cube and Double Cube rooms, so called because of their precise dimensions. Sir Philip Sidney, illustrious Elizabethan courtier and poet, wrote part of his magnum opus *Arcadia* here – the dado round the Single Cube Room illustrates scenes from the book – and the Double Cube room was the setting for the ballroom scene in Ang Lee's film, *Sense and Sensibility*. The easel **paintings** are what makes Wilton really special, however – the collection includes works by Van Dyck, Rembrandt, two of the Brueghel family, Poussin, Andrea del Sarto and Tintoretto. In the grounds, the famous **Palladian Bridge** has been joined by attractions including an adventure playground, garden centre and an audio-visual show on the colourful earls of Pembroke. Frequent city buses #60, #60A and #61 connect Wilton with Salisbury's centre.

Salisbury Plain and northwards

The Ministry of Defence is the landlord of much of **Salisbury Plain**, the hundred thousand acres of chalky upland to the north of Salisbury. Flags warn casual trespassers away from MoD firing ranges and tank training grounds, while rather stricter security cordons off such secretive establishments as the research centre at Porton Down, Britain's centre for chemical and biological warfare. As elsewhere, the army's presence has ironically saved much of the plain from modern agricultural chemicals, thereby inadvertently nurturing species that are all but extinct in more trampled landscapes.

Though now largely deserted except by forces families living in ugly, temporary-looking barracks quarters, Salisbury Plain once positively throbbed with communities. Stone Age, Bronze Age and Iron Age settlements left hundreds of burial mounds scattered over the chalklands, as well as major complexes at Danebury, Badbury, Figsbury, Old Sarum, and, of course, the great circle of **Stonehenge**. North of Salisbury Plain, beyond the A342 Andover–Devizes road, lies the softer Vale of Pewsey, traversed by the Kennet canal. **Marlborough**, to the north of the Vale, is the centre for another cluster of ancient sites, including the huge stone circle of **Avebury**, the mysterious grassy mound of **Silbury Hill** and the chamber graves of **West Kennet**. On the western edges of Wiltshire, Lacock and Bradford-on-Avon offer picturesque glimpses into a past, less stressed era of provincial life. Malmesbury, though in Wiltshire, is covered in the next chapter, as it feels more closely allied to the Cotswolds area than to the rest of the county, from which it's cut off by the M4 and the railway line.

Stonehenge

No ancient structure in England arouses more controversy than **Stonehenge** (daily: mid-March to May & Sept to mid-Oct 9.30am–6pm; June–Aug 9am–7pm; mid-Oct to mid-March 9.30am–4pm; £6.50; NT & EH), a mysterious ring of monoliths nine miles north of Salisbury. Bus #3 connects Stonehenge with Salisbury's bus and train stations six or seven times daily (20–35min). While archeologists argue over whether it was a place of ritual sacrifice and sun-worship, an astronomical calculator or a royal palace, the guardians of the site struggle to accommodate its year-round crowds who are resentful at no longer being able to walk among the stones: special access to the inner ring can be arranged on ☎01722/343834, and you can check dates and times at the website ⓦwww.english-heritage.org.uk/stonehenge. Annual summer solstice battles between the police and gatherings of druids and New Age travellers are a thing of the past now, and low-key solstice celebrations are permitted.

Conservation of Stonehenge, a UNESCO-designated World Heritage Site, is an urgent priority, and the current custodians are trying to address the dissatisfaction that many feel on visiting this landmark. Plans to re-route nearby roads and build a new visitors' centre have been afoot for years, but a lack of general consensus on the project and the daunting cost have led to interminable delays: in the meantime, visitors are issued with audioguides that dispense a range of information on the site.

What exists today is only a small part of the original prehistoric complex, as many of the outlying stones were probably plundered by medieval and later farmers for building materials. The **construction** of Stonehenge is thought to have taken place in several stages. In about 3000 BC the outer circular bank and ditch were created, just inside which was dug a ring of 56 pits, which at a later date were filled with a mixture of earth and human ash. Around 2500 BC the first stones were raised within the earthworks, comprising approximately forty great blocks of dolerite (bluestone), whose original source was Preseli in South Wales. Some archeologists have suggested that these monoliths were found lying on Salisbury Plain, having been borne down from the Welsh mountains by a glacier in the last Ice Age, but the lack of any other glacial debris on the plain would seem to disprove this theory.

It really does seem to be the case that the stones were cut from quarries in Preseli and dragged or floated here on rafts, a prodigious task which has defeated recent attempts to emulate it.

The crucial phase in the creation of the site came during the next six hundred years, when the incomplete bluestone circle was transformed by the construction of a circle of twenty-five **trilithons** (two uprights crossed by a lintel) and an inner horseshoe formation of five trilithons. Hewn from Marlborough Downs sandstone, these colossal stones (called sarsens), ranging from 13ft to 21ft in height and weighing up to thirty tons, were carefully dressed and worked – for example, to compensate for perspectival distortion the uprights have a slight swelling in the middle, the same trick as the builders of the Parthenon were to employ hundreds of years later. More bluestones were arranged in various patterns within the outer circle over this period.

The purpose of all this work remains baffling, however. The symmetry and location of the site (a slight rise in a flat valley with even views of the horizon in all directions), as well as its alignment towards the points of sunrise and sunset on the summer and winter solstices, tend to support the supposition that it was some sort of observatory or time-measuring device. The site ceased to be used at around 1600 BC, and by the Middle Ages it had already become a "landmark". Recent excavations have revealed the existence of a much larger settlement here than had previously been thought – in fact the most substantial Neolithic village of this period to be found on the British mainland – covering a wide area. Nothing is to be seen of the new finds as yet, though there are plans to re-create a part of the ancient complex.

There's a lot less charisma about the reputedly significant Bronze Age site of **Woodhenge** (dawn–dusk; free), two miles northeast of Stonehenge. The site consists of a circular bank about 220ft in diameter enclosing a ditch and six concentric rings of post holes, which would originally have held timber uprights, possibly supporting a roofed building of some kind. The holes are now marked more durably if less romantically by concrete pillars. A child's grave was found at the centre of the rings, suggesting that it may have been a place of ritual sacrifice.

Marlborough

A good base from which to explore Salisbury Plain is **MARLBOROUGH**, once an important staging post for travellers from London. It's a handsome place too: the wide High Street, a dignified assembly of Georgian buildings, has a fine Perpendicular church standing at each end and half-timbered cottages rambling up the alleyways behind. The famous public school is not especially old – it was established in 1843 – but incorporates an ancient coaching inn among its red-brick buildings.

Marlborough's **tourist office** is in the library at 91 High St (Mon 10am–8pm, Wed & Fri 9.30am–5pm, Thurs 9.30am–8pm, Sat 9.30am–4pm; ℡01672/512663, ⓦwww.visitkennet.co.uk), with several inns and **guesthouses** also along the High Street, including *Ivy House* at no. 43 (℡01672/515333, ⓦwww.ivyhousemarlborough.co.uk; ⑥), the antique *Castle and Ball* (℡01672/515201, ⓦwww.castleandball.com; ⑥), and the *Merlin Hotel* at no. 36–39 (℡01672/512151; ❸). **Eating** options in central Marlborough include Ask at 101 High St, which has some pavement seating for its snacks and full meals, and *Ivy House* for bistro dishes, while *Polly Tea Rooms*, 27 High St (daytime only), serves good snacks, cakes, chocolates and ice cream.

Silbury Hill, West Kennet and Avebury

The neat green mound of **Silbury Hill**, five miles west of Marlborough, is probably overlooked by the majority of drivers whizzing by on the A4. At 130ft it's no great height, but when you realize it's the largest prehistoric artificial mound in Europe, and was made by a people using nothing more than primitive spades, it commands more respect. It was probably constructed around 2600 BC, but like so many of the sites of Salisbury Plain, no one knows quite what it was for, though the likelihood is that it was a burial mound. You can't walk on the hill anyway, so having admired it briefly from the car park, cross the road to the footpath that leads half a mile to the **West Kennet Long Barrow** (free access; NT & EH). Dating from about 3250 BC, this was definitely a chamber tomb – nearly fifty burials have been discovered here.

Immediately to the west, the village of **AVEBURY** stands in the midst of a **stone circle** (free access; NT & EH) that rivals Stonehenge – the individual stones are generally smaller, but the circle itself is much wider and more complex. A massive earthwork 20ft high and 1400ft across encloses the main circle, which is approached by four causeways across the inner ditch, two of them leading into wide avenues that stretch over a mile beyond the circle. The best guess is that it was built soon after 2500 BC, and presumably had a similar ritual or religious function to Stonehenge. The structure of Avebury's diffuse circle is quite difficult to grasp, but there are plans on the site, and you can get an excellent overview at the **Alexander Keiller Museum**, at the western entrance to the site (daily 10am–4/6pm or dusk; £4.20, including Barn Gallery; NT & EH), which displays excavated material and explanatory information. Nearby, the **Barn Gallery** holds a permanent exhibition of Avebury and the surrounding country, and shows clips from recently discovered home-movies of Keiller excavating the stones aided by a bevy of nubile assistants. Having absorbed the contents of the various collections, you can wander round the peaceful circle, accompanied by sheep and cattle grazing unconcernedly among the stones. To the southeast, an avenue of standing stones leads half a mile beyond West Kennet towards a spot known as the Sanctuary, though there is little left to see here.

Back in the placid **village** of Avebury, you might drop into **Avebury Manor** (April–Oct: house Mon, Tues & Sun 2–4.40pm; garden Mon, Tues & Fri–Sun 11am–5pm; £4, garden only £3; NT), behind the Alexander Keiller Museum. This sixteenth-century house – incorporating later alterations – has four or five panelled and plastered rooms, for which you are issued with over-shoes to protect the wooden floors from the chalk dust, and a **garden** with topiary and medieval walls.

The Circle restaurant, next to the Barn Gallery, offers **snacks** and cream teas, while the *Red Lion* **pub** also serves reasonable meals and has a few en-suite **rooms** (☎01672/539266; ❺). Alternatively, you can wake up to views of the stones at *Manor Farm*, a B&B on the High Street (☎01672/539294; no credit cards; ❺), which has a private guests' sitting room. There's a **tourist office** (Easter–Oct Tues–Sun 9.30am–5pm; Nov–Easter Wed–Sun 9.30am–4.30pm; ☎01380/734669, ⓦwww.visitkennet.co.uk) in the Avebury Chapel Centre on Green Street, which sells local walking guides. Good **bus** routes connect Avebury with Salisbury and Marlborough.

Lacock

Photogenic **LACOCK**, ten miles northwest of Devizes, is the perfect English feudal village, albeit one gentrified by the National Trust to within a hair's breadth of natural life, and besieged by tourists all summer. Appropriately for such a regular TV and film location – its abbey starred in the recent *Harry Potter* films – the village has a fascinating museum dedicated to the founding father of photography, Henry Fox Talbot, a member of the dynasty which has lived in the local **abbey** since it passed to Sir William Sharington on the Dissolution of the Monasteries in 1539. Ten years later Sharington was arrested for colluding with Thomas Seymour, Treasurer of the Mint, in a plot to subvert the coinage: he narrowly escaped with his life by shopping his partner in crime – who was beheaded – and after a period of disgrace managed to buy back his estates. His descendant, William Henry Fox Talbot, was the first to produce a photographic negative, and the **Fox Talbot Museum**, in a sixteenth-century barn by the abbey gates (Jan to mid-Feb & Nov to mid-Dec Sat & Sun 11am–4pm; March–Oct daily 11am–5.30pm; £5.10, including abbey garden and cloisters, £3.60 in winter; NT), captures something of the excitement he must have experienced as the dim outline of an oriel window in the abbey steadily imprinted itself on a piece of silver nitrate paper. A copy of the postage-stamp-sized result is on display in the museum (the original is in Bradford's National Museum of Photography, Film and Television, see p.787). The **abbey** itself (April–Oct daily except Tues 1–5.30pm; £6.70, £8.30 including museum; NT) preserves a few monastic fragments amid the eighteenth-century Gothic, while the church of **St Cyriac,** in its grounds, contains the opulent tomb of the nefarious Sir William Sharington, buried beneath a splendid barrel-vaulted roof.

The village's delightfully Chaucerian-sounding hostelry, *At the Sign of the Angel*, is a good, if expensive, **hotel** and **restaurant** (℡01249/730230, Ⓦwww.lacock.co.uk;Ⓞ).

Bradford-on-Avon

With its buildings of mellow auburn stone, reminiscent of the townscapes just over the county border in Bath and the Cotswolds, **BRADFORD-ON-AVON** is the most appealing town in Wiltshire's northwest corner. Sheltering against a steep wooded slope, it takes its name from its "broad ford" across the Avon, though the original fording place was replaced in the thirteenth century by a **bridge** that was in turn largely rebuilt in the seventeenth century. The domed structure at one end is a quaint old jail converted from a chapel.

The local industry, based on textiles like that of its Yorkshire namesake, was revolutionized with the arrival of Flemish weavers in 1659, and many of the town's handsome buildings reflect the prosperity of this period. Yet Bradford's most significant building is the tiny **St Lawrence** on Church Street, an outstanding example of Saxon church architecture dating from about 700 AD. Its distinctive features are the carved angels over the chancel arch.

Trains call regularly at Bradford from Salisbury, Dorchester, Bath and Bristol; the **train station** is on St Margaret's Street close to the town centre. For easy biking along the Kennet and Avon Canal west to Bath you can **rent bikes** from Lock Inn Cottage, 48 Frome Rd (℡01225/867187). The well-equipped **tourist office** is at 50 St Margaret's St (Mon–Sat 10am–4/5pm, Sun 10/11am–3/4pm; ℡01225/865797, Ⓦwww.bradfordonavon.co.uk).

Bradford has a good range of **accommodation**, none more characterful than *Bradford Old Windmill*, a B&B up the hill at 4 Mason's Lane (℡01225/866842, Ⓦwww.bradfordoldwindmill.co.uk; closed Dec & Jan;Ⓞ), where seven choices of breakfast are available and vegetarian evening meals can be arranged (Mon, Wed, Thurs & Sat only; £25) with a day's notice. *Priory Steps*, closer to the centre on Newtown (℡01225/862230, Ⓦwww.priorysteps.co.uk;Ⓞ), is a family home converted from seventeenth-century weavers' cottages, with well-prepared dinners (by prior arrangement; £25) and excellent views over the rooftops. More cheaply, there's the *Riverside Inn,* 49 St Margaret's St (℡01225/863526, Ⓦwww .riversideboa.co.uk; ❸), with en-suite rooms overlooking the Avon, though it can get noisy on Friday and Saturday evenings, when there's live rock, jazz and blues downstairs. Other pubs include the *Bunch of Grapes* on Silver Street, which has good wines and beers and serves great meals.

Travel details

Buses

Details of minor and seasonal local bus services are frequently given in the text. For information on all other local and national bus services, contact Traveline ℡0871/200 2233, Ⓦwww .traveline.org.uk.

Bournemouth to: London (hourly; 2hr 40min); Salisbury (Mon–Sat every 30min, Sun 7; 1hr 10min); Southampton (11–14 daily; 45min–1hr 50min); Weymouth (5 daily; 1hr 20min); Winchester (6 daily; 1hr 15min–2hr).

Dorchester to: London (1 daily; 4hr); Weymouth (3–6 hourly; 30min).

Portsmouth to: London (15 daily; 2hr 15min–3hr 50min); Salisbury (1 daily; 1hr 35min); South-ampton (Mon–Sat 13 daily, Sun 6; 40–50min).

Salisbury to: Bournemouth (Mon–Sat every 30min, Sun 7; 1hr 10min); London (3 daily; 2hr 50min–4hr); Portsmouth (1 daily; 1hr 30min); Southampton (Mon–Sat 1–2 hourly, Sun 6; 45min–1hr); Winchester (Mon–Sat 5–7 daily; 1hr 20min).

Southampton to: Bournemouth (11–14 daily; 45min–1hr 50min); London (hourly; 2hr 35min–3hr); Portsmouth (Mon–Sat 13 daily, Sun 6; 40–50min); Salisbury (Mon–Sat 1–2 hourly, Sun 6; 45min–1hr); Weymouth (2 daily; 2hr 40min); Winchester (every 15–30min; 45min).

Winchester to: Alton (Mon–Sat hourly, Sun every 2hr; 40min); Bournemouth (3 daily; 1hr 15 min–1hr 35min); London (9 daily; 2hr); Salisbury (Mon–Sat 5–7 daily; 1hr 20min); Southampton (every 15–30min; 45min).

Trains

For information on all local and national rail services, contact National

Rail Enquiries ℡0845/748 4950, Ⓦwww.nationalrail.co.uk.

Bournemouth to: Brockenhurst (3–4 hourly; 15–25min); Dorchester (hourly; 45min); London Waterloo (2 hourly; 2hr); Poole (3 hourly; 10min); Southampton (3 hourly; 30–50min); Weymouth (hourly; 55min); Winchester (2–3 hourly; 45min–1hr).

Dorchester to: Bath (Mon–Sat 8 daily, Sun 3; 2hr); Bournemouth (hourly; 45min); Bradford-on-Avon (Mon–Sat 8 daily, Sun 3; 1hr 35min); Bristol (Mon–Sat 8 daily, Sun 3; 2hr 10min); Brockenhurst (hourly; 1hr); London Waterloo (hourly; 2hr 40min); Weymouth (1–2 hourly; 10–15min).

Poole to: Bournemouth (2–3 hourly; 10–15min); London Waterloo (1–2 hourly; 2hr 5min–2hr 50min); Weymouth (hourly; 45min).

Portsmouth to: London Waterloo (3–4 hourly; 1hr 35min–2hr 15min); Salisbury (hourly; 1hr 20min); Southampton (2 hourly; 45min–1hr); Winchester (hourly; 1hr).

Ryde (Isle of Wight) to: Shanklin (Mon–Sat every 20–40min, Sun hourly; 25min).

Salisbury to: Bath (hourly; 1hr); Bradford-on-Avon (hourly; 45min); Bristol (hourly; 1hr 20min); London Waterloo (2 hourly; 1hr 30min); Portsmouth (hourly; 1hr 20min); Southampton (1–2 hourly; 30min).

Southampton to: Bournemouth (3 hourly; 30–50min); Brockenhurst (2–3 hourly; 15–30min); London Waterloo (2–3 hourly; 1hr 20min); Portsmouth (2 hourly; 45min–1hr); Salisbury (1–2 hourly; 30min); Weymouth (hourly; 1hr 40min); Winchester (3–4 hourly; 15–30min).

Weymouth to: Bournemouth (hourly; 55min); London Waterloo (hourly; 2hr 50min–3hr 35min); Poole (hourly; 45min).

Winchester to: Bournemouth (3 hourly; 45min–1hr); London Waterloo (3–4 hourly; 1hr–1hr 15min); Portsmouth (hourly; 1hr); Southampton (4 hourly; 15–20min).

Oxfordshire, the Cotswolds and around

CHAPTER 4

Highlights

✳ Chiltern Hills Some 75 miles from tip to toe, these rolling, wooded hills hold some of the region's most handsome scenery . See p.293

✳ The Vale of White Horse The huge, prehistoric horse cut into the bright-white chalk of the Berkshire Downs is a stunning sight. See p.298

✳ Christ Church College, Oxford Oxford boasts many beautiful old buildings, with Christ Church holding several of the most fascinating. See p.307

✳ Falkland Arms, Great Tew Wonderful pub in the most charming of hamlets, deep in the heart of the Cotswolds. See p.334

✳ Chipping Campden, Gloucestershire Perhaps the most handsome of the Cotswolds towns, with honey-coloured stone houses flanking the superb church of St James. See p.335

▲ Christ Church College, Oxford

Oxfordshire, the Cotswolds and around

A rching around the peripheries of London, beyond the orbital M25, the "Home Counties" of England form London's commuter belt. Beyond the suburban sprawl, however, there is plenty to entice. The northwestern Home Counties – **Berkshire**, **Buckinghamshire** and **Hertfordshire** – are at their most appealing amidst the **Chiltern Hills**, a picturesque band of chalk uplands whose wooded ridges rise near Luton, beside the M1, and stretch southwest, petering out beside the River Thames near Reading. The hills provide an exclusive setting for many of the capital's wealthiest commuters, but for the casual visitor the obvious target is **Henley-on-Thames**, an attractive old town famous for its regatta and with a good supply of accommodation. Henley is also a handy base for further explorations, with the village of **Cookham** – and its Stanley Spencer Gallery – leading the way.

Traversing the Chilterns is the 85-mile-long **Ridgeway**, a prehistoric track – and now a national trail – that offers excellent hiking, though its finest portion is further to the west, across the Thames, on the downs straddling the Berkshire–Oxfordshire border. Here, the Ridgeway visits a string of prehistoric sites, the most extraordinary being the gigantic chalk horse that gives the **Vale of White Horse** its name. The Vale is dotted with pleasant little villages, but the nearby university city of **Oxford**, with its superb architecture, museums and lively student population, is the region's star turn. It's also close to **Woodstock**, the handsome little town abutting one of England's most imposing country homes, **Blenheim Palace**.

To the northeast of Oxford, well beyond the Chilterns, the plain landscapes of north Buckinghamshire hardly fire the soul, though modest **Buckingham** is pleasant enough and is also within easy striking distance of **Stowe Gardens**, which holds a remarkable collection of outdoor sculptures, monuments and follies. Travel east from Buckingham and you soon reach **Woburn**, home to another whopping stately home, **Woburn Abbey**, as well as **Woburn Safari Park**. It's another short hop from here into Bedfordshire, mostly flat agricultural

OXFORDSHIRE, THE COTSWOLDS & AROUND

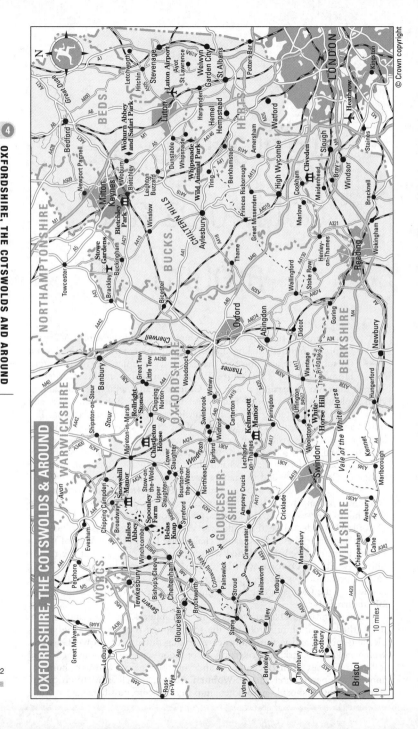

© Crown copyright

10 miles

0

land with a hint of the industrial Midlands, whose only real attraction is the town of **Bedford** with its John Bunyan connection. Back towards London, the county of Hertfordshire boasts the ancient and dignified town of **St Albans**, with Roman remains and a superb cathedral, though it's sadly marooned amidst a knot of motorways and unexciting new towns on the fringes of the capital.

Beyond Oxford lie the rolling hills and ridges of the **Cotswolds**, stretching northeast to southwest and covering much of west **Oxfordshire** and **Gloucestershire**. Dotted with picturesque villages made from the local honey-coloured stone, the Cotswolds became rich from the medieval wool trade, evidence of which remains all around in a multitude of beautiful old churches and handsome mansions. Unsurprisingly, the region attracts visitors by the coachload, though this should not deter you from visiting the Cotswolds in general and the engaging market town of **Chipping Campden**, the delightful village of **Northleach** and bustling **Cirencester** in particular. Ultimately, however, the Cotswolds' subtle charms only really reveal themselves when you take to the hills and valleys along its dense network of footpaths and trails, in particular the **Cotswold Way**, a hundred-mile national trail that runs along the edge of the Cotswold escarpment from Chipping Campden in the northeast to Bath in the southwest.

Heading west, the land drops sharply from the Cotswold escarpment down to **Cheltenham**, an appealing Regency spa town famous for its horse racing. The town's reputation as a bastion of blue-stockinged conservatism is fairly passé now, and it has developed a more sophisticated veneer in recent years, boasting some of the best restaurants and bars in the region. Cheltenham also makes a good base for a visit to **Gloucester**, with its superb cathedral and rejuvenated harbour area.

The area covered in this chapter is threaded by four **motorways**, the M4, M40, M1 and A1(M), which give swift access from all directions. Long-distance **buses** mostly stick to the motorways, providing an efficient service to all the larger towns, but local services between the villages are patchy, sometimes non-existent. There are **mainline train** services from London's Paddington Station to Oxford, Reading, Cheltenham, Gloucester and Bristol, and from London's St Pancras to St Albans and Bedford. In addition, trains from London's Paddington Station stop at several Cotswold towns en route to Worcester and Hereford. These main routes are supplemented by a number of branch lines.

The Chiltern Hills and Reading

The **Chiltern Hills** extend southwest from the workaday town of Luton, beside the M1, bumping across Buckinghamshire and Oxfordshire as far as the River Thames, just to the west of Reading. At their best, the hills offer handsome countryside, comprising a band of forested chalk hills with steep ridges and deep valleys interrupted by easy, rolling farmland. The Chilterns are also one of the country's wealthiest areas, liberally sprinkled with exclusive commuter hideaways-cum-country homes – though there are unappetizing suburban blotches too. For non-residents, an obvious target is **Henley-on-Thames**, a pleasant riverside town within easy striking distance of the area's key attractions, which offers a reasonable range of accommodation. Nearby highlights include the sumptuous country house and estate of **Cliveden** and the village of **Cookham**, home to the fascinating Stanley Spencer Gallery. Leave time also for suburban **Great Missenden**, home to the inventive

Roald Dahl Museum and Story Centre, and **Reading**, a busy modern town straddling the River Thames just beyond the Chilterns. Crossing the Chilterns to the north and west of Henley, the Ridgeway National Trail (see box p.299) offers splendid hiking, though the most diverting part of the trail is further to the west in the **Vale of White Horse** (see p.298).

Henley, Reading and Great Missenden are well served from London by **train** and there's a branch line up to Cookham from Maidenhead, but to get to Cliveden you'll need your own transport.

Henley-on-Thames

Three counties – Oxfordshire, Berkshire and Buckinghamshire – meet at **HENLEY-ON-THAMES**, which was long a favourite stopping place for travellers between London and Oxford. It's a good-looking, affluent commuter town, at its prettiest among the old brick and stone buildings that flank the short main drag, **Hart Street**. At one end of Hart Street is the Market Place and its large and fetching **town hall**, at the other stands the easy Georgian curves of **Henley Bridge**. Overlooking the bridge is the **parish church of St Mary**, whose sturdy square tower sports a set of little turrets worked in chequerboard flint and stone, a popular decorative motif hereabouts in the fifteenth and sixteenth centuries. Several operators run **boat trips** out along the Thames from the jetties just south of the bridge, including Hobbs & Sons (℡01491/572035, 🖳www.hobbs-of-henley.com), who offer hour-long jaunts from April to September for £6.50 (see also box opposite). Henley also possesses an imaginative **River and Rowing Museum** (daily 10am–5pm; £3.50; 🖳www.rrm.co.uk), a five- to ten-minute walk south along the riverbank from the foot of Hart Street via Thames Side. This focuses on three main themes: the history of the town, the development of rowing from the Greeks onwards, and the Thames both as a wildlife habitat and as a trading link. Inside the museum, a supplementary exhibition (£3.50 extra) is devoted to Kenneth Grahame's children's book *Wind in the Willows*. The book was set near Henley where Grahame (1859–1932) was sent to live with his grandmother, after his mother died from scarlet fever.

But above all, Henley is renowned for its **Royal Regatta**, the world's most important amateur rowing tournament, when the town gets all puffed up and excitable. Established in 1839, the regatta is effectively a parade ground for the rich, aristocratic and aspiring, whose champagne-swilling antics are inexplicably found thrilling by large numbers of the hoi polloi. The regatta, featuring past and potential Olympic rowers, begins on the Wednesday before the first weekend in July and runs for five days. Further information is available from the Regatta Headquarters on the east side of Henley Bridge (℡01491/572153, 🖳www.hrr.co.uk).

Practicalities

It takes about an hour to get to Henley by **train** from London's Paddington Station, but you normally have to change at Twyford. From Henley **train station**, it's a five-minute walk north to Hart Street, along Station Road and its continuation Thames Side. Henley is easy to reach by bus, too, with regular services from Oxford, Reading and London. **Buses** from Reading and points south and west mostly pull in on Hart Street, while those from the north and east – including Cookham – stop on Bell Street, immediately to the north of Hart Street. The **tourist office** (daily 10am–5pm, till 4pm in winter; ℡01491/578034, 🖳www.visithenley-on-thames.co.uk) is located in a refurbished old barn, in a courtyard across from the town hall.

Thames passenger boat services

Salter's Steamers runs **passenger boats** along the River Thames from mid-May to late September. There are services between Oxford and Abingdon, Reading and Henley, Henley and Marlow, and between Marlow, Cookham and Windsor. Prices are reasonable – Marlow to Cookham costs £6.50 one way, £9.70 return – and there are one or two boats daily on the more popular routes, three weekly on others. Further details are available from local tourist offices or direct from Salter Brothers on ☏01865/243421, ⊛www.salterssteamers.co.uk.

Henley has several first-rate **B&Bs**, most notably the smart and tastefully furnished *Alftrudis*, 8 Norman Ave (☏01491/573099, ⊛www.alftrudis.co.uk; no credit cards; ➍), which occupies a handsome Victorian town house in a quiet, leafy residential street just south of the centre off Reading Road, the A4155. Another excellent choice is *Lenwade*, 3 Western Rd (☏01491/573468, ⊛www .w3b-ink.com/lenwade; no credit cards; ➍), an attractive Edwardian house with six en-suite or private-bathroom guest rooms, comfortable furnishings and an unusual stained-glass window in the hallway. **Hotels** are thinner on the ground with the pick of the bunch being the distinctive ⚑ *Hotel du Vin*, in the creatively revamped old Brakspear's Brewery, right in the centre of town on New Street, one block north of Hart Street and fifty yards from the river (☏01491/848400, ⊛www.hotelduvin.com; ➐). The hotel is part of a small, upmarket chain and the rooms are kitted out in slick modernist style.

The *Hotel du Vin* also has the best **restaurant** in town, where the emphasis is on local – or at least British – ingredients, with mains about £15; the Yorkshire roast grouse in orange jus is especially delicious. The tastiest coffee in Henley is served up at *Bloc 2*, across from the town hall at the top of Hart Street, and, amongst a platoon of downtown **pubs**, the *Angel*, by the bridge, has the advantage of an outside deck overlooking the river. There are several outstanding country pubs within easy striking distance of Henley too, probably the best of them being the one-time hideout of the highwayman Dick Turpin, ⚑ *The Crooked Billet* (☏01491/681048), in **Stoke Row**, five miles west of Henley off the B481. With an open fireplace and low-beamed ceilings dating from the 1640s, this is the quintessential English pub, but the food, which is excellent, has all sorts of English, French and Italian flourishes. Main courses average around £17 and advance booking is strongly recommended.

Cookham

Heading east out of Henley on the A4155, it's eight leafy miles to the bustling riverside town of **Marlow**, then three more to tiny **COOKHAM**, former home of **Stanley Spencer** (1891–1959), one of Britain's greatest – and most eccentric – artists. The son of a Cookham music teacher, Spencer's art was inspired by the Bible and many of his paintings depict biblical tales transposed into his Cookham surroundings – remarkable, visionary works in which the village is turned into a sort of earthly paradise. Spencer made his artistic name in the 1920s, first as an official war artist and then for his *Resurrection: Cookham*, which attracted rave reviews when it was exhibited in London in 1927. No one minded much that his brand of Christianity was extremely unorthodox – he called his religious system the "Church of Me" – but in the 1930s his reputation temporarily dipped and he received endless critical flak when his work took an erotic turn. In part, this reflected his own changing circumstances; in 1937, he divorced his first wife, Hilda, in order to marry his mistress, Patricia Preece, but the latter exploited him financially and, so most contemporaries thought, regularly humiliated him. Spencer continued writing to Hilda throughout his troubled second marriage, a passionate correspondence that – bizarrely – continued after her death in 1950.

Much of Spencer's most acclaimed work is displayed in London's Tate Britain (see p.95), but there's a fine sample here at the **Stanley Spencer Gallery** (Easter–Oct daily 10.30am–5.30pm; Nov–Easter Sat & Sun 11am–4.30pm; £3; Ⓦwww.stanleyspencer.org.uk), which occupies the old Methodist Chapel on the High Street. Three prime exhibits are *View from Cookham Bridge*, the unsettling *Sarah Tubb and the Heavenly Visitors*, and the wonderful (but unfinished) *Christ Preaching at Cookham Regatta*. The permanent collection is enhanced by regular exhibitions of Spencer's paintings and the gallery also contains incidental Spencer letters, documents and memorabilia, including the pram in which he used to wheel his artist's equipment around the village. As a boy, Spencer worshipped in the chapel, and his home, Fernlea (no access), is on the High Street. The gallery has a leaflet detailing an hour-long walk round Cookham, visiting places with which he is associated.

Practicalities

From **Cookham train station**, which is on the Maidenhead–Marlow branch line, it's a fifteen-minute walk east along the High Street to the gallery. Maidenhead is on the London Paddington to Reading line. From Henley, you have to change trains twice to reach Marlow (at Twycross and Maidenhead). The antique, half-timbered *Bel & The Dragon* **pub**, just across the street from the Spencer Gallery, is a good spot for a pint, though Cookham is also a short drive from one of England's most acclaimed and proclaimed **restaurants**, Heston Blumenthal's ⚞ *Fat Duck*, on the High Street in **BRAY** (☎01628/580333, Ⓦwww.fatduck.co.uk; closed Sun eve). Vastly expensive it may be, but only here can you can taste such extraordinary delights as pig's trotter and truffle, snail porridge and egg and bacon ice cream; reservations are essential.

Cliveden

Perched on a ridge overlooking the River Thames about four circuitous miles east of Cookham, **Cliveden** is a grand Victorian mansion, whose sweeping Neoclassical lines were designed by Sir Charles Barry, architect of the Houses of Parliament. Its most famous occupant was **Nancy Astor**, the first woman to sit in the House of Commons and, together with her husband, the second Viscount Astor, a leading light of the "**Cliveden set**" – a weekly gathering of influential politicians who came here at weekends in the run-up to World War II. Reactionary to the core, their ability to appreciate the difficulties faced by Hitler was not readily understood by many of their compatriots, but this didn't stop Churchill appointing Astor a minister in his wartime cabinet. The second Viscount died in 1952, but the family scandals didn't end there, with the third Viscount outdoing his predecessor by getting enmeshed in the Profumo affair, which transfixed Britain in the early 1960s (see box opposite).

The National Trust now owns Cliveden and leases the house as a luxury **hotel** (☎01628/668561, Ⓦwww.clivedenhouse.co.uk; ➒), which boasts an extraordinarily lavish interior. Acres of wood panelling, portraits of past owners and fancy chimneypieces culminate in the French Dining Room, containing the complete fittings and furnishings of Madame de Pompadour's eighteenth-century dining room, bought as a job lot in Paris by one of the Astors. Most of the hotel is only open to guests, but visitors are permitted limited access

The Profumo affair

The **Profumo affair** was a complicated tale of sex and spies, which rocked the Conservative government of Harold Macmillan to its very core in 1963. The lynchpin of the whole scandal was **Stephen Ward**, a well-connected osteopath who acted as a sort of middleman, introducing women to the high and mighty. At the third Viscount Astor's invitation, Ward spent many a weekend at a cottage on Astor's Cliveden estate in the company of **Christine Keeler** who, at one of the many parties, was introduced to **John Profumo**, the Secretary of State for War. They proceeded to have an affair, but unluckily for the minister Keeler was also sleeping with a Russian naval attaché at the Soviet embassy – and this at the height of the Cold War. It's long been a matter of debate as to whether Keeler passed information from pillow to pillow and if, for that matter, Profumo spilt any secret beans, but Keeler's autobiography certainly insists that Ward was a Soviet spy. Whatever the truth, when the story broke in 1962, it created the most intense of scandals. Initially, Profumo denied the affair, but eventually he had to come clean, thereby polishing off his own political career and fatally undermining the credibility of the Harold Macmillan government. Perhaps inevitably, the fall guy was Ward, who was prosecuted for living off immoral earnings, but committed suicide on the very last day of the trial, before the jury reached their verdict, whilst Profumo decided to withdraw from public life and dedicate himself to charitable works. From the whole debacle, one quote has echoed down the years. At Ward's trial, the prosecution alleged that one of Keeler's friends, **Mandy Rice-Davies**, had received money from Viscount Astor for sex. Astor denied ever having relations with her, prompting Rice-Davies to respond "He would say that, wouldn't he?"

(April–Oct Thurs & Sun 3–5.30pm; £1 on top of grounds price; NT), with timed, same-day tickets issued on a first-come, first-served basis at the information kiosk, so arrive early to avoid disappointment. More satisfying and justifiably popular are the **grounds** (daily: mid-March to Oct 11am–6pm; Nov to late Dec 11am–4pm; £7.50; NT), where a large slice of broadleaf woodland is crisscrossed by footpaths and intercepted by several themed gardens – the water garden is perhaps the most striking. There are also superb views of the Thames, none better than from the Yew Walk just beyond the house. Free maps are issued at the reception desk at the car park.

Great Missenden

GREAT MISSENDEN, eighteen miles north of Henley – a couple less from Cliveden – may once have been a pretty Buckinghamshire village, but in recent years it's been enmeshed by suburbia and today its long main street of old brick houses is surrounded by the mundane. Don't despair, for it was here that **Roald Dahl** (1916–1990), arguably the greatest children's storywriter of all time, spent the later part of his life. Born in Wales, the son of Norwegian parents, Dahl had a spectacularly eventful war that included a harrowing air crash in the Libyan desert. After the war, his life was no less tragic, with one of his children dying of measles, another developing hydrocephalus, and his wife, Patricia Neal, suffering three strokes when she was pregnant in 1965. Despite – perhaps partly because of these troubles – Dahl produced a series of wonderful books, tales infused with menace and comedy, malice and eccentricity, most memorably *Charlie and the Chocolate Factory*, *The Twits*, *The BFG* and *The Witches*. Dahl's house remains in private hands, but Great Missenden comes up trumps with the **Roald Dahl Museum and Story Centre**, 81 High St (Tues–Sun 10am–5pm;

£5; ☎01494/892192, ⊛www.roalddahlmuseum.org), an unmissable treat for Dahl fans. As well as chronicling the author's life, the museum has a replica of the hut where Dahl wrote some of his best-known books, and explores the nature of creative writing, supported by hints from contemporary writers and a scattering of interactive games.

There are two **trains** hourly from London Marylebone to Great Missenden and the journey takes forty minutes; the museum is a five-minute walk from the station – veer right down the hill from the station and then turn right along the High Street. There are no trains from Henley – you have to go into London and out again.

Reading

READING, ten miles south of Henley, is a modern, prosperous town on the south bank of the River Thames. Guarding the western approaches to the capital, it has always been important, long a stopping-off point for kings and queens. Since the 1980s the town has reinvented itself, attracting a raft of IT companies that have made it the epicentre of England's own "Silicon Valley", running along the M4 corridor.

Reading also boasts a couple of Victorian curiosities: the **prison** (no public access), a severe-looking structure on Forbury Road, where Oscar Wilde was incarcerated in the 1890s and wrote his poignant *Ballad of Reading Gaol*; and a replica of the **Bayeux Tapestry** recording William the Conqueror's invasion of England in 1066. The original is in France, but in the 1880s no less than thirty-five embroiderers worked on this 70-metre-long copy, now displayed in a purpose-built gallery at the **Museum of Reading**, in the town hall, on the northeast side of the main shopping precinct (Tues–Sat 10am–4pm, Sun 11am–4pm; free; ⊛www.readingmuseum.org.uk).

Reading boasts a flourishing **arts scene**, with both the Reading Film Theatre (☎0118/378 7151, ⊛www.readingfilmtheatre.co.uk) and the Hexagon Theatre (☎0118/960 6060, ⊛www.readingarts.com) offering a good programme of concerts and shows, though the town's cultural highlight is the **Reading Festival** (⊛www.readingfestival.com), a three-day event held at the back end of August and featuring many of the big names of contemporary music.

With fast and frequent services from London Paddington, Reading **train station** is on the north side of town, a five- to ten-minute walk from the centre.

The Vale of White Horse

The **Vale of White Horse**, running east–west between Wantage, a modest market town about twenty-five miles northwest of Reading, and Faringdon, seventeen miles southwest of Oxford, is a shallow valley, whose fertile farmland is studded with tiny villages. It takes its name from the prehistoric figure cut into the chalk downs above two of its smaller hamlets – **Uffington** and **Woolstone**. Carved in the first century BC, the horse is the most conspicuous of a string of prehistoric remains that punctuates these open downs and includes burial mounds and Iron Age forts. The **Ridgeway National Trail** (see box opposite), running along – or near – the top of the downs, links several of these sites, offering wonderful, breezy views over the vale and skirting the White Horse itself. The Vale most readily lends itself to day-trips, but you might opt to stay locally in the attractive hostel on the ridge above **Wantage**, or in one of the Vale's quaint villages – tiny **Woolstone** is perhaps the most appealing. As for

The Iron Age inhabitants of Britain developed the **Ridgeway** as a major thoroughfare, a fast route that beetled across the chalky downs of modern-day Berkshire and Oxfordshire, negotiated the Thames and then traversed the Chiltern Hills. It was probably once part of a longer route extending from the Dorset coast to the Wash in Norfolk. Today, the Ridgeway is one of England's fourteen national trails, running from **Overton Hill**, near Avebury in Wiltshire, to **Ivinghoe Beacon**, 87 miles to the northeast near Tring. Crossing five counties, the trail avoids densely populated areas, keeping to the hills, except where the Thames slices through the trail at **Goring Gap**, marking the transition from the wooded valleys of the Chilterns to the more open Berkshire–Oxfordshire downs.

By and large, the Ridgeway is fairly easy hiking and over half of it is accessible to cyclists. The prevailing winds mean that it is best walked in a northeasterly direction. The trail is strewn with prehistoric monuments of one description or another, though easily the finest archeological remains are on the downs edging the **Vale of White Horse** and around **Avebury** (see p.286). There are several **hostels** within reach of the Ridgeway – most notably the *Court Hill Centre* near Wantage (see below) – and numerous B&Bs. Maps and detailed guides are available from the National Trails Office (☎01865/810224, ⓦwww.nationaltrail.co.uk).

public transport, there is an intermittent local **bus** service between the towns and villages of the Vale, but you'll need to plan ahead.

Wantage

Workaday **WANTAGE** is an unassuming, somewhat care-worn market town, whose crowded Market Place is overseen by a statue of its most famous son, Alfred the Great (849–99), the most distinguished of England's Saxon kings. Unveiled in 1877, the statue doesn't do Alfred any favours – though he must have been very strong indeed to stand any chance of lifting his over-large axe. From the south side of the Market Place a couple of alleys lead through to Church Street. This is the location of the **tourist office** (Mon–Sat 10am–4.30pm; ☎01235/771447, ⓦwww.wantage.com), which sells local hiking maps, and a modest **museum**.

From Wantage, it's a couple of miles south to the **Ridgeway** at the point where it begins one of its finest stretches, running seven miles west along the downs to White Horse Hill (see below). There is B&B **accommodation** in the villages below White Horse Hill (see p.300), or you could head for the *Court Hill Centre* **hostel** (☎01235/760253, ⓦwww.courthill.org.uk; dorm beds £16.50, doubles ❶; Easter to October), in a prime position just off the A338 two miles south of Wantage, and just a stone's throw away from the Ridgeway trail. The hostel consists of several converted timber barns set around a courtyard, with sixty beds in two- to thirteen-bedded rooms; advance reservations are strongly recommended.

White Horse Hill and around

White Horse Hill, overlooking the B4507 six miles west of Wantage, follows close behind Stonehenge (see p.284) and Avebury (see p.286) in the hierarchy of Britain's ancient sites, though it attracts nothing like the same number of visitors. Carved into the north-facing slope of the downs above the villages of Uffington and Woolstone, the 374-foot-long **horse** looks like something created with a few swift strokes of an immense brush, and there's been no lack

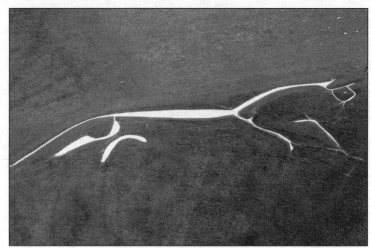

▲ The White Horse

of weird and wonderful theories as to its origins. Some have suggested it was a glorified signpost, created to show travellers where to join the Ridgeway; others that it represented the horse (or even the dragon) of St George. In Victorian times, the best-loved legend – popularized in a ballad by G.K. Chesterton – claimed that it was cut by King Alfred to celebrate his victory over the Danes at the battle of Ashdown, fought around here in 871 AD. In fact, burial sites excavated in the surrounding area point to the horse having some kind of sacred function, though frankly no one knows quite what. The first written record of the horse's existence dates from the time of Henry II, but it was cut much earlier, probably in the first century BC, making it one of the oldest chalk figures in Britain. A detailed study in 1994 showed that its creators dug out the soil to a depth of a metre and then filled the hollow with clear white chalk taken from a nearby hilltop.

Just below the horse is **Dragon Hill**, a small flat-topped hillock that has its own legend. Locals long asserted that this was where St George killed and buried the dragon, a theory proved, so they argued, by the bare patch at the top and the channel down the side, where blood trickled from the creature's wounds. Here also, at the top of the hill, is the Iron Age earthwork of **Uffington Castle**, which provides wonderful views over the Vale.

The Ridgeway runs alongside the horse and continues west to reach, after one and a half miles, **Wayland's Smithy**, a 5000-year-old burial mound encircled by trees. It is one of the best Neolithic remains along the Ridgeway, though heavy restoration has rather detracted from its mystery. In ignorance of its original function, the invading Saxons named it after Weland (hence Wayland), an invisible smith who, according to their legends, made invincible armour and shod horses without ever being seen.

The B4507 passes the narrow lane that leads – after 500 yards – to the car park just below the White Horse. There are no regular buses.

Woolstone and Uffington

About three-quarters of a mile below the White Horse car park, on the north side of the B4057, is the minuscule hamlet of **WOOLSTONE**, where the attractive *White Horse Inn* (℡01367/820726, ⓦwww.whitehorsewoolstone .co.uk; ❹) occupies a half-timbered, partly thatched old building. The inn offers both good-quality pub food and straightforward **accommodation**, mostly in a modern annexe. A mile or so to the north of Woolstone, the much larger village of **UFFINGTON** possesses an outstanding **B&B**, ⚲ *The Craven*, on Fernham Road (℡01367/820449, ⓦwww.thecraven.co.uk; ❹), in a simply delightful thatched cottage with the dinkiest of front doors. There are five infinitely cosy guest rooms here and breakfast is served in the old farmhouse kitchen. Uffington's most famous son was Thomas Hughes (1823–96), the author of *Tom Brown's School Days* – hence the village's pocket-sized Tom Brown's School Museum.

Oxford

When they think of **OXFORD**, visitors almost always imagine its **university**, revered as one of the world's great academic institutions, inhabiting honey-coloured stone buildings set around ivy-clad quadrangles. Much of this is accurate enough, but although the university dominates central Oxford both physically and mentally, the wider city has an entirely different character, its economy built on the **car plants** of Cowley to the south of the centre. It was here that Britain's first mass-produced cars were manufactured in the 1920s and, although there have been more downs than ups in recent years, the plants are still vitally important to the area.

Oxford started late, in Anglo-Saxon times, and blossomed even later, under the **Normans**, when the cathedral was constructed and Oxford was chosen as a royal residence. The origins of the university are obscure, but it seems that the reputation of **Henry I**, the so-called "Scholar King", helped attract students in the early twelfth century, their numbers increasing with the expulsion of English students from the Sorbonne in 1167. The first **colleges**, founded mostly by rich bishops, were essentially ecclesiastical institutions and this was reflected in collegiate rules and regulations – until 1877 lecturers were not allowed to marry and women were not granted degrees until 1920. There are **common architectural features**, too, with the private rooms of the students arranged around quadrangles (quads), as are most of the communal rooms – the chapels, halls (dining rooms) and libraries.

Though they share a similar history, each of the university's 39 colleges has its own character and often a particular label, whether it's the richest (St John's), most left-wing (Wadham and Balliol) or most public-school-dominated (Christ Church). Collegiate rivalries are long established, usually revolving around sports, and tension between the university and the city – "Town" and "Gown" – has existed as long as the university itself. Relations became especially fractious during the **Civil War**, when the colleges sided with Charles I (who turned Oxford into a Royalist stronghold) while the city backed the Parliamentarians. The privileges enjoyed by the colleges – until 1950 the university had two MPs of its own – have also stoked resentment and this still flares into the occasional confrontation, but a non-communicative coexistence is more typical. Given that thousands of tourists and foreign-language students also invade the city throughout the year, it is no surprise that Oxford's 140,000 permanent inhabitants often choose to keep themselves to themselves.

Despite – indeed, partly because of – its idiosyncrasies, Oxford should be high on anyone's itinerary, and can keep you occupied for several days. The university

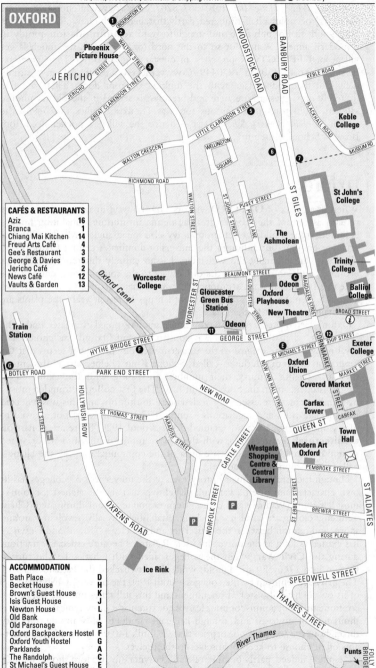

OXFORD

A34/M40, Woodstock, Blenheim & Chipping Norton

A & Banbury

JERICHO

Phoenix Picture House

Keble College

St John's College

The Ashmolean

Trinity College

Balliol College

Worcester College

Gloucester Green Bus Station

Odeon

Oxford Playhouse

New Theatre

Exeter College

Odeon

Train Station

Oxford Union

Covered Market

Carfax Tower

Town Hall

Modern Art Oxford

Westgate Shopping Centre & Central Library

Ice Rink

River Thames

Punts

FOLLY BRIDGE

CAFÉS & RESTAURANTS

Aziz	16
Branca	1
Chiang Mai Kitchen	14
Freud Arts Café	4
Gee's Restaurant	3
George & Davies	5
Jericho Café	2
News Café	12
Vaults & Garden	13

ACCOMMODATION

Bath Place	D
Becket House	H
Brown's Guest House	K
Isis Guest House	J
Newton House	L
Old Bank	I
Old Parsonage	B
Oxford Backpackers Hostel	F
Oxford Youth Hostel	G
Parklands	A
The Randolph	C
St Michael's Guest House	E

Faringdon & Vale of White Horse

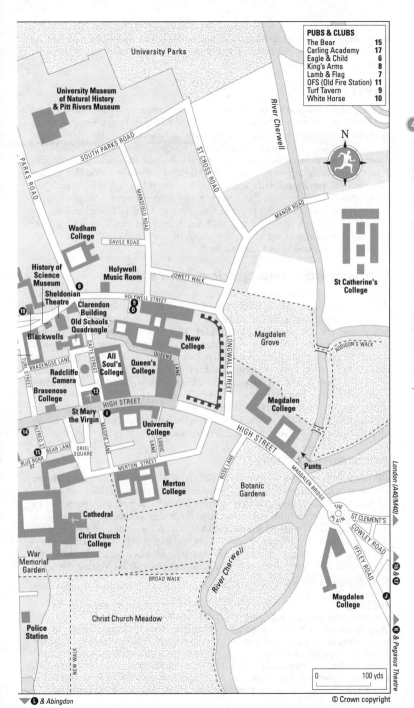

PUBS & CLUBS

The Bear	15
Carling Academy	17
Eagle & Child	6
King's Arms	8
Lamb & Flag	7
OFS (Old Fire Station)	11
Turf Tavern	9
White Horse	10

University Parks

University Museum of Natural History & Pitt Rivers Museum

River Cherwell

N

SOUTH PARKS ROAD

PARKS ROAD

MANSFIELD ROAD

ST CROSS ROAD

MANOR ROAD

Wadham College

SAVILE ROAD

St Catherine's College

History of Science Museum

Holywell Music Room

JOWETT WALK

Sheldonian Theatre

HOLYWELL STREET

Clarendon Building

Old Schools Quadrangle

Blackwells

CATTE STREET

BRASENOSE LANE

TURL STREET

New College

QUEENS LANE

Magdalen Grove

LONGWALL STREET

ADDISON'S WALK

All Soul's College

Queen's College

Radcliffe Camera

Brasenose College

HIGH STREET

Magdalen College

St Mary the Virgin

MAGPIE LANE

University College

LOGIC LANE

HIGH STREET

MAGDALEN BRIDGE

ALFRED ST

BEAR LANE

BLUE BOAR ST

ORIEL SQUARE

MERTON STREET

ROSE LANE

Punts

London (A40/M40)

Merton College

Botanic Gardens

Cathedral

Christ Church College

THE PLAIN

ST CLEMENT'S

COWLEY ROAD

War Memorial Garden

BROAD WALK

River Cherwell

IFFLEY ROAD

Magdalen College

Police Station

Christ Church Meadow

NEW WALK

London & Abingdon

0   100 yds

© Crown copyright

buildings include some of England's finest architecture, and the city can also boast some excellent museums and a good range of bars and restaurants. Getting there is easy, too: from London Paddington the journey takes just an hour by train, a little longer by bus.

Arrival

From Oxford **train station**, it's a five- to ten-minute walk east to the centre via Park End Street and its continuation Hythe Bridge Street. Long-distance and many county-wide buses terminate at the Gloucester Green **bus station**, in the city centre adjoining George Street. The Oxford Bus Company work in tandem with Stagecoach to operate most local and city buses, many of which terminate on the High Street and St Giles. The former also runs the **park-and-ride** scheme, with buses (Mon–Sat 6am–11pm, Sun 9am–7pm) travelling into the centre every fifteen minutes at peak times (every thirty minutes to an hour in the evening) from five large and clearly signed car parks on the main approach roads into the city. Parking costs are minimal, whereas parking in the city centre is – by municipal design – both inordinately expensive and hard to find.

Information and guided tours

The **tourist office** is plumb in the centre of town at 15 Broad St (Mon–Sat 9.30am–5pm, Sun 10am–4pm; ☏01865/252200, ⓦwww.visitoxford.org). They have a wealth of information about the city and its sights, little of which is issued free, though the **listings booklet** *This Month in Oxford* is a notable exception. The tourist office also offers excellent **guided walking tours**, including a two-hour gambol round the city centre and its colleges (several tours daily; £6.50). Further along Broad Street, the main Blackwell's bookshop (☏01865/333606) also runs specialist walking tours at £6.50 per adult. Their main offering is a literary tour of Oxford (2 weekly), but there are other, more infrequent offerings, like their Inklings Tour – Inklings being the group of writers, Tolkien and C.S. Lewis included, who met regularly in Oxford in the 1930s. In all cases, advance booking is recommended.

Accommodation

With supply struggling to keep pace with demand, Oxford's central **hotels** are almost invariably expensive, though nowhere near as pricey as those in London. There are, it's true, one or two inexpensive hotels in or near the centre, but by and large they are far from inspiring, and at the budget end of the market, you're better off choosing a **guest house** or **B&B**, which are plentiful if usually some way from the centre. Wherever you stay, book ahead in high season either direct or through the tourist office, which operates an efficient accommodation-booking service. Note also that hotels almost always cost less during the week than on the weekend.

Hotels

Bath Place 4 Bath Place ☏01865/791812, ⓦwww.bathplace.co.uk. This unusual, pink and blue hotel is tucked away down an old cobbled courtyard flanked by ancient buildings with higgledy-piggledy roofs. There are just fourteen rooms, each individually decorated in attractive, antique style – canopied beds, bare stone walls and so forth. The location is excellent – in the centre, off Holywell Street. ❻

Old Bank 92 High St ☏01865/799599, ⓦwww.oldbank-hotel.co.uk. Great location for a slick and sleek hotel, a glistening conversion of an old bank. All forty-plus bedrooms are decorated in crisp, modern style – all pastel shades and whites – and some have great views over All Souls College. ❽

Old Parsonage 1 Banbury Rd ☏ 01865/310210, ⓦ www.oldparsonage-hotel.co.uk. Arguably the best in town, this lovely hotel occupies a charming, wisteria-clad stone building, a former parsonage, by the church at the top of St Giles. The thirty-odd rooms are tastefully furnished in a bright modern manner, the only problem being the noise of the traffic. ❽

Parklands 100 Banbury Rd ☏ 01865/554374, ⓦ www.oxfordcity.co.uk. Pleasant fourteen-room hotel in a large Victorian house with a garden and bar. North of the centre, but connected to it by a frequent bus service. Good value. ❺

The Randolph 1 Beaumont St ☏ 0870/400 8200, ⓦ www.randolph-hotel .com. The most famous hotel in the city, long the favoured choice of the well-heeled visitor. As *The Randolph* occupies a large and well-proportioned brick building with a distinctive neo-Gothic interior – the carpeted staircase is especially handsome. Now part of a chain, but with impeccable service and well-appointed bedrooms with all mod cons. The rooms on the top floor are the quietest. Discounts are available at slack periods, but otherwise it's ❽

Guest houses and B&Bs

Becket House 5 Becket St ☏ 01865/724675. Modest but proficient bay-windowed guesthouse in a plain terrace close to the train station. Most rooms en suite. ❸

Brown's Guest House 281 Iffley Rd ☏ 01865/246822, ⓦ www.brownsguesthouse.co. uk. Well-maintained guesthouse in a pleasing Victorian property with fourteen rooms, mostly en suite. It's a little less than two miles southeast from the centre. ❸

Isis Guest House 45–53 Iffley Rd ☏ 01865/248894, ⓦ www.isisguesthouse.co.uk. From July to Sept, this college hall becomes a guest house with around forty single (£30, en-suite £38) and double rooms, about half of which are en suite. Located within easy walking distance of Magdalen Bridge. Good value, with rooms decorated in a brisk if frugal modern style. ❸

Newton House 82–84 Abingdon Rd ☏ 01865/240561, ⓦ www.oxfordcity.co.uk. Appealing, family-run guest house in two good-looking and well-kept Victorian town houses about ten minutes' walk south of the centre – well placed for evening strolls along the Thames. The guest rooms are decorated in a smart, traditional style. Thirteen rooms, mostly en-suite. ❸

St Michael's Guest House 26 St Michael's St ☏ 01865/242101. Often full, this friendly, well-kept B&B, in a cosy three-storey terrace house, has unsurprising furnishings and fittings, but a charming, central location. A real snip. ❸

Hostels

Oxford Backpackers Hostel 9a Hythe Bridge St ☏ 01865/721761; ⓦ www.hostels.co.uk. Independent hostel with quads and dorms. Fully equipped kitchen and laundry plus Internet facilities. Handy location between the train station and the centre; 24-hour access. Dorm beds £15–16.

Oxford Youth Hostel 2a Botley Rd ☏ 0870/7705970, ⓔ oxford@yha.org.uk. In a clumpy modern block next door to the train station, this popular YHA hostel has 187 beds divided into two-, four- and six-bedded rooms. There's 24-hour access, laundry, Internet access, and an inexpensive café. Open daily all year. Dorm beds including breakfast £17.

The City

The compact **centre** of Oxford is wedged in between the rivers Thames and Cherwell, just to the north of the point where they join. In theory, and on most maps, the Thames is known within the city as the "Isis", but few locals actually use the term. Central Oxford's principal point of reference is **Carfax**, a busy junction from where three of the city's main thoroughfares begin: the **High Street** runs east to Magdalen Bridge and the River Cherwell; **St Aldates** south to the Thames; and **Cornmarket** north to the broad avenue of St Giles. Many of the oldest **colleges** face onto the High Street or the side streets adjoining it, their mellow stonework combining to create the most beautiful part of Oxford, though the most stunning college of them all is **Christ Church**. All of the more visited colleges have restricted opening hours and some impose an admission charge, while others permit no regular public access at all. Of those that do open their doors, **college opening hours** are fairly consistent throughout the year, but there are sporadic term-time variations, especially at weekends. It's also worth noting that during the exam season, which stretches

On the river

Punting is a favourite summer pastime amongst both students and visitors, but handling a **punt** – a flat-bottomed boat ideal for the shallow waters of the Thames and Cherwell rivers – requires some practice. The punt is propelled and steered with a long pole, which beginners inevitably get stuck in riverbed mud: if this happens, let go and paddle back, otherwise you're likely to be pulled overboard. The Cherwell, though much narrower than the Thames and therefore trickier to navigate, provides more opportunities for pulling to the side for a picnic, an essential part of the punting experience.

There are two central **boat rental** places: Magdalen Bridge boathouse (☎01865/202643), beside the Cherwell at the east end of the High Street; and the Thames boat station at Folly Bridge (☎01865/243421), a five- to ten-minute stroll south of the centre along St Aldates. In summer, the queues soon build up at both, so try to get there early in the morning – at around 10am. At both boathouses, expect **to pay** about £12 per hour for a boat plus a £30 deposit, and remember that sometimes ID is required. Punts can take a maximum of five passengers – four sitting and one punting. Call the boathouses for opening times – which vary – or if there are any doubts about the weather. Both boathouses also rent out **chauffeured punts** (about £20 for 30min). and **pedaloes**, which cost less, but aren't as much fun. Alternatively, Salter's Steamers (☎01865/243421, ⓦwww.salterssteamers.co.uk) runs **passenger boats** along the Thames from Oxford's Folly Bridge to Abingdon, about eight miles to the south, between late May and late September. There are two boats daily in each direction with the return trip taking four hours (£14.90).

The other boats most commonly seen on the Thames belong to the university's **rowing clubs**, which started up in the early nineteenth century, when top hats were *de rigueur*. The first Oxford–Cambridge boat race – now staged in London – took place in 1829. Rowers mostly practise along the wide stretch of river to the south of Folly Bridge, which is also used for college races – the **Torpids**, held in February, and the **Eights**, in May. The latter are the more important and therefore attract the larger crowds.

---

from late April to early June, all the colleges have periods when they are closed to the public entirely. For more specific information, contact the relevant college – details are given in the text below.

South from Carfax to Modern Art Oxford

Too busy to be comfortable and too modern to be pretty, the **Carfax** crossroads is not a place to hang around, but it is overlooked by an interesting remnant of the medieval town, a chunky fourteenth-century **tower**, adorned by a pair of clocktower jacks dressed in vaguely Roman attire. The tower is all that remains of St Martin's Church, where legend asserts that William Shakespeare stood sponsor at the baptism of one of his friends' children. You can climb the **tower** (daily 10am–3.30/5.30pm; £2) for wide views over the centre, though other vantage points – principally St Mary's (see p.311) – have the edge.

Spreading down St Aldates from Carfax, Oxford's **Town Hall** is an ostentatious Victorian confection that reflects a municipal determination not to be overwhelmed by the university. A staircase on its south side gives access to the **Museum of Oxford** (Tues–Fri 10am–5pm, Sat & Sun noon–5pm; free), which often gets ignored, though it does make good use of photographs to tell the history of the city.

From the town hall, cross St Aldates and it's a few paces to Pembroke Street, which possesses the city's best contemporary art gallery, **Modern Art Oxford** (Tues–Sat 10am–5pm, Sun noon–5pm; free; ⓦwww.modernartoxford.org.uk).

The gallery has an excellent programme of temporary exhibitions, featuring international contemporary art in a wide variety of media, along with lectures, films, workshops and multimedia performances (not all of which are free).

Christ Church College and Cathedral

Doubling back along Pembroke Street, turn right down St Aldates and you'll spy the main facade of **Christ Church College** (Mon–Sat 9.30am–5.30pm, Sun 1–5.30pm; £5; ☎01865/286573, ⓦ www.chch.ox.ac.uk), whose distinctive Tom Tower was added by Christopher Wren in 1681 to house the weighty "Great Tom" bell. The tower lords it over the main entrance of what is Oxford's largest and arguably most prestigious college, but visitors have to enter from the south, a signed five-minute walk away – just beyond the tiny War Memorial Garden and at the top of **Christ Church Meadow**. Popular with strollers, the Meadow fills in the tapering gap between the rivers Cherwell and Thames; if you decide to delay visiting Christ Church College, either head east along Broad Walk for the Cherwell or keep straight down tree-lined (and more appealing) New Walk for the Thames.

The College

Albert Einstein and no fewer than thirteen British prime ministers, including William Gladstone, were educated at Christ Church and the college also claims the distinction of having been founded three times, firstly by Cardinal Wolsey in 1525, then by Henry VIII after the cardinal's fall from favour and finally, after the Reformation – when the second college was suppressed – in 1545, when it assumed its present name.

Entering the college from the south, it's a short step to the striking **Tom Quad**, the largest quad in Oxford, so large in fact that the Royalists penned up their mobile larder of cattle here during the Civil War. Guarded by the Tom Tower, the Quad's soft, honey-coloured stone makes a harmonious whole, but it was actually built in two main phases with the southern side dating back to Wolsey, the north finally finished in the 1660s. A wide stone staircase in the southeast corner of the Quad leads up to the **Dining Hall**, the grandest refectory in Oxford with a fanciful hammer-beam roof and a set of stern portraits of past scholars by a roll-call of well-known artists, including Reynolds, Gainsborough and Millais. Charles I held court here when the Parliamentarians were in control of London and, in one of those snippets of information beloved of academics, Lewis Carroll, former student and author of *Alice's Adventures in Wonderland*, ate eight thousand meals in this very hall.

The Cathedral

Just to the rear of the Tom Quad stands the **Cathedral**, which is also – in a most unusual arrangement – the college chapel. The Anglo-Saxons built a church on this site in the seventh century as part of St Frideswide Priory. The priory was suppressed in 1524, but the church survived, becoming a cathedral forty years later, though in between Wolsey knocked down the west end to make space for the Tom Quad. It's an unusually discordant church, with all sorts of bits and bobs from different periods, but it's fascinating all the same. The dominant feature is the sturdy circular columns and rounded arches of the Normans, but there are also early Gothic pointed arches and the chancel ceiling is a particularly fine example of fifteenth-century stone vaulting. The battered **shrine of St Frideswide**, in the Latin Chapel – to the far left (northeast) of the entrance – was destroyed during the Dissolution, but the pieces were found down an old well and gamely assembled by the Victorians. Today, it exhibits some of the earliest natural foliage in English sculpture, a splendid filigree of leaves dating from around 1290. The shrine is overlooked by an equally rare, two-storey, stone and timber **watching loft**, from where custodians would keep a close eye on the tomb of the saint, and by a cluttered but deeply coloured **stained-glass window** by Edward Burne-Jones. The window, crammed with biblical bodies, was completed in 1858, long before Jones got into his Pre-Raphaelite stride, but there are three examples from his later period along the rest of the back of the chancel, with the **St Catherine Window**, in the right-hand corner of the church, being the finest.

To the Canterbury Quad

A passage at the northeast corner of the Tom Quad leads through to the **Peckwater Quad**, whose pleasantries are overwhelmed by the whopping Neoclassical library. A few paces more and you're in the pocket-sized **Canterbury Quad**, where the **Picture Gallery** (May–Sept Mon–Sat 10.30am–5pm, Sun 2–5pm; Oct–April Mon–Sat 10.30am–1pm & 2–4.30pm; £2) is home to works by many of Italy's finest artists from the fifteenth to eighteenth centuries, including Leonardo da Vinci and Michelangelo. There's also a good showing by the Flemish and Dutch – Van Dyck, Frans Hals and so forth. The Canterbury Quad abuts **Oriel Square** with Merton College beckoning just beyond, or you can return to the college's south entrance for Christ Church Meadow (see p.307).

Merton College

Just a few yards from Christ Church, on Merton Street, stands **Merton College** (Mon–Fri 2–4pm, Sat & Sun 10am–4pm; free; ☎01865/276310, ⓦ www.merton.ox.ac.uk), historically the city's most important college. Balliol and University colleges may have been founded earlier, but it was Merton – opened in 1264 – which set the model for colleges in both Oxford and Cambridge, being the first to gather its students and tutors together in one place. Furthermore, unlike the other two, Merton retains some of its original medieval buildings, with the best of the thirteenth-century architecture clustered around **Mob Quad**, a charming courtyard with mullioned windows and Gothic doorways to the right of the Front Quad. The quad's **Library** is of interest too, built in the 1370s and the first library in England to store books upright on shelves as distinct from in piles. Much of the woodwork, including the panelling, screens and bookcases, dates from the Tudor period, but some fittings are original and there's a small display on one of the college's most distinguished alumni, Max Beerbohm. From the Mob Quad, an archway leads through to the **Chapel**, which dates from 1290. The chapel has never had a nave, leaving the choir as the main body of the church and the transepts as ante-chapels. In the latter is the curious funerary plaque of **Thomas Bodley** – founder of Oxford's most important library (see p.310) – his bust surrounded by ungainly, boyish-looking women in classical garb. The windows of the choir were donated by the egocentric Henry de Mamesfeld, who appears as a kneeling figure no less than 24 times. Famous Merton alumni include T.S. Eliot, Angus Wilson, Louis MacNeice and Kris Kristofferson.

University and Queen's colleges

From Merton, narrow Magpie Lane cuts through to the west end of **University College** (no set opening times; ☎01865/276602, ⓦ www.univ.ox.ac.uk), whose long sweeping facade and twin gateway towers spread along the High Street. Known as "Univ", the college claims Alfred the Great as its founder, but things really got going with a formal endowment in 1249, making it Oxford's oldest college – though nothing of that period survives. A year the college may prefer to forget is 1811, when it expelled **Percy Bysshe Shelley** for distributing a paper called *The Necessity of Atheism*. Guilt later induced the college to accept a memorial to the poet, who drowned in Italy in 1822: the white marble monument, showing the limp body of the poet borne by winged lions and mourned by the Muse of Poetry, occupies a shrine-like domed chamber in the northeast corner of the Front Quad. The college's most famous recent alumnus was Rhodes Scholar Bill Clinton, while the former Australian premier Bob Hawke also studied here as did Stephen Hawking, Clement Attlee and the current poet laureate, Andrew Motion.

Across the High Street from Univ stands **Queen's College** (no set opening times; ℡01865/279120, 🅦www.queens.ox.ac.uk), whose handsome Baroque buildings cut an impressive dash. The only Oxford college to have been built in one period (1682–1765), Queen's benefited from the skills of several talented architects, most notably Nicholas Hawksmoor and Christopher Wren. Wren designed (or at least influenced the design of) the college's most diverting building, the **Chapel**, whose ceiling is filled with cherubs amidst dense foliage.

Magdalen College and the University Botanic Gardens

Heading east along the High Street from Queen's, it's a short hop to **Magdalen College** (pronounced "Maudlin"; daily: late June to Sept noon–6pm, Oct to late June 1–6pm or dusk; £3; ℡01865/276000, 🅦www.magd.ox.ac.uk), whose gaggle of stone buildings is overshadowed by its chunky medieval bell tower. Steer right from the entrance and you soon reach the **Chapel**, which has a handsome reredos, though you have to admire it through the windows of an ungainly stone screen. The adjacent **cloisters**, arguably the finest in Oxford, are adorned by standing figures, some biblical and others folkloric, most notably a tribe of grotesques. Magdalen also boasts better **grounds** than most other colleges, with a bridge – at the back of the cloisters – spanning the River Cherwell to join **Addison's Walk**, which you can follow along the river and around a water meadow; rare wild fritillaries flower here in spring. Magdalen's alumni include Oscar Wilde, C.S. Lewis, John Betjeman, Julian Barnes and A.J.P. Taylor.

Across the High Street from Magdalen lie the **University of Oxford Botanic Gardens** (daily: March, April, Sept & Oct 9am–5pm; May–Aug 9am–6pm; Nov–Feb 9am–4.30pm; £3; 🅦www.botanic-garden.ox.ac.uk), whose greenery is bounded by a graceful curve of the Cherwell. First planted in 1621, the gardens comprise several different zones, from a lily pond, a bog garden and a rock garden through to borders of bearded irises and variegated plants. There are also six large **glasshouses** featuring tropical and desert species.

The gardens are next to **Magdalen Bridge**, where you can rent punts (see box on p.306).

New College

Doubling back along the High Street, cut up **Queen's Lane** and you'll dog-leg your way north to **New College** (daily: Easter to early Oct 11am–5pm; £2; mid-Oct to Easter 2–4pm; free; ℡01865/279555, 🅦www.new.ox.ac.uk). Founded in 1379, the college kicks off with an attractive **Front Quad**, though the splendid Perpendicular Gothic architecture of the original was spoiled by the addition of an extra storey in 1674. The adjoining **Chapel** has been mucked about too, yet it can still lay claim to being the finest in Oxford, not so much for its design as its contents. The ante-chapel contains some superb fourteenth-century stained glass and the west window – of 1778 – holds an intriguing (if somewhat unsuccessful) Nativity scene based on a design by Sir Joshua Reynolds. Beneath it stands the wonderful *Lazarus* by Jacob Epstein; Khrushchev, after a visit to the college, claimed that the memory of this haunting sculpture kept him awake at night. The entire east wall of the main chapel is occupied by a magnificent nineteenth-century stone reredos, consisting of about fifty canopied figures, mostly saints and apostles, with Christ Crucified as the centrepiece. An archway on the east side of the Front Quad leads through to the modest **Garden Quad**, with the thick flowerbeds of the **College Garden** beckoning beyond. The north side of the garden is flanked by the largest and best-preserved section of Oxford's medieval **city wall**, but the conspicuous earthen **mound** in the middle is a later decorative addition and not, disappointingly, medieval at all. Notable New College alumni include Tony Benn, the author John Fowles and arguably the finest cricket commentator of all time, Brian Johnston.

From the entrance to New College, it's the briefest of walks to the east end of Broad Street.

The Sheldonian Theatre and the Clarendon Building

The east end of Broad Street abuts much of Oxford's most monumental architecture, beginning with the **Sheldonian Theatre** (Mon–Sat 10am–12.30pm & 2–4.30pm; Nov–Feb closes 3.30pm; £2; ⑩ www.sheldon .ox.ac.uk), ringed by a series of glum-looking, pop-eyed classical heads. The Sheldonian was Christopher Wren's first major work, a reworking of the Theatre of Marcellus in Rome, semi-circular at the back and rectangular at the front. It was conceived in 1663, when the 31-year-old Wren's main job was as professor of astronomy. Designed as a stage for university ceremonies, nowadays it also functions as a concert hall, but the interior lacks any sense of drama, and even the views from the cupola are disappointing.

Wren's colleague Nicholas Hawksmoor designed the **Clarendon Building**, a domineering, solidly symmetrical edifice topped by allegorical figures that is set at right angles to – and lies immediately east of – the Sheldonian. The Clarendon was erected to house the University Press, but is now part of the **Bodleian Library** – the UK's largest after the British Library in London – with an estimated eighty miles of shelves distributed among its several buildings. The heart of the Bodleian is located straight across from the Clarendon in **the Old Schools Quadrangle**.

The Old Schools Quadrangle

Occupied by the **Bodleian Library**, the beautifully proportioned **Old Schools Quadrangle** was built in the early seventeenth century in the ornate Jacobean-Gothic style that distinguishes many of the city's finest buildings. On the quad's east side is the handsome **Tower of the Five Orders**, which gives a lesson in architectural design, with tiers of columns built according to the five classical styles – Tuscan, Doric, Ionic, Corinthian and Composite. On the west side is the library's main entrance and, although most of the complex is out of bounds to the general public, you can pop into the **Divinity School** (Mon–Fri 9am–5pm, Sat 9am–4.30pm; £2), one large room where, until the nineteenth century, degree candidates were questioned in detail about their subject by two interlocutors, with a professor acting as umpire. Begun in 1424, and sixty years in the making, the Divinity School boasts an extravagant vaulted ceiling, a riot of pendants and decorative bosses, altogether an exquisite example of late

Gothic architecture. However, this elaborate design was never carried right through – funding was a constant problem – and parts of the school were finished off in a much plainer style with the change being especially pronounced on the south wall.

You can also sign up for a forty-minute **guided tour** (Mon–Fri 9am–4.15pm, Sat 9am–3.30pm; £2.50) of the Bodleian, which includes visits to **Convocation House**, adjacent to the Divinity School, and **Duke Humfrey's Library**, immediately above. The former is a sombre wood-panelled chamber graced by a fancy fan-vaulted ceiling, completed in 1759 but designed to look much older. The latter is distinguished by its painted beams and carved corbels, dating from the fifteenth century, but restored and remodelled by Thomas Bodley over a century later.

The Radcliffe Camera

Behind the Old Schools Quadrangle rises Oxford's most imposing – or vainglorious – building, the Bodleian's **Radcliffe Camera** (formerly the Radcliffe Library; no public access), a mighty rotunda, built between 1737 and 1748 by James Gibbs, architect of London's St Martin-in-the-Fields church. There's no false modesty here. Dr John Radcliffe was, according to a contemporary diarist, "very ambitious of glory" and when he died in 1714 he bequeathed a mountain of money for the construction of a library – the "Radcliffe Mausoleum" as one wag termed it. Gibbs was one of the few British architects of the period to have been trained in Rome and his rotunda was thoroughly Italian in style, its limestone columns ascending to a delicate balustrade, decorated with pin-prick urns and encircling a lead-sheathed dome. For a less overpowering perspective, climb the tower of the church of St Mary the Virgin (see below) to the rear of the rotunda – from where there's also a charming view of All Souls College (see below).

St Mary the Virgin

Flanking the High Street just behind the Radcliffe Camera, **St Mary the Virgin** (daily 9am–5pm; free) is a hotchpotch of architectural styles, but mostly dates from the fifteenth century. The church's saving graces are its elaborate, thirteenth-century pinnacled spire and its distinctive Baroque **porch**, flanked by chunky corkscrewed pillars – and paid for by one of Archbishop Laud's friends in 1637. Curiously, the House of Commons cited the porch when they tried Laud, the Archbishop of Canterbury and religious adviser to Charles I, for high treason in 1640, the objection being that the porch was idolatrous, or at least too "Catholic". The real beef was Laud's sustained persecution of the Puritans and, although the trial dragged on and on, he was finally executed at the height of the Civil War in 1644. The church's interior is disappointingly mundane, though the carved poppy heads on the choir stalls are of some historical interest: the tips were brusquely flattened off when a platform was installed here in 1554 to stage the heresy trial of Cranmer, Latimer and Ridley, leading Protestants who had run foul of Queen Mary. In a desperate bid to avoid being burned at the stake, **Cranmer** (1489–1556) had previously confessed to heresy and at his public trial he was expected to repeat his recantation. Instead, Cranmer rounded on his accusers and confirmed his Protestant faith, an action which stunned Mary and gave new heart to her religious opponents. The church's other diversion is the **tower** (same times; £2.50), with wonderful views across to the Radcliffe Camera (see above) and east over **All Souls College** (Mon–Fri 2–4pm; free; ☎01865/279379, ⊛www.all-souls.ox.ac.uk), with its

▲ The Radcliffe Camera

twin mock-Gothic towers (the work of Hawksmoor) and conspicuous, brightly decorated sundial designed by Wren.

History of Science Museum, Trinity and Balliol

Back on Broad Street, the classical heads that shield the Sheldonian (see p.310) continue along the front of the **History of Science Museum** (Tues–Fri noon–5pm, Sat 10am–5pm, Sun 2–5pm; free; ⓦ www.mhs.ox .ac.uk), whose two floors display an amazing clutter of antique microscopes and astrolabes, sundials, quadrants and sextants. More obscure items include a thirteenth-century geared calendar and an "equatorium" for finding the position of the planets. The highlights are Elizabeth I's own astrolabe and Einstein's blackboard.

Across the street, **Trinity College** (no set opening times; free; ☎01865/279900, ⓦ www.trinity.ox.ac.uk) is fronted by three dinky lodge-cottages. Behind them the manicured lawn of the Front Quad stretches back to the richly decorated **Chapel**, awash with Baroque stuccowork. Its high altar is flanked by an exquisite example of the work of Grinling Gibbons – a distinctive performance, with cherubs' heads peering out from delicate foliage. Behind the chapel stands **Durham Quad**, an attractive ensemble of old stone buildings begun at the end of the seventeenth century. Recent Trinity alumni include Richard Burton, Terence Rattigan and the Labour Party politician, Anthony Crosland.

Next door, **Balliol College** (no set opening times; free; ☎01865/277777, ⓦ www.balliol.ox.ac.uk) is Trinity's arch-rival, the collegiate antipathy ritualized in the tradition of Gordouli, when Balliol students chant abuse at their adversaries across the wall, usually at unsociable hours of the night. It's historically appropriate: the Balliol family of Scotland founded Balliol in the 1260s as a penance after one of the family insulted the Bishop of Durham – and the Durham bishops had associations with Trinity. Nevertheless, despite its antiquity, Balliol has little to offer architecturally: remodelled and rebuilt in the nineteenth century, it now presents an unexceptional assembly of buildings, haphazardly gathered around two quads. Amongst many notable alumni are Adam Smith, Hilaire Belloc, Graham Greene and Aldous Huxley, plus a raft of politicians, including Harold Macmillan, Edward Heath, Denis Healey and Roy Jenkins.

Exeter College

From the south side of Broad Street, take Turl Street and you'll soon reach – on the left – the entrance to **Exeter College** (daily 2–5pm; free; ☎01865/279600, ⓦ www.exeter.ox.ac.uk), another medieval foundation whose original buildings were chopped about in the nineteenth century. On this occasion, however, the Victorians did create something of interest in the elaborate Neo-Gothic **Chapel**, whose intricate, almost fussy detail was conceived by Gilbert Scott in the 1850s. The chapel contains a fine set of stained-glass windows illustrating scores of biblical stories – St Paul on the road to Damascus and Samson bringing down the pillars of the Philistine temple for example – but their deep colours put the nave in permanent shade. The chapel also holds a superb **Pre-Raphaelite** tapestry, the *Adoration of the Magi*, a fine collaboration between William Morris and Edward Burne-Jones. Morris and Burne-Jones were both students here, as were J.R.R. Tolkien and Alan Bennett.

Cornmarket and the Oxford Union

Broad Street leads into the **Cornmarket**, a busy pedestrianized shopping strip lined by major stores. There's precious little here to fire the imagination, but **St Michael's Street** – the first turning on the right – is a pleasant residential street and the location of the **Oxford Union** (no public access), which occupies an inconsequential Victorian pile that belies its political importance. The Union is home to the university debating society, where scores of budding British politicians have flexed their oratorical muscles. It's also hosted a mixed bag of internationally famous celebrity speakers, among them Yasser Arafat, Archbishop Desmond Tutu, Ronald Reagan, Mother Teresa and Diego Maradona. The original debating hall, shaped rather like an upturned boat and now the Union library, is decorated with Pre-Raphaelite murals illustrating the Arthurian legend, created (but never completed) in the 1850s by William Morris, Rossetti, Burne-Jones and a few like-minded friends.

The Ashmolean

Occupying a mammoth Neoclassical building on the corner of Beaumont Street and St Giles, the **Ashmolean** (Tues–Sat 10am–5pm, Sun noon–5pm; free; ⓦ www.ashmolean.org) is the university's principal museum. It grew from and around the collections of the magpie-like **John Tradescant**, gardener to Charles I and an energetic traveller. During his wanderings, Tradescant built up a huge assortment of artefacts and natural specimens, which became known as Tradescant's Ark. He bequeathed all this to his friend and sponsor, the lawyer Elias Ashmole, who in turn gave it to the university. Tradescant's Ark (see below) has been added to ever since – though parts were hived off to the Pitt-Rivers Museum (see opposite) years ago – and today the Ashmolean possesses a vast and far-reaching collection covering everything from English glass to Russian icons and Egyptian mummies. In order to display the full collection, the museum is undergoing a major expansion which will create thirty new galleries. The redevelopment will not be completed until 2010 and in the meantime visitors have to take potluck as to what is on display and what isn't, though the Western Art and Egyptology sections should be largely unaffected. Pick up a **plan** at reception for the latest state of affairs.

The **Egyptian** rooms are not to be missed: in addition to well-preserved mummies and sarcophagi, there are unusual frescoes, rare textiles from the Roman and Byzantine periods and several fine examples of relief carving, such as those on the Taharqa shrine. Look out, too, for the superb Islamic ceramics in the **Islamic art** collection, while the **Chinese art** section boasts some remarkable early Chinese pottery with the simple monochrome pots of the Sung dynasty (960–1279) looking surprisingly modern. The archeologist Arthur Evans had close ties with the museum and he gifted it a stunning collection of **Minoan** finds from his years working at Knossos in Crete (1900–06): pride of place goes to the storage jars, sumptuously decorated with sea creatures and marine plants. A further highlight is the extraordinary **Alfred Jewel**, a tiny gold, enamel and rock crystal piece of uncertain purpose. The inscription translates as "Alfred ordered me to be made" – almost certainly a reference to King Alfred the Great.

The museum is also strong on **European art**. Amongst the **Italian** works, watch out for Piero di Cosimo's *Forest Fire* and Paolo Uccello's *Hunt in the Forest*, though Tintoretto, Veronese and Bellini feature prominently as well. **French paintings** make a strong showing too, with works by Pissarro, Monet, Manet and Renoir hanging alongside Cézanne and Bonnard, and there's a representative selection of eighteenth- and nineteenth-century **British artists**: Samuel Palmer's visionary paintings run rings around the rest, though there are lashings of Pre-Raphaelite stuff from Rossetti and Holman Hunt to assorted cohorts.

Finally, don't miss the treasures displayed from **Tradescant's Ark**. Amongst the assorted curiosities, a particular highlight is **Powhatan's mantle**, a handsome garment made of deerskin and decorated with shells. Powhatan was the father of Pocahontas, and this mantle therefore dates back to the earliest contacts between English colonists and the Native Americans of modern-day Virginia. Other prime pieces include Guy Fawkes' lantern, Oliver Cromwell's death mask and the peculiar armour-plated hat that Bradshaw, the president of the board of regicides, wore when he condemned King Charles I to death.

The University and Pitt-Rivers museums

From the Ashmolean, it's a brief walk north up St Giles to the *Lamb & Flag* pub, beside which an alley cuts through to the **University Museum of Natural History** (daily 10am–5pm; free; Ⓦwww.oum.ox.ac.uk) on Parks Road. The building, constructed under the guidance of John Ruskin, looks like a cross between a railway station and a church – and the same applies inside, where a High Victorian-Gothic fusion of cast iron and glass features soaring columns and capitals decorated with animal and plant motifs. Exhibits include some impressive fossil dinosaurs, though the museum's natural history displays are outdone by the **Pitt-Rivers Museum** (Mon noon–4.30pm; Tues–Sun 10am–4.30pm; free; Ⓦwww.prm.ox.ac.uk), reached through a door at the far end. Founded in 1884 from the bequest of grenadier guard turned archeologist Augustus Henry Lane-Fox Pitt-Rivers, this is one of the world's finest ethnographic museums and an extraordinary relic of the Victorian Age, arranged like an exotic junk shop with each bulging cabinet labelled meticulously by hand. The exhibits, brought to England by several explorers, Captain Cook among them, range from totem poles and mummified crocodiles to African fetishes and gruesome shrunken heads.

Eating and drinking

With so many students and tourists to cater for, Oxford has a wide choice of places to eat and drink. For a midday bite, one of the city's numerous **cafés** is ideal – some of the best are listed below and you'll find several others in the **Covered Market**, between the High Street and Cornmarket, an Oxford institution as essential to local shoppers as the Bodleian is to academics. There are also a couple of good cafés in Jericho, a much-gentrified former working-class area of terrace houses bordered by Walton Street. Jericho chips in with some of the city's most appealing **restaurants** too, but by and large Oxford's restaurant scene is pretty low-key – again some of the better options are listed below. Reasonable food is served at most **pubs**, but those listed have been singled out for their ambience or selection of beers rather than for their menus.

Cafés

George & Davies Little Clarendon St. Great little place offering everything from (delicious) ice cream to bagels and full breakfasts. The cow mural is good fun too. Daily till midnight.

News Café 1 Ship St. Breakfasts, bagels and daily specials, plus beer and wine in this brisk and efficient, spick and span café; as the name suggests, plenty of local and international newspapers are on hand too. Daily till 10pm.

Vaults & Garden Radcliffe Square. In an atmospheric stone-vaulted room attached to the church of St Mary the Virgin, this café serves up good-quality coffee and cake, as well as quiche-and-salad lunches. There's a small outside area, but it's a tad glum.

Restaurants

Aziz 228–230 Cowley Rd ☎01865/794945. Spacious and brightly decorated Bangladeshi restaurant, with delicious food, including an exceptional range of vegetarian dishes.

Reservations recommended at weekends. Closed Sun lunch; mains from £8.

Branca 111 Walton St ☎01865/556111. Large and informal brasserie-restaurant in proto-industrial premises offering a wide-ranging menu, though Italian dishes predominate. Excellent daily specials from £13.

Chiang Mai Kitchen 130a High St ☎01865/202233. Smart little place, down an alley bang in the centre off the High St, that's the best and most authentic Thai restaurant in town. All the classics are served – and then some – and it's particularly strong on vegetarian dishes. Mains average around £8.

Freud Arts Café 119 Walton St. Occupying a grand building in the style of a Roman temple, this fashionable café-bar serves straightforward Italian/Mediterranean food, with main courses from as little as £6. Live music some nights too. Open daily from 11am till late.

Gee's Restaurant 61 Banbury Rd ☎01865/553540. Chic conservatory setting for this well-established restaurant, where the inventive menu includes such items as chargrilled vegetables with polenta, roasted beetroot, a variety of steaks and a wide choice of breads. Strong on fish, too, with seafood main courses for around £16. Open daily for lunch and dinner plus Sat and Sun right through from noon to 10.30pm.

Jericho Café 112 Walton St ⊤01865/310840. Relaxed and relaxing neighbourhood café-restaurant, next door to the *Branca*, whose creative menu is strong on eastern Mediterranean dishes – try the mouth-smacking mezzes (from £11). Open daily for lunch and dinner.

Pubs

The Bear 6 Alfred St. Tucked away down a narrow side street in the centre of town, this popular pub has not been themed up – and a good job too. Offers a wide range of beers amidst and amongst its traditional decor.

Eagle & Child 49 St Giles. Known variously as the "Bird & Baby", "Bird & Brat" or "Bird & Bastard",

this pub was once the haunt of J.R.R. Tolkien and C.S. Lewis. It still attracts an interesting crowd, but the modern extension at the back rather detracts from the cloistered rooms at the front.

King's Arms 40 Holywell St. Prone to student overkill on term-time weekends, but otherwise reasonably pleasant, with snug rooms at the back and a reasonably good choice of beers.

Lamb & Flag St Giles. Generations of university students have hung out in this old pub, which comes complete with low-beamed ceilings and a series of cramped but cosy rooms.

Turf Tavern Bath Place, off Holywell St. Small, atmospheric seventeenth-century pub with a fine range of beers, and mulled wine in winter. Abundant seating outside.

White Horse 52 Broad St. A tiny, old pub with snug rooms, pictures of old university sports teams on the walls and real ales. It was used as a set for the *Inspector Morse* TV series.

Entertainment and nightlife

Oxford does not rate highly when it comes to contemporary **live music**, though devotees of **classical music** are well catered for, with the city's main concert halls and certain college chapels – primarily Christ Church, Merton and New College – offering a wide-ranging programme of concerts and recitals. As regards **theatre**, student productions dominate the city repertoire, but the quality of acting varies, particularly when they tackle Shakespeare, the favourite for the open-air college productions put on for tourists during the summer.

For classical music and theatre **listings**, consult *This Month in Oxford*, available free from the tourist office. The daily *Oxford Mail* newspaper also carries information on gigs and events. For more adventurous stuff – special club nights etc – watch out for flyers.

Live music and clubs

Carling Academy 190 Cowley Rd ⊤01865/813500, ⓦwww.oxford-academy.co.uk. Far and away Oxford's liveliest indie and dance venue, with a fast-moving programme of live bands and guest DJs.

OFS (Old Fire Station) 40 George St ⊤01865/297170, ⓦwww.oxfordtheatres.com. Multi-purpose venue hosting musicals and theatre, plus a separate café-bar featuring one-off DJ club nights.

Classical music and theatre

Holywell Music Room 32 Holywell St. This small, plain, Georgian building was opened in 1748 as the first public music hall in England. It

offers a varied programme, from straight classical to experimental, with occasional bouts of jazz. Programme details are posted outside and are available at the Oxford Playhouse (see below), which also sells its tickets.

New Theatre George St ⊤01865/320760, ⓦwww.newtheatreoxford.org.uk. Popular – and populist – programme of theatre, dance, pop music, musicals and opera, from Ross Noble to The Hollies and beyond.

Oxford Playhouse 11 Beaumont St ⊤01865/305305, ⓦwww.oxfordplayhouse.com. Professional touring companies perform a mixture of plays, opera and concerts at what is generally regarded as the city's best theatre.

Pegasus Theatre Magdalen Rd ⊤01865/722851, ⓦwww.pegasustheatre.org.uk. Low-budget,

avant-garde productions dominate the programme of this adventurous theatre.
Sheldonian Theatre Broad St ℡01865/277299. Some have criticized the acoustics here, but this is still Oxford's top concert hall. Its resident symphony orchestra is the Oxford Philomusica (℡01865/736 202, 🌐www.oxfordphil.com).

Listings

Bike rental Bikezone, 6 Lincoln House, Market St, off Cornmarket (℡01865/728877, 🌐www.bikezoneoxford.co.uk).
Bookshops The leading university bookshop is Blackwells (🌐www.blackwell.co.uk), with several outlets including three shops on Broad Street: Blackwells Music, Blackwells Art & Posters, and the main bookshop at 48–51 Broad St (℡01865/792792).
Buses Most local buses, including park-and-ride, are operated by the Oxford Bus Company (℡01865/785400, 🌐www.oxfordbus.co.uk), which also – amongst several companies – offers fast and frequent services to London Gatwick and Heathrow airports. Other local services are mostly in the hands of Stagecoach (℡01865/772250, 🌐www.stagecoach-oxford.co.uk).
Car rental Avis ℡0870/1539102; National ℡01865/240471.
Cinema The Odeon cinemas on Magdalen and George streets (both ℡0871/224 4007, 🌐www.odeon.co.uk) show the latest blockbusters, while the best art-house cinema is the Ultimate Picture Palace (UPP) on Jeune St, off Cowley Rd (℡01865/245288, 🌐www.ultimatepicturepalace.co.uk). The Phoenix Picture House, 57 Walton St (℡01865/512526, 🌐www.picturehouses.co.uk), shows mainstream and arts films, and regularly screens foreign-language films too.
Internet Free at the Central Library, Westgate Shopping Centre, at the west end of Queen Street (Mon–Thurs 9.15am–7pm, Fri & Sat 9.15am–5pm; ℡01865/815509).
Pharmacies Boots, 6 Cornmarket (℡01865/247461).
Post office At the top of St Aldates, near the corner with the High St.
Taxis Taxi ranks are liberally distributed across the city centre, with taxis lining up at the train station and on the High St. Alternatively, call Radio Taxis ℡01865/242424.

Around Oxford

As a base for exploring some of the more delightful parts of central England, Oxford is hard to beat. It's a short trip west to the Cotswolds (see p.326) and a brief haul south to both Vale of White Horse (see p.298) and the Chiltern Hills (see p.293). Alternatively, if you're heading north into the Midlands, Oxford is just 25 miles away from the likes of Buckingham (see p.319) and Stowe Landscape Gardens (see p.320). Nearer still, however – a brief bus ride north – is the charming little town of **Woodstock** and its imperious neighbour, **Blenheim Palace**, birthplace of Winston Churchill.

Woodstock

WOODSTOCK, eight miles north of Oxford, has royal associations going back to Saxon times, with a string of kings attracted by its excellent hunting. Henry I built a royal lodge here and his successor, Henry II, enlarged it to create a grand manor house-cum-palace, where the Black Prince was born in 1330. The Royalists used Woodstock as a base during the Civil War, but, after their defeat, Cromwell never got round to destroying either the town or the palace: the latter was ultimately given to (and flattened by) the Duke of Marlborough in 1704 when work started on Blenheim Palace of today. Long dependent on royal and then ducal patronage, Woodstock is now both a well-heeled commuter town for Oxford and a provider of food, drink and beds for visitors to Blenheim. It is also an extremely pretty little place, its handsome stone buildings gathered around the main square, at the junction of Market and High streets. This is also where you'll find the town's one specific sight, the **Oxfordshire Museum** (Tues–Sat 10am–5pm,

Sun 2–5pm; free), a well-composed review of the county's archeology, social history and industry.

The museum shares its premises with the town's **tourist office** (Mon–Sat 9.30/10am–5/5.30pm, plus March–Oct Sun 2–5pm; ℡01993/813276, ⓦwww.oxfordshirecotswolds.org), which has a useful range of information on the Cotswolds. Woodstock has several good **pubs**, but the bar of the *Bear Hotel*, an old coaching inn across from the museum with low-beamed ceilings and an open fire, is the most atmospheric. Part of the Macdonald **hotel** chain, the *Bear* (℡0870/400 8202, ⓦwww .bearhotelwoodstock.co.uk; ⑥) has fifty or so luxurious rooms kitted out in an attractive, country-house style. Just as enticing, maybe more so, is the nearby *King's Arms*, 19 Market St (℡01993/813636, ⓦwww.kings-hotel -woodstock.co.uk; ❼), with fifteen chic, pastel-painted rooms, and a great **restaurant**, with main courses starting at about £11. The baked nut loaf with mushroom and watercress sauce is especially tasty.

Stagecoach **bus #20** leaves Oxford bus station bound for Woodstock every thirty minutes or so (hourly on Sun); thereafter it continues onto Chipping Norton in the Cotswolds (see p.333).

Blenheim Palace

Nowadays, successful British commanders get medals and titles, but in 1704, as a thank-you for his victory over the French at the battle of Blenheim, Queen Anne gave **John Churchill, Duke of Marlborough** (1650–1722) the royal estate of Woodstock, along with the promise of enough cash to build himself a gargantuan palace. Marlborough was an exceptionally brilliant general – undoubtedly, one of Britain's all-time military greats – and this was but one of his victories. Nonetheless, the largesse shown him had more to do with the queen's fear of Louis XIV – and the relief she felt after the battle – than it did to a recognition of his genius, as events were to prove.

Work started promptly on **Blenheim Palace** (mid-Feb to Oct daily 10.30am–5.30pm, last admission 4.45pm; Nov to mid-Dec Wed–Sun same times; £16.50 including park, gardens & parking, £14 in winter; ⓦwww .blenheimpalace.com) with the principal architect being Sir John Vanbrugh, who was also responsible for Castle Howard in Yorkshire (see p.827). However, the duke's formidable wife, Sarah Jennings, who had wanted Christopher Wren as architect, was soon at loggerheads with Vanbrugh, while Queen Anne had second thoughts, stifling the flow of money. Construction work was halted and the house was only finished after the duke's death at the instigation of his widow, who ended up paying most of the bills and designing much of the interior herself. The end result is the country's grandest example of Baroque civic architecture, an Italianate palace of finely worked yellow stone that is more a monument than a house – just as Vanbrugh intended.

The **interior** of the main house is stuffed with paintings and tapestries, plus all manner of objets d'art, including furniture from Versailles and carvings by Grinling Gibbons. The Great Hall has assorted grisailles and murals that celebrate Marlborough's martial skills, though Horace Walpole, the eighteenth-century wit and social commentator, had it about right when he wrote that Blenheim resembled "the palace of an auctioneer who had been chosen King of Poland". Churchill fans may find more of interest in the **Churchill Exhibition**, which provides a brief introduction to Winston, accompanied by live recordings of some of his more famous speeches. Born here at Blenheim, Churchill (1874–1965) now lies buried alongside his wife in the graveyard of Bladon church just outside the estate.

Blenheim's formal **gardens** (same times as house; gardens, park & parking only £9.50/7.50), to the rear of the house, are divided into several distinct areas, including a rose garden and an arboretum, though the open **parkland** (daily 9am–5.30pm or dusk, last admission 45min before closing) is more enticing, leading from the front of the house down to an artificial lake, **Queen Pool**. Vanbrugh's splendid Grand Bridge crosses the lake to the **Column of Victory**, erected by Sarah Jennings and topped by a statue of her husband posing heroically in a toga. It's said that Capability Brown, who landscaped the park, laid out the trees and avenues to represent the battle of Blenheim.

There are two **entrances** to Blenheim, one just south of Woodstock on the Oxford road and another through the Triumphal Arch at the end of Park Street in Woodstock itself. Stagecoach **bus #20** runs to Blenheim Palace from Oxford's bus stations every thirty minutes (hourly on Sun).

North Buckinghamshire and Bedfordshire

A short drive northeast of Oxford, the untidy landscapes of **north Buckinghamshire** and **Bedfordshire** herald a transition between the satellite towns of London and the Midlands. Since World War II, the character of the region has been transformed by the attempt to solve London's overcrowding. Sprawling suburbs now festoon many of the small country towns of yesteryear and, in the 1960s, Milton Keynes swallowed thirteen villages to become the country's largest new town. Nonetheless, north Buckinghamshire does boast a couple of prime targets, in the shape of **Stowe Gardens**, dotted with a remarkable assortment of outdoor sculptures and follies, and the old World War II code-breaking centre of **Bletchley Park**. Meanwhile, Bedfordshire's most distinctive feature is the wriggling **River Ouse**, whose banks were once lined with dozens of watermills, though these were not nearly as important as the brickworks that long underpinned the local economy. The county is also home to the whopping country mansion of **Woburn Abbey** and nearby **Woburn Safari Park**, while **Bedford** itself is mainly of interest for its links with John Bunyan.

As regards public transport, local **buses** link all the larger towns and there is a fast and frequent **train** service from London to Bedford and Milton Keynes.

Buckingham and around

Unassuming **BUCKINGHAM** is tucked into a sharp bend in the River Ouse about 25 miles northeast of Oxford. It became the county town of Buckinghamshire in the tenth century and flourished during medieval times, but was bypassed by the Industrial Revolution and remained a forgotten backwater until a recent wave of incomers created the modern suburbs that surround it today. The town centre is at its prettiest along the wide, sloping Market Hill, in the middle of which is the **Old Gaol**, a chunky, stone structure that houses the tourist office (see below) and a modest local history museum. Otherwise, Buckingham is short on sights, though you might take a peek inside the sombre **Church of St Peter and St Paul**, which perches on the hill where the castle once stood – take Castle Street from the west end of Market Hill and you can't miss it.

There's no train service to Buckingham, but there are **bus** links from neighbouring towns, principally Milton Keynes. Buses stop on the High Street a few yards from the **tourist office** in the Old Gaol (Mon–Sat 10am–4pm; July & Aug also Sun noon–4pm; ℡01280/823020), which can book local **B&Bs**. Alternatively, the best **hotel** is the *Villiers*, in an imaginatively modernized old inn at 3 Castle St (℡01280/822444, ⓦwww.villiers-hotel.co.uk; ⓞ); most of the rooms flank the courtyard to the rear of the main building and are decorated in smart modern style. The best spot for **food** is the *Dipalee Indian Restaurant* (℡01280/813151) on Castle Street, with a good range of main courses for about £8.

Northwest of Buckingham: Stowe Gardens

Just three miles northwest of Buckingham off the A422, the extensive **Stowe Landscape Gardens** (March–Oct Wed–Sun 10am–5.30pm; Nov–Feb Sat & Sun 10.30am–4pm; £6.50; NT) contain an extraordinary collection of outdoor sculptures, monuments and decorative buildings by some of the greatest designers and architects of the eighteenth century. They worked at the behest of the prodigiously wealthy Temple and Grenville families, and later the dukes of Buckingham and Chandos. The thirty-odd structures that comprise this ornamental miscellany are spread over a sequence of separate, carefully planned landscapes, from the lake views of the Western and Eastern gardens to the wooded delights of the Elysian Fields and the gentle folds of the Grecian Valley, **Capability Brown**'s first large-scale design. The gardens were planned in detail, but the romantic rural idyll they represented was a fundamental break with the strictly formal garden tradition that had dominated Europe for decades. There was a political agenda too: the owners were Whigs, proudly committed to the constitutional monarchy and liberal, albeit class-based notions of political liberty, their *bêtes-noires* being the absolutist Stuarts, whom they had helped depose in the Glorious Revolution of 1688. Several of the monuments hammer home the Whig agenda, especially **The Temple of British Worthies**, whose fourteen busts represent a selection of those leading figures of whom the family approved. As for the architecture, several buildings are of particular interest, most memorably the Neo-Romanesque **Hermitage**, the eccentric **Gothic Temple**, the magnificent **Grecian Temple** (Temple of

▲ Temple of Concord and Victory, Stowe

Concord and Victory) and the beautifully composed **Palladian Bridge**, one of only three such bridges in the country.

At the heart of the gardens, the **main house**, with its whopping Neoclassical facade, is separate from the estate, as it is used by Stowe School, which offers fairly regular guided tours – ring ☏01280/818166 for the schedule.

East of Buckingham: Bletchley Park

Marooned on the edge of Milton Keynes thirteen miles east of Buckingham, **Bletchley Park** (April–Oct Mon–Fri 9.30am–5pm, Sat & Sun 10.30am–5pm; Nov–March daily 10.30am–4pm; £10 including audioguide; ☏01908/640404, ⓦwww.bletchleypark.org.uk) was known as "**Station X**" during World War II. The home of Britain's leading code breakers, Station X was where the British built the first program computer – Colossus – and it was here that they famously broke the German "**enigma**" code, the enigma machine being the main encoder for all communications within Hitler's armed forces. Much of Station X has survived, its scattering of Nissen huts spread over a leafy parcel of land that surrounds the original Victorian mansion. Inside are a variety of displays explaining and exploring the workings of Station X as well as the stolen enigma machine that was crucial in deciphering the German code. Visitors can explore Station X under their own steam, but there are also occasional excellent **guided tours** at no extra charge (call for times and to book).

With connections from Birmingham New Street, Bedford and London Euston, Bletchley Park **train** station is 300 yards from the park.

Woburn

Four miles or so east of Bletchley Park, on the peripheries of Milton Keynes, the little village of **WOBURN** makes a healthy living from its location beside Woburn Abbey and Safari Park. Little more than one main street lined with some sterling Georgian buildings, the village's most interesting feature is **St Mary's Church**, whose cumbersome stonework is guarded by a couple of peculiar – and peculiarly large – gargoyles, one of which looks like a prototype Tolkien hobgoblin. The interior is less distinctive but certainly impressive, refitted in fancy Gothic style by the Duke of Bedford in the 1860s and supplemented with an elaborate reredos a few years later. Woburn has several good **restaurants**, where you can prime up for – or unwind after – an excursion into the Abbey and the Safari Park. Amongst several options, *Nicholls Brasserie* (☏01525/290896) is a chic establishment with an imaginative menu that ranges from guinea fowl to fishcakes, with main courses averaging £14.

Woburn Abbey and Safari Park

The grandiloquent Georgian facade of **Woburn Abbey** (April–Oct daily 11am–5pm, last entry 1hr before closing; £10.50; ⓦwww.woburnabbey.co.uk) overlooks a huge chunk of parkland just to the east of the eponymous village. Called an abbey because it was built on the site of a Cistercian foundation, the house is the ancestral pile of the dukes of Bedford, whom Queen Victoria once dismissed as a dull lot. Judging from the family's penchant for canine portraits, she may have had a point, but the lavish state rooms also contain some fine paintings, including an exquisite set of **Tudor portraits**, most notably the famous *Armada Portrait* of Elizabeth I by George Gower. Elsewhere are works by Van Dyck, Velázquez, Gainsborough, Rembrandt and Reynolds, as well as a fine selection of Canalettos. The surrounding parkland, with its rolling hills and trees, was landscaped by Humphry Repton.

Another part of the duke's enormous estate is home to **Woburn Safari Park** (early March to late Oct daily 10am–6pm, last entry 5pm; £16/17.50; Nov to mid-March Sat & Sun 11am–3pm; £9.50; ☎01525/290407; ⓦwww .woburnsafari.co.uk), the largest drive-through wildlife reserve in Britain. The animals include endangered species such as the African white rhino and bongo antelope, and appear to be in excellent health. A posse of guards roams around looking for drivers in distress, but the main danger is an overheated engine rather than an attack by an enraged animal – the Safari Park is extraordinarily popular and in high season the traffic can achieve rush-hour congestion, so turn up as early as possible for a quieter experience. Note that the park may close in bad weather.

Bedford

BEDFORD, some twelve miles northeast of Woburn, has struggled to retain a modicum of character in the face of redevelopment, but the end result is pleasant enough, the town's neat and tidy centre hugging the north bank of the River Ouse. Bedford also makes the most of its connections with **John Bunyan** (1628–88), a blaspheming tinker turned Nonconformist preacher, who lived most of his life in and around the town. Bunyan fought for Parliament in the Civil War and became a well-known public speaker during Cromwell's Protectorate, but the Restoration proved disastrous for him. In 1660, he was arrested for breaking Charles II's new religious legislation, which restricted the activities of Nonconformist preachers, and he spent most of the next seventeen years in Bedford prison. During his incarceration, he wrote *The Pilgrim's Progress*, a seminal text whose simple language and powerful allegories were to have a profound influence on generations of Nonconformists – and it was they who championed a raft of progressive causes, most notably the campaign for the abolition of slavery.

Built in 1850 on the spot where Bunyan founded his first Independent Congregation, the **Bunyan Meeting Free Church** (Tues–Sat 10am–4pm), just east of the High Street on Mill Street, is still a Nonconformist church. It bears several memorials to Bunyan, beginning with the splendid bronze doors, decorated with ten finely worked panels inspired by *Pilgrim's Progress*. Inside, the stained-glass windows develop the theme, again depicting scenes from the book, plus one showing Bunyan scribbling away in prison. Next door, the homely **Bunyan Museum** (March–Oct Tues–Sat 11am–4pm; free) features extracts from his book and tracks through the author's life and times – including his notably insignificant military exploits. Bunyan spent the Civil War on garrison duty at nearby Newport Pagnell, where he never saw a shot fired in anger, though he did suffer the indignities of being poorly supplied – at one point, the garrison only had one pair of breeches for every two men.

Practicalities

Bedford is on the London St Pancras–Sheffield rail line with **trains** arriving at Midland Station, from where it's a ten-minute walk east to the centre. The **bus station** is on All Hallows and from here it's a couple of minutes' walk east to the short High Street, which runs north–south and crosses the River Ouse. The **tourist office** (May–Aug Mon–Sat 9am–4.30pm, Sun 10am–2pm; Sept–April Mon–Sat 9.30am–5pm ☎01234/215226, ⓦwww.bedford.gov.uk) is in the old town hall, just off the High Street on St Paul's Square. The town's best **hotel** is the *Swan*, down by the river on The Embankment at the foot of the High Street

(☎01234/346565, ⓦwww.bedfordswanhotel.co.uk; ❼), where the Georgian stonework conceals a lavish and tastefully modernized interior.

Bedford's large Italian community adds a bit of zip to the local **restaurant** scene. Pick of the bunch, serving some of the tastiest pizzas and pastas in town, is *Pizzeria Santaniello*, 9 Newnham St (☎01234/353742), immediately to the east of Mill Street's Bunyan Meeting Free Church. Further down Newnham Street, at no. 36, the *Cappuccino Bar* chips in with authentic coffee, ice cream, pizzas and snacks.

St Albans and around

Over in Hertfordshire, **ST ALBANS** is one of the most appealing towns on the peripheries of London, its blend of medieval and modern features grafted onto the site of **Verulamium**, the town founded by the Romans soon after their successful invasion of 43 AD. Boudicca and her followers burned this settlement to the ground eighteen years later, but reconstruction was swift and the town grew into a major administrative base. It was here, in 209 AD, that a Roman soldier by the name of Alban became the country's first Christian martyr, when he was beheaded for giving shelter to a priest. Pilgrims later flocked to the town that had come to bear his name, with the place of execution marked by a hilltop cathedral that was once one of the largest churches in the Christian world.

Not just a religious centre, St Albans also flourished as a trading town and a staging post on the route to London from the north, its economy buttressed by two local industries, brewing and straw-hat-making. In the nineteenth century, the coaching trade faded away with the coming of the railways, but when St Albans was connected to London by train in 1868, it rapidly reinvented itself as a prosperous and pleasant commuter town, a description that fits well today.

St Albans' best-known attraction is its **cathedral**, but the town also possesses the outstanding **Verulamium Museum**, home to several breathtaking Roman mosaics, as well as a pleasant riverside park, a number of charming old streets, and some excellent pubs. All the town's main sights are within easy walking distance of each other. The town is also just a short drive from the former home of George Bernard Shaw in **Ayot St Lawrence**, now a National Trust property.

The City

One good way to start a tour of the city is by climbing to the top of the fifteenth-century **clocktower**, plumb in the centre of town where the High Street and Market Place meet (Easter–Sept Sat & Sun 10.30am–5pm; 80p). The climb is a tight squeeze, but worth it for the view over the **cathedral** (daily 8.30am–5.45pm; donation requested; ⓦwww.stalbanscathedral.org.uk), a vast brick and flint edifice immediately to the south – and reached down a narrow passageway across from the foot of the tower. An abbey was constructed here in 1077 on the site of a Saxon monastery founded by King Offa of Mercia, and despite subsequent alterations – including the ugly nineteenth-century west front – the legacy of the Normans remains the most impressive aspect. The sheer scale of their design is breathtaking: the **nave**, almost 300 feet long, is the longest medieval nave in Britain, even if it isn't the most harmonious – the massive Norman **pillars** on the north side stand out from those in the later

Early English style opposite. Some of the Norman pillars retain thirteenth- and fourteenth-century paintings, the detail clear though the ochre colours are much faded. Two- and three-tone geometric designs decorate the Norman **arches** in the nave and at the central crossing, where the impact of the original design reaches its peak with the mighty Norman tower.

Behind the high altar an elaborate stone **reredos** (a clumsy construction compared with the splendid Gothic rood screen) hides the fourteenth-century **shrine of St Alban**. The tomb was smashed up during the Reformation, but the Victorians discovered the pieces and gamely put them all together again. Some of the carving on the Purbeck marble is now remarkably clear – look out for the scene on the west end depicting the saint's martyrdom.

Verulamium

From the abbey gateway, a few yards to the west of the cathedral's main entrance, Abbey Mill Lane leads down past the *Fighting Cocks* (one of England's oldest pubs) and across the trickle of the River Ver to **Verulamium Park**, whose sloping lawns and duck ponds occupy the site of the Roman city. The park holds a scattering of Roman remains, including fragments of the old city wall and the **Hypocaust** (Mon–Sat 10am–4pm, Sun 2–4pm; free), comprising the foundations of a town house complete with an *in situ* mosaic and the original underfloor heating system of the bath suite. However, this is small beer in comparison with the **Verulamium Museum** (Mon–Sat 10am–5.30pm, Sun 2–5.30pm; £3.30), which occupies an attractive circular building on the northern edge of the park. Inside, a series of well-conceived displays illustrate and explain life in Roman Britain, but these are eclipsed by the **mosaics**, a set of wonderful floor mosaics exhibited in one gallery and unearthed hereabouts in the 1930s and 1950s. Dating from about 200 AD, the Sea God Mosaic has created its share of academic debate, with some arguing it depicts a god of nature with stag antler horns rather than a sea god with lobster claws, but there's no disputing the subject of the Lion Mosaic, in which a lion carries the bloodied head of a stag in its jaws. The most beautiful of the five is the Shell Mosaic, a gorgeous work of art whose semicircular design depicts a beautifully crafted scallop shell within a border made up of rolling waves.

Just to the west, across busy Bluehouse Hill, the **Roman Theatre of Verulamium** (daily: March–Oct 10am–5pm; Nov–Feb 10am–4pm; £2) was built around 140 AD, but was reduced to the status of a municipal rubbish dump by the fifth century. Little more than a small hollow now, the site is still impressive enough and gives a real sense of how these theatres would once have looked.

From the theatre, you can walk back to the centre along **St Michael's Street**, over one of the prettier stretches of the Ver and past an antique watermill. At the end of St Michael's Street, steer right up the gently curving **Fishpool Street**, a quiet road lined with medieval inns and handsome Georgian houses that leads back to the clocktower.

Practicalities

Thameslink **trains** on the London King's Cross to Bedford line call at St Albans station, from where it's a ten-minute walk west up the hill along Victoria Street to the main drag – at a point just north of the clocktower. The **main street** comprises Chequer Street, which begins at the clocktower, and its northern continuation St Peter's Street. Running parallel, immediately to the west, is the Market Place, home of the **tourist office**, which is located in the town hall (Easter–Oct Mon–Sat 9.30am–5.30pm, plus Sun in summer school hols 10am–4pm; Nov–Easter Mon–Sat 10am–4pm; ℡01727/864511, ⒲www.stalbans.gov.uk).

St Albans has a couple of recommendable **places to stay**, including a very competent B&B, *Wren Lodge*, 24 Beaconsfield Rd (℡01727/855540; no credit cards; ❸), a well-maintained Edwardian house with four comfortable and attractively furnished bedrooms down near the station. A pricier option is the splendid *St Michael's Manor Hotel,* in a handsome Georgian house on Fishpool Street (℡01727/864444, ⒲www.stmichaelsmanor.com; ❻). Each of the thirty rooms here is tastefully decorated in a modern rendition of country-house style and the hotel sits in its own grounds with terraces where guests can take breakfast.

St Albans holds the headquarters of **CAMRA**, the real-ale campaigners (⒲wwwcamra.org.uk), and it's satisfying to see that excellent, hand-pumped brews are available in many a local **pub**. Good choices include the *Farmer's Boy*, a short stroll east of the clocktower at 134 London Rd, where they brew their own beers on site, and the antique *Ye Old Fighting Cocks*, on Abbey Mill Lane, which gets mighty crowded on sunny summer days, but still has lots of enjoyable nooks and crannies in which to nurse a pint. *The Goat*, on Sopwell Lane, just east of the cathedral off Holywell Hill (℡01727/833934) serves the best **bar food** in town.

Around St Albans: Ayot St Lawrence and Shaw's Corner

The tiny village of **AYOT ST LAWRENCE**, hiding among gentle hills in one of the prettiest corners of Hertfordshire, was the home of **George Bernard Shaw** from 1906 until his death in 1950. He lived in a trim Edwardian villa known as **Shaw's Corner** (mid-March to Oct Wed–Sun 1–5pm; £4.50; NT), which has been left pretty much as it was at the time of his demise, packed with literary bits and pieces, his personal effects and various press releases. Not one to mince his words, one of these releases implores his readers not to send him birthday cards as the "arrival of thousands of them together is a calamity that is not the less dreaded because it occurs but once a year". There's also the **shed** at the bottom of the garden where Shaw used to write, but this is little more than a cell, the only luxuries being a telephone and the hut's ability to revolve in order to maximize the available sunlight.

The village's other point of interest is the Greek Revival **church of St Lawrence**, built in the 1770s on the instructions of the local bigwig, Lyonel Lyde, who simultaneously turned the existing medieval church into a picturesque ruin to make the village more "romantic". When the bishop heard of these antics, he threw a fit, but it was too late. The ruined church is hidden among the trees opposite the village's excellent **pub**, the *Brocket Arms* (℡01438/820250, ⒲www.brocketarms.com; ❻), a cosy old place with low-beamed ceilings and a walled garden. They serve real ales here and the food is very good, featuring such delights as steak and ale pie with mash and marinaded venison. Visitors can eat either in the bar at lunchtimes or in the restaurant in the evening (Tues–Sat); mains start at £8. The *Brocket* also has half a dozen bedrooms decorated in a homely version of traditional style, with four-poster beds.

Ayot St Lawrence is eight miles north of St Albans via the B651; there's no **public transport**.

The Cotswolds

The limestone hills that make up the **Cotswolds** are preposterously photogenic, dotted with a string of picture-book villages built by wealthy cloth merchants. **Wool** was important here as far back as the Roman era, but the greatest fortunes were made between the fourteenth and sixteenth centuries, and it was at this time that many of the region's fine manors and churches were built. Largely bypassed by the Industrial Revolution, which heralded the area's commercial decline, much of the Cotswolds is technically speaking a relic, its architecture preserved in immaculate condition. Numerous **churches** are decorated with beautiful carving, for which the local limestone was ideal: soft and easy to carve when first quarried, but hardening after long exposure to the sunlight. The use of this **local stone** is a strong unifying characteristic across the region, though its colour modulates as subtly as the shape of the hills, ranging from a deep golden tone in Chipping Campden to a silvery grey in Winchcombe.

The consequence is that the Cotswolds have become one of the country's main tourist attractions, with many towns afflicted by plagues of tearooms and souvenir and antiques shops – this is morris dancing country. To see the Cotswolds at their best, you should visit off-season or perhaps avoid the most popular towns and instead escape into the hills themselves, though even in high season the charms of towns like **Chipping Campden** – "Chipping" as in *ceapen*, the old English for market – **Winchcombe** and **Northleach** are evident. As for **walking**, this might be a tamed landscape, but there's good scope for exploring the byways, either in the gentler valleys that are most typical of the Cotswolds or along the dramatic escarpment that marks the boundary with the Severn Valley. A national trail, the **Cotswold Way**, runs along the top of the ridge, stretching about one hundred miles from Chipping Campden past Cheltenham, Gloucester and Stroud as far as Bath. A number of prehistoric sites provide added interest along the route, with some – such as **Belas Knap** near Winchcombe – being well worth a diversion.

As regard to **public transport**, the **train** network comes close to ignoring the Cotswolds, the main exception being the Oxford to Worcester service, on which the slower trains stop at half a dozen of the region's villages and the town of Moreton-in-Marsh, though none of these are prime targets. As for the rest, you'll be reliant on the **bus** network, which does a good job connecting all the larger towns and villages, but not the smaller, more isolated places and nothing much at all on Sundays. All the region's tourist offices carry timetables and the larger ones sell an excellent synopsis of train and bus services in their *Explore the Cotswolds* brochure, with Oxfordshire County Council's *Public Transport Guide* filling in the gaps.

Burford and around

Twenty miles west of Oxford you get your first real taste of the Cotswolds at **BURFORD**, where the long and wide **High Street**, which slopes down to the bridge over the River Windrush, is simply magnificent – despite all the juggernauts. The street is flanked by a remarkable – and remarkably homogeneous – line of old buildings that exhibit almost every type of peccadillo known to the Cotswolds, from wonky mullioned windows and half-timbered facades with bendy beams through to spiky brick chimneys, fancy bow-fronted stone houses, and grand horse-and-carriage gateways. What's more, Burford also possesses the fascinating **church of St John the Baptist**, by the river and down a lane off the High Street. Of all the Cotswold churches, this has the most historical resonance with architectural bits and pieces surviving from every phase of its construction, beginning with the Normans and ending in the wool boom of the seventeenth century. Thereafter, it was pretty much left alone and, most unusually, its clutter of mausoleums, chapels and chantries survived the Reformation to create the jingle and jangle of today. The most impressive **mausoleum** is that of Lawrence Tanfield, James I's Chancellor of the Exchequer, who lies on his canopied table-tomb with his wife, both decked out in their Jacobean finery. Even more striking, however, is the **funerary plaque** of Edmund Harman, Henry VIII's barber and surgeon, stuck to the wall of the nave and sporting four Amazonian Indians, the first representation of Native Americans in Britain. It is not likely that Harman met any Amazonians as such, but rather he seems to have been linked to a Spanish company trading with South America.

Back outside, the **churchyard** is strewn with so-called "bale tombs", whose rounded tops symbolize wool, and a modern **plaque** just to the left of the entrance pays tribute to the three **Levellers**, who were shot in the churchyard on Cromwell's orders in 1649. Loyal members of Cromwell's New Model Army, the Levellers were an informal alliance of politicized soldiers who believed all men were born free and equal and possessed equal rights under the law. Although Cromwell vacillated in his attitude to them, in the end his belief in class and property rights won the day and he crushed them; the executions here in Burford were one of the last acts of the drama.

When you've finished exploring Burford, spare a few hours to follow the **footpath** east along the River Windrush through **Widford**, a hamlet with an idyllic medieval chapel built in the middle of a field on the site of a Roman villa, and on to **Swinbrook**, just under three miles from Burford. Here, the church of St Mary holds a monument showing six members of the Fettiplace family reclining comically on their elbows: the Tudor effigies rigid and stony-faced, their Stuart counterparts stylish and really rather camp.

Practicalities

Buses to Burford pull in along the High Street. One of the most useful services is the three or four times daily – once on Sundays – Swanbrook bus (℡01452/712386, ⊛www.swanbrook.co.uk) from Oxford to Gloucester via Burford, Northleach and Cheltenham. The **tourist office** is located just off the High Street on Sheep Street (March–Oct Mon–Sat 9.30am–5.30pm, Nov–Feb Mon–Sat 9.30am–4pm; ℡01993/823558, ⊛www.oxfordshirecotswolds.org).

Burford has two first-class **hotels**, kicking off with *The Bay Tree*, on Sheep Street (℡01993/822791, ⊛www.cotswold-inns-hotels.co.uk; ❽), which occupies a wisteria-clad stone house dating from the seventeenth century. There are twenty-odd rooms here – both in the main house and in a couple of annexes – and each is done out in a modern and sometimes lavish rendition of period style. The *Lamb Inn*, just along Sheep Street (℡01993/823155, ⊛www.cotswold-inns-hotels.co.uk; ❼), is another great choice and is, if anything, a tad more traditional than its neighbour from the bar's flagstoned floor and up. For something less expensive, head for *The Angel*, just off the High Street at 14 Witney St (℡01993/822714, ⊛www.theangelatburford.co.uk; ❻), where there are just three guest rooms decorated in a pleasant version of traditional style in another very old stone house. The *Angel* is also where you should **eat**: they offer a lively, creative menu with mains from £14; the roasted monkfish with mussels is especially delicious.

Socialist, artist, writer and craftsman **William Morris** (1834–1896) had a profound influence on his contemporaries and on subsequent generations. In some respects he was an ally of Karl Marx, railing against the iniquities of private property and the squalor of industrialized society, but where he differed from Marx was in his belief that machines necessarily enslave the individual, and that people would be liberated only through a sort of communistic, crafts-based economy. His prose/poem story *News from Nowhere* vaguely described his Utopian society, but his main legacy turned out to be the **Arts and Crafts Movement**.

Morris's career as an artist began at Oxford, where he met **Edward Burne-Jones**, who shared his admiration for the arts of the Middle Ages. After graduating they both ended up in London, painting under the direction of Dante Gabriel Rossetti, the leading light of the **Pre-Raphaelites** – a loose grouping of artists intent on regaining the spiritual purity characteristic of art before Raphael and the Renaissance "tainted" the world with humanism. In 1861 Morris founded **Morris & Co** ("The Firm"), whose designs came to embody the ideas of the Arts and Crafts Movement, one of whose basic tenets was formulated by its founder: "Have nothing in your houses that you do not know to be useful or believe to be beautiful." Rossetti and Burne-Jones were among the designers, though the former remains better known for his paintings of Jane Morris, William's wife and Rossetti's mistress, whom he turned into the archetypal Pre-Raphaelite woman. Morris's own designs for fabrics, wallpapers and numerous other products were to prove a massive influence in Britain, as evidenced by the success of the Laura Ashley aesthetic, a lineal descendant of Morris's rustic nostalgia.

Not content with his artistic endeavours, in 1890 Morris set up the **Kelmscott Press**, named after (but not located at) his summer home, whose masterpiece was the so-called *Kelmscott Chaucer*, the collected poems of one of the Pre-Raphaelites' greatest heroes, with woodcuts by Burne-Jones. Morris also pioneered interest in the architecture of the Cotswolds and, in response to the Victorian penchant for modernizing the region's churches and cottages, he instigated the **Society for the Protection of Ancient Buildings**, still an active force in preserving the country's architectural heritage today (ⓦ www.spab.org.uk).

Around Burford: Kelmscott Manor

Kelmscott Manor (April to late Sept Wed 11am–5pm, plus some Sats 2–5pm; £8.50; ⓣ01367/252486, ⓦ www.kelmscottmanor.co.uk), about eight miles south of Burford, is a place of pilgrimage for devotees of **William Morris** (see box above), who used this Tudor manor as a summer home from 1871 to his death in 1896. The simple beauty of the house is enhanced by the furniture, fabrics, wallpapers and tapestries created by Morris and his Pre-Raphaelite friends, including Burne-Jones and Rossetti. Entry is by timed ticket and it's wise to call ahead to confirm the opening hours. There are no buses and the easiest way to get there by **car** from Burford is to drive south on the A361 to Lechlade-on-Thames, from where you take the A417 east – and watch for the sign after a couple of miles. The car park is a ten-minute walk from the house.

Cirencester and around

CIRENCESTER, some twenty miles southwest of Burford, is a somewhat old-fashioned town on the southern fringes of the Cotswolds. It made an early start, when, as Corinium, it became a provincial capital and a centre of trade under the **Romans**. The town flourished for three centuries, and even had one of the largest forums north of the Alps, but the Saxons destroyed almost all of the Roman city and it only revived with the wool boom of the Middle Ages. Nowadays, with its handsome stone buildings, Cirencester is an affluent little place of 19,000 souls that lays claim to be the "Capital of the Cotswolds"; it's also within easy striking distance of **Malmesbury**, where the big deal is the Norman abbey.

The Town

Cirencester's heart is the delightful, swirling **Market Place**, packed with traders' stalls on Mondays and Fridays. An irregular line of eighteenth-century facades along the north side contrasts with the heavier Victorian structures opposite, but the parish church of **St John the Baptist** (Mon–Sat 9.30am–5pm, Sun 2.15–5pm; £2 suggested donation), built in stages during the fifteenth century, dominates. The extraordinary flying buttresses that support the tower had to be added when it transpired that the church had been constructed over a filled-in ditch. Its grand three-tiered south **porch**, the largest in England and big enough to function as the one-time town hall, leads to the nave, where slender piers and soaring arches create a superb sense of space, enhanced by clerestory windows that bathe the nave in a warm light. The church contains much of interest, including a colourful wineglass **pulpit**, carved in stone around 1450 and one of the few pre-Reformation pulpits to have survived in Britain. North of the chancel, superb fan vaulting hangs overhead in the **chapel of St Catherine**, who appears in a still vivid fragment of a fifteenth-century wall painting. In the adjacent **Lady Chapel** are two good seventeenth-century monuments, one to Humphrey Bridges and his family and the other to the dandified Sir William Master. Outside, one of the best views of the church is from the **Abbey Grounds**; site of the Saxon abbey, it's now a small park skirted by the modest River Churn and a fragment of the Roman city wall.

Few medieval buildings other than the church have survived in Cirencester. The houses along the town's most handsome streets – Park, Thomas and Coxwell – date mostly from the seventeenth and eighteenth centuries. One of those on Park Street, just to the west of the Market Place, houses the sleekly refurbished **Corinium Museum** (Mon–Sat 10am–5pm, Sun 2–5pm; £3.90), which mostly devotes itself to Roman and Saxon artefacts, including several wonderful **mosaic pavements**. There's a reconstruction of a Romano-British garden, as well as finds from a cemetery excavated at Lechlade-on-Thames in 1985. A yew hedge the height of telegraph poles runs along Park Street, concealing **Cirencester House**, the home of the Earl of Bathurst. At no point can you actually see the building (it's rather plain anyway), but the attached three-thousand-acre **park** is open to the public: you enter it from Cecily Hill, a lovely street except for the eccentric Victorian barracks. The park's polo pitches attract some of the country's top players, with games held almost daily between May and September.

Finally, the **Brewery Arts Centre** (Mon–Fri 10am–5pm, Sat 9.30am–5.30pm; free; ☎01285/657181, ⊛www.breweryarts.org.uk), just south of the Market Place off Cricklade Street, is occupied by more than a dozen resident artists, whose studios you can visit and whose work you can buy in the shop. The centre's theatre hosts high-calibre plays and concerts (from jazz to classical), and there is a busy café on the first floor.

Practicalities

Buses to Cirencester stop in the Market Place, where the **tourist office** (9.30/9.45am–5.30pm; Dec closes 5pm; ☎01285/654180, ⊛www.cotswold .gov.uk), in the Corn Hall, covers the whole of the Cotswolds and has a list of local **accommodation** pinned outside. The choicest **B&B** is in an old and attractively furnished Georgian house down a narrow alley just north of the Market Place at 107 Gloucester St (☎01285/657861; no cards; ●). Alternatively, a string of B&Bs line up along Victoria Road, a short walk east of the Market Place, including *The Ivy House*, in high-gabled Victorian premises at no. 2 (☎01285/656626, Ⓦwww.ivyhousecotswolds.com; ●); there are four guest rooms here, all en suite, and each is decorated in a modest but homely manner. More upmarket is the *Crown of Crucis* **hotel**, a much modified sixteenth-century former coaching inn with riverside gardens just two and a half miles east of town on the A417 in Ampney Crucis (☎01285/851806, Ⓦwww .thecrownofcrucis.co.uk; ●).

For **snacks**, you can't do much better than *Keith's Coffee Shop* on Black Jack Street, where they serve the best coffee in town, and the inexpensive *Coffee House*, in the Brewery Centre, which serves interesting vegetarian dishes (no credit cards; closed Sun). The best choice for a relaxing **evening meal** is *Harry Hare's* at 3 Gosditch St (☎01285/652375), just behind the church, which specializes in classy renditions of down-to-earth English dishes at moderate prices.

Cirencester has plenty of **pubs**, their clientele swollen by tweedy students from the nearby Royal Agricultural College. Try the *Kings Head* on the Market Place or, for **bar meals**, the *Waggon & Horses* on London Road.

Malmesbury

The small hill town of **MALMESBURY** lies on the periphery of the Cotswolds twelve miles south of Cirencester, just over the county boundary in Wiltshire. The town may have lost most of its good looks with a rash of modern development, but there's no gainsaying the stirring beauty of its partly ruinous Norman abbey, a majestic structure boasting some of the finest Romanesque sculpture in the country. Malmesbury's local celebrities include **Thomas Hobbes** (1588–1679), the moral and political philosopher whose most influential work, *Leviathan*, argued for the absolute power of the state, and **Elmer the Monk**, who in 1005 attempted to fly from the abbey tower with the aid of wings: he limped for the rest of his life, but won immortal fame as the "flying monk".

Malmesbury's **High Street** begins at the bottom of the hill by the old silk mills and heads north across the river and up past a jagged row of ancient cottages on its way to the octagonal **Market Cross**, built around 1490 to provide shelter from the rain. Nearby, the eighteenth-century **Tolsey Gate** leads through to the **Abbey** (daily 10am–4pm; free), which was once a rich and powerful Benedictine monastery. The first abbey burnt down in about 1050, the second was roughed up during the Dissolution, but the beautiful Norman **nave** of the abbey church has survived, its south porch sporting a multitude of exquisite if badly worn figures. Three bands of figures surround the doorway, depicting scenes from the Creation, the Old Testament and the life of Christ, while inside the porch the apostles and Christ are carved in a fine deep relief – stately figures in flowing folds surmounted by a flying angel. The tympanum shows Christ on a rainbow, supported by gracefully gymnastic angels. Within the main body of the church, the pale stone brings a dramatic freshness, particularly to the carving of the nave arches (look out for the Norman beak-heads) and of the clerestory. To the left of the high altar, the pulpit virtually hides the **tomb of King Athelstan**, grandson of Alfred the Great and the first Saxon to be recognized as king of England; the tomb, however, is empty and the location of the king's body is unknown. The abbey's greatest surviving treasures are housed in the **parvis** (room above the porch), reached via a narrow spiral staircase right of the main doorway, where pride of place is given to four

Flemish **medieval Bibles**, written on parchment and sumptuously illuminated with gilt ink and exquisite miniature paintings.

Buses to Malmesbury pull into the Market Place, a short walk from the **tourist office**, on the corner of Cross Hayes and Market Lane (Mon–Thurs 9am–4.50pm,Fri 9am–4.20pm,Easter–Sept also Sat 10am–4pm;℗01666/823748, ⓦwww.visitwiltshire.co.uk).There's no real reason to **stay the night**, though the *Old Bell* in Abbey Row (℗01666/822344, ⓦwww.oldbellhotel.com; ❼) provides a strong incentive: originally built as a guest house for the abbey, it has loads of atmosphere, pleasantly appointed rooms, and a good **restaurant**.

Northleach

Secluded in a shallow depression some ten miles north of Cirencester, **NORTHLEACH** is one of the most appealing and least developed villages in the Cotswolds.This, together with its location within easy reach of Oxford and the picturesque Windrush Valley, makes it a perfect base from which to explore the region. Rows of immaculate late-medieval cottages cluster around the village's **market place** with more of the same framing the adjoining **green**, but the most outstanding feature is the handsome Perpendicular **church of St Peter and St Paul**, erected in the fifteenth century at the height of the wool boom, when the surrounding fields of rich limestone grasses supported a vast population of sheep.The local breed, known as the Cotswold Lion, was a descendant of flocks introduced by the Romans, and by the thirteenth century had become the biggest sheep breed in the country, producing heavy fleeces that were exported to the Flemish weaving towns. The income from this lucrative trade, initially controlled by the clergy but later by a handful of wealthy merchants, financed the construction of four major churches in the region, of which those at Northleach and Burford (see p.326) are the most impressive – the others are in Cirencester (see p.328) and Chipping Campden (see p.335). Setting the tone, the porch of St Peter and St Paul is a suitably ostentatious affair overseen by a set of finely carved corbel heads, while beyond the beautifully proportioned nave is lit by wide clerestory windows.The floor of the nave is inlaid with an exceptional collection of **memorial brasses**, marking the tombs of the merchants whose endowments paid for the church. On several, you can make out the woolsacks laid out beneath the corpse's feet – a symbol of wealth and power that features to this day in the House of Lords, where a woolsack is placed on the Lord Chancellor's seat.

Two minutes' walk up along the High Street from the Market Place is Northleach's other main attraction, **Keith Harding's World of Mechanical Music** (daily 10am–6pm; £7.50; ⓦwww.mechanicalmusic.co.uk), comprising a bewildering collection of antique musical boxes, automata, barrel organs and mechanical instruments all stuffed into one room.The entrance fee includes an hour-long demonstration tour, of which the highlight is hearing the likes of Rachmaninov, Gershwin or Paderewski playing their own masterpieces on piano rolls. Finally, **walking trails** radiate out from Northleach in all directions either across the grassy hills or along the river.

Practicalities

There's a reasonably good **bus** service from Cirencester to Northleach (Mon–Sat every 2–3hr) and another linking Oxford, Burford, Northleach, Cheltenham and Gloucester (1–3 daily). The latter is operated by Swanbrook Bus (see p.327). Buses pull into the centre of the village beside the green.There is no tourist office but there are two smashing places to stay – one **B&B** and

one **hotel**. The B&B is *Cotteswold House* (℡01451/860493, Ⓦwww
.cotteswoldhouse.com; ❹), a wonderfully well-preserved stone cottage with
exposed stone arches and antique oak panelling right in the centre of the village
on the Market Place; there are three guest rooms here, all en suite. Alternatively,
head for the excellent ⚲ *Wheatsheaf Hotel* (℡01451/860244, Ⓦwww
.wheatsheaf.cotswoldsinns.com; ❺), a former coaching inn just along from the
Market Place on West End. The hotel's old stone exterior has been left intact,
but the public rooms have been remodelled in a bright and brisk modern style
and the same applies to the eight, en-suite guest rooms, though here the design
is softened by period furniture. The *Wheatsheaf's* **restaurant** is first-rate too,
offering delicious traditional English cuisine – roast rack of lamb, cod in beer
and so forth – with mains averaging £14.

Stow-on-the-Wold and around

Ambling over a steep hill some ten miles northeast of Northleach,
STOW-ON-THE-WOLD sucks in a disproportionate number of visitors for
its size and attractions, which essentially comprise an old **market place**
surrounded by cafés, pubs, antique and souvenir shops. The narrow walled
alleyways, or "tunes", running into the square were designed for funnelling
sheep into the market, which is itself dominated by an imposing Victorian hall
– but architecturally that is pretty much it.

Stow is, however, easy to reach by **bus** from the likes of Cheltenham and
Cirencester, with buses pulling in on the High Street, just off the main square,
where the **tourist office** (Mon–Sat 9.30am–4.30/5.30pm; ℡01451/831082,
Ⓦwww.cotswold.gov.uk) carries oodles of local information. They will also
book **accommodation**, of which there is a reasonable supply, including the
Tall Trees B&B (℡01451/831296; no credit cards; ❸), on the edge of town off
the Oddington road (A436), which has sweeping views and a cosy wood burner
in its modern sitting room annexe; there are five rooms here, two en suite.
There's only one **youth hostel** in the Cotswolds and it's here, in a
good-looking Georgian town house on the main square (℡0870/770 6050,
Ⓔstow@yha.org.uk; dorm beds £16). The hostel has fifty beds in four- to
eight-bedded rooms (no doubles) and is open all year.

For **food**, *The Royalist Hotel*, just off the main square on the corner of Park
and Digbeth streets, offers light meals in its *Eagle & Child* bar and also possesses
the more formal but extremely good *947AD* restaurant (℡01451/830670),
where a main course costs around £14. The best **teashop** in town is the
Cotswold Garden Tearoom, yards from the Royalist on Digbeth Street and offering
tasty home-made cakes and snacks.

Around Stow: Bourton-on-the-Water and the Slaughters

If anywhere can be described as the epicentre of Cotswold tourism, it has to be
BOURTON-ON-THE-WATER, some four miles south of Stow just to the
east of the A429. The reason for all the fuss are the five (allegedly very picturesque) mini-bridges that straddle the River Windrush as it courses through the
centre of the village. Add to this a few purpose-built attractions – a Model
Village here, a Dragonfly Maze there – and you have enough to attract an army
of tourist coaches.

Much more enticing, if still on the day-trippers' circuit, is the minuscule
hamlet of **LOWER SLAUGHTER** (as in *slohtre*, old English for "marshy
place"), just to the west of the A429, a mile or so from Bourton. Here, the River

Eye snakes its way through the village, overlooked by a string of immaculate and very old stone cottages. The village **church** blends in well, but in fact it's largely Victorian, and there is a small **museum** (and souvenir shop) in what was once a mill, but you're better off walking up the river valley to **UPPER SLAUGHTER**, another pretty little place buried deep in a wooded dell; the walk between the two takes about an hour.

There are several **places to stay** in the Slaughters, the most appealing being the *Lords of the Manor*, a luxurious and infinitely comfortable hotel in Upper Slaughter's old rectory (℡01451/820243, ⓦwww.lordsofthemanor.com; ⓢ).

Chipping Norton and around

The bustling market town of **CHIPPING NORTON**, eight miles east of Stow, is not the prettiest place in the Cotswolds by any means, but it is flanked to the north and east by one of the least explored and most scenic corners of the region, where the limestone uplands are patterned by long dry-stone walls and sprinkled with tiny stone villages. Pick of the scenic bunch is **Great Tew**, an extraordinarily picturesque hamlet with a delightful inn, but there are also the eerie – or at least idiosyncratic – prehistoric **Rollright Stones**. In the other direction, to the west, Chipping Norton is within easy striking distance of an especially handsome Jacobean country mansion, **Chastleton House**.

The Town

It was King John who granted a **wool fair** charter to Chipping Norton in the twelfth century, but the town reached its peak three hundred years later, when it acquired many of the stalwart stone buildings that now line up along the market square. Also paid for by wealthy wool merchants, **St Mary's Parish Church**, just below the square – and beyond a row of handsome almshouses – looks every inch the country church, the modesty of its tower offset by the long and slender windows of its beautiful Perpendicular Gothic nave. The vaulted porch is equally striking, if not for itself then for the large and inordinately ugly grinning devils and green men that peer down from the roof. By comparison, the interior is really rather routine, though the nave is well-lit and airy and the east window of the south aisle is a splendid affair, spiralling out from a central tulip; look out also for two superbly carved alabaster table-tombs commemorating two long-forgotten merchants and their wives, who passed on in the sixteenth century. Finally, the old **Bliss Tweed Mill** (no public access) recalls the textile mini-boom that Chipping Norton enjoyed in the nineteenth century. You can't miss its whopping chimneystack as you leave – or approach – the town on the A44.

Practicalities

Buses to Chipping Norton pull in on West Street, a few yards from the town hall. **Accommodation** is thin on the ground, but there are well-appointed and recently revamped rooms behind the Georgian facade of the *Crown and Cushion* (℡01608/642533, ⓦwww.crown-cushion.co.uk; ⓢ), a few yards from the town hall on the main square; curiously enough, the hotel was once owned by Keith Moon of The Who. More distinctively, *The Forge B&B* (℡01608/658173, ⓦwww.cotswolds-accommodation.com; ④) offers a handful of en-suite rooms in tastefully converted old stone premises, three miles southwest of town along the B4450 in the middle of tiny **Churchill**. The best – or at least the most authentic – **pub** in Chipping Norton is the *Chequers*, just down from the main square near St Mary's.

The Rollright Stones

Driving west from Chipping Norton along the A44, it only takes a few minutes to reach the signed country lane that leads off to the right to run past the **Rollright Stones**, a scattering of megalithic monuments in the fields to either side of the lane. The monuments consist of large natural stones moved here for some purpose or other – no one is sure – plus several burial chambers and barrows. The largest of them – and one of the most important stone circles in the country – is the **King's Men Stone Circle**, comprising over seventy irregularly spaced stones forming a circle thirty metres in diameter. Signed just off the lane, it's also the easiest to find. The circle gets its name from an old legend recounting the time a witch turned a king and his army (of unknown identity) into these gnarled rocks to stop them invading England. Volunteers sometimes staff a hut at the entrance, charging 50p for access and also providing a map of the surrounding prehistoric monuments – very useful as the majority are well-nigh impossible to track down otherwise.

Great Tew

GREAT TEW, about five miles east of Chipping Norton via the A361, is one of the most beautiful of all the Cotswold villages, its thatched cottages and honey-coloured stone houses weaving around grassy hillocks with woodland on all sides. Here also is one of England's most idyllic pubs, the ⚑ **Falkland Arms**, which rotates four guest beers in addition to its regular real-ale supplies, and sells a fine selection of single malts, herbal wines, snuff, and clay pipes you can fill with tobacco for a smoke in the flower-filled garden. Little has changed in the flagstone-floored **bar** since the sixteenth century, although the snug was recently converted into a small **dining room** serving delicious, homemade lunches and evening meals, except on Sunday evenings – with main courses starting from as little as £8. It's also a popular place **to stay** (☎01608/683653, Ⓦ www.falklandarms.org.uk; ⑤): there are half a dozen rooms, each sympathetically renovated and equipped with attractive furnishings and fittings, but it's pretty much essential to book ahead.

▲ The Falkland Arms, Great Tew

Chastleton House

About four miles west of Chipping Norton along the A44 – and beyond the turning for Stow-on-the-Wold (see p.332) – stands one of the region's prime country houses, **Chastleton House** (Wed–Sat: April–Sept 1–5pm, Oct 1–4pm; £7; timed tickets, pre-bookable on ℡01494/755560; NT). Built between 1605 and 1612 by Walter Jones, a wealthy Welsh wool merchant, this ranks among the most splendid Jacobean properties in the country, set amid ornamental gardens that include England's first-ever croquet lawn (the rules of this most eccentric of games were codified here in 1865). Inside, the house looks as if it's been in a time warp for four hundred years, with unwashed upholstery, unpolished wood panelling and miscellaneous clutter clogging some of the corners. This dishevelled air partly derives from the previous owners, the Jones family, who lost their fortune in the aftermath of the Civil War – they were Royalists – and never had enough cash to modernize thereafter. It's also a credit to the National Trust, who took on the property in 1991, but wisely decided to stick to the "lived-in look". It's the general flavour of the house that is of most appeal, but there are several highlights, notably the huge barrel-vaulted long gallery, acres of elaborate plasterwork and panelling, tapestries and exquisite glassware, and, in the beer cellar, the longest ladder (dated 1805) you're ever likely to come across. There's also a topiary garden, where the hedges are clipped into bulbous shapes reminiscent of squirrels and tortoises.

Chipping Campden

CHIPPING CAMPDEN, some fifteen miles northwest of Chipping Norton, gives a better idea than anywhere else in the Cotswolds as to what a prosperous wool town might have looked like in the Middle Ages. The short **High Street** is hemmed in by ancient houses, whose undulating, weather-beaten roofs jag against each other, while down below are twisted beams and mullioned windows. The seventeenth-century **Market Hall** has survived too, a barn-like affair in the middle of the High Street, where farmers once gathered to sell their harvests. From the High Street, it's a brief walk east past a splendid sequence of old stone houses to the **church of St James** (April–Oct Mon–Fri 10am–5pm, Sat 11am–5pm, Sun 2–5pm; Nov–March Mon–Sat 11am–3pm, Sun 2–4pm; free), the archetypal Cotswold wool church built in the fifteenth century, the zenith of the town's wool-trading days. Inside, the airy nave is bathed in light from the clerestory windows and there's a delicate and carefully considered balance between height and length. Here also is the ostentatious **funerary chapel** of the Hicks family, with the fancily carved marble effigies of Sir Baptist and Lady Elizabeth lying on their table-tomb overlooked by the standing figures of their daughter and son-in-law, Edward Noel, who came a fatal cropper fighting the Parliamentarians in the Civil War. Sir Baptist built himself a huge mansion next to the church in the 1610s, but this was burnt down shortly afterwards, leaving just two splendidly Baroque gatehouses and a pair of banqueting halls (no public access).

A fine panoramic view rewards those who make the short but severe hike up the Cotswold Way north from the High Street (along West End Terrace/Hoo Lane) to **Dover's Hill**. Since 1610 this natural amphitheatre has been the stage for an Olympics of rural sports, though the event was suspended last century when games such as shin-kicking became little more than licensed thuggery. A more civilized version, the **Cotswold Olimpick Games** (ⓦwww.olimpickgames.co.uk), has been staged here each June since 1951 with hammer-throwing and tug-of-war pulling plus a bit of shin-kicking for the overly-excited.

Practicalities

Inevitably, Chipping Campden heaves with day-trippers in the summer, so try to stay overnight and explore in the evening or at dawn, when the streets are empty and the golden hues of the stone at their richest. Getting here by **bus** is relatively easy from Cheltenham, Moreton-in-Marsh (for Chipping Norton and Oxford) and Stratford-upon-Avon, but other places usually require more effort. The town's **tourist office** is bang in the middle of town, on the High Street (daily 10am–5.30pm; ☎01386/841206, ⓦwww.chipping-campden.net). They will book accommodation on your behalf, a useful service in the height of the summer when **rooms** are in short supply. The town's best B&B by a long chalk is 🅰 *Badgers Hall* (☎01386/840839, ⓦwww.badgershall.com; ⑥), in an old stone house on the High Street, above their own tearoom. All the guest rooms are en suite and come complete with period detail – beamed ceilings and so forth; advance bookings are advised. There's also the plush, perhaps overly plush, *Cotswold House Hotel*, which occupies an immaculately maintained Regency town house and its older neighbours on The Square (☎01386/840330, ⓦwww.cotswoldhouse.com; ⑨); there are about thirty guest rooms here and each is kitted out in smart modern style.

Badgers Hall is the best **teashop** in town and the pick of the **pubs** is the 🅰 *Eight Bells Inn* (☎01386/840371, ⓦwww.eightbellsinn.co.uk), a particularly cosy spot in a charming old stone building on the way up to the church. The restaurant here is first-rate, trying wherever possible to source things locally; the menu encompasses dishes such as ham and cloves or pheasant and mushroom; main courses start at £9, less in the bar. If there's no room at the inn, try the half-timbered *Red Lion*, a pub and restaurant on the High Street, where a good range of English dishes is on offer, with main courses about £12.

Broadway and around

BROADWAY, five miles from Chipping Campden, is a particularly handsome little village at the foot of the steep escarpment that rolls along the western edge of the Cotswolds. It seems likely that the Romans were the first to settle here, but Broadway's high times were as a stagecoach stop on the route from London to Worcester. It's this former function that has defined much of the village's present appearance – its long and wide main street framed by stone cottages and shaded by chestnut trees. Broadway attracts more visitors than is good for it, but things quieten down in the evening and *The Olive Branch*, 78 High St (☎01386/853440, ⓦwww.theolivebranch-broadway.com; ⑤), is an extremely pleasant B&B in an old stone house and with half a dozen homely guest rooms. There are **bus** services to Broadway from Chipping Campden and Winchcombe (see p.337).

Tucked away down a country lane just over two miles south of Broadway, **Snowshill Manor** is a good-looking Cotswold manor house, which holds a veritable trove of exotic curiosities (April–Oct Wed–Sun noon–5pm; garden same months & days 11am–5.30pm; £7.70, gardens only £4.20; NT). Inspired as a boy by his grandmother's "wonderful" Chinese cabinet (now in the Zenith room of the house), the architect, craftsman and poet Charles Paget Wade (1883–1956) spent decades hunting down objects that were not "rare or valuable" but "of interest as records of various vanished handicrafts". The results of his forays – model carts, boneshaker bicycles, children's prams, wooden toys, beds, beetles, all kinds of musical instruments – were crammed into the house, while he himself lived in a cottage in the garden. Most dramatic is the arrangement of 26 Samurai warriors dating from the seventeenth to the nineteenth centuries in the Green Room. Note that there is a ten-minute walk to the house from the entrance to the grounds.

Winchcombe and around

From Broadway, it's about eight miles southwest to **WINCHCOMBE**, whose long main street is flanked by a fetching medley of stone and half-timbered buildings. Inconsequential today, Winchcombe was once an important Saxon town and one-time capital of the kingdom of Mercia. It flourished during the medieval cloth boom too, one of the results being **St Peter's**, the town's main church, a mainly fifteenth-century structure distinguished by the forty striking gargoyles that ring the exterior, a mixed crew of devils, beasts and the insane. It doesn't take long to explore Winchcombe, but the village does make a good base from which to hike to a trio of neighbouring attractions – **Spoonley Wood**, **Hailes Abbey** and **Belas Knap**.

Spoonley Wood

The mildly strenuous three-and-a-half-hour hiking loop from Winchcombe through Spoonley Wood to Spoonley Farm, two miles southeast of town, takes in a ruined Roman villa with a beautifully preserved **mosaic** *in situ*. The villa's existence was a well-kept secret until American travel writer Bill Bryson featured it in his chart-topping *Notes From A Small Island*. Since then, Winchcombe tourist office has been inundated with requests for its *Country Walks Around Winchcombe* booklet, which describes the route in detail. If you can't get hold of this, check OS Explorer Map 45. The footpath to Spoonley Farm starts in the same place as the Cotswold Way, opposite the church at the south end of the main street, but shortly after peels left towards **Sudeley Castle**, a much restored Tudor mansion with immaculate gardens. After crossing the castle grounds, it follows the contour of the hill to **Spoonley Wood**, site of the old villa; the mosaic is covered in sheets of plastic held down with stones, which you have to remove yourself (be sure to replace them afterwards). From the ruin, strike uphill as far as a farm track, which you can follow southwest, turning right at Cole's Hill towards Waterhatch Farm. The path then drops gently down to river level and wends its way back to Winchcombe.

Hailes Abbey

Hailes Abbey (daily: April–June & Sept 10am–5pm; July & Aug 10am–6pm; Oct 10am–4pm; £3.40; EH), a two-mile stroll or drive northeast of Winchcombe, was once one of England's great Cistercian monasteries. Pilgrims came here from all over the country to pray before the abbey's phial of Christ's blood, a relic shown to be a fake at the time of the Reformation, which also saw most of the thirteenth-century monastery demolished. The principal remains are an assortment of foundations, but some cloister arches survive, worn by wind and rain. The ruins may lack drama, but Hailes is still worth visiting for its **museum**, where you can examine thirteenth-century bosses at close quarters, and for the nearby **church**, which is older than the abbey and contains beautiful wall paintings dating from around 1300. The cartoon-like hunting scene was probably a warning to Sabbath-breakers.

Belas Knap

Up on the ridge overlooking Winchcombe to the south, the Neolithic long barrow of **Belas Knap** occupies one of the wildest spots in the Cotswolds. Dating from around 3000 BC, this is the best-preserved burial chamber in

England, stretching out like a strange sleeping beast cloaked in green velvet. The best way to get there is to **walk**, undertaking the two-mile climb up the Cotswold Way from Winchcombe. The path strikes off to the right near the entrance to Sudeley Castle and afterwards, when you reach the country lane at the top, turn right and then left for the ten-minute hike to the barrow. It's also possible to drive to Belas Knap along this same country lane: just follow the signs to the roadside pull-in where you can park before setting off for the briefest of hikes. South beyond Belas Knap, the country lane cuts an exhilarating route, scuttling over the hills and through dense woods on its way to Syreford – with the A40 (for Northleach, see p.331) a little further on.

Practicalities

Monday through Saturday only, there are three or four **buses** a day to Winchcombe from Cheltenham and Broadway; passengers arriving from Chipping Campden have to change at Broadway, though this can mean an awfully long wait. Winchcombe **tourist office**, in the town hall on the High Street (Mon–Sat 10am–5pm, Sun 10am–4pm; ☎01242/602925, ⓦwww .visitcotswoldsandsevernvale.gov.uk), has information on local hikes and attractions; they will also book accommodation.

Of the town's many **B&Bs**, one of the best is the excellent *Gower House*, 16 North St (☎01242/602616; no credit cards; ❸), which offers three extremely comfortable rooms – two en suite – in an attractively modernized, seventeenth-century house in the town centre. Alternatively, the *White Hart Inn*, in a good-looking old building on the High Street (☎01242/602359, ⓦwww .wineandsausage.co.uk; ❹), has eight spick and span rooms decorated in cosy, traditional-meets-folksy manner.

For **food**, the *White Hart Inn* is the place to go, its speciality being simple, British dishes in general and sausages in particular – not just any old sausage, but delicious gourmet versions, like venison and red wine or lamb, mint and apricot; you can eat either in the restaurant, where main courses start at about £8, or at the bar (from £4).

Cheltenham

Until the eighteenth century **CHELTENHAM** was like any other Cotswold town, but the discovery of a spring in 1716 transformed it into Britain's most popular **spa**. During Cheltenham's heyday, a century or so later, the royal, the rich and the famous descended in droves to take the waters, which were said to cure anything from constipation to worms. The super-rich have moved onto sunnier climes, but the town has maintained a lively, bustling atmosphere, holds lots of good restaurants and boasts some of England's best-preserved Regency architecture.

Cheltenham is also a thriving arts centre, famous for its festivals of **folk** (Feb), **jazz** (April/May), **science** (June), **classical music** (July) and **literature** (April and October) – for information on any of these check ⓦwww .cheltenhamfestivals.co.uk – and, of course, the **races** (see box, p.340). In addition, **Coopers' Hill**, six miles southwest on the A46 near the village of Brockworth, is the venue for the region's most bizarre competition. On the second bank holiday in May, a steep section of the Cotswold escarpment hosts the annual **Cheese Rolling Festival** (ⓦwww.cheese-rolling.co.uk), when a large Double Gloucester cheese is rolled down the one-in-two incline and

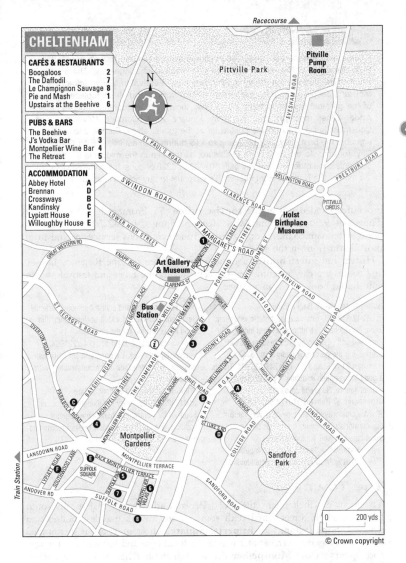

CHELTENHAM

CAFÉS & RESTAURANTS

Boogaloos	2
The Daffodil	7
Le Champignon Sauvage	8
Pie and Mash	1
Upstairs at the Beehive	6

PUBS & BARS

The Beehive	6
J's Vodka Bar	3
Montpellier Wine Bar	4
The Retreat	5

ACCOMMODATION

Abbey Hotel	A
Brennan	D
Crossways	B
Kandinsky	C
Lypiatt House	F
Willoughby House	E

© Crown copyright

chased by dozens of drunken folk; the first person to get down the hill is the winner. The damage to life and limb has resulted in the race being banned in the past, but it has been reinstated by popular demand, and now there are four races – three for men and one for women.

Arrival, information and accommodation

All long-distance **buses** arrive at the **bus station** in Royal Well Road, just west off the main drag, the Promenade. Cheltenham Spa **train station** is on Queen's Road, southwest of the centre; local buses run into town every fifteen minutes, otherwise it's a twenty-minute walk. Among the many leaflets and

Cheltenham races

Cheltenham racecourse, on the north side of town, a ten-minute walk from Pittville Park at the foot of Cleeve Hill, is Britain's main steeplechasing venue. The principal event of the season, the three-day **National Hunt Festival** in March, attracts forty thousand people a day, a fair proportion of them from Ireland, the birthplace of some of the greatest horses to have raced here, including the supreme steeplechaser, **Arkle**. Other meetings take place in January, April, October, November and December: a list of fixtures is posted up at the tourist office. For the cheapest but arguably the best view, pay £8 (rising to £15 during the Festival, £25 on Gold Cup Day) for entry to the Best Mate Enclosure, as the pen in the middle is known. For schedules and other information, call ⓣ01242/226226 or consult ⓦwww.cheltenham.co.uk. For the National Hunt Festival it's essential to buy tickets in advance.

brochures handed out at the **tourist office**, 77 Promenade (Mon, Tues & Thurs–Sat 9.30am–5.15pm, Wed 10am–5.15pm; ⓣ01242/522878, ⓦwww.visitcheltenham.co.uk), is one giving a rundown of bus services to and from most destinations in the area.

Hotels and **guest houses** abound, many of them in fine Regency houses, and rooms are easy to come by – except during the races and festivals, when you should book weeks in advance.

Abbey Hotel 14–16 Bath Parade ⓣ01242/516053, ⓦwww.abbeyhotel-cheltenham.com. Rooms here are attractively and individually furnished and wholesome breakfasts are taken overlooking the garden. Friendly service. 5

Brennan 21 St Luke's Rd ⓣ01242/525904. This is a good-value option in a small Regency building, on a quiet square. No credit cards. 3

Crossways 57 Bath Rd ⓣ01242/527683, ⓦwww.crosswaysguesthouse.com. Very central, this comfortable Regency house has period trimmings and well-equipped rooms. 5

Kandinsky Bayshill Road, Montpellier ⓣ01242/527788, ⓦwww.hotelkandinsky.com. With colourful and stylish bedrooms, Oriental decor and basement cocktail-bar/nightclub, this hotel is good value for the price. 7

Lypiatt House Lypiatt Rd ⓣ01242/224994, ⓦwww.lypiatt.co.uk. Victorian villa set in its own grounds, with open fires and a conservatory with a small bar. 5

Willoughby House 1 Suffolk Square ⓣ01242/522798, ⓦwww.willoughbyhouse.com. South of the centre, in a handsome Regency building, this hotel has ornately opulent rooms and a restaurant. 7

The Town

The focus of Cheltenham, the broad **Promenade**, sweeps majestically south from the High Street, lined with some of the town's grandest houses and smartest shops. It leads into **Imperial Square**, whose greenery is surrounded by proud Regency terraces that herald the handsome and harmonious terraces and squares of the **Montpellier** district, which stretches south in a narrow block to Suffolk Road, making a delightful detour.

Back in the centre, just to the north of the Promenade on Clarence Street, is the enjoyable **Cheltenham Art Gallery and Museum** (Mon–Sat 10am–5.20pm; free; ⓦwww.cheltenhammuseum.org.uk). This is very good on social history, with different eras represented by table displays of personal belongings and a typical dinner of the time. There's also a fine room dedicated to the Arts and Crafts Movement, containing several pieces by Charles Voysey and Ernest Gimson, two of the period's most graceful designers. Also on display is an array of rare Chinese ceramics, works by artists such as Stanley Spencer and Vanessa Bell, and a section devoted to Edward Wilson, a local man who died on Scott's ill-fated expedition to the Antarctic.

From the gallery, it's a brief stroll north to the **Holst Birthplace Museum**, at 4 Clarence Rd (mid-Jan to mid-Dec Tues–Sat 10am–4pm; £2.50; ⓦwww .holstmuseum.org.uk). Once the home of the composer of *The Planets*, the intimate rooms hold plenty of Holst memorabilia – including his piano – and also give a good insight into Victorian family life.

Pressing on, it's about ten minutes' walk to the **Pittville** district, where a certain Joseph Pitt planned to build his own spa. Work began on Pitt's grand scheme in the 1820s, but he went bust and most of Pittville is now parkland, though he did manage to complete the domed **Pump Room** (daily except Tues 10am–4pm) before he hit the skids. A lovely Classical structure with an imposing colonnaded facade, the Pump Room is now used as a concert hall, but you can still sample the **spa waters** from the marble fountain in the main auditorium for free – and very pungent they are too.

Eating and drinking

Cheltenham caters for all tastes and pockets and possesses some of the best **restaurants**, **bars** and **pubs** in the area, drawing in the punters from nearby Gloucester as well as the Cotswolds.

Cafés and restaurants

Boogaloos 16 Regent St. The salads and sandwiches are good at this coffee house, where you can either chill out in the relaxed sofa basement or join the crowd in the buzzing, brightly coloured upstairs rooms. Closed Sun.

The Daffodil 18–20 Suffolk Parade ☎01242/700055. Eat in the circle bar or auditorium of this former cinema, where the screen has been replaced with a hubbub of chefs. Great atmosphere and first-class Modern British food with main courses hovering around £15.

Le Champignon Sauvage Suffolk Rd ☎01242/573449. Top-notch French cuisine – including scrumptious desserts – at this chic and intimate restaurant. Two-course set menu £39, three courses £48. Book well ahead. Closed Sun & Mon.

Pie and Mash 10 Bennington St ☎01242/702785. As well as pie and mash, a range of other traditional English dishes is served here, and they're all organic. Local art in the upstairs bar and Nelly the singing Jack Russell provide entertainment. Closed daytime Tues & Wed, and all Sun & Mon.

Upstairs at the Beehive 1–3 Montpellier Villas ☎01242/702270. Friendly ambience and great French food in a lofty, blue-draped room above the pub (see below) make this a popular dining spot. Mains from £13. Reservations advised; closed Sun eve.

Pubs and bars

The Beehive 1–3 Montpellier Villas. Easygoing Cheltenham institution with games shed, courtyard garden and cosy snug.

J's Vodka Bar 6 Regent St. Killer drinks from a range of 24 vodkas, served to the accompaniment of DJs playing house and funk.

Montpellier Wine Bar Bayshill Lodge, Montpellier St. Stylish wine bar and restaurant, with lovely bow-fronted windows. Good breakfasts are also served, and Friday is fish night.

The Retreat 10–11 Suffolk Parade. Lively venue which caters to the business fraternity at lunchtimes and a Cheltenham Ladies' College set in the evening. Good lunches too. Closed Sun.

Gloucester

For centuries life was good for **GLOUCESTER**, just ten miles west of Cheltenham. The Romans chose this spot for a garrison to guard the River Severn and spy on Wales, and later for a *colonia* or home for retired soldiers – the highest status a provincial Roman town could dream of. Commercial success came with traffic up the Severn, which developed into one of the busiest trade routes in Europe, and the city's political importance hit its peak under the Normans, with William the Conqueror a regular visitor. Gloucester

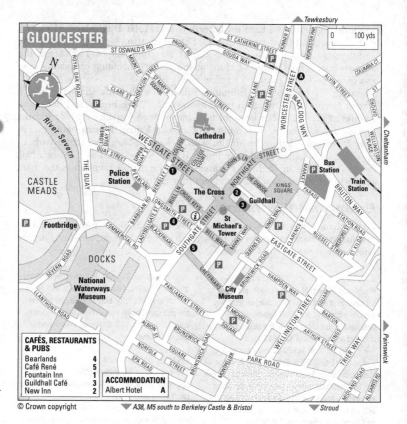

GLOUCESTER

▲ Tewkesbury

0   100 yds

ST CATHERINE STREET
ST OSWALD'S RD
PRIORY RD
GOUDA WAY
SKINNER STREET
WORCESTER PAR
COLUMBIA CT
ROYAL OAK ROAD
MOUNT ST
ST MARY'S SQUARE
ARCHDEACON STREET
CLARE ST
PITT STREET
PARK LANE
HARE LANE
WORCESTER STREET
BLACK DOG WAY
ALVIN STREET
Cheltenham

Cathedral

River Severn
LOWER QUAY ST
UPPER QUAY STREET
QUAY STREET
THE QUAY
WESTGATE STREET
COLLEGE COURT
ST JOHN'S LN
NORTHGATE STREET
Bus Station
Train Station
WELLINGTON PLACE
MARKET PARADE
BRUTON WAY
STATION ROAD

CASTLE MEADS

Police Station
BEARLAND
BERKELEY ST
KINGS SQUARE
KINGS WALK

The Cross
Guildhall

Footbridge
BARBICAN RD
LONGSMITH ST
LADYBELLGATE ST
BLACKFRIARS
BULL LN
CROSS KEYS
SOUTHGATE STREET
St Michael's Tower
BELL WALK
MARKET WAY
QUEENS ST
KINGS BARTON
CLARENCE ST
RUSSELL STREET
BEDFORD ST
ST KILDA
COMMERCIAL RD
EASTGATE STREET
STATION ROAD
Painswick

DOCKS
SEVERN ROAD
LLANTHONY ROAD
BRUNSWICK ROAD
HAMPDEN WAY
GREYFRIARS

National Waterways Museum
PARLIAMENT STREET
City Museum
ST MICHAEL'S SQUARE
WELLINGTON STREET
ARTHUR STREET
TRIER WAY

ALBION ST
BRUNSWICK SQUARE
NORFOLK SQUARE
SPA ROAD
MONTPELLIER
PARK ROAD
MIDLAND ROAD
ALL SAINTS RD
Stroud

CAFÉS, RESTAURANTS & PUBS	
Bearlands	4
Café René	5
Fountain Inn	1
Guildhall Café	3
New Inn	2

ACCOMMODATION	
Albert Hotel	A

© Crown copyright   ▼ A38, M5 south to Berkeley Castle & Bristol   ▼ Stroud

became a religious centre too, as exemplified by the construction of what is now the cathedral, but by the fifteenth century it was on the skids: navigating the Severn as far up as Gloucester was so difficult that most trade gradually shifted south to Bristol. In a brave attempt to reverse the city's decline, a canal was opened in 1827 to link Gloucester to Sharpness, on a broader stretch of the Severn further south. Trade picked up for a time, but it was only a temporary stay of economic execution.

Today, the **canal** is busy once again, though this time with pleasure boats, and the Victorian **docks** have undergone a facelift, their assorted warehouses turned into offices, apartments, a large antiques centre and a museum. The main reason for a visit, however, is Gloucester's magnificent **cathedral**, the city's one and only outstanding attraction. Given this, there is no strong reason to overnight here – a day trip (from Cheltenham) is sufficient.

Arrival, information and accommodation

Gloucester's **bus and train stations** are opposite one another on Bruton Way, a five-minute walk east of the city centre. The **tourist office** is handily located at 28 Southgate St (Mon–Sat 9.30am–5pm, plus Sun in July & Aug 11am–3pm; ☎01452/396572, ⊛www.gloucester.gov.uk/tourism). There's limited **accommodation** in the city centre, but you might consider the *Albert Hotel*,

northeast of the centre at 56 Worcester St ($\textcircled{T}$01452/502081, $\textcircled{W}$www
.alberthotel.com; $\textcircled{O}$). The hotel occupies a listed red-brick building from the
1830s and has homely modern rooms.

The City

Gloucester lies on the east bank of the Severn, its centre spread around a curve
in the river. **The Cross**, once the entrance to the Roman forum, marks the heart
of the city and the meeting-point of Northgate, Southgate, Eastgate and Westgate
streets, all Roman roads. **St Michael's Tower**, the remains of an old church,
overlooks it. The main shopping area lies east of the Northgate–Southgate axis,
with the **cathedral** and the **docks** the focus of interest, to the west.

The Cathedral

The superb condition of Gloucester **Cathedral** (daily 7.30am–6pm; suggested
donation £3; $\textcircled{W}$www.gloucestercathedral.org.uk) is striking in a city that has lost
so much of its history. The Saxons founded an abbey here, and four centuries
later, Benedictine monks arrived intent on building their own church; work
began in 1089. As a place of worship it shot to importance after the murder of
King Edward II at Berkeley Castle (see p.345) in 1327: Bristol and Malmesbury
supposedly refused to take his body, but Gloucester did, and the king's shrine
became a major place of pilgrimage. The money generated helped finance the
conversion of the church into the country's first and greatest example of the
Perpendicular style, crowned by the magnificent 225-foot tower. Henry VIII
recognized the church's prestige by conferring the status of cathedral.

Beneath the fourteenth- and fifteenth-century reconstructions, some Norman
aspects remain, best seen in the **nave**, which is flanked by sturdy pillars and
arches adorned with immaculate zigzag carvings. Only when you reach the
choir and transepts can you see how skilfully the new church was built inside
the old, the Norman masonry hidden beneath the finer lines of the Perpendicular panelling and tracery. The **choir** has extraordinary fourteenth-century
misericords, and also provides the best vantage point for admiring the **east
window**, completed in around 1350 and – at almost 80 feet tall – the largest
medieval window in Britain. Beneath it, to the left (as you're facing the east
window) is the **tomb of Edward II**, immortalized in alabaster and marble. In
the nearby **Lady Chapel**, delicate carved tracery holds a staggering patchwork
of windows, a stunning cliff face of stained glass. There are well-preserved
monuments here, too, but the tomb of Robert, duke of Normandy, in the **south
ambulatory**, is far more unusual. Robert, eldest son of William the Conqueror,
died in 1134, but the painted wooden effigy dates from around 1290. Dressed
as a crusader, he lies in a curious pose, with his arms and legs crossed, his right
hand gripping his sword ready to do battle with the infidel.

The innovative nature of the cathedral's design can also be appreciated in the
beautiful **cloisters**, completed in 1367 and featuring the first fan vaulting in the
country; the intricate quality of the work is outdone only by Henry VII's Chapel
in Westminster Abbey, which it inspired. The setting was used to represent the
corridors of Hogwart's School of Witchcraft and Wizardry in the *Harry Potter*
films. Back inside, the **north transept** holds the entrance to the **treasury**
(Mon–Fri 10.30am–4pm, Sat 10.30am–3.30pm; free), containing a mixed bag of
ecclesiastical bric-a-brac, and also serves as the entrance to the **upstairs galleries**
(April–Oct same days and times; £2). Here, an exhibition gives the low-down
on the east window and allows you to view it at close quarters, whilst the
Whispering Gallery enables you to pick up the tiniest sounds from across the

vaulting. You can also climb the **tower** for outstanding views of Gloucester (Wed–Fri 2.30pm, Sat 1.30pm & 2.30pm; £3).

Westgate and Southgate streets

From the cathedral, it's a brief stroll over to **Westgate Street**, quieter and many times more pleasant than its three Roman counterparts, and another short step to **Southgate Street**, from where Greyfriars runs east to the **City Museum**, housed in a Victorian building on Brunswick Road (Tues–Sat 10am–5pm; free). The museum has a diverting archeological collection, including several prize pieces, most notably the decorative bronze Birdlip mirror dating to about 50 AD and an exquisite set of bone and antler playing pieces – the Gloucester Tables Set – bearing designs representing everything from the signs of the Zodiac to biblical stories and dating to around 1100 AD.

The Gloucester Docks

From the museum, it's about 600 yards to the **Gloucester Docks**, whose fourteen capacious **warehouses** were built for storing grain following the opening of the Sharpness canal to the River Severn in 1827. Most of these warehouses have been turned into offices and shops, but the southernmost Llanthony Warehouse is now occupied by the **National Waterways Museum** (daily 10/11am–4/5pm; £7.50, £8.50 including boat trip; Ⓦwww.nwm .org.uk), which delves into every watery nook and cranny, from the engineering of the locks to the lives of the horses that trod the towpaths. The three floors contain plenty of atmospheric noises off, videos, accessible information and interactive displays. Out from the main building you can also practise "walking the wall" in the time-honoured manner of boatmen, who propelled their narrowboats through the tunnels by their feet, and explore the boats themselves moored up along the quayside.

Eating and drinking

Gloucester is no gourmet's paradise, but you'll find reliable if undemanding fare at the **café-bar** in the Guildhall on Eastgate Street; it's open until 11pm and always lively (closed Sun & Mon). Alternatively, there are well-prepared British and European dishes at *Bearlands*, a smart **restaurant** on Longsmith Street (☎01452/419966; closed Sun & Mon), where a two-course meal will set you back £23. Or head for *Café René*, Greyfriars, 31 Southgate St (☎01452/309340), whose walls and ceilings are covered with bottles: Desperate Dan Burgers and other more substantial dishes are on the menu and the Sunday barbecues in summer are worth going out of your way for.

Gloucester's best **pubs** are all within spitting distance of The Cross. The rambling fifteenth-century *New Inn* in Northgate Street has plenty of atmosphere, a splendid galleried courtyard and inexpensive meals, but for really tasty hot food at rock-bottom prices go to the *Fountain Inn*, down a narrow alley off Westgate Street; this pub pulls a sublime pint of Abbot ale and has tables in an adjacent courtyard – ideal for a sunny day. *Café René* (see above) hosts live blues, jazz and acoustic **music** in its cellar bar (Thurs–Sun).

Painswick, Uley and Berkeley Castle

Heading south from either Cheltenham or Gloucester, most visitors thump down the M5 bound for Bristol (see p.349) and/or Bath (see p.359). En route, however, there are three prominent diversions – the elaborate shrubbery of **Painswick's Rococo Garden**, the handsome hamlet of **Uley**, and a fully-fledged castle at **Berkeley**.

Painswick

Heading south from Cheltenham on the A46, it's ten miles to the congenial, old wool town of **PAINSWICK**, where ancient buildings jostle for space on narrow streets running downhill off the busy main street. The fame of Painswick's **church** stems not so much from the building itself as from the surrounding **graveyard**, where 99 yew trees, cut into bizarre bulbous shapes resembling lollipops, surround a collection of eighteenth-century table-tombs unrivalled in the Cotswolds. However, it's the **Rococo Garden** (mid-Jan to Oct daily 11am–5pm; £5.50; ⓦ www.rococogarden.co.uk), about half a mile north up the Gloucester road – and attached to Painswick House (no access) – that ranks as the town's main attraction. Created in the early eighteenth century and later abandoned, the garden has been restored to its original form with the aid of a painting dated 1748. Although there's usually some restoration in progress, it's a beautiful example – and the country's only one – of Rococo garden design, a short-lived fashion typified by a mix of formal geometrical shapes and more naturalistic, curving lines. With a vegetable patch as an unusual centrepiece, the Painswick garden spreads across a sheltered gully – for the best vistas, walk around anticlockwise. In February and March people flock to see the snowdrops that smother the slopes beneath the pond.

Bus #46 (Mon–Sat hourly, Sun 6 daily) links Cheltenham with Painswick, where the **tourist office** is housed in the library on the main street (April–Oct Tues–Sat 10am–5pm, Sun 10am–1pm; ☏ 01452/813552, ⓦ www.painswick-pc.gov.uk). The best **hotel** is *Cardynham House* on St Mary's Street (☏ 01452/814006, ⓦ www.cardynham.co.uk; ⑨), which has themed rooms, most with four-posters and one with not only its own lounge but even a private pool. You can eat well at the *Royal Oak* **pub**, also on St Mary's Street, which has a flowery courtyard and real ales.

Uley

Beyond Painswick, the A46 slips into the humdrum market town of Stroud, once the centre of the local cloth industry. From here, the B4066 cuts a glorious route southwest along the valley ridge, passing through **ULEY**, six miles out and half a mile from the Cotswold Way. Boasting one of the best settings in the region, the village **church** lords it over the small green and the *Old Crown* pub. **Uley Bury**, among the largest hill forts in Britain, extends along the ridge above the village. The path from the church takes you up the shortest and steepest route, though motorists can opt to drive up to the car park right by the fort. Fences prevent you from clambering on top of the bury, but you can walk around the edge – a distance of about two miles altogether – and take in some staggering views. The atmosphere peaks on a winter's day, when bracing winds blow across the ridge while mist gathers in the valley below.

Berkeley

Though secluded within a swathe of meadows and gardens, **Berkeley Castle** (April–Sept Tues–Sat 11am–4pm, Sun 2–5pm; Oct Sun 2–5pm; £7.50, grounds only £4; ⓦ www.berkeley-castle.com) dominates the little village of **BERKELEY**, about nine miles from Uley on the west side of the M5.

The stronghold has a turreted medieval look, its robust twelfth-century walls softened by later accretions acquired in its gradual transformation into a family home. The interior is packed with mementoes of its long history, including its grisliest moment when, in 1327, **Edward II** was murdered here – apparently by a red-hot poker thrust into his bowels. You can view the cell where the event took place, along with dungeons, dining room, kitchen, picture gallery and the Great Hall. Outside, the grounds include an Elizabethan terraced garden.

Within easy walking distance of the castle, in the village itself, is the **Jenner Museum** (April–Sept Tues–Sat 12.30–5.30pm, Sun 1–5.30pm; Oct Sun 1–5.30pm; £4.25; Ⓦ www.jennermuseum.com), dedicated to Edward Jenner, son of a local vicar and discoverer of the principle of **vaccination**. After studying in London, he returned here to practise as a doctor and conduct his experiments; the house's garden holds the thatched hut where he treated needy locals for free.

For a lunchtime stop near Berkeley, follow the narrow High Street out of the centre of the village for about a mile to reach the *Salutation*, an unpretentious country **pub** with a garden; it serves up bacon sandwiches and the like at lunchtimes.

Travel details

Buses

For information on all local and national bus services, contact Traveline Ⓣ 0871/200 2233, Ⓦ www.traveline .org.uk.

Bedford to: Buckingham (hourly; 1hr 40min).

Buckingham to: Bedford (hourly; 1hr 40min); Oxford (hourly; 1hr 30min).

Cheltenham to: Gloucester (Mon–Sat every 15min, Sun 2 hourly; 15–40min); London (11–13 daily; 2hr 35min–3hr 20min); Painswick (Mon–Sat hourly, Sun 6 daily; 30min).

Cirencester to: Cheltenham (Mon–Sat hourly; 45min); Gloucester (Mon–Sat 5 daily; 40min–1hr); Moreton-in-Marsh (Mon–Sat every 2–3hr; 1hr); Northleach (Mon–Sat every 2–3hr).

Gloucester to: Cheltenham (Mon–Sat hourly; 15–40min); Cirencester (6 daily; 1hr 40min); London (12 daily; 3hr 20min–3hr 50min).

Great Missenden to: London (every 30min; 40min).

Henley to: London (every 30min; 45min direct or 1hr, changing at Twyford); Oxford (hourly; 50min); Reading (hourly; 20min); Wantage (hourly; 1hr 40min).

Oxford to: Buckingham (hourly; 1hr 30min); Henley (hourly; 50min); London (up to 3 hourly; 1hr

15min); Reading (every 2hr; 1hr 30min); Wantage (hourly; 1hr).

Reading to: Henley (hourly; 20min); Oxford (every 2hr; 1hr 30min).

Wantage to: Henley (hourly; 1hr 40min); Oxford (hourly; 1hr).

Trains

For information on all local and national rail services, contact National Rail Enquiries Ⓣ 0845/748 4950, Ⓦ www.nationalrail.co.uk.

Bedford to: London (1–2 hourly; 30min–1hr); Oxford (hourly; 2hr 30min); St Albans (1–2 hourly; 40min).

Cheltenham to: Bristol (3 hourly; 45min–1hr); Gloucester (2–3 hourly; 10–15min); London (every 2hr; 2hr 10min).

Gloucester to: Bristol (hourly; 50min); Cheltenham (2–3 hourly; 10–15min); London (every 2hr; 1hr 50min).

Henley to: London (every 30min with 1 or 2 changes; 1hr).

Oxford to: Bedford (hourly; 2hr 30min); Birmingham (hourly; 1hr 30min); London (1–2 hourly; 1hr).

St Albans to: Bedford (1–2 hourly; 40min); London (14 daily; 20–40min).

5

Bristol, Bath and Somerset

CHAPTER 5

Highlights

* **Clifton Suspension Bridge**
Brunel's iconic construction
soars above the impressive
Avon Gorge. See p.357

* **Building of Bath Museum**
Get to grips with how Bath
came to assume its present
appearance – a fascinating
overview of the Georgian city.
See p.367

* **Wells Cathedral** A gem of
medieval masonry, not least
for its richly ornamented west
front. See p.370

* **Cheddar Gorge** Despite
the coach parties, a truly

impressive rockscape, with
opportunities for wild walks in
the Mendips. See p.373

* **Glastonbury Abbey**
Evocative and picturesque
ruins are a fitting setting for
a complexity of Christian
legends and Arthurian myths.
See p.375

* **Quantock Hills** Follow in the
footsteps of Coleridge and
Wordsworth on the wooded
slopes of this West Somerset
range. See p.379

▲ Wells Cathedral

Bristol, Bath and Somerset

The rural allure of England's West Country is encapsulated by the undulating green swards of **Somerset**, where tidy cricket greens and well-kept country pubs contrast with wilder, more dramatic landscapes. A world away from this bucolic charm, the main city hereabouts is **Bristol**, one of the most dynamic and cosmopolitan centres outside London, with a busy go-ahead vibe. The city's dense traffic and some hideous postwar architecture are more than compensated for by the surviving traces of its long maritime history, not to mention a great selection of pubs, clubs and restaurants.

Just a few miles away, the graceful, honey-toned terraces of Georgian **Bath** combine with the city's beautifully preserved Roman baths and a vivacious cultural scene to make an unmissable stop on any itinerary. Within easy reach to the south is the exquisite cathedral city of **Wells**, and the ancient town of **Glastonbury**, steeped in Christian lore and Arthurian legend, and popular with New-Age mystics. The nearby **Mendip Hills** are pocked by cave systems, such as **Wookey Hole** and **Cheddar Gorge**, while to the west, **Bridgwater** makes a useful base for exploring the **Quantock Hills** – best experienced on foot or on saddle.

Trains from London's Paddington Station provide easy access to Bristol, Bath and Bridgwater. From these centres, a network of **bus routes** connects with all the places covered in this chapter, with the exception of the heights of the Mendip and Quantock Hills. The M4 and M5 **motorways**, which meet outside Bristol, are the main through-routes for the region.

Bristol

On the borders of Gloucestershire and Somerset, **BRISTOL** has harmoniously blended its mercantile roots with an innovative, modern culture, fuelled in recent years by technology-based industries, a lively arts and media community and a large student population. Its vibrant youth scene ensures the region's best nightlife, while daytime sights range from medieval churches to cutting-edge attractions highlighting the city's scientific achievements.

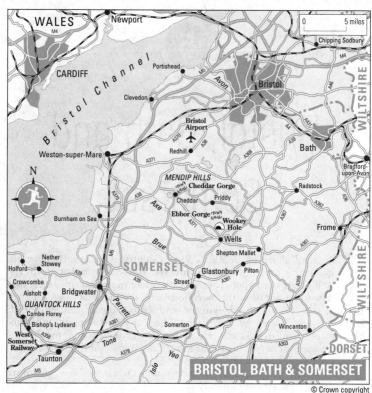

© Crown copyright

Weaving through its centre, the River Avon forms part of a system of waterways that made Bristol a great inland port, in later years booming on the transatlantic trafficking of such goods as rum, tobacco and slaves. In the nineteenth century the illustrious **Isambard Kingdom Brunel** laid the foundations of a tradition of engineering, creating two of Bristol's greatest monuments – the SS *Great Britain* and the lofty Clifton Suspension Bridge. More recently, spin-offs from the aerospace industry have placed the city at the forefront of the fields of communications, computing, design and finance.

Arrival, information and accommodation

Twice-hourly **trains** from London Paddington arrive at Bristol Temple Meads, a twenty-minute walk from the centre and served by frequent buses (#8, #8A and #9), which pass through the city centre on their way to Clifton. Alternatively, from behind the train station you can make use of the cycle-way linking Temple Meads with the SS *Great Britain* (taking in St Mary Redcliffe and Queen Square), or the river ferry that leaves for the centre every forty minutes (see p.357). The **bus station** in Marlborough Street has regular services from London with Bakers Dolphin, which also stop in Clifton, and National Express; Megabus services from London stop opposite Colston Hall, off The Centre – the name given to the busy traffic intersection at the heart of the modern city, where most local buses stop. **Bristol International Airport** is at Lulsgate, eight miles southwest of town on the A38 (℡0871/334 4444, Ⓦwww .bristolairport.co.uk); it is connected by bus to the train and bus stations, with services leaving every twenty minutes.

The main **tourist office** is in the at-Bristol complex, in the Explore foyer, Harbourside (Mon–Fri during school terms 10am–5pm, Sat, Sun & daily in school hols 10am–6pm; ℡0906/711 2191, Ⓦwww.visitbristol.co.uk), and offers an **accommodation** booking service (℡0845/408 0474; £3). There are also information desks in City Museum and Art Gallery, the British Empire and Commonwealth Museum, and in the Broadmead shopping centre.

Hotels and B&Bs

Arches 132 Cotham Brow ℡0117/924 7398, Ⓦwww.arches-hotel.co.uk. In an attractive area of town, accessible on bus #9 from the centre, this eco-friendly place has small but comfortable rooms with or without bath, and vegan or vegetarian breakfasts only. ❸

Downs View 38 Upper Belgrave Rd ℡0117/973 7046, Ⓦwww.downsviewguesthouse.co.uk. As the name implies, this B&B enjoys a good vista over Clifton Downs, though the views over the city from the back are even better. The cheaper rooms have shared bathrooms. ❸

Hotel du Vin Narrow Lewins Mead ℡0117/925 5577, Ⓦwww.hotelduvin.co.uk. Chic, warehouse conversion, centrally located, with solid comforts, contemporary decor and first-class food and wine. ❼

Victoria Square Victoria Square ℡0117/973 9058, Ⓦwww.vicsquare.com. With a choice location near Clifton Village, this Georgian hotel has smart, light rooms, though some are on the small side. Breakfast is taken overlooking the leafy square. Rates are higher on weekdays. ❺–❻

Walkabout St Nicholas Court, St Nicholas St ℡0117/945 9699, Ⓦwww.walkabout.eu.com.

Functional, no-frills hotel, cramped but clean, with all rooms en suite. The location in the heart of the pubs/clubs district makes for noisy weekends. No single rooms but some triples. Breakfast not included. ❷

Hostels and campsite

Bristol Backpackers 17 St Stephen's St ℡0117/925 7900, Ⓦwww.bristolbackpackers .co.uk. Friendly hostel in a handsome old building, with clothes-washing facilities, first-class showers and a late bar. Kitchen and cheap Internet access too, but the area can be noisy. Dorm beds £14. ❶

Bristol YHA Hayman House, 14 Narrow Quay ℡0870/770 5726, Ⓔbristol@yha.org.uk. Located in a refurbished warehouse on the quayside; most dorms have four beds (from £23, including breakfast). Kitchen, laundry, games room and bike storage available, and 24hr access. ❷

Brook Lodge Farm Cowslip Green, Redhill ℡01934/862311, Ⓦwww.brooklodgefarm.com. Nine miles southwest of Bristol, this is the nearest rural campsite to town, a mile southwest of the village of Redhill off the A38. Bikes can be rented, and there's an outdoor pool in summer. Closed for tents Nov–Feb.

The City

Once a quay-lined dock but now the traffic-ridden nucleus of the city, **The Centre** makes a good place to kick off an exploration of Bristol, just a few steps from the cathedral and the oldest quarter of town. At its southern end is a branch of the Floating Harbour, the waterway network that links up with the River Avon. You could cover Bristol's other central attractions on foot without too much sweat, but there are enough steep hills to make it worthwhile using the bus network for more distant sights, especially in the Clifton district, at the highest part of town, on the edge of the Avon Gorge.

College Green: the cathedral and Lord Mayor's Chapel

A short walk west of The Centre, the grassy expanse of **College Green** is dominated by the crescent-shaped Council House, which dates from 1956, and the contrasting medieval lines of **Bristol Cathedral** (daily 8am–5pm;

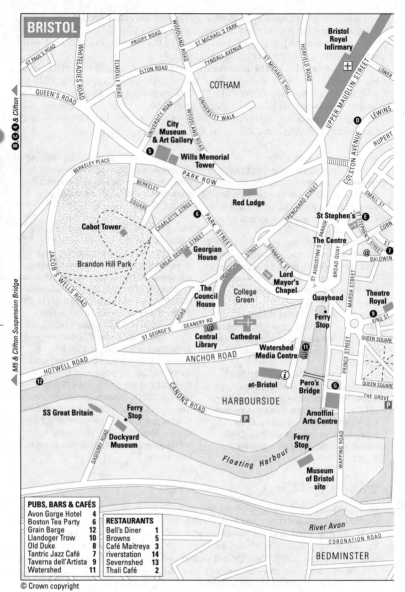

BRISTOL

COTHAM

Bristol Royal Infirmary

City Museum & Art Gallery **5**

Wills Memorial Tower

Red Lodge

Cabot Tower

Brandon Hill Park

Georgian House

6

St Stephen's **E**

The Centre

Lord Mayor's Chapel

The Council House

College Green

Quayhead

Theatre Royal

9

7

Central Library

Cathedral

Ferry Stop

Watershed Media Centre **11**

at-Bristol

Pero's Bridge **G**

HARBOURSIDE

SS Great Britain

Ferry Stop

Arnolfini Arts Centre

Dockyard Museum

Ferry Stop

Museum of Bristol site

Floating Harbour

12

River Avon

CORONATION ROAD

BEDMINSTER

PUBS, BARS & CAFÉS	
Avon Gorge Hotel	4
Boston Tea Party	6
Grain Barge	12
Llandoger Trow	10
Old Duke	8
Tantric Jazz Café	7
Taverna dell'Artista	9
Watershed	11

RESTAURANTS	
Bell's Diner	1
Browns	5
Café Maitreya	3
riverstation	14
Severnshed	13
Thali Café	2

© Crown copyright

Ⓦwww.bristol-cathedral.co.uk). Founded around 1140 as an abbey on the supposed spot of St Augustine's convocation with Celtic Christians in 603, this became a cathedral church with the Dissolution of the Monasteries. Among the many additions in subsequent centuries are the two towers on the west front, erected in the nineteenth century in a faithful act of homage to Edmund Knowle, architect and abbot of the cathedral at the start of the fourteenth

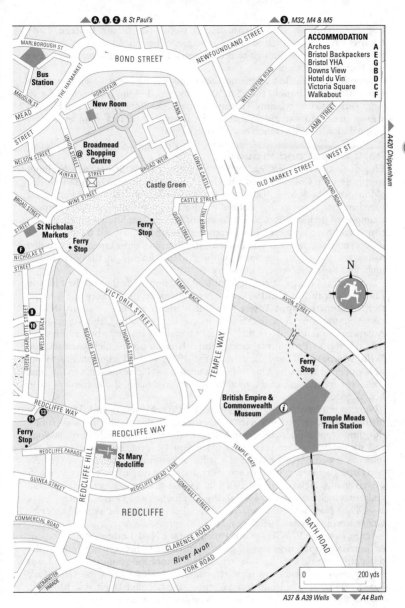

ACCOMMODATION

Arches	A
Bristol Backpackers	E
Bristol YHA	G
Downs View	B
Hotel du Vin	D
Victoria Square	C
Walkabout	F

▲ A420 Chippenham

MARLBOROUGH ST

BOND STREET

NEWFOUNDLAND STREET

Bus
Station

THE HAYMARKET

HORSEFAIR

WELLINGTON ROAD

MAUDLIN ST

MEAD
STREET

New Room

LAMB STREET

WEST ST

PENN ST

Broadmead
@ Shopping
Centre

UNION STREET

STREET

NELSON STREET

FAIRFAX

STREET

BROAD WEIR

LOWER CASTLE

OLD MARKET STREET

MIDLAND ROAD

BROAD STREET

WINE STREET

Castle Green

CASTLE STREET

St Nicholas
Markets

NICHOLAS ST

STREET

Ferry
Stop

Ferry
Stop

CASTLE HILL

QUEEN STREET

TOWER HILL

F

VICTORIA STREET

TEMPLE BACK

AVON STREET

N

QUEEN CHARLOTTE STREET

WELSH BACK

REDCLIFFE STREET

ST THOMAS STREET

TEMPLE WAY

Ferry
Stop

8

10

REDCLIFFE WAY

14 13

British Empire &
Commonwealth
Museum (i)

Temple Meads
Train Station

Ferry
Stop

REDCLIFFE WAY

REDCLIFFE HILL

REDCLIFFE PARADE

St Mary
Redcliffe

REDCLIFFE MEAD LANE

SOMERSET STREET

TEMPLE GATE

GUINEA STREET

BATH ROAD

COMMERCIAL ROAD

REDCLIFFE

CLARENCE ROAD

River Avon

YORK ROAD

BEDMINSTER PARADE

0		200 yds

century. The cathedral's interior offers a unique example among Britain's cathedrals of a German-style "hall church", in which the aisles, nave and choir rise to the same height. Abbot Knowle's **choir** offers one of the country's most exquisite illustrations of the early Decorated style of Gothic, while the adjoining **Elder Lady Chapel**, dating from the early thirteenth century, contains some fine tombs and eccentric carvings of animals, including a monkey playing the bagpipes accompanied by a ram on the violin. The ornate **Eastern Lady Chapel** has some of England's finest examples of heraldic glass. From the south transept, a door leads through to the **Chapter House**, a richly carved piece of late Norman architecture.

Opposite the cathedral, on the northeast side of the green, take a glance at the **Lord Mayor's Chapel** (Tues–Sat 10am–noon & 1–4pm), conspicuous by its large Perpendicular window. The interior has some lovely French and Flemish stained glass, and striking effigies of the thirteenth-century founders of the hospital of which the church once formed a part.

Park Street and around

Elegant Georgian streets lead off the shop-lined **Park Street**, which climbs steeply up from College Green. On Great George Street, the **Georgian House** (Mon–Wed, Sat & Sun 10am–5pm; free), is the former home of a local sugar merchant, its spacious and faithfully restored rooms filled with sumptuous examples of period furniture. The basement kitchens are fitted with equipment that would have been used in the early eighteenth century, and there's even an indoor pool, or rather a plunge bath, for morning dips. Upstairs, illustrated panels tell the engrossing story of the family's dealings in the West Indies, including their involvement in slavery.

From Great George Street, or from Berkeley Square further up the hill, you can access **Brandon Hill Park**, a sequestered pocket of greenery that is home to the landmark **Cabot Tower** (open daily until dusk; free), built in 1897 to commemorate the four-hundredth anniversary of John Cabot's voyage to America. You can climb up the 105-foot tower for the city's best panorama.

At the top of Park Street stands central Bristol's other chief landmark, the **Wills Memorial Tower**, erected in the 1920s to lend some stature to the newly opened university. One of the last great neo-Gothic buildings in England, the tower was the gift of the local Wills tobacco dynasty, the university's main benefactors.

Next to the tower, on Queen's Road, the **City Museum and Art Gallery** (daily 10am–5pm; free) occupies another building donated by the Wills family, this time Neoclassical. The ground-floor sections on local archeology, geology and natural history are pretty well what you'd expect, but the scope of the museum is occasionally surprising – it has an important collection of Chinese porcelain, glassware, stoneware and ivory, and some magnificent Assyrian reliefs carved in the eighth century BC. The second-floor gallery of paintings and sculptures includes work by English Pre-Raphaelites and French Impressionists, as well as a few choice older pieces, among them a portrait of Martin Luther by Cranach and Giovanni Bellini's unusual *Descent into Limbo*.

Across from the Wills Tower, on Park Row, the **Red Lodge** (Mon–Wed, Sat & Sun 10am–5pm; free) was originally a merchant's home when built in the sixteenth century, later became a finishing school for young ladies, and was subsequently England's first girls' reform school. Highlight is the Great Oak Room, featuring a splendid carved stone fireplace and lavish oak panelling. Behind the house, an Elizabethan knot-garden (an intricate, formal garden) has been recreated.

From The Centre to Broadmead

One of Bristol's oldest churches, **St Stephen's**, stands at the northern end of The Centre. Established in the thirteenth century, rebuilt in the fifteenth and thoroughly restored with plenty of Neo-Gothic trimmings in 1875, the parish church has some flamboyant tombs inside, mainly of various

The slave trade in Bristol

The statue of Edward Colston that stands in Bristol's Centre has more than once been the subject of graffiti attacks and calls for its removal. Although the eighteenth-century sugar magnate is known and revered as a great philanthropist – his name given to numerous buildings, streets and schools in Bristol – he is reviled by many as a leading light in the London-based Royal African Company, which held the monopoly on the **slave trade** until the market was opened in 1698. From that date until the abolition of the British slave trade in 1807, merchants throughout the country were able to participate in the "triangular trade" whereby vast numbers of slaves were shipped from West Africa to plantations in the Americas, the vessels returning to Europe with cargoes of sugar, cotton, tobacco and other slave-produced commodities. By the 1730s, Bristol, a leading transatlantic port, had become, along with London and Liverpool, one of the main beneficiaries of the trade, sending out a total of more than two thousand ships in search of slaves on the African coast; in 1750 alone, Bristol ships transported some eight thousand of the twenty thousand slaves sent that year to British colonies in the Caribbean and North America. The direct profits, together with the numerous spin-offs, helped to finance some of the city's finest Georgian architecture.

Bristol's primacy in the trade had already been long supplanted by Liverpool by the time opposition to the trade began to gather force: first the Quakers and Methodists, then more powerful forces voiced their discontent. By the 1780s the Anglican Dean Josiah Tucker and the Evangelical writer Hannah More had become active abolitionists, and Samuel Taylor Coleridge made a famous anti-slavery speech in Bristol in 1795.

Today, Bristol's Caribbean link is maintained by an active West Indian population largely concentrated in the St Paul's district – scene of a flamboyant carnival in early July. To learn more about the city's involvement in the slave trade, visit the small but informative exhibitions at the Georgian House (see opposite) and the British Empire and Commonwealth Museum (see p.357).

members of the merchant class who were the church's main patrons. Especially striking are those of Justice Snygge and Edmund Blanket, a fourteenth-century cloth merchant.

On nearby **Corn Street**, in the city's financial quarter, you'll find the Georgian Corn Exchange, designed by John Wood of Bath, and now holding the covered **St Nicholas markets**, good for all kinds of bric-à-brac as well as delis, cafés and juice bars. Outside the entrance stand four engraved bronze pillars, dating from the sixteenth and seventeenth centuries and transferred from a nearby arcade where they served as trading tables – thought to be the "nails" from which the expression "pay on the nail" is derived.

The area north of here holds the extensive, partly pedestrianized shopping centre of **Broadmead**, laid out on the ruins left by bombing in World War II. One older building miraculously survived the devastation however – the **New Room** (Mon–Sat 10am–4pm; free), accessible from both the central strip of Broadmead and from the Horsefair, to the north. Established by John Wesley in 1739, this was the country's first Methodist chapel, and today looks very much as Wesley left it, with a double-deck pulpit beneath a hidden upstairs window, from which the evangelist could observe the progress of his trainee preachers. Tours of the chapel and some of the rooms used by Wesley and his acolytes are available by prior arrangement (☎0117/926 4740, ⑯www.newroombristol .org.uk; £4), and include an entertaining introduction by an actor kitted out in Wesleyan garb.

King Street and Queen Square

King Street, a short walk southeast from The Centre, was laid out in 1633 and still holds some fine seventeenth- and eighteenth-century buildings, among them the **Theatre Royal**, the oldest working theatre in the country. Opened in 1766 and preserving many of its original Georgian features, the theatre hosted most of the famous names of its time, including Sarah Siddons, whose ghost is said to stalk the building.

Past the theatre, in a very different architectural style, the timber-framed **Llandoger Trow** pub derives its name from the flat-bottomed boats that were used to trade between Bristol and the Welsh coast. Traditionally the haunt of seafarers, it is reputed to have been the meeting place of Daniel Defoe and Alexander Selkirk, the model for Robinson Crusoe. The area around here bristles with pubs, restaurants and nightclubs, getting pretty lively at weekends and on summer evenings.

South of King Street, **Queen Square** is an elegant grassy area with a statue of William III by Rysbrack at its centre, reckoned to be the best equestrian statue in the country. The square was the site of some of the worst civil disturbances ever seen in England when the Bristolians rioted in support of the Reform Bill of 1832, burning houses on two sides of the square; among the surviving buildings was no. 37, where the first American consulate was established in 1792.

St Mary Redcliffe and the British Empire and Commonwealth Museum

The southeast corner of Queen Square leads to Redcliffe Bridge and the Redcliffe district, where the spire of **St Mary Redcliffe** (Mon–Sat 8.30/9am–4/5pm, Sun 8am–7.30pm) provides one of the distinctive features of the city's skyline. Described by Elizabeth I as "the goodliest, fairest, and most famous parish church in England", the church was largely paid for and used by merchants and mariners who prayed here for a safe voyage. The present building was begun at the end of the thirteenth century, though it was added to in subsequent centuries and the spire was constructed in 1872. Inside, memorials and tombs recall some of the figures associated with the building, including the arms and armour of Sir William Penn, admiral and father of the founder of Pennsylvania, on the north wall of the nave, and the Handel Window in the North Choir aisle, installed in 1859 on the centenary of the death of Handel, who composed on the organ here. The whale bone above the entrance to the Chapel of St John the Baptist is thought to have been brought back from Newfoundland by John Cabot. The poets Samuel Taylor Coleridge and Robert Southey were both married in St Mary, within six weeks of each other in 1795.

Above the church's north porch is the muniment room, where **Thomas Chatterton** claimed to have found a trove of medieval manuscripts; the poems, distributed as the work of a fifteenth-century monk named Thomas Rowley, were in fact dazzling fakes. The young poet committed suicide when his forgery was exposed, thereby supplying English literature with one of its most glamorous stories of self-destructive genius. The "Marvellous Boy" is remembered by a memorial stone in the south transept, and there is another one to his family, who were long associated with the church, in the churchyard.

A few minutes' walk away, Bristol's **Old Station** stands outside Temple Meads Station, the original terminus of the Great Western Railway linking London and Bristol. The terminus, like the line itself, was designed by Brunel in 1840, and was the first great piece of railway architecture. Part of the original building now houses the absorbing **British Empire and Commonwealth Museum** (daily 10am–5pm; £7.95), which focuses on the history of the empire and the Commonwealth that succeeded it, covering trade, slavery, and various of the cultures which it encompassed. Film, photographs and sound recordings help to fill out the picture, and there are exhibitions throughout the year on such themes as aboriginal art.

at-Bristol and the SS Great Britain

At the southern end of The Centre, **St Augustine's Reach**, part of the Floating Harbour, is flanked by pubs, clubs, and the **Arnolfini** and **Watershed** arts centres, both housed in refurbished Victorian warehouses and the venues for exhibitions and art-house films. Opposite the Arnolfini is the site for the new Museum of Bristol, due to open in 2010. There's a stop at the Quayhead for the **ferry service** that connects the various parts of the Floating Harbour including Temple Meads station, leaving every forty minutes (10.30am–5.50pm; £1.50 one way; £4.80 forty-minute return; £7 all-day ticket; ☎0117/927 3416, ⓦwww.bristolferry.com).

South and west of the Watershed, off Anchor Road, Bristol's Harbourside is the home of **at-Bristol** (daily: Mon–Fri during school terms 10am–5pm; Sat, Sun & school hols 10am–6pm; last entry 1hr before closing; £9), made up of two main attractions: Explore, an interactive science centre, and a planetarium. Although chiefly aimed at families and schoolkids, there's enough at **Explore** to occupy everyone for two or three hours, with plenty of hands-on, multi-media activities and general scientific wizardry. The spherical, stainless-steel **planetarium** has shows every 45 minutes (11am–2pm on weekdays during school terms, 11am–5pm on weekends & school hols), which should be booked when you buy your Explore tickets.

A quick ride on the ferry west, or a ten-minute walk, is one of Bristol's iconic sights, the **SS Great Britain** (daily 10am–4.30/6pm; last entry 1hr before closing; £10.50, including entry to the *Matthew* and the Dockyard Museum). Built in 1843 by Brunel, the SS *Great Britain* was the first propeller-driven, ocean-going iron ship, used initially between Liverpool and New York, then between Liverpool and Melbourne, circumnavigating the globe 32 times over a period of 26 years. Her ocean-going days ended in 1886 when she was caught in a storm off Cape Horn, and abandoned in the Falkland Islands. Salvaged from there and returned to Bristol in 1970, she is now berthed in the same dry dock in which she was built. Visitors can peer into the immense engine room, and see the cabins that have already been restored, their bunks occupied by eerily breathing mannequins. The adjacent **Dockyard Museum** fills in the background and history of the vessel, while alongside the ship is moored a much smaller affair: a replica of the **Matthew**, the vessel in which John Cabot sailed to America in 1497, rebuilt in time for the voyage to be re-enacted on the 500th anniversary.

Clifton

North and west of the Wills Tower (see p.354) extends **Clifton**, once an aloof spa resort and now Bristol's most elegant quarter. Clifton Village, its select enclave, is centred on the Mall, close to **Royal York Crescent**, the longest Georgian crescent in the country, offering splendid views over the steep drop to the River Avon below.

A few minutes' walk behind the Crescent is Bristol's most famous symbol, **Clifton Suspension Bridge**, 702-foot long and poised 245ft above high water. Money was first put forward for a bridge to span the Avon Gorge by a Bristol wine merchant in 1753, though it was not until 1829 that a competition was held for a design, won by Isambard Brunel on a second round, and not until 1864 that the bridge was completed, five years after Brunel's death. Hampered by financial difficulties, the bridge never quite matched the engineer's original ambitious design, which included Egyptian-style towers topped by sphinxes on each end. The original drawings of Brunel's designs are in the university's Brunel Collection and can be viewed on application, or you can see copies in the temporary **Visitor Centre**, located at the far side of the bridge (daily 10am–5pm; free), alongside other designs proposed by Brunel's rivals, some of them frankly bizarre.

Just above the bridge in Clifton, a small **Observatory** sits on an arm of **Clifton Downs** overlooking the gorge, and contains a working camera obscura (summer daily 10.30am–5.30pm; winter Sat & Sun 10.30am–5.30pm or dusk; £2). You can also buy a ticket (£2) for the 190-foot tunnel leading from here to the "Giant's Cave" set in the cliffs overlooking the gorge; it housed a Roman Catholic chapel in the fifteenth century. Both attractions may be closed in bad weather, however – check at ☎0117/974 1242. Adjoining the downs is **Bristol Zoo** (daily 9am–5/5.30pm; £11.50), renowned for its animal conservation work, and also featuring a collection of rare trees and shrubs.

Eating, drinking and nightlife

Bristol's numerous **pubs** and **restaurants** are nearly always buzzing – especially those around King Street and Corn Street. Nightlife is equally lively; for a full list of **clubs**, pick up a copy of *Venue*, the Bristol and Bath weekly listings magazine (£1.50), or consult the website ⓦwww.whatsonbristol.co.uk for details of events.

Restaurants

Bell's Diner 1 York Rd ☎0117/924 0357. In the villagey Montpelier quarter (10min from the bus station up Stokes Croft), this corner bistro offers a contemporary, inventive menu with award-winning food. Main dishes à la carte cost £15–20, and there's a tasting menu for £45. Closed Sun.

Browns 38 Queen's Rd ☎0117/930 4777. Spacious and relaxed place for breakfast, a late cocktail, seafood platter (£7.75) or superior burger (£9.75); it's housed in the former university refectory, a Venetian-style structure next to the City Museum.

Café Maitreya 89 St Mark's Rd ☎0117/951 0100. Tucked away in the multicultural Easton neighbourhood (bus #48/49 from Centre), this easy-going place is rated one of the country's best vegetarian restaurants, with a constantly changing menu of innovative dishes. Set menus are £17.50 and £21. Closed daytime and all Sun & Mon.

riverstation The Grove ☎0117/914 4434. A former river-police station artfully transformed, with the downstairs *Bar Kitchen* serving deli-type snacks and drinks (some tables on an outdoor deck), and a more formal upstairs restaurant offering Modern European dishes. Set lunches here cost £12 or £14.50, while main courses in the

evening are £14–19. Try to bag a table by the window for the dockside views.

Severnshed The Grove ☎0117/925 1212. Right next to *riverstation* with a waterside terrace, this serves light, tasty food, ranging from fish and chips "with Yorkshire caviar" (mushy peas) to vegetarian risotto. Two-course meals are offered for under £10 (Mon–Sat noon–3pm & 6–7pm).

Thali Café 12 York Rd ☎0117/942 6687. Dhaba-style Asian food in vibrant surroundings in the heart of Montpelier. There's not much choice: a combination of spicy dishes are served on a steel plate (around £7). Live acoustic music on Sun eve. Closed Mon.

Pubs, bars and cafés

Avon Gorge Hotel Sion Hill. On the edge of the Gorge in Clifton Village, the mediocre bar is compensated for by a broad terrace with magnificent views. Meals available.

Boston Tea Party 75 Park St. Cosy place in the centre of town for teas and coffees as well as soups and pies, with seating on two floors and a heated terrace garden.

Grain Barge Hotwell Rd. A floating pub, café and restaurant with a tranquil ambience, real ales and regular live music on Fri eves.

Llandoger Trow King St. Seventeenth-century tavern full of historical resonance (see p.356), with cosy nooks and armchairs.

Old Duke King St. Jolly, trad jazz pub with live bands nightly and lunchtime on Sun, and tables outside.

Tantric Jazz Café 39–41 St Nicholas St. Relaxed place that serves drinks and Mediterranean-style meals in the evenings, when there are live jazz and blues performances until late.

Taverna dell'Artista King St. A haunt of theatrical folk as well as a rowdy bunch of regulars, this Anglo-Italian dive offers wines, beers and pizzas until 2am. Closed daytime and all Sun & Mon.

Watershed St Augustine's Reach. A great bar and café in the arts complex overlooking the boats, with food available until 10pm (7pm on Sun). Free Internet access.

Venues and clubs

The Academy Frogmore St ☎0905/020 3999, ⓦwww.bristol-academy.co.uk. Near The Centre, this spacious, multi-level place stages almost nightly live gigs as well as club nights. Thurs is student night.

Bierkeller All Saints St, off Broadmead ☎0117/926 8514, ⓦwww.bristolbierkeller.co.uk. Live music from thrash metal to revival bands in this sweaty cellar venue. Live oompah band on Sat.

Blue Mountain 2 Stokes Croft ☎0117/924 6666. Excellent non-mainstream club with a relaxed feel, and stonking funk, hip-hop and drum'n'bass.

Colston Hall Colston Ave ☎0117/922 3686, ⓦwww.colstonhall.org. Major names appear in this stalwart of mainstream venues. Most of the events in the classical Proms Festival, at the end of May, take place here.

Fiddlers Willway St, Bedminster ☎0117/987 3403, ⓦwww.fiddlers.co.uk. Mainly folk, ska and world bands at this relaxed live music venue on the south side of the river, off Bedminster Parade.

The Fleece 12 St Thomas St ☎0117/945 0996, ⓦwww.fleecegig.co.uk. Stone-flagged ex-wool warehouse, now a loud and sweaty pub putting on live rock and tribute bands most nights.

St George's Great George St ☎0845/402 4001, ⓦwww.stgeorgesbristol.co.uk. This elegant Georgian church with near-perfect acoustics has regular lunchtime and evening concerts of classical, world and jazz music.

Thekla The Grove ☎0117/929 3301, ⓦwww.theklabristol.co.uk. Riverboat venue popular with students, staging regular live bands plus dub, funky house and indie club nights.

Vibes 3 Frog Lane, off Frogmore St ☎0117/934 9076, ⓦvibesbristol.co.uk. Lively gay club with comfy seating and a second dance space and bar open on Sat.

Listings

Bike rental Blackboy Hill Cycles, 180 Whiteladies Rd, Clifton ☎0117/973 1420.

Buses Local services ☎0845/602 0156, ⓦwww.firstgroup.com. In addition to National Express and Megabus (see p.34) services to London are run by Bakers Dolphin (☎01934/413000).

Car rental Avis, Rupert St ☎0870/608 6325 and airport ☎0870/608 6324; Speedway, 654 Fishponds Rd ☎0117/965 5555.

Hospital Bristol Royal Infirmary, Marlborough St ☎0117/923 0000.

Internet Free access at the Central Library, College Green (Mon, Tues & Thurs 9.30am–7.30pm, Wed 10am–5pm, Fri & Sat 9.30am–5pm, Sun 1–5pm; book at ☎0117/903 7234) and the Watershed, St Augustine's Reach (daily roughly 9.30am–11pm).

Police Rupert St ☎0845/456 7000.

Post office The Galleries, Wine St

Taxis Ranks at train and bus stations, and in The Centre. Call ☎0117/965 5999 or ☎0117/955 8558.

Bath

Though only twelve miles from Bristol, **BATH** has a very different feel from its neighbour – more harmonious, compact, leisurely and complacent. Jane Austen set *Persuasion* and *Northanger Abbey* here, it is where Gainsborough established himself as a portraitist and landscape painter, and the city's elegant crescents and Georgian buildings are studded with plaques naming Bath's eminent inhabitants from its heyday as a spa resort. Nowadays Bath ranks as one of Britain's top tourist cities – the Roman Baths are the busiest fee-charging

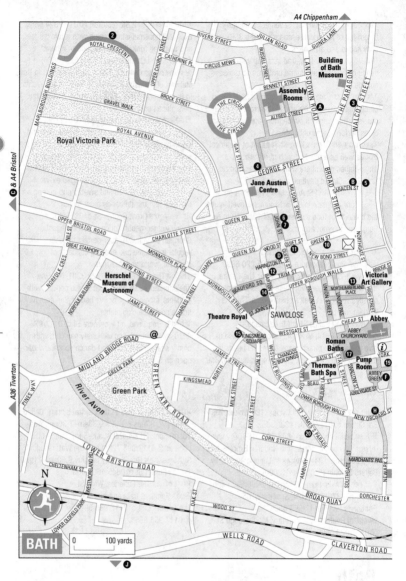

historic site outside London – yet the place has never lost the exclusive air those names evoke.

Bath owes its name and fame to its **hot springs** – the only ones in the country – which made it a place of reverence for the local Celtic population, though it had to wait for Roman technology to create a fully-fledged bathing establishment. The baths fell into decline with the departure of the Romans, but the town later regained its importance under the Saxons, its abbey seeing the coronation of the first king of all England, Edgar, in 973.

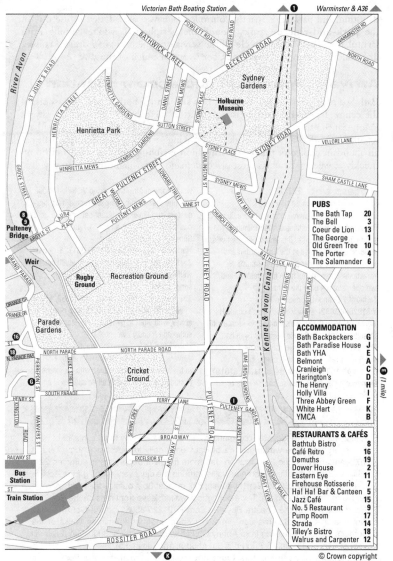

PUBS

The Bath Tap	20
The Bell	3
Coeur de Lion	13
The George	1
Old Green Tree	10
The Porter	4
The Salamander	6

ACCOMMODATION

Bath Backpackers	G
Bath Paradise House	J
Bath YHA	E
Belmont	A
Cranleigh	C
Harington's	D
The Henry	H
Holly Villa	I
Three Abbey Green	F
White Hart	K
YMCA	B

RESTAURANTS & CAFÉS

Bathtub Bistro	8
Café Retro	16
Demuths	19
Dower House	2
Eastern Eye	11
Firehouse Rotisserie	7
Ha! Ha! Bar & Canteen	5
Jazz Café	15
No. 5 Restaurant	9
Pump Room	17
Strada	14
Tilley's Bistro	18
Walrus and Carpenter	12

A new bathing complex was built in the sixteenth century, popularized by the visit of Elizabeth I in 1574, and the city reached its fashionable zenith in the eighteenth century, when **Beau Nash** ruled the town's social scene. It was at this time that Bath acquired its ranks of Palladian mansions and town houses, all of them built in the local **Bath stone**, which is still the city's leitmotif today.

The acres of parkland between the Georgian developments lend modern Bath a spacious feel, with theatrical vistas at every turn. The traffic, however, can be daunting, and parking is strictly controlled – drivers are advised to use one of the **park-and-ride** car parks around the periphery. If you're coming from Bristol, note that you can **cycle** all the way along the route of a disused railway line, following the course of the River Avon for much of the way.

Arrival, information and accommodation

Bath Spa **train station** and the city's **bus station** are both a short walk south of the centre. The **tourist office** is right next to the abbey on Abbey Churchyard (Mon–Sat 9.30am–5/6pm, Sun 10am–4pm; ☎0906/711 2000, ⓦwww.visitbath .co.uk), and offers an accommodation booking service (£3). Although Bath has an abundant choice of **places to stay**, most establishments are small and fill up quickly at weekends, when most places demand a two-night minimum stay.

Hotels and B&Bs

Bath Paradise House 88 Holloway ☎01225/317723, ⓦwww.paradise-house.co.uk. The wonderful view justifies the ten-minute uphill trudge from the centre to this lovely Georgian villa, while croquet or boules in the lush garden and open fires in the winter provide alternative attractions. Three rooms have four-posters, and two open straight onto the garden. ❼

Belmont 7 Belmont, Lansdown Rd ☎01225/423082, ⓦwww.belmontbath.co.uk. Huge rooms – though the single's a bit poky – some with en-suite shower, in a house designed by John Wood, very near to the Assembly Rooms, Circus and Royal Crescent. No credit cards. ❷

Cranleigh 159 Newbridge Hill ☎01225/310197, ⓦwww.cranleighguesthouse.com. A mile or so

west of the centre, this period Victorian house has fine views from the back rooms, two four-posters and seven breakfast options. The garden has a hot tub. Buses #17, #319 and #332 (#632 Sun). ❺

Harington's Queen St ☎01225/461728, ⓦwww .haringtons.co.uk. Very central hotel with small but well-equipped and quiet rooms, and friendly service. ❼

The Henry 6 Henry St ☎01225/424052, ⓦwww .thehenry.com. Excellent guest house close to the abbey, with eight large rooms (doubles are en suite) and friendly owners. ❺

Holly Villa 14 Pulteney Gardens ☎01225/310331, ⓦwww.hollyvilla.com. Neat and friendly B&B, close to the Kennet and Avon Canal, with six rooms (including a triple), nearly all en suite, and a small,

---

Tours in and around Bath

A tour with a knowledgeable commentary can be the best way to take in a lot of Bath in a short time. Free **walking tours** of Bath leave daily from Abbey Church Yard at 10.30am and 2pm (no 2pm tour on Sat; more frequent departures in summer; 2hr), while Bizarre Bath offers "comedy walks" around the city every evening from April to September (☎01225/335124; 1hr 30min; £7); meet at 8pm outside the *Huntsman Inn* on North Parade Passage). Two-hour "ghost walks" leave from outside the *Garrick's Head* pub next to the Theatre Royal at 8pm (☎01225/350512; April–Oct Mon–Sat, Nov–March Sun; £6;). The Jane Austen Centre arranges 90-minute walks in the author's footsteps, leaving from Abbey Church Yard (☎01225/443000; Sat & Sun all year at 11pm, also July & Aug Fri & Sat at 6pm; 1hr 30min; £5).

A plethora of open-top **bus tours** are available all year, leaving from Grand Parade or the bus station (all-day tickets about £10). Between Easter and October, various **river trips** can be made from Pulteney Bridge and weir (one-hour trips about £6), and there are cruises on the Kennet and Avon Canal from Sydney Wharf, near Bathwick Bridge.

Outside Bath, Mad Max Tours offers half- or full-day minibus **excursions** to Lacock, the pretty village of Castle Combe, Stonehenge, Avebury and the Cotswolds (☎07990/505970, ⓦwww.madmaxtours.co.uk; £15–30), while Scarper Tours conducts afternoon tours to Stonehenge (☎07739/644155, ⓦwww.scarpertours.com; £12.50).

flower-filled front garden. Closed 2 weeks in March & in Nov. No credit cards. ❸

🏃 **Three Abbey Green** 3 Abbey Green ☎01225/428558, ⓦwww.threeabbeygreen .com. Top-class B&B in a beautifully renovated Georgian house just steps from the abbey. The airy rooms are Wi-Fi-enabled; the more spacious ones overlooking a peaceful square are in a higher price category. ❺

Hostels and campsite

Bath Backpackers 13 Pierrepoint St ☎01225/446787, ⓦwww.hostels.co.uk. Aussie-run place right in the centre of things. There's no curfew, no lockout, a kitchen, Internet access and a "party dungeon". Breakfast is included in the price. Beds in 4–10-bed dorms cost £14–18.

Bath YHA Bathwick Hill ☎0870/770 5688, ℮bath@yha.org.uk. An Italianate mansion a mile from the centre, with gardens and panoramic views. Dorm beds (from £12.50 each) and double

rooms available, also evening meals. Buses #18, #410 or #418 from the bus station. ❶

Newton Mill Touring Centre ☎01225/333909, ⓦwww.campinginbath.co.uk. The nearest campsite, three miles west of the centre at Newton St Loe (bus #5 to Newton Mill), with the Bristol–Bath cycleway nearby. The site has a laundry, bar/restaurant, shop and hot showers.

🏃 **White Hart** Widcombe Hill, a ten-minute walk from the train station ☎01225/313985, ⓦwww.whitehartbath.co.uk. The comfiest of Bath's hostels has a kitchen, a first-class restaurant and a sunny courtyard. Dorm beds are £15, and a range of neat doubles and twins are available. Midnight curfew. ❷

YMCA International House, Broad St ☎01225/325900, ⓦwww.bathymca.co.uk. Clean and central, with lots of room, this place charges £13–15 for dorm beds, £25–29 for singles and £38–46 for doubles, with reductions for weekly stays; all prices include breakfast (but there's no kitchen). ❶–❷

The City

Although Bath could easily be seen on a day-trip from Bristol, it really deserves a stay of a couple of days. The city itself is chock-full of museums, but some of the greatest enjoyment comes simply from wandering the streets, with their pale gold architecture and sweeping vistas. With limited time you might consider viewing these on a walking or open-top bus tour (see box opposite).

The Roman Baths

Bath's focal point is the pedestrianized Abbey Church Yard, two interlocking squares usually milling with buskers, tourists and traders, and site of both the Baths and the abbey. Although ticket prices are high for the **Roman Baths** (daily: March–June, Sept & Oct 9am–6pm; July & Aug 9am–9pm; Nov–Feb 9.30am–5.30pm; last entry 1hr before closing; £10.25, £11.25 in July & Aug, £13.50 combined ticket with Fashion Museum; ⓦwww.romanbaths.co.uk), there's two or three hours' worth of well-balanced, informative entertainment here, with both hourly guided tours and audioguides available (both free), which allow you to wander at your own pace around the complex . Highlights are: the Sacred Spring, part of the temple of the local deity Sulis Minerva, where water still bubbles up at a constant 46.5°C; the open-air (but originally covered) Great Bath, its vaporous waters surrounded by nineteenth-century pillars, terraces and statues of famous Romans; the Circular Bath, where bathers cooled off, and the Norman King's Bath. Among a quantity of coins, jewellery and sculpture exhibited are the gilt bronze head of Sulis Minerva and a grand, Celtic-inspired gorgon's head from the temple's pediment. Models of the complex at its greatest extent give some idea of the awe which it must have inspired, while the graffiti salvaged from the Roman era – mainly curses and boasts – give a nice personal slant on this antique leisure centre. You can get a free glimpse into the baths from the next-door **Pump Room**, the social hub of the Georgian spa community and still redolent of that era, housing a formal tearoom and restaurant (see p.368).

▲ Bath's Roman baths

Bath Abbey

Although there has been a church on the site since the seventh century, **Bath Abbey** (Mon–Sat 9am–4.30/6pm, Sun 1–2.30pm & 4.30–5.30pm; requested donation £2.50) did not take its present form until the end of the fifteenth century, when Bishop Oliver King began work on the ruins of the previous Norman building, some of which were incorporated into the new church.

The bishop was said to have been inspired by a vision of angels ascending and descending a ladder to heaven, which the present facade recalls on the turrets flanking the central window. The west front also features the founder's signature in the form of carvings of olive trees surmounted by crowns, a play on his name.

Much of the building underwent restoration following the destruction that took place under Henry VIII; his daughter, Queen Elizabeth I, played a large part in the repairs. The interior is in a restrained Perpendicular style, and boasts splendid fan vaulting on the ceiling, which was not properly completed until the nineteenth century. The floor and walls are crammed with elaborate monuments and memorials, and traces of the grander Norman building are visible in the Norman Chapel.

Below the abbey, reached from a door to the right of the Choir, the **Heritage Vaults** (free) gives some background to the construction of the building, and displays examples of statuary and precious silver.

Thermae Bath Spa

Finally open after years of unseemly delay, **Thermae Bath Spa,** at the bottom of the elegantly colonnaded Bath Street (daily 9am–10pm; ☎0844/888 0844, Ⓦwww.thermaebathspa.com), allows you to take the local waters in much the same way that visitors to Bath have done throughout the ages, but with state-of-the-art spa facilities. The complex is heated by the city's thermal waters and offers every treatment from massages to dry flotation. Its centrepiece is the **New Royal Bath**, a sleekly futuristic "glass cube" designed by Nicholas Grimshaw, incorporating a curving indoor pool with massage jets, fragrant steam rooms and a rooftop pool with awe-inspiring views. From the main building, you can access the **Hot Bath**, originally designed by the younger John Wood and today surrounded by treatment rooms. Across from the New Royal Bath, a separate building holds the **Cross Bath**, site of a Celtic place of worship and now housing a second, much more intimate, open-air thermal pool, while a small visitor centre has displays relating to Bath's thermal waters and a film.

Tickets for the New Royal Bath are £20 for two hours, £30 for four hours and £50 for a full day; for the Cross Bath pool, they cost £12 for a 90-minute session. Towels, robes and slippers can be rented, but you'll need a bathing costume. The complex also houses an excellent **café-restaurant** with nourishing soups and salads.

To The Circus and the Royal Crescent

North of Hot Bath Street, Westgate Street and Sawclose are presided over by the **Theatre Royal**, opened in 1805 and one of the country's finest surviving Georgian theatres. Next door is the house where Beau Nash spent his last years, now a restaurant. Up from the Theatre Royal, off Barton Street, the graceful **Queen Square** was the first Bath venture of the architect **John Wood**, who with his son (see box, p.366) was chiefly responsible for the Roman-inspired developments outside the confines of the medieval city. Wood himself lived at no. 24, giving him a vista of the northern terrace's palatial facade.

Just north of the square, at 40 Gay St, the **Jane Austen Centre** (March–Oct daily 9.45am–5.30pm, July & Aug Thurs–Sat open till 8.30pm; Nov–Feb Mon–Fri & Sun 11am–4.30pm, Sat 9.45am–5.30pm; £6.50) helps you to tie the various Austen threads together with an overview of the author's connections with the city, illustrated by extracts from her writings, contemporary costumes, furnishings and household items. However, a lot of the displays have only a tangential link to Austen, so even die-hard fans may

Beau Nash and Bath's Golden Age

Bath's golden age was played out according to a strictly defined set of rules, both in architecture and social style. Among the arbiters of etiquette, none enjoyed greater prestige than **Richard "Beau" Nash**, an ex-army officer, ex-lawyer, dandy and gambler, who became Bath's Master of Ceremonies in 1704, conducting public balls of an unprecedented splendour. Wielding dictatorial powers over dress and behaviour, Nash orchestrated the social manners of the city and even extended his influence to cover road improvements and the design of buildings. In an early example of health awareness, he banned smoking in Bath's public rooms at a time when pipe-smoking was a general pastime among men, women and children. Less philanthropically, he also encouraged gambling and even took a percentage of the bank's takings. He was nonetheless generally held in high esteem and succeeded in establishing rules such as the setting of specific hours and procedure for all social functions. Balls were to begin at six and end at eleven and every ball had to open with a minuet "danced by two persons of the highest distinction present". White aprons were banned, gossipers and scandalmongers were shunned, and, most radical of all, the wearing of swords in public places was forbidden, a ruling referred to in Sheridan's play *The Rivals*, in which Captain Absolute declares, "A sword seen in the streets of Bath would raise as great an alarm as a mad dog." By such measures, Nash presided over the city's greatest period, during the first four decades of the eighteenth century. He lived in Bath until his death at the age of 87, by which time he had been reduced to comparative poverty.

As for Bath's distinctive Georgian style of architecture, this was largely the work of **John Wood** ("the elder", c. 1704–54) and his son, also called John Wood ("the younger", 1727–81), both champions of the Neolassical Palladianism that originated in Renaissance Italy. Their "speculative developments", designed to cater to the seasonal floods of fashionable visitors, were constructed in the soft oolitic limestone from local quarries belonging to **Ralph Allen** (c. 1694–1764), another prominent figure of the period. A deputy postmaster who made a fortune by improving England's postal routes, and later from Bath's building boom, Allen was nicknamed "the man of Bath", and is best remembered for Prior Park, the mansion he built outside the city based on the elder Wood's designs, and for his association with Pope, Fielding and other luminaries who were frequent visitors.

Next to the innovations of Nash and the creations of Allen and the two John Woods, the name of **William Oliver** should not be forgotten in the story of Georgian Bath. A physician and philanthropist, Oliver did more than anyone to boost the city's profile as a therapeutic centre, thanks to publications such as his *Practical Essay on the Use and Abuse of Warm Bathing in Gouty Cases* (1751), and by founding the Bath General Hospital to enable the poor to make use of the waters. He is remembered today by the Bath Oliver biscuit, which he invented.

find it disappointing. Austen herself, who wasn't entirely enamoured of the city, lived just down the road at 25 Gay St – one of a number of places the author inhabited while in Bath.

West of Queen Square, at 19 New King St, another typical Bath town house houses the small **Herschel Museum of Astronomy** (Feb to mid-Dec Mon, Tues, Thurs & Fri 1–5pm, Sat & Sun 11am–5pm; £3.50), where the musician and astronomer Sir William Herschel, in collaboration with his sister Caroline, discovered the planet Uranus in 1781. The museum displays contemporary furnishings, musical instruments, a replica of the telescope with which Uranus was identified and various knick-knacks from the Herschels' lives. In the basement, you can watch a short film relating the lustrous careers of the siblings, and observe celestial phenomena via computer links to telescopes around the world.

Up from Queen Square, at the end of Gay Street, is the elder John Wood's masterpiece, **The Circus**, consisting of three crescents arranged in a tight circle of three-storey houses, with a carved frieze running round the entire circle. Wood died soon after laying the foundation stone for this enterprise, and the job was finished by his son. The painter Thomas Gainsborough lived at no. 17 from 1760 to 1774.

The Circus is connected by Brock Street to the **Royal Crescent**, grandest of Bath's crescents, begun by the younger John Wood in 1767. The stately arc of thirty houses is set off by a spacious sloping lawn from which a magnificent vista extends to green hills and distant ribbons of honey-coloured stone. The interior of **No. 1 Royal Crescent**, on the corner with Brock Street, has been restored to reflect as nearly as possible its original Georgian appearance at the end of the eighteenth century (Tues–Sun: mid-Feb to Oct 10.30am–5pm; Nov 10.30am–4pm; £5). The furnishings, drapes and Laura Ashley-style wallpaper are all authentic or else faithful recreations, as explained by the attendants providing commentaries in each room.

At the bottom of the Crescent, Royal Avenue leads onto **Royal Victoria Park**, the city's largest open space, containing an aviary and botanical gardens.

The Assembly Rooms, the Paragon and Milsom Street

The younger John Wood's **Assembly Rooms**, east of The Circus on Bennett Street, were, with the Pump Room, the centre of Bath's social scene. A fire virtually destroyed the building in 1942, but it has now been perfectly restored and houses the **Fashion Museum** (daily 11am–4/5pm; £6.75, or £13.50 with the Baths), an entertaining collection of clothing from the Stuart era to the latest Milanese designs.

From the Assembly Rooms, Alfred Street leads to the area known as the **Paragon**. Here, accessed from the raised pavement, the Georgian-Gothic Countess of Huntingdon's Chapel houses the **Building of Bath Museum** (Tues–Sun 10.30am–5pm; £4), a fascinating exploration of the construction and architecture of Bath. This should ideally be an early stop in your explorations around the city – it both focuses on such specific features as the styles of doors, windows and interior decoration that you'll see on your wanderings, and allows you to view Bath in long-shot by means of a huge 1:500 scale model of the city. At the bottom of the Paragon, off George Street, lies **Milsom Street**, a wide shopping strand designed by the elder Wood as the main thoroughfare of Georgian Bath.

The river and Great Pulteney Street

East of the abbey, Grand Parade looks down onto the formal Parade Gardens and the River Avon. At the top of Grand Parade, the **Victoria Art Gallery** (Tues–Sat 10am–5pm, Sun 1.30–5pm; free) has an impressive exhibition space upstairs where you can see works by artists who worked locally, including Gainsborough, while subjects of the numerous portraits include Beau Nash; the ground-floor rooms are used for temporary exhibitions. Across the road, the flow of the river – a crucial ingredient in the city's charm – is interrupted by a graceful V-shaped weir just below the shop-lined **Pulteney Bridge**, an Italianate structure designed by the eighteenth-century Scottish architect Robert Adam. The bridge was intended to link the city centre with **Great Pulteney Street**, a handsome avenue originally planned as the nucleus of a large residential quarter on the eastern bank, but the work ran into financial difficulties, so the roads running off it now stop short after a few yards. There is, however, a lengthy vista to the imposing classical facade of the **Holburne Museum** at the end of the street (Feb to mid-Dec Tues–Sat 10am–5pm, Sun 11am–5pm; £4.50). The three-storey building contains an impressive range of decorative and fine art, mostly furniture, silverware, porcelain and paintings, including work by Stubbs and the famous *Byam Family* by Gainsborough, his biggest portrait. Behind Holburne House, **Sydney Gardens** make a delightful place to take a breather. When Holburne House was a bustling hotel, the pleasure gardens were the venue for concerts and fireworks, as witnessed by Jane Austen, a frequent visitor here – the family had lodgings across the street at 4 Sydney Place in the autumn of 1801. Today, the gardens' slopes are cut through by the railway and the Kennet and Avon Canal. From here, it's a pleasant one-and-a-half mile saunter along the canal to the *George* pub (see p.369).

If you want to explore the river itself, rent a skiff, punt or canoe from the **Victorian Bath Boating Station** at the end of Forester Road, behind the Holburne Museum (Easter–Sept daily 10am–6pm; £7 per person for 1hr, then £2 per hour).

Eating and drinking

Bath has a huge range of **eating** outlets, from expensive gourmet cuisine to decent, inexpensive cafés. Booking in the evening is advised at most places. Numerous congenial **pubs** also offer good-value food in atmospheric surroundings.

Restaurants and cafés

Bathtub Bistro 2 Grove St ☎01225/460593. Just off Pulteney Bridge, this place looks tiny from the outside but reveals several eating areas on three levels. By day you can have coffees and light snacks, and in the evenings the place smartens up, serving traditional English dishes for around £15.

Café Retro 18 York St ☎01225/339347. A cosy place near the abbey for a cappuccino and a bite, accompanied by a mellow soundtrack. Also open Thurs–Sat eves for inventive international dishes for around £12. The *Retro-to-Go* takeaway next door sells rolls and salads.

Demuths 2 North Parade Passage ☎01225/446059. Bath's favourite eaterie for veggies and vegans offers light bites (£6–7) or hot stews and curries (around £10) at lunchtime, and original and delicious dishes from around the world in the evenings (around £15). Organic beers and wines are available, and the ambience is smooth and civilized.

Dower House *Royal Crescent Hotel*, 16 Royal Crescent ☎01225/823333. Stately surroundings and modern English-based classics with Mediterranean elements make for a luxurious dining experience. Set menus help to lighten the cost (two meat-based or three vegetarian courses £45).

Eastern Eye 8 Quiet St ☎01225/422323. This designer curry house occupies a Georgian bank, with a spectacular vaulted ceiling. The food's good too, (mains around £8), and briskly served.

Firehouse Rotisserie 2 John St ☎01225/482070. Delicious, outsized Californian pizzas (about £11) and grills (£12–15) are the main items in this busy place with a pleasant woody interior on two floors. Closed Sun.

Ha! Ha! Bar & Canteen Beehive Yard, Walcot St. Drinks, nibbles and full meals (£7–10) in this modern lounge and outdoor terrace, also a great breakfast stop.

Jazz Café 1 Kingsmead Square. Big breakfasts, snack fodder and dishes such as Hungarian vegetable goulash (£7) are served at this boho-style greasy spoon. Beers and wines are served, newspapers are on hand, and there's some outside seating. Open until 6pm Mon–Wed, 9pm Thurs–Sat, and 4pm on Sun.

No. 5 Restaurant 5 Argyle St ☎01225/444499. Candles on the tables and prints on the walls set the tone here. French-inspired main courses are £14–18, and there's a good-value two-course lunch menu for £8.

Pump Room Abbey Church Yard ☎01225/444477. Splash out on an Eggs Benedict brunch, try the excellent lunchtime menu, or succumb to a Bath bun or a range of cream teas, all accompanied by a pianist or a classical trio. It's a bit hammy, and you may have to queue, but you get a good view of the Baths. Open daytime only, plus eves during the Bath Festival, Aug and Christmas, when three-course menus are around £21.

Bath's festivals

Bath has a great range of festivals throughout the year, offering talks, gigs and other events in often sumptuous surroundings. If you're visiting during one of these occasions, you'll find the city's mellow pace livened up a notch or two, though you should be aware that accommodation gets very scarce. Best of the bunch are: the **Bath International Music Festival** (ⓦwww.bathmusicfest.org.uk), held between mid-May and early June and featuring big names in classical music, jazz, folk and blues, plus fireworks, literary and art events and lots of busking; the **Bath Fringe Festival** (ⓦwww.bathfringe.co.uk), running from late May to early June, with the accent on art and performance; and **Bath Literature Festival** (ⓦwww.bathlitfest.org.uk), taking place over ten days in February/March. There's also an international guitar festival in July/August, a Jane Austen festival in late September and a film festival in October. For further information on each, call ⓣ01225/463362, click on ⓦwww.bathfestivals.org.uk, visit the festivals office at 2 Church St, Abbey Green, or check out the individual websites above.

Strada Sawclose ⓣ01225/337753. Italian standards are served in the elegant surroundings of Beau Nash's former home. Pizzas and pastas are £7–10, main courses are £10–14, and there are good-value lunchtime, pre- and post-theatre menus.

Tilley's Bistro 3 North Parade Passage ⓣ01225/484200. Informal, rather cramped French restaurant with different-sized portions (small £5–7, medium £6–9, large £10–17) to allow more samplings, and good set-price lunchtime menus. Closed Sun.

Walrus and Carpenter 28 Barton St ⓣ01225/314864. You'll find an extensive vegetarian menu in this warren of small rooms near the Theatre Royal – though organic and free-range steaks, burgers and poultry dishes are also available (£10–14). The atmosphere is friendly and funky.

Pubs

The Bath Tap 19–20 St James's Parade. Home of Bath's gay and lesbian scene, though without so much of the "scene". It's lively but relaxed, with a mixed crowd enjoying the karaoke and occasional cabaret, and there's food. Open until 2am Thurs–Sat for club nights in the basement.

The Bell 103 Walcot St. Excellent, easy-going pub with a great atmosphere. There's a beer garden, bar billiards, free Internet access and live music three times a week (Mon & Wed eve, plus Sun lunchtime).

Coeur de Lion Northumberland Place. Centrally located tavern on a flagstoned shopping alley, with a few tables outside. It's Bath's smallest boozer and a regular tourist stop, but persevere for the good lunchtime food.

The George Mill Lane, Bathampton. Popular canal-side pub twenty minutes' walk from the centre and with better than average bar food.

Old Green Tree Green St. Wood panelling, low ceilings and some great real ales make this minute place a popular stop among beer connoisseurs and pub fans.

The Porter Miles Buildings, George St. Part of *Moles* club (see below), serving good beer and veggie food in a grungy setting. There are tables outside and pool and table football in the *Cellar Bar*, where, in the evenings, there's free live music (Mon–Thurs), DJs (Fri & Sat) and comedy (Sun).

The Salamander 3 John St. Local brewery Bath Ales pub with a woody decor, a laid-back atmosphere and good food available at the bar or in the upstairs restaurant.

Nightlife and entertainment

First and foremost of the town-centre **clubs** is *Moles* (ⓣ01225/404445, ⓦwww.moles.co.uk) on George Street, a Bath institution which features a mix of live music and DJs playing club sounds. Other DJ-based venues include *Qube*, 1 South Parade (ⓣ01225/312800, ⓦwww.qubeclub.com), for anthems, party tunes and R'n'B, popular with students, and two Moroccan-style clubs, *Fez Club*, The Paragon (ⓣ01225/444162), and *Po Na Na*, 8 North Parade (ⓣ01225/424952), which attract big crowds for their varied indie, commercial, hip-hop and cheese nights. For gay and lesbian club nights, see the *Bath Tap*, p.369. For **live music**, head for *Moles* or the *Cellar Bar* in the next-door *Porter*, or try the *Porter Butt* pub at York Place, London Road (℡01225/425084), which has live bands most weekends playing roots, punk and ska.

Theatre and ballet fans should check out what's showing at the Theatre Royal on Sawclose (℡01225/448844, 🌐www.theatreroyal.org.uk), which stages fairly traditional productions in the main house and more experimental material in its Ustinov Studio. Big names in all genres of music play during the International Music Festival (see box, p.369), while for **concerts**, gigs and other events during the rest of the year, check *Venue*, the weekly listings magazine (£1.50), or *Bath Quarterly*, a free listings guide available from the tourist office.

Listings

Car rental Hertz, Windsor Bridge Rd ℡0870/850 2691; Thrifty, Bath Spa station ℡01225/442911. **Internet** @ Internet, 12 Manvers St (daily 9am–9pm); *Green Park Brasserie*, Green Park Station, off James St (Tues–Sat 10am–11pm, Sun noon–2.30pm).

Left luggage *Bath Backpackers* (see p.363) provides the only place in town to leave your bags (£2.50 per item per day).

Taxis Ranks at Orange Grove, near the abbey, and Bath Spa train station, or call Abbey Taxis ℡01225/444444 or Bath Taxis ℡01225/447777.

Wells, the Mendips and Glastonbury

Wells, twenty miles south of Bristol across the Somerset border and the same distance southwest from Bath, is a miniature cathedral city that has not significantly altered in eight hundred years. You could spend a good half-day kicking around here, and you might decide to make it an accommodation stop for visiting nearby attractions in the **Mendip Hills**, such as the **Wookey Hole** caves and **Cheddar Gorge**. On the southern edge of the range, and just a jump away from Wells, the town of **Glastonbury** has for centuries been one of the main Arthurian sites of the West Country, and is now the country's most enthusiastic centre of New-Age cults.

Wells

Technically England's smallest city, **WELLS** owes its celebrity entirely to its **cathedral** (daily 7am–6/7pm; suggested donation £5.50; 🌐www.wellscathedral .org.uk). Hidden from sight until you pass into its spacious close from the central Market Place, the building presents a majestic spectacle, the broad lawn of the former graveyard providing a perfect foreground. The west front teems with some three hundred thirteenth-century figures of saints and kings, once brightly painted and gilded, though their present honey tint has a subtle splendour of its own. Close up, the impact is slightly lessened, as most of the statuary is badly eroded and many figures were damaged by Puritans in the seventeenth century. The facade was constructed about fifty years after work on the main building was begun in 1180. The **interior** is a supreme example of early English Gothic, the long nave punctuated by a dramatic "scissor arch", one of three that were constructed in 1338 to take the extra weight of the newly built tower. Though some wax enthusiastic about the ingenuity of these so-called "strainer" arches, others argue that they're "grotesque intrusions" from an artistic point of view.

Other features worth scrutinizing are the narrative carvings on the **capitals and corbels** in the transepts – including men with toothache and an old man caught raiding an orchard. In the north transept, don't miss the 24-hour astronomical clock, dating from 1390, whose jousting knights charge each other every quarter-hour, as announced by a figure known as Jack Blandiver, who kicks a couple of bells from his seat high up on the right – on the hour he strikes the bell in front of him. Opposite the clock, a doorway leads to a graceful, much-worn flight of steps rising to the **Chapter House**, an octagonal room elaborately ribbed in the Decorated style. There are some gnarled old tombs to be seen in the aisles of the **Quire**, at the end of which is the richly coloured stained glass of the fourteenth-century **Lady Chapel**. The best way to see it all is on one of the **free guided tours**, which take place up to five times daily (twice daily in winter; none on Sun). If you want to take pictures, you have to buy a photographic permit (£3); the use of flash is banned in the Quire. Evensong takes place at 5.15pm (3pm on Sun).

The row of clerical houses on the north side of the cathedral green are mainly seventeenth- and eighteenth-century, though one, the **Old Deanery**, shows traces of its fifteenth-century origins. The chancellor's house is now a **museum** (Easter–Oct Mon–Sat 10am–5.30pm, Sun 11am–4pm; Nov–Easter daily 11am–4pm; £3), displaying, among other items, some of the cathedral's original statuary, as well as a good geological section with fossils from the surrounding area, including Wookey Hole (see p.372).

Beyond the arch, a little further along the street, the cobbled medieval **Vicars' Close** holds more clerical dwellings, linked to the cathedral by the Chain Gate and fronted by small gardens. The cottages were built in the mid-fourteenth century – though only no. 22 has not undergone outward alterations – and have been continuously occupied by members of the cathedral clergy ever since.

On the other side of the cathedral – and accessible through the cathedral shop – are the cloisters, from which you can enter the tranquil grounds of the **Bishop's Palace** (April–Oct daily except Sat 10.30am–6pm; Aug daily 10.30am–6pm; last entry at 5pm; £4), also reachable from Market Place through the Bishop's Eye archway. The residence of the Bishop of Bath and Wells, the palace was walled and moated as a result of a rift with the borough in the fourteenth century, and the imposing gatehouse still displays the grooves of the portcullis and a chute for pouring oil and molten lead on would-be assailants. On a less warlike note, look out for the bell attached to the side of the gatehouse, which swans and their cygnets have learned to ring when they're hungry. Within, the tranquil gardens contain the springs from which the city takes its name – and which still feed the moat as well as the streams flowing along the gutters of Wells's High Street – and the scanty but impressive remains of the **Great Hall**, built at the end of the thirteenth century and despoiled during the Reformation. Across the lawn, which is used for regular croquet matches in summer, stands the square **Bishop's Chapel** and the **Undercroft**, holding state rooms, displays relating to the history of the site and a café. Outside, a stroll along the rampart walk reveals glimpses of Glastonbury Tor to the south.

Practicalities

Wells is not connected to the rail network, but its **bus station**, off Market Street, receives buses from Bristol and Bath. The **tourist office** is on Market Place (April & Oct 10am–5pm, Sun 10am–4pm; May–Sept Mon–Sat 9am–5pm, Sun 10am–4pm; Nov–March Mon–Sat 10am–4pm; ☏01749/672552, ⊛www.wellstourism.com). Discounted tickets for Cheddar Gorge and Wookey Hole are sold here. Market Place is the scene of a small but busy **market** on Wednesday and Saturday, good for trinkets and locally sourced snacks. You can **rent bikes** – useful for visiting Wookey Hole – from Bike City, 38 Market St (☏01749/671711).

Accommodation

Ancient Gatehouse Hotel Sadler St
☎01749/672029, ⓦwww.ancientgatehouse.co.uk.
The fourteenth-century origins of this hostelry are
evident in the sagging floors and winding staircase,
but – apart from poor sound insulation – the Wi-Fi-
enabled rooms are comfortable; some have four-
posters and carved wooden ceilings, and four of
them overlook the cathedral. ❻

Canon Grange Cathedral Green
☎01749/671800, ⓦwww.canongrange.co
.uk. Beautifully located B&B, with three rooms
facing the west front of the cathedral. Breakfast,
which can cover various dietary requirements, is
taken overlooking the green. ❸

The Crown Market Place ☎01749/673457,
ⓦwww.crownatwells.co.uk. Fifteenth-century
coaching inn with an authentically antique flavour,
where William Penn was arrested in 1695 for illegal
preaching. Can be noisy from the bar and bistro
below. ❻

Swan Hotel Sadler St ☎01749/836300, ⓦwww
.swanhotelwells.co.uk. This rambling inn is
old-fashioned and shabby in places, but it has
character and some rooms have cathedral views. ❼

Eating and drinking

City Arms Cuthbert St. Formerly the city jail, this is
a good place for a drink or a full meal in its moderately priced restaurant. There's also seating in the
plant-filled courtyard.

Good Earth Priory Rd. Excellent organic
produce is on hand at this inexpensive
vegetarian café near the bus station, with pizzas
and flans to eat in and delicious takeaway
goodies. Expect queues at lunchtime. Closed eves
& all Sun.

Goodfellows 5 Sadler St ☎01749/673866. You
can pick up superb sandwiches and pastries at
the patisserie here (closed Sun), or a two-course
lunch with wine for £10. The restaurant at the
back is famed for its innovative seafood dishes
(£27 for a set-price dinner). Closed Tues eve and
all Sun & Mon.

Rugantino's 20 Sadler St ☎01749/672029.
Italian-run restaurant (attached to the *Ancient
Gatehouse Hotel*) in gorgeous medieval
surroundings. It's slightly formal, serving quality
Mediterranean fare; main courses are around £15
and a set evening menu is £21.50.

The Mendips

The **Mendip Hills**, rising to the north of Wells, are chiefly famous for **Wookey
Hole** – the most impressive of many caves in this narrow limestone chain – and
for **Cheddar Gorge**, where a walk through the narrow cleft might make a
starting point for more adventurous trips across the Mendips.

Wookey Hole

Hollowed out by the River Axe a couple of miles north of Wells, **Wookey
Hole** is an impressive cave complex of deep pools and intricate rock
formations, but it's folklore rather than geology that takes precedence on the
guided tours (daily 10am–4.30/5.30pm; £12.50). Highlight of the tour is the
alleged petrified remains of the Witch of Wookey, a "blear-eyed hag" who
was said to turn her evil eye on crops, young lovers and local farmers until
the Abbot of Glastonbury intervened; he dispatched a monk who drove the
witch into the inner cave, sprinkled her with holy water and turned her into
stone. Some substance was lent to the legend when an ancient skeleton – in
fact Romano-British – was unearthed here in 1912, together with a dagger,
sacrificial knife and a big rounded ball of pure stalagmite, the so-called
witch's ball. Beside her were found two skeletons, the remains of goats tied
to a stake. At the end of the hour-long guided tour, you can use your
ticket to visit a functioning Victorian paper mill by the river, and rooms
containing speleological exhibits. On a less earnest note, the range of
amusements includes a collection of gaudy, sometimes ghoulish, Edwardian
fairground pieces.

For food, drinks – including a great selection of Belgian beers – or a **place
for the night**, head for the ⚡ *Wookey Hole Inn* (☎01749/676677, ⓦwww
.wookeyholeinn.com; ❻), just along the street from the caves, and a reason in

itself to come here. In contrast with the traditional exterior, the five guest-rooms are furnished in contemporary style with widescreen TVs and CD players, and continental breakfast is delivered in a basket. At lunchtime you can just have a soup or a sandwich, while in the evening the **restaurant** (for which advance booking is essential; closed Sun eve) cooks up exquisite dishes (£12–20 for mains); there's also a sculpture garden, and regular live music.

A walkable couple of miles uphill west of Wookey Hole, **Ebbor Gorge** offers a wilder alternative to the more famous Cheddar Gorge, with tranquillity guaranteed on the wooded trails that follow the ravine up to the Mendip plateau.

Cheddar Gorge

Six miles west of Wookey on the A371, **Cheddar** has given its name to Britain's best-known cheese – most of it now mass-produced far from here – but the biggest selling point of this rather plain village is **Cheddar Gorge**, lying beyond the neighbourhood of Tweentown about a mile to the north.

Cutting a jagged gash across the Mendip Hills, the limestone gorge is an impressive geological phenomenon, though its natural beauty is undermined by the minor road running through it and by the Lower Gorge's mile of shops and parking areas. Beyond these, the first few curves of the gorge hold its most dramatic scenery, though each turn of the two-mile length presents new, sometimes startling vistas, which can be seen from the open-top bus that plies up and down between March and October (free to Cheddar Caves ticket-holders; see below). At its narrowest the road squeezes between cliffs towering almost five hundred feet above. Those in a state of honed fitness can climb the 274 steps of **Jacob's Ladder** to a **lookout tower** that offers views towards Glastonbury Tor and occasional glimpses of the sea and even Exmoor – if you don't want to tackle the muscle-wrenching climb you can reach the same spot with a great deal more ease via the narrow lane winding up behind the cliffs. There's a circular three-mile clifftop Gorge Walk, with marked paths branching off to such secluded spots as **Black Rock**, two miles west of Cheddar, and **Black Down**, at 1067ft the Mendips' highest peak. The tourist office can also provide details of the **West Mendip Way**, a forty-mile route extending from Uphill, near Weston-super-Mare, to Wells and Shepton Mallet.

Beneath the gorge, the **Cheddar Caves** (daily 10/10.30am–5/5.30pm; £14) were scooped out by underground rivers in the wake of the Ice Age, and subsequently occupied by primitive communities. The bigger of the two main groups, **Gough's Caves**, is a sequence of chambers with names such as Solomon's Temple, Aladdin's Cave and the Swiss Village, all arrayed with tortuous rock formations that resemble organ pipes, waterfalls and giant birds. **Cox's Caves** (same ticket), entered lower down the main drag, are floodlit to pick out the subtle pinks, greys, greens and whites in the rock, as well as a set of lime blocks known as "the Bells", which produce a range of tones when struck. The Crystal Quest, attached to Cox's Caves, is the kids' favourite, with high-tech light and laser effects playing on its gushing waterfall.

Practicalities

Cheddar's **tourist office** stands at the bottom of the gorge (Easter to mid-Sept daily 10am–5pm; mid-Sept to Oct daily 10.30am–4.30pm; Nov–Easter Sun 11am–4pm; ☎01934/744071, ⊛www.visitsomerset.co.uk). Among the village's handful of **B&Bs**, *Chedwell Cottage*, on Redcliffe Street (☎01934/743268; no credit cards; ❷), has three en-suite rooms and a garden, while another option is the **youth hostel**, opposite the fire station, off the Hayes (☎0870/770 5760,

@ cheddar@yha.org.uk; dorm bed from £14; call to check opening). There are two **campsites** nearby, most centrally *Cheddar Bridge Park,* a camping and caravan complex opposite the church on Draycott Road (℡01934/743048, @www.cheddarbridge.co.uk; no under-18s; closed Dec–Feb), while the fully equipped, family-orientated *Broadway House* lies on the northwestern outskirts of the village, off the A371 to Axbridge (℡01934/742610, @www .broadwayhouse.uk.com; closed mid-Nov to Feb).

Glastonbury

Six miles south of Wells, and reachable from there in twenty minutes on frequent buses, **GLASTONBURY** lies at the centre of the so-called **Isle of Avalon**, a region rich with mystical associations. At the heart of it all is the early Christian legend that the young Christ once visited this site, a story that is not as far-fetched as it sounds. The Romans had a heavy presence in the area, mining lead in the Mendips, and one of these mines was owned by **Joseph of Arimathea**, a well-to-do merchant said to have been related to Mary. It's not completely impossible that the merchant took his kinsman on one of his many visits to his property, during a period of Christ's life of which nothing is recorded. It was this possibility to which William Blake referred in his *Glastonbury Hymn*, better known as *Jerusalem*: "And did those feet in ancient times/Walk upon England's mountains green?"

Another legend relates how Joseph was imprisoned for twelve years after the Crucifixion, miraculously kept alive by the **Holy Grail**, the chalice of the Last Supper in which the blood was gathered from the wound in Christ's side. The Grail, along with the spear which had caused the wound, were later taken by Joseph to Glastonbury, where he founded the abbey and commenced the conversion of Britain.

Arrival, information and accommodation

Buses #375, #376 and #377 run up to four times hourly from Wells, dropping you outside the abbey on Magdalene Street. Round the corner on the High Street, housed in the Tribunal, Glastonbury's **tourist office** (Mon –Thurs & Sun 10am–4/5pm, Fri & Sat 10am–4.30/5.30pm; ℡01458/832954, @www.glastonburytic.co.uk) sells discounted tickets to such local attractions as Cheddar Caves and Wookey Hole. You can log on to the **Internet** across the road at the Assembly Rooms (Tues–Sat noon–5pm).

Glastonbury's **accommodation** takes in everything from medieval hostelry to backpacker hostel, with most places a brief walk from the town centre. There's also a decent **campsite** within sight of the Tor, the *Isle of Avalon* (℡01458/833618), ten minutes' walk up Northload Street on Godney Road.

> ### Glastonbury Festival
>
> Glastonbury is of course best known for its **music festival**, which takes place most years over three days at the end of June outside the nearby village of Pilton. Having started in the 1970s, the festival has become one of the biggest and best organized in the country, without shedding too much of its alternative feel. Bands range from huge acts like Coldplay and The Killers to up-and-coming indie groups and such old hands as The Who. Though ticket prices are steep (around £150) they are snapped up within hours when released in early April: for general information, contact the promoters on ℡01458/834596, or see @www.glastonburyfestivals.co.uk.

Hotels and B&Bs

1 Park Terrace Street Rd ☎01458/835845, ⊛www.no1parkterrace.co.uk. Large Victorian house, five minutes' walk from the centre, with rooms en suite or with shared facilities, Internet and Wi-Fi access, and evening meals available. ❸

3 Magdalene St ☎01458/832129, ⊛www.numberthree.co.uk. Beautifully furnished bedrooms make for a stylish stay in this Georgian house with a large walled garden, right next to the abbey. ❻

George & Pilgrims 1 High St ☎01458/831146, ⊛www.georgeandpilgrims.activehotels.com. This fifteenth-century oak-panelled inn brims with medieval atmosphere. ❹

Meadow Barn Middlewick Farm, Wick Lane ☎01458/832351, ⊛www.middlewickholidaycottages.co.uk. A mile and a half north of town, this Canadian-run place offers peace and quiet in rural surroundings, with an indoor pool, a steam room and Wi-Fi. Minimum two-night stay. ❸

Shambhala Healing Retreat Coursing Batch, near the Tor ☎01458/831797, ⊛www.shambhala.co.uk. Recharge your spiritual batteries in one of the retreat's Tibetan, Egyptian or Chinese guest rooms. Use of the Meditation Sanctuary is included in the price, and various types of massage and therapy are on offer. ❺

Hostels

Glastonbury Backpackers Market Place ☎01458/833353, ⊛www.glastonburybackpackers.com. Centrally located former coaching inn with lively café/bar, kitchen, pool table, Internet access and no curfew. Advance booking recommended. Dorm beds £14, doubles ❶

YHA Street Ivythorn Hill, Street ☎0870/770 6056, Ⓔstreet@yha.org.uk. The nearest YHA lies a couple of miles south of Glastonbury, but is easily accessed by bus (#375 or #376; alight at Marshalls Elm crossroads and follow signs). Camping pitches available. Call for opening details. Dorm beds from £12.

Glastonbury Abbey

Aside from its mythological origins, **Glastonbury Abbey**, with its entrance near the town centre on Magdalene Street (daily 9.30/10am–4.30/6pm; £4.50), can safely claim to be the oldest Christian foundation in England, dating back to the seventh century and possibly earlier. Three kings (Edmund, Edgar and Edmund Ironside) were buried here, and in the tenth century, funded by a constant procession of pilgrims, the Saxon church was enlarged by St Dunstan (later archbishop of Canterbury), under whom it became the richest Benedictine abbey in the country, with a widely renowned library. Further expansion took place under the Normans, though most of the additions were destroyed by fire in 1184. Rebuilt, the abbey was later a casualty of the Dissolution of the Monasteries in the 1530s, and the ruins, now hidden behind walls and nestled among grassy parkland, can only hint at its former extent. The most prominent and photogenic remains are the transept piers and the shell of the Lady Chapel, with its carved figures of the Annunciation, the Magi and Herod.

The abbey's **choir** introduces another strand to the Glastonbury story, for it holds what is alleged to be the tomb of **Arthur and Guinevere**. As told by William of Malmesbury and Thomas Malory, the story relates how, after being mortally wounded in battle, King Arthur sailed to Avalon where he was buried alongside his queen. The discovery of two bodies in an ancient cemetery outside the abbey in 1191 – from which they were transferred here in 1278 – was taken to confirm the popular identification of Glastonbury with Avalon. In the grounds, the fourteenth-century abbot's kitchen is the only monastic building to survive intact, with four huge corner fireplaces and a great central lantern above. Behind the main entrance to the grounds, look out for the thorn-tree that is supposedly from the original **Glastonbury Thorn** said to have sprouted from the staff of Joseph of Arimathea when he landed here to convert the country. The plant grew for centuries on a nearby hill known as Wyrral, or Weary-All, and despite being hacked down by Puritans, lived long enough to provide numerous cuttings whose descendants still bloom twice a year (Easter & Dec). Only at Glastonbury do they flourish, it is claimed – everywhere else they die after a couple of years.

The Town and Glastonbury Tor

At the bottom of Glastonbury's High Street, abbots once presided over legal cases in the fourteenth-century **Tribunal**; it later became a hotel for pilgrims, and now holds the tourist office and the small **Glastonbury Lake Village Museum**, which displays finds from the Iron Age villages that fringed the former marshland below the Tor (same hours as tourist office; £2, free to EH members).

Further up the High Street, take a glance at the fifteenth-century church of **St John the Baptist**: the tower is reckoned to be one of Somerset's finest, and the interior has a fine oak roof and stained glass illustrating the legend of St Joseph of Arimathea, both from the period of the church's construction. The Glastonbury thorn in the churchyard is the biggest in town.

At the top of the High Street, walk down Lambrook and Chilkwell streets to find, at the southeastern edge of the abbey grounds, the medieval **Abbey Barn**, centrepiece of the engaging **Somerset Rural Life Museum** (April–Oct Tues–Fri 10am–5pm, Sat & Sun 2–6pm; Nov–March Tues–Sat 10am–5pm; free), which illustrates a range of local rural occupations, from cheese- and cider-making to peat-digging, thatching and farming. A collection of heavy-duty farm machinery is on show in the fourteenth-century tithe barn, which originally held the produce of the abbey's 24 acres of arable estates. These included apple orchards, a residue of which exists in the adjacent Barn Orchard, where there are examples of twenty different types of cider apple trees.

Further down Chilkwell Street, the **Chalice Well** (daily 10am–4/5.30pm; £3) stands in the middle of a lush garden intended for quiet contemplation. The iron-red waters of the well – which is fondly supposed to be the hiding-place of the Holy Grail – were considered to have curative properties, making the town a spa for a brief period in the eighteenth century, and they are still prized (there's a tap in Wellhouse Lane).

From Chilkwell Street, turn left into Wellhouse Lane and immediately right for the footpath that leads up to **Glastonbury Tor**, at 521ft a landmark for miles around. The conical hill – topped by the dilapidated **St Michael's Tower**, sole remnant of a fourteenth-century church – commands stupendous views encompassing Wells, the Quantocks, the Mendips, the once-marshy Somerset Levels, and, on very clear days, the Welsh mountains. Pilgrims once embarked on the stiff climb here with hard peas in their shoes as penance – nowadays people come to feel the vibrations of crossing ley-lines.

You can save some legwork by taking advantage of the **Glastonbury Tor Bus** (daily: April–Sept 9.30am–7pm; Oct–March 10am–3pm; £2), which ferries people from the abbey car park to the base of the Tor every thirty minutes, with stops at the Rural Life Museum and Chalice Well; your ticket can be used all day.

Eating, drinking and entertainment

Wedged between the esoteric shops of Glastonbury's High Street are numerous **cafés** and informal **restaurants** serving inexpensive meals, usually with an accent on organic and vegetarian food. The Assembly Rooms (Ⓦwww .assemblyrooms.org.uk) is the venue for talks and musical and theatrical **performances**, usually on Friday and Saturday evenings, while big-name

▲ Glastonbury Tor

BRISTOL, BATH AND SOMERSET | Wells, the Mendips and Glastonbury

concerts, miracle plays and exhibitions are held in the abbey grounds – call ☎01458/832267 or see Ⓦwww.glastonburyabbey.com for details. Various talks and workshops are also held throughout the year at the Chalice Well (☎01458/831154, Ⓦwww.chalicewell.org.uk).

Blue Note Café 4 High St. A relaxed place to hang out over coffees and cakes with some seating in the courtyard. Sometimes open eves in summer. Inexpensive.

Glastonbury Backpackers Market Place. A convivial spot for drinks and snacks at all hours, with TVs showing live sport, DJs, bands on Fri & Sat eves, and karaoke on Sun.

Hawthorns 8 Northload St ☎01458/831255. Bar and restaurant with an eclectic menu, including a curry buffet at lunchtime, great vegetarian choices, and "Ethnic English" dishes. Moderate.

Hundred Monkeys 52 High St ☎01458/833386. Mellow café-restaurant with a courtyard. Tasty snacks include a renowned seafood soup. Stays open until 9pm Thurs–Sat eves for meals and live music. Closed Sun. Inexpensive–moderate.

Mocha Berry Market Place. Small café with a buzzy feel, serving up traditional grub such as sausage and mash and bubble and squeak. Inexpensive.

Who'd a Thought It 17 Northload St. Congenial pub with garden, serving excellent meals. Moderate.

Bridgwater and the Quantocks

Travelling west through the reclaimed marshland of the Somerset Levels, your route could take you through **Bridgwater**, a handy starting point for excursions into the gently undulating **Quantock Hills**, where snug villages nestle among scenic wooded valleys or "combes". Public transport is fairly minimal around here, but you can see quite a lot on the **West Somerset Railway** between Bishops Lydeard and the coastal resort of Minehead, which stops at some of the thatched, typically English villages along the west flank of the Quantocks, and there are **horse-riding** facilities at many local farms.

Bridgwater

Sedate **BRIDGWATER** has seen little excitement since it was embroiled in the Civil War and its aftermath, in particular the events surrounding the **Monmouth Rebellion** of 1685. Having landed from his base in Holland, the Protestant Duke of Monmouth, an illegitimate son of Charles II, was enthusiastically proclaimed king at Bridgwater, and was only prevented from taking Bristol by the encampment of the Catholic James II's army there. Monmouth turned round and attempted to surprise the king's forces on **Sedgemoor**, three miles outside Bridgwater. The disorganized rebel army was mown down by the royal artillery, Monmouth himself was captured and later beheaded, and a period of repression was unleashed under the infamous Judge Jeffreys, whose Bloody Assizes created a folk-memory in Somerset of gibbets and gutted carcasses displayed around the county.

The town was once one of Somerset's major ports and, despite some ugly outskirts, still has some handsome Georgian buildings around its centre. Bridgwater's most striking monument, though, is the thirteenth- to fourteenth-century **St Mary's Church**, immediately identifiable by its polygonal, angled steeple that soars over the town centre. Within, you can admire the oak pulpit and a seventeenth-century Italian altarpiece – the impressive hammer-beam roof, however, was added in the 1850s. Elsewhere in town – just round the corner from the red-brick Christ Church, where Coleridge preached in 1797 and 1798 – the **Blake Museum**, by the River Parrett on Blake Street (Tues–Sat 10am–4pm; free), shows relics, models and a video relating to the Battle of Sedgemoor. The sixteenth-century building is reputedly the birthplace of local hero Robert Blake, admiral under Oliver Cromwell, whose swashbuckling career against Royalists, Dutch and Spanish is chronicled and illustrated here. There's also an archeology section, and

Carnival at Bridgwater

A good time to be in Bridgwater is for the **carnival** celebrations, said to be the largest illuminated procession in Europe, attracting up to 150,000 people. The festivities usually take place on the nearest Thursday or Friday to Bonfire Night (one of the Catholic conspirators of the Gunpowder Plot hailed from nearby Nether Stowey; see below). Grandly festooned floats belonging to Somerset's seventy-odd carnival clubs roll through town, before heading off to do the same in various other local towns and villages, including Glastonbury and Wells. See Ⓦ www.somersetcarnivals.co.uk for dates.

material on local merchant, cartoonist and anti-slavery campaigner John Chubb, a friend of Coleridge.

Practicalities

Bridgwater's **tourist office**, in King's Square (Mon–Fri 8.45am–5pm; ℡ 01278/436438, Ⓦ www.somersetbythesea.co.uk), provides details of **accommodation** hereabouts. Central choices include the *Old Vicarage* right opposite St Mary's Church (℡ 01278/458891, Ⓦ www.theoldvicaragebridgwater .com; ❻), one of the town's oldest buildings, and the more up-to-date though unexciting *Tudor Hotel*, 27 St Mary St (℡ 01278/422093; ❸).

Both of the above-mentioned hotels serve teas, light lunches and full meals, while the *Tudor* also hosts live jazz on Thursday evenings. The Bridgwater Arts Centre on Castle Street (℡ 01278/422700, Ⓦ www.bridgwaterartscentre.co.uk) is worth seeking out for its concerts, films, plays and comedy.

The Quantock Hills

West of Bridgwater, crossed by clear streams and grazed by red deer, the **Quantock Hills** measure just twelve miles in length and are mostly 800 to 900-foot high. The secluded hamlets within the range are linked by a tangle of narrow lanes, connected by rather sporadic local **bus** services from Bridgwater and Taunton, Somerset's county town, and by a restored **steam railway** along the western edge of the range. There are unstaffed **information** points in various Quantock villages, or see Ⓦ www.quantockhills.com or Ⓦ www .quantockonline.co.uk, which also has walking itineraries.

Nether Stowey and around

On the northern edge of the hills, eight miles west of Bridgwater on the A39, the pretty village of **NETHER STOWEY** is best known for its association with **Samuel Taylor Coleridge**, who walked here from Bristol at the end of 1796 to join his wife and child at their new home. This "miserable cottage", as Sara Coleridge called it, was visited six months later by William Wordsworth and his sister Dorothy, who soon afterwards moved into the somewhat grander Alfoxden House, near Holford, a couple of miles down the road. The year that Coleridge and Wordsworth spent as neighbours was extraordinarily productive – Coleridge composed some of his best poetry at this time, including *The Rime of the Ancient Mariner* and *Kubla Khan*, and the two poets in collaboration produced the *Lyrical Ballads*, the poetic manifesto of early English Romanticism. Many of the greatest figures of the age made the trek down to visit the pair, among them Charles Lamb, Thomas De Quincey, Robert Southey, Humphry Davy and William Hazlitt, and it was the coming and going of these intellectuals that stirred the suspicions of the local authorities in a period when England was at war with France. Spies were sent to track them and Wordsworth was finally given notice to leave in June 1798, shortly before *Lyrical Ballads* rolled off the press. In **Coleridge Cottage** (April–Sept Thurs–Sun 2–5pm; £3.90; NT), not such an "old hovel" now, you can see the poet's parlour and reading room, and, upstairs, his bedroom and an exhibition room containing various letters and first editions. You can pick up leaflets here (or consult the website Ⓦwww .coleridgeway.co.uk) on the **Coleridge Way**, a walking route that supposedly follows the poet's footsteps between Nether Stowey and Porlock on the Exmoor coast (see p.426). Waymarked with quill signs, the 36-mile hike takes you through some of the most scenic parts of the Quantocks and Exmoor.

From Nether Stowey, a minor road winds south off the A39 to the highest point on the Quantocks at **Wills Neck** (1260ft); park at Triscombe Stone, on the edge of Quantock Forest, from where a footpath leads to the summit about a mile distant. Stretching between Wills Neck and the village of Aisholt, the bracken- and heather-grown moorland plateau of **Aisholt Common** is the heart of the Quantocks – the best place to begin exploring this central tract is near **West Bagborough**, where a five-mile path starts at Birches Corner. Lower down the slopes, outside Aisholt, the banks of **Hawkridge Reservoir** make a lovely picnic stop.

The Quantocks are notorious for confrontations between hunting parties and anti-hunt activists, but if you want to indulge in less contentious **pony-trekking**, contact *Mill Farm* at Fiddington, near Nether Stowey (see p.379).

Practicalities

There are a couple of good **accommodation** choices on Castle Street in Nether Stowey: *Stowey Brooke House*, at no. 18 (☎01278/733356, Ⓦwww .stoweybrookehouse.co.uk; no credit cards; ❸), handsomely renovated with all rooms en suite (one has its own sitting area), and the *Old Cider House* at no. 25 (☎01278/732228, Ⓦwww.theoldciderhouse.co.uk; ❸), which has fully equipped rooms and great evening meals – real ale walks in the area can be arranged. Alternatively, the *Rose & Crown* on St Mary Street offers comfortable en-suite rooms (☎01278/732265, Ⓦwww.roseandcrown-netherstowey.co.uk; ❸). This and the tile-fronted *George* next door also provide decent ales and bar **meals** – and the *George* has pool, table football and occasional live bands. **Campers** should head for *Mill Farm* (☎01278/732286, Ⓦwww.millfarm.biz), a couple of miles east of Nether Stowey outside the village of Fiddington; there's also a stables here, indoor and outdoor pools, and **bike rental**. Five miles further west along the A39, the village of Holford, a stop on the #14 bus from Bridgwater, has the *Plough Inn*, where Virginia and Leonard Woolf spent their honeymoon, today serving simple **snacks**.

Bishops Lydeard to Crowcombe

The other main road route fringing the Quantocks – the A358 heading northwest from Taunton – is accompanied for most of the way by the **West Somerset Railway**, a restored branch line running some twenty miles between the village of Bishops Lydeard, five miles out of Taunton, to Minehead on the Somerset coast (see p.425). Between mid-March and October (plus some dates in Dec & Feb), up to eight steam and diesel trains depart daily from Bishops Lydeard, stopping at renovated stations on the way (for timetables, call ☎01643/704996, or log on at Ⓦwww.west-somerset -railway.co.uk); the full ticket to Minehead costs £8.80 one way, £13 return. A special bus service links the terminus with Taunton's train station, or take bus #23 or #28A (both Mon–Sat).

BISHOPS LYDEARD itself is worth a wander, not least for **St Mary's** church, with a splendid tower in the Perpendicular style and carved bench-ends inside, one of them illustrating the allegory of a pelican feeding its young with blood from its own breast – a symbol of the redemptive power of Christ's blood. The church is constructed of the pink-red sandstone characteristic of Quantock villages; **COMBE FLOREY**, a couple of miles north, is almost exclusively built in this material. For over fifteen years (1829–45), the rector here was the unconventional cleric Sydney Smith, called "the greatest master of ridicule since Swift" by Macaulay; more recently it's been home to Evelyn Waugh. A little over three miles further along the A358, and the first stop on the West Somerset Railway (though the station lies around four miles west of the village), **CROWCOMBE** is another typical cob-and-thatch Quantock village, with a well-preserved Church House from 1515. Opposite, the parish church has some pagan-looking carved bench-ends from around the same time that are worth a look.

There's **camping**, plus one room **B&B** (❷), at *Quantock Orchard Caravan Park* (☎01984/618618, ⓦwww.quantockorchard.co.uk), south of Crowcombe towards Triscombe, which has a heated pool and also rents out **mountain bikes**. The cycle, hike or drive across the Quantocks from Crowcombe to Nether Stowey takes in some of the range's loveliest wooded scenery.

Travel details

Buses

For information on all local and national bus services, contact Traveline ☎0871/200 2233, ⓦwww.traveline .org.uk.

Bath to: Bradford-on-Avon (Mon–Sat every 30min, Sun every 2hr; 30min); Bristol (Mon–Sat every 12min, Sun every 30min; 55min); London (10 daily; 3hr–3hr 50min); Salisbury (Mon–Sat 10 daily, Sun 1; 1hr 15min); Wells (Mon–Sat hourly, Sun 7; 1hr 15min).

Bridgwater to: Glastonbury (Mon–Sat hourly, Sun 4; 50min–1hr 10min); Holford (Mon–Sat 4 daily, Sun 6; 30–50min); Nether Stowey (6 daily; 40min); Taunton (Mon–Sat every 30min, Sun every 2hr; 45min); Wells (Mon–Sat hourly, Sun 4; 1hr 10min–1hr 25min).

Bristol to: Bath (Mon–Sat every 12min, Sun every 30min; 50min); Glastonbury (hourly; 1hr 15min); London (1–2 hourly; 2hr 30min); Wells (1–2 hourly; 1hr).

Glastonbury to: Bridgwater (Mon–Sat hourly, Sun 4 daily; 50min–1hr 10min); Bristol (hourly; 1hr 10min); Wells (2–4 hourly; 15min).

Wells to: Bath (Mon–Sat hourly, Sun 7 daily; 1hr 15min); Bridgwater (Mon–Sat hourly, Sun 4; 1hr 10min–1hr 25min); Bristol (1–2 hourly; 1hr); Glastonbury (2–4 hourly; 15min); Wookey Hole (Mon–Sat 9 daily, Sun 4 daily; 10min).

Trains

For information on all local and national rail services, contact National Rail Enquiries ☎0845/748 4950, ⓦwww.nationalrail.co.uk.

Bath to: Bristol (2–3 hourly; 15min); London (1–2 hourly; 1hr 30min); Salisbury (1–2 hourly; 1hr).

Bristol to: Bath (2–3 hourly; 15min); Birmingham (every 30min; 1hr 30min); Bridgwater (hourly; 45min); Cheltenham (2–3 hourly; 40min–1hr); Exeter (1–2 hourly; 1hr); Gloucester (hourly; 50min); London (every 30min; 1hr 45min).

6

Devon and Cornwall

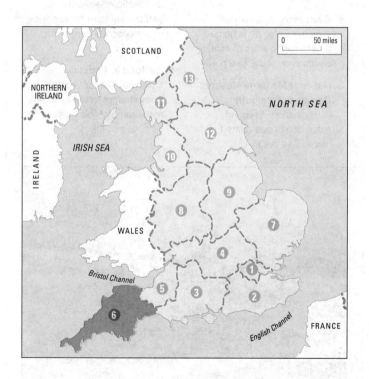

CHAPTER 6 # Highlights

* **Sidmouth Folk Week** Great folk and roots music from around the country, with plenty of workshops, ceilidhs and busking. See p.394

* **South West Coast Path** The ever-changing vistas ensure constant variety on Britain's longest waymarked path. See p.426

* **Eden Project, Cornwall** A disused clay pit is home to a fantastic array of exotic plants and crops. See p.434

* **National Maritime Museum Cornwall, Falmouth** A fascinating, all-round exhibition of sea-related items. See p.438

* **Lizard Point, Cornwall** This unspoiled headland is the starting point for some inspiring walks. See p.441

* **Tate St Ives, Cornwall** Iconic beachside showcase for local and contemporary art. See p.451

* **Surfing in Newquay** Ranks of Atlantic rollers draw enthusiasts from far and wide to the beaches here. See p.456

* **Seafood in Padstow, Cornwall** The local catch goes straight to the excellent restaurants of this bustling port. See p.459

▲ Surfing in Newquay

6

Devon and Cornwall

At the western extremity of England, the counties of **Devon and Cornwall** encompass everything from genteel, cosy villages to wild expanses of granite moorland and vast Atlantic-facing strands of golden sand. The combination of rural peace and first-class beaches has made the peninsula perennially popular with tourists, so much so that tourism has replaced the traditional occupations of fishing and farming as the main source of employment and income. Enough remains of these beleaguered communities to preserve the region's authentic character, however – even if this can be occasionally obscured during the summer season. Avoid the peak periods and you'll be seduced by the genuine appeal of this region.

Although the human history of the area has left its stamp, it's the natural landscape which exerts the strongest pull, and not just in the beauty of the long, deeply indented seaboard. Straddling the border between Devon and Somerset, **Exmoor** is one of the peninsula's three great moors, its heathery slopes much favoured by hunting parties as well as by hikers. For wilderness, however, nothing can beat the remoter tracts of **Dartmoor**, which takes up much of the southern half of inland Devon. The greatest of the West Country's granite massifs, most of Dartmoor retains its solitude in spite of its proximity to the only major cities at this end of the country, either of which would make a good touring base. Of the two, **Exeter** is by far the more interesting, dominated by the twin towers of its medieval cathedral and offering a rich selection of restaurants and nightlife. Much of the city was destroyed by bombing during World War II, though the largest city of Devon and Cornwall, **Plymouth**, suffered far worse, the consequence of its historic role as a great naval port. Bland postwar development inflicted almost as much damage as the Luftwaffe, although enough of Plymouth's Elizabethan core has survived to merit a visit, and the city, by capitalizing on its maritime associations, has succeeded in reviving its port area.

The coastline on either side of Exeter and Plymouth is within easy reach. Warmed by the Gulf Stream, and enjoying more hours of sunshine than virtually anywhere else in England, this part of the country can sometimes come fairly close to the atmosphere of the Mediterranean, and indeed Devon's principal resort, **Torquay**, styles itself the capital of the "English Riviera". St Tropez it ain't, but there's no denying a certain glamour, far removed from the old-fashioned charm of the seaside towns of **east Devon**, or the cliff-backed resorts of the county's northern littoral.

Cornwall, too, has its pockets of concentrated tourist development – chiefly at **Falmouth** and **Newquay**, the first of these a sailing centre, the second a mecca for surfers drawn to its choice of west-facing beaches. **St Ives**, also, has long attracted the crowds, though the town has a separate identity as a magnet

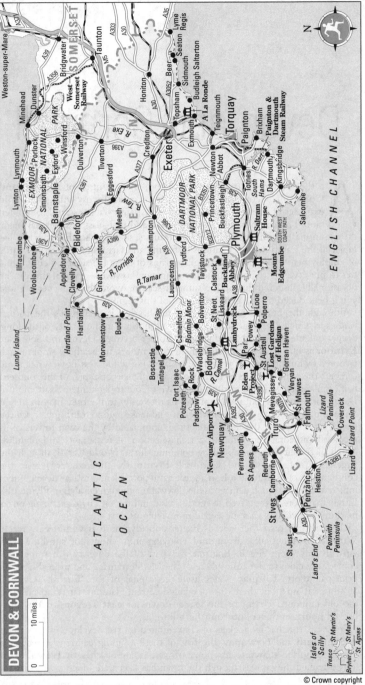

DEVON & CORNWALL

0   10 miles

N

for the arts. Despite the tourist incursions, this county is essentially less domesticated than its agricultural neighbour, in part due to the overbearing presence of the turbulent Atlantic, which is never more than half an hour's drive away. The restless waves give Cornwall's old fishing ports an almost embattled character, especially on the north coast, where the fortified headland of **Tintagel** – the most famous of the many places hereabouts to boast a connection with King Arthur and his knights – and the rock-walled harbour of **Boscastle** are typical of the county's craggy appeal, but the full elemental power of the ocean can best be appreciated on the twin pincers of **Lizard Point** and **Land's End**, where the splintered cliffs resound to the constant thunder of the waves. And there's another factor contributing to Cornwall's starker feel – unlike Devon, this county was once considerably industrialized, and is dotted with remnants of its now defunct mining industries, their ruins presenting a salutary counterpoint to the tourist-centred seaside towns. A disused clay pit, though, is the site of one of Cornwall's biggest success stories of recent times, the **Eden Project**, which imaginatively highlights the diversity of the planet's plant systems, with the help of science-fiction "biomes" where tropical and Mediterranean climates and conditions have been recreated.

The best way of exploring the coast of Devon and Cornwall is along the **South West Coast Path**, Britain's longest waymarked footpath, which allows the dauntless hiker to cover almost six hundred miles from the Somerset border to Poole in Dorset. Getting around by **public transport** in the West Country can be a convoluted and lengthy process, especially if you're relying on the often deficient bus network. By train, you can reach Exeter, Plymouth and Penzance, with a handful of branch lines wandering off to the major coastal resorts – though there's nothing like the extensive network the Victorians once enjoyed.

Devon

With its rolling meadows, narrow lanes and remote thatched cottages, **Devon** has long been idealized as a vision of a pre-industrial, "authentic" England, and a quick tour of the county might suggest that this is largely a region of cosy, gentrified villages inhabited mainly by retired folk and urban refugees. Certainly parts of Devon suffer from an excess of cloying gentility, but its stereotyped image has a positive side to it as well – chiefly that zealous care is taken to preserve the countryside and coast in the undeveloped condition for which they are famous. The county still offers an abundance of genuine tranquillity, from moorland villages with an appeal that goes deeper than the merely picturesque, to quiet coves on the spectacular coastline.

Devon has played a leading part in England's **maritime history**, and you can't go far without meeting some reminder of the great names of Tudor and Stuart seafaring, particularly in the two cities of **Exeter** and **Plymouth**. These days the nautical tradition is perpetuated on a domesticated scale by yachtspeople taking advantage of Devon's numerous creeks and bays, especially on its southern coast, where ports such as **Dartmouth** and **Salcombe** are awash with amateur sailors. Land-bound tourists flock to the sandy beaches and seaside resorts, of which **Torquay**, on the south coast, and **Ilfracombe**, on the north, are the busiest – though the most attractive are those which have retained something of their nineteenth-century elegance, such as **Sidmouth**, in east Devon. Other seaside villages retain a low level of fishing activity but otherwise live on a stilted olde worlde image, of which **Clovelly** is the supreme example. **Inland**, Devon is characterized by swards of lush pasture and a scattering of sheltered villages, the county's low population density dropping to almost zero on **Dartmoor**, the wildest and bleakest of the region's moors, and **Exmoor**, whose seaboard constitutes one of the West Country's most scenic littorals.

Exeter and Plymouth are on the main **rail** lines from London and the Midlands, with branch lines from Exeter linking the north coast at Barnstaple and the south-coast towns of Exmouth and Torquay. **Buses** fan out along the coasts and into the interior, though the service can be extremely rudimentary for the smaller villages.

Exeter

EXETER's sights are richer than those of any other town in Devon or Cornwall, the legacy of an eventful history since its Celtic foundation and the establishment here of the most westerly Roman outpost. After the Roman withdrawal, Exeter was refounded by Alfred the Great and by the time of the Norman Conquest had become one of the largest towns in England, profiting from its position on the banks of the River Exe. The expansion of the wool trade in the Tudor period sustained the city until the eighteenth century, and Exeter has maintained its status as commercial centre and county town, despite having much of its ancient centre gutted by World War II bombing. You're likely to pass through this transport hub for Devon at least once on your West Country travels, and Exeter's sturdy cathedral and the remnants of its compact old quarter would repay an extended visit.

Arrival, information and accommodation

Exeter has two **train stations**, Exeter Central and St David's, the latter a little further out from the centre of town, though connected by frequent city buses. South West trains on the London Waterloo–Salisbury line stop at both, as do trains on the Tarka Line to Barnstaple (see p.417) and those to Exmouth, though Exeter Central is not served by most other long-distance trains. **Buses** stop on Paris Street, which is opposite the **tourist office**, at Dix's Field, off Princesshay (Mon–Sat 9am–5pm, plus Sun 10am–4pm in July & Aug; ℡01392/665700, ⊛www.exeterandessentialdevon.com). There's a second visitor centre in The Quay House on Exeter's Quay (April–Oct daily 10am–5pm, Nov–Easter Sat & Sun 11am–4pm; ℡01392/271611). The **Internet** can be accessed at the library on Castle Street (Mon, Tues, Thurs & Fri 9.30am–7pm, Wed 10am–5pm, Sat 9.30am–4pm, Sun 11am–2.30pm), and the *New Horizon* café at 47 Longbrook St (daily 9am–9pm), where you can also nibble on Moroccan snacks.

Most of Exeter's B&B **accommodation** lies north of the centre, near the two stations.

Hotels and B&Bs

Abode Exeter Cathedral Yard ℡01392/319955, ⊛www.abodehotels.co.uk. Built in 1769 and reputedly the first inn in England to be described as a "hotel". Now part of an upmarket chain, it boasts a superb location, with contemporary bedrooms

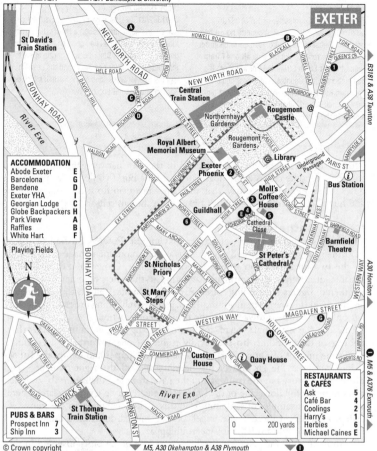

EXETER

St David's Train Station

New North Road

Central Train Station

Northernhay Gardens

Rougemont Castle

Rougemont Gardens

Royal Albert Memorial Museum

Exeter Phoenix

Library

Underground Passages

Bus Station

Moll's Coffee House

Guildhall

Cathedral Close

Barnfield Theatre

St Nicholas Priory

St Mary Steps

St Peter's Cathedral

Custom House

Quay House

St Thomas Train Station

River Exe

Playing Fields

Bonhay Road

ACCOMMODATION

Abode Exeter	E
Barcelona	G
Bendene	D
Exeter YHA	I
Georgian Lodge	C
Globe Backpackers	H
Park View	A
Raffles	B
White Hart	F

PUBS & BARS

Prospect Inn	7
Ship Inn	3

RESTAURANTS & CAFÉS

Ask	5
Café Bar	4
Coolings	2
Harry's	1
Herbies	6
Michael Caines	E

0 — 200 yards

© Crown copyright

and the celebrated *Michael Caines* restaurant on the ground floor (see p.392). **⓿**

Barcelona Magdalen Street ☏01392/281000, ⊛www.aliashotels.com. Stylish designer hotel installed in a red-brick Victorian eye hospital, with strong colours, light, spacious rooms, and a Mediterranean-style bistro. **⓿**

Bendene 15 Richmond Rd ☏01392/213526, ⊛www.bendene.co.uk. Smallish but comfortable rooms (most en suite), a heated outdoor swimming pool (summer only) and a handy location near Central Station are the main lures of this terrace house. No credit cards. **❸**

Georgian Lodge 5 Bystock Terrace ☏01392/213079, ⊛www.georgianlodge.com. Just up from Exeter Central Station, this has bright, neat rooms, most of them overlooking a quiet square. **❹**

Park View 8 Howell Rd ☏01392/271772, ⊛www.parkviewhotel.freeserve.co.uk. Conveniently located for St David's Station, this Georgian building has airy rooms overlooking a park, mostly en suite and with Wi-Fi access. **❸**

Raffles 11 Blackall Rd ☏01392/270200, ⊛www.raffles-exeter.co.uk. An elegant Victorian house whose rooms are furnished with Pre-Raphaelite etchings and other items from the owner's antique business. Breakfasts make use of the organic garden produce. **❹**

White Hart 65 South St ☏01392/279897, ⊛www.roomattheinn.info. Old coaching inn with period trappings and a lovely old bar, though rooms have a bland business ambience. Prices drop at weekends. **❸–❹**

Hostels

Exeter YHA 47 Countess Wear Rd ☎0870/770 5826, ⓔexeter@yha.org.uk. A country house two miles southeast of the centre, with dorm beds from £16 and bike rental. Take minibus #K or #T from High Street or South Street (#57 or #85 from the bus station) to the Countess Wear post office on Topsham Road, a fifteen-minute ride, then a ten-minute walk. Also reachable on the footpath alongside the River Exe from The Quay.

Globe Backpackers 71 Holloway St ☎01392/215521, ⓦwww.exeterbackpackers.co .uk. Clean and central (though a bit of a hike from the stations), this hostel has good showers and an upbeat atmosphere. Bunk-beds in dorms of six to ten cost from £15 for one night, and the seventh night is free for week-long stays. Facilities include kitchen and Internet access. ❶

⑥ The City

Most of Exeter's sights are concentrated in the area between the High Street and the river. The city is easily negotiated on foot, but if you envisage using the buses on an intensive one-day visit, pick up a bus map from the tourist office and buy a "Day Rider" all-day bus ticket from the bus station (£4).

Exeter Cathedral

The most distinctive feature of Exeter's skyline, **St Peter's Cathedral** (daily 9.30am–5pm; £3.50 suggested donation), is a stately monument made conspicuous by the two great Norman towers flanking the nave. Close up, it's the facade's ornate Gothic screen that commands attention: its three tiers of sculpted (and very weathered) figures – including Alfred, Athelstan, Canute, William the Conqueror and Richard II – were begun around 1360, part of a rebuilding programme which left only the Norman towers from the original construction.

Entering the cathedral, you're confronted by the longest unbroken **Gothic ceiling** in the world, its **bosses** vividly painted – one, towards the west front, shows the murder of Thomas à Becket. The **Lady Chapel** and **Chapter House** – respectively at the far end of the building and off the right transept – are thirteenth-century, but the main part of the nave, including the lavish rib-vaulting, dates from the full flowering of the English Decorated style, a century later. There are many fine examples of sculpture from this period, including, in the minstrels' gallery high up on the left side, angels playing musical instruments, and, below them, figures of Edward III and Queen Philippa.

Dominating the cathedral's central space are the organ pipes installed in the seventeenth century and harmonizing perfectly with the linear patterns of the roof and arches. In the **choir** don't miss the sixty-foot **bishop's throne** or the **misericords** – decorated with mythological figures dating from around 1260, they are thought to be the oldest in the country. Near the entrance stands a comparatively recent addition to the many medieval tombs and memorials lining the cathedral's walls: a monument to R.D. Blackmore, author of *Lorna Doone*. If you want to make sure you don't miss a thing, take one of the free **tours** (March–Oct Mon–Fri 11am & 2.30pm, Sat 11am; also July–Sept Mon–Sat 12.30pm). Photo permits cost £1.

Outside, a graceful statue of the theologian Richard Hooker surveys the **Cathedral Close**, a motley mixture of architectural styles from Tudor to Regency, though most display Exeter's trademark red-brick work. One of the finest buildings is the Elizabethan **Mol's Coffee House**, impressively timbered and gabled, now a map shop.

From the High Street to the river

Some older buildings are still standing amid the banal concrete of the modern town centre, including, on the pedestrianized **High Street**, the fourteenth-century **Guildhall** (Mon–Fri 11am–1pm & 2–4.30pm, Sat 10am–12.30pm; sometimes closed for functions, call ☎01392/265500 to check), claimed to be England's oldest municipal building in regular use. Fronted by an elegant Renaissance portico, the main chamber merits a glance for its arched roof timbers, which rest on carved bears holding staves, symbols of the Yorkist cause during the Wars of the Roses.

Around the corner from the High Street on Queen Street, the **Royal Albert Memorial Museum** is the closest thing in Devon to a county museum, but remains closed for a major refit until 2010. Behind the museum, Rougemont and Northernhay Gardens hold what remains of **Rougemont Castle**, now little more than a perimeter of red-stone walls. Off the top end of the High Street, the Princesshay shopping precinct holds the entrance to a network of **underground passages** (June–Sept & school hols Mon–Sat 9.30am–5.30pm, Sun 10.30am–4pm; Oct–May Tues–Fri 11.30am–5.30pm, Sat 9.30am–5.30pm, Sun 11.30am–4pm; £5), first excavated in the thirteenth century to bring water to the cathedral precincts, and now visitable on a guided **tour**; it's not recommended to claustrophobes.

In the opposite direction, High Street leads to Fore Street, off which **St Nicholas Priory** (Mon–Sat 10am–5pm), part of a small Benedictine foundation that became a merchant's home after the Dissolution, has been restored to what it might have looked like in the Tudor era. Across Fore Street, trailing down towards the river, cobbled **Stepcote Hill** was once the main road into Exeter from the west, though it is difficult to imagine this steep and narrow lane as a main thoroughfare. Another of central Exeter's ancient churches, **St Mary Steps**, stands surrounded by mainly Tudor houses at the bottom, with a fine seventeenth-century clock on its tower and a late Gothic nave inside.

Exeter's centre is bounded to the southwest by the River Exe, where the port area is now mostly devoted to leisure activities, particularly around **The Quay**. Pubs, shops and cafés share the space with handsomely restored nineteenth-century warehouses and the smart **Custom House**, built in 1681, its opulence reflecting the former importance of the cloth trade. Next door, the Quay House from the same period has an information desk and, upstairs, a video on Exeter's history. The area comes into its own at night, but is worth a wander at any time, and you can **rent bikes** and **canoes** at Saddles & Paddles on The Quay (☎01392/424241, ⊛www.sadpad.com) to explore the **Exeter Canal**, which runs five miles to Topsham and beyond.

Eating and drinking

Exeter is well supplied with **eateries** to suit every pocket. Good **pubs** are harder to find, though The Quay makes a lively spot to while away an evening over a pint or two.

Restaurants and cafés

Ask 5 Cathedral Close ☎01392/427127. This lovely old building facing the cathedral makes a superb setting for the standard pizzas and pastas (£6–9). Outdoor seating in the courtyard.

Café Bar Cathedral Yard ☎01392/223626. Opposite the cathedral, this is a casually modish spot for a coffee, lunch (toasties, salads, burgers and pastas) or a full evening meal (set menus for £12.50 and £15.50). There's live music on Fri and DJs on Sat, for which booking is advised.

Coolings Gandy St. Popular wine bar and bistro serving tasty lunches (around £7) – it's also open until late evening with a cellar bar open for cocktails on Fri & Sat.

Harry's 86 Longbrook St ☎01392/202234. In a converted church, this place offers good-value Mexican, Italian and American staples (most about £11) and usually attracts a cheery crowd.

Herbie's 15 North St ☎01392/258473. Serves up great wholefood dishes (average

£8) and organic beers, wines and ice cream. Closed all Sun & Mon eve.

Michael Caines *Abode Exeter* hotel, Cathedral Yard ☎01392/223638. Exeter's classiest restaurant offers sophisticated Modern European cuisine in sleek surroundings. Prices are fairly high (mains around £22), but there are reasonable fixed-price menus (£13 and £17.50) at lunchtime. Closed Sun.

Pubs

Prospect Inn The Quay. You can eat and drink sitting outside at this seventeenth-century waterside pub, which was the setting for TV drama *The Onedin Line*.

Ship Inn St Martin's Lane. Claiming to have once been Francis Drake's local, this pub also serves food (jacket potatoes, baps and baguettes) in the low-ceilinged bar adorned with knots and clay pipes, and main meals in the bistro upstairs.

Nightlife and entertainment

If you're not turned on by the brash **club complexes** on Exeter's Quay, you could opt instead for the mellower *Timepiece* on Little Castle Street (☎01392/493096), occupying a former prison, or the club nights at the subterranean *Cavern Club* (☎01392/495370, ⊛www.cavernclub.co.uk), with entrances on Queen and Gandy streets – though the latter is best known for **live bands**, mainly post-punk, dub, electro and indie. Off Gandy Street, live music is among the cultural pursuits at **Exeter Phoenix** (☎01392/667080, ⊛www.exeterphoenix.org.uk), an arts centre which also hosts art-house films, exhibitions and readings.

Of the town's **theatres**, the Northcott, near the university on Stocker Road (☎01392/493493, ⊛www.exeternorthcott.co.uk), and the Barnfield, on Barnfield Road (☎01392/270891, ⊛www.barnfieldtheatre.co.uk), have the best productions – both also have music performances in a range of genres. During two weeks in June and November, the **Exeter Festival** (☎01392/265200, ⊛www.exeter.gov.uk/festival) takes over various venues around town, featuring a range of cultural events, while, in March, **Vibraphonic**, based at the Phoenix, concentrates more on modern music.

The east Devon coast

The coast south and east of Exeter holds an architectural oddity, **A La Ronde**, as well as a string of old-fashioned seaside resorts, stretching towards the Dorset border. None of them is over-commercialized, though still best seen outside the summer peak, with **Sidmouth** and the neighbouring village of **Beer** being good choices for an overnight stop.

Frequent **trains** connect Exeter with Exmouth, while A La Ronde and Exmouth are both served by **bus** #57 from Exeter's bus station. For Budleigh Salterton and Sidmouth, take bus #157 from Exmouth; #52A and #52B connect Sidmouth directly with Exeter. The #899 service links Sidmouth with Beer (Mon–Sat), and the #X53 from Exeter stops in Beer (Sun only Nov–April) en route to the Jurassic Coast (see p.270).

A La Ronde

The Gothic folly of **A La Ronde** (Easter–Oct Mon–Wed, Sat & Sun 11am–5pm; £5.20; NT), a couple of miles outside Exmouth off the A376, was the creation of two cousins, Jane and Mary Parminter, who in the 1790s were inspired by their European Grand Tour to construct a sixteen-sided house possibly based on the Byzantine basilica of San Vitale in Ravenna. The end product is filled with mementoes of the Parminters' travels as well as a number of their more offbeat creations, such as a frieze made of feathers culled from game birds and chickens. In the upper rooms are a gallery and staircase completely covered in shells, too fragile to be visited, though part can be glimpsed from the completely enclosed octagonal room on the first floor – a closed-circuit TV system enables visitors to home in on details. Superb views extend over the Exe Estuary.

Exmouth and Budleigh Salterton

EXMOUTH started as a Roman port and went on to become the first of the county's resorts to be popularized by holiday-makers in the late eighteenth century. Overlooking lawns, rock pools and a respectable two miles of beach, Exmouth's Georgian terraces once accommodated such folk as the wives of Nelson and Byron – installed at nos. 6 and 19 The Beacon respectively (on a rise overlooking the seafront, above the public gardens). From Easter to October, Exmouth is linked by hourly **ferry** to Starcross, on the other side of the Exe estuary (£4.50 single fare), where you can pick up a bus to Torquay (see p.395). There's a **tourist office** on Alexandra Terrace (Easter–Oct Mon–Sat 10am–5pm; Nov–Easter Mon–Sat 10am–2pm; ℡01395/222299, ⓦwww.exmouthguide.co.uk).

Four miles east of Exmouth, bounded on each side by red sandstone cliffs, **BUDLEIGH SALTERTON** has a more genteel air – its thatched and whitewashed cottages attracted such figures as Noël Coward and P.G. Wodehouse, and John Millais painted his famous *Boyhood of Raleigh* on the shingle beach here (Sir Walter Raleigh was born in pretty East Budleigh, a couple of miles inland). Three miles east, **Ladram Bay** is a popular pebbly beach sheltered by woods and beautiful eroded cliffs. If you want to stay in the area, contact Budleigh's **tourist office** on Fore Street (Easter–Sept Mon–Sat 10am–5pm; Oct–Easter Mon–Thurs & Sat 10am–1pm, Fri 10am–3pm; ℡01395/445275, ⓦwww.visitbudleigh.com).

Sidmouth

Set amidst a shelf of crumbling red sandstone, cream-and-white **SIDMOUTH** is the chief resort on this stretch of coast and boasts nearly five hundred buildings listed as having special historic or architectural interest, among them the stately Georgian homes of **York Terrace** behind the Esplanade. Moreover, the **beaches** are better tended than many along this stretch, not only the mile-long main town beach but also Jacob's Ladder, a cliff-backed shingle-and-sand strip beyond Connaught Gardens to the west of town. To the east, the coast path climbs steep Salcombe Hill to follow cliffs that give sanctuary to a range of birdlife including yellowhammers and green woodpeckers, as well as the rarer grasshopper warbler. Further on, the path descends to meet one of the most isolated and attractive beaches in the area, **Weston Mouth**.

The **tourist office** is on Ham Lane, off the eastern end of the Esplanade (March & April Mon–Thurs 10am–4pm, Fri & Sat 10am–5pm, Sun 10am–1pm; May–July, Sept & Oct Mon–Sat 10am–5pm, Sun 10am–4pm; Aug Mon–Sat 10am–6pm, Sun 10am–5pm; Nov–Feb Mon–Sat 10am–1.30pm; ℡01395/516441, ⓦwww.visitsidmouth.co.uk). Among the town's vast range of **accommodation**, you can't beat ⚘*Rock Cottage* for location, a National Trust-owned B&B at the quieter, western end of the Esplanade on Peak Hill Road (℡01395/514253, ⓦwww.rockcottage.co.uk; no credit cards; ❺); the spacious, Edwardian rooms and veranda enjoy great sea views, and there's access to the beach. Two hundred yards from the seafront, *Rose Cottage* on Coburg Road

(☎01395/577179, Ⓦ www.rosecottage-sidmouth.co.uk; ❹) is equally alluring, a family-run guesthouse with comfy rooms, a garden and a beach hut. Most of the budget choices are a mile or so inland, around Alexandria and Salcombe roads – for example *Kyneton Lodge*, 87 Alexandria Rd (☎01395/513213; no credit cards; ❸; closed Dec–Jan), with three simple en-suite rooms and a guests' sitting room. The nearest **campsite** lies a mile and a half east of town at Salcombe Regis: *Salcombe Regis Camping and Caravan Park* (☎01395/514303, Ⓦ www.salcombe-regis.co.uk; closed Nov–Easter).

For **meals** in town, *Mocha Restaurant* on The Esplanade (☎01395/512882) serves jacket potatoes, paninis and hot lunches, including crab and a seafood platter for under £10 (daytime only, eves in July & Aug), while *Brown's Bistro and Wine Bar* at 33 Fore St (☎01395/516724; closed Mon & Tues in winter) offers a good-value early-evening menu. Among the **pubs**, *The Dove* on Fore Street, which has an open fire in winter, feels authentically local, while the agreeable *Swan Inn*, near the tourist office at 37 York St, is a fun place to be at festival time, with real ales, bar meals and a garden.

Beer

Eight miles east along the coast, the fishing village of **BEER** lies huddled within a small sheltered cove between gleaming white headlands. A stream rushes along a deep channel dug into Beer's main street, and if you can ignore the crowds in high summer much of the village looks unchanged since the time when it was a smugglers' eyrie. The area is best known for its quarries, which were worked from Roman times until the nineteenth century: **Beer stone** was used in many of Devon's churches and houses, and also went into the construction of some buildings in London. A mile or so west of the village, you can take a guided tour around **Beer Quarry Caves** (Easter–Sept daily 10am–6pm; Oct daily 11am–5pm; last tour 1hr before closing; £5.50), which includes a small exhibition of pieces carved by medieval masons. Take something warm to wear.

Bay View (☎01297/20489, Ⓦ www.bayviewbeer.com; no credit cards; ❷), overlooking the sea on Fore Street, is the best of the **B&Bs**, and east Devon's only **youth hostel** is half a mile northwest, at Bovey Combe, Townsend (☎0870/770 5690, ✉ beer@yha.org.uk; from £14; call to check opening). For **food**, head for the *Barrel o' Beer* pub (☎01297/20099), on Fore Street, where the moderately priced restaurant menu includes oysters and home-smoked fish, or, at the bottom of the street, the *Anchor Inn*, where you can have beers and snacks overlooking the sea in its cliff-top garden or choose from the range of seafood on offer in the separate restaurant.

The "English Riviera" region

The wedge of land between Dartmoor and the sea contains some of Devon's most fertile pastures, backing onto some of the West Country's most popular coastal resorts. Chief of these is **Torbay**, an amalgam of **Torquay**, **Paignton** and **Brixham**, together forming the nucleus of an area optimistically known as "**The English Riviera**". South of the Torbay conurbation, the port of **Dartmouth** offers a calmer alternative, linked by riverboat to historic and almost unspoiled **Totnes**. West of the River Dart, the rich agricultural district of **South Hams** extends as far as Plymouth, cleft by a web of rivers flowing off Dartmoor. The main town here is **Kingsbridge**, at the head of an estuary down which you can ferry to the sailing resort of **Salcombe**.

   Trains from Exeter to Plymouth run down the coast as far as Teignmouth before striking inland for Totnes – to get to Torbay, change at Newton Abbot. The frequent #X46 **bus** connects Exeter and Torquay in less than an hour. For the hinterland and points south and west along the coast, you can rely on a network of buses from Torquay, and travellers to Totnes and Dartmouth could make use of the **South Devon Railway** and **boats** along the River Dart.

Torquay

TORQUAY, the largest component of the super-resort of **Torbay**, comes closest to living up to the self-penned "English Riviera" sobriquet, sporting a mini-corniche and promenades landscaped with flowerbeds. The much-vaunted palm trees and the coloured lights that festoon the harbour by night contribute to the town's unique flavour, a slightly frayed combination of the exotic and the classically English. The most famous figures associated with Torquay – crimewriter Agatha Christie and traveller Freya Stark – have been joined in recent years by the fictional angst-ridden hotelier Basil Fawlty.

Arrival, information and accommodation

The **train station** is off Rathmore Road, next to the Torre Abbey gardens; most **buses** leave from outside the Pavilion, including the #X80 to Totnes and

▲ Torquay harbour

Plymouth, and the frequent #12 and #12A service linking Torquay with Paignton and Brixham. Torquay's well-organized **tourist office** is on Vaughan Parade, by the harbour (Mon–Sat 9.30am–5/5.30pm, plus Sun 10am–4pm June–Sept; ☎01803/211211, ⓦwww.englishriviera.co.uk). Tourist offices in Paignton and Brixham share the same times and telephone number.

Torquay has plenty of **accommodation**, but you'll need to book in advance during peak season. Most of the budget choices lie along and around Belgrave Road and, slightly further out, Avenue Road.

Allerdale 21 Croft Rd ☎01803/292667, ⓦwww.allerdalehotel.co.uk. The place to come for views and stately surroundings, with a long, sloping, lawned garden and a snooker room. Wi-Fi available. ❹

The Exton 12 Bridge Rd ☎01803/293561, ⓦwww.extonhotel.co.uk. Small, clean and quiet hotel, very close to Belgrave Road and a ten-minute walk from the train station. Evening meals available. ❸

Lanscombe House Cockington ☎01803/606938, ⓦwww.lanscombehouse.co.uk. A couple of miles west of the centre outside the touristy village of

Cockington, this elegant B&B offers rural seclusion, with airy rooms and a walled garden. ❺

Mulberry House 1 Scarborough Rd ☎01803/213639, ⓦwww.mulberryhousetorquay .co.uk. Clean white walls, antique pine furnishings and crisp bed linen set the tone in this Victorian guesthouse, and there's a good restaurant. ❺

Torquay Backpackers 119 Abbey Rd ☎01803/299924, ⓦwww.torquaybackpackers .co.uk. Central, cheap and friendly hostel with dorm beds for £12 a night (less in winter), and doubles with shared bathroom. A ten-minute walk from the station or a free pick-up service. ❶

The Town

Torquay's seafront is centred on the small **harbour** and marina off The Strand, where the mingling crowds can seem almost Mediterranean, especially at night. To one side stands the copper-domed **Pavilion**, an Edwardian building that originally housed a ballroom and assembly hall and is now refurbished with shops. Behind the Pavilion, limestone cliffs sprouting white high-rise hotels and apartment blocks separate the harbour area from Torquay's main beach, **Abbey Sands**. Good for chucking a frisbee about but too busy in summer for serious relaxation, it takes its name from **Torre Abbey**, sited in ornamental gardens behind the beachside road (daily 10am–5/6pm; £5.90). The Norman church that once stood here was razed by Henry VIII, though a gatehouse, tithe barn, chapter house and tower escaped demolition, and recent excavations have uncovered medieval walls. The present **Abbey Mansion** is a seventeenth- and eighteenth-century construction, now containing a suite of period rooms and a good museum, with collections of silver and glass, window designs by Edward Burne-Jones, illustrations by William Blake, and nineteenth-century and contemporary works of art.

A more down-to-earth collection can be viewed at **Torquay Museum**, a short walk up from the harbour at 529 Babbacombe Rd (Easter–Oct Mon–Sat 10am–5pm, also Sun in summer school hols 1.30–5pm; £3.95), which includes a section devoted to Agatha Christie, who was born and raised in Torquay, though most of the space here is given over to local history and natural history displays.

At the northern end of the harbour, **Living Coasts** (daily: Easter–Sept 10am–4.30/5.30pm; £6.75, or £14.50 with Paignton Zoo, see p.397) is home to a variety of fauna and flora found on British shores, including puffins, penguins and seals. You can see the animals in their carefully recreated habitats, and feed them at various intervals throughout the day. The rooftop café and restaurant have splendid panoramic views. Beyond here, the coast path leads round a promontory to reach some good sand beaches: **Meadfoot Beach** is one of the busiest, reached by crossing Daddyhole Plain, an open green space named after a large chasm in the adjacent cliff caused by a landslide, but locally attributed to the devil

("Daddy"). North of the Hope's Nose promontory, the coast path leads to a string of less crowded beaches, including **Babbacombe Beach** and, beyond, **Watcombe** and **Maidencombe**.

Eating, drinking and nightlife

Torquay has a surprisingly high standard of **restaurants**, with one of the best being the award-winning *Elephant*, 3 Beacon Terrace, right on the harbour (℡01803/200044), where you can enjoy fine – if slightly pretentious – dining in the intimate upstairs area (open eves Tues–Sat; closed Jan), or more rough-and-ready fare in the casual and considerably cheaper ground-floor brasserie (Tues–Sat all day, plus Sun lunch). Alternatively, the nearby *Orange Tree*, 14 Parkhill Rd (℡01803/213936; eves only), serves up Modern British and European dishes for around £16. Cheaper places are thick on the ground: try *Al Beb*, 64 Torwood St (℡01803/211755; closed lunchtime Mon, Wed, Thurs & Sun), which has an extensive menu, a North African ambience and belly-dancing (Fri & Sat). Also strong on atmosphere is the *Hole in the Wall* **pub** on Park Lane, which serves decent vegetarian dishes – it was the Irish playwright Sean O'Casey's boozer when he lived in Torquay.

Torquay has the hottest and rowdiest **nightlife** in Devon; the main clubs are all near the harbour, including, on Torwood Street, *The Venue* (℡01803/213903, Ⓦwww.venueclubbing.co.uk) and *Bohemia* (℡01803/292079), and *Valbonne's* on Higher Union Street (℡01803/290458, Ⓦwww.thevalbonne.co.uk). By the harbour, *Café Mambo* on The Strand (℡01803/291112, Ⓦwww.cafemambo .co.uk) has three floors including a patio, with Thai food on hand and nightly DJs playing chart, hip-hop and R&B. *Rocky's* (℡01803/292279), near the Pavilion on Rock Road (off Abbey Road), is a long-established gay club.

Paignton

Not so much a rival to Torquay as its complement, **PAIGNTON** lacks the gloss of its neighbour, but also its pretensions. Activity is concentrated at the southern end of the wide town beach, around the small harbour that nestles in the lee of the appropriately named Redcliffe headland. Otherwise, diversion-seekers could wander over to **Paignton Zoo** (daily: summer 10am–6pm, winter 10am–4.30pm or dusk, last entry 1hr before closing; £9.35, or £14.50 with Living Coasts, see opposite), a mile out on Totnes Road, or board the **Paignton & Dartmouth Steam Railway** at Paignton's Queen's Park train station near the harbour (℡01803/555872, Ⓦwww.paignton-steamrailway.co.uk). Running almost daily from Easter to October, plus a few dates in December, the line connects with Paignton's other main beach – **Goodrington Sands** – before trundling alongside the Dart estuary to Kingswear, seven miles away. If you can stomach the heavy-handed Victorian trappings, it's a pleasant way to view the scenic countryside, and you could make a day of it by using the ferry connection from Kingswear to Dartmouth (see p.400), then taking a river boat up the Dart to Totnes, from where you can catch any bus back to Paignton – a "Round Robin" ticket (£14.50) lets you do this.

Paignton's bus and train stations are next to each other off Sands Road. Five minutes away, the seafront has a **tourist office** (see p.396 for details).

Brixham

From Paignton, it's a fifteen-minute bus ride down to **BRIXHAM**, the prettiest of the Torbay towns. Fishing was for centuries Brixham's lifeblood, its harbour extending some way farther inland than it does now to afford a safe anchorage – a function performed today by an extensive breakwater. Indeed, at the beginning of the nineteenth century, this was the major fish market in the West Country, and it still supplies fish to restaurants as far away as London. The harbour is overlooked by an unflattering statue of William III, a reminder of his landing in Brixham to claim the Crown of England in 1688. Among the trawlers moored here is a full-size reconstruction of the **Golden Hind** (March–Oct daily 9am–4pm, with longer opening in summer; £3), in which Francis Drake circumnavigated the world – though it has no real connection with the port. The boat is surprisingly small, and below decks you can see the extremely cramped surgeon's and carpenter's cabins, and the only slightly grander captain's quarters.

From the quayside, steep lanes and stairways climb up to the older centre around Fore Street, where the bus from Torquay pulls in. East of the harbour, you can reach the promontory of **Berry Head** along a path winding up from the *Berry Head House Hotel*. Fortifications built during the Napoleonic wars are still standing on this southern limit of Torbay, which is now a conservation area, attracting colonies of nesting seabirds and affording fabulous views.

On the quayside, the town's **tourist office** (see p.396 for details) can help with finding **accommodation**. The best places are on King Street, overlooking the harbour: try *Sampford House* at no. 57 (☎01803/857761, ⓦwww .sampfordhouse.com; ❸), a B&B with smallish but smart en-suite rooms, or the classy *Quayside Hotel* (☎01803/855751, ⓦwww.quaysidehotel.co.uk; ❺), with two bars and a restaurant. There's a YHA **hostel** four miles away outside the village of Galmpton, on the banks of the Dart (☎0870/770 5962, ⓔriverdart @yha.org.uk; sporadic opening; from £14), a two-mile walk from Churston Bridge, accessible on frequent buses #12 or #12A and on the Paignton & Dartmouth Steam Railway (see p.397).

When it comes to **eating** options, Brixham offers fish and more fish – from the stalls selling cockles, whelks and mussels on the harbourside to the moderately expensive *Yard Arms* (☎01803/858266; closed Mon lunch; no kids), on Beach Approach off the quayside, a semi-formal bar and bistro with jazz sessions on Sunday evenings. Otherwise the local **pubs** serve decent food; try the *Sprat & Mackerel* by the harbour, or for a more relaxed pint, the *Blue Anchor* on Fore Street, with coal fires and low beams.

Totnes

Most of the Plymouth buses from Paignton and Torquay and trains from Exeter make a stop at **TOTNES**, on the west bank of the River Dart. The town has an ancient pedigree, its period of greatest prosperity occurring in the sixteenth century when this inland port exported cloth to France and brought back wine. Some handsome structures from that era remain, and there is still a working port down on the river, but these days Totnes has mellowed into a residential market town, enjoying an esoteric fame as a centre of the New Age arts-and-crafts crowd. With its arcaded High Street and secretive flowery lanes, Totnes has its syrupy side, partly the result of its proximity to the Torbay tourist hive, but so far its allure has survived more or less intact.

Arrival, information and accommodation

Totnes **train station** lies a few minutes north of the centre, while **buses** pull into The Plains at the bottom of the main street. Signposted off The Plains, the **tourist office** is in The Town Mill, near the Morrisons car park (Mon–Sat 9.30am–5pm; ☎01803/863168, ⓦwww.totnesinformation.co.uk). **Bike rental** is available from Hot Pursuit, 26 The Stables, Ford Road on Totnes Industrial

Estate, a short walk east of the station off Babbage Road (☎01803/865174, Ⓦwww.hotpursuit-cycles.co.uk).

You'll find a range of **accommodation** in and around town, though it can fill quickly. The nearest **campsite** is peaceful *Beara Farm*, five miles northwest of Totnes and close to the River Dart, on Colston Road, Buckfastleigh (☎01364/642234).

3 Plymouth Rd ☎01803/866917, Ⓦwww.mlfen .freeserve.co.uk. Friendly good-value B&B off the High Street, with simple rooms, with and without en-suite facilities, and a small roof terrace. No credit cards. Closed Nov–Feb. ❷

Cott Inn Shinner's Bridge ☎01803/863777, Ⓦwww.thecottinn.co.uk. Two miles west of Totnes on the A385, and close to Dartington, this place is outwardly almost unchanged since its construction in 1320, with snug bedrooms under the eaves. ❺

The Great Grubb Fallowfields, Plymouth Rd ☎01803/849071, Ⓦwww.thegreatgrubb .co.uk. Leather sofas, restful colours, healthy breakfasts and a patio are the main attractions at this B&B. No credit cards. ❹

Royal Seven Stars The Plains ☎01803/862125, Ⓦwww.royalsevenstars.co.uk. Atmospheric coaching inn, very central, where the clean rooms have character and charm. ❺

The Town

Totnes centres on the long main street that starts off as Fore Street, site of the town's **museum** (mid-March to Oct Mon–Fri 10.30am–5pm; £2), which occupies a four-storey Elizabethan house at no. 70. Showing how wealthy clothiers lived at the peak of Totnes's fortunes, it's packed with domestic objects and furniture, and also has a room devoted to local mathematician Charles Babbage, whose "analytical engine" was the forerunner of the computer. There are a number of other houses along Fore and High streets in an equally good state of preservation: the late-eighteenth-century, mustard-yellow **Gothic House**, a hundred yards up Fore Street on the left; 28 High St, overhung by some curious grotesque masks; and 16 High St, a house built by pilchard merchant Nicholas Ball, whose initials are carved outside. His wealth, inherited by his widow, was eventually bequeathed by her second husband, Thomas Bodley, to found Oxford's Bodleian Library.

Fore Street becomes the High Street at the **East Gate**, a much retouched medieval arch. Beneath it, Rampart Walk trails off along the old city walls, curling round the fifteenth-century **church of St Mary** (daily 9am–4.30pm), inside which you can admire the exquisitely carved rood-screen that stretches across the full width of the red sandstone building. Behind the church, the eleventh-century **Guildhall** (daily 10am–4.30pm; £1) was originally the refectory and kitchen of a Benedictine priory. Granted to the city corporation in 1553, the building still houses the town's Council Chamber, which you can see together with the former jail cells, used until the end of the nineteenth century, and the courtroom, which ceased to function only in 1974. **Totnes Castle** (daily: late March to June & Sept 10am–5pm; July & Aug 10am–6pm; Oct 10am–4pm; £2.50; EH) on Castle Street – leading off the High Street – is a classic Norman structure of the motte and bailey design, its simple crenellated keep atop a grassy mound offering wide views of the town and Dart valley.

Along the river

Totnes is the highest navigable point on the **River Dart** for seagoing vessels, and the quayside at the bottom of Fore Street is the departure point for cruises to Dartmouth, leaving between Easter and October from Steamer Quay, on the far side of the Dart (1hr 15min; £9 return; ☎01803/834488, Ⓦwww.riverlink .co.uk) – the best way to see the river's deep creeks. Riverside walks in either direction pass some congenial pubs, and near the railway bridge you can board a steam train of the **South Devon Railway** (April–Oct; ℡0845/345 1420, ⓦwww.southdevonrailway.org) on its run along the course of the Dart to Buckfastleigh, on the edge of Dartmoor (£9 return).

A walkable couple of miles north of Totnes, both rail and river pass near the estate of **Dartington Hall**, the arts and education centre set up in 1925 by US millionairess Dorothy Elmhirst and her husband. You can walk through the sculpture-strewn gardens and – when it's not in use – visit the fourteenth-century Great Hall, rescued from dereliction by the Elmhirsts. There's a constant programme of films, plays, concerts, dance and workshops; for details, call ℡01803/847070 or see ⓦwww.dartington.org.

Eating and drinking

You don't need to stray off the Fore Street/High Street axis to find good **places to eat** in Totnes, most of which are fairly laid-back. There are several decent **pubs** in town apart from *The Steampacket* listed below: both the *Castle Inn* on Fore Street and the *Bull Inn* at the top of the High Street have a lively atmosphere, bar meals and local ales.

Barrel House 58–59 High St ℡01803/863000. A café at street level, and upstairs a lounge in a former ballroom with chandeliers and cinema seats, where you can eat salads, burgers and moderately priced full meals. Regular events, from poetry readings to club nights.

Rumour 30 High St ℡01803/864682. With a buzzy atmosphere, this is good for coffees, snacks or good-value full meals – English or Mediterranean, including burgers and pizzas. Most mains are around £13. Closed Sun lunch.

The Steampacket St Peter's Quay ℡01803/863880. Riverside inn with a conservatory and patio, reached by walking west along The Plains. Good-value, well-prepared traditional meals and real ales are served. A jazz band plays every other Sunday lunchtime, when booking is advisable for the Sunday roast.

Willow 87 High St ℡01803/862605. Vegetarian and vegan food and organic wines are offered here, with an Indian menu on Wed night and live music on Fri night. Evening dishes cost around £8. The courtyard's good for lunches and teas. Closed Sun, also Mon, Tues & Thurs eves.

Dartmouth and around

South of Torbay, and eight miles downstream from Totnes, **DARTMOUTH** has thrived since the Normans recognized the potential of this deepwater port for trading with their home country. Today its activities embrace fishing, freight and a booming leisure industry, as well as the education of the senior service's officer class at the Royal Naval College, built at the start of the last century on a hill overlooking the port. Coming from Torbay, visitors to Dartmouth can save time and a long detour through Totnes by using the frequent ferries crossing the Dart estuary, either the Higher Ferry from the A379 (£1 one way, £2.50 for cars with passengers), or the Lower Ferry from Kingswear and the B3205 (£1 one way, £3.30 for cars with passengers); the last ones leave at around 10.45pm.

The Town

Behind the enclosed boat basin at the heart of town stands Dartmouth's most photographed building, the four-storey **Butterwalk**, built in the seventeenth century for a local merchant. Richly decorated with wood-carvings, the timber-framed construction overhangs the street on eleven granite columns, and is home to Dartmouth's small **museum** (Mon–Sat: April–Oct 10am–4pm; Nov–March noon–3pm; £1.50), mainly devoted to maritime curios, including old maps, prints and models of ships. Nearby **St Saviour's**, rebuilt in the 1630s from a fourteenth-century church, has long been a landmark for boats sailing upriver. The building stands at the head of Higher Street, the old town's central thoroughfare and the site of another tottering medieval structure, the *Cherub Inn*. More impressive is **Agincourt House** on the parallel Lower Street, built by a merchant after the battle for which it is named, then restored in the seventeenth century and again in the twentieth.

Lower Street leads down to **Bayard's Cove**, a short cobbled quay lined with well-restored eighteenth-century houses, where the Pilgrim Fathers stopped en route to the New World. A twenty-minute walk from here along the river takes you to **Dartmouth Castle** (late March to June & Sept daily 10am–5pm; July & Aug daily 10am–6pm; Oct daily 10am–4pm; Nov–March Sat & Sun 10am–4pm; £4; EH), one of two fortifications on opposite sides of the estuary dating from the fifteenth century. The castle was the first in England to be constructed specifically to withstand artillery, though was never tested in action, and consequently is excellently preserved. The site includes coastal defence works from the nineteenth century and from World War II. If you don't relish the return walk, you can take advantage of a **ferry** back to town (Easter–Oct continuous service 10am–4/5pm; £1.80).

Blackpool Sands and along the Dart

Continuing south along the coastal path brings you through the pretty hilltop village of **Stoke Fleming** to **Blackpool Sands** (45min from the castle), the best and most popular beach in the area. The unspoilt cove, flanked by steep, wooded cliffs, was the site of a battle in 1404 in which Devon archers repulsed a Breton invasion force sent to punish the privateers of Dartmouth for their raiding across the Channel.

From Dartmouth's quay there are regular ferries across the river to **Kingswear**, terminus of the **Paignton & Dartmouth Steam Railway** (see p.397), as well as various **cruises** around the harbour and up the River Dart to Totnes (see p.398), affording good views of the **Royal Naval College**. The river is also the best way to get to **Greenway House** (early March to mid-Oct Wed–Sat 10.30am–5pm; £5.20, or £4.40 if arriving by river; NT), birthplace of Walter Raleigh's three seafaring half-brothers, the Gilberts, and later rebuilt for Agatha Christie. At present it is only possible to visit the wooded grounds here, as well as a collection of contemporary art in the Barn Gallery, but the house will soon be open to display, among other things, Christie memorabilia. You can also arrive by road on a circuitous ten-mile route via Dittisham, but it gets very congested.

Practicalities

Dartmouth's **tourist office** is opposite the car park on Mayor's Avenue (Mon–Sat 9.30am–5pm; Easter–Oct also Sun 10am–2pm; ☎01803/834224, ⊛www.discoverdartmouth.com). The town's less expensive **accommodation** is scattered along Victoria Road, a continuation of Duke Street, though it's worth paying a little more for the views that the hill-top choices can boast, such as the spacious and elegant *Avondale* at 5 Vicarage Hill (☎01803/835831, ⊛www.avondaledartmouth.co.uk; no credit cards; ❺). More centrally, for character and funky charm you can't beat the rooms above the 🍴 *Café Alf Resco* on Lower Street (☎01803/835880, ⊛www.cafealfresco.co.uk; no credit cards; ❺), while for something a little different, there's the *Resnova Inn*, a barge moored in mid-river (☎0777/062 8967, ⊛www.resnova.co.uk; closed Jan & Feb; ❹–❺), which has seven cramped but comfy cabins with shared bathroom – guests are ferried to and from town by arrangement.

As for **eating**, the *Café Alf Resco* (open until 2pm) is good for breakfasts, snack lunches and steaming coffees, and has outdoor tables where live music evenings take place monthly in summer, with food on offer; Internet access is also available. The *Resnova Inn* (closed Mon & Tues daytime) is open for breakfast, lunch and dinner, with the menu covering everything from bangers and mash (£8.50) to lobster (around £18). Dartmouth's top restaurant is the *New Angel*, 2 South Embankment (℡01803/839425; closed Sun eve & all Mon), run by celebrity chef John Burton-Race; it provides high-class seafood in an informal atmosphere, with great riverside views. The ancient *Cherub Inn*, 13 Higher St, is one of the most atmospheric **pubs** in town, and serves meals in a small restaurant upstairs.

The South Hams

The area between the Dart and Plym estuaries, the **South Hams**, holds some of Devon's comeliest villages and most striking coastline. Frequent buses from Dartmouth and Totnes run to **Kingsbridge**, at the top of the Kingsbridge estuary, the "capital" of the region and the hub of local services to the South Hams villages. However, you'll spend more time in the yacht resort of **Salcombe**, near the mouth of the estuary and connected to Kingsbridge by a ferry in summer, and on the less crowded coast hereabouts.

Kingsbridge

Fine Tudor and Georgian buildings distinguish the busy market town of **KINGSBRIDGE**, especially along the steep Fore Street, where the colonnaded Shambles is largely Elizabethan on the ground floor, its granite pillars supporting an upper floor added at the end of the eighteenth century. There are various **markets** throughout the year at the town hall and on The Quay; the latter is right by the **tourist office**, which has information on the whole region (Mon–Sat 9am–5/5.30pm; summer also Sun 10am–4pm; ℡01548/853195, ⓦwww.kingsbridgeinfo.co.uk).

For a snack or full **meal**, the boldly coloured ⚓ *Pig Finca Café*, The Quay (℡01548/855777; closed Tues eve and all Sun & Mon), has a courtyard, sofa-filled lounge and regular live roots and world music (usually Wed & Fri). The organically sourced Mediterranean dishes average around £10.

Salcombe and around

Once a nondescript fishing village, **SALCOMBE** is now a full-blown sailing and holiday resort, its calm waters strewn with small craft and the steep streets awash with leisurewear. There's still some fishing activity here, and a few working boatyards, and you can bone up on boating and local history at **Salcombe Maritime Museum** on Market Street, off the north end of the central Fore Street (Easter–Oct 10.30am–12.30pm & 2.30–4.30pm; £1.50).

From the quay off Fore Street, a **ferry** provides transport to the beach at South Sands (Easter–Oct every 30min; £2.70), while the ferry across to **East Portlemouth** (Easter–Oct continuous service until 7pm; Nov–Easter every 30min until 5.30pm; £1.20) enables you to follow the coastal path east to the craggily photogenic **Gammon Point** and, half a mile further, Devon's most southerly tip at **Prawle Point**. Around four miles east, at the far end of Lannacombe Bay, the headland of **Start Point** has a raw elemental grandeur – an inspiring spot for a picnic.

Salcombe's **tourist office** is on Market Street (Easter to late July and early Sept to Oct daily 10am–5pm; late July to early Sept daily 9am–6pm;

Nov–March Mon–Sat 10am–3pm; ☎01548/843927, ⓦwww
.salcombeinformation.co.uk). Most of the **B&Bs** are above Fore Street, enjoying
excellent estuary views: try *Rocarno* on Grenville Road (☎01548/842732,
ⓔrocarno@aol.com; ❷), or *Ria View*, Devon Road (☎01548/842965, ⓦwww
.salcombebandb.co.uk; closed Dec–Easter; ❹), the latter with bright, en-suite
rooms, two of them with harbour views; neither place accepts credit cards.
Campers have a good choice in the area, for example *Alston Farm*
(☎01548/561260, ⓦwww.alstoncampsite.co.uk), signposted off the A381
Malborough road, or *Higher Rew* at Rew Cross (☎01548/842681,
ⓦwww.higherrew.co.uk; closed Nov–Easter), a mile southwest of Salcombe
and about the same distance from South Sands beach.

Back in town, fish is top of the **menu** at *Dusters Bistro* at 51 Fore St
(☎01548/842634; eves only, open weekends only in winter), and there's live
jazz on Sundays (Easter–Sept), though you'll find lower prices and a more
family-friendly atmosphere at *Captain Flints*, 82 Fore St, which specializes in
pastas and pizzas (closed in winter).

Sharpitor

At **SHARPITOR**, a couple of miles south of Salcombe, the National Trust
runs **Overbeck's Museum** (mid-March to mid-July & Sept daily except Sat
11am–5.30pm; mid-July to Aug daily 11am–5.30pm; Oct Mon–Thurs & Sun
11am–4pm; garden open Mon–Thurs & Sun 10/11am–4/5.30pm; £5.80; NT),
which is mainly given over to natural history and shares its building with a
spacious **youth hostel** (☎0870/770 6016, ⓔsalcombe@yha.org.uk; call to
check opening; from £14). You can reach the site from Salcombe on the ferry
to South Sands (see p.402), from where it's a ten-minute climb.

South of Sharpitor, the six-mile hike from Bolt Head to Bolt Tail takes you
along a ragged coast where shags and cormorants swoop over the rocks, and
wild thyme and sea thrift grow underfoot.

Plymouth and around

PLYMOUTH's predominantly bland and modern face belies its great
historic role as a naval base, a position it has held since the sixteenth century
when it was the home port of such national heroes as John Hawkins – known
as chief architect of the Elizabethan navy (and also the first English slave-
trader) – and his kinsman, Francis Drake. It was from here that the latter
sailed to defeat the Spanish Armada in 1588, and 32 years later the port was
the last embarkation point for the Pilgrim Fathers, whose New Plymouth
colony became the nucleus for the English settlement of North America. The
city's Devonport dockyards made it a target in World War II, when the
Luftwaffe reduced the old centre to rubble, apart from the compact area
around the **Barbican**. Subsequent reconstruction, spurred on by growth that
has made Plymouth by far Devon's biggest town, has done nothing to
enhance the place. That said, it would be difficult to spoil the glorious vista
over **Plymouth Sound**, the basin of calm water at the mouth of the
combined Plym, Tavy and Tamar estuaries, which has remained largely
unchanged since Drake played his famous game of bowls on the Hoe before
joining battle with the Armada. And you could also spend a couple of hours
wandering around the Elizabethan warehouses and inns of the Barbican,
where a gamut of restaurants specialize in freshly caught seafood.

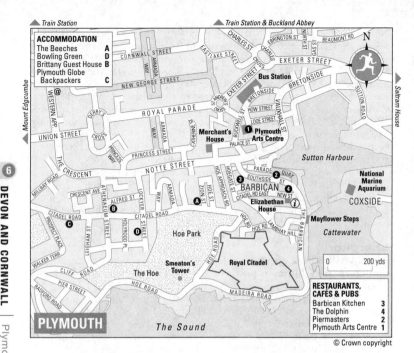

© Crown copyright

Although this area is easy to stroll around, you could also make use of the regular and frequent circular **bus** service (#25) for getting around the town, with stops at the train station, Sutton Harbour and the Hoe. Plymouth makes a good starting point for forays onto Dartmoor, and a base for visiting a trio of elegant **country houses** with both aesthetic appeal and historical resonance, though transport connections are not always easy.

Arrival, information and accommodation

Plymouth's **train station** is a mile north of the Hoe off Saltash Road; the **bus station** is near the harbour at Bretonside and has **left-luggage lockers**. The **tourist office**, at 3 The Barbican (April–Oct Mon–Sat 9am–5pm, Sun 10am–4pm; Nov–March Mon–Fri 9am–5pm, Sat 10am–4pm; ☎01752/306330, ⓦ www.visitplymouth.co.uk), can provide details of tours of the city and surrounding areas. **Internet** access is available from the *Plymouth Internet Café*, 32 Frankfort Gate (Mon–Sat 9am–5pm; ☎01752/221777).

Plymouth has plenty of choice when it comes to **accommodation**: try first the row of B&Bs edging the Hoe on Citadel Road if you want to be near the sights.

The Beeches 175 Citadel Rd ☎01752/266475. A good choice on this row close to the Barbican, with views over the Hoe and all rooms en suite except for a couple of singles. No credit cards. ❷
Bowling Green 9–10 Osborne Place, Lockyer St ☎01752/209090, ⓦ www.bowlingreenhotel.com. Smart establishment with bright rooms overlooking Francis Drake's fabled haunt on the Hoe. ❹
Brittany Guest House 28 Athenaeum St ☎01752/262247, ⓦ www.brittanyguesthouse .co.uk. Easy-going place with en-suite rooms, a choice of breakfasts and a car park (a bonus around here). ❸

The City

A good place to start a tour of the city is **Plymouth Hoe**, an immense esplanade
studded with reminders of the great events in the city's history, including a rather
portly statue of Sir Francis Drake gazing grandly out to the sea – appropriately,
there's a bowling green back from the brow. Resplendent in fair weather, with
glorious views over the sea, the Hoe can also attract some pretty ferocious winds,
making it well-nigh impossible to explore in wintry conditions.

In front of the memorials the red-and-white-striped **Smeaton's Tower**
(Tues–Sat: 10am–noon & 1–3/4.30pm; £2) was erected in 1759 by the renowned
engineer John Smeaton on the treacherous Eddystone Rocks, fourteen miles out
to sea. When replaced by a larger lighthouse in 1882, it was reassembled here,
where it gives the loftiest view over Plymouth Sound. Following the seafront
round to the east, past the formidable seventeenth-century Royal Citadel, you'll
reach the old town's quay at **Sutton Harbour**, where the **Mayflower Steps**
commemorate the sailing of the 102 Pilgrim Fathers and a nearby plaque lists their
names and professions. Nowadays, the harbour is the starting point for **boat trips**,
ranging from one-hour tours around the Sound to a four-hour cruise up the
Tamar to the Cornish village of Calstock.

The **Barbican** district, which edges the harbour, is the heart of old Plymouth.
Most of the buildings are now shops and restaurants, but off the quayside, New
Street holds some of the oldest buildings, among them the **Elizabethan House**
(mid-Feb to March Tues–Sat 10am–noon & 1–3pm; April–Sept Tues–Sat
10am–5pm; £1.50), a captain's dwelling retaining most of the original
architectural features, including a lovely old pole staircase. Above the tourist
office at 3 The Barbican, the **Mayflower Centre** (Mon–Sat 10am–4pm, Sun
11am–3pm; £2) traces the story of the Pilgrim Fathers, and explains much of
the history of the Barbican area.

Cross the bridge over Sutton Harbour to reach the grand **National Marine
Aquarium** (daily 10am–5/6pm; last entry 1hr before closing; £9.50). On four
levels, the complex represents a range of marine environments from moorland
stream to coral reef and deep-sea ocean, including sharks and an extensive
collection of seahorse species. Talks and presentations take place throughout the
day, and the feeding times – carried out by divers – are among the highlights.
Back in the centre of town, the handsome timber-framed, mainly seventeenth-
century **Merchant's House Museum**, 33 St Andrew's St (mid-Feb to March
Tues–Sat 10am–noon & 1–3pm; April–Sept Tues–Sat 10am–5pm; £1.50), goes
into various aspects of Plymouth's history.

Eating and drinking

You'll find an eclectic range of **restaurants and pubs** in and around
Plymouth's Barbican area, where the nightlife can get pretty raucous.

harbour; it's plain but elegant, with lunchtime specials for around £7.50 and evening mains about £19.50. Closed Sun.

Plymouth Arts Centre 38 Looe St ☎01752/206114, ⒲www.plymouthac.org.uk. This place has an inexpensive vegetarian restaurant (closed all Sun & Mon eve), worth sampling even if you're not here for the regular exhibitions, films and live performances.

Around Plymouth

One of the best local excursions from Plymouth is to **Mount Edgcumbe**, where woods and meadows provide a welcome antidote to the urban bustle, and are within easy reach of a fabulous beach. East of Plymouth, the aristocratic opulence of **Saltram House** includes some fine art and furniture, while to the north of town you can visit Drake's old residence at **Buckland Abbey**.

Mount Edgcumbe

Lying on the Cornish side of Plymouth Sound and visible from the Hoe, **Mount Edgcumbe** features a Tudor house, landscaped gardens and acres of rolling parkland and coastal paths. The **house** (Easter–Sept Mon–Thurs & Sun 11am–4.30pm; £5) is a reconstruction of the bomb-damaged Tudor original, though inside the predominant note is eighteenth century, the rooms elegantly restored with authentic Regency furniture. Far more enticing than the house however, are the **grounds**, which include impeccable gardens divided into French, Italian and English sections – the first two a blaze of flowerbeds adorned with classical statuary, the last an acre of sweeping lawn shaded by exotic trees. The **park**, which is free and open all year, covers the whole of the peninsula facing the estuary and the sea, including a part of the Cornish Coastal Path. From the peninsula's two headlands, Rame Head and Penlee Point, extensive views show Plymouth in its best light.

You can reach the house by the passenger **ferry** to Cremyll, leaving at least hourly from Admiral's Hard, a small mooring in the Stonehouse district of town, reachable on bus #34 from Royal Parade; in summer there's also a direct motor launch between the Mayflower Steps and the village of **Cawsand**, an old smugglers' haunt two hours' walk from the house. Cawsand itself is just a mile from the southern tip of the huge **Whitsand Bay**, a good bathing beach, though subject to dangerous shifting sands and fierce currents.

Saltram House

Showing little of its Tudor origins, **Saltram House** (mid-March to Sept daily except Fri noon–4.30pm: £8.40, including garden; NT), two miles east of Plymouth off the A38, is Devon's largest country house. The mansion features work by the great architect Robert Adam and fourteen portraits by **Joshua Reynolds** (1723–92), who was born nearby in Plympton. The showpiece, however, is the **Saloon**, a fussy but exquisitely furnished room dripping with gilt and plaster, and set off by a huge Axminster carpet especially woven for it in 1770. Saltram's landscaped **garden** (daily except Fri 11am–4/4.30pm; £4.20) provides a breather from this riot of interior design, though it's marred by the proximity of the road. You can get here on the hourly #22 bus (not Sun) from Royal Parade to Merafield Road, from where it's a fifteen-minute signposted walk.

Buckland Abbey

Six miles north of Plymouth, close to the River Tavy and on the edge of Dartmoor, stands **Buckland Abbey** (mid-Feb to mid-March & Nov Sat & Sun

2–5pm; mid–March to Oct daily except Thurs 10.30am–5.30pm; Dec Thurs–Sun 11am–5pm; £7.40, grounds only £3.90; NT), once the most westerly of England's Cistercian abbeys. After its dissolution Buckland was converted to a family home by the privateer Richard Grenville (cousin of Walter Raleigh), from whom the estate was acquired by Sir Francis Drake in 1582, the year after he became mayor of Plymouth. It remained his home until his death, but the house reveals few traces of Drake's residence, as he spent most of his retirement years plundering on the Spanish main. There are, however, numerous maps, portraits and mementoes of his buccaneering exploits on show, most famous of which is Drake's Drum, which was said to beat a supernatural warning of impending danger to the country. More eye-catching are the architectural embellishments in the oak-panelled **Great Hall**, dated 1576 but previously the nave of the abbey, while the majestic grounds contain a fine fourteenth-century **monastic barn**, buttressed and gabled and larger than the abbey itself. To get here from Plymouth, take any bus to Tavistock, changing at Yelverton for the hourly #55, or, on Sunday, take the #48 direct from Royal Parade.

Dartmoor

The longer one stays here the more does the spirit of the moor sink into one's soul, its vastness, and also its grim charm. When you are once out upon its bosom you have left all traces of modern England behind you, but on the other hand you are conscious everywhere of the homes and the work of the prehistoric people... If you were to see a skin-clad, hairy man crawl out from the low door, fitting a flint-tipped arrow on to the string of his bow, you would feel that his presence there was more natural than your own.

Arthur Conan Doyle, *The Hound of the Baskervilles*

Occupying the main part of the county between Exeter and Plymouth, **Dartmoor** is southern England's greatest expanse of wilderness, some 365 square miles of raw granite, barren bogland, sparse grass and heather-grown moor. It was not always so desolate, as testified by the remnants of scattered Stone Age settlements and the ruined relics of the area's nineteenth-century tin-mining industry. Today desultory flocks of sheep and groups of ponies are virtually the only living creatures to be seen wandering over the central fastnesses of the National Park, with solitary birds – buzzards, kestrels, pipits, stonechats and wagtails – wheeling and hovering high above.

The core of Dartmoor, characterized by tumbling streams and high tors chiselled by the elements, is **Dartmoor Forest**, which has belonged to the Duchy of Cornwall since 1307, though there is almost unlimited public access as long as certain guidelines are followed – for instance, you are not allowed to park overnight in unauthorized places, and no vehicles are allowed farther than

Dartmoor's firing ranges

A significant portion of northern Dartmoor, containing some of its highest tors and most famous beauty spots, has been appropriated by the **Ministry of Defence**. The firing ranges are marked by red and white posts; when firing is in progress, red flags or red lights signify that entry is prohibited. As a general rule, if no warning flags are flying by 9am between April and September, or by 10am from October to March, there is to be no firing on that day; alternatively, check at ☎0800/458 4868 or ⓦ www.dartmoor-ranges.co.uk.

© Crown copyright

fifteen yards from the road. Camping is permitted out of sight of houses and roads, but fires are strictly forbidden. Though networks of signposts or painted stones do exist to guide **walkers**, map-reading abilities are a prerequisite for any but the shortest walks, and a good deal of experience is essential for longer distances – it's not uncommon for search parties to have to look for hikers gone astray. Two- to six-hour guided walks are listed in the *Dartmoor Visitor* newspaper, available free from National Park visitor centres in Dartmoor's major towns and villages, and from information points in smaller villages. The *Dartmoor Visitor* also has info on camping and other accommodation, events, facilities for disabled travellers, and military firing-range schedules (see box, p.407); ask at visitor centres about **riding** facilities on the moor.

Princetown, at the heart of the moor, has the Dartmoor National Park's main information centre and a selection of stores, pubs and places to stay. A few other villages, such as **Postbridge** and **Widecombe**, have B&Bs and shops, though for the widest choice of accommodation you have to go to the towns and villages circling the moor – chief among them **Tavistock**, **Lydford** and **Okehampton**. It would not be impossible to base yourself in Exeter or

Plymouth, neither more than an hour's ride from the central **Two Bridges**, at the intersection of the B3212 and B3357, which gives access to some of Dartmoor's wildest tracts. Always plan ahead and book places to stay – availability can be extremely restricted in high season.

Getting around

From June to late September, the Transmoor **bus** (#82) runs twice daily Monday to Saturday and five times daily on Sundays between Moretonhampstead and Plymouth, stopping at Two Bridges and Princetown; at weekends the service links up with Exeter, and the full Exeter–Plymouth route also operates on Sundays during winter. Also from Exeter, the #173 goes to Castle Drogo and nearby Chagford (not Sun), on the northeast side of the moor, and #X9 and #X90 go to Okehampton. From Plymouth, #86 takes in Tavistock and Lydford en route to Okehampton. Bus #98 connects Princetown with Tavistock up to six times daily (not Sun), while the infrequent #179 links Okehampton, Chagford and Moretonhampstead (not Sun). On Sundays between Easter and October, there is also the useful **Dartmoor Freewheeler** service, a minibus that carries bikers and their bikes on a trailer (maximum 12 bikes) for free on four routes onto the moor: contact Princetown's **National Park information centre** or consult their website for details (see below). Apart from these, there's little except the occasional Sunday service in summer and once-weekly runs to remote villages.

There are also a couple of **train** services: Exeter to Okehampton on summer Sundays (late May to late Sept; 5 daily; 45min), and the Tamar Valley Line between Plymouth and Gunnislake (5 daily; 45min), five miles southwest of Tavistock. The **Sunday Rover** ticket (£6 valid all day) covers all transport on the moor, including the two rail lines, as well as most other bus services throughout Devon, and gives reduced-price admission to several local attractions.

Princetown and Wistman's Wood

PRINCETOWN owes its growth to the proximity of Dartmoor Prison, a high-security jail originally constructed for POWs captured in the Napoleonic wars. The grim presence seeps into the village, some of whose functional grey stone houses – as well as the parish church of St Michael – were built by French and American prisoners. What Princetown lacks in beauty is amply compensated for by the surrounding countryside, the best of which lies immediately to the north.

On the village's central green, information on all of Dartmoor is supplied by the main **National Park information centre** (daily 10am–4/5pm; ☎01822/890414, ⓦ www.dartmoor-npa.gov.uk). One of the best **places to stay** is *Duchy House*, two hundred yards from the centre on Tavistock Road (☎01822/890552, ⓔ duchyhouse@aol.com; closed Nov; no credit cards; ❷), which has rooms with and without private bath. Two pubs on Princetown's central square offer pricier accommodation: the *Railway Inn* (☎01822/890240; ❺), with all rooms en suite, and, under the same management, the *Plume of Feathers* (ⓦ www.theplumeoffeathers.co.uk; ❺), with shared bathrooms; the latter claims to be the oldest building in town, and also has dormitory accommodation in two bunkhouses (£12) as well as a convenient **campsite** – standard bar food is always available.

Northeast of Princetown, two miles north of the crossroads at Two Bridges, the dwarfed and misshapen oaks of **Wistman's Wood** are an evocative relic of the original Dartmoor Forest, cluttered with lichen-covered boulders and a dense undergrowth of ferns. The gnarled old trees are alleged to have been the site of druidic gatherings, a story unsupported by any evidence but quite plausible in this solitary spot.

Postbridge and Bellever Forest

Three miles northeast of Two Bridges, the largest and best preserved of Dartmoor's **clapper bridges** crosses the East Dart river at **POSTBRIDGE**. Used by tin-miners and farmers since medieval times, these simple structures consist of huge slabs of granite supported by piers of the same material; another more basic example is at Two Bridges. Postbridge has a useful tourist office in the car park near the bridge (Easter–Oct daily 10am–5pm; Nov & Dec Sat & Sun 10am–4pm; ☏01822/880272), which can point out local walks.

If you're not content with strolling up and down the river, you might decide to venture south through **Bellever Forest** to the open moor where **Bellever Tor** (1453ft) affords outstanding views. On the edge of the forest, a couple of miles south of Postbridge on the banks of the East Dart river, lies one of Dartmoor's two **YHA hostels** (☏0870/770 5692, ⓔbellever @yha.org.uk; from £14) – it's on a minor road from Postbridge, accessible on the rare #98 from Tavistock (not Sun), or else walk the mile from Postbridge. Close to Bellever Forest, *Runnage Farm* (☏01822/880222, ⓦwww .runnagecampingbarns.co.uk) offers **camping barns** (£6.50), a bunkhouse (£10) and outdoor camping facilities, as well as bikes for rent.

Two miles northeast of Postbridge, the solitary *Warren House Inn* offers warm, fire-lit comfort and **meals** in an unutterably bleak tract of moorland.

Grimspound and Hound Tor

To the east of the B3212, reachable on a right turn towards Widecombe-in-the-Moor, the Bronze Age village of **Grimspound** lies below Hameldown Tor, about a mile off the road. Inhabited some three thousand years ago, when Dartmoor was fully forested and enjoyed a considerably warmer climate than it does today, this is the most complete example of Dartmoor's prehistoric settlements, consisting of 24 circular huts scattered within a four-acre enclosure. A stone wall nine-feet thick surrounds the huts, several of which have raised

▲ Clapper bridge

bed-places, and you can see how the villagers ensured a constant water supply by enclosing part of a stream with a wall. Grimspound itself is thought to have been the model for the Stone Age settlement in which Sherlock Holmes camped in *The Hound of the Baskervilles*, while **Hound Tor**, an outcrop three miles to the southeast, was the inspiration for Conan Doyle's tale – according to local legend, phantom hounds were sighted racing across the moor to hurl themselves on the tomb of a hated squire following his death in 1677. There's a **camping barn** here, *Great Houndtor*, with two upstairs sleeping areas, a cooking area and showers (℡0870/770 8868 or 01647/221202; £5).

Buckland-in-the-Moor and the southeastern moor

Four miles east of the crossroads at Two Bridges, **Dartmeet** marks the place where the East and West Dart rivers merge after tortuous journeys from their remote sources. Crowds home in on this beauty spot, but the valley is memorably lush and you don't need to walk far to leave the car park and ice-cream vans behind. From here the Dart pursues a more leisurely course, joined by the River Webburn near the pretty moorland village of **BUCKLAND-IN-THE-MOOR**, one of a cluster of moorstone-and-thatched hamlets on this southeastern side of the moor.

Four miles north is another candidate for most popular Dartmoor village, **WIDECOMBE-IN-THE-MOOR**, set in a hollow amid high granite-strewn ridges. Its **church of St Pancras** provides a famous local landmark, its pinnacled tower dwarfing the fourteenth-century main building, whose interior boasts a beautiful painted rood-screen. Look out here too for the carved one-eared rabbits above the communion rail. The nearby **Church House** was built in the fifteenth century for weary churchgoers from outlying districts, and was later converted into almshouses. Widecombe's other claim to fame is the traditional song, *Widdicombe Fair*: the **fair** is still held annually on the second Tuesday of September.

You could **stay** in Widecombe at the elegant *Old Rectory* (℡01364/621231, Ⓔrachel.belgrave@care4free.net; no credit cards; ❸), opposite the post office and set in a lovely garden, or, half a mile south, at *Higher Venton Farm* (℡01364/621235, Ⓦwww.ventonfarm.com; no credit cards; ❸), a peaceful thatched longhouse where evening meals are served. There is **camping** at *Cockingford Farm*, one and a half miles south of Widecombe (℡01364/621258; closed mid-Nov to mid-March). A quarter of a mile south of *Higher Venton Farm*, you'll find the Shilstone Rocks **pony-trekking** centre (℡01364/621281, Ⓦwww.dartmoorstables.com), for tuition and excursions.

South of Buckland, the village of **HOLNE** is another rustic idyll surrounded on three sides by wooded valleys. The vicarage here was the birthplace of Charles Kingsley, author of *The Water Babies* and such Devon-based tales as *Westward Ho!* – a window commemorates him in the village church. The next-door *Church House Inn*, which once accommodated Oliver Cromwell, offers excellent **meals** and **rooms** (℡01364/631208, Ⓦwww.church-house-inn .co.uk; ❸). On the edge of Holne, on the route of the Two Moors Way, there's a **camping barn** at *The Stone Barn*, with good facilities (℡01364/631544), backing onto a small camping field.

The northeastern moor

The peaceful village of **MORETONHAMPSTEAD**, lying on the north-eastern edge of the moor, makes an attractive entry point to the moor from

Exeter. Local **information** is handled by a visitor information point at 10 The Square (Easter–Oct daily 9.30am–5pm; Nov–Easter Fri–Sun 10am–4.30pm; ☎01647/440043). There's classy **accommodation** on the western edge of the village in Court Street: the *Old Post House*, at no. 18 (☎01647/440900, ⓦwww.theoldposthouse.com; no credit cards; ③), is a friendly B&B which has four en-suite rooms, including a family room, while *Cookshayes*, at no. 33 (☎01647/440374, ⓦwww.cookshayes.co.uk; ②), has a large garden and offers good home cooking. The village also has a first-rate, centrally located vegetarian **hostel**, *Sparrowhawk Backpackers*, at 45 Ford St (☎01647/440318, ⓦwww .sparrowhawkbackpackers.co.uk), with dorm beds (£14) and private rooms sleeping four (①).

Moretonhampstead has a historic rivalry with neighbouring **CHAGFORD**, a Stannary town (a chartered centre of the tin trade) that also enjoyed prosperity as a centre of the wool industry. Standing on a hillside above the River Teign, and with a fine fifteenth-century church, it makes a great base for the area, with a selection of pubs and **accommodation**, such as the ancient *Three Crowns Hotel*, facing the church (☎01647/433444, ⓦwww.chagford-accom.co.uk; ⑤), some of whose comfortable rooms are subject to noise from the church clock. A quieter alternative is the sixteenth-century *Cyprian's Cot*, 47 New St (☎01647/432256, ⓦwww.cyprianscot.co.uk; no credit cards; ③), where you can warm your bones by an inglenook fireplace. There's also a renowned **restaurant** in the village, *22 Mill Street* (☎01647/432244, ⓦwww.22millstreetrestaurant.co.uk; closed Sun eve and all Mon), which offers top-quality Modern European cuisine; two-course set menus are £21 for lunch and £33 for dinner. For diners only, there are also two en-suite rooms available (⑤).

Numerous **walks** can be made in the immediate vicinity, for instance to Fernworthy Reservoir, four miles to the southwest along signposted narrow lanes, or downstream along the Teign to the twentieth-century extravaganza of **Castle Drogo** (early to mid-March Sat & Sun 11am–4pm; mid-March to early Nov daily except Tues 11am–4/5pm; Dec Sat & Sun noon–4pm; grounds early to mid-March Sat & Sun 10.30am–4.30pm; mid-March to early Nov daily 10.30am–4.30/5.30pm; early Nov to late Dec Fri–Sun 11am–4pm; £7.40, grounds only £4.75; NT), which occupies a stupendous site overlooking the Teign Gorge. Having retired at the age of 33, grocery magnate Julius Drewe unearthed a link that suggested his descent from a Norman baron, and set about creating a castle befitting his pedigree. Begun in 1910, to a design by **Sir Edwin Lutyens**, it was not completed until 1930, but the result was an unsurpassed synthesis of medieval and modern elements. The croquet lawn is available for use (June–Sept), with mallets for rent.

Paths lead from Drogo east to **Fingle Bridge**, one of Dartmoor's most noted beauty spots, where shaded green pools hold trout and the occasional salmon. The *Fingle Bridge Inn* here has an adjoining **restaurant** (closed Sun eve).

Okehampton and around

The main centre on the northern fringes of Dartmoor, **OKEHAMPTON** grew prosperous as a market town for the medieval wool trade, and some fine old buildings survive between the two branches of the River Okement that meet here, among them the prominent fifteenth-century tower of the **Chapel of St James**. Across the road from the seventeenth-century town hall, a granite archway leads into the **Museum of Dartmoor Life** (Easter–Oct Mon–Sat 10.15am–4.30pm; £3), an excellent overview of habitation on the moor since earliest times. Loftily perched above the West Okement on the other side of town, **Okehampton Castle** (daily: late March to June & Sept 10am–5pm; July & Aug 10am–6pm; £3; EH) is the shattered hulk of a stronghold laid waste by Henry VIII; its ruins include a gatehouse, Norman keep and the remains of the Great Hall, buttery and kitchens. Four miles east of Okehampton at Sticklepath (bus #X9, #179, #510 or #670), **Finch Foundry** (mid-March to Oct Mon & Wed–Sun 11am–5pm; £3.90; NT) is a Victorian forge with working machinery and demonstrations.

Practicalities

Okehampton's station, which provides a useful Sunday **rail** connection from Exeter (between late May and late Sept) lies a fifteen-minute walk up Station Road from Fore Street in the town centre, where the **tourist office** (Easter–Oct Mon–Sat 10am–5pm, Nov–Easter Mon, Fri & Sat 10am–4.30pm; ☎01837/53020, ⓦwww.okehamptondevon.co.uk) sits next to the museum. East along Fore Street, the *Fountain Hotel* (☎01837/53900; ❸), an old beamed coaching inn, offers very central **accommodation** in characterful rooms, while the Victorian *Meadowlea*, 65 Station Rd (☎01837/53200, ⓦwww .meadowleaguesthouse.co.uk; ❷) provides good-value B&B near the station. If you prefer rural surroundings, try the comfortable and spacious *Upcott House* on Upcott Hill, half a mile north of the centre (☎01837/53743, ⓦwww .upcotthouse.com; no credit cards; ❷). Okehampton's **youth hostel** (☎0870/770 5978, ⓔokehampton@yha.org.uk; closed Dec & Jan; from £14) provides bunkrooms in a converted goods shed at the station, **rents bikes** and offers a range of outdoor activities including rock climbing and pony trekking.

Dartmoor's northern tors

A seven-mile, three-hour walk from Okehampton skirts the east of the MoD's Okehampton Range, brings you within view of the highest points on the moor, then plunges you into the recesses of the East Okement River, before rounding Belstone Common and returning north to Okehampton via the village of Belstone. From Okehampton, follow signs for Ball Hill and the East Okement Valley from the Mill Street car park south of the centre, passing under the graceful arches of the **Fatherford Viaduct**, which carries the Exeter–Okehampton railway. Follow a well-defined path for about a mile through Halstock Wood, sloping down diagonally until meeting the East Okement River, which you can cross at **Chapel Ford** – a good spot for a pause.

Walk up the eastern bank of the East Okement for five hundred yards before passing through an opening in the hedge, leaving the valley to head towards **Winter Tor**, a little more than a mile due south of the ford. At the tor, carry on up to the top of the ridge, from which a splendid panorama unfolds, with Dartmoor's highest peaks of **Yes Tor** (2028ft) and **High Willhays Tor** (2039ft) about three miles southwest. To the east the great bowl of Taw Marsh can be seen.

Follow the rock-strewn ridge northwards, to the rocky pinnacles of **Belstone Common**. Between **Higher Tor** and **Belstone Tor** you'll pass **Irishman's Wall**, the vestige of an attempt to enclose part of the moor against the wishes of the locals, who waited until the wall was nearly complete before gathering to push the structure down. Carry on heading north, descending sharply towards the **Nine Stones** cairn circle, seven hundred yards below Belstone Tor. This Bronze Age burial ground was popularly held to be the petrified remains of nine maidens turned to stone for dancing on Sunday (there are in fact twelve stones). A little way north, a track brings you northeast to the village of Belstone, half a mile away.

From Belstone, follow the road signed "Okehampton Indirect"; you can either continue on this road to Okehampton or, after half a mile or so, turn left beyond Cleave House, descend to the East Okement river and follow it northwards.

The nearest **campsite** is at the small *Betty Cottles Inn* (℡01837/55339, Ⓦwww .bettycottles.co.uk), two miles southwest of town on the B3260.

Okehampton has no great choice when it comes to **eating**, though the *White Hart Hotel* on Fore Street has bar meals, pastas, pizzas and fixed-price three-course dinners, while *Panache*, across Fore Street in Red Lion Yard is good for coffees and inexpensive lunches, with some outdoor tables (closed Sun). Best of all is 🍴 *The Pickled Walnut*, a cellar restaurant hidden behind the church on Fore Street (℡01837/54242; closed eves Mon–Wed & all day Sun): the menu is international and reasonably priced, and the atmosphere is mellow. For **riding** on the moor, contact Skaigh Riding Stables (℡01837/840917, Ⓦwww .skaighstables.co.uk; closed Oct–March).

The western moor

Southwest from Princetown, walkers can trace the grassy path of the defunct rail line to **Burrator Reservoir**, four miles away; flooded in the 1890s to provide water for Plymouth, this is the biggest stretch of water on Dartmoor. The wooded lakeside teems with wildlife, and the boulder-strewn slopes are overlooked by the craggy peaks of **Sharpitor** (1312ft) and **Sheep's Tor** (1150ft). From here, the best walk is to strike northwest to meet the valley of the **River Walkham**, which rises in a peat bog at Walkham Head, five miles north of Princetown, then scurries through moorland and woods to join the River Tavy at Double Waters, two miles south of Tavistock. The fast-flowing water attracts herons, kingfishers and other colourful birdlife, to be seen darting in and out of dense woods of alder, ash and sycamore.

The river crosses the B3357 Tavistock road four miles west of Princetown at **MERRIVALE**, a tiny settlement amounting to little more than a **pub**, the *Dartmoor Arms*. Merrivale makes another good starting point for moorland walks – it's only half a mile west of one of Dartmoor's most important prehistoric sites, the **Merrivale Rows**. Just a few yards from the B3357, the upright stones form a stately procession, stretching 850ft across the bare landscape. Dating from between 2500 BC and 750 BC, and probably connected with burial rites, the rows are known locally as "Potato Market" or "Plague Market" in memory of the time when provisions for plague-stricken Tavistock were deposited here. A mile to the southwest, on the western slopes of the Walkham valley, the sphinx-like pinnacle of **Vixen Tor** looms over the barren moor.

Tavistock and around

Five miles west of Merrivale, the main town of the western moor, **TAVISTOCK**, owes its distinctive Victorian appearance to the building boom that followed the discovery of copper deposits here in 1844. Originally, however, this market and Stannary town on the River Tavy grew around what was once the West Country's most important Benedictine abbey, established in the eleventh century and, at the time of its dissolution, owning land as distant as the Isles of Scilly. Some scant remnants survive in the churchyard of **St Eustace**, a mainly fifteenth-century building with stained glass from William Morris's studio in the south aisle.

Tavistock's **tourist office**, in the town hall on Bedford Square (April–Oct daily 9.30am–5pm; Nov–March Mon, Tues, Fri & Sat 10am–4.30pm; ℡01822/612938) can supply you with information on the western moor. Among the town's good range of **accommodation**, try *Kingfisher Cottage*, Mount Tavy Road (℡01822/613801, Ⓔkingfisher.cott@fsnet.co.uk; no credit cards; ❸), a small B&B, and, about half a mile east of Tavistock off the

B3357 Princetown Road, *Mount Tavy Cottage* (℡01822/614253, 🌐www
.mounttavy.freeserve.co.uk; ❹), set in a lush garden and serving organic breakfasts; self-catering accommodation is also available here. For a luxurious splurge,
there's *Browns* on West Street, off Bedford Square (℡01822/618686, 🌐www
.brownsdevon.co.uk; ❼), a plush boutique hotel. For **camping** head two miles
east of Tavistock to *Higher Longford*, Moorshop (℡01822/613360, 🌐www
.higherlongford.co.uk), on the B3357 towards Merrivale. **Bikes** can be rented
from Tavistock Cycles, Paddons Row, Brook Street (℡01822/617630), and
Dartmoor Cycles, 6 Atlas House, West Devon Business Park, next to Morrisons
supermarket (April–Oct; ℡01822/618178).

North of Tavistock, a four-mile lane wanders up to **Brent Tor**, 1130ft high
and dominating Dartmoor's western fringes. Access to its conical summit is
easiest along a path gently ascending through gorse on its southwestern side,
leading to the small church of St Michael at the top. Bleak, treeless moorland
extends in every direction, wrapped in silence that's occasionally pierced by the
shrill cries of stonechats and wheatears. A couple of miles eastwards, **Gibbet
Hill** looms over Black Down and the ruined stack of the abandoned Wheal
Betsy silver and lead mine.

Lydford

Six miles north of Tavistock, the village of **LYDFORD** boasts the sturdy but
small-scale Lydford Castle, a Saxon outpost, then a Norman keep and later used
as a prison. The chief attraction here, though, is **Lydford Gorge** (mid-Feb to
late March Fri–Sun 11am–3.30pm; late March to Sept daily 10am–5pm; Oct
daily 10am–4pm; Nov & Dec Sat & Sun 11am–3.30pm; £5.20; NT), whose
main entrance is a five-minute walk downhill. Two routes – one above, one
along the banks – follow the ravine burrowed through by the River Lyd as far
as the hundred-foot White Lady Waterfall, coming back on the opposite bank.
The full course would take you roughly two hours at a leisurely pace, though
there is a separate entrance at the south end of the gorge if you only want to
visit the waterfall. In winter, when the river can flood, the waterfall is the only
part of the gorge open.

Back in the village, the picturesque *Castle Inn* sits right next to the castle, and
provides a fire-lit sixteenth-century bar where you can drink and snack amid
curios and memorabilia, and also has an extensive beer garden. The inn offers
en-suite **accommodation** in low-ceilinged oak-beamed rooms
(℡01822/820242; ❹), and there's a separate **restaurant** too. Cheaper rooms are
available at *Heathergate* (℡01822/820486, 🌐www.heathergate-lydford.co.uk;
no credit cards; ❸), a working farm less than a mile west of Lydford on the
Coryton road. The renowned *Dartmoor Inn* (℡01822/820221, 🌐www
.dartmoorinn.com; closed Sun eve & Mon lunchtime), on the A386 opposite
the Lydford turning, serves superior bar meals and pricier British and European
dishes – evening meals usually need booking – and offers three spacious,
antique-furnished rooms (❼).

North Devon

From Exeter the A377 runs alongside the scenic Tarka Line railway to **North
Devon**'s major town, **Barnstaple**. Within easy reach of here, the resorts of
Ilfracombe and **Woolacombe** draw the crowds, though the fine sandy
beaches surrounding the latter give ample opportunity to find your own space.

West of the river port of **Bideford**, the precipitous village of **Clovelly** is one of Devon's most famous beauty spots, while stormy **Hartland Point** offers dramatic scenery and inspiring coastal walks. For a complete break and further scope for stretching the legs and clearing the lungs, head over to the tiny island of **Lundy**, twelve miles out to sea, reachable from Ilfracombe or Bideford.

Barnstaple

BARNSTAPLE, at the head of the Taw estuary, makes an excellent north Devon base, being well connected to the resorts of Bideford Bay, Ilfracombe and Woolacombe, as well as to the western fringes of Exmoor. The town's centuries-old role as a marketplace is perpetuated in the daily bustle around the huge timber-framed **Pannier Market** off the High Street, alongside which runs **Butchers Row**, its 33 archways now converted to a variety of uses. Also off the High Street, in the pedestrianized area, lies Barnstaple's **parish church**, itself worth a look, and the fourteenth-century **St Anne's Chapel**, converted into a grammar school in 1549 and later numbering among its pupils John Gay, author of *The Beggar's Opera*; it's now closed to the public (though can be visited as part of a guided tour – ask at the tourist office for details). At the end of Boutport Street on The Square, make time to visit the **Museum of North Devon** (Mon–Sat 9.30am–5pm; free), a lively miscellany including wildlife displays and a collection of eighteenth-century pottery for which the region was famous. The museum lies alongside the Taw, where footpaths make for a pleasant riverside stroll, with the colonnaded eighteenth-century **Queen Anne's Walk** – built as a merchants' exchange – providing some architectural interest and housing the **Barnstaple Heritage Centre** (April–Oct Tues–Sat 10am–5pm; Nov–March Tues–Fri 10am–4.30pm, Sat 10am–3.30pm; £3.50), which traces the town's social history by means of reconstructions and touch-screen computers.

Practicalities

Barnstaple's friendly and helpful **tourist office** is inside the Museum of North Devon (Mon–Sat 9.30am–5pm; ☎01271/375000, ⓦwww.staynorthdevon .co.uk). You can **rent bikes** from Tarka Trail Cycle Hire at the train station (April–Oct; ☎01271/324202, ⓦwww.tarkatrail.co.uk).

Places to stay in town include *The Old Post Office*, 22 Pilton St (☎01271/859439, ⓦwww.theoldpostoffice-pilton.co.uk; no credit cards; ④), half a mile north of the centre, with just one large en-suite double room overlooking a garden, and, a couple of miles southeast of the centre on Landkey Road, *Mount Sandford* (☎01271/342354; no credit cards; ③), an elegant, porticoed Regency building. Outside town, you could have a more interesting stay at *Broomhill Art Hotel*, Muddiford, signposted two miles north of Barnstaple off the A39 – a striking combination of gallery, restaurant and hotel (☎01271/850262, ⓦwww.broomhillart.co.uk; no credit cards; ③), where the en-suite rooms look onto a sculpture garden. Half-board only is available at weekends.

By day, you can pick up coffees and **snacks** at the *Old School Coffee House* (closed Sun), a building dating from 1659 on Church Lane, near St Anne's Chapel, and from *Jan's Kitchen* on Butchers Row (closed Sun), which serves superb breakfasts, panini and pasties. Out of town, the **restaurant** at the *Broomhill Art Hotel* (see above) lays on delicious bar meals, Mediterranean-style fixed-price lunches for £13 and dinners for £19 (closed Mon & Tues).

Rated by many as one of the finest pieces of nature writing in the English language, Henry Williamson's *Tarka the Otter* (1927), which relates the travels and travails of a young otter, is frequently recalled in north Devon. The Exeter–Barnstaple rail route, which for half of its length follows the Taw valley – where parts of the book are set – has been dubbed the **Tarka Line,** while Barnstaple itself forms the centre of the figure-of-eight traced by the **Tarka Trail**, which tracks the otter's wanderings for a distance of over 180 miles. To the north, the trail penetrates Exmoor then follows the coast back, passing through Williamson's home village of Georgeham on its return to Barnstaple. South, the path takes in Bideford (see p.418), following a disued rail line to Meeth, and continuing as far as Okehampton (see p.412), before swooping up via Eggesford, the point at which the Tarka Line enters the Taw valley.

Twenty-one miles of the trail follow a former rail line that's ideally suited to **bicycles**, and up to two bikes can be carried free on Tarka Line trains, for which advance booking is recommended (☎08457/000125); there are bike rental shops at Barnstaple (see opposite), and Bideford (see p.419). A good ride from Barnstaple is to **Great Torrington** (fifteen miles south), where you can eat at the *Puffing Billy* pub, formerly the train station.

Tourist offices sell a *Tarka Trail* booklet and give out free leaflets on individual sections of the trail.

Ilfracombe and around

The most popular resort on Devon's northern coast, **ILFRACOMBE** is essentially little changed since its evolution into a Victorian and Edwardian tourist centre, with any large-scale development restricted by the surrounding cliffs. In summer, the place is heaving, but you can always escape on a coastal tour, cruise to Lundy Island (see box, p.421) or fishing trip from the harbour. For walkers, the coast path follows the attractive stretch east of town beyond the grassy cliffs of Hillsborough to a succession of unspoiled coves and inlets characterized by jagged slanting rocks and heather-covered slopes.

From Barnstaple, **buses** #3, #30 and #301 run several times an hour to Ilfracombe (only #3 on Sun), while from Minehead and Lynton "Exmoor Coastlink" #300 runs to the town up to six times daily (weekends only in winter). The Ilfracombe **tourist office** is at the Landmark on the seafront (Easter–Oct daily 10am–5pm; Nov–Easter Mon–Fri 10am–5pm, Sat 10am–4pm; ☎01271/863001, www.visitilfracombe.co.uk).

Smartest choice among Ilfracombe's extensive **accommodation** is *Westwood*, Torrs Park (☎01271/867443, www.west-wood.co.uk; ❺), in a quiet area west of the centre: a B&B that's more like a small boutique hotel, with three sleekly contemporary rooms and serves organic breakfasts. On the east side of town, off Hillsborough Road, *The Towers*, Chambercombe Park (☎01271/862809, www.thetowers.co.uk; no credit cards; ❹), is a roomy Victorian villa with sea views from most of its rooms. There's also an excellent **hostel**, *Ocean Backpackers*, near the bus station and harbour at 29 St James Place (☎01271/867835, www.oceanbackpackers.co.uk), offering dorm beds at £12 and two double rooms (❶).

Woolacombe, Croyde and Saunton Sands

Five miles west of Ilfracombe, a cluster of hotels, B&Bs and villas makes up the summer resort of **WOOLACOMBE**, at the northern end of one of the West Country's top beaches, **Woolacombe Sands**, a broad, west-facing expanse much favoured by surfers and families alike. The beach can get crowded around here, but you'll always find space at the quieter southern end, **Putsborough Sands**, a choice swimming spot bracketed by **Baggy Point**, where from September to November the air is a swirl of gannets, shags, cormorants and shearwaters. Woolacombe Bay is bounded to the north by **Morte Point**, a rocky promontory named after the menacing sunken reef of Morte Stone. A break in the rocks makes space for the pocket-sized **Barricane Beach**, famous for the tropical shells washed here from the Caribbean by the Atlantic currents, and a popular swimming spot.

South of Baggy Point, **CROYDE** is another surfers' delight, more compact than Woolacombe, with its beach tucked out of sight of buildings. Shops in the village and stalls on the sand rent surfboards and wetsuits. South of Croyde Bay, **Saunton Sands** is a magnificent long stretch of coast pummelled by ranks of classic breakers and beloved of longboarders.

Practicalities

Woolacombe is linked to Barnstaple by bus #303, and to Ilfracombe by #3B. Bus #308 connects Barnstaple to Croyde, via Saunton. There's no service between Woolacombe and Croyde. Woolacombe's **tourist office** is on the Esplanade (Easter–Oct Mon–Sat 10am–5pm, Sun 10am–3pm; Nov–Easter Mon–Sat 10am–1pm; ☎01271/870553, ⓦwww.woolacombetourism.co.uk).

In Woolacombe, *Sandunes* is one of a number of **B&Bs** on Beach Road (☎01271/870661, ⓦwww.sandwool.fsnet.co.uk; no credit cards; ❺), minutes from the beach; two rooms have large balconies with views. In Croyde, the friendly *Parminter*, 16 St Mary's Rd (☎01271/890030, ⓔjim@parminter.co.uk; no credit cards; ❸), has large rooms in two converted barns. Most local **campsites** are around Morte Point, including *North Morte Farm*, Mortehoe (☎01271/870381, ⓦwww.northmortefarm.co.uk; closed Nov–March), with caravans for rent, panoramic sea views and access to Rockham Beach.

For **refreshments** in Woolacombe, surfers and day-trippers gather at the *Red Barn*, a bar/restaurant just behind the beach (closed Sun eve), while great food and a buzzy atmosphere can be found further up at the stylish *West Beach*, Beach Road (☎01271/870877; open only eves Fri & Sat in winter), where the focus is on locally caught fish; there's occasional live music and it stays open late in summer, when there are barbecues on its patio deck. Croyde's hangouts of choice are *The Thatch* pub and *The Blue Groove*, a contemporary café/restaurant – both on Hobbs Hill.

Bideford Bay

BIDEFORD BAY (sometimes called Barnstaple Bay) takes in the full variety of Devon, from the twee village of **Clovelly** to the savage windlashed rocks of **Hartland Point**. Low-key **Bideford** is a useful transit centre, with some decent accommodation, bus connections to all the towns on the bay and regular boats for Lundy.

Bideford

Like Barnstaple, nine miles to the east, the estuary town of **BIDEFORD** formed an important link in the north Devon trade network, mainly due to its **bridge**, which still straddles the River Torridge. First built in 1300, the bridge was reconstructed in stone in the following century, and subsequently reinforced and widened, hence the irregularity of its 24 arches, no two of which have the same span.

From the Norman era until the eighteenth century, the port was the property of the Grenville family, whose most celebrated scion was **Richard Grenville**, commander of the ships that carried the first settlers to Virginia, and a major player in the defeat of the Spanish Armada. Grenville also featured in *Westward Ho!*, the historical romance by **Charles Kingsley** who wrote part of the book in Bideford.

Bideford's **tourist office** lies at the northern end of the quay in Victoria Park (Easter–Sept Mon–Sat 10am–5pm, Sun 10am–1pm, till 4pm July & Aug; Oct–Easter Mon, Tues, Thurs & Fri 10am–4.30pm, Wed & Sat 10am–1pm; ☎01237/477676, ⊛www.torridge.gov.uk). You can pick up information and tickets here (also sold on the quayside) for coastal cruises and the boat to Lundy (see box, p.421). Bideford Bicycle Hire, Torrington Street (☎01237/424123), two hundred yards south of the old bridge on the far riverbank, **rents bikes** for exploring the Tarka Trail.

The town's best **accommodation** choice is the Georgian *Mount* on Northdown Road (☎01237/473748, ⊛www.themountbideford.co.uk; ●), set in its own walled garden and linked to the centre by a footpath, while the *Royal Hotel* (☎01237/472005, ⊛www.royalbideford.co.uk; ●), just over the old bridge on Barnstaple Street, mixes corporate and traditional styles; its oak-panelled Kingsley Room is named after Charles Kingsley who penned much of *Westward Ho!* here.

For a daytime **snack** or full Mediterranean-style evening **meal**, head for *Cafecino Plus*, 26 Mill St (closed Mon eve & Sun), a lively café/bistro serving snacks and offering free Wi-Fi. You'll find a pair of first-class **pubs** a couple of miles downstream in the port of Appledore, where the *Royal George* and *Beaver Inn* on Irsha Street serve great seafood and enjoy wonderful estuary views.

Clovelly

The picturesque village of **CLOVELLY** must have featured on more biscuit tins and tourist posters than anywhere else in the West Country. It was put on the map in the second half of the nineteenth century by two books: Charles Dickens' *A Message From the Sea* and, inevitably, *Westward Ho!* – Charles Kingsley's father was rector here for six years. Though the antique tone of the village has been preserved by strict regulations limiting hotel and holiday accommodation, its excessive quaintness and the regular stream of visitors on summer days make it impossible to see beyond the artifice.

Holding shops, snack bars and an audio-visual show, the **visitor centre** (daily 9/9.30am–4/6pm; ⊛www.clovelly.co.uk) charges £5.50 for access to the village, including the car park (there's nowhere else to leave your motor). Below the centre, the cobbled, traffic-free main street plunges down past neat, flower-smothered cottages where sledges are tethered for transporting goods – the only way to carry supplies since the use of donkeys ceased.

At the bottom lies Clovelly's stony beach and tiny harbour, snuggled under a cleft in the cliff wall. The jetty here was built in the fourteenth century to shelter the coast's only safe harbour between the Taw estuary and Boscastle in Cornwall. If you can't face the steep return climb, take the Land Rover that leaves about every fifteen minutes from behind the *Red Lion* (Easter–Oct 9am–5.30pm; £2.20) back to the top of the village. It is here, immediately below the visitor centre, that Hobby Drive begins, a three-mile **walk** along the cliffs through woods of sycamore, oak, beech, rowan and the occasional holly, with grand views over the village.

You can reach Clovelly by **bus** #319 (not Sun), which traces a route from Barnstaple and Bideford to Hartland. Of the old village's two pricey **hotels**, the

▲ Clovelly

luxurious *Red Lion* enjoys the best position, right on the harbour (℡01237/431237, ⓔredlion@clovelly.co.uk; ❼). Halfway down the main street, *Donkey Shoe Cottage* (℡01237/431601, ⓦwww.donkeyshoecottage.co.uk; no credit cards; ❷) offers much more modest **B&B** accommodation, though still needs plenty of advance booking in summer. You'll find better value for money and greater availability a twenty-minute walk up from the visitor centre in Higher Clovelly: right at the top, near the A39 junction, try the two-hundred-year-old *East Dyke Farmhouse*

(☎01237/431216, ✉steve.goaman@virgin.net; no credit cards; ❷), whose rooms have fridges and private bathrooms and there's a beamed and flagstoned dining room. Clovelly's best **eating** option is the *Red Lion*, which offers snacks in its Harbour Bar, and full meals in its upstairs restaurant.

Hartland Point and around

You could drive along minor roads to **Hartland Point**, ten miles west of Clovelly, but the best approach is on foot along the coastal path. Shortly before arriving, the path touches at the only sandy beach along this stretch of coast, **Shipload Bay**. The headland presents one of Devon's most dramatic sights, its jagged black rocks battered by the sea and overlooked by a solitary lighthouse 350ft up. South of Hartland Point, the saw-toothed rocks and near-vertical escarpments defiantly confront the waves, with spectacular waterfalls tumbling over the cliffs.

This sheer stretch of coast has seen dozens of shipwrecks over the centuries, though many must have been prevented by the sight of the tower of fourteenth-century **St Nectan's** – a couple of miles south of the point in the village of **STOKE** – which acted as a landmark to sailors before the construction of the lighthouse. At 128ft, it is the tallest church tower in north Devon, and the

Lundy Island

There are fewer than twenty full-time residents on **Lundy**, a tiny windswept island twelve miles north of Hartland Point. Now a refuge for thousands of marine birds, Lundy has no cars, just one pub and one shop – indeed little has changed since the Marisco family established itself here in the twelfth century, making use of the shingle beaches and coves to terrorize shipping along the Bristol Channel. The family's fortunes only fell in 1242 when one of their number, William de Marisco, was found to be plotting against the king, whereupon he was hanged, drawn and quartered at Tower Hill in London. The castle erected by Henry III on Lundy's southern end dates from this time.

Today the island is managed by the Landmark Trust. Unless you're on a specially arranged diving or climbing expedition, **walking** along the interweaving tracks and footpaths is really the only thing to do here. The grass, heather and bog is crossed by dry-stone walls and grazed by ponies, goats, deer and the rare soay sheep. The shores – mainly cliffy on the west, softer and undulating on the east – shelter a rich variety of **birdlife**, including kittiwakes, fulmars, shags and Manx shearwaters, which often nest in rabbit burrows. The most famous birds, though, are the **puffins** after which Lundy is named – from the Norse *lunde* (puffin) and *ey* (island). They can only be sighted in April and May, when they come ashore to mate. Offshore, **grey seals** can be seen all the year round.

Between April and October, the MS *Oldenburg* sails to Lundy up to four times a week from Ilfracombe, less frequently from Bideford, taking around two hours from both places. Day-return tickets cost £29, open returns around £50; to reserve a place, call ☎01271/863636 (day-returns can also be booked from local tourist offices). **Accommodation** in a range of idiosyncratic properties on the island can be booked up months in advance, and B&B is only available in houses that have not already been taken for weekly rentals. Since B&B bookings can only be made within two weeks of the proposed visit, this limits the options, though outside the holiday season it's still possible to find a double room for under £60 per night. **Bookings** for weekly rentals must be made through the Landmark Trust's office (☎01628/825925, ⊕www.landmarktrust.org.uk), or call ☎01271/863636 for shorter B&B stays. There's also a **campsite** on the island open from April to October. More information can be found on the island's website, ⊕www.lundyisland.co.uk.

wagon-roofed interior boasts a finely carved rood-screen and a Norman font. Opposite, tea and home-made scones are served at *Stoke Barton Farm* (Easter–Sept Tues–Thurs, Sat & Sun).

Half a mile east of the church, gardens and lush woodland surround **Hartland Abbey** (Easter to late May Wed, Thurs & Sun 2–5pm; late May to early Oct also Mon & Tues; grounds Easter to early Oct daily except Sat noon–5pm; £8.50, grounds only £6.50), an eighteenth-century country house incorporating the ruins of an abbey dissolved in 1539, and displaying fine furniture, old photographs and recently uncovered frescoes. There's a nice walk through the grounds to the beach here.

HARTLAND itself, further inland, holds little appeal beyond its three pubs and café, but on the coast, **Hartland Quay** deserves a linger: once a busy port, financed in part by the mariners Raleigh, Drake and Hawkins, it was mostly destroyed by storms in the nineteenth century, and now holds a solitary pub and hotel, surrounded by beautiful slate cliffs. About one mile south of here, **Speke's Mill Mouth** is a select surfers' beach.

Accommodation options in the area are scattered, and you'll need your own transport unless you stay in Hartland itself (bus #319 from Barnstaple), where you'll find a small, friendly B&B at ⚘ *2 Harton Manor*, The Square, off Fore Street (℡01237/441670, ⓦwww.twohartonmanor.co.uk; no credit cards; ❸), with two congenial rooms above an artist's studio. For proximity to the sea, you can't do better than the *Hartland Quay Hotel*, Hartland Quay (℡01237/441218, ⓦwww.hartlandquayhotel.com; ❺), but if you want to be nearer Shipload Bay and Hartland Point (and the coast path), try *West Titchberry Farm* (℡01237/441287; no credit cards; ❷), for which drivers should follow signs for Hartland Light-house. In nearby Stoke, *Stoke Barton Farm* (see above) provides basic **camping** facilities (℡01237/441238; closed Nov–Easter).

Exmoor

A high bare plateau sliced by wooded combes and splashing rivers, **Exmoor** can be one of the most forbidding landscapes in England, especially when its sea mists fall. When it's clear, though, the moorland of this National Park reveals rich displays of colour and an amazing diversity of wildlife, from buzzards to the unique **Exmoor ponies**, a species closely related to prehistoric horses. In the treeless heartland of the moor around **Simonsbath**, in particular, it's not difficult to spot these short and stocky animals, though fewer than twelve hundred are registered, and of these only about two hundred are free-living on the moor. Much more elusive are the **red deer**, England's largest native wild animal, of which Exmoor supports England's only wild population. The effect of hunting through the centuries has accounted for a drastic depletion in numbers, though they have a strong recovery rate, and about two and half thousand are thought to inhabit the moor today; their annual culling is a regular point of issue among conservationists and nature-lovers.

Endless permutations of **walking routes** are possible along a network of some six hundred miles of footpaths and bridleways. In addition, the National Park Authority and other local organizations have put together a programme of guided walks, graded according to distance, speed and duration and costing £3–5 per person. Contact any of the local visitor centres or the National Park base at Dulverton (see opposite) for details. **Horseback** is another option for getting the most out of Exmoor's desolate beauty, and stables are dotted throughout the area – the most convenient are mentioned below; expect to pay £15–20 an hour. Whether walking or riding, bear in mind that over seventy percent of the National Park is privately owned and that access is theoretically restricted to public rights of way; special permission should certainly be sought before camping, canoeing, fishing or similar. Check the website Ⓦwww .activeexmoor.com for **organized activity** operators on Exmoor.

There are four obvious inland bases, all on the Somerset side of the county border: **Dulverton** in the southeast, site of the main information facilities; **Simonsbath** in the centre; **Exford**, near Exmoor's highest point of Dunkery Beacon, and **Winsford**, close to the A396 on the east of the moor. Exmoor's coastline offers an alluring alternative to the open moorland, all of it accessible via the **South West Coast Path**, which embarks on its long coastal journey at **Minehead**, though there is more charm to be found farther west at the sister villages of **Lynmouth** and **Lynton**, just over the Devon border.

Getting around

Minehead is the northern terminus of the **West Somerset Railway** (see p.380), but otherwise you have to rely on infrequent local **buses** for public transport. On the coast, the most useful route is the #300 (Easter–Oct daily; Nov–Easter Sat & Sun only) connecting Minehead with Lynton and Ilfracombe, while the #39 runs frequently between Minehead and Porlock and #398 links Minehead, Dunster, Dulverton and Tiverton, where there's a main-line train station; both the latter services operate all year, but not on Sun. In summer, the #400 Exmoor Explorer vintage bus service, which is open-top in fine weather, links Minehead, Dunster, Exford and Porlock (May–Sept Sat & Sun; late July to late Aug also Tues & Thurs), while winter sees a few once- or twice-weekly community buses connecting Dulverton, Minehead and Lynton. If you're planning to make good use of the buses, buy a "First Day Southwest" ticket from the bus driver (one-day's off-peak travel £6.20).

Dulverton

The village of **DULVERTON**, on the southern edge of the National Park, is the Park Authority's headquarters and so makes a good introduction to Exmoor. Information on the whole moor is available at the **visitor centre**, 7 Fore St (daily: April–Oct 10am–5pm; Nov–March 10.30am–3pm; Ⓣ01398/323841, Ⓦwww .exmoor-nationalpark.gov.uk). Dulverton's best **accommodation** is *Town Mills* (Ⓣ01398/323124, Ⓦwww.townmillsdulverton.co.uk; ❹), an old mill house in the centre of the village, or try the nearby *Lion Hotel* in Bank Square (Ⓣ01398/324437, Ⓦwww.lionhoteldulverton.com; ❺), with beams and four-posters. Alternatively, there's the less traditional *Tongdam*, a Thai restaurant at 26 High St (Ⓣ01398/323397, Ⓦwww.tongdamthai.com), offering two doubles with shared bathroom (❸) and a suite with a sitting room and private bathroom (❻). A mile north of Dulverton, *Northcombe Farm* (Ⓣ01398/323602) has two **camping barns** (£7.50) as well as basic camping facilities. Both the *Lion* and *Tongdam* offer moderately priced **meals**, while further down the High Street, *Lewis's Tea Rooms* serves teas and snacks. Moorland **horse riding** and tuition is offered at West Anstey Farm (Ⓣ01398/341354), a couple of miles west of Dulverton.

Winsford, Exford and Dunkery Beacon

Just west of the A396, five miles north of Dulverton, **WINSFORD** lays good claim to being the moor's prettiest village. A scattering of thatched cottages ranged around a sleepy green, it is watered by a confluence of streams and

Walks from Dulverton and Tarr Steps

The most popular short walk from Dulverton goes along the east bank of the Barle to the seventeen-span medieval bridge at **Tarr Steps**, five miles to the northwest. You could combine this walk with a hike up **Winsford Hill**, a circular route of less than four hours from Tarr Steps. Follow the riverside path upstream from Tarr Steps, turning right after about half a mile along Watery Lane, a rocky track that deteriorates into a muddy lane near Knaplock Farm. Stay on the track until you reach a cattle-grid, on open moorland. Turn left here, cross a small stream and climb up Winsford Hill, a heather moor whose 1400-foot summit is invisible until you are almost there. At the top, from where there are views as far as Dartmoor, you can see the **Wambarrows**, three Bronze Age burial mounds. If you want a refreshment stop, descend the hill on the other side to the village of Winsford.

A quarter-mile due east of the barrows, the ground drops sharply by more than two hundred feet to the Punchbowl, a bracken-grown depression resembling an amphitheatre. Keep on the east side of the B3223 which runs up Winsford Hill, following it south for a mile, until you come across the **Caractacus Stone**, an inscribed stone just by Spire Cross. The stone is thought to date from between 450 and 650, the damaged inscription reading "Carataci Nepos" – that is, "kinsman of Caractacus", the first-century British king.

Continue south on the east side of the road, cross it after about a mile, and pass over the cattle grid on the Tarr Steps road, from which a footpath takes you west another one and a half miles back to Tarr Steps. The *Tarr Farm* restaurant here provides food, refreshment and pricey accommodation (℡01643/851507, ⓦwww .tarrfarm.co.uk; ⑦).

rivers – one of them the Exe – giving it no fewer than seven bridges. On Halse Lane, *Karslake House* (℡01643/851242, ⓦwww.karslakehouse.co.uk; no under-12s; ⑨) offers excellent **B&B** and serves evening meals (not Sun or Mon eves), and there's a well-equipped **campsite** a mile southwest of the village at *Halse Farm* (℡01643/851259, ⓦwww.halsefarm.co.uk; closed Nov to mid-March). The thatched and rambling old *Royal Oak* serves drinks, snacks and full restaurant **meals**, and also offers plush accommodation (℡01643/851455, ⓦwww.royaloak-somerset.co.uk; ⑥–⑦).

The hamlet of **EXFORD**, an ancient crossing-point on the River Exe four miles northwest of Winsford, is popular with hunting folk as well as with walkers here for the four-mile hike to **Dunkery Beacon**, Exmoor's highest point at 1700ft. There's a good range of **accommodation**, including *Exmoor Lodge*, a friendly B&B on Chapel Street (℡01643/831694, ⓦwww .smoothhound.co.uk; ⑨), and the village also holds Exmoor's main YHA **hostel**, a rambling Victorian house in the centre (℡0870/770 5828, ⓔexford @yha.org.uk; from £13). Two and a half miles northwest of Exford off the Porlock Road, *Westermill Farm* (℡01643/831238, ⓦwww.westermill.com) provides a tranquil **campsite** on the banks of the Exe.

Exmoor Forest and Simonsbath

At the heart of the National Park stands **Exmoor Forest**, the barest part of the moor, scarcely populated except by roaming sheep and a few red deer – the word "forest" denotes simply that it was a hunting reserve. In the middle of it stands the village of **SIMONSBATH** (pronounced "Simmonsbath"), at a crossroads between Lynton, Barnstaple and Minehead on the River Barle. The village was home to the Knight family, who bought the forest in 1818 and, by introducing tenant farmers, building roads and importing sheep, brought systematic agriculture to an area that had never before produced any income. The Knights also built a wall round their land – parts of which can still be seen – as well as the intriguing Pinkworthy (pronounced "Pinkery") Pond, four miles to the northwest, whose exact function remains unexplained.

Simonsbath would make a useful base for hikes on the moor, but there are only two **accommodation** possibilities: the *Exmoor Forest Inn* (℡01643/831341, Ⓦ www.exmoorforestinn.co.uk; ❺), with numerous hunting trophies and old-fashioned rooms, and the *Simonsbath House Hotel* (℡01643/831259, Ⓦ www.simonsbathhouse.co.uk; ❻), former home of the Knights and now a cosy bolt-hole offering elegant rooms and a good but fairly expensive **restaurant**. In a converted barn next to the hotel, *Boevey's* offers coffees and lunches (closed Dec & Jan), while a couple of miles southwest of the village on the Brayford Road is the *Poltimore Arms* at **Yarde Down**, a classic country **pub** serving excellent food.

Minehead and around

A chief port on the Somerset coast, **MINEHEAD** quickly became a favourite Victorian watering-hole with the arrival of the railway, and it has preserved an upbeat holiday-town atmosphere ever since. Steep lanes link the two quarters of **Higher Town**, on North Hill, containing some of the oldest houses, and **Quay Town**, the harbour area. It's in Quay Town that the **Hobby Horse** performs its dance in the town's three-day May Day celebrations, snaring maidens under its prancing skirt and tail in a fertility ritual resembling the more famous festivities at the Cornish port of Padstow (see p.457).

The **tourist office** is midway between Higher Town and Quay Town at 17 Friday St, off the Parade (Mon–Sat 10am–12.30pm & 1.30–4/5pm, plus Sun 10am–1pm in July & Aug; ℡01643/702624, Ⓦ www.minehead.co.uk). If you want to **stay** in Minehead, try the *Old Ship Aground* right by the harbour on Quay Road (℡01643/702087; ❸), or, nearer the centre, just up from the tourist office, *Kildare Lodge* on Townsend Road (℡01643/702009; ❹), a comfortable, reconstructed Tudor inn designed by a pupil of Lutyens. There's a YHA **hostel** a couple of miles southeast, outside the village of Alcombe (℡0870/770 5968, Ⓔ minehead@yha.org.uk; from £12), in a secluded combe on the edge of Exmoor. Minehead is crammed with **places to eat**, mostly very mediocre. However, you could do a lot worse than an evening at the *Queen's Head*, on Holloway Street, off the Parade and near the tourist office; it's a free house with a range of ales and bar meals, as well as darts and pool.

Dunster

As well as being the start of the South West Coast Path (see box, p.426), Minehead is a terminus for the **West Somerset Railway**, which curves eastwards into the Quantocks as far as Bishops Lydeard (see p.380). The area's major attraction, the old village of **DUNSTER**, is about a mile from the line's first stop, three miles inland. Dunster's main street is dominated by the towers and turrets of its **castle** (castle: late March to Oct Mon–Wed, Sat & Sun 11am–4/5pm; grounds: March–Dec daily 10/11am–4/5pm; £7.80, grounds only £4.30; NT). Most of its fortifications were demolished after the Civil War, after which time the castle became something of an architectural showpiece, and Victorian restoration has made it more like a Rhineland *schloss* than a Norman stronghold.

On a tour of the castle you can see various portraits of the Luttrells, owners of the house for six hundred years; a bedroom once occupied by Charles I; a fine seventeenth-century carved staircase; and a richly decorated banqueting hall. The grounds include terraced gardens and riverside walks, all overlooked by a hilltop folly, **Conygar Tower**, dating from 1776.

Despite the influx of seasonal visitors, Dunster village preserves relics of its wool-making heyday; the octagonal **Yarn Market**, in the High Street below the castle, dates from 1609, while the three-hundred-year-old **water mill** at the end of Mill Lane is still used commercially for milling the various grains which go to make the flour and muesli sold in the shop (April, May & Oct daily except Fri 11am–4.45pm; June–Sept daily 11am–4.45pm; £2.85; NT) – the café, overlooking its riverside garden, is a good spot for lunch. For somewhere to **stay**, try the traditional *Yarn Market Hotel*, 25–31 High St (☎ 01643/821425, ⓦ www.yarnmarkethotel.co.uk; ⑤), with rooms overlooking the Yarn Market and a restaurant. There's a **National Park Centre** at the top of Dunster Steep by the main car park (Easter–Oct daily 10am–5pm, some weekends in winter 10.30am–3pm; ☎ 01643/821835).

Porlock

The real enticement of **PORLOCK**, six miles west of Minehead, is its extraordinary position in a deep hollow, cupped on three sides by the hogbacked hills of Exmoor. The thatch-and-cob houses and dripping charm of the village's long main street have led to invasions of tourists, some of whom are also drawn by the place's literary links. According to Coleridge's own less than reliable testimony, it was a "man from Porlock" who broke the opium trance in which he was composing *Kubla Khan*, while the High Street's beamed *Ship Inn* prides itself on featuring prominently in the Exmoor romance *Lorna Doone* and, in real life, having sheltered the poet Robert Southey, who staggered in rain-soaked after an Exmoor ramble. There's little specific to do in Porlock, but the

Doverhay Manor Museum (May–Sept Mon–Fri 10am–1pm & 2–5pm, Sat 10am–noon & 2.30–4.30pm; free), in a fifteenth-century house at the eastern end of the High Street, holds a degree of interest, with a couple of cramped rooms showing traditional domestic and agricultural tools of Exmoor – including a man-trap – together with some material on the local wildlife. The most impressive items here though are the beautiful window and huge fireplace on the ground floor.

Porlock's **tourist office** is at West End, High Street (April–Oct Mon–Sat 10am–5pm, Sun 10am–1pm; Nov–Easter Tues–Fri 10.30am–1pm, Sat 10am–4pm; ☎01643/863150, ⓦwww.porlock.co.uk). The best **accommodation** in town is on the High Street, where the Victorian *Lorna Doone Hotel* (☎01643/862404, ⓦwww.lornadoonehotel.co.uk; ❷) offers three sizes of rooms, all with private bath and TV. Further down, the thatched, sixteenth-century *Myrtle Cottage* (☎01643/862978, ⓦwww.myrtleporlock.co .uk; ❸) has small en-suite rooms and a patio. The *Lorna Doone* serves snacks, meals and teas, and the *Whortleberry Tearoom* (closed Mon & Tues), also on the High Street, offers whortleberry jam on muffins among other homemade goodies. Porlock has a central **campsite**, *Sparkhayes Farm* (☎01643/862470; closed Nov–Feb), signposted off the main road near the *Lorna Doone*.

Two miles west over the reclaimed marshland, the tiny harbour of **PORLOCK WEIR** gives little inkling of its former role as a hard-working port trafficking with Wales. It's a peaceful spot, giving onto a bay that enjoys the mildest climate on Exmoor, and there's a top-notch – and very expensive – **restaurant**, *Andrew's on the Weir* (☎01643/863300, ⓦwww.andrewsontheweir.co.uk; closed Mon & Tues), which cooks up local lamb and seafood to perfection and also offers luxury **accommodation** (❼). An easy two-mile stroll west from Porlock Weir along the South West Coast Path brings you to **St Culbone**, a tiny church – claimed to be the country's smallest – sheltered within woods once inhabited by a leper colony.

Lynton and Lynmouth

West from Porlock, the road climbs 1350ft in less than three miles, though cyclists and drivers might prefer the gentler and more scenic toll-road alternative to the direct uphill trawl (cars £2.50). Nine miles along the coast, on the Devon side of the county line, the Victorian resort of **LYNTON** perches above a lofty gorge with splendid views over the sea. Almost completely cut off from the rest of the country for most of its history, the village struck lucky during the Napoleonic wars, when frustrated Grand Tourists – unable to visit their usual continental haunts – discovered in Lynton a domestic piece of Swiss landscape. Coleridge and Hazlitt trudged over to Lynton from the Quantocks, but the greatest spur to the village's popularity came with the publication in 1869 of R.D. Blackmore's Exmoor melodrama *Lorna Doone*, a book based on the outlaw clans who inhabited these parts in the seventeenth century. Since then the area has become indelibly associated with the swashbuckling romance.

Opposite the school on Market Street, one of the oldest houses in the village is home to the **Lyn and Exmoor Museum** (Easter–Oct Mon–Fri 10am–12.30pm & 2–4.30pm, Sun 2–4pm; £1.50), holding a motley selection of relics from the locality and a reconstructed Exmoor kitchen c.1800. Lynton's imposing **town hall** on Lee Road epitomizes the Victorian–Edwardian accent of the village. It was the gift of publisher George Newnes, who also donated the nearby **cliff railway** connecting Lynton with Lynmouth (daily 10am–5/7pm; £3 return). The device is an ingenious hydraulic system, its two

Walks from Lynton and Lynmouth

As well as the draws of the coastal path, there are several popular walks inland in this region. The one-and-a-half-mile tramp to **Watersmeet**, for example, follows the East Lyn River to where it's joined by Hoar Oak Water, a tranquil spot transformed into a roaring torrent after a bout of rain. From the fishing lodge here – now owned by the National Trust and open as a café and shop in summer – you can branch off on a range of less-trodden paths, such as the three-quarters-of-a-mile route south to **Hillsford Bridge**, the confluence of Hoar Oak and Farley Water.

North of Watersmeet, a path climbs up **Countisbury Hill** and the higher **Butter Hill** (nearly 1000ft) giving riveting views of Lynton, Lynmouth and the north Devon coast, and there's also a track leading to the lighthouse at **Foreland Point**, close to the coastal path. East from Lynmouth you can reach the point via a fine sheltered shingle beach at the foot of Countisbury Hill – one of a number of tiny coves that are easily accessible on either side of the estuary.

From Lynton, an undemanding expedition takes you west along the North Walk, a mile-long path leading to the **Valley of the Rocks**, a steeply curved heathland dominated by rugged rock formations. At the far end of the valley, herds of wild goats range free, as they have done here for centuries.

carriages counterbalanced by water tanks, which fill up at the top, descend, and empty their load at the bottom.

Five hundred feet below, **LYNMOUTH** lies at the junction and estuary of the East and West Lyn rivers, in a spot described by Gainsborough as "the most delightful place for a landscape painter this country can boast". Shelley spent nine weeks here with his 16-year-old bride Harriet Westbrook in the summer of 1812, during which time he wrote his polemical *Queen Mab* – two different houses claim to have been the Shelleys' love-nest. R.D. Blackmore, author of *Lorna Doone*, stayed in **Mars Hill**, the oldest part of the town, its creeper-covered cottages framing the cliffs behind the Esplanade. In summer, the harbour offers boat trips and fishing expeditions, and at the back of the village you can explore the **Glen Lyn Gorge**, a wooded valley, with walks, waterfalls and displays of waterpower (Easter–Oct daily 10am–3/6pm; £4). The gorge was the conduit of ferocious floodwaters streaming off Exmoor in 1952, a disaster that almost washed away the village and is recalled here.

You can also ask at the gorge (or call) about **boat trips** from Lynmouth harbour with Exmoor Coast Boat Cruises (Easter–Sept; ☎01598/753207); the hour-long excursion to Woody Bay and back (£10) allows you to view the abundant birdlife on the cliffs between April and July.

Practicalities

The local **tourist office** is in Lynton's town hall (Easter–Oct Mon–Sat 9.30am–5pm, Sun 10am–4pm; Nov–Easter Mon–Sat 10am–4pm, Sun 10am–2pm; ☎0845/660 3232, ⓦlynton-lynmouth-tourism.co.uk).

Lynton has the better choice of budget **B&Bs**, among them the friendly, Victorian *Turret Hotel*, 33 Lee Rd (☎01598/753284, ⓦwww.turrethotel.co.uk; no under-14s; ❸), one of a row of guest houses lining this street; built by the same engineer who built the cliff railway, it has six spacious rooms. A more central choice is 🪑 *St Vincent Hotel* (☎01598/752244, ⓦwww.st-vincent -hotel.co.uk; ❺; closed Nov–March), a whitewashed Georgian house on Castle Hill with spacious, beautifully furnished bedrooms and a good **restaurant** specializing in French and Belgian recipes using local meat and fish (eves only; closed Mon), with two- and three-course menus at £24 and £27. For food, you'll find lower prices at *The Greenhouse*, an informal eatery on Lee Road (closed Mon) that serves everything from hot baguettes to Madagascar duck.

In **Lynmouth**, central **accommodation** choices include the posh *Shelley's*, right next to the Glen Lyn Gorge (℡01598/753219, ⓦwww.shelleyshotel .co.uk; ⑤), where you can sleep in the room occupied by the poet – he apparently left without paying his bill. Among other options, try *Tregonwell*, 1 Tors Rd (℡01598/753369, ⓦwww.smoothhound.co.uk; ③), a Victorian B&B overlooking the East Lyn and with a tea garden in the front, or, at the top of a steep path, *Sea View Villa*, 6 Summer House Path (℡01598/753460, ⓦwww .seaviewvilla.co.uk; ⑥), with elegant rooms and splendid views; evening meals and picnics are also available. For **food**, you'll find loads of atmosphere and fairly expensive prices at the traditional *Rising Sun* inn, Harbourside, or for cheaper eats, try the nearby *Rock House Hotel*, which has a tea garden, snacks at the bar and meals in its restaurant.

Cornwall

When D.H. Lawrence wrote that being in **Cornwall** was "like being at a window and looking out of England", he wasn't just thinking of its geographical extremity. Virtually unaffected by the Roman conquest, Cornwall was for centuries the last haven for a **Celtic culture** elsewhere eradicated by the Saxons – a land where princes communed with Breton troubadours, where chroniclers and scribes composed the epic tales of Arthurian heroism, and where itinerant monks from Welsh and Irish monasteries disseminated an elemental and visionary Christianity. Primitive granite crosses and a crop of Celtic saints remain as traces of this formative period, and though the Cornish language had ebbed away by the eighteenth century, it is recalled in Celtic place names that in many cases have grown more exotic as they have become corrupted over time.

Cornwall's formerly thriving **industrial economy** is far more conspicuous than in neighbouring Devon. Its more westerly stretches in particular are littered with the derelict stacks and castle-like ruins of the engine-houses that once powered the region's **copper** and **tin mines**, while deposits of **china clay** continue to be mined in the area around St Austell, as witnessed by the conical spoil heaps thereabouts. Also prominent throughout the county are the grey Nonconformist chapels that reflect the impact of Methodism on Cornwall's mining communities.

Nowadays, of course, Cornwall's most flourishing industry is tourism, though its impact has been uneven across the county: **Land's End** for example is cluttered with a tacky leisure complex while Cornwall's other great promontory, **Lizard Point**, remains undeveloped. All the stops are pulled out in the thronged resorts of **Falmouth**, site of the impressive National Maritime Museum, and **Newquay**, the southwest's chief surfing centre, though the effects of mass tourism have been more destructive in smaller, quainter places, such as **Mevagissey**, **Polperro**, **Mousehole** and **Padstow**, whose underlying charm can be hard to make out in full season. Other villages, such as **Charlestown,**

Port Isaac and **Boscastle**, are hardly touched, however, and you couldn't wish for anything more remote than **Bodmin Moor**, a tract of wilderness in the heart of Cornwall – and even **Tintagel**, site of what is fondly known as King Arthur's castle, has preserved its sense of desolation. Near **St Austell**, the spectacular and high-profile **Eden Project** has pointed the way to a less destructive and exploitative form of crowd-pulling, while other places – such as **St Ives**, **Fowey** and **Bude** – have reached a happy compromise with the seasonal influx, or else are saved from saturation by sheer isolation, as is the case with the **Isles of Scilly**. Throughout the county, though, it only requires a shift of a few miles to escape the crowds, and there are enough good beaches around for everyone to find a space.

The best way to reach the quietest spots is along the **South West Coast Path** (see box on p.426), but a car is almost indispensable for anyone wanting to see a lot in a short time, as the system of **public transport** is limited to a couple of branch lines off the main rail line to Penzance, and a thin network of local bus services.

From Looe to Veryan Bay

The southeast strip of the Cornish coast from Looe to Veryan Bay holds a string of medieval harbour towns tarnished by various degrees of commercialization, but there are also a few spots where you can experience the best of Cornwall, including some wonderful coastline. The main rail stop is **St Austell**, the capital of Cornwall's china clay industry, though there is a branch line connecting nearby Par with the north coast at Newquay. To the east of St Austell Bay, the touristy **Polperro** and **Looe** are easily accessible by bus from Plymouth, and there's a rail link to Looe from Liskeard. The estuary town of **Fowey**, in a niche of Cornwall closely associated with the author Daphne du Maurier, is most easily reached by bus from St Austell and Par, as is **Mevagissey**, to the west.

Looe

LOOE was drawing crowds as early as 1800, when the first "bathing-machines" were wheeled out, but the arrival of the railway in 1879 was what really packed its beaches. Though the village now touts itself as something of a shark-fishing centre, most people come here for the sand, the handiest stretch being the beach in front of East Looe, the busier half of the river-divided town. Away from the river mouth, you'll find a cleaner spot to swim a mile eastwards at **Millendreath**. Most of Looe's attractions are in boating and bathing, and in summer, you'll find various **boating and fishing trips** advertised on the long quayside, spread along the river parallel to the main Fore Street. The main diversion in the village is the **Old Guildhall Museum** (Easter & late May to Sept daily except Sat 11.30am–4.30pm; £1.50), a diverse collection of maritime models and exhibits, though none so interesting as the building itself, a fifteenth-century construction preserving its prisoners' cells and raised magistrates' benches.

East Looe's **tourist office** is at the Guildhall on Fore Street (Easter–Sept daily 10am–5pm; Oct–Easter unstaffed Mon–Fri 10am–noon; ☎01503/262072, ⓦwww.looecornwall.com). The best **accommodation** here enjoys lofty views: on East Cliff, try the friendly *Marwinthy* (☎01503/264382, ⓦwww .marwinthy.co.uk; no credit cards; ❷), with old-fashioned rooms, some en suite; or on Barbican Hill there's the more up-to-date *Haven House* (☎01503/264160,

For fresh, local seafood, the town has a couple of quality **restaurants** right next to each other on the harbourside: the oak-beamed *Old Sail Loft* (☎01503/262131; closed Tues lunch & Wed lunch in winter) and the more formal *Trawlers* (☎01503/263593; eves only; closed Sun & Mon), though prices are steep. For simpler dishes, try the inexpensive *Grapevine* on Fore Street (☎01503/263913; closed Sun eve & all Mon), which has a pleasant secluded courtyard.

Polperro

Looe is linked by hourly #573 buses (5 on Sun) with neighbouring **POLPERRO**, a smaller and quainter place, but with a similar feel. From the bus stop and car park at the top of the village, it's a five- or ten-minute walk alongside the River Pol to the pretty harbour. The surrounding cliffs and the tightly packed houses rising on each side of the stream have an undeniable charm, and the tangle of lanes is little changed since the village's heyday of smuggling and pilchard fishing, though its straggling main street – The Coombes – is now an unbroken row of tourist shops and food outlets.

Polperro's best **places to stay** include: *The Cottles* on Longcoombe Lane, above the car park at the top of the village (☎01503/272578, ⓦwww .cottles-polperro.co.uk; ❹), with a conservatory and decking, and reflexology, reiki, aromatherapy and other treatments offered; and the central but relatively secluded *Old Mill House*, an agreeable old pub on Mill Hill offering tastefully decorated rooms (☎01503/272362, ⓦwww.oldmillhouseinn.co.uk; ❸). There's a separate **restaurant** at the *Old Mill*, though you'll find a more sophisticated menu at *Couches Great House* (☎01503/272554; closed daytime except Sun lunch), a modern-looking place with contemporary dishes and fairly high prices. You can get chunky crab sandwiches at the snug *Blue Peter* **pub** on The Quay, where there's live music at weekends.

Fowey and around

The ten-mile stretch west from Polperro to Polruan is one of the most scenic parts of the coastal path in south Cornwall, giving access to some beautiful secluded sand beaches. There are frequent ferries across the River Fowey from Polruan, giving a fine view of the quintessential Cornish port of **FOWEY** (pronounced "Foy"), a cascade of neat, pale terraces at the mouth of one of the peninsula's greatest rivers. The major port on the county's south coast in the fourteenth century, Fowey finally became so ambitious that it provoked Edward IV to strip the town of its military capability, though it continued to thrive commercially and was as the leading port for china clay shipments in the nineteenth century. The harbour today is crowded with yachts and other craft, giving the town a brisk, purposeful character lacking in many of Cornwall's south-coast ports.

Fowey's steep layout centres on the church of **St Fimbarrus**, a distinctive fifteenth-century construction that marks the end of the ancient **Saints' Way footpath** from Padstow, linking the north and south Cornish coasts. Beside St Fimbarrus on South Street, the **Literary Centre**, at the back of the tourist office (and sharing the same times; free), is worth a glance; it's mainly devoted to Daphne du Maurier, who spent her most creative years in and around Fowey. Fans can join a guided walk around scenes described in her books – contact the tourist office for details – while the nine-day **Daphne du Maurier Festival**

▲ Polperro

each May delves more deeply into her life and work (℡0845/094 0428, ⓦwww.dumaurierfestival.co.uk).

Below St Fimbarrus, Fore Street, Lostwithiel Street and the **Esplanade** fan out from Trafalgar Square, the last leading to a footpath that gives access to some splendid walks around the coast. Past the remains of a blockhouse that once supported a defensive chain hung across the river's mouth, you'll soon reach the small beach of **Readymoney Cove** – so-called either because it was where smugglers buried their ill-gotten gains, or because it was where the flotsam of shipwrecks came ashore. Close by stand the ruins of **St Catherine's Castle**, built on the orders of Henry VIII, and offering fine views across the estuary.

Other scenic hikes include the **Hall Walk**, a circular four-mile ramble north of Fowey, passing a memorial to "Q", alias Sir Arthur Quiller-Couch, who lived on Fowey's Esplanade between 1892 and 1944, and whose writings helped popularize the place he called "Troy Town". Details of this and other local excursions are available from the tourist office. Further afield, you can reach the riverside hamlet of **Golant**, three miles north and just over a mile east of the Iron Age fort of **Castle Dore**, which features in Arthurian romance as the residence of King Mark of Cornwall, husband of Iseult.

Coastwalkers can trace the rocky shore westwards to **Gribbin Head** (less than four miles), near which stands Menabilly House, where Daphne du Maurier lived for 24 years – it was the model for the Manderley of *Rebecca*. The house is not open to the public, but the coast path takes you down to the twin coves of Polridmouth, where Rebecca met her watery end.

Practicalities

Separated from eastern routes by its river, Fowey is most accessible by hourly #25 and #25B **buses** from St Austell and Par train stations. Travellers to or from the west might make use of the **ferry** linking Fowey with Mevagissey (see p.435), which operates three to six times daily between late April and September (35min; £6; Ⓦwww.mevagissey-ferries.co.uk). The **tourist office** is at 5 South St (Mon–Sat 9.30am–5.30pm, Sun 10am–4.30pm; Ⓣ01726/833616, Ⓦwww.fowey.co.uk).

Most of the town's pubs offer **B&B**; try the *Ship Inn* on Trafalgar Square (Ⓣ01726/832230; ❸) or the *Safe Harbour*, right at the town's bus stop on Lostwithiel Street (Ⓣ01726/833379, Ⓦwww.cornwall-safeharbour.co.uk; ❹), which has less character but good views and parking. At the top of the scale, there's the *Old Quay House*, 28 Fore St (Ⓣ01726/833302, Ⓦwww.theoldquayhouse .com; ❾), a boutique hotel with creamily opulent rooms – those with estuary views and patios cost extra. Outside Fowey, *Coombe Farm* (Ⓣ01726/833123, Ⓦwww.coombefarmbb.co.uk; no credit cards; ❸) provides perfect rural isolation twenty minutes' walk from town, at the end of a lane off the B3269 – and there's a bathing area just 300m away. There's a YHA **hostel** outside Golant at *Penquite House*, a Georgian mansion with views over the valley (Ⓣ0870/770 5832, Ⓔgolant@yha.org.uk; from £15.50); tipis and bikes are available.

Fowey has some first-rate seafood **restaurants**; among the finest is the elegant but relaxed *Q*, by the waterside at the sumptuous *Old Quay House* (see above), specializing in Modern British cuisine at fairly high prices, and also offering a more moderately priced snack menu at lunchtime. Also on Fore Street, *Sam's* at no. 20 (no booking; no credit cards) has an eclectic menu from burgers to bouillabaisse and a fun atmosphere, while up the road at no. 41, *The Other Place* has takeaway items at the counter on the ground floor and a smart restaurant upstairs (Ⓣ01726/833636; Fri & Sat only in winter). Fowey is also well provided with fine **pubs** – the *Ship Inn* and the *King of Prussia* on the quayside are both worth a lingering drink or meal.

St Austell Bay

It was the discovery of china clay, or kaolin, in the downs to the north of **St Austell Bay** that spurred the area's growth in the eighteenth century.

An essential ingredient in the production of porcelain, kaolin had until then only been produced in northern China, where a high ridge, or *kao-ling*, was the sole known source of the raw material. Still a vital part of Cornwall's economy, the clay is now mostly exported for use in the manufacture of paper, as well as paint and medicines. The conical spoil heaps are a feature of the local landscape, the great green and white mounds making an eerie sight.

The town of **ST AUSTELL** itself is fairly unexciting, but makes a useful stop for trips in the surrounding area. The town's nearest link to the sea is at **CHARLESTOWN**, two miles south and an easy downhill walk from the centre of town. This unassuming and unspoilt port is named after the entrepreneur Charles Rashleigh, who in 1791 began work on the harbour in what was then a small fishing community, widening its streets to accommodate the clay wagons daily passing through. The wharves are still used, loading clay onto vessels that appear oversized beside the tiny jetties, and also providing a backdrop for the location filming that frequently takes place here – you'll often see period sailing vessels moored here too. Behind the harbour, the **Shipwreck & Heritage Centre** (March–Oct daily 10am–5/6pm; £5.95) is entered through tunnels once used to convey the clay to the docks, and shows a good collection of photos and relics as well as tableaux of historical scenes.

The Eden Project

A disused clay pit four miles northeast of St Austell is home to Cornwall's highest-profile attraction – the **Eden Project** (April–Oct daily 9.15am–6pm or 9pm during summer school hols; Nov–March daily 10am–4.30pm; last entry 90min before closing; £14; ⓦwww.edenproject.com). Occupying a 160-foot-deep crater whose awesome scale only reveals itself once you have passed the entrance at its lip, the project showcases the diversity of the planet's plant life in an imaginative, sometimes wacky, but refreshingly ungimmicky style. The whole site is stunningly landscaped with an array of various crops and flowerbeds, but at centre stage are the vast geodesic "biomes", or conservatories made up of eco-friendly, Teflon-coated, hexagonal panels. One cluster holds groves of olive and citrus trees, cacti and other plants more usually found in the warm, temperate zones of the Mediterranean, southern Africa and southwestern USA, while the larger group contains plants from the tropics, including teak and mahogany trees. There's a waterfall and river gushing through, and things can get pretty steamy – you can take cool refuge in an air-conditioned bunker halfway along the course. Equally impressive are the external grounds (described as "Picasso meeting the Aztecs"), where plantations of bamboo, tea, hops, hemp and tobacco are interspersed with brilliant displays of flowers. The whole "living theatre" presents a constantly changing spectacle, and should ideally be visited in different seasons. Look out for news about the latest planned addition to the site: a third covered biome, using cutting-edge design and technology, dedicated to the warm desert regions and the impact of climate change.

Allow at least half a day for a full exploration, but arrive early – or take advantage of the extended opening in summer – to avoid congestion. There are timed "story-telling" sessions, and abundant good food is on hand. In summer, the grassy arena sees performances of a range of music – from Peter Gabriel to Hot Chip – and in winter a skating rink is set up; consult the website for all details.

The most useful **bus routes** to Eden are #T9, #27B (Sun only) and #527 from St Austell station all year. Bus #27B also links the site with Truro, and #527 connects it with Newquay, as does #T10 in summer, and there's also the summer-only #T11 from Truro and Falmouth (Mon–Fri once daily). Drivers will find the site signposted on most roads in the area, and there's a useful network of routes for walkers and cyclists, who can claim a £4 reduction off the adult entry fee.

On each side of the dock the coarse sand and stone **beaches** have small rock pools, above which cliff walks lead around St Austell Bay. Eastwards, you soon arrive at overdeveloped **Carlyon Bay**, whose main resort is **Par**. The beaches here get clogged with clay – the best swimming is to be found by pressing on to the sheltered crescent of **Polkerris**.

Practicalities

Trains on the main London–Penzance line serve St Austell, with most services stopping at Par, which is also connected to Newquay on the north coast. Hourly #25 **buses** link St Austell with Charlestown, Par and Fowey (on Sun #25B).

Charlestown is the most attractive **place to stay** hereabouts: try *T'Gallants* (℡01726/70203, ⓦwww.t-gallants.co.uk; ❹), a smart Georgian B&B at the back of the harbour where cream teas are served in the garden, or *Broad Meadow House*, behind the Shipwreck Centre on Quay Road (℡01726/76636, ⓦwww .broadmeadowhouse.com; no credit cards; ❸), which offers B&B as well as "tent and breakfast" (April–Oct; up to £20 per person), with family-size tents provided in a meadow by the sea, to which breakfast is brought in the morning; limited camping in small tents is also available. St Austell Bay has a range of official **campsites**, mostly closed October to Easter, including *Carlyon Bay* (℡01726/812735, ⓦwww.carlyonbay.net), near the beach at Bethesda and just a mile and a half from the Eden Project.

Behind *T'Gallants* in Charlestown, the *Rashleigh Arms* offers real ales and a lunchtime carvery, and the *Harbourside Inn* also has a range of **food**.

Mevagissey to Veryan Bay

MEVAGISSEY was once known for the construction of fast vessels, used for carrying contraband as well as pilchards. Today the tiny port might display a few stacks of lobster pots, but the real business is tourism, and in summer the maze of back streets is saturated with day-trippers, converging on the inner harbour and overflowing onto the large sand beach at **Pentewan** a mile to the north.

A couple of miles north of Mevagissey lie the **Lost Gardens of Heligan** (daily: March–Oct 10am–6pm; Nov–Feb 10am–5pm; last entry 90min before closing; £8.50), a fascinating resurrection of a Victorian garden which had fallen into neglect and was rescued from a ten-foot covering of brambles by Tim Smit, the visionary instigator of the Eden Project (see box opposite). The abundant palm trees, giant Himalayan rhododendrons, immaculate vinery and glasshouses scattered about all look as if they've been transplanted from warmer climes; a boardwalk takes you past interconnecting ponds, through a jungle and under a canopy of bamboo and ferns down to the Lost Valley, where there are lakes, wild flower meadows and leafy oak, beech and chestnut rides.

Past the headland to the south of Mevagissey, the small sandy cove of **Portmellon** retains little of its boat-building activities but is freer of tourists. Further still, the village of **GORRAN HAVEN**, which was formerly known for its crab-fishing, has a neat rock-and-sand beach and a footpath that winds round to the even more attractive **Vault Beach**, half a mile south. South of here juts the most striking headland on Cornwall's southern coast, **Dodman Point**, cause of many a wreck and topped by a stark granite cross built by a local parson as a seamark in 1896. The promontory holds the substantial remains of an Iron Age fort, with an earthwork bulwark cutting right across the point.

Curving away to the west, the elegant parabola of **Veryan Bay** is barely touched by commercialism. Just west of Dodman Point lies one of Cornwall's most beautiful coves, **Hemmick Beach**, an excellent swimming spot with rocky outcrops affording a measure of privacy. Visually even more impressive is **Porthluney Cove**, a crescent of sand backed by green pastures and the battlemented **Caerhays Castle** (mid-March to May Mon–Fri noon–4pm; gardens mid-Feb to May daily 10am–5pm; last entry 1hr before closing; house £5.50, garden £5.50, combined ticket £9.50), built in 1808 by John Nash and surrounded by beautiful gardens.

A little further on, the minuscule and whitewashed **Portloe** is fronted by jagged black rocks that throw up fountains of seaspray, giving it a bracing, on-the-edge feel. Sequestered inland, **VERYAN** has a pretty village green and pond, but is best known for its curious circular white houses built in the nineteenth century by one Reverend Jeremiah Trist. A lane from Veryan leads down to one of the cleanest swimming spots on Cornwall's southern coast, **Pendower Beach**. Two-thirds of a mile long and backed by dunes, Pendower joins with the neighbouring **Carne Beach** at low tide to create a long sandy continuum.

Practicalities

From St Austell's bus and train station, **buses** #26, #25B (Sun only, not Heligan) and #526 leave for Mevagissey and Heligan, with some #526 buses continuing to Gorran Haven. Veryan and Portloe are reachable on #T51 from Truro (not Sun). You can find local information at Mevagissey's **tourist office** on St George's Square (Easter–May, Sept & Oct Mon–Fri 10am–3pm; June–Aug Mon–Sat 10am–5pm, Sun 11am–4pm; ☎0870/443 2928, ⓦwww .mevagissey-cornwall.co.uk). **Bike rental** is available from Pentewan Valley Cycle Hire (☎01726/844242), on the B3273 outside Pentewan.

Right in the heart of Mevagissey, the best **accommodation** option is the fifteenth-century *Fountain Inn* (☎01726/842320, ⓦwww.staustellbrewery.co.uk; ❸) on Cliff Street, off East Quay; alternatively, try *The Old Parsonage*, 58 Church St (☎01726/843709, ⓦwww.oldparsonage.net), ❹), a B&B with simply furnished rooms with private facilities. You might appreciate the coast better by staying in Portmellon, where the weathered old *Rising Sun Inn* (☎01726/843235; ❺; closed Jan & Feb) confronts the sea. In Veryan, head for the *Elerkey Guest House* (☎01872/501261, ⓦwww.elerkey.com; ❸), an ex-farmhouse with a spacious garden and adjoining art gallery; it's the first on the left after the church. There's a YHA **hostel** (☎0870/770 5712, ⓔboswinger@yha.org.uk; from £13) in a former farmhouse at Boswinger, a remote spot half a mile from Hemmick Beach. Difficult to reach without your own transport, it's about a mile from the bus stop at Gorran Church Town, served infrequently by #526 buses.

There's no shortage of **restaurants** in Mevagissey, most specializing in fish – for something a bit different, try the Portuguese *Alvorada*, 17 Church St (closed daytime, plus all Mon–Wed & Sun Oct–Feb; ☎01726/842055), offering an inventive menu (fixed price in winter: £21 for five courses). The *Fountain Inn* and the *Ship Inn* on Fore Street both offer **pub** grub, and Portmellon's *Rising Sun* serves Cornish sausages as well as fresh fish.

Truro, Falmouth and St Mawes

Lush tranquillity collides with frantic tourist activity around the estuary basin of **Carrick Roads**. Connected by river to the estuary, **Truro** is a stop on the main rail line to Penzance and the region's main transport centre. At the end of a branch line from Truro and at the mouth of the Carrick Roads, **Falmouth** is the major resort around here, and the site of one of Cornwall's mightiest castles, **Pendennis**. Its sister fort lies across the Carrick Roads in **St Mawes**, the main settlement on the **Roseland peninsula**, a luxuriant backwater of woods and sheltered creeks between the River Fal and the sea.

Truro

Cornwall's county town, **TRURO**, presents a mixture of different styles, from the graceful Georgian architecture that came with the tin-mining boom of the 1800s to its modern shopping centre. Further blurring the town's overall identity, and its dominant feature, is Truro's faux-medieval **Cathedral** (Mon–Sat 7.30am–6pm, Sun 9am–7pm), at the bottom of Pydar Street. Completed in 1910, it was the first Anglican cathedral to be built in England since St Paul's in London, though it incorporates part of the fabric of a much older parish church. The airy interior's best feature is its Neo-Gothic baptistry, complete with emphatically pointed arches and elaborate roof vaulting. To the right of the choir, St Mary's aisle is a relic of the original Perpendicular building, other fragments of which adorn the walls, including – in the north transept – a colourful Jacobean memorial to local Parliamentarian John Robartes and his wife. To get the full picture, join a **guided tour** of the cathedral (April–Oct Mon–Thurs & Sat 11am, Fri 11.30am, plus weekdays at 2pm during school hols).

Truro's other unmissable attraction is the **Royal Cornwall Museum** (Mon–Sat 10am–5pm; free), housed in an elegant Georgian building on River Street. The wide-ranging exhibits include minerals, Celtic inscriptions and paintings by Cornish artists. From Town Quay, Enterprise Boats runs scenic **river cruises** to Falmouth and St Mawes up to five times daily between May and October (£10 return; ☎01326/374241, ⌨www.enterprise-boats.co.uk).

Practicalities

Buses stop nearby at Lemon Quay, or near the train station on Richmond Hill, and Truro's **tourist office** is in the Italianate City Hall on Boscawen Street; (Mon–Fri 9am–5pm; Easter–Oct also Sat 9am–5pm; ☎01872/274555, ⌨www .truro.gov.uk). Best hotel **accommodation** in the centre of town is the *Royal Hotel* at the bottom of Lemon Street (☎01872/270345, ⌨www .royalhotelcornwall.co.uk; ❻), with a bright, modern feel and a good, informal brasserie. Among the **B&Bs**, try *Bay Tree*, a restored Georgian house at 28 Ferris Town (☎01872/240274, ⌨www.baytree-guesthouse.co.uk; no credit cards; ❸), where rooms have shared bathrooms. There's also a central and comfortable **hostel**, *Truro Backpackers Lodge*, at 10 The Parade (☎01872/260857 or 0781/375 5210, ⌨www.trurobackpackers.co.uk), with dorm beds (£15) and single and double rooms (❶), while there's an excellent **campsite**, *Carnon Downs*, three miles southwest of Truro on the A39 Falmouth road (☎01872/862283, ⌨www .carnon-downs-caravanpark.co.uk).

Truro's best **restaurants** are fairly centrally located. For coffees, vegetarian lunches and a choice of organic wines and Belgian beers, head for *Lettuce & Lovage*, 15 Kenwyn St (☎01872/272546; closed eves & all Sun), while *Saffron*, 5 Quay St (☎01872/263771; closed Sun, also Mon eve Jan–May), also serves inexpensive lunches as well as a good-value early-evening menu and seafood specials. The *One Eyed Cat*, a cool and contemporary restaurant and "drinkery" in a converted church at 116 Kenwyn St (☎01872/222122) has pastas, pizzas and seafood dishes on the menu and DJs at weekends. Among the **pubs**, you'll find good ale and decent bar meals at the *Wig and Pen*, on the corner of Frances and Castle streets, and at the *Globe Inn*, next door.

Falmouth

The construction of Pendennis Castle on the southern point of Carrick Roads in the sixteenth century prepared the ground for the growth of **FALMOUTH**, then no more than a fishing village. Falmouth's prosperity was assured when in 1689 it became chief base of the fast Falmouth Packets, which sped mail to the Americas, and the port has maintained its allure for sailors ever since. Recent years have seen the growth of a local arts scene, and the castle alone is reason enough to brave the waves of tourist traffic that engulf the town every summer, drawn to the lush beaches stretching south of town.

The Town

From the **Prince of Wales Pier**, embarkation point for ferries to St Mawes and Truro as well as a plethora of other boat trips in summer, Falmouth's long **High Street** and its continuations Market and Church streets are a busy parade of humdrum bars and cafés. At is southern end, Arwenack Street holds the Tudor remains of **Arwenack House** (closed to the public), residence of the Killigrews, an important local dynasty. The peculiar granite pyramid in front, dating from 1737, was probably intended to commemorate the family, though its exact significance has never been clear. On the seafront opposite stands Falmouth's chief attraction, the **National Maritime Museum Cornwall** (daily 10am–5pm; £7.50), an impressive collection of vessels from all over the world. Many of these are suspended in mid-air in the Flotilla Gallery, the cavernous centre-piece of the museum, which can be viewed from three different levels. Panels on the walkways explain the finer points of boat design, while smaller lateral galleries focus on boat-building and repairing, Falmouth's packet ships and Cornwall's various other links with the sea, including fishing. A lighthouse-like lookout tower offers excellent views over the harbour and estuary.

Pendennis Castle and Falmouth's beaches

A few minutes' walk west of the museum, **Pendennis Castle** stands sentinel at the tip of the promontory that separates Carrick Roads from Falmouth Bay (late March to June & Sept Mon–Fri & Sun 10am–5pm, Sat 10am–4pm; July & Aug Mon–Fri & Sun 10am–6pm, Sat 10am–4pm; Oct–March daily 10am–4pm; £5.50; EH). The extensive fortification shows little evidence of its five-month siege by the Parliamentarians during the Civil War, which ended only when half its defenders had died and the rest had been starved into submission. Though this is a less-refined contemporary of the castle at St Mawes (see opposite), its site wins hands down, facing right out to sea on its own pointed peninsula, the stout ramparts offering the best all-round views of Carrick Roads and Falmouth Bay. Jousting displays, concerts and drama productions are occasionally staged in the grounds in summer.

If you want to swim in the area, head for the long sandy bay round Pendennis Point, south of the centre, where a succession of sheltered **beaches** are backed by expensive hotels. From the popular **Gyllyngvase Beach**, you can reach the more attractive **Swanpool Beach** by cliff path, or walk a couple of miles further on to **Maenporth**, from where there are some fine cliff-top walks.

Practicalities

Falmouth's **tourist office** is off the Prince of Wales Pier at 11 Market Strand (March–Oct Mon–Sat 9.30am–5.15pm, plus July & Aug Sun 10.15am–1.45pm; Nov–Feb Mon–Fri 9.30am–5.15pm; ☎01326/312300, ⓦwww.acornishriver .co.uk). You can access the **Internet** at Q Bar, 15a Killigrew St (daily 9am–5pm).

For central budget **accommodation**, look no further than the *Arwenack Hotel*, 27 Arwenack St (℡01326/311185, Ⓦwww.falmouthtownhotels.co.uk; no credit cards; ❸), with basic, good-value rooms, including two with good views. Most other options are south of the centre, near the train station and beach area: try the Victorian *Melvill House Hotel*, 52 Melvill Rd (℡01326/316645, Ⓦwww.melvill-house-falmouth.co.uk; ❸), a few minutes' walk from the beach, with sea or harbour views from its en-suite rooms; or *Gyllyngvase House Hotel*, a staid but comfortable choice on Gyllyngvase Road (℡01326/312956, Ⓦwww.gyllyngvase.co.uk; ❺), two minutes from the sea, with views from two of its rooms. The very clean and friendly *Falmouth Lodge* backpackers' **hostel** is also near the beach at 9 Gyllyngvase Terrace (℡01326/319996, Ⓦwww .falmouthbackpackers.co.uk; dorm beds from £16, doubles ❶), with a kitchen and Internet access. Among the overdeveloped caravan parks on the coast south of Falmouth, the **campsite** at *Tregedna Farm* is more tent-friendly, two and a half miles from town and half a mile from Maenporth Beach and the coast path (℡01326/250529, Ⓦwww.tregednafarmholidays.co.uk; closed Oct–Easter).

As for **restaurants**, Arwenack Street has *South Side* at no. 35–37 (℡01326/212122), which has comfy sofas and everything from tapas and burgers to steaks on the menu, and the cool, contemporary *Hunky Dory* at no. 46 (℡01326/212997; closed daytime), offering a fusion of European and Asian food including seafood and vegetarian. Away from the bustle, you can tuck in to grills and pizzas right on Gyllyngvase Beach at the lively *Gylly Beach Café* (℡01326/312884), which has occasional live music.

The *Quayside Inn*, on Arwenack Street, is the pick of the **pubs**, with harbour-side tables and live music at weekends. Drivers or boaters might venture out of town to the *Pandora Inn* at Restronguet, four miles north of Falmouth, where you can drink by the river; superior bar food is available at lunchtime, or you can eat fresh seafood in the upstairs restaurant (℡01326/372678).

St Mawes and the Roseland peninsula

Stuck at the tip of a prong of land at the bottom of Carrick Roads, the secluded, unhurried village of **ST MAWES** has an attractive walled seafront lying below a hillside of villas and abundant gardens. Just out of sight at the end of the seafront stands the small and pristine **St Mawes Castle** (late March to June & Sept daily except Sat 10am–5pm; July & Aug daily except Sat 10am–6pm; Oct daily 10am–4pm; Nov–March Mon & Fri–Sun 10am–4pm; £4; EH), built during the reign of Henry VIII. The castle owes its excellent condition to its early surrender to Parliamentary forces during the Civil War, a move that hastened the bloody subjugation of Pendennis Castle over in Falmouth. Both castles adhere to the same cloverleaf design, with a round central keep surrounded by robust gun emplacements, but this is the more attractive of the pair. The dungeons and gun installations contain various artillery exhibits as well as some background on local social history.

Moving away from St Mawes, you could spend a pleasant afternoon poking around the **Roseland peninsula**. Between Easter and October, a twice-hourly passenger **ferry** (daily 10am–5pm; £5 return) crosses from the village to the southern arm of the peninsula, which holds the twelfth- to thirteenth-century church of **St Anthony-in-Roseland** and the **lighthouse** on St Anthony's Head, marking the entry into Carrick Roads. Two and a half miles north of St Mawes, the scattered hamlet of **ST JUST-IN-ROSELAND** holds the strikingly picturesque church of St Just, right next to the creek and surrounded by palms and subtropical shrubbery, its gravestones tumbling down to the water's edge.

The easiest way to visit St Mawes and the Roseland peninsula is on one of the frequent ferries from Falmouth's Prince of Wales Pier (£7 return). By road, the fastest road route from Truro, Falmouth and west Cornwall involves crossing the River Fal on the chain-driven **King Harry Ferry** (every 20min: April–Sept Mon–Sat 7.30am–9.20pm, Sun 10am–8.20pm; Oct–March Mon–Sat 7.20am–7.20pm, Sun 10am–6.20pm; £4.50 per car, 50p per bike, 20p per foot passenger; ☏01872/862312). The latter docks close to **Trelissick Garden** (mid-Feb to Oct daily 10.30am–5.30pm; Nov to mid-Feb daily 11am–4pm; £5.80; NT), which is celebrated for its hydrangeas and other Mediterranean species, and has a splendid woodland walk along the Fal (free access all year). In summer, ferries from Falmouth, St Mawes and Truro also stop here, as does the year-round bus #T16 (not Sun) from Truro.

Practicalities

Though lacking Falmouth's range of accommodation, St Mawes makes an attractive – if pricey – **place to stay**. The best budget choices are a ten-minute walk up from the seafront on Newton Road and all are run by the same family: *Newton Farm* (☏01326/270427; ❸), with shared bathroom, and, with en-suite facilities, *Little Newton* (☏01326/270664; ❸) and *Lower Meadow* (☏01326/270036; ❺); all have spacious rooms and friendly hosts. For location – and very steep rates – book in at the *Tresanton Hotel* (☏01326/270055, ⓦwww.tresanton.com; ❾), an exclusive Mediterranean-style retreat. You can eat and drink at the *Victory Inn,* a fine old oak-beamed **pub** just off the seafront.

The Lizard peninsula

The **Lizard peninsula** – from the Celtic *lys ardh,* or "high point" – preserves a thankfully undeveloped if sometimes bleak appearance. If this flat and treeless expanse can be said to have a centre, it is **Helston**, a junction for buses running from Falmouth and Truro to the spartan villages of the peninsula's interior and the tiny fishing ports on its coast. By public transport, you can reach Helston on **bus** #2 from Penzance, #T1 from Truro and #T4 from Falmouth. From Helston, #T2 with the east-coast settlements of **St Keverne** and **Coverack**, and #T34 goes via **Mullion** to the village of **The Lizard**. The infrequent #T3 "Lizard Rambler" links Helston, St Keverne, Coverack and Helford. Neither #T3 nor #T4 runs on Sundays in winter.

Along the River Helford

To the north of the peninsula, the snug hamlets sprinkled in the valley of the **River Helford** are a complete contrast to the rugged character of most of the Lizard. At the river's mouth stands **MAWNAN**, whose granite church of **St Mawnan-in-Meneage** is dedicated to the sixth-century Welsh missionary St Maunanus – Meneage (rhyming with "vague") means "land of monks".

Upstream, outside the village of Gweek, the **National Seal Sanctuary** (daily: summer 10am–5pm, winter 10am–4pm; £10.95) is a rehabilitation and release centre for the increasing number of injured seals being rescued from around Cornwall and beyond. Most entertaining are the seal pups, which can be seen during the winter months.

On the south side of the estuary, **Frenchman's Creek**, one of a splay of creeks and arcane inlets running off the river, was the inspiration for Daphne

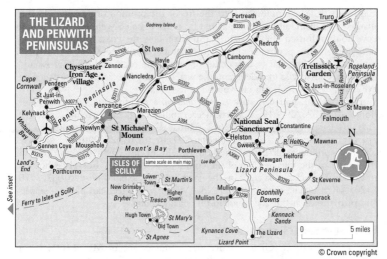

THE LIZARD
AND PENWITH
PENINSULAS

Portreath
Truro
Godrevy Island
St Ives
Hayle
Redruth
Camborne
Chysauster Zennor
Iron Age
Cape village Nancledra
Cornwall Pendeen
St Just-in-
Penwith
Kelynack
Penzance
Marazion
Newlyn St Michael's
Mount
Whitesand Bay
Sennen Cove Mousehole
Land's
End Porthcurno

Trelissick
Garden
Roseland
Peninsula
St Just-in-Roseland
St Mawes
Falmouth
National Seal
Sanctuary
Helston
Gweek
Mawnan
R. Helford
Helford
Mawgan
Lizard Peninsula
St Keverne

ISLES OF
SCILLY
same scale as main map
Lower
Town
St Martin's
New Grimsby
Bryher
Tresco
Higher
Town
Hugh Town
St Mary's
Old Town
St Agnes

Loe Bar
Porthleven

Mullion
Mullion Cove
Goonhilly
Downs
Coverack

Kennack
Sands
Kynance Cove
The Lizard
Lizard Point

0   5 miles

N

© Crown copyright

DEVON AND CORNWALL | The Lizard peninsula

6

du Maurier's novel of the same name. Her evocation of it holds true: "still and soundless, surrounded by the trees, hidden from the eyes of men".

You can get over to the south bank by the seasonal ferry (Easter–Oct) from Helford Passage to **Helford**, an agreeable old smugglers' haunt worth a snack-stop – the *Shipwright's Arms* has pub lunches and a garden overlooking the river.

St Keverne and Coverack

South of Helford, the broad, windswept plateau of **Goonhilly Downs** is interrupted by ranks of wind turbines and the futuristic saucers of Goonhilly Satellite Station. The minor B3293 ends at the inland village of **ST KEVERNE**, whose tidy square is flanked by two inns and a church. Forking right onto the B3294, you'll come to **COVERACK**, a fishing port in a lovely sheltered bay, with a range of **accommodation**. Among the B&Bs, try *Fernleigh* (①01326/280626, Ⓔsudan-ann03@hotmail.co.uk; no credit cards; ❸), on Chymbloth Way, a turn-off from Harbour Road, whose amiable proprietors can cook up a homely three-course meal for around £15. Alternatively, you can stay right above the harbour in the en-suite rooms of the *Paris Hotel* (①01326/280258 Ⓦwww.pariscoverack.com; ❹). There's a YHA **hostel** just west of Coverack's centre overlooking the bay (①0870/770 5780, Ⓔcoverack@yha.org.uk; closed Nov–March; £18), and a **campsite** outside the village, *Little Trevothan* (①01326/280260, Ⓦwww.littletrevothan.com; closed Nov–Feb).

The *Paris Hotel* provides good **meals**; otherwise nip across to the *Lifeboat House Seafood Restaurant* (①01326/280899; closed Mon & Oct–Easter), with superb fresh fish; it's pricey and often fully booked, but you can always pick up first-rate fish and chips from the attached takeaway. Ask about **windsurfing** courses at the Coverack Windsurfing Centre, below the post office at Cliff Cottage, (April–Oct; ①01326/280939, Ⓦwww.coverack.co.uk).

Around Lizard Point

Mainland Britain's southernmost village, called simply **THE LIZARD**, is a nondescript but much visited place, with a handful of shops and B&Bs. A road and footpath lead a mile south to the tip of the promontory, **Lizard Point**, marked by a plain lighthouse. Sheltered from the ceaselessly churning sea, a tiny cove holds a disused lifeboat station. You can follow the coast path a mile or so northwest to the peninsula's best-known beach, **Kynance Cove**, with sheer hundred-foot cliffs, stacks and arches of serpentine rock, and offshore islands. The beach has a wild grandeur, and the water quality is excellent – but keep an eye on the tide, which can cut you off at its flood.

In The Lizard, you can **stay** at: *Caerthillian*, a comfortable Victorian guest house (℡01326/290019, ⓌWww.thecaerthillian.co.uk; no credit cards; ❸); *Parc Brawse House* (℡01326/290466, Ⓦwww.cornwall-online.co.uk /parcbrawsehouse; ❸); and *Penmenner House* (℡01326/290370, Ⓦwww .cornwall-online.co.uk/penmennerhouse-thelizard; no credit cards; ❸), all in the centre of the village. One of the country's newest YHA **hostels** is housed in a classic Victorian villa right on the coast next to the lighthouse (℡0870/770 6120, Ⓔlizard@yha.org.uk; closed Nov–March; £18). You can pick up snacks and **pub meals** at the *Top House* in the village centre.

Mullion and around

Four miles north of Kynance Cove, the inland village of **MULLION** has a fifteenth- to sixteenth-century church dedicated to the Breton **St Mellane** (or Malo), with a dog-door for canine churchgoers. A lane leads a mile and a quarter west to **Mullion Cove**, where a tiny beach is sheltered behind a lovely harbour and more rock stacks. A mile or two north, the sands at **Polurrian** and **Poldhu**, are better, however, and attract surfers. At the cliff edge at Poldhu, the **Marconi Monument** marks the spot from which the first transatlantic radio transmission was made in 1901.

Back in Mullion, behind an enclosed garden at the top of Nansmellyon Road, *The Old Vicarage* (℡01326/240898, Ⓦwww.cornwall-online.co.uk /mullionoldvicarage; no credit cards; ❺) provides elegant **accommodation** in four spacious rooms, while *Campden House* offers plainer B&B north of the centre on The Commons, just a few minutes from Poldhu beach (℡01326/240365; no credit cards; ❸). In the village centre, you'll find **refreshment** at the sixteenth-century *Old Inn*, Churchtown, which serves bar food and real ales, and has outdoor tables.

Helston and around

The main transport hub and centre for the Lizard peninsula, the unassuming town of **HELSTON** is best known for its **Furry Dance** (or Flora Dance), which dates from the seventeenth century. Held on May 8 (unless this falls on a Sun or Mon, when the procession takes place on the nearest Sat), it's a stately procession of top-hatted men and summer-frocked women performing a solemn dance through the town's streets and gardens. You can learn something about it and absorb plenty of other local history and lore in the eclectic **Helston Folk Museum** (Mon–Sat 10am–1pm, closes 4pm school hols; £2, free on Sat), housed in former market buildings behind the Guildhall on Church Street.

For a drink or a snack, seek out the 🍴 *Blue Anchor*, 50 Coinagehall St, a fifteenth-century monastery rest house, now a snug **pub** with flagstone floors and mellow Spingo beer brewed on the premises in three strengths. Next door, *No. 52* provides **meals** (closed daytime & Sun) as well as good-sized **rooms** (℡01326/569334, Ⓦwww.spingoales.com; ❸) – ask in the pub if there's no reply.

Three miles southwest of Helston, **PORTHLEVEN** is a sizeable port that once served to export tin ore from the inland mines. There are plenty of good

6

beaches within easy reach: the best for swimming are around **Rinsey Head**, three miles north along the coast, including the sheltered **Praa Sands**. One and a quarter miles south of Porthleven, strong currents make it unsafe to swim at the beautiful **Loe Bar**, a strip of shingle which separates the freshwater **Loe Pool** from the sea. The elongated pool is one of two places claiming to be where the sword Excalibur was restored to its watery source (the other is on Bodmin Moor), and there's a path running along its western shore as far as Helston, five miles north, making an excellent **walk**.

The Penwith peninsula

Though more densely populated than the Lizard, the **Penwith peninsula** is a more rugged landscape, with a raw appeal that is still encapsulated by the headland of **Land's End**, despite the commercial paraphernalia superimposed there. The seascapes, the quality of the light and the slow tempo of the local fishing communities made this area a hotbed of artistic activity towards the end of the nineteenth century, when the painters of **Newlyn**, near **Penzance**, established a distinctive school of painting. More innovative figures – among them Ben Nicholson, Barbara Hepworth and Naum Gabo – were soon afterwards to make **St Ives** one of England's liveliest cultural communities, and their enduring influence is illustrated in the Tate St Ives, showcasing the modern artists associated with the locality.

Penwith is far more easily toured than the Lizard, with a road circling its coastline and a better network of public transport from the two main towns, St Ives and Penzance, which have most of the accommodation. From Penzance – the terminus for **rail** services from London and Birmingham – **buses** #1 and #1A go straight to Land's End, whereas the #6, #345, #346 and #504 take in Newlyn and Mousehole. North of Land's End, the headland of Cape Cornwall is served by the circular #345 (not Sun); otherwise walk from St Just, reachable on the #17, #17A, #17B, #345 and #509. The open-top, summer-only #300 is a good way to view the coast between St Ives and Land's End. St Ives can be reached by branch rail line or numerous buses from Penzance and Truro.

Hikers might consider walking the eight miles separating Penzance from St Ives along the old St Michael's Way, a waymarked pilgrim's route for which the tourist office in both towns can provide a free route map.

Penzance and around

Occupying a sheltered position at the northwest corner of Mount's Bay, **PENZANCE** has always been a major port, but most traces of the medieval town were obliterated by a Spanish raiding party at the end of the sixteenth century. Today, much of the town has a graceful Georgian character, and it makes an attractive base, though it does get very busy in summer.

Arrival, information and accommodation

Penzance's **train** and **bus stations** are next to each other on the seafront. Drivers can leave their cars during excursions to the Isles of Scilly at Avalon **car park** near the harbour, which can be accessed from 33 Regent Terrace and South Place (℡01736/364622; £5 per day). The **tourist office** (Mon–Fri 9am–5pm, plus May–Sept Sat 9am–4pm, Sun 10am–2pm; ℡01736/362207, Ⓦwww .visit-westcornwall.com) is next to the bus station. For **bike rental** head for the Cycle Centre, 1 New St (℡01736/351671). Penzance Computers, 36B Market Jew St, provides **Internet** access (Mon–Sat 9am–6pm, Sun noon–4pm).

Accommodation

Abbey Hotel Abbey St, off Chapel St
℡01736/366906, 🖰www.theabbeyonline.com.
Pamper yourself at this seventeenth-century
boutique hotel owned by former model Jean
Shrimpton and her husband. Lashings of old-
fashioned comfort, superb views and an excellent
restaurant. **❼**

Cornerways 5 Leskinnick St ℡01736/364645,
🖰www.penzance.co.uk/cornerways. Small, friendly
B&B very close to the bus and train stations, with
simply furnished en-suite rooms. Evening meals
and packed lunches are available. **❸**

Penzance Arts Club Chapel House, Chapel St
℡01736/363761, 🖰www.penzanceartsclub.co.uk.
Formerly the Portuguese embassy, this has seven
tastefully decorated rooms and lots of Bohemian
ambience. There's a good café/restaurant in the
basement, plus cabaret, DJs and film nights. **❺**

Penzance Backpackers Alexandra Rd
℡01736/363836, 🖰www.pzbackpack.com. Tidy
and friendly hostel with dorm beds as well as
doubles, self-catering, laundry and Internet
facilities. Dorm beds £14, doubles **❶**

Penzance YHA Castle Horneck, Alverton
℡0870/770 5992, ✉penzance@yha.org.uk.
Housed in a Georgian mansion out of town, a
two-mile hike from the station up Market Jew St
into Alverton Rd, then turn right at the *Pirate Inn* (or
take bus #5 or #6 from Penzance station as far as
the *Pirate Inn*). Dorm beds from £15.50.

Union Hotel Chapel St ℡01736/362319, 🖰www
.unionhotel.co.uk. Soak up the atmosphere at this
classic Georgian hotel, centrally located. **❹**

The Town

Climbing up from the harbour and the train and bus stations, **Market Jew Street** (from *Marghas Jew*, meaning "Thursday Market") is Penzance's main traffic artery. At the top, in front of the silver-domed Victorian **Market House**, stands a statue of **Humphry Davy** (1778–1829), the local woodcarver's son who pioneered the science of electrochemistry and invented the life-saving miners' safety-lamp. Turn left here into **Chapel Street**, which has some of the town's finest buildings, including the flamboyant **Egyptian House**, built in 1835 to house a geological museum but subsequently abandoned until its restoration 30 years ago. Across the street, the **Union Hotel** dates from the seventeenth century, and originally held the town's assembly rooms; the news of Admiral Nelson's victory at Trafalgar and the death of Nelson himself were first announced from the minstrels' gallery here in 1805.

Off Chapel and Market Jew streets in Princes Street, an old telephone exchange houses a modern art gallery and education centre, **The Exchange** (Mon–Sat 10am–5pm, Sun 11am–4pm, closed Mon & Tues in winter; free), worth a visit for its sleek design and regular exhibitions. You'll find a more traditional collection of art at **Penlee House Gallery and Museum** (Mon–Sat: Easter–Sept 10am–5pm; Oct–April 10.30am–4.30pm; £3, free on Sat), off Morrab Road (walk up from the Promenade or down from Alverton Street, a continuation of Market Jew Street). The gallery holds the biggest collection of the works of the Newlyn School – impressionistic harbour scenes, sometimes sentimentalized but often bathed in an evocatively luminous light. There are frequent exhibitions, and also displays on local history.

On the seafront, bulging out of the Promenade into Mount's Bay, the Art Deco **Jubilee Pool** (mid-May to mid-Sept daily 10am–7pm; £3.85) is a tidal, salt-water (though chlorinated) open-air swimming pool, built to mark the Silver Jubilee of George V in 1935. It's a classic example of the style. Non-swimmers can stroll around (£1.30) to get a closer view of the pool and bay.

From the Promenade, it's an easy walk to **NEWLYN**, Cornwall's biggest fishing port, lying immediately south of Penzance. The newly refurbished **art gallery**, near the harbour at 24 New Rd (Mon–Sat 10am–5pm, Sun 11am–4pm, closed Mon & Tues in winter; free), concentrates on contemporary art.

Eating and drinking

Penzance has a decent range of **restaurants** scattered about town, as well as modern bars and traditional **pubs**.

Admiral Benbow Chapel St. Crammed with gaudy ships' figureheads and other nautical items, this pub offers standard bar meals and heaps of atmosphere.

Archie Brown's Bread St. You can get tasty and inexpensive vegetarian and wholefood dishes at this café above a health shop off the pedestrianized Causeway Head. Occasionally open for special theme nights, otherwise open daytime only and closed Sun.

Blue Snappa 18 Market Place. At the top of Market Jew Street this congenial café-bar serves great breakfasts, ciabattas, salads, wraps and moderately priced evening meals. Closed Sun eve.

Coco's Chapel St. Good for coffees, cakes, beers and tapas, and Helford River mussels are also on the menu. Main courses cost around £12.

Harris's 46 New St ☏01736/364408. Quality but expensive Modern British cuisine can be sampled at this formal restaurant. Main courses average at £18.50. Closed Sun, plus Mon in winter.

Turk's Head Chapel St. The town's oldest inn, reputed to date back to the thirteenth century, with a maze of low-ceilinged rooms and a garden. Food served.

St Michael's Mount

The medieval chimneys and towers of **St Michael's Mount** (late March to Oct Mon–Fri & Sun 10.30am–5/5.30pm; Nov to late March guided tours Tues & Fri at 11am & 2pm, book at ☏01736/710507; £6.40; NT) are a prominent feature of Mount's Bay. The fortress-isle lies a couple of hundred yards offshore of the village Marazion, five miles east of Penzance and reachable on frequent buses from the bus station. A vision of the archangel Michael led to the building of a church on this granite pile around the fifth century, and within three centuries a Celtic monastery had been founded here. The present building originated as a chapel, constructed in the eleventh century by Edward the Confessor. It was then handed over to the Benedictine monks of Brittany's Mont St Michel, whose island abbey – also founded after a vision of St Michael – was the model for this one. The complex was appropriated by Henry V during the Hundred Years' War, and it became a fortress after its dissolution a century later. After the Civil War, when it was used to store arms for the Royalist forces, it became the residence of the St Aubyn family, who still live in the castle.

A good number of the fortress's buildings date from the twelfth century, but the later additions are more interesting, such as the battlemented **chapel** and the seventeenth-century decorations of the **Chevy Chase Room**, so called after the medieval hunting ballad, which is illustrated by a simple plaster frieze on the walls. Other rooms are crowded with paintings and general memorabilia.

At low tide the promontory can be approached on foot via a cobbled causeway; at high tide there are boats from Marazion (£1.50).

Mousehole to Land's End

Accounts vary as to the derivation of the name of **MOUSEHOLE** (pronounced "Mowzle"), though it may be from a smugglers' cave just south of town. In any case, the name evokes perfectly this minuscule harbour, cradled in the arms of a granite breakwater three miles south of Penzance. The village attracts more visitors than it can handle, so hang around until the crowds have departed before exploring its tight tangle of lanes. Among them, you'll come across Mousehole's oldest house, the fourteenth-century **Keigwin House**, a survivor of the sacking of the village by Spaniards in 1595. Finish off with a drink at the harbourside *Ship Inn*, which also has **meals** and en-suite **rooms** (☏01736/731234; ❺).

Eight miles west round the coast, **PORTHCURNO** is one of Penwith's best bathing spots. The name means "Port Cornwall", but its beach of tiny white

The **Isles of Scilly** are a compact archipelago of about a hundred islands 28 miles southwest of Land's End, none of them bigger than three miles across, and only five of them inhabited – **St Mary's**, **Tresco**, **Bryher**, **St Martin's** and **St Agnes**. Free of traffic, theme parks and crowds, they offer a welcome respite from the mainland tourist trail.

In the annals of folklore, the Scillies are the peaks of the submerged land of Lyonnesse, a fertile plain that extended west from Penwith before the ocean broke in, drowning the land and leaving only one survivor to tell the tale. Geologically, the islands form part of the same granite mass as Land's End, Bodmin Moor and Dartmoor, and, though they rarely rise above a hundred feet and are largely treeless, possess a remarkable variety of landscape. Each one has a distinctive character, at every turn revealing new perspectives over the extraordinary rocky seascape. The energizing briny air is thronged with the cries of seabirds, while the **beaches** are well-nigh irresistible, ranging from minute coves to vast untrammelled strands – though swimmers must steel themselves for the chilly water. The waters hereabouts, free of plankton or silt, are said to be among the clearest in Britain, offering some of the country's best **diving** sites; non-divers too can go snorkelling among the seals. Contact the tourist office for details of operators offering tuition and equipment hire.

For all information, contact the **tourist office** on Hugh Street, Hugh Town, St Mary's (Easter–Oct Mon–Fri 8.30am–6pm, Sat 8.30am–5pm, Sun 9am–2pm; Nov–Easter Mon–Fri 9am–5pm; ☎01720/422536, ⓦwww.simplyscilly.co.uk). Between May and September, on Wednesday and Friday evenings, islanders gather to watch the **gig races**, performed by six vessels over thirty feet long, and some over a hundred years old. The usual route starts at Nut Rock, to the east of Samson, and finishes at St Mary's Quay. You can follow the race from launches that leave about twenty minutes before the start of each race – see boards on St Mary's Quay or contact the tourist office.

Getting there

The islands are accessible by sea or air. **Boats** to St Mary's, operated by Isles of Scilly Travel (☎0845/710 5555, ⓦwww.islesofscilly-travel.co.uk), depart from Penzance's South Pier between Easter and October, the crossing taking about two and three-quarter hours. Saver returns, subject to certain restrictions, cost £76. The main departure points for **flights** (also operated by Isles of Scilly Travel) are Land's End (near St Just), Newquay, Exeter, Bristol and Southampton: in winter, there are departures only from Land's End and Newquay. From Land's End, a Saver return fare costs £109. British International (☎01736/363871, ⓦwww.islesofscillyhelicopter .com) also runs helicopter flights (20min) to St Mary's and Tresco from the heliport a mile east of Penzance. Short break returns are around £120.

Accommodation, eating and drinking

Although you can get a taste of the islands' highlights on a day-trip from Penzance, the Scillies deserve a much longer visit. Apart from the high cost of reaching them, the chief drawback is the shortage of **accommodation**, making advance booking essential in summer and school holidays. The vast majority of places to stay are on St Mary's, while Bryher, St Martin's and St Agnes each have three or four B&Bs only, and Tresco has just two very swanky choices. Prices are generally steep, especially at the trio of elite **hotels**: Tresco's *Island Hotel* (☎01720/422883, ⓦwww.tresco.co .uk), Bryher's *Hell Bay Hotel* (☎01720/422947, ⓦwww.hellbay.co.uk), and St Martin's *St Martin's on the Isle* (☎01720/422090, ⓦwww.stmartinshotel.co.uk), all ❾ and closed in winter.

As for **B&Bs**, most are in the ❹–❺ category in summer, less in the low season. Note that many offer – and often insist on – a dinner, bed and breakfast package, which is (apart from on St Mary's) the most convenient option in any case, considering the tiny choice of places to eat on the off-islands. Many close in winter, but there's usually enough to cater for the trickle of visitors who come in these months. The alternatives are a **self-catering** deal, almost always available only by the week (you'll need to book some time in advance), and **camping**. There are very basic sites on St Mary's, Bryher, St Martin's and St Agnes, mostly unsheltered and all closed in winter; camping elsewhere is not allowed.

Groceries are available on all five inhabited islands (though cost more than on the mainland), and there are places to eat on each, though only St Mary's has any great choice. The best **restaurants** are attached to the above-mentioned hotels, though there are a few other places worth seeking out. In addition, each island also has at least one **pub** serving food, among which special mention should be made of the New Inn on Tresco, which also provides high-quality restaurant meals, and the Turk's Head on St Agnes, famous for its pasties.

Exploring the islands

Apart from beach and sea, the main attractions of the Isles of Scilly include Cornwall's greatest concentration of **prehistoric remains**, some fabulous **rock formations**, and masses of **flowers**, nurtured by the equable climate and long hours of sunshine (the archipelago's name means "Sun Isles"). Along with tourism, the main source of income here is flower-growing, and the heaths and pathways of the islands are also dense with a profusion of wild flowers, from marigolds and gorse to sea thrift, trefoil and poppies, not to mention a host of more exotic species introduced by visiting foreign vessels.

The majority of the resident population of just over two thousand is concentrated on the biggest island, **St Mary's**, which has the lion's share of facilities in its capital, **Hugh Town**, and the richest trove of prehistoric sites. The island has a limited bus service, but cycling is the ideal way to get around – and you can **rent bikes** from St Mary's Bike Hire on The Strand, Hugh Town (☎01720/422289, or 07796/638506 in winter).

The "off islands", as the other inhabited members of the group are known, are always accessible on inter-island launches. The largest, **Tresco**, presents an appealing contrast between the orderly landscape around the remains of its ancient abbey and the bleak, untended northern half. The exuberant **Tresco Abbey Gardens** (daily 10am–4pm; £9), hosting an impressive collection of subtropical plants, are the archipelago's most popular visitor attraction. West of Tresco, **Bryher** has the smallest population, the slow routines of island life quickening only in the tourist season. The bracing, back-to-nature feel here is nowhere more evident than on the exposed western shore, where **Hell Bay** sees some formidable Atlantic storms. East of Tresco, **St Martin's** has a reputation as the least striking of the Scillies with the most introverted population, but its white-sand beaches are as majestically wild as any – Par Beach deserves a special mention – there are stunning views from its cliffy north-eastern end, and the surrounding waters are much favoured by scuba enthusiasts. On the southwest rim of the main group, the tidy lanes and picturesque cottages of **St Agnes** are nicely complemented by the weathered boulders and craggy headlands of its indented shoreline.

A visit to the isles would be incomplete without a sortie to the **uninhabited islands**, sanctuaries for seals, puffins and a host of other marine birdlife. On the largest of them, **Samson**, you can poke around prehistoric and more recent remains that testify to former settlement. Some of the smaller islets also repay a visit for their delightfully deserted beaches, though the majority amount to no more than bare rocks. This chaotic profusion of rocks of all shapes and sizes, each bearing a name, is densest at the archipelago's extremities – the **Western Rocks**, lashed by ferocious seas and the cause of innumerable wrecks over the years, and the milder **Eastern Isles**.

shells suggests privacy and isolation rather than the movement of ships. Steep steps lead up from here to the cliff-hewn **Minack Theatre**, created in the 1930s and since enlarged to hold 750 seats (though the basic Greek-inspired design has remained intact). The spectacular backdrop of Porthcurno Bay makes this one of the country's most inspiring theatres. The summer season lasts seventeen weeks from May to September, presenting a gamut of plays, opera and musicals, with tickets costing just £7–8.50 (℡01736/810181, 🖰www.minack.com). Bring a cushion and a rug. The **Exhibition Centre** (daily: Easter–Sept 9.30am–5.30pm; Oct–Easter 10am–4pm; closed during performances; £3) allows you to view the theatre and illustrates the story of its creation.

The peculiar white pyramid on the shore to the east of Porthcurno marks the spot where the first transatlantic cables were laid in 1880. On the headland beyond lies an Iron Age fort, **Treryn Dinas**, close to the famous rocking stone called **Logan's Rock**, a seventy-ton monster that was knocked off its perch by a nephew of playwright Oliver Goldsmith and a gang of sailors in 1824. Somehow they replaced the stone, but it never rocked again.

Land's End

The best way to reach **Land's End** is unarguably on foot along the coastal path. Although nothing can completely destroy the potency of this approach to the extreme western tip of England, the theme park behind this majestic headland comes close to violating irreparably the spirit of the place. The trivializing **Land's End Experience** (daily from 10am, closing times vary: call ℡0870/458 0099 to check; £10) substitutes a tawdry panoply of lasers and unconvincing sound effects for the real open-air experience, though the location is still a public right of way (you'll have to pay to use the car park, however; £3), and once past the theme park, nature takes over. Turf-covered cliffs sixty feet high provide a platform to view the Irish Lady, the Armed Knight, Dr Syntax Head and the rest of the Land's End outcrops, beyond which you can spot the Longships lighthouse, a mile and a half out to sea, sometimes the Wolf Rock lighthouse, nine miles southwest, and even the Isles of Scilly, 28 miles away.

Whitesand Bay to Pendeen

To the north of Land's End the rounded granite cliffs fall away at **Whitesand Bay** to reveal a glistening mile-long shelf of beach that offers the best swimming on the Penwith peninsula. The rollers make for good surfing and boards can be rented at **Sennen Cove**, the more popular southern end of the beach. There are a few **B&Bs** here, including *Myrtle Cottage* (℡01736/871698; no credit cards; ❸), which also has a cosy teashop open to non-residents. If you don't mind staying a short distance inland, there's *Whitesands Hotel* (℡01736/871776, 🖰www.whitesandshotel.co.uk; ❺), with five themed rooms and a deck with hammocks and barbecues in summer. The **restaurant** and grill is open to all and has pizzas, pastas, and meat and seafood dishes (around £11–15).

Cape Cornwall, three miles northward, shelters another good beach, overlooked by an old mining chimney. Half a mile inland the grimly grey village of **ST JUST-IN-PENWITH** was a centre of the tin and copper industry, and the rows of trim cottages radiating out from Bank Square are redolent of the close-knit community that once existed here. The tone is somewhat lightened by the grassy open-air theatre where miracle plays were staged; it was later used by Methodist preachers as well as Cornish wrestlers. St Just has limited **accommodation**, though there is the *Commercial Hotel* on Market Square (℡01736/788455, 🖰www.commercial-hotel.co.uk; ❹), which has en-suite rooms, and the village has a YHA **hostel** on its outskirts (℡0870/770 5906, ✉landsend@yha.org.uk; from £14) – take the left fork past the post office. There's also an excellent secluded **campsite**, just outside the hamlet of Kelynack a couple of miles south of St Just: *Kelynack Caravan and Camping Park* (℡01736/787633, ⓦwww.kelynackcaravans.co.uk; closed Nov–Easter), one of the few sheltered sites on Penwith, which also has bunks in small dorms available all year (£12). *Kegen Teg*, at 12 Market Square, serves good coffees, teas and **meals** (℡01736/788562; closed eves, also Jan & Feb). Just off Bank Square, the traditional *Star Inn* is the best of the **pubs**.

A couple of miles north of St Just, outside **PENDEEN**, you can get a close-up view of the Cornish mining industry at **Geevor Tin Mine** (daily except Sat 9/10am–4/5pm; last entry 1hr before closing; £7.50), where you can tour the surface machinery, explore an underground mine and visit the museum.

Zennor and around

East of Pendeen, the landscape is all rolling moorland and an abundance of granite, the chief building material of **ZENNOR**. D.H. Lawrence and Frieda came to live here in 1916 and were soon joined by John Middleton Murry and Katherine Mansfield, with the hope of forming a writers' community. The new arrivals soon left for a more sheltered haven near Falmouth, but Lawrence stayed on to write *Women in Love*, spending in all a year and a half in Zennor before being given notice to quit by the local constabulary, who suspected Lawrence and his German wife of unpatriotic sympathies. His Cornish experiences were later described in *Kangaroo*.

At the bottom of the village, the **Wayside Museum** is dedicated to Cornish life from prehistoric times (Easter–Oct daily 10.30/11am–5/5.30pm; £3). At the top of the lane, the **church of St Sennen** displays a sixteenth-century bench-carving of a mermaid who, according to local legend, was so entranced by the singing of a chorister that she lured him down to the sea, from where he never returned.

Next to the church, a fairly level path leads less than a mile northwest to the sea at **Zennor Head**, where there is some awe-inspiring cliff scenery above the sandy **Pendour Cove** (the fabled home of Zennor's mermaid). A couple of miles southeast of Zennor, located on a windy hillside off the minor road to Penzance, the Iron Age village of **Chysauster** (late March to June & Sept daily 10am–5pm; July & Aug 10am–6pm; Oct daily 10am–4pm; £2.50; EH) is the best-preserved ancient settlement in the southwest. Dating from about the first century BC, it contains two rows of four buildings, each consisting of a courtyard with small chambers leading off it, and a garden that was presumably used for growing vegetables.

Back in the village, the *Tinners Arms* is a cosy **place to eat** and **drink**. If you don't mind sleeping up to six to a room, the ⚸ *Old Chapel Backpackers Hostel* makes a fun **place to stay**, right next to the Wayside Museum (℡01736/798307, ⓦwww.zennorbackpackers.co.uk); dorm beds cost from £15, and there's a family room (❷), too. Sea views from the rooms and a congenial atmosphere are added attractions, and a café provides meals for guests and others.

St Ives

East of Zennor, the road runs four hilly miles on to the steeply built town of **ST IVES**, a place that has smoothly undergone the transition to holiday haunt from its previous role as a major fishing port. Virginia Woolf, who spent every summer here to the age of 12, described St Ives as "a windy, noisy, fishy, vociferous, narrow-streeted town; the colour of a mussel or a limpet; like a bunch of rough shell fish clustered on a grey wall together." By the time the pilchard reserves dried up around the early years of the last century, the town was beginning to attract a vibrant **artists' colony**, precursors of the wave later headed by Ben Nicholson, his wife Barbara Hepworth, Naum Gabo and the potter Bernard Leach, who in the 1960s were followed by a third wave including Terry Frost, Peter Lanyon and Patrick Heron.

Arrival and information

To reach St Ives by **train**, change at St Erth on the main line to Penzance or there are direct services from Penzance. Regular and frequent **buses** connect Penzance with St Ives, which you can reach from Truro on #14, #14B, and National Express buses. The train station is off Porthminster Beach, just south of the bus station on Station Hill. The **tourist office** is in the Guildhall, in the narrow Street-an-Pol, two minutes' walk away (June–Sept Mon–Fri 9am–5.30pm, Sat 9am–5pm, Sun 10am–4pm; Oct–May Mon–Fri 9am–5pm, Sat 10am–1pm; ☎01736/796297, ⓦwww.visit-westcornwall.com). Among the places where you can rent **surfing equipment** are Porthmeor Beach and the surf specialists on Fore Street and by the harbour. The **St Ives Festival** of folk, jazz and blues, which also takes in classical music and theatre, takes place over two weeks in September (ⓦwww.stivesseptemberfestival.co.uk).

Accommodation

Even with West Cornwall's greatest concentration of hotels and guest houses, St Ives can still run short of available **accommodation** in peak season, and advance booking is essential. Most of the places listed below are central, and the majority offer one or two parking spaces.

Hotels and B&Bs

Cornerways The Square ☎01736/796706, ⓦwww.cornerwaysstives.com. Daphne du Maurier once stayed in this tastefully modern cottage conversion, which has friendly management and airy rooms with black slate bathrooms. No credit cards. ⑤

Kynance 24 The Warren ☎01736/796636, ⓦwww.kynance.com. A good choice among the many B&Bs in this area of town near Porthminster Beach. The top-floor rooms have good views but get booked up early. Two-night minimum stay, one week in summer. No under-7s. Closed mid-Oct to mid-April. ④

Primrose Valley Porthminster Beach ☎01736/794939, ⓦwww.primroseonline.co.uk. Edwardian villa just above Porthminster Beach. Rooms, some with balconies, are fresh and light. One-week minimum stay in July and Aug. ⑦

Tre-Pol-Pen 4 Tre-pol-pen, Street-an-pol ☎01736/794996, ⓦwww.trepolpen.co.uk. In the heart of town (opposite the tourist office), this B&B has three bright, modern rooms, with en-suite or private bathrooms and friendly management. No under-12s. ⑤

Hostel and campsites

Ayr Higher Ayr ☎01736/795855, ⓦwww.ayrholidaypark.co.uk. Large complex with caravans and holiday homes, half a mile west of the centre above Porthmeor Beach, with good sea views. It's near the coast path, and buses #8B and the summer-only #300 to Land's End pass close by.

Higher Chellew Nancledra ☎01736/364532, ⓦwww.higherchellewcamping.co.uk. Out-of-town site, cheaper than the *Ayr*, with basic but clean facilities including washing machines. It's on the B3311, equidistant between St Ives and Penzance. Closed Oct–Easter.

St Ives Backpackers The Stennack ☎01736/799444, ⓦwww.backpackers.co.uk/st-ives. Restored Wesleyan chapel school from 1845, usefully located in the centre of St Ives opposite the cinema, that's now a comfortable and clean hostel, with barbecues and parties in summer. Dorms have four, six or eight beds for £17 per night in peak season, and there are also double and twin rooms (①).

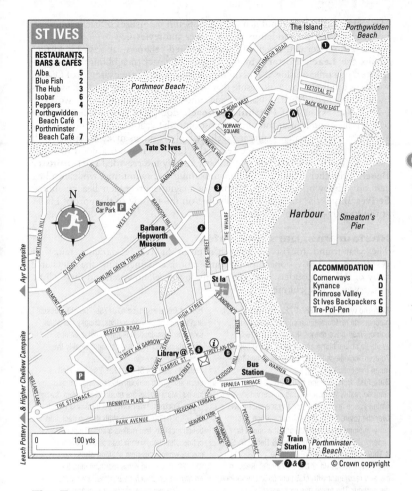

ST IVES

**RESTAURANTS,
BARS & CAFÉS**

Alba	5
Blue Fish	2
The Hub	3
Isobar	6
Peppers	4
Porthgwidden Beach Café	1
Porthminster Beach Café	7

ACCOMMODATION

Cornerways	A
Kynance	D
Primrose Valley	E
St Ives Backpackers	C
Tre-Pol-Pen	B

0   100 yds

© Crown copyright

The Town

Dozens of galleries are sandwiched between the town's restaurants and bars, but the only unmissable one is the **Tate St Ives**, overlooking Porthmeor Beach on the north side of town (March–Oct daily 10am–5.20pm; Nov–Feb Tues–Sun 10am–4.20pm; closes two or three times a year for about ten days – call ☏01736/796226 to check; £5.75, or £8.75 with Hepworth Museum). The airy, gleaming-white building is the perfect setting for the various paintings, sculptures and ceramics on display, most of which date from the period 1925 to 1975, though there are also specially commissioned contemporary works on view. The museum's rooftop **café** is one of the best places in town for tea and cake.

A short distance away on Barnoon Hill, the **Barbara Hepworth Museum** (same times as Tate; £4.75, or £8.75 with the Tate) gives another insight into the local arts scene. One of the foremost non-figurative sculptors of her time, Hepworth lived in the building from 1949 until her death in a studio fire in 1975. Apart from the sculptures, which are arranged in positions chosen by

Hepworth in the house and garden, the museum has masses of background on her art, from photos and letters to catalogues and reviews.

Devotees of Bernard Leach's Japanese-inspired ceramics can visit his former studio, the **Leach Pottery**, in the Higher Stennack neighbourhood, three-quarters of a mile outside St Ives on the Zennor road. Some examples of Leach's work are on display here, alongside that of his wife, Janet Leach, as well as pieces by Shoji Hamada, Michael Cardew and other more contemporary artworks.

The wide expanse of **Porthmeor Beach** dominates the northern side of St Ives, the stone houses tumbling almost onto the yellow sands. Unusually for a town beach, the water quality is excellent, and the rollers make it popular with surfers (boards available for rent below the Tate); there's also a good open-air café here. South of the station, the broader, usually less crowded **Porthminster Beach** is another favourite spot for sunbathing and swimming, while, heading east out of town, you'll find a string of magnificent golden beaches lining **St Ives Bay** – the strand is especially fine on the far side of the port of Hayle, at the mouth of the eponymous river.

Restaurants, bars and cafés

The year-round tourist industry has given St Ives a dazzling range of **restaurants**, mostly concentrating on seafood, and including the inevitable array of fast-food outlets. **Bar life** is fairly low-level, however, and there's little in the way of café culture.

Alba The Wharf ☎01736/797222. Sleekly modern harbourside restaurant in a converted lifeboat house. Fixed-price menus (£13.50 and £16.50), available at lunchtime and in the evening before 7.30pm, include seafood, Cornish beef and free-range roast chicken.

Blue Fish Norway Lane ☎01736/794204. Top seafood restaurant with a long conservatory-style eating space and an outdoor terrace with views over the town. There are set-price lunch and early-evening menus (£12), and the paella is superb. Closed Mon–Wed in Nov & Dec, also Sun & Thurs Jan to mid-Feb. Expensive.

The Hub 4 Wharf Rd ☎01736/799099. Relaxed bar and restaurant with first-floor patio overlooking the harbour. The menu has inexpensive soups, *moules-frites*, burgers and salads. No evening meals in winter.

Isobar Tregenna Place ☎01736/799199. Cocktail and tapas bar serving coffees, chunky ciabattas, salads and seafood. DJs play most evenings downstairs and there's a club and weekly live music upstairs.

Peppers 22 Fore St ☎01736/794014. Mellow pizza and pasta parlour, also serving fish and steaks. Most pizzas are around £8. Closed daytime.

Porthminster Café Porthminster Beach ☎01736/795352. With its sun deck and beach location, this makes a superb spot for coffees, lunches, cream teas and full evening meals, when innovative seafood dishes cost £17–20. Under the same management, the *Porthgwidden Beach Café* in the Downalong area of town offers a smaller range of similar food. Late Oct to Easter closed all Mon and eves Sun, Tues & Wed.

Cornwall's north coast

Though generally harsher than the county's southern seaboard, the north Cornish coast is punctuated by some of the finest beaches in England, the most popular of which are to be found around **Newquay**, the surfers' capital. Other major holiday centres are to be found down the coast at the ex-mining town of **St Agnes** and north around the Camel estuary, where the port of **Padstow** makes a good base for some remarkable beaches as well as a fine inland walk. North of the Camel, the coast is an almost unbroken line of cliffs as far as the Devon border, the gaunt, exposed terrain making a melodramatic setting for **Tintagel**, though the wide strand at **Bude** attracts legions of surfers and family holiday-makers.

▲ The Barbara Hepworth Museum

Newquay is the terminus for the cross-peninsula **train** route from Par, while the main line to Penzance stops at Redruth (connected to St Agnes on **bus** #315) and Camborne (connected to Truro on bus #40 and to Falmouth on #41). Bus #T1 plies between Perranporth, St Agnes and Truro, while #403 (not Sun) and the summer-only #501 (not Sat) connect St Agnes with Newquay (the #403 also goes to Truro); #89, #90, #585, #586, #587 and #597 also link Newquay with Truro (and #89 and #90 go to Falmouth). Bus #521 connects Newquay with St Austell, #555 runs between Padstow and Bodmin, and #556 tracks the coast between Newquay and Padstow. North of here, bus #584 serves Polzeath and Port Isaac, #594 goes to Boscastle and Tintagel, and #595 connects Boscastle and Bude. Finally, Okehampton and Exeter are linked to Bude by #X9 and to Newquay by #510, while National Express coaches run daily between Penzance, St Ives, Camborne, Redruth, Newquay, Bodmin and Plymouth.

St Agnes and around

East of St Ives Bay, surfers and other beach cognoscenti congregate at **Portreath** and, three miles further up the coast, **Porthtowan**, which together enjoy some of the cleanest water on this stretch. A couple of miles east of Porthtowan, **ST AGNES** makes a useful stopover for exploring the area. Though surrounded by ruined engine houses, the village gives little hint of the conditions in which its population once lived, the uniform grey ex-miners' cottages now fronted by immaculate flower-filled gardens, and its steep, straggling streets busy in summer with troops of holiday-makers.

At the end of a steep valley below St Agnes, **Trevaunance Cove** is the site of several failed attempts to create a harbour for the town and now has a fine sandy beach. West of the village lies one of Cornwall's most famous vantage points, **St Agnes Beacon**, 630ft high, from which views extend inland to Bodmin Moor and even across the peninsula to St Michael's Mount. To the northwest, the headland of **St Agnes Head** has the area's largest colony of breeding kittiwakes, and the nearby cliffs also shelter fulmars and guillemots, while grey seals are a common sight offshore.

Practicalities

The St Agnes **tourist office** is housed in a gift shop at 5 Churchtown (Mon–Sat 9.30am–5.30pm, Sun 10am–5pm; ☏01872/554150, ⓦwww.st-agnes.com). Well connected by bus to Truro, St Ives, Redruth and Newquay, the town has a good choice of **accommodation**, including the eighteenth-century 🜨 *Malthouse* in Peterville, the lower part of the village, a former brewing-house where you'll find three rooms with a shared bathroom, big breakfasts and a relaxed atmosphere (☏01872/553318, ⓦwww.themalthousestagnes.co.uk; no credit cards; ❸). Near the centre on Penwinnick Road, *Penkerris* (☏01872/552262, ⓦwww.penkerris .co.uk; ❸) is a spacious creeper-clad house, with log fires in winter, a big garden and good home-cooked dinners. At Trevaunance Cove, the whitewashed *Driftwood Spars* (☏01872/552428, ⓦwww.driftwoodspars.com; ❺) is a well-restored seventeenth-century inn with a range of rooms – front-facing ones with a balcony cost more. You can have bar food or full **meals** in the fish restaurant here, and there's live music at weekends. Back in St Agnes, the *Tap House* **pub** on Peterville Square attracts a young and lively crowd, has Far Eastern dishes as well as pizzas on the menu and also hosts regular live music.

Perranporth

Past the old World War II airfield three miles north of St Agnes, the resort of **PERRANPORTH** lies at the southern end of Perran Beach, a three-mile expanse of sand enhanced by caves and natural rock arches. It's very popular with surfers – boards and equipment are available to rent in summer.

Right next to the beach, the fairly basic **rooms** at the *Seiners' Arms* are worth booking for the location (℡01872/573118, Ⓦwww.ccinns.com; ⑤), though you'll have a quieter time at the small *Tide's Reach Hotel*, also close to the beach on Ponsmere Road (℡01872/572188, Ⓦwww.tidesreachhotel.com; ⑤), offering bright, en-suite rooms and a restaurant. On the cliff-top at the southern end of Perranporth beach, a YHA **hostel** (℡0870/770 5994, Ⓔperranporth@yha.org .uk; from £15) occupies a former coastguard station and enjoys superb views.

The huge *Seiners' Arms* has tables outside for a drink and a **meal**, though the best choice for refreshment around here is the tropical-looking ⚘ *Watering Hole*, right on the beach and a great place for breakfasts, burgers and steaks, or just for a drink; there's usually a live band at weekends and barbecues in summer.

Newquay

It is difficult to imagine a lineage for **NEWQUAY** that extends more than a few decades, but the "new quay" was built in the fifteenth century in what was already a long-established fishing port more colourfully known as Towan Blistra. The town was given a boost in the nineteenth century when its harbour was expanded for coal import and a railway was constructed across the peninsula for china clay shipments. With the trains came a swelling stream of seasonal visitors, drawn to the town's superb position on a knuckle of cliffs overlooking fine golden sands and Atlantic rollers, natural advantages which have made Newquay the premier resort of north Cornwall.

Arrival, information and accommodation

Newquay's **airport**, is five miles northeast of town at St Mawgan (℡01637/860600, Ⓦwww.newquaycornwallairport.com; buses #556 and #T10). The town's **train station** is off Cliff Road, just east of the centre, and the **bus station** is on Manor Road. Five minutes from the bus station, Newquay's **tourist office** on Marcus Hill (June–Aug Mon–Sat 9.30am–5.30pm, Sun 9.30am–3.30pm; Sept–May Mon–Fri 9.30am–4.30pm, plus Sat 9.30am–12.30pm Easter–May & Sept; ℡01637/854020, Ⓦwww.newquay.co.uk) has **Internet** access. The town has a plethora of **accommodation** in every category, though vacancies can still be scarce in July and August.

Hotels and B&Bs

Harbour Hotel North Quay Hill ℡01637/873040, Ⓦwww.theharbour.uk.com. Small, luxurious hotel with fantastic views from its stylish rooms, all of which have balconies. ⑦

Pengilley Guest House 12 Trebarwith Crescent ℡01637/872039, Ⓦwww.pengilley-guesthouse .com. Very close to the main town beach, this amiable B&B has tasteful en-suite rooms. No credit cards. ③

Rockpool Cottage 92 Fore St ℡01637/870848, Ⓦwww.rockpoolcottage.co.uk. Run by a former surfing champion, this B&B is convenient for the town centre and Fistral Beach. Breakfast is served in your room, where there are mini-fridges and en-suite bathrooms with good showers. Closed Jan–Easter. ③

Trewinda Lodge 17 Eliot Gardens ℡01637/877533, Ⓦwww.trewindalodge.co.uk.

Friendly B&B close to the train station and Tolcarne Beach, with access at all times. The owner, who runs a surf school, can give informed advice to surfers. No credit cards. ③

Hostels and campsites

Matt's Surf Lodge 110 Mount Wise Rd ℡01637/874651, Ⓦwww.matts-surf-lodge.co.uk. Set slightly further out than other hostels, this place has free tea and coffee available all day and a licensed bar. In summer, dorm beds are from £20 and en-suite double rooms ②, but winter prices are much lower.

Porth Beach Porth ℡01637/876531, Ⓦwww .porthbeach.co.uk. Located behind Porth Beach to the east of town, this campsite has good washing facilities. No same-sex groups. Closed Nov–Feb.

Reef Surf Lodge 10–12 Berry Rd ℡01637/879058, Ⓦwww.reefsurflodge.info.

Surfing in Newquay

Newquay's surfing buzz is infectious enough to tempt scores of non-surfheads to try their hand every summer. Close to the centre of town, the sheltered beaches of **Towan**, **Great Western** and **Tolcarne** are suitable for beginners with bodyboards, while further to the north **Watergate Bay** is slightly more exposed, so good for intermediates. Experts should head for **Fistral Bay** to the west of the town, which enjoys fast hollow waves, especially when the wind comes from the southwest, and is the venue for competitions. The beach is under lifeguard surveillance; conditions are most dangerous at low tide, especially mid-afternoon on the spring tide. For surf reports and webcam images, see any one of a number of websites – for example ⓦwww.a1surf.com or ⓦmagicseaweed.com.

You can rent or buy **surfing equipment** from Newquay's beach stalls or a range of outlets in town; boards cost £5–15 a day, wetsuits around the same. The town has plenty of opportunities for **surf tuition**; anything from a two-and-a-half-hour session (around £25) to a week (around £130). The British Surfing Association (☎01736/876474, ⓦwww.britsurf.co.uk) provides a list of approved schools, clubs and events, and offers courses at both Fistral and Lusty Glaze beaches, while Dolphin Surf School (☎01637/873707, ⓦwww.surfschool.co.uk), Reef Surf School (☎01637/879058, ⓦwww.reefsurfschool.com) and the women-only Hibiscus (☎01637/879374, ⓦwww.hibiscussurfschool.co.uk) also offer accommodation. For **kite-surfing, land yachting, surf canoeing, paragliding** and other activities, head for The Extreme Academy on Watergate Bay (☎01637/860840, ⓦwww.watergatebay.co.uk).

If you can, try to arrange your visit to Newquay to coincide with one of the surfing competitions and events that run all through the year – contact the tourist office (see p.455) for details.

Central, upmarket hostel, with fully-equipped bunkrooms and adjoining bathrooms. Prices in summer start at £30 but drop in low season. There's food, live entertainment and a surf centre for tuition and rental.

Trevelgue Trevelgue Rd ☎0845/130 1515, ⓦwww.trevelgue.co.uk. Beyond Porth Beach, this place separates its caravan and family sites from groups. There's a restaurant, a large indoor pool and nightly entertainment in summer, though minimal facilities in winter, if the site opens at all.

The town and beaches

Aside from the allure of the sea, there's little specific to see in Newquay. The centre of town is a somewhat tacky parade of shops and fast food outlets, partly pedestrianized, from which lanes lead to ornamental gardens and sloping lawns on the cliff-tops. At the bottom of Beach Road, adjacent to the small harbour, the **Blue Reef Aquarium** (daily 10am–4/5pm; £7.95) allows you to view tropical fish from an underwater tunnel; there are also tours, talks and feeding sessions. Below the aquarium, in the crook of the massive Towan Head, **Towan Beach** is the most central of the seven miles of firm sandy beaches that follow in an almost unbroken succession. You can reach all of them on foot, though for some of the further ones, such as **Porth Beach**, with its grassy headland, or the extensive **Watergate Bay**, two and a half miles north of the centre, you could make use of bus #556 to Padstow or the summer-only #T10. The beaches can all be unbearably crowded in full season, and all are popular with surfers, particularly Watergate and – west of Towan Head – **Fistral Bay**, the largest of the town beaches. On the other side of East Pentire Head from Fistral, **Crantock Beach** – reachable over the Gannel River by ferry or upstream footbridge – is usually less crowded, and has a lovely backdrop of dunes and undulating grassland.

Eating

Although most of Newquay's numerous **eateries** are pretty bland, recent years have seen an influx of more stylish places, some of them out of town.

Beach Hut Bistro and Bar Watergate Bay ☎01637/860877. Trendy hangout for surfers and a good venue for a sundowner. Breakfasts, snacks and daily specials are available all year, but the restaurant, where main courses cost £10–15, is closed Nov–Easter.

Café Irie 38 Fore St ☎01637/859200. Funky, lattice-windowed cottage serving all-day breakfasts, soups, veggie food, cream teas and – during summer school hols – inexpensive evening meals, usually to a mellow music accompaniment. Closed Mon–Thurs Nov–Easter. No credit cards.

The Chy Beach Rd ☎01637/873415. Sleek, contemporary setting for steaks, a mixed grill or seafood medley (around £14) upstairs, or sandwiches, salads, and burgers (£10) downstairs. There's a spacious terrace, DJs at weekends and Wi-Fi Internet.

Fifteen Watergate Bay ☎01637/861000. Overlooking the beach, this contemporary-looking place set up by TV chef Jamie Oliver showcases the culinary talents of trainee chefs. The mainly Italian but locally sourced dishes are inventive and delicious; set menus are £24.50 at lunchtime, £50 (£90 including select wines) in the evening, and breakfasts are also worth sampling.

Drinking and nightlife

Newquay is easily Cornwall's biggest centre for **nightlife**, drawing in crowds from around the county at weekends. Among the **pubs** offering an amenable atmosphere are the *Red Lion*, North Quay Hill, with weekly live music and meals available, and the spacious, Aussie-themed *Walkabout Inn* on Beachfield Avenue, which has great waterside views and gets loud and crowded in the evening. As for **clubbing**, the town's current hot spots are: *Berties* on East Street (☎01637/870369, ⓦwww.bertiesclub.com), which has its own lodge if you want to stay over; *Sailors* on Fore Street (☎01637/872838, ⓦwww.sailorsnightclub.com); *The Beach* on Beach Road (☎01637/872194, ⓦwww.beachclubnewquay.com); and *The Barracuda*, 27–29 Cliff Rd (☎01637/875800, ⓦbarracudanewquay.com), which also has regular live acts. These mainstream places tend to be fairly glittery and get overwhelmed in summer, though you can sometimes hear more alternative sounds at the *Koola Club* on Beach Road (☎01637/873415, ⓦwww.thekoola.com).

Padstow and around

The small fishing port of **PADSTOW** is nearly as popular as Newquay, but has a very different feel. Enclosed within the estuary of the Camel – the only river of any size that empties on Cornwall's north coast – the town long retained its position as the principal fishing port on this coast, and still has something of the atmosphere of a medieval town. Its chief annual festival is also a hangover from times past, the **Obby Oss**, a May Day romp when one of the locals garbs themselves as a horse and prances through the town preceded by a masked and club-wielding "teaser" – a spirited if rather institutionalized re-enactment of old fertility rites.

On the hill overlooking Padstow, the **church of St Petroc** is dedicated to Cornwall's most important saint, a Welsh or Irish monk who landed here in the sixth century, died in the area and gave his name to the town – "Petrock's Stow". The building has a fine fifteenth-century font, an Elizabethan pulpit and some amusing carved bench-ends. The walls are lined with monuments to the local Prideaux family, who still occupy nearby **Prideaux Place**, an Elizabethan manor house with grand staircases, richly furnished rooms full of portraits, fantastically ornate ceilings and formal gardens (Easter & mid-May to early Oct

The Camel Trail and the Saints' Way

The old railway line between Padstow and Wadebridge has been converted into an excellent **cycle track** that forms part of the **Camel Trail**, a fifteen-mile traffic-free path that follows the river up as far as Wenfordbridge, on the edge of Bodmin Moor, with a turn-off for Bodmin. The five-mile Padstow–Wadebridge stretch offers glimpses of a variety of birdlife, especially around the small **Pinkson Creek**, habitat of terns, herons, curlews and egrets.

You can **rent bikes** from Trail Bike Hire (℡01841/532594, ⊛www.trailbikehire.co.uk) and Padstow Cycle Hire (℡01841/533533, ⊛www.padstowcyclehire.com), both on South Quay, by the start of the Camel Trail. Outside Wadebridge, Bridge Bike Hire (℡01208/813050, ⊛www.bridgebikehire.co.uk) has a greater stock, though it's still advisable to reserve.

Padstow also marks one end of the thirty-mile cross-peninsula **Saints' Way**, linking up with Fowey on Cornwall's south coast (see p.431). Leaflets and books detailing the walk are available from the tourist offices at Padstow, Bodmin and Fowey.

Mon–Thurs & Sun 1.30–5pm, last tour at 4pm; grounds open from 12.30pm; £7, grounds only £2), all of which have been used as settings for a plethora of films, such as *Twelfth Night* and *Oscar and Lucinda*. The grounds contain an ancient deer park, and give good views over the Camel estuary.

The harbour is jammed with launches and boats offering cruises in Padstow Bay, while a regular **ferry** (summer daily 8am–7.30pm; winter Mon–Sat 8am–4.30pm; £3 return) carries people across the river to **ROCK** – close to the low-slung **church of St Enodoc** (John Betjeman's burial place) and to the good beaches around Polzeath. The ferry leaves from the harbour's North Pier except at low water when it goes from near the war memorial downstream.

The coast on the **south side** of the estuary also offers some good **beach** country, which you can reach on bus #556, though walking would enable you to view some terrific coastline. Out of Padstow, the rivermouth is clogged by **Doom Bar**, a sand bar that was allegedly the curse of a mermaid who had been mortally wounded by a fisherman who mistook her for a seal. Apart from thwarting the growth of Padstow as a busy commercial port, the bar has scuppered some three hundred vessels, with great loss of life. Round **Stepper Point** you can reach the sandy and secluded **Harlyn Bay** and, turning the corner southwards, **Constantine Bay**, the area's best surfing beach. The dunes backing the beach and the rock pools skirting it make this one of the most appealing bays on this coast; it boasts good water quality too, though the tides can be treacherous and bathing hazardous near the rocks. Surfers are attracted to other beaches in the neighbourhood, too, but the surrounding caravan sites can make these claustrophobic in summer – the sands around **Porthcothan**, south of Constantine, might offer more seclusion.

Three or four miles further south lies one of Cornwall's most dramatic beaches, **Bedruthan Steps**. Said to be the stepping-stones of a giant called Bedruthan (a figure conjured into existence in the nineteenth century), these slate outcrops can be readily viewed from the cliff-top path, at a point which drivers can reach on the B3276. Steps lead down to the broad beach below (closed in winter), which has dangerous tides and thunderous waves and is not advised for swimming.

Practicalities

Padstow's **tourist office** is on the harbour (Easter–Oct Mon–Sat 9.30am–5pm, Sun 10am–4pm; Nov–Easter Mon–Fri 10am–4pm, Sat & Sun 10am–2pm; ℡01841/533449, ⊛www.padstowlive.com), and offers **Internet** access.

Central **accommodation** includes *Cullinans*, a B&B at 4 Riverside (℡01841/532383, ⓔcullinan@madasafish.com; no credit cards; ❸), a three-storey building right on the harbour; the top bedroom has a French window leading onto a balcony. A short walk uphill, the elegant Edwardian *Treverbyn House*, Treverbyn Road (℡01841/532855, ⓦwww.treverbynhouse.com; ❺), has beautifully furnished rooms with great views, while nearby *Pendeen House*, 28 Dennis Rd (℡01841/532724, ⓦwww.pendeenhousepadstow.co.uk; ❹), has a more minimalist feel, with pristine, en-suite rooms. There's a YHA **hostel** four miles west of Padstow, excellently sited above the beach at Treyarnon Bay (℡0870/770 6076, ⓔtreyarnon@yha.org.uk; from £15.50); take bus #556 to Constantine then walk for half a mile. The nearest **campsite** is ⚑ *Dennis Cove* (℡01841/532349; closed Oct–Easter), picturesquely situated alongside the estuary about a ten-minute walk south of town; generally quiet and well tended, with great views, it sits right above the Camel Trail.

Foodies know Padstow best for its high-class **restaurants**, particularly those associated with star chef Rick Stein, whose *Seafood Restaurant*, at Riverside, is one of England's top fish restaurants – and expensive, with most main courses around £29 (though cod, chips and mushy peas cost a more reasonable £17.50). The waiting list for a table here can be months long, though a weekday reservation out of season can mean booking only a day or two ahead, and there's always the chance of a cancellation if you turn up on spec. The TV chef also runs *St Petroc's Bistro* at 4 New St, which has a lighter, more restricted version of the *Seafood Restaurant's* menu (mains around £16), and the casual *Rick Stein's Café* nearby at 10 Middle St, which serves snacks at lunch and moderately priced evening meals. Alternatively, you can always opt for the food served at *Stein's Fish and Chips* on South Quay or his **deli** next door. All three of the main establishments also offer attractive accommodation (❻–❽). For information and reservations for eating and sleeping, call ℡01841/532700 or go to ⓦwww.rickstein.com.

The best alternative restaurant to the Stein empire is *No. 6* at 6 Middle St, a Georgian town house with stylish modern decor, where a gourmet three-course meal costs £45. Otherwise, you can eat and drink well in Padstow's **pubs**, such as the *Shipwright's* on the harbour's north side, or the eighteenth-century *Old Ship* on Mill Square, both with outdoor seating.

Polzeath to Port Isaac

Facing west into Padstow Bay, the beaches around **Polzeath** are the finest in the vicinity, pelted by rollers which make **Hayle Bay**, in particular, one of the most popular **surfing** venues in the West Country. A mile south of Polzeath, **Daymer Bay** is more favoured by the windsurfing crowd. All the gear can be rented from shops on the beach, where you can get information on tuition, and there are campsites and bars in the vicinity.

The *Seascape Hotel* offers about the only solid-walled **accommodation** around here, beautifully sited a few yards up from Polzeath's beach (℡01208/863638, ⓦwww.seascapehotel.co.uk; closed Nov–Easter; ❻). The nearest **campsite**, *Valley Caravan Park* (℡01208/862391, ⓦwww.valleycaravanpark.co.uk), lies 150m from the beach, signposted up the lane behind the shop; it has a stream running through it attracting ducks and geese. The *Waterfront* (℡01208/869655), a relaxed **café/restaurant** just back from the beach, has a first-floor terrace and an eclectic menu.

Heading east, the coastal path brings you through cliff-top growths of feathery tamarisk, which flower spectacularly in July and August. From the headland of

Pentire Point, views unfold for miles over the offshore islets of **The Mouls** and **Newland**, with their populations of grey seals and puffins. Half a mile east, the scanty remains of an Iron Age fort stand on **Rump's Point**, from where the path descends a mile or so to **Lundy Bay**, a pleasant sandy cove surrounded by green fields. Climbing again, you pass the shafts of an old antimony mine on the way to **Doyden Point**, which is picturesquely ornamented with a nineteenth-century castle folly once used for gambling parties.

Beyond the inlet of **Port Quin**, the next settlement of any size is **PORT ISAAC**, wedged in a gap in the precipitous cliff-wall and dedicated to the crab and lobster trade. Only seasonal trippers ruffle the surface of life in this cramped harbour town, whose narrow lanes focus on a pebble beach where rock pools are exposed at low tide. The village makes a good place to **stay**: you can enjoy great views from both *The Gallery*, 44 Fore St (℡01208/881032, ⓦwww .bed-and-breakfast-port-isaac.co.uk; ❹), which has stylish, contemporary rooms and a large garden, and the elegant Victorian *Bay Hotel*, 1 The Terrace (℡01208/880380, ⓦwww.bayhotelportisaac.co.uk; ❺), where two of the rooms have spa baths.

Food-wise, Port Isaac is most famous for crab, which you can sample from stalls at the harbour or from the excellent **restaurant** at the *Slipway Hotel* on the quayside. The bar here is a congenial place for a pint, as is the neighbouring *Golden Lion*, which has a cellar bistro. In serene **Port Gaverne**, the next cove to the east, the snug *Port Gaverne Inn* offers bar food as well as fine dining in a separate restaurant.

Tintagel

East of Port Isaac, the coast is wild and unspoiled, making for some steep and strenuous walking, and interspersed with some stupendous strands of sandy beaches such as that at **Trebarwith** – a surfers' favourite. Two miles further north, the rocky littoral provides an appropriate backdrop for the black, forsaken ruins of **Tintagel Castle** (daily: Easter–Sept 10am–6pm; Oct 10am–5pm; Nov–Easter 10am–4pm; £4.70; EH). It was the medieval chronicler Geoffrey of Monmouth who first popularized the notion that this was the **birthplace**

▲ Tintagel Castle

Did **King Arthur** really exist? If he did, it's likely that he was an amalgam of two figures; a sixth-century Celtic warlord who united local tribes in a series of successful battles against the invading Anglo-Saxons, and a local Cornish saint. Whatever his origins, his role was recounted and inflated by poets and troubadours in later centuries, and elaborated by the unreliable twelfth-century chronicler Geoffrey of Monmouth, who made Arthur the conqueror of Western Europe, and was the first to record the belief that **Tintagel** was his birthplace. The Arthurian legends were crystallized in Thomas Malory's epic, *Morte d'Arthur* (1485), further romanticized in Tennyson's *Idylls of the King* (1859–85) and resurrected in T.H. White's saga, *The Once and Future King* (1937–58).

Although there are places throughout Britain and Europe which claim some association with Arthur, it's England's West Country, and **Cornwall** in particular, that has the greatest concentration of places boasting a link. Here, influenced by tales from Celtic Brittany and Wales, the legends have established deep roots, so that, for example, the spirit of Arthur is said to be embodied in the Cornish chough – a bird now almost extinct. Cornwall's most famous Arthurian site is **Tintagel**, the king's supposed birthplace and where Merlin reputedly lived in a cave (a rock near Mousehole, south of Penzance also claims this honour). Nearby Bodmin Moor is dotted with such places as "King Arthur's Bed" and "King Arthur's Downs", while Camlan, the battlefield where Arthur was mortally wounded fighting against his nephew Mordred, is associated with **Slaughterbridge**, near Camelford – which is also sometimes identified as Camelot itself. Also on the moor, **Dozmary Pool** was apparently where the knight Bedivere was dispatched by the dying king to return the sword Excalibur to the mysterious hand emerging from the water (though some sources claim this happened at **Loe Pool** in Mount's Bay). According to legend, Arthur's body was carried after the battle to **Boscastle**, northeast of Tintagel, from where a funeral barge transported it to Avalon.

Cornwall is also the presumed home of **King Mark**, at the centre of a separate cycle of myths which later became interwoven with the Arthurian one. It was Mark who sent the knight Tristan to Ireland to fetch his betrothed, Iseult; his headquarters is supposed to have been at **Castle Dore**, north of Fowey. Out beyond Land's End, the fabled, vanished country of **Lyonnesse** was the birthplace of Tristan (according to Malory and Spenser's *Faerie Queene*) – and some sources name this as Arthur's native land.

---

of **King Arthur**, son of Uther Pendragon and Ygrayne, but by that time local folklore was already saturated with tales of King Mark of Cornwall, Tristan and Iseult, Arthur and the knights of Camelot. Tintagel is certainly a plausibly resonant candidate for the abode of the Once and Future King, but the **castle** ruins in fact belong to a Norman stronghold occupied by the earls of Cornwall, who after sporadic spurts of rebuilding allowed it to decay, most of it having been washed into the sea by the sixteenth century. However, remains of a Celtic monastery that occupied this site in the sixth century can still be seen. A visitor centre fills you in on the story.

The best approach to the site is South West Coast Path from **Glebe Cliff** to the west, where the parish **church of St Materiana** sits in isolation; drivers, however, should park in the village of **TINTAGEL**, from which there's easy access on foot. For the most part a dreary collection of cafés and B&Bs, Tintagel has one other item of genuine interest: the **Old Post Office** on Fore Street (daily: Easter to Sept 11am–5.30pm; Oct 11am–4pm; £2.70; NT), a slate-built, rickety-roofed construction dating from the fourteenth century, now restored to its appearance in the Victorian era when it was used as a post office.

Buses stop on the main Fore Street close to the **tourist office** on Bossiney Road (daily 10/10.30am–4/5pm; ☎01840/779084, ⓦwww .visittintagelandboscastle.com). The village has plenty of **accommodation**, most of it fairly basic. The best B&Bs are a few minutes' walk along Atlantic Road: *Pendrin House* (☎01840/770560, ⓦwww.pendrinhouse.co.uk; ❸) and *Bosayne* (☎01840/770514, ⓦwww.bosayne.co.uk; ❹). Nearer the castle, and within sight of it, is *Castle View*, 2 King Arthur's Terrace (☎01840/770421, ⓔcastleviewbandb@aol.com; no credit cards; ❶), which has small rooms with a shared bathroom and a no-breakfast option. Three-quarters of a mile outside the village at Dunderhole Point, past St Materiana, the offices of a former slate quarry now house a YHA **hostel**, which has great views of the coastline (☎0870/770 6068, ⓔtintagel@yha.org.uk; closed Nov–March; from £12). At the end of Atlantic Road, the *Headland* site offers scenic **camping** (☎01840/770239, ⓦwww.headlandcaravanpark.co.uk; closed Nov–Easter). There's no shortage of cafés and tearooms in Tintagel, and both the *Old Malt House* and the *Tintagel Arms Hotel* on Fore Street have decent **restaurants**.

Boscastle

Three miles east of Tintagel, the port of **BOSCASTLE** lies compressed within a narrow ravine drilled by the rivers Jordan and Valency and ending in a twisty harbour. The tidy riverfront bordered by thatched and lime-washed cottages was the scene of a devastating flash flood in 2004, but most of the damage has now been repaired. Above and behind, you can see more seventeenth- and eighteenth-century houses on a circular walk that traces the valley of the Valency for about a mile to reach Boscastle's graceful **parish church** (pick up a leaflet showing the route from the tourist office). A mile and a half further up the valley lies another church, **St Juliot's**, restored by Thomas Hardy when he was plying his trade as a young architect. It was while he was working here that he met Emma Gifford, whom he married in 1874, a year after the publication of *A Pair of Blue Eyes*, the book that kicked off Hardy's literary career. It opens with an architect arriving in a Cornish village to restore its church, and is full of descriptions of the country around Boscastle.

Boscastle's **tourist office** is in the main car park in the lower village (daily 10/10.30am–4/5pm; ☎01840/250010, ⓦwww.visittintagelandboscastle.com). One of the most appealing **places to stay** locally is *St Christopher's* (☎01840/250412, ⓦwww.st-christophers-boscastle.co.uk; no credit cards; ❺), a restored Georgian manor house at the top of the High Street, but for a real Hardy experience, head for the ⚘ *Old Rectory*, on the road to St Juliot (☎01840/250225, ⓦwww.stjuliot.fsnet.co.uk; no under-12s; ❺; closed Dec to mid-Feb), where you can stay in Hardy's or Emma's bedroom, or in a converted stable, and roam the extensive grounds. There's also a YHA **hostel**, right on the harbourfront (☎0870/770 5710, ⓔboscastle@yha.org.uk; closed Nov–March; from £15.50), housed in a former stables. You can eat at one of the village's excellent **pubs**: in upper Boscastle, the *Napoleon* has a good seafood bistro and a spacious lawned garden, while the *Cobweb*, down near the harbour, rates highly on atmosphere and has bar food; both have live music evenings.

Bude and around

There is little distinctively Cornish in Cornwall's northernmost town of **BUDE**, four miles west of the Devon border. Built around an estuary surrounded by a fine expanse of sands, the town has sprouted a crop of holiday homes and hotels, though these have not unduly spoilt the place nor the magnificent cliffy coast surrounding it.

Of the excellent beaches hereabouts, the central and clean **Summerleaze** grows to immense proportions at low tide, though bathers can save themselves a lengthy trudge by taking advantage of a sea-water swimming pool near the cliffs. The mile-long **Widemouth Bay**, two and a half miles south of Bude, also draws the holiday hordes – though bathing can be dangerous near the rocks at low tide. Surfers congregate five miles down the coast at **Crackington Haven**, wonderfully situated between 430-foot crags at the mouth of a lush valley. The cliffs hereabouts are characterized by remarkable zigzagging strata of shale, limestone and sandstone, a mixture which erodes into vividly contorted detached formations.

To the north of Bude, acres-wide **Crooklets** is the scene of **surfing** and life-saving demonstrations and competitions, while the pristine expanse of **Sandy Mouth**, a couple of miles further, has rock pools beneath encircling cliffs. It's a short walk from here to another surfers' delight, **Duckpool**, a tiny sandy cove flanked by jagged reefs at low tide and dominated by the three-hundred-foot **Steeple Point**.

Between Duckpool and the Devon border stretch five miles of strenuous but exhilarating coast. The only village along here is **MORWENSTOW**, just south of **Henna Cliff**, at 450ft the highest sheer drop of any sea cliff in England after Beachy Head, affording magnificent views along the coast and beyond Lundy to the Welsh coast.

Practicalities

Bude's **tourist office** is in the car park off the Crescent (April–Sept Mon–Fri 10am–5pm, Sat & Sun 10am–4pm; Oct–March Mon–Fri 10am–4pm, Sat 10am–1pm; ☎01288/354240, ⦿www.visitbude.info). There's a cluster of **B&Bs** overlooking the golf course on Burn View, among them *Palms* at no. 17 (☎01288/353962, ⦿www.palms-bude.co.uk; no credit cards; ❸), with small, neat, en-suite rooms. If you're prepared to spend a little more, you'll find better places outside town, including two places near Widemouth Bay: *Elements* (☎01288/352386, ⦿www.elements-life.co.uk; ❺), a self-styled "surf hotel" on the coast road near Upton, with a gym and sauna though smallish rooms, and *Bangors Organic*, a stylish B&B a mile inland at Poundstock (☎01288/361297, ⦿www.bangorsorganic.co.uk; ❼), with spacious, beautifully designed modern rooms. There's a friendly backpackers' **hostel** not far from the beaches at 57 Killerton Rd (☎01288/354256, ⦿www.northshorebude.com; from £12), with a large garden, **Internet** access and some double rooms (❶). The nearest of the numerous **campsites** around Bude is *Upper Lynstone Caravan and Camping Park* (☎01288/352017, ⦿www.upperlynstone.co.uk; closed Nov–Easter), three-quarters of a mile south of the centre on the coastal road to Widemouth Bay.

For style, location and cuisine, Bude's best **place to eat** is ⚲ *Life's a Beach*, right on Summerleaze Beach, a café by day and a romantic (and expensive) bistro in the evening, worth booking ahead (☎01288/355222; closed in winter weekday lunch and all Mon & Tues); fish features strongly on the menu. In town, try the *Atlantic Diner*, 5–7 Belle Vue (closed Mon, plus most eves in winter; no credit cards), popular with shoppers and surfers alike for its inexpensive burgers, steaks, curries and ice creams. *Bangors Organic* (see above) has an excellent restaurant open to non-residents, where you can enjoy a three-course evening meal (£28) using organic, home-grown ingredients – call to check opening.

There's a choice of **surfing equipment rental** outlets, including Zuma Jay on Belle Vue Lane. On a different note, the **Bude Jazz Festival** attracts a range of stonking sounds from around the world for a week in August or September (ⓦwww.budejazzfestival.co.uk).

Bodmin and Bodmin Moor

Bodmin Moor, the smallest and mildest of the West Country's great moors, has some beautiful tors, torrents and rock formations, but much of its fascination lies in the strong human imprint, particularly the wealth of relics left behind by its **Bronze Age** population, including such important sites as **Trethevy Quoit** and the stone circles of the **Hurlers**. Separated from these by some three millennia, the churches in the villages of **St Neot**, **Blisland** and **Altarnun** are among the region's finest examples of fifteenth-century art and architecture.

The biggest centre in the area, **Bodmin**, stands outside the moor but can provide a useful base, with a good choice of accommodation and easy access – main-line trains stop just outside town and there are regular bus connections to Padstow and St Austell. The north moor village of **Camelford** also has good accommodation, and is connected by bus #584 to Port Isaac and by #594 to Tintagel and Boscastle. The only regular services on the moor, however, are #225, running three or four times daily on weekdays between Launceston and Altarnun, and #274 between Liskeard and St Neot on weekdays. Otherwise, there's the Corlink community bus scheme, which must be booked (call ☎0845/850 5556 at least 1hr before) for journeys between Bodmin, Blisland, Bolventor and Camelford (not Sun).

Bodmin

The town of **BODMIN** lies on the western edge of Bodmin Moor, equidistant from the north and south Cornish coasts and the Fowey and Camel rivers, a position that encouraged its growth as a trading town. It was also an important ecclesiastical centre after the establishment of a priory by St Petroc, who moved here from Padstow in the sixth century. The priory disappeared but Bodmin retained its prestige through its church, **St Petroc's**, situated at the end of Fore Street (open for services and April–Sept Mon–Sat 11am–3pm; at other times call ☎01208/73867). Dating from the fifteenth century, and still Cornwall's largest church, it contains an extravagantly carved twelfth-century font and an ivory casket that once held the bones of the saint, while the southwest corner of the churchyard contains a sacred well.

West of here on Berrycoombe Road, the notorious **Bodmin Jail** (daily 10am–dusk; £5) recalls the public executions that were guaranteed crowd-pullers until 1862, from which time the hangings continued behind closed doors until 1909. The jail finally closed in 1927. You can visit part of the original eighteenth-century structure, including the condemned cell and some grisly exhibits chronicling the lives of the inmates. There's a good café and **bike rental** here (☎01208/74170).

Further up Berrycoombe Road, there's access to a cycleway and footpath that after a mile links up to the main route of the **Camel Trail** (see p.458) at Boscarne Junction. From the station here, steam locomotives of the **Bodmin & Wenford Railway** run to the main-line station at Bodmin Parkway between March and October (☎0845/125 9678, ⓦwww.bodminandwenfordrailway.co.uk; £7.50–10 return). The trains make a stop at the restored old station on St Nicholas Street, and at Colesloggett, a good starting point for rambles in **Cardinham Woods**.

From Parkway it's less than two miles' walk to one of Cornwall's most celebrated country houses, **Lanhydrock** (house mid-March to Oct Tues–Sun 11am–5/5.30pm; gardens open daily 10am–6pm or dusk; £9.40, grounds only £5.30; NT), originally seventeenth-century but rebuilt in 1881. Inside the granite exterior, the fifty-odd rooms include a long picture gallery with a plaster ceiling depicting scenes from the Old Testament, and servants' quarters that reveal the daily workings of a Victorian manor house. The grounds hold magnificent beds of magnolias, azaleas and rhododendrons, and a huge area of wooded parkland bordering onto the River Fowey.

Practicalities

Three miles outside town, Bodmin Parkway **train station** has a regular bus connection to the centre; all **buses** pull in on Mount Folly, site of the local **tourist office** (Easter–Oct Mon–Sat 10am–5pm; Nov–Easter Mon–Fri 10am–5pm; ☎01208/76616, ⑩www.bodminlive.com), which also offers **Internet** access. There's comfortable **B&B** accommodation at *Higher Windsor Cottage*, 18 Castle St (☎01208/76474, ⑩www.higherwindsorcottage.co.uk; no under-10s; no credit cards; ❸), and *Bedknobs*, further up the same street at Polgwyn (☎01208/77553, ⑩www.bedknobs.co.uk; ❺), a Victorian villa in an acre of wooded garden.

Off Fore Street, the *Hole in the Wall* **pub** in Crockwell Street, formerly a debtors' prison, has a backroom bar, an upstairs **restaurant** and a courtyard. Wholesome snacks are also served at the tiny *Bara Café*, just across from St Petroc's at 14 Honey St (closed Sun except during summer school hols).

Bodmin Moor

Just ten miles in diameter, **Bodmin Moor** is a wilderness on a small scale, its highest tor rising to just 1375ft from a platform of 1000ft. Yet the moor conveys a sense of loneliness quite out of proportion to its size, with scattered ancient remains providing in places the only distraction from an empty horizon. Aside from its tors, the main attractions of the landscape are the small Dozmary Pool, a site steeped in myth, and a quartet of rivers – the Fowey, Lynher, Camel and De Lank – that rise from remote moorland springs and effectively bound the moor to the north, east and south.

Blisland and the western moor

BLISLAND stands in the Camel valley on the western slopes of Bodmin Moor, three miles northeast of Bodmin. Georgian and Victorian houses cluster around a village green and a church whose well-restored interior has an Italianate altar and a startlingly painted screen. On **Pendrift Common** above the village, the gigantic **Jubilee Rock** is inscribed with various patriotic insignia commemorating the jubilee of George III's coronation in 1809. From this seven-hundred-foot vantage point you look eastward over the De Lank Gorge and the boulder-crowned knoll of **Hawk's Tor**, three miles away. On the shoulder of the tor stand the Neolithic **Stripple Stones**, a circular platform once holding 28 standing stones, of which just four are still upright.

Blisland lies just a couple of miles east of the **Merry Meeting** crossroads, a point near the end of the Camel Trail. On Blisland's village green, you can sample good **ales and food** at the *Blisland Inn*, with outdoor tables.

Jamaica Inn, Dozmary Pool and Altarnun

On the A30 midway between Bodmin and Launceston, outside the uninspiring village of **Bolventor** in the heart of the moor, **Jamaica Inn** is one of the chief points of interest locally for walkers and sightseers alike. A staging-post even before the main road was first laid here in 1769, the inn was described by Daphne du Maurier as being "alone in glory, four square to the winds", though it has lost much of its romance since its development into a rather bland hotel and restaurant complex (℡01566/86250, ⓦwww.jamaicainn.co.uk; ⑤). One corner exhibits the room where the author stayed in 1930, soaking up inspiration for her smugglers' yarn. Adjacent to the hotel, the **Smuggler's Museum** (daily 9/11am–4/6pm; £3.75) shows the diverse ruses used for concealing contraband.

The inn's car park makes a useful place to leave your vehicle and venture forth on foot. Just a mile south, **Dozmary Pool** is famous in Arthurian mythology (see box on p.461). The diamond-shaped lake has been known to run dry in summer, dealing a bit of a blow to the legend that it is bottomless.

Four miles northeast of Bolventor, the granite-grey village of **ALTARNUN** lies snugly sheltered beneath the eastern heights of the moor. Its prominent **church**, St Nonna's, contains a fine Norman font and 79 bench-ends carved at the beginning of the sixteenth century, depicting saints, musicians and clowns. The *King's Head* here has beams, saggy ceilings and a resident ghost; plain **rooms** (℡01566/86241; ②) as well as a range of **food and drink** are available.

Camelford and the northern tors

The northern half of Bodmin Moor is dominated by its two highest tors, both of them easily accessible from **CAMELFORD**, a town once associated with King Arthur's Camelot, while Slaughterbridge, which crosses the River Camel north of town, is one of the contenders for his last battleground. The town has resisted trading on the Arthurian myths, but does have a couple of museums providing some diversion: the **British Cycling Museum** (Mon–Thurs & Sun 10am–5pm, phone ahead for times on Fri & Sat ℡01840/212811; £3.35), housed in the old station one mile north of town on the Boscastle Road, is a cyclophile's dream, containing some four hundred examples of bikes through the ages and a library of books and manuals. The collection may be of special interest to bikers on Route 3 on the National Cycle Way, which runs through Camelford. Meanwhile, the more conventional **North Cornwall Museum** (April–Sept Mon–Sat 10am–5pm; £2.50) in Camelford's centre contains domestic items and exhibits showing the development of the local slate industry, and also has a **tourist office** (same hours; ℡01840/212954).

Although it lacks excitement, Camelford makes a useful touring base. Among its **accommodation** are the thirteenth-century, slate-hung *Darlington Inn* on Fore Street (℡01840/213314; ③) and the *Countryman Hotel*, at 7 Victoria Rd (℡01840/212250, ⓦwww.thecountrymanhotel.co.uk; ④), close to the National Cycle Way. There's **camping** at *Lakefield Caravan Park*, Lower Pendavey Farm (℡01840/213279, ⓦwww.lakefieldcaravanpark.co.uk; closed mid-Oct to March), which also offers **horse riding**. For a **meal**, try the modern *Raval's* on Fore Street (℡01840/213888; closed Mon & Tues in winter), which has snacks by day and fuller evening meals. The *Mason's Arms* on Market Place has bar food and a beer garden.

Rough Tor, the second highest peak on Bodmin Moor at 1311ft, is four miles southeast of Camelford. The hill presents a different aspect from every angle: from the south an ungainly mass, from the west a nobly proportioned mountain. A short distance to the east are Little Rough Tor, where there are the remains of an Iron Age camp, and Showery Tor, capped by a prominent formation of piled rocks.

Easily visible to the southeast, **Brown Willy** is, at 1375ft, the highest peak in Cornwall, as its original name signified – Bronewhella, or "highest hill". Like Rough Tor, Brown Willy shows various faces, its sugarloaf appearance from the north sharpening into a long multi-peaked crest as you approach. The tor is accessible by continuing from the summit of Rough Tor across the valley of the De Lank, or, from the south, by footpath from Bolventor. The easiest ascent is by the worn path which climbs steeply up from the northern end of the hill.

St Neot and the southeastern moor

Seven miles east of Bodmin, on the southern edge of the moor, **ST NEOT** is one of the region's prettiest villages. Its fifteenth-century **church** contains some of the most impressive stained-glass windows of any parish church in the country, the oldest glass being the fifteenth-century **Creation Window**, at the east end of the south aisle. Next along, **Noah's Window** continues the sequence, but the narration soon dissolves into windows portraying patrons and local bigwigs, while others present cameos of the ordinary men and women of the village.

This side of the moor is greener and more thickly wooded than the northern reaches, due to the confluence of a web of rivers into the Fowey. One of the best-known local beauty spots is a couple of miles east, below Draynes Bridge, where the Fowey tumbles through the **Golitha Falls**, less a waterfall than a series of rapids. Dippers and wagtails flit through the trees, and there's a pleasant woodland walk you can take to the dam at the Siblyback Lake reservoir just over a mile away.

North of Siblyback Lake, **Twelve Men's Moor** holds some of Bodmin Moor's grandest landscapes. The quite modest elevations of **Hawk's Tor** (1079ft) and the lower **Trewartha Tor** appear enormous from the north, though they are overtopped by **Kilmar**, highest of the hills on the moor's eastern flank at 1280ft. A quarter-mile northwest of **Minions**, Cornwall's highest village, you can see **The Hurlers**, a wide complex of three circles dating from about 1500 BC. The purpose of these stark upright stones is not known, though they owe their name to the legend that they were men turned to stone for playing the Celtic game of hurling on the Sabbath. A further half-mile or so north, **Stowe's Hill** is the site of the moor's most famous stone pile, **The Cheesewring**, a precarious pillar of balancing flat granite slabs that have been marvellously eroded by the wind. The disused Cheesewring Quarry, gouged out of the hillside nearby, is a centre for rock-climbing. Three miles south of Minions stands another Stone Age survivor, **Trethevy Quoit**, a chamber tomb nearly nine feet high, surmounted by a massive capstone. Originally enclosed in earth, the stones have been stripped by centuries of weathering to create Cornwall's most impressive megalithic monument.

Travel details

Buses

For information on all local and national bus services, contact Traveline ℡0871/200 2233, ⓦwww.travelinesw.com.

Bodmin to: Newquay (4 daily; 30–50min); Padstow (Mon–Sat hourly, Sun 6 daily; 55min); Plymouth (3 daily; 1hr); St Austell (Mon–Sat hourly, Sun 5 daily; 50min).

Exeter to: Bristol (4–5 daily; 1hr 40min–2hr); Newquay (3–6 daily; 3hr 20min); Penzance (3–4 daily; 4hr 30min–5hr); Plymouth (Mon–Sat hourly, Sun every 1–2hr; 1hr 15min); Sidmouth (Mon–Sat 2–3 hourly, Sun 1–2 hourly; 40–50mins); Torquay (Mon–Sat 8 daily, Sun 3; 50min); Truro (3–4 daily; 3hr–3hr 50min).

Falmouth to: Helston (Mon–Sat hourly, Sun 2–4; 25min–1hr 10min); Penzance (Mon–Sat 7–8 daily, Sun 1; 1–2hr); St Austell (2 daily; 1hr 10min); Truro (Mon–Sat 3–4 hourly, Sun hourly; 35–50min).

Newquay to: Bodmin (4 daily; 30–50min); Exeter (3–6 daily; 3hr 20min); Padstow (Mon–Sat hourly, Sun 5; 1hr 20min); Plymouth (3–4 daily; 1hr 30min–2hr); St Austell (every 1–2hr; 1hr); Truro (Mon–Sat 6–7 hourly, Sun 2 hourly; 50min–1hr 25min).

Penzance to: Falmouth (Mon–Sat 7–8 daily, Sun 1; 1hr–1hr 45min); Helston (Mon–Sat hourly, Sun 6 daily; 50min); Plymouth (7 daily; 2hr 35min–3hr 30min); St Austell (5 daily; 1hr 35min–2hr 15min); St Ives (Mon–Sat 3–5 hourly, Sun hourly; 30–50min); Truro (Mon–Sat 1–2 hourly, Sun 5 daily; 1hr–1hr 30min).

Plymouth to: Bodmin (3 daily; 1hr); Exeter (Mon–Sat hourly, Sun every 1–2hr; 1hr 15min); Falmouth (2 daily; 2hr 30min); Newquay (3–4 daily; 1hr 30min–1hr 50min); Penzance (7 daily; 3hr 15min); St Austell (6 daily; 1hr 20min); St Ives (4 daily; 2hr 45min); Torquay (Mon–Sat every 30min, Sun 6 daily; 1hr 40min–2hr); Truro (6 daily; 1hr 50min).

St Austell to: Bodmin (Mon–Sat hourly, Sun 5 daily; 50min); Exeter (3 daily; 2hr 50min); Falmouth (2 daily; 1hr); Newquay (every 1–2hr; 1hr 10min); Penzance (5 daily; 2hr); Plymouth (6 daily; 1hr 20min); St Ives (2 daily; 1hr 30min); Truro (Mon–Sat 1–2 hourly, Sun every 2hr; 40min).

St Ives to: Penzance (Mon–Sat 3–5 hourly, Sun hourly; 30–50min); Plymouth (4 daily; 3hr); St Austell (2 daily; 1hr 45min); Truro (Mon–Sat hourly, Sun 6 daily; 1hr 10min–1hr 40min).

Torquay to: Exeter (Mon–Sat 8 daily, Sun 3; 50min); Plymouth (Mon–Sat every 30min, Sun 6 daily; 1hr 50min–2hr 10min).

Truro to: Exeter (3–4 daily; 3hr 10min–4hr); Falmouth (Mon–Sat 3–4 hourly, Sun hourly; 35–50min); Newquay (Mon–Sat 6–7 hourly, Sun 2 hourly; 50min–1hr 25min); Penzance (Mon–Sat 1–2 hourly, Sun 5 daily; 1hr–1hr 30min); Plymouth (6 daily; 2hr); St Austell (Mon–Sat hourly, Sun every

2hr; 40min); St Ives (Mon–Sat hourly, Sun 6 daily; 1hr–1hr 35min); St Mawes (Mon–Sat hourly, Sun 3 daily; 1hr).

Trains

For information on all local and national rail services, contact National Rail Enquiries ☏0845/748 4950, Ⓦwww.nationalrail.co.uk.

Barnstaple to: Exeter (Mon–Sat 11 daily, Sun 6 daily; 1hr–1hr 30min).

Bodmin to: Exeter (1–2 hourly; 1hr 40min); Penzance (1–2 hourly; 1hr 25min); Plymouth (1–2 hourly; 45min).

Exeter to: Barnstaple (Mon–Sat hourly, Sun 6 daily; 1hr–1hr 30min); Bodmin (1–2 hourly; 1hr 45min); Bristol (1–2 hourly; 1hr 20min); Exmouth (1–2 hourly; 30min); Liskeard (every 1–2hr; 1hr 30min); London (1–2 hourly; 2–3hr); Par (hourly; 2hr); Penzance (every 1–2hr; 3hr 10min); Plymouth (1–2 hourly; 1hr); Torquay (1–2 hourly; 30min–1hr); Totnes (1–2 hourly; 40min); Truro (hourly; 2hr 15min).

Falmouth to: Truro (hourly; 25min).

Liskeard to: Exeter (every 1–2hr; 1hr 30min); Looe (hourly, not Sun in winter; 30min); Penzance (1–2 hourly; 1hr 35min); Plymouth (1–2 hourly; 30min); Truro (hourly; 50min).

Newquay to: Par (4–8 daily, not Sun in winter; 50min).

Par to: Exeter (hourly; 2hr); Newquay (4–8 daily, not Sun in winter; 50min); Penzance (hourly; 1hr 15min); Plymouth (1–2 hourly; 50min).

Penzance to: Bodmin (1–2 hourly; 1hr 25min); Exeter (every 1–2hr; 3hr); Plymouth (1–2 hourly; 2hr); St Ives (most via St Erth; 1–2 hourly, not Sun in winter; 25–45min); Truro (1–2 hourly; 40min).

Plymouth to: Bodmin (1–2 hourly; 40min); Exeter (1–2 hourly; 1hr); Liskeard (1–2 hourly; 30min); Par (1–2 hourly; 50min); Penzance (1–2 hourly; 2hr); Truro (hourly; 1hr 15min).

St Ives to: Penzance (via St Erth; 1–2 hourly, not Sun in winter; 30min–1hr).

Torquay to: Exeter (1–2 hourly; 45min).

Truro to: Exeter (1–2 hourly; 2hr 15min); Falmouth (hourly; 25min); Liskeard (1–2 hourly; 50min); Penzance (1–2 hourly; 45min); Plymouth (hourly; 1hr 20min).

7

East Anglia

CHAPTER 7 # Highlights

* **Orford** Solitary hamlet with a splendid coastal setting that makes for a wonderful weekend away. See p.487

* **The Aldeburgh Festival** The region's prime classical music festival washes over the ears every June for two and a half weeks. See p.488

* **Southwold** A postcard-pretty seaside town that is perfect for walking and bathing – without an amusement arcade in sight. See p.490

* **Norwich Market** This open-air market is the region's biggest and best for everything from whelks to wellies. See p.497

* **Holkham Bay and beach** Wide bay holding Norfolk's finest beach – acres of golden sand set against hilly dunes. See p.509

* **Ely** Isolated Cambridgeshire town, with a true fenland flavour and a magnificent cathedral. See p.515

* **Cambridge** Fine architecture, dignified old churches and manicured quadrangles jostle for prime position in the compact city centre. See p.518

▲ Holkham Beach

East Anglia

S trictly speaking, **East Anglia** is made up of just three counties – Suffolk, Norfolk and Cambridgeshire – which were settled by Angles from Schleswig-Holstein in present-day Germany in the fifth century, though in more recent times it's come to be loosely applied to parts of Essex too. As a region it's renowned for its wide skies and flat landscapes, and of course such generalizations always contain more than a grain of truth – if you're looking for mountains, you've come to the wrong place. Nevertheless, East Anglia often fails to conform to its stereotype: parts of Suffolk are positively hilly, and its coastline can induce vertigo; the north Norfolk coast holds steep cliffs as well as wide sandy beaches; and even the pancake-flat fenlands are broken by wide, muddy rivers and hilly mounds, on one of which perches Ely's magnificent cathedral. Indeed, the whole region is sprinkled with fine medieval churches, the legacy of the days when this was England's most progressive and prosperous region.

Heading into East Anglia from the south almost inevitably takes you through **Essex**, whose proximity to London has turned much of the county into an unappetizing commuter strip. Amidst the suburban gloom, there are, however, several worthwhile destinations, most notably **Colchester**, once a major Roman town and now a likeable sort of place with an imposing castle, and the handsome hamlets of the bucolic Stour River Valley on the Essex–Suffolk border. Essex's Dedham is one of the prettiest of these villages, but the prime attraction hereabouts is Suffolk's Flatford Mill, famous for its associations with the painter John Constable.

Pushing on deeper into **Suffolk**, the county boasts a string of extremely pretty, well-preserved little towns – **Lavenham** is the prime example – which enjoyed immense prosperity from the thirteenth to the sixteenth century, the heyday of the wool trade. Elsewhere, **Bury St Edmunds** can boast not just the ruins of its once-prestigious abbey, but also some fine Georgian architecture on its grid-plan streets, while even the much maligned county town of **Ipswich** has more to offer than it's generally given credit for. Nevertheless, for many visitors it's the north Suffolk coast that steals the local show. In **Southwold**, with its comely Georgian high street, Suffolk possesses a delightful seaside resort, elegant and relaxing in equal measure, while neighbouring **Aldeburgh** hosts one of the best music festivals in the country.

Norfolk, as everyone knows thanks to Noël Coward, is very flat. It's also one of the most sparsely populated and tranquil counties in England, a remarkable turnaround from the days when it was an economic and political powerhouse – until, that is, the Industrial Revolution simply passed it by. Its capital, **Norwich**, is still East Anglia's largest city, renowned for its Norman cathedral

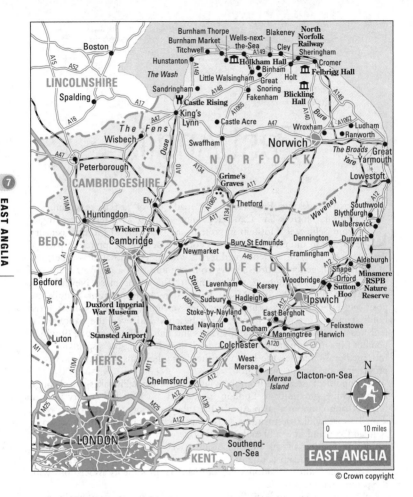

© Crown copyright

and castle, and for its high-tech Sainsbury Centre, exhibiting a challenging collection of twentieth-century art. The most visited part of Norfolk is, however, the **Broads**, a unique landscape of reed-ridden waterways that has been intensively exploited by boat-rental companies for the last thirty years. Almost as popular, the **Norfolk coast** holds a string of busy, very English seaside resorts – **Great Yarmouth**, **Cromer**, **Sheringham** and **Hunstanton** to name but four – but for the most part it's charmingly unspoilt, with marshes, creeks and tidal flats studded with tiny flintstone villages, most enjoyably Blakeney and Cley. Meanwhile, sheltering inland, are two outstanding stately homes – **Blickling Hall** and **Holkham** – with a couple more within easy striking distance of **King's Lynn**, a strange, almost disconcerting mixture of fenland town and ancient seaport.

Cambridge is the one place in East Anglia everyone visits, principally because of its world-renowned university, whose ancient colleges boast some of the finest medieval and early modern architecture in the country. The rest of

Cambridgeshire is pancake-flat fenland, for centuries an inhospitable marshland but now rich alluvial farming land. The one star turn here is the cathedral town of **Ely**, settled on one of the few areas of raised ground in the fens and an easy and popular day-trip from Cambridge.

Getting around

East Anglia's **train** network is at its best to and from London, with quick and frequent services from the capital to all of the region's major towns. One main line links Colchester, Ipswich and Norwich, another Cambridge and Ely. These services are supplemented by a number of cross-country branch lines, most usefully between Peterborough, Ely and Norwich and Ipswich, Bury St Edmunds and Cambridge. Once you get away from the major towns, however, you'll have to rely on local **buses**, whose services, run by a multitude of companies, are very patchy. Indeed, in parts of north Norfolk and inland Suffolk, you may find the only way to get about is by your own transport. The largest regional bus operator is **First** (@www.firstgroup.com), which sells several sorts of bus pass, valid for unlimited travel on all their Norfolk and Suffolk bus routes. Their one-day Network Ticket costs £10, seven days £25; both are available at major bus stations and from bus drivers.

Given the prevailing flatness of the terrain, hiking in East Anglia is less strenuous than in most other English regions, and there are several **long-distance footpaths**. The main one is the **Peddars Way**, which runs north from Knettishall Heath, near Thetford, to the coast at Holme, near Hunstanton, where it continues east as the **Norfolk Coast Path** to Cromer – 93 miles in total (see @www.nationaltrail.co.uk for both). At Cromer, you can pick up the 56-mile **Weavers' Way**, which wends its way through the Broads to Great Yarmouth.

Colchester

If you visit anywhere in Essex, it should be **COLCHESTER**, a busy sort of place with a castle, a university and a large army base, fifty miles or so northeast of London. More than anything else, Colchester prides itself on being England's oldest town and there is indeed documentary evidence of a settlement here as early as the fifth century BC. By the first century AD, it was the region's capital under **King Cunobelin** – better known as Shakespeare's Cymbeline – and when the **Romans** invaded Britain in 43 AD they chose Colchester (Camulodunum) as their new capital, though it was soon eclipsed by London, becoming a retirement colony for legionaries instead. The first Roman temple in the country was erected here, and in 60 AD the colony was the target of Boudicca's abortive revolt (see box p.475). A millennium later, the conquering Normans built one of their mightiest strongholds in Colchester, but the conflict that most marked the town was the **Civil War**. In 1648, Colchester was subjected to a gruelling siege by the Parliamentarian army led by Lord Fairfax; after three months, during which the population ate every living creature within the walls, the town finally surrendered and the Royalist leaders were promptly executed for their pains.

Today, Colchester makes a potential base for further exploration of the surrounding countryside – particularly the Stour valley towns of Constable country (see p.475), within easy reach a few miles to the north.

Arrival, information and accommodation

Colchester has two **train stations**, one for local services and the other, Colchester North, for mainline trains from London, Ipswich and Harwich ferry port. From the mainline station, it's a fifteen-minute walk south into town – follow the ring road, then take North Station Road and its continuation, North Hill, until you reach the west end of the High Street. The **bus station** is off Queen Street, a couple of minutes' walk from the High Street and yards from both the castle and the **tourist office**, at 1 Queen St (Mon–Sat 10am–5pm; ☎01206/282920, ⓦwww.visitcolchester.com), which can supply free town maps and book accommodation.

Colchester has its fair share of city-centre hotels, including the dependable, half-timbered *Best Western Rose & Crown*, on East Street (☎01206/866677, ⓦwww.bw-roseandcrown.co.uk; ❹), a ten-minute walk east of the tourist office, via the High Street and East Hill. The hotel dates back to the fourteenth century and guests choose between the oak-beamed rooms in the original building or the attractively furnished rooms in the modern wing. The pick of the town's **B&Bs** is the *Old Manse*, 15 Roman Rd (☎01206/545154; ❷), with three pleasant guest rooms, set in a well-maintained, bay-windowed Victorian house on a quiet cul-de-sac; it's on the east side of the castle, a couple of minutes' walk from the tourist office.

The Town

At the heart of Colchester is its **castle**, or rather what remains of the medieval stronghold, a ruggedly imposing, honey-coloured keep, set in attractive parkland stretching down to the River Colne. Begun less than ten years after the Battle of Hastings, the keep was the largest in Europe at the time, and was built on the site of the Temple of Claudius – the one that Boudicca had attacked many centuries before (see box opposite). Inside the keep, a **museum** (Mon–Sat 10am–5pm, Sun 11am–5pm; £5.10) holds an excellent collection of Romano-British archeological finds, including a miscellany of coins, tombstones, statues and mosaics. Highlights are the so-called Colchester vase, decorated with gladiators and a hunting scene, and a fine if armless bronze of Mercury, the messenger of the gods. The museum also covers the history of the town and runs regular **guided tours** (45min; £2), giving access to the Roman vaults, the Norman chapel and the castle roof, which are otherwise out of bounds. Outside, down towards the river in Castle Park, is a section of the old **Roman walls**, whose battered remains are still visible around much of the town centre. They were erected after Boudicca had sacked the city and, as such, are a case of too little too late.

The castle stands at the eastern end of the wide and largely pedestrianized **High Street**, which follows pretty much the same route as it did in Roman times. The most arresting building here is the flamboyant **town hall**, built in 1902 and topped by a statue of St Helena, mother of Constantine the Great and daughter of Old King Cole of nursery-rhyme fame – after whom, some say, the town was named.

Looming above the western end of the High Street is the town landmark, "**Jumbo**", a disused nineteenth-century water tower, considerably more imposing than the nearby **Balkerne Gate**, which marked the western entrance to Roman Colchester. Built in 50 AD, this is the largest surviving Roman gateway in the country, though with the remains at only a touch over six feet in height, it's far from spectacular. The gate is joined to another section of the town's Roman walls, though here the effect is spoiled by the neighbouring ring road.

Boudicca

Boudicca – aka Boadicea – was the wife of Prasutagus, chief of the Iceni tribe of Norfolk, who allied himself to the Romans during their conquest of Britain in 43 AD. Five years later, when the Iceni were no longer useful, the Romans attempted to disarm them and, although the Iceni rebelled, they were soon brought to heel. On Prasutagus's death, the Romans confiscated his property and when Boudicca protested, they flogged her and raped her daughters. Enraged, Boudicca determined to take her revenge, quickly rallying the Iceni and their allies before setting off on a rampage across southern Britain in 60 AD.

As the ultimate symbol of Roman oppression, the **Temple of Claudius** in Colchester was the initial focus of hatred, but, once Colchester had been razed, Boudicca soon turned her sights elsewhere. She laid waste to London and St Albans, massacring over seventy thousand citizens and inflicting crushing defeats on the Roman units stationed there. She was far from squeamish, ripping traitors' arms out of their sockets and torturing every Roman and Roman collaborator in sight. The Roman governor Suetonius Paulinus eventually defeated her in a pitched battle, which cost the Romans just four hundred lives and the Britons untold thousands. Boudicca knew what to expect from the Romans, so she opted for suicide, thereby ensuring her later reputation as a patriotic Englishwoman, who died fighting for liberty and freedom – claims which Boudicca would have found incomprehensible.

Eating and drinking

Colchester's **oysters** have been highly prized since Roman times and the local vineyards have an equally long heritage, so it's no surprise to find the town has a good choice of first-rate **restaurants**. One of the best places in town is *The Hub*, 19 Head St (℡01206/564977), at the west end of the High Street, which offers contemporary, broadly Mediterranean dishes with main courses from around £13. Alternatively, try the *The Lemon Tree*, 48 St John's St, which runs east off Head Street, parallel to the High Street (℡01206/767337; closed Sun), where main courses, such as marinated, free-range chicken on aubergine, hover around £13.

For top-quality seafood, head about six miles south out of town to the oyster fisheries at **West Mersea**, on Mersea Island. Here, ⚐ *The Company Shed*, 129 Coast Rd (℡01206/382700), serves the freshest of oysters without any frills at rickety tables; the season runs from September to May.

The Stour Valley and the old wool towns of south Suffolk

Five miles or so north of Colchester, the **Stour River Valley** forms the border between Essex and Suffolk, and signals the beginning of East Anglia proper. Compared with much of the region it is positively hilly, a handsome landscape of farms and woodland latticed by dense, well-kept hedges and the thick grassy banks that once kept the Stour in check. The valley is dotted with lovely little villages too, where rickety, half-timbered Tudor houses and elegant Georgian dwellings cluster around medieval churches, proud buildings with square, self-confident towers. The Stour's prettiest villages are concentrated along its lower reaches – to the east of the A134 – in Dedham Vale, with **Stoke-by-Nayland**

and **Dedham** arguably the most appealing of them all. The vale is also known as "**Constable Country**" as it was the home of John Constable (1776–1837), one of England's greatest artists, and the subject of his most famous works. Inevitably, there's a Constable shrine – the much-visited complex of old buildings down by the river at **Flatford Mill**.

The villages along the River Stour and its tributaries were once busy little places at the heart of East Anglia's weaving trade, which boomed from the thirteenth to the fifteenth century. By the 1490s, the region produced more cloth than any other part of the country, but in Tudor times production shifted to Colchester, Ipswich and Norwich and, although most of the smaller settlements continued spinning cloth for the next three hundred years or so, their importance slowly dwindled. Bypassed by the Industrial Revolution, south Suffolk had, by the late nineteenth century, become a remote rural backwater, an impoverished area whose decline had one unforeseen consequence: with few exceptions, the towns and villages were never prosperous enough to modernize, and the architectural legacy of medieval and Tudor times survived. The two best-preserved villages are **Lavenham** and **Kersey**, both of which heave with sightseers on summer weekends. Nearby **Sudbury** is also attractive and boasts an excellent museum devoted to the work of Thomas Gainsborough, another talented English artist who spent much of his time painting the local landscape.

Seeing the region by **public transport** is problematic – distances are small (Dedham Vale is only about ten miles long), but buses between the villages are infrequent and you'll find it difficult to get away from the towns. By **train**, you need to make for Sudbury, which is on a branch line off the London Liverpool Street–Colchester mainline; change at Marks Tey. For walkers, **footpaths** criss-cross the area, with some of the most enjoyable being in the vicinity of Dedham village. All the local tourist offices sell easy-to-use walking leaflets.

East Bergholt and Flatford Mill

"I associate my careless boyhood to all that lies on the banks of the Stour," wrote **John Constable**, who was born the son of a miller in **EAST BERGHOLT**, nine miles northeast of Colchester in 1776. The house in which he was born has long since disappeared, so it has been left to **Flatford Mill**, a mile or so to the south, to take up the painter's cause. The mill was owned by his father and was where Constable painted his most famous canvas, *The Hay Wain* (now in London's National Gallery, see p.89), which created a sensation when it was exhibited in 1824. To the chagrin of many of his contemporaries, Constable turned away from the landscape-painting conventions of the day, rendering his scenery with a realistic directness that harked back to the Dutch landscape painters of the seventeenth century. Typically, he justified this approach in unpretentious terms, observing that, after all "no two days are alike, nor even two hours; neither were there ever two leaves of a tree alike since the creation of the world." The mill itself – not the one he painted, but a Victorian replacement – is not open to the public, but the sixteenth-century thatched **Bridge Cottage** (Jan & Feb Sat & Sun 11am–3.30pm; March & April Wed–Sun 11am–5pm; May–Sept daily 10am–5.30pm; Oct daily 11am–4pm; Nov & Dec Wed–Sun 11am–3.30pm; free, except for parking; NT), which overlooks the scene, has been painstakingly restored and stuffed full of Constabilia. Unfortunately, none of the artist's paintings is displayed here, but there's a pleasant riverside tearoom to take in the view. Beyond stands **Willy Lott's Cottage** (also closed to the public), which does actually feature in *The Hay Wain*.

▲ Flatford Mill

In summer, the National Trust organizes **guided walks** around the sites of Constable's paintings (£2.50; call ☏01206/298260 for details), but there are many other pleasant walks to be had along this deeply rural bend in the Stour. One footpath connects the mill to the **train station** at Manningtree, two miles to the east, and another runs over to the village of Dedham, a mile and a half to the west. Alternatively, you can rent a **rowing boat** from beside the bridge and potter peacefully along the river. There's a **B&B** here too, *Flatford Granary* (☏01206/298111, ⓦwww.granaryflatford.co.uk; ❸), in the annexe to the old granary that was once owned by Constable's father. The en-suite rooms are cottage-style affairs with beamed ceilings and folksy furniture.

Dedham

Constable went to school in **DEDHAM**, just upriver from Flatford Mill and one of the region's most attractive villages, with a string of ancient timber-framed houses lining its wide main street. The only sights as such are **St Mary's Church**, an early-sixteenth-century structure that Constable painted on several occasions, and the **Sir Alfred Munnings Art Museum**, in Castle House (Easter–July & Sept Wed & Sun 2–5pm; Aug Wed, Thurs, Sat & Sun 2–5pm; £4; ⓦwww.siralfredmunnings.co.uk), just south of the village on the road to Ardleigh. A locally born academician, Munnings (1875–1959) is barely remembered today, but in his time he was well known for his portraits of horses. In the 1940s, Munnings became a controversial figure when, as President of the Royal Academy, he savaged almost every form of modern art there was. Few would say his paintings were inspiring, but seeing them is a pleasant way to fill a rainy afternoon.

Monday through Saturday, there's a twice-daily Network Colchester **bus** (☏01206/764029) from Colchester to Dedham, though both services depart in the late afternoon; on Sundays, First buses (☏01206/366911) run the same route every couple of hours. Dedham possesses one of Essex's best

pubs, ✻ *The Sun Inn*, on the High Street (☎01206/323351, ⓦwww.thesun inndedham.com; ❺, weekends ❼), an ancient place of panelled walls and plank floors, where they serve real ales and delicious Modern British food – for example, celeriac, braised black cabbage and calf's liver; main courses begin at about £9. They also have five immaculate en-suite **rooms** decorated in a creative blend of country inn and boutique hotel, from four-poster beds through to billowy, caramel-cream curtains. The inn's main competitor is the recently revamped, notably plush *Maison Talbooth* (☎01206/322367, ⓦwww .maison-talbooth.co.uk; ❽), which occupies a good-looking Victorian country house near the A12 a couple of minutes' drive southwest of the village on the road to Stratford St Mary. A third option is *Dedham Hall* (☎01206/323027, ⓦwww .dedhamhall.demon.co.uk; ❻), in an old manor house set in its own grounds on the east side of the village off Brook Street, a continuation of the High Street; be sure to ask for a room in the house itself. The restaurant here – *The Fountain House* (closed Sun & Mon) – serves very good Modern British cuisine, with a three-course set menu costing £31.

Stoke-by-Nayland, Nayland and Wissington

Heading northwest from Dedham, the B1029 dips beneath the A12 to reach the byroad to Higham, an unremarkable hamlet where you pick up the road to **STOKE-BY-NAYLAND**, four miles further west. This is the most pictur-esque of villages, where a knot of half-timbered, pastel-painted cottages snuggle up to one of Constable's favourite subjects, **St Mary's Church** (daily 9am–5pm; free), with its pretty brick and stone-trimmed tower. The doors of the south porch are covered by the beautifully carved figures of a medieval Jesse Tree and, although the interior is sombre and severe, it does boast a magnificent, soaring tower arch. The village also has a pair of great old **pubs**, beginning with *The Angel* (☎01206/263245, ⓦwww.theangelinn.net; ❹), where there's real ale, quality bar food and six, cosy, en-suite guest **rooms**. The food at *The Crown* (☎01206/262001, ⓦwww.eoinns.co.uk; ❺) is, however, even better, being an adventurous amalgamation of British and European dishes with the ingredients sourced locally wherever possible – try the pork belly with leek mash; main courses cost in the region of £12–15. At time of writing, *The Crown* does not do accommodation, but this is about to change with the construction of eleven new rooms. The pick of several other options in and near the village is *Thorington Hall* (☎01206/337329; ❷; Easter–Sept), a handsome seventeenth-century country house with four somewhat frugal guest rooms; it's located a little over a mile east of Stoke back towards Higham.

Southwest from Stoke-by-Nayland, it's two miles back to the River Stour at **NAYLAND**, a workaday little place where the most distinctive feature is the church of St James, whose square tower and copper-green spire poke high into the sky. Inside, Constable's *Christ Blessing the Bread and Wine* is one of only two attempts he made at a religious theme – and, dating from 1809, it was completed long before he found his artistic rhythm. There's more ecclesiastical hoopla in the fine, largely Norman church of St Mary a mile or so to the southwest at tiny **WISSINGTON**, where the nave is decorated with a rare series of thirteenth-century frescoes.

Sudbury

With a population of around 12,000, **SUDBURY** – the fictional "Eatanswill" of Dickens' *Pickwick Papers* – has doubled in size in the last thirty years, to become by far the most important town in this part of the Stour Valley. A handful of timber-framed houses harks back to its days of wool-trade prosperity, but its three Perpendicular churches were underwritten by another local industry, **silk weaving**, which survives on a small scale to this day. Sudbury's most famous export, however, is **Thomas Gainsborough** (1727–1788), the leading English portraitist of the eighteenth century, whose statue, with brush and palette, stands on Market Hill, the town's predominantly Victorian market place. A superb collection of the artist's work is on display a few yards away in the house where he was born – **Gainsborough's House**, at 46 Gainsborough St (Mon–Sat 10am–5pm; £4; ⊛www.gainsborough.org). Gainsborough left Sudbury when he was just 13, moving to London where he was apprenticed to an engraver, but it seems he was soon moonlighting and the earliest of his surviving portrait paintings – his *Boy and Girl*, a remarkably self-assured work dated to 1744 – is displayed here. In 1752, Gainsborough moved on to Ipswich, where he quickly established himself as a portrait painter to the Suffolk gentry with one of his specialities being wonderful "conversation pieces", so-called because the sitters engage in polite chitchat – or genteel activity – with a landscape as the backdrop. Seven years in Ipswich was followed by a move upmarket to Bath, where he painted high-society figures, which he continued when he moved back to London in 1774. During his years in Bath, Gainsborough developed a fluid, flatteringly easy style that was ideal for his aristocratic subjects, who posed in becoming postures painted in soft, evanescent colours. Examples of Gainsborough's later work on display include the *Portrait of Harriet, Viscountess Tracy* (1763) and the particularly striking *Portrait of Abel Moysey, MP* (1771). In his later years, the artist also dabbled with romantic paintings of country scenes – as in *A Wooded Landscape with Cattle by a Pool* – a playful variation of the serious landscaping painting he loved to do best; the rest, he often said, just earned him a living. Gainsborough never bothered with assistants, with one exception, his nephew **Gainsborough Dupont**, whose work has a room devoted to it on the top floor.

Practicalities

Sudbury is just seven miles northwest of Nayland along the A134. It's accessible by **train** from Colchester, fourteen miles away (for some services, change at Marks Tey), and is the hub of **bus** services to and from neighbouring towns and villages including Colchester and Ipswich. Once you've seen Gainsborough's house, there's little reason to spend the night, but if you do decide to stay, the **tourist office** in the town hall at the east end of Market Hill (Mon–Fri 9am–5pm, Sat 10am–2.45/4.45pm; ☎01787/881320, ⊛www.visit-suffolk.org .uk) can provide **accommodation** details.

Lavenham

LAVENHAM, some eight miles northeast of Sudbury off the A134, was once a centre of the region's wool trade and is now one of the most visited villages in Suffolk, thanks to its unrivalled ensemble of perfectly preserved half-timbered houses. The whole place has changed little since the demise of the wool industry, owing in part to a zealous local preservation society, which has carefully maintained the village's antique appearance by banning from view such modern frivolities as advertising hoardings and TV aerials.

The village is at its most beguiling in the triangular **Market Place**, an airy spot flanked by pastel-painted, medieval dwellings whose beams have been bent into all sorts of wonky angles by the passing of the years. It's here you'll find Lavenham's most celebrated building, the pale-white, timber-framed

Guildhall of **Corpus Christi** (March–Oct Tues–Sun 11am–5pm; Nov Sat & Sun 11am–4pm; £3.75; NT), erected in the sixteenth century as the headquarters of one of Lavenham's four guilds. In the much-altered interior (used successively as a prison and workhouse), there are exhibitions on timber-framed buildings and the wool industry, though most visitors head straight for the walled garden and the teashop. Back outside on Market Place, the view down Prentice Street from beside the *Angel Hotel* is one of Lavenham's most exquisite – a line of creaky timber-framed dwellings dipping into the deep green countryside beyond. The other building worthy of special notice is the Perpendicular **church of St Peter and St Paul** (daily: May–Sept 8.30am–5.30pm; Oct–April 8.30am–3.30pm; free), which is sited a short walk southwest of the centre, at the top of Church Street. Local merchants endowed the church with a nave of majestic proportions and a mighty flint tower, at 141ft the highest for miles around, partly to celebrate the Tudor victory at the Battle of Bosworth in 1485 (see p.631), but mainly to vaunt their wealth.

Practicalities

Monday through Saturday, there's an hourly **bus service** linking Colchester, Bury St Edmunds, Lavenham and Sudbury. Lavenham **tourist office** is plumb in the centre, just south off the Market Place on Lady Street (April–Oct daily 10am–5pm; Nov–March Sat & Sun 11am–3pm; ☎01787/248207, ⊛www.visit-suffolk .org.uk). They can help with **accommodation** – rooms get mighty tight in the high season – and sell a detailed, street-by-street walking guide. To cater for its many visitors, Lavenham has a veritable battery of **B&Bs** one of the most luxurious of which is *Lavenham Priory*, in a rambling old house – and former priory – on Water Street (☎01787/247404, ⊛www.lavenhampriory.co.uk; ●). There are half a dozen en-suite guest rooms here, each kitted out in a fancy version of period style – four-poster beds are de rigueur. Less expensive B&Bs include the dinky *Angel Gallery*, 17 Market Place (☎01787/248417, ⊛www .lavenham.co.uk/angelgallery; ●), with three straightforward guest rooms situated above an art shop, and ⚘ *The Guinea House*, 16 Bolton St (☎01787/249046, ⊛www.guineahouse.co.uk; no credit cards; ●), whose two low-beamed guest rooms are cosy and folksy in equal measure; there are great breakfasts here too – don't stint on the sausages. Amongst several **hotels**, *The Swan* (☎01787/247477, ⊛www.theswanatlavenham.co.uk; ●) is a splendid if somewhat dandified old inn on the High Street, which incorporates a warren of lounges and courtyard gardens not to mention an authentic Elizabethan Wool Hall. Rather more modest, but much more informal, is the ancient *Angel Hotel*, on the Market Place (☎01787/247388, ⊛www.theangelhotel-lavenham.co.uk; ●), where there are eight, en-suite guest rooms with a retro/period appearance.

The *Angel Hotel* serves excellent **food** in its bar and in its restaurant – tasty, unpretentious English cuisine with dishes such as steak and ale pie, a snip at just £8. Alternatively, the chic and smart ⚘ *Great House* restaurant, on Market Place (☎01787/247431; closed Sun eve & Mon), specializes in classic French cuisine, with main courses around £17. It's received rave reviews all over the place, so book ahead.

Kersey and Hadleigh

Seven miles southeast of Lavenham off the A1141, minuscule **KERSEY** is one of the most photographed villages in Suffolk. Another old wool town, it seems to have dodged just about every historical bullet since the seventeenth century and now comprises little more than one exquisite street of timber-framed houses, which dips in the middle to cross a ford that's inhabited by a family of fearless ducks. Prime real estate today, Kersey's more populous past is recalled by the large and austere parish **church of St Mary**, visible for miles around, perched on high ground above the village. There's nowhere to stay, but there is one good **pub**, the ancient, half-timbered *Bell Inn*.

From Kersey, it's a couple of miles southeast to the market town of **HADLEIGH**, a positive metropolis compared to Kersey, but nevertheless everything of interest is within a stone's throw of the **church of St Mary** (daily: May–Sept 9am–5.30pm; Oct–April 9am–3.30pm). The church, one block west of the elongated High Street, is mainly fifteenth century, a good-looking replacement for several earlier versions. Legend asserts that **Guthrum**, the Danish chieftain and arch-rival of Alfred the Great, was buried underneath the south aisle in 889, but his remains have never been definitively identified. Opposite the church, across the graveyard, is the half-timbered Guildhall, every bit as immaculate as Lavenham's, with the earliest sections dating from 1438. Behind the church is the extravagantly ornate **Deanery Tower**, a fifteenth-century gatehouse whose palace was never completed. In the garret room at the top of the tower, the Oxford Movement, which opposed liberal tendencies within the Anglican Church and sought to promote Anglo-Catholicism, was founded in 1833 by local rector Hugh Rose.

Hadleigh is easy to reach by **bus** with regular services from Sudbury, Lavenham, Ipswich and Colchester, though Sundays can be a bit tricky. Several Hadleigh-bound buses pass through Kersey too.

Bury St Edmunds

Appealing **BURY ST EDMUNDS**, ten miles north of Lavenham, started out as a Benedictine monastery, founded to accommodate the remains of Edmund, the last Saxon king of East Anglia, who was tortured and beheaded by the marauding Danes in 869. Almost two centuries later, England was briefly ruled by the kings of Denmark and the shrewdest of them, **King Canute**, made a gesture of reconciliation to his Saxon subjects by granting the monastery a generous endowment and building the monks a brand-new church. It was a popular move and the abbey prospered, so much so that before its dissolution in 1539, it had become the richest religious house in the country. Most of the abbey disappeared long ago, and nowadays Bury is better known for its graceful Georgian streets, its flower gardens and its sugar-beet plant than for its ancient monuments. However, it's still an amiable, eminently likeable place, one of the prettiest towns in Suffolk, and one with good transport connections on to Cambridge, Colchester, Ipswich and Norwich.

The Town

The town centre has preserved much of its Norman street plan, a gridiron in which Churchgate was aligned with – and sloped up from – the abbey's high altar. It was the first planned town of Norman Britain and, for that matter, the first example of urban planning in England since the departure of the Romans. At the heart of the town, beside the abbey grounds, is **Angel Hill**, a broad, spacious square partly framed by Georgian buildings, the most distinguished being the ivy-covered **Angel Hotel**, which features in Dickens' *Pickwick Papers*. Dickens also gave readings of his work in the **Athenaeum**, the Georgian assembly rooms at the far end of the square. A twelfth-century wall runs along the east side of Angel Hill, with the bulky fourteenth-century **Abbey Gate** forming the entrance to the abbey gardens and ruins beyond.

The **abbey ruins** themselves (open access) are like nothing so much as petrified porridge, with little to remind you of the grandiose Norman complex that once dominated the town. Thousands of medieval pilgrims once sought solace at St Edmund's altar and the cult was of such significance that the barons of England gathered here to swear that they would make King John sign their petition – the Magna Carta of 1215. Today, the only significant remnants are on the far side of the abbey gardens, behind the more modern cathedral (see below), and they comprise the rubbled remains of a small part of the old **abbey church** integrated into a set of unusual Georgian houses. In front, across the green, is the imposing **Norman tower**, once the main gateway into the abbey and now a solitary monument with dragon gargoyles and fancily decorated capitals.

Incongruously, the tower is next to the front part of Bury's Anglican **Cathedral of St James** (daily 8.30am–6pm; £3 donation requested), with chancel and transepts added as recently as the 1960s. It was a toss-up between this church and **St Mary's** (Mon–Sat 10am–4pm, 3pm in winter; free), further down Crown Street, as to which would be given cathedral status in 1914. The presence of the tomb of the resolutely Catholic Mary Tudor in the latter was the clinching factor.

Bury's **main commercial area** is on the west side of the centre, a five-minute walk up Abbeygate Street from Angel Hill. There's been some intrusive modern planning here, but dignified Victorian buildings flank both **Cornhill** and **Buttermarket**, the two short main streets, as well as the narrower streets in between. Also between the two is **Bury St Edmunds Art Gallery** (Tues–Sat 10.30am–5pm; £1; @www.burystedmundsartgallery.org), which features a lively programme of temporary exhibitions focusing on contemporary fine and applied art. Of some interest, too; is the Cornhill's flint-walled **Moyse's Hall**, one of the few surviving Norman houses in England, while the streets to the south are lined by an attractive medley of architectural styles, from elegant Georgian town houses to Victorian brick terraces. You'll see the best by strolling along Guildhall Street and turning left down Churchgate, which brings you back to Angel Hill.

Practicalities

From Bury St Edmunds' **train station**, it's ten minutes' walk south to Angel Hill via Northgate Street. The **bus station** is on St Andrew Street North, just north of Cornhill. The town's **tourist office**, at 6 Angel Hill (Easter–Oct Mon–Sat 9.30am–5.30pm, plus May–Sept Sun 10am–3pm; Nov–Easter Mon–Fri 10am–4pm, Sat 10am–1pm; ☎01284/764667, @www.stedmundsbury .gov.uk), provides free town maps and has a useful range of leaflets.

The pick of the town's **hotels** is the immaculately maintained 🎄 *Angel*, on Angel Hill (☎01284/714000, @www.theangel.co.uk; ❼), a former coaching inn with wood-panelling, thick carpets and suitably plush rooms. A good alternative is the *Chantry Hotel*, 8 Sparhawk St (☎01284/767427, @www .chantryhotel.com; ❺), with fifteen smart, modern guest rooms in two converted Georgian town houses, located just to the south of the abbey ruins off Honey Hill. The town also has a very distinctive **B&B**, *The Old Cannon*, 86 Cannon St (☎01284/768769, @www.oldcannonbrewery.co.uk; ❹), where the five guest rooms, all en suite and each decorated in a bright and cheerful manner, are sited in a former brewery; Cannon Street is on the north side of the centre – to get there, take Abbeygate Street from Angel Hill, then turn right along Lower Baxter Street and its continuation Garland Street.

For **restaurants**, ✻ *Maison Bleue*, 31 Churchgate St (☎01284/760623; closed Sun & Mon), is an excellent option with a wide range of wonderfully fresh seafood from crab through to sardines and skate; main courses kick off at £12. ✻ *The Old Cannon* (see opposite) is a good second choice, offering a delicious range of dishes, using locally sourced ingredients wherever possible, in both its bar and restaurant; main courses, such as pheasant in a redcurrant and ale sauce, cost around £13. Otherwise, fill up on coffee, cakes and **snacks** at the *Scandinavia Coffee House*, 30 Abbeygate St. Of the **pubs**, don't miss the *Nutshell* (closed Sun), on The Traverse at the top of Abbeygate, which, at sixteen feet by seven and a half, claims to be Britain's smallest, and even better, serves real ales. Finally, the **Theatre Royal**, at the junction of Crown and Westgate streets (☎01284/769505, ⓦ www.theatreroyal.org), offers a year-round programme of cultural events, from Shakespeare to pantomime.

Ipswich and around

IPSWICH, situated at the head of the Orwell estuary some twenty-five miles southeast of Bury St Edmunds, was a rich trading port in the Middle Ages, but its appearance today is mainly the result of a revival of fortunes in the Victorian era – give or take some clumsy postwar development. The two surviving reminders of old Ipswich – **Christchurch Mansion** and the splendid **Ancient House** – plus the recently renovated **quayside** are all reason enough to spend at least an afternoon here. The town can also make a convenient base from which to explore the attractive villages of **Framlingham** and **Dennington**, and the nearby Anglo-Saxon burial site at **Sutton Hoo**.

The Town

Cornhill, the ancient Saxon market place, is still the town's focal point, a likeable urban space flanked by a bevy of imposing Victorian edifices – the Italianate town hall, the old Neoclassical Post Office and the pseudo-Jacobean Lloyds building. From here, it's just a couple of minutes' walk south to Ipswich's most famous building, the **Ancient House**, on Buttermarket, just north of St Stephen's Lane. The building's exterior was decorated around 1670 in extravagant style, a riot of pargeting and stucco work that together make it one of the finest examples of Restoration artistry in the country. There are plasterwork reliefs of pelicans and nymphs as well as representations of the four continents known at the time: Europe is symbolized by a Gothic church, America a tobacco pipe, Asia an Oriental dome and Africa, eccentrically enough, by an African astride a crocodile. Since the house is now a shop, you're free to take a peek inside to view yet more of the decor, including the hammer-beam roof on the first floor.

From the Ancient House, it's a short hop north to the gates of **Christchurch Mansion** (daily 10am–5pm; free), a handsome, if much-restored Tudor building sporting seventeenth-century Dutch-style gables and set in 65 acres of parkland – an area larger than the town centre itself. The mansion's labyrinthine interior is worth exploring, with period furnishings and a good assortment of paintings by Constable and Gainsborough, as well as more contemporary art exhibitions.

On the other side of the town centre, about half a mile southeast of Cornhill, the **Wet Dock** was the largest dock in Europe when it opened in 1845. Today, after an imaginative redevelopment, it's flanked by apartments and offices, pubs, hotels and restaurants, many converted from the old marine warehouses. Walking round the Wet Dock is a pleasant way to pass an hour or so – look out, in particular, for the proud Neoclassical **Customs House** on Neptune Quay. Once weekly in July and August, **boat trips** run from Orwell Quay beside the Wet Dock down the River Orwell to Pin Mill, a rural picnic spot on the west bank of the river; operated by Orwell River Cruises (℡01473/836680, ⒲www .orwellrivercruises.com), the trips last two and a half hours and cost £9.

Practicalities

Ipswich **train station** is on the south bank of the river, about ten minutes' walk from Cornhill along Princes Street. The **bus station** is more central, a short walk from Cornhill – and near the **tourist office**, which is located in the converted St Stephen's Church, off St Stephen's Lane (Mon–Sat 9am–5pm; ℡01473/258070, ⒲www.visit-suffolk.org.uk).

Ipswich has one really good **hotel**, the *Salthouse Harbour*, in an imaginatively converted old warehouse, down by the Wet Dock at 1 Neptune Quay (℡01473/226789, ⒲www.salthouseharbour.com; ❼). It has great views over the docks from its upper floors and the rooms are decorated in modern, minimalist style. The hotel **brasserie** is good too, with a surprisingly varied menu – from liver and parsnips to daily seafood specials: main courses average around £12.

Northeast of Ipswich: Sutton Hoo, Framlingham and Dennington

Beyond Ipswich, the obvious target is the Suffolk coast (see p.487), but en route it's well worth stopping at **Sutton Hoo**, where a National Trust exhibition hall provides an outstanding introduction to the **Anglo-Saxon burial mounds** that decorate the surrounding fields. From here, it's another hop to two pleasant villages, **Framlingham**, with its impressive castle, and **Dennington**, which has an intriguing old church.

Sutton Hoo

At **SUTTON HOO** in 1939, a local archeologist by the name of Basil Brown investigated one of a group of burial mounds on a sandy ridge above the east bank of the River Deben. Much to everyone's amazement, including his own, he unearthed the forty-oar burial ship of an Anglo-Saxon warrior king, packed with his most valuable possessions, from a splendid iron and tinted-bronze helmet through to his intricately worked gold and jewelled ornaments. There's been much academic debate about the burial ship ever since, not least as to the identity of the body, though Raedwald, king of East Anglia, who died around 625 AD, remains the favourite. A series of supplementary digs has since explored the other burial mounds, but these were robbed centuries ago and have revealed little. Much of the Sutton Hoo treasure is now in London's British Museum (see p.104), but a scattering of artefacts – ship's rivets, belt buckles, a horse harness and so forth – can be seen in the **Sutton Hoo exhibition hall** (Jan to mid-March, Nov & Dec Sat & Sun 11am–4pm; mid-March to Oct Wed–Sun 11am–5pm, plus early April, July & Aug Mon & Tues 11am–5pm; £5.90; ℡01394/389700; NT), which explains the history and significance of the finds. Afterwards, you can wander out onto the burial site itself, about 500 yards away.

▲ Helmet, Sutton Hoo treasure

Located some ten miles east of Ipswich, on the far side of the River Deben, Sutton Hoo is clearly signed from the A12 at Woodbridge. The site is beside the B1083 road between Melton and Bawdsey; there is no public transport, but trains go from Ipswich to Melton station, from where it's a (dreary) mile and a half walk.

Twelve miles north of Sutton Hoo, **FRAMLINGHAM** boasts a magnificent **castle** (April–Sept daily 10am–6pm; Oct–March Mon & Thurs–Sun 10am–4pm; £4.70; EH), whose severe, turreted walls date from the twelfth century. The original seat of the dukes of Norfolk, the fortress is little more than a shell inside, but the curtain-wall, with its thirteen towers, has survived almost intact, a splendid example of medieval military architecture, topped by ornamental Tudor chimney stacks. Footpaths crisscross the earthen banks encircling the castle, and from the internal wall walkways there are sweeping views across to the imposing red-brick mass of Framlingham College. Unfortunately nothing remains of the castle's Great Hall where Mary Tudor was proclaimed Queen of England in 1553.

Next to the castle, the drowsy little village is a real pleasure, its elongated main street, **Market Hill**, flanked by a harmonious ensemble of sedate old buildings. The parish **church of St Michael** is also intriguing, its finely crafted hammer-beam roof sheltering several wonderful, sixteenth-century tombs belonging to the Howard family, who owned the castle at the time. They were a turbulent clan. During the reign of Henry VIII, both Thomas Howard, the Duke of Norfolk, and his son Henry Howard, the Earl of Surrey, schemed away, determined to be the leading nobles of their day. They brought down the powerful Chancellor of the Exchequer, Thomas Cromwell, in 1540 and their position seemed secure when the king married one of their kin, Catherine, later the same year. But the Howards had over-reached themselves. In 1542, the king had Catherine beheaded for adultery and, from his deathbed in 1547, he ordered Henry Howard to be executed. The same fate would have befallen Howard's father had the king lived a few days longer.

Also on Market Hill is *The Crown Hotel* (☏01728/723521, ⓦwww.theframcrown.com; ❻), a traditional seventeenth-century **inn** with roaring fires, wood-panelling and snug bedrooms. *The Crown* has a **restaurant**, but the best place to eat is the ⚔ *Station Hotel*, on the south side of the village on Station Road (☏01728/723455). There's nothing pretentious about the setting – it's a country kitchen in an old railway building – but the food, locally sourced wherever possible, is a treat: try the pigeon breasts, puy lentils and green bean salad. Main courses average around £12 and reservations are advised in the evening.

A mile north of Framlingham, along the B1120, is the well-established **Shawsgate Vineyard** (April–Sept Mon–Sat 9am–5pm, Sun 10am–4pm; ☏01728/724060, ⓦwww.shawsgate.co.uk), one of several local vineyards to offer free tastings.

Dennington

A couple of miles north of Framlingham along the B1116, the hamlet of **DENNINGTON** is home to another intriguing church. This is **St Mary's** (daily 10am–5pm; free), a sturdy medieval edifice, whose benches and pews sport a fantastical series of carvings – wild and folkloric figures and beasts. In particular, there is a rare representation of a **sciapod**, a mythical creature that avoided sunlight by shading itself with its one, large foot. The sciapod died if it smelt contaminated air, so it carried sniffable fresh fruit everywhere it went. Equally unusual is a rare pyx canopy over the altar (the pyx was the vessel in which the Holy Sacrament was kept) – one of only two such surviving canopies in Europe.

The Suffolk coast

The **Suffolk coast** feels detached from the rest of the county: the road and rail lines from Ipswich to the seaport of Lowestoft funnel traffic a few miles inland for most of the way, and patches of marsh and woodland make the separation still more complete. The coast has long been plagued by erosion and this has contributed to the virtual extinction of the local fishing industry, and, in the case of **Dunwich**, almost destroyed the whole town. What is left, however, is undoubtedly one of the most unspoilt shorelines in the country – if, that is, you set aside the Sizewell nuclear power station. Highlights include the sleepy isolation of minuscule **Orford** and several genteel resorts, most notably **Southwold**, which has evaded the lurid fate of so many English seaside towns. There are scores of delightful **walks** hereabouts too, easy routes along the coast that are best followed with either the appropriate OS Explorer Map or the simplified Footpath Maps available at most tourist offices. The Suffolk coast is also host to East Anglia's most compelling cultural gathering, the **Aldeburgh Festival**, which takes place every June.

Local buses shunt up and down the coast linking Ipswich and Norwich with all of Suffolk's coastal towns and villages, but services are infrequent – just two or three times daily and nothing on Sundays – and time-consuming as you often have to change buses at least once: for example, it takes three hours and two changes to get from Orford to Southwold.

Orford and Orford Ness

Some twenty miles from Ipswich, on the far side of Tunstall Forest, two medieval buildings dominate the tiny, eminently appealing village of **ORFORD**. The more impressive is the twelfth-century **castle** (April–Sept daily 10am–6pm; Oct–March Mon & Thurs–Sun 10am–4pm; £4.70; EH), built on high ground by Henry II, and under siege within months of its completion from Henry's rebellious sons. Most of the castle disappeared centuries ago, but the lofty keep remains, its impressive stature hinting at the scale of the original fortifications. Orford's other medieval edifice is **St Bartholomew's church**, where Benjamin Britten premiered his most successful children's work, *Noye's Fludde*, as part of the 1958 Aldeburgh Festival (see box on p.488).

From the top of the castle keep, there's a great view across **Orford Ness National Nature Reserve**, a six-mile-long shingle spit that has all but blocked Orford from the sea since Tudor times. The spit's assorted mud flats and marshes harbour sea lavender beds, which act as feeding and roosting areas for wildfowl and waders. The National Trust offers **boat trips** (early April to June & Oct Sat only; July–Sept Tues–Sat; outward boats between 10am and 2pm, last ferry back 5pm; £6.50, NT members £3.70; ☏01394/450057) across to the Ness from Orford Quay, four hundred yards down the road from the church, and a five-mile hiking trail threads its way along the spit. En route, the trail passes the occasional, abandoned **military building**. Some of the pioneer research on radar was carried out here, but the radar station was closed at the beginning of World War II because of the threat of German bombing – though the military stayed on until the 1980s. There are also plenty of **walks** to be had around Orford itself. One of the best is the five-mile hike north along the river wall that guards the west bank of the River Alde, returning via Ferry Road, a narrow country lane.

Orford's gentle and unhurried air is best experienced by **staying** overnight at the excellent 🪶 *Crown & Castle Hotel*, in a modest-looking building on

the main square, Market Hill (℡01394/450205, ⓦwww.crownandcastlehotel
.co.uk; ⓖ). Inside, the hotel is stylish with pastel-painted guest rooms and top-
of-the-range beds, and there's a superb **restaurant**, where the emphasis is on
local ingredients. Main courses – grilled plaice with toasted almonds and
grapes, for example – average around £13 and reservations are advised. The
village is also home to the 🍴 *Butley Orford Oysterage* (℡01394/450277,
ⓦwww.butleyorfordoysterage.co.uk), where they catch and smoke their own
fish and shellfish. The end results can be bought at their shop and sampled at
their down-to-earth **café/restaurant** (daily noon–2pm, plus eves April, May
& mid-Sept to Oct Wed–Sat only, June to mid-Sept daily, Nov–March Fri &
Sat only), which is especially famous for its fresh oysters. For a **pint**, it's the
Crown & Castle again or the *Jolly Sailor Inn*, down near the quay.

Aldeburgh

Well-heeled **ALDEBURGH**, just along the coast from Orford, is best known
for its annual arts festival, the brainchild of composer **Benjamin Britten**
(1913–76), who is buried in the village churchyard alongside the tenor Peter
Pears, his lover and musical collaborator. They lived by the seafront in Crag
House on Crabbe Street – named after the poet, George Crabbe, who
provided Britten with his greatest inspiration (see box below). Outside of

---

Benjamin Britten and the Aldeburgh Festival

Born in Lowestoft in 1913, **Benjamin Britten** was closely associated with Suffolk for
most of his life. The main break was during World War II when, as a conscientious
objector, Britten exiled himself to the USA. Ironically enough, it was here that Britten
first read the work of the nineteenth-century Suffolk poet, George Crabbe, whose *The
Borough*, a grisly portrait of the life of the fishermen of Aldeburgh, was the basis of
the libretto of Britten's best-known opera, *Peter Grimes*. The latter was premiered in
London in 1945 to great acclaim.

In 1947 Britten founded the English Opera Group and the following year launched
the **Aldeburgh Festival** as a showpiece for his own works and those of his contemporaries. He lived in the village for the next ten years and it was during this period
that he completed much of his best work as a conductor and pianist. For the rest of
his life he composed many works specifically for the festival, including his masterpiece for children, *Noye's Fludde*, and the last of his fifteen operas, *Death in Venice*.

By the mid-1960s, the festival had outgrown the parish churches in which it
began, and moved into a collection of disused malthouses, five miles west of
Aldeburgh on the River Alde, just south of the small village of **Snape**. **Snape
Maltings** (ⓦwww.snapemaltings.co.uk) were subsequently converted into one of
the finest concert venues in the country and, in addition to the concert hall, there's
now a recording studio, a music school, various craft shops and galleries, a
tearoom, and a pub, the *Plough & Sail*. Consequently, even if there's nothing
specific on, it's worth calling into the complex to nose around.

The Aldeburgh Festival takes place every June for two and a half weeks. Core
performances are still held at the Maltings, but a string of other local venues are
pressed into service as well. Throughout the rest of the year, the Maltings hosts a
wide-ranging programme of musical and theatrical events, including the three-day
Britten Festival in October. For more information, contact **Aldeburgh Music**
(℡01728/687110, ⓦwww.aldeburgh.co.uk), which operates two box offices, one at
Snape Maltings, the other on Aldeburgh High Street (same number & website).
Tickets for the Aldeburgh Festival itself usually go on sale to the public towards the
end of March, and sell out fast for the big-name recitals.

June, when the festival takes place, Aldeburgh is the quietest of places, with just a small fishing fleet selling its daily catch from wooden shacks along the pebbled shore, but there was an almighty rumpus – Barbours at dawn – when Maggi Hambling's thirteen-foot-high *Scallop* sculpture appeared on the beach in 2003. Made of steel, Hambling described the sculpture as a conversation with the sea and a suitable memorial to Britten; others compared it to a mantelpiece ornament gone wrong.

Aldeburgh's wide **High Street** and its narrow sidestreets run close to the beach, but this was not always the case – hence their garbled appearance. The sea swallowed most of what was once an extensive medieval town long ago and today Aldeburgh's oldest remaining building, the sixteenth-century, red-brick, flint and timber **Moot Hall**, which began its days in the centre of town, now finds itself on the seashore. Several **footpaths** radiate out from Aldeburgh, with the most obvious trail leading north along the coast to Thorpeness, and others going southwest to the winding estuary of the **River Alde**, an area rich in wildfowl.

Practicalities

Aldeburgh's festival box office (see box opposite) shares its High Street premises with the village **tourist office** (April–Sept daily 9am–5.30pm; Oct–March Mon–Sat 9am–5pm; ☎01728/453637, ⓦwww.suffolkcoastal .gov.uk/tourism). They have local bus timetables and can book **accommodation**, though during the festival you'll need to reserve well in advance. The town boasts several splendidly sited **hotels**, including the family-owned *Wentworth* (☎01728/452312, ⓦwww.wentworth-aldeburgh .com; ❼), which occupies a good-looking Edwardian mansion just along the seafront from the Moot Hall. The hotel has thirty-five well-appointed guest rooms in a modern version of country-house style with lots of creams and whites. Amongst local **B&Bs**, the pick is ⚹ *Ocean House*, 25 Crag Path (☎01728/452094, ⓦwww.oceanhousealdeburgh.co.uk; ❺), in an immaculately maintained Victorian dwelling right on the seafront in the centre of town; there are just two guest rooms here – so advance booking is well-nigh essential – and both of them come complete with period furnishings. The full English breakfasts, with homemade bread, are delicious too. Finally, there's a YHA **hostel** in the old village school on Heath Walk in the hamlet of **Blaxhall** (☎0870/770 5702, ✉blaxhall@yha.org.uk; dorm beds £14, doubles ❶). The hostel has forty beds in two- to six-bedded rooms, a self-catering kitchen, a café and a laundry. Blaxhall is a couple of miles southwest of the concert facilities at Snape Maltings (see box opposite).

Pride of the gastronomic crop is ⚹ *The Lighthouse*, 77 High St (☎01728/453377), a relaxed and informal **restaurant** in cosy premises that serves breakfast, lunch and dinner seven days a week. Prominence is given to locally sourced ingredients, but the menu features both Modern British and Mediterranean-style dishes, from cod with a cheese sauce to venison tagine with couscous; a set two-course lunch costs £12.50, a tad more in the evening. Aldeburgh also has two outstanding **fish-and-chip shops** – the original take-away ⚹ *Fish & Chip Shop* at 226 High St, and its sister, *The Golden Galleon*, where you can sit in just along the street at no. 137.

Dunwich and Minsmere

One-time seat of the kings of East Anglia, a bishopric and formerly the largest port on the Suffolk coast, the ancient city of **DUNWICH**, about twelve miles up the coast from Aldeburgh, reached its peak of prosperity in the twelfth century. Over the last millennium, however, something like a mile of land has been lost to the sea, a process that continues at the rate of about a yard a year. As a result, the whole of the medieval city now lies under water, including all twelve churches, the last of which toppled over the cliffs in 1919. All that survives today are fragments of the Greyfriars monastery, which originally lay to the west of the city and now dangles at the sea's edge. For a potted history of the lost city, head for the **museum** (daily: April–Sept 11.30am–4.30pm; Oct noon–4pm; free) in what's left of Dunwich – little more than one small street of terraced houses built by the local landowner in the nineteenth century.

A sprawling, coastline **car park** gives ready access to this part of the seashore. From the car park, it's a short stroll to the village and the remains of Greyfriars, beyond which you can hike along the coast to **Dunwich Heath**, where the coastguard cottages house a National Trust shop and tearoom (times vary, call ☏01728/648501 for details). The heath is itself next to the **Minsmere RSPB Nature Reserve** (daily 9am–9pm or dusk; £5), where terns nest on the beach in summer, avocets prod around in the wetland, and marsh harriers circle up above. In the autumn, it's a gathering place for wading birds and waterfowl which arrive here by the hundred, and it's also home to a small population of bitterns, one of England's rarest birds. You can rent binoculars from the RSPB **visitor centre** (daily 9am–4/5pm; ☏01728/648281) and strike out on the trails to the birdwatching hides.

Dunwich's one remaining **pub**, the *Ship Inn* (☏01728/648219, ⓦwww .shipinndunwich.co.uk), with its low wooden beams and open fire, is a good place for a drink; the inn also has a few rooms (⑥).

Southwold

Perched on robust cliffs just to the north of the River Blyth, **SOUTHWOLD** gained what Dunwich lost, and by the sixteenth century it had overtaken all its local rivals to become a busy fishing port. In turn, Southwold lost most of its fishery to Lowestoft, up the coast, and today, although a small fleet still brings in herring, sprats and cod, the town is primarily a seaside resort, a genteel and eminently appealing little place with none of the crassness of many of its competitors. There are fine old buildings, a long sandy beach, open heathland, a dinky harbour and even a little industry – in the shape of the Adnams brewery – but no burger bars and certainly no amusement arcades. This gentility was not to the liking of **George Orwell**, who lived for a time at his parents' house at 36 High St (a plaque marks the spot). Orwell heartily disliked the town's airs and graces, and has left no trace of his time here – apart from disguised slights in a couple of early novels.

The Town

Southwold's breezy **High Street** is framed by attractive, mainly Georgian buildings, which culminate in the pocket-sized Market Place. From here, it's a brief stroll along East Street to the curious **Sailors' Reading Room** (daily: April–Sept 9am–5pm; Oct–March 9am–3.30pm; free), decked out with model ships and nautical texts, and the bluff above the **beach**, where row upon row of candy-coloured huts face the sea. Queen Street begins at the Market Place too, quickly leading to **South Green**, the prettiest of several greens dotted across town. In 1659, a calamitous fire razed much of Southwold and when the town was rebuilt the greens were left to act as firebreaks. Beyond South Green, both Ferry Road and the ferry footpath lead down to the **harbour**, at the mouth of the River Blyth, an idyllic spot, where fishing smacks rest against old wooden jetties and nets are spread out along the banks to dry. A harbourside footpath leads to a tiny passenger **ferry** (Easter–May Sat & Sun 10am–12.30pm & 2–4.30pm; June–Aug daily 10am–12.30pm & 2–4.30pm; 40p), which crosses the river to Walberswick (see p.492). Turn right after the *Harbour Inn* and right again to walk back into town across **Southwold Common**. The whole circular walk takes about thirty minutes.

Back on Market Place, it's a couple of hundred yards north along Church Street to East Green, with the Adnams Brewery on one side and the stumpy lighthouse on another. Close by is Southwold's architectural pride and joy, the **church of St Edmund** (daily: June–Aug 9am–6pm; Sept–May 9am–4pm; free), a handsome fifteenth-century structure whose solid symmetries are balanced by its long and elegantly carved windows. Inside, the slender, beautifully proportioned nave is distinguished by its panelled roof, embellished with praying angels, and its intricate rood-screen. The latter carries paintings of the apostles and the prophets, though Protestants defaced them during the Reformation. Beyond the screen, the choir stalls carry finely carved human and animal heads as well as grotesques – look out for the man in the throes of toothache. Look out also for "**Southwold Jack**", a brightly painted, medieval effigy of a man in armour nailed to the wall beside the font. No one knows when or why this very military carving was moved into the church – it certainly doesn't fit in – but the betting is that he was once part of a clock, nodding belligerently as he struck the hours.

From the church, it's a short walk north to the **pier**, the latest incarnation of a structure that dates from 1899. Built as a landing stage for passenger ferries, the pier has had a troubled history: it has been repeatedly damaged by storms, was hit by a sea-mine and then partly chopped up by the army as a protection against German invasion in World War II.

Practicalities

Apart from on Sunday, Southwold is easy to reach by **bus**, with services from the likes of Norwich and Aldeburgh. Buses pull into the Market Place, yards from the **tourist office**, at 69 High St (April–Oct Mon–Fri 10am–5pm, Sat 10am–5.30pm, Sun 11am–4pm; Nov–March Mon–Fri 10.30am–3pm, Sat 10am–4.30pm; ℡01502/724729, Ⓦwww.visit-southwold.co.uk), which has details of local attractions and sells walking maps. The town has two well-known **hotels** beside the Market Place, both owned and run by Adnams. The smarter of the two is 🍴 *The Swan* (℡01502/722186, Ⓦwww.adnams.co.uk; ❼), which occupies a splendid Georgian building with lovely period rooms both in the main house and in the garden annexe behind, though some are a little on the small side. *The Crown*, just along the High Street (℡01502/722275, Ⓦwww .adnams.co.uk; ❼), costs slightly less and has fourteen spick-and-span bedrooms, all en suite, decorated in contemporary style. The best **B&B** in town was the delightful *Acton Lodge*, 18 South Green (℡01502/723217, Ⓦwww.southwold .ws/actonlodge; no credit cards; ❺), which occupies a grand Victorian house complete with its own Neo-Gothic tower, though at the time of writing it was up for sale. Alternatively, there's a string of **guesthouses** along the seafront, including the attractive *Home @ 21*, in a well-kept Victorian house at 21 North Parade (℡01502/722573, Ⓦwww.northparade.southwold.info; ❺). Incidentally, General Booth, the founder of the Salvation Army, was a regular visitor to 28 North Parade, the house with the mini-tower just along the street.

Southwold has two outstanding **places to eat**. 🍴 *The Crown*'s front bar serves delicious informal meals, with daily fish and meat specials, and has an enlightened wine list where all the choices are available by the glass. Expect to pay £14 or so for a main course – tope fillet baked in saffron yogurt for example; you'll have to make a booking if you want to eat in the adjacent restaurant, which is pricier, slightly more adventurous and just as terrific. The main gastronomic competitor is *Sutherland House*, in antique premises at 56 High St (☎01502/724544; closed Mon); the menu here has a strong emphasis on local ingredients and main courses start at £10. For a **drink**, sample Adnams' brews in *The Crown*'s wood-panelled back-bar or stroll along to the *Red Lion* on South Green.

Around Southwold: Walberswick and Blythburgh

Just across the River Blyth from Southwold lies the leafy little village of **WALBERSWICK**, another once-prosperous port now fallen (or risen) into well-heeled tranquillity. For many years it was the home of the English Impressionist painter Philip Wilson Steer (1860–1942) and, warming to the same theme, it's now a seaside escape with an arty undertow. There's not much to see as such, but a network of **footpaths** head inland to – and across – a nature reserve, or you can stroll south along the coast to Dunwich (see p.489). The *Bell Inn*, an old village pub close to the riverfront offers bar food and Adnams beer, but it's trumped by *The Anchor* (☎01502/722112, ⓦwww.anchoratwalberswick .com; ⓞ) another five minutes' walk away on The Street, the village's main drag. *The Anchor* has a handful of comfortable if somewhat plain guest rooms, but the big deal is the food and drink – the beer menu is extensive, featuring many Belgian imports, and there's a good range of English dishes with main courses beginning at £8; one tasty offering is beer-battered haddock, chips and pease pudding. There are two ways for walkers to get to Walberswick from Southwold – either via the ferry (see p.491) or over the bridge about a mile further inland. The footpath to the bridge begins on Station Road, a westerly continuation of Southwold's High Street.

Up until the sixteenth century, **BLYTHBURGH**, five miles west of Southwold, was a thriving port at the head of a wide estuary, but the silting up of the River Blyth slowly strangled the town, reducing it to an inconsequential hamlet. The **church of the Holy Trinity** (daily 9am–5pm), a handsome flint and stone structure dating from the 1440s, recalls the village's salad days – its sheer bulk earning it the title "Cathedral of the Marshes". Inside, the light and airy nave is decorated with carved angels and brightly painted flower patterns similar to St Edmund's in Southwold. The bench-ends depict the Seven Deadly Sins with gusto and, in another echo of Southwold, there's a "Jack-o'-the-Clock" here, too.

Norwich

One of the five largest cities in Norman England, **NORWICH** once served a vast hinterland of East Anglian **cloth producers**, whose work was brought here by river and then exported to the Continent. Its isolated position beyond the Fens meant that it enjoyed closer links with the Low Countries than with the rest of England – it was, after all, quicker to cross the North Sea than to go cross-country to London. The local textile industry, based on worsted cloth (named after the nearby village of Worstead), was further enhanced by an influx of Flemish and Huguenot weavers, who made up more than a third of the population in Tudor times. By 1700, Norwich was the second richest city in the country after London.

With the onset of the Industrial Revolution, however, Norwich lost ground to the northern manufacturing towns – the city's famous mustard company, Colman's, is one of its few industrial success stories – and this, together with its continuing geographical isolation, has helped preserve much of the ancient street plan and many of the city's older buildings. Pride of place goes to the beautiful **cathedral** and the sterling **castle**, but the city's hallmark is its medieval **churches**, thirty or so squat flintstone structures with sturdy towers and sinuous stone tracery round the windows. Many are no longer in regular use and are now in the care of the **Norwich Historic Churches Trust** (Ⓦwww.norwichchurches.co.uk), whose excellent website describes each church in precise detail and gives opening times.

Norwich's relative isolation has also meant that the population has never swelled to any great extent and today, with just 130,000 inhabitants, it remains an easy and enjoyable city to negotiate. Yet Norwich is no provincial backwater. In the 1960s, the foundation of the **University of East Anglia** (UEA) made it more cosmopolitan and bolstered its arts scene, while in the 1980s it attracted new high-tech companies, who created something of a mini-boom, making the city one of England's wealthiest. As East Anglia's unofficial capital, Norwich also lies at the hub of the region's **transport** network, serving as a useful base for visiting the Broads and as a springboard for the north Norfolk coast.

Arrival and information

Norwich's grandiose **train station** is on the east bank of the River Wensum, ten minutes' walk from the city centre along Prince of Wales Road. Long-distance **buses** terminate at the Surrey Street Station, also little more than ten minutes' walk from the town centre, but this time to the south off Surrey Street (though some stop in the centre on Castle Meadow too). **First** (Ⓦwww.firstgroup.com), the largest regional bus company, sell Network Tickets valid for unlimited travel on all their Norfolk and Suffolk bus routes (£10 for one day, £25 for seven). These passes can be purchased at the bus station, from any bus driver and at the **tourist office**, which is in the glassy Forum building overlookng the Market Place (April–Oct Mon–Sat 9.30am–6pm, Sun 10.30am–4.30pm; Nov–March Mon–Sat 9.30am–5.30pm; Ⓣ01603/727927, Ⓦwww.visitnorwich.co.uk).

The best way to see the city is on **foot**, or by **riverbus** (April–Sept 4 daily; £4 return). The latter runs from the Thorpe Road Quay, opposite the train station, to the Elm Hill Quay near the cathedral, providing an inexpensive means of cruising Norwich's central waterway. The journey takes about fifteen minutes and the boats are operated by City Boats (Ⓣ01603/701701, Ⓦwww.cityboats.co.uk), who also offer longer cruises out from Norwich and into the Norfolk Broads.

Accommodation

As you might expect, Norwich has **accommodation** to suit all budgets, though there's precious little in the city centre. Most **B&Bs** and **guesthouses** are strung along **Earlham Road**, a tedious, mostly Victorian street running west towards the university, UEA.

3 Princes St B&B 3 Princes St ☎01603/662693, ⓦwww.3princes-norwich.co.uk. Great location, up a narrow lane yards from the cathedral, this B&B looks pretty dour from the outside – it occupies a plain brick Georgian terraced house – but the four guest rooms are attractively furnished with a comely mix of modern and period furnishings and fittings. Continental breakfast. ⑤

By Appointment 25 St George's St ☎01603/630730, ⓦwww.byappointmentnorwich .co.uk. Here at Norwich's smallest hotel – a restaurant with five en-suite rooms up above – the bedrooms have beamed ceilings and heavy-drape curtains and the whole caboodle is jam-packed with antiques. ⑥

Earlham Guest House 147 Earlham Rd ☎01603/454169, ⓦwww.earlham-guesthouse.co .uk. The nine rooms are homely and spick and span at this family-run guest house, located in a Victorian building three-quarters of a mile from the centre. ③

Maid's Head Hotel Tombland ☎0870/609 6110, ⓦwww.foliohotels.com/maidshead. Not everyone's cup of tea perhaps, but this chain hotel has its idiosyncrasies – a rabbit warren of a place with all sorts of architectural bits and pieces, from the mock-Tudor facade to the ancient, wood-panelled bar, though there is also a clumpy modern extension. The rooms are comfortable in a standard-issue sort of way and the location, bang in the centre opposite the cathedral, can't be beat. ⑤

The City

Norwich is tucked into a wide bend of the River Wensum and has an irregular street plan, a Saxon legacy, that can make orientation difficult. There are, however, three obvious landmarks to help you find your way – the **cathedral** with its giant spire, the Norman **castle** on its commanding mound and the distinctive **clocktower** of City Hall. The cathedral and the castle are the town's premier attractions and the latter also holds one of the region's most satisfying collections of fine art. Note that **Sunday** can be a disastrous day to visit if you want to see anything other than the cathedral: the majority of museums and attractions are closed, not to mention most of the restaurants.

The cathedral

Norwich Cathedral (daily: mid-May to mid-Sept 7.30am–7pm; mid-Sept to mid-May 7.30am–6pm; free; ⓦwww.cathedral.org.uk) is distinguished by its prickly octagonal spire, which rises to a height of 315ft, second only to Salisbury. The exterior is best viewed from the Lower Close (see p.496), to the south, where the thick curves of the flying buttresses, the rounded excrescences of the ambulatory chapels – unusual in an English cathedral – and the straight symmetries of the main trunk can all be seen to perfection.

The **interior** is pleasantly light thanks to a creamy tint in the stone and the clear glass windows of much of the **nave**, where the thick pillars are a powerful legacy of the Norman builders who began the cathedral in 1096. Look up to spy the nave's fan vaulting, delicate and geometrically precise carving adorned by several hundred roof **bosses** recounting – from east to west – the story of the Old and New Testaments from the Creation to the Last Judgement. Pushing on down the south (right) side of the ambulatory, you soon reach **St Luke's Chapel** where the cathedral's finest work of art, the *Despenser Reredos*, is a superb painted panel commissioned to celebrate the crushing of the Peasants' Revolt of 1381. Across the aisle, encased by the choir, is the **bishop's throne**, a sturdy stone structure placed directly behind the high altar. Norman bishops were barons as much as religious leaders, and to emphasize their direct relationship with Almighty God they usually put their thrones behind the high altar. Most were relocated during the Reformation, but this one occupies its original position. Here in Norwich, the bishop also had a spiritual prop: a flue runs down from the back of the throne to a reliquary recess behind in the ambulatory, the idea being that divine essences would be transported up to him.

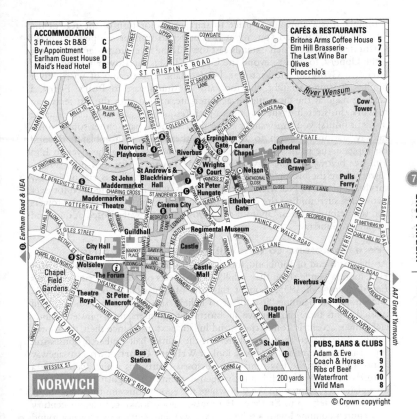

Accessible from the south aisle of the nave are the cathedral's unique **cloisters**. Built between 1297 and 1450, and the only two-storey cloisters left standing in England, they contain a remarkable set of sculpted **bosses**, similar to the ones in the main nave, but here they are close enough to be scrutinized without binoculars. The carving is fabulously intricate and the dominant theme is the **Apocalypse**, but look out also for the bosses depicting green men, originally pagan fertility symbols.

The cathedral precincts

Outside, in front of the main entrance, stands the medieval **Canary Chapel**. This is the original building of Norwich School, whose blue-blazered pupils are often visible during term-time – the rambling school buildings are adjacent. A statue of the school's most famous boy, **Horatio Nelson**, faces the chapel, standing on the green of the **Upper Close**, which is guarded by two ornate and imposing medieval gates, **Erpingham** and, a hundred yards or so to the south, **Ethelbert**. Beside the Erpingham gate is a memorial to **Edith Cavell**, a local woman who was a nurse in occupied Brussels during World War I. She was shot by the Germans in 1915 for helping allied prisoners to escape, a fate that made her an instant folk hero; her grave is outside the cathedral ambulatory. Both gates lead onto the old Saxon market place, **Tombland**, a wide and busy thoroughfare whose name derives from the Saxon word for an open space.

Tombland is a convenient place to start an exploration of the rest of the city centre, but instead you might first prefer to wander the pedestrianized **Cathedral Close**, which extends east towards the river from – and including – the Upper Close. Just beyond the Upper Close is the **Lower Close**, where attractive Georgian and Victorian houses flank a scattering of wispy silver birches. Keeping straight, the footpath continues east to **Pull's Ferry**, a landing stage at the city's medieval watergate, named after the last ferryman to work this stretch of the river. It's a picturesque spot and from here (during daylight hours) you can wander along the riverbank path either south to the railway station or north to Bishopgate, then back to Tombland. Beyond Bishopgate, the path continues north and then west along the river to Elm Hill (see below). On the way you pass **Cow Tower**, a fifty-foot-high watch-tower where the bishop's retainers collected river tolls. This is one of the few surviving pieces of Norwich's **fortified walls**, which once stretched for over two miles, surrounding the city and incorporating thirty such circular towers and ten defensive gates. Up until the 1790s, the gates were closed at dusk and all day on Sundays.

From Tombland to Elm Hill and St Andrew's Hall

At the north end of Tombland, fork left into Wensum Street and cobbled **Elm Hill**, more a gentle slope than a hill, soon appears on the left. Priestley, in his *English Journey* of 1933, thought this part of Norwich to be overbearingly Dickensian, proclaiming "it difficult to believe that behind those bowed and twisted fronts there did not live an assortment of misers, mad spinsters, saintly clergymen, eccentric comic clerks, and lunatic sextons." Since then, the tourist crowds have sucked the atmosphere, but the quirky half-timbered houses still appeal and while you're here take a look at **Wright's Court**, down a passageway at no. 43, one of the few remaining enclosed courtyards which were once a feature of the city. Elm Hill quickly opens out into a triangular square centred on a plane tree, planted on the spot where the eponymous elm tree once stood. It then veers left up to **St Peter Hungate**, a good-looking, fifteenth-century flint church equipped with a solid square tower and gentle stone tracery round its windows.

Turn right at the church and it's just a few yards to **St Andrew's Hall** and **Blackfriars Hall**, two adjoining buildings that were originally the nave and chancel, respectively, of a Dominican monastery church. Imaginatively recycled, the two halls are now used for a variety of public events, including concerts, weddings and antique fairs; the crypt of the former now serves as a café (Mon–Sat 10am–4.30pm).

Maddermarket

Heading south from St Andrew's Hall, cut along Bridewell Alley to get to Bedford Street and then Lobster Lane, which leads west to Pottergate's **St John Maddermarket** (April–Oct Tues–Sat 10.30am–5pm; free), one of thirty medieval churches standing within the boundaries of the old city walls. Most are redundant and are rarely open to the public, but this is one of the more accessible, courtesy of dedicated volunteers. Apart from the stone trimmings, the church is almost entirely composed of **flint rubble**, the traditional building material of east Norfolk, an area chronically short of decent stone. The exterior is a good example of the Perpendicular style, a sub-division of English Gothic which flourished from the middle of the fourteenth to the early sixteenth century and is characterized by straight vertical lines – as you might expect from the name – and large windows framed by flowing, but plain, tracery. By comparison, the interior is something of a disappointment, its furnishings and fittings thoroughly remodelled at the start of the twentieth century. It's from this period that the heavy-duty oak altar canopy and the extensive wood panelling date.

Back outside, the arch under the church tower leads through to the **Maddermarket Theatre**, built in 1921 in the style of an Elizabethan playhouse. Incidentally, Maddermarket is named after the yellow flower that the weavers used to make red vegetable dye, or madder.

The Market Place

From Pottergate, several narrow alleys lead through to the city's **Market Place**, site of one of the country's largest open-air markets (closed Sun), with stalls selling everything from bargain-basement clothes to local mussels and whelks. Four very different but equally distinctive buildings oversee the market's stripy awnings, the oldest of them being the fifteenth-century **Guildhall**, a capacious flint and stone structure begun in 1407. Opposite, commanding the heights of the Market Place, are the austere **City Hall**, a lumbering brick pile with a landmark clocktower built in the 1930s in a Scandinavian style – it bears a striking resemblance to Oslo's city hall – and **The Forum**, a large, flashy, glassy structure completed in 2001. The latter is home to the city's main library and the tourist office (see p.493).

On the south side of Market Place is the finest of the four buildings, **St Peter Mancroft** (Mon–Sat 10am–3.30pm; free), whose long and graceful nave leads to a mighty stone tower, an intricately carved affair surmounted by a spiky little spire. The church once delighted John Wesley, who declared "I scarcely ever remember to have seen a more beautiful parish church," a fair description of what remains an exquisite example of the Perpendicular style with the slender columns of the nave reaching up towards the delicate groining of the roof. Completed in 1455, the open design of the nave was meant to express the mystery of the Christian faith with light filtering in through the stained-glass windows in a kaleidoscope of colours. Some of the original glass has survived, most notably in the east window, which boasts a cartoon strip of biblical scenes from the Virgin nursing the baby Jesus, through to the Crucifixion and Resurrection.

Back outside and just below the church is the **Sir Garnet Wolseley** pub, sole survivor of the 44 alehouses that once crowded the Market Place – and stirred the local bourgeoisie into endless discussions about the drunken fecklessness of the working class. Opposite the pub, on the far side of **Gentlemen's Walk**, the city's main promenade, which runs along the bottom of the Market Place, is the **Royal Arcade**, an Art Nouveau extravagance from 1899. The arcade has been beautifully restored to reveal the swirl and blob of the tiling, ironwork and stained glass, though it's actually the eastern entrance, further from Gentlemen's Walk, which is the fanciest section.

The castle

Perched high on a grassy mound in the centre of town – with a modern shopping mall drilled into its side – the stern walls of **Norwich Castle**, replete with conspicuous blind arcading, date from the twelfth century. To begin with they were a reminder of Norman power and then, when the castle was turned into a prison, they served as a grim warning to potential law-breakers. Now refurbished in lavish style, the castle holds the **Castle Museum and Art Gallery** (Mon–Fri 10am–4.30pm, Sat 10am–5pm, Sun 1–5pm; £6.50 all zones, £4.50 per zone), which is divided into three zones.

The **Art and Exhibitions** zone is the pick, scoring well with its temporary displays and boasting an outstanding selection of work by the **Norwich School**. Founded in 1803, and in existence for just thirty years, this school of landscape painters produced – for the most part – richly coloured, formally composed land- and seascapes in oil and watercolour, paintings whose realism harked back to the Dutch landscape painters of the seventeenth century. The leading figures were **John Crome** (1768–1821) – aka "Old Crome" – and **John Sell Cotman** (1782–1842), who is generally acknowledged as one of England's finest watercolourists. Both have a gallery to themselves and, helpfully, there's also a gallery given over to those Dutch painters who influenced them.

The **castle keep** itself is no more than a shell, its gloomy walls towering above a scattering of local archeological finds and some gory examples of traditional forms of punishment. More unusual is a bloated model **dragon**, known as Snap, which was paraded round town on the annual guilds' day procession – a folkloric hand-me-down from the dragon St George had so much trouble finishing off. To see more of the keep, join one of the regular **guided tours** that explore the battlements and the dungeons.

Finally, a long, dark (and one-way) tunnel leads down from the Castle Museum to the **Royal Norfolk Regimental Museum** (Tues–Fri 10am–4.30pm, Sat 10am–5pm; £3.10, but included in the all-zone castle ticket), which tracks through the history of the regiment with remarkable candour – including an even-handed account of the regiment's police-keeping role in Northern Ireland. The exit leaves you below the castle on Market Avenue.

King Street

East of the castle, **King Street** possesses one or two surprises, beginning with the **Dragon Hall**, at no. 115–123 (Mon–Fri 10am–5pm, Sun 11am–4pm; closed Sat; £5), an extraordinarily long, half-timbered showroom built for the cloth merchant Robert Toppes in the fifteenth century. You get a good impression of the bowed and bent building from the outside, but enthusiasts can pop in to have a closer look at the complex network of wooden beams that support the roof – there's nothing much else to see. A right turn opposite the hall up St Julian's Alley leads to **St Julian's Church** (daily 7.30am–4/5pm; free) and an adjoining monastic cell, thatched and standing in open countryside as late as the mid-nineteenth century. One of the smallest of the city's religious foundations, this was the retreat of St Julian, a Norwich woman who took to living here after experiencing visions of Christ in 1373. Her mystical *Revelations of Divine Love* – written after twenty years' meditation on her visions – was the first widely distributed book written by a woman in the English language, and has been in print ever since.

Doubling back along King Street, it takes about ten minutes to get back to the cathedral.

The University

The **University of East Anglia** (UEA) occupies a sprawling campus on the western outskirts of the city beside the B1108. Its buildings are resolutely modern, an assortment of concrete-and-glass blocks of varying designs, some quite ordinary, others like the prize-winning "ziggurat" halls of residence, designed by Denys Lasdun, eminently memorable. The main reason to visit is the high-tech **Sainsbury Centre for Visual Arts** (Tues–Sun 10am–5pm, Wed till 8pm; free; ⓦwww.scva.org.uk), built by Norman Foster in the 1970s.

The interior houses one of the most varied collections of sculpture and painting in the country, donated by the family which founded the Sainsbury supermarket chain, in which the likes of Degas, Seurat, Picasso, Giacometti, Bacon and Henry Moore rub shoulders with Mayan and Egyptian antiquities. The centre also runs a first-rate programme of temporary exhibitions (for which admission may be charged).

Buses #25, #26 and #27 run frequently to UEA from Castle Meadow.

Eating and drinking

There are plenty of **cafés and restaurants** in the city centre, and many of them are very good value. Decent **pubs**, though, are harder to find, partly because previously serviceable places have been turned into ersatz "traditional" drinking dens for students.

Cafés and restaurants

Britons Arms Coffee House 9 Elm Hill. Homemade quiches, tarts, cakes and scones plus pies and salads in quaint Elm Hill premises. Closed Sun, plus Mon in winter.

Elm Hill Brasserie 2 Elm Hill ⊕01603/624847. New kid on the gastronomic block, this intimate, one-room bistro-brasserie, housed in an old shop, offers a creative menu with a French twist. Daily specials, written on a blackboard, are well considered and reasonably priced at around £12 per main course. Closed Sun & Mon.

The Last Wine Bar 70 St George's St ⊕01603/626626. Imaginatively converted old shoe factory, a couple of minutes' walk north of the river, holding a relaxed and very amenable wine bar in one section and an excellent restaurant in the other. The food is firmly British, with the likes of braised lamb shank with carrots and parsnips in a rosemary jus (around £13). Closed Sun.

Olives 40 Elm Hill. In antique, half-timbered premises, this agreeable café serves up a good line in salads and light meals – and it's not part of a chain (hurrah). Closed Sun.

Pinocchio's 11 St Benedict's St ⊕01603/613318. Relaxed Italian restaurant in a bright and lively conversion of what was once a general store. The menu covers all the classics and then some, and prices are very reasonable with pizzas from £8. Closed Sun.

Pubs, bars and clubs

Adam & Eve Bishopgate. There's been a pub on this site for seven hundred years and it's still a top spot for the discerning drinker with a changing range of real ales and an eclectic wine list supplied by Adnams.

Coach & Horses Bethel St. Pleasant city-centre pub with lived-in furnishings and fittings. Good for a quiet drink.

Ribs of Beef 24 Wensum St. Boisterous riverside drinking haunt popular with students and townies alike.

Waterfront 139–141 King St ⊕01603/508050, ⓦwww.waterfrontnorwich.com. Norwich's principal club and alternative music venue, with gigs and DJs most nights. Sponsored by UEA's student union.

Wild Man 29 Bedford St. Long-established city-centre watering hole – a popular student hangout.

Entertainment

As well as its fair share of multi-screen **cinemas** showing Hollywood blockbusters, Norwich has the excellent art-house **Cinema City**, in Suckling House on St Andrew's Plain (⊕01603/622047, ⓦwww.picturehouses.co.uk). The city also has several noteworthy **theatres**: the Theatre Royal, on Theatre Street (⊕01603/630000, ⓦwww.theatreroyal.co.uk), has a wide-ranging programme of mainstream and more adventurous plays and dance; the amateur Maddermarket, St John's Alley, off Pottergate (⊕01603/620917, ⓦwww.maddermarket .co.uk), offers an interesting range of modern theatre; and Norwich Playhouse, on St George's Street (⊕01603/612580, ⓦwww.norwichplayhouse.co.uk) chips in with just about everything from blues concerts to panto.

Three **rivers** – the Yare, Waveney and Bure – meander across the flatlands to the east of Norwich, converging on Breydon Water before flowing into the sea at Great Yarmouth. In places these rivers swell into wide expanses of water known as "**broads**", which for years were thought to be natural lakes. In fact they're the result of extensive peat cutting, several centuries of accumulated diggings made in a region where wood was scarce and peat a valuable source of energy. The pits flooded when sea levels rose in the thirteenth and fourteenth centuries to create the **Norfolk Broads**, now one of the most important wetlands in Europe – a haven for many birds such as kingfishers, grebes and warblers – and the county's major tourist attraction.

The Broads' delicate **ecological balance** suffered badly during the 1970s and 1980s. The careless use of fertilizers poisoned the water with phosphates and nitrates encouraged the spread of algae; the decline in reed cutting – previously in great demand for thatching – made the broads partly unnavigable; and the enormous increase in pleasure-boat traffic began to erode the banks. National Park status was, however, accorded to the area in 1988, and efforts are now well under way to clear the waters and protect the ecosystem. Co-ordinating the clean up is the **Broads Authority** (Ⓦ www.broads-authority.gov.uk), which maintains a series of information centres throughout the region. At any of these, you can pick up a free copy of the *Broadcaster*, a useful newspaper guide to the Broads as a whole.

The region is crisscrossed by roads and rail lines, but the best – really the only – way to see the Broads is **by boat**, and you could happily spend a week or so exploring the 125 miles of lock-free navigable waterways, visiting the various churches, pubs and windmills en route. Of the many **boat rental** companies, Blakes Holiday Boating (Ⓣ 0870/220 2498, Ⓦ www.blakes.co.uk) and Broads Tours Ltd (Ⓣ 01603/782207, Ⓦ www.broads.co.uk) are both well-established and have rental outlets at **Wroxham**, seven miles to the northeast of Norwich and easy to reach by train, bus and car. Prices for cruisers start at around £700 a week for four people in peak season, but less expensive, short-term rentals are widely available, too. **Houseboats** are much cheaper than cruisers, but they are, of course, static.

Trying to explore the Broads by car is pretty much a waste of time, but cyclists and walkers can take advantage of the region's network of footpaths and cycle trails. There are Broads Authority **bike rental** points dotted around the region and **walkers** might consider the 56-mile Weavers' Way, a long-distance footpath that winds through the best parts of the Broads on its way from Cromer to Great Yarmouth, though there are many shorter options too.

As for specific sights, one prime target for landlubbers and boaters alike is **Toad Hole Cottage** (April, May & Oct Mon–Fri 10.30am–1pm & 1.30–5pm, Sat & Sun 10.30am–5pm; June–Sept daily 9.30am–6pm; free), an old eel-catcher's cottage holding a small exhibit on the history of the trade, which was common hereabouts until the 1940s. The cottage is at How Hill, close to the hamlet of **Ludham**, six miles east of Wroxham on the A1062. Behind the cottage is the narrow River Ant, where there are hour-long, wildlife-viewing **boat trips** in the *Electric Eel* (June–Sept daily 10am–5pm, hourly; £4.50; reservations on Ⓣ 01692/678763). Another enjoyable boat trip is on the *Helen of Ranworth*, a former reed lighter that makes two-hour excursions (Easter to Oct 1 daily; £5.50; reservations on Ⓣ 01603/270453) out into the Broads from **Ranworth**, a tiny hamlet about twelve miles east of Norwich via the A1151 and B1140. Most trips visit the isolated ruins of **St Benet's Abbey** (open access; free).

▲ Boating on the Broads

Great Yarmouth

First and foremost, **GREAT YARMOUTH**, about twenty miles east of Norwich, is a seaside resort, its promenade a parade of amusement arcades and rainy-day attractions, deserted in winter, heaving in summer. But it's also a port with a long history and, despite extensive wartime bomb damage, it retains a handful of sights that give some idea of the place Daniel Defoe thought "far superior to Norwich".

Yarmouth was a major trading port by the fourteenth century, its economy underpinned by its control of the waterways leading inland to Norwich. It also benefited from **fishing**, especially during the nineteenth century when there was a spectacular boom in the herring industry. The fishing finally fizzled out in the 1960s, but the timely discovery of **gas and oil** deposits off the Norfolk coast helped mitigate the effects and have since made the town a major base for the offshore gas industry, second only to Aberdeen for North Sea oil.

The Town

Arriving by train or car from Norwich, initial impressions are favourable thanks to the appealing silhouette of the **church of St Nicholas**, which boasts one of the widest naves in the country and, consequently, an impressive west front. The church stands just to the north of the broad **Market Place**, which served as the centre of medieval Yarmouth, but is now mostly undistinguished. The one exception, at the square's northeast corner, is the **Hospital for Decayed Fishermen**, almshouses built in 1702 and opening out into a lovely little courtyard flanked by Dutch gables, the central cupola topped by a chilly looking statue of the fishermen's friend himself, St Peter. Close by, at 26 Church Plain and now a restaurant, is Sewell House, the childhood home of Anna Sewell (1820–1878), author of *Black Beauty*.

One especially interesting feature of the old town is its parallel narrow alleys – locally "**rows**" – which were built to connect South Quay, running beside the River Yare, with the town centre just to the east. Sixty-nine rows have survived, and English Heritage maintains two seventeenth-century row houses, the **Old Merchant's House** in Row 117 and the **Row 111 House** next door (April–Sept daily noon–5pm; £3.50; EH). The first holds furnishings and fittings illustrating the life of local folk in the 1870s, the other is kitted out as it would have looked in the early 1940s. Of the town's several other museums, the most interesting is the **Norfolk Nelson Museum**, nearby at 26 South Quay (April–Sept Mon–Fri 10am–5pm, Sat & Sun 1–4pm; Oct–March Mon–Fri 10am–4pm, Sun 1–4pm; £3), devoted to the eponymous admiral, who was a regular visitor to Yarmouth; it has a particularly good feature on Nelson's early life in Norfolk.

Row houses or not, the vast majority of visitors make a beeline for the wide sandy **beach** and the gimcrackery of **Marine Parade**, the seafront promenade where you'll find the usual suspects – gardens, huts, waxworks, crazy golf, an aquarium and a pier. The beach was also the unlikely setting for many of the most dramatic events in Dickens' *David Copperfield*.

Practicalities

It's a five- to ten-minute walk east from Great Yarmouth **train station** to the central Market Place – cross the river by the footbridge and you'll find yourself on North Quay, from where The Conge leads straight through to the square. Long-distance **buses** terminate on Market Gates, just off the Market Place. The **tourist office** is on the seafront at 25 Marine Parade (Easter–Sept Mon–Sat 9.30am–5pm, Sun 10am–5pm; Oct Mon–Fri 9.30am–4.30pm, Sat & Sun 10am–4pm; Nov–Easter Mon–Fri 9.30am–4.30pm; ☎01493/846346, ⊛www .great-yarmouth.co.uk). They have a long list of hotels and B&Bs and an **accommodation** booking service, which is especially useful in the height of the summer. Yarmouth's **youth hostel** is in a large Victorian house near the beach – and half a mile northeast of the Market Place – at 2 Sandown Rd (☎0870/770 5840, ⊜gtyarmouth@yha.org.uk; dorm beds £12, doubles ❶). It has forty beds in two- to ten-bedded rooms, a café and a self-catering kitchen; advance reservations are advised. Far and away the best **restaurant** in town is the *Seafood Restaurant*, 85 North Quay (☎01493/856009; closed Sun), which does a superb fish soup and Mediterranean-influenced seafood dishes; mains cost around £17.

The north Norfolk coast

Beyond Great Yarmouth, the first thirty-odd miles of the **north Norfolk coast** is dominated by beach, with barely a village, never mind an estuary or a harbour, in sight. The first place of any note is **Cromer**, a workaday seaside town whose bleak and blustery cliffs have drawn tourists for over a century. A few miles to the west is another well-established resort, **Sheringham**, but thereafter the shoreline becomes a ragged patchwork of salt marshes, dunes and shingle spits which form an almost unbroken series of nature reserves supporting a fascinating range of flora and fauna. It's a lovely stretch of coast and the villages bordering it, such as **Cley**, **Blakeney** and **Wells-next-the-Sea**, are prime targets for an overnight stay. The other major attractions hereabouts are a short distance inland, including Little Walsingham, an ancient hamlet that was the country's most important place of pilgrimage throughout the medieval period, and a string of stately homes, such as **Felbrigg** and **Holkham Hall**, which are among the finest in the region.

Cromer and Sheringham are the only places accessible by **train**, with an hourly service (every 2hr on winter Sundays) from Norwich on the Bittern Line. Local **bus** services fill in (most of) the gaps, connecting all the towns and many of the villages. There's also the **Coasthopper bus** (see p.532). The Coasthopper Rover ticket (£7) gives a day's unlimited travel on the route. For **walkers**, the **Norfolk Coast Path** runs from Hunstanton to Cromer (where it joins the Weavers' Way, which presses on to Great Yarmouth), an exhilarating route through the dunes and salt marshes; a National Trail guide covers the route in detail, otherwise you'll need the appropriate OS Explorer map.

Cromer and around

Dramatically poised on a high bluff, **CROMER** should be the most memorable of the Norfolk coastal resorts, but its fine aspect is undermined by a shabbiness in its streets and shopfronts – an "atrophied charm" as Paul Theroux called it. The tower of **St Peter and St Paul**, at 160ft the tallest in Norfolk, attests to the port's medieval wealth, but it was the advent of the railway in the 1880s that heralded the most frenetic flurry of building activity. A bevy of grand Edwardian hotels was constructed along the seafront and for a moment Cromer became the most fashionable of resorts, but the gloss soon wore off and only the dishevelled **Hotel de Paris** has survived as a reminder of all the bustles and top hats. While you're here, be sure to take a stroll out onto the **pier**, and, of course, don't forget to grab a **crab** – J.W.H. Jonas, in the centre at 7 Chapel St, has some fine specimens.

Somewhat miraculously Cromer has managed to retain its rail link with Norwich; the **train station** is a five-minute walk west of the centre. **Buses** terminate on Cadogan Road, next to the **tourist office** (daily 10am–4pm; closed 1–2pm Nov to mid-March; ☎01263/512497, ⓦwww.visitnorthnorfolk .com), which is itself just 200 yards from the cliff-top promenade. An hour or two in Cromer is probably enough, though the **beach** is first-rate and the cliff-top walk exhilarating. There's no shortage of inexpensive **accommodation** – the tourist office has all the details – but it's hard to beat the enticing

Beachcomber B&B, a cosy place with five en-suite rooms conveniently located near the centre at 17 Macdonald Rd (℡01263/513398, Ⓦwww.beachcomber-guesthouse.co.uk; no credit cards; ❸).

Felbrigg Hall

Felbrigg Hall (mid-March to Oct Mon–Wed, Sat & Sun 1–5pm; £7.50, including park & garden; NT), situated just a couple of miles southwest of Cromer off the A148, is a charming Jacobean mansion. The main facade is particularly appealing, the soft hues of the ageing limestone and brick intercepted by three bay windows, which together sport a large, cleverly carved inscription – "Gloria Deo in Excelsis" – in celebration of the reviving fortunes of the family who then owned the place, the Windhams. The interior is splendid too, with the studied informality of both the dining and drawing rooms enlivened by their magnificent seventeenth-century plasterwork ceilings plus sundry *objets d'art*. Many of the **paintings** were purchased by William Windham II, who undertook his Grand Tour in the 1740s – hence the two paintings of the Battle of the Texel by Willem van de Velde the Elder, and the six oils and twenty-odd gouaches of Rome and southern Italy by Giovanni Battista Busiri.

The surrounding **parkland** (daily dawn to dusk; free) divides into two, with woods to the north and open pasture to the south. Footpaths crisscross the park and a popular spot to head for is the medieval **church of St Margaret's** in the southeastern corner, which contains a fine set of brasses and a fancy memorial to William Windham I and his wife by Grinling Gibbons. Nearer the house, the extensive **walled garden** (mid-March to May Mon–Wed, Sat & Sun 11am–5pm; June–Oct daily 11am–5pm; garden only £3.50) features flowering borders and an octagonal dove house, while the stables have been converted into particularly pleasant **tearooms**.

Blickling Hall

Blickling Hall (mid-March to late July, Sept & Oct Wed–Sun 1–5pm; late July to Aug daily except Tues 1–5pm; house & gardens £8.50, gardens only £5.50; NT), set in a sheltered, wooded valley ten miles south of Cromer via the A140, is another grand Jacobean pile. Built for Sir Henry Hobart, a Lord Chief Justice, the hall dates from the 1620s and although it was extensively remodelled over a century later, the modifications respected the integrity of the earlier design. As a result, the long facade, with its slender chimneys, high gables and towers, remained – and remains – the apotheosis of Jacobean design. Inside, highlights include a superb plasterwork ceiling in the Long Gallery and an extraordinarily grand main staircase. There's also a gargantuan tapestry depicting Peter the Great defeating the Swedes, given to one of the family by no less than Catherine the Great. The earthly remains of the last of the male Hobarts are stashed away in a weird pyramidal mausoleum that is located in the **parkland** (daily dawn to dusk) that encircles the house.

Sheringham

SHERINGHAM, a popular seaside town four miles west of Cromer, has an amiable, easy-going air and makes a reasonable overnight stop, though frankly you're still only marking time until you hit the more appealing places further to the west. One of the distinctive features of the town is the smooth beach pebbles that face and decorate the houses, a **flinting technique** used frequently in this part of Norfolk – the best examples here are just off the High Street. The downside is that the power of the waves, which makes the pebbles smooth, has also forced the local council to spend thousands rebuilding the sea defences. The resultant mass of reinforced concrete makes for a less than pleasing seafront – one reason to head, instead, for **Sheringham Park** (daily dawn to dusk; free, but parking extra; NT), the 770-acre woodland park a couple of miles southwest of the town, laid out by Humphry Repton in the early 1800s. The park boasts wonderful battalions of rhododendrons and azaleas, at their best in late May to early June, and a series of lookout posts from which you can admire the view down to the coast. The other out-of-town jaunt is on the **North Norfolk Railway**, whose steam and diesel trains operate along the five miles of track southwest from Sheringham to the modest market town of Holt (April & Oct most days; May–Sept daily; Nov–March limited service; all-day ticket £9.50; ☎01263/820800, ⓦwww.nnrailway.co.uk).

Practicalities

Sheringham's two **train stations** are opposite each other on either side of Station Road. The main station, the terminus of the Bittern Line from Norwich, is just to the east, the North Norfolk Railway station is to the west. The **tourist office** (March–Oct Mon–Sat 10am–5pm, Sun 10am–4pm; ☎01263/824329, ⓦwww.visitnorthnorfolk.com) is in between them on Station Approach – and from here it's a five-minute walk north to the seafront, down Station Road and its continuation, the High Street. There are plenty of **B&Bs**, with one of the best being the unassuming *Two Lifeboats*, 2 High St (☎01263/822401, ⓦwww.twolifeboats.co.uk; ④), a small, traditional hotel on the promenade; most of the ten en-suite bedrooms have sea views.

The tastiest **fish and chips** for miles around are served up at *Dave's*, at 50 High St and 7 Cooperative St. The *Sweet Shop*, 14 High St, sells Ronaldo's ice cream in a mouthwatering battery of flavours, from chocolate and ginger to cinnamon and lavender.

Cley and Blakeney Point

Travelling west from Sheringham, the A149 meanders through a pretty rural landscape offering occasional glimpses of the sea and a shoreline protected by a giant shingle barrier erected after the catastrophic flood of 1953. After seven miles you reach **CLEY-NEXT-THE-SEA**, once a busy wool port but now little more than a row of flint cottages and Georgian mansions set beside a narrow, marshy inlet that (just) gives access to the sea. The original village was destroyed in a fire in 1612, which explains why Cley's fine medieval **church of St Margaret** is located half a mile inland at the very southern edge of the current village, overlooking the green. The Black Death brought church construction to a sudden halt here, hence the contrast between the stunted, unfinished chancel and the splendid nave, which boasts several fine medieval brasses and some folksy fifteenth-century bench-ends depicting animals and grotesques. Cley's other great draw – housed in an old forge on the main street – is the excellent **Cley Smoke House**, selling local smoked fish amongst other delicacies, while nearby **Picnic Fayre** has long been one of the finest delis in East Anglia.

It's about 400 yards east from the village to the mile-long byroad that leads to the shingle mounds of **Cley beach**. This is the starting point for the four-mile hike west out along the spit to **Blakeney Point**, a nature reserve famed for its colonies of terns and seals. The seal colony is made up of several hundred common and grey seals, and the old lifeboat house, at the end of the spit, is now a National Trust information centre. The shifting shingle can make walking difficult, so keep to the low-water mark – which also means that you won't accidentally trample any nests. The easier alternative is to take one of the boat trips to the point from Blakeney or Morston (see below). The Norfolk Coast Path passes close to Cley beach, too, and then continues along the edge of the **Cley Marshes**, which attract a wide variety of waders – and, of course, the accompanying "twitchers".

As for a **place to stay**, Cley holds the outstanding ⚲ *Cley Mill B&B* (☎01263/740209, 🖩 www.cleymill.co.uk; ❼), which occupies a converted windmill complete with sails and a balcony offering wonderful views over the surrounding salt marshes and seashore. The guest rooms, both in the windmill and the adjoining outhouses, are decorated in attractive period style and the best, like the Stone Room, have splendid beamed ceilings; self-catering arrangements are possible as well. At peak times, there's a minimum two-night stay.

Blakeney and Binham Priory

Just a mile west of Cley, **BLAKENEY** is delightful. Once a bustling port exporting fish, corn and salt, it's now a lovely little place with pebble-covered cottages sloping up from a narrow harbour. Crab sandwiches are sold from stalls at the quayside, the meandering high street is flanked by family-run shops, and footpaths stretch out along the sea wall to east and west, offering fine views over the salt marshes. The only sight as such is the **church of St Nicholas**, beside the A149 at the south end of the village, whose sturdy tower and nave are made of flint rubble with stone trimmings, the traditional building materials of north Norfolk. Curiously, the church has a second, much smaller tower at the back. In the nineteenth century this was used as a lighthouse to guide ships into harbour, but its original function is unknown. Inside, the oak and chestnut hammer-beam roof and the delicate rood-screen are the most enjoyable features of the nave, which is attached to a late thirteenth-century chancel, the only survivor from the original Carmelite friary church. With its seven stepped lancet windows, the east window is a rare example of Early English design, though the stained glass is much later.

Blakeney **harbour** is linked to the sea by a narrow channel, which wriggles its way through the salt marshes. The channel is, however, only navigable for a few hours at high tide – at low tide the harbour is no more than a muddy creek (ideal for a bit of quayside crabbing and mud sliding). Depending on the tides, there are **boat trips** from either Blakeney or **Morston quay**, a mile or two to the west, to both Blakeney Point (see p.505) – where passengers have a couple of hours at the point before being ferried back – and to the seal colony just off the point. The main operators advertise departure times on blackboards by the quayside or you can reserve in advance with Beans Boats (☎01263/740505, 🖩 www.beansboattrips.co.uk) or Bishop's Boats (☎01263/740753, 🖩 www.norfolksealtrips.co.uk). Both the seal trips and those to Blakeney Point cost £7.50.

Practicalities

For **accommodation**, the quayside ⚲ *Blakeney Hotel* (☎01263/740797, 🖩 www.blakeney-hotel.co.uk; ❾) is one of the most charming seaside hotels in Norfolk, a rambling building with high-pitched gables and pebble-covered walls. The hotel has a heated indoor swimming pool, a secluded garden, and cosy lounges with exquisite sea views; it also serves outstanding lunches, afternoon teas and dinners. The cheaper rooms can be poky and somewhat airless, so it's worth paying a little more for one with splendid views across the harbour and the marshes. Less expensive options include the *Manor Hotel* (℡01263/740376, Ⓦwww.blakeneymanor.co.uk; ❺), which occupies a low-lying courtyard complex a few yards to the east of the harbour; the *King's Arms* (℡01263/740341, Ⓦwww.blakeneykingsarms.co.uk; ❹), a traditional pub with low, beamed ceilings and seven, modest, modern en-suite bedrooms just back from the quay on Westgate; and the *White Horse* (℡01263/740574, Ⓦwww.blakeneywhitehorse.co.uk; ❺), an old pub in the centre of the village just up from the quay with nine recently revamped guest rooms kitted out in bright and cheerful modern style. Finally, *Morston Hall Hotel* (℡01263/741041, Ⓦwww.morstonhall.com; ❾) is set in an attractive country house of traditional flint-and-brick, a couple of miles west of Blakeney on the A149. The well-appointed bedrooms are decorated in traditional style with modern touches, and the gardens are immaculate. For longer stays, *Quayside Cottages* (℡01462/768627, Ⓦwww.blakeneycottages.co.uk) rents some charming Blakeney cottages from £500 per week in high season, half that in winter.

Both the *White Horse* and the *King's Arms* serve first-rate **bar food** with local seafood the principal speciality; the former also has an excellent **restaurant**, where the menu is very British featuring such delights as haddock fish cakes with red onion and caper salad; main courses average £12.

Binham Priory

The substantial remains of **Binham Priory** (open access; free; EH) boast a handsome rural setting about four miles southwest of Blakeney, on the edge of the hamlet of Binham. The Benedictines established a priory here in the late eleventh century, but long before its suppression in 1540, the priory had gained a bad reputation, its priors renowned for their irresponsibility. One of the worst was William de Somerton, who funded his dabblings in alchemy by selling the church silverware and then the vestments in the fourteenth century. Neither were the monks a picture of contentment – one became insane through excessive meditation, so the prior had him flogged and then kept in solitary confinement until his death. Today, the ruins focus on the **priory church**, whose nave was turned into the parish church during the Reformation. Inside, the nave arcades are a handsome illustration of the transition between the Norman and Early English styles, a triple bank of windows that sheds light on the spartan interior. Among the fittings, look out for the delicately carved font and the remains of the former rood-screen kept at the back of the church. The Protestants whitewashed the screen and then covered it with biblical texts, but the paint is wearing thin and the saints they were keen to conceal have started to pop up again.

Wells-next-the-Sea

Despite its name, **WELLS-NEXT-THE-SEA**, some eight miles west of Blakeney, is situated a good mile or so from open water. In Tudor times, before the harbour silted up, this was one of the great ports of eastern England, a major player in the trade with the Netherlands. Those heady days are long gone and although today it's the only commercially viable port on the north Norfolk coast, this is hardly a huge advantage. More importantly, Wells is also one of the county's more attractive towns, and even though there are no specific sights among its narrow lanes, it does make a very good base for exploring the surrounding coastline.

The town divides into three distinct areas, starting with **The Buttlands**, a broad rectangular green on the south side of town, lined with oak and beech trees and framed by a string of fine Georgian houses; it takes its unusual name from the time it was used for archery practice (a butt being the earthen mound behind the target). North from here, across Station Road, lie the narrow lanes of the town centre with **Staithe Street**, the minuscule main drag, flanked by quaint old-fashioned shops. Staithe Street leads down to the **quay**, a somewhat forlorn affair inhabited by a couple of amusement arcades and fish-and-chip shops, and the mile-long byroad that scuttles north to the **beach**, a handsome sandy tract backed by pine-clad dunes. The beach road is shadowed by a high flood defence and a tiny narrow-gauge **railway**, which scoots down to the beach every twenty minutes or so (Easter–Oct from 10.30am; 90p each way).

Buses to Wells stop on The Buttlands, a short stroll from the **tourist office** at the foot of Staithe Street (mid-March to late May & mid-Sept to Oct daily 10am–2pm; late May to mid-Sept daily 10am–5pm; ☎01328/710885, ⓦwww .visitnorthnorfolk.com). Several of the best **B&Bs** are along Standard Road, which runs up from the eastern end of the quayside. First choice here is *The Normans* (☎01328/710657, ⓦwww.thenormansatwells.co.uk; ❻), in a handsome Georgian red-brick mansion and with four spacious and tastefully decorated rooms; the TV lounge has a log fire and racks of games and the first-floor look-out window provides a wide view over the marshes – binoculars are provided. Similarly enticing, and also on Standard Road, is *Fern Cottage* (☎01328/710306, ⓦwww.ferncottage.co.uk; ❺), a dinky little Georgian house with two immaculate period guest rooms; there is a minimum stay of two nights. There's also a **campsite**, the sprawling and extremely popular *Pinewoods Caravan and Camping Park*, right by the beach (☎01328/710439, ⓦwww .pinewoods.co.uk; closed Nov to mid-March).

There are two smashing **pubs** in town – *The Crown* and *The Globe* – both of which are on The Buttlands and do tasty bar food. *The Globe* also has a restaurant.

Holkham Hall and Holkham Bay

One of the most popular outings from Wells is to **Holkham Hall** (June–Sept Mon–Thurs & Sun noon–5pm; £7; ⓦwww.holkham.co.uk), three miles to the west and a stop on the Coasthopper bus (see p.532). This grand and self-assured (or vainglorious) stately home was designed by the eighteenth-century architect William Kent for the first earl of Leicester and is still owned by the family. The severe sandy-coloured Palladian exterior belies the warmth and richness of the interior, which retains much of its original decoration, notably the much-admired marble hall, with its fluted columns and intricate reliefs. The rich colours of the state rooms are an appropriate backdrop for a fabulous selection of **paintings**, including canvases by Van Dyck, Rubens, Gainsborough and Gaspar Poussin. One real treat is the Landscape Room where around twenty landscape paintings are displayed in the cabinet style of the eighteenth century. Most depict classical stories or landscapes, a poetic view of the past that enthralled the English aristocracy for decades.

The **grounds** (Easter–Oct Mon–Sat 7am–7pm, Sun 9am–7pm; Nov–Easter Mon, Wed & Fri 7am–7pm, Tues & Thurs 10am–7pm; free) are laid out on sandy, saline land, much of it originally salt marsh. The focal point is an eighty-foot-high obelisk, atop a grassy knoll, from where you can view both the hall to the north and the triumphal arch to the south. In common with the rest of the north Norfolk coast, there's plenty of **birdlife** to observe – Holkham's lake attracts Canada geese, herons and grebes and several hundred deer graze the open pastures.

The footpaths latticing the estate stretch as far as the A149, from where a half-mile byroad – Lady Anne's Drive – leads north across the marshes from opposite the *Victoria Hotel* to **Holkham Bay**, which boasts one of the finest beaches on this stretch of coast, with golden sand and pine-studded sand dunes. Warblers, flycatchers and redstarts inhabit the drier coastal reaches, while waders paddle about the mud and salt flats.

Little Walsingham

For centuries **LITTLE WALSINGHAM**, five miles south of Wells (and not to be confused with adjoining Great Walsingham), rivalled Bury St Edmunds and Canterbury as the foremost pilgrimage site in England. It all began in 1061 when the Lady of the Manor, a certain Richeldis de Faverches, was prompted to build a replica of the **Santa Casa** (Mary's home in Nazareth) here – inspired, it is said, by visions of the Virgin Mary. Whatever the reason for her actions, it brought instant fame and fortune to this little Norfolk village and every medieval king from Henry III onwards made at least one trip, walking the last mile barefoot. Both the Augustinians and the Franciscans established themselves here and all seemed set fair when **Henry VIII** followed in his predecessors' footsteps in 1511. However, pilgrim or not, it didn't stop Henry from destroying the shrine in the Dissolution of the 1530s, and at a stroke the village's principal trade came to a halt. Pilgrimages resumed in earnest after 1922, when the local vicar, one Alfred Hope Patten, organized an Anglo-Catholic pilgrimage, the prelude to the building of an Anglican shrine in the 1930s to the chagrin of the diocesan authorities. Today the village does good business out of its holy connections and the narrow-gauge **steam railway** from Wells (late March to Oct daily 3–5 each way; 30min; £7 return; ☏01328/711630, ⓦwww.wellswalsinghamrailway.co.uk).

Little Walsingham now has a number of **shrines** catering to a variety of denominations – there's even a Greek Orthodox Church – though the main one is the **Anglican shrine**, beside Holt Road – and a few yards to the east of the main square, Common Place. It's a strange-looking building, rather like a cross between an English village hall and an Orthodox church, and inside lies a series of small chapels and a Holy Well with healing waters as well as the idiosyncratic Holy House – Santa Casa – which contains the statue of Our Lady of Walsingham.

Shrines apart, Little Walsingham has an attractive centre, beginning with the **Common Place**, whose half-timbered buildings surround a quaint octagonal structure built to protect the village **pump** in the sixteenth century. The **High Street** extends south from here, overlooked by antique brick and half-timbered houses, several of which are given over to shrine shops and religious bookstores. The High Street is also flanked by the impressive, but badly weathered, fifteenth-century **abbey gatehouse** of the old Augustinian priory – look up and you'll spy Christ peering out from a window – though the **ruins** beyond, whose landscaped grounds stretch down to the River Stiffkey, can only be reached from Common Place through the **Shirehall Museum** (April–Oct daily 10am–4.30pm, plus Feb daily 10am–4pm for snowdrop walks; £3 for grounds & museum). Adjoining the south end of the High Street is the town's second square, **Friday Market Place**, a pretty little rectangle of very old houses. Beyond here, about 200 yards out on the Fakenham road, is a second set of ecclesiastical **ruins** – the porridge-like stonework of the old Franciscan Friary (no access).

Monday through Saturday, there's an hourly **bus** service from Wells to Little Walsingham's Anglican shrine, but on Sundays it only runs five times daily. The **train station** (for the steam train from Wells, see p.509) is a five-minute walk from Common Place: from the station, turn left along Egmere Road and take the second major right down Bridewell Street. The **tourist office** is part of the Shirehall Museum, on Common Place (Easter–Sept Mon–Sat 10am–4.30pm; ℡01328/820510). They have details of local **accommodation**, but note that during major **pilgrimages** – in particular the national pilgrimage on the late May Bank Holiday – vacant rooms are thin on the ground. The best local choice is the *Black Lion Hotel*, an old inn on Friday Market (℡01328/820235, Ⓦwww.blacklionwalsingham.com; ❺), with a handful of comfortable en-suite rooms. The **place to eat** is the *Norfolk Riddle Restaurant*, 2 Wells Rd (℡01328/821903), a combined fish-and-chip shop and restaurant supplied – and owned – by local farmers and fishermen.

Burnham Market and Burnham Thorpe

Heading west from Wells on the A149, it's about five miles to the pretty little village of **BURNHAM MARKET**, where an attractive medley of Georgian and Victorian houses surrounds a dinky little green. The village attracts a well-heeled, north London crowd, in no small measure because of the *Hoste Arms* (℡01328/738777, Ⓦwww.hostearms.co.uk; ❼), an old coaching inn overlooking the green that has been intelligently and sympathetically modernized to offer some of the best restaurant and bar food on the coast. The seafood is the big deal here and main courses average around £16, less at lunch times. The guest rooms are round the back and range from the small (verging on the cramped) to the much more expansive (and expensive). The same people also own the village's recently refurbished *Railway Inn*, in the old station on Creake Road (same details), and several local cottages.

A mile or so to the southeast, along a narrow country road, **BURNHAM THORPE** was the birthplace of **Horatio Nelson**, who was born in the village's parsonage on September 29, 1758. Nelson joined the navy at the tender age of 12, and was sent to the West Indies, where he met and married Frances Nisbet, retiring to Burnham Thorpe in 1787. Back in action by 1793, his bravery cost him first the sight of his right eye, and shortly afterwards his right arm. His personal life was equally eventful – famously, his infatuation with Emma Hamilton, wife of the ambassador to Naples, caused the eventual break-up of his marriage. His finest hour was during the Battle of Trafalgar in 1805, when he led the British navy to victory against the combined French and Spanish fleets, a crucial engagement that set the scene for Britain's century-long domination of the high seas. The victory didn't do Nelson much good – he was shot in the chest during the battle and even the kisses of Hardy failed to revive him. Thereafter, Nelson was placed in a barrel of brandy and the pickled body shipped back to England, where he was laid in state at Greenwich and then buried at St Paul's (see p.113).

Nelson's parsonage was demolished years ago, but the admiral is still celebrated in the village's **All Saints Parish Church**, where the lectern is made out of timbers taken from Nelson's last ship, the *Victory*, the chancel sports a Nelson bust, and the south aisle has a small exhibition on his life and times. It was actually Nelson's express wish that he should be buried here, but to no avail. The other place to head for here is the village **pub** (no prizes for guessing the name; Sept–June closed Mon), where Nelson held a farewell party for the locals in 1793. They have kept modernity at bay here – from the old wooden benches through to the serving hatch and tiled floor – and the bar food is first rate: try the venison sausages and mash.

Burnham Deepdale, Brancaster Staithe and Titchwell

From Burnham Market, it's a couple of miles west to tiny **BURNHAM DEEPDALE**, where *Deepdale Farm* (☎01485/210256, ⓦwww .deepdalefarm.co.uk; dorm beds from £12.50, doubles ❷), situated just off the A149, is a lively and very amiable set-up, operating a combined campsite, **café**, art gallery and eco-friendly **hostel** in creatively renovated former stables. Behind the hamlet to the north stretches a tract of lagoon, sandspit and creek that pokes its head out into the ocean, attracting thousands of wildfowl. This is prime **walking territory** and *Deepdale Farm*'s information centre sells hiking maps and will advise on routes. There's also a smashing pub-cum-hotel nearby, ⚓ *The White Horse* (☎01485/210262, ⓦwww .whitehorsebrancaster.co.uk; ❻), just west along the A149 in the hamlet of **BRANCASTER STAITHE**. A dapper little place, there are great views across the marshes from the rear of the premises and the food – especially the fish – is excellent with main courses starting at around £10. There are fifteen en-suite bedrooms here, each kitted out in smart modern style with a scattering of nautical knick-knacks – model boats and so forth.

Pushing on west from Brancaster Staithe, it's a couple of miles more to minuscule **TITCHWELL**, the site of the Titchwell Marsh RSPB Reserve (ⓦwww.rspb.org.uk) and the roadside *Titchwell Manor Hotel* (☎01485/210221, ⓦwww.titchwellmanor.com; ❻), whose thirty ultra-modern rooms occupy a rambling Victorian brick house and an adjacent garden complex.

From Titchwell, it's just six miles more to Hunstanton.

Hunstanton

The Norfolk coast pretty much ends at **HUNSTANTON**, a Victorian seaside resort that grew up to the southwest of the original fishing village – now **Old Hunstanton**. Like Great Yarmouth (see p.501), the place has its fair share of amusement arcades, crazy golf, and entertainment complexes – not to mention England's largest joke shop, The World of Fun – but it has also hung on to its genteel origins, and its sandy beaches, backed by stripy gateau-like cliffs, are among the cleanest in the county.

Hunstanton **tourist office** is in the town hall (daily: April–Sept 10am–5pm; Oct–March 10.30am–4pm; ☎01485/532610) on the wide sloping green that serves as the resort's focal point. They have a long list of **B&Bs** with the nicest (and priciest) among the cottages of Old Hunstanton. There's also a **YHA hostel** in a pair of Victorian town houses at 15 Avenue Rd (☎0870/770 5872, Ⓔhunstanton@yha.org.uk; dorm beds £14, doubles ❶), a brief walk south of Hunstanton green. It has forty beds, in two- to eight-bedded rooms, a cycle store, garden and self-catering kitchen; advance booking is advised.

Sandringham House

Built in 1870 on land purchased by Queen Victoria for her son, the future Edward VII, **Sandringham House** (April–Oct daily from 11am; last entry 4.45pm, Oct 4pm; closed for two weeks late July or early Aug; £9; ⓦwww .sandringhamestate.co.uk) is located off the A149 about eight miles south of

Hunstanton. The house is billed as a private home, but few families have a drawing room crammed with Russian silver and Chinese jade. The **museum** (same times), housed in the old coach and stable block, contains an exhibition of royal memorabilia from dolls to cars, but much more arresting are the beautifully maintained **gardens** (same dates daily from 10.30am; last entry 5pm, Oct 4pm), a mass of rhododendrons and azaleas in spring and early summer. The estate's sandy soil is also ideal for game birds, which was the attraction of the place for the terminally bored Edward, whose tradition of posh shooting parties is still followed by the royals.

Local **buses** #40 and #41 make the journey to Sandringham from Hunstanton, as does the Coasthopper (see p.532).

Castle Rising

In remarkably good condition, the shell of the twelfth-century keep of **Castle Rising** (April–Oct daily 10am–6pm; Nov–March Wed–Sun 10am–4pm; £3.85; EH) stands at the centre of extensive earth works four miles south of Sandringham along the A149. Towering over the surrounding flatlands, it's a powerful, imposing structure and some of its finer architectural details have survived as well, most notably its precise blind arcading and the interior galleries gouged out of the original defensive walls. The adjacent village is laid out on a grid plan and contains a quadrangle of beautiful seventeenth-century **almshouses**, whose elderly inhabitants still go to church in red cloaks and pointed black hats, the colours of the original benefactor, the Earl of Northampton.

Bus #41 (Mon–Sat hourly, Sun every 2hr), linking Hunstanton with King's Lynn, stops off at the *Black Horse* pub in the village.

King's Lynn and around

An ancient port, **KING'S LYNN** straddles the canalized mouth of the River Great Ouse a mile or so before it slides into The Wash. Before the river was tamed, the town occupied an improbably marshy location, but it was strategically placed for easy access to seven English counties. Consequently, the town's merchants grew rich importing fish from Scandinavia, timber from the Baltic and wine from France, while exporting wool, salt and corn to the Hanseatic ports. The good times came to an end when the focus of maritime trade moved to the Atlantic seaboard, but its port struggled on until it was reinvigorated in the 1970s by the burgeoning trade between the UK and its EU partners. Much of the old centre was demolished during the 1950s and 1960s to make way for commercial development and, as a result, Lynn lacks the concentrated historic charm of towns such as Bury St Edmunds and Lavenham. Nonetheless it does have a clutch of well-preserved buildings, including the oldest guildhall in the country, which taken together are well worth a couple of hours. In addition, King's Lynn's lively, open-air **markets** attract large fenland crowds – there's one on the Saturday Market Place every Saturday and two others on the Tuesday Market Place, on Tuesdays and Fridays – and the town is also within comfortable striking distance of both the ruined Norman priory and castle of **Castle Acre** and the prehistoric flint mines of **Grimes Graves**, which are also an easy detour if you're heading onto Ely (see p.515) or Cambridge (see p.518).

Arrival, information and accommodation

From the **train station**, it's a short walk west along Waterloo Street to Railway Road, the principal north–south thoroughfare, which borders the eastern edge of the town centre on the east bank of the river. The **bus station** is nearer the centre, about 150 yards to the west of Railway Road. The **tourist office** is by the river, bang in the centre in the Custom House on Purfleet Quay (Mon–Sat 10am–4/5pm, Sun noon–4/5pm; ℡01553/763044, ⓦ www.west-norfolk .gov.uk). They have the details of a number of **B&Bs**, with one of the best being *The Bank House*, an intelligently converted Georgian town house down by the river and the tourist office on King's Staithe Square (℡01553/660492, ⓦ www.thebankhouse.co.uk; ⑤); there are five en-suite guest rooms here, each decorated in an unfussy, homely manner. Alternatively, *The Old Rectory*, 33 Goodwins Rd (℡01553/768544, ⓦ www.theoldrectory-kingslynn.com; ❸), occupies a good-looking nineteenth-century villa and has four attractively decorated en-suite guest rooms; Goodwins Road is on the southern edge of town, east off London Road (the A148). There's also a small, central YHA **hostel** in old stone premises on College Lane, yards from both the tourist office and the river (℡0870/770 5902, ⓔkingslynn@yha.org.uk; dorm beds £12). It has 35 beds in one- and three- to ten-bedded rooms, and advance reservations are advised.

The Town

King's Lynn's historic core lies in the two blocks between the High Street and the quayside. A good place to begin is the **Saturday Market Place**, the older and smaller of the town's two marketplaces, presided over by the hybrid **church of St Margaret**, which contains two of the most fanciful medieval brasses in East Anglia. These are the Walsoken brass, adorned with country scenes, and the Braunche brass, named after a certain Robert Braunche and depicting the lavish feast he laid on for Edward III. Across the square is Lynn's prettiest building, the **Trinity Guildhall**, its wonderful chequered flint and stone facade dating to 1421 and repeated in both the Elizabethan addition to the left and in the adjoining Victorian town hall. Next door to the Guildhall is the entrance to the **Tales of the Old Gaol House** (April–Oct Mon–Sat 10am–5pm; Nov–March Tues–Sat 10am–4pm; £2.80), which incorporates a series of eighteenth-century cells within a small museum on local baddies. There's also access to the Guildhall undercroft, which displays an exhibition on the town's rich collection of civic regalia. This is actually more stimulating than you might think, since the treasures include King John's cup and sword, which were gifted to the town prior to the king's ill-fated and ill-timed dash across The Wash. The king and his retinue were caught by the incoming waters and, although they saved themselves, they lost the crown jewels – and people have been looking for them ever since.

Of the medieval warehouses that survive along the quayside, the most evocative is the former **Hanseatic Warehouse**, built around 1475, whose half-timbered upper floor juts unevenly over the cobbles of St Margaret's Lane. The other architectural highlight is a short stroll north, at the end of the gentle Georgian curve of Queen Street. It's here you'll find the splendid **Custom House**, erected in 1683 in a style clearly influenced by the Dutch. There are classical pilasters, petite dormer windows and a roof-top balustrade, but it's the dinky little cupola that catches the eye. The Custom House holds the tourist office (see above) and overlooks **Purfleet Quay**, a short and stumpy harbour once packed with merchant ships.

Beyond the Custom House, King Street, with its much wider berth, continues where Queen Street ends. On the left, just after Ferry Lane, stands Lynn's most precious building, **St George's Guildhall**, dating from 1410 and one of the oldest surviving guildhalls in England. It was a theatre in Elizabethan times and is now part of the King's Lynn Arts Centre (see below). Beyond the Guildhall is the **Tuesday Market Place**, with the pastel-pink *Duke's Head Hotel*, dating from 1689, and the Neoclassical **Corn Exchange** (also now an art centre; see below) standing out against an otherwise unspectacular assemblage.

Eating, drinking and entertainment

The best **café** in town is *Crofters Coffee Shop* (closed Sun), located in the undercroft of St George's Guildhall at the King's Lynn Arts Centre, 29 King St. They serve tasty salads and light meals plus sandwiches and soups. There are two quality restaurants, kicking off with the *Riverside*, 27 King St (℡01553/773134; closed Sun), in a handsomely converted, fifteenth-century warehouse overlooking the river from the back of the arts centre. The menu here is inventive, mixing British and Italian dishes and styles, with main courses starting at £14. A second choice is *Maggie's*, 11 Saturday Market Place (℡01553/771483; closed Sun & Mon), where the menu is firmly Modern British – spinach stuffed lamb, for instance – with two courses costing £20.

Entertainment in Lynn revolves around the **King's Lynn Arts Centre**, 29 King St (℡01553/764864, ⓦwww.kingslynnarts.co.uk), which stages a wide range of performances and exhibitions both here and in several other downtown venues, including the old Corn Exchange, on Tuesday Market Place.

East of King's Lynn: Castle Acre

The solitary hamlet of **CASTLE ACRE** spreads over one of the few hilltops in Norfolk some twenty miles east of King's Lynn, just off the A47. Inevitably, the hill attracted the military attention of the Normans, and one of William I's most trusted lieutenants, a certain William Warenne, built a fortified manor house here shortly after the Conquest; this was turned into a fully fledged **castle** (open access; free; EH) in the 1140s. Most of the stonework disappeared centuries ago, but the Norman **earthworks** have survived in fine fettle and are some of the most complete in England, with the steep mound of the keep and the banks and deep ditches of the bailey still easy to discern and to clamber over.

The castle is at one end of the village and at the other, in an open field a five- to ten-minute walk away, stand the substantial medieval ruins of **Castle Acre Priory** (April–Sept daily 10am–6pm; Oct–March Mon & Thurs–Sun 10am–4pm; £4.70; EH), founded by Warenne's son in 1090. The most significant remains of this, one of the earliest Cluniac monasteries in England, are the gatehouse, with its chequered flint and stone facade, and the west front of the priory church, an excellent illustration of the way different medieval styles were blended together, with the Norman doorway and delicate blind arcading set beneath an arching Early English window.

The village, which has maintained much of its Norman street plan, zeroes in on its green, where the *Castlegate Coffee Shop* serves up a range of inexpensive snacks and light meals.

Southeast of King's Lynn: Grimes Graves

Located 25 miles or so southeast of King's Lynn via the A10 and the A134, **Grimes Graves** is the earliest significant industrial site in Europe, dating from around 2000 BC (March & Oct Mon & Thurs–Sun 10am–5pm; April–Sept daily 10am–6pm; £2.90; EH). The site lies on a slice of open heathland that looks as if it has been bombarded by giant golf balls, the shallow indentations the results of Stone Age flint mining. The mines were not identified as such until they were excavated in the 1870s, though they owe their collective name to the Anglo-Saxons, who called them after one of their gods, Grim. English Heritage has opened one of the shafts and visitors can descend no less than thirty feet by ladder.

Ely and around

Perched on a mound of clay above the River Great Ouse about thirty miles south of King's Lynn, the attractive little town of **ELY** – literally "eel island" – was to all intents and purposes a true island until the draining of the fens in the seventeenth century. Up until then, the town was encircled by treacherous marshland, which could only be crossed with the help of the local "fen-slodgers" who knew the firm tussock paths. In 1070, **Hereward the Wake** turned this inaccessibility to military advantage, holding out against the Normans and forcing William the Conqueror to undertake a prolonged siege – and finally to build an improvised road floated on bundles of sticks. Centuries later, the Victorian writer Charles Kingsley resurrected this obscure conflict in his novel *Hereward the Wake*. He presented the protagonist as the Last of the English who "never really bent their necks to the Norman yoke and … kept alive those free institutions which were the germs of our British liberty" – a heady mixture of nationalism and historical poppycock that went down a storm.

Since then, Ely has always been associated with Hereward, which is really rather ridiculous as Ely is, above all else, an ecclesiastical town and a Norman one to boot. The Normans built the **cathedral**, a towering structure visible for miles across the flat fenland landscape and Ely's main sight. It's easy to see the town on a day-trip from Cambridge, but Ely does make a pleasant night's stop in its own right. It's also relatively close to Cambridgeshire's most important ecclesiastical sight – namely the cathedral at **Peterborough** – not to mention the undrained and unmolested **Wicken Fen.**

Arrival, information and accommodation

Ely is a major rail intersection, receiving direct trains from as far afield as Liverpool, Norwich and London King's Cross, as well as from Cambridge, just twenty minutes to the south. From Ely **train station**, it's a ten-minute walk to the cathedral, straight up Station Road and its continuation Back Hill and then The Gallery. **Buses** (from King's Lynn and Cambridge) stop on Market Street immediately north of the cathedral. The **tourist office**, in Oliver Cromwell's House at 29 St Mary's St (April–Oct daily 10am–5.30pm; Nov–March Mon–Fri & Sun 11am–4pm, Sat 10am–5pm; ☎01353/662062, ⓦwww.eastcambs.gov.uk/tourism), issues free town maps and will help with accommodation.

Ely has several appealing **B&Bs**, with first choice being *Cathedral House*, in an attractive Georgian town house a brief stroll from the cathedral at 17 St Mary's St (☎01353/662 124, ⓦwww.cathedralhouse.co.uk; no credit cards; ④). All the guest rooms here are en suite and each comes complete with period details, though they all tend to be a tad spartan. A second option is *Sycamore House*, which occupies an attractive and well-maintained detached house on the

southwest edge of town at 91 Cambridge Rd (℡01353/662139, ⓦwww
.sycamoreguesthouse.co.uk; no credit cards; ❹); they have four en suite, guest
rooms and all are decorated in a cheerful, vaguely retro style.

Ely Cathedral

Ely Cathedral (June–Sept daily 7am–7pm; Oct–May Mon–Sat 7.30am–6pm,
Sun 7.30am–5pm; Mon–Sat £5.20, Sun free; ⓦwww.cathedral.ely.anglican
.org) is one of the most impressive churches in England, but the **west facade**,
where visitors enter, has been an oddly lopsided affair ever since one of the
transepts collapsed in a storm in 1701. Nonetheless, the remaining transept,
which was completed in the 1180s, is an imposing structure, its dog-tooth
windows, castellated towers and blind arcading possessing all the rough, almost
brutal charm of the Normans. The cathedral is actually seen to best advantage
from its south side, from where the crenellated towers of the west facade can be
seen to balance the prickly finials to the east with the church's distinctive
lantern nudging up in between.

The first things to strike you as you enter the **nave** are the sheer length of the
building and the lively nineteenth-century painted ceiling, largely the work of
amateur volunteers. The nave's procession of plain late-Norman arches, built
around the same time as those at Peterborough (see p.518), leads to the
architectural feature that makes Ely so special, the **octagon** – the only one of
its kind in England – built in 1322 to replace the collapsed central tower. Its
construction, employing the largest oaks available in England to support some
four hundred tons of glass and lead, remains one of the wonders of the medieval
world, and the effect, as you look up into this Gothic dome, is simply
breathtaking. From April to October, **Octagon Tower tours** (£3.20 extra;
reservations & schedule ℡01353/660344) depart two to four times daily from
the desk at the entrance, venturing up into the octagon itself.

When the central tower collapsed, it fell eastwards onto the **choir**, the first three
bays of which were rebuilt at the same time as the octagon in the Decorated style
– in contrast to the plainer Early English of the choir bays beyond. In the floor of
the choir, a commemorative plaque marks the site of the shrine of **St Ethelreda**,
founder of the abbey in 673, who, despite being twice married, is honoured liturgi-
cally as a virgin. The shrine once attracted pilgrims from far and wide, but it was
destroyed during the Reformation. At the east end of the cathedral is the
thirteenth-century **presbytery**, where there are two medieval **chantry chapels**,
the more charming of which (on the left) is an elaborate Renaissance affair dated
to 1488. The other marvel is the **Lady Chapel**, a separate building accessible via
the north transept. It lost its sculpture and its stained glass during the Reformation,
but its fan vaulting remains, an exquisite example of English Gothic. Retracing
your steps, the south triforium near the main entrance holds the **Stained Glass
Museum** (Mon–Fri 10.30am–5pm, Sat 10.30am–5/5.30pm, Sun noon–4.30/6pm;
£3.50), an Anglican money-spinner exhibiting examples of this applied art from
1200 to the present day.

At the back of the cathedral, on its south side, is a fine ensemble of medieval
domestic architecture, a higgledy-piggledy assortment of old stone, brick and
half-timbered buildings that runs south from the **Infirmary complex**, abutting
the presbytery, to the Prior's buildings near the sturdy **Porta gate**, once the
principal entrance to the monastery complex. Many of the buildings are used
by the King's boarding school – where the cathedral's choristers are trained –
others by the clergy. You can't go in any of them but it's still a pleasant area to
stroll; a free map and brochure are available from the cathedral.

The rest of the town

The rest of Ely is pleasant and pretty enough, but hardly compelling after the wonders of the cathedral. To the north of the church is the **High Street**, a slender thoroughfare lined by Georgian buildings and old-fashioned shops that makes for an enjoyable browse. If you push on past the Market Place at its east end, then Forehill and its continuation Waterside lead down to the riverside **Babylon Gallery** (Tues–Sat 10am–4pm, Sun 11am–4pm; free; ☎01353/616375, ⓦwww.babylongallery.co.uk), where an imaginative programme of temporary exhibitions featuring contemporary art and craft is displayed in an attractively renovated old brewery warehouse. Alternatively, head west from the cathedral entrance across the Palace Green to **Oliver Cromwell's House** at 29 St Mary's St (April–Oct daily 10am–5.30pm; Nov–March Mon–Fri & Sun 11am–4pm Sat 10am–5pm; £4), a timber-framed former vicarage, which holds a small exhibition on the Protector's ten-year sojourn in Ely, when he was employed as a tithe collector.

Eating and drinking

Amongst a battalion of **tearooms**, the most engaging is *The Almonry*, on the High Street, which offers smashing views of the cathedral from its outside area. The food hardly fires the palate, but it's competent enough – and the same stricture applies to the *Steeplegate Tea Rooms*, also backing onto the cathedral grounds at 16–18 High St (closed Sun). The best **restaurant** in town is

---

The Fens – and Wicken Fen

One of the strangest of all English landscapes, the **Fens** cover a vast area of eastern England from just north of Cambridge right up to Boston in Lincolnshire. For centuries, they were an inhospitable wilderness of quaking bogs and marshland, punctuated by clay islands on which small communities eked out a livelihood cutting peat for fuel, using reeds for thatching and living on a diet of fish and wildfowl. Piecemeal land reclamation took place throughout the Middle Ages, but it wasn't until the seventeenth century that the systematic draining of the fens was undertaken – amid fierce local opposition – by the Dutch engineer **Cornelius Vermuyden**. This wholesale draining had unforeseen consequences: as it dried out, the peaty soil shrank to below the level of the rivers, causing frequent flooding, and the region's **windmills**, which had previously been vital in keeping the waters at bay, compounded the problem by causing further shrinkage. The engineers had to do some rapid backtracking and the task of draining the fens was only completed in the 1820s following the introduction of **steam-driven pumps**, leviathans which could control water levels with much greater precision. Drained, the fens now comprise some of the most fertile agricultural land in the Europe.

At **Wicken Fen National Nature Reserve** (daily dawn to dusk; ☎01353/720274; £5, including cottage; NT), nine miles south of Ely via the A10 and A1123, you can visit one of the few remaining areas of undrained fenland. Its survival is thanks to a group of Victorian entomologists who donated the land to the National Trust in 1899, making it the oldest nature reserve in the UK. The seven hundred acres are undrained but not uncultivated – sedge and reed cutting are still carried out to preserve the landscape as it is – and the reserve is readily explored by means of several easy and clearly marked **footpaths**, one of which – the easiest – is a three-quarter-of-a-mile stroll along a boardwalk. The boardwalk trail passes one of the last surviving fenland wind pumps and the reserve holds about ten bird-watching hides. At the main entrance, there's a **visitor centre** (Tues–Sun 10am–5pm) and an antique fenland thatched **cottage** (April–Oct Sun only 2–5pm). The visitor centre organizes a variety of events and guided walks – call ahead for details.

The Boathouse, an expansive modern place down by the river at 5 Annesdale (☎01353/664388). The menu, which features local, seasonal ingredients, is firmly British with the likes of pheasant and skate, mutton and – the house speciality – sausages and mash; mains average £13, but the sausages cost £10.

Ely has two excellent **pubs** on Silver Street, a right turn off The Gallery, which runs south from the cathedral's main entrance. These are the relaxed and welcoming *Fountain* at no. 1, and the infinitely cosy *Prince Albert*, at no. 62. Both serve real ales.

Northwest of Ely: Peterborough

Booming **PETERBOROUGH**, some thirty-odd miles northwest of Ely, has shaken off its dusty history as a brick-making town and attracted a raft of high-tech industries, whose employees now occupy the sprawling, leafy suburbs that surround its compact centre. For the casual visitor, however, it has but one distinct – and unmissable – attraction, its superb Norman **cathedral** (Mon–Fri 9am–6.30pm, Sat 9am–5pm, Sun 7.30am–5pm; £3.50 suggested donation; ⓦwww.peterborough-cathedral.org.uk). A site of Christian worship since the seventh century, the first two churches here were destroyed – the original Saxon monastery by the Danes in 870, its replacement by fire in 1116. Work on the present structure began a year after the fire and was largely completed within the century. The one significant later addition is the thirteenth-century **west facade**, one of the most magnificent in England, made up of three grandiloquent, deeply recessed arches, though the purity of the design is marred slightly by an incongruous central porch added in 1370.

The **interior** is a wonderful example of Norman architecture. Round-arched rib vaults and shallow blind arcades line the nave, while up above the painted wooden ceiling, dating from 1220, is an exquisite example of medieval art, one of the most important in Europe. There are several notable tombs in the cathedral, too, beginning with that of **Catherine of Aragon**, who is buried in the north aisle of the presbytery under a slab of black Irish marble. Catherine was Henry VIII's first wife and the king's determination to divorce her in favour of Anne Boleyn precipitated the English Reformation. The marriage was finally declared void in 1533, but much to the king's chagrin, Catherine insisted till her death (in 1536) that she remained Henry's lawful wife. Mary Queen of Scots was also interred here, in the south aisle, after her execution in 1587, but 25 years later she was transferred to Westminster Abbey.

With frequent connections in all directions – including Ely – Peterborough is easy to reach by rail. The **train station** is a short, signposted walk across the pedestrianized town centre from the cathedral, while the **tourist office** is in the lovely little close that surrounds the cathedral at no. 3–5 (July–Sept Mon–Sat 9am–5pm, Sun noon–4pm; Oct–June Mon–Sat 10am–4pm; ☎01733/452336, ⓦwww.peterborough.gov.uk). There are, as you would expect, lots of **cafés** in the town centre and one of the most agreeable is *Beckets*, a traditional little place serving tasty snacks in the Cathedral Precincts.

Cambridge and around

On the whole, **CAMBRIDGE** is a much quieter and more secluded place than Oxford, though for the visitor what really sets it apart from its scholarly rival is "**The Backs**" – the green sward of land that straddles the languid River Cam, providing exquisite views over the backs of the old colleges. At the front, the handsome facades of these same colleges dominate the layout of the city centre, lining up along the main streets. Most of the older colleges date back to the late thirteenth and early fourteenth centuries and are designed to a similar plan with the main gate leading through to a series of "courts," typically a carefully manicured slab of lawn surrounded on all four sides by college residences or offices. Many of the buildings are extraordinarily beautiful, but the most famous is **King's College**, whose magnificent **King's College Chapel** is one of the great statements of late Gothic architecture. There are 31 university colleges in total, each an independent, self-governing body, proud of its achievements and attracting – for the most part at least – a close loyalty from its students, amongst whom privately educated boys remain hopelessly over-represented. This intrinsic elitism is amplified by all sorts of eccentric (some say charming) rules and regulations and by an arcane vocabulary unfamiliar to ordinary mortals. "Heads of house" are heads of college – whether they be "Masters", "Provosts", "Principals", "Presidents" or "Wardens" – and most of them are elected by the "Fellows", graduates or senior members with teaching responsibilities. "The Other Place" is Oxford; "bedders" are college domestics; and "porters" man the gates and keep good order. There are **three terms** – Michaelmas (Oct–Dec), Lent (Jan–March) and Easter (April–June) – and the students' biggest annual knees-up, the "May balls", are held in June.

Cambridge is an extremely compact place, and you can **walk** round the centre, visiting the most interesting colleges, in an afternoon. A more thorough exploration, covering more of the colleges, a visit to the fine art of the **Fitzwilliam Museum** and a leisurely afternoon on a **punt**, will, however, take at least a couple of days. If possible, avoid coming in high summer, when the students are replaced by hordes of sightseers and posses of foreign-language students, though you can still miss the crowds by getting up early – the tourists only start to appear in numbers from around 10am.

Some history

Tradition has it that Cambridge was founded in the late 1220s by scholastic refugees from Oxford, who fled the town after one of their number was lynched by hostile townsfolk – though the first proper college wasn't founded until 1271. Rivalry has existed between the two institutions ever since – epitomized by the annual Boat Race on the River Thames – while internal tensions between "**town and gown**" have inevitably plagued a place where, from the late fourteenth century onwards, the university has tended to control local life. The first (but by no means the last) rebellion against the scholars occurred during the Peasants' Revolt of 1381, and had to be put down with armed troops by the Bishop of Norwich.

In the sixteenth century, Cambridge became a centre of **church reformism**, educating some of the most famous Protestant preachers in the country, including Cranmer, Latimer and Ridley, all of whom were martyred in Oxford by Mary Tudor. Later, during the Civil War, Cambridge once again found itself at the centre of events: **Oliver Cromwell** was both a graduate of Sidney Sussex and the local MP, though the university itself was largely Royalist. After the Restoration, the university regained most of its privileges, but by the eighteenth century it was in the doldrums, better known, as Byron put it, for its "din and drunkenness" than for its academic record.

The university finally lost its ancient **privileges** over the town in Victorian times, when the latter expanded rapidly thanks to the arrival of the railway. The town's population quadrupled between 1800 and 1900 and meanwhile the university expanded too, with the number of students increasing by leaps and bounds following the broadening of the curriculum to include new subjects such as natural science and history. Change was slower in coming in the battle for **equality of the sexes**. The first two women's colleges were founded in the 1870s, but it was only in 1947 that women were actually awarded degrees, and one or two colleges held out against accepting women students until the 1980s. In the meantime, the city and university acquired a reputation as a **high-tech centre** of excellence, known locally as "Silicon Fen". Cambridge has always been in the vanguard of scientific research – its alumni have garnered no fewer than ninety Nobel prizes – and it has now become a major international player in the lucrative electronic communications industry.

Arrival, information and getting around

Cambridge **train station** is a mile or so to the southeast of the city centre, off Hills Road. It's an easy but tedious twenty-minute walk into the centre, or take local bus #3 to the **bus** stop on Emmanuel Street, which is itself yards from the Drummer Street long-distance **bus station**. **Stansted**, London's third airport, is just thirty miles south of Cambridge on the M11; there are hourly trains from the airport to the city, and regular bus services too. Arriving by **car**, you'll find much of the city centre closed to traffic and on-street parking well-nigh impossible to find; for a day-trip, at least, the best option is a **park-and-ride** car park; they are signposted on all major approaches.

Cambridge's well-equipped **tourist office** is bang in the centre of town in the old library, on Wheeler Street, off King's Parade (Mon–Fri 10am–5.30pm, Sat 10am–5pm, plus April–Sept Sun 11am–3pm; ☎0871/226 8006, ⓦwww.visitcambridge.org). They issue free city maps, have lots of leaflets on local attractions and can book accommodation (see opposite).

The city centre is small enough to walk round comfortably, so apart from getting to and from the train station, you shouldn't have to use the city's buses. On the other hand, **cycling** is an enjoyable way of getting around and has long been extremely popular with locals and students alike. There are **bike rental**

▲ Punting on the Cam

Messing about on the water

The quintessential Cambridge activity, **punting** is a good deal harder than it looks. First-timers find themselves zigzagging across the water and "punt jams" are very common on the stretch of the River Cam beside The Backs in summer. **Punt rental** is available at several points, including the boatyard at Mill Lane (beside the Silver Street bridge), at Magdalene Bridge, and at the Garret Hostel Lane bridge at the back of Trinity College. It costs around £14 an hour (most places charge a deposit), and punts can hold up to six people. Alternatively, you can hire a **chauffeured punt** from any of the rental places for about £10 per person per hour.

Cambridge is also famous for its **rowing clubs**, which are clustered along the north bank of the river across from Midsummer Common. For their convenience, this stretch of water is punt-free. The most important inter-college races are the **May Bumps**, which, confusingly, take place in June.

outlets dotted all over town (see p.531), but when and wherever you leave your bike, padlock it to something immovable as bike theft is not infrequent. The tourist office runs very popular **walking tours** of the centre and its key colleges (1–4 daily; 2hr; £10; reservations on ☎01223/457574); book well in advance in summer.

Accommodation

Cambridge is short of central accommodation and those few **hotels** that do occupy prime locations are expensive. That said, Chesterton Lane and its continuation, Chesterton Road, the busy street running east from the top of Magdalene Street, have several reasonably priced hotels and guesthouses. There are lots of **B&Bs** on the outskirts of town, with several near the train station, and it's here you'll also find the **YHA hostel**. In high season, when vacant rooms are often thin on the ground, the tourist office's efficient **accommodation booking service** can be very useful (☎01223/457581, Ⓦ www.visitcambridge.org).

Arundel House Hotel 53 Chesterton Rd ☎01223/367701, Ⓦ www.arundelhousehotels .co.uk. One of the better mid-range hotel choices, in a converted row of late-Victorian houses overlooking the river and Jesus Green. Neat and tidy rooms, but mundane modern furnishings. ❻

Cambridge Garden House Hotel Granta Place, Mill Lane ☎01223/259988, Ⓦ www .cambridgegardenhouse.com. Outstanding hotel, the city's best, in a strikingly modern 1960s building a couple of minutes' walk from the centre. The foyer is wide and open, the breakfasts are first-rate, and some rooms have balconies overlooking the river (though the views are hardly riveting). ❼

Cambridge YHA 97 Tenison Rd ☎0870/770 5742, Ⓔ cambridge@yha.org.uk. This well-equipped hostel has laundry and self-catering facilities, a cycle store, a games room and a small courtyard garden. There are one hundred beds in two- to eight-bedded rooms and advance reservations are advised. It's located close to the train station – Tenison Road is a right turn a couple of hundred yards down Station Road. Dorm beds £17.50, doubles ❶

City Roomz Station Rd ☎01223/304050, Ⓦ www .cityroomz.com. This popular hotel is in an imaginatively converted granary warehouse, right outside the train station. Most of the rooms are bunk-style affairs done out in the manner of a ship's cabin, and there are a few doubles too. All rooms are en suite, with shower and TV. ❸

Crowne Plaza Hotel Cambridge 20 Downing St ☎0870/400 9180, Ⓦ www.ichotelsgroup.com. Immaculately tailored behind a dignified facade, this sleek and slick hotel is first-rate. The foyer is adventurously designed and the rooms are resolutely modern in efficient chain-hotel style. Great central location too. ❼

Lensfield Hotel 53 Lensfield Rd ☎01223/355017, Ⓦ www.lensfieldhotel.co.uk.

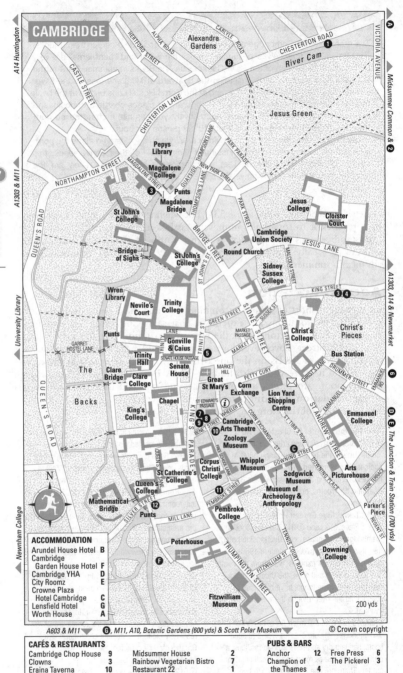

CAMBRIDGE

CHESTERTON ROAD
River Cam
Alexandra Gardens
Jesus Green
CARLYLE ROAD
VICTORIA AVENUE
ALPHA ROAD
HERTFORD STREET
CASTLE STREET
CHESTERTON LANE
THOMPSON'S LANE
NEW PARK STREET
PARK PARADE
Pepys Library
Magdalene College
NORTHAMPTON STREET
MAGDALENE STREET
QUAYSIDE
Punts
Magdalene Bridge
Jesus College
Cloister Court
St John's College
QUEEN'S ROAD
Bridge of Sighs
St John's College
BRIDGE STREET
Round Church
Cambridge Union Society
JESUS LANE
Sidney Sussex College
MALCOLM STREET
KING STREET
Wren Library
Nevile's Court
Trinity College
ST JOHN'S STREET
GREEN STREET
SIDNEY STREET
SUSSEX ST
Christ's College
Christ's Pieces
Bus Station
University Library
Punts
GARRET HOSTEL LANE
TRINITY LANE
Gonville & Caius
TRINITY ST
MARKET PASSAGE
MARKET ST
HOBSON STREET
CHRIST'S LANE
DRUMMER STREET
EMMANUEL RD
The
Clare Bridge
Trinity Hall
Clare College
SENATE HOUSE PASSAGE
Senate House
MARKET HILL
Great St Mary's
Corn Exchange
PETTY CURY
ST TIBB'S ROW
ST ANDREW'S STREET
Emmanuel College
Backs
King's College
Chapel
ST EDWARD'S PASSAGE
KING'S PARADE
WHEELER ST
Lion Yard Shopping Centre
CORN EXCHANGE ST
Cambridge Arts Theatre
Zoology Museum
Whipple Museum
EMMANUEL ST
Arts Picturehouse
QUEEN'S ROAD
Corpus Christi College
St Catherine's College
Queens' College
FREE SCHOOL LANE
BENE'T STREET
DOWNING STREET
DOWNING PLACE
Sedgwick Museum
Museum of Archeology & Anthropology
PEMBROKE STREET
Pembroke College
PARK TERRACE
Parker's Piece
REGENT ST
Mathematical Bridge
SILVER STREET
Punts
MILL LANE
Peterhouse
TRUMPINGTON STREET
TENNIS COURT ROAD
Downing College
FITZWILLIAM STREET
Fitzwilliam Museum

0   200 yds

© Crown copyright

ACCOMMODATION

Arundel House Hotel	B
Cambridge Garden House Hotel	F
Cambridge YHA	D
City Roomz	E
Crowne Plaza Hotel Cambridge	C
Lensfield Hotel	G
Worth House	A

A14 Huntingdon
A1303 & M11
A1303 A14 & Newmarket
The Junction & Train Station (700 yds)
Midsummer Common & 2
A603 & M11
M11, A10, Botanic Gardens (600 yds) & Scott Polar Museum
Newnham College

CAFÉS & RESTAURANTS

Cambridge Chop House	9	Midsummer House	2
Clowns	3	Rainbow Vegetarian Bistro	7
Eraina Taverna	10	Restaurant 22	1
Michaelhouse Café	5	Trockel, Ullmann und Freunde	11

PUBS & BARS

Anchor	12	Free Press	6
Champion of the Thames	4	The Pickerel	3
Eagle	8		

Well-kept, medium-sized hotel in Victorian premises on the inner ring road, just round the corner from the Fitzwilliam Museum. The hotel's pleasantly appointed guest rooms are decorated in frilly retro style. ⑥

Worth House 152 Chesterton Rd ☎01223/316074, ⓦwww.worth-house.co.uk. Very recommendable B&B in a tastefully upgraded Victorian house, about twenty minutes' walk from the centre. Four bedrooms, all en suite. ③

The City

Cambridge's **main shopping street** is Bridge Street, which becomes Sidney Street, St Andrew's Street and finally Regent Street; the other main thoroughfare is the procession of St John's Street, Trinity Street, King's Parade and Trumpington Street. The university developed on the land west of this latter route along the banks of the River Cam, and now forms a continuous half-mile parade of **colleges** from Peterhouse to Magdalene, with sundry others scattered about the periphery. The **Fitzwilliam Museum**, holding the city's finest art collection, is along Trumpington Street just south of Peterhouse. The account below starts with **King's College**, whose **chapel** is the university's most celebrated attraction, and covers the rest of the city in a broadly clockwise direction.

King's College and King's College Chapel

Henry VI founded **King's College** (term time: Mon–Fri 9.30am–3.30pm, Sat 9.30am–3.15pm, Sun 1.15–2.15pm; rest of year: Mon–Sat 9.30am–4.30pm, Sun 10am–5pm; ☎01223/331100, ⓦwww.kings.cam.ac.uk) in 1441, but he was disappointed with his initial efforts, so four years later he cleared away half of medieval Cambridge to make room for a much grander foundation. His plans were ambitious, but the Wars of the Roses – and bouts of royal insanity – intervened and by the time of his death in 1471 very little had been finished and work on what was intended to be Henry's **Great Court** hadn't even started. This part of the site remained empty for no less than three hundred years and the Great Court complex of today – facing King's Parade from behind a long stone screen – is largely Neo-Gothic, built in the 1820s to a design by William Wilkins.

Henry's workmen did, however, start on the college's finest building, the much-celebrated **King's College Chapel** (same times; £4.50), on the north side of today's Great Court. Committed to canvas by Turner and Canaletto, and eulogized in no fewer than three sonnets by Wordsworth, it's now best known for its **boys' choir**, whose members process across the college grounds during term time in their antiquated garb to sing evensong (Tues–Sat at 5.30pm) and carols on Christmas Eve. Begun in 1446 and over sixty years in the making, the chapel is an extraordinary building. From the outside, it seems impossibly slender, its streamlined buttresses channelling up to a dainty balustrade and four spiky

---

College admission charges and opening times

In summertime at least, all the more visited colleges impose an **admission charge**, partly to control the number of tourists and partly to raise cash. It is, however, a creeping trend, so don't be surprised if other, lesser-known colleges follow suit. **Opening times** are fairly consistent throughout the year, though there are sporadic term-time variations and it's also worth noting that during the exam season, which stretches from late April to mid-June, all the colleges have periods when they are closed to the public. Where there are no set opening hours, you're usually allowed to tour the grounds at any time during the day. For more specific information, call the relevant college – **phone numbers** are given in the text.

turrets, but the exterior was, in a sense at least, a happy accident – its design predicated by the carefully composed interior. Here, in the final flowering of the Gothic style, the high and handsome **nave** boasts an exquisite ceiling, whose fan-tail tracery is a complex geometry of extraordinary complexity and delicacy. Below, it is flooded with kaleidoscopic patterns of light that filter in through copious stained-glass windows. Paid for by Henry VIII, the **stained glass** was largely the work of Flemish glaziers, with the lower windows portraying scenes from the New Testament and the Apocrypha, and the upper windows the Old Testament. Henry VIII also paid for the dark and clumpy wooden **choir organ screen**, one of the earliest examples of Italian Renaissance woodcarving in England, but the **choir stalls** beyond date from the 1670s. Above the **altar** hangs Rubens' tender *Adoration of the Magi*. Finally, an exhibition in the side **chantries** puts more historical flesh on Henry's grand plans.

King's enjoyed an exclusive supply of students from one of the country's public schools – in this case, Eton – and until 1851 claimed the right to award its students degrees without taking any examinations. The first non-Etonians were only accepted in 1873. Times have changed since those days, and, if anything, King's is now one of the more progressive colleges, having been one of the first to admit women in 1972. Among its most famous alumni are E.M. Forster, who described his experiences in *Maurice*, film director Derek Jarman, poet Rupert Brooke and John Maynard Keynes, whose economic theories did much to improve the college's finances when he became the college bursar.

From King's Parade to Gonville and Caius College

Originally the town's medieval High Street, **King's Parade** is dominated by King's College and Chapel, but the higgledy-piggledy shops and cafés opposite are an attractive foil to William Wilkins's architectural screen. At the northern end of King's Parade is **Great St Mary's** (daily 9am–6pm except during services; free), the university's pet church, a sturdy Gothic structure dating from the fifteenth century. Its tower (Mon–Sat 9.30am–4.30pm, Sun noon–4.30pm; £2.50) offers a good overall view of the colleges and a bird's-eye view of **Market Hill**, east of the church, where food and bric-a-brac stalls are set out daily. Opposite the church stands **Senate House**, an exercise in Palladian classicism by James Gibbs, and the scene of graduation ceremonies on the last Saturday in June, when champagne corks fly around the rabbit-fur collars and black gowns. It's not usually open to the public, though you can wander around its precincts if the gate is open.

The northern continuation of King's Parade is Trinity Street, a short way along which, on the left, is the cramped main entrance to **Gonville and Caius College** (no set opening hours; free; ☎01223/332 400, ⓦwww.cai.cam.ac.uk), known simply as Caius (pronounced "keys"), after the sixteenth-century co-founder John Keys, who latinized his name as was then the custom with men of learning. The design of the college owes much to Keys, who placed three gates on two adjoining courts, each representing a different stage on the path to academic enlightenment: the **Gate of Humility** is at the main entrance; the **Gate of Virtue**, sporting the female figures of Fame and Wealth, fronts Caius Court; and the exquisite **Gate of Honour**, capped with sundials and decorated with classical motifs, leads to Senate House Passage and the Senate House (see above).

Trinity Hall, Clare College and Clare Bridge

Senate House Passage continues west beyond Caius College's Gate of Honour to Trinity Lane and **Trinity Hall** (daily 9.15am–noon & 2–5.30pm; free; ☎01223/332500, ⓦwww.trinhall.cam.ac.uk) – not to be confused with Trinity

College (see below) – where the Elizabethan library retains several of its original chains, designed to prevent students from purloining the texts. A few yards to the south is the much more diverting **Clare College** (daily 10.30am–4.30pm; free, but £2 in summer; ☎01223/333200, ⓦwww.clare.cam.ac.uk), whose alumni include David Attenborough and Siegfried Sassoon. The college's plain period-piece courtyards, completed in the early eighteenth century, lead to one of the most picturesque of all the bridges over the Cam, **Clare Bridge**. Beyond lies the **Fellows' Garden**, one of the loveliest college gardens open to the public (times as college). Back at the entrance to Clare, it's a few steps more to the North Gate of King's College, beside King's College Chapel (see p.523).

Trinity College

Trinity College, on Trinity Street (daily 10am–5pm; Nov–Feb free, but otherwise £2.20; ☎01223/338400, ⓦwww.trin.cam.ac.uk), is the largest of the Cambridge colleges and also has the largest courtyard. It comes as little surprise then that its list of famous alumni is probably longer than any of its rivals: literary greats, including Dryden, Byron, Tennyson, Thackeray and Vladimir Nabokov; the Cambridge spies Blunt, Burgess and Philby; prime ministers, including Balfour and Baldwin; Isaac Newton, Lord Rutherford, Vaughan Williams, Pandit Nehru, Bertrand Russell and Ludwig Wittgenstein; and not to mention a trio of (much less talented) royals, Edward VII, George VI and Prince Charles.

A statue of Henry VIII, who founded the college in 1546, sits in majesty over Trinity's **Great Gate**, his sceptre replaced long ago with a chair leg by a student wit. Beyond lies the vast asymmetrical expanse of **Great Court**, which displays a fine range of Tudor buildings, the oldest of which is the fifteenth-century clocktower – the annual race against its midnight chimes is now common currency thanks to the film *Chariots of Fire*. The centrepiece of the court is a delicate fountain, in which, legend has it, Lord Byron used to bathe naked with his pet bear – the college forbade students from keeping dogs.

On the far side of the Great Court, walk through "**the screens**" – the narrow passage separating the Hall from the kitchens – to reach **Nevile's Court**, where Newton first calculated the speed of sound. The west end of Nevile's Court is enclosed by one of the university's most famous buildings, the **Wren Library**, which was completed in 1695 (Mon–Fri noon–2pm, plus Sat during term time 10.30am–12.30pm; free). Viewed from the outside, it's impossible to appreciate the scale of the interior thanks to Wren's clever device of concealing the internal floor level by means of two rows of stone columns. In contrast to many modern libraries, natural light pours into the white stuccoed interior, which contrasts wonderfully with the dark lime-wood bookcases, also Wren-designed and housing numerous valuable manuscripts including Milton's *Lycidas*, Wittgenstein's journals and A.A. Milne's *Winnie the Pooh*.

St John's College

Next door to Trinity, **St John's College**, on St John's Street (March–Oct daily 10am–5.30pm; Nov–Feb Sat & Sun 10am–5.30pm; £2.80; ☎01223/338600, ⓦwww.joh.cam.ac.uk), sports a grandiloquent Tudor gatehouse, which is distinguished by the coat of arms of the founder, Lady Margaret Beaufort, the mother of Henry VII, held aloft by two spotted, mythical beasts. Beyond, three successive courts lead to the river, but there's an excess of dull reddish brickwork here – enough for Wordsworth, who lived above the kitchens on F staircase, to describe the place as "gloomy". The arcade on the far side of Third Court leads through to the **Bridge of Sighs**, a chunky, covered bridge built in 1831 but in most respects very unlike its Venetian namesake. The bridge is best viewed from the much older – and much more stylish – Wren-designed bridge a few yards to the south. The Bridge of Sighs links the old college with the fanciful nineteenth-century **New Court**, a crenellated Neo-Gothic extravaganza topped by a feast of dinky stone chimneys and pinnacles.

From the Round Church to Magdalene College

Back on St John's Street, it's a few seconds' walk to Bridge Street and the **Round Church** (Tues–Sat 10am–5pm, Sun 1–5pm; £2), built in the twelfth century on the model of the Holy Sepulchre in Jerusalem. It's a curious-looking structure, squat with an ill-considered late medieval extension to the rear, but the Norman pillars of the original church remain, overseen by sturdy arcading and a ring of finely carved faces.

Set back from the street, down a footpath beside the church, is the Cambridge **Union Society**, a bastion of male-dominated debating culture, founded in 1815 and finally opened to women in the 1960s. The society likes to think of itself as a miniature House of Commons – its debating chamber is designed as such – and its debates continue to attract many of the leading politicians and speakers of the day. These are presided over by the Union's officers, who tend to be made up of the university's more ambitious, conservative elements. In the normal scheme of things, election to the Union presidency leads about twenty years later to a place in Cabinet – the last Tory administration barely contained a minister who hadn't been Union president at either Oxford or Cambridge.

From the Round Church, it only takes a minute or two to stroll up to **Magdalene Bridge** and then to **Magdalene College** (no set opening hours; free; ☏01223/332100, ⓦwww.magd.cam.ac.uk) – pronounced "maudlin" – which was founded as a hostel by the Benedictines, became a university college in 1542 and was the last of the colleges to admit women, finally succumbing in 1988. The main focus of attention, here, is the **Pepys Library** (mid-Jan to mid-March, Oct & Nov Mon–Sat 2.30–3.30pm; late April to Aug Mon–Sat 11.30am–12.30pm & 2.30–3.30pm; free), in the second of the college's ancient courtyards. Samuel Pepys, a Magdalene student, bequeathed his entire library to the college, where it has been displayed ever since in its original red-oak bookshelves – though his famous diary, which also now resides here, was only discovered in the nineteenth century.

Jesus College

Doubling back down Bridge Street, take Jesus Lane, the first left after the Round Church, to get to **Jesus College** (daily 10am–5pm; free; ☏01223/339339, ⓦwww.jesus.cam.ac.uk), whose intimate cloisters are reminiscent of a monastery – appropriately, as the Bishop of Ely founded the college on the grounds of a suppressed Benedictine nunnery in 1496. The main red-brick gateway is approached via a distinctive walled walkway strewn with bicycles and known as "the Chimney". Beyond, much of the ground plan of the nunnery has been preserved, especially around **Cloister Court**, the first court on the right after the entrance and the prettiest part of the college, dripping with ivy and, in summer, overflowing with hanging baskets. Entered from the Cloister Court, the college **chapel** occupies the former priory chancel and looks like a medieval parish church; it was imaginatively restored in the nineteenth century, using ceiling designs by William Morris and Pre-Raphaelite stained glass. The poet Samuel Taylor Coleridge was the college's most famously bad student, absconding in his first year to join the Light Dragoons, and returning only to be kicked out for a combination of bad debts and unconventional opinions.

Sidney Sussex College and Christ's College

Near Jesus, Malcolm Street cuts off Jesus Lane to reach King Street and its continuation **Hobson Street**, named after the owner of a Cambridge livery stable, who would only allow customers to take the horse nearest the door – hence "Hobson's choice". Leading off Hobson Street is the pleasant shopping **arcade** that occupies the Victorian red-bricks of tiny Sussex Street. The arcade leads through to **Sidney Sussex College** (no set opening times; free; ☎01223/338800, ⓦwww.sid.cam.ac.uk), whose sombre, mostly mock-Gothic facade glowers over Sidney Street. The interior is fairly unexciting too, though the long, slender **chapel** is noteworthy for its fancy marble floor, hooped roof and Baroque wood panelling, as well as for being the last resting place of the skull of its most famous alumnus, Oliver Cromwell. Originally buried with much pomp and circumstance in Westminster Abbey, Cromwell's body was exhumed after the Restoration on the orders of Charles II, and then dragged through the streets of the capital, before being hung on a gibbet and decapitated. It was then stuck on a post, where it remained for a couple of decades, before it was blown down in a storm. The skull then disappeared from historical view until, finally, a Suffolk family donated it to Sidney Sussex in 1960. It was subsequently buried somewhere in the chapel – in a secret location so as to avoid the attentions of latter-day admirers and detractors alike.

Just to the south of Sidney Sussex College, along Sidney Street, you hit the hustle and bustle of the town's central shopping area, which is dominated by the **Lion Yard shopping centre**. Opposite, the turreted gateway of **Christ's College** (daily 9.30am–4.30pm; free; ☎01223/334900, ⓦwww.christs.cam .ac.uk) features the coat of arms of the founder, Lady Margaret Beaufort, who also founded St John's. Passing through First Court you come to the Fellows' Building, attributed to Inigo Jones, whose central arch gives access to the **Fellows' Garden** (Mon–Fri 9.30am–noon & 2–4pm; free). The poet John Milton is said to have either painted or composed beneath the garden's elderly mulberry tree, though there's no definite proof that he did either; another of Christ's famous undergraduates was Charles Darwin, who showed little academic promise and spent most of his time hunting.

Emmanuel College

Just to the south of Christ's College, on St Andrew's Street, **Emmanuel College** dates from 1584 (no set opening times; free; ☎01223/334200, ⓦwww .emma.cam.ac.uk). Here, the college's stolid Neoclassical facade hides a neat and trim Front Court, where the **chapel** was designed by Wren in a simple Classical style, its wood-panelled nave set beneath a fancy stucco ceiling. Emmanuel trained a new generation of Protestant clergy on the heels of the Reformation, and Emmanuel men were numbered among the Pilgrims who settled New England, which not only explains the derivation of the place name Cambridge in Massachusetts but also accounts for Harvard University – **John Harvard**, another alumnus, is remembered by a memorial window in the chapel.

Downing Street and the university museums

Opposite Emmanuel, **Downing Street** and its continuation **Pembroke Street** cut west to King's Parade and Trumpington Street. To either side is a rambling assortment of large, mostly Victorian buildings, some of which are taken over by a group of scientific and specialist museums. Each museum is connected to one of the university faculties and forms an important resource for students, but is also open to the public. First up, on the left, is the

Sedgwick Museum of Earth Sciences (Mon–Fri 10am–1pm & 2–5pm, Sat 10am–4pm; free), which displays fossils and skeletons of dinosaurs, reptiles and mammals, plus one of the oldest geological collections in the world. In the same complex is the **Museum of Archaeology and Anthropology** (Tues–Sat 10.30am–4.30pm; free; ⓦ www.museum.archanth .cam.ac.uk), which is probably the pick of the bunch for the non-specialist, covering the development of the city from prehistoric times to the nineteenth century and, better still, holding a superb ethnographical gallery. This is centred on a soaring fifty-foot native totem pole and many of the exhibits derive from the "cabinets of curiosities" collected by eighteenth-century explorers. Several pieces were gathered on Captain Cook's first voyage to the South Pacific between 1768 and 1771.

A little further down – and on the opposite side of – Downing Street is the **Museum of Zoology** (Mon–Fri 10am–4.45pm; free), some of whose exhibits were donated by Darwin. Next up, with its entrance round the corner on Free School Lane, is the **Whipple Museum of the History of Science** (Mon–Fri 12.30–4.30pm; free), crammed with hundreds of scientific instruments from the fourteenth century onwards.

Queens' College

At the west end of Pembroke Street, turn right up King's Parade and then first left along Silver Street to get to **Queens' College** (mid-March to mid-May Mon–Fri 11am–3pm, Sat & Sun 10am–4.30pm; late June to Sept daily 10am–4.30pm; Oct Mon–Fri 1.45–4.30pm, Sat & Sun 10am–4.30pm; Nov to mid-March daily 1.45–4.30pm; £2 in summer, otherwise free; ⓣ01223/335511, ⓦ www.queens.cam.ac.uk), which is accessed through the visitors' gate on Queens' Lane. This is one of the most popular colleges with university applicants, and it's not difficult to see why. In the **Old Court** and the **Cloister Court**, Queens' possesses two fairy-tale Tudor courtyards, with the first of the two the perfect illustration of the original collegiate ideal with kitchens, library, chapel, hall and rooms all set around a tiny green. Cloister Court is flanked by the Long Gallery of the President's Lodge, the last remaining half-timbered building in the university, and, in its southeast corner, by the tower where Erasmus is thought to have beavered away during his four years here, probably from 1510 to 1514. Be sure to pay a visit to the college **Hall**, off the screens passage between the two courts, which holds mantel tiles by William Morris, and portraits of Erasmus and one of the college's co-founders, Elizabeth Woodville, wife of Edward IV. Equally eye-catching is the wooden **Mathematical Bridge** over the River Cam (viewable for free from the Silver Street Bridge), a copy of the mid-eighteenth-century original, which – so it was claimed – would stay in place even if the nuts and bolts were removed.

Pembroke College and Peterhouse College

Doubling back to Trumpington Street, **Pembroke College** (no set opening times; free; ⓣ01223/338100, ⓦ www.pem.cam.ac.uk) contains Wren's first ever commission, the **chapel**, paid for by his Royalist uncle, erstwhile Bishop of Ely and a college fellow, in thanks for his deliverance from the Tower of London after seventeen years' imprisonment. It holds a particularly fine, though modern, stained-glass east window and a delicate fifteenth-century marble relief of St Michael and the Virgin, the product of an unusually skilled Early English workshop. Outside the library there's a statue of a toga-clad William Pitt the Younger, who entered the college at fifteen and was prime minister ten years later. Pitt is just one of a long list of college alumni, which includes poets Edmund Spenser, Thomas Gray and Ted Hughes.

Across the street and just along from Pembroke is the oldest and smallest of the colleges, **Peterhouse** (no set opening times; free; ☏01223/338200, Ⓦwww.pet.cam.ac.uk), founded in 1284. Few of the original buildings have survived, the principal exception being the thirteenth-century **Hall**, whose interior was remodelled by William Morris; it is entered from the main court. Peterhouse used the church next door – Little St Mary's – as the college chapel until the present one, a sterling, somewhat overblown structure, was plonked in the main court in 1632.

The Fitzwilliam Museum

Of all the museums in Cambridge, the **Fitzwilliam Museum**, on Trumpington Street (Tues–Sat 10am–5pm, Sun noon–5pm; free; Ⓦwww .fitzmuseum.cam.ac.uk), stands head and shoulders above the rest. The building itself is a grandiloquent interpretation of Neoclassicism, built in the mid-nineteenth century to house the vast collection bequeathed by Viscount Fitzwilliam in 1816. Since then, the museum has been gifted a string of private collections, most of which follow a particular specialism, and consequently the Fitzwilliam says much about the changing tastes of the British upper class. The **Lower Galleries,** on the ground floor, contain a wealth of antiquities including Egyptian sarcophagi and mummies, fifth-century BC black- and red-figure Greek vases, plus a bewildering display of early European ceramics. Further on, there are sections dedicated to armour, glass and pewterware, medals, portrait miniatures and illuminated manuscripts, and – right at the far end – galleries devoted to Far Eastern applied arts and Korean ceramics.

The **Upper Galleries** concentrate on painting and sculpture, with an eclectic assortment of mostly nineteenth- and early twentieth-century European paintings. There are two rooms of French paintings, with works by Picasso, Matisse, Monet, Renoir, Delacroix, Cézanne and Degas, and two rooms of Italian works by the likes of Fra Filippo Lippi and Simone Martini, Titian and Veronese. Two further rooms feature British paintings, with works by William Blake, Constable and Turner, Hogarth, Reynolds, Gainsborough and Stubbs, and one is devoted to Dutch art, displaying paintings by Frans Hals and Ruisdael. The twentieth-century gallery is packed with a fascinating selection including pieces by Lucian Freud, David Hockney, Henry Moore, Ben Nicholson and Barbara Hepworth.

Scott Polar Research Museum and Botanic Gardens

Past the Fitzwilliam Museum, turn left along busy Lensfield Road for the **Scott Polar Research Museum** (Tues–Fri 11am–1pm & 2–4pm, Sat noon–4pm; free), founded in 1920 in memory of the explorer, Captain Robert Falcon Scott (1868–1912), with displays from the expeditions of various polar adventurers, plus exhibitions on native cultures of the Arctic. There's more of general interest near at hand in the shape of the **University Botanic Gardens** (daily: Feb, March & Oct 10am–5pm; April–Sept 10am–6pm; Nov–Jan 10am–4pm; £3; Ⓦwww.botanic.cam.ac.uk), whose entrance is on Bateman Street, about 500 yards to the south of Lensfield Road via Panton Street. Founded in 1760 and covering forty acres, the gardens are second only to Kew with glasshouses as well as bountiful outdoor displays. The outdoor beds are mostly arranged by natural order, but there's also a particularly unusual series of chronological beds, showing when different plants were introduced into Britain.

Eating and drinking

Even at Cambridge, students are not the world's greatest restaurant goers, so although the downtown **takeaway** and **café** scene is fine, decent **restaurants** are a little thin on the ground. On any kind of budget, the myriad Italian places – courtesy of Cambridge's large Italian population – will stand you in good stead; otherwise, choose carefully, particularly in the more touristy areas, where quality isn't always all it should be. Happily, Cambridge abounds in excellent **pubs**, and our list rounds up some of the best traditional student and local drinking haunts.

Cafés and restaurants

Cambridge Chop House 2 King's Parade
☎01223/359506. The cafés facing King's College have always been low-key and downbeat, but this flashy new place represents a move upmarket – and is perhaps the face of things to come. Large, bistro-style premises and an emphasis on locally produced, seasonal ingredients, with mains, like beef chop, mushrooms and new potatoes, costing £13–20.

Clowns 54 King St. Italian-style cappuccino and cakes, sandwiches and snacks, plus newspapers to browse. Off the tourist route and not part of a chain – bonuses in anyone's books. Daily 8am–late.

Eraina Taverna 2 Free School Lane
☎01223/368786. Packed Greek taverna, which satisfies the hungry hordes with huge platefuls of stews and grills, as well as pizzas, curries and a whole host of other menu madness. Try to avoid getting stuck in the basement, though at weekends (when you'll probably have to queue) you'll be lucky to get a seat anywhere. Mains from £6.

Michaelhouse Café Trinity St. Good-quality café food – snacks, salads and so forth – in an attractively renovated medieval church. Great, central location too. Closed Sun.

Midsummer House Midsummer Common, on the south side of the river, beside the footbridge just to the east of Victoria Avenue ☎01223/369299. Lovely riverside restaurant with conservatory, specializing in top-notch French-Mediterranean cuisine; main courses, such as braised turbot with peanuts and pistachios, squash and asparagus, begin at about £18. Reservations essential. Tues 7–9.30pm & Wed–Sat noon–1.30pm & 7–9.30pm.

Rainbow Vegetarian Bistro 9a King's Parade
☎01223/321551. Vegetarian restaurant with main courses – ranging from couscous to lasagne and Indonesian *gado-gado* – for around £8. Organic wines served with meals. Handy location, opposite King's College. Tues–Sat 10am–10pm.

Restaurant 22 22 Chesterton Rd
☎01223/351880. One of the best restaurants in Cambridge, a candlelit town house offering a good-value, fixed-price menu (at around £27). Expect dishes like sautéed squid with chorizo and a steamed sea bream and shellfish broth. Closed lunchtimes & all day Sun & Mon.

Trockel, Ulmann und Freunde 13 Pembroke St. Café food at its best in bright, creatively decorated premises. The baguettes have imaginative fillings – humous and avocado, for example; the soups are hot and tasty; and the cakes are simply delicious. Tends to get jam-packed during term time. Closed Sun.

Pubs and bars

Anchor 12 Silver St. Very popular riverside tourist haunt with an outdoor deck – and adjacent punt rental.

Champion of the Thames 68 King St. Gratifyingly old-fashioned central pub with decent beer and a student/academic clientele.

Eagle 8 Bene't St. An ancient inn with a cobbled courtyard where Crick and Watson sought inspiration in the 1950s, at the time of their discovery of DNA. It's been tarted up since and gets horribly crowded, but is still worth a pint of anyone's time.

Free Press 7 Prospect Row. Classic, superbly maintained backstreet local with real ale brews and delicious bar food: nothing frozen, but all freshly prepared stuff from sandwiches and snacks at lunchtimes to heartier meals at night. To get there, proceed south down St Andrew's Street, turn left along Park Terrace, which runs beside the grassy expanse of Parker's Piece; then, turn right onto Parkside, cross over the road and take Melbourne Place, a narrow, pedestrian alley that intersects with Prospect Row.

The Pickerel 30 Magdalene St. Once a brothel and one of several pubs competing for the title of the oldest pub in town, *The Pickerel* has a lively atmosphere and offers a good range of beers beneath its low beams.

Entertainment

The **performing arts** scene is at its busiest and best during the university's term time, with numerous student **drama** productions, **classical concerts** and **gigs**, culminating in the traditional whizzerama of excess following the exam season. Apart from the places highlighted below, each college and several churches contribute to the performing arts scene too, with the **King's College choir** being, of course, the most famous attraction (see p.523), though the choral scholars who perform at the chapels of St John's and Trinity are also exceptionally good. For upcoming events, ask for details at the tourist office (see p.520), which issues various **listings** leaflets and brochures for free.

June and July are the busiest times in Cambridge's calendar of **events**. The fortnight of post-exam celebrations, which take place in the first two weeks of June – and are confusingly known as **May Week** – herald the ball and garden-party season, and include boat races, known as the "May Bumps", on the River Cam by Midsummer Common. The large and extremely popular **Midsummer Fair**, descendant of the town's famous medieval Stourbridge Fair, discontinued in 1934, takes place in late June on Midsummer Common, with funfair rides and much more besides. There are also free jazz and brass band performances in the city's parks and, at the end of July, the three-day **Cambridge Folk Festival** (Ⓦwww.cambridgefolkfestival.co.uk), one of the longest-running folk festivals in the world, is held in neighbouring Cherry Hinton.

Arts Picturehouse 38–39 St Andrew's St ☎0871/704 2050, Ⓦwww.picturehouses.co.uk. Art-house cinema with an excellent, wide-ranging programme.

Cambridge Arts Theatre 6 St Edward's Passage, off King's Parade ☎01223/503333, Ⓦwww .cambridgeartstheatre.com. The city's main repertory theatre, founded by John Maynard Keynes, and launch pad of a thousand-and-one famous careers; offers a top-notch range of cutting-edge and classic productions.

Cambridge Corn Exchange Wheeler St ☎01223/357851, Ⓦwww.cornex.co.uk. Revamped nineteenth-century trading hall, now the main city-centre venue for opera, ballet, musicals and comedy as well as regular rock and folk gigs.

Junction Clifton Rd, near the train station ☎01223/511511, Ⓦwww.junction.co.uk. Rock, indie, jazz, reggae or soul gigs, plus theatre, comedy and dance at this popular arts and entertainments venue.

Listings

Airport London Stansted Airport ☎0870/000 0303, Ⓦwww.stanstedairport.com.

Bike rental Mikes Bikes, 28 Mill Rd (☎01223/312591); and H. Drake, near the train station at 56–60 Hills Rd (☎01223/363468).

Bookshops Cambridge University Press has a shop at 1 Trinity St; Borders is at 12–13 Market St; and Waterstones at 22 Sidney St. For secondhand books try the shops down St Edward's Passage off King's Parade: G. David, at no.16, is an antiquari-an's and hardback hunter's paradise; the Haunted

Bookshop, at no. 9, is better for first editions, travel and illustrated books.

Car rental Europcar ☎01223/233644; Hertz ☎01223/309842.

Pharmacies Boots: 4 St Andrews St ☎01223/321459; 28 Petty Cury ☎01223/350213.

Post office The main office is at 9–11 St Andrew's St.

Taxis There are ranks at the train and bus stations. Alternatively, call Diamond Taxis ☎01223/523523.

Around Cambridge: Duxford Imperial War Museum

Just eight miles south of Cambridge, and clearly visible from the M11 (Junction #10), the giant hangars of the **Duxford Imperial War Museum** dominate the eponymous airfield (daily: mid-March to late Oct 10am–6pm; late Oct to mid-March 10am–4pm; £16; ℡01223/835000, ⓦwww.duxford.iwm.org.uk). Throughout World War II, East Anglia was a centre of operations for the RAF and the USAF, with the region's flat, unobstructed landscape dotted by dozens of airfields, amongst which Duxford was one of the more important. In total, the museum holds over 150 historic aircraft, a wide-ranging collection of civil and military planes from the Sunderland flying boat to Concorde and the Vulcan B2 bombers, which were used for the first and last time in the 1982 Falklands conflict; the Spitfires, however, remain the most enduringly popular. Most of the planes are kept in full working order and are taken out for a spin several times a year at **Duxford Air Shows**, which attract thousands of visitors. There are usually four air shows a year and advance bookings are strongly recommended – call ahead or consult the museum website, as you should also for details of the bus service linking Duxford with Cambridge bus station.

Travel details

Buses

For information on all local and national bus services, contact Traveline ℡0871/200 2233, ⓦwww.traveline.org.uk. The Norfolk **Coasthopper bus** runs from Cromer to Hunstanton – with some services continuing to/from Great Yarmouth and King's Lynn – via a whole gaggle of coastal towns and villages, including Blakeney, Sheringham, Wells and the Burnhams. Frequencies vary on different stretches of the route and there are more services in the summer than in the winter, but on the more popular stretches buses appear every thirty minutes or hour, much less frequently on Sundays. The operator is Norfolk Green ℡01553/776980, ⓦwww.norfolkgreen.co.uk.

Cambridge to: Bury St Edmunds (hourly; 1hr); Colchester (7 daily; 3hr 30min); Ely (every 30min; 50min); Ipswich (8 daily; 3–4hr); London (hourly; 2hr); Peterborough (hourly; 2hr 20min); Stansted Airport (hourly; 50min).

Colchester to: Bury St Edmunds (hourly; 2hr); Cambridge (7 daily; 3hr 30min); Ipswich (hourly; 1–2hr); Sudbury (hourly; 50min).

Ely to: Cambridge (every 30min; 50min); King's Lynn (7 daily; 2hr); Peterborough (every 2hr; 2hr).

Ipswich to: Aldeburgh (hourly; 1hr 30min); Bury St Edmunds (every 2hr; 2hr); Colchester (hourly; 1–2hr); Orford (every 2hr; 1hr 20min).

King's Lynn to: Bury St Edmunds (3 daily; 2hr 15min); Ely (7 daily; 2hr); Great Yarmouth (hourly; 2hr 30min); Norwich (hourly; 1hr 45min); Peterborough (hourly; 1hr 20min).

Norwich to: Bury St Edmunds (hourly; 2–3hr); Great Yarmouth (hourly; 30min); King's Lynn (hourly; 1hr 45min); Sheringham (every 30min; 1hr 20min).

Peterborough to: Cambridge (hourly; 2hr 20min); Ely (every 2hr; 2hr); King's Lynn (hourly; 1hr 20min).

Trains

For information on all local and national rail services, contact National Rail Enquiries ℡0845/748 4950, ⓦwww.nationalrail.co.uk.

Cambridge to: Bury St Edmunds (8 daily; 40min); Ely (hourly; 15min); Ipswich (6 daily; 1hr 20min); King's Lynn (hourly; 45min); London (every 30min; 1hr); Norwich (hourly; 1hr); Peterborough (hourly; 50min); Stansted Airport (10 daily; 40min).

Colchester to: Ipswich (2 hourly; 25min); London (2 hourly; 50min); Norwich (hourly; 1hr).

Ely to: King's Lynn (hourly; 30min); London (hourly; 1hr); Peterborough (hourly; 30min).

Ipswich to: Bury St Edmunds (10 daily; 30min); Ely (7 daily; 1hr); London (every 30min; 1hr 10min); Norwich (hourly; 45min); Peterborough (7 daily; 1hr 50min).

Norwich to: Cromer (every 1–2hr; 50min); Ely (hourly; 50min); Great Yarmouth (hourly; 30min); London (hourly; 2hr); Peterborough (hourly; 1hr 30min); Sheringham (every 1–2hr; 1hr).

Peterborough to: Bury St Edmunds (6 daily; 1hr); Cambridge (hourly; 50min); London (2 hourly; 1hr); Norwich (hourly; 1hr 30min).

8

The West Midlands and the Peak District

CHAPTER 8

Highlights

* **The theatres, Stratford-upon-Avon** The place to see Shakespeare's plays performed by the pre-eminent Royal Shakespeare Company. See p.543

* **Mappa Mundi, Hereford Cathedral** This antique map, dating to around 1000, provides a riveting insight into the medieval mind. See p.555

* **Hay-on-Wye** Deep in the countryside, this dinky little town has more secondhand bookshops than anywhere else in the world. See p.561

* **Ironbridge Gorge** The first iron bridge ever constructed arches high above the River Severn. See p.564

* **Ludlow** A postcard-pretty country town with half-timbered houses and a sprawling castle. See p.572

* **Buxton** Good-looking former spa town that makes an ideal base for exploring the Peak District. See p.594

* **Hassop Hall Hotel, Hassop** Perhaps the most charming of all the Peak District's country hotels and a great base for some hiking. See p.607

▲ Ironbridge Gorge

The West Midlands and the Peak District

W
ith justification, the small country towns and untrammelled scenery of the **West Midlands** are the apple of the tourist eye, but there's no disputing the urban epicentre of the region – **Birmingham**, Britain's second city, once the world's greatest industrial metropolis with a slew of factories that powered the Industrial Revolution. Long saddled with a reputation as a culture-hating, car-loving backwater, Birmingham has redefined its image in recent years, initiating some ambitious architectural and environmental schemes, jazzing up its museums and industrial heritage sites and giving itself a higher profile on the nation's cultural map than it's ever had before. It's not an especially good-looking city, it must be admitted, but it does hold several excellent attractions and it's certainly lively, with its nightlife encompassing everything from Royal Ballet productions to all-night grooves, and a great spread of restaurants and pubs in between. To some extent change was forced on Birmingham by the decline in its manufacturing base – it lost over a third of its manufacturing jobs between 1974 and 1983 – but things were even worse in the **Black Country**, that knot of industrial towns clinging to the western side of the city. This area has found it difficult to re-route itself through the maze of post-industrialization and more amply fulfils the negative stereotypes once attached to Birmingham.

The counties to the south and west of Birmingham and beyond the Black Country – **Warwickshire, Worcestershire, Herefordshire** and **Shropshire** – comprise a rural stronghold that maintains an emotional and political distance from the conurbation. The left-wing politics of the big city seem remote indeed when you're in Shrewsbury, but in fact it's only seventy miles from one to the other. For the most part, the four counties constitute a quiet, unassuming stretch of pastoral England whose beauty is rarely dramatic, but whose charms become more evident the longer you stay. Of the four counties, **Warwickshire** is the least obviously scenic, but draws by far the largest number of visitors, for – as the road signs declare at every entry point – this is "Shakespeare Country". The prime target is, of course, **Stratford-upon-Avon**, with its handful of Shakespeare-related sites and world-class theatre, but spare time also for the diverting town of Warwick, which has a superb church and a whopping castle.

Neighbouring **Worcestershire**, which stretches southwest from the urban fringes of the West Midlands, holds two principal places of interest, **Worcester**,

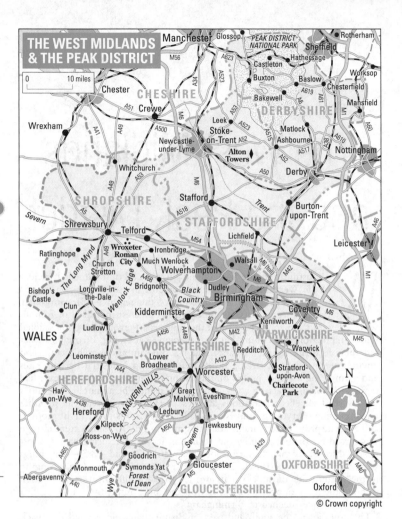

which is graced by a mighty cathedral, and **Great Malvern**, a mannered inland resort spread along the rolling contours of the **Malvern Hills** – prime walking territory. From here, it's west again for **Herefordshire**, a large and sparsely populated county that's home to several charming market towns, most notably picture-postcard **Ledbury** and **Hay-on-Wye**; the latter has the largest concentration of secondhand bookshops in the world. There's also **Hereford**, where the remarkable medieval Mappa Mundi map is displayed, and pocket-sized Ross-on-Wye, which is within easy striking distance of an especially scenic stretch of the **Wye River Valley**. Next door, to the north, rural **Shropshire** weighs in with **Ludlow**, one of the region's prettiest towns, awash with antique half-timbered buildings, and the amiable county town of **Shrewsbury**, which is also close to the hiking trails of the **Long Mynd**. Shropshire has a fascinating industrial history, too, for it was here in the **Ironbridge Gorge** that British industrialists built the world's first iron bridge and pioneered the use of coal as a smelting fuel. These were two key events in the Industrial Revolution and, appropriately, the gorge's industrial heyday is recalled by a phalanx of museums.

To the east of Shropshire, sprawling north of the Birmingham conurbation, is **Staffordshire**, where **Lichfield** makes a good hand of its links with **Samuel Johnson**. Beyond lies **Derbyshire**, whose northern reaches incorporate the region's finest scenery in the rough landscapes of the **Peak District National Park**. The latter offers great opportunities for moderately strenuous walks, as well as the comely former spa town of **Buxton**, the limestone caverns of **Castleton** and the so-called "Plague Village" of **Eyam**, not to mention the grandiose stately pile of **Chatsworth House**, a real favourite hereabouts.

Birmingham, the region's **public transport hub**, is easily accessible by **train** from London Euston, Liverpool, Manchester, Leeds, York and a score of other towns. It is also well served by the National Express **bus** network, with dozens of buses leaving every hour for destinations all over Britain. Local **bus** services are excellent around the West Midlands conurbation and very good in the Peak District, but fade away badly in amongst the villages of Herefordshire and Shropshire.

Stratford-upon-Avon

Despite its worldwide fame, **STRATFORD-UPON-AVON** is at heart an unassuming market town with an unexceptional pedigree. Its first settlers forded, and later bridged, the River Avon, and developed commercial links with the farmers who tilled the surrounding flatlands. A charter for Stratford's weekly market was granted in the twelfth century, a tradition continued to this day, and the town later became an important stopping-off point for stagecoaches between London, Oxford and the north. Like all such places, Stratford had its clearly defined class system and within this typical milieu John and Mary **Shakespeare** occupied the middle rank, and would have been forgotten long ago had their first son, **William**, not turned out to be the greatest writer ever to use the English language. A consequence of their good fortune is that this ordinary little town is nowadays all but smothered by package-tourist hype and, in the summer at least, its central streets groan under the weight of thousands of tourists. Don't let that deter you: the **Royal Shakespeare Company** offers superb theatre, and dodging the multitudes is possible by avoiding the busiest attractions – principally the Birthplace Museum. Moreover, Stratford still has the ability to surprise and delight, whether in the excellence of some of its restaurants or by the gentle river views beside the lovely **Holy Trinity Church**.

Arrival, information and getting around

Stratford **train station** is on the northwest edge of town, ten minutes' walk from the centre. Two companies operate train services to Stratford, and on both routes the town is the end of the line: Central Trains runs hourly services from Birmingham (Moor Street and Snow Hill stations); and Chiltern Railways operate a service every two hours from London Marylebone (via Warwick). Local **bus services** arrive and depart from Bridge Street bang in the centre; National Express services and most other long-distance and regional buses pull into the Riverside station on the east side of the town centre, off Bridgeway.

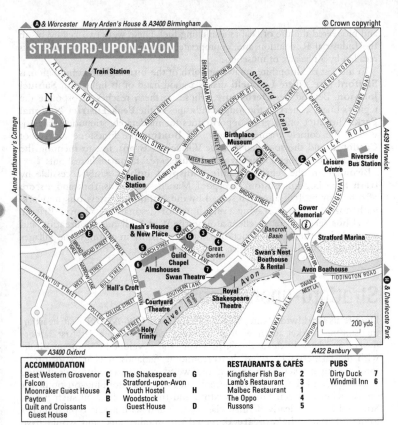

STRATFORD-UPON-AVON

ACCOMMODATION				RESTAURANTS & CAFÉS		PUBS	
Best Western Grosvenor	C	The Shakespeare	G	Kingfisher Fish Bar	2	Dirty Duck	7
Falcon	F	Stratford-upon-Avon		Lamb's Restaurant	3	Windmill Inn	6
Moonraker Guest House	A	Youth Hostel	H	Malbec Restaurant	1		
Payton	B	Woodstock		The Oppo	4		
Quilt and Croissants		Guest House	D	Russons	5		
Guest House	E						

The **tourist office** (April–Sept Mon–Sat 9am–5.30pm, Sun 10.30am–4pm; Oct–March Mon–Sat 9am–5pm, Sun 10am–3pm; ☏0870/160 7930, ⓦwww .shakespeare-country.co.uk) is handily located by the bridge at the junction of Bridgeway and Bridgefoot. They have oodles of information on local attractions and operate an accommodation-booking service (see opposite), which is very useful during the height of the summer when rooms can be in short supply. They also issue bus and train timetables and sell bus and theatre tickets as well as the all-in ticket for the five **Shakespeare Birthplace Trust** properties (£14), or a **Three In-Town Shakespeare Property Ticket** (£11) for the three Trust properties in the town centre; both tickets are also available from the sites themselves.

The best way to see Stratford is on **foot**, but the tourist office does have the details of a veritable raft of guided walking and bus tours.

Accommodation

As one of the most popular tourist destinations in England, Stratford's **accommodation** is a tad pricey and often gets booked up well in advance. Indeed, in peak months, and during the Shakespeare birthday celebrations around April 23, it's pretty much essential to book ahead. The town has a dozen or so **hotels**, the pick of which occupy old half-timbered buildings right in the centre, but most visitors choose to stay in a **B&B**. These have sprung up in every part of Stratford, but there's a particular concentration to the southwest of the centre around Grove Road, Evesham Place and Broad Walk. The tourist office operates an efficient and extremely useful accommodation booking hotline (℡0870/160 7930, ⓦwww.shakespeare-country.co.uk).

Hotels

Best Western Grosvenor Warwick Rd ℡01789/269213, ⓦwww.bwgh.co.uk. Close to the canal, just a couple of minutes' walk from the town centre, the *Grosvenor* occupies a row of pleasant, two-storey Georgian houses. The interior is crisp and modern and there's ample parking at the back. Discounted short-break deals available. ⑥

Falcon Chapel St ℡0870/832 9905, ⓦwww.legacy-hotels.co.uk. Handily situated in the middle of town, this hotel has a half-timbered facade dating from the sixteenth century, though most of the rest is an unremarkable modern rebuild. Substantial discounts are commonplace, but the rack rate is ⑦

Payton 6 John St ℡01789/266442, ⓦwww.payton.co.uk. On the north side of the town centre, a couple of minutes' walk from the Birthplace Museum, this comfortable hotel occupies an attractive Georgian town house on a quiet residential street. Family-run, the hotel has five comfortable rooms, all en suite. A good bet and very affordable. ⑤

The Shakespeare Chapel St ℡01789/294997, ⓦwww.mercure.com. Now part of a chain, this old hotel, with its mullion windows and half-timbered facade, is one of Stratford's best known. The interior has low beams and open fires and represents a fairly successful amalgamation of the old and new. Right in the centre of town. ⑥

Guest houses and B&Bs

Moonraker Guest House 40 Alcester Rd ℡01789/268774, ⓦwww.moonrakerhouse.com.

This amenable place, in a large suburban house, has seven en-suite guest rooms, each decorated in smart modern-meets-period style (canopied beds, mini-chandeliers and so forth). Great breakfasts, too – either full English or vegetarian. Just beyond the train station, about 900 yards from the centre. ⑤

Quilt and Croissants Guest House 33 Evesham Place ℡01789/267629, ⓦwww.quiltcroissants.co.uk. Amiable B&B in a bow-windowed, Victorian terrace house a short walk from the centre. Seven neat and trim single and double rooms, most en suite. Delicious homemade breakfasts, too. ②

Woodstock Guest House 30 Grove Rd ℡01789/299881, ⓦwww.woodstock-house.co.uk. A smart and neatly kept B&B five minutes' walk from the centre, by the start of the path to Anne Hathaway's Cottage (see p.545). It has five extremely comfortable bedrooms, all en suite. No credit cards. ③

Hostel

Stratford-upon-Avon Youth Hostel Hemmingford House, Alveston ℡0870/770 6052, Ⓔstratford@yha.org.uk. This hostel occupies a rambling Georgian mansion on the edge of the pretty village of Alveston. There are dormitories, double and family rooms, some of which are en suite, plus laundry, cycle hire, Internet access, car parking and self-catering facilities. Breakfasts and evening meals are on offer too. It's located two miles east of the town centre on the B4086 and served by regular bus from Stratford's Riverside bus station. Open all year. Dorm beds £20, doubles ①

The Town

Spreading back from the River Avon, Stratford's **town centre** is flat and compact, its mostly modern buildings filling out a simple gridiron just two blocks deep and four blocks long. Running along the northern edge of the centre is **Bridge Street**, the main thoroughfare lined with shops and chock-a-block with local buses. At its west end Bridge Street divides into Henley Street, home of the **Birthplace Museum**, and Wood Street, which leads up to the market place. It also intersects with High Street, which – along with its continuation Chapel and Church streets – cuts south to pass most of the old buildings that the town still possesses. From here, it's a short hop to the charming **Holy Trinity Church**, where Shakespeare lies buried, and then only a few minutes back along the river past the **theatres** to the foot of Bridge Street. In itself, this circular walk only takes about fifteen minutes, but it takes all day if you potter around the attractions. In addition, there are two outlying

Over the past hundred years or so, the deification of **William Shakespeare** (1564–1616) has been dogged by a loony backlash among a fringe of revisionist scholars and literary figures known as "**Anti-Stratfordians**". According to these heretics, the famous plays and sonnets were not written by a wool merchant's son from Stratford at all, but by someone else, and William Shakespeare was merely a nom de plume. The American novelist Henry James, among the most notorious arch-sceptics, once claimed that he was "haunted by the conviction that the divine William is the biggest and most successful fraud ever practised on a patient world."

A variety of candidates has been proposed for the authorship of Shakespeare's works, and they range from the faintly plausible (Christopher Marlowe, Ben Jonson, and the Earls of Rutland, Southampton and Oxford) to the manifestly whacko (Queen Elizabeth I, King James I and Daniel Defoe, author of *Robinson Crusoe*, who was born six years after publication of the first Folio). The wildest theories, however, have been reserved for Francis Bacon. In his book *The Great Cryptogram*, American congressman Ignatius Donnelly postulated that the word "honorificabilitudinitatibus", which crops up in *Love's Labours Lost*, was actually an anagram for the Latin "Hi ludi F Baconis nati tuiti orbi" ("These plays, F. Bacon's offspring, are preserved for the world"). Others have rallied around the Earl of Oxford's banner; Sigmund Freud maintained that Oxford wrote the plays, and Orson Welles agreed, saying that otherwise there were "… some awfully funny coincidences to explain away".

Lying at the root of the authorship debate are several **unresolved questions** that have puzzled scholars for years. How could a man of modest background from the provinces have such an intimate knowledge of royal protocol? How could he know so much about Italy without ever having travelled there? Why was he allowed to write potentially embarrassing love poems to one of England's most powerful aristocrats? Why did he not leave a library in his will, when the author of the plays clearly possessed an intimate knowledge of classical literature? And why, given that Shakespeare was supposedly a well-known dramatist, did no death notice or obituary appear in publications of the day?

The speculation surrounding Shakespeare's work stems from the lack of definite information about his life. The few details that have been preserved come mostly from official archives – birth, marriage and death certificates and court records. From these we know that on April 22 or 23, 1564, a certain John Shakespeare, variously

Shakespearean properties, **Anne Hathaway's Cottage** in Shottery and **Mary Arden's House** in Wilmcote – though you have to be a really serious sightseer to want to see them all.

The Birthplace Museum

Top of everyone's bardic itinerary is the **Birthplace Museum**, on Henley Street (April, May, Sept & Oct daily 10am–5pm; June–Aug Mon–Sat 9am–5pm, Sun 9.30am–5pm; Nov–March Mon–Sat 10am–4pm, Sun 10.30am–4pm; £7), comprising an unappetizing modern visitor centre and the heavily-restored, half-timbered building where the great man was born. The visitor centre pokes into every corner of Shakespeare's life and times, making the most of what little hard evidence there is. His will is interesting in so far as he passed all sorts of goodies to his daughters and chums, but precious little to his wife – the museum commentary tries to gainsay this apparent meanness, but fails to convince. Next door, the half-timbered birthplace dwelling is actually two buildings knocked into one. The northern, much smaller and later part was the house of Joan, Shakespeare's sister, and it adjoins the main family home, bought by John Shakespeare in 1556 and now returned to something like its original described as a glove-maker, butcher, wool merchant and corn trader, and his wife, Mary, had their first son, William. We also know that the boy attended a local grammar school until financial problems forced him into his father's business, and that, at the age of 18, he married a local woman, **Anne Hathaway**, seven years his senior, who five months later bore a daughter, Susanna, the first of three children. Several years later, probably around 1587, the young Shakespeare was forced to flee Stratford after being caught poaching on the estate of Sir Thomas Lucy at nearby Charlecote. Five companies of players passed through the town on tour that year, and it is believed he **absconded** with one of them to London, where a theatre boom was in full swing. *Henry VI*, Shakespeare's first play, appeared soon after, followed by the hugely successful *Richard III*. Over the next decade, Shakespeare's output was prodigious. Thirty-eight plays appeared, most of them performed by his own theatre troupes based in the **Globe** (see p.122), a large timber-framed theatre overlooking the south bank of the River Thames, in which he had a one-tenth share.

Success secured Shakespeare the patronage of London's fashionable set, among them the dashing young courtier, Henry Wriothesley, 3rd Earl of Southampton, with whom the playwright is believed to have had a passionate affair (Southampton is thought to have been the "golden youth" of the Sonnets). The ageing Queen Elizabeth I, bewigged and bedecked in opulent jewellery, regularly attended the Globe, as did her successor, James I, whose Scottish ancestry and fascination with the occult partly explain the subject matter of *Macbeth* – Shakespeare knew the commercial value of appealing to the rich and powerful. This, as much as his extraordinary talent, ensured his plays were the most acclaimed of the day, earning him enough money **to retire** comfortably to Stratford, where he largely abandoned literature in the last years of his life to concentrate on business and family affairs.

Ultimately, the sketchy details of Shakespeare's life are of far less importance than the plays, sonnets and songs he left behind. Whoever wrote them – and despite all the conjecture, William Shakespeare almost certainly did – the body of work attributed to this shadowy historical figure comprises some of the most inspired and exquisite English ever written. The greatest irony is not that *King Lear* and *The Tempest* were penned by a provincial middle-class merchant's son, but that of all the many visitors who pass through Stratford each year, the majority appear to be more interested in the writer himself than in what he wrote.

appearance. It includes a glover's workshop, where Shakespeare's father beavered away, though some argue that he was a wool merchant or a butcher. Neither is it certain that Shakespeare was born in this building nor that he was born on April 23, 1564 – it's just known that he was baptized on April 26, and it's an irresistible temptation to place the birth of the national poet three days earlier, on St George's Day. Despite these uncertainties, the house has been attracting visitors for centuries and upstairs one of the old mullioned windows, now displayed in a glass cabinet, bears the scratch-mark signatures of some of them, including those of Thomas Carlyle and Walter Scott.

Nash's House and New Place

Follow **High Street** south from the junction of Bridge and Henley streets, and you'll soon come to another Birthplace Trust property, **Nash's House** on Chapel Street (April, May, Sept & Oct daily 11am–5pm; June–Aug Mon–Sat 9.30am–5pm, Sun 10am–5pm; Nov–March daily 11am–4pm; £3.75). Once the property of Thomas Nash, first husband of Shakespeare's granddaughter, Elizabeth Hall, the house's ground floor is kitted out with a pleasant assortment of period furnishings. Upstairs, one display provides a potted history of Stratford, including a scattering of archeological bits and pieces, and another focuses on the house with a cabinet of woodcarvings made from the **mulberry tree** that once stood outside. Reputedly planted by Shakespeare, the tree was chopped down in the 1750s by the owner, a certain Reverend Francis Gastrell, because he was fed up with all the pilgrims. An enterprising woodcarver bought the wood and carved Shakespearean mementoes from it – hence the carvings in the cabinet.

The adjacent gardens contain the bare foundations of **New Place** (same hours), Shakespeare's last residence, which was demolished by the same Reverend Gastrell, but for different reasons – Gastrell was in bitter dispute with the town council over taxation. A replacement mulberry tree has been planted beside the foundations of New Place and there are others in the adjacent **Great Garden** (March–Oct Mon–Sat 9am–dusk, Sun 10am–dusk; Nov–Feb Mon–Sat 9am–4pm, Sun noon–4pm; free), a formal affair of topiary, lawns and flowerbeds. A gated path leads into the Great Garden from New Place, but the main entrance is on Chapel Lane.

On the other side of Chapel Lane stands the **Guild Chapel**, whose chunky tower and sturdy stonework shelter a plain interior enlivened by some rather crude stained-glass windows and a faded mural above the triumphal arch. The adjoining King Edward VI **Grammar School**, where it's assumed Shakespeare was educated, incorporates a creaky line of fifteenth-century **almshouses** running along Church Street.

Hall's Croft

At the end of Church Street, turn left along Old Town Street for Stratford's most impressive medieval house, the Birthplace Trust's **Hall's Croft** (April, May, Sept & Oct daily 11am–5pm; June–Aug Mon–Sat 9.30am–5pm, Sun 10am–5pm; Nov–March daily 11am–4pm; £3.75). The former home of Shakespeare's elder daughter, Susanna, and her doctor husband, John Hall, the immaculately maintained Croft, with its creaking wooden floors, beamed ceilings and fine kitchen range, holds a good-looking medley of period furniture and – mostly upstairs – a fascinating display on **Elizabethan medicine**. Hall established something of a reputation for his medical know-how and after his death some of his case notes were published in a volume entitled *Select Observations upon English Bodies*. You can peruse extracts from Hall's book – noting that Joan Chidkin of Southam "gave two vomits and two stools" after being "troubled with trembling of the arms and thighs" – and then suffer vicariously at the displays of eye-watering forceps and other implements. The best view of the building itself is at the back, in the neat walled garden.

Holy Trinity Church

Beyond Hall's Croft, Old Town Street steers right to reach the handsome **Holy Trinity Church** (March & Oct Mon–Sat 9am–5pm, Sun 12.30–5pm; April–Sept Mon–Sat 8.30am–6pm, Sun 12.30–5pm; Nov–Feb Mon–Sat 9am–4pm, Sun 12.30–5pm free), whose mellow, honey-coloured stonework dates from the thirteenth century. Enhanced by its riverside setting and flanked by the yews and weeping willows of its graveyard, the dignified proportions of this quintessentially English church are the result of several centuries of chopping and changing, culminating in the replacement of the original wooden spire with today's stone version in 1763. At the entrance, on the second set of doors, the **Sanctuary Knocker** is a reminder of medieval times when local criminals could seek refuge from the law here, but only for 37 days. This, so local custom dictated, was long enough for them to negotiate a deal with their persecutors. Inside, the nave is flanked by a fine set of stained-glass windows, some of which are medieval, and bathed in light from the clerestory windows up above. Quite unusually, you'll see that the nave is built on a slight skew from the line of the chancel – supposedly to represent Christ's inclined head on the cross. In the north aisle, beside the transept, is the **Clopton Chapel**, where the large wall-tomb of George Carew is a Renaissance extravagance decorated with military insignia appropriate to George's job as master of ordnance to James I. But poor old George is long forgotten, unlike William Shakespeare, who lies buried in the **chancel** (£1.50), his remains overseen by a sedate and studious memorial plaque and effigy added just seven years after his death.

The theatres and the Gower Memorial

Doubling back from the church, turn right into the **park** just before you reach Southern Lane and you can stroll along – or at least near – the river bank, past the dinky little **chain ferry** (50p) across the Avon, en route to the Royal Shakespeare Company's two main **theatres**, the Swan Theatre and the Royal Shakespeare Theatre – though both are currently closed during rebuilding. There was no theatre in Stratford in Shakespeare's day and indeed the first home-town festival in his honour was only held in 1769 at the behest of London-based David Garrick. Thereafter, the idea of building a permanent home in which to perform Shakespeare's works slowly gained momentum, and finally, in 1879, the first Memorial Theatre was opened on land donated by local beer baron Charles Flower. A fire in 1926 necessitated the construction of a new theatre, and the ensuing architectural competition, won by Elisabeth Scott, produced the **Royal Shakespeare Theatre**, a cinema-like, red-brick edifice that lasted until 2007, when work started on the creation of a much grander structure. This new theatre is scheduled to be completed in 2010 and the revamped Swan, a replica "in-the-round" Elizabethan stage just round the back, will be reopened at the same time. In the meantime, a third RSC auditorium, **The Courtyard Theatre**, a few yards away on Southern Lane, will host all the major performances.

In front of the Royal Shakespeare Theatre, the manicured lawns of a small riverside park stretch north as far as **Bancroft Basin**, where the Stratford canal meets the river. The basin is usually packed with narrowboats and in the small park on the far side, over the little hump-backed pedestrian bridge, is the finely sculpted **Gower Memorial** of 1888 in which a seated Shakespeare is

---

Tickets for the RSC

As the **Royal Shakespeare Company** (information: ☏01789/403444, ⊛www.rsc.org.uk) works on a repertory system, you could stay in Stratford for a few days and see three or four different plays. Neither would they all have to be Shakespearean: the RSC does indeed focus on the great man's plays, but it offers other productions too, from new modern writing through to plays written by Shakespeare's contemporaries. With two of the company's auditoria, the Swan and the **Royal Shakespeare Theatre**, closed for rebuilding, the RSC currently performs in the **Courtyard Theatre,** where tickets start at £5 for a restricted view, rising to £30 for the best seats in the house. Tickets can be bought online (⊛www.rsc.org.uk); by phone (☏0844/800 1110); at Stratford tourist office (see p.538); and in person at the Courtyard Theatre box office. Many performances are sold out months in advance and although there's always the off-chance of a last-minute return or stand-by ticket (for unsold seats), don't bet on it. Finally, some people find the Courtyard Theatre's seats very uncomfortable – take a cushion.

HAMLET.

▲ Gower Memorial

surrounded by characters from his plays. To round things off, stroll over to the Boathouse, on Swan's Nest Lane, where **Avon Boating** (April–Oct 9am–dusk; ☏01789/267073, ⊛www.avon-boating.co.uk) rents out rowing boats, punts and canoes for a couple of pounds a time; they also offer thirty-minute river trips (£4).

Anne Hathaway's Cottage

Anne Hathaway's Cottage (April–Oct Mon–Sat 9/9.30am–5pm, Sun 9.30/10am–5pm; Nov–March daily 10am–4pm; £5.50), also operated by the Birthplace Trust, is located just over a mile west of the centre in the well-heeled suburb of Shottery. The cottage – actually an old farmhouse – is an immaculately maintained, half-timbered affair with a thatched roof and dinky little chimneys. This was the home of Anne Hathaway before she married Shakespeare in 1582, and the interior holds a comely combination of period furniture, including a superb, finely carved four-poster bed. The garden is splendid too, crowded with bursting blooms in the summertime. The adjacent orchard and **Shakespeare Tree Garden** features a scattering of modern sculptures and over forty trees, shrubs and roses mentioned in the plays, with each bearing the appropriate quotation inscribed on a plaque. The most agreeable way to get to the cottage from the town centre is on the signposted **footpath** from Evesham Place, at the south end of Rother Street.

Mary Arden's House

The Birthplace Trust also owns **Mary Arden's House** (daily: April & May 10am–5pm; June–Aug 9.30am–5pm; Sept & Oct 11am–5pm; Nov–March 10am–4pm; £6), three miles northwest of the town centre in the village of Wilmcote. Mary was Shakespeare's mother and the only unmarried daughter of her father, Robert, at the time of his death in 1556. Unusually for the period, Mary inherited the house and land, thus becoming one of the neighbourhood's most eligible women – John Shakespeare, eager for self-improvement, married her within a year. The house is a well-furnished example of an Elizabethan farmhouse and, though the labelling is rather scant, a platoon of guides fills in the details of family life and traditions.

Eating and drinking

Stratford is used to feeding and watering thousands of visitors, so finding refreshment is never difficult. The problem is that many places are geared up to serve the day-tripper as rapidly as possible – not a recipe for much gastronomic delight. That said, there is a scattering of very good **restaurants**, several of which have been catering to theatre-goers for many years, and a handful of **pubs** and **cafés** offering good food, too. The best restaurants are concentrated along Sheep Street, running up from Waterside.

Restaurants and cafés

Kingfisher Fish Bar 13 Ely St. The best fish-and-chip shop in town. Takeaway and sit-down. A five-minute walk from the theatres. Closed Sun.

Lamb's Restaurant 12 Sheep St ☎01789/292554. Smart and immensely appealing restaurant serving a mouth-watering range of stylish English and continental dishes in antique premises – beamed ceilings and so forth. Daily specials at around £8, other main courses £14–16. The best place in town. Closed Mon lunchtime.

Malbec Restaurant 6 Union St ☎01789/269106. Smart and intimate restaurant serving top-quality seafood and meat dishes, often with a Mediterranean slant. Mains around £15.

The Oppo 13 Sheep St ☎01789/269980. International cuisine in a busy but amiable atmosphere and pleasant old premises. The dishes of the day, chalked up on a board inside, are good value at around £7, otherwise mains average £12.

Russons 8 Church St ☎01789/268822. Excellent, good-value cuisine, featuring interesting meat and vegetarian dishes on the main menu and an extensive blackboard of daily specials. Cosy little place too. Main courses around £11. Closed Sun & Mon.

Pubs

Dirty Duck 53 Waterside. The archetypal actors' pub, stuffed to the gunwales every night with a vocal entourage of RSC employees and hangers-on. Traditional beers in somewhat spartan premises plus a terrace for hot-weather drinking.

Windmill Inn Church St. Popular pub with rabbit-warren rooms and low-beamed ceilings. Flowers beers too.

Listings

Bike rental Spencer Clarke Cycles, 3 Guild St ☎01789/205057, ⓦwww.cycling-tours.org.uk. Cycle rental and Cotswold cycling tours.

Car rental Hertz, Station Road ☎01789/298827.
Pharmacy Boots, 11 Bridge St ☎01789/292173.
Post office Henley St (Mon–Sat 9am–5.30pm).

Warwick

Pocket-sized **WARWICK**, just eight miles northeast of Stratford and easily reached by bus and train, is famous for its massive **castle**, but it also possesses several charming streetscapes erected in the aftermath of a great fire in 1694, not to mention an especially fine church chancel. An hour or two is quite enough time to nose around the town centre, though you'll need the whole day if, braving the crowds and the medieval musicians, you're also set on exploring the castle and its extensive grounds: either way, Warwick is the perfect day-trip from Stratford.

The castle

Towering above the River Avon at the foot of the town centre, **Warwick Castle** (daily: April–Sept 10am–6pm; Oct–March 10am–5pm; £17.95; parking £2.50–5; ⓦwww.warwick-castle.co.uk) is often proclaimed the "greatest medieval castle in Britain". This claim is valid enough if bulk equals greatness, though even so, much of the existing structure is the result of extensive nineteenth-century tinkering. It's likely that the first fortress on this site was raised by Ethelfleda, daughter of Alfred the Great, in about 915 AD, but things really took off with the Normans, who built a large motte and bailey towards the end of the eleventh century. Almost three hundred years later, the eleventh Earl of Warwick turned the stronghold into a formidable stone castle, complete with elaborate gatehouses, multiple turrets and a keep. The earl and his descendants played a prominent part in the Hundred Years' War – one of their number was the executioner of **Joan of Arc** – and they all brought prisoners back to Warwick pending ransom negotiations.

The **entrance** to the castle is through the old stable block at the bottom of Castle Street. Beyond, a footpath leads round to the imposing moated and mounded **East Gate**. Over the footbridge – and beyond the protective towers – is the main **courtyard**. You can stroll along the ramparts and climb the towers, but most visitors head straight for one or other of the special displays installed inside the castle's many chambers and towers. One of the most popular of these displays is the "Royal Weekend Party, 1898", an extravaganza of waxwork nobility hobnobbing in the private apartments which were rebuilt in the 1870s after fire damage. The **grounds** are much more enjoyable, acres of woodland and lawn inhabited by peacocks and including a large glass **conservatory**. A footbridge leads over the River Avon to **River Island**, the site of jousting tournaments and other such medieval hoopla.

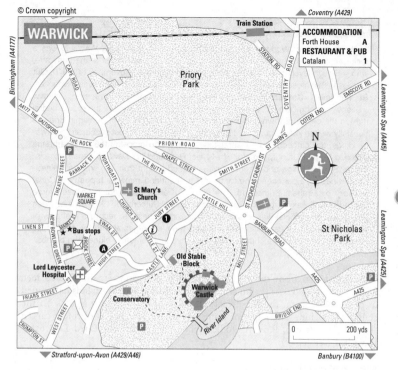

The town centre

Re-emerging from the castle at the stables, **Castle Street** leads up the hill for a few yards to its junction with the High Street. Turn left and it's a brief stroll to another remarkable building, the **Lord Leycester Hospital** (daily except Mon: April–Oct 10am–5pm; Nov–March 10am–4pm; £4.90), a tangle of half-timbered buildings that lean at fairy-tale angles against the old West Gate. The complex represents one of Britain's best-preserved examples of domestic Elizabethan architecture. It was established as a hostel for old soldiers by Robert Dudley, Earl of Leicester – a favourite of Queen Elizabeth I – and incorporates several beamed buildings, principally the Great Hall and the Guildhall, as well as a wonderful galleried courtyard and an intimate chantry chapel. There's a **tearoom** too, plus a modest regimental museum – appropriately enough as retired servicemen (and their wives) still live here. Known as "Brethren", the veterans are distinguished by their black cloaks and silver boar pendants, which they don for ceremonial occasions.

Doubling back along the High Street, turn left up Church Street – opposite Castle Street – for **St Mary's Church** (daily: April–Oct 10am–6pm; Nov–March 10am–4.30pm; £1 donation suggested), which was rebuilt in a weird Gothic-Renaissance amalgam after the fire of 1694. One part remained untouched, however – the **chancel**, a glorious illustration of the Perpendicular style with a splendid vaulted ceiling of flying and fronded ribs. On the right-hand side of the chancel is the **Beauchamp Chapel**, which contains several beautiful tombs, exquisite works of art beginning with that of Richard Beauchamp, Earl of Warwick, who is depicted in an elaborate suit of armour

At the outbreak of World War II, **Coventry**, eleven miles north of Warwick, was a major engineering centre and its factories attracted the attentions of the Luftwaffe, who well-nigh levelled the town in a huge bombing raid on November 14, 1940. Out of the ashes arose what is now Coventry's one sight of note, Basil Spence's **St Michael's Cathedral** (daily 9am–5pm; £3 donation requested; ⓦwww .coventrycathedral.org.uk), raised alongside the burnt–out shell of the old cathedral right in the centre of town and dedicated with a performance of Benjamin Britten's specially written *War Requiem* in 1962. One of the country's most successful postwar buildings, the cathedral's pink sandstone is light and graceful, the main entrance adorned by a stunningly forceful *St Michael Defeating the Devil* by Jacob Epstein. Inside, Spence's high and slender nave is bathed in light from the soaring stained-glass windows, a perfect setting for the magnificent and immense **tapestry** of *Christ in Glory* by Graham Sutherland. The choice of artist could not have been more appropriate. A painter, graphic artist and designer, Sutherland (1903–80) had been one of Britain's official war artists, his particular job being to record the effects of German bombing. A canopied walkway links the new cathedral with the old, whose shattered nave flanks the church tower and spire that somehow eluded the bombs.

of Italian design from the tip of his swan helmet down to his mailed feet. Richard is guarded by a griffin and a bear and he lies with his hands half joined in prayer so that, on the Resurrection, he could see the holy figures on the ceiling above him. The adjacent tomb of Ambrose Dudley is of finely carved alabaster, as is that of Robert Dudley, who also founded the **Lord Leycester Hospital** (see p.547).

Practicalities

From Warwick **train station**, on the northern edge of town, it's about ten minutes' walk to the centre via Station and Coventry roads. More conveniently, **buses** stop on Market Street, close to the Market Square, from where it's a couple of minutes' walk east to St Mary's Church. The **tourist office** is in the old Court House at the corner of Castle and Jury streets (daily 9.30am–4.30pm; ☏01926/492212, ⓦwww.warwick-uk.co.uk). They have a list of local hotels and B&Bs, but with Stratford so near and easy to reach, there's no special reason to stay. That said, *Forth House*, 44 High St (☏01926/401512, ⓦwww .forthhouseuk.co.uk; ⑤), is an excellent **B&B** with two en-suite and very comfortable guest rooms in a listed sixteenth-century property a short walk from the tourist office. For a bite to **eat**, try the *Catalan*, 6 Jury St (closed Tues eve & all day Sun), a slick, modern café-restaurant, which offers tasty tapas and light lunches during the day, and Mediterranean-inspired food at night, with main courses from £10; it's located just along from the tourist office.

Worcestershire

In geographical terms, **Worcestershire** can be compared to a huge saucer, with the low-lying plains of the Severn Valley and the Vale of Evesham, Britain's foremost fruit-growing area, rising to a lip of hills, principally the Malverns in the west and the Cotswolds to the south. In character, the county divides into two broad belts. To the north lie the industrial and overspill towns – Droitwich and Redditch for instance – that have much in common with the Birmingham conurbation, while the south is predominantly rural. Marking the transition between the two is **Worcester** itself, whose main claim to fame is its splendid cathedral. The south holds the county's finest scenery in the **Malvern Hills**, excellent walking territory much loved by that most English of composers, **Edward Elgar**, and home to the amiable former spa town of **Great Malvern**. South Worcestershire's rural lifestyle is famously portrayed in *The Archers*, the BBC's long-running radio soap, which attracts a massive and extraordinarily dedicated audience. From Great Malvern, it's a short drive southeast to Tewkesbury, across the border in Gloucestershire, with its splendid Norman abbey.

The proximity of Birmingham ensures Worcestershire has a good network of **trains** and **buses**, though services are spasmodic amongst the villages in the south of the county. There's an excellent regional public transport information line covering all of the West Midlands – Centro (☎0121/200 2787, Ⓦwww.centro.org.uk) – or you can resort to the usual national numbers for bus (☎0871/200 2233, Ⓦwww.traveline.org.uk) and rail (☎0845/748 4950, Ⓦwww.nationalrail.co.uk).

Worcester and around

Bang at the geographical heart of the county, **WORCESTER** is something of an architectural hotchpotch, its half-timbered Tudor and stone Georgian buildings standing cheek by jowl with some fairly charmless modern developments. Postwar clumsiness apart, the biggest single influence on the city has always been the **River Severn**, which flows along Worcester's west flank. It was the river that drew the Romans here and river trade that made it an important settlement as early as Saxon times. The river's major drawback is its propensity to breach its banks, inundating parts of the city in murky water, though this has at least limited development along the riverside, where a leafy footpath passes below the mighty bulk of the **cathedral**, Worcester's star turn by a long chalk.

The cathedral

Towering above the River Severn, the soaring sandstone of **Worcester Cathedral** (daily 8am–6pm; free, £3 donation requested; Ⓦwww.worcestercathedral.org.uk) comprises a rich stew of architectural styles dating from 1084. The bulk of the church is firmly medieval, from the Norman transepts through to the late Gothic cloister, though the Victorians did have a good old hack at the exterior. Inside, the cavernous **nave** is unexceptional except for its two west bays, which are an unusual – and unusually fine – example of the transitional period, when the rounded Norman arch was being supplanted by the pointed arches of Early English Gothic. They date to the 1160s. The pillars of the nave are decorated with bunches of fruit, initially carved by stonemasons from Lincoln, most of whom succumbed to the Black Death, leaving inferior successors to finish the job.

Moving on, the **choir**, built between 1220 and 1260, is a beautiful illustration of the Early English style, with a forest of slender pillars rising above the intricately worked choir stalls. Here also, in front of the high altar, is the **table-tomb** of England's most reviled monarch, **King John**, who died in 1216. Much-loathed, perhaps rightly so, but John certainly would not have appreciated the lion that lies at his feet biting the end of his sword – a reference to the curbing of his power by the barons when they obliged him to sign the Magna Carta. Just beyond the tomb – on the right – is **Prince Arthur's**

Chantry, a delicate lacy confection of carved stonework built in 1504 to commemorate Arthur, King Henry VII's son, who died at the age of 15 in Ludlow. He was on his honeymoon with Catherine of Aragon, who was soon passed on – with such momentous consequences – to his younger brother, Henry. The chantry is liberally plastered with heraldic and symbolic depictions of the houses of York and Lancaster, united by the Lancastrian Henry VII after his victory at Bosworth Field and subsequent marriage to Elizabeth, daughter of the Yorkist king Edward IV.

A stairway beside the chantry leads down to the **crypt**, the oldest part of the cathedral and the largest Norman crypt in the country. In addition, a doorway on the south side of the nave leads to the **cloisters**, with their delightful roof bosses, and the circular, largely Norman **chapter house**, which has the distinction of being the first such building constructed with the use of a central supporting pillar.

Royal Worcester Porcelain

Tucked away behind the cathedral on Severn Street, the **Royal Worcester Porcelain** complex (Mon–Sat 9am–5.30pm, Sun 11am–5pm) contains factory shops, a visitor centre, a substantial porcelain museum (same times; £5), and the factory itself (1hr guided tours Mon–Fri only, reservations required on ☎01905/746000, ⓦwww.worcesterporcelainmuseum.org; £5, £9 with museum). Beginning in the mid-eighteenth century, porcelain manufacture was long the city's main industry and Royal Worcester its leading light. Traditionally, the company's wares were ornate to a fault, but they also kept abreast of fashions – as they continue to do today. Among the pieces exhibited in the museum, keep an eye out for Dorothy Doughtey's bird pieces and an extravagant vase celebrating Wellington and his Prussian ally Blucher, whose timely help proved crucial at the Battle of Waterloo.

The Commandery

From the Royal Worcester complex, it's a brief walk north via Severn Street to the **Commandery** (Mon–Sat 10am–5pm, Sun 1.30–5pm; £5.25), on the far side of the busy Sidbury dual carriageway. This is the town's main history museum, its varied displays occupying Worcester's oldest building, a rambling, half-timbered structure dating from the early sixteenth century. Its moment of fame came when **King Charles II** used the building as his headquarters during the battle-cum-siege of Worcester in 1651. Charles II's father – King Charles I – had been executed in 1649 and England had become a Commonwealth, run by Parliament. Two years later Charles II landed in Scotland, raised an army and then marched south bent on seizing the English Crown. In the event, Oliver Cromwell outwitted and trapped Charles and his army here in Worcester. However, much to Cromwell's chagrin, Charles managed to escape Parliament's clutches and reach safety in France by fleeing in disguise – no mean feat considering the would-be king was six feet and two inches tall, about ten inches above the average. Recently refurbished, the highlight of the Commandery is the **painted chamber**, whose walls are covered with intriguing cameos recalling the building's original use as a monastery hospital. Each of the cameos relates to a saint with healing powers – for starters St Roch nursing plague victims and St Erasmus, the patron saint of stomach diseases, having his bowels winched out by his tormentors. There's also a painting of St Thomas à Becket being stabbed in the head by a group of knights, enough to make him the saint who specialized in headaches.

Practicalities

Worcester has two **train stations**. The handiest for the city centre is Foregate Street (from London Paddington and Hereford), from where it's about half a mile south to the cathedral along Foregate Street and its continuation The Cross and the High Street. The other train station, Shrub Hill, is located further out, about a mile to the northeast of the cathedral. The **bus station** is at the back of the sprawling Crowngate shopping mall, on The Butts, about 600 yards northwest of the cathedral. The **tourist office** (Mon–Sat 9.30am–5pm; ☎01905/726311, ⓦwww.visitworcester.com) is in the Guildhall towards the cathedral end of the High Street. An extravagant structure built in the 1720s, the **Guildhall** comes complete with trumpeting cherubs, allegorical figures and niche statues of Charles I, Charles II and Queen Anne.

There's no overriding reason to overnight in Worcester, but there are several appealing places **to stay**, including the likeable *Diglis House Hotel*, in an attractive Georgian building beside the river and just behind the cathedral on Severn Street (☎01905/353518, ⓦwww.diglishousehotel.co.uk; ⑥). The hotel has a vaguely old-fashioned air – and is not the worse for that – and each of the twenty-odd rooms is comfortable and well appointed. Amongst several central B&Bs, the pick is *Burgage House*, 4 College Precincts (☎01905/25396, ⓦwww.burgagehouse.co.uk; no credit cards; ⑨), which occupies a delightful Georgian town house on a cobbled lane beside the cathedral.

For **food**, there are several recommendable cafés and restaurants dotted along Friar Street, a short walk east of the cathedral, as well as its northerly continuation, New Street. One of them is the pastel-painted *Saffron's Bistro*, 15 New St (☎01905/610505), where an imaginative menu features such delights as monkfish and tiger prawns in a wine sauce; main courses here average £14, less for the vegetarian dishes.

Around Worcester: Lower Broadheath

One of Worcestershire's most famous sons was **Sir Edward Elgar** (1857–1934), the first internationally acclaimed English composer for almost two hundred years. Elgar built his reputation on a series of lyrical works celebrating his abiding love of the Worcestershire countryside, quintessentially English pieces amongst which the most famous is the *Enigma Variations*. Elgar was born in **LOWER BROADHEATH**, a hamlet just four miles west of Worcester off the A44, and it's here you'll find the **Elgar Birthplace Museum** (daily 11am–5pm, last admission 4.15pm; £5; ⓦwww.elgarfoundation.org). This comprises a modern **visitor centre**, exploring Elgar's life and times with the assistance of some fascinating old photographs, and – just behind at the end of the path – the modest brick **cottage** where he was born. Inside the cottage, the cramped rooms contain several of Elgar's musical scores, personal correspondence in his spidery handwriting, press cuttings, and miscellaneous mementoes. The museum also organizes an imaginative programme of special events from illustrated talks to Elgar concerts and recitals. Lower Broadheath is not, however, of any scenic interest and if you want to see the green, quilted landscapes that inspired Elgar you'll have to push on to The Malverns.

Great Malvern and the Malvern Hills

One of the most exclusive and prosperous areas of the Midlands, **The Malverns** is the generic name for a string of towns and villages stretched along the eastern lower slopes of the **Malvern Hills**, which rise spectacularly out of the flatlands a few miles to the southwest of Worcester. About nine miles from north to south

– between the A44 and the M50 – and never more than five miles wide, the hills straddle the Worcestershire–Herefordshire boundary. Of ancient granite rock, they are punctuated by over twenty summits, mostly around 1000 feet high, and in between lie innumerable dips and hollows. It's easy if energetic walking country, with great views, and there's an excellent network of hiking trails, most of which can be completed in a day or half-day.

Amongst The Malverns, it's **GREAT MALVERN** which grabs the attention, its pocket-sized centre clambering up the hillside with the crags of North Hill beckoning beyond. The Benedictines chose this hilly setting for one of their abbeys and although Henry VIII closed the place down in 1538, the **Priory Church** (daily: 9am–5pm; free) has survived, the crisp symmetries and elaborate decoration of its exterior witnessing the priory's former wealth. Inside, the sternly Norman nave sweeps down to the chancel, which came later, a fine example of Perpendicular Gothic, its sinuous tracery serving to frame a simply fabulous set of **stained-glass windows** dating from the end of the fifteenth century. Amongst them, pride of place goes to the great east window, a giant flash of colour with several easily decipherable Biblical scenes, such as Palm Sunday and the Crucifixion. The north transept window is also of special interest as it holds both a portrait of Prince Arthur, Henry VII's son – the same Arthur who is commemorated in Worcester Cathedral (see p.549) – and a rare "Coronation of Mary" set against a blue sky background. These coronation windows were once a common feature of English monastery churches, but the Protestants, inflamed by such idolatry, hunted almost all of them down.

Malvern Museum

A couple of minutes' walk away, hard by the top of Church Street, the modest **Malvern Museum** (Easter–Oct daily except for most Wed 10.30am–5pm; £1) is housed in the delicately proportioned Priory Gatehouse, but it concentrates on Great Malvern's days as a spa town. The spring waters hereabouts became popular at the end of the eighteenth century, but it was to be the Victorians who packed the place out – and built the grand stone houses that still line many of the town's streets. The museum has a goodly selection of old cartoons showing patients packed into cold wet sheets before hopping gaily away from their crutches and wheelchairs – exaggerated claims perhaps, but poor hygiene did bring on a multitude of skin complaints and the relief the spa waters brought was real enough. You can still sample the waters at ♨ *St Ann's Well Café* (☎01684/560285; June & Sept daily except Mon; Oct–May Sat & Sun only), a cosy little vegetarian café in an attractive Georgian building a steep fifteen-minute walk up the wooded hillside from the top of town; the signposted path begins on the far side of the main road across from the *Foley Arms Hotel*.

Hiking The Malverns

Great Malvern tourist office (see p.553) sells hiking maps and issues half a dozen free **Trail Guide leaflets**, which describe circular routes up to and along the hills that rise behind the town. The shortest trail is just one and a half miles, the longest four. One of the most appealing is the 2.5-mile hoof up to the top – and back – of **North Hill** (1307ft), from where there are panoramic views over the surrounding countryside; this hike takes in *St Ann's Well Café* (see above). Alternatively, the one-way hike along the top of the ridge is a sterner test that takes all day and is ten miles long. On the way, you'll pass through the vague remains of a brace of Iron Age hill forts. It's best to start at the southern end – at **Chase End Hill** – and work your way north.

Back at the museum, it's a short walk down the hill to Grange Road, where the **Malvern Theatres** (℡01684/892277, Ⓦwww.malvern-theatres.co.uk) is the key venue for the wide range of special events the town puts on each year.

Practicalities

With its dainty ironwork and quaint chimneys, Great Malvern's infinitely rustic **train station** has fast and frequent connections with Birmingham and Worcester. It's located half a mile or so from the town centre – take Avenue Road and then **Church Street**, the steeply sloping main drag. The **tourist office** is at the top of Church Street, across from the Priory Church (daily 10am–5pm; ℡01684/892289, Ⓦwww.malvernhills.gov.uk/tourism).

Accommodation is plentiful. Amongst the **hotels**, the pick is *The Abbey* (℡01684/892332, Ⓦwww.sarova.com; ◉), a rambling, creeper-clad Victorian hotel with mock-Tudor timbering, handsome stone doorways and plush rooms, all set behind the Priory Church on Abbey Road – but note that the hotel's lumpy modern wing is unappetizing; the hotel is part of a small chain. One very recommendable **B&B** is *The Copper Beech House*, in a large Victorian house near the train station at 32 Avenue Rd (℡01684/565013, Ⓦwww.copperbeechhouse .co.uk; ◉), offering a handful of well-appointed en-suite rooms decorated in plush, semi-period style. Further afield, a mile or two to the south along the A449 in **MALVERN WELLS**, is the *Cottage in the Wood Hotel* (℡01684/575859, Ⓦwww.cottageinthewood.co.uk; ◉), which occupies an extensively modernized old mansion with superb views out across the flatlands down below; the thirty-odd rooms are divided between the main house and two well-appointed annexes and each is decorated in bright, often vintage style.

With most visitors apparently eating where they sleep, the **restaurant** scene in Great Malvern is not as varied as you might expect – try the smart and chic *Anupam* Asian restaurant at 85 Church St (℡01684/573814), where main courses average around £10.

Tewkesbury

The small market town of **TEWKESBURY**, over in Gloucestershire, fourteen miles southeast of Great Malvern, is hemmed in by the Avon and Severn rivers, which converge nearby, and the threat of floods has always curbed its expansion. Important throughout the Middle Ages, it was bypassed by the Industrial Revolution and today, although it possesses a raft of old timber-framed buildings, especially on Church Street, the town can't help but feel a little neglected and would not really merit a visit were it not for its superb Norman abbey.

Tewkesbury Abbey

The site of **Tewkesbury Abbey** (Mon–Sat 7.30am–5.30/6pm, Sun 7.30am–7pm; suggested donation £3; Ⓦwww.tewkesburyabbey.org.uk) was first selected for a Benedictine monastery in the eighth century, but virtually nothing of the Saxon complex survived a Danish raid, and the Normans began work on a replacement in 1092. The job took about sixty years to complete, with some additions made in the fourteenth century. Two hundred years later the Dissolution brought about the destruction of most of the monastic buildings, but the abbey itself survived thanks to a buy-out in which the local people paid Henry VIII £453 for the property.

The sheer scale of the abbey's exterior makes a lasting impact: its colossal **tower** is the largest Norman tower in the world, while the west front's soaring recessed arch – 65 feet high – is the only exterior arch in the country to boast such impressive proportions. In the nave, fourteen stout Norman pillars steal the show, graceful despite their size, and topped by a fourteenth-century ribbed and vaulted ceiling, studded with gilded bosses (look for the musical angels). On the blue and scarlet **choir** roof the bosses include a ring of shining suns (emblem of the Yorkist cause), said to have been put there by Edward IV after the defeat of the Lancastrians at Tewkesbury in 1471, the last important battle of the Wars of the Roses: the battlefield, known as Bloody Meadow, is off Lincoln Green Lane, southwest of the abbey. South of the choir is the **Milton Organ**, played by the poet when he was secretary to Oliver Cromwell at Hampton Court and bought by the townspeople in 1727. The abbey's medieval tombs celebrate Tewkesbury's greatest patrons, the Fitzhamons, De Clares, Beauchamps and Despensers, who turned the building into something of a mausoleum for the nobility. The Despensers have the best monuments, particularly Sir Edward, standard-bearer to the Black Prince, who died in 1375 and is shown as a kneeling figure on the roof of the **Trinity Chapel** to the right of the high altar. Nearby, in the ambulatory behind the high altar, the macabre so-called **Wakeman Cenotaph**, carved in the fifteenth century but of otherwise uncertain origin, represents a decaying corpse being consumed by snakes and other creatures.

Practicalities

There are hourly **buses** from Great Malvern to Tewkesbury and the journey takes about an hour, though you do have to change at Upton upon Severn. After you have visited the abbey, you might take a **pint** at The Berkeley Arms, an ancient half-timbered pub just along from the abbey on Church Street. There's a good **delicatessen**, *1471*, at 102 Church St, next door to the **tourist** office (April–Oct Mon–Sat 9.30am–5pm, Sun 10am–4pm; Nov–March closed Sun; ☏01684/855040, ⓦwww.visitcotswoldsandsevernvale.gov.uk).

Herefordshire

Over the Malvern Hills from Worcestershire, the rolling agricultural landscapes of **Herefordshire** have an easy-going charm, but the finest scenery hereabouts is along the banks of the **River Wye**, which wriggles and worms its way across the county linking most of the places of interest. Plonked in the middle of the county on the Wye is **Hereford**, a sleepy, rather old-fashioned sort of place whose proudest possession, the cathedral's remarkable Mappa Mundi map, was almost flogged off in a round of ecclesiastical budget cuts back in the 1980s. Hereford is also close to the superb Norman church of tiny **Kilpeck**, to the southwest, and, to the east, the delightful little town of **Ledbury**, sitting on the edge of the Malvern Hills and distinguished by its Tudor and Stuart half-timbered buildings – sometimes called "**Black and Whites**". Moving on, the southeast corner of the county has one attractive town, **Ross-on-Wye**, a genial little place with a picturesque river setting. Ross is also an ideal base for explorations into one of the wilder portions of the **Wye River Valley**, around a well-known beauty spot, **Symonds Yat Rock**. To the west of Hereford, hard by the Welsh border, the key attraction is **Hay-on-Wye**, which – thanks to the purposeful industry of Richard Booth (see p.561) – has become the world's largest repository of secondhand books, on sale in around thirty bookshops.

Herefordshire possesses one **rail line**, linking Ledbury and Hereford with points north to Shrewsbury and east to Great Malvern and Worcester. Otherwise, you'll be restricted to the tender mercies of the county's **buses**, which provide a reasonable service between the villages and towns, except on Sundays when there's almost nothing at all. All the local tourist offices have bus timetables and there's **bus information** on ☎0870/608 2608 and ⓦwww .herefordshire-buses.tbctimes.co.uk.

Hereford

Founded by the Saxons in the seventh century, **HEREFORD** – literally "army ford" – was long a border garrison town held against the Welsh, its military importance guaranteed by its strategic position beside the River Wye. It also became a religious centre after the Welsh murdered the Saxon king Ethelbert near here in 794. These were bloody times, so in itself the murder was pretty routine, but legend asserts that Ethelbert's ghost kept on turning up to insist his remains be interred here in Hereford – and eventually it got its way. Ethelbert's posthumous antics made him a military martyr and a Saxon cult soon grew up around his name, prompting the construction of the town's first cathedral. The Welsh were, however, having none of this and, in 1055, they attacked Hereford and burnt the cathedral to the ground.

Today, with the fortifications that once girdled the city all but vanished, it's the second **cathedral**, dating from the eleventh century, which forms the main focus of architectural interest. It lies just to the north of the River Wye at the heart of the city centre, whose compact tangle of narrow streets and squares is clumsily boxed in by the ring road. Taken as a whole, Hereford makes for a pleasant – if not exactly riveting – overnight stay and is also within easy striking distance of **Kilpeck**, with its exquisite Norman church, and pocket-sized **Ledbury**, one of the county's prettiest towns.

The cathedral

Hereford Cathedral (daily 9.15am–5.30pm; £4 donation suggested; ⓦwww .herefordcathedral.org) is a curious building, an uncomfortable amalgamation of architectural styles, with bits and pieces added to the eleventh-century original by a string of bishops and culminating in an extensive – and not especially sympathetic – Victorian refit. From the outside, the sandstone **tower** is the dominant feature, constructed in the early fourteenth century to eclipse the Norman western tower, which subsequently collapsed under its own weight in 1786. The crashing masonry mauled the **nave** and its replacement lacks the grandeur of most other English cathedrals, though the forceful symmetries of the long rank of surviving Norman arches and piers more than hints at what went before. The **north transept** is, however, a flawless exercise in thirteenth-century taste, its soaring windows a classic example of Early English architecture and a handsome home for the delicately carved table-tomb of a certain St Thomas Cantilupe. Across the church, the **south transept** is largely Norman, its chunky stonework interrupted by an old fireplace, one of the few still surviving within an English church, and decorated by an intricately carved *Adoration of the Magi*, a sixteenth-century bas-relief triptych from Germany.

The Mappa Mundi and Chained Library

In the 1980s, the cathedral's finances were so stretched that a plan was drawn up to sell its most treasured possession, the **Mappa Mundi**. There was an awful lot of cultural huffing and puffing about this controversial proposal, but the government and John Paul Getty Jnr rode to the rescue, with the oil tycoon stumping up a million pounds to keep the map here and install it in a brand-new building. Made of sandstone, this **New Library** – located next to the cathedral at the west end of the cloisters – blends in seamlessly with the other, older buildings close by. Inside, the **Mappa Mundi and Chained Library Exhibition** (April–Oct Mon–Sat 10am–4.30pm, plus May–Sept Sun 11am–3.30pm; Nov–March Mon–Sat 10am–3.30pm, but some closures for maintenance in Jan; £4.50) begins with a series of interpretative panels that lead to the Mappa, displayed in a dimly lit room. Dating to about 1300, and 64 by 52 inches in size (1.58 x 1.33 metres), the map is quite simply remarkable – and it provides an extraordinary insight into the medieval mind. It is indeed a map (as we know it) in so far as it suggests the general geography of the world – with Asia at the top and Europe and Africa below, to left and right respectively – but it also squeezes in history, mythology and theology. At the top of the map, Christ sits in judgment with the saved on one side, the damned on the other – hell is represented by the jaws of a dragon. The rest of the border contains representations of the twelve winds and the repeated monogram "MORS" – for death. Inside the border, at the top of the earth, is the Garden of Eden, shown as an island, and in the centre is the walled city of Jerusalem. Britain is at the bottom on the left with Hereford – and several other cathedral cities – labelled in Latin, as are almost all the other inscriptions. In total, the three continents are adorned by over five hundred drawings, some signifying towns and cities, others biblical events, plants, birds and animals as well as a menagerie of mythological creatures – from the manticoras (man-headed-lions) and the essedones (cannibals), through to the blemyae (who have heads in their chests).

As if this wasn't enough, the New Library also holds the **Chained Library**, a remarkably extensive collection of books and manuscripts dating from the eighth to the eighteenth century. A selection is always on display. The cathedral also owns a copy of the **Magna Carta** – or, to be exact, one of the revised versions drawn up after the original of 1215 and complete with clauses reworded in the king's favour – and this is frequently on display in the Chained Library too.

The rest of the city

After the Mappa, Hereford's other attractions can't help but seem rather pedestrian. Nonetheless, the **Hereford Museum and Art Gallery**, in a flamboyant Victorian building opposite the cathedral on Broad Street (Tues–Sat 10am–5pm, plus April–Sept Sun 10am–4pm; free), does hold a mildly diverting collection of geological remains, local history and Victorian art spruced up with several interactive exhibits. From the gallery, Broad Street continues up and round into the main square, **High Town**, which is fringed by several good-looking Georgian buildings.

Practicalities

From Hereford **train station**, it's about half a mile southwest to the main square, High Town – via Station Approach, Commercial Road and its continuation Commercial Street. The long-distance **bus station** is just off Commercial Road, but most local and some regional buses stop in St Peter's Square, at the east end of High Town. The **tourist office** is directly opposite the cathedral, at 1 King St (Mon–Sat 9am–5pm, plus mid–May to mid–Sept Sun 10am–4pm; ℡01432/268430, ⊛www.visitherefordshire.co.uk). They stock oodles of local leaflets and issue the free *Herefordshire Visitor Guide*, which has comprehensive accommodation listings.

Easily the best **hotel** in town is the ☆ *Castle House*, an immaculate refurbished Georgian mansion just a couple of minutes' walk from the cathedral on Castle Street (℡01432/356321, ⊛www.castlehse.co.uk; ❽). The hotel has a chic waterside terrace at the rear and each of the rooms is decorated in a plush modern version of Georgian style. Hereford also has a substantial number of **B&Bs**, arguably the pick of which is *Charades*, 34 Southbank Rd (℡01432/269444, Ⓦ www.charadeshereford.co.uk; ◑), with five comfortable, en-suite guest rooms in a large Victorian house a ten- to fifteen-minute walk northeast from the centre. To get there, take Commercial Street and then Commercial Road, cross the railway bridge and Southbank is the second on the right.

There are several appealing **places to eat** just north of the cathedral on pedestrianized Church Street. One of the best is *Nutters* (closed Sun), a vegetarian café just off Church Street on Capuchin Yard. There's also *Cafe @allsaints*, in the old church at the top of Broad Street (closed Sun), where they serve a tasty range of well-conceived veggie dishes – ricotta pie with salad leaves for instance – at around £6. The smartest restaurant in town is at the *Castle House Hotel* (see oppoiste), where the emphasis is on local ingredients – Hereford beef and Gloucestershire pork for instance; main courses start at £13.

Don't leave town without sampling the favourite local tipple, **cider**. Every pub in town serves the stuff with one of the most enjoyable being *The Barrels*, a traditional place, five minutes' walk southeast of High Town, at 69 St Owen's St. *The Barrels* is also the home pub of the local Wye Valley Brewery (Ⓦ www .wyevalleybrewery.co.uk), whose trademark **bitters** are much acclaimed.

Around Hereford: Kilpeck

The lonely hamlet of **KILPECK**, nine miles southwest of Hereford off the A465, boasts the red sandstone **Church of St Mary and St David**, arguably the most perfectly preserved Norman church in Britain. Here, the full vitality of Saxon-Norman sculpture is revealed, principally around the south door where Oriental-looking warriors gaze out, and birds, dragons, green men, a phoenix and all sorts of mythical monsters hoop the tympanum's Tree of Life. Up above, running right round the church, a superb set of no less than ninety tiny **corbel** sculptures features all manner of curiosities from grotesques and animal heads to musicians and acrobats, with barely a saint or religious figure in sight. The sculptors, who may or may not have had some sort of decorative plan, seem to have been inspired by pagan Viking carving, reminders of the Normans' Scandinavian ancestry – William the Conqueror was the descendant of a Viking chief who seized Normandy in the tenth century. The Victorians restored the corbel sculptures, but removed the more sexually explicit, with the exception of the genital-splaying **sheila-na-gig** on the apse to the right of the south doorway – food for thought. Inside, the church is plain and frugal, but there are several exquisite carvings here too, much more serene than the corbels and at their finest in the pious saints decorating the chancel arch.

Kilpeck was originally a frontier settlement, but the old village disappeared ages ago as did the **castle**, now no more than an overgrown hump at the top of the church graveyard.

Ledbury

Heading east from Hereford, it's an easy fifteen miles along the A438 to **LEDBURY**, a good-looking little town glued to the western edge of the Malvern Hills. The focus of the town is the Market Place, home to the dinky **Market House**, a Tudor beamed building raised on oak columns and with herringbone pattern beams. From beside it, narrow **Church Lane** – not to be confused with adjacent Church Street – runs up the slope framed by an especially fine ensemble of half-timbered Tudor and Stuart buildings. Among

▲ Kilpeck Church

them is the Butcher Row House Museum and, pick of the bunch, the so-called **Painted Room** (Easter–Sept Mon–Fri 11am–4pm, & June–Sept Sun 2–5pm; free), in the town council offices, featuring a set of bold symmetrical floral frescoes painted on wattle-and-daub walls sometime in the sixteenth century. At the far end of the lane stands **St Michael's parish church**, whose strong and angular detached spire pokes high into the sky. The nucleus of the adjacent church is Norman – note the sturdy round pillars and the chancel's porthole windows – but there are early Gothic flourishes too, most importantly the nave's long and slender windows. Otherwise, the most interesting features are the funerary monuments, including the spectacular seventeenth-century **Skynner Tomb**, where five sons and five daughters kneel in honour of their parents, beneath the canopied slab on which their parents also kneel, she in a hat that looks fancy enough to wear at Ascot.

Practicalities

Ledbury **train station** is inconveniently situated on the northern edge of town, about three-quarters of a mile from the Market Place – straight along the A438. **Buses** stop on the Market Place, across from the **tourist office** (Easter to Oct daily 10am–5pm; Nov to Easter Mon–Sat 10am–4pm; ☎01531/636147, ⓦ www.visitherefordshire.co.uk).

Accommodation is thin on the ground, but the *Feathers Hotel* (☎01531/635266, ⓦ www.feathers-ledbury.co.uk; ❼) occupies a smashing "Black and White" on the High Street, footsteps from the Market Place. It possesses nineteen comfortable if somewhat aesthetically pedestrian rooms, plus a leisure spa. There's also an excellent B&B, ⚸ *The Barn House*, right in the centre of the village on New Street (☎01531/632825, ⓦ www.thebarnhouse.net; ❺), but set in its own grounds, in a handsome half-timbered barn and redbrick house. There are three guest rooms here, one en suite. Similarly stylish is *The Verzon*, in an appealing Georgian redbrick villa, again in its own grounds, but four miles west of Ledbury on the A438 in the hamlet of **Trumpet** (☎01531/670381, ⓦ www.theverzon .co.uk; ❽). This hotel has just eight guest rooms kitted out in immaculate modern-meets-period style and a **restaurant** that has a reputation for quality for its Modern British (with a hint of French) cuisine; mains cost £15. Back in Ledbury, there's also the exemplary *Malthouse Restaurant*, Church Lane (☎01531/634443; dinner only except Sat, plus closed all day Sun & Mon), which offers a creative menu featuring local ingredients – main courses average around £16. A few doors away, the charming *Prince of Wales* **pub** is a great place to sink a beer amidst its snug, low-beamed rooms.

Ross-on-Wye

Pocket-sized **ROSS-ON-WYE**, perched above a loop in the river sixteen miles southeast of Hereford and eleven miles southwest of Ledbury, is a relaxed, easy-going town with an artsy/New Age undertow. It's also the obvious base for exploring one of the more dramatic sections of the **Wye River Valley**.

Ross's jumble of narrow streets zeroes in on the **Market Place**, which is shadowed by the seventeenth-century **Market House**, a sturdy two-storey sandstone structure that sports a medallion bust of a bewigged Charles II, placed here at the instigation of the pioneering seventeenth-century town planner, John Kyrle. A local man, Kyrle did much to improve the town's amenities and his reputation was such that the poet Alexander Pope singled him out for praise in one of his *Moral Essays*.

Veer right at the top of the Market Place, then turn left up Church Street to reach Ross's other noteworthy building, the mostly thirteenth-century **St Mary's Church**, whose sturdy stonework culminates in a slender, tapering spire. In front of the church, at the foot of the graveyard, is a plain but rare **Plague Cross**, commemorating the three hundred or so townsfolk who were buried here by night without coffins during a savage outbreak of the plague in 1637. Inside, the church holds two distinctive **table-tombs**, one of which

– that of a certain William Rudhall (d.1530) – is a late example of the wonderful alabaster sculptures created by the specialist masons of Nottingham, whose work was prized right across medieval Europe. Beside the church, to the right of the entrance, **The Prospect** is a neat public garden offering pleasant views over the river.

If you've strolled around town but still have time to spare, strike out along one of the many well-defined **footpaths** that thread their way through the riverine fields and woods bordering the Wye. A collection of leaflets giving detailed descriptions of several circular routes is available at the tourist office (see below).

Practicalities

There are no trains to Ross, but the **bus station** is handily located on Cantilupe Road, from where it's a couple of minutes' walk west to the Market Place. The **tourist office** is equally convenient, located a few yards west of the Market Place on the corner of High and Edde Cross streets (Easter–Sept Mon–Sat 9.30am–5.30pm, plus mid-July to mid-Sept Sun 10am–4pm; Oct–Easter Mon–Sat 9.30am–4.30pm; ☎01989/562768, ⓦwww.visitherefordshire.co.uk). **Bikes** can be rented from Revolutions, 48 Broad St (☎01989/562639, ⓦwww.wyenot.com/revolutions/).

Ross is strong on **B&Bs** with one of the best being the *Linden House*, in a fetching, three-storey Georgian building opposite St Mary's at 14 Church St (☎01989/565373, ⓦwww.lindenguesthouse.com; ❸). The seven guest rooms, half of which are en suite, are cosily decorated in a modern style and the breakfasts are delicious – both traditional and vegetarian. Another excellent if pricier choice is the *Old Court House B&B*, near the tourist office at 53 High St (☎01989/762275, ⓦwww.wyenot.com; ❹). This occupies a sympathetically modernized, old town house with grand fireplaces and an idiosyncratic, warren-like layout.

For **food**, *Nature's Choice*, 17 Broad St (Mon–Thurs 10am–5pm, Fri & Sat 10am–9pm, Sun 10am–2pm; ☎01989/763454), is a pleasant café-restaurant selling a tasty range of organic foods – scones, tea cakes and nachos during the day, salads, quesadillas and other California-style stuff at night, when main courses average around £9. Of the **pubs**, the *Crown & Sceptre*, on the Market Place, offers a goodly range of brews, but the traditional *Man of Ross*, at the top of Wye Street across from the tourist office, wins on atmosphere.

The Wye River Valley

Heading **south from Ross** along the B4234, it's just five miles to the sullen sandstone mass of **Goodrich Castle** (March–Oct daily 10am–5pm; Nov–Feb Wed–Sun 10am–4pm; £4.90; EH), which commands wide views over the hills and woods of the **Wye River Valley**. The castle's strategic location beside a busy river crossing point guaranteed its importance as a border stronghold from the twelfth century onwards. Today, the substantial ruins incorporate a Norman keep, a maze of later rooms and passageways and walkable ramparts, complete with murder holes, the slits through which boiling oil or water was poured onto the attackers down below. During the Civil War, a determined Royalist garrison held on until the Parliamentarians cast themselves a special cannon, "Roaring Meg", which soon brought victory – a great achievement considering the unreliability of the technology: large cannons had the unfortunate habit of blowing up as soon as anyone fired them.

The castle stands next to tiny **Goodrich** village, from where it's around a mile and half southeast along narrow country lanes to the solitary *Welsh Bicknor Hostel* (☎0870/770 6086, ⓔwelshbicknor@yha.org.uk; Easter–Oct; dorm beds

£14, doubles **❶**), in a Victorian rectory above the River Wye. The hostel, in 25-acre grounds, has 76 beds in anything from two- to ten-bed rooms, and provides evening meals on request; advance booking is recommended.

Symonds Yat Rock and Symonds Yat East

From Goodrich, it's a couple of miles south along narrow country roads to the signposted turning that wriggles its way up to the top of **Symonds Yat Rock**, one of the region's most celebrated viewpoints, rising high above a wooded, hilly loop in the Wye. At the foot of the rock – a two-mile drive away – is **SYMONDS YAT EAST**, a pretty little hamlet that straggles along the east bank of the river. It's a popular spot and one that offers both canoe rental and regular, forty-minute **boat trips** with Kingfisher Cruises (April–Sept; ℡01600/891063, Ⓦwww .fweb.org.uk/kingfisher). There's also a first-rate **pub/B&B** here, the *Saracens Head Inn* (℡01600/890345, Ⓦwww.saracensheadinn.co.uk; **❺**), where the ten guest rooms are decorated in slick modern style – all wooden floors and pastel-painted walls. The **restaurant** is excellent too, featuring an Anglo-French menu with mains costing £13–19.

The road to the village is a dead end, so you have to double back to regain Goodrich.

Hay-on-Wye

Straddling the Anglo-Welsh border some twenty miles west of Hereford, the hilly little town of **HAY-ON-WYE** is known to most people for one thing – **books**. Hay saw its first bookshop open in 1961 and has since become a bibliophile's paradise, with just about every spare inch of the town being given over to the trade, including the old cinema and the ramshackle stone castle. As a consequence, many of Hay's inhabitants are now outsiders, which means that it has little indigenous feel, but there again when the hill farmers come into town on the razzle Hay gets a bit of a (welcome) jolt. In summer, the town plays

---

The King of Hay

Richard Booth, whose family originates from the Hay area, opened the first of his Hay-on-Wye secondhand bookshops in 1961. Since then, and with extraordinary panache, he has attracted a bevy of other booksellers to the town, turning it into the greatest market of used books in the world. There are now over thirty such shops in this minuscule town, the largest of which – Booth's own – contains around half a million volumes.

Whereas many of the region's country towns have seen their populations ebb in recent decades, Hay has **boomed** on the strength of its bibliophilic connections. Booth regards this success as a prototype for other endangered communities, placing the emphasis firmly on local initiatives and unusual specialisms. He is unequivocal in his condemnation of government regeneration programmes, which, he asserts, have done little to stem the flow of jobs and people out of the region. This healthy distaste for bureaucracy, coupled with Booth's self-promotional skills and Hay's geographical location slap bang on the Anglo–Welsh border, led him to declare Hay independent of the UK in 1977, with himself, naturally enough, as King. In a flurry of activity, he appointed his own ministers and offered "official" government scrolls, passports and car stickers to bewitched visitors. Although this proclamation of independence carried no official weight, most of the locals rallied behind **King Richard** and were delighted with the publicity – and the visitors. With Hay's success now assured, Booth no longer has to be so publicity-hungry, but he remains an important and popular local figure.

host to a succession of riverside parties and travelling fairs, the pick of which is the prestigious **Hay Festival of literature and the arts** (box office ℡0870/990 1299, Ⓦwww.hayfestival.com), held over ten days at the back end of May, when London's literary world decamps here en masse.

Arrival and information

Buses to Hay stop yards from the centre of town on Oxford Road beside the main car park. The adjacent **tourist office** (daily: Easter–Oct 10am–1pm & 2–5pm; Nov–Easter 11am–1pm & 2–4pm; ℡01497/820144, Ⓦwww.hay-on -wye.co.uk) issues free town maps and free leaflets outlining what, in general terms at least, each of the town's bookshops stock and their specialisms, if any. The tourist office also sells an exhaustive range of hiking books and maps, and will arrange accommodation.

Accommodation

Accommodation in and around Hay is plentiful, though things get booked up long in advance during the Hay Festival (see above). There are a handful of hotels, but the town's **B&Bs** and **guest houses** are far more numerous. Of several campsites, the handiest is the no-frills *Radnors End* (℡01497/820780), in a pleasant setting five minutes' walk from the town centre across the Wye bridge on the Clyro road.

In Hay

La Fosse Guest House Oxford Rd ℡01497/820613, Ⓦwww.lafosse.co.uk. This agreeable B&B is in an old three-storey cottage a brief walk east of the tourist office at the junction of Lion and Oxford roads. There are four en-suite guest rooms, each kitted out with homely furnishings and fittings. ❸

Old Black Lion Lion St ℡01497/820841, Ⓦwww.oldblacklion.co.uk. Town centre pub with ten en-suite guest rooms decorated in a cheerful, modern style. ❺

Start Bed and Breakfast Hay Bridge ℡01497/821391, Ⓦwww.the-start.net. One of the best B&Bs in town, occupying a much modernized old house, just across the bridge from the town centre. Has three cheerful en-suite guest rooms. ❸

Out of town

Llangoed Hall Hotel Llyswen ℡01874/754525, Ⓦwww.llangoedhall.com. This exceptional hotel, set in its own Wye Valley grounds eight miles southwest of Hay in Llyswen, has 23 smooth and polished guest rooms decorated in a style suitable for a country mansion that was extensively refashioned in the 1910s. ❾

Lower House Cusop Dingle ℡01497/820773, Ⓦwww.lowerhousegardenhay.co.uk. Sympathetically updated, eighteenth-century country home, with beamed ceilings and immaculate gardens, located just one mile from the centre of Hay – either an easy walk along the Offa's Dyke footpath, or the briefest of drives. Two double rooms. Minimum two-night stay. ❺

Old Post Office B&B Llanigon ℡01497/820008, Ⓦwww.oldpost-office .co.uk. First-rate B&B in a seventeenth-century former post office, complete with wood floors and beamed ceilings. There are three rooms here, two en suite, and the vegetarian breakfasts are delicious; Llanigon is a couple of miles south of Hay along a country lane – take the Brecon road and watch for the signs. No credit cards; two nights minimum stay on the weekend. ❹

The Town

Hay has an attractive riverside **setting**, amidst rolling forested hills, and its narrow, bendy streets are lined with a particularly engaging assortment of old stone houses, but before you start ambling round the town, visit the tourist office (see above) to pick up the free leaflet that gives the lowdown on all of Hay's bookshops together with a street plan. Across the street from the tourist office, a signed footpath leads up the slope to the **castle**, a careworn Jacobean mansion built into the walls of an earlier medieval fortress. The bookseller Richard Booth (see box, p.561) owns the castle and its southern extremities are given over to a pair of bookshops: **Castle Street Books** (℡01497/820160), which has a large stock of remaindered books; and **Hay Castle Bookshop** (℡01497/820503 ⓦwww.richardbooth.demon.co.uk), a trusty collection focused on fine art, cinema, antiquarian and photography. From here, the footpath twists its way round the western flank of the castle to meet the steps that lead down to Castle Street, home to The **Pound Bookshop**, at no. 9 (℡01497/821572, ⓦwww.bookends.uk.com), where all the books cost £1.

Castle Street slopes up to the main square, High Town, just beyond which is Lion Street, where **Richard Booth's Bookshop**, at no. 44 (℡01497/820322, ⓦwww.richardbooth.demon.co.uk), is a huge, musty, bookish warehouse of a place offering almost unlimited browsing potential. At the foot of Lion Street is the town's main landmark, the ornate, somewhat Ruritanian Victorian **clocktower**.

Eating and drinking

As regards **food**, *Shepherds*, 9 High Town, is an appealing café with a good line in snacks and mouth-watering, locally made ice cream. There's also the hard-to-beat *Granary* (℡01497/820790), a combined café, bar and restaurant opposite the clocktower on Broad Street. Here they serve delicious wholefood snacks and soups as well as filling main meals (£7–9) with the emphasis on local organic produce; they have a roadside terrace, too, where hikers can kick off their boots and sink a leisurely pint. For something a tad more formal, head for the restaurant of the *Old Black Lion*, Lion Street, where an imaginative menu does its best to feature locally sourced ingredients; main courses start at about £12 – half that in the adjoining bar. The pub also serves up its own **beer** – Black Lion bitter.

Canoeing and hiking around Hay-on-Wye

Hay-on-Wye's environs are readily and pleasantly explored by **kayak or canoe** along the River Wye. In four to six days, it's possible to paddle your way downriver from Hay to Ross-on-Wye (see p.559), overnighting in tents on isolated stretches of river bank, or holing up in comfortable B&Bs and pubs along the way. Hay's Paddles & Pedals, 15 Castle St (℡01497/820604, ⓦwww.paddlesandpedals.co.uk), is a reputable outfit for **kayak and canoe rental**, full of good ideas and advice. Rental of life jackets and other essential equipment (such as waterproof canisters to carry your gear) is included in the price, which works out at around £40 per canoe for 24 hours, with discounts for longer trips. In addition, Paddles & Pedals will transport their customers to and from the departure and the finishing points by minibus.

Hundreds of visitors come to Hay to go **hiking** and the surrounding countryside is latticed with footpaths. One of them is the **Offa's Dyke Path**, a long-distance hiking trail which runs north/south along – or near – the Welsh–English border, from Prestatyn to Chepstow, both of which are in Wales, passing through Hay-on-Wye along the way. Some 180 miles long, the path takes its name from the ditch King Offa of Mercia (broadly central England) had cut along the Anglo–Welsh frontier in the eighth century. Unlike Hadrian's Wall, it was never guarded or patrolled, acting as a boundary marker, not a defensive work. For all that, it was an extraordinary enterprise, though there's precious little to actually see today – the dyke merged with its surroundings centuries ago. The Offa's Dyke Path cuts a varied course, traversing open moorland and agricultural land but also weaving through deep wooded valleys. To the south of Hay it slips through the Black Mountains of Wales, making Hay as good a place as any to sample a section. Hay tourist office can supply the prospective hiker with everything from maps to specialist guidebooks; alternatively, consult ⓦwww.ramblers.org.uk.

Shropshire

One of England's largest and least populated counties, **Shropshire** (ⓦwww
.shropshiretourism.com) stretches from its long and winding border with Wales
to the very edge of the urban Black Country. Its most unique attraction is
industrial: it was here that the Industrial Revolution made a huge stride forward
with the spanning of the River Severn by the very first **iron bridge**. The
assorted industries that subsequently squeezed into the **Ironbridge Gorge** are
long gone, but a series of **museums** celebrate their craftsmanship – from tiles
through to iron. The River Severn also flows through the county town of
Shrewsbury, whose antique centre holds dozens of old half-timbered buildings,
though **Ludlow**, further to the south, has the edge when it comes to handsome
Tudor and Jacobean architecture. In between the two lie some of the most
beautiful parts of Shropshire, namely the twin ridges of **Wenlock Edge** and the
Long Mynd, both of which are prime hiking areas, readily explored from the
attractive little town of **Church Stretton**.

Yet, for all its attractions, Shropshire remains well off the main tourist routes,
one factor protecting the county's isolation being the paucity of its **public
transport**. Shrewsbury and Telford are connected to Birmingham, whilst
Ludlow, Craven Arms and Church Stretton are connected to Shrewsbury on the
Hereford line, but that's about the limit of the **train** services, whilst rural **buses**
tend to connect the county's outlying villages on just a few days of the week.
One recent step forward has been the creation of the **Shropshire Hills
Shuttle bus** service (ⓦwww.shropshirehillsshuttles.co.uk) aimed at the tourist
market and operating every weekend from April to October. The shuttle has
two routes, the more useful of which noses round the Long Mynd and the
Stiperstones and drops by Church Stretton; buses are hourly and an adult Day
Rover ticket, valid on the whole route, costs just £4. Bus timetables are available
at most Shropshire tourist offices and on the website.

Ironbridge Gorge

Both geographically and culturally, **Ironbridge Gorge**, the collective title
for a cluster of small villages huddled in the wooded Severn Valley to the
south of new-town Telford, looks to the cities of the West Midlands conurbation rather than rural Shropshire. Ironbridge Gorge was the crucible of the
Industrial Revolution, a process encapsulated by its famous span across the
Severn – the world's first **iron bridge**, engineered by Abraham Darby and
opened on New Year's Day, 1781. Darby was the third innovative industrialist
of that name – the first Abraham Darby started iron-smelting here back in
1709 and the second invented the forging process that made it possible to
produce massive single beams in iron. Under the guidance of such creative
figures as the Darbys and Thomas Telford, the area's factories once churned
out engines, rails, wheels and other heavy-duty iron pieces in quantities
unmatched anywhere else in the world. Manufacturing has now all but
vanished, but the surviving monuments make the gorge the most extensive
industrial heritage sight in England – and one that has been granted
World Heritage Site status by UNESCO.

The Gorge contains several museums and an assortment of other industrial
attractions spread along a five-mile stretch of the River Severn Valley. A
thorough exploration takes a couple of days, but the **highlights** – the iron
bridge itself, the Museum of Iron and the Jackfield Tile Museum – are easily
manageable on a day-trip. Each museum and attraction charges its own

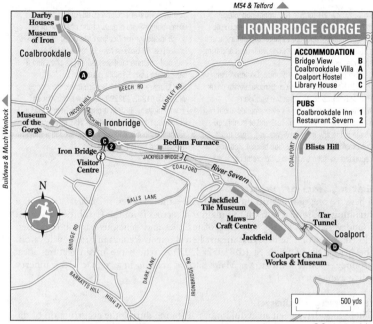

IRONBRIDGE GORGE

ACCOMMODATION
Bridge View	**B**
Coalbrookdale Villa	**A**
Coalport Hostel	**D**
Library House	**C**

PUBS
Coalbrookdale Inn	**1**
Restaurant Severn	**2**

© Crown copyright

admission fee, but if you're intending to visit several, then buy a **passport ticket** (£14), which allows access to each of them once in any calendar year. Passport tickets are available at all the main sights and at the Visitor Information Centre (see below), which also issues local maps and information. **Parking** is free at most of the sights, but not in Ironbridge village itself.

Arrival, getting around and information

Every two hours or so, Monday through Saturday only, there is a **bus** from Shrewsbury bus station to Ironbridge village, at the heart of the gorge; the journey takes an hour and a half. The problem is that once you have reached Ironbridge village, there are no connecting buses along the gorge except on weekends from April to October, when the **Gorge Connect bus** shuttles along the gorge from Coalbrookdale in the west to Coalport (for Telford) in the east, taking in Ironbridge village on the way. Departures are every half-hour (9am–5pm) and each journey you make, no matter how short or long, costs 50p. Alternatively, **bike** rental is available from the Bicycle Hub (Tues–Sat 10am–5pm; ☎01952/883249, ⊛www.thebicyclehub.co.uk) in the same complex as Jackfield Tile Museum (see p.567).

The **Ironbridge Visitor Information Centre** (Mon–Fri 9am–5pm, Sat & Sun 10am–5pm; ☎01952/884391, ⊛www.ironbridge.org.uk) is located in the old toll house at the south end of the iron bridge in Ironbridge village.

Accommodation

Most visitors to the gorge come for the day, but there are several pleasant **B&Bs** in Ironbridge village, which is where you want to be. There's also a hostel in Coalport.

Bridge View 10 Tontine Hill, Ironbridge village ☎01952/432541, ⊛www.ironbridgeview.co.uk. Sympathetically updated eighteenth-century house a stone's throw from the bridge with neat and trim en-suite rooms. ❸

Coalbrookdale Villa 17 Paradise, Coalbrookdale ☎01952/433450, ⊛www.coalbrookdalevilla.co.uk. This B&B occupies an attractive Victorian ironmaster's house set in its own grounds about half a mile up the hill from the west end of Ironbridge village in the tiny hamlet of Paradise, close to Coalbrookdale iron foundry (see below). Sedately decorated en-suite bedrooms. No credit cards. ❹.

Coalport Hostel Coalport ☎0870/770 5882, ⊛ironbridge@yha.org.uk. At the east end of the gorge in the former Coalport China factory, this YHA hostel has 80 beds in two- to ten-bedded rooms. Has self-catering facilities, laundry, a shop and a café. Dorm beds £15.50, doubles ❶

The Library House 11 Severn Bank, Ironbridge village ☎01952/432299, ⊛www.libraryhouse .com. Enjoyable B&B in a charming Georgian villa just yards from the iron bridge. Has three well-appointed double bedrooms decorated in a modern rendition of period style. ❺.

Eating and drinking

There is one good **pub** in the gorge – the excellent *Coalbrookdale Inn*, a smashing traditional pub on the main road across from the Coalbrookdale iron foundry. It offers a tasty selection of real ales and delicious bar food (kitchen closed Sun eve). The best **restaurant** hereabouts is *Restaurant Severn*, yards from the bridge at 33 High St (☎01952/432233), where the menu features local produce – some homegrown. Mains such as venison in a cognac and cranberry sauce average around £16.

Ironbridge village

There must have been an awful lot of nail-biting during the construction of the **iron bridge** over the River Severn in the late 1770s. No one was quite sure how the new material would wear and although the single-span design looked sound, many feared the bridge would simply tumble into the river. To compensate, Abraham Darby used more iron than was strictly necessary, but the end result still manages to appear stunningly graceful, arching between the steep banks with the river far below. The settlement at the north end of the span was promptly renamed **IRONBRIDGE**, and today its brown-brick houses climb prettily up the hill from the bridge. The village is also home to the **Museum of the Gorge** (daily 10am–5pm; £2.75), located in a church-like, Neo-Gothic old riverside warehouse about 500 yards west of the bridge along the main road. This provides an introduction to the industrial history of the gorge and gives a few environmental pointers too.

Coalbrookdale iron foundry

At the roundabout just to the west of the Museum of the Gorge, turn right for the half-mile trip up to what was once the gorge's big industrial deal, the **Coalbrookdale iron foundry**, which boomed throughout the eighteenth and early nineteenth century, employing up to four thousand men and boys. The foundry has been imaginatively converted into the **Museum of Iron** (daily 10am–5pm; £5.25, £6.50 including Darby Houses, see below), with a wide range of displays on iron-making in general and the history of the company in particular. There are superb examples of Victorian and Edwardian ironwork here, including the intricate castings – stags, dogs and even camels – that became the house speciality. Also in the complex, across from the foundry beneath a protective canopy, are the ruins of the **furnace** where Abraham Darby pioneered the use of coke as a smelting fuel in place of charcoal.

From the foundry, it's about 100 yards up to the two **Darby Houses** (late March to early Nov daily 10am–5pm; £3.75) – Dale House and Rosehill – both attractively restored, old ironmasters' homes with Georgian period rooms and a scattering of items that once belonged to the Darby family.

The Tar Tunnel

Heading east from the iron bridge, it's a third of a mile along the river to the battered brick-and-stone remains of the **Bedlam furnace** (open access; free), one of the first furnaces to use coke rather than charcoal. It was kept alight round-the-clock and at night its fiery silhouette scared passers-by half to death – hence the name. From here, it's a mile to the turning for Blists Hill (see p.568) and another 500 yards or so to the **Tar Tunnel** (April–Oct daily 10am–5pm; £1.75), built to transport coal from one part of the gorge to another, but named for the bitumen that oozes naturally from its walls.

Jackfield

Beside the Tar Tunnel, a **footbridge** crosses the Severn to reach **JACKFIELD**, now a sleepy little hamlet whose brown-brick cottages string prettily along the river, but once a sooty, grimy place that hummed to the tune of two large tile factories, Maws and Craven Dunnill. Both were built in the middle of the nineteenth century to the latest industrial design, a fully integrated manufacturing system that produced literally thousands of tiles at breakneck speed. Ahead of their time – and well ahead of their competitors – the two factories boomed from the time of their construction until the 1920s, and they have both survived in good condition. From the footbridge, it's a couple of minutes' walk west to the first of the two, which has been sympathetically converted into the **Maws Craft Centre** (Ⓦwww.mawscraftcentre.co.uk), holding over twenty arts, craft and specialist shops, selling everything from flowers to decorative plasterwork with belly-dancing lessons as a possible add-on. A short walk away, the former Craven Dunnill factory has become the excellent **Jackfield Tile Museum** (daily 10am–5pm; £5.25), whose exhibits begin by providing a potted history of Jackfield and its two factories. Upstairs, beyond a series of period rooms related to the factory, is the superb "Style Gallery", where cabinet after cabinet illustrates the different styles of tile produced here, from Art Deco and Art Nouveau through to Arts and Crafts and the Aesthetic Movement. The adjacent "Tiles Everywhere Gallery" is perhaps even better, displaying some exquisite examples of tilework retrieved from all over the UK, including a tiled wall from Covent Garden tube station. The museum plans to expand the displays whenever possible and also offers tile-making workshops. Incidentally, tiles are still produced here by Craven Dunnill (Ⓦwww.cravendunnill-jackfield .co.uk) – there are boxes of new tiles down by reception.

Coalport

Back at the Tar Tunnel, a canal towpath leads east in a couple of minutes to **Coalport China works**, a large brick complex holding a youth hostel (see opposite) and the **Coalport China Museum** (daily 10am–5pm; £5.25). The museum kicks off with a couple of rooms crammed full with Coalport wares, the particular highlight being the gaudy and ornate pieces manufactured in the company's Victorian heyday, from around 1820 to 1890 – the company moved production to Stoke-on-Trent in 1926. There's also a workshop, where potters demonstrate their skills, and a Social History Gallery, which explores the hard life of the factory's workers, whose health was constantly at risk from the factory's lead-saturated dust. The museum also includes two **bottle-kilns**, those distinctive conical structures that were long the hallmark of the pottery industry.

In the base of one is a small display of fine Coalport pieces, whilst the other explains how the kilns worked – though quite how the firers survived the conditions defies the imagination.

Blists Hill Victorian Town

Doubling back along the river, it's a third of a mile west from Coalport to the clearly signed, mile-long side road that cuts up to the gorge's most popular attraction, the rambling **Blists Hill Victorian Town** (daily 10am–5pm; £9.50). This encloses a substantial number of reconstructed Victorian buildings, most notably a school, a candle-maker's, a doctor's surgery, a gas-lit pub, and wrought-iron works. Jam-packed on most summer days, it's especially popular with school parties, who keep the period-dressed employees very busy.

Much Wenlock

Heading west from Ironbridge village along the northern bank of the River Severn, it's only a couple of miles to the A4169 and three more to **MUCH WENLOCK**, a tiny little town where a medley of Tudor, Jacobean and Georgian buildings dots the High Street – and pulls in the day-trippers by the score. At the foot of the High Street is the **Guildhall**, sitting pretty on sturdy oak columns, but the town's architectural high point is **Wenlock Priory** (March–April & Sept–Oct Wed–Sun 10am–5pm; May–Aug daily 10am–5pm; Nov–Feb Thurs–Sun 10am–4pm; £3.40; EH) a short stroll away – turn left at the Guildhall and then first right along the Bull Ring. The Saxons built a monastery at Much Wenlock, but today's remains mostly stem from the thirteenth and fourteenth centuries when its successor, a Cluniac monastery founded here in the 1080s, reached the height of its wealth and power. Set amidst immaculate gardens and fringed by woodland, the ruins are particularly picturesque, from the peeling stonework of the old priory church's transepts to the shattered bulk of **St Michael's chapel** next to the bare foundations of the church's west door. Of special note also is the **Chapter House**, where a trio of immaculately preserved, dog-tooth decorated Norman arches have survived along with some delicate false arcading on the inside walls – the Cluniacs were particularly fond of this decorative design.

It only takes an hour or so to look round the town, but the **tourist office**, at the foot of the High Street (Mon–Sat 10.30am–5pm; ☎01952/727679, ⓦ www.muchwenlockguide.info), does carry lots of local information, including details of hikes along Wenlock Edge.

Wenlock Edge

Attracting hikers from all over the region, the beautiful and deeply rural **Wenlock Edge** is a limestone escarpment that runs twenty-odd miles southwest from Much Wenlock to the A49. The south side of the escarpment is a gently shelving slope of open farmland, while the thickly wooded north side scarps steeply down to the Shropshire plains. Much of the Edge is owned by the National Trust, and a network of waymarked **trails**, graded by colour according to length and difficulty, winds through the woodland from a string of car parks along the **B4371**, which hugs the first part of the ridge from Much Wenlock to **Longville-in-the-Dale**. The paths are easy to follow, but it's still a good idea to pick up the appropriate OS map and a copy of the National Trust's very helpful and free *Walks along Wenlock Edge* leaflet. The latter should be available from Much Wenlock tourist office (see above) and *Wilderhope Manor* (see opposite).

To explore Wenlock Edge, you'll need your own transport and the most obvious base is Ironbridge village (see p.566). Alternatively, you might head for one of the YHA's most distinctive – if somewhat spartan – **hostels**, *Wilderhope Manor* (☎0870/770 6090, ✉wilderhope@yha.org.uk; dorm beds £14, doubles ❶). The hostel occupies a remote Elizabethan mansion next to a farm about one mile off the B4371 – the turning is clearly signed on the edge of Longville-in-the-Dale. Facilities include a self-catering kitchen, a laundry and a cycle store, and breakfasts and evening meals are on offer; there are seventy beds in three- to ten-bedded rooms.

Shrewsbury and around

SHREWSBURY, the county town of Shropshire some twelve miles northwest of Much Wenlock, sits in a tight and narrow loop of the River Severn, a three-hundred-yard spit of land being all that prevents the town centre from becoming an island. It would be difficult to design a better defensive site and the Britons were quick to erect a fort here once the Roman legions had hot-footed it out of their colony in the fifth century. Later, the Normans built a stone castle, which Edward I decided to strengthen and expand, though by then the local economy owed as much to the Welsh wool trade as it did to all these military shenanigans. In Georgian times, Shrewsbury became a fashionable staging post on the busy London to Holyhead route, boasting a lively social season, patronized by the sort of people who could afford to send their offspring to the famous Shrewsbury School. However, those heady days are long gone and nowadays Shrewsbury is an easy-going, middling market town, whose jingle and jangle of narrow lanes, courtyards and alleys fills out the hilly neck of land that comprises the centre. It's the overall feel of the place that is its main appeal, though **St Mary's Church** and its immediate environs are particularly pleasing. Shrewsbury is also within easy striking distance of the substantial ruins of **Wroxeter Roman City**, though you'll need your own transport to get there easily.

Arrival, information, orientation and accommodation

Shrewsbury **train station** stands at the narrow neck of the loop in the river that holds the town centre; long-distance **buses** mostly pull into the Raven Meadows bus station, off the Smithfield Road, five minutes' walk southwest from the train station, further into the centre. The **tourist office** is a five-minute walk south up the hill from the train station, off High Street and on The Square (May–Sept Mon–Sat 9.30am–5.30pm, Sun 10am–4pm; Oct–April Mon–Sat 10am–5pm; ☎01743/281200, ⊛www.visitshrewsbury.com).

The labyrinthine streets of the town centre can be baffling, but fortunately it's too small an area to be lost for long. As a general guideline, Castle Gates/Castle Street runs from the train station up to **Pride Hill**, a short pedestrianized street that intersects with St Mary's Street at one end and High Street at the other. The Square off the High Street is at the heart of the town centre.

The best **hotel** in town is the *Prince Rupert*, which occupies a cannily converted old building bang in the centre on Butcher Row, off Pride Hill (☎01743/499955, ⊛www.prince-rupert-hotel.co.uk; ❻). There are over seventy bedrooms here and although some are a tad too fancy for most tastes – ornate bed-head canopies and so forth – the rooms are undeniably comfortable. Among central **B&Bs**, one good choice is the *College Hill Guest House*, in a well-maintained Georgian town house at 11 College Hill, just south of The Square (☎01743/365744; no credit cards; ❸).

The Town

Poking up above the mansion-like train station, the careworn ramparts of Shrewsbury **castle** are but a pale reminder of the mighty medieval fortress that once dominated the town, largely because the illustrious Thomas Telford turned the castle into the private home of a local bigwig in the 1780s. **Castle Gates** winds up the hill from the station into the heart of the river loop where the medieval town took root. Here, off Pride Hill, several half-timbered buildings are dotted along **Butcher Row**, which leads into the quiet precincts of **St Alkmund's Church**, from where there's a charming view of the fine old buildings of **Fish Street**.

St Mary the Virgin

Close to St Alkmund's is the most interesting of the town's churches, **St Mary the Virgin** (Mon–Fri 10am–4/5pm, Sat 10am–4pm; free), whose sombre exterior is partly redeemed by its slender spire. Inside, the church is unusual in so far as it exhibits both the rounded arches beloved of the Normans in the nave and the pointed arches of Early English Gothic in the choir and the transepts. The nave also boasts a splendid panelled roof, featuring angels with musical instruments, while the east window of the chancel, with its filigree tracery rising high above the high altar, represents the apogee of the Decorated style and dates to the 1330s. The stained glass of this east window comprises a superlative **Tree of Jesse**, one of the finest in the country with Jesse – the supposed father of David, King of the Israelites – at the bottom with his genealogical tree rising above him, its branches inhabited by Biblical characters. Look out also – in the chapel off the north transept – for the funerary plaque commemorating a bewigged **Admiral John Benbow** (1653–1702), who rose through the ranks to become one of Britain's finest admirals – hence the plaque's ship-of-the-line.

To the English Bridge and Shrewsbury Abbey

From St Mary's, it's the briefest of walks to the High Street, on the far side of which, in the narrow confines of The Square, is the **Old Market House**, a heavy-duty stone structure built in 1596. From The Square, High Street snakes down the hill to become **Wyle Cop**, lined with higgledy-piggledy ancient buildings and leading to the **English Bridge**, which sweeps across the Severn in grand Georgian style. Beyond the bridge, on Abbey Foregate, is the stumpy redstone mass of the **Abbey Church** (Mon–Sat 10am–4pm & Sun 11.30am–2.30pm; free), all that remains of the Benedictine abbey that was a major political and religious force hereabouts until the Dissolution. The **church** is still in use as a place of worship, hence its good condition, but the interior is fairly pedestrian, the best features being the doughty Norman columns of the nave and the soaring triumphal arch.

Eating and drinking

For daytime **food**, try the inexpensive *Goodlife Wholefood Restaurant* (closed Sun), on Barracks Passage, just off – and about halfway along – Wyle Cop; they specialize in salads and vegetarian dishes with main courses costing around £5. In the evening, many locals swear by *Osteria da Paolo*, a homely Italian place offering mouth-watering dishes from its premises down a narrow alley off Hills Lane near the Welsh Bridge on the north side of the town centre (Mon–Wed dinner only, closed Sun; ☎01743/243336); main courses here average around £10.

Amongst Shrewsbury's many **pubs**, one of the most distinctive is the *Loggerheads*, an ancient place – perhaps a little too authentically so – with several small rooms and great real ales; it's located near St Alkmund's Place at 1 Church St. Other recommendable pubs include the *Three Fishes*, in an ancient building on Fish Street, and the cosy *Coach & Horses*, on Swan Hill just south of The Square.

Around Shrewsbury: Wroxeter Roman City

Heading east from Shrewsbury ring road along the **B4380**, which follows the course of **Watling Street**, the former Roman military road that linked the Welsh borders with London, Canterbury and Dover, it's about three miles to **Wroxeter Roman City** (March–Oct daily 10am–5pm; Nov–Feb Wed–Sun 10am–4pm; £4.10; EH), originally Roman Britain's fourth largest city, **Viroconium**. The site was first settled by the Cornovii, but it was the Emperor Nero who really got things going in 58 AD as part of his drive to conquer Wales, building a fort here at the point where Watling Street crossed the River Severn. In the event, the Welsh proved intractable and, when there was another imperial visit sixty years later, this time by the Emperor Hadrian, the focus was on security and the garrison was doubled. Hadrian also ordered the construction of a grand set of municipal buildings and today the ruins of his civic centre are still impressive, particularly the large chunk of masonry that once enclosed part of the main baths. You will, however, need a vivid imagination to picture the ruins as a teeming Roman metropolis, even though a modest museum helps fill in the gaps.

Church Stretton and the Long Mynd

Beginning about ten miles south of Shrewsbury, the upland heaths of the **Long Mynd**, some ten miles long and between two and four miles wide, run parallel to and just to the west of the A49. This is prime walking territory and the heathlands are latticed with footpaths, the pick of which offer sweeping views over the border to the Black Mountains of Wales. Nestled at the foot of the Mynd beside the A49 is **CHURCH STRETTON**, a tidy little village and popular day-trippers' destination that makes an ideal base for hiking the area. The village also possesses the dinky parish **church of St Laurence**, parts of which – especially the nave and transepts – are Norman. Look out also for the fertility symbol over the side door, just to the left of the entrance – it's a (badly weathered) sheila-na-gig comparable to the one in Kilpeck (see p.557).

Practicalities

Church Stretton is easy to reach from Shrewsbury and Ludlow by **train** or **bus**. Most buses stop in the centre of the village along the High Street, but some pull in beside the train station, close to the A49 – and about 600 yards east of the High Street. The **tourist office** is on Church Street (April–Sept Mon–Sat 9.30am–5pm; Oct–March Mon–Sat 9.30am–12.30pm & 1.30–5pm; ☎01694/723133, ⊛www.churchstretton.co.uk), west of the High Street. They stock an excellent range of local hiking leaflets and booklets, have information on off-road cycle routes and will book accommodation on your behalf. Of the many **hikes** beginning in the village, a selection is described in Ian Jones's excellent *Twenty Church Stretton Circular Walks*, which is available at the tourist office.

There's no shortage of good-value **accommodation** in and around Church Stretton. One particularly recommendable **B&B** is the first-rate ⅍ *Jinlye* (☎01694/723243, ⊛www.jinlye.co.uk; ❺), in an attractively modernized and extended stone cottage on Castle Hill on the edge of All

Stretton, one mile north of Church Stretton. There are six splendid guest rooms here, each decorated in a homely, vaguely period style. In Church Stretton itself, *Brookfields Guesthouse*, Watling Street North (℡01694/722314, ⓦwww.churchstretton-guesthouse.co.uk; ❹), is a comfortable B&B in a large bay-windowed Edwardian house with seven, well-appointed en suite guest rooms. It's situated a five-minute walk east then north of the train station; Watling Street runs parallel to – and just to the east of – the A49. Hostellers have choices too – either *Wilderhope Manor* (see p.569), in Longville-in-the-Dale, about seven miles east of Church Stretton along the B4371, or *Bridges Long Mynd* (℡01588/650656; dorm beds £13), a small YHA **hostel** along country lanes in a converted village school just five miles west of Church Stretton on the western edge of the hamlet of **Ratlinghope**. The *Bridges* hostel has 37 beds in five- to ten-bedded rooms, a café, camping facilities and a self-catering kitchen. Both hostels are splendid bases for hiking, the first for Wenlock Edge (see p.568), the second for either the Long Mynd or the **Stiperstones**, a remote range of boggy heather dotted with ancient cairns and earthworks.

Ludlow

LUDLOW, perched on a hill nearly thirty miles south of Shrewsbury, is one of the most picturesque towns in the West Midlands, if not in England – a gaggle of beautifully preserved black-and-white half-timbered buildings packed around a craggy stone castle, with rural Shropshire forming a drowsy backdrop. These are strong recommendations in themselves, but Ludlow scores even more points by being something of a gastronomic hideyhole with a clutch of outstanding restaurants.

The castle

Close to the Welsh border, the Saxons were the first to recognize the site's defensive qualities, but it was the Normans who got down to business when Roger Montgomery turned up here with his men in 1085. Over the next few decades, Montgomery's fortifications were elaborated into an immense **Castle** (Jan Sat & Sun 10am–4pm; Feb–July & Sept–Dec daily 10am–4/5pm; Aug daily 10am–7pm; £4; ⓦwww.ludlowcastle.com), strong enough to keep the Welsh at bay and the seat of the Lord President of the Council of the Marches, as the borders were then known. Surviving the attentions of the Parliamentary troops in the Civil War, the rambling and imposing ruins that remain today include towers and turrets, gatehouses and concentric walls as well as the remains of the 110-foot Norman **keep** and an unusual **Round Chapel** built in 1120. With its spectacular setting above the rivers Teme and Corve, the castle also makes a fine open-air auditorium during the **Ludlow Festival** (℡01584/872150, ⓦwww.ludlowfestival.co.uk), two weeks of assorted musical and theatrical fun running from the end of June to early July.

The rest of town

The castle entrance abuts **Castle Square**, an airy rectangle, whose eastern side leads into four narrow lanes – take the one on the left, Church Street, and you'll soon reach the gracefully proportioned **Church of St Laurence** (late March to late Dec Mon–Sat 10am–5.30pm, Sun 12.30–5pm; late Dec to late March Mon–Sat 11am–4pm, Sun 1–4pm; free), whose interior is distinguished by its stained-glass windows. Amongst them, two of the most exquisite are the north wall's fifteenth-century Annunciation window and the east window, where the men in blue are members of the Palmers' Guild. Founded in the middle of the thirteenth century, and dissolved in 1551, the guild dominated the economy of medieval Ludlow and its members often undertook pilgrimages to Jerusalem. Thus, one window panel shows the Palmers on their pilgrimage, another the enthusiastic welcome they receive on their return. The church also holds an especially fine set of misericords. Carved in oak, they run the gamut from royal emblems and religious scenes to the folkloric and seemingly profane – green men, devils, a fox preaching to geese, a witch, a mermaid and a woman disappearing into the mouth of hell, bottom first. Back outside the church, it's a few paces to the **Bull Ring**, home of the **Feathers Hotel**, a fine Jacobean building with the fanciest wooden facade imaginable.

To the south of Castle Square, the gridiron of streets laid out by the Normans has survived intact, though most of the buildings date from the eighteenth century. It's the general appearance that appeals rather than any special sight, but steeply sloping **Broad Street** is particularly attractive, flanked by many of Ludlow's five hundred half-timbered Tudor and red-brick Georgian listed buildings, its north end framed by the high and mighty **Butter Cross**, a Neoclassical extravagance from 1744. At the foot of Broad Street is Ludlow's only surviving medieval **gate**, which was turned into a house in the eighteenth century.

Practicalities

From Ludlow **train station**, on the Shrewsbury–Hereford line, it's a fifteen-minute walk southwest to the castle – just follow the signs. Most **buses** stop on Mill Street, just off Castle Square. Ludlow's **tourist office**, on Castle Square (Mon–Sat 10am–5pm, Sun 10.30am–5pm; Oct–March closed Sun; ☎01584/875053, ⓦ www.ludlow.org.uk), sells a wide range of maps and books on local hikes.

Accommodation is plentiful, though rooms still get scarce during the festival. One excellent choice is ⚜ *Dinham Hall Hotel*, handily located close to the castle in a rambling, bow-windowed eighteenth-century stone mansion that has previously seen service as a boarding house for Ludlow School (☎01584/876464, ⓦ www.dinhamhall.co.uk; ➐). The hotel has just thirteen guest rooms, each of which is decorated in an appealing, but never overdone modern version of period style. Similarly enticing is ⚜ *Mr Underhill's*, Dinham Weir (☎01584/874431, ⓦ www.mr-underhills .co.uk; ➐), in the jumble of old riverside buildings below and behind the castle walls beside the River Teme. The six guest rooms here are decorated in smooth modern style with lots of pastel shades and river views. One other, less expensive option in the town centre is the *Wheatsheaf Inn*, a quaint little pub with five en-suite rooms at the foot of Broad Street (☎01584/872980, ⓦ www.wheatsheaf-ludlow.co.uk; ➌).

In recent years, Ludlow and its environs have become something of a gastronomic hotspot with the establishment of a string of much lauded **restaurants**. Predictably enough, none of these prime places come cheap, but you might treat yourself by going to ⚜ *Mr Underhill's* (see above; reservations essential), where the menu is carefully and skilfully crafted – no wonder it gets rave reviews again and again; set menus kick off at around £40. If that sounds too wallet-wilting, head for the popular *Olive Branch*, in the centre on the Bull Ring, whose speciality is inexpensive daytime light meals and salads, or try the superior pub food (not Sun) at the antique *Unicorn Inn*, on the north side of town on Lower Corve Street, a continuation of the Bull Ring; main courses here begin at £9.

Birmingham

If anywhere can be described as the first purely industrial conurbation, it has to be **BIRMINGHAM**. Unlike the more specialist industrial towns which grew up across the north and the Midlands, including the **Black Country**, that clutch of towns immediately to the west of Birmingham, "Brum" – and its "Brummies" – turned its hand to every kind of manufacturing, gaining the epithet "the city of 1001 trades". It was here also that the pioneers of the Industrial Revolution – James Watt, Matthew Boulton, William Murdock, Josiah Wedgwood, Joseph Priestley and Erasmus Darwin (grandfather of Charles) – formed the **Lunar Society**, an extraordinary melting-pot of scientific and industrial ideas. They conceived the world's first purpose-built factory, invented gas lighting and pioneered both the distillation of oxygen and the mass production of the steam engine. Thus, a modest Midlands market town mushroomed into the nation's economic dynamo with the population to match: in 1841 there were 180,000 inhabitants, three times that number just fifty years later.

Now the second largest city in Britain, with a population of over one million, Birmingham has long outgrown the squalor and misery of its boom years and today its industrial supremacy is recalled – but only recalled – in a crop of excellent **heritage museums** and an extensive network of **canals**. It also boasts a thoroughly multiracial population that makes this one of Britain's most cosmopolitan cities. The recent shift to a post-manufacturing economy has been symbolized by an intelligent and far-reaching revamp of the city centre that has included the construction of a glitzy **Convention Centre** and an extravagant revamping of the **Bull Ring**, while the enormous **National Exhibition Centre** (NEC) now inhabits the outskirts near the International Airport. Birmingham has also launched a veritable raft of cultural initiatives, enticing a division of the **Royal Ballet** to take up residence here, and building a fabulous new concert hall for the **City of Birmingham Symphony Orchestra**. Nevertheless, there's no pretending that Birmingham is packed with interesting sights – it isn't – though along with its first-rate restaurant scene and nightlife, it's well worth at least a couple of days.

Arrival, information and city transport

Birmingham's **International Airport** is eight miles east of the city centre off the A45 and near the M42 (Junction 6); the terminal is beside Birmingham International train station, from where there are regular services into **New Street train station**, right in the heart of the city. New Street train station is where all inter-city and the vast majority of local services go, though trains on the Stratford-upon-Avon, Warwick, Worcester and Malvern lines mostly use **Snow Hill** and **Moor Street stations**, both about ten minutes' signposted walk from New Street to the north and east respectively. National Express **coach** travellers are dumped in the grim surroundings of **Digbeth coach station**, from where it's a ten-minute uphill walk to the Bull Ring.

Maps, loads of local leaflets, theatre and concert tickets, and transport information are provided by all of the city's **tourist offices**. The main office is located at 150 New St, at the back of the Rotunda, beside the Bull Ring (Mon–Sat 9.30am–5.30pm, Sun 10.30am–4.30pm; ☎0870/225 0127, ⓦwww .beinbirmingham.com). A second, smaller office occupies a kiosk in front of New Street station, at the junction of New Street and Corporation Street (Mon–Sat 9am–5pm, Sun 10am–4pm; same number). There is a third tourist

12, 13, Sparkhill, Custard Factory, Birmingham Intl. Airport & NEC, M42, M6 & A45 Coventry

Aston, M6 & A38 Lichfield

Museum of the Jewellery Quarter

Moseley, 15, 16, M5 & A38

A456 Kidderminster

M5

Map labels

GROSVENOR ST
FOX ST
NEW CANAL STREET
OXFORD STREET
REA STREET
Coach Station
JENNENS ROAD
GROSVENOR ST
COLESHILL ST
NELSON ST
BAGOT STREET
ALBERT ST
MERIDEN STREET
BORDESLEY STREET
COVENTRY ST
BRADFORD STREET
DIGBETH
City Markets
JAMES WATT QUEENSWAY
LANCASTER CIRCUS QUEENSWAY
DALTON ST
THE PRIORY QUEENSWAY
Police Station
Victoria Law Courts
General Hospital
NEWTON ST
CORPORATION STREET
STEELHOUSE LANE
Moor Street Station
St Martin's Church
Selfridges
MOOR ST
PARK ST
MOAT LANE
City Markets
WHITTALL STREET
WEAMAN ST
SNOW HILL Q-WAY
LIVERY STREET
BULL STREET
HIGH STREET
CARRS LANE
Bull Ring
Rotunda
EDGBASTON STREET
PERSHORE STREET
St Chad's Catholic Cathedral
ST CHAD'S CIRCUS
QUEENSWAY
Snow Hill Train Station
SNOW HILL CIRCUS
UNION ST
NEW STREET
Arcadian Centre
CHINESE QUARTER
HURST STREET
St Philip's Anglican Cathedral
TEMPLE ROW
CANNON STREET
NEEDLESS ALLEY
New Street Station
Old Rep. Theatre
Hippodrome Theatre
GREAT CHARLES STREET QUEENSWAY
EDMUND STREET
CHURCH STREET
COLMORE ROW
BENNETT'S HILL
TEMPLE ST
HILL STREET
Council House
STEPHENSON STREET
Alexandra Theatre
LIVERY STREET
CORNWALL STREET
NEWHALL STREET
MARGARET ST
Waterhall Gallery
Birmingham Museum & Art Gallery
CHAMBERLAIN SQUARE
Town Hall
VICTORIA SQUARE
PARADISE ST
JOHN BRIGHT ST
ELLIS ST
BLUCHER STREET
St Paul's
ST PAUL'S SQUARE
LUDGATE HILL
LIONEL STREET
FLEET STREET
Library
PARADISE FORUM
PINFOLD ST
NAVIGATION STREET
SUFFOLK STREET QUEENSWAY
BRUNEL ST
RBSA
LIVERY STREET
BROOK ST
JAMES ST
SUMMER ROW
CAMBRIDGE STREET
QUEENSWAY
Hall of Memory
Repertory Theatre
CENTENARY SQUARE
BROAD STREET
COMMERCIAL STREET
HOLLIDAY STREET
The Mailbox
VITTORIA ST
CHARLOTTE STREET
GEORGE STREET
GRAHAM STREET
NEWHALL HILL
JEWELLERY QUARTER
Birmingham & Fazeley Canal
International Convention Centre & Symphony Hall
Gas St Basin
BRIDGE STREET
GAS ST
BERKLEY STREET
GRANVILLE STREET
Boat Trips
FREDERICK STREET
NEWHALL HILL
LEGGE LANE
ALBION STREET
CARVER STREET
POPE STREET
CAMDEN STREET
SAND PITS
SUMMER HILL TERRACE
SUMMERHILL ST
SHEEPCOTE STREET
KING EDWARDS RD
Ikon Gallery
Sea Life Centre
BRINDLEY PLACE
National Indoor Arena
Birmingham Main Line Canal
Crescent Theatre
BROAD STREET
FIVE WAYS
GROSVENOR ST WEST
SHERBORNE STREET
RYLAND STREET
TENNANT ST
BISTON ST

BIRMINGHAM

ACCOMMODATION

Back to Backs Houses	F
Copthorne Birmingham	A
Hyatt Regency Birmingham	B
Malmaison	C
Radisson SAS	E
Travelodge	D

CAFÉS & RESTAURANTS

Brasserie de Malmaison	C
Chez Jules	8
Chung Ying	11
Deolali	15
Edwardian Tea Room	6
Kababish	16
Metro Bar and Grill	5
The Oriental	10
Purnells	4
Royal Naim	13

PUBS & BARS

Actress & Bishop	3
Factory Club	12
The Jam House	14
The Old Fox	7
Old Joint Stock	9
Tap & Spile	2
Tarnished Halo	1

0   200 yds

© Crown copyright

575

8

office in the National Exhibition Centre (NEC). All of the tourist offices operate a hotel bed booking service at no charge. There's also a dedicated ticket hotline (☎0121/202 5000).

To see Birmingham at its best, you really need to stay in the centre, but most of the less expensive accommodation is scattered around the suburbs. This may mean you'll be dealing with Birmingham's excellent local transport system, whose **trains**, **metro** and **buses** delve into almost every urban nook and cranny. Various companies provide these services, but they are co-ordinated by **Centro**, which operates a regional public transport information line, **Centro Hotline** (☎0121/200 2787, ⊛www.centro.org.uk). A One Day **Network Card**, valid on all services, can be purchased from bus drivers and at train and metro stations at a cost of £5.80; if you avoid peak-time travel, the price drops to £4.70, but then it's known as the Daytripper.

One thing that may confuse is the name of the **inner ring road**: it's called the Queensway, but individual stretches keep their other names too, for example: Great Charles Street, Queensway.

Accommodation

As you might expect, central Birmingham is liberally sprinkled with chain **hotels**, from glitzy tower blocks through to more modest red-brick, but it's in the vicinity of the Gas Street Basin and Centenary Square that you really want to stay. The prize for originality, however, goes to the National Trust, who rent out three reasonably priced "**cottages**" – actually restored old terraced-houses – in the city centre on the edge of the Chinese Quarter. The tourist office (see p.574) publishes a free booklet detailing all of the city's hotels and also operates a **hotel room booking service** at no charge. Even better, they are often aware of special deals and discounts, which can slash costs considerably, especially at the weekend.

Hotels

Copthorne Birmingham Paradise Circus ☎0121/200 2727, ⊛www.millenniumhotels.co.uk. It may look rather like a Rubik cube from the outside, but this is a great hotel, partly because its 212 modern bedrooms are neat and trim, and partly because its location – plum in the centre beside Centenary Square – can't be bettered. It's expensive during the week, but weekends bring prices down to more affordable levels. **❼**, weekends **❻**

Hyatt Regency Birmingham 2 Bridge St ☎0121/643 1234, ⊛www.hyatt.com. The sleek, black skyrise that towers above Centenary Square is a luxury Hyatt hotel. The central location is hard to beat, the city views from the guest rooms on the upper floors are superlative, and the public area has some pleasant Art Deco touches. Less positively, the rooms are decorated in uninspiring chain-hotel style and you can't open the windows. Discounts are commonplace, but rack rate is **❻**, **❼** at weekends.

Malmaison 1 Wharfside St, The Mailbox ☎0121/246 5000, ⊛www.malmaison -birmingham.com. This impeccably stylish,

designer hotel offers first-class accommodation of wit and substance – no wonder it's next door to Harvey Nichols. Every convenience and a central location. **❼**

Radisson SAS 12 Holloway Circus ☎0121/654 6000, ⊛www.birmingham.radissonsas.com. Smart new hotel in a tall and sleek skyrise within a few minutes' walk of the centre. The interior is designed in routine modern-minimalist style, but the green amoeba-like pattern etched onto the acres of glass adds an air of distinction, as do the floor-to-ceiling windows of many of the bedrooms. **❻**

Travelodge 230 Broad St ☎0871/984 6064, ⊛www.travelodge.co.uk. Workaday central chain hotel, but prices are very reasonable and it's within easy walking distance of lots of restaurants, bars and clubs. **❹**

National Trust Cottages

🏃 **Back to Backs Houses** 52 Inge St ☎0870/458 4422, ⊛www .nationaltrustcottages.co.uk. The National Trust has refurbished a small block of nineteenth-century back-to-back workers' houses just to the south of the city centre along Hurst Street (see p.582). In part of the complex, it has installed three small "cottages" – really terraced houses – and kitted them out in a sympathetic modern version of period style, including en-suite facilities, and these can be rented out for two nights or longer. The cottages have a convenient, central location and make for the most distinctive place to stay in town. Each accommodates two guests. Costs vary with the season: a two-night stay costs £125 in January, rising to £275 in Aug.

The City

Many visitors get their first taste of central Birmingham at **New Street Station**, whose unreconstructed ugliness – piles of modern concrete – makes a dispiriting start, though there are plans afoot to give the place a thoroughgoing face lift. Things do, however, soon get better if you cut up east from the station to the newly developed **Bull Ring**, once itself a 1960s eyesore, but now a gleaming new shopping mall distinguished by the startling design of its leading store, **Selfridges**. Head west along pedestrianized **New Street** from here and it's a brief stroll to the elegantly revamped **Victoria Square**, with its tumbling water fountain, and the adjacent **Chamberlain Square**, where pride of place goes to the **Birmingham Museum and Art Gallery**, the city's finest museum, complete with a stunning collection of Pre-Raphaelite art. Beyond, further west still, is the glossy **International Convention Centre**, from where it's another short hop to the **Gas Street Basin**, the prettiest part of the city's serpentine canal system. Close by is canalside **Brindley Place**, a smart, brick and glass complex sprinkled with slick cafés and bars and holding the enterprising **Ikon Gallery** of contemporary art.

From Brindley Place, it's a short walk southeast to **The Mailbox**, the immaculately rehabilitated former postal sorting office with yet more chic bars and restaurants, or you can head north along the old towpath of the **Birmingham and Fazeley canal** as far as Newhall Street. The latter is within easy walking distance of the Georgian delights of **St Philip's Cathedral** and – in the opposite direction – the **Jewellery Quarter**, which holds an excellent museum and scores of jewellery workshops and retail outlets.

The Bull Ring and Selfridges

A few steps from New Street Station, Rotunda Square marks the intersection of New and High streets, taking its name from the soaring **Rotunda**, a handsome and distinctive cylindrical tower that is the sole survivor of the notorious **Bull Ring** shopping centre, which fulfilled every miserable cliché of 1960s town planning until its demolition in 2001. The new Bull Ring shopping centre that has sprung up in its place would be a textbook example of safe yet uninspired contemporary planning were it not for two strokes of real invention. In the redevelopment, the architects split the Bull Ring shops into two separate sections and in the gap there is now an uninterrupted view of the medieval spire of St Martin's – an obvious contrast between the old and the new perhaps, but still extraordinarily effective. The second coup was the design of **Selfridges'** new store, a billowing organic swell protruding from the Bull Ring's east side, and seen to good advantage from the wide stone stairway that descends from Rotunda Square to St Martin's. Reminiscent of an inside-out octopus, Selfridges shimmers with an architectural chain mail of thousands of silver discs, altogether a bold and hugely successful attempt to create a popular city landmark. It was designed by Future Systems (responsible for the media centre at Lord's cricket ground in London) to resemble a sequinned dress, hence its nickname – the "Bobbles Building".

▲ Selfridges, Birmingham

St Martin's Church and the city markets

Nestling at the foot of the Bull Ring, the newly scrubbed and polished **St Martin's Church** (daily 10am–5pm; free) is a fetching amalgamation of the Gothic and the Neo-Gothic, its mighty spire poking high into the sky. The church has had some hard times, bombed by the Luftwaffe and attacked by the Victorians, but the interior, with its capacious three-aisled nave, is saved from mediocrity by a delightful Burne-Jones stained-glass window, a richly coloured, finely detailed affair whose panes sport angels, saints, biblical figures and scenes; it's in the south transept.

Across from the church are Birmingham's three main **markets** – two selling fresh produce, one indoor (Mon–Sat 9am–5.30pm), the other outdoor (Tues–Sat 9am–5.30pm), with the **Rag Market** (Tues, Thurs, Fri & Sat 9am–5pm) in between. There was a time when the Rag Market was crammed with every sort of material you could imagine and then some, but although its heyday is past it still musters up all sorts of knick-knacks, always sold at bargain-basement prices.

New Street, Victoria and Chamberlain squares

Stretching west from the Bull Ring, **New Street** is a busy, bustling pedestrianized thoroughfare, lined with shops and stores. At its west end, New Street opens out into the handsomely refurbished **Victoria Square**, whose centrepiece is a large and particularly engaging water fountain designed by Dhruva Mistry. The fountain's large and distinctive female figure is affectionately known as "the floozy in the Jacuzzi" by the locals – but there's no such term of endearment for Antony Gormley's rusting *Iron Man* lurking nearby, and leaning at a precarious angle like a Saturday-night drunk. The waterfall outdoes poor old Queen Victoria, whose **statue** is glum and uninspired, though the thrusting self-confidence of her bourgeoisie is very apparent in the flamboyant **Council House** behind her, its assorted gables and cupolas, columns and towers completed in 1879.

Across the square, and very different, is the **town hall** of 1834, whose classical design – by Joseph Hansom, who went on to design Hansom cabs – was based on the Roman temple in Nîmes. The building's simple, flowing lines contrast with much of its surroundings, but it's an appealing structure all the same, erected to house public meetings and musical events in a flush of municipal pride and now, after a recent re-fit, a performing arts and community venue.

Victoria Square leads into **Chamberlain Square**, in the middle of which is a dinky Neo-Gothic memorial in honour of **Joseph Chamberlain** (1836–1914), who made himself immensely popular hereabouts by taking the city's gas and water supplies into public ownership. His political career ultimately took him from the Birmingham mayor's office to national prominence as leader of the Liberal Unionists and figurehead of the resistance to Irish home rule.

The Birmingham Museum and Art Gallery

The **Birmingham Museum and Art Gallery** (BM&AG) occupies a rambling, Edwardian building on Chamberlain Square (Mon–Sat 10/10.30am–5pm, Sun 12.30–5pm; free; ⓦwww.bmag.org.uk). It possesses a multifaceted collection divided into several sections, but the bulk is spread over one long floor – Floor 2 – which is where you'll find the fine art, which attracts most attention. Note, however, that the paintings mentioned below are not always on display; the BM&AG's collection is too large for it all to be exhibited at any one time, so paintings are regularly rotated and key paintings are often moved to (and from) the Round Room, at the start of Floor 2. Furthermore, the whole show can be disturbed by temporary exhibitions. Be sure to pick up a plan at reception.

The BM&AG holds one of the world's most comprehensive collections of **Pre-Raphaelite** work and this is found in Rooms 14 and 17–19. Founded in 1848, the Pre-Raphaelite Brotherhood consisted of seven young artists, of whom Rossetti, Holman Hunt, Millais and Madox Brown are the best known. The name of the group was selected to express their commitment to honest observation, which they thought had been lost with the Renaissance. Many of the Brotherhood's most important paintings are (usually) displayed here, including **Dante Gabriel Rossetti**'s (1828–82) seminal *Beata Beatrix* (1870), a stirring portrait of the fourteenth-century Italian poet Dante's beloved Beatrice, but commonly thought to be a tribute to **Rossetti**'s wife, Elizabeth Siddal, who died in 1862. Here also is **Ford Madox Brown**'s (1821–93) powerful image of emigration, *The Last of England* (1855). There's actually a lot more going on in Brown's painting than first meets the eye. On one level, it is a sentimental portrayal of a migrant family, but to Brown the family also symbolized the yeomen of England – as evidenced by their possessions – whose enforced emigration was a result of poor government, and thus a national outrage. Political sub-texts aside, the group's dedication to realism (as they conceived it) was unyielding and **Hunt**, for example, visited the Holy Land to prepare a series of religious paintings including his extravagant *The Finding of the Saviour in the Temple*. By 1853, the Brotherhood had effectively disbanded, but a second wave of artists carried on in its footsteps. The most prominent of them was **Edward Burne-Jones** (1833–98), who has an entire room to himself (Room 14). It's his *Star of Bethlehem* which catches the eye most, one of the largest watercolours ever painted, a mysterious, almost magical piece with earnest Magi and a film-star-like Virgin Mary.

The rest of the art section, though not quite as memorable, contains a very good collection of eighteenth- and nineteenth-century British art, including an extensive sample of **watercolour** landscapes as well as some especially fine, bucolic paintings by **David Cox** (1783–1859), Constable's Birmingham contemporary. There's also a significant sample of **European** paintings from the likes of Jan van Scorel and Lucas Cranach through to the Impressionists. Look out also for Sir Peter Lely's iconic portrait of a thoughtful and determined *Oliver Cromwell* in Room 24.

Sharing Floor 2 is the **industrial art section**, which kicks off with the **Industrial Gallery**, set around an expansive atrium whose wrought-iron columns and balconies clamber up towards fancy skylights. The gallery holds small but choice selections of ceramics, metalwork and jewellery, plus a wonderful sample of locally produced stained glass retrieved from defunct churches across Birmingham. Here also is the **Edwardian Tea Room**, one of the more pleasant places in Birmingham for a cuppa (see p.583).

Moving on, Floor 1's cavernous **Gas Hall** is an impressive venue for touring art exhibitions, while the **Waterhall Gallery** (same times), inside the Council House, just across Edmund Street from the main museum building, showcases modern and contemporary art including the likes of Francis Bacon and Bridget Riley.

Centenary Square

From the north side of Chamberlain Square, walk through the hideously ugly **Paradise Forum** shopping and fast-food complex to get to **Centenary Square**, where there's an unusual World War I war memorial, the **Hall of Memory** (Mon–Sat 10am–4pm; free). Erected in 1923, to commemorate those 13,000 Brummies who had died in World War I, the memorial is an architectural hybrid, a delightful mix of Art Deco and Neoclassical features, whose centrepiece is a domed Remembrance chamber. From the memorial, a grassy lawn stretches over to the showpiece **Symphony Hall** and **International Convention Centre** (ICC) with the **Birmingham Repertory Theatre** on the right.

Gas Street Basin and The Mailbox

From the ICC, it's a brief stroll along Broad Street to Gas Street, on the left, which leads down to **Gas Street Basin**, the hub of Birmingham's intricate canal system. There are eight canals within the city's boundaries, comprising no less than 32 miles of canal. The highpoint of canal construction was the late eighteenth century, when almost all heavy goods were transported by water. In the middle of the nineteenth century, the railways made the canals uneconomic, but they struggled on until the 1970s when tourism – and narrowboats – gave them a new lease of life. Much of Birmingham's surviving canal network slices through the city's grimy, industrial bowels, but certain sections have been immaculately restored with Gas Street Basin leading the way. At the junction of the Worcester and Birmingham and Birmingham Main Line canals, the Basin, with its herd of brightly painted narrowboats, is edged by a delightful medley of old brick buildings. There's a good pub here too – the *Tap & Spile* (see p.584) – and in summer a **water bus service** plies the central part of the canal system (May, June & Sept Sat & Sun 10am–4pm; July & Aug daily 10am–5pm; every 45min; day pass £3.50 or 50p per stop).

Follow the towpath along the canal southeast from the Basin and you soon reach **The Mailbox**, a talented reinvention of Birmingham's old postal sorting office complete with restaurants, hotels, and some of the snazziest shops in the city – including Jaeger and Harvey Nichols.

Brindley Place and the Ikon Gallery

Doubling back to the Basin, it's a short walk northwest along the canal towpath to the bars, shops and offices of waterside **Brindley Place**, named after James Brindley the eighteenth-century engineer who was responsible for many of Britain's early canals. It's an aesthetically pleasing development where you'll also find the city's celebrated **Ikon Gallery** (Tues–Sun 11am–6pm; free; ⊛www.ikon-gallery.co.uk), housed in a rambling Victorian building and one of the country's most imaginative venues for touring exhibitions of contemporary art.

Along the Birmingham & Fazeley Canal to St Paul's Square

Just beyond Brindley Place, in front of the huge dome of the National Indoor Arena (NIA), the **canal** forks: the Birmingham & Fazeley leads northeast (to the right) and the Birmingham Main Line Canal cuts west (to the left), though to complicate matters the latter has a spur loop here, going under Sheepcote Street. Also beside the main canal junction is the shell-like **National Sea Life Centre** (daily 10am–5/6pm; ☎0121/643 6777, ⊛www.sealifeeurope.com), which can't help but raise a few eyebrows, given the city's inland location. Nevertheless, it's an enterprising educational venture, offering Birmingham's landlubbers an opportunity to view and even touch many unusual varieties of fish and sea life – it's so popular with kids that bookings are advised during school holidays.

Beyond the main canal fork, the first part of the **Birmingham & Fazeley Canal** has been attractively restored, its antique brick buildings cleaned of accumulated grime and leading past the quaint **Scotland Street Locks**. Further on, however, things take a grittier aspect as the canal bores beneath the city centre amidst its industrial tangle. Emerging at **Newhall Street** by means of a flight of (unsigned) steps, about half a mile from the main canal junction, you're a stone's throw from **St Paul's Square**, where an attractive ensemble of old houses flank the **church of St Paul's**. Dating to the 1770s, the rational symmetries of St Paul's are an excellent illustration of Neoclassical design, though to the people who paid for it (by public subscription), there was much more to the building than aesthetics: gone were the mysteries of the medieval church, replaced by a church of the Enlightenment and one that proved popular with the new industrialists – both Matthew Boulton and James Watt had family pews here, though Watt never actually turned up. St Paul's Square is one of the more agreeable parts of the centre and here also, beside the square in Dakota House, on Brook Street, you'll find the **Royal Birmingham Society of Artists** (RBSA; Mon–Sat 10.30am–5.30pm, Sun 1–5pm; free), which offers an inventive range of fine and applied art exhibitions.

The Square is on the edge of the Jewellery Quarter and a short haul from Colmore Row and St Philip's Cathedral (see p.582).

The Jewellery Quarter

Birmingham's long-established **Jewellery Quarter** lies to the northwest of the city centre, beginning just beyond St Paul's Square. Buckle-makers and toy-makers first colonized this area in the 1750s, opening the way for hundreds of silversmiths, jewellers and goldsmiths. There are still around five hundred jewellery-related companies in the district today with most of the **jewellery shops** concentrated along Vittoria Street and its northerly continuation, Vyse Street. The quarter's information centre, at the start of Vyse Street, will help if you're looking for somewhere or something in particular. The prime attraction hereabouts is the engrossing **Museum of the Jewellery Quarter**, 75–79 Vyse St (Easter to Oct Tues–Sun 11.30am–4pm; Nov to Easter Tues–Sat 11.30am–4pm; free), a five-minute walk north of the Vittoria Street/Warstone Lane intersection. The museum occupies a former jewellery maker's, which closed down in the early 1980s but – and this is what makes it so distinctive – the owners just shut up shop, leaving everything intact and untouched, down to the dirty tea cups. Not only that, but the owners were hardly keen investors and the bulk of the furnishing and fittings in use when they closed date back to the 1950s if not beyond. The museum details the rise and fall of the jewellery trade in Birmingham, but it's the old factory that steals the show. Here, the atmosphere and conditions of the old works are intriguing – the jewellers were wedged into tiny, hot and noisy spaces to churn out hundreds of earrings, brooches and rings. Their modern counterparts use the old machines to show how some of the most common designs were produced.

From the museum, it's a couple of minutes' walk back along Vyse Street to the Jewellery Quarter **train station** and **metro stop**, on the Snow Hill line.

St Philip's Cathedral

A few minutes' walk southeast of St Paul's Square, on the other side of the ring road, is **Colmore Row**, where a string of fancily carved High Victorian stone buildings provide a suitable backdrop for **St Philip's Cathedral** (late July to early Sept Mon–Fri 7.30am–5pm, Sat & Sun 8.30am–5pm; early Sept to late July Mon–Fri 7.30am–6.30pm, Sat & Sun 8.30am–5pm; free; Ⓦwww .birminghamcathedral.com), a bijou example of English Baroque. Consecrated in 1715, St Philips was initially a parish church that served as an overspill for St Martin's (see p.578). It was, however, in a more genteel location than the older church and when, in 1905, the Church of England decided to establish a new diocese in Birmingham, they made St Philip's the cathedral. The church is a handsome affair, its graceful, galleried interior all balance and poise, its harmonies unruffled by the Victorians, who enlarged the original church in the 1880s, when four new stained-glass windows were commissioned from local boy **Edward Burne-Jones**, a leading light of the Pre-Raphaelite movement. The windows are typical of his style – intensely coloured, fastidiously detailed and distinctly sentimental. Three – the *Nativity*, *Crucifixion* and *Ascension* – are at the east end of the church beyond the high altar, the fourth – the *Last Judgement* – is directly opposite.

St Philip's Cathedral lies just to the west of the city centre's pedestrianized core with chain stores and shopping precincts bunching up along Corporation, New and High streets before reaching some sort of retail climax at the Bull Ring (see p.577).

East of the Bull Ring: the Custard Factory

Below the Bull Ring, **Digbeth** – once the main thoroughfare through medieval Birmingham – falls away to the southeast. Jammed with traffic and jostled by decrepit industrial buildings, it's hardly enticing, but there are two reasons to venture out here. The first is the bus station on the right; the second – on the left just along and off Gibb Street – is the arts complex that occupies the old **Alfred Bird Custard Factory**. The factory is a homely affair set around a friendly little courtyard and the **arts complex** (Ⓦwww.custardfactory.com) offers a fascinating variety of workshops and has gallery space for temporary exhibitions of modern art. There are a couple of groovy cafés and bars here too (see pp.584 & 585).

Southwest of the Bull Ring: the Back to Backs

The sheer scale of the industrial boom that gripped nineteenth-century Birmingham is hard to grasp, but the raw statistics speak for themselves: in 1811, there were just 85,000 Brummies, a century later there were literally ten times more. Inevitably, Birmingham's infrastructure could barely cope, particularly in terms of **housing** with the city's newest inhabitants crowded into every conceivable nook and cranny. The concomitant demand for cheap housing spawned the **back-to-back**, quickly erected dwellings that were one room deep and two, sometimes three floors high, built in groups ('courts') around a courtyard where the communal privies were located. Even by the standards of the time, this was pretty grim stuff, especially as overcrowding was the rule rather than the exception, and as early as the 1870s Birmingham council banned the construction of any more, though it took several decades to clear the back-to-backs that had already been built. The last Birmingham courts were bulldozed in the 1970s, but one set survived and this, the **Birmingham Back to Backs**, 55–63 Hurst St (Tues–Sun 10am–5pm; 1hr guided tours on timed ticket; bookings on ☎0121/666 7671; £5), a short walk southwest of the Bull Ring, has now been repaired and restored by the National Trust. The NT's guided tour wends its way through four separate homes, each of which represents a different period from the early nineteenth century onwards. The tour is very informal, with tidbits about the families who lived here and lots of period bygones to touch and feel. There is also a room devoted to the history of the back-to-back and you can even stay here – part of the court has been turned into NT "cottages" (see p.576).

Eating and drinking

Central Birmingham has a bevy of first-rate **restaurants** with a string of smart, new venues springing up in the slipstream of the burgeoning conference and trade-fair business, particularly in and around The Mailbox. There's also a concentration of decent, reasonably priced restaurants in the Chinese Quarter, just south of New Street Station, on and around Hurst Street. Birmingham's gastronomic speciality is the **balti**, a delicious and astoundingly inexpensive Kashmiri stew cooked and served in a small wok-like dish called a *karahi*, with naan bread instead of cutlery. Although balti houses have opened up within the city centre, the original and arguably the best balti houses are in the gritty suburbs of **Balsall Heath/Moseley**, a couple of miles to the south of the centre, and **Sparkhill**, about three miles to the southeast. A few of these are listed here – but note that many are unlicensed, so you may want to take your own booze.

City centre **pubs** vary as much as you'd expect. The liveliest, catering for a mixed bag of conference delegates and Brummies-out-on-the-ale, are liberally sprinkled along Broad Street, in the immediate vicinity of the Convention Centre, and in Brindley Place. Most of these are decorated in sharp, modern style, but there are more traditional places hereabouts as well – as there are in other parts of the city centre.

Cafés and restaurants

Brasserie de Malmaison The Mailbox, 1 Wharfside St ☎0121/246 5000. Slick and smart brasserie offering a varied menu of both French and English dishes. Prides itself on its use of local ingredients. Part of the *Malmaison* hotel (see p.576). Mains £11–18. Open daily

Chez Jules 5a Ethel St, off New St ☎0121/633 4664. Cosy, very recommendable, medium-priced French restaurant in the city centre, with especially good lunchtime deals. The lamb dishes are particularly tasty. A two-course lunch costs £8, main courses £10–15 in the evening. Closed Sun.

Chung Ying 16–18 Wrottesley St ☎0121/622 5669. Arguably the best Cantonese dishes in the Chinese Quarter, and always busy. Mains £8–11. Open daily.

Deolali 23a St Marys Row, Moseley ☎0121/442 2222. No flock wallpaper here in this slick Indian restaurant with beamed ceilings and bare brick walls. Excellent food with the emphasis on southern India. Mains from around £10. Evenings only; closed Sun.

Edwardian Tea Room At the Birmingham Museum and Art Gallery, Chamberlain Square. This café has a great location in one of the large and fancily decorated halls of the museum's industrial section – hence all the cast-iron columns – but the food is canteen-style routine. Daytimes only.

Kababish 29 Woodbridge Rd, Moseley ☏0121/449 5556. Cosy, inventively decorated restaurant specializing in northern Indian and Kashmiri dishes, including balti. Many locals swear by the place. Mains from £7. Evenings only.

Metro Bar and Grill 73 Cornwall St ☏0121/200 1911. Slick, very-modern-Brummie bar-cum-restaurant serving Modern British cuisine with bar plates at just £6. The long, curved mirror on the back wall adds elan. Mains from £14. Closed Sun.

🏃 **The Oriental** The Mailbox, 128 Wharfside St ☏0121/633 9988. Large and smart restaurant decorated in a sort of pan-Asian style and with a smashing location, down by the canal in The Mailbox. Has a wide-ranging menu featuring Malay, Thai and Chinese dishes. A place to experiment – the Malay cuisine is the least familiar to most Brits. Main courses average a very reasonable £9. Daily from noon.

🏃 **Purnells** 55 Cornwall St ☏0121/212 9799. Smooth and polished restaurant recently opened by much lauded chef, Glynn Purnell. The premises are Victorian red-brick, but the interior is all modernist – prestige dining with a three-course à la carte meal costing £40. "Brill cooked in coconut milk with Indian red lentils" gives the flavour of the menu. Closed Sat lunchtime and all day Sun & Mon; open till 1am. Reservations essential.

Royal Naim 417 Stratford Rd, Sparkhill ☏0121/766 7849. Twice named Brum's best balti house – as good as it gets. Main courses from £6. Daily from noon.

Pubs and bars

Actress & Bishop 35 Ludgate Hill ☏0121/236 7426, 🌐www.surgemusic.com. Popular bar in a fashionable part of town with a strong line-up of local bands.

Factory Club Custard Factory, Gibb St, off Digbeth. Great bar located in a laid-back arts complex that was once a custard factory. Turns into a club late at night – see opposite.

🏃 **The Jam House** 3 St Paul's Sq ☏0121/200 3030, 🌐www.thejamhouse.com. Jazz, funk, blues and swing joint pulling in artists from every corner of the globe. Daily except Mon from 6pm.

The Old Fox Hurst Street. Over-modernized but popular pub, with an excellent selection of beers and a boisterous atmosphere. At least the great long windows (of 1891) have survived the updaters.

🏃 **Old Joint Stock** 4 Temple Row West. This delightful pub has the fanciest decor in town – with busts and a balustrade, a balcony and chandeliers, all dating from its days as a bank. A stone's throw from St Philip's Cathedral.

Tap & Spile 10 Gas St. Charming traditional pub with rickety rooms and low-beamed ceilings beside the canal on Gas Street Basin. Once the hangout of weathered canal men, it now attracts tourists and locals in equal measure.

Tarnished Halo 21 Ludgate Hill. Great name for this jam-packed bar where students hang out in numbers.

Nightlife and entertainment

Nightlife in Birmingham is thriving, and the **club scene** is recognized as one of Britain's best, spanning everything from word-of-mouth underground parties to meat-market mainstream clubs. There's a particular emphasis on special nights with leading DJs turning up at different venues on different nights. **Live music** is strong in the city, too, with big-name concerts at several major venues and other, often local bands appearing at some clubs and pubs. Birmingham's showpiece **Symphony Orchestra** and **Royal Ballet** are the spearheads of the city's resurgent **classical scene**. The social calendar also gets an added fillip from a wide range of upmarket **festivals**, including the **Jazz Festival** (☏0121/454 7020, 🌐www.birminghamjazzfestival.com) for two weeks in July and the three-day **Artsfest** (☏0121/464 5678, 🌐www.artsfest.org.uk) of film, dance, theatre and music in September.

For current **information** on all events, performances and exhibitions, pick up a free copy of the excellent, fortnightly *What's On*, Birmingham's definitive listings guide – or consult 🌐www.wowbirmingham.co.uk. The guide is available at all city tourist offices and many public venues.

Clubs

Air Heath Mill Lane, off Digbeth ☎0845/009 8888, ⓦwww.airbirmingham.com. Shiny, high-tech superclub host to hundreds of house- and trance-hungry clubbers.

Factory Club Custard Factory, Gibb Square, off Digbeth, ☎0121/224 7502, ⓦwww.factoryclub .co.uk. Eclectic and frequently impeccable music policy, plus juicy live events. One of the best nights out in town. Part of the arts complex that inhabits the old Alfred Bird Custard Factory (see p.582).

The Nightingale Essex House, Kent St ☎0121/622 1718, ⓦwww.nightingaleclub.co.uk. The king of Brum's gay clubs, but popular with straights too. Five bars, three levels, two discos, a café-bar and even a garden. Just south of The Mailbox (see p.580).

Waterworks Jazz Club Gough St ☎0121/445 5668, ⓦwww.waterworksjazz.com. Specialist jazz joint just off the inner ring road near Holloway Circus.

Classical music, theatre and dance

Birmingham Repertory Theatre Centenary Square, Broad St ☎0121/236 4455, ⓦwww .birmingham-rep.co.uk. Mixed diet of classics and new work, featuring local and experimental writing.

The Crescent Theatre Sheepcote Street, Brindley Place ☎0121/643 5858, ⓦwww.crescent-theatre .co.uk. Adventurous theatre group and venue for visiting companies.

Hippodrome Theatre Hurst St ☎0870/730 1234, ⓦwww.birminghamhippodrome.com. Lavishly refurbished, the Hippodrome is home to the Birmingham Royal Ballet. Also features touring plays and big pre- and post-West End productions, plus a splendiferous Christmas pantomime.

National Exhibition Centre (NEC) Bickenhill Parkway ☎0871/945 6000, ⓦwww.necgroup .co.uk. The NEC's arena hosts major pop concerts. Ten miles east of the centre beside the M42; train from New Street to Birmingham International Station.

Old Rep Theatre Station St ☎0121/303 2323, ⓦwww.oldreptheatre.org.uk. One of Britain's oldest repertory theatres, with regular performances from the imaginative Birmingham Stage Company.

Symphony Hall International Convention Centre, Broad St ☎0121/780 3333, ⓦwww.thsh.co.uk. Acoustically one of the most advanced concert halls in Europe, home of the acclaimed City of Birmingham Symphony Orchestra (CBSO), as well as a venue for touring music and opera.

Town Hall Broad St ☎0121/780 3333, ⓦwww .thsh.co.uk. Newly refitted and refurbished, the old Town Hall offers a very varied programme of pop, classical and jazz music through to modern dance and ballet.

Listings

Cricket Warwickshire County Cricket Club play at one of England's most famous grounds, Edgbaston, just to the southwest of the city centre on Edgbaston Road (☎0121/446 4422, ⓦwww.thebears.co.uk).

Football Birmingham has two top-flight football teams: Aston Villa, who play at Villa Park, just north of the centre in Aston (☎0800/612 0970, ⓦwww .avfc.premiumtv.co.uk); and Birmingham City, based at St Andrew's, Small Heath (☎0844/557 1875, ⓦwww.blues.premiumtv.co.uk).

Internet Free Internet and email access at Birmingham Central Library, on Chamberlain Square (Mon–Fri 9am–8pm & Sat 9am–5pm; ☎0121/303 4511).

Pharmacy Boots, 65 High St ☎0121/212 1330.

Post office 1 Pinfold St at Victoria Square (Mon–Sat 9am–5.30pm).

Public transport Centro Hotline ☎0121/200 2787, ⓦwww.centro.org.uk.

Taxis Toa Taxis ☎0121/427 8888.

Staffordshire

Spreading north from the Birmingham conurbation, the miscellaneous and low-key landscapes of **Staffordshire** don't enthral too many people. Nonetheless, the county does pack in coachloads of visitors on account of **Alton Towers** (☎0870/520 4060, ⓦwww.altontowers.com; closed mid–Nov to March), the nation's most popular amusement park, with several million visitors annually howling and screaming for all they are worth. The white-knuckle rides take much more money than do the hoteliers in the cathedral city of **Lichfield**, at the southern end of Staffordshire, both the main historic attraction and the county's most agreeable town. Lichfield is easy to reach by **rail** and **bus** from Birmingham and other major cities.

Lichfield

Located some sixteen miles to the north of Birmingham, the pocket-sized town of **LICHFIELD** is a slow-moving, amenable kind of place that demands a visit for two reasons – its magnificent sandstone **cathedral** and its associations with local lad turned genius, **Samuel Johnson.**

The cathedral

Begun in 1085, but substantially rebuilt in the thirteenth and fourteenth centuries, **Lichfield Cathedral** (daily 8am–5pm; free, but donation requested) is unique in possessing three spires – an appropriate distinction for a bishopric that once extended over virtually all of the Midlands. The church stands on the site of a shrine built for the relics of St Chad, a much-venerated English bishop noted for his humility, who died here in Lichfield in 672.

The cathedral's **west front** is adorned by over one hundred statues of biblical figures, English kings and the supposed ancestors of Christ, some of them dating back to the thirteenth century, but mostly Victorian replacements of originals destroyed by Cromwell's troops. Even the central spire was demolished during the skirmishes – Lichfield suffered more damage in the Civil War than any other cathedral. Extensive and painstaking rebuilding and restoration work began immediately after the Restoration in 1660 and has gone on ever since, although the bulk of the work was only completed at the end of the nineteenth century.

Inside, the three-aisled **nave** is supported by two long lines of pointed Gothic arches set beneath a heavy-duty arcaded gallery, which renders the celerestory windows insignificant. The whole effect is rather gloomy, but there's still enough light to admire the soaring vaulted roof, which extends without interruption into the choir, looking like the rib-cage of a giant beast – a distinctly eerie experience. The **south transept** is earlier than the nave, dating to the 1220s, but the main item of interest here is unreservedly Victorian and imperialist. The transept's **St Michael's Chapel** is dedicated to the Staffordshire Regiment and its railings are decorated with replica Zulu shields to celebrate their involvement in the Zulu War; the sphinx-topped monument does the same for another vainglorious campaign, not – as you might expect – in Egypt, but the First Sikh War in India in the 1840s. Beyond the transepts, the first three bays of the choir are the oldest part of the church, completed in the Early English style of the twelfth century, but thereafter the choir is resolutely middle Gothic. On the south side of the **choir** a narrow stone stairway leads up to a fine **minstrels' gallery** and the **St Chad's Head Chapel**, where the head of the saint was once displayed to cheer up the faithful. Most impressive of all, however, is the **Lady Chapel**, at the far end of the choir, which boasts a set of magnificent sixteenth-century windows, purchased from a Cistercian abbey in Belgium in 1802.

The cathedral's greatest treasure, the **Lichfield Gospels**, is displayed in the **chapter house**, off the north side of the choir. A rare and exquisite example of Anglo-Saxon artistry dating to the eighth century, this illuminated manuscript contains the complete gospels of Matthew and Mark, and a fragment of the gospel of Luke, written in Latin and embellished with elaborate decoration. Different pages are exhibited at different times, but a particular favourite is the gorgeous Carpet Page, showing a decorative cross whose blend of Coptic, Celtic and Oriental influences make it the equal of the more famous Irish Book of Kells and Lindisfarne Gospels (see p.915). The fact that the book ends midway through St Luke means it's almost certainly one of a pair – and rare book specialists have long been on the look-out for the other volume.

The rest of the town centre

Encircling the cathedral is **The Close**, which, with its good-looking medley of Tudor, Georgian and Victorian buildings, is the prettiest place in town. From The Close, it's a short walk along **Dam Street** – past the gloomy waters of the Minster Pool – to the **Market Square**, where there's a peculiar little statue of a puck-nosed Boswell and a much better one honouring **Samuel Johnson**, who looks suitably intellectual. The plinth below the statue is carved with three key scenes from Johnson's life. The most revealing shows Johnson making a public penance in Uttoxeter Market Place for the sin – as he saw it – of refusing to work on his father's Uttoxeter bookstall fifty years before.

At the back of the Market Place stands **St Mary's Church**, unremarkable in itself and now home to the **Lichfield Heritage Centre** (Mon–Sat 10am–5pm, Sun 10am–4pm; £3.50), which tracks through the city's history, with an

Samuel Johnson

Eighteenth-century England's most celebrated wit and critic, **Samuel Johnson**, was born above his father's bookshop on Lichfield's Market Place in 1709. From Lichfield he went to Pembroke College, Oxford, which he left in 1731 without having completed his degree. Disgruntled with academia, Johnson returned to Staffordshire as a teacher, before settling in Birmingham for three years, a period that saw his first pieces published in the *Birmingham Journal*.

In 1735 Johnson married Elizabeth Porter, a Birmingham friend's widow twenty years his senior, returning to his home district to open a private school in the village of Edial, just outside Lichfield. The school was no great success, so after two years the Johnsons abandoned the project and went to London along with the young David Garrick, their star pupil. Journalism and essays were the mainstay of the Johnsons' penurious existence until publisher Robert Dodsley asked Samuel to consider compiling a **Dictionary of the English Language**, a project that nobody had undertaken before, and which was to occupy him for eight years prior to its publication in 1755. Massively learned and full of mordant wit ("lexicographer: a writer of dictionaries; a harmless drudge"), the dictionary is one of Johnson's greatest legacies, although he was financially and emotionally stretched to breaking point by the workload it imposed. The dictionary was widely acclaimed, but, despite his increasing celebrity, money problems continued to dog him – in 1759 he wrote the novel *Rasselas* in one week, in order to raise money for his mother's funeral. Nevertheless, Johnson's financial bacon was saved shortly afterwards when, in the early 1760s, the new king, George III, granted him a bursary of £300 per year.

In 1763 Johnson met **James Boswell**, a pushy young Scot who clung tenaciously to the cantankerous older man until he learned to like him. Their journey to Scotland resulted in one of the finest travel books ever written, *A Journey to the Western Isles of Scotland* (1775), in which Johnson's fascinated incredulity at the native way of life makes for absorbing reading. Other publications from his final decade included a preface to Shakespeare's plays, a series of political tracts and the magnificent *Lives of the English Poets*. However, the work by which he is now best known is not one that he wrote himself – it's Boswell's *The Life of Samuel Johnson*, commenced on its subject's death in 1784, published in 1791 and still one of the English language's most full-blooded biographies. Johnson was buried in Westminster Abbey.

illuminating section on the Civil War. On the outside wall of the church several **plaques** commemorate noteworthy incidents. One of them is a memorial to the unfortunate Edward Wightman, who was burnt at the stake for heresy on this very spot in 1612 – the last Englishman to be so punished for this particular crime.

Also on the Market Place is the **Samuel Johnson Birthplace Museum** (April–Sept daily 10.30am–4.30pm; Oct–March daily noon–4.30pm; free). The great man's father – Michael – was a bookseller and this house, a narrow four-storey affair, was both the family home and his place of work. The museum's ground floor still serves as a bookshop – with copies of Boswell's biography and many of Johnson's works – whilst up above, on the first floor, a video provides a well-considered potted introduction to its subject. Thereafter, a series of modest displays explores Johnson's life and times. Of particular interest is the biting letter he sent to a certain Lord Chesterfield, after the latter falsely claimed credit for sponsoring Johnson's dictionary. The top floor holds a small collection of personal memorabilia, including Johnson's favourite armchair, his chocolate pot (chocolate was a real Georgian delicacy), bib holder, shoe buckles and ivory writing tablets.

Practicalities

Lichfield has two **train stations**: Lichfield City, with regular connections to and from Birmingham New Street, is about five minutes' walk south of the centre; while Lichfield Trent Valley, served by mainline trains from London Euston, is on the eastern fringe of the city, about twenty minutes' walk from the centre. The **bus station** is opposite Lichfield City Station. The **tourist office** shares premises with the Lichfield Garrick Theatre (see below), on Castle Dyke, just to the south of the Market Square via Baker's Lane (Mon–Sat 9am–5pm; ☎01543/412112, ⊛www.visitlichfield.com).

Once you've seen the sights, there's no strong reason to hang around, but Lichfield does have a reasonable supply of affordable **B&Bs**. One of the most central is *The Bogey Hole*, with just four guest rooms, in an old and well-kept house near the cathedral at 21 Dam Street (☎01543/264303; no credit cards; ❸). As regards **cafés** and **restaurants**, *Chapters*, next to the cathedral on the south side of The Close, is an old-fashioned café with a pleasant atmosphere and inexpensive home-made food. For something more substantial, head for **Bird Street**, two short blocks west of the Market Square, where there is a whole slew of restaurants. Amongst them, *Eastern Eye*, at 19 Bird St (☎01543/415047), is a smart, modern Asian restaurant serving all the classics, from tandoori through to kormas and dansaks; main courses start from as little as £6. Finally, the **Lichfield Garrick Theatre** (☎01543/412121, ⊛www.lichfieldgarrick.com), right in the centre on Castle Dyke, offers a lively programme of comedy, music, dance and theatre.

Derbyshire and the Peak District

In 1951, the hills and dales of the **Peak District**, at the southern tip of the Pennine range, became Britain's first National Park. Wedged between **Derby**, Manchester and Sheffield, it is effectively the backyard for the fifteen million people who live within an hour's drive of its boundaries, though somehow it accommodates the huge influx with minimum fuss.

Landscapes in the Peak District come in two forms. The brooding high moorland tops of **Dark Peak**, fifteen miles east of central Manchester, take their name from the underlying gritstone, known as millstone grit for its former use – a function commemorated in the millstones demarcating the park boundary. Windswept, mist-shrouded and inhospitable, the flat tops of these peaks are nevertheless a firm favourite with walkers on the **Pennine Way**, which meanders north from the tiny village of **Edale** to the Scottish border (see box, p.598). Altogether more forgiving, the southern limestone hills of the **White Peak** have been eroded into deep forested dales populated by small stone villages and often threaded by walking trails, some of which follow former rail routes. The limestone is riddled with complex cave systems around **Castleton** and under the region's largest centre, **Buxton**, a charming former spa town just outside the park's boundaries and at the end of an industrialized corridor that reaches out from Manchester. One of the country's most distinctive manorial piles, **Chatsworth House**, stands near **Bakewell**, a town famed locally not just for its cakes but also for its **well-dressing**, a possibly pagan ritual of thanksgiving for fresh water that takes place in about thirty local villages each summer. The well-dressing season starts in early June and continues through to mid-September; a specialist leaflet, available at most tourist offices, gives the low-down on when and where.

There's no obvious **route** around the Peaks, but the one outlined below comes in from the south – from Derby – and then cuts up to Buxton before looping round in a clockwise direction to Castleton, Hathersage, Baslow, Bakewell and points in between. The nearest motorway is the **M1** – come off at either junction 29 or 30 and you're within easy striking distance of Baslow, on the way to which you'll pass **Chesterfield**, a workaday town famous for the conspicuous **crooked spire** of the church of Our Lady and All Saints. To Midlanders, the spire announces the start of the Peak District and although Chesterfield doesn't have much else of immediate appeal, it does have a notable Thursday morning open-air flea market. The town's **tourist office**, opposite the spire (Mon–Sat 9am–5pm; ☎01246/345777), is also a good place to stock up on Peak District information.

As for a **base**, Buxton is your best bet by a (fairly) long chalk, though if you're after the hiking and cycling you'll probably prefer one of the area's villages.

Public transport

There are frequent **trains** (ⓦwww.nationalrail.co.uk) south from Manchester to end-of-the-line Buxton, and Manchester–Sheffield trains cut through Edale and Hathersage. The main **bus** access is via the Trent Barton bus company's TransPeak (ⓦwww.transpeak.co.uk) service from Nottingham to Manchester via Derby, Matlock, Bakewell and Buxton; otherwise First (ⓦwww.firstgroup .com) bus #272 runs regularly from Sheffield to Castleton, via Hathersage and Hope, and TM Travel (ⓦwww.tmtravel.co.uk) bus #65 connects Sheffield to Buxton via Eyam every hour or two. If you're not planning on walking or driving between towns and villages, you'll need the essential, encyclopedic *Peak District Bus Timetable* as well as the free *Derbyshire Train Times* booklet, both of which are available at local tourist and National Park information offices. Buses are more widespread than you might imagine, though there are limited winter and Sunday services, and often only sporadic links between the smaller villages. Various **one-day bus passes** allow unlimited travel to and within specified zones. It's a complicated system, but broadly speaking the South Yorkshire Peak Explorer (£7.50) covers the chunk of the park in Yorkshire; the Peak Wayfarer (£8.80), and the Derbyshire Wayfarer (£8.80) cover the rest. For all Peak District bus **timetable** information call ☎0871/200 2233.

The Peak District has a wide network of dedicated cycle lanes and trails, sometimes along former railway lines, and the National Park Authority (for contact details, see below) operates three **cycle rental** outlets: at Ashbourne (℡01335/343156); Derwent (℡01433/651261); and Parsley Hay, Buxton (℡01298/84493).

Information

The main **Peak District National Park Authority office** is at Aldern House, Baslow Road in Bakewell (℡01629/816200, Ⓦwww.peakdistrict.gov .uk). They operate a string of **visitor centres**, whose services supplement a host of town and village tourist offices. A variety of **maps** and **trail guides** is widely available across the Peaks, but for the non-specialist it's hard to beat the **Grate Little Guides**, a series of leaflets which provide hiking suggestions and trail descriptions for a dozen or so localities in a clear and straightforward style. They cost £1.80 each and are on sale at almost every tourist office and information centre, but note that the maps printed on the leaflets are best used in conjunction with an OS map. Be sure also to pick up a copy of the free and official **Peak District paper**, crammed with useful information and local news. Finally, there are two official Peak District **websites**, Ⓦwww .visitpeakdistrict.com and Ⓦwww.peak-experience.org.uk.

Accommodation

As you might expect, there's a plethora of **accommodation** in and around the National Park, mostly in B&Bs, though one of the area's distinctive features is the quality of its **country hotels** – like the ones in Ashford in the Water (see p.607), Baslow (see p.604) and Hassop (see p.607). The greatest concentration of first-rate hotels and B&Bs is, however, in the town of Buxton. The Peak District also holds numerous campsites and half a dozen or so youth hostels as well as a network of YHA-operated **camping barns**. These are located in converted farm buildings and provide simple and inexpensive self-catering accommodation for between six and twenty-four people. For further details, consult Ⓦwww.yha.org.uk.

Derby

The proximity of the Peak District might lead you to think that **DERBY**, 25 miles northeast of Lichfield, could prove to be an interesting stopping-off point. Sadly, the city is an unexciting place, though its workaday centre has recently been spruced up and it does hold several long and handsome nineteenth-century stone terraces, and it has one prime attraction – Derby Museum and Art Gallery, where there's an outstanding collection of paintings by Joseph Wright (see p.593). There's also a fine **Cathedral** (daily 8.30am–6pm; free), whose pinnacled, medieval tower soars high above its modest, mostly Victorian surroundings on Queen Street – just north along Irongate from the spacious, central Market Place. Attached to the tower, the main body of the church is firmly Georgian, its wide and graceful nave sweeping down to a splendidly ornate wrought-iron rood-screen. Here also, south of the chancel, is the magnif-icent table-tomb of Bess of Hardwick, her calm face presiding over the most intricate of alabaster carving; for more on Bess, see p.623.

Derby Museum and Art Gallery

Of the city's several museums, easily the best is the attractively laid-out **Derby Museum and Art Gallery** at the top of the Strand (Mon 11am–5pm, Tues–Sat 10am–5pm, Sun 1–4pm; free), a couple of minutes' walk west from the cathedral via Irongate and then Sadlergate. Amongst a string of separate displays, the

▲ Hiking in the Peak District

museum exhibits a splendid collection of Derby **porcelain**, several hundred pieces tracking through its different phases and styles from the mid-eighteenth century until today. Royal Crown Derby, founded in 1878, is still in production and the museum holds a healthy sample of their fancifully ornate ware – but really this is something of an acquired taste. Upstairs, there's a period room devoted to Charles Edward Stuart – aka **Bonnie Prince Charlie** – who

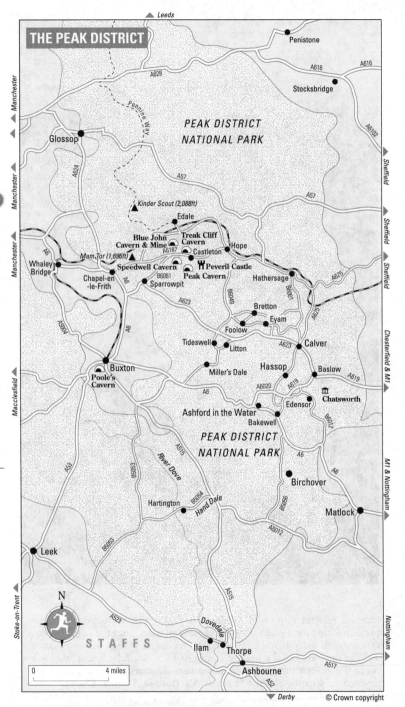

THE PEAK DISTRICT

Leeds

Penistone

A628

A616   A616

Stocksbridge

A6102

PEAK DISTRICT
NATIONAL PARK

Glossop

Pennine Way

A57

A57

Kinder Scout (2,088ft)

Edale

Blue John   Treak Cliff
Cavern & Mine   Cavern

Hope

Mam Tor (1,696ft)   Castleton

Whaley   A6187
Bridge   Speedwell Cavern   Peveril Castle

Chapel-en   B6061   Peak Cavern
-le-Frith   Sparrowpit   Hathersage

A623   B6049

Bretton

Eyam

Foolow

Tideswell   Litton   A623   Calver

Miller's Dale   Hassop   Baslow

Buxton   A6   A6020   A619   A619

Poole's   A619
Cavern   Edensor   Chatsworth

Ashford in the Water   B6012

Bakewell

PEAK DISTRICT
NATIONAL PARK   A6

A515   Birchover

River Dove   B6056

Hartington   Hand Dale   Matlock

A5012

Leek

A523

N

STAFFS

Ilam   Thorpe

Dovedale

Ashbourne

A52

A53   A53N4   A6   A624   A6   B5053   B5054   B5053   A517   A525   A6   Sheffield   Sheffield   Sheffield   Chesterfield & M1   M1 & Nottingham   Nottingham   Stoke-on-Trent   Macclesfield   Manchester   Manchester   Manchester

0   4 miles

592

Derby   © Crown copyright

attempted to seize the throne from George II in the Jacobite Rebellion of 1745. Advancing south from Scotland, Charles and his army got as far as Derby, spreading panic in London, but, unable to press their advantage, it was here they turned round for the long and dismal retreat that ended with their defeat at the bloody battle of Culloden.

In addition, the museum possesses a first-rate collection of the work of **Joseph Wright** (1734–97), a local artist generally regarded as one of the most talented English painters of his generation. Wright's bread and butter came from portraiture, though his attempt to fill the boots of Gainsborough, when the latter moved from Bath to London, came unstuck – his more forceful style did not satisfy his genteel Bath customers and Wright soon hightailed it back to Derby. Typical of his style is his portrait of *Sir Richard Arkwright*, looking uncompromising and very porky. Wright was one of the few artists of his period to find inspiration in technology and his depictions of the scientific world were hugely influential – as in his *The Alchemist Discovering Phosphorus* and *A Philosopher Lecturing on the Orrery*.

Practicalities

With fast and frequent connections to many major cities – including Sheffield, Nottingham and Birmingham – Derby **train station** is a mile to the southeast of the city centre: follow Midland Road and turn right onto London Road at the end, though it's a dreary walk, so best advice is to take a taxi. The **bus station** is more convenient, just off the inner ring road on Morledge, about five minutes' walk southeast of the Market Place, which is where you'll find the **tourist office** (Mon–Fri 9.30am–5.30pm, Sat 9.30am–5pm, Sun 10.30am–2.30pm; ℡01332/255802, ⓦwww.visitderby.co.uk). For a bite to **eat**, there are several good places on **Sadler Gate** including *Café B*, metres from the Derby Museum and serving the best coffee in town.

Ashbourne and around

Sitting pretty on the edge of the Peaks twelve miles northwest of Derby, **ASHBOURNE** is an amiable little town, whose stubby, cobbled **Market Place** is flanked by a happy ensemble of old stone buildings. Hikers tramp into town from the neighbouring dales to hang around the square's cafés and pubs, and stroll down the hill to take a peek at the suspended wooden beam spanning Church Street. Once a common feature of English towns, but now a rarity, these **gallows** were not warnings to malcontents, but advertising hoardings.

Walk west along Church Street from here and you soon leave the bustling centre for a quieter part of town, all set beneath the soaring spire of **St Oswald's Church**, an imposing lime- and ironstone structure dating from the thirteenth century. Something of an architectural muddle, the interior of the church is intriguing nonetheless, its columns decorated with all sorts of weathered sculptures and graced by handsome stained-glass windows, the best of which are exquisite examples of early-twentieth-century Arts and Crafts design. In the east aisle of the north transept, the **Cockayne Chapel** is named after the eponymous clan of local landowners who lie buried here. Of the five main table-tombs in and just outside the chapel the earliest dates from 1483, the latest from 1592, and taken together they illustrate changing fashions culminating in the elaborate ruffs and hats popular with the Elizabethans. The most striking tomb is that of Sir John (d.1447) and his son, Edmund, with its delicately carved alabaster figures – John in his suit of armour, Edmund in a fancy cloak and belted doublet.

Practicalities

There are no trains to Ashbourne, but the town is easy to reach by **bus** from Derby, Buxton and Manchester. From the bus station, it's a couple of minutes' walk to the Market Place. The **tourist office**, on the Market Place (March–Oct daily 10am–5pm; Nov–Feb Mon–Sat 10am–4pm; ☎01335/343666, ⊛www .visitpeakdistrict.com), has reams of hiking maps and guides, including the first-rate *Grate Little Guide to Dovedale* (see p.590). They can also advise on accommodation, though Ashbourne is best regarded as a pit-stop rather than as a base for further wanderings.

Ashbourne boasts a first-rate **delicatessen**, *Patrick & Brooksbank*, 22 Market Place (Mon–Sat 9am–5pm; ☎01335/342631), which has a superb selection of takeaway food, including local cheeses and hams – perfect for a picnic. The best **café** in town is inside the Bennetts store, at 19 St John St (closed Sun).

Around Ashbourne: Dovedale

The **River Dove** wriggles its way across the Peak District, cutting a circuitous course from the high hills of Derbyshire to the flatlands southwest of Derby, where it joins the River Trent. The Dove is at its scenic best just four miles north of Ashbourne in the stirring two-mile gorge that comprises **Dovedale** – confusingly, other parts of the river are situated in different dales. To get to Dovedale, head north from Ashbourne along the A515 and then follow the signs to the car park, which is on a narrow country road just beyond the hamlet of Thorpe – and a mile or so before you reach minuscule **Ilam**. The **hike** along the gorge is a real pleasure and easy to boot, the only problem being the bogginess of the valley after rain, but be warned that the place heaves with visitors on summer weekends and bank holidays. If you do decide to hike here, be sure to pick up a map and trail guide from Ashbourne tourist office (see above).

Hartington

Best approached from the east, through the boisterous scenery of Hand Dale, **HARTINGTON**, thirteen miles north of Ashbourne via the A515, is one of the prettiest villages in the Peaks, its easy ramble of stone houses zeroing in on a tiny duck pond. The village is also within easy walking distance of the River Dove as well as a sequence of handsome limestone dales – Biggin Dale is perhaps the pick. In addition, Hartington has several **B&Bs**, the most recommendable of which is the *Bank House Guest House*, in an attractive old building on the Market Place (☎01298/84465; no cards; ❸). There's also a **youth hostel** (☎0870/770 5848, ✉hartington@yha.org.uk; dorm beds £17.50, doubles ❶), whose 130 beds – in one- to eight-bedded rooms – are squeezed into a seventeenth-century manor house, Hartington Hall. The hostel is about 300 yards from the centre of the village and is very well equipped. Facilities include a self-catering kitchen, a café and Internet access.

Buxton

BUXTON, twenty miles north of Ashbourne, may have had its doldrums, but now it's on the way up, its centre revamped and reconfigured with imagination and flair. It holds a string of excellent hotels and B&Bs, which makes it a perfect base for exploring much of the Peaks National Park, and it also boasts the outstanding **Buxton Festival** (☎01298/70395; ⊛www .buxtonfestival.co.uk), running for two weeks in July. This features a full programme of classical music, opera and literary readings, and it has spawned the first-rate **Buxton Festival Fringe** (⊛www.buxtonfringe.com), also in July, with the emphasis on contemporary music, theatre and film. The biggest festival is, however, the **Gilbert & Sullivan Festival** (℡ 01422/323252 ⓦ www .gs-festival.co.uk,), a three-week affair in August mainly featuring amateur troupes and attracting an enthusiastic audience.

Buxton has a long history as a **spa**, beginning with the Romans, who happened upon a spring from which 1500 gallons of pure water gushed every hour at a constant 28°C. Impressed by the recuperative qualities of the water, the Romans came here by the chariot load, setting a trend that was to last hundreds of years. One of the most famous visitors was Mary, Queen of Scots, who was allowed by her captors to visit Buxton for the treatment of her rheumatism, another was Daniel Defoe, who loved the place. The spa's salad days came at the end of the eighteenth century with the **fifth Duke of Devonshire**'s

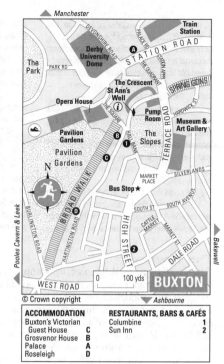

BUXTON

© Crown copyright

ACCOMMODATION		RESTAURANTS, BARS & CAFÉS	
Buxton's Victorian		Columbine	1
Guest House	C	Sun Inn	2
Grosvenor House	B		
Palace	A		
Roseleigh	D		

8

grand design to create a northern answer to Bath or Cheltenham, a plan ultimately thwarted by the climate, but not before some distinguished buildings had been erected, most memorably The Crescent. Neither was Victorian Buxton a laggard for although it may not have had quite the elan of its more southerly rivals, it still flourished, creating the raft of handsome stone houses that edge the town centre today. The stickiest years came after the town's thermal baths were closed for lack of custom in 1972, but Buxton hung on to emerge as the most appealing town in the Peaks.

Arrival, information and accommodation

Hourly trains from Manchester Piccadilly to Buxton pull into the **train station,** two minutes' walk from The Crescent on Station Road. The **TransPeak bus**, running every two hours between Manchester and Nottingham, stops in Buxton's Market Place, as do buses from Sheffield. Buxton **tourist office** is in The Crescent (daily: April–Oct 9.30am–5pm; Nov–March 10am–4pm; ℡ 01298/25106, ⓦ www.visitbuxton.co.uk) in what used to be the old Mineral Baths – hence the small display on Buxton's mineral water. They operate an accommodation booking service and have plentiful information on the town in particular and the Peaks in general.

Buxton town centre is liberally sprinkled with first-rate **B&Bs** and **hotels**. Several of the best choices are located on the pedestrianized Broad Walk, where a string of distinguished Edwardian and Victorian stone houses face out onto the Pavilion Gardens. Finding somewhere to stay is rarely a problem, except during the Buxton Festival (see opposite), when advance reservations are well-nigh essential.

Buxton's Victorian Guest House 3a Broad Walk
℡ 01298/78759, ⓦ www.buxtonvictorian.co.uk.
Cosy B&B with a handful of well-appointed rooms
decorated in crossover traditional/modern style.
Breakfasts feature local produce wherever feasible.
Occupies one of the grand Victorian houses
flanking Broad Walk. ❺

Grosvenor House 1 Broad Walk ℡ 01298/72439,
ⓦ www.grosvenorbuxton.co.uk. There are eight
en-suite guest rooms here in this handsome
Victorian town house beside the Pavilion Gardens,
each decorated in a modern rendition of period
style. Tasty breakfasts, plus evening meals by prior
arrangement. ❹

Palace Palace Rd ℡ 01298/22001, ⓦ www
.paramount-hotels.co.uk/palace. Built to
impress, the *Palace* was the pride of the Victorian
spa, its sweeping stone facade, with its pediments,

pilasters, balconies and imposing central tower,
lording it over the town centre from the high
ground of Palace Road. The hotel is a little
careworn today, but there's no gainsaying the
grandness of the entrance lobby and the soaring
staircase beyond. The bedrooms are very comfortable and although the decor is modern, many have
a quirky antique charm, as do the long, echoing
corridors. Substantial discounts are commonplace
– ring ahead to check. ❻

Roseleigh 19 Broad Walk ℡ 01298/24904,
ⓦ www.roseleighhotel.co.uk. This classic
three-storey gritstone Victorian town house,
overlooking Pavilion Gardens, is an excellent place
to stay, its neat and trim public rooms decorated in
attractive Victorian style, the en-suite bedrooms
beyond similarly well appointed. Family-run and
very competitively priced. ❹

The Town

The centrepiece of Buxton's hilly, compact centre is **The Crescent**, a broad
sweep of Georgian stonework commissioned by the fifth Duke of Devonshire
in 1780 and modelled on the Royal Crescent in Bath. It's recently been
refurbished, but remains empty while the townsfolk discuss its future, one good
idea being the creation of a brand-new thermal baths. Facing The Crescent, the
old **Pump Room** of 1894 provides space for art and crafts exhibitions, while
the adjacent water **fountain**, supplied by St Ann's Well, is still used to fill many
a local water bottle. For a better view of The Crescent, clamber up **The Slopes**,
a narrow slice of park that rises behind the Pump Room dotted with decorative
urns and a war memorial.

At the west end of The Crescent, the appealing old stone buildings of **The
Square** – though square it isn't – nudge up to the grandly refurbished **Buxton
Opera House**, an Edwardian extravagance whose twin towers, cherubs and
tiffany glass date from 1903. Stretching back from the Opera House are the
Pavilion Gardens, a slender string of connected buildings distinguished by
their wrought-iron work and culminating in a large and glassy dome. The
pavilions are actually a good deal more interesting from outside than from
within, reason enough to wander off into the adjoining park, also known as the
Pavilion Gardens, whose immaculate lawns and neat borders are graced by a
bandstand, ponds, dinky little footbridges and fountains.

Back at the Opera House, it's impossible not to notice the enormous **dome**
of what was originally the Duke of Devonshire's stables and riding school,
erected in 1789. For decades, the building was used as a hospital, but it's now
part of Derby University.

The Market Place and the Museum and Art Gallery

From the south end of The Square, the fetching stone terrace that comprises
Hall Bank scuttles up to the wide, breezy but somewhat traffic-choked **Market
Place**. There's nothing much here to hold the eye, but it's only a few yards back
down the hill along Terrace Road to the first-rate **Buxton Museum and Art
Gallery** (Tues–Fri 9.30am–5.30pm, Sat 9.30am–5pm & Easter–Sept Sun
10.30am–5pm; free). The museum begins well with its ground floor largely
devoted to enterprising temporary displays featuring the work of local

contemporary artists. There's also a period room dedicated to two Victorian archeologist-cum-geologists – William Boyd Dawkins (1837–1929) and Wilfred Jackson (1880–1978) – who spent decades exploring and explaining the Peaks. Upstairs, the large proficient "Wonders of the Peak" display tracks through the history of the region from its geological construction through the Romans and on to the Victorians. One of the most diverting sections looks at the prehistoric hilltop forts that lie dotted over the Peaks, while another examines the relics left by the Anglo-Saxons, most notably the incised Crosses at Eyam and Bakewell. Best of all, however, is the section dealing with the **petrifactioners**, who turned local semi-precious stones into ornaments and jewellery designed to tickle the fancy of the visitors who arrived here in numbers after the duke had put Buxton on the tourist map. By the 1840s, Buxton had no less than fourteen petrifactioners' shops, selling every stone trinket imaginable from plates and stone eggs to vases and obelisks. A variety of materials were used, but the two favourites were Blue John fluorspar (for more on which see p.599) and Ashford black marble, actually a dark limestone – and the museum displays a superb collection of both.

Poole's Cavern

The Peaks are riddled with cave systems and around half a dozen have become popular tourist attractions. One is **Poole's Cavern** (daily: March–Oct 9.30am–5pm; Nov–Feb 10am–4pm; £6.75; Ⓦ www.poolescavern.co.uk), whose impressively large chambers are home to a host of orange and blue-grey stalactites and stalagmites. The cavern is located about a mile to the southwest of central Buxton just off Green Lane. Guided tours of the caves depart every twenty minutes.

Eating and drinking

Buxton has several good places to eat, but the best **restaurant** in town is the ⚘ *Columbine*, a small and intimate place in the centre at 7 Hall Bank (Mon–Sat 7–10pm, but closed most Tues in winter; ☎01298/78752). The menu here is short but imaginative with main courses – such as saddle of monkfish with crab risotto – averaging £12; pre-theatre dinners are available by prior reservation from about 5pm. An excellent second choice is the *Sun Inn*, a fine old pub with antique beamed rooms just south of the Market Place at 33 High St. They offer fine ales and first-rate bar food – beef in ale, for instance, at £7.50, chicken, ham & meat pies £8. The *Sun Inn* is also the best place for a **pint**.

Castleton

The agreeable little village of **CASTLETON**, ten miles northeast of Buxton, lies on the northern edge of the White Peak, its huddle of old stone cottages ringed by hills and set beside a babbling brook. As a base for local walks, the place is hard to beat and the hikers resting up in the quiet Market Place, just off the main drag behind the church, have the choice of a healthy spread of local accommodation and services. Overseeing the whole caboodle is **Peveril Castle** (April–Oct daily 10am–5pm; Nov–March Mon & Thurs–Sun 10am–4pm; £3.50; EH), from which the village takes its name. William the Conqueror's illegitimate son William Peveril raised the first fortifications here to protect the king's rights to the forest that then covered the district, but most of the remains – principally the ruinous square keep – date to the 1170s. After a stiff climb up to the keep, you can trace much of the surviving curtain wall, which commands great views of the Hope Valley down below with the swollen mass of Mam Tor mountain rising to the west.

The Peak and Speedwell caverns

The limestone hills pressing in on Castleton are riddled with water-worn **cave systems** and four of them have been developed as tourist attractions. They can all be reached by car or on foot, the latter by means of a three-and-a-half-mile circular trail that begins in the village and takes two hours. The tourist office (see opposite) has the leaflet and sells the maps, though most visitors settle for just one set of caves – either the Peak Cavern or the Treak Cliff Cavern (see below) will do very nicely.

Peak Cavern is the handiest of the four (April–Oct daily 10am–5pm; Nov–March Sat & Sun 10am–5pm; £6.75, combined with Speedwell £11.50; ⓦ www.peakcavern.co.uk), tucked into a gully at the back of Castleton, its gaping mouth once providing shelter for a rope factory and a small village. Daniel Defoe, visiting in the eighteenth century, noted the cavern's colourful local name, the **Devil's Arse**, a reference to the fiendish fashion in which its interior contours twisted and turned.

Not too far away, 700 yards or so west from the village along the main road, is **Speedwell Cavern** (daily 10am–5pm; £7.25, combined with Peak £11.50; ⓦ www.speedwellcavern.co.uk). At 600 feet below ground, this is the deepest of the cave systems, but the main drama comes with the means of access – down a hundred dripping steps and then by boat through a quarter-mile-long claustrophobic tunnel that was blasted out in search of lead. At the end lies the Bottomless Pit, a pool where 40,000 tons of mining rubble were once dumped without raising the water level one iota.

The Treak Cliff and Blue John caverns

The other two caves are the world's only source of the sparkling fluorspar known as **Blue John**. Highly prized for ornaments and jewellery since Georgian times, this semi-precious stone comes in a multitude of hues from

The Pennine Way

The 268-mile-long **Pennine Way** (ⓦ www.nationaltrail.co.uk) was the country's first long-distance footpath, officially opened in 1965. It stretches north from the boggy plateau of the Peak District's Kinder Scout, through the Yorkshire Dales and Teesdale, crossing Hadrian's Wall and the Northumberland National Park, before entering Scotland to fizzle out at the village of Kirk Yetholm. People had been using a similar route for over thirty years before the official opening, inspired by Tom Stephenson, secretary of the Ramblers' Association, who had first identified the need for such a long-distance path in the 1930s. His idea was to stick to the crest of the Pennines where practicable and link up existing tracks, bridleways and footpaths, only descending to the valleys for overnight accommodation and services. The problem was that much of the route lay on private land, so years of negotiation and re-routing were necessary before the Pennine Way could be officially declared open.

Now it's one of the **most popular** walks in the country, either taken in sections or completed in two to three weeks, depending on your level of fitness and experience. It's a challenge in the best of weather, since it passes through some of the most remote countryside in England. You must certainly be properly equipped, able to use a map and compass and be prepared to follow local advice about current diversions and re-routing; changes are often made to avoid erosion of the existing trail. The National Trail Guides, *Pennine Way: South* and *Pennine Way: North*, are essential, though some still prefer to stick to Wainwright's *Pennine Way Companion*. Information centres along the route – like the one at Edale village – stock a selection of guides and associated trail leaflets and can offer advice.

blue through deep red to yellow, depending on its hydrocarbon impurities. Before being cut and polished, it is soaked in pine resin, a process originally carried out in France, where the term *bleu et jaune* (after its primary colours) provided its English name. The **Treak Cliff Cavern** (daily: 10am–5pm; £6.80; Ⓦwww.bluejohnstone.com), some 400 yards north from Speedwell, contains the best examples of the stone *in situ* and a good deal more in the shop. This is also the best cave to visit in its own right, dripping – literally – with stalactites (some up to 100,000 years old), flowstone and bizarre rock formations, all visible on an entertaining forty-minute walking tour through the main cave system. Water collected in one of the caves is used to make tea in the café at the entrance – it's much purer than the stuff that pours from local taps.

Further afield, just two miles or so west of Castleton off the B6061, tours of **Blue John Cavern** (daily: April–Oct 9.30am–5.30pm; Nov–March 9.30am–dusk; £7; Ⓦwww.bluejohn-cavern.co.uk) dive deep into the rock, with narrow steps and sloping paths following an ancient watercourse. The tour leads through whirlpool-hollowed chambers to Lord Mulgrave's Dining Room, a cavern where the eponymous lord and owner once put on a banquet for his miners. A goodly sample of Blue John is on sale at the cavern gift shop.

Practicalities

Easily the most scenic approach to Castleton is from Sparrowpit, about five miles to the west on the A623, with the road wiggling through the dramatic Winnats Pass. However, the principal **bus** service to Castleton arrives from the east – from Sheffield and Hathersage (First bus #272; hourly). In the opposite direction, several operators combine to link Buxton with Castleton, but buses are few and far between, one or two a day if that. The nearest **train station** is at Hope, a couple of miles or so to the east of Castleton along the valley. The station is on the Manchester Piccadilly–Sheffield line and there are trains every hour or two; bus #272 links Hope with Castleton. The **Castleton Information Centre** (daily 9.30/10am–5pm, ☎01433/620679, Ⓦwww.visitpeakdistrict .com), a combined museum, community centre and tourist office, stands beside the car park on the west side of the village, just off the main street, which dog-legs through the village doubling as the A6187. They operate an accommodation booking service, have oodles of local information and sell **hiking leaflets** and maps: a string of walking routes take you up from Castleton to the swollen hilltops that rise up in every direction. Most of the trails are easy to follow in good weather, but you will need an appropriate OS map and one of the trail leaflets issued by the tourist office.

Accommodation and eating

Accommodation is plentiful, but should be booked in advance at holiday times. Cream of the **B&B** crop is *Bargate Cottage*, in a modernized old cottage at the top end of the Market Place (☎01433/620201, Ⓦwww.bargatecottage .co.uk; no credit cards; ❸). They have three well-kept en-suite rooms, each kitted out in frilly modern style, and the breakfasts are first-rate. Another inexpensive option is the *Cryer House*, just off the Market Place opposite the church on Castle Street (☎01433/620244; ❸). This B&B occupies a former rectory and has just two guest rooms, plus a pleasant conservatory. Finally, the **youth hostel** (☎0870/770 5758, Ⓔcastleton@yha.org.uk; dorm beds £13, doubles ❶) is housed in Castleton Hall, a capacious old stone mansion on the Market Place. The hostel is well equipped with a self-catering kitchen, a café, cycle store and drying room, and its 140 beds are parcelled up into two- to six-bedded rooms, many of which are en suite.

For **food**, Castleton's pubs are its gastronomic mainstay and there's nowhere better than *The George*, on Castle Street, yards from the Market Place, which offers tasty bar food at affordable prices.

Edale village

There's almost nothing to **EDALE** village, some five miles from Castleton, except for a slender, half-mile trail of stone houses, which march up the main street from the train station with a couple of pubs, an old stone church and a scattering of B&Bs on the way – and it's this somnambulant air that is of immediate appeal. Walkers arrive in droves throughout the year to set off on the 268-mile **Pennine Way** (see box p.598) across England's backbone to Kirk Yetholm on the Scottish border; the route's starting-point is signposted from outside the *Old Nag's Head* at the head of the village.

An excellent **circular walk** (9 miles; 5hr) uses the first part of the Pennine Way, leading up onto the bleak gritstone, table-top of **Kinder Scout** (2088ft), below which Edale cowers. The route cuts west from the *Old Nag's Head* along a packhorse route once used by Cheshire's salt exporters to reach the campsite and **camping barn** at *Upper Booth Farm* (see p.601). From here, you climb the path called Jacob's Ladder and then continue half a mile west to the carved medieval **Edale Cross**. Backtracking a couple of hundred yards, the Pennine Way branches north along the broken edge of the plateau to **Kinder Downfall**, Derbyshire's highest cascade. This was the site of the Kinder Scout Trespass of 1932, when dozens of protesters walked onto unused but private land, five subsequently receiving prison sentences. It was the turning-point in the fight for public access to open moorland, leading, three years later, to the formation of the Ramblers' Association. At Kinder Downfall turn east then southeast across the often boggy peat towards the wind-sculpted **Wool Pack** rocks, then across to the eastern rim, where a path to the south along Grindslow Knoll and down into Edale avoids Grindsbrook Clough, the highly eroded route of the original Pennine Way. It can be extremely wet up here among the bare furrows of peat – as long-distance walker John Hillaby recorded on his *Journey Through Britain*. Hillaby had to resort to removing his footwear to make his way across the sodden top of Kinder Scout, which to his mind looked as if it was "entirely covered in the droppings of dinosaurs".

Practicalities

Edale village is about five miles northwest of Castleton by road, slightly more by footpath. There are regular **trains** from Manchester, Sheffield and Hathersage to Edale station, and there is also a patchy **bus** service from Castleton. From Edale train station, it's 400 yards or so up the road to the **Peak National Park's Moorland Centre** (April–Sept Mon–Fri 9.30am–5.30pm, Sat & Sun 9.30am–5pm; Oct–March Mon–Fri 10am–3pm, Sat & Sun 9.30am–4.30pm; ☏01433/670207). They sell all manner of trail leaflets and hiking guides and can advise about local accommodation. The nearest **youth hostel**, the *Edale YHA Activity Centre* (☏0870/770 5808, ✉edale@yha.org.uk; dorm beds £12.50, doubles ❶), lies two miles east of Edale train station at Rowland Cote, Nether Booth. It's clearly signed from the road into Edale or you can hoof it there across the fields from behind the information centre. There are 150 beds in two- to ten-bedded rooms and a good range of facilities from a laundry and a café through to a self-catering kitchen. They also offer an extensive programme of outdoor pursuits, but these need to be booked in advance, as does accommodation. Naturally enough, the hostel is popular with Pennine Way walkers – as is the **camping barn** at *Upper Booth Farm* (☎01433/670250, ⓦwww.upperboothcamping.co.uk) on the way to Kinder Scout (see p.600).

Those without hair shirts, or with more money, will do better at one of Edale's several **B&Bs**, the pick of which is *Stonecroft*, a detached Victorian house with two pleasantly comfortable guest rooms in the village near the church (☎01433/670262, ⓦwww.stonecroftguesthouse.co.uk; ❹). As for **food**, the hiker-friendly *Rambler*, yards from the train station at the bottom of the village, serves filling bar food.

Hathersage

Hilly **HATHERSAGE**, five miles east of Castleton and just eleven from Sheffield, has a hard time persuading people not to pass straight through into the heart of the Peaks. This little town is, however, worth at least an hour of anyone's time, the prime target being the much restored **church of St Michael and All Angels**, a good-looking stone structure perched high on the hill on its eastern edge. The views out over the surrounding countryside are delightful and, enclosed within a miniature iron fence in the churchyard, opposite the porch, is the **grave** – or at least what legend asserts to be the grave – of Robin Hood's old sparring partner, **Little John**. In typically English style, Little John wasn't "little" at all and, although no one can be sure if he actually existed, one of the church's Georgian vicars couldn't resist opening up the tomb to check it out. He unearthed the skeleton of a giant of a man, over 7ft tall, quite enough encouragement for the vicar to display a green cap, longbow and arrows in the church, though sadly there is no sign of them today. Hathersage's other claim to fame is its association with Charlotte Brontë's **Jane Eyre**. The title of the book was borrowed from a certain James Eyre, a former landlord of Hathersage's *George Hotel*, and the book's "Morton" takes its name from the landlord – James Morton – who met Charlotte off the stagecoach from Haworth when she came to stay here in 1845. Charlotte was visiting a friend, whose brother was the local vicar, and Charlotte was doubtless shown the Eyre brasses, inside the church beside the table-tomb of Robert Eyre (d.1459) – another prompt for the title.

In the 1800s, Hathersage became a **needle-making centre** with a string of factories billowing out dust and dirt. The needle grinders were the best paid among the factory workers, but most of them didn't last long – the metallic dust simply killed them off. Those dangerous days are long gone, but the metal-working tradition has been revived by the Sheffield designer David Mellor, who has set up his factory in the distinctive **Round Building**, a comely gritstone edifice with a sweeping lead roof. The attached Country Shop (☎01433/650220, ⓦwww.davidmellordesign.co.uk) sells the full range of Mellor cutlery, tableware and kitchenware – but you do pay for the quality. The factory is about half a mile south of town on the B6001, beyond the train station.

Practicalities

Hathersage is on the Manchester–Sheffield rail line and from the town's **train station** it's about 500 yards north to the scattering of shops, banks and pubs that comprise the centre, strung along the main street, which doubles as the A6187. Among several **buses** to Hathersage, one of the most useful is the frequent First bus #272 linking Sheffield and Castleton. In Hathersage, this service stops on the main street outside the *George Hotel* (☎01433/650436, ⓦwww .george-hotel.net; ❼), a one-time coaching **inn** with an immaculate interior that remains very much the place to stay – don't be deterred by the discordant stone facade. At the other end of the spectrum, Hathersage **youth hostel** (☎0870/770 5852, ⓔhathersage@yha.org.uk; advance reservations required; dorm beds £12, doubles ❶) occupies a rambling Victorian house on the main road just to the west of the *George*. It has forty beds, in two- to six-bedded rooms, and a good range of facilities, including a self-catering kitchen. The *George* also has a first-rate **restaurant** featuring a canny amalgamation of traditional and modern dishes with main courses averaging around £16.

Eyam

Within a year of September 7, 1665, the lonely lead-mining settlement of **EYAM** (pronounced "Eem"), five miles south of Hathersage, had lost almost half of its population of 750 to the bubonic plague, a calamity that earned it the enduring epithet "The Plague Village". The first victim was one George Vicars, a journeyman tailor who is said to have released some infected fleas into his lodgings from a package of cloth he had brought here from London. Acutely conscious of the danger to neighbouring villages, **William Mompesson**, the village rector, speedily organized a self-imposed quarantine, arranging for food to be left at places on the parish boundary. Payment was made with coins left in pools of disinfecting vinegar in holes chiselled into the old boundary stones – and these can still be seen at **Mompesson's Well**, half a mile up the hill to the north of the village and accessible by footpath. The rector closed the church and held services in the open air at a natural rock arch to the south of the village – and every year since 1906, on the last Sunday in August, a commemorative service has been held here, at Cucklet Delph. Mompesson himself survived the plague, though his wife did not – poor reward for a man whose endeavours prevented the plague from spreading across the Peaks.

The village

Long, thin and hilly, Eyam is little more than one main street – Church and then Main Street – which trails west up from **The Square**, which is itself really no more than a crossroads overlooked by a few old stone houses. First up of interest along Church Street is the comely **church of St Lawrence** (Easter–Sept

▲ Eyam village church

Mon–Sat 9am–6pm, Sun 1–5.30pm; Oct–Easter Mon–Sat 9am–4pm, Sun 1–5.30pm; free), of medieval foundation but extensively revamped in the nineteenth century. In the church graveyard a few feet from the entrance stands a conspicuous, eighth-century carved **Celtic cross** and close by is the distinctive **table-tomb** of Mompesson's wife, whose sterling work nursing sick villagers is recalled every Remembrance Day when red roses are left beside her tomb. Rather more cheerful is the grave of one Harry Bagshawe (d. 1927), a local cricketer whose tombstone shows a ball breaking his wicket with the umpire's finger raised above, presumably – on this occasion – to heaven. Bagshawe lies buried round the back of the church on the right-hand side of this part of the graveyard. Inside the church, informative panels reveal more of the village's plague history, highlighting a number of associated sites in and around the place. The most harrowing of these is the **Riley Graves**, in open country half a mile east of The Square, where a certain Elizabeth Hancock buried her husband, three sons and three daughters within the space of six days in 1666.

Much nearer at hand, immediately to the west of the church, are the so-called **plague cottages**, where plaques explain who died where and when – it was here that Vicars met his maker. Another short hop brings you to **Eyam Hall** (guided tours: July & Aug Wed, Thurs & Sun noon–4pm; £6.25; ⓦwww .eyamhall.co.uk), which was built for Thomas Wright a few years after the plague ended, possibly in an attempt to secure his position as the squire of the depleted village. Wright's heirs have lived in it ever since, building up a mildly diverting collection of furnishings, family portraits, tapestries, costumes and incidental bygones. Some of the adjacent farm buildings have been turned into a **Craft Centre** (Tues–Sun 11am–5pm; free) with a restaurant and gift shop.

From the hall, it's a few minutes' walk along Main Street and up Hawkhill Road – follow the signs – to the modest Methodist chapel that now houses the **Eyam Museum** (mid-March to Oct Tues–Sun 10am–4.30pm; £1.75). This tracks through the history of the village and has a good section on the bubonic plague – its transmission, symptoms and social aftermath.

Practicalities

Buses to Eyam all stop on The Square, and one or two also run along Main/ Church Street. There are surprisingly few places to stay, the pick of a handful of **B&Bs** being *Crown Cottage*, in a pleasantly maintained old stone building on Main Street (☎01433/630858, ⓦwww.crown-cottage.co.uk; ❸). There are four homely guest rooms here, three doubles and one twin. The most appealing alternative is the well-equipped **youth hostel** (☎0870/770 5830, ⓔeyam@yha.org.uk; £14, doubles ❶), which occupies an idiosyncratic Victorian house, whose ersatz medieval towers and turrets overlook Eyam from amidst wooded grounds on Hawkhill Road, a stiff, half-mile ramble up from Eyam Museum (see above). The hostel has a café, self-catering facilities, a cycle store and a lounge; the sixty beds are parcelled up into two- to ten-bedded rooms and advance reservations are recommended.

The best **place to eat** is the *Miner's Arms*, in antique premises just off The Square on Water Lane, which serves filling bar meals as well as very enjoyable and moderately priced traditional British dinners in its restaurant every evening except Sunday.

Around Eyam: Foolow and Bretton

Keep going west out of Eyam along Main Street and you're soon into open countryside, a quick flash of scenery before you reach – after almost two miles – the pretty little hamlet of **FOOLOW** with a village green, duck pond and

The plague

As the residents of Eyam began to drop like flies from the **plague** in the autumn of 1665, they resorted to **home remedies** and desperate snatches from folkloric memory to stave off the inevitable. There was little understanding in the seventeenth century of why or how the disease spread: Daniel Defoe, in his later journal of London's plague, recorded how the lord mayor ordered the destruction of all the city's pets, believing them to be responsible. Others, thinking it to be a miasma, kept coal braziers alight day and night in the hope that the smoke would push the infection back into the sky from where it was thought to have come. In isolated Eyam, with the plague among them and no way out through the self-imposed cordon, the locals improvised with great invention but little effect. Applications of cold water, herb infusions and draughts of brine or lemon juice were tried; poultices applied; bleeding by leeches was commonplace; and when all else failed, **charms and spells** were wheeled out – the plucked tail of a pigeon laid against the sore supposedly drew out the poison. All, of course, had no effect and the death toll mounted, though occasionally there was coincidental success: one 14-year-old girl mistakenly drank a pitcher of discarded bacon fat, left by her bedside; the fever passed and she recovered.

The horrors of plague-ridden England were recorded in a children's **nursery rhyme**, whose gruesome verse has been popular ever since:

Ring a ring o' roses
A pocket full of posies
Atishoo, atishoo
We all fall down

The "roses" are the patches which developed on the victim's chest soon after contracting the disease; the "posies" are herbs or flowers, carried as charms; as the fever took hold, sneezing ("atishoo, atishoo") was a common symptom; until, chillingly, at death's door, "we all fall down".

cross. From Foolow, a mile-long country lane cuts north, climbing up to a windswept ridge, where **BRETTON** is little more than a pub – the appealing *Barrel Inn* (☎01433/630856, ⓦwww.thebarrelinn.co.uk.; ❹), an old low-slung stone building with beamed ceilings, good ales, top-quality bar food and panoramic views. The inn also offers a handful of unassuming but perfectly comfortable rooms. Hikers can reach Bretton direct from Eyam, but it's a stiff and steep two-mile hoof; there are no buses.

Baslow

BASLOW, some four miles southeast of Eyam, is an inconclusive little village, whose oldest stone cottages string prettily along the River Derwent. The only building of note is **St Anne's Church** whose stone spire pokes up above the Victorian castellations of its nave in between the river and the busy junction of the A623/A619. Baslow may be inconsequential, but it is handy for the nearby Chatsworth estate (see opposite), especially if you're travelling by bus, and it possesses one of the Peak's finest **hotels**, *Fischer's Baslow Hall* (☎01246/583259, ⓦwww.fischers-baslowhall.co.uk; ❽), a mile or so out of the village back towards Eyam along the A623. In its own grounds, the hall is picture-postcard perfect, a handsome Edwardian building made of local stone with matching gables and a dinky canopy over the front door. The interior is suitably lavish and the service attentive with rooms both in the main building and in the Garden House annex next door. The **restaurant** is superb too, and has won several awards for its imaginative cuisine – Modern British at its best, with set meals costing £65. Alternatively, you can pop back into Baslow for a bite at the excellent *Avant Garde Café*, where they serve a delicious range of salads and light meals in bright, modern surroundings; the café is opposite St Anne's Church.

Chatsworth House

Fantastically popular, **Chatsworth House** (mid-March to late Dec daily 11am–5.30pm, last admission 4.30pm; gardens till 6pm, last admission 5pm; house & gardens £13.50, gardens only £7.45; Ⓦ www.chatsworth.org), just south of Baslow via the A619, was built in the seventeenth century by the first Duke of Devonshire. It has been owned by the family ever since and several of them have done a bit of tinkering – the sixth duke, for instance, added the north wing in the 1820s – but the end result is remarkably harmonious. The house is seen to best advantage from the **B6012**, which meanders across the estate to the west of the house, giving a full view of its vast Palladian frontage, whose clean lines are perfectly balanced by the undulating partly wooded **parkland**, which rolls in from the south and west. The B6012 also gives access to the immaculately maintained estate village of **EDENSOR**, whose sturdy stone houses are well worth a look in their own right; a signed turning off the same road leads to the house itself.

Many visitors forgo the house altogether, concentrating on the gardens instead – an understandable decision given the predictability of the assorted baubles accumulated by the family over the centuries. Nonetheless, amongst the maze of grandiose rooms and staircases, there are several noteworthy highlights, including the ornate ceilings of the **State Apartments**, daubed with strikingly energetic cherubs. In the apartments is the **State Bedroom**, where pride of place goes to the four-poster in which King George II breathed his last, and the anachronistic **Oak Room**, kitted out with overpoweringly heavy oak panelling in the 1840s. There's also the showpiece **Great Dining Room**, which has its table set as it was for the visit of George V and Queen Mary in 1933. And then there are the paintings. Amongst many, Frans Hals, Tintoretto, Veronese and Van Dyck all have a showing and there's even a Rembrandt – *A Portrait of an Old Man* – hanging in the chapel. The sixth duke also added a **Sculpture Gallery** to show all the tackle he had acquired on his travels, mostly large-scale Italian sculptures, but here also is the Chatsworth tazza, probably the largest Blue John vase in the world; for more on this semi-precious stone, see p.599.

Back outside, the **gardens** are a real treat and owe much to the combined efforts of Capability Brown, who designed them in the 1750s, and Joseph Paxton (designer of London's Crystal Palace), who had a bash seventy years later. Amongst all sorts of fripperies, there are water fountains, a rock garden, an artificial waterfall, a grotto and a folly as well as a nursery and greenhouses. Afterwards, you can wend your way to the **café** in the handsomely converted former stables.

Getting to Chatsworth

The best way to get to Chatsworth House is **on foot** along one of the footpaths that lattice the estate. It's easy walking and the obvious departure point is Baslow on the northern edge of the estate. The *Grate Little Guide* (see p.590) to Chatsworth describes an especially pleasant four-mile loop, taking in the house and beginning and ending in Baslow. There are no buses to Chatsworth House

| Derbyshire and the Peak District

Bakewell is a popular starting point for short **hikes** into the easy landscapes that make up the town's surroundings, with one of the most relaxing excursions being a four-mile loop along the banks of the River Wye to the south of the centre. Chatsworth (see p.605) is within easy hiking distance too – about seven miles there and back – and so is Ashford in the Water (see opposite), a brief hike away to the northwest along the Wye. Rather more ambitious – and one of the best-known hikes in the National Park – is the **Monsal Trail**, which cuts eight miles north and then west through some of Derbyshire's finest limestone dales using part of the old Midland Railway line. The trail begins at Coombs viaduct, one mile southeast of Bakewell, and ends at Blackwell Mill Junction, three miles east of Buxton.

itself – the nearest you'll get is Edensor, from where it's about a one-mile walk east across the park to the house, but buses are few and far between.

Bakewell and around

BAKEWELL, flanking the banks of the River Wye four miles southwest of Baslow – and twelve miles east of Buxton – is famous for its **Bakewell Pudding**. Known throughout the rest of the country as a Bakewell Tart, this is a wonderful slippery, flaky, almond-flavoured confection – now with a dab of jam – invented here around 1860 when a cook botched a recipe for strawberry tart. Almost a century before this fortuitous mishap, the Duke of Rutland set out to turn what was then a remote village into a prestigious spa, thereby trumping the work of his rival, the Duke of Devonshire, in Buxton. The frigidity of the water made failure inevitable, leaving only the prettiness of **Bath Gardens** at the heart of the town centre, beside the crossroads Rutland Square, as a reminder of the venture.

Famous tart apart, Bakewell is an undemanding place today, its main streets too crowded by traffic – and tourists – to be much fun, though it is within easy striking distance of several first-rate attractions, primarily Chatsworth (see p.605). In town, there is some interest in the web of narrow shopping streets around **Water Street**, just off the main drag near Rutland Square, as well as in the nearby **riverside walkway**, but the most agreeable part of Bakewell trails up the hill at the west end of the centre. Here, strolling up North Church Street, with its line of comely stone cottages, you soon reach **All Saints Church**, the result of centuries of architectural fiddling from the Normans onwards. Outside, in the churchyard, is a rare **Saxon cross**, carved with decorative circles and scrolls, and inside, in the south transept's Vernon Chapel, are the **tombs** of the Vernons/Manners, local bigwigs who long ruled the Bakewell roost. The finest is that of George Manners (d.1623), whose alabaster effigy is set above his kneeling children plus the baby he lost at birth, all wrapped up in swaddling clothes.

Practicalities

Bakewell doesn't have a train station, but there are regular **buses** from a string of towns and villages including Baslow, Buxton, Manchester, Derby, Sheffield and Nottingham. All services stop on – or very close to – central Rutland Square. The **tourist office** is just a couple of hundred yards off the square, down the main drag – Bridge Street – in the recycled Old Market Hall (daily: Easter–Oct 9.30am–5.30pm; Nov–Easter 10am–5pm; ☎01629/816558). They are very well equipped with public transport timetables and have a multitude of local biking and hiking leaflets, maps and guides. There's no overriding reason to overnight in Bakewell, but there is a wide selection of **B&Bs**. One good choice is *Avenue House*, whose three cosily furnished, en-suite rooms are in a spacious Victorian building just south of the centre on Haddon Road (℡01629/812467, Ⓦwww.bakewell-bed-breakfast.co.uk; no credit cards; ➋); Haddon Road doubles as the A6.

Bakeries all over town claim to make Bakewell Pudding to the original recipe, but probably the most authentic are served up at the *Old Original Bakewell Pudding Shop*, on the main street a few yards from Rutland Square. They sell the pudding in several sizes, from the small and handy to the gargantuan, enough to keep the average family going for a whole day. There are several good **restaurants** in the town, most notably *Renaissance*, in a pleasantly renovated old beamed building on Bath Street immediately north of the main drag (℡01629/812687). The emphasis here is on French cuisine with à la carte and set meals – a three-courser costs £29.

Bakewell is also a ten-minute drive from one of the area's most popular restaurants, ✳ *The Druid Inn* (℡01629/650302), an unpretentious place occupying an old stone building in the village of **Birchover**. The menu here consistently receives rave reviews – two recent offerings are, for example, scallops and sea squid risotto (£16) and Druid ale, steak, kidney and potato pie (£10). Reservations are well-nigh essential. To get to the *Druid* from Bakewell, take the A6 south and then turn right along the B5056, following the signs to Birchover thereafter.

Around Bakewell: Hassop and Ashford in the Water

Hidden away in the heart of the Peaks, about three miles north of Bakewell on the B6001, the tiny hamlet of **HASSOP** has a rugged, solitary feeling. It is also home to one of the region's finest **hotels**, the wonderful ✳ *Hassop Hall* (℡01629/640488, Ⓦwww.hassophall.co.uk; ➏), a handsome stone manor house whose long stone facade ripples with elegant bay windows. The interior has kept faith with the Georgian architecture too – modernization has been kept to a subtle minimum – and the views out over the surrounding parkland are delightful. The hotel **restaurant** (reservations required) is also first class with a two-course set meal costing £30.

Minuscule **ASHFORD IN THE WATER**, just over a mile to the west of Bakewell along the River Wye, is one of the prettiest and wealthiest villages in the Peaks, its old stone cottages nuzzling up to a quaint medieval church. It was not always so. Ashford was once a poor lead-mining settlement with sidelines in milling and agriculture, hence the name of the (impossibly picturesque) Sheepwash Bridge. There was, however, a bit of a boom when locals took to polishing the dark limestone found on the edge of the village (and nowhere else), turning it into so-called Ashford black marble – much to the delight of Buxton's petrifactioners (see p.597). Ashford also possesses an outstanding **hotel**, the plush *Riverside House* (℡01629/814275, Ⓦwww.riversidehousehotel .co.uk; ➒), which occupies a handsome Georgian building by the banks of the Wye. There are fifteen extremely well-appointed rooms here and the hotel takes justifiable pride in both its gardens and its restaurant.

Travel details

Buses

For information on all local and national bus services, contact Traveline ☎0871/200 2233, ✆www.traveline .org.uk. Operated by the Trent Barton bus company, the TransPeak bus service (✆www.transpeak.co.uk) runs from Nottingham to Manchester via Derby, Matlock, Bakewell and Buxton every 2 hours daily. The whole journey takes 3 hours 30 minutes.

Birmingham to: Buxton (2 daily; 4hr); Cambridge (3 daily; 3hr 25min); Coventry (every 20min; 1hr); Great Malvern (2 daily; 1hr 30min); Hereford (2 daily; 2hr 20min); Liverpool (6 daily; 3hr); London (hourly; 3hr); Ludlow (hourly; 2hr 10min); Manchester (hourly; 2hr 30min); Nottingham (6 daily; 1hr 30min); Oxford (5 daily; 1hr 30min); Ross-on-Wye (2 daily; 1hr 30min); Shrewsbury (2 daily; 1hr 20min); Stratford-upon-Avon (every 2hr; 1hr); Worcester (hourly; 1hr 30min).

Buxton to: Ashbourne (4 daily; 2hr); Birmingham (2 daily; 4hr); Derby (3 daily; 1hr 30min).

Derby to: Buxton (3 daily; 1hr 30min).

Great Malvern to: Birmingham (2 daily; 1hr 30min); Hereford (1 daily; 40min); Stratford-upon-Avon (5 daily; 3hr 50min); Tewkesbury (Mon–Sat hourly; 1hr); Worcester (7 daily; 35min).

Hay-on-Wye to: Hereford (4 daily; 1hr); Ross-on-Wye (5 daily; 2hr).

Hereford to: Birmingham (2 daily; 2hr 20min); Great Malvern (1 daily; 40min); Hay-on-Wye (4 daily; 1hr); Ludlow (4 daily; 4hr); Ross-on-Wye (hourly; 40min); Shrewsbury (2 daily; 3hr 30min); Worcester (2 daily; 1hr).

Ludlow to: Birmingham (hourly; 2hr 10min); Hereford (4 daily; 4hr); Shrewsbury (6 daily; 1hr 20min); Worcester (2 daily; 2hr 15min).

Ross-on-Wye to: Birmingham (2 daily; 1hr 30min); Hay-on-Wye (5 daily; 2hr); Hereford (hourly; 40min).

Shrewsbury to: Birmingham (2 daily; 1hr 20min); Hereford (2 daily; 3hr 30min); Ludlow (6 daily; 1hr 20min); Stratford-upon-Avon (2 daily; 2hr 30min).

Stratford-upon-Avon to: Birmingham (every 2hr; 1hr); Great Malvern (5 daily; 3hr 50min); Shrewsbury (2 daily; 2hr 30min).

Tewkesbury to: Cheltenham (Mon–Sat every 20min, Sun hourly; 30min); Gloucester (Mon–Sat hourly; 30–40min); Great Malvern (Mon–Sat hourly; 1hr).

Worcester to: Birmingham (hourly; 1hr 30min); Great Malvern (7 daily; 35min); Hereford (2 daily; 1hr); Ludlow (2 daily; 2hr 15min).

Trains

For information on all local and national rail services, contact National Rail Enquiries ☎0845/748 4950, ✆www.nationalrail.co.uk.

Birmingham New Street to: Birmingham International (every 15–30min; 15min); Derby (hourly; 45min); Great Malvern (every 30min; 1hr); Hereford (hourly; 1hr 50min); Leicester (hourly; 50min); Lichfield (every 15min; 45min); London (every 30min; 1hr 30min); Shrewsbury (hourly; 1hr 20min); Worcester (every 30min; 1hr).

Birmingham Snow Hill to: Stratford-upon-Avon (Mon–Sat hourly; 50min); Warwick (Mon–Sat hourly; 40min).

Derby to: Birmingham (hourly; 45min); Leicester (hourly; 30min); London (hourly; 1hr 50min); Nottingham (every 30min; 30min).

Hereford to: Birmingham (hourly; 1hr 40min); Great Malvern (hourly; 30min); London (hourly; 2hr 40min); Ludlow (hourly; 30min); Shrewsbury (hourly; 1hr); Worcester (1–2 hourly; 40min).

Shrewsbury to: Birmingham (hourly; 1hr 20min); Church Stretton (every 30min; 15min); Hereford (hourly; 1hr); Ludlow (hourly; 30min); Telford (every 30min; 20min).

Stratford-upon-Avon to: Birmingham Snow Hill (Mon–Sat hourly; 50min); London Marylebone (every 2hr; 2hr 25min); Warwick (Mon–Sat hourly; 30min).

Worcester to: Birmingham (every 30min; 40min–1hr); Hereford (hourly; 50min).

9

The East Midlands

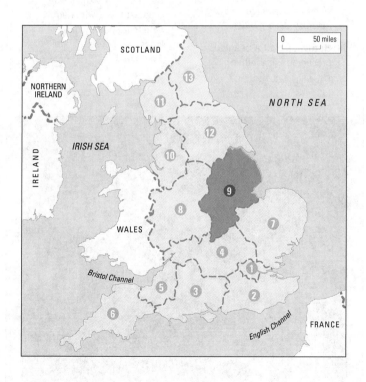

CHAPTER 9

Highlights

* **World Service Restaurant, Nottingham** Hard-to-beat Modern British restaurant with oodles of gastronomic and decorative flair. See p.620

* **Rufford Abbey Country Park** Well off the usual tourist track, Rufford offers a ceramic gallery, a bird sanctuary, a mill and a sculpture garden with lots of relaxed strolling in between. See p.622

* **Hardwick Hall** A beautifully preserved Elizabethan mansion that was once the home of the illustrious Bess of Hardwick. See p.623

* **Lincoln Cathedral** One of the finest medieval cathedrals in the land, seen to fine advantage on a rooftop guided tour. See p.645

* **Stamford** Lincolnshire's prettiest town, with narrow streets framed by old limestone houses. See p.653

▲ Lincoln Cathedral

The East Midlands

M any tourists bypass the five counties of the **East Midlands** – Nottinghamshire, Leicestershire, Northamptonshire, Rutland and Lincolnshire – on their way to more obvious destinations, an understandable mistake given that the region is short on star attractions. And it's true that the first three of these counties are pockmarked by industrialization, from the coal mines of northern Nottinghamshire to the hosiery industry of Leicester, and their county towns – **Nottingham**, **Leicester** and **Northampton** – have been badly bruised by postwar town planning. Nevertheless, embedded in the modernity are a few historical landmarks and even though these are the frills rather than the substance, Nottingham does have enough character to give it an aesthetic edge. Furthermore, the countryside surrounding these three towns can be delightful, with rolling farmland punctuated by wooded ridges and flowing hills, all sprinkled with prestigious country homes, pretty villages and old market towns. In **Nottinghamshire**, Byron's **Newstead Abbey** is intriguing, though the Elizabethan **Hardwick Hall** (just over the border in Derbyshire but covered in this chapter) is even better, whilst the eastern reaches of the county hold two appealing market towns – **Southwell** and **Newark**. Heading south, **Leicestershire** offers the fascinating mansion of **Calke Abbey** and lies adjacent to the easy countryside of **Rutland**, the region's smallest county, where you'll find two more pleasant country towns, **Oakham** and **Uppingham**, not to mention the even more picturesque village of **Lyddington**. Rutland and **Northamptonshire** benefit from the use of limestone as the traditional building material and rural Northamptonshire is studded with handsome old stone villages and small towns – most notably **Fotheringhay** and **Oundle** – as well as a battery of country estates, the best known of which is **Althorp**, the final resting place of Princess Diana.

Lincolnshire is very different in character from the rest of the region, an agricultural backwater that remains surprisingly remote – locals sometimes call it the "forgotten" county. This was not always the case: throughout medieval times the county flourished as a centre of the wool trade with Flanders, its merchants and landowners becoming some of the wealthiest in England. Reminders of the high times are legion, beginning with the majestic cathedral that graces **Lincoln**, in part at least a dignified old city which, with its cobbled lanes and ancient buildings, well deserves an overnight stay. Equally enticing is the splendidly intact stone town of **Stamford**, while out in the sticks, the most distinctive feature is **The Fens**, whose pancake-flat fields, filling out much of the south of the county and extending deep into East Anglia, have been regained from the marshes and the sea. Fenland villages are generally short of

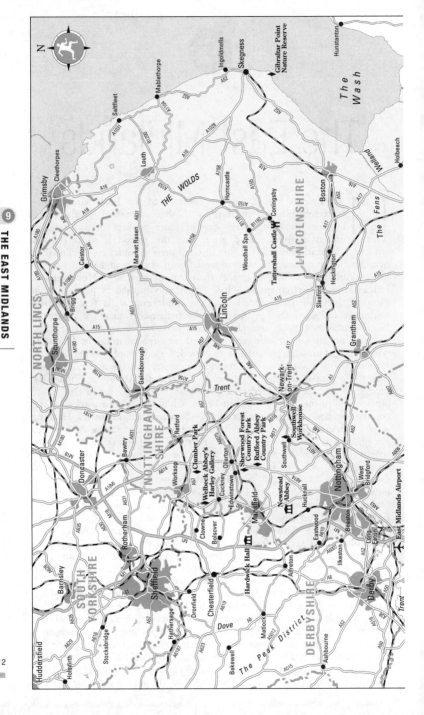

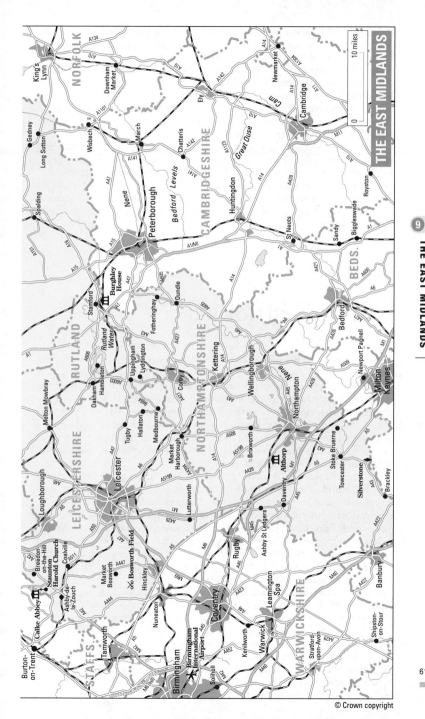

THE EAST MIDLANDS

10 miles

0

© Crown copyright

charm, but their **parish churches**, whose spires regularly interrupt the wide-skied landscape, are simply stunning, the most impressive of the lot being St Botolph's in the otherwise humdrum town of **Boston**.

In north Lincolnshire, the gentle chalky hills of the **Lincolnshire Wolds** contain the county's most diverse scenery, including woodland clustered round **Woodhall Spa**, and a string of sheltered valleys concentrated in the vicinity of **Louth**, an especially fetching country town. To the east of the Wolds is the **coast**, whose long sandy beach extends, with a few marshy interruptions, from Mablethorpe to **Skegness**, the region's main resort. The coast has long attracted thousands of holiday-makers from the big cities of the East Midlands and Yorkshire, hence its trail of bungalows, campsites and caravan parks – though significant chunks of the seashore are now protected as **nature reserves**.

As for **public transport**, travelling between the cities of the East Midlands by train or bus is simple and most of the larger towns have good regional links, too; but things are very different in the country with bus services distinctly patchy.

Nottinghamshire

With a population of around 280,000, **Nottingham** is one of England's big cities. A long-time manufacturing centre for bikes, cigarettes, pharmaceuticals and lace, it is, however, more famous for Nottingham Forest football team, for the Trent Bridge cricket ground and for its association with **Robin Hood**, the legendary thirteenth-century outlaw. Hood's bitter enemy was, of course, the Sheriff of Nottingham, but unfortunately his home and lair – the city's imposing medieval castle – is long gone, and today Nottingham is at its most diverting in the Lace Market, whose cramped streets are crowded with the mansion-like warehouses of the city's Victorian lacemakers.

The city is flanked to the south by the commuter villages of the Nottinghamshire Wolds and to the north by the gritty towns and villages of what was, until it was decimated in the late 1980s, the Nottinghamshire coalfield. Both are unremarkable, but encrusted within the old coalfield are the thin remains of **Sherwood Forest**, the bulk of which is contained within **The Dukeries**, named after the five dukes who owned most of this area and preserved at least part of the ancient broad-leaved forest. Three of the four remaining estates that comprise the Dukeries – Worksop, Welbeck and Thoresby – are still in private hands, though **Welbeck** does hold the pleasing Harley Art Gallery and Thoresby Hall has recently been turned into a Warner resort hotel. The fourth estate, **Clumber Park**, is very different, now owned by the National Trust and offering charming woodland walks. Also within the confines of the former coalfield are two fascinating country houses, **Newstead Abbey**, one-time home of Byron, and the wonderful Elizabethan extravagance of **Hardwick Hall**. Moving on, eastern Nottinghamshire is agricultural, its most important town being **Newark**, an agreeable, low-key kind of place straddling the River Trent. Newark has a castle, but the main attraction hereabouts is the fine Norman church at nearby **Southwell**.

Born in Middlesbrough, **Brian Clough** (1935–2004) was a prolific goal-scoring footballer whose career was cut short by injury. He soon turned to football management, his most remarkable achievements coming with **Nottingham Forest**, with whom he won two European cups. His ability to motivate his players was second to none, but his immense popularity in Nottingham was as much to do with his forthright personality and idiosyncratic utterances. Duncan Hamilton's excellent *Provided You Don't Kiss Me: 20 Years with Brian Clough* reveals the man in all his complexity, but a couple of quotes give the flavour:

"I wouldn't say I was the best manager in the business, but I was in the top one."

"We talk about it for twenty minutes and then we decide I was right." (on what happened if a player disagreed with him).

Fast and frequent **trains** connect Nottingham with, among many destinations, London, Birmingham, Newark, Lincoln and Leicester. Countywide **bus** services radiate out from the city, too, making Nottingham an obvious base for a visit.

Nottingham and around

Controlling a strategic crossing point over the River Trent, the Saxon town of **NOTTINGHAM** was built on one of a pair of sandstone hills whose 130-foot cliffs looked out over the river valley. In 1068, William the Conqueror built a castle on the other hill, and the Saxons and Normans traded on the low ground in between, the **Market Square**. The castle was a military stronghold and royal palace, the equal of the great castles of Windsor and Dover, and every medieval king of England paid regular visits. In August 1642, **Charles I** stayed here too, riding out of the castle to raise his standard and start the Civil War – not that the locals were overly sympathetic. Hardly anyone joined up, even though the king had the ceremony repeated on the next three days.

After the Civil War, the Parliamentarians slighted the castle and, in the 1670s, the ruins were cleared by the Duke of Newcastle to make way for a **palace**, whose continental – and, in English terms, novel – design he chose from a pattern book, probably by Rubens. Beneath the castle lay a market town which, according to contemporaries, was handsome and well kept – "One of the most beautiful towns in England," commented **Daniel Defoe**. In the second half of the eighteenth century, however, the city was transformed by the expansion of the lace and hosiery industries, and within the space of fifty years, Nottingham's population increased from ten thousand to fifty thousand, the resulting slum becoming a hotbed of radicalism. In the 1810s, a recession provoked the hard-pressed workers into action. They struck against the employers and, calling themselves **Luddites** after an apprentice-protester by the name of Ned Ludd, raided the factories to smash the knitting machines. The Luddites were beaten into submission, but this was but the first of several troubled periods, the most dramatic of which came during the **Reform Bill** riots of 1831, when the workers set fire to the duke's palace in response to his opposition to parliamentary reform.

The worst of Nottingham's slums were cleared in the early twentieth century, when the city centre assumed its present structure, with the main commercial area ringed by alternating industrial and residential districts. Thereafter, crass

postwar development added tower blocks, shopping centres and a ring road, resulting in a cityscape that is dishearteningly familiar if you've seen a few other English commercial centres. The flavour of this postwar industrial city was best described by Nottingham's own **Alan Sillitoe** in his perceptive and forceful novel, *Saturday Night, Sunday Morning*.

Arrival, information and accommodation

Nottingham **train station** is on the south side of the city centre, a five- to ten-minute walk from the Market Square – just follow the signs. Most long-distance **buses** arrive at the **Broad Marsh Bus Station**, down the street from the train station on the way to the centre, but some – including services to north Nottinghamshire – pull in at the **Victoria Bus Station**, a five-minute walk north of the Market Square. **East Midlands Airport** is located 18 miles southwest of the city; Skylink buses into town pull in across the street from the train station.

Nottingham's new(ish) **trams** link the train station with the Market Square but otherwise are not especially useful for tourists. The city's **tourist office** is on the Market Square, on the ground floor of the Council House, 1 Smithy Row (Mon–Fri 9am–5.30pm, Sat 9am–5pm & Sun 10am–4pm; ☎0115/915 5330, ⓦ www.visitnottingham.com).

As you might expect of a big city, Nottingham has a good range of accommodation, with the more expensive **hotels** concentrated in the centre, the cheaper places and the **B&Bs** mostly located on the outskirts and beside the main approach roads. Finding a room is rarely difficult, and the tourist office can always help out.

Accommodation

Greenwood City Lodge 5 Third Ave, off Sherwood Rise ☎0115/962 1206, ⓦ www .greenwoodlodgecityguesthouse.co.uk. Attractive guest house in a quiet corner of the city, down a narrow lane about a mile north of the city centre. Six bedrooms decorated in smart Victorian style. Nottingham's most distinctive accommodation. ❺

Harts Hotel Standard Hill, Park Row ☎0115/988 1900, ⓦ www.hartshotel.co.uk. Chic hotel, with comfort and style in equal measure: ultra-modern fixtures and fittings, Egyptian cotton bed linen and so forth. It's quite pricey, but first-rate

all the same and the quiet location – near both the castle and the Market Square – is hard to beat. ❼

Lace Market Hotel 29 High Pavement ☎0115/852 3232, ⓦ www.lacemarkethotel.co.uk. Great location, footsteps from St Mary's Church, this smart hotel has just over forty slick modern rooms decorated in sharp minimalist style – and all within a tastefully modernized Georgian house. ❼

Rutland Square Hotel Rutland St, off St James's St ☎0115/941 1114, ⓦ www.forestdale.com. Enticing and tastefully furnished modern chain hotel in a good location, just by the castle. Ninety-odd rooms. ❻

The City

Nottingham's busy, bustling centre attracts shoppers by the coach load, but its most distinctive features are its handsome **Market Square**, the **castle** and the **Lace Market** district with its fetching Victorian architecture. All are within easy walking distance of each other.

The Market Square and the castle

The **Market Square** is still the heart of the city, an airy open plaza whose shops, offices and fountain are overlooked by the grand Neo-Baroque **Council House**, completed as part of a make-work scheme in 1928. From here, it's a five-minute walk west up Friar Lane to **Nottingham Castle** (daily: March–Sept 10am–5pm, Oct–Feb 11am–4pm; £3.50), whose heavily restored

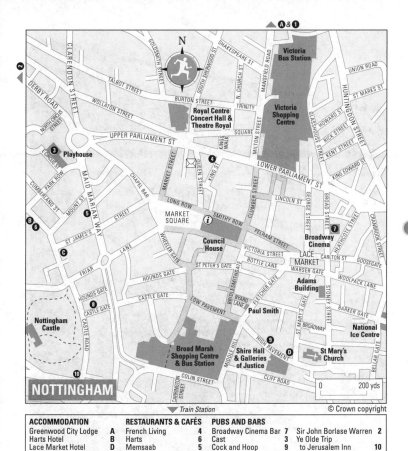

NOTTINGHAM

ACCOMMODATION		RESTAURANTS & CAFÉS		PUBS AND BARS	
Greenwood City Lodge	A	French Living	4	Broadway Cinema Bar	7
Harts Hotel	B	Harts	6	Cast	3
Lace Market Hotel	D	Memsaab	5	Cock and Hoop	9
Rutland Square Hotel	C	World Service	8	Lincolnshire Poacher	1

Sir John Borlase Warren	2		
Ye Olde Trip			
to Jerusalem Inn	10		

medieval gateway stands above a folkloric **bronze of Robin Hood**, with plaques depicting legendary scenes from his life on the wall behind. Beyond the gateway, gardens slope up to the squat, seventeenth-century ducal **palace**, which – after remaining a charred shell for forty years – was opened as the country's first provincial museum in 1878. The mansion occupies the site of the medieval castle's upper bailey, and round the back, just outside the main entrance, two sets of steps lead down into the maze of ancient **caves** that honeycomb the cliff beneath. One set is currently open for guided tours (Mon–Sat 2–3 daily; call ☎0115/915 3676 for times; £2); it leads into **Mortimer's Hole**, a three-hundred-foot shaft along which, so the story goes, the young Edward III and his chums crept in October 1330 to capture the queen mother, Isabella, and her lover, Roger Mortimer. The couple had already polished off Edward III's father, the hapless Edward II, and were intent on usurping the Crown, but the young Edward proved too shrewd for them and Mortimer came to a sticky end.

The interior of the ducal mansion holds the **Castle Museum and Art Gallery**, where a particular highlight is the "Story of Nottingham", a lively, well-presented

▲ Castle Museum and Art Gallery, Nottingham

and entertaining account of the city's development. Elsewhere in the museum, look out for a small but exquisite collection of late medieval **alabaster carvings**, an art form for which Nottingham once had an international reputation. It's worth walking up to the top floor, too, for a turn round the main **picture gallery**, a handsome and spacious room where a curious assortment of mostly English nineteenth-century romantic paintings are displayed. The works are regularly rotated, but look out for the evocative canvases of Nottingham's own Richard Parkes Bonington (1802–1828), Laslett John Pott's (1837–98) melodramatic *Mary Queen of Scots being led to her Execution*, and the cheerily folksy Nottingham cityscapes of Arthur Spooner (1873–1962). One surprise is a typical industrial scene by Lowry (see p.674), entitled *Industrial Panorama*.

The Lace Market

A few minutes' walk away, on the east side of the Market Square up along Victoria Street, is the **Lace Market**, whose narrow lanes and alleys are flanked by an attractive assortment of Victorian factories and warehouses – a particular shame then that the spaceship-like National Ice Centre interrupts the area's architectural flow. **Stoney Street** is the Lace Market at its most appealing with pride of place going to the imposing **Adams Building**, whose handsome stone and brick facade combines both Neo-Georgian and Neo-Renaissance features. Adjoining **Broadway** doesn't lag far **behind**, with a line of homogeneous red-brick and sandstone-trimmed buildings that perform a neat swerve halfway along the street. One feature that many of the buildings share is the long attic windows, designed to light what were once the mending and inspection rooms. At the heart of the Lace Market is the church of **St Mary**, a good-looking, mostly fifteenth-century Gothic structure built on top of the hill that was once the Saxon town. The church abuts High Pavement, the administrative centre of Nottingham in Georgian times, and here you'll find **Shire Hall**, whose Neoclassical columns, pilasters and dome date from 1770. The facade also bears the marks of a real Georgian cock-up: to the left of the entrance, at street level, the mason carved the word "Goal" onto an arch and then had to have a second bash, turning it into "Gaol"; both versions are clearly visible. The hall now houses the **Galleries of Justice** (April to early Sept Tues–Sun 10am–4pm; early Sept to March Tues–Fri 10am–3pm, Sat & Sun 11am–4pm; also Mon 10am–3/4pm in school hols; £8.95; ⓦwww.nccl.org.uk), whose child-friendly "Crime and Punishment" tour features lots of role-play. Alternatively, you can wander round the building independently to see two superbly preserved Victorian courtrooms, an Edwardian police station, some spectacularly unpleasant old cells, a women's prison with bath house and a prisoners' exercise yard.

Nearby, on Byard Lane, is the first shop of local lad **Paul Smith**, a major success story of contemporary British fashion.

Eating

Nottingham boasts at least half a dozen top-quality **restaurants**, where the elaborate menus attempt to balance unusual ingredients in unusual combinations. There are lots of more straightforward places too – primarily Italian and Asian – plus a slew of **cafés** and **café-bars**. Almost without exception, the latter have adopted the same formula – angular and ultra-modern furnishings and fittings – and the vast majority stick to coffees and snacks rather than more substantial offerings.

French Living 27 King St ☎0115/958 5885. Authentic French cuisine served in an intimate, candle-lit basement. Daytime snacks and baguettes in the ground floor café too. Evening main courses from £10. Closed Sun & Mon.

Harts Standard Court, Park Row ☎0115/947 7694. One of the city's most acclaimed restaurants, occupying part of the old general hospital and serving an international menu of carefully presented meals. Attractive pastel/ modernist decor and attentive service;

reservations well-nigh essential. Mains from about £15.

Memsaab 12 Maid Marian Way t0115/957 0009. One of a new breed of Indian restaurants (to Nottingham at least) – no burgundy wallpaper here, but crisp modern decor and bags of space. The food – canny amalgamations of different Indian cooking styles from different regions – is exquisite. A large and imaginative menu with main courses starting from as little as £10.

World Service Newdigate House, Castle Gate ⊕0115/847 5587. Chic restaurant with bags of (vaguely Asiatic) flair in charming premises up near the castle. A Modern British menu, featuring such delights as pork cutlets with onion marmalade and rack of lamb with butternut squash tarte tatin, is prepared with imagination and close attention to detail. In the evenings, main courses start at around £16, but there are great deals at lunchtimes with two-course set meals costing £12, or £16 for three courses.

Drinking and nightlife

Nottingham's **nightclub** scene is boisterous, with places moving in and out of fashion all the time, though two current hot spots are *Stealth*, in the centre on Goldsmith Street (Ⓦwww.stealthattack.co.uk), and *Blueprint*, out at 76 Vale Road in Colwick (Ⓦwww.blueprintclub.co.uk). The **pubs** around Market Square have a tough edge to them, especially on the weekend, but within a few minutes' walk there are several lively and more enjoyable and relaxing drinking-holes. For **live music**, both popular and classical, most big names play at the Royal Centre Concert Hall on South Sherwood Street (⊕0115/989 5555, Ⓦwww.royalcentre-nottingham.co.uk). The Broadway, in the Lace Market at 14 Broad St (⊕0115/952 6611, Ⓦwww.broadway.org.uk), is the best **cinema** in the city, featuring the pick of mainstream and avant-garde films, and there's **theatre** at the Nottingham Playhouse, on Wellington Circus (⊕0115/941 9419, Ⓦwww.nottinghamplayhouse.co.uk).

Pubs and bars

Broadway Cinema Bar Broadway Cinema, 14 Broad St. Informal, fashionable (in an arty sort of way) bar serving an eclectic assortment of bottled beers to a cinema-keen clientele. The bar food is, however, very average.

Cast Wellington Circus. The bar of the Nottingham Playhouse is a popular, easy-going spot with courtyard seating on summer nights. Patrons have the advantage of looking at a piece of modern art too – Anish Kapoor's whopping, reflective *Sky Mirror*. There's also an attached deli and (pretty average) restaurant.

Cock and Hoop 25 High Pavement, Lace Market. One of the few pubs in the centre to have avoided being made over for a younger clientele. It's a curious little split-level bar that verges on the

smart, with its thick carpets and comfortable chairs. Real ales, too.

Lincolnshire Poacher 161 Mansfield Rd. Very popular and relaxed pub, popular with an older clientele, offering a wide selection of bottled and real ales.

Sir John Borlase Warren 1 Ilkeston Road, Canning Circus, half a mile up the hill from the city centre along Derby Road. Pulling in a mixed bag of students and locals, this rambling old pub has character and a lively and (usually) friendly atmosphere.

Ye Olde Trip to Jerusalem Inn Below the castle in Brewhouse Yard. Carved into the castle rock, this ancient inn may well have been a meeting point for soldiers gathering for the Third Crusade. Its cave-like bars, with their rough sandstone ceilings, are delightfully secretive.

Around Nottingham: Eastwood

D.H. Lawrence (1885–1930) was born in the coal-mining village of **EASTWOOD**, about eight miles west of Nottingham. The mine closed years ago, and Eastwood is something of a post-industrial eyesore, but Lawrence's childhood home has survived, a tiny, red-brick terraced house refurbished as the **D.H. Lawrence Birthplace Museum**, 8a Victoria St, off Nottingham Road (daily 10am–4/5pm; Mon–Fri free, Sat & Sun £2). None of the furnishings and fittings are Lawrence originals, which isn't too surprising considering the family moved out when he was two, but it's an appealing evocation of the period interlaced with biographical insights into the author's early life. Afterwards, enthusiasts can follow the three-mile **Blue Line Walk** round those parts of Eastwood with Lawrence associations – his family moved house on several occasions and Lawrence only left Eastwood in 1908. The walk takes an hour or so, and a brochure is available at the museum.

Buses leave Nottingham's Victoria Bus Station every twenty minutes for the thirty-minute journey to Eastwood.

Northern Nottinghamshire

Rural **northern Nottinghamshire**, with its gentle rolling landscapes and large ducal estates, was transformed in the nineteenth century by **coal** – deep, wide seams of the stuff – that spawned dozens of collieries, and colliery towns, stretching north across the county and on into Yorkshire. Almost without exception, the mines have closed, their passing marked only by the old pit-head winding wheels left, bleak and solitary, to commemorate the thousands of men who laboured here. The suddenness of the pit closure programme imposed by the Conservative government in the 1980s knocked the stuffing out of the area and only now is it beginning to revive. One prop has been the tourist industry, for the countryside in between these former mining communities holds several enjoyable attractions, the best-known of which is **Sherwood Forest** – or at least the patchy remains of it – supposedly the one-time haunt of Robin Hood. Lord Byron is a pip-squeak in the celebrity stakes by comparison, but his family home – **Newstead Abbey** – is here too. National Trust-owned **Clumber Park** is a great place for some pleasant woodland walks, while the delightful **Harley Gallery** of art in Welbeck Abbey estate, and **Hardwick Hall**, a stunningly handsome Elizabethan mansion, also make well-worthwhile excursions.

Reaching the first three of these attractions by **bus** from Nottingham is easy enough, but to get to the last two – the Harley Gallery and Hardwick Hall – you'll need your own transport.

Newstead Abbey

In 1539, **Newstead Abbey,** ten miles north of Nottingham on the A60 (house: April–Sept daily noon–5pm: grounds daily 9am–6pm or dusk; £6, grounds only £3; ⓦ www.newsteadabbey.org.uk), was granted by Henry VIII to Sir John Byron, who demolished most of the church and converted the monastic buildings into a family home. In 1798, **Lord Byron** inherited the estate, then little more than a ruin. He restored part of the complex during his six-year residence (1808–14), though most of the present structure dates from later renovations, which maintained much of the shape and feel of the medieval original while creating the warren-like mansion that exists today.

Inside, a string of intriguing period rooms includes everything from a Neo-Gothic Great Hall to the Henry VII bedroom, fitted with carved panels and painted house screens imported from Japan. Some of the rooms are pretty much as they were when Byron lived here – notably his bedroom and dressing room – and in the library is a small collection of the poet's possessions, from letters and manuscripts through to his pistols and boxing gloves. In the west gallery, look out also for the painting of Byron's favourite dog, **Boatswain**, a perky beast who was buried just outside the house – a conspicuous memorial, with its absurdly extravagant inscription, marks the spot. The surrounding **gardens** are delightful, a secretive and subtle combination of walled garden, lake, Gothic waterfalls, yew tunnels and Japanese-style rockeries, complete with idiosyncratic pagodas.

There's a fast and frequent **bus** service leaving every twenty minutes or so from Nottingham's Victoria Bus Station to the gates of Newstead Abbey, a mile from the house; the journey takes about 25 minutes.

Rufford Abbey Country Park

Council-run country parks may be ten-a-penny, but **Rufford Abbey Country Park** (daily dawn–dusk; main facilities daily 10.30am–5pm; free, but weekend car parking fee £3) shows just how things should be done. Though the abbey and later country house are now largely gone, the former stable block holds a café, a much better-than-average craft shop and a first-rate ceramics gallery. At the back of the stables are the gardens, both informal and formal, and an outstanding **Sculpture Garden**, which manages to be both accessible and contemporary with sculptures such as the eerily lifelike, concrete *Man and Sheep on a Bench*. Elsewhere in the park, footpaths lead to a lake and a mill, a bird sanctuary and a wetland area. It's also host to a lively programme of special events and temporary art exhibitions.

Rufford is right beside the A614 about eighteen miles north of Nottingham and reached on hourly Stagecoach **bus** #33 from Nottingham's Victoria Bus Station.

Sherwood Forest Country Park

Most of **Sherwood Forest**, once a vast royal woodland of oak, birch and bracken covering all of northern Nottinghamshire, was cleared in the eighteenth century and nowadays it's difficult to imagine the protection it provided for generations of outlaws, the most famous of whom was **Robin Hood**. There's no "true story" of Robin's life – the earliest reference to him, in Langland's *Piers Plowman* of 1377, treats him as a fiction – but to the balladeers of fifteenth-century England, who invented most of Hood's folklore, this was hardly the point. For them, Robin was a symbol of yeoman decency, a semi-mythological opponent of corrupt clergymen and evil officers of the law; in the early tales, although Robin shows sympathy for the peasant, he has rather more respect for the decent nobleman, and he's never credited with robbing the rich to give to the poor. This and other parts of the legend, such as Maid Marion and Friar Tuck, were added later.

Robin Hood may lack historical authenticity, but it hasn't discouraged the county council from spending thousands of pounds sustaining the **Major Oak**, the creaky tree where Maid Marion and Robin are supposed to have plighted their troth. The Major Oak is on a pleasant one-mile trail that begins beside the visitor centre at the main entrance to **Sherwood Forest Country Park** (daily dawn–dusk; free, but weekend car parking fee £3), which comprises 450 acres of oak and silver birch crisscrossed with footpaths. The visitor centre is half a mile north of the village of Edwinstowe, itself just two miles northwest of Rufford Park and twenty-odd miles north of Nottingham via the A614.

Stagecoach **bus** #33 runs hourly from Nottingham's Victoria Bus Station to Edwinstowe via Rufford.

Clumber Park

Six miles along the A614 north of Ollerton, Edwinstowe's immediate neighbour, is the main entrance to **Clumber Park** (daily dawn–dusk; free, parking for non-NT members £4.50), four thousand acres of park and woodland lying to the south of industrial Worksop. The estate was once the country seat of the dukes of Newcastle, and it was here in the 1770s that they constructed a grand mansion overlooking Clumber Lake. The house was dismantled in 1938, when the duke sold the estate, and today the most interesting survivor of the lakeside buildings – located about two and a half miles from the A614 – is the Gothic Revival **chapel** (daily 10am–4/5.30pm; free; NT), an imposing edifice with a soaring spire and an intricately carved interior built for the seventh duke in the 1880s. Close by, the old **stable block** now houses a National Trust office, shop and **café** (same hours as chapel), and there's **bike rental** (April–Oct & winter weekends) just behind the chapel. The woods around the lake offer some delightful strolls and bike rides through planted woodland interspersed with the occasional patch of original forest.

Bus #33 runs up the west side of Clumber Park en route to Worksop; ask the driver to stop at Carburton for the 2.5-mile walk to the Clumber Park NT office. The whole excursion takes a full day.

Welbeck Abbey's Harley Gallery

To the west of Clumber Park lies **Welbeck Abbey estate**, which remains firmly in ducal hands. The estate's old gas works, built on the edge of the duke's property in the 1870s, has been imaginatively turned into the **Harley Gallery** (Tues–Sun 10am–5pm; free; Ⓦ www.harleygallery.co.uk). The gallery is mainly devoted to temporary exhibitions featuring the work of local living artists, all well presented and intelligently arranged, but there's also a permanent exhibition on the ducal family, variously named Cavendish, Portland and Newcastle. It's a small display – just one room – but includes an appealing assortment of family knick-knacks, from portraits, timepieces and rare books through to silverware and paintings. Locally at least, the most famous of the line was the Fifth Duke of Portland (1800–1879), known as the "burrowing duke" for the maze of gaslit tunnels he built underneath his estate. Naturally enough, many thought he was bonkers, but the truth may well be far more complex – an issue explored in Mick Jackson's novel *The Underground Man*, wherein the duke is portrayed as a shy man haunted by his obsessions. Another school of thought puts his burrowing down to the disfiguring effects of a skin disease. The tunnels are not, however, open to the public.

The gallery's **café** serves reasonably tasty light snacks and there's a large garden centre across the car park. The entrance to the Harley Gallery is on the A60, two miles north of the hamlet of Cuckney – and about five miles from Clumber Park's west entrance. There are no buses to the gallery from Nottingham.

Hardwick Hall

Born the daughter of a minor Derbyshire squire, Elizabeth, Countess of Shrewsbury (1527–1608) – aka **Bess of Hardwick** – became one of the leading figures of Elizabethan England, renowned for her political and business acumen. She also had a penchant for building and her major achievement, **Hardwick Hall** (mid-March to Oct: house Wed, Thurs, Sat & Sun noon–4.30pm; gardens Wed–Sun 11am–5.30pm; house & gardens £9, gardens only £4.50; NT), begun when she was 62, has survived in amazingly good condition. The house was the epitome of fashionable taste, a balance of symmetry and ingenious detail in which the rectangular lines of the building are offset by line upon line of window – there's actually more glass than stone – whilst up above her giant-sized initials (E.S.) hog every roof line. Inside, the ground floor is relatively routine, but it's here that the hall's extensive collection of sixteenth- and seventeenth-century needlework is displayed, including several pieces by Mary, Queen of Scots, who was held in custody by the Earl of Shrewsbury for years. He moaned about the expense incessantly, one of the reasons for the souring of his relationship with Bess, a deterioration that prompted their estrangement.

On the top floor, the **High Great Chamber**, where Bess received her most distinguished guests, boasts an extraordinary plaster frieze, a brightly painted, finely worked affair celebrating the goddess Diana, the virgin huntress – it was, of course, designed to please the Virgin Queen herself. Next door, the **Long Gallery** is simply breathtaking, like an indoor cricket pitch only with exquisite furnishings and fittings from the splendid chimneypieces and tapestries through to a set of portraits, including one each of the queen and Bess. Bess and her chums could exercise here while keeping out of the sun – at a time when any hint of a tan was considered plebeian.

Outside, the **garden** makes for a pleasant wander and, beyond the ha-ha (the animal-excluding ditch and low wall), rare breeds of cattle and sheep graze the surrounding **parkland** (daily 8am–6pm; free). Finally – and rather confusingly – there's **Hardwick Old Hall** (mid-March to Oct Wed, Thurs, Sat & Sun 10am–6pm; £3.90; EH), next to Hardwick Hall. It was Bess's previous home, but is now little more than a broken-down if substantial ruin.

The easiest way to reach Hardwick is along the M1; come off at Junction 29 and follow the signs from the roundabout at the top of the slip road – a three-mile trip. Note, however, that Hardwick is not signed from the motorway itself.

Eastern Nottinghamshire

Without coal, **eastern Nottinghamshire** escaped the heavy-duty industrialization that fell upon its county neighbours in the late nineteenth century. It remains a largely rural area today, its undulating farmland, punctuated by dozens of pint-sized villages, rolling seamlessly over to the River Trent, the boundary with Lincolnshire. By and large, it's a prosperous part of the county and by no means unpleasant, but for the casual visitor the attractions are distinctly low-key, being essentially confined to **Southwell** and **Newark**, both of which are easy to reach by public transport from Nottingham.

Southwell

SOUTHWELL, some fourteen miles northeast of Nottingham, is a sedate and well-heeled backwater distinguished by **Southwell Minster** (Mon–Sat 8am–7pm or dusk, Sun same hours depending on services; free but £3 donation suggested; ⓦ www.southwellminster.co.uk), whose twin towers are visible for miles around, and by the fine Georgian mansions facing it along Church Street. The Normans built the minster at the beginning of the twelfth century and, although some elements were added later, their design predominates, from the imposing west towers through to the dog-tooth-decoration of the doorways and the bull's-eye windows of the clerestory. Inside, the proud and forceful arcaded **nave**, with its sturdy columns, marches up to the **north transept**, where there is a remarkably fine alabaster tomb of a long forgotten churchman, one Archbishop Sandys, who died in 1588. The red-flecked alabaster effigy of Sandys is so precise that you can see the furrows on his brow and the crow's feet round his eyes; his children are depicted kneeling below and it's assumed that Sandys was one of the first bishops to marry – and beget – after the break with Rome changed the rules. The nave's Norman stonework ends abruptly at the transepts with the inelegance of the fourteenth-century **rood-screen**, beyond which lies the Early English **choir** and the extraordinary **chapter house**. The latter is embellished with naturalistic foliage dating from the late thirteenth century, some of the earliest carving of its type in England. To wet your whistle, the minster's **café** is in the modern annexe just outside the entrance to the church.

About a mile from the minster, out on the road to Newark, stands **Southwell Workhouse** (mid-March to early April & Oct Sat & Sun noon–5pm; early April to July & Sept Thurs–Sun noon–5pm; Aug daily except Tues noon–5pm; £5.50; NT), a substantial three-storey brick building that looks like a prison, but is in fact a rare survivor of the Victorian workhouses that once dotted every corner of the country. They were built as result of the New Poor Law of 1834, which made a laudable attempt to provide shelter for the destitute. However, the middle classes were concerned that the workers would take advantage of free shelter, so conditions were made hard – as a matter of policy – and the "workhouses" were much feared. Most were knocked down or redeveloped years ago, but Southwell remained almost untouched, though its bare rooms and barred windows make the whole experience rather depressing.

There are regular NCT (Nottingham City Transport) **buses** to Southwell from Queen Street, in central Nottingham.

Newark

From Southwell, it's eight miles east to **NEWARK**, an amiable old river port and market town that was once a major staging point on the Great North Road. Fronting the town as you approach from the west are the gaunt riverside ruins of **Newark Castle** (daily dawn–dusk; free), all that's left of the mighty medieval fortress that was pounded to pieces during the Civil War by the Parliamentarians. Opposite, just across the street to the north, is **The Ossington**, a flashy structure whose Tudor appearance is entirely fraudulent – it was built in the 1880s as a temperance hotel by a local bigwig, in an effort to save drinkers from themselves. In the opposite direction, a pleasant riverside walk leads round the foot of the castle, past ancient houses, to the busy town **lock**. From here, it's just five minutes east through a network of narrow lanes and alleys to the **Market Place**, an expansive square framed by attractive Georgian and Victorian facades and home to the mostly thirteenth-century church of **St Mary Magdalene** (Mon–Sat 8.30am–4.30pm, May–Sept also Sun 2–4.30pm). It's a handsome church, with a massive spire (236ft) towering over the town centre, and a well-proportioned nave cheered by some brightly restored roof paintings and a fancy reredos. Look out also for a pair of medieval Dance of Death **panel paintings** behind the reredos in the choir's Markham Chantry Chapel. One panel has a well-to-do man slipping his hand into his purse, the other shows a carnation-carrying skeleton pointing to the grave – an obvious reminder to the observer of his or her mortality.

Newark has two **train stations**: Newark Castle on the Nottingham to Lincoln line is on the west side of the River Trent, a five-minute walk from the castle; while the larger Newark Station, on the main London to Edinburgh line, is on Lincoln Road, off Northgate, a ten-minute walk southwest of the castle. Regular buses from Nottingham pull into the **bus station**, on Lombard Street, from where it's a five-minute walk north along Castlegate to the castle. Newark **tourist office** is in front of the castle on Castlegate (daily 9am–5pm, Oct–March till 4pm; ℡01636/655765).

For **food**, either head for the excellent *Gannets*, 35 Castlegate, a first-rate coffee bar serving delicious daytime snacks and meals, or go to *Café Bleu*, opposite at 14 Castlegate (℡01636/610141), a brilliant French/Modern British restaurant serving top-class meals (main courses average £12–15) from an inventive menu – try the lasagne of wild mushrooms with squash and truffle dressing or the sea trout and pak choi. It's one of the best restaurants in the county, with an outside terrace and frequent live jazz; the decor – all pastel-painted cheerfulness – is appealing too.

Leicestershire and Rutland

The compact county of **Leicestershire** is one of the more anonymous of the English shires, though **Leicester** itself is saved from mediocrity by its role as a focal point for Britain's Asian community. Beyond the city, the western part of the county has more to offer than the east, for although its rolling landscapes are blemished by a series of industrial settlements, **Ashby-de-la-Zouch** is a pleasing little town graced by the substantial remains of its medieval castle. Near here too are **Calke Abbey**, a dishevelled country house set in its own estate just over the border in Derbyshire, and the trim charms of **Market Bosworth**, the site of the Battle of Bosworth Field, the climactic engagement of the Wars of the Roses. In the east of the county, the farmland is studded with long-established market towns. None of them are particularly enthralling, unless you're a fan of pork pies – genial **Melton Mowbray** is undisputably the pork pie capital of the world.

To the east of Leicestershire lies England's smallest county, **Rutland**, re-instated in its own right in 1997 following 23 unpopular years of merger with its larger neighbour. As part of their spirited publicity campaign to revive their ancient county, Rutland's canny burghers issued "passports" to locals and created quite a stir, breaking through the profound apathy that characterizes the English attitude to local government. Rutland has three places of note: **Oakham**, the county town, and **Uppingham**, both rural centres with some elegant Georgian architecture, and the prettier, tiny stone hamlet of **Lyddington**.

Getting around Leicestershire and Rutland can be problematic. **Train** lines radiate out from Leicester, most usefully to Oakham, and there's a good network of **bus** services between the market towns, but these fade away in the villages where, if there is a bus at all, it only runs once or twice a day.

Leicester

At first glance, **LEICESTER** seems a resolutely modern city, but further inspection reveals traces of its medieval and Roman past, situated immediately to the west of the downtown shopping area near the River Soar. The Romans chose this site to keep an eye on the rebellious Corieltauvi and developed Leicester's precursor, Rate Corioneltavori, as a fortified town – kitted out by Emperor Hadrian with huge public buildings – on the Fosse Way, the military road running from Lincoln to Cirencester. Subsequently, in the eighth century, the Danes colonized the town and later still its medieval castle became the base of the earls of Leicester, the most distinguished of whom was **Simon de Montfort**, who forced Henry III to convene the first English Parliament in 1265. Since the late seventeenth century, Leicester has been a centre of the **hosiery trade** and it was this industry that attracted hundreds of Asian immigrants to settle here in the 1950s and 1960s. Today, about a third of Leicester's population is **Asian** and the city elected England's first Asian MP, Keith Vaz, in 1987. Leicester's Hindus celebrate two massive autumn **festivals**, Navrati and Diwali, while the city's sizeable Afro-Caribbean community holds England's second biggest street festival (after the Notting Hill Carnival; see *Festivals & events* colour section), the Leicester Caribbean Carnival, on the first weekend in August.

Arrival, information and accommodation

Leicester **train station** is on London Road just to the southeast of the city centre, while **St Margaret's bus station** is on the north side of the centre, just off Gravel Street. The centre is signed from both – the large Haymarket shopping centre, between the two, is an easy landmark. The **tourist office** is a short walk to the south of the Haymarket at 7–9 Every St, on Town Hall Square (Mon–Wed & Fri 9am–5.30pm, Thurs 10am–5.30pm, Sat 9am–5pm; premium-rate line ☏0906/294 1113, ⊛www.goleicestershire.com).

With other more enticing cities nearby, there's no strong reason to overnight here, but Leicester does have a good crop of business **hotels** close to the centre, within walking distance of the train station. The tourist office also has a substantial list of competitively priced **B&Bs**, though most are out of the centre. They will help fix you up with somewhere to stay, but things rarely get tight except during the Navrati and Diwali festivals.

Accommodation

Best Western Belmont House Hotel De Montfort St ☏0116/254 4773, ⊛www.belmonthotel.co.uk. Proficient chain hotel in a modernized and extended Georgian property about 300 yards south of the train station via London Road. Popular with business folk. Weekend discounts. ❼

Holiday Inn 129 St Nicholas Circle ☏0870/400 9048, ⊛www.holiday-inn.com/leicester. Smart chain hotel, which manages to overcome its unfortunate location – in the middle of the ring road – by creating a relaxed and self-enclosed environment. Comfortable rooms, indoor pool and extensive fitness facilities. Weekend discounts. ❼

Spindle Lodge Hotel 2 West Walk ☏0116/233 8801, ⊛www.spindlelodge.com. Well-maintained hotel in a pleasantly converted, three-storey, ivy-clad Victorian town house on a quiet residential street. Ten minutes' walk from the train station – head south on London Road, turn right onto De Montfort Street and then left onto Regent Road; *Spindle Lodge* is at the junction of Regent Road and West Walk. ❹

The City

Most of Leicester's more important attractions are dotted around the centre within easy walking distance of each other. There's nothing outstanding but pride of municipal place goes to the fine art of the **New Walk Museum and Art Gallery**.

The Haymarket and around

The most conspicuous building in Leicester's crowded centre is undoubtedly the large, modern **Haymarket shopping centre**, but the proper landmark is the Victorian **clocktower** of 1868, standing in front of the Haymarket and marking the spot where seven streets meet. One of the seven is Cheapside, which leads to Leicester's open-air **market** (Mon–Sat), one of the best of its type in the country and the place where the young Gary Lineker, now the UK's best-known football pundit, worked on the family stall. Good-hearted Gary remains a popular figure hereabouts and has been made a freeman of the city, which gives him the right to graze his sheep in front of the town hall. Another of the seven streets is Silver Street (subsequently Guildhall Lane), which leads to **St Martin's Cathedral**, a much modified, eleventh-century structure incorporating a fine, ornately carved medieval entrance porch. Next door is the **Guildhall** (Feb–Nov Mon–Wed & Sat 11am–4.30pm, Sun 1–4.30pm; free), a half-timbered building that has served, variously, as the town hall, prison and police station. The most interesting part of a visit is the rickety Great Hall, its beams bent with age, but there are a couple of old cells too, plus the town gibbet on which the bodies of the hanged were publicly displayed until the 1840s.

The Jewry Wall

From the Guildhall, it's a short walk west to St Nicholas Circle, a large roundabout that is part of the ring road. Go round it to the right – there's a walkway – and you'll see, on the right behind the church, the **Jewry Wall**, a chunk of Roman masonry some 18ft high and 73ft long that was originally part of Hadrian's public baths. The project was a real irritation to the emperor: the grand scheme was spoilt by the engineers, who miscalculated the line of the aqueduct that was to pipe in the water, and so bathers had to rely on a hand-filled cistern replenished from the river – which wasn't what he had in mind at all.

To St Mary de Castro and the Jain Centre

From the Jewry Wall, keep on going round St Nicholas Circle – with the *Holiday Inn* on the left – then veer down the first major street on the right and opposite you'll see the entrance to **Castle Gardens**, a narrow strip of a park that runs alongside a canalized portion of the Soar. The gardens are a pleasant spot, incorporating the overgrown mound where Leicester's Norman castle motte once stood. At the far end, you emerge on The Newarke; turn left and follow the road round, and in a minute or two you'll reach **Castle View**, a narrow lane spanned by the **Turret Gateway**, a rare survivor of the city's medieval castle. Just beyond the gateway is **St Mary de Castro** (Easter–Oct Sat 2–5pm), a dignified old church where Chaucer may have got married. The church's dainty crocketed spire presides over a harmonious mix of architectural styles, including several Norman features such as the dog-tooth decorated doorways and a five-seater sedilia in the chancel.

Behind the church, along the ring road, you can see the distinctive and substantial **Magazine Gateway** (no access), a combined medieval gateway and arsenal that is now ignominiously stranded between the two carriageways. Take the underpass beneath the ring road, head right along Oxford Street and you'll soon reach the **Jain Centre** (℡0116/254 1150, ⓦwww.jaincentre .com), which occupies a remodelled Congregational chapel dating from the nineteenth century. The rites and beliefs of followers of the Jain faith focus on an extreme reverence for all living things – traditional customs include the wearing of gauze masks to prevent the inhalation of passing insects. The temple, one of very few of its kind in Western Europe, has a splendidly garish white marble facade, and visitors may enter the lobby – or, better, view the interior by prior appointment.

New Walk Museum and Art Gallery

From the Jain Centre, it's about ten minutes' walk east to the **New Walk Museum and Art Gallery**, 55 New Walk (Mon–Sat 10am–5pm, Sun 11–5pm; free), easily the best of the city's museums. To get there from the Jain Centre, go back to the beginning of Oxford Street, turn right onto Newarke Street and keep going straight until you intersect with – and turn right onto – New Walk, a pedestrianized promenade that runs out from the centre to Victoria Park. The museum covers a lot of ground, from the natural world to geology and beyond, but one highlight is its extensive collection of Ancient Egyptian artefacts, featuring mummies and hieroglyphic tablets brought back to Leicester in the 1880s. It also holds an enjoyable collection of paintings, including works by British artists such as Hogarth, Francis Bacon, Stanley Spencer and Lowry as well as a whole raft of mawkishly romantic Victorian paintings, such as Charles Green's *The Girl I Left Behind Me* (1880). In addition, and this is something of a surprise, there's an outstanding collection of German Expressionist works, mostly sketches, woodcuts and lithographs by the likes of Otto Dix and George Grosz. In particular, look out for the latter's 1919 rallying-call sketch of the coffins of the two murdered leftists, Rosa Luxemburg and Karl Liebknecht.

From the museum, it takes about ten minutes to walk back to the Haymarket.

Belgrave and the National Space Centre

Beginning about a mile to the northeast of the centre, the cramped terraced houses of the **Belgrave** neighbourhood are the focus of Leicester's Asian community. Both Belgrave Road and its northerly continuation, Melton Road, are lined with Indian and Pakistani goldsmiths and jewellers, sari shops, Hindi music stores and curry houses. It's never dull down here, but Sunday afternoons are particularly enjoyable, when locals have time to stroll the streets in their finest gear. Belgrave celebrates two major Hindu festivals: **Diwali**, the Festival of Light, held in October or November, when six thousand lamps are strung out along the Belgrave Road and 20,000 people come to watch the switch-on alone; and **Navrati**, an eight-day celebration in October held in honour of the goddess Ambaji.

On the edge of Belgrave, just off the A6 two miles north of the city centre, the **National Space Centre** (term time Tues–Sun 10am–5pm; school hols daily 10am–5pm; last entry 90min before closing; £12, children (5–16) £10; ℡0116/261 0261, ⓦwww.spacecentre.co.uk) is devoted to space, science and astronomy, with a string of themed galleries exploring everything from the planets to orbiting earth. The emphasis is on the interactive, which makes the place very popular with children. Bus #54 links the train station and the Haymarket with Abbey Lane, a five-minute walk from the centre

Eating, drinking and entertainment

People come from miles around to eat at the **Indian restaurants** along Belgrave Road. The pick are clustered at the start of the road, just beyond the flyover to the northeast of the centre, and it's here you'll find the famous 🍴 *Bobby's*, at no. 154 (☎0116/266 0106; closed Mon). Run by Gujaratis, this bright, modern restaurant and takeaway is strictly vegetarian and uses no garlic or onions; try their delicious house speciality, the multi-flavoured Bobby's Special Chaat. Alternatively, the *Sayonara Thali*, at no. 49 (☎0116/266 5888), specializes in set thali meals, with several different dishes, breads and pickles served together on large steel plates, while the *Chaat House*, opposite the *Sayonara* at no. 108 (☎0116/266 0513), does wonderful *masala dosas* and other south Indian snacks. The best restaurant in the city centre is the *Opera House*, 10 Guildhall Lane (☎0116/223 6666), in lovely old premises and with a creative menu featuring dishes such as ravioli with wild mushrooms (mains £13–20).

Leicester's excellent **Phoenix Arts Centre**, in the city centre on Newarke Street (☎0116/255 4854, ⓦwww.phoenix.org.uk), features a first-rate mix of comedy, music, theatre and dance, whilst doubling up as an independent cinema.

Western Leicestershire

Give or take the odd industrial blip, most of the western part of the county – to the west of the A6 – is rural, its small towns and villages dotted over undulating countryside. The key attractions here are best visited as day-trips, beginning with **Market Bosworth**, a pleasant little spot near the site of **Bosworth Field**, where Richard III came an unpleasant cropper. Nearby, there's a good castle at **Ashby-de-la-Zouch**, a fine hilltop church at **Breedon-on-the-Hill**, and **Calke Abbey**, technically over the boundary in Derbyshire and not an abbey at all, but an intriguing country house whose faded charms witness the declining fortunes of the landed gentry.

With the exception of Calke Abbey, all the places mentioned above are easy to reach by **bus** from Leicester.

Market Bosworth

The thatched cottages and Georgian houses of tiny **MARKET BOSWORTH**, some fifteen miles west of Leicester, fan out from a dinky market square that was an important trading centre throughout the Middle Ages. From the sixteenth to the nineteenth century, the dominant family hereabouts was the Dixies, merchant-landlords who mostly ended up at the local church of **St Peter** (daily 8.30am–dusk; free), a good-looking edifice with a castellated nave and a sturdy square tower, a five-minute walk east of the Market Place. Heavily revamped by the Victorians, the church's interior is fairly routine, but the chancel does hold the charming early-eighteenth-century **tomb** of John Dixie, one-time rector, who is honoured by a long hagiographic plaque and the effigy of his weeping sister. John apart, the Dixies were not universally admired, however, and the young Samuel Johnson, who taught at the **Dixie Grammar School** – its elongated facade still abuts the Market Place – disliked the founder, Sir Wolstan Dixie, so much that he recalled his time there "with the strongest aversion and even a sense of horror".

Market Bosworth is best known for the **Battle of Bosworth Field**, fought on hilly countryside a couple of miles south of town in 1485. This was the last and most decisive battle of the Wars of the Roses, an interminably long-winded and bitterly violent conflict amongst the nobility for control of the English Crown. The victor was Henry Tudor, subsequently Henry VII, the vanquished Richard III, who famously died on the battlefield. In desperation, Shakespeare's villainous Richard cried out "A horse, a horse, my kingdom for a horse," but in fact the defeated king seems to have been a much more phlegmatic character. Taking a glass of water before the fighting started, he actually said, "I live a king: if I die, I die a king." The **exhibition centre** (daily 10am–5pm; £6) provides a lively account of the battle and its historical context. From here, the two-mile circular Battle Trail explores the battlefield with explanatory plaques filling out the details on the way – and good fun it is, too.

There are hourly **buses** from Leicester to Market Bosworth, then it's a two-mile walk to the battlefield visitor centre along an unsigned footpath – either get directions locally or pack the appropriate Ordnance Survey map (Landranger 140). Afterwards, have a **pint** at the traditional *Old Black Horse Inn*, on Market Bosworth's Market Place.

Ashby-de-la-Zouch

ASHBY-DE-LA-ZOUCH, fourteen miles northwest of Leicester, takes its fanciful name from two sources – the town's first Norman overlord was Alain de Parrhoet la Souche, while the rest simply means "place by the ash trees". Nowadays, Ashby is far from rustic, but it's still an amiable little place. Its principal attraction, the **castle** (April–June & Sept–Oct Thurs–Mon 10am–5pm; July & Aug daily 10am–6pm; Nov–March Thurs–Mon 10am–4pm; £3.50; EH), stands just off the town's main drag, Market Street. Originally a Norman manor house, the stronghold was the work of Edward IV's chancellor, Lord Hastings, who received his licence to crenellate in 1474. But Hastings didn't enjoy his new home for long. Just nine years later, he was dragged from a Privy Council meeting to have his head hacked off on a log by the order of Richard III, his crime being his lacklustre support for the Yorkist cause. Today, the rambling ruins include substantial leftovers from the old fortifications, as well as the shattered remains of the great hall, solar and chapel, but the star turn is the hundred-foot-high **Hastings Tower**, a self-contained four-storey stronghold that has survived in reasonably good nick. This tower house represented the latest thinking in castle design: it provided a secure inner fastness for Hastings and his retinue both against any outside enemy and his own mercenaries – who, experience had shown elsewhere, were often a threat to their employer – while also providing much better accommodation than was previously available. Improved living quarters reflecting the power and pride of the nobility were built all over England at this time and this is a rare survivor – witness the large windows on the upper floors, accessible via the tower's well-worn spiral staircase.

There are regular **buses** to Ashby's Market Street from Leicester.

Breedon-on-the-Hill

It's five miles northeast from Ashby to the village of **BREEDON-ON-THE-HILL**, which sits in the shadow of the large, partly quarried hill from which it takes its name. A steep footpath and a winding, half-mile lane lead up from the village to the summit, where the fascinating church of **St Mary and St Hardulph** (daily 9.30am–4pm, sometimes later in summer; free) occupies the site of an Iron Age hill fort and an eighth-century Anglo-Saxon monastery. Mostly dating from the thirteenth century, the church is kitted out with Georgian pulpit and pews as well as a large and distinctly rickety box pew. Much rarer are a number of **Anglo-Saxon carvings**, both individual saints and prophets and wall friezes, where a dense foliage of vines is inhabited by a tangle of animals and humans. The friezes are quite extraordinary, and the fact that the figures look Byzantine rather than Anglo-Saxon has fuelled much academic debate. The church has something else too, in the form of a set of fine alabaster tombs occupied by members of the Shirley family, who long ruled the local roost. One is an especially imposing affair with the kneeling family up above and a skeleton down below. Most **buses** from Ashby pull into the village at the bottom of the hill.

Calke Abbey and Staunton Harold Church

The eighteenth-century facade of **Calke Abbey** (house: mid-March to Oct Mon–Wed, Sat & Sun 12.30–5pm; gardens: mid-March to early July & early Sept to Oct Mon–Wed, Sat & Sun 11am–5pm, early July to early Sept daily 11am–5pm; £8, garden only £5; NT) is all self-confidence, its acres of dressed stone and three long lines of windows polished off with an imposing Greek Revival portico. This all cost oodles of money and the Harpurs, and then the Harpur-Crewes, who owned the estate, were doing very well until the finances of the English country estate changed after World War I. Then, at a time when country houses were being demolished by the score, the Harpur-Crewes simply hung on, becoming the epitome of faded gentility and refusing to make all but the smallest of changes to the house – though they did finally plump for electricity in 1962. The last Harpur-Crewe to live here, Charles, died in 1981 and the estate passed in its entirety to the National Trust. Very much to their credit, the Trust decided not to bring in the restorers and have kept the house in its dishevelled state – and this is its real charm.

▲ Calke Abbey

A visit starts in one of the old agricultural outbuildings, from where it's a short stroll to the **house**, whose entrance hall adroitly sets the scene, its walls decorated with ancient, moth-eaten stuffed heads from the family's herd of prize cattle. Beyond is the Caricature Room, whose walls are lined (up to three or four deep) with satirical cartoons, some by the leading cartoonists of their day, including Gillray and Cruikshank. Further on, there are: more animal heads and glass cabinets of stuffed birds in the capacious Saloon; an intensely cluttered Miss Havisham-like Drawing Room; a chaotic at-home School Room; and, indicating that eccentricity was a family trait, a state bed given to the Harpurs by the daughter of George II in 1734, then left in its packaging until the National Trust arrived 250 years later. After you've finished in the house, you can wander out into the **gardens** and pop into the Victorian estate **church**.

There's no public transport to Calke Abbey, and motorists must follow a long-winded one-way system: from Ashby, take the B587 Melbourne Road and follow the signs – the entrance is at the village of Ticknall to the north of the house; the exit is to the south. Back towards Ashby on the B587, spare a little time for **Staunton Harold Church** (early June to Aug Wed–Sun 1–4.30pm; April to early June, Sept & Oct Sat & Sun 1–4.30pm only; free, but £1 donation requested; NT), a political rant of a building in which the local lord, the reactionary Robert Shirley, expressed his hatred of Oliver Cromwell. There's no missing Shirley's intentions as he carved them above the church door: "In the year 1653 when all things sacred were throughout the nation either demolished or profaned…" and so he goes on. Whatever the politics, it was certainly an audacious – probably foolhardy – gesture, and sure enough Cromwell had the last laugh when an unrepentant Shirley died in prison three years later. The church itself is a good-looking affair, largely in the Perpendicular style with delightful painted ceilings and wood panelling.

Eastern Leicestershire and Rutland

For the casual visitor at least, there's nothing compelling about **eastern Leicestershire**, though the scenery is pleasant enough, with open farmland broken up by hills and ridges, and one middling town worth a pit stop: **Melton Mowbray**. Things improve over in neighbouring **Rutland** with a brace of amiable country towns – **Oakham** and **Uppingham** – and the postcard-pretty hamlet of **Lyddington**.

Melton Mowbray, Oakham and Stamford are on the Leicester–Peterborough **train** line and there are reasonably frequent **buses** to and between all the destinations mentioned above, except Lyddington.

Melton Mowbray

MELTON MOWBRAY, some fifteen miles northeast of Leicester, is famous for **pork pies**, an unaccountably popular English snack made (with some honourable exceptions – see p.634) of compressed balls of meat and gristle encased in wobbly jelly and thick pastry. The pie was the traditional repast of the fox-hunting fraternity, for whom the town of Melton, lying on the boundary of the region's most important hunts – Belvoir, Cottesmore and Quorn – was long a favourite spot. The antics of some of the aristocratic huntsmen are legend – in 1837 the Marquis of Waterford literally painted the town's buildings red, hence the saying. If you want to sample the genuine traditional hunters' pie, head to **Dickinson & Morris** (closed Sun), just off the pedestrianized Market Place on Nottingham Street – and a superior product it is too, as are the sausages the same company sells next door.

Most of Melton Mowbray is Victorian or modern red brick, but a brief walk south from the central Market Place, in its own close, stands the medieval **church** of **St Mary** (Mon–Sat 10am–noon & 2–4pm; free), which is distinguished by its impressive size (150ft long, with a tower soaring to over 100ft) and by some of its detail. The clerestory is an especially fine illustration of the Perpendicular style, its 48 windows encircling the church and bathing the interior with a gentle light.

The frequent **train** services that run from Leicester to Oakham and Stamford stop at Melton Mowbray; there are also regular **buses** between Nottingham, Melton and Oakham. From Melton train station, it's a five-minute walk north to the Market Place; buses stop a short walk to the north of the Market Place.

Oakham

Some twenty miles east of Leicester and ten southeast of Melton Mowbray, prosperous **OAKHAM** is Rutland's county town. It has a long history as a commercial centre, its prosperity bolstered by Oakham School, a late-sixteenth-century foundation that's now one of the country's more exclusive private schools. The town's stone terraces and Georgian villas are too often interrupted by the mundanely modern to assume much grace, but Oakham does have its architectural moments – particularly in the L-shaped **Market Place**, where a brace of sturdy awnings shelter the old water pump and town stocks. A few steps from the north side of the Market Place stands **Oakham Castle** (Mon–Sat 10.30am–1pm & 1.30–5pm, Sun 2–4pm; free), comprising a banqueting hall that was originally part of a fortified house dating back to 1191. Surrounded by the grassy banks of what was once a motte and bailey castle, the hall is a good example of Norman domestic architecture, and inside the whitewashed walls are covered with **horseshoes**, the result of an ancient custom by which every lord or lady, king or queen, is obliged to present an ornamental horseshoe when they first set foot in the town.

Oakham School is housed in a series of impressive ironstone buildings that frame the west edge of the Market Place. On the right-hand side of the school, a narrow lane allows you to see a little more of the buildings on the way to **All Saints' Church**, whose heavy tower and spire rise high above the town. Dating from the thirteenth century, the church is an architectural hybrid, but the airy interior is distinguished by the intense medieval carvings along the columns of the nave and choir, with Christian scenes and symbols set alongside dragons, grotesques, devils and demons. Finally, spare a few minutes for the assorted agricultural tools and mementoes of the **Rutland County Museum**, on Catmose Street (Mon–Sat 10.30am–5pm, Sun 2–4pm; free), a brief signposted walk from the Market Place via the High Street.

Practicalities

Oakham **train station** lies on the west side of town, a five-minute walk from the Market Place. **Buses** connect the town with Leicester, Nottingham and Melton Mowbray, and arrive on John Street, west of the Market Place. A thorough exploration of Oakham only takes an hour or so, but if you do decide to stay the best **hotel** in town is the distinctive *Lord Nelson's House Hotel*, 11 Market Place (☏01572/723199, ⓦwww.nicksrestaurant.co.uk; ⑤), with a handful of bedrooms decorated in attractive period style. For something more extravagant, the opulent *Hambleton Hall* (☎01572/756991, ⓦwww.hambletonhall.com; ⓪) occupies an imposing Baronial Gothic mansion, overlooking Rutland Water three miles east of Oakham: its gardens are particularly impressive, and the restaurant is outstanding. Back in Oakham, one of the best places to eat is *Nelson's* excellent and affordable **restaurant** *Nicks* (closed Mon), with a tasty modern menu featuring local ingredients; mains here cost about £17 in the evening, less at lunch. Alternatively, try neighbouring *Don Paddy Sanchez*, 8 Market Place (☎01572/822255), a combined craft shop and café-restaurant, where the cured-fish platter is especially good value (at £7). For a **drink**, the *Wheatsheaf* is a traditional pub with a good range of beers (and a garden) across from All Saints' Church at 2–4 Northgate.

Uppingham and around

The town of **UPPINGHAM**, seven miles south of Oakham, has the uniformity of style Oakham lacks, its narrow, meandering High Street flanked by bow-fronted shops and ironstone houses, mostly dating from the eighteenth century. It's the general appearance that pleases, rather than any individual sight, but the town is famous as the home of **Uppingham School**, a bastion of privilege whose imposing, fortress-like building stands at the west end of the High Street. Founded in 1587, the school was distinctly second-rate until the middle of the nineteenth century, when a dynamic headmaster, the Reverend Edward Thring, grabbed enough land to lay out some of the biggest playing fields in England – fitness being, of course, an essential attribute for the rulers of the British Empire.

Uppingham has one especially good **hotel**, the *Lake Isle*, in a tastefully modernized eighteenth-century town house at 16 High St East (☎01572/822951, ⓦwww.lakeislehotel.com; ⓪). The hotel **restaurant** is outstanding too, offering a superb and varied menu from guinea fowl to local venison, with main courses averaging around £15. For a **drink**, head for *The Vaults*, on the tiny Market Place.

Lyddington

Situated two miles southeast of Uppingham, **LYDDINGTON** is a sleepy little village of honey-coloured cottages straggling along a meandering main street, all backed by plump hills and broadleaf woodland. Early in the twelfth century, the Bishop of Lincoln, whose lands once extended south as far as the Thames, chose this as the site of a small palace – one of thirteen he erected to accommodate himself and his retinue while away on episcopal business. Confiscated during the Reformation, **Lyddington Bede House**, on Church Lane (April–Oct Thurs–Mon 10am–5pm; £3.30; EH), next door to the ironstone bulk of St Andrew's Church, was later converted into almshouses by Lord Burghley and has since been beautifully restored by English Heritage. The highlight is the light and airy Great Chamber, with its exquisitely carved oak cornices, but look out also for the tiny ground-floor rooms, which were occupied by impoverished locals for centuries.

Of the village's **pubs**, the most convivial is *The Old White Hart*, a traditional village inn with beamed ceilings on Main Street (☎01572/821703, ⓦwww .oldwhitehart.co.uk; ⓪). The inn has four pleasantly decorated, modern-style **rooms** and serves delicious food, both in the bar and in the **restaurant**, where main courses average around £12 (kitchen closed Sun evenings).

HALLATON, back over the border in Leicestershire, some five miles southwest of Uppingham along winding country lanes, is an agreeable village, whose High Street is flanked by a fetching medley of buildings, from antique ironstone houses to dinky thatched cottages. Every Easter Monday the **Hare Pie Scramble and Bottle Kicking** contest disturbs this peaceful scene, when the inhabitants of Hallaton and nearby Medbourne fight for pieces of pie before proceeding to kick small barrels of ale around a hill and across a stream, as has been the custom for several hundred years – though no one seems to know why. For a **pint** and a ploughman's, head for the *Bewicke Arms* beside the green.

Northamptonshire

Northamptonshire is one of the region's most diverse counties – so diverse in fact that even many Midlanders can't recall what is actually in it and what isn't. Even so, its superabundance of stately homes and historic churches has given it a tag as the "County of Spires and Squires" and there's also a good scattering of charming unspoilt villages, the most picturesque of which are built of local limestone. By contrast, however, three of the county's four big towns – Wellingborough, Corby and Kettering – are primarily industrial and whatever charms they offer to their inhabitants, there's not much to attract the regular tourist. Yet the county town, **Northampton**, does something to bridge the gap, its busy centre possessed of several fine old buildings and an excellent museum devoted to shoe-making, the industry that long made the place tick.

Gentle hills, farmland and patchy woodland stretch right across the county, with the prime tourist attraction being **Althorp**, family home of the Spencers and the burial place of Diana, Princess of Wales. Runners-up by a long chalk are the Anglo-Saxon church at **Brixworth**, the canalside village of **Stoke Bruerne** and postcard-pretty **Ashby St Ledgers**, one-time haunt of Guy Fawkes and his incendiary cronies. East Northamptonshire's star turn is the good-looking country town of **Oundle**, which makes the best base for visiting the delightful hamlet of **Fotheringhay**. The county also has a notable **long-distance footpath**, the seventy-mile **Nene Valley Way**, which follows the looping course of the river right across the county. Nene Way brochures are available at or from Northampton tourist office (see p.638).

Getting to Northampton by **public transport** is no problem, but to reach the villages and stately homes, you'll mostly need your own vehicle – or some careful planning around patchy bus services.

Northampton

Spreading north from the banks of the River Nene, **NORTHAMPTON** is a workaday modern town whose appearance largely belies its ancient past. Throughout the Middle Ages, this was one of central England's most important centres, a flourishing commercial hub whose now demolished castle was a popular stopping-off point for travelling royalty. A fire in 1675 burnt most of the medieval city to a cinder, and the Georgian town that grew up in its stead was itself swamped by the Industrial Revolution, when Northampton swarmed with boot- and shoemakers. Their products shod almost everyone in the Empire – from Australia to Canada – as well as the British army, though things did go badly awry during the Crimean War. The army ordered two boat-loads of Northampton boots in preparation for the Russian winter, but – for reasons that remain obscure – insisted that all the left boots be shipped in one vessel, the right ones in another. Unfortunately, one of the boats sank en route – and the soldiers were left perplexed by the ways of the army commissariat. Equally perplexed were the Northampton tailors who clothed **Errol Flynn**, while he was in repertory here in 1933. Always a charmer, Flynn dressed well, but he hightailed it out of town after just a year, leaving a whopping tailor's debt behind him.

Northampton's compact **centre** is at its most appealing on and around its main plaza, Market Square, which is where you'll find the town's finest buildings, notably All Saints' Church and the Guildhall. Half a day is enough for a quick gambol round the sights, but if you're tempted to stay the night there's a reasonable supply of downtown hotel accommodation.

The Town

Northampton's expansive, cobbled **Market Square** has a bustling, self-confident air, its sides flanked by a comparatively harmonious mixture of the old and the new. From here, either of a couple of narrow lanes leads through to the church of **All Saints** (Mon–Fri 9.30am–1pm; free), whose unusually secular appearance stems from its finely proportioned, pillared portico as well as its towered cupola. A statue of a bewigged Charles II in Roman attire surmounts the portico, a (flattering) thank-you for his donation of a thousand tons of timber after the Great Fire of 1675 had incinerated the earlier church. Inside, the elegant interior looks more like a ballroom than a church, from the sweep of its timber galleries through to its Neoclassical pillars and a ceiling coated in delicately sculpted plasterwork.

Behind the church is one of Lutyens' less inspiring monuments, a plain, blunt **war memorial** dating from 1926, and, just beyond that, in St Giles' Square, is the **Guildhall**, a flamboyant Victorian edifice constructed in the 1860s to a design by Edward Godwin. Godwin was one of the period's most inventive architects and his Gothic exterior, with its high-pointed windows and dinky turrets and towers, sports kings and queens plus scenes central to the county's history – look out for Mary, Queen of Scots' execution, the Great Fire and the battle of **Naseby**. Fought a few miles to the north of town in 1645, Naseby was a crucial engagement in the Civil War. It pretty much sealed the fate of King Charles and blooded Parliament's (later Cromwell's) New Model Army, a volunteer force driven by religious conviction (rather than money) that was soon to be the scourge of the Lord Protector's enemies.

The **Northampton Museum and Art Gallery** (Mon–Sat 10am–5pm, Sun 2–5pm; free), a few yards south of the Guildhall on Guildhall Road, celebrates the town's industrial heritage with a fabulous collection of **shoes**. Along with silk slippers, clogs and high-heeled nineteenth-century court shoes, there's one of the four boots worn by an elephant during the British Expedition of 1959, which retraced Hannibal's putative route over the Alps into Italy. There's celebrity footwear too, such as the giant DMs Elton John wore in *Tommy*, plus whole cabinets of heavy-duty riding boots, pearl-inlaid raised wooden sandals

▲ Stoke Bruerne

from Ottoman Turkey, and a couple of cabinets showing just how long high heels have been in fashion. Moving on, the top floor is given over to an excellent display charting the town's history from Roman days to the present, paying particular attention to the significance of the shoe industry, which employed no less than half the town's population in 1920.

Practicalities

From Northampton **train station**, which has regular services from Birmingham and London Euston, it's a ten-minute walk east to the Market Square. Buses pull into the **bus station** on Greyfriars, behind the over-large Grosvenor shopping centre, immediately to the north of the Market Square. At time of writing, the **tourist office** is in transit, but it will end up across from All Saints' Church on George Row (℡01604/838800, ⓦwww.explorenorthamptonshire.co.uk).

For **accommodation**, the *Best Western Lime Trees Hotel*, 8 Langham Place, Barrack Road (℡01604/632188, ⓦwww.limetreeshotel.co.uk; ⑨), occupies attractive Georgian premises a little more than half a mile north of the centre on the A508. As for **food**, *The Vineyard*, just east of the Market Square at 7 Derngate (℡01604/633 978), is a smart little place specializing in seafood; mains begin at £13.

Western Northamptonshire

The verdant countryside of **west Northamptonshire**, falling to the west of the A508, is dotted with stately homes, amongst which the most diverting is **Althorp**, the last resting place of Diana, Princess of Wales. The area also possesses the canal locks and narrowboats of tiny **Stoke Bruerne**, on the Grand Union Canal, and a rare and fine Saxon church at **Brixworth**. The best of the county's limestone villages lie further to the east, but there is a sprinkling here too, with **Ashby St Ledgers**, not far from Althorp, being an especially picturesque spot.

Stoke Bruerne

Heading south out of Northampton on the A508, it's about eight miles to the village of **STOKE BRUERNE**, which sits beside a flight of seven locks on the Grand Union Canal. By water at least, the village is very close to England's longest navigable tunnel, the one-and-three-quarter-miles-long **Blisworth Tunnel**, constructed at the beginning of the nineteenth century. Before the advent of steam tugs in the 1870s, boats were pushed through the tunnel by "legging" – two or more men would push with their legs against the tunnel walls until they emerged to hand over to waiting teams of horses. This exhausting task is fully explained in the village's excellent **museum** (Easter–Oct daily 10.30am–4.30pm; Nov–Easter Wed–Fri 10.30am–3.30pm, Sat & Sun 10.30am–4.30pm; £4.75), which is housed in a converted canalside corn mill. The museum delves into two hundred years of canal history with models, exhibits of canal art and spit-and-polish engines.

There are two good places to **eat** near the museum – the moderately priced *Bruerne's Lock Restaurant*, and the *Old Chapel Tea Rooms*, which features snacks and meals with a Mediterranean slant as well as displays of local art. Over the canal bridge, the *Boat Inn* **pub** (℡01604/862428, ⊛www.boatinn.co.uk) is jam-packed with narrowboat trinkets and serves a good pint. The pub operates **narrowboat cruises** through the Blisworth Tunnel (Easter–Sept; 30min; £3) as well as longer canal trips; advance booking is advised as sailings do not take place every day.

Althorp

Some six miles northwest of Northampton off the A428, the ritzy mansion of **Althorp** (July & Aug daily 11am–5pm, last admission 4pm; £12.50; ℡01604/770107, ⊛www.althorp.com) is the focus of the Spencer estate. The Spencers have lived here for centuries, but this was no big deal until one of the tribe, **Diana**, married Prince Charles in 1981. The disintegration of the marriage and Diana's elevation to sainthood is a story known to millions – and most perceptively analysed by B. Campbell in her book, *Diana, Princess of Wales: How Sexual Politics Shook the Monarchy*. The public outpouring of grief following Diana's death in 1997 was quite astounding, and Althorp became the focus of massive media attention as the coffin was brought up the M1 motorway from London to be buried on an island in the grounds of the family estate. Today, visitors troop round the **Diana exhibition**, in the old stable block, as well as the adjacent Althorp house, where there's a large collection of priceless paintings, including works by Gainsborough, Van Dyck and Rubens. From the house, a footpath leads round a lake in the middle of which is the islet (no access) where Diana is buried.

There are no scheduled **buses** from Northampton to Althorp – you need a car to get here.

Ashby St Ledgers

The **Gunpowder Plot**, which so dismally failed to blow the Houses of Parliament to smithereens in 1605, was hatched in **ASHBY ST LEDGERS**, immediately to the west of the M1 off the A361, about seven miles northwest of Althorp. Since those heated conversations, nothing much seems to have

The Gunpowder Plot

Born in York, **Guy Fawkes** (1570–1606) was a young convert to Catholicism, and his enthusiasm for the old faith induced him to leave Elizabeth I's Protestant England to fight in the Spanish army – against the "heretics" of the Netherlands – in 1593. There he established a reputation as a brave and determined soldier, catching the eye of leading Catholics back home. Cowed by Elizabeth for decades, these same Catholics viewed the queen's death, in 1603, and the accession of **James I** with some optimism, but their hopes were dashed when the new king proved unsympathetic to the Catholic cause. A small group, under the leadership of one **Robert Catesby**, decided that this called for desperate measures and, keen to recruit a military man, one of them popped over to the Netherlands to seek out Fawkes, who signed up and returned to England like a shot. The plan was simple – almost amazingly so: first the conspirators rented a cellar under Parliament and then Fawkes filled it with barrels of gunpowder, enough to blow Parliament sky high. But on November 4, 1605, the eve of the planned attack, the authorities discovered this so-called **Gunpowder Plot** and Fawkes was promptly tortured into giving away the names of his co-conspirators. Fawkes was tried and executed in January 1606, but he is burnt in effigy all over the country on **Bonfire Night**, November 5.

happened here, and the village's one and only street, flanked by handsome limestone cottages and a patch of ancient grazing land, still leads to the conspiratorial **manor house** (no access), a beautiful Elizabethan complex set around a wide courtyard. The adjacent **church**, dedicated to St Mary and St Leodegarius (hence Ledger), looks a little stodgy, but its modest fourteenth-century stonework holds some wonderful, if faded, medieval **murals**. Those above and to the side of the rood-loft depict the Passion of Christ, from Palm Sunday onwards, but the clearest is the large painting in the nave of St Christopher carrying the infant Jesus. Tradition asserts that St Christopher was a giant of a man, who earned his living carrying travellers across a river. He did, however, fail in his attempt to carry Jesus, who became impossibly heavy owing to the sins of the world he bore; Christopher became a Christian and was later installed as the patron saint of travellers.

The *Olde Coach House Inn*, at the start of the village, is a delightful country **pub** with a good range of ales and food.

Brixworth

Located just six miles north of Northampton off the A508, **BRIXWORTH** would be an inconsequential village were it not for **All Saints' Church** (usually open daily 10am–5pm; free), one of England's finest surviving Anglo-Saxon churches, dating from around 680 AD. From a distance, its most striking feature is its unusual cylindrical stair-turret, added to the western tower in the ninth century as part of a plan to fortify the church against Viking raids. Closer inspection, however, reveals something even rarer. The church is mostly limestone, but scores of Roman tiles, probably salvaged from a nearby villa, frame the windows and doorways, often mortared in at irregular angles. Inside, the uncluttered **nave** is whitewashed except for certain key features, including the **great arch** spanning the nave. Built around 1400, this arch replaced a Saxon wall with three arches that had previously separated the nave from the chancel; look carefully at each end of the later arch and you'll spot the remains of the Saxon stonework. At the far end of the church, the rounded **apse**, modelled on a Roman basilica, was once encased by an ambulatory, but this was closed off during restoration work in the nineteenth century – note the two small and blocked doorways low down on either side of the apse arch. During the refurbishment, the Victorians found fragments of bone, thought to be St Boniface's larynx, buried under the apse. The bones were Brixworth's most important reliquary and they may well have been hidden here for safekeeping when Viking raids were at their peak.

Eastern Northamptonshire

The River Nene wriggles and worms its way across **east Northamptonshire** passing through a string of small villages and towns. Amongst them, handsome **Oundle**, about 30 miles northeast of Northampton and seven miles west of Peterborough (see p.518), is the most diverting, with historic **Fotheringhay**, a few miles further along the river, running a close second.

Oundle

Arguably Northamptonshire's prettiest town, pocket-sized **Oundle** slopes up gently from the River Nene, its congregation of old limestone houses zeroing in on the congenial **Market Place**. Preserving much of its medieval layout, Oundle boasts some of the finest seventeenth- and eighteenth-century streetscapes in the Midlands, and is a suitably exclusive setting for one of England's better-known private schools, **Oundle School**, which has been running since 1556 and owns many of the town's most prized buildings. Above all it's the general appearance of the place that appeals rather than anything in particular, the exception being the parish church of **St Peter** (Mon–Sat 9am–5pm, Sun between services; free), whose magnificent two-hundred-foot Decorated spire soars high above the centre, though the interior – give or take the odd stained-glass window – is unremarkable.

Buses from Peterborough and Northampton stop on the Market Place, a short walk from the **tourist office**, at 14 West St (Mon–Sat 9am–5pm, plus Easter–Aug Sun 1–4pm; ☎01832/274333, ⦻www.explore northamptonshire.co.uk). The best place **to stay** in town is the seventeenth-century *Talbot Hotel*, just along from the Market Place on New Street (☎01832/273621, ⦻www.thetalbot-oundle.com; ⑥). The hotel has thirty-five plush bedrooms, mostly decorated in a modern rendition of antique style, but its main claim to fame is its oak staircase, which was brought here from Fotheringhay Castle (see p.642) and is thought to be the very one that Mary, Queen of Scots, walked down on the way to her execution. Apparently the queen's executioner stayed at the *Talbot* and both his and Mary's ghost are said to wander the upper floor. To avoid an apparition – and save some money – try instead the immaculate *Ashworth House*, a spick-and-span little stone guest house, five minutes' walk from the Market Place at 75 West St (☎01832/275312, ⦻www.ashworthhouse.co.uk; ❸).

The *Talbot* has the best **restaurant** in town – try the beef and Ruddles ale pie for just £8 – and there's a first-rate deli too, *Trendalls* (closed Sun), on the Market Place, which is good for baguettes and sandwiches of all descriptions.

Fotheringhay

Nestling by the River Nene just four miles northeast of Oundle, the tiny hamlet of **FOTHERINGHAY** has long been left to its own devices, but its medieval heyday is recalled by the magnificent church of **St Mary and All Saints** (dawn–dusk; free), which rises mirage-like above the green riverine meadows. Begun in 1411 and a hundred and fifty years in the making, the church is a paradigm of the Perpendicular, its exterior sporting wonderful arching buttresses, its nave lit by soaring windows and the whole caboodle topped by a splendid octagonal lantern tower. The interior is a tad bare, but there are two fancily carved medieval pieces to inspect – a painted pulpit and a sturdy stone font. On either side of the altar are the tombs of Elizabeth I's ancestors, the dukes of York, Edward and Richard. Elizabeth found the tombs in disarray in 1573 and promptly had them rebuilt in a smooth white limestone that still looks like new.

Fotheringhay Castle witnessed two key events – the birth of Richard III in 1452 and the beheading of Mary, Queen of Scots, in 1587. On the orders of Elizabeth I, Mary was executed in the castle's Great Hall with no one to stand in her defence – apart, that is, from her dog, which is said to have rushed from beneath her skirts as her head hit the deck. Not long afterwards, the castle fell into disrepair and nowadays only a grassy **mound** and ditch remain to mark its position; it's signposted down a short and narrow lane on the bend of the road as you come into the village from Oundle.

Fotheringhay has an excellent **pub–restaurant**, *The Falcon* (☎01832/226254), which occupies a neat stone building with a modern patio. They offer a delicious and imaginative menu here – lamb shank and artichoke for example – with main courses costing around £13.

Lincolnshire

The obvious place to start a visit to **Lincolnshire** is **Lincoln** itself, an old and easy-paced city whose cathedral, the third largest in England, remains the county's outstanding attraction. Northeast and east of here, the Lincolnshire **Wolds** band the county, their gentle green hills harbouring the pleasant market town of **Louth**. In this vicinity also is **Woodhall Spa**, a former Edwardian resort of studied gentility that served as the base of the Dambusters as they prepared for their Ruhr raid in 1943. The Wolds are flanked by the coast, so different from the rest of Lincolnshire, its brashness encapsulated by the resort of **Skegness**, though there are unspoilt stretches too, most notably at the **Gibraltar Point Nature Reserve**.

Beguiling **Stamford**, in the southwest corner of the county, makes an alternative base: it's an attractive town, whose narrow streets are flanked by a handsome ensemble of antique stone buildings, and on its doorstep stands one of the great monuments of Elizabethan England, **Burghley House**. From here, it's a short hop east into **The Fens**, which are readily explored along the A17, a road that runs close to the old fenland port of **Boston**, now Lincolnshire's second town. On any tour of the Fens you'll pass some of the county's most imposing medieval **churches**. Several are worth a special visit – particularly **St Botolph's** in Boston, **St Andrew's** in Heckington and **St Mary Magdalene's** in Gedney – and are seen to best advantage, like all the other churches of this area, in the pale, watery sunlight of the fenland evening. The other chief town of southern Lincolnshire is Grantham, the unremarkable birthplace of **Margaret Thatcher** – her childhood home is at the top of the main street at 2 North St.

Getting around Lincolnshire by public transport can be difficult. Lincoln is the hub of the county's limited **rail** network, with regular services to Heckington, Boston and Skegness. There are also links to Newark, in Nottinghamshire, which is on the main line from London to the northeast. In addition, reasonable **bus** services run between Lincoln and the county's larger market towns, like Louth and Boston, but you'll struggle to get to the villages without your own transport. For **information** on all aspects of the county, check the Lincolnshire Tourist Board's very helpful website (Ⓦ www.visitlincolnshire.com).

Lincoln

Reaching high into the sky from the top of a steep hill, the triple towers of the mighty cathedral in **LINCOLN** are visible for miles across the surrounding flatlands. This conspicuous spot was first fortified by the Celts, who called their settlement Lindon, "hillfort by the lake", a reference to the pools formed by the

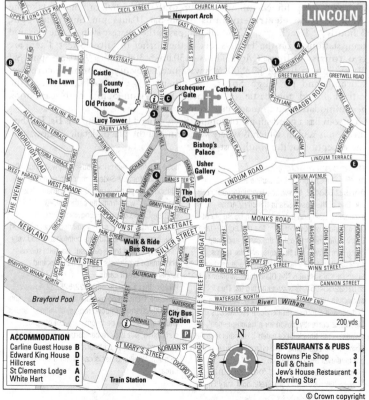

ACCOMMODATION
Carline Guest House   **B**
Edward King House   **D**
Hillcrest   **E**
St Clements Lodge   **A**
White Hart   **C**

RESTAURANTS & PUBS
Browns Pie Shop   3
Bull & Chain   1
Jew's House Restaurant   4
Morning Star   2

© Crown copyright

River Witham in the marshy ground below. In 47 AD the Romans occupied Lindon and built a fortified town, which subsequently became, as Lindum Colonia, one of the four regional capitals of Roman Britain.

Today, only fragments of the Roman city survive, mostly pieces of the third-century town wall, and these are outdone by reminders of Lincoln's medieval heyday, which began during the reign of William the Conqueror with the construction of the **castle** and **cathedral**. Lincoln flourished, first as a Norman power-base and then as a centre of the wool trade with Flanders, until 1369, when the wool market was transferred to neighbouring Boston. It was almost five hundred years before the city revived, the recovery based upon its manufacture of agricultural machinery and drainage equipment for the neighbouring fenlands. As the nineteenth-century city spread south down the hill and out along the old Roman road – the Fosse Way – so Lincoln became a place of precise class distinctions: the **Uphill** area, spreading north from the cathedral, became synonymous with middle-class respectability, **Downhill** with the proletariat. It's a distinction that remains – locals selling anything from secondhand cars to settees still put Uphill in brackets to signify a better quality of merchandise.

Arrival, information and accommodation

Both Lincoln **train station**, on St Mary's Street, and the **bus station**, close by off Melville Street, are located "Downhill" in the city centre. From either, it's a very steep, fifteen-minute walk up to the cathedral, or you can take the **Walk & Ride electric minibus** (Mon–Sat 10am–5pm, Sun noon–5pm; 3 hourly; £1 each way, £2.50 all-day pass); the nearest stop to the bus and train stations is on the High Street at the corner of Silver Street. There are two **tourist offices** (Mon–Thurs 9.30am–5.30pm, Fri 9.30am–5pm, Sat 10am–5pm; ℡01522/873800, ⊕www.lincoln.gov.uk), one on the corner of Cornhill and the High Street, the other at 9 Castle Hill, between the cathedral and the castle (also opens Sun 10am–5pm); both can book accommodation and guided city tours.

Lincoln has a good supply of competitively priced **hotels** and **B&Bs**. The best location is Uphill, which is where you'll find all the places detailed below, with the exception of the youth hostel.

Accommodation

Carline Guest House 1–3 Carline Rd ℡01522/530422, ⊕www.carlineguesthouse.co .uk. One of the best B&Bs in the city, Carline occupies a neat and trim Edwardian house about ten minutes' walk down from the cathedral – take Drury Lane from in front of the castle and keep going. Breakfasts are first-rate, and the rooms smart and tastefully furnished. No credit cards. ❸

Edward King House The Old Palace, Minster Yard ℡01522/504050, ⊕www.ekhs.org.uk. This distinctive B&B, located immediately below the cathedral in a former residence of the bishops of Lincoln, is currently closed for a much-needed revamp – but check it out when it reopens in 2008. Some of the bedrooms have charming views over the medieval Bishop's Palace.

Hillcrest 15 Lindum Terrace ℡01522/510182, ⊕www.hillcrest-hotel.com. Traditional, very English hotel in a large red-brick house that was originally a Victorian rectory. Sixteen comfortable rooms with all mod cons plus a large, sloping garden. About ten minutes' walk from the cathedral. ❺

St Clements Lodge 21 Langworth Gate ℡01522/521532. In a brisk, modern house a short walk from the cathedral, this comfortable and very friendly B&B has three pleasant, en-suite rooms. Homemade breakfasts – great haddock and kippers. No credit cards. ❸

White Hart Bailgate ℡01522/526222 ⊕www .whitehart-lincoln.co.uk. Antique former coaching inn with charming public rooms, all hidden nooks and crannies. The bedrooms are not quite as distinctive, but they're comfortable enough and many overlook the cathedral. Great Uphill location. Weekend deals can slash the normal price. ❻

The City

For the visitor, almost everything of interest is confined to the Uphill part of city, clustering around the cathedral and castle.

The cathedral

Not a hill at all, charming **Castle Hill** is a wide, short and level cobbled street that links Lincoln's castle and cathedral. Its east end is marked by the arches of the medieval **Exchequergate**, beyond which soars the glorious west front of **Lincoln Cathedral** (May–Sept Mon–Fri 7.15am–8pm, Sat & Sun 7.15am–6pm; Oct–April Mon–Sat 7.15am–6pm, Sun 7.15am–5pm; access restricted during services; £4 including guided tour – see box below; Ⓦ www.lincolncathedral.com), a sheer cliff-face of blind arcading mobbed by decorative carving. Most striking of all is the extraordinary band of twelfth-century carved panels that depict biblical themes with passionate intimacy, their inspiration being a similar frieze at Modena Cathedral in Italy. The west front's apparent homogeneity is, however, deceptive, and further inspection reveals two phases of construction – the small stones and thick mortar of much of the facade belong to the original church, completed in 1092, whereas the longer stones and finer courses date from the early thirteenth century. These were enforced works, for in 1185 an earthquake shattered much of the Norman church, which was then rebuilt under the auspices of **Bishop Hugh of Avalon**, the man responsible for most of the present cathedral, with the notable exception of the (largely) fourteenth-century central tower.

The cavernous **interior** is a fine example of Early English architecture, with the nave's pillars conforming to the same general design yet differing slightly, their varied columns and bands of dark Purbeck marble contrasting with the oolitic limestone that is the building's main material. Looking back up the nave from beneath the **central tower**, you can also observe a major medieval cock-up: Bishop Hugh's roof is out of alignment with the earlier west front, and the point where they meet has all the wrong angles. It's possible to pick out other irregularities, too – the pillars have bases of different heights, and there are ten windows in the nave's north wall and nine in the south – but these are deliberate features, reflecting a medieval aversion to the vanity of symmetry. Also medieval is the use of pre-Christian imagery, especially on and around the **rood screen** at the top of the nave, where there's a veritable menagerie of demons and gargoyles peering out of the foliage.

Beyond the rood screen lies **St Hugh's Choir**, its fourteenth-century misericords carrying an eccentric range of carvings, with scenes from the life of Alexander the Great and King Arthur mixed up with biblical characters and folkloric parables. Further on is the open and airy **Angel Choir**, completed in 1280 and dotted with stone table-tombs, its roof embellished by dozens of finely carved statuettes, including the tiny Lincoln Imp (see p.647). Finally, a corridor off the choir's north aisle leads to the wooden-roofed **cloisters** and

---

Guided tours of Lincoln Cathedral

There are two different **guided tours** offered by the cathedral, both free with the price of admission. The first – the **Floor Tour** (Mon–Sat 2–3 daily) – is a quick gambol round the cathedral's salient features, while the second, the ninety–minute **Roof Tour** (Mon–Sat 1–2 daily), takes in parts of the church otherwise out of bounds. Both are very popular, so it's a good idea to book in advance on ☎01522/561600.

the polygonal **chapter house**, where Edward I and Edward II convened gatherings that pre-figured the creation of the English Parliament.

The Bishop's Palace

Hidden behind a gated wall immediately to the south of the cathedral on Minster Yard are the ruins of what would, in its day, have been the city's most impressive building. This, the medieval **Bishop's Palace** (April–Oct daily 10am–5pm; Nov–March Mon & Thurs–Sun 10am–4pm; £3.60; EH), once consisted of two grand halls, a lavish chapel, kitchens and ritzy private chambers, but today the most coherent survivor is the battered and bruised Alnwick Tower – where the entrance is. The damage was done during the Civil War when a troupe of Roundheads occupied the palace until they themselves had to evacuate the place after a fierce fire. Nonetheless, the ruins are suitably fetching, with wide views over the surrounding flatlands. The adjoining gardens are immaculate, and abut an elevated terrace holding one of Europe's most northerly vineyards.

The castle

From the west front of the cathedral, it's a quick stroll across Castle Hill to **Lincoln Castle** (April–Sept Mon–Sat 9.30am–5.30pm, Sun 11am–5.30pm; Oct–March Mon–Sat 9.30am–4pm, Sun 11am–4pm; £3.90). Intact and forbidding, the **castle walls** incorporate bits and pieces from the twelfth to the nineteenth centuries with the wall walkway offering great views over town. The earliest remains are those of the **Lucy Tower**, built on the steep grassy mound to the left of the main entrance and originally the site of a Norman motte. The castle was turned into a prison in the 1820s and some of the prisoners were unceremoniously buried here inside the tower wall at the top of the mound – a sad and lonely spot if ever there was one, especially as the tombs were only allowed to carry the prisoners' initials. The castle wall encloses a large central courtyard, part of which is occupied by the old **prison**, a dour red-brick structure that holds one of the four surviving copies of the **Magna Carta** (see p.927) as well as a truly remarkable **prison chapel**. Here, the prisoners were locked in high-sided cubicles, where they could see the preacher and his pulpit but not their fellow inmates. Neither was this approach just applied to chapel visits: the prisoners were kept in perpetual solitary confinement, and were compelled to wear masks when they took to the exercise yard. This system was founded on the pseudo-scientific theory that defined crime as a contagious disease, but unfortunately for the theorists, their so-called Pentonville System of "Separation and Silence", which was introduced here in 1846, drove so many prisoners crazy that it was abandoned thirty years later; nobody ever bothered to dismantle the chapel.

The rest of the city

The rest of **Uphill Lincoln** is scattered with historic remains, notably several chunks of Roman wall, the most prominent of which is the second-century **Newport Arch** straddling Bailgate and once the main north gate into the city. There's also a bevy of medieval stone houses, most notably on and around the aptly named **Steep Hill** as it cuts down from the cathedral to the city centre. In particular, look out for the tidily restored twelfth-century **Jew's House**, a reminder of the Jewish community that flourished in medieval Lincoln. A rare and superb example of domestic Norman architecture, it now houses the *Jew's House Restaurant* (see opposite).

Straddling Danesgate just below the Bishop's Palace, **The Collection** (daily 10am–5pm; free) occupies two buildings – a striking modern structure built to display the city's extensive collection of archeological artefacts, from prehistoric times onwards, and a good-looking 1920s edifice, also known as the **Usher Gallery**, which focuses on fine art. The fine-art collection includes some charming paintings of the cathedral and its environs, the best being those by William Logsdail (1859–1944), and a Lincoln view by Lowry. The gallery also holds an eclectic collection of coins, porcelain, watches and clocks. Dating from the seventeenth century, the timepieces were given to the gallery by its benefactor, James Ward Usher, a local jeweller and watchmaker who made a fortune on the back of the **Lincoln Imp**: first, in the 1880s, he devised the legend and then he sold the little trinkets and novelties to match – with such success that the imp became the city's emblem. His story has a couple of imps hopping around the cathedral, until one of them is turned to stone for trying to talk to the angels carved into the roof of the Angel Choir. His chum made a hasty exit on the back of a witch, but the wind is still supposed to haunt the cathedral awaiting their return.

Eating and drinking

Lincoln's **café** and **restaurant** scene is a little patchy, but there are a couple of excellent places within shouting distance of the cathedral. First stop must be ☀ *Browns Pie Shop*, yards from the cathedral at 33 Steep Hill (☎01522/527330). It's not a pie shop at all, but an excellent restaurant whose creative menu puts the emphasis on British ingredients; a main course here will cost you about £12, but save room for the earth-shattering puddings. A second recommendable spot, just beyond the foot of Steep Hill, is the smart and marginally more expensive *Jew's House Restaurant*, 15 The Strait (☎01522/524851), where again much emphasis is placed on local ingredients.

As for **pubs**, there are a pair of amiable and traditional locals near the cathedral – the *Bull & Chain*, on Langworthgate, and the *Morning Star*, close by on Greetwellgate. The former has a garden; the latter features real ales. For somewhere rowdier, there's a whole string of places on Bailgate.

The Wolds and the coast

The rolling hills and gentle valleys of the **Lincolnshire Wolds**, a narrow band of chalky land running southeast from Caistor to just outside Skegness, stand out amidst the more mundane agricultural landscapes of north Lincolnshire. A string of particularly appealing valleys is concentrated in the vicinity of **Louth**, which, with its striking church and old centre, is easily the most enticing of the region's towns – with the added advantage of being fairly close to the coast. A few miles to the south of Louth, the Wolds dip down to the wooded heathland surrounding the once fashionable hamlet of **Woodhall Spa**, and it's south again to the imposing red-brick **Tattershall Castle**, north Lincolnshire's main historical attraction. East of the Wolds lies the coast, with its bungalows, campsites and caravans parked beside a sandy beach that extends, with a few marshy interruptions, north from **Skegness**, the main resort, to Mablethorpe and ultimately Cleethorpes. South of Skegness, the **Gibraltar Point Nature Reserve** is a welcome diversion from the bucket-and-spade/amusement-arcade commercialism.

Louth and around

Henry VIII described the county of Lincolnshire as "one of the most brutal and beestlie of the whole realm", his contempt based on the events of 1536, when thousands of northern peasants rebelled against his religious reforms. In Lincolnshire, this insurrection, the **Pilgrimage of Grace**, began in the northeast of the county at **LOUTH**, 25 miles from Lincoln, under the leadership of the local vicar, who was subsequently hanged, drawn and quartered for his pains. There's a commemorative plaque in honour of the rebels beside Louth's church of **St James** (April to Christmas Mon–Sat 10.30am–4pm, Christmas to March Mon, Wed, Fri & Sat 8am–noon; free), which is the town's one outstanding building, its soaring Perpendicular spire, buttresses, battlements and pinnacles set on a grassy knoll just to the west of the centre. The interior is delightful too, the sweeping symmetries of the nave illuminated by slender windows and capped by a handsome Georgian timber roof decorated with dinky little angels. The roof of the tower vault is, if anything, even finer, its intricate stonework an exercise in geometrical precision.

Next to the church, the well-tended gardens and Georgian houses of **Westgate** make it one of Louth's prettiest streets. Afterwards, it doesn't take long to explore the rest of the town centre, whose cramped lanes and alleys – focusing on the **Cornmarket** – are flanked by red-brick buildings mostly dating from the nineteenth century.

Practicalities

Handling regular weekday services from Boston and Lincoln, Louth's **bus station** is at the east end of Queen Street, a couple of minutes' walk from the Cornmarket: head west along Queen Street and turn right onto the Market Place to get there. The **tourist office** is in the New Market Hall off Cornmarket (Mon–Sat 9am–4.30pm; ☎01507/609289).

The best **hotel** by a long chalk is the excellent, family-run *Priory*, 149 Eastgate (☎01507/602930, ⓦwww.theprioryhotel.com; ❺), in a handsomely maintained Georgian villa dating from 1818 with extensive gardens; the hotel is located east of the centre, about ten minutes' walk from the Cornmarket. Its **restaurant** (non-residents Fri & Sat only; closed Sun) is also the best place in town to eat, serving good-quality Modern British cuisine with main courses from £13. Don't ignore the church's **café** and its homemade cakes – locals set out early to get a slice of lemon-drizzle. And for a drink head to the antique *Wheatsheaf Inn* on Westgate.

The Saltfleetby-Theddlethorpe dunes

An enjoyable short excursion from Louth takes you east along the B1200 across nine miles of fen farmland to the **coast**. This byroad is built over an old Roman road that was used to transport salt inland from the seashore salt pans, once a lucrative source of income for local traders. At the coast, turn right along the main A1031 and, after about half a mile, take the (poorly signed) gravel track on the left through the **Saltfleetby-Theddlethorpe Dunes National Nature Reserve**. Comprising over five miles of sand dune, salt and freshwater marsh, the reserve is at its prettiest in midsummer, when the dunes sprout buckthorn bushes and sea heather flowers, forming a carpet of violet spreading down towards the sea. A network of trails navigates the dunes and lagoons, with the latter attracting hundreds of migratory wildfowl in spring and autumn.

Woodhall Spa

Heading south from Louth along the A153, it's fourteen miles to **Horncastle**, which was once famous for its horse fairs – as described in George Borrow's *Romany Rye*. A further seven miles along the B1191 brings you to **WOODHALL SPA**, an elongated village surrounded by a generous chunk of woodland. Here, the main street – **The Broadway** – is lined with Victorian/Edwardian houses and shops, reminders of the time when the spring water of this isolated place, rich in iodine and bromine, was a popular tipple. The tiny **Cottage Museum** (same times as tourist office, see below; £1.50; ⓦwww.woodhallspa-museum. co.uk), on Iddesleigh Road off The Broadway, outlines the development of the spa and also has a section on the **Dambusters**, who were based at a nearby mansion, **Petwood**, on Stixwould Road, which is now a luxury hotel (see below). The mansion was built in 1905 for the furniture millionaires, the Maples, then requisitioned by the RAF during World War II, and turned into the Officers' Mess of 617 Squadron, the Dambusters, famous for their bombing raid of May 16, 1943. The raid was planned to deprive German industry of water and electricity by breaching several Ruhrland dams, a mission made possible by Barnes Wallis's famous bouncing bomb. A rusting specimen stands outside the hotel, which also contains the old Officers' Bar, kitted out with memorabilia from bits of aircraft engines to newspaper cuttings.

Another unexpected delight is Woodhall Spa's **Kinema**, set deep in the woods, yet only five minutes' walk from The Broadway – just follow the signs. Opened in 1922, the Kinema is one of England's few remaining picture houses where the film is projected from behind the screen, and at weekends a 1930s organ rises in front of the screen to play you through the ice-cream break. For details of what's showing, call ⓣ01526/352166 or check ⓦwww .thekinemainthewoods.co.uk.

Woodhall Spa's **tourist office** is inside the Cottage Museum (Easter–Oct Mon–Fri 10am–5pm, Sat & Sun 10.30am–4.30pm; ⓣ01526/353775). The smartest **hotel** hereabouts is the ⚡*Petwood* (ⓣ01526/352411, ⓦwww.petwood .co.uk; ❼), set in immaculate gardens, its handsome half-timbered gables and stone facades sheltering a fine panelled interior and fifty large, well-appointed bedrooms decorated in un-fussy modern style. Otherwise, the *Oglee Guest House*, in Edwardian premises off The Broadway at 16 Stanhope Ave (ⓣ01526/353512, ⓦwww.ogleeguestghouse.com; ❷), is a pleasant alternative; all its rooms are en suite and the breakfasts are tasty.

Tattershall Castle

From Woodhall Spa, it's about four miles southeast to **Tattershall Castle** (early March & Nov to early Dec Sat & Sun noon–4pm; April–Sept Mon–Wed, Sat & Sun 11am–5.30pm; Oct Mon–Wed, Sat & Sun 11am–4pm; £4.50; NT), whose massive, moated, red-brick keep dominates the fenland from beside the main road between Sleaford and Skegness. There's been a castle here since Norman times, but it was Ralph Cromwell, the Lord High Treasurer, who built the present quadrangled tower in the 1440s. A veteran of Agincourt, Cromwell was familiar with contemporary French architecture and it was to France that he looked for his basic design – in England, keeps had been out of fashion since the thirteenth century. Cromwell's quest for style explains Tattershall's contradictions. The castle walls are sixteen feet thick and rise to a height of one hundred feet, but there are no fewer than three ground-floor doorways with low-level windows to match. It's a medieval keep as fashion accessory, a theatricality that continues inside the castle with the grand chimneypieces, though otherwise the interior is almost entirely bare – give or take the occasional Flemish tapestry. The adjacent church of the **Holy Trinity** (April–Sept daily 10am–5pm; free) is a high and mighty fifteenth-century structure, whose soaring nave, with its slender columns and pointed windows, is bright but austere. It now houses a volunteer-run **café**, serving excellent homemade cakes.

Skegness

SKEGNESS, some 26 miles east of Tattershall, has been a busy resort ever since the railways reached the Lincolnshire coast in 1875. Its heyday was pre-1960s, before the Brits began to take themselves off to sunnier climes, but it still attracts tens of thousands of city-dwellers who come for the wide, sandy beaches and for a host of attractions ranging from nightclubs to bowling greens. Every inch the traditional English seaside town, Skegness gets the edge over many of its rivals by keeping its beaches sparklingly clean and its parks spick-and-span. Indeed, the resort has a tradition of keeping ahead of its competitors: in 1908 it came up with the ground-breaking "Skegness is So Bracing" slogan beneath a picture of a jolly fisherman, and it was here in 1936 that ex-showman Billy Butlin opened his first Butlin's Holiday Camp. All that said, the seafront, with its rows of souvenir shops and amusement arcades, can be dismal, especially on rainy days, and you may well decide to sidestep the whole affair by heading south three miles along the coastal road to the **Gibraltar Point National Nature Reserve** (daily dawn–dusk; free). Here, a network of clearly signed footpaths patterns a narrow strip of salt and freshwater marsh, sand dune and beach that attracts an inordinate number of birds, both resident and migratory.

Skegness' Bus and **train stations** are next door to each other about ten minutes' walk from the seashore – cut across Lumley Square and go straight up the High Street to the landmark clocktower. The **tourist office** (April–Oct daily 9.30am–5pm; Nov–March Mon–Fri 9.30am–4.30pm; ☎01754/899887, ⓦwww.visitlincolnshire.com) is only yards from the clocktower, on Grand Parade. Skegness has scores of **hotels**, **B&Bs** and **guest houses**: one of the most appealing is the *Best Western Vine Hotel*, Vine Road (☎01754/610611, ⓦwww.thevinehotel.com; ❹), a rambling, ivy-clad old house set in its own grounds on a quiet residential street about three-quarters of a mile from the clocktower.

The Lincolnshire Fens

The Lincolnshire section of **The Fens**, that great chunk of eastern England extending from Boston to Cambridge, encompasses some of the most productive farmland in Europe. With the exception of the occasional hillock, this pancake-flat, treeless terrain has been painstakingly reclaimed from the marshes and swamps that once drained into the Wash, a process that has taken almost two thousand years. In earlier times, outsiders were often amazed by the dreadful conditions hereabouts – as one medieval chronicler put it: "There is in the middle part of Britain a hideous fen which [is] oft times clouded with moist and dark vapours having within it divers islands and woods as also crooked and winding rivers." These dire conditions spawned the distinctive culture of the so-called **fen slodgers**, who embanked small portions of marsh to create pastureland and fields, supplementing their diets by catching fish and fowl and gathering reed and sedge for thatching and fuel. Their economy was threatened by the large-scale land reclamation schemes of the late fifteenth and sixteenth centuries, and time and again the fenlanders sabotaged progress by breaking down the banks and dams. But the odds were stacked against the saboteurs, and a succession of great landowners eventually drained huge tracts of the fenland; by the end of the eighteenth century the fen slodgers' way of life had all but disappeared. Nevertheless, the Lincolnshire Fens remain a distinctive area of introverted little villages, with just one significant settlement, the old port of **Boston**.

Boston

As it approaches The Wash, the muddy River Witham weaves its way through **BOSTON** (a corruption of Botolf's stone, or Botolph's town), which was named after the Anglo-Saxon monk-saint who first established a monastery here, overlooking the main river crossing point in 645 AD. In the thirteenth and fourteenth centuries, the settlement expanded to become England's second largest seaport, its flourishing economy dependent on the wool trade with Flanders. Local merchants, revelling in their success, decided to build a church that demonstrated their wealth, the result being the magnificent church of **St Botolph**, whose 272-foot tower still presides over the town and its surroundings. The church was completed in the early sixteenth century, but by then Boston was in decline as trade drifted west towards the Atlantic and the Witham silted up. The town's fortunes only revived in the late eighteenth century when, after the nearby fens had been drained, it became a minor agricultural centre with a modest port that has, in recent times, been modernized for trade with the EU. A singular mix of fenland town and seaport, Boston is an unusual little place that is at its liveliest on **market days** – Wednesday and Saturday.

The Town

Mostly flanked by Victorian red-brick buildings, the mazy streets of Boston's cramped and compact centre, on the east side of the River Witham, radiate out from the **Market Place**, a dishevelled square of irregular shape. Just to the west looms the massive bulk of **St Botolph's** (daily 8.30am–4.30pm; free), whose exterior masonry is embellished by the high-pointed windows and elaborate tracery of the Decorated style. Most of the structure dates from the fourteenth century, but the huge and distinctive **tower**, whose lack of a spire earned the church the nickname the "Boston Stump", is of later construction. The octagonal lantern is later still, added in the sixteenth century and graced by flying buttresses and pointy pinnacles. Visible from twenty miles away, it once sheltered a beacon that guided travellers in from the fens and the North Sea. A tortuous 365-step spiral **staircase** (closed on Sun) leads to a balcony near the top, from where the panoramic views over Boston and the fens amply repay both the price of the ticket (£2.50) and the effort of the climb. Down below, St Botolph's light and airy **nave** is an exercise in the Perpendicular, all soaring columns and high windows. The sheer purity of design is stunning, its virtuosity heightened by the narrowness of the annexe-like chancel and the elegance of the Decorated arch that partly screens it from view. Indeed, the chancel is comparatively dowdy, though it does boast some intriguing fourteenth-century **misericords**, bearing a lively mixture of vernacular scenes such as organ-playing bears, a pair of medieval jesters squeezing cats in imitation of bagpipes and a schoolmaster birching a boy, watched by three more awaiting the same fate.

The church's most famous vicar was **John Cotton** (1584–1652), who helped stir the Puritan stew during his twenty-year tenure, encouraging a stream of Lincolnshire dissidents to head off to the colonies of New England to found their "New Jerusalem". Cotton emigrated himself in 1633 and soon became the leading light among the Puritans of Boston, Massachusetts. The Cotton connection was finally commemorated here in the Stump by the creation of the **Cotton Chapel**, at the west end of the nave, in 1857. The most interesting relic from Cotton's sojourn here is not, however, in the chapel at all, but in the nave in the form of the ornate **pulpit** from which he pounded out his three-hour sermons.

Boston had been alive to religious dissent before Cotton arrived and, in 1607, several of the **Pilgrim Fathers** were incarcerated here after their failed attempt to escape religious persecution by slipping across to Holland. They were imprisoned for thirty days in the old **Guildhall** (currently closed for refurbishment) on South Street, a brief walk south from St Botolph's back through the Market Place. A creaky affair, the Guildhall incorporates an antique Council Chamber, the court where the Pilgrim Fathers were tried and sentenced, as well as the cells where they were locked up.

Practicalities

It's ten minutes' walk east from Boston **train station** to the town centre – head straight out of the station along Station Street and keep going until you hit the river and cross the bridge. The **bus station** is also to the west of the river, just five minutes' walk away from the Market Place on Lincoln Lane. The **tourist office** (Mon–Sat 9.30am–5pm; ☎01205/356656, ⓦwww.boston.gov.uk) is in the new Haven Gallery, a brief walk south of the Market Place along the river at 2 South Square. They have a list of **B&Bs**, including the *Bramley House*, 267 Sleaford Rd (☎01205/354538; ❷), which occupies an attractively converted eighteenth-century farmhouse, a mile west of town beyond the train station. Another good choice is the much-enlarged Victorian *Fairfield Guest House* at 101 London Rd (☎01205/362869; no credit cards; ❷), about two miles south of the centre; it has sixteen guest rooms (mostly en suite), all decorated in bright and cheerful style.

Heckington

The village of **HECKINGTON**, thirteen miles west of Boston, has a tidy little centre that drapes around the church of **St Andrew** (Mon–Sat 9am–5pm or dusk in winter; free), a splendid example of the Decorated style, with a pinnacled spire and elaborate canopied buttresses framing the flowing tracery of the windows. Inside, the original fourteenth-century chancel fittings have survived, including the battered tomb of the founder, Richard de Potesgrave, and an **Easter Sepulchre**, whose folksy and energetic carved figures are set against a dense undergrowth of foliage. The sepulchre, one of the finest in England, was built to accommodate the host between Good Friday and Easter morning. The **sedilia** is intriguing too, boasting a cartoon strip of domestic scenes on the subject of food – a man eating fruit, a woman feeding the birds and suchlike. Heckington has one other attraction, its unique eight-sailed **windmill**, located a short stroll from the church and worth visiting when it's in operation (Easter to mid–July Thurs–Sun noon–5pm; mid–July to mid–Sept daily noon–5pm; mid–Sept to Easter Sun 2–5pm; £1.50; ☎01529/461919). In between the windmill and the church, on the High Street, is the village's best **pub**, the *Nag's Head*, while the **train station** (on the Skegness–Grantham line) is opposite the windmill.

Gedney to Sutton Bridge

Travelling southeast on the A17 from Heckington, it's about twenty-two miles to the scattered hamlet of **GEDNEY**, where the massive tower of **St Mary**

Magdalene (daily dawn–dusk; free) intercepts the fenland landscape. Seen from a distance, the church seems almost magical, or at least mystical, its imposing lines so much in contrast with its fen-flat surroundings. Close up, the nave is simply beautiful, its blend of Early English and Perpendicular features culminating in a phalanx of elongated windows, which soar above the exquisite Renaissance alabaster effigies of Adlard and Cassandra Welby, facing each other on the south wall near the chancel.

There's more ecclesiastical excitement just a mile or two to the east in **LONG SUTTON**, a modest farming centre that limps along the road until it reaches its trim Market Place. Here, the church of **St Mary** (daily dawn–dusk; free) has preserved many of its Norman features, with its arcaded tower supporting the oldest lead spire in the country, dating from around 1200. Look out also for the striking medieval stained glass in the chancel aisle. Long Sutton once lay on the edge of the five-mile-wide mouth of the **River Nene**, where it emptied into The Wash. This was the most treacherous part of the road from Lincoln to Norfolk, and locals had to guide travellers across the obstacle on horseback, not always without mishap. In 1205, **King John** was caught by the rising tide, losing his jewels and baggage train in the quicksands somewhere between Long Sutton and Terrington St Clement in Norfolk. In 1831, the River Nene was embanked and then spanned with a wooden bridge at **Sutton Bridge**, a hamlet just two miles east of Long Sutton. The present swing bridge, with its nifty central tower, was completed in 1894.

The marshy shores of **The Wash** remain wild and desolate. There are several access points, but the best is near Sutton Bridge – from the car park on the east side of the mouth of the Nene. This marks the start of the five-mile-long **Peter Scott Walk** running east along the seashore to King's Lynn (see p.512), and named after the famous naturalist, who spent long periods in a renovated lighthouse near the mouth of the Nene. To do the whole walk, you'll need proper maps and hiking gear.

Stamford

STAMFORD is delightful, a handsome little limestone town of yellow-grey seventeenth- and eighteenth-century buildings edging narrow streets that slope up from the River Welland. It was here that the Romans forded this important river, establishing a fortified outpost that the Danes subsequently selected for one of their regional capitals. Later the town became a centre of the medieval wool and cloth trade, its wealthy merchants funding a series of almshouses known as "**callises**" – after Calais, the English-occupied port through which most of them traded. Indeed, Stamford **cloth** became

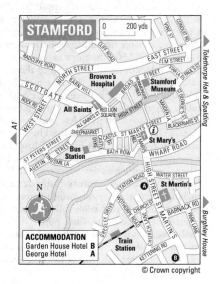

© Crown copyright

famous throughout Europe for its quality and durability, a reputation confirmed when Cardinal Wolsey used it for the tents of the "Field of the Cloth of Gold", the grand conference between Henry VIII and Francis I of France held outside Calais in 1520. Stamford was also the home of William Cecil, Elizabeth I's chief minister, who built his splendid mansion, **Burghley House**, close by. The town survived the collapse of the wool trade, prospering as an inland port after the Welland was made navigable to the sea in 1570, and, in the eighteenth century, as a staging point on the Great North Road from London. More recently, Stamford escaped the three main threats to old English towns – the Industrial Revolution, wartime bombing and postwar development – and was designated the country's first Conservation Area in 1967. Thanks to this, its unspoilt streets readily lend themselves to period drama- and film-making.

The Town

Above all, it's the harmony of Stamford's architecture that pleases, rather than any specific sight. There are, nevertheless, a handful of buildings of some special interest amongst the web of narrow streets that make up the town's compact centre.

Around the centre

Start your exploration at the church of **St Mary** (no regular opening hours), set beside a pristine close of proud Georgian buildings just above the main bridge on St Mary's Place. The church, with its splendid spire, has a small, airy interior, which incorporates the Corpus Christi chapel, whose intricately embossed, painted and panelled roof dates from the 1480s.

Across the street from St Mary's, several lanes thread up to the carefully preserved **High Street**, from where Ironmonger Street leads north again to the wide and handsome **Broad Street**, the site of the **Stamford Museum** (Mon–Sat 10am–5pm, April–Sept also Sun 2–5pm; free). This features a tasteless exhibit comparing the American midget Tom Thumb with **Daniel Lambert**, the Leicester fat man who died at Stamford in 1809, aged 39 and weighing 52st 11lb (336kg). After Lambert's death his clothes were displayed in a local inn, which Tom Thumb, otherwise Charles Stratton, visited several times to perform a few party tricks, such as standing in Lambert's waistcoat armhole.

Nearby, also on Broad Street, is **Browne's Hospital** (June–Sept Sat & Sun 11am–4pm; £2.50), the most extensive of the town's almshouses, dating from the late fifteenth century. Not all of the complex is open to the public, but it's still worth visiting with the first room – the old dormitory – capped by a splendid wood-panelled ceiling. The adjacent chapel holds some delightfully folksy misericords and upstairs, the audit room is illuminated by a handsome set of stained-glass windows. Here also is a small feature on one of the inmates, a certain George Spencer, who lived here from 1945 until his death in 1963. After his demise, Spencer was found to have stuffed a cake tin with his savings – enough to refurbish a goodly slice of the hospital.

From Browne's, it's a few paces more to Red Lion Square, which is overlooked by the church of **All Saints** (daily dawn–dusk; free). Several centuries in the making, this is a happy amalgamation of Early English and Perpendicular features and one that takes full advantage of its position, perched on a small hillock. Entry is via the south porch, itself an ornate structure with a fine – if badly weathered – crocketed gable, and, although much of the interior is routinely Victorian, the carved capitals are of great delicacy. There's also an engaging folkloric carving of the Last Supper behind the high altar.

High Street St Martin's

Down the slope from St Mary's, across the reedy River Welland on **High Street St Martin's**, is the **George Hotel**, a splendid old coaching inn whose Georgian facade supports one end of the gallows that span the street – not a warning to criminals, but a traditional advertising hoarding. Along – and across – the street, the plain and sombre, late-fifteenth-century church of **St Martin** (daily 9.30am–4pm; free) shelters the magnificent tombs of the lords Burghley, with a recumbent William Cecil carved beneath twin canopies, holding his rod of office and with a lion at his feet. Just behind, the early eighteenth-century effigies of John Cecil and his wife show the couple as Roman aristocrats, propped up on their elbows, she to gaze at him, John to stare across the nave commandingly.

Burghley House

Burghley House (late March to late Oct daily except Fri 11am–5pm, last admission 4.30pm; £10.40, including grounds; Ⓦ www.burghley.co.uk), an extravagant Elizabethan mansion standing in parkland landscaped by Capability Brown, is located a mile and a half or so to the east of Stamford, either out along the Barnack Road or by footpath from High Street St Martin's. Completed in 1587 after 22 years' work, the house sports a mellow-yellow ragstone exterior, embellished by dainty cupolas, a pyramidal clocktower and skeletal balustrading, all to a plan by **William Cecil**, the long-serving adviser to Elizabeth I. A shrewd and cautious man, Cecil steered his queen through all sorts of difficulties, from the wars against Spain to the execution of Mary, Queen of Scots, vindicating Elizabeth's assessment of his character when she appointed him secretary of state in 1558: "You will not be corrupted with any manner of gifts, and will be faithful to the state."

With the notable exception of the Tudor kitchen, little remains of Burghley's Elizabethan interior. Instead, the house bears the heavy hand of John, fifth Lord Burghley, who toured France and Italy in the late seventeenth century, commissioning furniture, statuary and tapestries, as well as buying up old Florentine and Venetian paintings, such as Paolo Veronese's *Zebedee's Wife Petitioning our Lord*. To provide a suitable setting for his old masters, John brought in Antonio Verrio and his assistant Louis Laguerre, who between them covered many of Burghley's walls and ceilings with frolicking gods and goddesses. These gaudy and gargantuan murals are at their most engulfing in the **Heaven Room**, an artfully painted classical temple that adjoins the **Hell Staircase**, where the entrance to the inferno is through the gaping mouth of a cat.

Practicalities

From Stamford **train station, which has** frequent services from Cambridge, Leicester and Oakham, it's a five-minute walk north to the town centre, on the other side of the River Welland. The **bus station** is in the centre, on the north side of the river, on Sheepmarket, off All Saints' Street. The **tourist office** is also bang in the centre, in the Stamford Arts Centre at 27 St Mary's St (Mon–Sat 9.30am–5pm, April–Oct also Sun 10.30am–4pm; ☎01780/755611, Ⓦ www .southwestlincs.com). They have a full list of local accommodation, including a battery of **B&Bs** (❷), though most of these are on the outskirts of town. Stamford has several charming **hotels**, the most celebrated of which is the ⚔ *George Hotel*, 71 High St St Martin's (☎01780/750750, Ⓦ www .georgehotelofstamford.com; ❼), an intelligently refurbished coaching inn with flagstone floors and antique furnishings, whose most appealing rooms overlook a cobbled courtyard. Further up the street, the attractive *Garden House Hotel* (☎01780/763359, ⓦwww.gardenhousehotel.com; ⑥) occupies a tastefully modernized eighteenth-century building with twenty smart bedrooms.

For food, it has to be the *George Hotel* – either in the smart and polished **restaurant**, where the emphasis is on British ingredients served in imaginative ways (main courses from around £13), or in the moderately priced and informal *Garden Lounge*. The *York Bar* serves inexpensive and delicious bar food, but only at lunchtimes (closed Sun).

In summer (June–Aug), Tolethorpe Hall, a graceful Elizabethan mansion not far from town, hosts the **Stamford Shakespeare Company**'s open-air performances (☎01780/756133, ⓦwww.stamfordshakespeare.co.uk); the audience is protected from the elements by a vast marquee.

Travel details

Buses

For information on all local and national bus services, contact Traveline ☎0871/200 2233, ⓦwww.traveline.org.uk.

Leicester to: Lincoln (hourly; 1hr 40min); Northampton (hourly; 1hr); Nottingham (every 30min; 1hr 40min); Oakham (hourly; 1hr 10min); Stamford (hourly; 2hr).

Lincoln to: Boston (hourly; 1hr 30min); Leicester (hourly; 1hr 30min); Louth (every 1–2hr; 40min); Northampton (hourly; 3hr); Nottingham (hourly; 2hr 30min); Oakham (hourly; 2hr 20min); Skegness (hourly; 1hr 45min).

Northampton to: Leicester (hourly; 1hr); Lincoln (hourly; 3hr); Nottingham (hourly; 2hr); Oundle (every 1–2hr; 2hr); Stamford (hourly; 2hr 30min–2hr 50min).

Nottingham to: Leicester (every 30min; 1hr 40min); Lincoln (hourly; 2hr 30min); Newark (hourly; 30min); Northampton (hourly; 2hr).

Oakham to: Leicester (hourly; 1hr 10min); Lincoln (hourly; 2hr 20min); Nottingham (every 1–2hr; 1hr 30min); Stamford (every 30min; 20min).

Stamford to: Leicester (hourly; 2hr); Northampton (hourly; 2hr 30min–2hr 50min); Oakham (every 30min; 20min).

Trains

For information on all local and national rail services, contact National Rail Enquiries ☎08457/484950, ⓦwww.nationalrail.co.uk.

Leicester to: Birmingham (every 30min; 1hr); Lincoln (hourly; 1hr 40min); London St Pancras (every 30min; 1hr 30min); Melton Mowbray (hourly; 15min); Nottingham (every 30min; 20min); Oakham (hourly; 30min); Stamford (hourly; 50min).

Lincoln to: Boston (hourly; 1hr); Cambridge (hourly; 1hr); Heckington (every 2hr; 1hr); Leicester (hourly; 1hr 40min); London (hourly; 2hr 15min); Newark (hourly; 25min); Nottingham (hourly; 45min); Peterborough (hourly; 1hr 20min); Skegness (hourly; 1hr 40min).

Northampton to: Birmingham (every 30min; 1hr); London Euston (every 30min; 1hr 10min–1hr 40min).

Nottingham to: Birmingham (2–3 hourly; 1hr 20min); Leicester (every 30min; 20min); Lincoln (hourly; 1hr 15min); London St Pancras (hourly; 1hr 40min); Newark (hourly; 30min); Oakham (hourly, change in Leicester; 1hr).

Stamford to: Cambridge (hourly; 1hr 20min); Leicester (hourly; 40min); Oakham (hourly; 10min); Peterborough (hourly; 15min).

10

The Northwest

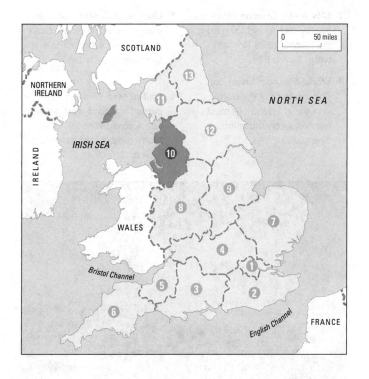

CHAPTER 10

Highlights

✳ **Imperial War Museum North, Manchester** A startlingly modern exploration of the reasons for, and effects of, war. See p.674

✳ **Café society, Manchester** Legendary café-bars set the tone for England's second city. See p.676

✳ **City walls, Chester** Survey the handsome old town from the heights of its Roman walls. See p.684

✳ **World Museum Liverpool** The wonders of the world, on view at Liverpool's most family-friendly museum. See p.692

✳ **Blackpool Tower** Blackpool's bold answer to the Eiffel Tower lights up the skyline of the UK's favourite resort. See p.702

✳ **National Football Museum, Preston** For armchair fans and fanatics alike – England's national game laid bare. See p.703

✳ **Lancaster Castle** From the dungeons to the ornate court rooms, the castle tour is a historical tour-de-force. See p.705

✳ **Calf of Man** Weather permitting, don't miss a boat ride across to the Isle of Man's remote bird sanctuary. See p.719

▲ Blackpool

The Northwest

Within the **northwest** of England lie some of the ugliest and some of the most beautiful parts of the country. The least attractive zones are to be found in the urban sprawl that engulfs the country's third and sixth largest conurbations, Manchester and Liverpool, but even here the picture isn't unrelievedly bleak, as the cities themselves have an ingratiating appeal. **Manchester**, in particular, surprises many first-time visitors, who don't expect to see much beyond a dour ("satanic") industrial cityscape. Where once only a handful of Victorian Gothic buildings lent any grace to the city, Manchester today has been transformed by a rebuilding programme that puts it in the vanguard of modern British urban design. Quite apart from a clutch of top-class visitor attractions – including The Lowry and the Imperial War Museum North – where Manchester really scores is in the buzz of its thriving café and club scene, which places it at the leading edge of the country's youth culture. **Liverpool**, set on the Mersey estuary, is perhaps less appealing at first glance, though its revitalized dockside, Georgian town houses, grand civic buildings and museums, and burgeoning café and restaurant scene soon change perceptions. Long-overdue redevelopment is also transforming the very fabric of the city, a process kick-started by the city's role as European Capital of Culture in 2008.

The southern suburbs of Manchester bump up into the steep hills of the Pennine range, but to the southwest the city slides into undulating, pastoral

Getting around

Manchester's international **airport** picks the city out as a major UK point of arrival, and there are direct train services from the airport to Liverpool, Blackpool, Lancaster, Leeds and York, as well as to Manchester itself. Both Manchester and Liverpool are well served by **trains**, with plentiful connections to the Midlands and London, and up the west coast to Scotland. There's also a frequent rail and bus service between both cities, and from each to Chester, allowing an easy triangular loop between Greater Manchester, Merseyside and Cheshire. The major east–west rail lines in the region are the direct routes between Manchester, Leeds and York, and between Blackpool, Bradford, Leeds and York. In addition, the Morecambe/Lancaster–Leeds line slips through the Yorkshire Dales (with possible connections at Skipton for the famous Settle–Carlisle line; see p.798); further south, the Manchester–Sheffield line provides a rail approach to the Peak District. Regional **rover tickets** are available for unlimited travel between Liverpool, Manchester, the Peak District, Lancashire and Cumbria – the validity varies from pass to pass (consult ⓦ www.nationalrail.co.uk) but flexi-tickets (4 days travel in 8) start at £52.

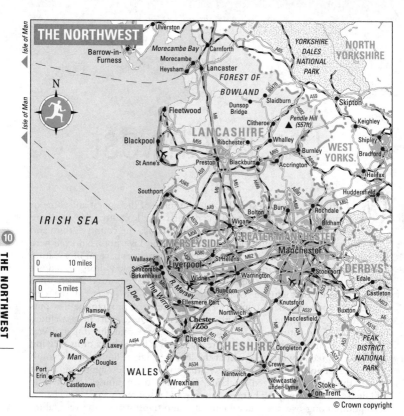

© Crown copyright

Cheshire, a county of rolling green countryside, whose dairy farms churn out the crumbly-white Cheshire cheese. The county town, **Chester**, with its complete circuit of town walls and partly Tudor centre, is as alluring as any of the country's northern towns, capturing the essence of what has always been one of England's wealthiest counties.

Lancashire, which historically lay directly to the north of Cheshire, reached industrial prominence in the nineteenth century primarily due to the cotton-mill towns around Manchester and to the thriving port of Liverpool. Today, neither of those cities is part of the county, and Lancashire's oldest town, and major commercial and administrative centre, is **Preston** – home of the national museum of England's favourite game, football – though tourists are perhaps more inclined to linger in the charming towns and villages of the nearby **Ribble Valley**. Meanwhile, along the coast to the west and north of the major cities stretches a line of **resorts** – from Southport to **Morecambe** – which once formed the mainstay of the northern British holiday trade before their client base disappeared on cheaper, sunnier holidays to Florida and the Mediterranean. Only **Blackpool** is really worth visiting for its own sake, a rip-roaring resort which has stayed at the top of its game by supplying undemanding entertainment with more panache than its neighbours. For anything more culturally invigorating you'll have to continue north to the historically important city of **Lancaster**, with its Tudor castle. Finally, the semi-autonomous **Isle of Man**, only 25 miles off the coast and served by ferries from Liverpool and Heysham (or short flights from various regional airports), provides a terrain almost as rewarding as that of the Lake District but without the seasonal overcrowding.

Manchester

Few cities in the world have embraced social change so heartily as **MANCHESTER**. From engine of the Industrial Revolution to test-bed of contemporary urban design, the city has no realistic English rival outside of London. Its pre-eminence expresses itself in various ways, most swaggeringly in the success of Manchester United, the richest football club in the world, but also in a thriving music and cultural scene that has given birth to world-beaters as diverse as the Hallé Orchestra and Oasis. Moreover, the city's cutting-edge concert halls, theatres, clubs and café society are boosted by one of England's largest student populations and a blooming gay community, whose spending power has created a pioneering **Gay Village**. For inspiration, Manchester's planners look to Barcelona – another revitalized industrial powerhouse – and scoff at many local rivals.

Specific attractions may be a little thin on the ground, but the city centre does possess the enjoyable **Manchester Art Gallery** as well as the extensive **Museum of Science and Industry**, which is itself next door to the canal footpaths of the creatively revamped **Castlefield** district. Further out, there's another good art gallery – the **Whitworth** – to the south of the city centre, and to the west, on the **Salford Quays**, there are two more prestigious sights, The **Lowry** arts centre, complete with a handsome selection of L.S. Lowry paintings, and the stirring and stunning **Imperial War Museum North**.

Some history

Despite a **history** stretching back to Roman times, and pockets of surviving medieval and Georgian architecture, Manchester is first and foremost a **Victorian manufacturing city** with imposing warehouses and towering office buildings to match. Its rapid growth was the equal of any flowering of the Industrial Revolution anywhere – from little more than a village in 1750 to the world's major cotton centre in only a hundred years. The spectacular rise of **Cottonopolis**, as it became known, came from the manufacture of vast quantities of competitively priced imitations of expensive Indian calicoes, using water and then steam-driven machines developed in the late eighteenth and nineteenth centuries. The statistics are daunting: in 1751 one thousand tons of raw cotton was imported into Manchester, 45,000 by the time of the Battle of Waterloo and no less than a billion tons when the industry peaked in 1914; the population grew to match and spread across the Lancashire hinterland as production was concentrated in peripheral towns like Bolton and Oldham, while Manchester itself focused on warehousing and distribution. This staggeringly rapid industrialization brought immense wealth for a few but a life of misery for the majority. The discontent this engendered amongst the working class came to a head in 1819 when eleven people were killed at **Peterloo**, in what began as a peaceful demonstration against the oppressive **Corn Laws**, which kept the price of barley, wheat, oats and rye at artificially high levels in deference to the interests of the landed aristocracy. Things were, however, even worse when the 23-year-old **Friedrich Engels** came here in 1842 to work in

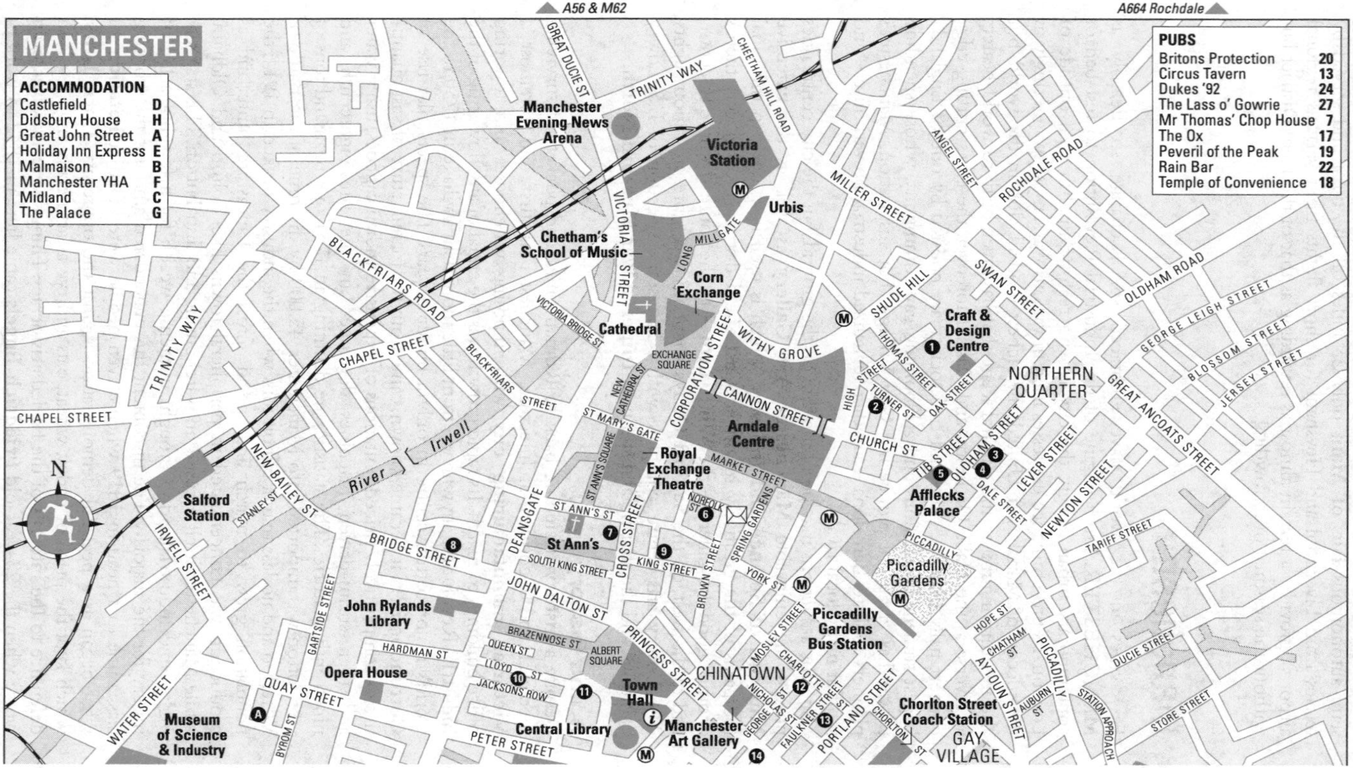
A56 & M62
A664 Rochdale
MANCHESTER
ACCOMMODATION
Castlefield D
Didsbury House H
Great John Street A
Holiday Inn Express E
Malmaison B
Manchester YHA F
Midland C
The Palace G
PUBS
Britons Protection 20
Circus Tavern 13
Dukes '92 24
The Lass o' Gowrie 27
Mr Thomas' Chop House 7
The Ox 17
Peveril of the Peak 19
Rain Bar 22
Temple of Convenience 18
N
Manchester Evening News Arena
Victoria Station
Urbis
Chetham's School of Music
Corn Exchange
Cathedral
Craft & Design Centre
NORTHERN QUARTER
Arndale Centre
Royal Exchange Theatre
Afflecks Palace
Salford Station
St Ann's
Piccadilly Gardens
Piccadilly Gardens Bus Station
John Rylands Library
Opera House
Town Hall
CHINATOWN
Chorlton Street Coach Station
GAY VILLAGE
Central Library
Manchester Art Gallery
Museum of Science & Industry
River Irwell
GREAT DUCIE ST
TRINITY WAY
CHEETHAM HILL ROAD
ANGEL STREET
ROCHDALE ROAD
MILLER STREET
VICTORIA STREET
MILLGATE
LONG MILLGATE
SHUDE HILL
SWAN STREET
OLDHAM ROAD
GEORGE LEIGH STREET
BLOSSOM STREET
JERSEY STREET
GREAT ANCOATS STREET
BLACKFRIARS ROAD
VICTORIA BRIDGE ST
CHAPEL STREET
BLACKFRIARS STREET
EXCHANGE SQUARE
NEW CATHEDRAL ST
CORPORATION STREET
WITHY GROVE
THOMAS STREET
HIGH STREET
TURNER ST
OAK STREET
CANNON STREET
CHURCH ST
TIB STREET
OLDHAM STREET
LEVER STREET
DALE STREET
NEWTON STREET
TARIFF STREET
ST MARY'S GATE
MARKET STREET
ST ANN'S SQUARE
ST ANN'S ST
NORFOLK ST
SPRING GARDENS
NEW BAILEY ST
STANLEY ST
DEANSGATE
CROSS STREET
BRIDGE STREET
SOUTH KING STREET
KING STREET
BROWN STREET
YORK ST
PICCADILLY
IRWELL STREET
JOHN DALTON ST
GARTSIDE STREET
BRAZENNOSE ST
HARDMAN ST
QUEEN ST
ALBERT SQUARE
LLOYD ST
JACKSONS ROW
PRINCESS STREET
MOSLEY STREET
CHARLOTTE ST
NICHOLAS ST
GEORGE ST
FAULKNER STREET
PORTLAND STREET
CHORLTON ST
HOPE ST
CHATHAM ST
AYTOUN STREET
AUBURN ST
DUCIE STREET
STATION APPROACH
STORE STREET
QUAY STREET
BYROM ST
WATER STREET
PETER STREET

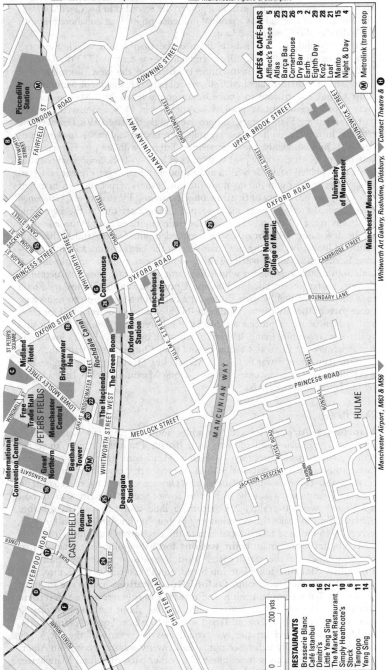

663

© Crown copyright

CAFÉS & CAFÉ-BARS
Affleck's Palace	5
Atlas	25
Barça Bar	23
Cornerhouse	26
Dry Bar	3
Earth	2
Eighth Day	29
Kro2	28
Loaf	21
Manto	15
Night & Day	4

Ⓜ Metrolink (tram) stop

RESTAURANTS
Brasserie Blanc	9
Café Istanbul	8
Dimitri's	16
Little Yang Sing	12
The Market Restaurant	1
Simply Heathcote's	10
Stock	6
Tampopo	11
Yang Sing	14

0   200 yds

▲ A635 Ashton-under-Lyme

▲ Manchester Apollo & Stockport

Whitworth Art Gallery, Rusholme, Didsbury, ▼ Contact Theatre & Ⓗ

Manchester Airport, M63 & M56 ▼

Old Trafford, A56 & Chester ▼

▲ Salford Quays

Ⓔ & Chester

Ⓔ PIDMO WHARF

his father's cotton plant: the grinding poverty he recorded in his *Condition of the Working Class in England* was a seminal influence on his later collaboration with Karl Marx in the *Communist Manifesto*.

Waterways and railway viaducts formed the matrix into which the city's principal buildings were and still are embedded – as early as 1772 the Duke of Bridgewater had a canal cut to connect the city to the west Lancashire coal mines, and in 1830 the Manchester–Liverpool railway opened. The **Manchester Ship Canal**, constructed to entice ocean-going vessels into Manchester and away from burgeoning Liverpool, was completed in 1894, and played a crucial part in sustaining Manchester's competitiveness. By the late 1950s, however, the city was in trouble, with the docks, mills, warehouses and canals in dangerous decline. Quite suddenly, the city seemed littered with empty factories and warehouses, all set cheek by jowl with rows of back-to-back houses, whose slate roofs and cobbled back alleys glistened in the seemingly ever-present rain – an image of gritty hardship and no-nonsense northerners perpetuated, to an extent at least, by the popularity of Britain's longest-running TV soap opera, *Coronation Street*. Sporadic efforts were made to pull Manchester out of the economic doldrums in the 1960s and 1970s, but the main engine of change turned out to be the devastating **IRA bomb**, which exploded outside the Arndale shopping centre in June 1996, wiping out a fair slice of the city's commercial infrastructure. Rather than simply patching things up, the city council embarked on an ambitious rebuilding scheme, which also came to embrace the construction of the various facilities needed to host the **Commonwealth Games**, held here in 2002. Emboldened by their success, the council have gone on to rejuvenate other parts of the city centre, with once-blighted areas now reclaimed for retail and residential use, a process assisted by the burgeoning fashion for loft and apartment city-centre living. It's very much work in progress, but it's impossible not to admire the drive and vision behind it all. Only one blot stains the city's modern reputation: it was in Greater Manchester, Stockport to be precise, that a certain Roy Brooke invented the Sing-along Machine in 1975, later adapted by the Japanese into Karaoke.

Arrival

Manchester Airport, located ten miles south of the city centre, is an increasingly popular point of entry into Britain. From the airport, there are trains (daily 6am–11pm every 10–15min; 11pm–6am every 30min to 1hr) direct to Manchester's principal station, Manchester Piccadilly; some of these services also continue onto Manchester's Deansgate and Oxford Road train stations. Train tickets from the airport to any of these three city stations cost £2.80 one way off-peak, £2.90 return, a little more on weekdays before 9.30am. You can make the same journey by bus (Skyline/Stagecoach bus #43; every 10–15min) and taxi; the taxi fare to the city centre is around £18.

Manchester's three main **train stations** form the points of a triangle that encloses much of the city centre. Most long-distance services pull into **Piccadilly Station**, facing London Road, on the east side of the centre, with some services continuing onto **Oxford Road Station**, just to the south of the centre. Trains from Lancashire and Yorkshire mostly terminate at **Victoria Station** on the north side of the centre. It takes about ten minutes to walk from either Victoria or Oxford Road stations to Albert Square, plumb in the middle of town, and on the way you'll pass by several of the city's key attractions; Piccadilly is further out, a dull twenty-minute hoof from Albert Square. All three stations are connected to other parts of central Manchester via the **Metroshuttle** free bus service; Piccadilly and Victoria are also on the **Metrolink** tram line.

Most long-distance **buses** use **Chorlton Street Coach Station**, about halfway between Piccadilly train station and Albert Square, though some regional buses drop passengers in nearby **Piccadilly Gardens** instead.

Information

The **Manchester Visitor Information Centre** is in the back of the Town Hall, bang in the centre of town on St Peter's Square (Mon–Sat 10am–5.30pm, Sun 10.30am–4.30pm; ☏0871/222 8223, ⓦwww.visitmanchester.com). They supply a free pocket map of the city centre and a free short-breaks city guide as well as various other useful leaflets and brochures. You can also buy National Express bus tickets, check rail timetables, and book guided tours. They reserve accommodation, too, and are often knowledgeable about special deals and discounts; for more on accommodation, see p.666.

To find out **what's on** in the city, check out the *Manchester Evening News* or consult their website, ⓦwww.manchestereveningnews.co.uk.

City transport

About thirty minutes' walk from top to bottom, central Manchester is compact enough to cover on **foot**, though most visitors take to the bus as soon as it starts raining. The **Metroshuttle** free bus service weaves its way across central Manchester on three routes: Service 1 (Mon–Sat 7am–7pm, Sun 10am–6pm) runs east–west linking Piccadilly Station with Piccadilly Gardens, the Royal Exchange and Deansgate; Service 2 (same times) travels north–south between Victoria and Oxford Road train stations via Deansgate, Princess and Whitworth streets; and Service 3 (Mon–Sat 7am–7pm) links Piccadilly Station with Oxford Street, Peter Street and ultimately Salford Central Station. Metroshuttle buses run every five to ten minutes.

There is also the **Metrolink** tram network (ⓦwww.metrolink.co.uk), which whisks through the city centre bound for the suburbs. There are two routes: one links central Manchester with Bury in the north and Altrincham in the south, the other travels west to Eccles via Salford Quays, the location of the Imperial War Museum North (see p.674). Metrolink has **eight city-centre stops**, the most useful of which are at Piccadilly Station, Piccadilly Gardens, St Peter's Square, Market Street and Victoria Station; note that the Manchester Central convention centre stop is extraordinarily difficult to find – it's amongst the tangle of elevated rail lines to the rear of the complex. Metrolink trams run every five to fifteen minutes daily from 6am (Sun 7am) to midnight (Sun 10.30pm). **Tickets** must be purchased from the automatic machines at Metrolink stops before the start of a journey; prices are reasonable with short hops costing about 60p and the return fare from central Manchester to Salford

---

Guided walks

Manchester's blue-badge guides offer a varied, year-round programme of **guided walks** (2hr; £5), covering everything from pop music and pubs to Peterloo and Cottonopolis heritage tours. Advance bookings are advised either in person at the Visitor Centre in St Peter's Square (☏0871/222 8223, ⓦwww.visitmanchester.com). There are usually two or three walks a week. Note, however, that at time of writing Manchester's *Coronation Street* film set is not open for tours.

Quays, for example, being £1.90 at the weekend and in the evening, £2.70 at peak times.

Accommodation

In the last few years, there's been a boom in the number of city-centre **hotels**, particularly among the budget chains, which means you have a good chance of finding a smart, albeit formulaic, en-suite room in central Manchester for around £60–70 at almost any time of the year – except when Manchester United are playing at home, when hotel prices can rocket into the stratosphere. Otherwise, hotel prices tend to be higher during the week than at the weekend. Manchester's **youth hostel** occupies a prime central location in Castlefield – book well in advance. There is rarely any pressing need to use the Visitor Centre's **accommodation booking service**, but they can often get good rates and know of the best deals.

Hotels

Castlefield Liverpool Rd ☏0161/832 7073, ⓦwww.castlefield-hotel.co.uk. Large, very modern, red-brick, warehouse-style hotel handily located near the foot of Deansgate in Castlefield, opposite the Science and Industry Museum. Nicely appointed rooms, and attached leisure club and pool (free to guests). ❼

Didsbury House Didsbury Park, Didsbury Village ☏0161/448 2200, ⓦwww.didsburyhouse.co.uk. Located about four miles south of the centre in well-heeled Didsbury village – buses into the centre are fast and frequent – this is a slick and stylish conversion of Victorian premises with 27 immaculate/verging-on-minimalist guest rooms. Great breakfasts too. Privately owned. ❼

Great John Street Great John St ☏0161/831 3211, ⓦwww.greatjohnst.co.uk. Deluxe hotel in an imaginatively refurbished old school building not far off Deansgate. Holds thirty individually designed, spacious and comfortable suites, some split-level with nifty scholastic names – "Headmaster's Office" and so forth. At the heart of the hotel is a bar-cum-restaurant, equipped with an open fire and wide sofas, and the gallery breakfast room is up above. Rooftop garden too. Substantial discounts are legion, but the rack-rate is ❾

Holiday Inn Express Waterfront Quays, Salford Quays ☏0161/868 1000 or 0870/400 9670, ⓦwww.hiexpress.co.uk. Reasonably large rooms in a great quay location, but in a standard-issue modern tower block. Convenient for The Lowry and even Old Trafford. Take the Metrolink tram to the Salford Quays tram stop. ❺

Malmaison 12 Gore St, Piccadilly ☏0161/278 1000, ⓦwww.malmaison-manchester.com. A couple of minutes' walk from Piccadilly Station, the ornate Edwardian facade of this handsome hotel hides the Malmaison group's trademark sleek interior lines and contemporary design. There's a gym, sauna, bar and brasserie, plus substantial weekend discounts depending on availability. ❼

Midland Peter St ☏0161/236 3333, ⓦwww.qhotels.co.uk. Once the terminus hotel for Central Station (now the Manchester Central convention centre) and the place where Rolls met Royce for the first time, this building was the apotheosis of Edwardian style. A recent refit has returned the public areas to much of their former glory and the bedrooms up above are in immaculate chain style. A full raft of leisure facilities too. ❼

The Palace Oxford Rd ☏0161/288 1111, ⓦwww.principal-hotels.com. Occupying one of the city's grandest Victorian buildings, a terracotta-clad extravagance built to a design by Alfred Waterhouse as the Refuge Assurance HQ in 1891, *The Palace* is part of a small chain of deluxe English hotels. The public rooms have all the stately grandeur you might expect, the foyer coming complete with ersatz Roman pillars and columns. Great location too, opposite the Cornerhouse arts centre. Has 250 plush rooms and suites. From ❻

Hostel

Manchester YHA Potato Wharf, Castlefield ☏0161/839 9960, ⓦwww.yhamanchester.org.uk. Excellent hostel overlooking the canal that runs close to the Museum of Science and Industry. There are 34 rooms in total (thirty four-bunk and four six-bunk rooms) and all of them are en-suite. Facilities include Internet access, laundry, self-catering and a café. You can pay a little extra to use one of the four-bunk rooms as a double. Dorm beds £20.50, doubles ❷

The city centre

If Manchester can be said to have a centre, it's **Albert Square** and the cluster of buildings surrounding it – the Town Hall, the Central Library and the *Midland Hotel*, originally built in the railway age to host visitors to Britain's greatest industrial city. South of here, the former Central Station now functions as **Manchester Central** convention centre, with the Hallé Orchestra's home, **Bridgewater Hall**, just opposite. **Chinatown** and the **Gay Village** are just a short walk to the east, while to the northeast, the revamped **Piccadilly Gardens** provides access to the so-called **Northern Quarter**, the funkiest of the regenerated inner-city areas. To the southwest is the **Castlefield** district, site of the **Museum of Science and Industry**. The central spine of the city is **Deansgate**, which runs from Castlefield to the cathedral and, in its northern environs, displays the most dramatic core of urban regeneration in the country, centred on the unalloyed modernity of **Exchange Square**.

Albert Square

Until recently at least, Manchester's only real claim to architectural merit was its panoply of **Neo-Gothic** buildings and monuments, most of which date from the city's salad days in the second half of the nineteenth century. One of the more fanciful is the shrine-like, canopied **monument** to Prince Albert, Queen Victoria's husband, perched prettily in the middle of the trim little square that bears his name – **Albert Square**. The monument was erected in 1867, six years after Albert's death, supposedly because the prince had always shown an interest in industry, but perhaps more to curry favour with the grieving queen. Overlooking the prince is Alfred Waterhouse's magnificent, Neo-Gothic **Town Hall** (Mon–Fri 9am–5pm; free), whose mighty clocktower, completed in 1877, pokes a sturdy finger into the sky, soaring high above its complementary gables, columns and arcaded windows. The interior is similarly imposing with its echoing stone-vaulted corridors arching above acres of mosaic, much of which sport appropriate motifs – industrious bees, cotton flowers and so forth. Be sure also to pop inside the first-floor Great Hall, which boasts stylish iron candelabras, stained-glass windows, a double hammer-beam roof and wall paintings by Ford Madox Brown, depicting decisive moments in Manchester's history.

St Peter's Square and around

Just to the south of the Town Hall, facing **St Peter's Square**, the circular **Central Library** (Mon–Thurs 10am–8pm, Fri & Sat 9am–5pm) was built in 1934 as the largest municipal library in the world, a self-consciously elegant, classical construction with a domed reading room. The library is an impressive sight, but Lutyens' mournful **Cenotaph**, in the middle of St Peter's Square, now passes virtually unnoticed amid the swooshing trams.

Footsteps away, over on Peter Street, the grandiose **Midland Hotel** of 1903 is distinguished by the intricacies of its exterior tilework, all fancily fronded and fluted and incorporating a set of heraldic lions. The hotel's earlier visitors ventured out for an evening's entertainment to the **Free Trade Hall**, a few yards to the west along Peter Street and the home of the city's Hallé Orchestra for over a century (until Bridgewater Hall was completed in 1996). The Italianate facade of the Free Trade Hall amazingly survived intense wartime bombing and is now a protected part of the *Radisson Edwardian Hotel*, whose modern tower block rises up behind at a (fairly) discrete distance. The Free Trade Hall was originally built on St Peter's Fields,

Agitation for social and parliamentary reform in the early nineteenth century was concentrated in Britain's booming industrial cities, led by radical orators, among them **Henry Hunt**, who addressed massed rallies of working men and women the length and breadth of the country. Such a meeting was planned for **St Peter's Fields** in Manchester for August 16, 1819, with Hunt as main speaker, and though rumours spread throughout the city about the possibility of trouble, the local magistrates seemed content to let the rally take place. Indeed, in the weeks before the event, many local people practised marching in orderly file so as to look respectable on the day – and on the day itself, a crowd of almost 80,000 turned up in its Sunday best, with women and children much in evidence, hardly the revolutionary rabble feared by reactionaries. But as Hunt began to speak the magistrates had a change of heart, sending in their special constables (mostly recruited from the ranks of local businessmen) to arrest him. As pandemonium erupted, Hunt gave himself up to avoid further trouble, but with the special constables now under siege from the crowd, the cavalry were sent in.

Panic broke out as people tried to escape from the swords of the mounted soldiers, who cleared the fields in ten minutes in what the press speedily dubbed "**Peterloo**". Over 400 people were wounded, over a hundred by sword cuts, the rest by the stampeding crowd, and the final reckoning saw eleven dead, including two women and one child. Home Secretary Lord Sidmouth later congratulated the Manchester authorities on their handling of the situation and the government passed the draconian Six Acts, restricting the right of public meeting. Protests were widespread, even among the government's own supporters, and Peterloo became the catalyst for yet more agitation, culminating in the **1832 Reform Act** and the subsequent rise of the egalitarian Chartist movement.

the site of the "Peterloo Massacre" (see box, above). In 1974 and 1976, the **Lesser Free Trade Hall**, a smaller room upstairs from the main hall, witnessed performances from the Sex Pistols that electrified Tony Wilson and assorted musicians from the likes of the Buzzcocks and Joy Division. Only about forty people actually went to the first concert, though hundreds of Mancunians claim they did.

Manchester Art Gallery

Presiding over the northeast corner of St Peter's Square on Mosley Street is Charles Barry's porticoed **Manchester Art Gallery** (Tues–Sun 10am–5pm; free; ⓦ www.manchestergalleries.org), which displays an invigorating collection of eighteenth- and nineteenth-century art on the middle of the gallery's three floors. The paintings are, however, divided by theme – Face and Place, Expressing Passion and so on – rather than by artist (or indeed school of artists), which makes it difficult to appreciate the strength of the collection, especially when it comes to its forte, the Pre-Raphaelite Brotherhood. Pre-Raphaelite highlights include the highly charged eroticism of Rossetti's *Astarte Syrinca* (Gallery 8) and Holman Hunt's *The Light of the World* (Gallery 5), a painting of Jesus standing at the door (of the soul) that was familiar to generations of evangelical Protestants. There's much else – views of Victorian Manchester, a Turner or two, a pair of Gainsboroughs, the preposterous historicism of Alexander Wagner and last but not least Stubbs' famous *Cheetah and Stag with Two Indians*. Floor 2 features temporary exhibitions and a Gallery of Craft and Design, while the Ground Floor's Manchester Gallery is devoted to a visual history of the city.

South to Bridgewater Hall and Deansgate Locks

South of St Peter's Square, **Lower Mosley Street** runs past **Manchester Central** convention complex, the main part of which occupies what was, until 1969, a train station. Across the street from the complex rises **Bridgewater Hall**, Britain's finest concert hall, balanced on shock-absorbing springs to guarantee the clarity of the sound.

Pressing on, the apartment block at the corner of Lower Mosley Street and Whitworth Street West bears the name of the site's previous occupant, the fabulously famous – and musically seminal – **Hacienda Club**, the spiritual home of Factory Records, which opened in 1982 and finally closed in 1997. In its 1980s heyday, the club showcased live performances by an army of important bands, many from Manchester, including the likes of the Happy Mondays, Stone Roses, Oasis and The Smiths, and pioneered and popularized a new dance craze – "house"; the rest is, as they say, history. If you missed it all, go see Michael Winterbottom's 2002 movie *24 Hour Party People*. Ian Brown of the Stone Roses also did his bit for local tourism, pronouncing "Manchester has got everything except a beach."

Turn right along Whitworth Street West and you'll soon spot the string of café-bars and restaurants that have been shoehorned along the Rochdale canal's **Deansgate Locks**, a pattern repeated along and across the street in the old railway arches abutting Deansgate Station. Look up and you can't help but see the striking **Beetham Tower**, easily the tallest skyscraper in Manchester and home to a glitzy *Hilton* hotel.

Castlefield

Best approached along Castle Street, just to the west of Deansgate Station, the remarkable tangle of railway viaducts and canals that lie sandwiched between Water Street, Liverpool Road and Deansgate make up the pocket-sized district of **Castlefield**. It was here that the country's first man-made canal, the Bridgewater Canal, brought coal and other raw materials to the city's warehouses throughout the eighteenth century; the railways followed later, cementing Castlefield's once pre-eminent economic position, which only declined after World War II. By the early 1960s, the district was a real eyesore, but thereafter an influx of money allied to a fair amount of speculative vision cleaned it all up, creating Britain's first "urban heritage park" in 1982, now complete with cobbled canalside walks, an outdoor events arena, a youth hostel (see p.666) and attractive café-bars – all set in the shadows of the sterling engineering work of the Victorian viaducts.

Curiously enough, Castlefield was also where Manchester started as the **Roman fort** of Mamucium in 79 AD; the Romans abandoned their settlement in around 410 AD and the scant remains – mainly defensive ditches plus a couple of replica walls – are now on display in open ground between the Rochdale Canal and Liverpool Road.

The Museum of Science and Industry

From the remains of the Roman fort, it's a couple of hundred yards north to the extremely popular **Museum of Science and Industry**, whose several different sections spread out along Liverpool Road (daily 10am–5pm; free, but admission charge for special exhibitions; ☎0161/832 2244, ⊛www.msim.org .uk). One of the most impressive museums of its type in the country, it mixes technological displays and special blockbuster exhibitions with trenchant analysis of the social impact of industrialization. A free map of the museum is issued at the entrance, with key points of interest including the **Power Hall**, which trumpets the region's remarkable technological contribution to the Industrial Revolution by means of a hall full of steam engines, some of which are fired up daily. There's more steam just outside the Power Hall in the shape of a working replica of Robert Stephenson's *Planet*, whose original design was based on the *Rocket*, the work of Robert's father George. Built in 1830, the *Planet* reliably attained a scorching 30mph but had no brakes; the museum's version does, and uses them at weekends (noon–4pm), dropping passengers a couple of hundred yards away at the **Station Building**, the world's oldest passenger railway station. It was here that the *Rocket* arrived on a rainy September 15, 1830, after fatally injuring Liverpool MP William Huskisson at the start of the inaugural passenger journey from Liverpool.

Elsewhere, the **1830 Warehouse** features a sound-and-light show that delves into the history of the city's warehouses whose immense storage capacity was essential to Manchester's economy, whilst the **Air and Space Hall**, which barely touches on Manchester at all, features vintage planes, cutaway engines and space exploration displays.

North along Deansgate to the John Rylands Library

Deansgate cuts through the city centre from the Rochdale Canal to the cathedral (see opposite), its architectural reference points ranging from Victorian industrialism to post-millennium pouting. The first major point of interest is the former **Great Northern Railway Company's Goods Warehouse**, a great sweep of brickwork dating back to the 1890s that flanks Deansgate between Great Bridgewater and Peter streets. Now incorporated into a modern retail and leisure development called "Great Northern", the warehouse was originally an integral part of a large and ambitious trading depot with road and rail links up above and a canal way down below street level.

Continuing north along Deansgate from Peter Street, turn right down either Queen or Brazennose streets for the minute's stroll to tiny **Lincoln Square**, named after its statue of the American President. During the American Civil War, Union ships blockaded Confederate ports, cutting off the supply of cotton to Manchester and causing a surge in unemployment across northern England. Nonetheless, Manchester, which was dead-set against slavery, sent a letter of support to Lincoln, whose grateful and very moving letter of reply is quoted on the statue.

Across Deansgate, opposite Brazennose Street, is the **John Rylands Library** (Mon–Sat 10am–5pm & Sun noon–5pm; free), the city's supreme example of Victorian Gothic, though a recent refurbishment has added an unbecoming modern entrance wing to the original building. The library takes its name from John Rylands (1801–1888), an extremely wealthy textile merchant, who – despite all the gossip – married the Cuban-born Enriqueta Tennant (1843–1908), when he was 74 and she was 32. After his death, Enriqueta decided to build a library as a memorial to her husband. The architect she employed, Basil Champneys, opted for a cloistered Neo-Gothicism of narrow stone corridors, delicately crafted stonework, stained-glass windows and burnished wooden panelling, all modified by splashes of Art Nouveau – for example in the radiator grills and light fittings. The library has survived in superb condition, but it's no longer a general-purpose library, housing instead specialist collections of rare books and manuscripts.

St Ann's Square and the Royal Exchange

Slender **St Ann's Square** is tucked away off the eastern side of Deansgate, a couple of blocks up from the Rylands Library. Flanking the square's southern side is **St Ann's Church** (daily 9.45am–4.45pm), a trim sandstone structure whose Neoclassical symmetries date from 1709, though the stained-glass windows are firmly Victorian. The church is fronted by a **statue** of nineteenth-century Free Trader Richard Cobden, joint leader, with John Bright, of the Anti-Corn-Law League, which finally forced the repeal in 1846 of the oppressive Corn Laws (see p.935).

At the other end of the square is the **Royal Exchange**, which houses the much lauded **Royal Exchange Theatre**, a theatre-in-the-round whose steel-and-glass cat's cradle is plonked under the building's immense glass-vaulted roof. Formerly the Cotton Exchange, this building employed seven thousand people until trading finished on December 31, 1968 – the old trading board still shows the last day's prices for American and Egyptian cotton. Look out also for **Barton Arcade**, a stunning Victorian glass-domed shopping gallery across from the Royal Exchange that leads through from St Ann's Square to Deansgate.

Exchange Square

A pedestrian high street – **New Cathedral Street** – runs north from St Ann's Square to **Exchange Square**, which, with its water features, public sculptures and massive department stores (primarily Selfridges and Harvey Nichols), has been the focus of the ambitious city-centre rebuilding programme that followed the IRA bomb of 1996. On the southeast side of the square stands the whopping **Arndale Centre**, once a real Sixties' eyesore, but now modernized and clad in glass.

Exchange Square may be overloaded with modern shops and stores, but in contrast its western corner – straight ahead from New Cathedral Street – abuts two old half-timbered **pubs**, the *Old Wellington Inn* and *Sinclair's Oyster Bar*, both were carefully moved to this new location in the 1990s.

Manchester Cathedral and Chetham's School of Music

Manchester Cathedral (Mon–Sat 10am–4.30pm, plus May–Sept Sun 11.30am–4pm; free), standing just beyond Exchange Square from the end of New Cathedral Street, dates back to the fifteenth century, though in truth its Gothic lines have been hacked about too much to have any real architectural coherence. Actually, it's surprising it's still here at all: in 1940, a 1000lb bomb all but destroyed the interior, knocking out most of the stained glass, which is why it's so light inside today.

The cathedral's choristers are trained in **Chetham's School of Music** (℡0161/834 7961, ⓦwww.chethams.org.uk), on the far side of the cathedral on Long Millgate. This fifteenth-century manor house became a school and a free public library in 1653 and was subsequently turned into a music school in 1969. There are free recitals during term time and, although there's no public access to most of the complex, you can visit the oak-panelled **Library** (Mon–Fri 9am–12.30pm & 1.30–4.30pm; free), with its handsome carved eighteenth-century bookcases. Along the side corridor is the main **Reading Room**, where Marx and Engels beavered away on the square table that still stands in the windowed alcove.

Urbis and Victoria Train Station

Directly opposite Chetham's – you can hardly miss it – is the six-storey glasswork of **Urbis** (Mon–Wed & Sun 10am–6pm, Thurs–Sat 10am–8pm; free except for special exhibitions; ⓦwww.urbis.org.uk), a huge and distinctive sloping structure completed in 2002 as a museum and exhibition centre.

The emphasis here is very much on urban life and modern culture – from punk through to graffiti and beyond. Manchester, as the world's first industrial city, is given due prominence.

Behind Urbis, down the slope, is **Victoria Station**, the most likeable of the city's several stations with its long, gently curving stone facade. Pop inside for a look at the Art Deco ticket booths and the immaculate tiled map of the Lancashire and Yorkshire Railway network as it was in the 1920s.

To Piccadilly Gardens and the Northern Quarter

For years, the bleak expanse of **Piccadilly Gardens**, to the east of the Arndale Centre and about ten minutes' walk from Victoria Station, interrupted the architectural flow of the city centre, but a recent beautification project has dramatically enhanced its character. Japanese architects have restyled the area, adding trees, a fountain and water jets, and a pavilion at one end to screen off the traffic. The gardens remain a major local transport hub and gateway to the still shabby but improving **Oldham Street**, which has been adopted by "alternative" entrepreneurs who have dubbed it the **Northern Quarter**. Traditionally, this is Manchester's garment district and you'll still find shops and wholesalers selling high-street fashions, shop fittings, mannequins and hosiery, but there are also new design outlets, lots of music stores, and some funky bars and cafés. For offbeat contemporary shopping, pop into **Affleck's Palace**, 52 Church St (Ⓦwww.afflecks-palace.co.uk). There are more skills and crafts on display in the excellent **Manchester Craft and Design Centre**, 17 Oak St (Mon–Sat 10am–5.30pm, plus Sun in Dec same hours; free; Ⓦwww .craftanddesign.com) – a great place to pick up ceramics, fabrics, earthenware, jewellery and decorative art, or just sip a drink in the café.

Chinatown and the Gay Village

From Piccadilly Gardens, it's a short walk to **Chinatown**, whose grid of narrow streets stretch north–south from Charlotte to Princess Street between Portland and Mosley streets, with the inevitable **Dragon Arch**, at Faulkner and Nicolas, providing the focus for the annual Chinese New Year celebrations. Close by, just to the southeast, the side-roads off Portland Street lead down to the Rochdale Canal, where Canal Street is the heart of Manchester's thriving **Gay Village**. The pink pound has filled this part of the city with canalside cafés, clubs, bars and businesses, thereby rescuing what had previously been a decaying warehouse district.

One block west of the Gay Village, at the junction of Oxford Road and Whitworth Street, stands the **Cornerhouse** (Ⓣ0161/200 1500, Ⓦwww.cornerhouse.org), the dynamo of the Manchester arts scene. In addition to screening art-house films, the Cornerhouse has three floors of gallery space devoted to contemporary and local artists' work as well as a popular café and bar.

Oxford Road and points south

Beginning at Whitworth Street, **Oxford Road** cuts a direct route south from the city centre, slicing through a string of Manchester University buildings, one of which houses the **Manchester Museum**, before reaching, after about a mile, the enjoyable **Whitworth Art Gallery**.

An endless stream of **buses** runs down Oxford Road from the stops outside the *Palace Hotel*, at the corner of Whitworth Street, putting both the museum and the gallery within easy reach.

The Manchester Museum

From the Whitworth Street/Oxford Road intersection, it's a ten-minute hoof south to the Gothic Revival home of the **Manchester Museum** (Mon & Sun 11am–4pm, Tues–Sat 10am–5pm; free; ⓦwww.museum.manchester.ac.uk), whose diverse collection spreads over five floors. One floor has displays on rocks, minerals and prehistoric life, a second focuses on meteorites and two more concentrate on animal life, the human body and biomedical research. A final floor boasts an excellent section on **Ancient Egypt** with captivating displays investigating burial practices and techniques. The museum has been undertaking pioneering work in Egyptology since the 1890s.

The Whitworth Art Gallery

Another half-mile away to the south is the university's **Whitworth Art Gallery** (Mon–Sat 10am–5pm, Sun noon–4pm; free; ⓦwww.whitworth.manchester .ac.uk), which occupies a large red-brick building at the corner of Oxford and Denmark roads. The gallery is formed of two distinct halves, pre-1880s and modern, with the former collection incorporating a strong assembly of watercolours by Turner, Constable, Cox and Blake as well as Gillray engravings, and Hogarth prints. There are also several diverting oddities, most notably Ford Madox Brown's *Execution of Mary Queen of Scots* – his first and not entirely successful attempt at a large-scale historical work. The modern collection concentrates on post-1880 British staples, with Moore and Hepworth setting off contributions from lesser-known artists. Look for works by Paul Nash (one of the organizers of the London Surrealist exhibition of 1936), the World War II artist John Piper and those of Stephen Conroy, a contemporary figurative painter whose subjects resonate with Victorian imagery. Given Manchester's cotton connections, it is perhaps not too surprising that the gallery also displays the country's widest range of textiles outside London's Victoria and Albert Museum.

Salford Quays: The Lowry and the Imperial War Museum North

After the Manchester Ship Canal opened in 1894, **Salford docks** played a pivotal role in turning Manchester into one of Britain's busiest seaports. By the 1970s, however, trade had well-nigh collapsed and the docks were forced to close in 1982, leaving a slew of post-industrial mess just a couple of miles to the west of the city centre. Since then, an extraordinarily ambitious redevelopment has transformed **Salford Quays**, as it was rebranded, into a hugely popular waterfront residential and leisure complex, with its own gleaming new apartment blocks, shopping mall and arts centre, **The Lowry**, amongst whose various delights are art galleries that feature the works of the centre's namesake, L.S. Lowry. Also on the quays is the much praised **Imperial War Museum North**, with its splendidly thoughtful displays on war in general and its effects on the individual in particular.

To get to the quays by public transport, take the **Metrolink** tram (Eccles line) from the city centre to the Harbour City tram stop, from where it is a five-minute walk to both The Lowry and the Imperial War Museum; for details of Metrolink tram stops in the city centre, see p.665.

The Lowry

Perched on the water's edge, **The Lowry** (☎0870/787 5780, ⓦwww.thelowry .com) is the quays' shiny steel arts centre, where you seem to be able to do just about anything, from watching the theatre to getting married. A small part of

The Lowry, the **Galleries** (Mon–Fri & Sun 11am–5pm, Sat 10am–5pm; free, but donation requested), is devoted to displays of fine art. There are some sixteen different exhibitions held here each year, but most of them showcase a selection of **Lowry paintings**, quite rightly given that no artist is more closely associated with Salford. The earlier paintings of **Lawrence Stephen Lowry** (1887–1976) have a sense of desolation and melancholia in their portrayal of Manchester mill workers, but later he modified his outlook, repeating earlier paintings but changing the greys and sullen browns for lively reds and pinks. Lowry also expanded his repertoire as he grew older, capturing mountain scenes and seascapes in broad sweeps of his brush, and painting full-bodied realistic portraits that are far less known than his internationally famous matchstick crowds. A twenty-minute film – *Meet Mr Lowry* – puts further flesh on the artistic bones.

Imperial War Museum North

A footbridge spans the Manchester Ship Canal to link The Lowry with the startling **Imperial War Museum North** (March–Oct daily 10am–6pm, Nov–Feb daily 10am–5pm; free; ⓦwww.north.iwm.org.uk), which raises a giant steel fin into the air, all to the design of Daniel Libeskind. The interior is just as striking, its angular lines serving as a dramatic backdrop to the displays, which kick off with the Big Picture, when the walls of the main hall are transformed into giant screens to show regularly rotated, fifteen-minute, surround-sound films. Among the hundreds of artefacts displayed in the main hall are five so-called "iconic objects", including the artillery piece that fired the first British shell in World War I and a fire tender used when Manchester was blitzed in World War II. In addition, there are all sorts of themed displays in six separate exhibition areas – the "Silos" – focusing on everything from women's work in the two world wars to war reporting and the build-up to the Iraq conflict of 2003. It's an ambitious and carefully conceived museum with a mixture of the personal and the general that is nothing less than superb.

Old Trafford

From the War Museum, it's about three quarters of a mile southeast to **Old Trafford**, the self-styled "Theatre of Dreams" and home of **Manchester United** (ⓦwww.manutd.com), arguably the most famous football team in the world. The club's following is such that only season-ticket holders can ever attend games, but **guided tours** of Old Trafford and its museum (daily 9.30am–4.30pm; advance booking essential; £10) placate out-of-town fans who want to gawp at the silverware and sit in the dug-out. To get here by public transport, take the Metrolink tram to Old Trafford Station and walk up Warwick Road to Sir Matt Busby Way. Incidentally, the city's poorer soccer cousins, **Manchester City** (ⓦwww.mcfc.co.uk), who have been almost entirely overshadowed by their neighbour's success for years, have finally evacuated their old inner-city ground, Maine Road – the "Theatre of Base Comedy", according to soccer commentator Stuart Hall – and moved to the spanking new City of Manchester Stadium on the east side of the city. The move has coincided with a change in City's fortunes and the team are now up with the best of them.

Eating and drinking

Second only to London in the breadth and scope of its **cafés** and **restaurants**, Manchester has something to suit everyone, from a cheap curry to a night out in a celebrity-chef hotspot. Moreover, at both ends of the market, your money goes a lot further than it does in London, and smart in Manchester doesn't often

▲ Imperial War Museum North

mean snobby – the city is much too egalitarian for that. The bulk of Manchester's eating and drinking places are scattered around the **city centre**, but the **Rusholme** district, a couple of miles south of the centre, possesses the city's widest and best selection of Asian restaurants in a "golden mile" of curry houses that extends along the main drag, **Wilmslow Road**. From Rusholme, it's another couple of miles, again along the Wilmslow Road, to **Didsbury**, a leafy, well-heeled suburb very different from Rusholme and equipped, along with nearby **West Didsbury**, with several excellent Modern British restaurants.

Most city-centre **pubs** dish up something filling at lunchtime, but for a more modish snack or drink, European-style **café-bars** are everywhere, especially in the new city-centre developments, in the **Northern Quarter**, and in the **Gay Village** on the Rochdale Canal.

Cafés and café-bars

Manchester's **café-bar scene** is its pride and joy, with most of the places below fielding a very definite crowd and atmosphere. Many of those in the Gay Village, the Northern Quarter and Castlefield are laid-back, easygoing joints, though evenings always see the atmosphere ratcheted up a notch or two, while among the half-dozen places along Deansgate Locks (Whitworth Street West) the emphasis is more on serious partying. Lots of café-bars have outdoor seating, and take advantage of relaxed licensing laws to offer drinks without food. As a general rule, the places listed below are open daily from 11am or noon until around midnight, often later at the weekend or if there's music, but we have also included a couple of daytime-only **cafés**.

Affleck's Palace 52 Church St, Northern Quarter. Five floors of hip/alternative/indie boutiques, with the pick of the cafés on the top floor, where you can grab a coffee and a grilled sandwich. Daytime only; closed Sun.

Atlas 376 Deansgate. Squeezed into an old red-brick building that pokes its nose out from beneath a railway arch, the *Atlas* is kitted out in slick, modern style, complete with large urban patio. Justly known for its quality focaccia sandwiches, it's also the place for Sunday brunch, a bottle of beer or a decent glass of wine. Light meals and lunches from £4.

Barça Bar Arches 8 & 9, Catalan Square. Love or hate it – and plenty of people do both – this trendy Castlefield café-bar does have a great location, tucked into the old railway arches off Castle St, a stone's throw from the Rochdale Canal. Best on the weekend.

Cornerhouse 70 Oxford St. Slick ground-floor bar and first-floor café-bar in Manchester's premier arthouse cinema and arts centre. Tasty, inexpensive snacks and light meals – from around £5 – though the service is patchy.

Dry Bar 28–30 Oldham St. The first of the designer café-bars on the scene, started by Factory Records and the catalyst for much of what has happened since in the Northern Quarter. Still as cool (though not always easy) as they come.

Earth 16–20 Turner St. Gourmet vegan and organic food and drink – stuffed pancakes,

pies, bakes, juices and deli delights – in a stylish Northern Quarter pit-stop with Buddhist leanings. Daytime only; closed Sun & Mon.

Eighth Day 107–111 Oxford Rd. Manchester's oldest organic-vegetarian café has got spanking new premises on its old Oxford Rd site – shop, takeaway and juice bar upstairs, café/restaurant downstairs. Daytime only; closed Sun.

Kro2 Oxford House, Oxford Rd. Half the students in Manchester crowd into this good-natured café-bar, sited in glassy modern premises close to the Mancunian Way overpass and opposite the university. Offers imaginative value-for-money food and on a sunny day you'll struggle to find table space outside. There are four other *Kro* outlets in the city, three further out along Oxford Road.

Loaf Deansgate Locks, Whitworth St West. Large queues at the weekend for this designer-industrial café-bar, not nearly so crowded during the day when you can grab an outdoor table underneath the arches and soak up the weak Manchester sun.

Manto 46 Canal St. Gay Village stalwart that has gone through several incarnations since it was established in 1990. *Manto* attracts a chic crowd, which laps up the cool sounds and club nights. Inexpensive fusion dishes served daily from noon till 8pm.

Night & Day 26 Oldham St. Unpretentious café-bar with a late licence and live music most nights from local musicians; club nights too. Details on ⓦ www.nightnday.org.

Restaurants

There's been a revolution in Manchester's dining scene in recent years, with long-standing city-centre **restaurants** being joined by a host of fashionable brasseries and celebrity-chef ventures. Paul Heathcote (the only vaguely local boy), Gary Rhodes and Raymond Blanc, among others, are all associated with various Manchester restaurants (they don't necessarily do the cooking) and if you are in the city for any length of time, you should go to at least one of them to see what all the fuss is about. Otherwise, downtown's **Chinatown** can always be counted upon for a budget lunch or a late-night meal, and there is another gaggle of recommendable restaurants along and off Deansgate. It also pays to visit the **suburbs**, particularly those of south Manchester, where Asian (Rusholme) and Mediterranean/Modern British (Didsbury Village and West Didsbury) restaurants are very à la mode. Taxis aren't particularly expensive to any of these places, or you can easily take a bus.

City centre

Brasserie Blanc 55 King St ☏ 0161/832 1000. Raymond Blanc's brasserie, housed in sleek modern premises near the Royal Exchange, is the city's best spot for reasonably priced classic and regional French cooking. Mains average around £13.

Café Istanbul 79 Bridge St ☏ 0161/833 9942. Delicious Turkish dishes, including a great *meze* selection, and an extensive wine list. Main courses average around £12. Open daily from noon.

Dimitri's 1 Campfield Arcade, Deansgate ☏ 0161/839 3319. Pick and mix from the Greek/ Spanish/Italian menu (particularly good for vegetarians), or grab a sandwich, an arcade table and sip a drink – Greek coffee to Lebanese wine. Snacks around £4, tapas £5.

Little Yang Sing 17 George St ☏ 0161/228 7722. Celebrated basement restaurant (forerunner to the larger *Yang Sing*) where the emphasis is on down-to-earth Cantonese cooking – dim sum, rice and noodle dishes – with lots of choice under £8.

The Market Restaurant 104 High St ☏ 0161/834 3743. First-rate Northern Quarter restaurant with a regularly changing menu that throws its Modern British weight around in adventurous, eclectic fashion, with main courses for around £13–18. Also a very good wine and beer list. Reservations absolutely essential. Closed all day Mon, Tues & Sun, plus lunchtime Sat.

Simply Heathcote's Jackson's Row ☏ 0161/835 3536. This large, popular first-floor restaurant occupies part of an old and classily revamped warehouse. Minimalist decor sets the tone and the menu, the handiwork of Lancastrian chef Paul Heathcote, mixes Mediterranean and local flavours and ingredients, so expect updated working-class dishes alongside the Parmesan shavings. Mains before 7pm hover around (a very reasonable) £9, £13 later on.

Stock 4 Norfolk St ☏ 0161/839 6644. Superior Italian cooking – the fish is renowned – accompanied

by a wine list of serious intent. It's housed in the city's old stock exchange, hence the name. Dress smart – everyone else does. Main courses average £18, less at lunchtimes and from 5 to 7pm. Closed Sun.

Tampopo 16 Albert Square ☏ 0161/819 1966. Basement noodle bar with long benches and a fast turnover. Noodle dishes are Japanese, Thai, Malaysian or Indonesian with most dishes under £7. One of a small chain.

Yang Sing 34 Princess St ☏ 0161/236 2200. The *Yang Sing* is one of the best Cantonese restaurants in the country, with thoroughly authentic food, from a lunchtime plate of fried noodles to the full works. Stray from the printed menu for the most interesting dishes; ask the friendly staff for advice. Main courses from £10.

Rusholme

Royal Darbar 65–67 Wilmslow Rd ☏ 0161/224 4392. Award-winning Asian food in plain but friendly surroundings. The house speciality is *nihari*, a slow-cooked lamb dish, while other homestyle choices appear on Sun. Take your own booze. Main courses from as little as £9.

Sanam 145–151 Wilmslow Rd ☏ 0161/224 8824. One of Rusholme's earliest Asian arrivals, now over thirty years old, the *Sanam* serves all the usual dishes plus award-winning *gulab juman*. Drop by the *Sanam* takeaway sweet centre at 169 Wilmslow Rd on the way home. No alcohol allowed. Mains from £9.

Shere Khan 52 Wilmslow Rd ☏ 0161/256 2624. A Rusholme standard-bearer, this big Indian brasserie gets packed at the weekends, but always maintains its high standards. The open grill dispenses marvellous kebabs, and the wide-ranging menu is also strong on *karahi* and *biryani* dishes. Main courses from £11.

Didsbury and West Didsbury

Lime Tree 8 Lapwing Lane, West Didsbury ☏ 0161/445 1217. Bundles of Modern British joy, with a menu that chargrills and oven-roasts as if its life depended on it. Organic salmon is a signature dish, or else you could be chowing down on such delights as crispy duckling or courgette and leek cheesecake. Very fashionable, reservations recommended. Main courses cost £13 and up in the evening, less at lunch times. Closed lunchtimes Tues–Fri & Sun.

No.4 4 Warburton St, Didsbury ☏ 0161/445 0448. Tucked away off the main road, this cottage-style bolt-hole has two floors of intimate dining. Omelettes and open sandwiches at lunch (around £5) give way to seasonally changing Modern British dinners, with main courses from £12. Closed Sun eve & all day Mon.

Pubs

As you might expect, Manchester has a full complement of **pubs**, from Victorian classics to modern designer joints in imaginatively recycled old buildings. Inevitably, there are also the off-the-shelf contemporary chains – Irish theme-bars and the like – but these are easy to avoid. As far as **beer** goes, Boddington's is the big deal hereabouts, though independent local brewers Hydes, Holts and Robinson's all have their adherents and proponents.

Britons Protection 50 Great Bridgewater St. Cosy, old pub with a couple of small rooms and all sorts of Victorian decorative detail – most splendidly the tiles. Also has a backyard beer garden.

Circus Tavern 86 Portland St. Manchester's smallest pub – a Victorian drinking-hole that's many people's favourite city-centre pit-stop. You may have to knock on the door to get in; once you do, you're confronted by the landlord in the corridor pulling pints.

Dukes '92 Castle St. Classily revamped former stable block (for canal horses) with art on the walls, terrace seating and a good selection of beers. Serves great-value food too, including a wide range of pâtés and cheeses.

The Lass o' Gowrie 1 Charles St. Outside, glazed tiles and Victorian styling; inside, stripped floors and a microbrewery.

Mr Thomas' Chop House 52 Cross St. Victorian classic with a Dickensian feel to its nooks and crannies, which office workers, hardcore daytime drinkers, old goats and students all call home. There's good-value, traditional English "chop-house" food (oysters, bubble and squeak and so on) served in the ornate dining-and-drinking room at the rear.

The Ox 71 Liverpool Road. Pleasant and popular old boozer that dates back to Victorian times – as does some of the tile work. Good range of cask ales along with well-above-average bar food.

Peveril of the Peak 127 Great Bridgewater St. The pub that time forgot – one of Manchester's best real ale houses, with a youthful crowd and some superb Victorian glazed tilework outside.

Rain Bar 80 Great Bridgewater St. Pub or bar? Experience both, drinking inside the stripped-wood pubby interior, up in the swish bar, or out on the canalside terrace. Good range of beers, a decent menu and summer barbecues.

Temple of Convenience Great Bridgewater St. Subterranean public toilet turned into a cramped and crowded bar. Lots of students love it; others find it rather gruesome.

Nightlife

For the last thirty years or so, Manchester has been vying with London as Britain's capital of **youth culture**, spearheaded by the success of its musical exports, from the sainted Morrissey to Badly Drawn Boy, Joy Division and Oasis. Banks of fly-posters advertise what's going on in the numerous **clubs**, which, as elsewhere, frequently change names and styles on different nights of the week, though it has to be said that clubbing is not quite what it was when the "Madchester" scene was at its peak in the early 1990s. The most enduring clubs are listed below; you can expect to pay £5–15 cover depending on what's on. Many of the city's groovier café-bars also host regular club nights.

Manchester also has an excellent pub and club **live music** scene, with tickets for local bands usually under £5, more like £10–15 for someone you've heard of. Mega-star gigs take place either at one of the city's major venues, also listed below. For the broadest coverage of Manchester's musical happenings, check out the local daily, the *Manchester Evening News*.

Manchester has one of Britain's most vibrant gay scenes, centred beside the Rochdale Canal between Princess and Chorlton streets, in the so-called **Gay Village**. The café-bars and clubs here are among the city's best, though some claim that the area's increased popularity – with straight as well as gay visitors – has somewhat diluted its essence. Amongst gay-specific events, one of the best is **Gayfest**, held every August bank holiday in and around the village. Other events, including an annual arts festival held every May, are co-ordinated by **queerupnorth** (information on ☏0161/234 2942, ⊛www.queerupnorth.com). For further information, try the **Lesbian and Gay Foundation** (daily 6–10pm; ☏0845/330 3030, ⊛www.lgfoundation.org.uk), which can put you in touch with the dozens of other organizations and services operating out of – or in constant communication with – the Gay Village.

Smaller live-music and club venues

Band on the Wall 25 Swan St ☏0161/834 1786, ⊛www.bandonthewall.org. Legendary Northern Quarter joint with a great reputation for its live bands – from world and folk to jazz and reggae – plus tasty club nights to boot. Featured early performances from the Buzzcocks and Joy Division. Currently closed for a thorough-going revamp – should reopen in 2009.

The Brickhouse Arch 66, Whitworth St West ☏0161/236 4418, ⊛www.brickhouse-nightclub .com. Rotating Indie and pop in a relaxed atmosphere geared up for an older crowd. Fri & Sat from 10.30pm.

Manchester Academy Oxford Rd ☏0161/275 2930, ⊛www.manchesteracademy.net. Academy 1 is on the university campus, opposite the medical school, Academy 2 & 3 are inside the Students' Union building on Oxford Rd. All three are popular student venues featuring both new and established bands.

Manchester Roadhouse 8 Newton St, Piccadilly ☏0161/237 9789, ⊛www.theroadhouselive.co.uk. Regular and varied gigs by local bands plus a succession of club nights.

The Ritz Whitworth St West ☏0161/236 4355, ⊛www.ritznightclub.co.uk. A one-time ballroom specializing in retro nights; student nights too.

Sankey's Soap Beehive Mill, Jersey St, Ancoats ☏0161/236 5444, ⊛sankeys.info. Many people's favourite night out, brought to you by the legendary Tribal Gathering crew, popular for their sleazy house music; other club night specials too. Ancoats is an inner-city suburb beginning about half a mile north of Piccadilly Station.

Star & Garter 18–20 Fairfield St ☏0161/273 6726, ⊛www.starandgarter.co.uk. Thrash/punk pub venue for loud, young bands and club nights. It's located about 200 yards from the short-stay car park at the back of Piccadilly Station.

Stadium venues

Manchester Central Petersfield ☏0161/834 2700, ⊛www.manchestercentral.co.uk. Mid-sized city-centre indoor stadium.

Manchester Apollo Stockport Rd, Ardwick Green ☏0870/991 3913, ⊛www.alive.co.uk /apollo. Huge theatre auditorium for all kinds of concerts.

Manchester Evening News Arena 21 Hunt's Bank, beside Victoria Station ☏0844/847 8000, ⊛www.menarena.com. Indoor stadium seating 20,000 and hosting all the big names.

Arts and culture

Manchester is blessed with the north's most highly prized **orchestra**, the Hallé, which is resident at Bridgewater Hall. Other acclaimed names include the BBC Philharmonic and the Manchester Camerata chamber orchestra (⊛www .manchestercamerata.com), who perform **concerts** at a variety of venues across the city. The Cornerhouse is the local "alternative" **arts** mainstay and the best art-house **cinema** in town, while a full range of mainstream and fringe **theatres** produces a lively, year-round programme of events.

Concerts and music

Bridgewater Hall Lower Mosley St ☎0161/907 9000, Ⓦwww.bridgewater-hall.co.uk. Home of the Hallé Orchestra and the Manchester Camerata; also sponsors a full programme of chamber, pop, classical and jazz concerts.

The Lowry Pier 8, Salford Quays ☎0870/787 5780, Ⓦwww.thelowry.com. Full, year-round programme of music events, from opera to country.

Royal Northern College of Music (RNCM) 124 Oxford Rd ☎0161/907 5555, Ⓦwww.rncm.ac.uk. Stages top-quality classical and modern-jazz concerts, including performances by Manchester Camerata.

Opera House Quay St ☎0161/828 1700, Ⓦwww.manchesteroperahouse.org.uk. Major venue for touring West End musicals, drama, comedy and concerts.

Theatre, cinema and the arts

Contact Theatre 15 Oxford Rd ☎0161/274 0600, Ⓦwww.contact-theatre.org. One of the most innovative theatre companies in town, housed in provocatively designed premises and showcasing mostly modern works. Just west of Oxford Road, a five-minute walk from the Oxford Road/Brunswick Street junction.

 Cornerhouse 70 Oxford St ☎0161/200 1500, Ⓦwww.cornerhouse.org. Engaging centre for contemporary arts. For films, the three screens are your best bet for art-house releases, special screenings and cinema-related talks and events. There are also changing art exhibitions, recitals, talks, bookshop, café and bar.

Dancehouse Theatre 10 Oxford Rd ☎0161/237 9753, Ⓦwww.thedancehouse.co.uk. Home of the Northern Ballet School and the eponymous theatre troupe; venue for dance, drama and comedy.

Green Room 54–56 Whitworth St West ☎0161/615 0500, Ⓦwww.greenroomarts.org. Rapidly changing fringe programme that includes theatre, dance, mime and cabaret.

Library Theatre Central Library, St Peter's Square ☎0161/236 7110, Ⓦwww.librarytheatre.com. Classic drama and new writing in an intimate theatre at the Central Library.

Royal Exchange Theatre St Ann's Square ☎0161/833 9833, Ⓦwww.royalexchange.co.uk. The theatre-in-the-round in the Royal Exchange is the most famous stage in the city, and there's a Studio Theatre (for works by new writers) alongside the main stage.

Stand-up comedy

The Comedy Store Arches 3 & 4, Deansgate Locks, Whitworth St West. Bookings on ☎0844/826 0001, Ⓦwww.thecomedystore.co.uk. Showcase for the best in nationwide stand-up comedy talent, with gigs most nights. Bar and brasserie too.

Listings

Airport ☎0161/489 3000, Ⓦwww.manchesterairport.co.uk.

Internet Internet access free at the Central Library, St Peter's Square (Mon–Thurs 9am–8pm, Fri & Sat 9am–5pm).

Pharmacy Boots, 11–13 Piccadilly Gardens (☎0161/834 8244) and 20 St Ann's St (☎0161/839 1798).

Post office 26 Spring Gardens.

Taxis Mantax ☎0161/230 3333; Taxifone ☎0161/236 9974.

Transport information For all Greater Manchester bus and train services, call GMPTE on ☎0871/200 2233, Ⓦwww.gmpte.com.

Chester and around

In 1779 Boswell wrote to Samuel Johnson: "Chester pleases me more than any town I ever saw" – and although **CHESTER**, forty miles southwest of Manchester across the Cheshire Plain, has greatly changed since then, it still has much to recommend it. A glorious two-mile ring of medieval and Roman walls encircles a kernel of Tudor and Victorian buildings, all overhanging eaves, mini-courtyards, and narrow cobbled lanes, which culminate in the unique raised arcades called "**The Rows**". Taken altogether, Chester has enough in the way of sights, restaurants and atmosphere to make it an enjoyable base for a couple of days; the most obvious excursion is to its much-vaunted **zoo**.

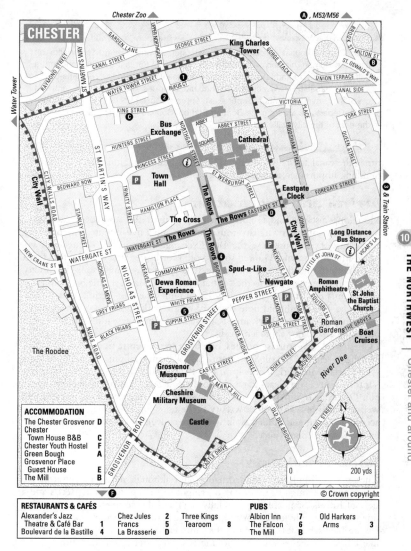

CHESTER

Chester Zoo ▲   **Ⓐ** , M53/M56 ▲

Water Tower ◄

King Charles Tower

Bus Exchange

Cathedral

Town Hall

Eastgate Clock

The Cross

The Rows

City Wall

Long Distance Bus Stops

Dewa Roman Experience

Newgate

Roman Amphitheatre

St John the Baptist Church

Spud-u-Like

Grosvenor Museum

Roman Gardens

Boat Cruises

The Roodee

Cheshire Military Museum

Castle

River Dee

N

0   200 yds

© Crown copyright

ACCOMMODATION

The Chester Grosvenor	**D**
Chester Town House B&B	**C**
Chester Youth Hostel	**F**
Green Bough	**A**
Grosvenor Place Guest House	**E**
The Mill	**B**

RESTAURANTS & CAFÉS				**PUBS**			
Alexander's Jazz Theatre & Café Bar	**1**	Chez Jules	**2**	Three Kings Tearoom	**8**	Albion Inn	**7**	Old Harkers Arms	**3**
Boulevard de la Bastille	**4**	Francs	**5**			The Falcon	**6**		
		La Brasserie	**D**			The Mill	**B**		

The fabric of the city is permeated with two thousand years of history. In 79 AD the Romans built Deva Castra here, their largest known fortress in Britain. Later, Ethelfleda, the daughter of King Alfred the Great, extended and refortified the place, only for it to be brutally sacked by William the Conqueror. Thereafter, trade routes to Ireland made Chester the most prosperous port in the northwest, though its enthusiasm for Charles I during the English Civil War did result in a two-year siege by the Parliamentarians. By the middle of the eighteenth century, however, the silting of the port had forced the Irish trade to be rerouted through Liverpool and Chester slipped into a genteel decline, which accidentally ensured the survival of many of its old buildings. In Victorian

Both Chester tourist offices (see below) offer a variety of **guided walks** on assorted Roman, historic and ghost trails. They cost £5, last between one and a half and two hours and take place throughout the year. In addition, **Bithells Boats** (☏01244/325394, ⊛www.chesterboat.co.uk) operates **river cruises** – either a quick thirty-minute gambol (£6 per adult) or more substantial two-hour excursions (£12). Departures are from the Boating Station, Souters Lane, The Groves, just to the east of the city walls.

times, the canal and railway networks made Chester a regional trading centre of middling importance, a status it retains today.

Arrival and information

Most long-distance and regional **buses** pull in at the stops on Vicar's Lane, opposite one of the town's two tourist offices and a five-minute walk from the city centre. Local buses use the Bus Exchange right in the centre of town, between Princess and Hunter streets, off Northgate Street. From the **train station**, to the northeast of the centre, it's a good ten-minute walk down City Road and Foregate Street to the central Eastgate Clock. A shuttle bus (Mon–Sat 8am–6pm, free with rail ticket; every 15min) links the train station with the Bus Exchange. Drivers should note that city-centre parking is thin on the ground, which makes Chester's **Park and Ride** scheme attractive – just follow the signs on any of the major approach roads.

Chester has two **tourist offices**, one bang in the centre in the Town Hall on Northgate Street (April–Sept Mon–Sat 9.30am–5.30pm, Sun 10am–4pm; Oct–March Mon–Fri 10am–4pm, Sat 10am–5pm), a second – the Chester Visitor Centre – on Vicar's Lane, just to the east of the town centre (same hours plus Oct–March Sun 10am–4pm). They share the same telephone number and website (☏01244/351 609, ⊛www.visitchester.co.uk). At either, you can book accommodation and guided walks (see box above), and pick up a copy of the handy *Chester Visitor Guide*.

Accommodation

Chester is a popular tourist destination and although most of its visitors are day-trippers, enough of them stay overnight to sustain dozens of **B&Bs** and a slew of **hotels**. Standards are generally high and the competition keeps prices down to reasonable levels. For most of the year, finding a vacant room presents few problems, but at the height of the summer and on high days and holidays – like Chester Races – advance booking is strongly recommended either direct or via the tourist office.

Hotels and B&Bs

The Chester Grosvenor Eastgate St
☏01244/324024, ⊛www.chestergrosvenor.co.uk. Superbly appointed luxury hotel in an immaculately maintained Victorian building plumb in the centre of town. Extremely comfortable bedrooms and a whole host of facilities, not least a full-blown spa. Discounts common at the weekend. ❽

Chester Town House B&B 23 King St
☏01244/350021, ⊛www.chestertownhouse.co.uk.

High-standard B&B in a comfortably furnished seventeenth-century town house on a curving, cobbled central street off Northgate St. There are five en-suite rooms and private parking. ❹

Green Bough 60 Hoole Road
☏01244/326241, ⊛www.greenbough .co.uk. Award-winning, small, friendly, family-run hotel with all sorts of thoughtful details – soft carpeting, comfortable beds, and plasma TV screens in each guest room or suite. Great

breakfasts too, plus three-course evening meals for £45 and a rooftop garden. One mile northeast of the city centre en route to the M53/M56. **7**

Grosvenor Place Guest House 2 Grosvenor Place ☎01244/324455, ⓦ www.grosvenorplacechester .co.uk. Pleasant town-house B&B in an attractive location near the Grosvenor Museum. All rooms are en suite. **3**

The Mill Milton St ☎01244/350035, ⓦ www .millhotel.com. Sensitive warehouse conversion on the canal between St Oswald's Way and Hooley Way, not far from the train station. Has its own car park and a nice waterside café-bar. Spick-and-span modern rooms, some with waterside balcony. **5**

Youth hostel

Chester Youth Hostel Hough Green House, 40 Hough Green ☎0870/770 5762, ⓔchester@yha .org.uk. Twenty minutes' walk southwest of the centre, this Victorian house has a cafeteria, self-catering and laundry facilities, and a shop. Over 100 beds in two- to ten-bedded rooms; dorm beds £17.50 including breakfast.

The City

Central Chester is a delightful spot, its easy charms readily explored on foot. There are two special highlights, **The Rows**, the picturesque galleries that run above the central shops, and the ancient **city wall**, from the top of which there are fetching views of Chester's environs. It's usually sufficient to get round the sights under your own steam, but the city's tourist offices do offer a variety of **walking tours** (see box opposite).

The Rows

Intersecting at **The Cross**, where the town crier welcomes visitors to the city (May–Aug Tues–Sat at noon), the four main thoroughfares of central Chester are lined by **The Rows**, galleried shopping arcades that run along the first floor of a wonderful set of half-timbered buildings with another set of shops down below at street level. This engaging tableau, which extends for the first 200 or 300 yards of each of the four main streets, is a blend of genuine Tudor houses and Victorian imitations that are hard to separate out. There's no clear explanation of the origin of The Rows – they were first recorded shortly after a fire wrecked Chester in 1278 – but it seems likely that the hard bedrock that lies underneath the town centre prevented its shopkeepers and merchants from constructing the cellars they required, so they built upwards instead. The finest Tudor buildings are on **Watergate Street**, though **Bridge Street** is perhaps the more picturesque and there's one real curiosity here: the **Spud-u-Like** snack bar doesn't look like much from the outside, but wander in and take the steps down to the cellar and you'll spy the substantial remains of a **Roman hypocaust** (under-floor heating system), whose carved stone pillars and mini-pool date from the first century AD. Opposite *Spud-u-Like*, an alley leads through to the child-friendly **Dewa Roman Experience** (Mon–Sat 9am–5pm, Sun 10am–5pm; £4.75), which attempts to evoke the flavour of Roman Chester with a galley, a reconstruction of a Roman street and some underground remains. Back at The Cross, it's a brief walk along **Eastgate Street** to one of the old town gates, above which is perched the filigree **Eastgate Clock**, raised in honour of Queen Victoria's Diamond Jubilee.

The Town Hall and the Cathedral

North of The Cross, along **Northgate Street**, rises the Neo-Gothic **Town Hall**, whose acres of red and grey sandstone look over to the **Cathedral** (Mon–Sat 9am–5pm, Sun 12.30–4pm; £4), a much modified red sandstone structure dating back to the Normans and for most of its history a Benedictine abbey dedicated to St Werburgh, an Anglo-Saxon princess who became Chester's patron saint. The **nave**, with its massive medieval pillars, is suitably imposing, and on one side it sports a splendid sequence of Victorian Pre-Raphaelite mosaic panels that illustrate Old Testament stories in melodramatic style. Close by, the **north transept** is the oldest and most Norman part of the church – hence the round-headed arch and arcade – and the adjoining **choir** holds an intricately carved set of fourteenth-century choir stalls with some especially beastly misericords. Look out also for the funerary **plaque** of a certain Frederick Philips (1720–1785), stuck on one of the pillars in the south transept. Poor old Philips had been a colonial bigwig in New York, but his loyalty to the British cost him dear during the American War of Independence, when he lost all his possessions and was obliged to hot-foot it back to England. Doors in the north wall of the nave lead into the old abbey buildings, principally the sixteenth-century **cloisters**, which enclose a small garden whose focal point is an imaginative and striking bronze **sculpture** by Stephen Broadbent of the Woman of Samaria, offering Jesus water at the well.

Around the city walls

East of the cathedral, steps provide access to the top of the **city walls**, a two-mile girdle of medieval and Roman handiwork that is the most complete in Britain – though in places the wall is barely above street level. You can walk past all its towers, turrets and gateways in an hour or so, and most have a tale or two to tell. The fifteenth-century **King Charles Tower** in the northeast corner is so named because Charles I stood here in 1645 watching his troops being beaten on Rowton Moor, two miles to the southeast, while the earlier **Water Tower** at the northwest corner, once stood in the river – evidence of the changes brought about by the gradual silting of the River Dee. South from the Water Tower you'll see **The Roodee**, England's oldest racecourse, laid out on a silted tidal pool where Roman ships once unloaded wine, figs and olive oil from the Mediterranean and slate, lead and silver from their mines in North Wales. Races are still held here throughout the year – the tourist office has the details.

The Grosvenor Museum and Chester Castle

Scores of sculpted tomb panels and engraved headstones once propped up the wall to either side of the Water Tower, evidence of some nervous repair work undertaken when the Roman Empire was in retreat. Much of this stonework was retrieved by the Victorians and is now on display at the **Grosvenor Museum**, 27 Grosvenor St (daily 10am–5pm; free), which also has interesting background displays on the Roman Empire in general and Roman Chester in particular. The assorted centurial stones, altars and tombstones are themselves in a separate room and together they form the largest collection from a single Roman site in Britain. The finest, and a splendid piece it is too, is the carving of a wounded barbarian, the surviving piece of a memorial to a Roman cavalryman.

Close by, on Castle Street, the **Cheshire Military Museum** (daily 10am–5pm; £3) inhabits part of the same complex as **Chester Castle** (no public access), built by William the Conqueror, though most of what you see today is resolutely Georgian and used as courts and offices. From the castle, it's an easy five- to ten-minute stroll east to one of the old city gates, **Newgate**, for the Roman Gardens and the Roman Amphitheatre.

The Roman Gardens and Roman Amphitheatre

Immediately to the east of Newgate, a footpath leads into the **Roman Gardens** (open access), where a miscellany of Roman stonework – odd bits of pillar, coping stones and incidental statuary – is on display amidst the surrounding greenery. Footsteps away, along Little St John Street, is the shallow, partly excavated bowl that marks the site of the **Roman Amphitheatre** (open access); it is estimated to have held seven thousand spectators, making it the largest amphitheatre in Britain, but frankly it's not much to look at today. The Roman garrison was 6000 strong in its heyday, and the amphitheatre was used by soldiers of the Twentieth Legion for weapons training as well as for entertainment.

St John the Baptist church and The Groves

A few yards from the amphitheatre, in Grosvenor Park, lurks the red sandstone **church of St John the Baptist** (daily 9.30am–5pm; free), which was founded by the Saxon king Ethelred in 689 and briefly served as the cathedral of Mercia. Rebuilt in its entirety by the Normans and largely untouched thereafter, it's an impressive structure, the solid Norman pillars of the nave rising to a Transitional triforium and Early English clerestory. The east portion of the church was abandoned at the Reformation and left to crumble, creating the echoing ruins of today.

Behind the ruins, steps lead down to **The Groves**, a partly pedestrianized esplanade that stretches out along the muddy River Dee, complete with bandstand, slender iron footbridge of 1923 and ancient willow trees. It's from here that Bithells Boats organize their river cruises (see p.682). The Groves leads round to the foot of Lower Bridge Street, from where you can regain the town centre.

Around Chester: Chester Zoo

Chester's most popular attraction is **Chester Zoo** (daily: April–Sept 10am–6pm; Oct–March 10am–4.30/6pm; last admission 1hr before closing; £14.95, £10.95 in winter, children 3–15 years £10.95/£7.95; ⓦwww.chesterzoo.org), one of the best in Europe. It is also the second largest in Britain (after London's), spreading over 100 landscaped acres, with new attractions opening all the time. The zoo is well known for its **conservation projects** and has had notable success with its Asiatic lions, jaguars and giant komodo dragons – Chester being the only British zoo to support these creatures. Animals are grouped by region in large paddocks viewed from a maze of pathways, from the monorail or from the water bus, with main attractions including the baby animals (elephants, giraffes and orang-utans), the rainforest habitat, the bat cave and the Chimpanzee Forest with the biggest climbing frame in the country. The zoo entrance is signposted off the A41 just to the north of Chester. To get there by public transport, take bus #1 (Mon–Sat every 20min, Sun hourly) from the Bus Exchange.

Eating and drinking

You can't walk more than a few paces in downtown Chester without coming across somewhere to eat and drink, as often as not housed in a medieval or Tudor building. Given the number of day-trippers, it's not surprising that standards are very variable, but there are a clutch of first-class **restaurants** and several delightful **pubs**.

Cafés and restaurants

Alexander's Jazz Theatre and Café Bar 2 Rufus Court ☎01244/340005, ⓦwww.alexandersjazz .com. Continental-style café-bar with inexpensive tapas and live music or comedy most nights.
Boulevard de la Bastille 39 Bridge St Row. One of the nicest of the arcade cafés, with tables

looking over the street and doing a roaring trade in breakfasts, pastries and sandwiches. Sandwiches from as little as £1.70.
Chez Jules 71 Northgate St ☎01244/400014. Classic brasserie menu – salade niçoise to vegetable cassoulet, Toulouse sausage to rib-eye steak – at this popular spot,

housed in an attractive black and white, half-timbered building. In the evenings, main courses begin at about £9, but they also do a terrific-value, two-course lunch for £7.90. Closed Sun eve.

Francs 14 Cuppin St ⓣ01244/317952. Excellent bistro with good-value set meals. You can also just drop in for a coffee and cake. Plat du jour £4; à la carte mains £12–14.

La Brasserie Chester Grosvenor Hotel, Eastgate St ⓣ01244/324024. The Grosvenor's smart but informal brasserie is a great place for a coffee and pastry, or inventive French and fusion cooking. Main courses average £15. Daily 7am–10pm.

Three Kings Tearoom 90 Lower Bridge St. Behind the cutest of antique shops, an amenable little tearoom with pleasantly fuddy-duddy decor and tasty food – a filling salad and sandwich combo costs about £4. Open Tues–Sun 10am–4pm.

Pubs and bars

Albion Inn corner of Albion and Park streets. A true English Victorian terraced pub in the shadow of the city wall – no fruit machines or muzak. Good old fashioned decor too, plus tasty bar food and a great range of ales.

The Falcon Lower Bridge St. This half-timbered building started out as an aristocrat's town house, but now it's a traditional pub with a good range of draught beers.

The Mill Milton St. Ale lovers flock to this converted Victorian corn mill to sample an excellent range of brews in a lively atmosphere.

Old Harkers Arms 1 Russell St, below the City Road bridge. Canalside real ale pub imaginatively sited in a former warehouse about 500 yards northeast of Foregate St. Quality bar food too.

Liverpool and around

Once the empire's second city, **LIVERPOOL** spent too many of the twentieth-century postwar years struggling against adversity. Things are looking up, as economic and social regeneration brightens the centre and old docks, and the city's stint as European Capital of Culture for 2008 has transformed the view from outside. Some may sneer at the very concept of Liverpudlian "culture", but this is a city with a Tate Gallery of its own, a series of innovative museums and a fascinating social history. Acerbic wit and loyalty to one of the city's two football teams (Liverpool and Everton) are the linchpins of Scouse culture, although Liverpool also makes great play of its musical heritage, which is reasonable enough from the city that produced The Beatles.

Liverpool gained its charter from King John in 1207, but remained a humble fishing village for half a millennium until the booming slave trade prompted the building of the first dock in 1715. From then until the abolition of slavery in Britain in 1807, Liverpool was the apex of the **slaving triangle** in which firearms, alcohol and textiles were traded for African slaves, who were then shipped to the Caribbean and America where they were in turn exchanged for tobacco, raw cotton and sugar. After the abolition of the trade, the port continued to grow into a seven-mile chain of docks, not only for freight but also to cope with wholesale European **emigration**, which saw nine million people leave for the Americas and Australasia between 1830 and 1930. Immigration from the Caribbean, China and especially Ireland in the wake of the potato famine in the 1840s resulted in one of Britain's earliest multi-ethnic communities, described by Carl Jung as "the pool of life".

The docks had lost their pre-eminence by the middle of the twentieth century and, although the arrival of car manufacturing plants in the 1960s stemmed the decline for a while, during the 1970s and 1980s Liverpool became a byword for British economic malaise. However, the waterfront area of the city was granted **UNESCO World Heritage** status in 2004, which spurred further redevelopment, and refurbishment of the city's magnificent municipal and industrial buildings.

Visitors have to plan ahead if they are to get around the sights in two or three days. The **River Mersey** provides one focus, whether crossing on the famous ferry to the **Wirral** peninsula or on a tour of the attractions in **Albert Dock**, such as **Tate Liverpool**. The associated **Beatles** sights can easily occupy another day. If you want a **cathedral**, they've "got one to spare" as the song goes; plus there's a fine showing of British art in the celebrated **Walker Art Gallery**, a multitude of exhibits in the terrific **World Museum Liverpool**, and a revitalized arts and nightlife urban quarter centred on **FACT**, Liverpool's showcase for film and the media arts.

Arrival and information

Mainline trains pull in to **Lime Street Station**, while the suburban **Merseyrail** system (for trains from Chester) calls at four underground stations in the city, including Lime Street, Central (under the main post office on Ranelagh Street) and James Street (for Pier Head and the Albert Dock). National Express **buses** use the station on Norton Street, just northeast of Lime Street, and local buses depart from Queen Square and Paradise Street.

Liverpool **airport** – officially named after John Lennon – is eight miles southeast of the city centre. From outside the main entrance, the **Airlink #500 bus** (every 20–30min: 5.10am to midnight; £2) runs into the city centre, stopping at all major bus terminals and at Lime Street; a **taxi** to Lime Street costs around £12. Most **ferries** – from the Isle of Man, Dublin and Belfast – dock at the terminals just north of Pier Head, not far from James Street Merseyrail station, though Norfolkline arrivals are over the water on the Wirral at Twelve Quays, near Woodside ferry terminal (ferry or Merseyrail to Liverpool).

Tourist information – including the free, comprehensive *Liverpool Visitor Guide* – is available from the **central tourist office**, currently named **The 08 Place**, at 36–38 Whitechapel (Mon–Sat 9/10am–6pm, Sun 11am–4pm; ☏0151/233 2008 or 0151/233 2459, accommodation line ☏0844/370 0123; ⓦwww.visitliverpool.com, www.liverpool08.com). There are smaller offices in the Anchor Courtyard at the **Albert Dock** (daily 10am–5/5.30pm) and at the **airport** (daily 5am to midnight; ☏0151/907 1057). Other **websites** include ⓦwww.liverpoolmuseums.org.uk, ⓦwww.artinliverpool.com and ⓦwww.liverpool.com.

City transport and tours

Liverpool city centre is surprisingly compact and you'll easily be able to get around on foot. Even the walk from the Metropolitan Cathedral through the centre to Albert Dock will take less than half an hour. For an overview take City Sightseeing's open-top **Liverpool Bus Tour** (April–Dec every 30–90min, 10am–4/5pm; 24hr ticket £6; ⓦwww.city-sightseeing.com). Meanwhile, everyone should take a **ferry across the Mersey** at some point (see p.694), if only to be able to say that they've sung *that* song in its proper environment; longer **cruises** (selected days May to mid-Oct; 6hr; £32) run from Woodside along the Manchester Ship Canal to Salford Quays (trip back by bus). The local transport authority is **Merseytravel** (enquiry line ☏0871/200 2233, ⓦwww.merseytravel.gov.uk), which has travel centres at Queen Square and the Paradise Street Interchange. A daily off-peak **Saveaway ticket** (£4.30) gives you unlimited travel on city buses, trains and ferries, and if you're here for any length of time, consider buying a "Your Ticket for Liverpool" **visitor card** (£19.99; ☏0844 870 0123, ⓦwww.yourticketforliverpool.com), which gives free and discounted tickets to attractions over three days.

The tourist offices have details of guided **walking tours** of the city (most Easter–Sept; from £3), or pick up one of the self-guided trails around sights

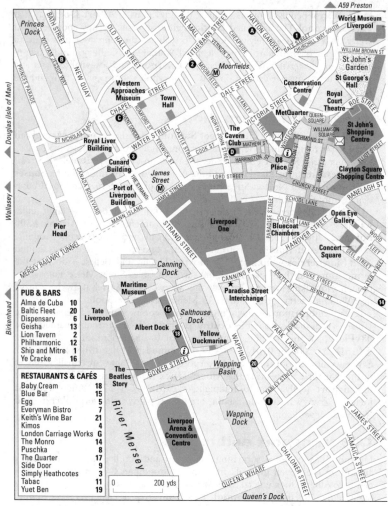

PUB & BARS

Alma de Cuba	10
Baltic Fleet	20
Dispensary	6
Geisha	13
Lion Tavern	2
Philharmonic	12
Ship and Mitre	1
Ye Cracke	16

RESTAURANTS & CAFÉS

Baby Cream	18
Blue Bar	15
Egg	5
Everyman Bistro	7
Keith's Wine Bar	21
Kimos	4
London Carriage Works	G
The Monro	14
Puschka	8
The Quarter	17
Side Door	9
Simply Heathcotes	3
Tabac	11
Yuet Ben	19

associated with Liverpool's Jewish or Irish heritage. With children in tow, don't miss a trip on the amphibious half-truck-half-boat **Yellow Duckmarine** (daily from 10.30/11am; peak time £11.95, off-peak £9.95; ☎0151/708 7799, ⓦwww.theyellowduckmarine.co.uk), which departs from Gower Street, in front of Albert Dock.

Accommodation

There's a good choice of central accommodation, from small-scale guest houses to boutique hotels and business-oriented four-stars. Budget chains are well represented, too, with *Premier Travel Inn*, *Ibis*, *Express by Holiday Inn*, *Campanile* and others all with convenient city-centre locations, including down by Albert

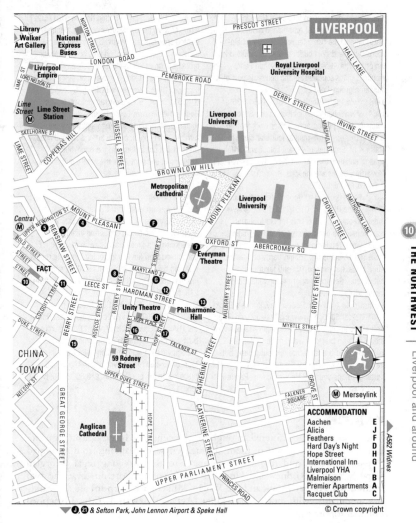

ACCOMMODATION

Aachen	E
Alicia	J
Feathers	F
Hard Day's Night	D
Hope Street	H
International Inn	G
Liverpool YHA	I
Malmaison	B
Premier Apartments	A
Racquet Club	C

© Crown copyright

▼ **J, 21 & Sefton Park, John Lennon Airport & Speke Hall**

Dock. The two best **hostels** are reviewed below, while both **universities** – John Moores University (℡0151/231 3511, ⓦwww.ljmu.ac.uk/conferences; from around £17.50 room only) and the University of Liverpool (℡0151/794 6440, ⓦwww.liv.ac.uk/conferenceservices; £34 with breakfast) – have hundreds of good-value single rooms available during the Easter holidays and from late June to early September.

Hotels, guest houses and apartments

Aachen 89–91 Mount Pleasant ℡0151/709 3477, ⓦwww.aachenhotel.co.uk. The best and most popular of the Mount Pleasant budget choices, a range of value-for-money rooms (with and without en-suite showers), big "eat-as-much-as-you-like" breakfasts, and a late bar. ❸

Feathers 113–125 Mount Pleasant ℡0151/709 9655, ⓦwww.feathers.uk.com.

A converted, modernized terrace of Georgian houses, with a variety of refurbished rooms in warm tones. Late bar, 24hr reception, and help-yourself hot-and-cold buffet breakfast included in the price. The *Alicia*, overlooking Sefton Park, around 3 miles southeast of the centre, is part of the same group. Both ⑤

Hard Day's Night North John St ☎0151/236 1964, ⓦwww.harddaysnighthotel.com. Specially commissioned photographs and artwork feature large in this up-to-the-minute four-star close to Mathew St. Splashes of vibrant colour and artful lighting enhance the elegant decor. The Lennon and McCartney suites are the tops. Breakfast not included. ⑦ suites ⑨

🏃 **Hope Street** 40 Hope St (entrance on Hope Place) ☎0151/709 3000, ⓦwww.hopestreethotel.co.uk. This former Victorian warehouse has been given a stunningly chic makeover – retaining its original brickwork and cast-iron columns but adding hardwood floors, huge beds, flat-screen TVs and luxurious bathrooms. Service is spot-on. Breakfast not included. ⑦, suites ⑨

Malmaison 7 William Jessop Way, Prince's Dock ☎0151/229 5000, ⓦwww.malmaison.com. The first purpose-built hotel in this chain has gone for industrial and black as well as the trademark plum. Bar and brasserie are opulently dark, but bedrooms are on the small side; low-level lighting guides you to slate wet rooms. Parking nearby. ⑦

Premier Apartments 9 Hatton Garden ☎0115/227 9467, ⓦwww.premierapartments.com. Centrally located spacious one- and two-bedroom apart-ments in a modern glass building. Wi-Fi, superior breakfasts (from the Delifonseca delicatessen on Stanley St) and parking are available. ⑥

Racquet Club Hargreaves Building, 5 Chapel St ☎0151/236 6676, ⓦwww.racquetclub.org.uk. Boutique-style town-house hotel with just eight rooms, each mixing good linen and traditional furniture with contemporary art and all mod cons. Breakfast is not included in the price, but is available courtesy of *Ziba*, the hotel's cutting-edge Modern British restaurant. ⑦

Hostels

🏃 **International Inn** 4 South Hunter St, off Hardman St ☎0151/709 8135, ⓦwww.internationalinn.co.uk. Converted Victorian warehouse in a great location, with modern accommodation for 100 in heated, en-suite rooms sleeping two to ten people. All facilities, and Internet access in adjacent café. Dorm beds from £15, twin rooms ①

Liverpool YHA 25 Tabley St, off Wapping ☎0870/770 5924, ⓔliverpool@yha.org.uk. One of the YHA's best, just south of Albert Dock, purpose-built and decorated with Beatles memorabilia. Accommodation is in smart en-suite two-, three-, four- or six-bed rooms, with licensed café and breakfast in the price. Dorms £16.50–24.50, twin rooms ②–④

The City

The main sights are scattered throughout the centre of Liverpool but you can easily walk between most of them, through cityscapes ranging from revamped shopping arcades and restyled city squares to the surviving regal Georgian terraces around Rodney and Hope streets. If you're short on time, the two **cathedrals**, **Albert Dock** and the **World Museum Liverpool** are the stand-out highlights, with both the **Walker Art Gallery** and **Tate Liverpool** essential for art fans.

Lime Street and St George's Hall

Emerging from **Lime Street Station** – of which the cast-iron train shed was the largest in the world on its completion in 1867 – you can't miss **St George's Hall**, one of Britain's finest Greek Revival buildings and a testament to the wealth generated from transatlantic trade. Now primarily an exhibition venue, but once Liverpool's premier concert hall and crown court, its vaulted Great Hall features a floor tiled with thirty thousand precious Minton tiles (usually covered over), while the Willis organ is the third largest in Europe. You can take a self-guided **tour** (Tues–Sat 10am–5pm, Sun 1–5pm; free) or contact the hall (☎0151/225 6909) for details of the guided tours.

Liverpool's **Walker Art Gallery** on William Brown Street (daily 10am–5pm; free; ⓦwww.thewalker.org.uk) houses one of the country's best provincial art collections. The art is up on the first floor, but don't miss the ground-floor

The Beatles in Liverpool

Mathew Street, ten minutes' walk west of Lime Street Station, is where *The Cavern* used to be – once the womb of Merseybeat, it has become a little enclave of Beatles nostalgia, most of it bogus and typified by the **Cavern Walks Shopping Centre**, with a bronze statue of the boys in the atrium. *The Cavern* itself saw 275 Beatles' gigs between 1961 and 1963 and was where the band was first spotted by Brian Epstein; the club closed in 1966 and was partly demolished in 1973, though a latter-day successor, the **Cavern Club** at 10 Mathew St, complete with souvenir shop, was rebuilt on half of the original site, using, it's claimed, the original bricks. The **Cavern Pub**, immediately across the way, boasts a coiffed Lennon lounging against the wall and an exterior "Wall of Fame", highlighting both the names of all the bands who appeared at the club between 1957 and 1973 (etched into the bricks) and brass discs commemorating every Liverpool chart-topper since 1952 – the city has produced more UK number No. 1 singles than any other. The soul of Beatlemania is embodied at **The Beatles Shop**, 31 Mathew St (ⓦwww.thebeatleshop.co.uk), with the "largest range of Beatles gear in the world". Around the corner, on Stanley Street, lurks the **Eleanor Rigby statue**, inspired by the song.

For a personal and social history of the group, you'll have to head to the Albert Dock for **The Beatles Story** in the Britannia Vaults (daily 10am–6pm; £9.99; ⓦwww.beatlesstory.com), which entertainingly traces The Beatles' rise from the early days at *The Cavern* to their disparate solo careers. Then it's on to the two houses where John Lennon and Paul McCartney grew up, both now saved for the nation by the National Trust. At **20 Forthlin Rd**, home of the McCartney family from 1955–1964, visitors are guided round the 1950s terraced house where John and Paul wrote songs and contemporary photographs by Paul's brother Mike are displayed. **Mendips**, the rather more genteel house where John Lennon lived between 1945 and 1963 with his Aunt Mimi and Uncle George, was bought by Yoko Ono and presented to the National Trust. It's been similarly preserved, its rooms and environs the source of inspiration for some of Lennon's finest early songs. The houses are only accessible on pre-booked minibus tours, which run from both the city centre and Speke Hall (from the city centre: early to mid-March Wed–Sun 10am, 12.30pm & 3pm, mid-March to Oct Wed–Sun 10am & 10.50am, Nov Wed–Fri 3pm; from Speke Hall: mid-March to Oct 2.30pm & 3.20pm; Nov Sat & Sun 3pm; £15, NT members £7; ☎0151/427 7231, information line ☎0844/800 4791). The price includes access to Speke Hall garden and grounds.

Dedicated pilgrims will undoubtedly want to see all the other famous Beatles' landmarks, like Strawberry Fields (a Salvation Army home), Penny Lane (an ordinary suburban street) and the Casbah Coffee Club (early basement hangout of the lads). This is best done on an **organized Beatles tour**, and the two best options are listed below, though note that these tours only show you the exteriors of the Lennon and McCartney homes.

Beatles tours

Phil Hughes ☎0151/228 4565 or 07961/511223, ⓦwww.tourliverpool.co.uk. Small (8-seater) minibus tours with a guide well versed in The Beatles and Liverpool life. Three-and-a-half-hour tours run daily on demand (£14; private tour £70), with city-centre pick-ups/drop-offs and free refreshments.

Magical Mystery Tour ☎0151/236 9091, ⓦwww.cavernclub.org or book at tourist offices. Two-hour tours (£12.95) on board a multi-coloured Mystery Bus, departing daily throughout the year from the 08 Place and Albert Dock.

Sculpture Gallery, where John Gibson's *Tinted Venus* (1851–56) takes pride of place, nor the Craft and Design Gallery, where the Walker displays changing exhibits from its large applied-art collection – glassware, ceramics, fabrics, precious metals and furniture, largely retrieved from the homes of the city's early industrial businessmen.

The Walker had its origins in the collection of one such person, eminent Liverpudlian William Roscoe (1753–1831), who acquired much of the early Renaissance art now on display, most notably the masterful *Christ Discovered in the Temple* (1342) by Simone Martini. Liverpool's explosive economic growth in the eighteenth and nineteenth centuries is reflected in much of the Walker's collection, as British painting begins to occupy centre stage – notably works by George Stubbs, England's greatest animal painter (and native Liverpudlian). With Victorian art the Walker shifts up another gear, with John Everett Millais' *Isabella* (1848) one of the first Pre-Raphaelite works, followed by a succession of splendid classical pieces by other members of the Brotherhood. Meanwhile, Victorian taste for melodrama is encapsulated in a work by W.F. Yeames whose English Civil War subject might not be immediately familiar but whose title undoubtedly is – *And when did you last see your father?* (1878). Impressionists and Post-Impressionists, including Degas, Sickert, Cézanne and Monet, drag the collection into more modern times and tastes, before the Walker embarks on its final round of galleries of contemporary British art. Paul Nash, Lucian Freud, Ben Nicholson, David Hockney and John Hoyland all have work here, much of it first displayed in (and subsequently purchased from) the Walker's biennial John Moores Exhibition (the next of which will run from the end of September 2008 until January 2009).

World Museum Liverpool

Further along William Brown Street the World Museum Liverpool (daily 10am–5pm; free; @www.worldmuseumliverpool.org.uk) is the city's major family attraction. The dramatic six-storey atrium provides access to an eclectic series of themed exhibits of broad appeal – from natural history to ethnographical collections, insects to antiquities, dinosaurs to space rockets. Stand-out sections for children include the Bug House (no explanation required), plus excellent hands-on natural history and archeology discovery centres. The planetarium and theatre have free daily shows, with times posted at the information desk.

The cathedrals and around

On the hill behind Lime Street, off Mount Pleasant, rises the idiosyncratically shaped Catholic Metropolitan Cathedral of Christ the King (daily 8am–5/6pm; donation requested; @www.liverpoolmetrocathedral.org.uk), denigratingly known as "Paddy's Wigwam" or the "Mersey Funnel". Built in the wake of the revitalizing Second Vatican Council, it was raised on top of the tentative beginnings of Sir Edwin Lutyens' grandiose project to outdo St Peter's in Rome. World War II brought building work to a halt in 1941, and following subsequent financial constraints the crypt was not completed until 1958. The present building, to Sir Frederick Gibberd's spectacular Modernist design, is anchored by sixteen concrete ribs supporting the landmark stained-glass lantern, and was consecrated in 1967. Ceremonial steps mark the approach from Mount Pleasant/Hope Street, with a café-bar at the bottom and four huge bells at the top.

At the other end of the aptly named Hope Street, the Anglican Liverpool Cathedral (daily 8am–6pm; donation requested; @www.liverpoolcathedral .org.uk) looks much more ancient but was actually completed eleven years later, in 1978, after 74 years in construction. The last of the great British Neo-Gothic structures, Sir Giles Gilbert Scott's masterwork claims a smattering of superlatives: Britain's largest and the world's fifth-largest cathedral, the world's tallest Gothic arches and the highest and heaviest bells. The stark interior is lightened by the beautiful stone tracery in the finely detailed Lady Chapel – the first part of the cathedral to be completed, in 1910 – while the Great Space **film and audio tour** (£4.75) makes more of the building's history, symbolism and architecture. On a clear day a trip up the 330-foot **tower** (£4.25, £6.75 combined ticket with the Great Space) is rewarded by views to the Welsh hills. For food, there's a choice of mezzanine café-bar and the *Refectory* restaurant.

A couple of minutes' walk from the Anglican Cathedral, **59 Rodney Street** (mid-March to Oct Wed–Sun & Nov weekends 11am–4.15pm, timed tours only, call ☎0151/709 6261; £5.20; NT) was the home and studio of photographer Edward Chambré Hardman. The National Trust has restored the rooms where he lived for forty years (1948–88), and presents a wide selection of his Liverpool photographs.

The city centre

After years of neglect, Liverpool's city centre is slowly being rebuilt or refashioned, often to quite dramatic effect. Some of the most strident changes have been made in the former warehouse and factory district between Bold Street and Duke Street (an area now known as the **Ropewalks**), where apartments, urban spaces, café-bars and shops have sprouted in recent years. **Concert Square**, just off Bold Street, occupies space once taken up by a factory which was levelled to provide room for warehouse-style bar developments. **FACT** at 88 Wood St (ⓦwww.fact.co.uk) – that's Film, Art and Creative Technology – provides a cultural anchor for the neighbourhood with its galleries for art, video and new-media exhibitions (Tues–Sun 11am–6pm; free), community projects, cinema screens, café and bar. Further down Wood Street, the **Open Eye Gallery**, at nos. 28–32 (Tues–Sat 10.30am–5/5.30pm; free; ⓦwww.openeye.org.uk), features several temporary exhibitions a year, concentrating on photography, installation and video work.

Nearby School Lane throws up the beautifully proportioned **Bluecoat Chambers**, originally built in 1717 as an Anglican boarding school for orphans. An integral part of Liverpool's cultural life for years, it has now been enlarged as The Bluecoat (ⓦwww.thebluecoat.org.uk) to incorporate artists' studios and retail units. The associated **Bluecoat Display Centre** (access from College Lane) features contemporary craft in its gallery and shop (ⓦwww .bluecoatdisplaycentre.com).

Diverting towards **Queen Square**, one of the city centre's surviving Victorian warehouses, on the corner of Whitechapel and Queen Square, is occupied by the **Conservation Centre** (Mon–Sat 10am–5pm, Sun noon–5pm; free; ⓦwww.conservationcentre.org.uk). This is where Liverpool's museums and galleries undertake their restoration work and give visitors a chance to identify fabrics and furniture beetles or learn how to get the rust off a gold disc.

En route to the Pier Head, the **Western Approaches Museum** at 1 Rumford Street, off Chapel Street (Mon–Thurs & Sat 10.30am–4.30pm; £4.75; ⓦwww.liverpoolwarmuseum.co.uk) reveals an underground labyrinth of rooms, formerly headquarters for Battle of the Atlantic during World War II. The massive Operations Room vividly displays all the technology of a 1940s' nerve centre – wooden pushers and model boats, chalkboards and ladders.

Pier Head, Mersey Ferry and the Three Graces

Though the tumult of shipping which once fought the current here has gone, the **Pier Head** landing stage remains the embarkation point for the

Mersey Ferry (☎0151/330 1444, ⊛www.merseyferries.co.uk) to Woodside (for Birkenhead) and Seacombe (Wallasey). Straightforward ferry shuttles (£2.20 return) operate during the morning and evening rush hours. At other times the boats run circular fifty-minute "river explorer" **cruises** (hourly: Mon–Fri 10am–3pm, Sat & Sun 10am–6pm; £5.10), which you can combine with a visit to the Spaceport space exploration visitor attraction at Seacombe (see opposite).

The view back across the Mersey to the Liverpool skyline is one of the city's glories. Dominating the waterfront are the so-called **Three Graces** – namely the Port of Liverpool Building (1907), Cunard Building (1913) and, most prominently, the 322-feet-high **Royal Liver Building** (1910), topped by the "Liver Birds", a couple of cormorants which have become the symbol of the city. Development of the waterfront area is ongoing – the cruise liner terminal at Princes Dock was opened in 2007 and a new Mersey ferry terminal should be operational by the end of 2008. Boats will be travelling the extension to the Leeds and Liverpool canal in 2009, and the following year will see opening of the new Museum of Liverpool.

Albert Dock

Albert Dock, five minutes' walk south of Pier Head, was built in 1846 when Liverpool's port was a world leader. It started to decline at the beginning of the twentieth century, as the new deep-draught ships were unable to berth here, and last saw service in 1972. A decade later the site was given a complete refit, emerging as a type of rescued urban heritage that's been copied throughout the country, but rarely as successfully as here. Bars, restaurants, shops and museum collections are bolstered by the high-profile Beatles Story (see box, p.691); there's pay parking – follow the Convention Centre signs – and frequent buses arrive at the Paradise Street Interchange from Queen Square bus station.

The **Merseyside Maritime Museum** (all museums and galleries daily 10am–5pm; free; ⊛www.liverpoolmuseums.org.uk/maritime) fills one wing of the Dock; allow at least two hours to peruse the various galleries. The basement houses **Seized**, giving the lowdown on smuggling and revenue collection, with plenty of interactive opportunities, along with **Emigrants to a New World**, an illuminating display detailing Liverpool's pivotal role as a springboard for over nine million emigrants. To cater for them, short-stay lodging houses sprang up all over the centre, as illustrated in an 1854 street scene, while on board the ships – there's a walk-through example – people were packed into dark, noisy ranks of bunks where they "puffed, groaned, swore, vomited, prayed, moaned and cried". Other galleries showcase maritime paintings and models, and tell the story of the Battle of the Atlantic and of the three ill-fated liners – the *Titanic*, *Lusitania* and *Empress of Ireland*. Finally, the brand new **International Slavery Museum** on the third floor manages to be both challenging and chilling. The number of slaves shipped to sugar plantations in the Americas over 400 years ran into millions; their conditions, deprivations and legacy are explored in three distinct areas. Life in Africa delves into the culture of West Africa, where a full-size re-creation of a Nigerian Igbo compound is prominent, while the Middle Passage Gallery tells dehumanizing stories of slavery through screen dramatizations and displays of manacles, chains, instruments of torture and a model of a Caribbean plantation. Lastly, contemporary issues of equality, freedom and racial injustice are examined via caricatures, film and music, focusing on key players such as Martin Luther King Jr and the Black Panther Party. The Black Achievers Wall emphasizes the positive.

Also on the Dock, **Tate Liverpool** (June–Aug daily 10am–5.50pm; Sept–May Tues–Sun 10am–5.50pm; free, special exhibitions usually £5;

▲ Albert Dock

@www.tate.org.uk/liverpool) is the country's national collection of modern art in the north. Popular retrospectives and an ever-changing display of individual works are its bread and butter, and there's also a full programme of events, talks and tours – the daily tour at noon is free. Break up visits with espressos in the Tate's dockside café-bar.

Speke Hall

Located near Liverpool's airport, six miles southeast of the centre, **Speke Hall** (mid-March to Oct Wed–Sun 1–5.30pm, plus Nov to mid-Dec Sat & Sun 1–4.30pm; gardens Tues–Sun 11am–5.30pm or dusk; £6.80, gardens only £4.10; NT; ☎0151/427 7231) is one of the country's finest examples of Elizabethan timbered architecture. Dating from 1530, and sitting in an oasis of rhododendrons, the house encloses a beautifully proportioned courtyard overlooked by myriad diamond panes. There are secret priest and spy holes, a wealth of seventeenth-century and Victorian furniture plus ornamental gardens and woodland walks. Any bus to the airport from the city centre runs within half a mile of the entrance.

The Wirral: Spaceport, Port Sunlight and Lady Lever Art Gallery

Across the Mersey lies **The Wirral**, the peninsula that sits between Liverpool and Chester, flanked by the Irish Sea and the River Dee. A trip on the Mersey ferry to its Seacombe Terminal at Wallasey brings you right to **Spaceport** (Tues–Sun 10.30am–6pm, last entry at 4.30pm; £8.50, with ferry £11.50; @www.spaceport.org.uk), where you can blast off in a space pod to the six galleries of hands-on exploration of all aspects of space flight and the universe. Allow two hours, especially if you want to stop for the thirty-minute planetarium show.

Merseyrail trains run under the Mersey and out as far as **Port Sunlight**, a garden village created in 1888 by industrialist William Hesketh Lever for the workers at his soap factory. The project, similar in scope to those of Titus Salt at Saltaire near Bradford and John Cadbury at Bournville in Birmingham, reveals one of the more benign aspects of Merseyside's industrial past. It's explored at the **Sunlight Vision Museum**, 95 Greendale Rd (daily 10am–4.30/5pm; £3.75; Ⓦwww.portsunlightvillage.com), from where a self-guided trail runs through the village, past the houses, church, theatre and gardens. Off Greendale Road, a little further from Port Sunlight Station, the **Lady Lever Art Gallery** (daily 10am–5pm; free; Ⓦwww.ladyleverartgallery.org.uk) houses an eclectic collection of English eighteenth-century furniture and paintings, Pre-Raphaelite paintings by artists such as Rossetti and Ford Madox Brown, Wedgwood china, porcelain and assorted Chinese artefacts. There's also a nice café.

Eating, drinking and nightlife

Liverpool's dining scene has a choice of classy **restaurants** alongside a fine selection of **cafés** and budget places to eat. Most are in three distinct areas – at Albert Dock, around Hardman and Hope streets, and along Berry and Nelson streets, heart of Liverpool's **Chinatown**. Failing those, take a short taxi ride out to **Lark Lane** in Aigburth, close to Sefton Park, where a dozen eating and drinking spots pack into one short street.

Liverpool's **pubs and bars** stay open later than most, with many serving until 1am or 2am. In the Ropewalks area, Fleet Street, Slater Street and Wood Street have seen most development, with the action centred on Concert Square. Victoria Street in the business district is another fast-developing area for bars and nightlife, with another tranche of places down at Albert Dock.

The city's dance **clubs** are mainly notable for their lack of pretence, fashion playing second string to dancing and drinking. The evening paper, the *Liverpool Echo* and the monthly *Liverpool.com* (Ⓦwww.liverpool.com) have events **listings**.

Cafés, bistros and café-bars

Baby Cream Edward Pavilion, Albert Dock. Hedonistic lounge bar that's always fun – a stylish crowd nibbles the "tear-and-share" food and sips cocktails.

Blue Bar Edward Pavilion, Albert Dock ☏0151/702 5830. Brick-vaulted café-bar with dockside tables and big sofas inside – its offshoot *Baby Blue* private members' lounge bar attracts the Liverpool soccerati and other celebs.

Egg 16 Newington St. Up on the third floor, this informal and rather purple café serves excellent vegan and vegetarian food, with good set-meal deals.

Everyman Bistro 5–9 Hope St. Long-standing theatre-basement hangout with homemade quiche, pies and bakes, pizza and salad-type meals, at around a tenner for two courses. It's also known for its beers and wines, and the bar closes at midnight, or 2am on Fri & Sat. Closed Sun.

Keith's Wine Bar 107 Lark Lane ☏0151/728 7688. An old favourite, as much for its good-value

bistro food (pasta, salads, risotto) as its wine selection.

Kimos 46 Mount Pleasant. A student fave for mountainous portions of Middle Eastern/Mediterranean-style grills, kebabs, platters and salads – there's a fine range of breakfasts, too.

The Quarter 7 Falkner St ☏0151/707 1965. A great lunch place between the two cathedrals, with some seats outside on the Georgian terrace. Serves an Italian bistro menu, including gourmet pizza, but you can just stop by for coffee and cake.

Tabac 126 Bold St. Contemporary café-bar, serving a wide-ranging menu from breakfast onwards.

Restaurants

London Carriage Works 40 Hope St ☏0151/705 2222. One of Liverpool's finest, a see-and-be-seen Modern British restaurant in the city's coolest designer hotel. You'll need a reservation (book well in advance for weekends). Expensive.

The Monro 92–94 Duke St ☏0151/707 9933. A gastropub makeover for one of the city's oldest hostelries means this is now a place for serious British eating at a reasonable price. Moderate.

Puschka 16 Rodney St ☎0151/708 8698. Contemporary English dining from a seasonally changing menu – locals like its relaxed atmosphere and there's usually a good vegetarian choice. Closed Mon, and for lunch Tues–Fri. Expensive.

Side Door 29a Hope St ☎0151/707 7888. The intimate Georgian town-house restaurant has settled on a winning combination of Mediterranean food and reasonable prices – with a bargain pre-theatre menu of £14.95. Closed Sun. Moderate.

Simply Heathcotes Beetham Plaza, 25 The Strand ☎0151/236 3536. Lancastrian magic behind a wall of glass– locally sourced ingredients (lamb, Goosnargh duckling, black pudding), light lunches, grills, Sunday brunch and other delights, in many people's favourite Liverpool restaurant. Expensive.

Yuet Ben 1 Upper Duke St ☎0151/709 5772. Specialist in Beijing-style food, with a superb range of dishes including barbecued ribs that experts drool over. Dinner only; closed Mon. Moderate.

Pubs and bars

Alma de Cuba St Peter's Church, Seel St. Far more candles than when it was a church, but the mirrored altar is still the focus of this bar's rich and dark Cuban-themed interior. The mezzanine restaurant has even more dripping candles.

Baltic Fleet 33a Wapping. Restored no-nonsense, quiet pub with age-old shipping connections, near the YHA and near Albert Dock. Good food on offer.

Dispensary 67 Renshaw St. Sympathetic recreation of a Victorian pub using rescued and antique wood. A good place for real ales.

Geisha 7 Myrtle St. Luxurious quasi-industrial venue on an Eastern theme, with huge curving bar. Dim sum, sushi and noodles downstairs and balcony restaurant.

Lion Tavern 67 Moorfields. Real ale in superbly restored Victorian surroundings, from the tiles to the stained-glass rotunda. Also excellent cheese and pâté lunches (Mon–Fri).

Philharmonic 36 Hope St. Liverpool's finest traditional watering-hole where the main attractions – the beer aside – are the mosaic floors, tiling, gilded wrought-iron gates and the marble decor in the gents.

Ship and Mitre 133 Dale St. For the biggest real ale choice in Liverpool – twelve guest beers, plus ciders and imported lagers – visit this renowned Art Deco free house.

Ye Cracke 13 Rice St. Crusty backstreet pub off Hope Street, much loved by the young Lennon, and with a great jukebox, and cheap-as-chips food (daytime only).

Clubs and live music

Barfly 90 Seel St ☎0870/907 0999, ⓦwww .barflyclub.com. Great indie/rock gigs and a wide variety of club nights – Chibuku and Circus are the big nights out.

Carling Academy 11–13 Hotham St ☎0151/707 3200, ⓦwww.liverpool-academy.co.uk. A good roster of contemporary, indie and rock gigs.

Cavern Club 10 Mathew St ☎0151/236 1965, ⓦwww.cavernclub.org. The self-styled "most famous club in the world" has live bands Wed to Sun.

Classical music, theatre and cinema

The Royal Liverpool Philharmonic Orchestra, ranked with Manchester's Hallé as the northwest's best, dominates the city's **classical music** scene. **Theatre** is well entrenched in the city at a variety of venues, while independent **cinema** has found a home at FACT, the city's creative technology centre.

Annual **festivals** include ship visits and events at the Mersey Maritime Festival (June); a celebration of African arts and music in Africa Oye (June; ⓦwww .africaoye.com); the **Summer Pops** (July), when the Royal Philharmonic and top pop names take the stage; the **Liverpool International Street Festival** (July/August; ⓦwww.brouhaha.uk.com), which involves performances by a host of European theatre, music and dance groups; and **Beatles Week** (last week of August) and the **Mathew Street Festival** (August bank holiday; ⓦwww .mathewstreetfestival.co.uk), with half a million visitors dancing to hundreds of local, national and tribute bands.

Everyman Theatre and Playhouse 5–9 Hope St ☎0151/709 4776, ⓦwww.everymanplayhouse .com. A launchpad of local talent, presenting everything from Shakespeare to Jarman, plus concerts, exhibitions, dance and music.

Liverpool Arena and Convention Centre King's Dock ☎0844/800 0400, ⓦwww.accliverpool .com. Liverpool's newest venue hosts large-scale concerts and sports fixtures as well as conventions.

Liverpool Empire Lime St ☎0870/606 3536, ⓦwww.liverpool-empire.co.uk. The city's largest theatre, a venue for touring West End shows, and large-scale opera and ballet productions – Welsh National Opera and English National Ballet both perform regularly.

Philharmonic Hall Hope St ☎0151/709 3789, ⓦwww.liverpoolphil.com. Home of the Royal Liverpool Philharmonic Orchestra, and with a full programme of other concerts. Shows classic films once a month.

Picturehouse at FACT Wood St ☎0871/704 2063, ⓦwww.picturehouses.co.uk. The city's only independent cinema screens, for new films, re-runs and festivals.

Royal Court Theatre Roe St ☎0870/787 1866, ⓦwww.royalcourtliverpool.co.uk. Art Deco theatre and concert hall, which sees regular plays, music and comedy acts.

Unity Theatre 1 Hope Place ☎0151/709 4988, ⓦwww.unitytheatreliverpool.co.uk. Puts on the city's most adventurous range of contemporary works.

Listings

Airport ☎0870/129 8484, ⓦwww .liverpoolairport.com.
Car rental Avis ☎0870/608 6311; Europcar ☎0151/486 7111; Hertz ☎0151/486 7444.
Ferries Isle of Man Steam Packet Company for ferries/Sea Cats to Isle of Man ☎0871/222 1333, ⓦwww.steam-packet.com; Mersey Ferries ☎0151/330 1444, ⓦwww.merseyferries.co.uk; Norfolkline ☎0870/600 4321, ⓦwww .norfolkline-ferries.co.uk.
Hospital Royal Liverpool University Hospital, Prescot St ☎0151/706 2000; NHS Walk-in Centre 52 Great Charlotte Row ☎0151/285 3535.
Internet Cafe Latte.net, 4 South Hunter St ☎0151/708 9610 (Mon–Fri 8am–7pm, Sat & Sun 9am–5.30pm).
Pharmacy Boots, Clayton Sq Shopping Centre ☎0151/709 4711; Moss Pharmacy, 68–70 London Rd ☎0151/709 5271 (daily until 11pm).

Police Canning Place ☎0151/709 6010.
Post office City-centre office at St John's Precinct.
Shopping Cavern Walks on Mathew St (☎ 0151/236 9082) is favoured by the WAGs for its boutiques, with the likes of Vivienne Westwood, Cricket and Drome, while the designer-led Met Quarter (☎0151/224 2390, ⓦwww.metquarter .com) focuses on the independent Flannels store. Liverpool One (due for completion in 2009) promises to be the largest retail outlet in Europe, housing large department stores. The Heritage Market at Stanley Dock (☎0151/207 7227, ⓦwww.heritagemarket.co.uk) attracts around 200 stalls, including food, retro clothing and antiques, every Sun. Farmers' markets take place on the third Sunday of the month by the suitcase sculpture on Hope St.
Taxis Mersey Cabs ☎0151/298 2222.

Blackpool

Shamelessly brash **BLACKPOOL** is the archetypal British seaside resort, its "Golden Mile" of piers, fortune-tellers, amusement arcades, tram and donkey rides, fish-and-chip shops, candyfloss stalls, fun pubs and bingo halls making no concessions to anything but low-brow fun-seeking of the finest kind. From ukelele-strumming George Formby and his "little stick of Blackpool rock" to today's predatory, half-dressed gangs of stag and hen parties, few visitors, then or now, are in any doubt about the point of a holiday here. There are seven miles of wide sandy beach backed by an unbroken chain of hotels and guest houses, attracting sixteen million people each year.

Wealthy visitors were already summer holidaying in Blackpool at the end of the eighteenth century, and while it took a day to get there from Manchester by carriage and two days from Yorkshire, the town remained a select destination. It was the coming of the railway in 1846 that made Blackpool what it is today: within thirty years, there were piers, promenades and theatres for the thousands who descended. Blackpool's own "Eiffel Tower" on the seafront and other refined diversions were built to cater to the tastes of the first influx, but it was the Central Pier's "open-air dancing for the working classes" that heralded the crucial change of accent. Suddenly Blackpool was favoured destination for the "Wakes Weeks", when whole Lancashire mill towns descended for their annual holiday.

Where other British holiday resorts have suffered from the rivalry of cheap foreign packages, Blackpool has gone from strength to strength by shrewdly providing exactly what its visitors want. Underneath the populist veneer there's a sophisticated marketing approach, which balances ever more elaborate rides and attractions with well-grounded traditional entertainment. And when other resorts begin to close up for the winter, Blackpool's main season is just beginning, as over half a million light bulbs are used to create the **Illuminations** which decorate the promenade from the beginning of September to early November. The first static display took place in 1912, and it has been an annual event since 1949. Lately, Blackpool has been looking to extend its attractions further, with plans under way to transform the seafront promenade into a "people's playground" and bestow new entertainment complexes and leisure parks upon the town. Inevitable references are made to the "British Las Vegas", but while laser shows, glass domes and resort-style hotels might all follow, they are intended to complement, not supplant, the town's Victorian heritage.

Arrival and information

Blackpool's main train station is **Blackpool North** (direct trains from Manchester and Preston), with the **bus station** just a few steps away down Talbot Road; alternatively, trains also run hourly from Preston direct to **Blackpool Pleasure Beach** (on the Blackpool South Line). There are **car parks** signposted all over town (including on Albert Road, Talbot Road, Bank Street and Central Drive), and it's best to use them since on-street parking is only short-term. Blackpool's **airport** (ⓦwww.blackpoolinternational.com) – which handles regular flights to over 25 European destinations – lies two miles south of the centre; there are buses from the bus station or it's a £5 taxi ride.

The main **tourist office** is at 1 Clifton St (Mon–Sat 9am–5pm; ⓣ01253/478222, ⓦwww.visitblackpool.com), on the corner of Talbot Road, and sells **discounted admission tickets** for all major Blackpool attractions (except the Pleasure Beach), as well as Travel Cards (1/3/5/7-day, £5.75/14/20/22) for use on local buses and trams.

Accommodation

Bed-and-breakfast prices are generally low (from £20 per person, even less on a room-only basis or out of season), but rise at weekends and during the Illuminations. In peak season, it's simply a matter of looking for vacancy signs or asking the tourist office for help – anything cheap between North and Central piers is guaranteed to be noisy; for more peace and quiet (an unusual request in Blackpool, it has to be said), look for places along the North Shore, beyond North Pier (the grid west of Warbreck Hill Road has hundreds of options).

The Big Blue Ocean Boulevard, Blackpool Pleasure Beach ⓣ0845/367 3333, ⓦwww .bigbluehotel.com. American-resort-style accommodation, with spacious family rooms with games consoles and separate children's area, plus boutique-style, dark-wood executive rooms featuring sofas, fireplaces and excellent bathrooms. There's a contemporary bar and brasserie, parking and a gym. It's next to the Pleasure Beach (and its train station), and most rooms look out on the rides. Parking. ⑥

Boltonia 124–126 Albert Rd ⓣ01253/620248, ⓦwww.boltoniahotel.co.uk. The choices on Albert Road, between the Tower and Central Pier, mark a qualitative step up from your basic Blackpool boarding houses. The *Boltonia* is not far from the

Winter Gardens, on a corner plot that lets lots of light into the rooms – all have en-suite showers, though the superior rooms are a bit more spacious. Parking available. ❸

The Imperial North Promenade ☎01253/623971, ⓦwww.paramount-hotels.co.uk. The politicians' conference favourite, a four-star hotel with sea-facing rooms, pool and gym, the famous oak-panelled *No. 10 Bar*, *Palm Court* restaurant, and parking. It's a short tram ride away from the Tower and the rest of the sights. Special online room-only deals from £69. ❼

Number One 1 St Lukes Rd ☎01253/343901, ⓦwww.numberoneblackpool.com. There's no other B&B quite like it – an extraordinarily lavish boutique experience hosted by the ultra-amiable Mark and Claire. There are just three extravagantly appointed rooms here, though very

nearby is their larger seafront outfit, *Number One South Beach* (4 Harrowside West ☎01253/343900, ⓦwww.numberonesouthbeach.co.uk), whose 14 rooms reflect the new Blackpool – contemporary style, low carbon footprint, Modern British restaurant and bar. There's parking at both, and either is handy for the Pleasure Beach. ❼, *South Beach* ❽

Raffles 73–77 Hornby Rd ☎01253/294713, ⓦwww.raffleshotelblackpool.co.uk. Nice place back from Central Pier and away from the bustle, with well-kept rooms, bar, and traditional tearooms attached. Some parking available. Winter rates are a good deal. ❹

Ruskin Albert Rd ☎01253/624063, ⓦwww.ruskinhotel.com. At the prom end of Albert Road, the *Ruskin* exudes repro-Victorian style and offers smart rooms with decent bathrooms. Bar and brasserie, and parking available. ❺

The Town

With seven miles of beach – the tide ebb is half a mile, leaving plenty of sand at low tide – and accompanying promenade, you'll want to jump on and off the electric trams if you plan to get up and down much between the piers. Most of the town-centre shops, bars and cafés lie between Central and North piers.

Blackpool Pleasure Beach

The major event in town is **Blackpool Pleasure Beach** on the South Promenade (March–Oct daily from 11am though times vary, check website for details; ⓦwww.blackpoolpleasurebeach.com), just south of South Pier. Entrance to the amusement park is free, but you'll have to fork out for the superb array of "white knuckle" rides including the "Big One", the world's fastest roller coaster (85mph), and the outrageous suspended looping roller coaster that is "Infusion". After these, the wonderful array of antique wooden roller coasters – "woodies" to aficionados – seems like kids' stuff, but each is unique. The original "Big Dipper" was invented at Blackpool in 1923 and still thrills, as does the "Wild Mouse" (1958) and,

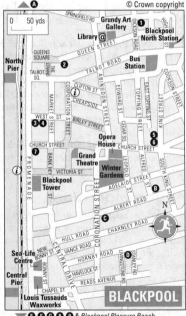

© Crown copyright

BLACKPOOL

ACCOMMODATION		CAFÉS & RESTAURANTS		PUBS & CLUBS	
The Big Blue	E	Harry Ramsden's	7	Funny Girls	1
Boltonia	B	Kwizeen	5	Mitre	4
The Imperial	A	Robert's		The Syndicate	6
Number One	F	Oyster Bar	3		
Number One South Beach	G	Septembers	2		
Raffles	D	White Tower	8		
Ruskin	C	Yamato	9		

❺,❻,❼,❽,❾ & Blackpool Pleasure Beach

Blackpool – behind the scenes

There's an alternative Blackpool behind the resort's facade – one of history, heritage and (whisper it softly) even culture.

Start at **Robert's Oyster Bar** (92 The Promenade), whose original panelled "Oyster Rooms" are still visible at the back of the adjacent pizza takeaway. There's more evidence of Victorian and Edwardian Blackpool in the **Mitre** pub (just around the corner, West St), "Blackpool's smallest pub", where for the price of a pint you can examine the collected black-and-white yesteryear photos. Down the prom and up Victoria Street leads directly to the **Winter Gardens** (Coronation St), which opened to fanfares in 1878. Scene of party political conferences over the decades, the Gardens house a motley set of cafés, bars and amusements these days, but don't miss seeing the extraordinary Spanish Hall Suite (in the form of a carved galleon) and the **Opera House** honours board, where Lillie Langtry, George Formby and Vera Lynn repose alongside contemporary entertainment giants like Darren Day and Joe Longthorne. The splendid **Grand Theatre** around the corner (Church St) is also worth a look, and has an ornate café and bar of its own.

From in front of the Opera House, follow Abingdon Street to Queen Street and the porticoed Central Library, next to which the **Grundy Art Gallery** (Mon–Sat 10am–5pm; free) might tempt you in to see its Victorian oils and watercolours, contemporary art and special exhibitions. Walking down Queen Street to the promenade you reach **North Pier**, the first pier to be opened (1863) on the Blackpool seafront and now a listed building. At this point, let chance and the trams dictate the final part of the tour – Blackpool, incidentally, had the world's first permanent electric street tramway (1885). Head northbound and you can get off at the **Imperial Hotel** (North Promenade), whose wood-panelled *No. 10 Bar* is covered with photographs and mementoes of every British prime minister since Lloyd George. Or, if the south-bound tram arrives first, stay on as far as Central Pier until you see *McDonald's* (corner of Chapel St), which only has one photograph on display, but a most extraordinary one – it's hard to say who looks more surprised, the staff on duty one day in October 2002 or their unexpected customers, Bill Clinton and Kevin Spacey.

best of all, the "Grand National" (1935), whose 3300-foot twin track races you against a parallel car. Before each one sets off, the public-service announcement intones "Please do not wave your hands in the air" – when any self-respecting woodie rider knows that's exactly what you have to do. Recuperate in the park's champagne and oyster bar, which adds a bit of class to the otherwise relentless barrage of fairground noise, shrieking, music and fast food. There are charges for individual rides but best value is to buy an unlimited-ride wristband (£15–28 depending on the season, cheaper if booked online).

The seafront and the tower

Pleasure Beach aside, most of the big-ticket attractions are found near the **Central Pier**, with its 108-foot-high revolving Big Wheel. You'll need a bulging wallet if you plan to do the lot, from **Sea–Life Centre** (Ⓦ www.sealife. co.uk) to **Doctor Who Museum** (Ⓦ www.doctowhoexhibitions.com), but they are all undeniably slick and entertaining, and open daily for most of the year. For a taste of what Blackpool attractions used to be like, visit **Louis Tussauds Waxworks** (Ⓦ www.louistussaudswaxworks.co.uk), though even here these days it's not so much Churchill and Margaret Thatcher, but rather "pint-sized pop princess" Kylie, Gordon Ramsay, and Posh and Becks.

Blackpool's elegant cast-iron **piers** strike a more traditional note. They're covered with arcades and amusements, while much of what passes for evening family entertainment – TV comics and variety shows – takes place in the various pier theatres. Between Central and North piers stands the 518-foot **Blackpool Tower** (June–Oct daily 10am–11pm; Nov–May daily 10am–6pm; £15.95, £9.95 after 7pm; ⓦwww.theblackpooltower.co.uk), erected in 1894 when it was thought that the northwest really ought not to be outdone by Paris. Paying the hefty entrance fee is the only way to ride up to the top for the stunning view and an unnerving walk on the see-through glass floor. The all-day ticket covers all the other tower attractions, including the gilt Edwardian ballroom, with its Wurlitzer organ tea dances and big-band evenings, plus aquarium, children's entertainers, indoor adventure playground, cafés and amusements. From the very early days, there's also been a Moorish-inspired **circus** (2hr shows included in the entry ticket; two daily performances) between the tower's legs.

If you've seen and been on everything mentioned so far you'll have been here for days, spent a fortune and thoroughly enjoyed yourself. These, it has to be said, are just the A-list attractions – indefatigable holiday-makers also take in Blackpool's zoo and model village on East Park Drive, or any one of a number of pleasure flights, go-kart rinks, donkey rides, children's play areas, ten-pin bowling alleys, games arcades and other jollifications.

Eating

Eating out revolves around the typical British seaside fare of fish and chips, available all over town. Given the sheer volume of customers, other restaurants don't have to try too hard: you'll have no trouble finding cheap roasts, pizzas, Chinese or Indian food, but might struggle if you're seeking a bit more sophistication. For a quieter night out, head the few miles south to genteel **St Annes** (a taxi's best), where Wood Street has a line of agreeable bars and restaurants.

Harry Ramsden's 60–63 The Promenade ☏01253/294386. The celebrated Yorkshire chippie chain has the town's pre-eminent (and priciest) fish and chips. Moderate.

Kwizeen 49 King St ☏01253/290045. Best restaurant in town is this friendly, contemporary bistro with a seasonally changing menu that places a real emphasis on locally sourced produce, from Blackpool tomatoes and Lancashire cheese to Fylde farm ostriches and Goosnargh duck. Mains are £13, though there's a bargain two-course weekday lunch. Closed Sat lunch & Sun, 2 weeks Feb and 1 week Aug. Expensive.

Septembers 17 Queen St ☏01253/299200. Sleek champagne bar upstairs, dining room below, for tapas and Spanish-Mediterranean mains, paella to seabass. Closed Mon & Tues, Wed lunch & Sun dinner. Expensive.

White Tower Ocean Blvd, Blackpool Pleasure Beach ☏01253/336365. Blackpool's posh night out and the closest the town gets to Vegas – a lounge-style restaurant with prom views (great for the Illuminations), snappy service and a contemporary bistro-style menu. Tues–Sat dinner only, plus Sun lunch. Expensive.

Yamato 28 Wood St, St Annes ☏01253/782868. A teppanyaki restaurant that's well worth the trip to watch the amiable chefs work their magic at the communal grill-tables. There's sushi too and some good-value set menus. Moderate.

Drinking, nightlife and entertainment

If you like your nightlife late, loud and libidinous, summertime Blackpool has few English peers. In all the **pubs and clubs**, young men can expect to have their attire and demeanour given the once-over by the hired hulks at the door, while "girls" and "ladies" can expect free drinks and entry and a lot of largely good-natured amorous jousting. Provided you don't expect too much sophistication, or snobby metropolitan ways, you'll have a great time. There's a plethora of theme bars, Irish to Australian, and any number of places for

karaoke or **dancing** – local opinion favours *The Syndicate*, 120–140 Church St
(Ⓦwww.thesyndicate.com), the UK's biggest club, which features star DJs
throughout the year. *Funny Girls*, a transvestite-run bar at 5 Dickson Rd, off
Talbot Road (Ⓣ0870/350 2665, Ⓦwww.funnygirlsshowbar.co.uk), has nightly
shows that attract long (gay and straight) queues. Otherwise, entertainment is
based very heavily on family shows, musicals, veteran TV comedians, magicians,
ice shows, tribute bands, crooners and stage spectaculars put on at a variety of
end-of-pier and **Pleasure Beach** (Ⓦwww.blackpoolpleasurebeach.com)
theatres, or at historic venues such as the **Grand Theatre** (Ⓣ01253/290190,
Ⓦwww.blackpoolgrand.co.uk) and **Opera House** (Ⓣ0870/380111, Ⓦwww
.blackpoollive.com), both on Church Street.

Preston and around

With the siren draws of the Lakes, the Peak District and the Yorkshire Dales so
close, the rest of Lancashire often gets bypassed in the rush to the surrounding
national parks, and more's the pity. It's true, the old cotton towns of north and
east Lancashire might not be first on everyone's must-see list, but in **Preston**,
25 miles northwest of Manchester, the county has one of England's oldest
towns, containing two fine museums and some appealing Georgian and
Victorian remnants. North of the town, rural Lancashire is at its most bucolic
in the villages of the **Ribble Valley**, particularly in the **Forest of Bowland**, to
which the gateway is the small market town of **Clitheroe**.

Preston

Strategically placed on the banks of the River Ribble, **PRESTON** was already
an important market town in Anglo-Saxon times and received its royal charter
in 1179 – origin of the Preston Guild celebrations, which since 1542 have taken
place every twenty years (the next in 2012). The town changed hands in the
Civil War and saw action during the Jacobite rebellions, while Charles Dickens
gathered material here for *Hard Times*, his coruscating attack on the factory
system. True, there's little to show for such a long history save the nickname,
"Proud Preston", but as the administrative and commercial centre of Lancashire,
it's a useful shopping and service centre.

Some handsome Victorian public buildings do survive, most notably the
majestic Greek Revivalist **Harris Museum and Art Gallery** (Mon–Sat
10am–5pm; free; Ⓦwww.harrismuseum.org.uk) in the central Market Square.
Aside from exploring the "Story of Preston", the permanent collection focuses
on fine art and decorative art, while temporary exhibitions often explore links
with the town's significant Asian population. On either side of the Harris lies
the modern shopping area, converging on Fishergate, the main street through
town, while for a change in emphasis, cross Fishergate to explore the handsome
Georgian development of **Winckley Square**, once home to the town's richest
cotton magnates. Beyond the square, the ground drops away to the River
Ribble and **Avenham Park**, one of the country's best examples of a landscaped
Victorian park.

If you needed any more incentive to stop it would be to make your way to
the ground of Preston North End – one of Britain's oldest football clubs and
winners of the first Football League championship – for the marvellous
National Football Museum on Sir Tom Finney Way, Deepdale Stadium
(Tues–Sat 10am–5pm, Sat matchday until 3pm, midweek matchday until

7.30pm, Sun 11am–5pm, also open Mon on bank and school hols; free; Ⓦwww
.nationalfootballmuseum.com). On one level, this is simply an unparalleled
collection of football memorabilia, but you really don't have to know anything
about football to enjoy the museum, since "the true story of the world's greatest
game" is backed by fascinating material on football's origins, its social importance, the experience of fans through the ages, and other relevant themes.

For the football museum, it's a ten-minute ride on bus #19 (every 5min) from
Preston **bus station**, right in the town centre. The **train station** has regular
services to Lancaster, Manchester and Blackpool; a bus connects the train station
to the town centre and bus station; otherwise, just follow Fishergate into the
centre, a ten-minute walk. The **tourist office** is in the Guild Hall, on Lancaster
Road (Mon–Sat 10am–5.30pm; ☏01772/253731, Ⓦwww.visitpreston.com),
just round the corner from the Harris Museum.

The Ribble Valley

When the nineteenth-century Lancashire cotton weavers enjoyed a rare break
from their industry they took to the bucolic retreats of the **Ribble Valley**, north
of Preston. In stark contrast to the conurbations to the south, the valley parades a
stream of small market towns and isolated villages set among verdant fields and
rolling hills. Much of the northwestern part of the region is occupied by thinly
populated grouse moorland known as the **Forest of Bowland**. **Public transport**
is limited to the train service from Manchester and Blackburn, or buses from
Preston, to the market town of **Clitheroe** on the forest's southern fringes; from
here, buses run out to Dunsop Bridge and **Slaidburn** (with connections on to
Settle in Yorkshire), the three tiny villages in the heart of the region. Hikers can
also follow the course of the river from its source to the estuary along the seventy-
mile **Ribble Way**, which passes through Clitheroe. For more **information**,
contact Clitheroe tourist office (☏01200/425566, Ⓦwww.ribblevalley.gov.uk).

Clitheroe

A tidy little market town on the banks of the River Ribble, **CLITHEROE** is
best seen from the terrace of its empty **Norman keep** which towers above the
Ribble Valley floor. From here, the small centre is laid out before you and, if
there's little else specific to see, you can at least spend an hour or two browsing
around the shops and old pubs. There's been a **market** in town since the
thirteenth century: the current affair is held off King Street every Tuesday,
Thursday and Saturday.

One obvious target is **Pendle Hill**, a couple of miles to the east, where the
ten **Pendle Witches** allegedly held the diabolic rites that led to their hanging
in 1612. The evidence against them came mainly from one small child, but
nonetheless a considerable mythology has grown up around the witches, whose
memory is perpetuated by a hilltop gathering each Halloween. The Clitheroe
tourist office can provide a self-drive leaflet guiding you around the locality.
With a car, you could also run out to the Roman museum at **Ribchester**
(southwest) and the ruined Cistercian abbey at **Whalley** (pronounced "Worley",
a few miles south of Clitheroe), in which case you could stop for a meal at the
excellent *Three Fishes* (☏01254/826888), a gastropub in rolling countryside just
outside Whalley on the Mitton road.

The Forest of Bowland

Heading northwest from Clitheroe on the B6478 brings you to the **Forest of
Bowland** (Ⓦwww.forestofbowland.com) – although the name "forest" is used

here in its traditional sense of "a royal hunting ground". It's designated an Area of Outstanding Natural Beauty, of remote fells and farmland and a preserve of rare birds like the hen harrier, ring ouzel and merlin. The website has details of guided walks and events in the area, from dawn-chorus safaris to night-time bat watches. At the duck-riddled riverside hamlet of **DUNSOP BRIDGE**, an old drover's track (now a very minor road) known as the **TROUGH OF BOWLAND** begins its fifteen-mile slog across the tops to Lancaster, winding through heather- and bracken-clad hills. Those in the know make their way the couple of miles south to the *Inn at Whitewell* (℡01200/448222, ⓦwww.innatwhitewell.com; ⓘ), which combines cosy, traditionally furnished rooms with fabulous food in its restaurant (dinner only, reservations essential) and a welcoming bar. Work up an appetite at the **BOWLAND WILD BOAR PARK** (daily 10.30/11am–4/5.30pm; £4.50, winter £3; ⓦwww.wildboarpark.co.uk), signposted down the Chipping road from Dunsop Bridge, where wild boar and longhorn cows roam free in the woodland by the River Hodder.

Northeast of Dunsop Bridge it's a couple of miles to **SLAIDBURN**, where old stone cottages fronted by a strip of aged cobbles set the tone. The village buildings are largely untouched by modern intrusion – a single family has owned much of the village for 200 years – and Slaidburn has a real nineteenth-century air about it. There's an even older **inn**, the *Hark to Bounty* (℡01200/446246, ⓦwww.harktobounty.co.uk; ⓢ), with reasonable rooms but better known for its good bar food, and a popular **youth hostel** (℡0870/770 6034, ⓔslaidburn@yha.org.uk; from £13), itself a former inn, with beamed ceilings and an open fire.

Lancaster and around

LANCASTER, Lancashire's county town, dates back at least as long ago as the Roman occupation, though only scant remains survive from that period. A Saxon church was later built within the ruined Roman walls as Lancaster became a strategic trading centre, and by medieval times ships were using the River Lune and the coastal routes to Cumbria. A castle on the heights above the river defended the town from attack and provided a focus for the dispensing of regional justice. Lancaster became an important port on the slave trade triangle, and it's the legacy of predominantly Georgian buildings from that time that gives the town its character, particularly in the leafy areas around the castle. It's no surprise that many people choose to spend a night here on the way to the Lakes or Dales to the north. It's also an easy side-trip the few miles west to the resort of **Morecambe** and to neighbouring **Heysham village**, with its ancient churches.

The City

The site of **Lancaster Castle** (daily: tours every 30min 10.30am–4pm; £5; ⓦwww.lancastercastle.com) has been the city's focal point since Roman times. The Normans built the first castle here in around 1093 in an attempt to protect the region from marauding Scots armies, and it was added to throughout medieval times, becoming a crown court and prison in the thirteenth century, a role it still fulfils today. Currently, about a quarter of the battlemented building can be visited on an entertaining hour-long tour, though court sittings sometimes affect the schedules. The tour begins around the back in the grandiose eighteenth-century Shire Hall, and then moves on to the eight-foot-thick walls of the thirteenth-century Adrian's Tower, which encircle a room hung with manacles and leg-irons. You may also see and hear something of the hangman's art: public executions were carried out at the castle until 1865.

A two-minute walk down the steps between the castle and the neighbouring **Priory Church of St Mary** brings you to the seventeenth-century **Judges' Lodgings** (Easter–June & Oct Mon–Fri 1–4pm, Sat & Sun noon–4pm; July–Sept Mon–Fri 10am–4pm, Sat & Sun noon–4pm; £3), once used by visiting magistrates. Rooms on the ground and first floors house quality furniture by Gillows of Lancaster, one-time boat builders who, in the early eighteenth century, took to cabinet-making with the tropical timber that came back as ballast in their boats. The top floor is given over to a **Museum of Childhood**, with memory-jogging displays of toys and games, and a period (1900) schoolroom.

Down on the banks of the **River Lune** – which lent Lancaster its name – one of the eighteenth-century quayside warehouses is taken up by part of the **Maritime Museum** (daily 11am/12.30pm–4/5pm; £3). The museum's ample coverage of life on the sea and inland waterways of Lancashire is complemented by the **City Museum** on Market Square back in town (Mon–Sat 10am–5pm; free), which explores the city's history from Neolithic to Georgian times. The grandiose **Town Hall** faces Dalton Square at the top of town, whose **Queen Victoria Memorial** bears a sculpted frieze that's a roll-call of the Victorian great and good – including Lancaster's own Richard Owen, natural scientist, first Superintendent of London's National Science Museum and coiner of the word "dinosaur".

For a panorama of the town, Morecambe Bay and the Cumbrian fells, take a bus from the bus station (or a steep 25-minute walk up Moor Lane) to **Williamson Park** (daily 10am–4/5pm; free; Ⓦ www.williamsonpark.com), Lancaster's highest point. The grounds were laid out among old stone quarries by cotton workers, put out of work by the cotton famine caused by the American Civil War. Funded by local statesman and lino magnate Lord Ashton, the park's centrepiece is the 220-foot-high **Ashton Memorial**, a Baroque folly raised by his son in memory of his second wife.

Practicalities

From either the **train station** on Meeting House Lane, or the **bus station** on Cable Street, it's a five-minute walk to the **tourist office** at 29 Castle Hill (Mon–Sat 10am–4/5pm; ☏ 01524/32878, Ⓦ www.citycoastcountryside.co.uk). Annual **events and festivals** include the Lancaster jazz festival (Sept) and spectacular Bonfire Night celebrations (Sat nearest Nov 5). For **canal cruises**, including the scheduled waterbus service to Carnforth, contact Lancaster Canal Packet Boats (☏ 01524/389410, Ⓦ www.budgietransport.co.uk).

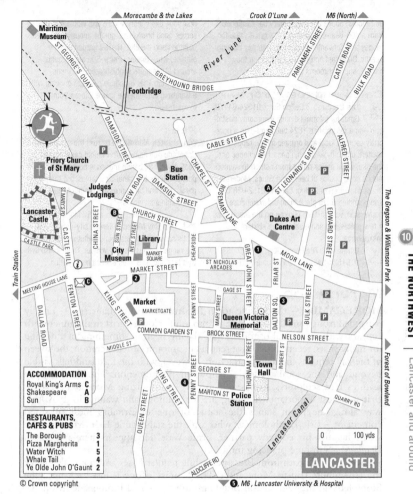

© Crown copyright

5, M6 , Lancaster University & Hospital

The main cultural destination is **Dukes** on Moor Lane (℡0845/344 0642, ⓦwww.dukes-lancaster.org), the city's principal arts centre, with cinema and theatre (including open-air performances in Williamson Park in summer). Five hundred metres up the hill from here, **The Gregson**, 33 Moorgate (℡01524/849959, ⓦwww.gregson.co.uk), is an enterprising arts and community centre with a good café and bar open to the public.

Accommodation

Royal King's Arms 75 Market St ℡01524/32451, ⓦwww.oxfordhotelsandinns.com. Fifty prettily furnished rooms with smart bathrooms, plus a bar and brasserie. Ask for a castle view. **6**

Shakespeare 96 St Leonard's Gate ℡01524/841041, ⓔtheshakespearelancaster @talktalk.net. Hard-working hosts maintain

seven cosy en-suite rooms (including two singles) in this popular town-house hotel on a central street near several long-stay car parks. No credit cards. **4**

Sun 63 Church St ℡01524/66006, ⓦwww .thesunhotelandbar.co.uk. The city centre's only four-star hotel has eight very handsome rooms (some with king-sized beds, all with fine bathrooms) above a contemporary bar fashioned from a 300-year-old building – it's great value for money and conveniently located, with pay parking nearby. Breakfast and meals available in the bar. ❹, superior rooms ❺

Cafés and restaurants

🏃 **The Borough** 3 Dalton Sq ☎01524/64170. Great for informal dining, this roomy gastro-pub – in a refurbished 1824 building – has a rigorously sourced local and organic menu. Tapas-style platters offer smoked fish, Lancashire cheese and the like, while mains range from ostrich to salmon. Also a good choice of beers and wines. Moderate.

Pizza Margherita 2 Moor Lane ☎01524/36333. Longstanding pizza place in an old warehouse conversion, with sixteen choices on the menu, plus a few pastas and some salad-type starters. Inexpensive.

🏃 **Whale Tail** 78a Penny St ☎01524/845133. Tucked up a yard on the first floor, this cheery veggie and wholefood café serves good breakfasts, quiche, moussaka, baked potatoes and the like. There's garden seating outside, while dinner (Thurs–Sun night, mains around £9) is more sophisticated, the menu ranging from Thai vegetable cakes to gnocchi with a Garstang blue-cheese sauce. Closes 3pm. Inexpensive.

Pubs

Water Witch Aldcliffe Rd (across the canal bridge). Canalside pub named after an old canal packet boat. A youthful crowd munches burgers, shoots pool and hogs the canal-side tables, but there are meals, too, and an impressive range of real ales and continental lagers.

🏃 **Ye Olde John O'Gaunt** 53 Market St, near the City Museum. Terrific city-centre local that's serious about its drinks, whether real ale or the range of whiskies and vodkas. There's also live trad jazz and R&B, plus a small beer garden.

Morecambe

MORECAMBE – the seaside town five miles west of Lancaster – rapidly expanded from a small fishing village into a full-blown resort in the nineteenth century with the arrival of the railway. Having been in something of a decline for many years, recent times have seen a fair amount of regeneration; the sweep of the bay remains the major attraction, however, with the Lakeland fells visible beyond and the local sunsets a renowned phenomenon. The **Stone Jetty** features bird sculptures, games and motifs – recognizing Morecambe Bay as Britain's most important wintering site for wildfowl and wading birds. A little way along the prom stands the statue of one of Britain's most treasured comedians – Eric Bartholomew, who took the stage name **Eric Morecambe** when he met his comedy partner, Ernie Wise. He appears here in famous Bring-Me-Sunshine prancing mode.

There's a cycle path from Lancaster, while regular buses and trains also make the ten-minute trip to Morecambe. The **tourist office** is just back from the Stone Jetty, in the Old Station Buildings on the Central Promenade (Mon–Sat 9.30am–4/5pm, Sun 10am–4pm; ☎01524/582808, ⓦ www.citycoastcountryside .co.uk.co.uk), and can provide information about seasonal **guided walks** taking in the town's Art Deco heritage. The notable Art Deco *Midland Hotel* (ⓦ www.midlandhotelmorecambe.co.uk) – a crumbling ruin on the prom for many years – is due to re-open in 2008 after a stylish refit, while the tourist office also operates a room-booking service for other local **guest-houses and hotels**, most of which are ranged along the seafront, and – at the budget end of the market at least – tend to be resolutely old-fashioned in style. **The Platform** arts centre (☎01524/582803, ⓦ www.lancaster.gov.uk /platformanddome) shares the same building as the tourist office.

Heysham

The main historic interest on the Lancashire side of Morecambe Bay is at **HEYSHAM**, three miles southwest of Morecambe – you can walk here along the promenade from the resort. Largely known for its ferry port (services to

▲ Eric Morecambe statue

Belfast and the Isle of Man) and unsightly nuclear power station, Heysham's hidden gem is the shoreside **Heysham Village**, centred on a group of charming seventeenth-century cottages and barns. Proudest relic is the well-preserved Viking hog's-back tombstone in Saxon **St Peter's Church**, set in a romantic churchyard below the headland. Just up the lane, on the headland itself, the even earlier ruins of **St Patrick's Chapel** occupy a superb vantage-point over the bay and to the Lakeland hills beyond. Once you've seen these, all that remains is to step back into one of the village tearooms for a glass of nettle beer, a local speciality dating from the Victorian era.

The Isle of Man

The **Isle of Man**, almost equidistant from Ireland, England, Wales and Scotland, is one of the most beautiful spots in Britain, a mountainous, cliff-fringed island just thirty-three miles by thirteen, into which are shoehorned wooded glens, sandy beaches and scores of standing stones and Celtic crosses. It takes some effort to reach, and the weather is hardly reliable, factors that have seen tourist numbers fall since its Victorian heyday. This means, though, that the Isle of Man has been spared the worst excesses of the British tourist trade: there's peace and quiet in abundance, walks around the unspoilt hundred-mile coastline, rural villages and steam trains straight out of a 1950s picture-book – a yesteryear ensemble if ever there was one.

The capital, **Douglas**, is atypical of an island that prides itself on its Celtic and Norse heritage, and it's the vestiges of the distant past – the castles at the former capital **Castletown** and the west coast port of **Peel** – that make the most obvious destinations. Elsewhere, **Port Erin** has one of the island's best beaches, while to the north **Laxey** is an attractive proposition for its huge waterwheel and the meandering train ride to the barren summit of **Snaefell**, the island's highest peak. From Snaefell's summit you get an idea of the range of the Manx scenery, the finest parts of which are to be found in the seventeen officially designated **National Glens**, most of them linked by the 100-mile **Raad Ny Foillan** (Road of the Gull) coastal footpath, which passes several of the island's numerous hill forts, Viking ship burials and Celtic crosses. The island's wildlife, meanwhile, is best seen on a boat trip to the **Calf of Man**, an islet off the southwest coast where breeding birds and seals are easily seen.

The island's main tourist draw, however, is the **TT (Tourist Trophy) motorcycle races** (held in the two weeks around the late-May bank holiday), a frenzy of speed and burning rubber that's shattered the island's peace annually since 1907. Thousands of bikers swamp the place to watch a non-stop parade of maniacs hurtling round the roads on a 37-mile circuit at speeds averaging 126mph. This is only the most famous of a summer-long list of **rallies and races** on the island's roads, and if you want to stay at these times (exact dates available from the Isle of Man tourist office), you must book accommodation well in advance.

Some history

St Patrick is said to have come to the island in the fifth century AD, bringing Christianity, though it was the arrival of the **Vikings**, who established garrisons here in the eleventh century, which changed the face of the Isle of Man. They reigned as **Kings of Mann** – the name derived from that of the island's ancient sea-god, Mannannan Mac Lir (Son of the Sea). The Scots under Alexander wrested power from the Norsemen in 1275, the beginning of an ultimately unsuccessful 130-year struggle with the English for control of the island. During the English **Civil War**, James Stanley, seventh Earl of Derby and Lord of Man, raised an army to support Charles II, but in his absence a local militia offered the island to Cromwell, provided the traditional rights of the islanders – long infringed upon by English overlords – were maintained. It was a shortlived insurrection: with the restoration of the monarchy, the leaders of the militia were executed and the island returned to Crown control.

The **distinct identity** of the island remained intact, however, and many true Manx inhabitants, who comprise a shade under fifty percent of its 80,000 population, insist that the Isle of Man is not part of England, nor even of the UK. Indeed, although a Crown dependency, the island has its own government, **Tynwald**, arguably the world's oldest democratic parliament, which has run continuously since 979 AD. Tynwald consists of two chambers, the 24-member House of Keys (directly elected every five years) and the Legislative Council (eight members elected by the Keys, plus three ex-officio members). To further complicate matters, the island maintains a unique associate status in the EU, neither contributing nor receiving funds but enjoying the same trading rights. The island has its own sterling currency (worth the same as the mainland currency), its own laws (though they generally follow Westminster's), an independent postal service, and a Gaelic-based language which is taught in schools and seen on dual-language road signs. The island also produces four-horned sheep and, of course, its own tailless version of the domestic cat, as well as famously good kippers and queenies (scallops).

The first regular steamship service from England commenced in 1819, and **tourism** began to flourish during the late-Victorian and Edwardian eras. At its height – at the beginning of the twentieth century – tourism was bringing in half a million visitors a year, but in recent times the real money-spinner has been the **offshore finance industry**, exploiting the island's low income tax and absence of capital gains tax and death duties. Given its financial expertise,

ISLE OF MAN

Point of Ayre
Ayres Visitor Centre

A10   A16

Bride

A10

Andreas

A10

Jurby

Ramsey
Bay

St Jude

A9

Sulby   The Grove Museum
Ballaugh   Churchtown   A3   Ramsey
A3   Maughold
Head

I R I S H   S E A

Kirk
Michael   Maughold
Tholt-y-Will   A14   Balajora
Glen
Sulby   Glen Mona
Reservoir
A3   B10   Snaefell   Manx
Snaefell   Mountain   Electrical
(2036 ft)   Railway   Railway

A4   B10

St Patrick's Isle   B12   A18
Cronk-y-   Laxey
Voddy   Great Laxey Wheel   Old Laxey
Peel   A1   Tynwald
St John's   A1   Greeba
A27   Greeba   A2
Glen Maye   A23
A1   Union
Niarbyl   Dalby   Foxdale   Crosby   Mills   Onchan
A36   Glen Vine   A2
A24   A24   Douglas Bay
Niarbyl   Braaid   DOUGLAS
Bay   A36   St Mark's   Newtown
A27   Port Soderick
Grenaby   Steam
Bradda   Santon   Railway
Head   Port   Colby Ballabeg   Rushen Abbey
Erin   Ballasalla   I R I S H   S E A
Cregneash   A5
Village   Port
Folk Museum   St Mary   Derbyhaven
Calf   Cregneash   Castletown
of Man   Sound Visitor Centre   0   5 miles
Spanish
Head

© Crown copyright

the Isle of Man is also playing a major role in the development of **e-banking and e-commerce**, while low taxes have provided incentives for the **filming** of an increasing number of movies.

Getting to the island

Most visitors from England arrive at Douglas on **ferries** or the quicker **fastcraft** (Sea Cats), both run by the Isle of Man Steam Packet Company (℡0871/222 1333, ⓦwww.steam-packet.com), from either Heysham or Liverpool. Heysham (ferry 3hr 30min) has the most frequent service, with two or three sailings a day throughout the year. Liverpool manages one or two fastcraft services a day (2hr 30min) down to one daily at weekends in December. **Fares** start at £15 one way for foot passengers, £110 return for drivers.

An increasing number of airlines offer **flights** to the island from around twenty British and Irish regional airports, with regular prices starting from £29 one way. Services are with A2B (Belfast, Blackpool; ⓦwww.a2bairways.com); Aer Arran (Dublin; ⓦwww.aerarran.com); Flybe (Birmingham, London

Gatwick, Manchester, Southampton; Ⓦwww.flybe.com); Eastern Airways (Newcastle, Bristol, Birmingham; Ⓦwww.easternairways.com); EuroManx (Belfast City, London City, Manchester, Liverpool; Ⓦwww.euromanx.com); Loganair (Glasgow, Edinburgh; Ⓦwww.loganair.co.uk); and Manx2 (Blackpool, Belfast City, Belfast International, Leeds Bradford, Gloucester M5; Ⓦwww.manx2.com).

Getting around the island

With a car you could see almost everything in a couple of days, but don't miss a trip on one of the two century-old rail services which still provide the best **public transport** (Ⓦwww.iombusandrail.info) to all the major towns and sights except for Peel. The carriages of the **Steam Railway** (April–Oct, regular daily services from Douglas, 10.15am–4.15pm; £9 return to Port Erin) rock their fifteen-mile course from Douglas to Castletown, Port St Mary and Port Erin at a spirited pace. Resembling a tramway more than a train, the **Manx Electric Railway** (April–Oct daily 9.40am–4.40pm; some later departures in summer; £8 return to Ramsey) runs for seventeen miles from Douglas's Derby Castle Station to Ramsey via Laxey. The trains are the most enjoyable way to get to Laxey, Ramsey, Castletown and Port Erin but **buses** are often quicker – bus routes are given in the text where appropriate. There's also the Snaefell Mountain Railway from Laxey to the top of the island's highest mountain, Snaefell; see p.715 for details.

The "**Island Explorer**" ticket gives one (£12), three (£24), five (£35) or seven (£40) days' unlimited travel on all public transport on the island.

Douglas

DOUGLAS, heart of the offshore finance industry, also has the vast majority of the island's hotels and best restaurants, and it makes as good a base as any, since all roads lead here. A mere market town as late as 1850, with one pier and an undeveloped seafront, Douglas was a product of Victorian mass tourism and displays many similarities to Blackpool, just across the water: candy coloured five-storey terraces back the two-mile-long curve of the promenade and its tram tracks, and the town even makes an attempt to emulate the illuminations. There's an excellent museum and truly dramatic bay views from the promenade, but if you just see Douglas you won't have seen the best of the island.

Arrival, orientation and information

All flights arrive at **Ronaldsway Airport** at Ballasalla, ten miles south of Douglas, close to Castletown. Buses (every 30min–1hr: 7.15am–11pm) connect the airport with Douglas as well as Castletown/Port St Mary, while a taxi to Douglas costs around £20. Ferries and Sea Cats dock by the **Sea Terminal** at the southern end of the Douglas waterfront. Fifty yards beyond the forecourt taxi rank, the Lord Street **bus terminal** is the hub of the island's dozen or so bus routes.

North Quay runs 300 yards west from the bus terminal alongside the river and fishing port to Douglas Station, the northern terminus of the **Steam Railway** to Port Erin. The waterfront (progressively Loch, Central and Queen's promenades) runs two miles north to Derby Castle Station for the **Electric Railway** to Laxey and Ramsey – take the horse-drawn tram along the promenade or bus #24, #24a, #26 or #26a from North Quay.

The **Welcome Centre** in the Sea Terminal building (Mon–Sat 8am–6pm, Sun 9am–2pm; ☏01624/686766 or 01624/662525) has island-wide transport information and sells Island Explorer **travel tickets**. There's a smaller office at the airport, open to meet flight arrivals. The main **websites** for information are Ⓦwww.gov.im and www.visitisleofman.com. The twelve heritage sites and museums are run under the umbrella of Manx National Heritage (Ⓦwww.gov.im/mnh). They all have individual admission charges, though a **4 Site Ticket** (£11, available from any attraction) will save you some money; NT and EH members get in free.

Accommodation

B&Bs are packed in along Douglas's seafront and up the roads immediately off Harris Promenade, particularly along Broadway, Castle Mona Avenue, Empress Drive and Empire Terrace. Prices start from under £40 for a double and a sea-view room can be had for £50. However, note that many places demand a two-night minimum stay in the summer. There's also an increasing number of boutique-style **hotels** in renovated seafront buildings, with significantly higher prices.

Admiral House Loch Promenade ☎01624/629551, Ⓦwww.admiralhouse.com. At the ferry terminal end of the prom, this club-like retreat features rooms in bold colours and equipped with elegant bathrooms. The town's most expensive restaurant, *Ciapelli's* (closed Sun) is on the ground floor. ❼

Birchfield House York Rd ☎01624/673000, Ⓦwww.birchfieldhouse.com. The most distinctive of Douglas' guest houses offers sunny spacious rooms loaded with antiques, all creature comforts, and luxurious bathrooms. It's run by the island's celeb-chef Kevin Woodford, and dinner in the library costs £35. ❽

Claremont 18–19 Loch Promenade ☎01624/698800, Ⓦwww.sleepwellhotels.com. Promenade hotel with a good bar-brasserie, and rooms in contemporary style with all mod cons. The less expensive nearby *Rutland* and *Chesterhouse* hotels are part of the same group (see the website), and similarly styled. ❼

Cunard Aparthotel 28–29 Loch Promenade ☎01624/6676728, Ⓦwww.cunard-accom.com. Modern spacious apartments sleeping from 2 to 7, with laminate flooring and fully equipped kitchens. Apartment 9 has the best view. ❻

Dreem Ard Ballanard Rd, 2 miles west of the centre ☎01624/621491. Tranquil, out-of-town B&B with three en-suite rooms, including a family room

and large garden suite with its own dressing room and sitting area. No credit cards. ❸, suite ❹

Glen Mona 6 Mona Drive, off Central Promenade ☎01624/676755, Ⓦwww.glenmona-iom.co.uk. Modern rooms in a nice, family-run guest house just off the prom. ❹

Regency Queen's Promenade ☎01624/680680, Ⓦwww.regency.iom-1.net. A contemporary facelift has retained the decorative oak panelling in the public rooms while kitting out guest quarters in style. Similar rooms also available in the associated *Hotel Penta* further down the prom (book through the *Regency*), plus two-room suites and apartments. ❻, suites/apartments ❼

🏃 **Sefton** Harris Promenade ☎01624/645500, Ⓦwww.seftonhotel.co.im. Next to the Gaiety Theatre, this four-star has sleek, spacious rooms offering a sea view or a balcony over the impressive internal water garden. Facilities include pool, gym, Internet access, free bikes, bar and restaurant. Book online and you save yourself a tenner. ❼

Welbeck Mona Drive, off Central Promenade ☎01624/675663, Ⓦwww.welbeckhotel.com. Mid-sized family-run hotel 100yd up the hill off the seafront. Accommodation is nicely decorated (modern furniture), with six two-person self-catering apartments (breakfast not included in the apartments). ❺, deluxe rooms/apartments ❻

The Town

Douglas's seafront vista has changed little since Victorian times, and is still trodden by heavy-footed carthorses pulling **trams** (May–Sept, from 9am; £2 return, Island Explorer ticket valid). On Harris Promenade the opulent **Gaiety Theatre** sports a lush interior that can be seen on fascinating ninety-minute-long tours each Saturday at 10.30am (April–Sept only; £6.50; information and box office ☎01624/694555). Further up Harris Promenade, approaching Broadway, the spruced-up **Villa Marina** gardens display more Victorian elegance, with their colonnade walk, lawns and bandstand. There's a monthly **farmers' market** here on the first Saturday of the month.

In the streets nearer the harbour, an attempt has been made to preserve Douglas's "historic quayside". There's not much to it, save a few old pubs, and you might as well head up Victoria Street, past the Manx Legislative Building, to the **Manx Museum**, on the corner of Kingswood Grove and Crellin's Hill (Mon–Sat 10am–5pm; free). The museum makes a good start for anyone wanting to get to grips with Manx culture and heritage before setting off around the island, kicking off with a National Gallery of Manx painters. Other rooms reveal Neolithic standing stones, Celtic grave markers and other artefacts, notably some excellent displays relating to Viking burials and runic crosses. More recently there are collections of smutty postcards from the 1930s, artefacts made by World War I internees and displays about the TT races, not forgetting the island's natural history and environment.

Out on Douglas Head – the point looming above the southern bay – the town's Victorian **camera obscura** has been restored for visits (Easter week, plus May–Sept Sat 1–4pm, Sun and bank hols 11am–4pm, weather permitting; £2; ☎01624/686766).

Eating, drinking and entertainment

Douglas has the best choice of **cafés and restaurants** on the island, with plenty of inexpensive places to grab a bite to eat as well as some more sophisticated dining options. Manx-brewed beer is on sale at most **pubs** and brews such as "Old Bushy Tail" soon revive flagging spirits, while for a more fashionable night out, the **bar scene** in Douglas is ever improving. The **Villa Marina and Gaiety Theatre** complex (☎01624/694555) is the hub of most entertainment, from orchestral concerts to rock gigs, tea dances to theatrical productions.

Cafés and café-bars

Alpine Café 5 Regent St. This bright and breezy chalet-style café serves a good selection of breakfasts, sandwiches, cakes and daily specials.

C'est La Vie 28 Victoria St. Good-looking café-bar with dishes ranging from bangers and mash to spicy Indonesian noodles. A busy lunchtime spot, though they serve food until 8.45pm. Closed Sun.

Greens Douglas Station, North Quay. Plant-filled vegetarian café in the ticket office serving drinks and snacks until 5pm, with hot lunches and a veggie buffet from noon to 2.30pm. Closed Sun.

Spill the Beans 1 Market Hill. Douglas's best coffee house, with a choice of brews plus muffins, croissants, cakes and pastries. Closes at 5pm, and all Sun.

Restaurants

Café Tanroagan 9 Ridgeway St ☎07624/472411. The best fish and seafood on the island, in a relaxed, contemporary restaurant. Visiting film crews and actors all make a beeline here, for fish (straight off the boat) either given an assured Mediterranean twist or served simply. Dinner reservations essential. Closed Sun. Expensive.

Highlander Inn Main Rd, A1, Greeba, 5 miles west of Douglas ☎01624/852609. A popular night out is this family-run restaurant offering an imaginative menu and a real fire. Reservations advised. Closed Sun & Mon. Moderate.

Paparazzi 26 Loch Promenade ☎01624/673222. Locals like this large pizzeria-trattoria with Sicilian beer and a few more unusual specialities alongside the traditional pizzas, pastas and Italian dishes. Moderate.

Pubs and bars

Bar George Hill St. A fashionable haunt housed in a converted Sunday School, opposite St George's church. Closed Sun.

Queen's Hotel Queen's Promenade. The best place for an alfresco drink is this old seafront pub at the top end of the promenade, where the picnic tables look out over the sweeping bay.

Rovers Return 11 Church St. Cosy old local where you can try the local Manx beers.

Airport Ronaldsway Airport, flight enquiries ☎01624/821600, ⓦwww.iom-airport.com.

Bicycle rental Eurocycles, 8a Victoria Rd, off Broadway ☎01624/624909. Closed Sun.

Car rental Most outfits have offices at the airport or can deliver cars to the Sea Terminal. Contact: Athol ☎01624/822481, ⓦwww.athol.co.im; Mylchreests ☎01624/823533, ⓦwww .mylchreests.com; or Ocean Ford ☎01624/820830, ⓦwww.oceanford.com.

Cruises Seasonal cruises, from Villier steps by the Sea Terminal, Douglas promenade, to Port Soderick or Laxey on the MV *Karina*. Departures daily April–Sept, weather permitting; call ☎01624/861724 or 07624/493592.

Hospital Noble's Hospital, Strang ☎01624/650000.

Internet Feegan's Lounge, 8 Victoria St (Mon–Sat 9am–6pm).

Outdoor activities Gemini Charter Boat (☎01624/832761 or 07624/483328) for fishing and bird/seal/shark watching trips all year round. Quad Bike Trail Rides, Ballacraine Farm. A1 road, St John's (☎01624/801219) for a ninety-minute moorland ride for £40. The Venture Centre Lewaigue Farm, Maughold (☎01624/814240, ⓦwww.adventure-centre.co.uk) provides half-multi- or full-day activities with self-catering bunkhouse accommodation available.

Pharmacies Boots, 14 Strand St ☎01624/616120; John Atkinson, 2 Granville St ☎01624/673402.

Police Douglas Police Station, Glencrutchery Rd ☎01624/631212.

Post office Main post office is at 6 Regent St ☎01624/686141.

Telephones Using a UK-registered mobile phone in the Isle of Man incurs international call rates for making and receiving calls. Some pay-as-you-go phones may not permit calls from the Isle of Man either.

Laxey

Filling a narrow valley, the straggling village of **LAXEY**, seven miles north of Douglas, spills down from its train station to a small harbour and long, pebbly beach, squeezed between two bulky headlands. The Manx Electric Railway from Douglas drops you at the station used by the Snaefell Mountain Railway (see below). Passengers disembark and then head inland and uphill to Laxey's pride, the **"Lady Isabella" Great Laxey Wheel** (April–Oct daily 10am–5pm; £3.30), smartly painted in red and white. With a diameter of over 72ft it's said to be the largest working waterwheel in the world. You can stroll around the various buildings and bits of machinery before climbing up to the top of the wheel for the full effect. Otherwise Laxey is at its best down in **Old Laxey**, around the harbour, half a mile below the station, where large car parks attest to the popularity of the beach and river.

Hourly **buses** #3 and #3A run to Laxey from Douglas. The *Mines Tavern*, by the station, serves **meals** (lunch and dinner), while down at the harbour, **drinking** is done at the *Shore Hotel*, a nice pub by the bridge.

Snaefell, Tholt-y-Will Glen and Sulby Glen

Every thirty minutes, the tramcars of the **Snaefell Mountain Railway** (May–Oct daily 10.15am–3.45pm; £7.80 return) begin their thirty-minute wind from Laxey through increasingly denuded moorland to the island's highest point, the top of **Snaefell** (2036ft) – the Vikings' "Snow Mountain" – from where you can see England, Wales, Scotland and Ireland on a clear day. The four and a half miles of track were built in seven months over the winter of 1895 by two hundred men. At the summit, most people are content to pop into the café and bar and then soak up the views for the few minutes until the return journey. But with a decent map and a clear day, you could walk back instead, following trails down the mountain to Laxey (the easiest and most direct route), Sulby Glen or the Peel–Ramsey road.

The road route up, the A18 from Douglas or Ramsey, also makes for a great ride, since it forms part of the TT course. Where the A18 and A14 (Snaefell–Sulby) meet, just below the summit, there's an isolated railway halt where drivers and hikers can pick up the mountain railway for a truncated ride to the summit and back. Three miles below the summit, down the A14, which sweeps past **Sulby Reservoir**, the road drops into **Tholt-y-Will Glen**, one of the island's more picturesque corners, with its gushing river and walks through the verdant plantations.

The A14 continues north to join the A3 Ramsey road, along a fine route – above the river – through **Sulby Glen**, with bracken-clad hills flanking the road. At the junction, the *Sulby Glen Hotel* (℡01624/897240, ⓦwww.sulbyglenhotel.net; ❹) has Manx beer and food (except Sun and Mon nights).

Maughold, Ramsey and the north

The Manx Electric Railway trains stop within a mile and a half of **MAUGHOLD**, seven miles northeast of Laxey, a tiny hamlet just inland from the cliff-side lighthouse at **Maughold Head**. It's an isolated spot which only adds to the attraction of Maughold's parish church, in whose grounds is maintained an outstanding collection of early Christian and Norse **carved crosses** – 44 pieces, dating from the sixth to the thirteenth century, and ranging from fragments of runic carving to a six-foot-high rectangular slab. Look inside the church, too, at the old parish cross, fourteenth-century in date and sporting the earliest known picture of the Three Legs of Mann apart from that on the twelfth-century Sword of State. Bus #16 comes direct to Maughold from Ramsey (not Sun).

RAMSEY marks the northern terminus of the Electric Railway, 45 minutes beyond Laxey. The Victorian tourist boom left behind the island's only iron pier and a solitary grand terrace along the front, but the bulk of the town, by the harbour – once more important than that in Douglas – is a dispiriting swatch of build-by-numbers modernity. Apart from the weekly Saturday **farmers' market**, the only real attraction is **The Grove Museum** (April–Sept daily 10am–5pm; £3.30), a mile north on the A9. This, once the summer home of a Merseyside shipping magnate, tells the story of three generations of the Gibb family, whose Victorian furniture, handiwork and domestic paraphernalia is all still there. There's a very nice conservatory café too.

You really need a car to see any more of the island beyond Ramsey. Due north at the end of the A16 is the **Point of Ayre** lighthouse, at the northeastern tip of the island, built in 1818. There's a car park here, where you could leave your vehicle and walk west along the coastal footpath the two miles to the **Ayres Visitor Centre** (end May to Sept Tues–Sun & bank hol Mon 2–5pm; free), which acts as an interpretation centre for the surrounding Ayres National Nature Reserve. It's an important coastal habitat of lichen heath, dune grassland and marsh, with common sightings of terns, oystercatchers, cormorants and ringed plovers.

St John's

The trans-island A1 (and hourly bus #5 or #6 from Douglas) follows a deep twelve-mile-long furrow between the northern and southern ranges from Douglas to Peel. A hill at the crossroads settlement of **ST JOHN'S**, nine miles along it, is the original site of **Tynwald**, the ancient Manx government, which derives its name from the Norse *Thing Völlr*, meaning "Assembly Field". Nowadays the word refers to the Douglas-based House of Keys and Legislative

Council, but acts passed in the capital only become law once they have been proclaimed here on July 5 (ancient Midsummer's Day) in an annual open-air parliament that also hears the grievances of the islanders. Tynwald's four-tiered grass mound – made from soil collected from each of the island's parishes – stands at the other end of a processional path from the stone **St John's Church**, which traditionally doubled as the courthouse. Until the nineteenth century the local people arrived with their livestock and stayed a week or more – in true Viking fashion – to thrash out local issues, play sports, make marriages and hold a fair. Now Tynwald Day begins with a service in the chapel, followed by a procession to the mound where the offices of state are carried out, after which a fair and concerts begin.

Peel and around

The main settlement on the west coast, **PEEL** (bus #5 or #6 hourly from Douglas) immediately captivates, with its fine castle rising across the harbour and a popular sandy beach running the length of its eastern promenade. It's a town of some antiquity and its enduring appeal is as one of the most "Manx" of all the island's towns, with an age-old Tuesday market in the marketplace above the harbour and a wood-smoke-belching kipper factory along the harbourside. Archeological evidence indicates that **St Patrick's Isle**, which guards the harbour, has had a significant population since Mesolithic times. What probably started out as a flint-working village on a naturally protected spot gained significance with the foundation of a monastery in the seventh or eighth century, parts of which remain inside the ramparts of the red sandstone **Peel Castle** (April–Oct daily 10am–5pm; £3.30). The site became the residence of the Kings of Mann until 1220, when they moved to Castle Rushen in Castletown.

It's a fifteen-minute walk from the town around the river harbour and over the bridge to the castle. On the way, you'll have passed the excellent harbourside **House of Manannan heritage centre** (daily 10am–5pm; £5.50, combined ticket with Peel Castle £7.70) named after the island's ancient sea-god. You should allow at least two hours to get around the museum, which concentrates strongly on participatory exhibits – whether it's listening to Celtic legends in a replica roundhouse, examining the contents and occupants of a life-sized Viking ship, walking through a kipper factory or steering a steamer.

If you're looking for something more than the seafront cafés and fish-and-chip shops, then head for the **pub** opposite the House of Mannannan: the *Creek Inn* serves a delicious array of specials. Locals also like the *Marine Hotel*, a pub on the seafront, with bar meals and a bistro.

Out of town, it's a five-mile drive south down the A27 to reach **Dalby**, from where you can take the minor road to the little headland of **Niarbyl**, framed by clear water and fronted by a flat pebbled beach, above which sits a picture-perfect thatched cottage. Scenes from the movie *Waking Ned* were filmed here, and there's a café and visitor centre to tempt the passing trade.

Port Erin

Plans for the southern branch of the Steam Railway beyond Castletown included the speculative construction of the new resort of **PORT ERIN**, at the southwestern tip of the island, 75 minutes' ride from Douglas. The aspect certainly demanded a resort: a wide, fine sand beach backing a deeply indented bay sits beneath green hills, which climb to the tower-topped headland of Bradda Head to the northwest.

A century on, an arm of holiday apartments stretches out towards the headland, while the far side of town is marked by the breakwater and small harbour. Families relish the beach and nearby coves, and the timewarped atmosphere, which appears to have altered little in forty years. For a stretch of the legs, head up the promenade past the golf club to the entrance of **Bradda Glen**, where you can follow the path out along the headland to Bradda Head.

Practicalities

The **train station** is on Station Road, a couple of hundred yards above and back from the beach. **Buses** #1 and #2 from Douglas/Castletown, and #8 from Peel/St John's, stop on Bridson Street, across Station Road and opposite the *Cherry Orchard* hotel.

For **accommodation**, the best B&B is *Rowany Cottier* (℡01624/832287; no credit cards; ❸), a detached house overlooking the bay, opposite the entrance to Bradda Glen. Or there's the *Cherry Orchard* on Bridson Street (℡01624/833811, ⓦ www.cherry-orchard.com; ❼, winter ❺), a couple of hundred yards back from the promenade, which has a range of self-catering or serviced **apartments** sleeping up to six people. These are available by the night, and guests have the use of a pool, Jacuzzi, gym, sauna, restaurant and bar.

There are a couple of beachfront **cafés** serving daytime snacks and meals. Come the evening, your choice is between bistro **meals** at the *Bay Hotel* down by the beach; or bar meals at either the *Falcon's Nest* on the promenade or the *Station Hotel* (closed Mon). The **Port Erin Arts Centre** in Victoria Square (℡01624/835858, ⓦ www.erinartscentre.com) has a full programme of concerts, films and exhibitions.

Port St Mary and around

Two miles east of Port Erin, the fishing harbour still dominates little **PORT ST MARY**, with its houses strung out in a chain above the busy dockside. The best beach is away to the northeast, reached from the harbour along a well-worked Victorian path that clings to the bay's rocky edge.

From Port St Mary, a minor road runs out along the Meayll peninsula towards **Cregneash**, the oldest village on the island, part of which now forms the **Cregneash Village Folk Museum** (April–Oct daily 10am–5pm; £3.30), a picturesque cluster of nineteenth-century thatched crofts. This was a real Gaelic-speaking village until well into the twentieth century, but is now peopled with spinners, weavers, turners and smiths dressed in period costumes; there's a café and information centre, and a chance to walk through the seasonal crops in the field and watch the horses at work. The local views are stunning and it's only a short walk south to **The Chasms**, a headland of gaping rock cliffs swarming with gulls and razorbills.

The footpath continues around **Spanish Head**, the island's southern tip, to the turf-roofed **Sound Visitor Centre** (daily 10/11am–4/5pm; free), which also marks the end of the road from Port St Mary. There's an excellent café, with windows looking out across The Sound to the Calf of Man, a small islet now preserved as a bird sanctuary – see opposite for access details.

Practicalities

Regular **steam trains** run to Port Erin or back to Douglas from Port St Mary, with the station a ten-minute walk from the harbour along High Street, Bay View Road and Station Road; hourly **buses** from the harbour serve the same places. Nicest **accommodation** is at ☂ *Aaron House*, high up on

The Promenade (℡01624/835702, Ⓦwww.aaronhouse.co.uk; ⑤), a lovingly recreated Victorian experience combining brass beds and clawfoot slipper baths (and chamber pot should you need it), with home-made scones and jam in the parlour and splendid breakfasts. You'll be well looked after, and the bay views from the front are superb.

Food options include *The Port* (℡01624/832064; dinner only; closed Sun night & Mon) on Athol Street, down by the harbour, which serves fresh fish specials daily, and *Horizons* on Bay View Road (℡01624/834040; closed Tues & Sun eve), with a more cosmopolitan menu. Or you can eat for less at the *Station Hotel*, by the Steam Railway stop, where Thai food is on offer on Friday and Saturday nights.

Calf of Man

It really is worth making the effort to visit the **Calf of Man**, a craggy 600-acre heathland island off the southwest coast that is preserved as a bird sanctuary. Resident wardens monitor the seasonal populations of kittiwakes, puffins, choughs, razorbills, shags, guillemots and others, while grey seals can be seen all year round basking on the rocks. Paths run across the island, out to the bird observatory, the lighthouses and various derelict buildings – bring something to eat and drink, and pack warm clothes in case the weather changes.

Charter **boats** to the island operate from Port St Mary, but the most reliable scheduled service (weather permitting) is from the pier at **Port Erin** (Easter–Sept daily; £10; usually at 10.15am, 11.30am and 1.30pm; ℡01624/832339); always call in advance as landing numbers are limited.

Castletown and around

From the twelfth century until 1869, **CASTLETOWN** was the island's capital, but then the influx of tourists and the increase in trade required a bigger harbour and Douglas took over. Its sleepy harbour and low-roofed cottages are dominated by **Castle Rushen** (April–Oct daily 10am–5pm; £4.80), formerly home to the island's legislature and still the site of the investiture of new lieutenant-governors. The rooms – entertainingly furnished in medieval and seventeenth-century styles – may seem unending, but it's worth pressing on to the rooftop viewpoint to admire the town below and the view beyond.

Across the central Market Square and down Castle Street in tiny Parliament Square you'll find the **Old House of Keys**. Built in 1821, this was the site of the Manx parliament, the Keys, until 1874 when it was moved to Douglas. The frock-coated Secretary of the House meets you at the door and shows you into the restored debating chamber, where visitors are included in a highly entertaining participatory session of the House, guided by a hologram Speaker. The visits are conducted on the hour (April–Oct daily 10am–noon & 2–5pm; £3.30). The **Nautical Museum** on the harbourside (April–Oct daily 10am–5pm; £3.30) reveals the *Peggy*, a boat built in 1791, walled up in her original cellar, and the architectural conceits of her somewhat eccentric owner George Quayle.

Practicalities

The **train station** is five minutes' walk from the centre of Castletown, out along Victoria Road from the harbour; **buses** #8 (from Peel/Port Erin) and #1 (from Douglas) stop in the main square. Best place for **food** is *The Garrison*, across from the hotel at 5 Castle St (℡01624/824885; closes Sun at 5pm), a tapas bar with a sunny courtyard. Out of town, at **Santon**, about

5 miles northeast of Castletown, the *Mount Murray Hotel and Country Club* (℡01624/661111, Ⓦwww.mountmurray.com; Ⓞ) is the highest-rated rural hotel on the island, with its own golf course, pool, health club, bar and restaurant.

Rushen Abbey

The island's most important medieval religious site, **Rushen Abbey** (April–Oct daily 10am–5pm; £3.30) lies two miles north of Castletown at Ballasalla ("place of the willows"). A Cistercian foundation of 1134, it was abandoned by its "White Monks" in the 1540s and in more recent times the site was used as a school and later a hotel, with tea dances held in the abbey grounds. The excavated remains themselves – low walls, grass-covered banks and a sole church tower from the fifteenth century – would hold only specialist appeal were it not for the excellent interpretation centre, which explains much about daily life in a Cistercian abbey. The **Silverburn Trail** runs from Castletown to the abbey, and there are pleasant walks in the surrounding area too, including a crossing of the fourteenth-century packhorse bridge known as the **Monks' Bridge**, just upstream of the abbey gardens. Ballasalla is a stop on the Steam Railway, with the abbey a few minutes' walk from the village.

Travel details

Buses

For information on all local and national bus services, contact Traveline ℡0871/200 2233, Ⓦwww.traveline .org.uk.
Chester to: Liverpool (every 20min; 1hr 20min); Manchester (3 daily; 1hr).
Lancaster to: Carlisle (4–5 daily; 1hr 10min); Kendal (hourly; 1hr); Leeds (1 daily; 3hr); London (2–3 daily; 5hr 30min); Manchester (2 daily; 2hr); Windermere (hourly; 1hr 45min).
Liverpool to: Blackpool (1 daily; 2hr); Chester (hourly; 1hr); Leeds (hourly; 2hr 40min); London (5 daily; 4hr); Manchester (hourly; 1hr); Preston (2 daily; 1hr).
Manchester to: Birmingham (6 daily; 3hr); Blackpool (5 daily; 1hr 40min); Chester (3 daily; 1hr); Leeds (6 daily; 2hr); Liverpool (hourly; 40min); London (every 1–2hr; 4hr 30min–6hr 45min); Newcastle (6 daily; 5hr); Sheffield (4 daily; 2hr 40min).

Trains

For information on all local and national rail services, contact National Rail Enquiries ℡0845/748 4950, Ⓦwww.rail.co.uk.

Blackpool to: Manchester (hourly; 1hr 10min); Preston (hourly; 30min).
Chester to: Birmingham (5 daily; 2hr); Liverpool (2 hourly; 45min); London (3 daily; 3hr 30min); Manchester (2 hourly; 1hr–1hr 20min).
Lancaster to: Carlisle (every 30min–1hr; 1hr); Manchester (every 30min–1hr; 1hr); Morecambe (every 30min–1hr; 10min); Preston (every 20–30min; 20min).
Liverpool to: Birmingham (hourly; 1hr 40min); Chester (2 hourly; 45min); Leeds (hourly; 2hr); London (hourly; 2hr 40min); Manchester (hourly; 50min); Newcastle (8 daily; 4–5hr); Preston (14 daily; 1hr 5min); Sheffield (hourly; 1hr 45min); York (hourly; 2hr 20min).
Manchester to: Barrow-in-Furness (Mon–Sat 7 daily, Sun 3 daily; 2hr 15min); Birmingham (hourly; 1hr 30min); Blackpool (hourly; 1hr 10min); Buxton (hourly; 50min); Carlisle (8 daily; 1hr 50min); Chester (every 30min; 1hr–1hr 20min); Lancaster (hourly; 1hr); Leeds (hourly; 1hr); Liverpool (every 30min; 50min); London (hourly; 2hr 40min); Newcastle (10 daily; 3hr); Oxenholme (4–6 daily; 40min–1hr 10min); Penrith (2–4 daily; 2hr); Preston (every 20min; 55min); Sheffield (hourly; 1hr); York (hourly; 1hr 35min).

Cumbria and the Lakes

0   50 miles

SCOTLAND

NORTHERN
IRELAND

IRELAND

IRISH SEA

WALES

Bristol Channel

NORTH SEA

English Channel

FRANCE

Highlights

▲ Borrowdale

Cumbria and the Lakes

The **Lake District** is England's most hyped scenic area, and for good reasons. Within an area a mere thirty miles across, sixteen major lakes are squeezed between the steeply pitched faces of the country's highest mountains, an almost alpine landscape that's augmented by waterfalls and picturesque stone-built villages packed into the valleys. Most of what people refer to as the Lake District – or simply the Lakes – lies within the **Lake District National Park**. This, in turn, falls entirely within the northwestern county of **Cumbria**, formed in 1974 from the historic counties of Cumberland and Westmorland, and the northern part of Lancashire. Consequently Cumbria contains more than just its lakes, stretching south and west to the **coast**, and north to its county town of **Carlisle**, a place that bears traces of a pedigree that stretches back beyond the construction of Hadrian's Wall. To the east, **Penrith** and the **Eden Valley** separate the Lakes from the near wilderness of the northern Pennines.

Before Neolithic peoples began to colonize the region around five thousand years ago, most of the now bare uplands were forested with pine and birch, while the valleys were blanketed with thickets of oak and alder. As these first settlers learned to shape flints into axes, they began to clear the upland forests, a process accelerated by the road-building Romans. An even greater impact was made by the Norse Vikings in the ninth and tenth centuries, who farmed the land extensively and left their mark on the local dialect: a mountain here is referred to as a "fell", a waterfall is a "force", streams are "becks", a mountain lake is a "tarn", while the suffix "-thwaite" indicates a clearing.

Two factors spurred the first waves of **tourism** here: the reappraisal of landscape brought about by such painters as Constable and the writings of **Wordsworth** and his contemporaries, and the turmoil of the French Revolution, which put paid to the idea of the continental Grand Tour. At the same time, as the war pushed food prices higher, farmers began to reclaim the hillsides, a tendency sanctioned by the General Enclosure Act of 1801. Most of the characteristic dry-stone walls were built at this time, a development that alarmed Wordsworth, who wrote in his *Guide to the Lakes* that he desired "a sort of national property, in which every man has a right and interest who has an eye to perceive and a heart to enjoy." His wish finally

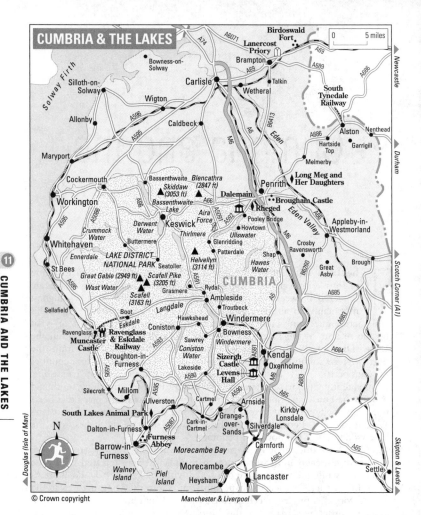

came to fruition in 1951 when the government designated 880 square miles of the Lake District as England's largest national park.

On any scale, the **National Park** has been wildly successful, attracting millions of visitors every year. This, of course, has come at some price, mainly in terms of traffic and environmental pressure, which a forward-thinking integrated transport strategy is attempting to alleviate. There's always been a severe contrast, too, between the touristed villages of the Lakes and the old industrial towns of coastal **West Cumbria**, which have struggled in the past to attract visitors and investment. However, regeneration has been dramatic in recent years, with the reviving fortunes of places like Whitehaven giving tourists ever more reason to stray from the Lakes.

National Express **coaches** connect London and Manchester with Windermere, Ambleside, Grasmere and Keswick. **Trains** leave the West Coast main line at **Oxenholme**, north of Lancaster, for the branch line service to Kendal and Windermere. The only other places directly accessible by train are Penrith, further north on the West Coast line, and the towns along the Cumbrian coast. Of the lakes themselves, Windermere, Coniston Water, Derwent Water and Ullswater have useful **cruise and ferry** services, while the summer-season **Cross Lakes Shuttle** (information from Mountain Goat ☏015394/45161, ⓦwww.mountain-goat .com, or see ⓦwww.lake-district.gov.uk) – integrating boats and buses – connects Bowness-on-Windermere with Hawkshead, Hill Top (Beatrix Potter house), Coniston Water and Grizedale Forest.

The one-day Stagecoach **Explorer Ticket** (£9; ⓦwww.stagecoachbus.com /northwest) is valid on the entire local bus network (and available from the driver), while other combination bus-and-boat tickets offer a variety of good deals. The two main bus services are the #555 (Kendal–Windermere–Ambleside–Grasmere–Keswick, with connections to Lancaster and Carlisle) and the open-top #599 (Kendal–Windermere–Bowness–Ambleside–Grasmere), but all routes and timetables are available on the Stagecoach website or by contacting **Traveline** (☏0871/200 2233, ⓦwww.traveline.org.uk), which can advise about all the region's bus, coach, rail and ferry services.

The Lake District

Although the **Lake District** might appear too popular for its own good, tourist numbers are concentrated in fairly specific areas, and it's relatively easy to escape the crowds even on the busiest of days. Given a week you could easily see most of the famous settlements and lakes – a circuit taking in the towns of Ambleside, Windermere and Bowness, all on **Windermere**, the Wordsworth houses and sites in pretty villages such as **Hawkshead** and **Grasmere**, and the more dramatic northern scenery near **Keswick** and **Ullswater** would give you a fair sample of the whole. But it's away from the crowds that the Lakes really begin to pay dividends, in the dramatic valleys of **Langdale** and **Eskdale**, and the lesser-visited lakes of **Wast Water** and **Buttermere**. Of course, it's only when you start to walk and climb around the Lakes that you can really say you've explored the region. Four peaks top out at over 3000ft – including **Scafell Pike**, the highest in England – but there are hundreds of other mountains, crags and fells to roam.

For more **information** about all aspects of the Lakes, visit ⓦwww .lake-district.gov.uk, while the official site of Cumbria Tourism, ⓦwww .golakes.co.uk, has links to all sorts of themed holiday ideas. It's wise to book accommodation ahead at any time of year, though local tourist offices pride themselves on always being able to find a bed for anyone arriving without a reservation. For farmhouse accommodation, a Cumbrian speciality, check the websites ⓦwww.farmstayuk.co.uk and ⓦwww.luxuryinafarm.co.uk, while campsites are all covered in depth on the excellent ⓦwww .lakedistrictcamping.co.uk.

Bad weather can move in quickly, even in summer, so before a hike always check the **weather forecast** – many hotels and outdoor shops post a daily forecast – or check on ☏0870/055 0575 (recorded 24hr line) or

Ⓦwww.lake-district.gov.uk/weatherline. Long-distance **hikers and cyclists** following the Coast-to-Coast, Sea-to-Sea, Cumbria Way and Dales Way routes, all of which cut through the region, can call on the **door-to-door baggage services** of Coast-to-Coast Packhorse (Ⓣ017683/71777, Ⓦwww.cumbria.com/packhorse) or Sherpa Van (Ⓣ0871/520 0124, Ⓦwww.sherpavan.com). Typically, you'll pay around £6 per bag per day, for it to be delivered to your next overnight accommodation.

Kendal and around

The self-billed "Gateway to the Lakes" (though nearly ten miles from Windermere), limestone-grey **KENDAL** is the largest of the southern Cumbrian towns, with a population of 25,000. It offers rewarding rambles along the River Kent and around the "yards" and "ginnels" on both sides of Highgate and Stricklandgate, the main streets, and while the old Market Place long since succumbed to development, traditional stalls still do business outside the Westmorland Shopping Centre every Wednesday and Saturday.

The **Kendal Museum**, on Station Road (hours may vary but currently Thurs–Sat noon–5pm; closed Christmas week; £2.80; Ⓦwww.kendalmuseum.org.uk), holds the district's natural history and archeological finds, and town history displays. These are bolstered by the reconstructed office, pen-and-ink drawings and personal effects of **Alfred Wainwright** (1907–91), always known as "AW", Kendal's former borough treasurer (and honorary clerk at the museum). Born in Blackburn, Lancashire, his lifelong love of the Lakes began with his first visit in 1930. Wainwright moved to Kendal in 1941, and by 1952, dissatisfied with the accuracy of existing maps, he embarked on his series of highly personal walking guides, painstakingly handwritten with mapped routes and delicately drawn views. They have been hugely popular guidebooks ever since, which many treat as gospel in their attempts to "bag" ascents of the 214 fells he recorded. When he died, Wainwright's ashes were scattered on his favourite fell – Haystacks in Buttermere.

The town's other two museums are at the Georgian **Abbot Hall** (Mon–Sat 10.30am–4/5pm; closed mid-Dec to mid-Jan; gallery & exhibitions £5, museum £3.75, combined ticket £7.50), by the river near the parish church. The main hall houses the **Art Gallery** (Ⓦwww.abbothall.org.uk), whose upper floors host temporary art exhibitions; the lower-floor galleries are more locally focused, concentrating in particular on the works of the eighteenth-century "Kendal School" of portrait painters, most famously George Romney. Across the way, the former stables contain the **Museum of Lakeland Life and Industry** (Ⓦwww.lakelandmuseum.org.uk), where reconstructed seventeenth-, eighteenth- and nineteenth-century house interiors stand alongside workshops which exhibit rural trades and crafts, from spinning and weaving to shoe-making and tanning. There's also a room devoted to the life and work of the children's writer Arthur Ransome, a must for *Swallows and Amazons* fans.

Climb every mountain

Kendal mintcake, a tooth-challenging, energy-giving, solid block of sugar and peppermint oil, was apparently invented by accident in the mid-nineteenth century. The familiar retro-packaged Romney's brand (from Kendal) is on sale throughout the Lakes, and its proudest boast is still that Kendal mintcake was carried to the top of Everest on Hillary's ascent of 1953.

Practicalities

Kendal's **train station** is the first stop on the Windermere branch line, just three minutes from the **Oxenholme** main-line station and a ten-minute walk from the centre. The **bus station** is on Blackhall Road (off Stramongate), while the **tourist office** (Mon–Sat 10am–5pm; ☎01539/725758, ⓦwww .lakelandgateway.info) is in the town hall on Highgate.

B&Bs are ranged along Milnthorpe Road, a few minutes south of the centre – walk straight down Highgate and Kirkland – including *The Headlands*, 53 Milnthorpe Rd (☎01539/732464; ❸), which offers a pick-up service from the bus or train stations. The best hotel in town is the *Riverside* on Stramongate Bridge (☎01539/734861, ⓦwww.riversidekendal.co.uk; ❻), fashioned from one of the old town tanneries, while there's a **youth hostel** at 118 Highgate (☎0870/770 5892, ⓔkendal@yha.org.uk; dorm beds from £14, includes breakfast), attached to the Brewery Arts Centre (see below). Five miles west of town at Crosthwaite, the ⅄ *Punch Bowl Inn* (☎01539/568237, ⓦwww .the-punchbowl.co.uk; ❸) is a super-stylish operation – the earth-toned rooms have exposed beams and superb bathrooms, while the unstuffy restaurant serves fine seasonal Modern British food (meals from around £30).

For inexpensive veggie **meals** and riverside seating visit *Waterside Wholefood* on Gulfs Road, by the river at the bottom of Lowther Street. There are good-value lunches and tapas, as well as more expensive meals, at ⅄ *Cortez*, 101 Highgate (☎01539/723123; closed Sun lunch), an agreeable place serving contemporary Spanish cuisine, while the best restaurant in town is generally acknowledged to be the *New Moon*, 129 Highgate (☎01539/729254; closed Sun & Mon), an easy-going contemporary bistro using locally sourced ingredients.

For evening entertainment, the ⅄ **Brewery Arts Centre**, 122 Highgate (☎01539/725133, ⓦwww.breweryarts.co.uk), is the town's central focus. Its *Grain Store Restaurant* and lively *Vats Bar* serve coffee and cake, light lunches, gourmet pizzas and a more elaborate dinner menu; the centre also has a cinema, theatre, galleries and concert hall. There's live music throughout the year and a renowned annual **jazz and blues festival** each November.

Sizergh Castle and Levens Hall

Three miles south of Kendal stands **Sizergh Castle** (Easter–Oct Mon–Thurs & Sun 1–5pm; gardens open same days from 11am; £6.70, gardens only £4.50; NT; bus #555) tucked away off the A591 amid acres of parkland. Home of the Strickland family for eight centuries, the stately home owes its "castle" epithet to the fourteenth-century peel-tower at its core, one of the best examples of the towers built throughout the region as safe havens during the protracted border raids of the Middle Ages. The Great Hall underwent significant changes in Elizabethan times, when extensions were added to the house and most of its rooms were panelled in oak, with their ceilings layered in elaborate plasterwork.

Two miles south of Sizergh, **Levens Hall** (Easter to mid-Oct Mon–Thurs & Sun noon–5pm; gardens open 10am; £9.50, gardens only £6.50; ⓦwww .levenshall.co.uk; bus #555) is more uniform in style than Sizergh, since the bulk of it was built or refurbished in the classic Elizabethan manner between 1570 and 1640. The dining room here is panelled not with oak but with goat's leather, printed with a deep green floral design – one goat was needed for every forty or so squares. Upstairs, the bedrooms offer glimpses of the beautifully trimmed **topiary gardens** below, where yews in the shape of pyramids, peacocks and top hats stand between colourful bedding plants.

Windermere town and around

WINDERMERE town was all but non-existent until 1847 when a railway terminal was built here, making England's longest lake (after which the town is named) an easily accessible resort. Windermere remains the transport hub for the southern lakes, but there's precious little else to keep you in the slate-grey streets. All the traffic pours a mile downhill to Windermere's older twin town, Bowness, actually on the lake, though stay long enough to make the twenty-minute stroll up through the woods to **Orrest Head** (784ft), from where there's a 360° panorama sweeping from the Yorkshire fells to Morecambe Bay – the path begins just to the left of the *Windermere Hotel* on the A591, across from Windermere train station.

You should also make time for the **Lake District Visitor Centre at Brockhole** (Easter–Oct daily 10am–5pm; grounds & gardens open all year; free, parking fee charged; ☏015394/46601), a lakeshore mansion three miles northwest of Windermere. It's the headquarters of the Lake District National Park and, besides the permanent natural history and geological displays, the centre hosts a full programme of guided walks, children's trails and activities, special exhibitions and lectures. The landscaped gardens are a real treat and there's also a nice café with an outdoor terrace. **Buses** between Windermere and Ambleside run past the visitor centre, or you can get here by Windermere Lake Cruises **launch** (Easter–Oct, hourly service) from either Waterhead, near Ambleside (£6 return), or Bowness (£7.50 return).

Practicalities

All **buses** stop outside Windermere **train station**, with the **tourist office** (daily 9am–5pm; ☏015394/46499, ⊛www.lakelandgateway.info) just a hundred yards away at the top of Victoria Street. For **bike rental**, contact Country Lanes at the train station (☏015394/44544, ⊛www.countrylanes.co.uk; from £15), which provides route maps for local rides. Mountain Goat, near the tourist office on Victoria Street (☏015394/45161, ⊛www.mountain-goat.com) offers **minibus tours** (half-day from £21, full-day £34) that get off the beaten track, departing daily from Windermere and other Lakeland towns. Good places to look for B&Bs are on High Street and neighbouring Victoria Street at the top of town near the tourist office, with other concentrations just to the south on College Road, Oak and Broad streets.

B&Bs, guesthouses and hotels

Archway 13 College Rd ☏015394/45613, ⊛www.the-archway.com. Four trim rooms in a Victorian house known for its breakfasts – try the great pancakes, kippers, home-made yoghurt and granola. ❸

Ashleigh 11 College Rd ☏015394/42292, ⊛www.ashleighhouse.com. Choose from one of five tasteful rooms that have been furnished in welcoming country pine. ❸

Boston House The Terrace ☏015394/43654, ⊛www.bostonhouse.co.uk. Beautifully restored Victorian Gothic house, a minute's walk from the tourist office, down a private drive off the A591. Five elegant rooms with four-posters and bright-as-a-button bathrooms. ❺

Brendan Chase 1–3 College Rd ☏015394/45638, ⊛www.placetostaywindermere.co.uk. Popular place with a friendly welcome and eight comfortable rooms (some en-suite) – family/group rooms sleep up to five. No credit cards. ❷

Coach House Lake Rd ☏015394/44494, ⊛www.lakedistrictbandb.com. Five classy rooms with wrought-iron beds, gleaming bathrooms and elegant touches – plus use of a local leisure club. ❹

Holbeck Ghyll Holbeck Lane, off A591, 3 miles north ☏015394/32375, ⊛www.holbeck-ghyll.co.uk. Luxurious rooms either in the main house or in the lodge or suites in the grounds – sherry decanter in every room, seven acres of gardens, and Michelin-starred Anglo-French food. Price – from around £240 – includes dinner. ❾

Festivals & events

From musical events to carnivals, England's festivals illustrate the richness of the country's history and depth of its diversity, while others celebrate a particular skill or interest. Some, of course, are no more than an excuse for a bizarre day out and a booze-up – the sight of the entire population of a village scrambling around a field after a barrel, or chasing a cheese downhill, is not easily forgotten.

Glastonbury

When Michael Eavis held a rock festival on his Somerset farm in 1970 (audience of two thousand, ticket price a quid, headliners T-Rex), he had no idea that it would eventually turn into England's biggest summer music and arts bash. Four decades on, the annual Glastonbury Festival of Performing Arts (to give it its full title) sees Worthy Farm inundated by almost 200,000 revellers, hell-bent on enjoying themselves whatever the weather – just as well, since late-June downpours are notorious for turning the three-day festival into a mudbath. Many complain that Glasto has moved away from its hippy roots, as high ticket prices, state-of-the-art security and even proper toilets have become the norm. But despite the contemporary buzz and headlining superstars, the "alternative" Glastonbury spirit is never far away – in the vast campsite village, organic cafés, circus fields, healing areas or performance tents. For more details, see p.374.

Glastonbury ▲
Notting Hill Carnival ▼

Notting Hill Carnival

Europe's greatest street party takes place over the last weekend of August (Sunday and bank holiday Monday). Born out of despair following the Notting Hill race riots of 1958, it started as little more than a few church-hall events and a carnival parade, inspired by the Caribbean roots of many of the area's residents. These days, up to a million revellers turn out for the two-day event, following a three-mile procession around the suburb which takes up to ten hours to complete. At its heart are the truck-borne sound systems and *mas* (masquerade) bands, behind which the masqueraders dance in outrageous costumes. There are also live music stages,

The weird and wonderful

England has been accumulating festivals from the time of the pre-Roman Druids. For a taste of the country at its most idiosyncratic, steer towards one of the numerous local celebrations that perpetuate ancient customs, the origins and meanings of which have often been lost or conveniently misplaced. The May Day frolics of the **Padstow Obby Oss**, in Cornwall, can be traced back to fertility rites in the distant past, while other events are grounded in ceremony, like **Swan Upping** (third week in July), the traditional registering of cygnets on the River Thames, or the medieval **rushbearings** of the Lake District, where reeds fashioned into crosses and garlands are carried in procession through the streets to church. However, some events do nothing more than celebrate English regional eccentricity: witness Gloucestershire's **Brockworth Cheese Rolling** contest; Cheshire's annual **World Worm-Charming Championships**; Leicestershire's annual **bottle-kicking** competition; or Yorkshire's **World Coal-Carrying Championship**. There's a full list of England's weird and wonderful celebrations in our festivals and events calendar on pp.47–50.

▲ Accordionist at the Padstow Obby Oss

and numerous sound systems, with the partying fuelled by cans of Red Stripe, curried goat and Jamaican patties. It's not quite Rio, but not staid old England either. For more details, see ⓦwww.rbkc.gov.uk.

Glyndebourne

Glyndebourne, Britain's only unsubsidized opera house, is situated near the village of Glynde, three miles east of Lewes in East Sussex. Founded in 1934, the Glyndebourne season (mid-May to August) is an indispensable part of the high-society calendar, with exclusive ticket prices to match. On one level, Glyndebourne is

▲ Swan Upping on the Thames
▼ Cheese rolling, Brockworth

elitist, its lawns thronged with gentry and corporate bigwigs bingeing on champagne and smoked salmon – the productions have long intervals to allow an unhurried repast. On the other hand, its musical values are the highest in the country, using young talent rather than expensive star names, and taking the sort of risks Covent Garden wouldn't dream of – for example, *Porgy and Bess* is now taken seriously as an opera largely as a result of a great Glyndebourne production. For ticket details, see p.207.

Glyndebourne ▲
Bonfire Night, Lewes ▼

Bonfire Night

"Remember, remember, the fifth of November", goes the old rhyme, "gunpowder, treason and plot" – and remember it the English certainly do, with night-time fireworks and fires across the nation commemorating the foiling of the 1605 Gunpowder Plot to blow up Parliament. Atop every bonfire is hoisted an effigy known as the "guy", after Guy Fawkes, one of the failed conspirators – an anonymous concoction of sticks and old clothes stuffed with newspaper suffices for most fires, but some effigies might represent resented contemporary or local figures (as, famously, at Lewes in East Sussex, which puts on the most dramatic show in the country – see p.206). Elsewhere, the best fireworks displays are the organized community affairs, some truly spectacular, though the traditional family or local bonfire usually rustles up some sparklers, rockets and flares. Although it's November 5 that is technically Bonfire Night (or Guy Fawkes Night), many prefer to hold their bonfire on the nearest weekend, while the proximity of Halloween (October 31) has had a knock-on effect – expect ghouls and ghosts, fires and fireworks, from the end of October onwards.

Miller Howe Rayrigg Rd, A592 ☎ 015394/42536, ⓦ www.millerhowe.com. Gorgeous Edwardian house in an elevated position above Windermere, featuring antique- and art-filled rooms and landscaped gardens. Rates (from around £300) include a theatrically presented dinner, plus early morning tea and lavish breakfast. Closed Jan. ❾
Queen's Head A592, Troutbeck, 3 miles north ☎ 015394/32174, ⓦ www.queensheadhotel.com. Although some prefer Troutbeck's traditional *Mortal Man* inn, the style is more contemporary and the food is great at the nearby *Queen's Head*, a refurbished old coaching inn that oozes atmosphere. Two-night minimum stay at weekends. ❼

Hostels

Lake District Backpackers' Lodge High St, across from the tourist office ☎ 015394/46374, ⓦ www.lakedistrictbackpackers.co.uk. Twenty beds in small dorms (available as private rooms on request) and a laid-back atmosphere. The price includes a tea-and-toast breakfast, and you can find out about local tours or work opportunities. No

credit cards. Dorm beds from £11.50, or £15.50 per person in a private room.
Windermere YHA High Cross, Bridge Lane, 1 mile north of Troutbeck Bridge ☎ 0870/770 6094, ⓔ windermere@yha.org.uk. Old mansion with lake views and mountain bike rental. A YHA shuttle-bus (£2.50) runs from Windermere train station (meeting arriving trains) and Ambleside YHA. Dorm beds £14–16.50, depending on season.

Cafes and restaurants

First Floor Lakeland Ltd, behind the train station ☎ 015394/88200. The daytime café inside the home furnishings/design store provides superior snacks, sandwiches and daily specials. Moderate.
Lamplighter Bar *Oakthorpe Hotel*, High St ☎ 015394/43547. A favoured local spot at night, where bistro meals (gammon, fresh fish, rack of lamb) are provided at value-for-money prices. Closed Sun & Mon lunch. Moderate.
Lighthouse Main Rd ☎ 015394/88260. Contemporary café-bar with a street-side terrace, seats in the bar and a first-floor dining room. Moderate.

Bowness and the lake

BOWNESS-ON-WINDERMERE – to give it its full title – is undoubtedly the more attractive of the two Windermere settlements, spilling back from its lakeside piers in a series of terraces lined with guesthouses and hotels. There's been a village here since the fifteenth century and a ferry service across the lake for almost as long – these days, though, you could be forgiven for thinking that Bowness begins and ends with **The World of Beatrix Potter** in the Old Laundry on Crag Brow (daily 10am–4.30/5.30pm; £6; ⓦ www.hop-skip-jump .com). It's unfair to be judgmental – you either like Beatrix Potter or you don't – but it's safe to say that the elaborate 3D story scenes, Peter Rabbit garden, audio-visual "virtual walks", themed tearoom and gift shop here find more favour with children than the more sight Potter attractions at Hill Top and Hawkshead. The other main sight is the **Windermere Steamboat Museum** (ⓦ www.steamboat.co.uk), a fifteen-minute walk north of the centre on Rayrigg Road. This is currently undergoing a major restoration (though parts may be open during the works – check the website for details), which will

Windermere cruises

Windermere Lake Cruises (ⓦ www.windermere-lakecruises.co.uk) operates services to Lakeside at the southern tip (£8 return) or to Brockhole and Waterhead (for Ambleside) at the northern end (£7.70 return). There's also a direct service from Ambleside to the Lake District Visitor Centre at Brockhole (£6 return), and a shuttle service across the lake between Pier 3 at Bowness and Ferry House, Sawrey (£3.50 return). The company also operates an enjoyable circular **cruise around the islands** (departs several times daily from Bowness; £6; 45min), while a 24-hour **Freedom-of-the-Lake** ticket costs £14. Services on all routes are frequent between Easter and October (every 30min–1hr at peak times), and reduced during the winter – but there are sailings every day except Christmas Day.

rejuvenate its collection of historic water craft, including the world's oldest mechanically driven boat and the steam-launch that was the inspiration for Captain Flint's houseboat in Arthur Ransome's *Swallows and Amazons*.

The lake itself – simply **Windermere** (from the Norse, "Vinandr's Lake", and thus never "*Lake* Windermere") – is the heavyweight of Lake District waters, at ten and a half miles long, a mile wide in parts and a shade over two hundred feet deep. Rowing boats are available for rent by the lakeside piers, while Windermere Lake Cruises operates modern cruisers and vintage steamers throughout the year. The traditional **ferry service** is the chain-guided contraption across the water from Ferry Nab on the Bowness side (a ten-minute walk from the cruise piers) to Ferry House, Sawrey (Mon–Sat 7am–10pm, Sun 9am–10pm; departures every 20min; 50p, cars £3), providing access to Beatrix Potter's former home at Hill Top and to Hawkshead beyond.

Practicalities

The open-top #599 **bus** from Windermere train station stops at the lakeside piers, also the terminus for the #517 (to Troutbeck and Ullswater). For onward routes to Ambleside and Grasmere you have to return first to Windermere station, though the useful **Cross-Lakes Shuttle** (daily Easter–Sept, plus Oct weekends) provides a direct connecting boat-and-minibus service from Bowness Pier 3 to Hill Top (£7.70 return), Hawkshead (£9), Grizedale (£11.40) and Coniston Water (£15.30). Windermere Canoe & Kayak (☎015394/44451, ⓦ www.windermerecanoekayak.co.uk), on Ferry Nab Road (on the way to the Sawrey ferry), is the place to rent bikes, canoes and kayaks.

Bowness Bay Information Centre is near the piers on Glebe Road (daily 9.30/10am–4/5.30pm; ☎015394/42895). Crag Brow and then Lake Road is the main thoroughfare up from the lake towards Windermere, on and off which you'll find much of the accommodation and services; pedestrianized **Ash Street**, at the foot of Crag Brow, is where to look for restaurants and bars, from fish and chips to tapas.

B&Bs, guesthouses and hotels

Above The Bay 5 Brackenfield ☎015394/88658, ⓦ www.abovethebay.co.uk. An elevated house in a residential area, just off the Kendal road, a 5min walk from the water. Three spacious rooms open onto a private terrace with stunning lake views. No credit cards. ❹

Gilpin Lodge Crook Rd, B5284, 2 miles southeast ☎015394/88818, ⓦ www.gilpinlodge.co.uk. A renowned country-house retreat with fourteen elegant rooms, some with four-posters, others with whirlpool baths or private patios; six more contemporary suites, sited lodge-style in the grounds, have private gardens with hot tubs. Rates (from £250) include breakfast and dinner in the Michelin-starred restaurant. ❾

Linthwaite House Crook Rd, B5284, 1 mile south ☎015394/88600, ⓦ www.linthwaite.com. Contemporary boutique style grafted onto an ivy-covered country house set high above Windermere – very comfortable rooms feature muted fabrics, Shaker-style furniture, king-sized beds and flat-screen TVs. Rates vary according to outlook and size (from around £200) and include dinner. ❾

Montclare House Crag Brow ☎015394/42723, ⓦ www.montclareguesthouse.co.uk. Attractive en-suite B&B accommodation above a coffee shop that's about the best value in Bowness – two spacious family rooms have bunk beds. No credit cards. ❸

New Hall Bank Fallbarrow Rd ☎015394/43558, ⓦ www.newhallbank.com. Detached Victorian house with a lake view (and just a few yards from the *Hole in't Wall* pub), whose room views get better the higher you go. ❺

Cafés, pubs and restaurants

2 Eggcups 6a Ash St ☎015394/45979. Serves the best sandwich in Bowness, plus other blackboard specials. Daytime only, closed Thurs. Inexpensive.

 Hole in't Wall Fallbarrow Rd ☎015394/43488. For a drink or bar meal you can't beat the town's oldest hostelry (named after the hole the beer used to be passed through); cosy in winter when the fires are lit, and pleasant in summer when you can sit outside. Inexpensive.

Jackson's Bistro St Martin's Sq ℡ 015394/46264. The local choice for a family meal or romantic night out – classic bistro dishes, including a good-value three-course *table d'hôte* menu available all night. Dinner only. Moderate.

Around Bowness

A mile and a half south of Bowness, there's the rare chance to visit a house designed by one of the major exponents of the Arts and Crafts Movement. Mackay Hugh Baillie Scott's **Blackwell** (daily 10.30am–4/5pm; closed Jan to mid-Feb; £5.45; ⓦ www.blackwell.org.uk) was built in 1900 as a lakeside holiday home, and Lakeland motifs (particularly trees, flowers, birds and berries) are visible in virtually every nook and cranny, from the stonework to the stained glass. You'll also have the chance to see changing exhibitions of Arts and Crafts furniture and other contemporary pieces, and there's an informative introductory talk (usually weekdays at 2.30pm), plus tearoom, craft shop and gardens. Parking is available; alternatively, walk from Bowness (about 25min).

From Bowness piers, boats head to the southern reaches of Windermere at Lakeside, which is also the terminus of the **Lakeside and Haverthwaite Railway** (Easter–Oct 6–7 daily; £5.20 return; ℡ 015395/31594, ⓦ www .lakesiderailway.co.uk), whose steam-powered engines chuff along four miles of track through the forests of Backbarrow Gorge. The boat arrivals at Lakeside connect with train departures throughout the day, and you can buy a joint boat-and-train ticket (£12.60 return) at Bowness if you fancy the extended tour. Also on the quay at Lakeside is the **Aquarium of the Lakes** (daily 9am–5/6pm; £7.50; ⓦ www.aquariumofthelakes.co.uk), an entertaining natural history exhibit centred on the fish and animals found along a Lakeland river, including a walk-through tunnel aquarium containing huge carp and diving ducks. Enthusiastic staff are on hand to explain what's going on and, again, there's a joint ticket available with the boat ride from Bowness (£14.35 return). Alternatively contact Country Lanes bike rental on the quayside for a bike-and-boat day out (ⓦ www.countrylanes.co.uk; from £15, which includes the boat ride from Bowness).

Ambleside

Five miles northwest of Windermere, **AMBLESIDE** is at the heart of the southern Lakes region, making it a first-class base for walkers, who are

---

Walks from Ambleside

A couple of good walks are possible straight from the town centre. First, from the footbridge across the river in Rothay Park you can strike up across **Loughrigg Fell** (1099ft). Dropping down to Loughrigg Terrace (2hr), overlooking Grasmere, you then cut south at Rydal on the A591 and follow the minor road back along the River Rothay to Ambleside – a total of 6 miles (4hr).

The walk over **Wansfell to Troutbeck** and back (6 miles; around 4hr) is a little tougher. Stock Ghyll Lane runs up the left bank of the tumbling stream to **Stock Ghyll Force,** one of the more attractive waterfalls in the region. The path then rises steeply to **Wansfell Pike** (1581ft) and down into Troutbeck village, where you can have lunch either at the *Mortal Man* or the nearby *Queen's Head*, both just a short walk from the village centre. The return cuts west onto the flanks of Wansfell and around past the viewpoint at **Jenkin Crag** back to Ambleside.

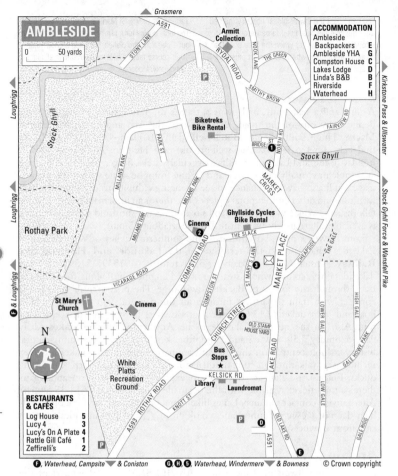

AMBLESIDE

0 ___ 50 yards

ACCOMMODATION
Ambleside
 Backpackers   E
Ambleside YHA   G
Compston House C
Lakes Lodge   D
Linda's B&B   B
Riverside   F
Waterhead   H

RESTAURANTS
& CAFÉS
Log House   5
Lucy 4   3
Lucy's On A Plate 4
Rattle Gill Café   1
Zeffirelli's   2

Grasmere

Armitt
Collection

Biketreks
Bike Rental

Ghyllside Cycles
Bike Rental

St Mary's
Church

Cinema

Rothay Park

Stock Ghyll

White
Platts
Recreation
Ground

Bus
Stops

Library

Laundromat

Kirkstone Pass & Ullswater

Stock Ghyll Force & Wansfell Pike

Stock Ghyll

F, Waterhead, Campsite ▼ & Coniston   **G**,**H**,**5**, Waterhead, Windermere ▼ & Bowness

catered for by a large number of outdoors shops. The town centre consists of a cluster of grey-green stone houses, shops, pubs and B&Bs hugging a circular one-way system, which loops round just south of the narrow gully of stony Stock Ghyll.

For some background on Ambleside's history, stroll a couple of minutes along Rydal Road to the **Armitt Collection** (daily 10am–5pm; £2.50; Ⓦwww .armitt.com), which catalogues the very distinct contribution to Lakeland society made by writers and artists from John Ruskin to Beatrix Potter. The rest of town lies a mile south at **Waterhead**, overlooked by the grass banks and spreading trees of Borrans Park. Two or three little cafés by Waterhead pier have outdoor seats, and you can take drinks from the bar onto the lawns of both the *Wateredge Inn* and *Waterhead* hotel.

Practicalities

Walking up to Ambleside from the ferry piers at Waterhead takes about fifteen minutes, while all **buses** stop on Kelsick Road, opposite the library. The **tourist**

office is on Market Cross (daily 9am–5pm; ☎015394/32582, ⓦwww
.lakelandgateway.info); further online information is avalialbe at ⓦwww
.amblesideonline.co.uk. There's **bike rental** from Biketreks on Rydal Road
(☎015394/31245, ⓦwww.biketreks.net), or Ghyllside Cycles on The Slack
(☎015394/33592, ⓦwww.ghyllside.co.uk).

Lake Road, running between Waterhead and Ambleside, is lined with **B&Bs**,
with other concentrations on central Church Street and Compston Road.
Zeffirelli's **cinema** (ⓦwww.zeffirellis.com) has four screens at two locations in
town, while annual festivals include the traditional procession to the church
known as the Rushbearing (July), and the famous annual **Ambleside Sports**
gathering (traditional wrestling to fell-running) on the Thursday before the first
Monday in August.

B&Bs, guesthouses and hotels

Compston House Compston Rd ☎015394/32305,
ⓦwww.compstonhouse.co.uk. There's a breezy
New York air in this traditional Lakeland house,
with American-style themed rooms and breakfasts
of pancakes and maple syrup if you wish. ❹

Lakes Lodge Lake Rd ☎015394/33240,
ⓦwww.lakeslodge.co.uk. A dozen spacious
rooms, stylishly kitted out, with upgraded
bathrooms and a good buffet breakfast served in
the informal café-style breakfast room. Two-night
minimum at weekends. ❻

Linda's B&B Compston Rd ☎015394/32999. The
cheapest rates in town. Guests can use the kitchen,
while two of the four rooms (all share a bathroom)
can sleep three or four. No credit cards. ❷

Riverside Under Loughrigg
☎015394/32395, ⓦwww.riverside-at
-ambleside.co.uk. Charming guesthouse on a
quiet lane, half-a-mile (10min walk) from town
(across Rothay Park). Six large, light country-pine
style rooms available, including a river-facing
four-poster. ❺

Waterhead Waterhead ☎015394/32566, ⓦwww
.elh.co.uk. Contemporary town-house-style
accommodation provides the Lakes' classiest
four-star lodgings – there's a champagne menu in
each slate-and-marble bathroom, plus garden-bar
and positively metropolitan restaurant. It's very
close to the lake, opposite the Waterhead piers. ❻

Hostels

Ambleside Backpackers Old Lake Rd
☎015394/32340, ⓦwww
.englishlakesbackpackers.co.uk. Midway between

lake and town, this independent backpackers' is a
secluded property with a decent kitchen and
Internet. Dorm beds from £16.

Ambleside YHA Waterhead, A591, 1 mile south
☎0870/770 5672, ✉ambleside@yha.org.uk. The
YHA's flagship regional hostel, a huge lakeside
affair with small dorms, twins, doubles and family
rooms, plus bike rental, Internet, licensed café and
private jetty. Dorm beds from £20, including
breakfast, rooms ❸

Cafés and restaurants

Log House Lake Rd ☎015394/31077. The New
Zealand chef presents an inventive menu – crispy
squid to Vietnamese roast duck – in an
eye-catching Norwegian log cabin, a 5min walk
from the town centre. Lunch is cheaper (and there
are two B&B rooms too). Closed Mon (& also Sun
in winter). Expensive.

Lucy's on a Plate Church St
☎015394/31191. Really enjoyable bistro
offering a daily-changing menu with tons of
choice. *Lucy 4* on St Mary's Lane, just over the
way, is its moderately priced tapas bar offshoot.
Expensive.

Rattle Gill Café Bridge St ☎015394/34360.
Squeeze into this little streamside café for tasty
veggie wholefood dishes, salads and sandwiches.
Daytime only. Inexpensive.

Zeffirelli's Compston Rd ☎015394/33845.
Famous for its wholemeal-based pizzas, but
also serving inventive pastas and veggie food –
there's a sun-trap terrace, upstairs jazz bar (with
live music a couple of nights a week) and a dinner
with cinema-ticket special for screenings at Zeff's
two cinemas. Moderate.

Great Langdale

Three miles west of Ambleside along the A593, Skelwith Bridge marks the start
of **Great Langdale**, a U-shaped glacial valley overlooked by the prominent
rocky summits of the **Langdale Pikes**, the most popular of the central

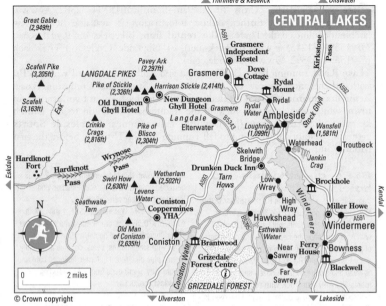

Thirlmere & Keswick   Ullswater

CENTRAL LAKES

Great Gable (2,949ft)

Scafell Pike (3,205ft)

Pavey Ark (2,297ft)

LANGDALE PIKES

Pike of Stickle (2,326ft)   Harrison Stickle (2,414ft)

Grasmere Independent Hostel

Grasmere   Dove Cottage

Rydal Mount

Rydal

Kirkstone Pass

A591

A592

Scafell (3,163ft)

Old Dungeon Ghyll Hotel

New Dungeon Ghyll Hotel   Grasmere

Langdale   Elterwater

Rydal Water   Ambleside

Stock Ghyll

Crinkle Crags (2,816ft)

Pike of Blisco (2,304ft)

Loughrigg (1,099ft)   Wansfell (1,581ft)

Hardknott Fort

Hardknott Pass

Wrynose Pass

Swirl How (2,630ft)

Wetherlam (2,502ft)

Skelwith Bridge

Drunken Duck Inn

Tarn Hows

Waterhead   Troutbeck

Jenkin Crag

Levens Water

Low Wray   Brockhole

Seathwaite Tarn

Coniston Coppermines YHA

High Wray

Hawkshead

Windermere

Miller Howe

Windermere

A591

N

0   2 miles

Old Man of Coniston (2,635ft)

Coniston   Brantwood

Grizedale Forest Centre

Esthwaite Water

Near Sawrey

Far Sawrey

Ferry House   Bowness

Blackwell

Coniston Water

GRIZEDALE FOREST

Esk

Eskdale

Kendal

B5343

B5285

© Crown copyright   Ulverston   Lakeside

Lakeland fells. The #516 Langdale Rambler **bus** from Ambleside's Kelsick Road runs to Elterwater (17min) and on up to the head of the valley (30min), passing all the accommodation reviewed below.

Half a mile northwest of its namesake water, pretty **ELTERWATER** is fringed by sheep-filled common land and centred on a tiny village green overlooked by the excellent *Britannia Inn* (☎015394/37210, ⊛www.britinn .co.uk; ⑥), with comfortable rooms and good food served in the bar or dining room – come on a summer's day and the terrace is packed. The local **youth hostel**, *Elterwater YHA* (☎0870/770 5816, Ⓔelterwater@yha.org.uk; dorm beds from £13.50), is a converted farmhouse and barn, just across the bridge from the pub – it's not at all fancy, but is sited in great walking country (hiking and activity weekends are held here year-round).

A **footpath** from Elterwater (signposted as the Cumbria Way) runs all the way up the valley; drivers follow the minor B5343 and should make for either of the valley's main car parks. Three miles from Elterwater, at **Stickle Ghyll** car park, Harrison Stickle (2414ft), Pike of Stickle (2326ft) and Pavey Ark (2297ft) form a dramatic backdrop, though many walkers aim no further than **Stickle Tarn**, an hour's climb up a wide path from Stickle Ghyll. Another obvious target is the sixty-foot waterfall of **Dungeon Ghyll**, around thirty minutes' stiff climb from the car park – the "dungeon" in question is a natural cave. The other car park, a mile further west up the valley road by the **Old Dungeon Ghyll Hotel**, is the starting-point for a series of more hardcore hikes to resonant Lakeland peaks like Crinkle Crags (2816ft) or Bowfell (2960ft), though curiously named **Pike o'Blisco** (2304ft) is the easier prospect – a five-mile, three-hour round trip from the car park, rewarded by marvellous views.

The comfortable **rooms** at the Victorian *New Dungeon Ghyll Hotel* (☎015394/37213, ⊛www.dungeon-ghyll.com; ⑥) feature dramatic fell views. You can eat here, or at the adjacent *Sticklebarn Tavern* (☎015394/37356), which has big breakfasts and inexpensive bar meals available year-round, as well as simple **bunk-barn accommodation** (£11 per night). However, the best-known accommodation in the valley is the peerless 🎋 *Old Dungeon Ghyll Hotel* (☎015394/37272, ⓦwww.odg.co.uk; ⑥), at the end of the B5343, seven miles northeast of Ambleside. It's a traditional, comfortable mountain inn, well known to walkers and climbers. Dinner (around £25, reservations essential) is served in the dining room, but all the action is in the stone-flagged **hikers' bar**, which serves real ales and filling chips-with-everything meals.

Grasmere and around

Four miles northwest of Ambleside, the village of **GRASMERE** consists of an intimate cluster of grey-stone houses on the old packhorse road that runs beside the babbling River Rothay. It's set back from one of the most alluring of the region's small lakes, itself called Grasmere, but it loses some of its charm in summer thanks to the hordes who descend on the trail of the village's most famous former resident, **William Wordsworth** (1770–1850). The poet, his wife Mary, sister Dorothy and other members of his family are buried beneath the yews in **St Oswald's churchyard**, around which the river makes a sinuous curl. At the rear entrance to the churchyard, the schoolhouse where Wordsworth once taught is now Sarah Nelson's Gingerbread Shop. There's little else to the village, save its gift shops, galleries, tearooms and hotels, though the **lake** is just a ten-minute walk away, past the tourist office, down Redbank Road; tremendous views unfold from **Loughrigg Terrace**, on its southern reaches. The full four-mile circuit of Grasmere and adjacent **Rydal Water** takes around two hours, though as the route passes Wordsworth haunts Rydal Mount and Dove Cottage, it could be turned into an all-day sightseeing venture.

Practicalities

Grasmere is on the main #555 and #599 **bus** routes, which both stop on the village green. On-street parking is extremely limited, so aim straight for the main car park on Redbank Road, by the garden centre. Note that as well as the recommended backpackers' hostel, there are two official YHA hostels close to the village (*Butharlyp Howe* and *Thorney How*, details on ⓦwww.yha.org.uk). For something a bit different contact Full Circle (☎01539/821278, ⓦwww.lake-district-yurts.co.uk; open Easter–Dec), who have three eco-friendly yurts in the Rydal Hall grounds, a couple of miles south of the village. The big event of the year is the Grasmere Lakeland Sports and Show (third or fourth Sun in Aug), a great day out showcasing traditional Cumbrian sports and activities.

Accommodation

🥾 **Grasmere Independent Hostel**
Broadrayne Farm, A591 ☎015394/35055, ⓦwww.grasmerehostel.co.uk. Just north of the village, past the *Travellers' Rest* pub, this stylish backpackers' is the top budget choice and the best of its kind in the Lakes – 24 beds in small, carpeted en-suite rooms, impressive kitchen, laundry facilities and sauna, not to mention gracious hosts. Dorm beds from £16.50.

Harwood Red Lion Sq ☎015394/35248, ⓦwww.harwoodhotel.co.uk. Genial family-run hotel with eight smartly furnished rooms with varied village outlooks, and a coffeehouse and deli below. Two-night minimum stay at weekends. Limited private parking. ④

How Foot Lodge Town End ☎015394/35366, ⓦwww.howfoot.co.uk. Spacious Victorian villa, just yards from Dove Cottage, with six rooms, one with its own sun lounge. Guests get a discount on dinner at the nearby *Villa Colombina* restaurant. Parking. Closed Jan. ④

Lancrigg Vegetarian Country House Easedale Rd ☎015394/35317, ⓦwww.lancrigg.co.uk. Relaxed country-house retreat, half a mile

William Wordsworth was not the first to praise the Lake District – Thomas Gray wrote appreciatively of his visit in 1769 – but it is Wordsworth that dominates its literary landscape. Born in Cockermouth in 1770, he was sent to school in Hawkshead before a stint at Cambridge, a year in France and two in Somerset. In 1799 he returned to the Lake District, settling in the Grasmere district, where he spent the last two-thirds of his life with his sister Dorothy, who not only transcribed his poems but was an accomplished diarist as well.

Wordsworth and fellow poets **Samuel Taylor Coleridge** and **Robert Southey** formed a clique that became known as the "Lake Poets", a label based more on their fluctuating friendships and their shared passion for the region than on any common subject matter in their writings. A fourth member of the Cumbrian literary elite was the critic and essayist **Thomas De Quincey**, chiefly known today for his *Confessions of an English Opium-eater*. One of the first to fully appreciate the revolutionary nature of Wordsworth's and Coleridge's collaborative *Lyrical Ballads*, De Quincey became a long-term guest of the Wordsworths in 1807, taking over Dove Cottage from them in 1809.

Inspired by Wordsworth's writings and by the terrain itself, the social philosopher and art critic **John Ruskin** also made the Lake District his home, settling at Brantwood, outside Coniston, in 1872. Much of Ruskin's feeling for the countryside permeated through to two other literary immigrants, **Arthur Ransome**, also a Coniston resident and writer of the children's classic *Swallows and Amazons*, and **Beatrix Potter**, whose favourite Lakeland spots feature in her children's stories. Potter, in fact, is the only serious Lakeland rival to Wordsworthian dominance, with her former home at Hill Top in Near Sawrey, her husband's office in Hawkshead and a museum in Bowness all packed with international visitors throughout the year.

northwest of the village. A dozen variously sized rooms have been carved from the well-worn interior (one the former library); a vegetarian four-course dinner is included in the price. ⑧

🏃 **Moss Grove Organic** Corner of College St, opposite the *Wordsworth Hotel* ☎015394/35251, ⓦ www.mossgrove.com. A Victorian-era hotel redesigned on organic, low-impact lines – luxurious rooms have extraordinary handmade beds of reclaimed timber, wool carpets, duck-down duvets and natural wood blinds. The feel is less hotel and more private house party – there are only eleven rooms and you're encouraged to forage in the kitchen for a superior buffet-style breakfast. Two-night minimum stay at weekends. Parking. ⑧

Raise View White Bridge ☎015394/35215, ⓦ www.raiseviewhouse.co.uk. There are lovely fell views from every corner of this amiable guest house, plus a warm welcome and very comfortable rooms (including a single in the eaves). Parking. No credit cards. ⑤

White Moss House Rydal Water, A591, 1 mile south ☎015394/35295, ⓦ www.whitemoss.com. The ivy-clad house has antique-filled rooms in the

main house and two more in a cottage suite with lake views. It's a glorious spot, to which regulars return year after year, and the breakfast is wonderful. Closed Dec & Jan. ⑥

Wordsworth Hotel College St ☎015394/35592, ⓦ www.thewordsworthhotel.co.uk. Four-star choice in the village centre, with updated rooms, a heated pool, Jacuzzi and gym, conservatory and terrace. There's a good bistro and bar (*Dove & Olive Branch*) and excellent restaurant (*Prelude*), so consider a dinner, bed and breakfast deal. Parking. ⑧

Cafés and restaurants

🏃 **Jumble Room** Langdale Rd ☎015394/35188. Funky café-restaurant with an organic touch and a menu that ranges the world – from Thai prawns to local game pie. Closed Mon & Tues and occasional other days in winter. Expensive.

Rowan Tree Church Bridge, Stock Lane ☎015394/35528. The main draw here is the outdoor terrace, on a lazy bend in the river opposite Grasmere church. A daytime tearoom menu gives way to Med-style dining at night, including pizza and pasta. Moderate.

Villa Colombina Town End ℡ 015394/35268. Informal, authentic Italian café-restaurant, by Dove Cottage, serving pizza, pasta, steak and chicken, plus daily blackboard specials. Closed Jan and occasional other days in winter. Moderate.

Dove Cottage

On Grasmere's southeastern outskirts, just off the A591, stands **Dove Cottage** (daily 9.30am–5.30pm; closed early Jan to early Feb; £6.50, though prices may rise; ⓦ www.wordsworth.org.uk; buses #555 and #599), home to William and Dorothy Wordsworth from 1799 to 1808 and where Wordsworth wrote some of his best poetry. Guides bursting with anecdotes lead you around rooms that reflect Wordsworth's guiding principle of "plain living but high thinking" and are little changed now but for the addition of electricity and internal plumbing. This maxim, however, was only temporary, as Wordsworth was raised in comfortable surroundings and returned to a relatively high standard of living when he moved to Rydal Mount. Most of the furniture in the cottage belonged to the Wordsworths, while in the upper rooms are various other possessions, including a pair of William's ice skates. In good weather, the garden is open for visits as well. In the adjacent **museum** are paintings, manuscripts (including that of "Daffodils") and personal effects once belonging to the Wordsworths (most poignantly Mary's wedding ring), plus mementoes of Southey, Coleridge and Thomas De Quincey. The museum ticket allows entry to any special **exhibitions** currently running, detailed on the website, while the Wordsworth Trust sponsors readings, family activities and other events throughout the year.

Rydal Mount

Another mile and a half southeast along the A591 from Grasmere, **Rydal Mount** (March–Oct daily 9.30am–5pm; Nov–Feb daily except Tues

▲ Dove Cottage

10am–4pm, closed for three weeks in Jan; £5, gardens only £2.50; ⓦwww
.rydalmount.co.uk) was the home of William Wordsworth from 1813 until his
death in 1850. The house is now owned by descendants of the poet and you're
free to wander around what is essentially still a family home – summer concerts
feature poetry readings by Wordsworth family members and there are recent
family photos on display alongside more familiar portraits of the poet and his
circle. In the drawing room and library is the only known portrait of Dorothy,
while memorabilia includes William's black leather sofa, his inkstand and
dispatch box. For many, the highlight is the **garden**, which has been preserved
as Wordsworth designed it, complete with terraces where he used to declaim his
poetry. Buses #555 and #599 pass the house on the way to Grasmere from
Windermere and Ambleside.

Coniston and around

Coniston Water is not one of the most immediately imposing of the lakes,
yet it has a quiet beauty which sets it apart from the more popular destinations. The nineteenth-century art critic and social reformer John Ruskin
made the lake his home, and today his isolated house, **Brantwood**, on the
northeastern shore, provides the most obvious target for a day-trip. However,
the plain village of **Coniston**, to the west, grows on visitors after a while,
especially those who base themselves here for some of the central Lakes' most
rewarding walking. **Arthur Ransome** was a frequent visitor, his local
memories and experiences providing much of the detail in his famous
Swallows and Amazons children's books.

Coniston village

The slate-grey village of **CONISTON** (a derivation of "King's Town") hunkers
below the craggy and coppermine-riddled bulk of **The Old Man of Coniston**
(2628ft), which most fit walkers can climb in under two hours – from the
bridge in the village, follow the path up past the *Sun Hotel* towards the
Coppermines hostel. Having climbed the fell, and then studied **John Ruskin's
grave**, which lies in St Andrew's original churchyard beneath a beautifully
worked Celtic cross, you'll have seen all that Coniston has to offer, save for the
excellent **Ruskin Museum** on Yewdale Road (Easter to mid-Nov daily
10am–5.30pm; mid-Nov to Easter Wed–Sun 10am–3.30pm; £4.25; ⓦwww
.ruskinmuseum.com). This combines local history and geology exhibits with a
fascinating look at Ruskin's life and work through his watercolours, manuscripts
and personal memorabilia.

Coniston Water

Coniston Water is hidden out of sight, half a mile southeast of the village.
Here, the *Bluebird Café* sells ices, snacks and drinks, while at the adjacent
Coniston Boating Centre (☏015394/41366) there are rowing boats,
sailing dinghies, canoes, electric launches and motorboats. From the pier, the
sumptuously upholstered **Steam Yacht Gondola** (Easter–Oct hourly
departures 11am–4pm, weather permitting; £6 return; ☏015394/41288,
ⓦwww.nationaltrust.org.uk/gondola), built in 1859, departs on hour-long
circuits of the lake, though you can also stop off at Ruskin's Brantwood. The
other lake service is the **Coniston Launch** (Easter–Oct hourly
10.30am–4.30pm; Nov–Easter up to 4 daily depending on the weather;
☏015394/36216, ⓦwww.conistonlaunch.co.uk), which operates wooden
solar-powered boats on three routes around the lake, north (£5.40 return),

south (£7.80) or mid-lake (£6.60), all calling at Brantwood. You can stop off at any pier en route, and local walk leaflets are available. Special **cruises** (Easter–Oct; call for times; £7.50–9) concentrate on the various sites associated with *Swallows and Amazons* and Donald Campbell, or show you the lake in the evening.

Brantwood

Nestling among trees on a hillside above the eastern shore of Coniston Water, two and a half miles by road from Coniston (off B5285), **Brantwood** (mid-March to mid-Nov daily 11am–5.30pm; mid-Nov to mid-March Wed–Sun 11am–4.30pm; £5.95, gardens only £4, combined Coniston Launch ticket available; ⓦwww.brantwood.org.uk) was home to John Ruskin from 1872 until his death in 1900.

Both art critic and moralist, Ruskin was champion of J.M.W. Turner and the Pre-Raphaelites and foremost Victorian proponent of the supremacy of Gothic architecture. He bought Brantwood in 1871, sight unseen, complaining when he saw it that it was "a mere shed". The views captivated him, however, and he spent the next twenty years adding to the house and laying out its gardens. His **study** – hung with handmade paper to his own design – and **dining room** boast superlative lake views, bettered only by those from the **Turret Room** where he used to sit in later life in his bathchair. The surviving Turners from Ruskin's own art collection are on show, and other exhibition rooms and galleries display Ruskin-related arts and crafts, while the excellent *Jumping Jenny Tearooms* – named after Ruskin's boat – has an outdoor terrace with lake views. The lovingly restored **gardens** are well worth exploring too – free guided walks take place several times a week – while Thursday is "activity day", always a good time to visit.

Practicalities

Buses – principally the #505 "Coniston Rambler" from Windermere, Ambleside and Hawkshead and the #12 from Ulverston – stop on the main road through Coniston village. A Ruskin Explorer ticket (from £12) gets you return bus travel on the #505, plus use of the Coniston Launch and entry to Ruskin's house – buy the ticket on the bus. The Cross-Lakes Shuttle minibus service from Bowness runs as far as the Coniston Launch pier (for Brantwood and lake services) at the *Waterhead Hotel*, half a mile out of the village. There's a **tourist office** (daily 9.30am–5pm; ☎015394/41533, ⓦwww.conistontic .org) right in the centre by the main car park, while best places for a bite to eat are the *Black Bull* **pub**, which brews its own Bluebird beer, and the *Meadowdore Café* (open until late in summer).

Accommodation

Bank Ground Farm Coniston Water, east side
℡015394/41264, ⓦwww.bankground.com. On the
lakeshore just north of Brantwood, this beautifully
set farmhouse was the model for Holly Howe Farm
in *Swallows and Amazons*. Country-style rooms in
the main house, many with sweeping views (room
8 is best), plus self-catering holiday cottages and
converted barn. ❹

Beech Tree Guesthouse Yewdale Rd
℡015394/41717. Friendly vegetarian place 150yd
north of the village on the Ambleside road, with
charming rooms (not all en-suite). Parking. No
credit cards. ❸

Black Bull Inn Coppermines Rd, by the bridge
℡015394/41335, ⓦwww.conistonbrewery.com/
blackbull.htm. The village's best pub has a variety
of rooms available in the main building or in the
renovated cottages attached. Hearty bar meals
served, with homemade soup, local lamb, sausage
and trout as mainstays. Weekends, 2-night
minimum stay. ❺

Coniston Coppermines YHA ℡0870/770 5772,
Ⓔcoppermines@yha.org.uk. *Holly How* might be
the closer YHA hostel to the village, but it's
Coppermines that is the hikers' favourite, set
dramatically in the mountains a steep mile or so
from the village. Follow the "Old Man" signs or take
the small road between the *Black Bull* and the
Co-op. Closed Nov–March & some other days in
summer season. Dorm beds from £13.

Meadowdore Café Hawkshead Old Rd
℡015394/41638, ⓦwww.meadowdore-café.co.uk
High-quality B&B above the café – two en-suite
rooms, and one with a lovely private bathroom, all
tastefully furnished. Breakfast is served all day in
the café. ❸

Yew Tree Farm A593, 2 miles north
℡015394/41433, ⓦwww.yewtree-farm
.com. Hiker-friendly accommodation in a peaceful
seventeenth-century farmhouse with munching
sheep and tearoom – Beatrix Potter once owned
the house and furnished its parlour (and you
might have seen the house in the Renée
Zellweger film, *Miss Potter*, when it doubled as
Hill Top). Three cosy oak-panelled rooms (one
en-suite) available, plus an excellent breakfast.
No credit cards. ❸

Hawkshead and around

HAWKSHEAD, midway between Coniston and Ambleside, wears its beauty
well, its patchwork of cottages and cobbles backed by woods and fells and barely
affected by modern intrusions. Huge car parks at the village edge take the strain,
and when the crowds of day-trippers leave, Hawkshead regains its natural
tranquillity.

The village was an important wool market at the time William Wordsworth
was studying at **Hawkshead Grammar School** (Easter–Oct Mon–Sat
10am–12.30pm & 1.30–5pm, Sun 1–5pm; £1), founded in 1585; this is now
a small museum, located near the main car park. However, most visits to
Hawkshead focus on the **Beatrix Potter Gallery** on Main Street
(Easter–Oct daily except Fri 10.30am–4.30pm; £4, discount available for
Hill Top visitors; NT), occupying rooms once used by the author's solicitor
husband. It's a hugely popular attraction, containing an annually changing
selection of her original sketchbooks, drawings, watercolours and manuscripts,
though the less devoted might find displays on her life as keen naturalist,
conservationist and early supporter of the National Trust more

> ## Beatrix Potter, the movie
>
> You'll find it hard to travel around the Lakes and not notice the effect of the 2007 film
> *Miss Potter* (starring Renée Zellweger and Ewan McGregor), the Beatrix Potter biopic
> largely filmed in Cumbria. It's bringing in even more tourists than ever to places like
> Hill Top and the Beatrix Potter Gallery, while location sites like Yew Tree Farm,
> Loughrigg Tarn, Loweswater and Derwent Water are making the most of their fleeting
> fame – the website ⓦwww.visitmisspotter.com has all the location and film details,
> while tour guides involved in the filming offer a full-day Miss Potter Film Tour
> (ⓦwww.lakedistrictfilmtours.co.uk).

diverting – Potter bequeathed her farms and land in the Lake District to the Trust on her death.

The most popular local walk from Hawkshead is to one such piece of land, **Tarn Hows**, a body of water surrounded by spruce and pine and circled by paths and picnic spots. It takes about an hour to walk around the tarn, and you can always make the half-mile diversion to the tearoom at nearby Yew Tree Farm. Tarn Hows is two miles from Hawkshead (or Coniston) on country lanes and paths, or can be reached by a minor road off the Hawkshead–Coniston B5285 – drivers have to pay to use the National Trust car park.

Practicalities

The main **bus service** to Hawkshead is the #505 Coniston Rambler between Windermere, Ambleside and Coniston, while the seasonal **Cross-Lakes Shuttle** runs from Hawkshead down to the Beatrix Potter house at Hill Top and on to Sawrey for boat connections back to Bowness. There is a YHA hostel, but it's a mile away from the village by Esthwaite Water and largely used by families.

B&Bs, guesthouses and hotels

Ann Tyson's Cottage Wordsworth St
ⓉT 015394/36405, Ⓦwww.anntysons.co.uk.
Whether or not Wordsworth briefly boarded here, as some contend, the old cobbled street has changed little since his era. Today there are three B&B rooms in the main house and two superior rooms in what used to be an old chapel. ❹, superior rooms ❺

Drunken Duck Inn Barngates crossroads, 2 miles north, off B5285 ⓉT 015394/36347, Ⓦwww.drunkenduckinn.co.uk. Superb restaurant-with-rooms in a beautifully located 400-year-old inn. The cuisine is cutting-edge Modern British (dinner around £35 excluding drinks and service;

reservations essential), the rooms eminently stylish, the views divine. ❼, superior rooms ❽

King's Arms Market Sq ⓉT 015394/36372, Ⓦwww.kingsarmshawkshead.co.uk. Bags of character in this old inn, with nine rooms retaining their oak beams and idiosyncratic proportions. It's also the best pub in the village, with good-value meals. ❺

Yewfield Hawkshead Hill, 2 miles west off B5285 ⓉT 015394/36765, Ⓦwww.yewfield .co.uk. Splendid vegetarian guest house set amongst organic vegetable gardens, orchards and wildflower meadows. The house is a Victorian Gothic beauty, filled with Oriental artefacts and art from the owners' travels, and breakfast is a treat. Closed mid-Nov to Jan. ❺

Grizedale Forest

Grizedale Forest extends over the fells separating Coniston Water from Windermere. The best starting point is the **Grizedale Forest Centre** (daily 10/11am–4/5pm; free, parking fee charged; ⓉT 01229/860010, Ⓦwww .forestry.gov.uk/grizedale), three miles southwest of Hawkshead – the Cross-Lakes Shuttle (from Bowness via Hawkshead) runs here in the morning, picking up return visitors later in the day. There's a good café, craft shop, and activity areas at the centre, while **Grizedale Mountain Bikes** (9am–4.30/5pm; ⓉT 01229/860369, Ⓦwww.grizedalemountainbikes.co.uk)

Fishing on Esthwaite Water

Hawkshead's lake, Esthwaite Water, was loved by Wordsworth who rambled and fished here as a boy. At **Esthwaite Water Trout Fishery** (Ⓦwww.hawksheadtrout .com), on the southwest side, there's loch-style day-fishing from boats (including for beginners), catching wild rainbow and brown trout. Tuition, barbecue and picnic facilities are also available.

has bikes available to explore the waymarked trails through the forest. These extend for between two and fourteen miles, with the longest, the **Silurian Way**, linking most of a remarkable series of ninety-odd stone and wood **sculptures** that are scattered among the trees. The challenging 10-mile North Face Trail also gets rave reviews from serious mountain-bikers. More adventurous still is the forest high-ropes course known as **Go Ape** (Feb–Oct daily, Nov weekends only, closed Dec & Jan; advance bookings required on ☎0870/444 5562, ⓦwww.goape.co.uk; £25; minimum age 10), which has you frolicking in the tree canopy for a couple of hours – fantastic fun involving zip-wires, Tarzan-swings, tree platforms and other aerial manoeuvres.

Hill Top

It's two miles from Hawkshead, down the eastern side of Esthwaite Water on the B5285, to the hamlet of Near Sawrey, the site of Beatrix Potter's beloved **Hill Top** (Easter–Oct Mon–Wed, Sat & Sun 10.30am–4.30pm; £5.40, timed entry; garden entry free on Thurs & Fri when house is closed; NT). A Londoner by birth, Potter bought the farmhouse here with the proceeds from her first book, *The Tale of Peter Rabbit*, and retained it as her study long after she moved out following her marriage in 1913. Its furnishings and contents have been kept as they were during her occupancy – a condition of Potter's will – and the small house is always busy with visitors; in summer, arrive early and expect to have to queue. The seasonal Cross-Lakes Shuttle boat-and-bus service runs directly here from Bowness, or you can walk up from the Sawrey ferry pier through the woods to the house in about an hour.

Keswick and Derwent Water

Standing on the shores of **Derwent Water** at the junction of the main north–south and east–west routes through the Lake District, the small market town of **KESWICK** makes a good base for exploring delightful Borrowdale to the south or the heights of Skiddaw (3053ft) and Blencathra (2847ft), which loom over the town to the north. It's a bustling place with plenty of accommodation, and some good pubs and cafés, while several bus routes radiate from the town, getting you to the start of even the most challenging hikes.

Arrival, information and accommodation

Buses use the terminal in front of the large Booths supermarket, off Main Street. Disc zones in town allow an hour or two's free parking, but you'll have to use the large signposted car parks if you're staying for the day. The **tourist office** is in the Moot Hall on Market Square (daily 9.30am–4.30/5.30pm; ☎017687/72645) and there's online information at ⓦwww.keswick.org and ⓦwww.dokeswick.com. George Fisher, at 2 Borrowdale Rd (ⓦwww .georgefisher.co.uk), is one of the most celebrated **outdoors stores** in the Lakes, with a daily weather information service and terrific hiker's café, *Abraham's*. **Guided walks** – from lakeside rambles to mountain climbs – depart from the Moot Hall (Easter–Oct daily 10.15am; £8, longer walks £10; ⓦwww .hillwalker.ic24.net); just turn up with a packed lunch. For **bike rental**, there's Keswick Mountain Bikes on Southey Lane (☎017687/75202, ⓦwww .keswickmountainbikes.co.uk; from £17).

Standard **B&Bs** cluster along Bank and Stanger streets, near the post office, and around Southey, Blencathra and Eskin streets in the grid near the start of the A591 Penrith road. Smarter **guest-houses** line the street known as The

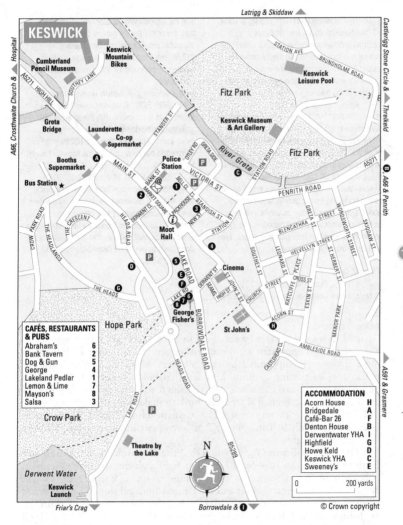

Heads, overlooking Hope Park, a couple of minutes south of the centre on the way to the lake.

B&Bs, guesthouses and hotels

Acorn House Ambleside Rd ☎017687/72553, ⓦwww.acornhousehotel.co.uk. Handsome eighteenth-century house with nine generously sized rooms, 5min from the centre. Parking. ④

Bridgedale 101 Main St ☎017687/73914. Keswick's most amenable landlady makes her rooms suit all requirements – whether you're looking for an early breakfast, a room-only deal,

en-suite room or cycle storage, you'll find it here. There's also a summer tea-garden out back. No credit cards. ③

Café-Bar 26 26 Lake Rd ☎017687/80863, ⓦwww.cafebar26 .co.uk. Three stylish rooms offer a central chintz-free base. Downstairs is the best of the town's café-bars, with squishy sofas, good lunches (not Mon) and a decent range of wines and beers. ③, weekends ④

Highfield The Heads ℡017687/72508, ⓦwww
.highfieldkeswick.co.uk. Beautifully restored
Victorian hotel whose stylish "feature rooms"
include two turret rooms and even a converted
chapel. There's also parking and a decent
restaurant with a daily changing menu (dinner
included in the price). ❼

🏃 **Howe Keld** 5–7 The Heads
℡017687/72417, ⓦwww.howekeld.co.uk.
Welcoming guest house whose rooms have fell
views and pretty fabrics. It also has a reputation for
great breakfasts (vegetarian specialities included,
from rissoles to pancakes and syrup). Parking. ❹
Sweeney's 18-20 Lake Rd ℡0500/600725,
ⓦwww.lakedistrictinns.co.uk. Four bright en-suite
rooms (including two large twin/family rooms)
above a contemporary bar-brasserie. Fell views
from some windows, a good breakfast and the
town's most spacious beer garden out back. Free
parking nearby. ❹, weekends ❺

Hostels

Denton House Penrith Rd ℡017687/75351,
ⓦwww.vividevents.co.uk. Keswick's cheapest bed

is at the independent backpackers', 10min walk
from the centre (by the railway bridge, just after
the ambulance/fire station). Dorm beds from
£12.50, breakfast £3 (when available, usually
weekends), plus outdoor activities and tours. No
credit cards.
Derwentwater YHA Barrow House, Borrowdale
℡0870/770 5792, ⓔderwentwater@yha.org.uk.
Based in an old mansion with fifteen acres of
grounds sloping down to the lake, a couple of
miles south of Keswick along the B5289 – the
Borrowdale bus runs past and the Keswick Launch
stops nearby. Dorm beds from £13.95.

🏃 **Keswick YHA** Station Rd ℡0870/770
5894, ⓔkeswick@yha.org.uk. Keswick's
town YHA, in a converted woollen mill on the river,
has a new contemporary look after a major
overhaul. Facilities and rooms are bang up-to-date,
while a restaurant and bar offer good-value meals.
Dorm beds from £17.50 (May–Sept from £19),
breakfast included.

The Town

Granted its market charter by Edward I in 1276 – **market day** is Saturday –
Keswick was an important wool and leather centre until around 1500, when
these trades were supplanted by the discovery of local graphite. With the
Italian idea of putting graphite into wooden holders, Keswick became an
important pencil-making town, and remained so until the late eighteenth
century, when the French discovered how to make pencil graphite cheaply
and broke Keswick's monopoly. The **Cumberland Pencil Museum** at
Greta Bridge (daily 9.30am–5pm; £3; ⓦwww.pencilmuseum.co.uk) tells the
story entertainingly.

In Fitz Park, on Station Road, you'll find the **Keswick Museum and Art
Gallery** (Easter–Oct Tues–Sat 10am–4pm; free), a gloriously quirky Victorian
collection including (amongst other things) a set of lion's teeth, ancient
dental tools, a 600-year-old cat and the famous "musical stones" which sound
in tune when you strike them. Make time, too, for a couple of churches:
St John's, on St John's Street in the centre, where the novelist Sir Hugh
Walpole (of Herries novels fame) is buried; and **Crosthwaite Church**, a
fifteen-minute walk northwest of town over Greta Bridge, resting place of
the poet Robert Southey.

Local walks

Latrigg (1203ft), north of town, gets the vote for a quick climb (45min) to
a fine viewpoint, while south of town the best half-day walk is to **Walla Crag**
(1234ft) and back (5 miles; 4hr), via the wooded peninsula of **Friar's Crag**
on Derwent Water. Also, you shouldn't miss Keswick's most mysterious
landmark, **Castlerigg Stone Circle**, where 38 hunks of volcanic stone, the
largest almost eight feet tall, form a circle a hundred feet in diameter, set
against a magnificent mountain backdrop. It probably had an astronomical or
time-keeping function when it was erected, four or five thousand years ago,

but no one really knows. From the end of Station Road, take the Threlkeld rail line path (signposted by the *Keswick Country House Hotel*) and follow the signs. The rail path itself continues all the way to **Threlkeld**, three miles from Keswick, a delightful riverside walk with the promise of a drink at the end in one of Threlkeld's old pubs.

Derwent Water

The shores of **Derwent Water** lie five minutes' walk south of the centre along Lake Road and through the pedestrian underpass. It's among the most attractive of the lakes, ringed by crags and studded with islets, and is most easily seen by hopping on the **Keswick Launch** (regular departures Easter–Nov daily, Dec–Easter weekends only; £8 round-trip, £1.50 per stage; ☎017687/72263, ⓦ www.keswick-launch.co.uk), which runs right around the lake calling at several points en route. There's also an enjoyable one-hour **evening cruise** (£8.50) from May Day bank holiday until mid-September.

You can jump off the launch at any of the half a dozen piers on Derwent Water for a stroll, but if you've only got time for one hike, make it up **Cat Bells** (take the launch to Hawes End), a superb vantage point (1481ft) above the lake's western shore – allow two and a half hours for the scramble to the top and a return to the pier along the wooded shore.

Eating, drinking and entertainment

Many of Keswick's **cafés** and **restaurants** cater to a walking crowd, which means large portions and few airs. Several of the **pubs** also have meals worth investigating, while there's a fair amount of entertainment in Keswick throughout the year, including the **jazz festival** and mountain festival (ⓦ www .keswickmountainfestival.co.uk), both in May, **beer festival** in June, and the traditional **Keswick Agricultural Show** (August bank holiday). The **Theatre by the Lake** on Lake Road (☎017687/74411, ⓦ www.theatrebythelake.com) hosts drama, concerts and exhibitions, as well as a renowned annual literature festival, Words By The Water (March, ⓦ www.wayswithwords.co.uk).

▲ Derwent Water

Bassenthwaite Lake

Keswick's other lake is **Bassenthwaite**, a couple of miles northwest of town – there are regular buses from the bus station along its eastern shore, including the #73/73A Caldbeck Rambler. You'll win any pub quiz if you know that Bassenthwaite is actually the only lake in the Lake District (all the others are known as waters or meres). Families will enjoy both **Mirehouse** stately home (ⓦwww.mirehouse.com) and **Trotters World of Animals** (ⓦwww.trottersworld.com), the latter a pioneering wildlife conservation project. There's also the unique attraction of the **Lake District ospreys** (ⓦwww.ospreywatch.co.uk), which nest and breed each year on the Bassenthwaite shore below Dodd Wood. From a viewing platform at the wood you'll get to see the ospreys fishing and feeding (usually April to late Aug/Sept), or you can get even closer with the nest-cam at nearby **Whinlatter Forest Park**, west of Keswick along the B5292 (the Cockermouth–Buttermere road).

Cafés and restaurants

Lakeland Pedlar Henderson's Yard, Bell Close, off Main St ☏017687/74492. Keswick's best café serves tasty veggie food – from breakfast burritos to veg crumble or chilli. Daytime only (sometimes until till 9pm in school holidays). Moderate.

Lemon and Lime 31 Lake Rd ☏017687/73088. A good choice if you can't decide on a cuisine – there's round-the-world tapas-style starters, followed by mains ranging from burgers and steaks to noodles and Thai curries. Moderate.

Mayson's 33 Lake Rd ☏017687/74104. Licensed, self-service restaurant, good for lasagne, moussaka, pies, curries and stir-fries (until 9pm in summer). Inexpensive.

Salsa 1 New St ☏017687/75222. Billed as a "Mexican bistro" – have a drink in the downstairs bars and then move upstairs for fajitas, tacos, ribs and wraps. Dinner only. Moderate.

Pubs

Bank Tavern 47 Main St. A local reputation for good bar meals means that every table is often occupied.

Dog and Gun 2 Lake Rd. Top pub in town, with old slate floors, oak beams, a changing selection of real ales and good food – the house special is a Hungarian goulash with dumplings, perfect after a gruelling day on the fells.

George St John's St. Keswick's oldest coaching inn has bags of character – snug bars lined with portraits, pictures and curios, with wooden settles in front of the fire. Classic pub meals or a fancier menu available in the restaurant.

Borrowdale

It is difficult to overstate the beauty of **Borrowdale**, with its river flats and yew trees, lying at the head of Derwent Water and overshadowed by Scafell Pike, the highest mountain in England, and Great Gable, reckoned as one of the finest-looking. Climbs up both these peaks start from the head of the valley near Seatoller, accessible on the #77A (along the west side of Derwent Water) and #79 Borrowdale Rambler (along the B5289) **buses** from Keswick. Accommodation in the valley also makes a good rustic alternative to staying in Keswick.

A couple of miles south of Keswick, the pier at Ashness Gate provides access to a narrow road branching south off the B5289 for the steep climb to the photogenic **Ashness Bridge**. The minor road ends two miles further south at **Watendlath**, where you'll find an idyllic little tarn and tearooms. Back on the B5289, a signposted path heads to the **Lodore Falls**, a diversion only really worth it after sustained wet weather, while further south is the 1900-ton **Bowder Stone**, a house-sized lump of rock scaled by way of a wooden ladder and worn to a shine on top by thousands of pairs of feet. Beyond lies the straggling hamlet of **Rosthwaite**, which is a popular base for local hikes and mountain climbs. Two or three local B&Bs include *Yew Tree*

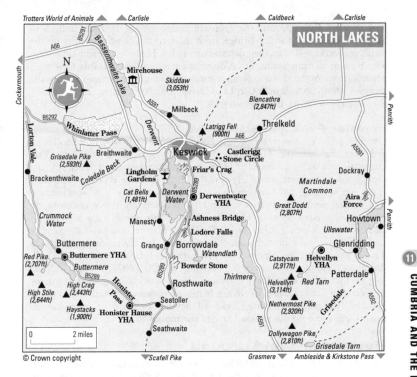

Trotters World of Animals ▲▲ ▲ Carlisle   ▲ Caldbeck   ▲ Carlisle

Cockermouth ◀

A66   B5291

Bassenthwaite Lake

N

Mirehouse 🏛

Skiddaw
(3,053ft) ▲

Blencathra
(2,847ft) ▲

Penrith ▶

B5292

Whinlatter Pass

Millbeck

Derwent

A591

Latrigg Fell
(900ft) A66

Threlkeld

A66

A5091

Griesdale Pike
(2,593ft) ▲   Braithwaite

Keswick ● Castlerigg
Stone Circle

Brackenthwaite   Coledale Beck

Lingholm
Gardens

Friar's Crag

Dockray

Cat Bells ▲
(1,481ft)

Derwent
Water   ● Derwentwater
YHA

Martindale
Common

Aira 🦌
Force

Crummock
Water

Manesty

Ashness Bridge

Great Dodd
(2,807ft) ▲

Howtown

Penrith ▶

Lodore Falls

Ullswater

Buttermere

Grange   Borrowdale

Watendlath

Glenridding

Red Pike ● Buttermere YHA
(2,707ft) ▲

Buttermere

B5289

Bowder Stone

Thirlmere

Catstycam
(2,917ft) ▲ Helvellyn
YHA ●

Patterdale

Honister Pass

Rosthwaite

Helvellyn   Red Tarn
(3,114ft) ▲

A592

High Crag
High Stile ▲(2,443ft)
(2,644ft) ▲

Seatoller

Nethermost Pike
(2,920ft) ▲

Grisedale

Haystacks
(1,900ft) ▲ Honister Hause
YHA ●

A591

Seathwaite

Dollywagon Pike
(2,810ft) ▲   Grisedale Tarn

0   2 miles

© Crown copyright   ▼ Scafell Pike   Grasmere ▼   Ambleside & Kirkstone Pass ▼

⑪

Farm (☎017687/77675, 🌐www.borrowdaleherdwick.co.uk; closed Dec & Jan; no credit cards; ❸), favoured on occasion by Prince Charles on incognito walking trips to the Lakes. There are also comfortable **rooms** at the hiker-friendly *Royal Oak Hotel* (☎017687/77214, 🌐www.royaloakhotel .co.uk; ❻,includes dinner) and the neighbouring *Scafell Hotel* (☎017687/77208, 🌐www.scafell.co.uk; ❻), which has a formal restaurant as well as the attached *Riverside Bar* – effectively the local **pub** – with cheaper bar meals. Best address though is *Hazel Bank* (☎017687/77248, 🌐www.hazelbankhotel .co.uk; ❽), a country house hotel set in serene gardens just outside the village, where a candlelit dinner is included in the price.

Another mile up the valley, eight from Keswick, the #79 bus route ends its run at the old farming and quarrying settlement of **Seatoller**, where there's a car park and visitor **information point** (daily 10am–5pm; ☎017687/77714) – call them in advance and you can arrange to ride out through Borrowdale by rental bike and go back to Keswick by bus. *Seatoller House* (☎017687/77218, 🌐www.seatollerhouse.co.uk; ❻ with dinner, except Tues; closed Dec–Feb) has rooms in an atmospheric seventeenth-century farmhouse right by the road, while virtually next door is the welcoming 𝒴 *Yew Tree* café-restaurant-bar (☎017687/77634; closed Mon & Jan to mid-Feb), where daytime sandwiches, pies and omelettes give way to African evening specials like Cape Malay curry, grilled ostrich and beef skewers.

It's twenty minutes' walk from Seatoller down the minor road to **Seathwaite**, where there's a farmhouse **campsite** and camping barn, and a basic café at Borrowdale Trout Farm (open daily Easter–Sept), which serves all-day breakfasts and meals of fresh and smoked salmon and trout. For England's highest peak, **Scafell Pike** (3205ft), the approach is through the farmyard and up to **Styhead Tarn** via Stockley Bridge; from the tarn the classic ascent is up the thrilling Corridor Route, then descending via Esk Hause – an eight-mile (6hr) loop walk in all from Seathwaite. A direct approach to **Great Gable** (2949ft) is possible from Styhead Tarn, though most people start out from Seathwaite campsite, climb up Sourmilk Ghyll and then approach via Green Gable (2628ft), also an eight-mile, six-hour return walk.

Honister Pass and Slate Mine

Overlooked by the steep Borrowdale Fells, the B5289 cuts west at Seatoller, up and over the dramatic **Honister Pass** (bus #77A comes this way). Slate quarrying was well established at Honister by the mid-eighteenth century and though full commercial quarrying ceased in 1986 the mine is now in operation again as a working and heritage enterprise. To get an idea of what traditional slate mining entailed, you can don a hard hat and lamp to join one of the hugely informative guided tours of **Honister Slate Mine** (tours daily at 10.30am, 12.30pm & 3.30pm; £9.75; ☎017687/77230, ⓦwww.honister-slate-mine.co .uk), which lead you through narrow tunnels into illuminated, dripping caverns. There's also a dramatic Alpine-style **Via Ferrata** (2 departures daily; £20, all-day pass including mine tour £32; bookings on ☎017687/77714) – or "Iron Way" – that, following a safety briefing, allows visitors to be guided to the top of Fleetwith Pike (2126ft), above the mines, by means of a fixed cableway and harness. This requires a strong head for heights, as you'll be following the miners' old route up the exposed face of the mountain.

Buttermere and around

From Honister Pass, the B5289 follows Gatesgarthdale Beck for three miles and makes a dramatic descent into the **Buttermere Valley**. The direct bus is the #77 via Whinlatter Pass; the #77A comes the long way around through Borrowdale. At Buttermere village there are no facilities save a seasonal café, a large car park and two **hotels**: the comfortable *Bridge Hotel* (☎017687/70252, ⓦwww.bridge-hotel.com; ❽, includes dinner) and the smaller, more romantic *Fish Hotel* (☎017687/70253, ⓦwww.fishhotel.com; ❺) – both serve reasonable meals, while the *Bridge* has a popular flagstoned bar. The **youth hostel**, *Buttermere YHA* (☎0870/770 5736, Ⓔbuttermere@yha.org.uk; dorm beds from £17.50, includes breakfast), overlooks the lake on the road to Honister Pass, while a few hundred yards in the other direction, overlooking Crummock Water, *Wood House* (☎017687/70208, ⓦwww.wdhse.co.uk; no credit cards; ❺) is quite the nicest **B&B** hereabouts, with elegant rooms with views.

The village – set between the two expanses of Buttermere and neighbouring **Crummock Water** – makes a good walking base, with a particularly easy two-mile hike out along Crummock Water's southwestern edge to the 125-foot **Scale Force** falls. The four-mile, round-lake stroll circling Buttermere itself shouldn't take more than a couple of hours; you can always detour up Scarth Gap to **Haystacks** (1900ft) if you want more of a climb and some views.

The scenery flattens out as the road heads north from Crummock Water and into the pastoral **Lorton Vale**, with Cockermouth just a few miles beyond. A minor road leads directly to minuscule **Loweswater**, one of the less frequented lakes, around which there's a gentle, four-mile (2hr) walk. En route, you'll pass the ⚹ *Kirkstile Inn* (☎01900/85219, ⓦwww.kirkstile.com; ❺, family suites ❼), a welcoming sixteenth-century place with contemporary rooms, cosy bar (with own-brewed beer), beer garden and restaurant. Back on the main route to

Cockermouth, there are two more excellent accommodation options, namely *New House Farm* (℡01900/85404, ⓦwww.newhouse-farm.co.uk; ❼), a mile south of Low Lorton – a meticulously restored seventeenth-century farmhouse offering quality B&B – and *Winder Hall* (℡01900/85107, ⓦwww.winderhall .co.uk; ❽), in Low Lorton itself, an elegant country house with excellent food.

Wast Water

Nothing prepares you for the first sight of **Wast Water**, England's deepest lake and Lakeland's most remote corner. Awesome screes plunge to its eastern shore, separating the lake from Eskdale to the south, while the highest peaks in the country – Great Gable and the Scafells – frame Wasdale Head, the tiny settlement at its head. The only road (there are no bus services) winds from the main coastal A595, via the hamlet of **Nether Wasdale** (where there are two small hotels on the green) before meeting the lake at its southwestern tip at the *Wasdale Hall* **youth hostel** (℡0870/770 6082, Ⓔwastwater@yha.org.uk; from £13), a country house set in its own lakeside grounds.

The minor road then hugs the shore of the lake, ending three miles away at **Wasdale Head**, a Shangri-La-like clearing between the mountain ranges, where you'll find the marvellous ⚜ *Wasdale Head Inn* (℡01946/726229, ⓦwww.wasdale.com; ❼), one of the most celebrated of all Lakeland inns, with legendary breakfasts, a great public bar and hearty four-course dinners. Nearby, there's **B&B**, walking advice and packed lunches from hiker-friendly *Lingmell House* (℡019467/26261, ⓦwww.lingmellhouse.co.uk; no credit cards; ❹; closed Jan), on the track to the church. The peaks of Pillar, Scafell and Great Gable are popular hiking targets from here, as is the route over the pass into Borrowdale or south over the fells to Eskdale.

Eskdale

Eskdale is perhaps the prettiest of the unsung Lakeland valleys, and can be accessed from the Cumbrian coast by the Ravenglass and Eskdale Railway (see p.755), which drops you at Dalegarth Station, right in the heart of superb walking country around the dead-end hamlet of **Boot**. There's a good café and bike rental available at the station, while three miles beyond Boot and 800 feet up, the remains of granaries, bath houses and the commandant's quarters for **Hardknott Roman Fort** (always open; free access) command a strategic and panoramic position. Beyond, over the narrow switchbacks of **Hardknott Pass**, the road drops to Cockley Beck, before making the equally alarming ascent of Wrynose Pass – this is the route back to Langdale and Ambleside.

The traditional accommodation choice in Boot is the *Boot Inn* (℡019467/23224, ⓦwww.bootinn.co.uk; ❺), though it's the first-rate ⚜ *Woolpack Inn* (℡019467/23230, ⓦwww.woolpack.co.uk; ❺), a mile east of the village on the Hardknott Pass road, that really stands out – cosy rooms, a beer garden with views, ale from the pub's own brewery and excellent food (dinner reservations advised).

Cockermouth

The attractive small town and market centre of **COCKERMOUTH**, midway between the coast and Keswick, is yet another station on the Wordsworth trail: the **Wordsworth House** on Main Street (Easter–Oct Mon–Sat 11am–4.30pm; £4.90, admission by timed ticket; NT; ⓦwww.wordsworthhouse.org.uk) is where William and Dorothy were born and spent their first few years. The building has been beautifully restored, but rather than a pure period piece it's presented as a functioning eighteenth-century home – with a costumed cook willing to share recipes in the kitchen and a clerk completing the ledger with quill and ink. It's an education, in the best sense, and a really excellent visit. Afterwards, follow your nose and you're likely to stumble upon **Jennings Brewery**, on Brewery Lane near the river. At Cumbria's best-known beer-maker, the hour-and-a-half-long tour (£4.95; booking advisable; ☎0845/129 7190; ⓦwww.jenningsbrewery.co.uk) culminates in a real-ale tasting session.

Practicalities

There's stylish **accommodation** at *Six Castlegate*, 6 Castlegate (☎01900/826749, ⓦwww.sixcastlegate.co.uk; ❹), and *Croft House*, 6–8 Challoner St (☎01900/827533, ⓦwww.croft-guesthouse.com; closed Jan; ❹), both renovated Georgian houses, or out of town (two mile southeast) you'll pass a quiet night at the *Old Homestead* at Byresteads Farm, Hundrith Hill Road, off the B5292 (☎01900/822223, ⓦwww.byresteads.co.uk; ❹), a beautifully restored seventeenth-century farmhouse offering quality B&B.

Merienda **café**, 7A Station St (☎01900/822790, ⓦwww.merienda.co.uk; daytime only, though open Fri night for tapas and music), is the best place for breakfasts, sandwiches and light meals, or drive out to the *Old Stackyard Tearooms* (☎01900/822777, ⓦwww.wellingtonjerseys.co.uk), a mile out of town, for a family farm tearoom and walks on the local nature reserve. Vegetarians come from far and wide for the fine-dining experience that is the *Quince and Medlar*, 13 Castlegate (☎01900/823579, ⓦwww.quinceandmedlar.co.uk; dinner only, closed Sun & Mon), while top **pub** is *The Bitter End* on Kirkgate, housing Cumbria's smallest brewery.

Ullswater

Much of the appeal of **Ullswater**, Cumbria's second longest lake at over seven miles long, derives from its serpentine shape. The chief lakeside settlements, Glenridding and Patterdale, are less than a mile apart at the southern tip of Ullswater, not otherwise notable except as bases for one of the most popular scrambling routes in the country – up the considerable heights of **Helvellyn**. The main **public transport** is the #108 Patterdale Rambler bus service from Penrith, which runs via Pooley Bridge, Aira Force and Glenridding to Patterdale. The #517 Kirkstone Rambler bus from Glenridding/Patterdale

Climbing Helvellyn

The climb to the summit of **Helvellyn** (3114ft), the most popular of the four 3000-foot mountains in Cumbria, forms part of a day-long circuit from either Glenridding or Patterdale. The most frequently chosen approach is via the infamous **Striding Edge**, an alarming, undulating rocky ridge offering the most direct access to the summit. The classic return is via the less demanding and less exposed **Swirral Edge**, where a route leads down to **Red Tarn** – the highest Lake District tarn – then follows the beck down to Glenridding past Helvellyn youth hostel; the Swirrel Edge route is also the best way *up* Helvellyn if you don't fancy Striding Edge. Either approach makes for around a seven-mile (5–6hr) round walk, though a good alternative descent is to follow the flat ridge south from Helvellyn, past **Nethermost Pike and Dollywagon Pike**, after which there's a long scree scramble down to **Grisedale Tarn** and then the gentlest of descents down **Grisedale Valley** to the Patterdale–Glenridding road – a good six hours all told for the entire circuit.

continues south over the Kirkstone Pass to Bowness (daily in summer school hols, weekends and bank hols Easter–Oct).

Glenridding and Patterdale

The former mining village of **GLENRIDDING** is the best base, featuring several inexpensive **B&Bs**, including *Beech House*, on the main road (℡017684/82037, Ⓦ www.beechhouse.com; ④). However, it's at the *Inn on the Lake* (℡017684/82444, Ⓦ www.innonthelakeullswater.com; ⑥) that you really begin to appreciate Ullswater's charms, with 15 acres of gardens stretching down to the water, alongside a lake-view restaurant and the informal *Ramblers Bar*. The helpful **tourist office** (Easter–Oct daily 9.30am–5.30pm; Nov–Easter Sat & Sun 9.30am–3.30pm; ℡017684/82414) is in the main car park, and there's **camping** and **bunkhouse** accommodation (from £8) half a mile away up the valley at *Gillside Caravan & Camping* (℡017684/82346, Ⓦ www.gillsidecampingandcaravansite.co.uk; closed Nov–Feb). Hikers wanting an early start on Helvellyn stay at *Helvellyn YHA* (℡0870/770 6110, Ⓔ helvellyn@yha.org.uk; from £13), a mile and a half up the valley road from Glenridding. There's another good hostel in **PATTERDALE** (℡0870/770 5986, Ⓔ patterdale@yha.org.uk; from £14; Nov–March restricted opening), whose only **pub**, the *White Lion* (℡017684/82214; ③), also has a few rooms available.

Around the lake

At **Gowbarrow Park**, three miles north of Glenridding, the hillside still blazes green and gold in spring, as it was doing when the Wordsworths visited in April 1802; it's thought that Dorothy's recollections of the visit in her diary inspired William to write his famous "Daffodils" poem. The car park and tea rooms here mark the start of a brief walk up to **Aira Force** (40min round-trip), a seventy-foot fall that's spectacular in spate.

The lake itself is traversed by the **Ullswater Steamers** (℡017684/82229, Ⓦ www.ullswater-steamers.co.uk), which have year-round services from Glenridding to Howtown, halfway up the lake's eastern side (£7.90 return; 35min), and from Howtown to the pretty village of Pooley Bridge, at the northern end of the lake (£7.20; 20min). Alternatively, you can buy a ticket between Glenridding and Pooley Bridge that effectively makes a round-the-lake cruise (£11; 2hr).

Howtown is tucked into a little clearing at the foot of beautiful Fusedale, where the *Howtown Hotel* has a pocket-sized hikers' bar around the back. A minor road from here hugs the eastern shore of the lake the four miles to **Pooley Bridge**, passing the incomparable *Sharrow Bay* (℡017684/86301, Ⓦ www.sharrowbay.com; ⑨ with dinner) on the way, one of England's finest country-house hotels – afternoon tea here is a famously lavish affair. Pooley Bridge itself has several local campsites and three pubs, while three miles to the north the welcoming *Gate Inn* at **Yanwath** (℡01768/862386) is a highly recommended gastropub.

The Cumbrian coast

South and west of the national park, the Cumbrian coast attracts much less attention than the spectacular scenery inland, but it would be a mistake to write it off. It splits into two distinct sections, the most accessible being the **Furness**

peninsulas area (Ⓦwww.lake-district-peninsulas.co.uk), just a few miles from Windermere, where varied attractions include the sleepy resort of **Grange-over-Sands**, the monastic priory at **Cartmel** and the enjoyable market town of **Ulverston**. Parts of this region share nearby Lancashire's industrial heritage and in the ship-building port of **Barrow-in-Furness** it's possible to see a slow revival that's only just starting to pay dividends in terms of tourism – though the dramatic ruins of nearby **Furness Abbey** have been attracting visitors for almost two hundred years.

The **Cumbrian coast** itself is generally judged to begin at Silecroft near Millom and stretches for more than sixty miles to the small resort of Silloth, on the shores of the Solway Firth. North of Silecroft the estuary village of **Ravenglass** is access point for the **Ravenglass and Eskdale Railway**, while en route to the wide beach and headland of **St Bees** you have the option of calling in at the visitor centre at **Sellafield** nuclear reprocessing plant. If you had to pick just one coastal destination, however, the attractive Georgian port of **Whitehaven** would be the clear winner.

Grange-over-Sands and around

Before the coming of the railways, the main route to the Lake District was the "road across the sands" from near Lancaster to **GRANGE-OVER-SANDS**, travellers being led by monks from Cartmel Priory and then, from the sixteenth century, by a royally appointed guide. The tradition continues today with one guide left, who leads the way around the slip sands and hidden channels which claimed so many lives between the fourteenth and nineteenth centuries. The eight-mile walk takes the best part of a day and departures are usually every other week between May and September. Further details are available from the Grange **tourist office**, which is located in Victoria Hall on Main Street (daily 10am–4/5pm; Ⓣ015395/34026, Ⓦwww.grange-over-sands.com).

Grange itself is a genteel place, with some grand yesteryear hotels and floral gardens fronted by a mile-long esplanade with fine views of the marshy bay. The local train line towards Lancaster offers a pleasant half-day out, running you across the rail causeway in five minutes to the pretty bayside settlement of **Arnside**, where a couple of pubs look back at Grange. From the next stop, **Silverdale** (another 5min), you can walk back around the headland to Arnside in around two hours, past isolated stony coves and through the shoreline woods. Or, film buffs can stay on for one more stop to **Carnforth** (under 20min from Grange; Ⓦwww.carnforthstation.co.uk), the station where Celia Johnson and Trevor Howard came over all misty-eyed in the classic David Lean film *Brief Encounter*. The station has been restored in 1940s style, while the refreshment room replicates the tearoom film set.

Cartmel and around

Sheltered several miles inland from Morecambe Bay, **CARTMEL** grew up around its twelfth-century Augustinian priory and is still dominated by the proud **Church of St Mary and St Michael** (daily 9am–3.30/5.30pm; free), the only substantial remnant to survive the Dissolution. Everything else in the village is modest in scale, centred on the attractive **market square**, beyond the church, with its Elizabethan cobbles, water pump and fish slabs. On the square, the **Cartmel Village Shop** is known to aficionados for the quality of its sticky-toffee pudding.

A couple of miles west of the village, on the B5278, one of Cumbria's most interesting country estates, **Holker Hall** (Easter–Oct Mon–Fri & Sun

10am–5.30pm; £9.25, gardens only £5.95; @www.holker-hall.co.uk) is still in use by the Cavendish family who've owned it since the late-seventeenth century. Only the **New Wing** of the house, rebuilt following a fire in 1871, is open to the public; the real showpieces here are the cantilevered staircase and the library, which is stocked with more than 3000 leather-bound books, some of whose spines are fakes, constructed to hide electric light switches added later. The highly impressive 23-acre **gardens**, both formal and woodland, are the highlight for many. A celebrated annual garden **festival** (June), as well as spring and winter markets, is held here. There is also an excellent food hall-deli and café (no charge for entry), both of which are also open when the hall is otherwise closed.

Practicalities

Trains stop at Cark-in-Cartmel, two miles southwest of the village proper; **buses** from here or from Grange-over-Sands train station run to the village. There's no tourist office, but the local **website**, @www.cartmelvillage.com, can fill you in on history, sights, events and businesses. **Cartmel Races** (@www.cartmel -steeplechases.co.uk) fill the village twice a year (last weekend in May and August). Otherwise, **accommodation** should be easy to find though you will need to book in advance for Cartmel's extraordinary *L'Enclume* on Cavendish Street (℡015395/36362, @www.lenclume.co.uk; ❼; closed first 2 weeks Jan; restaurant closed all Mon, plus Tues & Wed lunch), a highly individual Michelin-starred restaurant-with-rooms. Also on Cavendish Street is the more traditional *Cavendish Arms* (℡015395/36240, @www.thecavendisharms.co.uk; ❹), a sixteenth-century inn which retains many of its original features, while there's organic farmhouse B&B at genial *Howbarrow Farm* (℡015395/36330, @www .howbarroworganic.co.uk; ❸), a couple of miles west of the village.

Ulverston

The railway line winds westwards to **ULVERSTON**, a close-knit market town which formerly prospered on the cotton, tanning and iron-ore industries. It's an attractive place, enhanced by its dappled grey limestone cottages and a jumble of cobbled alleys and traditional shops zigzagging off the central **Market Place**. Stalls are still set up here and in the surrounding streets every Thursday and Saturday; on other days (not Wed or Sun), the **market hall** on New Market Street is the centre of commercial life.

Ulverston's most famous son is Stan Laurel (born Arthur Stanley Jefferson), the whimpering, head-scratching half of the comic duo, celebrated in a mind-boggling collection of memorabilia at the **Laurel and Hardy Museum** (daily 10am–4.30pm, closed Jan; £3; @www.laurel-and-hardy-museum.co.uk), up an alley at 4c Upper Brook St, near Market Place. The copy of Stan's birth certificate (16 June 1890, in Foundry Cottages, Ulverston) lists his father's occupation as "comedian" – young Arthur Stanley could hardly have become anything else. It's also worth checking to see what's on at the **Lanternhouse**, on The Ellers (@www.lanternhouse.org), just off the A590 at the bottom of Market Street and across Tank Square (a traffic roundabout). A group of multimedia artists known as Welfare State International occupy this award-winning conversion of an old school, presenting imaginative exhibitions, installations and concerts relating to the "celebratory arts".

The 70-mile **Cumbria Way** long-distance footpath from Ulverston to Carlisle starts from The Gill, at the top of Upper Brook Street – a waymarker spire marks the start. There's also an increasingly popular annual walking festival held each spring (April/May), with lots of walks and events held over ten days, from one-mile strolls to all-day hikes. For a day walk, pick up the leaflet at the tourist office detailing an 11-mile circular country-and-coast hike from town.

Practicalities

Ulverston **train station**, serving the Cumbrian coast railway, is only a few minutes' walk from the town centre – head down Prince's Street and turn right at the main road for County Square. **Buses** arrive on nearby Victoria Road, while the **tourist office** is in Coronation Hall on County Square (Mon–Sat 9am–5pm; ☎01229/587120, Ⓦwww.ulverston.net).

Trinity House Hotel, 200 yards downhill from the station, on the corner of Prince's Street and the main A590 (☎01229/588889, Ⓦwww.trinityhousehotel .co.uk; ❺), has spacious **accommodation** in a handsome Georgian building. There's also the terrific 🦌 *Walker's Hostel* on Oubas Hill (☎01229/585588, Ⓦwww.walkershostel.co.uk; no credit cards; from £16), fifteen minutes' walk from the centre on the A590 near Canal Head, at the foot of the Hoad Monument: there are thirty beds in small rooms (you won't have to share with strangers), with vegetarian breakfasts (included) and evening meals available (£10). One of the nicest **places to eat** is the moderately priced *Farmers Arms* pub in Market Place, where fish is always a good choice, while the *World Peace Café*, 5 Cavendish St (daytime only, closed Sun & Mon), is a relaxed organic veggie place and meditation centre.

Barrow-in-Furness and around

BARROW-IN-FURNESS grew around a booming iron industry in the mid-nineteenth century. Steelworks and shipbuilding followed, making Barrow one of England's busiest ports, and the town still makes a handsome living from orders for military hardware. Yet even Barrow's most enthusiastic supporters could hardly claim the town as attractive: recession in the 1980s emptied many of the proud Victorian buildings and left the centre rough at the edges. However, there's been a significant amount of town-centre regeneration in recent years, while some of the older buildings still retain the capacity to surprise – the splendid sandstone Gothic town hall for one.

For visitors, the best move is straight to the **Dock Museum** (Tues–Fri 10/10.30am–4/5pm, Sat & Sun 11am–4.30/5pm; Nov–Easter also closed Tues; free; Ⓦwww.dockmuseum.org.uk), on North Road, half a mile from the centre. Located in the dried-out graving dock where ships were once repaired, the museum tells the history of Barrow – which is also the history of modern shipbuilding. A series of family events every summer add focus to a visit.

Ruined **Furness Abbey** (April–Oct daily 10am–6pm; Nov–March Thurs–Sun 10am–4pm; £3.50; EH) lies a mile and a half out of Barrow on the Ulverston road, hidden in a wooded vale. Founded in 1124, the abbey's industry was remarkably diverse – it owned sheep on the local fells, controlled fishing rights, produced grain and leather, smelted iron, dug peat for fuel and manufactured salt. By the fourteenth century it had become such a prize that the Scots raided it twice, though it survived until April 1536, when Henry VIII chose it to be the first of the large abbeys to be dissolved. The *Abbey Tavern* at the entrance serves drinks at tables scattered about some of the ruined outbuildings.

The attacks by the Scots goaded Furness Abbey into protecting itself with Piel Castle on **Piel Island**, now also in ruins. This is reached from Roa Island, three miles southeast of Barrow down the A5087 – turn off at Rampside (signposted

"Lifeboat station") – from where there's a seasonal weather- and tide-dependent **ferry** across to Piel Island. Apart from the ruins of a massive keep and the lifeboat station, it's the island's only commercial building, the *Ship Inn*, which draws people over here – the landlord is traditionally known as the King of Piel.

Whatever you feel about zoos, you're likely to be positively surprised by the **South Lakes Animal Park** (daily 10am–4.30/5pm; £10.50, Nov–Feb prices reduced; ⓦwww.wildanimalpark.co.uk), five miles north of Barrow, just outside Dalton-in-Furness. An award-winning conservation zoo, it relies on ditches and trenches (not cages) for the most part to contain its animals and is split into separate habitat areas, ranging from the Australian bush to a tropical rainforest. It's quite something to encounter free-roaming kangaroos in rural Cumbria, while the Sumatran tiger-feeding (encouraging them to climb and jump for their meal) is unique in Europe.

Ravenglass and Muncaster

The single main street of **RAVENGLASS**, twenty miles or so up the coast from Barrow, preserves a row of characterful nineteenth-century cottages facing out across the estuarine mud flats and dunes. Despite appearances, the village dates back to the arrival of the Romans, who established a supply post here in the first century AD for the northern legions manning Hadrian's Wall. Nothing remains, save the ruins of the "Roman Bath House", just past the station and off to the right, 500 yards up a single-track lane.

Cumbrian coastal-line trains stop at Ravenglass, which is also the starting point for the enjoyable **Ravenglass and Eskdale Railway** (March–Oct, at least 7 trains daily; trains also most winter weekends, plus Christmas, New Year and Feb half-term hols; £10.20 return; ☎01229/717171, ⓦwww .ravenglass-railway.co.uk). Opened in 1875 to carry ore from the Eskdale mines to the coastal railway, the 15-inch-gauge track winds seven miles up through the Eskdale Valley to Dalegarth Station near Boot. The full return

▲ Ravenglass and Eskdale Railway

The main blot on the Cumbrian coast is Sellafield nuclear reprocessing plant, midway between Ravenglass and Whitehaven. It's a significant local employer – thousands of jobs currently depend on its existence – which enjoys high-level bipartisan political support. Surprisingly perhaps, the **Sellafield Visitors' Centre** (daily 10am–4pm; free; Ⓦwww.go-experimental.com) is about as even-handed as you could expect, allowing you to make up your own mind about the pros and cons of nuclear power. The pro-nuke argument points to the benefits of "clean" nuclear power – no greenhouse gas emissions – while critics question the entire reprocessing system, pointing to the lethal maritime and atmospheric discharges (virtually all European radioactive pollution comes from reprocessing) and the manifest dangers of waste transportation and treatment. In the end, the bare statistics do much to undermine the visitor centre's relentlessly open and upbeat approach. The Sellafield site contains more than 200 separate nuclear facilities, including redundant defence work (ie weapons) sites and Calder Hall, the world's first fully commercial nuclear power station (1957–2003). The long-term clean-up contract, under the auspices of the Nuclear Decommissioning Authority (NDA) and designed to return Sellafield to a "safe, passive state", will cost billions of pounds and won't be complete until 2150.

journey, without a break, takes an hour and forty minutes, though a really good day out is to take your bike up on the train and cycle back from Dalegarth down the traffic-free **Eskdale T-Rail** (8.5 miles, 2hr) – or there's bike rental at Dalegarth station.

A mile east of Ravenglass on the A595 spreads the estate of **Muncaster Castle** (Feb half-term hols to first week of Nov; £9.50, £7 without castle entrance; ☎01229/717614, Ⓦwww.muncaster.co.uk). Apart from the ghost-ridden rooms of the castle itself (Mon–Fri & Sun noon–5pm), there are also seventy acres of well-kept **grounds and gardens**, as well as an **owl centre** (a breeding centre for endangered species) and **meadow vole maze** (each daily 10.30am–6pm or dusk), where you'll learn about the Muncaster voles, follow the hiking trails, and see entertaining bird displays (daily 2.30pm) or wild herons feeding (4.30pm, 3.30pm in winter). The castle is closed in winter, though the grounds remain open for the illuminated Darkest Muncaster experience (open until 9pm, not Jan; £5).

The best local **accommodation** is at ⚘ *The Pennington* (☎01229/717222, Ⓦwww.thepennington.co.uk; ❼), a restored seafront hotel in Ravenglass that belongs to the castle; it also has an excellent restaurant. At Muncaster Castle itself, there are also B&B rooms see above for contact details; ❺) in the converted stable block, while the *Ratty Arms* (☎01229/717676) at Ravenglass mainline train station is the place for a bar meal and pint of real ale.

St Bees

The coastal village of **ST BEES** saw a nunnery established as early as the seventh century that was succeeded by **St Bees Priory** in the twelfth century, which still stands. Long sands lie a few hundred yards west of the village (there's a massive car park there, plus tearoom and pub), while the steep, sandstone cliffs of **St Bees Head** to the north are good for windy walks and birdwatching. The headland's lighthouse marks the start of Alfred Wainwright's 190-mile **Coast-to-Coast Walk** to Robin Hood's Bay.

St Bees is on the Cumbrian coast train line and lies just five miles south of Whitehaven, from where there's a regular bus service. There's good

accommodation at ⚥ *Fleatham House*, High House Road (℡01946/822341, Ⓦwww.fleathamhouse.com; ⑤), a lovely retreat set in its own grounds just five minutes' walk from the station (first left off Main Street). It's very informal – tea and cakes are offered on arrival, with dinner available in the attached restaurant (not Sun; also open to non-residents). Several other B&Bs are found locally, and there are three nice rooms at *Platform 9*, a romantic railway-themed bistro at the station (℡01946/822600, Ⓦwww.platform9.co.uk; ⑤).

Whitehaven

Some fine Georgian houses mark out the centre of **WHITEHAVEN**, one of the few grid-planned towns in England. The economic expansion that forced this planning was as much due to the booming slave trade as to the more widely recognized coal traffic, and all the local history is covered entertainingly in **The Beacon** (under refurbishment at time of writing but open for 2008; Ⓦwww .thebeacon-whitehaven.co.uk), an enterprising museum on the harbour, with interactive exhibitions on all floors. The **harbour** itself sits at the heart of a renaissance project that has spruced up the quayside and provided new promenades, sculptures and heritage trails. The whole waterfront comes alive during the biennial **maritime festival** in June, held on odd-numbered years.

For all the changes round the harbour, it's Whitehaven's Georgian streets and neatly painted houses that make it one of Cumbria's most distinguished towns. There's a **market** held here every Thursday and Saturday, which adds a bit of colour. Otherwise, stroll up Lowther Street to the **Rum Story** (daily 10am–4.30pm; £5.45; Ⓦwww.rumstory.co.uk), housed in the eighteenth-century shop, courtyard and warehouses of the Jefferson's rum family. You could easily spend a couple of hours here, discovering Whitehaven's links with the Caribbean and learning all about rum, the Navy, temperance and the hideousness of the slaves' Middle Passage, amongst other matters. Also on Lowther Street, don't miss Michael Moon's secondhand **bookshop** at no. 19 (closed Wed Jan–Easter, and closed Sun all year), a bookworm's treasure-trove.

Practicalities

From the **train station** (services to St Bees/Ravenglass, and Maryport/ Carlisle) you can walk around the harbour to The Beacon in less than ten minutes. Buses use a variety of stops around town – Duke Street for St Bees and Ravenglass, Lowther Street for Cockermouth and Carlisle. The **tourist office** is in the Market Hall on Market Place (Mon–Sat 9.30/10am–4/5pm, plus July & Aug Sun 11am–3pm; ℡01946/598914, Ⓦwww .rediscoverwhitehaven.com), just back from the harbour. Whitehaven is the start of the 140-mile **C2C cycle route** to Sunderland/Newcastle – a metal cut-out at the harbour marks the spot.

For **accommodation**, the best central B&B is the *Corkickle Guest House*, 1 Corkickle (℡01946/692073; no credit cards; ③), five minutes' walk from the centre – keep on up Lowther Street to find the row of Georgian town houses. Two miles north of town, *Moresby Hall* (℡01946/696317, Ⓦwww .moresbyhall.co.uk; ⑥) also provides B&B, this time in an attractive mansion with walled gardens, and sea and fell views. For **meals**, *Zest Harbourside* on West Strand (℡01946/66981) is a waterside café-bar doing mix-and-match tapas-style dishes. The sister restaurant, *Zest*, on Low Road (℡01946/692848; dinner only Wed–Sat), three-quarters of a mile out of the centre (on the B5349 Whitehaven–St Bees road), is good for moderately priced Modern British cuisine.

Maryport

MARYPORT sports splendid views of the Solway Firth and the Scottish hills across the water, and boasts a history going back to Roman times. That's taken care of in the excellent **Senhouse Roman Museum** (July–Oct daily 10am–5pm; closed certain days other months; £2.50; Ⓦwww .senhousemuseum.co.uk), high on a hill above the harbour, ten minutes' walk from the centre. Maryport's modern history dates from its eighteenth-century heyday as an industrial port – it's named after the wife, Mary, of local lord and entrepreneur Humphrey Senhouse. The most appealing part of town is the harbour and marina, now smartly landscaped and featuring the **Lake District Coast Aquarium** (daily 10am–5pm; £5; Ⓦwww.lakedistrict-coastaquarium .co.uk), on the South Quay. The streets behind the harbour are slowly reviving, but still show evidence of Maryport's long decline since the Great Depression of the 1930s. For a glimpse of better days, walk uphill to **Fleming Square** (on the way to the Roman museum), where the surviving cobbles are still surrounded by Georgian houses.

East Cumbria: Penrith and the Eden Valley

The Lake District might end abruptly with the market town and transport hub of **Penrith**, ten miles northeast of Ullswater, but Cumbria doesn't. To the east, the **Eden Valley** splits the Pennines from the Lake District fells, and boasts a succession of hardy market towns, prime among which is the former county town of **Appleby-in-Westmorland**. This lies on the magnificent **Settle to Carlisle railway**, connecting Cumbria with the Yorkshire Dales (see p.798). The other great local feat of engineering – the M6, following the main London–Penrith–Glasgow rail line – misses the best of the valley, yet remains one of the most attractive sections of motorway in the country. Northeast of Penrith, the A686 leads you imperceptibly from Cumbria into Teesdale via a string of offbeat attractions and the high town of **Alston** – making a superbly scenic approach to Hexham and Hadrian's Wall.

Penrith and around

Once a thriving market town on the main north–south trading route, **PENRITH** today suffers from undue comparisons with the improbably pretty settlements of the nearby Lakes. The brisk streets have more in common with the towns of the North Pennines than the stone villages of south Cumbria, and even the local building materials emphasize the geographic shift. Its deep-red buildings were erected from the same rust-red sandstone used to construct

Potty Penrith

Potfest (Ⓦwww.potfest.co.uk), Europe's biggest ceramics show, takes place in Penrith over two consecutive weekends (late July/early August), with **Potfest in the Park** held in the grounds of Hutton-in-the-Forest country house, followed by the highly unusual **Potfest in the Pens**. This sees potters displaying their creations in the unlikely setting of the cattle-pens at Penrith's cattle market, where the public can talk to the artists and even sign up for classes.

Penrith Castle (daily 7.30am–dusk; free) in the fourteenth century, as a bastion against raids from the north; it's now a romantic, crumbling ruin, opposite the train station. The town itself is at its best in the narrow streets, arcades and alleys off **Market Square**, and around **St Andrew's churchyard**, where the so-called "Giant's Grave" is actually a collection of tenth-century Viking crosses and Viking-influenced "hogsback" tombstones.

Practicalities

Penrith **train station** is five minutes' walk south of Market Square and the main street, Middlegate, while the **bus station** is on Albert Street, behind Middlegate. There are **car parks** signposted around town, though spaces are hard to come by on Tuesdays (market day). The **tourist office** is on Middlegate (Mon–Sat 9.30/10am–4/5pm, until 6pm July & Aug, plus Sun 1–4.45pm Easter–Oct; ☎01768/867466, ⓦwww.visiteden.co.uk), and shares its seventeenth-century schoolhouse premises with a small local museum. Eden Arts (☎01768/899444, ⓦwww.edenarts.co.uk) can provide details of events in and around town, including **Edenfest**, a three-day summer music festival in the Deer Park, off the A6 at Brougham.

The bulk of the standard **B&Bs** line noisy Victoria Road (the continuation of King Street running south from Market Square). However, Portland Place, behind the town hall, has a more refined row of **guesthouses**, including the excellent *Brooklands*, 2 Portland Place (☎01768/863395, ⓦwww .brooklandsguesthouse.com; ❹). The traditional choice in town is the *George Hotel*, an old coaching inn by Market Square (☎01768/862696, ⓦwww.georgehotelpenrith.co.uk; ❺), but for something more contemporary drive out fifteen miles southeast to ⚑ *Crake Trees Manor* at Crosby Ravensworth (☎01931/715205, ⓦwww.craketreesmanor.co.uk; ❺), a super-stylish barn conversion in the Eden Valley, with quality B&B and local walks. There's a local pub there, or it's a ten-minute drive to the renowned bar meals at the *Greyhound* in Shap, on the A6 (☎01931/716474, ⓦwww .greyhoundshap.co.uk).

Around Penrith

Several attractions lie close to town, the nearest being the ruins of **Brougham Castle** (Easter–Sept daily 10am–6pm; Oct Mon & Thurs–Sun 10am–4pm; £2.80; EH), a mile and a half south of Penrith in a pretty spot by the River Eamont. Three miles southwest of town, the country house of **Dalemain** (Feb half-term hol & Easter–Oct Mon–Thurs & Sun, house 11.15am–4pm, gardens 10.30am–5pm; Nov, Dec & Feb–Easter gardens and tearoom only Mon–Thurs 11am–4pm; £6.50, gardens only £4.50, though prices may rise; ⓦwww.dalemain.com) started life in the twelfth century as a fortified tower, but has subsequently been added to by successive generations, culminating with a Georgian facade grafted onto a largely Elizabethan house. You're given the run of the public rooms, which the family still uses – hence the photographs and contemporary portraits alongside those of the ancestors – while the servants' corridors and pantries offer a glimpse of life "below stairs".

You also shouldn't miss **Rheged** (daily 10am–5.30pm; ⓦwww.rheged.com; free) at Redhills on the A66, a couple of minutes' drive from the M6 (junction 40); express buses between Penrith and Keswick stop outside. Billed as Europe's largest earth-covered building, it takes its name from the ancient kingdom of Cumbria and features a spectacular atrium-lit underground visitor centre, which fills you in on the region's culture, history and food by way of exhibitions, local art and craft displays, family activities, food hall, restaurant and café.

There's also a giant-format cinema screen showing *Rheged: The Movie*, documenting a Cumbrian journey through time, as well as the separate **National Mountaineering Exhibition**, presenting an entertaining history of mountain-climbers and climbing. Several other big-screen presentations also play here daily. Admission to one film or the Mountaineering Exhibition costs £5.95, while seeing each extra film costs £4.

Penrith to Alston

The main routes north from Penrith are the M6 and the rail line to Carlisle, but if you're heading for Hadrian's Wall the highly scenic A686 provides an alternative trans-moor route into the North Pennines, via Alston.

The prehistoric stone circle known as **Long Meg and her Daughters** is just outside Little Salkeld, off the A686, six miles north of Penrith and just over a mile's walk from Langwathby on the Settle to Carlisle railway. Standing outside a ring of stones nearly 400ft in diameter, Long Meg is the tallest stone at 18ft and has a profile like the face of an austere old lady. Little Salkeld itself is the location of the prettily sited **Little Salkeld Watermill** (daily 10.30am–5pm; closed Jan; free; ⓦ www.organicmill.co.uk), producer of organic flour – the wholefood veggie tearoom here is worth a stop – while you can also detour into **Langwathby** for the idiosyncratic **Eden Ostrich World** (Feb half-term hol–Oct daily 10am–5pm; Nov–Feb closed Tues; £5.45, cheaper in winter; ⓦ www.ostrich-world.com); chick-hatching season is May to October, though there's always something to do and see. For a good meal, there's the *Highland Drove* pub at nearby Great Salkeld (ⓣ 01768/898349, ⓦ www.highland-drove-co.uk), whose restaurant specialises in Eden Valley and regional produce.

Back on the A686, it's also worth making a point of stopping **Melmerby**'s marvellous *Village Bakery* (daily until 5pm; ⓣ 01768/881811, ⓦ www.village-bakery.com), a pioneer in organic baking, with a café with garden seating serving fine breakfasts, lunches and light meals. Having covered an initial stretch of smooth vales and aromatic pine woods, the road then winds steeply up the bracken-strewn slopes of **Hartside Top** (1900ft), which has a welcome café at its summit (closed weekdays Nov–March). Come here on a Sunday and you'll see half of the region's bikers parked up watching the other half zoom by.

Alston

Seven miles below Hartside Top, **ALSTON** commands the head of the South Tyne Valley. It no longer has a market to back up its claim to being the highest market town in England, but still has its market cross, beside the cobbled curve

Women wanted

Alston hit the headlines in 2005 when a group of local young men – despairing at the paucity of suitable mates – launched the **Alston Moor Regeneration Society** in an attempt to attract women to move to this isolated rural outpost. Their lonely hearts plea struck a chord, as the national press ran with the story and Channel 4 made a documentary on "the town that's looking for love". Gimmick or not, the campaign said something serious about the problems facing many similar towns in the UK, where young locals move away for work – though whether or not Alston really is "the Ibiza of the north" (one of the enticements offered) is for you to decide.

of the steep main road, Front Street. It's a tidily restored town, and the convenient location between Cumbria and the northeast, and position as a hiking and biking hub, makes it a popular stopover. Families also come for the narrow-gauge **South Tynedale Railway** (Easter week & June–Sept almost daily; rest of the year Sat & Sun only; £5 return, day-ticket £8; ☏01434/382828, ⓦwww.strps.org.uk), whose steam engines follow the route of an old coal-carrying branch of the Carlisle to Newcastle line.

The South Tynedale **train station** lies just down the Hexham road, five minutes' walk from the centre; the **tourist office** is inside the town hall (Easter–Oct Mon–Sat 10am–5pm, Sun 10am–4pm; ☏01434/382244, ⓦwww.visiteden.co.uk). There's plenty of local **accommodation** in all price ranges, starting with country-house B&B at *Lowbyer Manor* (☏01434/381230, ⓦwww.lowbyer.com; ❹), a Georgian house with an effusive welcome, just a hundred yards or so beyond the train station. *Alston House* (☏01434/382200, ⓦwww.alstonhouse.co.uk; ❹), at the foot of town on the main road, also has B&B rooms, as well as moderately priced bistro meals served in the café or bar. A town youth hostel caters for Pennine Way walkers, while a couple of miles east on the Nenthead road, the *Lovelady Shield Country House* (☏0871/288 1345, ⓦwww.lovelady.co.uk; ❾ including dinner) is a beautiful Georgian establishment in mature grounds that serves excellent food. Or you can drive the four miles southeast to **Garrigill** (also on the Pennine Way from Alston), a cute hamlet set around a green, where the *George & Dragon* has flagstoned floors, a roaring fire, real ale and bar meals.

Appleby-in-Westmorland

One-time county town of Westmorland, **APPLEBY-IN-WESTMORLAND** is protected on three sides by a lazy loop in the River Eden. The fourth was defended by the now privately owned **Appleby Castle**, whose Norman keep was restored by Lady Anne Clifford, who, after her father's death in 1605, spent 45 years trying to claim her rightful inheritance. It's currently closed to the public, but you can pursue the Lady Anne trail at the lovely **almshouses** she founded. These are on Boroughgate, the town's backbone, which runs from High Cross, former site of the cheese market outside the castle, down to Low Cross, previously a butter market but now home of the general Saturday market. **St Lawrence's Church** meanwhile, at Low Cross, holds the tombs of Lady Anne Clifford and her mother.

Appleby Horse Fair

The town changes its character completely every June when the **Appleby Horse Fair** takes over nearby Gallows' Hill, as it has done since 1750. Britain's most important gypsy gathering draws hundreds of chrome-plated caravans and more traditional horse-drawn "bow-tops", as well as thousands of tinkers, New-Age travellers and sightseers. Historically, the main day of the fair was the second Wednesday of June (the official day for horse trading), but now most of the action takes place between the previous Thursday and the Tuesday, culminating on the Tuesday evening with the showpiece trotting races. It's a vaguely anarchic event all round, and something happens most years that causes unrest – in 2007 a horse drowned, to general consternation, during the ritual morning horse-washing in the River Eden. But, on the whole, the town remains supportive of the fair and it's certainly a unique sight, with the main road closed so that trotting horses can be displayed, and hair-raising stunts and fortune-telling *de rigueur* for the week.

The **Settle to Carlisle Railway** is the best way to get to Appleby, although **bus services** from Penrith are frequent enough. The **tourist office**, in the Moot Hall on Boroughgate (April–Oct Mon–Sat 9.30am–5pm, Sun 11–3pm; Nov–March Mon–Thurs 10am–1pm, Fri & Sat 10am–3pm; ☎01768/351177, ⓦwww.applebytown.org.uk), is ten minutes' walk from the station, across the river.

🛏 *Rutter Mill Cottage* (☎01768/353243; no credit cards; ❹), three miles south of town at Great Asby, is set by the side of tumbling **Rutter Falls**, next to a ford and footbridge, and offers one highly attractive B&B room and two very smart cottages (by the week). Otherwise, there are a couple of **B&Bs** on Bongate, 500yd (10min walk) from town, over the river from Low Cross, then south along the Brough road. Also along here you'll find the *Royal Oak* (☎01768/351463; ❹), an aged inn with some comfortable rooms. The top hotel in town is the *Tufton Arms* on Market Square (☎01768/351593, ⓦwww .tuftonarmshotel.co.uk; ❻). **Cafés and tearooms** in town soak up much of the passing trade, while there's decently priced brasserie-style food at the *Royal Oak*.

Carlisle and around

The county capital of Cumbria and its only city, **CARLISLE** is also the repository of much of the region's history, its strategic location having been fought over for more than 2000 years. The original Celtic settlement was superseded by a Roman town, whose first fort was raised here in 72 AD. Carlisle thrived during the construction of Hadrian's Wall and then, long after the Romans had gone, the Saxon settlement was repeatedly fought over by the Danes and the Scots – the latter losing it eventually to the Normans. The struggle with the Scots defined the very nature of Carlisle as a border city: William Wallace was repelled in 1297 and Robert the Bruce eighteen years later, but Bonnie Prince Charlie's troops took Carlisle in 1745 after a six-day siege, holding it for six weeks before surrendering to the Duke of Cumberland.

It's not surprising, then, that Carlisle still trumpets itself as the "great border city", and it's well worth taking the time to explore its historic centre. If you've a couple of days to spare you can also tour the locality: nearby **Talkin Tarn**, the ruins of **Lanercost Priory** and the only surviving bit of Hadrian's Wall in Cumbria, at **Birdoswald Fort**, are all worth a stop. Heading on, Edinburgh is under two hours north, while Carlisle is also the terminus of the historic Settle to Carlisle Railway.

The City

Carlisle's main thoroughfare, **English Street**, is pedestrianized as far as the expansive **Green Market** square, formerly heart of the medieval city, though a huge fire in 1392 destroyed its buildings and layout. The Lanes shopping centre on the east side of the square – its "alleys" lit through a cast-iron-and-glass roof – stands where the medieval city's lanes once ran. Otherwise, the only historic survivors are the **market cross** (1682), the Elizabethan former **town hall** behind it, which now houses the tourist office and, at the southern end of Fisher Street, the timber-framed **Guildhall** (1405).

It's only a few steps along to **Carlisle Cathedral** (Mon–Sat 7.30am–6.15pm, Sun 7.30am–5pm; free, donation requested), founded in 1122 but embracing a

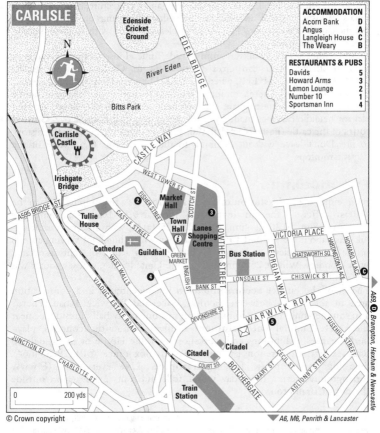

considerably older heritage. Christianity was established in sixth-century Carlisle by St Kentigern (often known as St Mungo), who became the first bishop and patron saint of Glasgow. Parliamentarian troops during the Civil War destroyed all but two powerful arches of the original eight bays of the Norman nave, but there's still much to admire in the ornate fifteenth-century choir stalls and the glorious **East Window**, which features some of the finest pieces of fourteenth-century stained glass in the country (although two-thirds of it is a faithful nineteenth-century restoration). Opposite the main entrance, the reconstructed **Fratry**, or monastic building, houses the *Prior's Kitchen*, a daytime café (closed Sun) using space that was once the monks' dining hall.

For more on Carlisle's history, head for the **Tullie House Museum and Art Gallery** (Mon–Sat 10am–4/5pm, Sun noon–4/5pm; £5.50; Ⓦwww .tulliehouse.co.uk), reached up Castle Street or through the cathedral grounds, via Abbey Street. This takes a highly imaginative approach to Carlisle's turbulent past, with special emphasis put on life on the edge of the Roman Empire – climbing a reconstruction of part of Hadrian's Wall, you learn about catapults and stone-throwers, while other sections elaborate on domestic life, work and burial practices. Down in the underground Millennium Gallery are innovative displays devoted to local geology, archeology and architecture, contrasted with a glass "Whispering Wall" in which are embedded recordings of stories and tales by the locals themselves. The café is pleasant, too, with terrace seating overlooking the gardens.

Using either a public walkway from outside Tullie House, or the eye-catching Irishgate Bridge, you can cross Castle Way to **Carlisle Castle** (daily: 9.30/10am–4/6pm; £4; EH), where, in 1568, Elizabeth I kept Mary Queen of Scots as her "guest". There's a military museum located in the former armoury, but much more interesting are the excellent displays in the **keep**, and the elegant heraldic carvings made by prisoners in a second-floor alcove. **Guided tours** of the castle (Easter–Oct daily; ask at the entrance) help bring the history to life. Don't leave without climbing to the battlements for a view of the Carlisle rooftops.

Practicalities

From either the **train station** or the **bus station**, it's a five-minute walk to the **tourist office** in the old town hall (Mon–Sat 9.30/10am–4/5.30pm, plus May–Aug Sun 10.30am–4pm; ☎01228/625600, ⓦwww.historic-carlisle.org .uk). Ask about the **guided tours** in summer, which highlight varying aspects of the city – medieval and modern Carlisle, say, or a tour of sights associated with Woodrow Wilson, 28th president of the United States, whose mother was born in Carlisle.

Most of the budget **accommodation** is concentrated in a conservation area in the streets between Victoria Place and Warwick Road. There's also summer-only YHA accommodation in a university hall of residence near the castle. Cultural **entertainment** revolves around the concerts, plays, performances, exhibitions and workshops at Tullie House or the associated Stanwix Arts Theatre on Brampton Road (box office ☎01228/534664). The big annual music fest is **Brampton Live** every July (ⓦwww .bramptonlive.net), a three-day world, folk and roots extravaganza outside the city at Brampton.

Accommodation

Acorn Bank Wetheral, 4 miles east of Carlisle, off A69 ☎01228/561434, ⓦwww.acornbank.co .uk. Two lovely rooms available at a country guest house in a pretty village. The owners (former restaurateurs) also offer dinner on request (£25), as well as cookery demonstrations. No credit cards. ⑥

Angus 14 Scotland Rd ☎01228/523546, ⓦwww .angus-hotel.co.uk. Prices are reasonable at this small family-owned hotel with moderately priced bistro (dinner only; closed Sun), a 15min walk from the centre. Parking nearby. ④

Langleigh House 6 Howard Place ☎01228/530440, ⓦwww.langleighhouse.co.uk. Nicely presented Victorian town-house B&B with eight rooms, including a family room that sleeps four. Parking. No credit cards. ⑤

The Weary Castle Carrock, Brampton, 8 miles east of Carlisle ☎01228/670230, ⓦwww.theweary.com. The inn with the "wow" factor – traditional eighteenth-century outside, utterly contemporary (yet unstuffy and informal) inside. The sleek rooms hit all the right buttons (big beds, rich colours and fabrics, DVD/CD players, bathrooms with glass basins and inset bath-side TV screens), while a handsome designer bar-restaurant and conservatory provides classy Modern British meals. ⑦

Restaurants

Davids 62 Warwick Rd ☎01228/523578. Formal Modern British restaurant that draws on Mediterranean ingredients for its seasonally changing offerings, from Cumbrian lamb to swordfish. Lunch is cheaper and set mid-week menus provide value for money. Closed Sun & Mon. Expensive.

The Lemon Lounge 18 Fisher St ☎01228/546363. Easy-going cellar bistro with a sun-trap outdoor terrace, where you can roam the gastronomic world – Thai curry, Mediterranean pasta, salads and the like. Closed Sun & Mon. Moderate.

Number 10 10 Eden Mount ☎01228/524183. Agreeable town-house restaurant, serving a seasonally changing Modern British menu. Most mains cost £12–16, though the midweek set menu is good value. Dinner only, closed Sun & Tues. Expensive.

Pubs

Howard Arms 107 Lowther St. Extravagantly tiled on the outside and with nice little snug rooms and real ale inside.
Sportsman Inn Heads Lane, at the back of Marks and Spencer. Cosy old local backing onto St Cuthbert's churchyard.

Around Carlisle

Eight miles east of Carlisle, the small market town of **Brampton** is at the centre of several outlying attractions that can make a fine day's tour from the city. Two miles south of Brampton, on the minor B6413 (Castle Carrock road), **Talkin Tarn** is the city's traditional bolthole, a pretty lake set within 120 acres of meadow and woodland. There's a car park and boathouse tearoom, with the tarn ringed by an easy (30min) footpath; many locals come out in the summer to sail, kayak or fish.

A similar distance to the northeast of Brampton (just north of the A69, at Low Row), the highly attractive ruins of **Lanercost Priory** (Easter–Sept daily 10am–5pm; Oct Mon & Thurs–Sun 10am–4pm; Nov weekends only 10am–4pm; £3; EH), occupy a lovely spot in deep countryside. The Augustinian priory dates from 1166 – though carved stones found here date back to Roman times – and you can view the remains of a medieval undercroft and the Prior's Tower, with its brick fireplace and ovens *in situ*. The adjacent priory church (daily 9am–dusk) is still used as the district's parish church; the nearby *Abbey Bridge Inn* is the local hostelry.

A little further east, signposted from the A69 five miles beyond Brampton and fifteen from Carlisle – **Birdoswald Fort** (Easter–Oct daily 10am–4.30pm; £4.10; EH; ⓦ www.birdoswaldromanfort.org.uk) is the area's real highlight. One of sixteen forts along Hadrian's Wall, it has all tiers of the Roman structure intact – the east gateway, in particular, is one of the best preserved on the wall – while a drill hall and other buildings have been excavated. There's a tearoom and picnic area at the fort, while its residential study centre is available to overnight hikers and others as a summer-only YHA **youth hostel** (☎0870/770 6124, ⓔbirdoswald@yha.org.uk; from £15.50), open July to September only. The seasonal **Hadrian's Wall Bus** (see p.896) connects Carlisle with Brampton (20min), Lanercost (30min) and Birdoswald (40min), before running on to the rest of the Hadrian's Wall sights.

Travel details

Buses

For information on all local and national bus services, contact Traveline ☎0871/200 2233, ⓦwww.traveline.org.uk.
Carlisle to: Keswick (3 daily; 1hr 10min); Windermere/Bowness (3 daily; 2hr 20min).
Cross Lake Shuttle (Lake District): up to 9 daily services; launch from Bowness connects with minibus from Sawrey to Hill Top (5min) and

Hawkshead (13min) – first and last bus of the day also runs to Grizedale (25min). Service daily Easter–Sept, plus Oct weekends.
Kendal to: Ambleside (hourly; 40min); Cartmel (7 daily; 1hr); Grasmere (hourly; 1hr); Keswick (hourly; 1hr 30min); Lancaster (hourly; 1hr); Windermere/Bowness (hourly; 30min).
Keswick to: Ambleside (hourly; 45min); Buttermere (2 daily; 30min); Carlisle (3 daily; 1hr 10min); Cockermouth (every 30min–1hr; 30min); Grasmere (hourly; 40min); Honister (Easter–Oct 4 daily;

40min); Kendal (hourly; 1hr 30min); Rosthwaite (every 30min–1hr; 25min); Seatoller (every 30min–1hr; 30min); Windermere (hourly; 1hr).
Windermere to: Ambleside (hourly; 15min); Bowness (every 20–30min; 15min); Carlisle (3 daily; 2hr 20min); Grasmere (every 20–30min; 30min); Kendal (hourly; 25min); Keswick (hourly; 1hr).

Trains

For information on all local and national rail services, contact National Rail Enquiries ☎08457/484950, ⓦwww.rail.co.uk.

Appleby-in-Westmorland to: Carlisle (6 daily; 40min).

Carlisle to: Appleby (6 daily; 40min); Barrow-in-Furness (5 daily; 2hr 20min); Lancaster (every 30min–1hr; 1hr); Newcastle (hourly; 1hr 20min–1hr 40min); Whitehaven (hourly; 1hr 10min).

Windermere to: Kendal (hourly; 15min) and Oxenholme (hourly; 20min) for onward services to Lancaster and Manchester, or Penrith and Carlisle.

12

Yorkshire

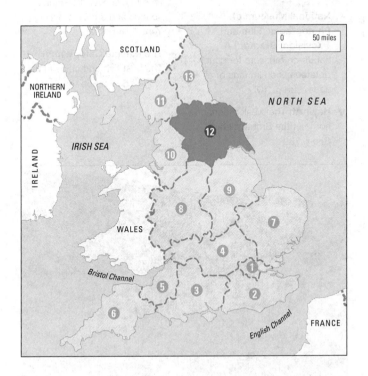

CHAPTER 12

Highlights

* **Millennium Galleries, Sheffield** Centrepiece of revamped Sheffield – terrific exhibitions with hothouse gardens attached. See p.774

* **Shopping in Leeds** Shop till you drop in the markets, malls and arcades of Yorkshire's most fashionable city. See p.782

* **National Museum of Photography, Film and Television, Bradford** A hands-on museum for couch potatoes and film fans of all ages. See p.787

* **Haworth** The bleak moorland home of the Brontë sisters. See p.789

* **Malham** Make the breathtaking hike from Malham village to the glorious natural amphitheatre of Malham Cove. See p.797

* **Turkish Baths, Harrogate** The ultimate in personal pampering. See p.813

* **Jorvik, York** Travel through time to discover the sights, sounds and smells of Viking York. See p.823

* **The Magpie Café, Whitby** The best fish and chips in the world? See p.854

▲ Malham Cove

Yorkshire

t's easy to be glib about **Yorkshire** – for much of the country, England's largest county is shorthand for "up north" and all its clichéd connotations, from flat caps and factories to tightfisted locals. For their part, many Yorkshire born-and-bred are happy to play to the prejudice of southerners, adopting an attitude roughly on a par with that of Texans or Australians in strongly suggesting that there's really nowhere else worth considering. In its sheer size at least, Yorkshire does have a case for primacy, while its most striking characteristics – from dialect to landscape – derive from a long history of settlement, invention and independence that's still a source of pride today. For every grim suburb and moribund mill there are acres of rolling valley, national park upland and glorious coast, riddled with Viking place names, medieval abbeys, English Civil War battle sites, and the country homes of nobles and industrialists. As for Yorkshire's other boasts (the beer's better, the air's cleaner, the people are friendlier than "down south" and so on), visitors can make up their own minds.

Yorkshire was once divided into three regions called **"ridings"** (North, East and West), from the Old Norse for "third part", which correspond roughly with the modern divisions of North, East and West Yorkshire, plus South Yorkshire which abuts the Peak District and East Midlands. Differently named administrative authorities confuse the issue further for locals, but for visitors the divisions are a handy guide to the main cities and attractions – South Yorkshire for Sheffield, West Yorkshire for Leeds, Bradford and Haworth, East Yorkshire for Hull, and North Yorkshire for York, moors, dales and coast.

The number-one destination is undoubtedly history-soaked **York**, for centuries England's second city until the Industrial Revolution created new

Regional transport

Fast **train** services on the East Coast main line link York to London, Newcastle and Edinburgh. Leeds is also served by regular trains from London, and is at the centre of the integrated Metro bus and train system that covers most of West and South Yorkshire. There are also train services to Scarborough (from York) and Whitby (from Middlesbrough), while the **Settle–Carlisle** line, to the southern and western Yorkshire Dales, can be accessed from Leeds. The **North Country Rover** ticket (any four days in eight; £68) covers unlimited train travel north of Leeds, Bradford and Hull and south of Newcastle and Carlisle. Picturesque private lines with steam trains make good days out, notably the **Keighley and Worth Valley Railway** line to Haworth and the **North Yorkshire Moors Railway** between Pickering and Grosmont.

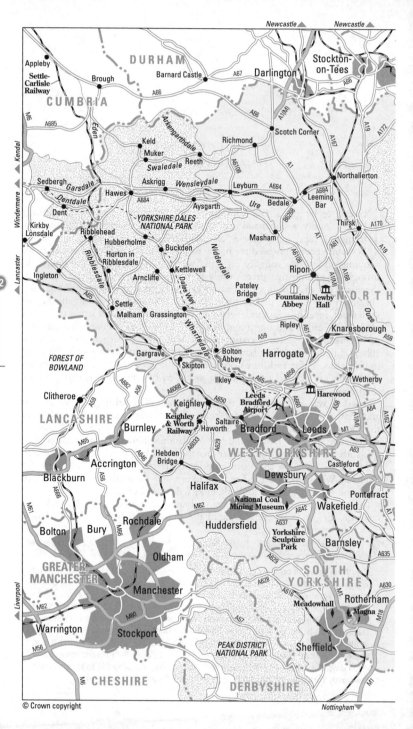

© Crown copyright

Nottingham ▼

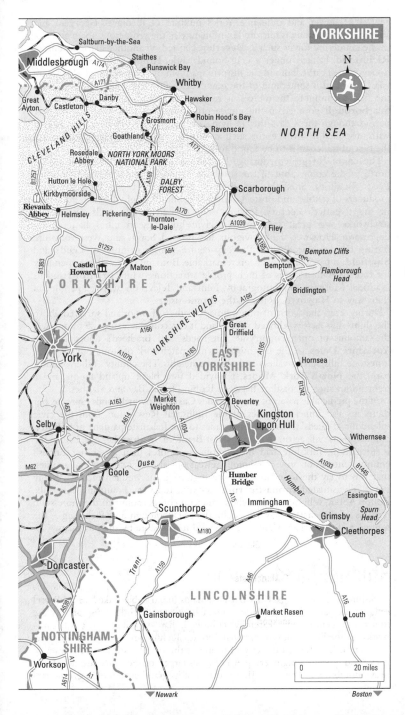

centres of power and influence. York's mixture of medieval, Georgian and Victorian architecture is mirrored in miniature in the prosperous north and east of the county by towns such as **Beverley**, centred on another soaring minster; **Richmond**, banked under a crag-bound castle; **Ripon**, gathered around its honey-stoned cathedral; and the historic spa town of **Harrogate**. The Yorkshire coast, too, retains something of the grandeur of the days when its towns were the first to promote themselves as resorts: places such as **Bridlington** and **Scarborough** boomed in the nineteenth century and again in the postwar period, though these days they're living on past glories. It's in smaller resorts with unspoiled historic centres such as **Whitby** and **Robin Hood's Bay** that the best of the coast is to be found today.

The engine of growth during the Industrial Revolution was not in the north of the county, but in the south and west. By the nineteenth century, Leeds, Bradford, Sheffield and their satellites were the world's mightiest producers of textiles and of steel. Ruthless economic logic devastated the area in the twentieth century, leaving only disused textile mills, abandoned steelworks and great soot-covered civic buildings in cities battered by depression. However, a new vigour has infused South and West Yorkshire during the last decade, and the city-centre transformations of **Leeds** and **Sheffield** in particular have been remarkable. Both are now making open play for tourists with a series of high-profile attractions, while **Bradford** and its National Museum of Photography, Film and Television waylays people on their way to **Haworth**, home of the Brontë sisters.

During even the worst of times, broad swathes of moorland survived above the slum- and factory-choked valleys, and it can come as a surprise to discover the amount of open countryside on Leeds' and Bradford's doorsteps. The **Yorkshire Dales**, to the northwest, form a patchwork of stone-built villages, limestone hills, serene valleys and majestic heights. The county's other national park, the **North York Moors**, is divided into bleak upland moors and a tremendous rugged coastline between Robin Hood's Bay and Staithes.

Of the predictable roster of stately homes **Castle Howard** stands supreme, but there are also imperious relics of the Industrial Revolution, from the civic splendour of Leeds' town hall and arcades to the Italianate pastiche of **Saltaire**, a millworkers' village on the outskirts of Bradford. In an earlier age, before the Reformation, Yorkshire had more monastic houses than any other English county, centres not only of religious retreat but also of a commercial acumen that was to lay the foundations of the region's great woollen industry. Many beautifully situated **monastic ruins** survive today at Fountains, Rievaulx, Bolton Abbey, Whitby and elsewhere, graceful counterpoints to the more solid remains of the **castles** at York, Richmond, Scarborough and Pickering – the foremost of more than twenty castles raised in Yorkshire by the Normans.

Sheffield and around

Yorkshire's second city, **SHEFFIELD** remains inextricably linked with its steel industry, in particular the production of high-quality cutlery. As early as the fourteenth century, the carefully fashioned, hard-wearing knives of hard-working Sheffield enjoyed national repute. Technological advances in steel production later turned the city into one of the country's foremost centres of heavy and specialist engineering. An obvious target for the Luftwaffe, it suffered heavy bombing in World War II, yet several of its grand civic buildings emerged remarkably unscathed. However, more damaging than bombs to the city's pre-eminence was the steel industry's subsequent downturn, which by the 1980s had tipped parts of Sheffield into dispiriting decline.

The subsequent economic and cultural revival has been rapid, with the centre in particular – the part, after all, that most tourists see – utterly transformed by flagship architectural projects. As a city-break destination, Sheffield can't fail to surprise, and with the Peak District so close (over a third of the city lies within its boundary), it's easy to escape for the day. A glut of sports facilities (including the Ski Village, Europe's largest artificial ski resort) backs Sheffield's claim to be considered "National City of Sport". Meanwhile, the city's two universities and large student population lend the alternative shopping, café and nightlife scene a welcome edge.

Steel, of course, still underpins much of what Sheffield is about. The city that gave the world *The Full Monty* – the black comedy about five former steel workers carving out a new career as a striptease act – also boasts **Meadowhall** shopping centre, located in an old steelworks and billed as one of Europe's biggest malls. Museum collections tend to specialize in the region's industrial heritage, which is complemented by the startling science-and-adventure exhibits at **Magna** built on a disused steelworks at nearby **Rotherham**, the former coal and iron town a few miles northeast of the city.

Arrival, information and accommodation

Parking is signposted throughout the city from the ring road. Sheffield's **train station** is on the eastern edge of the city centre, by Sheffield Hallam University, with the bus and coach station, known as **Sheffield Interchange**, about two hundred yards to the north – the two are clearly linked, while following Howard Street from the station takes you straight up to the city centre, emerging at Millennium Square. The **tourist office** is just north of here, at 14 Norfolk Row (Mon–Fri 10am–5pm, Sat 10am–4pm; ℡0114/221 1900, Ⓦwww.sheffieldtourism.co.uk and www.spinsheffield.com).

Most local **buses** depart from High Street or Arundel Gate, while the **Supertram** system (Ⓦwww.supertram.com) connects the city centre with Meadowhall (northeast), Middlewood (northwest) and Halfway (southeast). For fare and timetable information, visit the **Mini Interchange** travel centre on Arundel Gate, behind the Crucible Theatre (Mon–Sat 7am–7pm; ℡01709/515151 or 0114/201 2675, Ⓦwww.sypte.co.uk). A Day Tripper (£5) gives unlimited travel on buses, trains and trams throughout South Yorkshire.

Sheffield has a fair amount of mid-range central **accommodation** – even so, the tourist office's room-booking service can come in handy (℡0871/700 0121), especially if you're looking for cheaper B&Bs on the outskirts. Self-catering student rooms in the Devonshire Quarter (late June to mid-Sept) can be booked through the University of Sheffield (℡0114/289 3500, Ⓦwww.victoriahall.com; from £25 per night), while a night in the central *Ibis* or *Premier Travel Inn* costs from £50.

Hotels and guest houses

Bristol Blonk St ℡0114/220 4000, Ⓦwww.hotel-bristol.co.uk. Breezy, informal business hotel near the river, quays and markets, with a good bar and restaurant. All rooms are stylishly furnished, some with futons – handy for families. Parking. ❻

Houseboat Hotels Victoria Quays ℡0114/232 6556 or 07974/590264, Ⓦwww.houseboathotels.com. Something a little bit different – two moored houseboats, available by the night, very nicely styled, both with en-suite bathrooms and kitchens. Tea and coffee are provided, continental breakfast can be arranged (£5 extra), parking is included, and there's use of the nearby *Hilton*'s leisure centre. They're rented exclusively, for two people ❹ or four people from £86.

Novotel 50 Arundel Gate ☎0114/278 1781,
Ⓦwww.accorhotels.com. A classy refurbishment
has made this designer four-star, right by
Millennium Square, an attractive option. Weekend
rates are reduced considerably. Indoor pool and
parking. **❼**
St Paul's 119 Norfolk St ☎0114/278 2000,
Ⓦwww.mercure.com/sheffield. An up-to-the-
minute hotel on Millennium Square, with restaurant

adjoining the Winter Gardens. Bedrooms are
minimalist and neutral in tone. Leisure facilities
include indoor pool, spa and sauna. **❽**
Westbourne House 25 Westbourne Rd, Broomhill
☎0114/266 0109, Ⓦwww.westbournehousehotel
.com. Victorian town house, a mile out of the centre
(and 10min from the bars and restaurants of
Ecclesall Rd), with individually furnished light and
white rooms. **❺**

The City

New-look Sheffield is at its best around the landmark **Town Hall**, at the
junction of Pinstone and Surrey streets. Completed in 1897, it's topped by the
figure of Vulcan, the Roman god of fire and metalworking, and the facade
sports a fine frieze depicting traditional Sheffield industries. The adjacent **Peace
Gardens** feature central water jets that whoosh up intermittently to send
children giddy with delight, while rising to the east, a minute's walk away, is the
main symbol of the city regeneration, the stunning **Winter Gardens** (daily
8am–6pm; free), an arched steel-and-wood glasshouse almost 200 feet long and
over 60 feet high. It's a spectacular public space, filled with plants and shrubs –
the central Norfolk pines will eventually touch the roof.

Sheffield's **Millennium Galleries** (Mon–Sat 10am–5pm, Sun 11am–5pm;
free, visiting exhibitions £4; Ⓦwww.sheffieldgalleries.org.uk) back onto the
gardens and contain two permanent displays, both specific to Sheffield and its
heritage. In the **Metalworks Gallery** you can discover why the eighteenth-
century city's natural endowments (a fast water supply, forests for charcoal and
gritstone deposits) ensured the rapid development of the cutlery industry. Not
surprisingly, the gallery contains the most extensive collection of Sheffield
cutlery in the world, from sixteenth-century knives to designer cleavers. There's
also the highly diverting **Ruskin Gallery**, based on the collection founded by
John Ruskin in 1875 to improve the working people of Sheffield. A library of
classic nineteenth-century texts ("the working man's Bodleian") is complemented
by an intriguing selection of watercolours, sketches, minerals, paintings and
medieval illuminated manuscripts, and contrasts with Keiko Mukaide's stunning
wall-length clouds and water sculpture.

The rest of central Sheffield divides into neat areas, touted rather grandly as
"quarters". Southeast of the Winter Gardens, clubs and galleries exist alongside
arts and media businesses in the **Cultural Industries Quarter**. North of the
stations, near the River Don, **Castlegate** has a traditional indoor **market**
(closed Sun) while the spruced-up warehouses and cobbled towpaths in the
neighbouring canal basin, **Victoria Quays**, house several high-tech businesses,
restaurants, hotels and leisure facilities.

Closer to the Town Hall, at the end of Fargate, the city's **Cathedral of
St Peter and St Paul** retains elements of its fifteenth-century origins, and is
enhanced by its late twentieth-century lantern tower and colourful glass.
Cutler's Hall, opposite on Church Street, is an imposing reminder of the
importance of the cutlery trade – the Company of Cutlers guild was established
here as early as 1624 to regulate the affairs of the industry. South of here, down
Fargate and across Peace Gardens, the pedestrianized **Moor Quarter** draws in
shoppers, though it's the **Devonshire Quarter**, east of the gardens and centred
on Division Street, that is the trendiest shopping area.

Sheffield's other attractions are all on the city outskirts. Fifteen minutes'
walk north of the cathedral, the **Kelham Island Museum** on Alma Street

(Mon–Thurs 10am–4pm, Sun 11am–4.45pm; £4; Ⓦ www.simt.co.uk) reveals the breadth of the city's industrial output. Many of the old machines are still working, arranged in period workshops where craftspeople demonstrate some of the finer points of cutlery production. You can then put the city's life and times into perspective a mile or so west at the **Weston Park Museum** (Mon–Sat 10am–5pm, Sun 11am–5pm; free; Ⓦ www .sheffieldgalleries.org.uk), where the imaginatively themed and family friendly galleries draw together the city's extensive archeology, natural history, art and social history collections. Catch bus #51 or #52 from High Street and get off at the Children's Hospital/Weston Park stop. Also on this side of the city are the lovely **Botanical Gardens** (Mon–Fri 8am–dusk, Sat & Sun 10am–dusk, pavilions 11am–3.30/5pm; free), where there are nineteen acres of Victorian landscaping, some impressively restored glass pavilions and an early nineteenth-century bear pit. There are two entrances – one on Clarkehouse Road (bus #50 or #59 from High St), the other on Thompson Road (buses #81 to 86 from High St).

Rotherham: Magna

About six miles northeast of Sheffield, across the M1, **ROTHERHAM** sees itself as just as much a gateway to Yorkshire as its bigger neighbour. The town centre has been improved over recent years, and locals point to its churches as its proudest feature. Certainly, the medieval parish church is particularly fine, while in the Chapel of Our Lady on Rotherham Bridge, the town has one of only four surviving examples in England of a medieval bridge chantry. For most visitors, however, these pale in comparison with **Magna** (daily 10am–5pm; closed Mon Nov–March; April–Oct £9.95, Nov–March £9; Ⓦ www.visitmagna.co.uk), the UK's first science adventure centre, housed in a former steelworks building on Sheffield Road (A6178) in Templeborough, just off the M1 a mile from the Meadowhall shopping complex. You can get here on bus #69 from either Sheffield or Rotherham Interchanges, or it's a fifteen-minute taxi ride from Sheffield. Signs from the M1 (junctions 33 or 34) direct drivers straight there.

Entering the bowels of the building confronts you immediately with the half-light, invasive noise and arcane hardware of a massive steelworks. The vast internal space comfortably holds four gadget-packed **pavilions**, themed on the basic elements of earth, air, fire and water. In these you're encouraged to get your hands on a huge variety of interactive exhibits, games and machines – operating a real JCB, filling diggers and barrows, blasting a rock face, firing a water cannon, or investigating a twister. On the hour, everyone decamps to the main hall for the **Big Melt** when the original arc furnace is used in a bone-shaking light and sound show that has visitors gripping the railings. The whole experience is an excellent day out – there are free tours of the premises most days, a very large children's play park, plus café and restaurant. Bring warm clothes if you're coming in winter.

Eating and drinking

Sheffield has plenty of great **café-bars** and good-value **restaurants** – there's no trouble finding something to eat in the city, while just south of the centre, London Road is lined with good, authentic southeast Asian restaurants. For the best insight into what makes Sheffield tick as a party destination take a night-time walk along **Division Street** and **West Street** where competing theme and retro bars go in and out of fashion. Town and gown meet at the fancy retail-restaurant-and-leisure development known as West:One (end of Devonshire St, at Fitzwilliam St), while locals and students also frequent the bars and pubs of Ecclesall Road (the so-called "golden mile"), out of the centre to the southwest – best take a taxi.

Cafés and café-bars

Blue Moon Café 2 St James St ☎0114/276 3443. Relax in the skylit dining room, next to the cathedral, and tuck into homemade vegetarian/vegan food, including pies, burritos, a cold-counter selection and organic beers. Closes 8pm; closed Sun.

Eat Crucible Theatre, Tudor Sq, 55 Norfolk St ☎0114/249 6008. Everything from sandwiches and salads to sharing platters and bistro classics, with most things priced between £5 and £12. Food until 7.30pm; closed Sun.

The Forum 127–129 Devonshire St ☎0114/272 0569. Long the mainstay of the Devonshire Quarter, *The Forum* has a great menu and laid-back clientele – breakfast from 10am, bar till 1am. A sinuous sun-terrace overlooks the green.

Restaurants

Antibo West:One, Unit 10, Fitzwilliam St ☎0114/272 7222. Classy, contemporary Italian restaurant with on-the-mark pizzas and pastas (around £9) and daily fish specials (£16), swordfish to seabass. Expensive.

Nonna's 535–541 Ecclesall Rd ☎0114/268 6166. Where the Sheffield beautiful hang out, a glam see-and-be-seen Italian bar and restaurant with a great reputation. Restaurant reservations advised. The deli and ice-cream parlour round the corner in Hickmott Rd (closed Mon & Tues) are worth a visit, too. Expensive.

Sheiks 274 Glossop Rd ☎0114/275 0555. Small, family-run Lebanese restaurant with extensive hot and cold mezze menu and good early evening deals. Dinner only. Moderate.

Vietnamese Noodle Bar 200–202 London Rd ☎0114/258 3608. Out of the centre, but really worth the trip for terrific Vietnamese and Chinese food. Always busy. Inexpensive.

Pubs and bars

Bluwater 18–19 The Arches, Victoria Quays. Sheffield's nicest spot for an alfresco drink, by the canal boats on the quayside.

Crystal 23-32 Carver St. A former scissor factory provides stunning premises for an airy bar-restaurant-patio, good for food, great for a night out, with a bar until 1.30am.

Devonshire Cat 49 Wellington St, Devonshire Green. Renowned ale-house with a beer menu on every table and good cheap food with drinks matched to every selection. For a bit more tradition, take a walk out (15min from the centre) to the *Fat Cat*, 23 Alma St, the cosier, older sister pub, also famed for its umpteen real ales and imported bottles.

Frog & Parrot 94 Division St. A boisterous pub with big windows onto the Division Street scene, lots of beers (including the hellishly strong Roger & Out) and a good jukebox.

Takapuna 52–54 West St. The cool crowd has moved out west to stylish *Takapuna*, for eating, greeting and drinking, with DJs and club nights an added incentive. The bar stays open until 2am.

The Washington 79 Fitzwilliam St. A favoured hangout for musicians, just two minutes across the green from Division St.

Nightlife, music and the arts

Friday's *Sheffield Telegraph* lists the week's performances, events, concerts and films, or there's *Exposed*, a free monthly listings magazine, available from cafés, restaurants, shops and bars across the city.

Clubs and live music

The Boardwalk 39 Snig Hill ☎0114/279 9090, ⓦwww.theboardwalklive.co.uk. Popular venue for indie bands, rock, folk and blues.

The Casbah 1 Wellington St ☎0114/275 6077. As in "Rock the . . .", which tells you what to expect – a stroll down punk/rock memory lane, with current indie and alternative nights as well.

Fuel Arundel Gate ⓦwww.fuel-sheffield.co.uk. Sheffield's gay "superclub" – glam decor, resident drag queen, star DJs – is the city's most reliable night out for gay and lesbian visitors.

Leadmill 6–7 Leadmill Rd ☎0114/221 2828, ⓦwww.leadmill.co.uk. In the Cultural Industries Quarter, this place hosts live bands and DJs most nights of the week.

Theatre, cinema and concerts

Crucible, Lyceum & Studio Tudor Sq ☎0114/249 6000, ⓦwww.sheffieldtheatres.co.uk.

Sheffield's theatres put on a full programme of theatre, dance, comedy and concerts. The Crucible, of course, has hosted the World Snooker Chamionships for 30 years. It also presents the annual Music in the Round festival of chamber music (May), and the Sheffield Children's Festival (late June or July).

Sheffield City Hall Barker's Pool ☎0114/278 9789, ⓦwww.sheffieldcityhall.com. Year-round programme of classical music, opera, mainstream concerts, comedy and club nights.

The Showroom 7 Paternoster Row ☎0114/275 7727, ⓦwww.showroom.org.uk. The biggest independent cinema outside London also has a relaxed café-restaurant on one side and a great bar on the other.

Listings

Hospital Royal Hallamshire Hospital, Glossop Rd (☎0114/271 1900), with NHS Walk-In centre.
Internet At Central Library, Surrey St ☎0114/273 4712 (Mon 10am–8pm, Tues & Thurs–Sat 9.30am–5.30pm, Wed 9.30am–8pm), and Mailboxes, Devonshire Green ☎0114/272 0777 (Mon–Fri 9am–5.30pm, Sat 9am–1pm), behind The Forum.
Laundry Sharrow Vale Launderette, 283 Sharrow Vale Rd ☎0114/266 3374.
Pharmacy Boots, 4–6 High St ☎0114/276 8333.

Police West Bar ☎0114/220 2020.
Post office 9 Norfolk Row.
Sports Sheffield Ski Village, Vale Rd ⓦwww .sheffieldskivillage.co.uk, is Europe's largest all-season ski resort, for skiing, boarding and snow-blading, plus bar and bistro. There's an Olympic-sized pool, plus leisure pool and slides at Ponds Forge, Sheaf St ⓦwww.ponds-forge .co.uk. Or visit The Foundry, 45 Mowbray St ⓦwww.cragx.com, a terrific indoor climbing centre.

Leeds and around

Yorkshire's commercial capital, and one of the fastest-growing cities in the country, **LEEDS** has undergone a radical transformation in recent years. There's still a true northern grit to its character, and in many of its dilapidated suburbs, but the grime has been removed from the impressive Victorian buildings and the city is revelling in its renaissance as a booming financial, commercial and cultural centre. An early market town, wool was traded here in medieval times by the monks of nearby Kirkstall Abbey. By the eighteenth century, the advent of canals and technical innovations such as the harnessing of steam power turned what had been a cottage industry into a dynamic large-scale economy. Leeds quickly boomed beyond its capacity to support its burgeoning population, and while the textile barons prospered, the city acquired a reputation for grimness that proved hard to shake off. In 1847 Charles Dickens described Leeds as "the beastliest place, one of the noisiest I know".

The renowned **shops, restaurants, bars and clubs** provide one focus of a visit to contemporary Leeds – it's certainly Yorkshire's top destination for a day or two of conspicuous consumption and indulgence. It's also long been the region's **cultural** centre, home to Opera North, the noted West Yorkshire Playhouse and a triennial international piano competition that ranks among the world's top musical events. Museums start with the hugely impressive **Royal Armouries**, which hold the national arms and armour collection, while the **City Art Gallery** has one of the best collections of British twentieth-century art outside London. The city itself deserves the best part of two days, longer if you plan to see any of the outlying attractions, which include the fascinating **Thackray Museum** of medicine, medieval **Kirkstall Abbey** and the art collection and grounds at **Temple Newsam**.

Leeds can also serve as the base for seeing some of West Yorkshire's most notable attractions, the prime example being **Harewood**, one of the country's great Georgian piles, which deserves a day's visit of its own. Two other trips out of the city make equally good excursions, depending on your interests – at the **National Coal Mining Museum** the north's industrial past is brought sharply into focus, while the bucolic **Yorkshire Sculpture Park** presents the country's greatest showing of sculptors Henry Moore and Barbara Hepworth.

Arrival, transport and information

Leeds Bradford Airport is eight miles northwest of the city; there's a bus (£2) every thirty minutes to the centre, or a taxi costs £17–20. National and local Metro trains use **Leeds Station** off City Square, which also houses the Gateway Yorkshire tourist office in the Arcade (Mon 10am–5.30pm, Tues–Sat 9am–5.30pm, Sun 10am–4pm; ☏0113/242 5242, ⓦwww.leeds.gov.uk, www .leedsliveitloveit.com). The **bus station** occupies a site to the east, behind Kirkgate Market, on St Peter's Street. Drivers will eventually be fed onto the City Centre Loop road and **parking** is available in the myriad signposted pay-and-display car parks.

The **Metro Travel Centres** at the bus and train stations have up-to-date service details for local transport or call **Metroline** (daily 7am–10pm; ☏0113/245 7676, ⓦwww.wymetro.com). **Passes** are available, and include bus/train day rovers and a good-value family day rover.

Accommodation

There's a good mix of **accommodation**, including inexpensive guest houses near the university campus, plenty of budget hotel chains, central business hotels and stylish designer or boutique hotels. Cheaper lodgings lie out to the northwest in the student area of Headingley, though these are a bus or taxi ride away. For **short breaks** and weekends away contact the tourist office's special booking line on ☏0800/808050. Rooms in self-catering **student apartments** at Clarence Dock (☏0113/343 6100, ⓦwww.universallyleeds.co.uk), near the Royal Armouries, are available every summer holiday (mid-July to mid-Sept; 2-night minimum stay costs £48, £21 a night thereafter).

42 The Calls 42 The Calls ☏0113/244 0099, ⓦwww.42thecalls.co.uk. Converted riverside grain mill, where rooms come with great beds and sharp bathrooms, though the cheapest rates are for the smallest "studio" rooms. Breakfast not included. Weekend rates start from £89 a night. ❼

Butlers/Boundary Cardigan Rd, Headingley, 1.5 miles northwest. Adjacent, associated hotels in a leafy suburban street offer good-value accommodation: cosy, smart, traditionally furnished en-suite rooms at *Butlers* (☏0113/274 4755, ⓦwww.butlershotel.co.uk) and cheaper lodgings at the *Boundary* (☏0113/275 7700, ⓦwww.boundaryhotel.co.uk), not all en-suite but nicely done with IKEA-style furnishings. Parking. Boundary ❷, Butlers ❸, superior rooms ❹

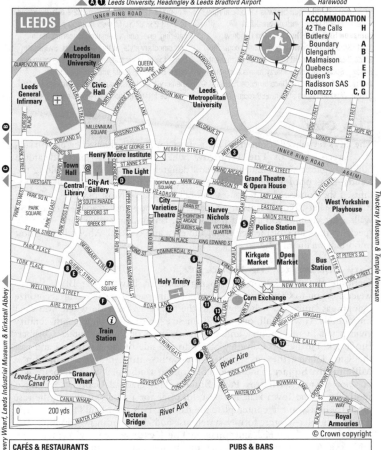

LEEDS

N

12

YORKSHIRE | Leeds and around

Brewery Wharf, Leeds Industrial Museum & Kirkstall Abbey

Thackray Museum & Temple Newsam

© Crown copyright

Glengarth 162 Woodsley Rd ☎0113/245 7940, ⓦwww.glengarthhotel.co.uk. The best of the bunch on Woodsley Rd, just behind the university, about a mile from the centre. Rooms are fairly basic, but a bit of care has been taken with the decor, and there's a friendly welcome. Negotiable prices for multi-night stays. Parking. ❷

Malmaison 1 Swinegate ☎0113/398 1000, ⓦwww.malmaison.com. Classy restored premises with the signature Malmaison style – plum and aubergine decor, big beds, power showers – plus brasserie and bar. Breakfast not included; weekend deals from £99. ❼

Quebecs 9 Quebec St ☎0113/244 8989, ⓦwww.theetoncollection.com. The ultimate city boutique lodgings, in the former Leeds and County Liberal Club. The glorious Victorian oak panelling and stained glass remain, offset by chic rooms with enormous beds, plumped pillows, and lovely bathrooms. Breakfast not included; weekend rates from £75. Very limited parking. ❼

Queen's City Sq ☎0845/074 0052, ⓦwww .qhotels.co.uk. Refurbished four-star Art Deco landmark, right in front of the station, with restaurant and parking. Rates are fairly flexible – even during the week you can sometimes get a

room from £75 (the code below is the official rate), while weekend prices include breakfast. **❼**
Radisson SAS No.1 The Light, The Headrow ⓣ0113/236 6000, ⓦ www.radissonsas.com. The Grade II-listed former HQ of the Leeds Permanent Building Society features snazzy rooms and suites that reflect high-tech, Art Deco or modern Italian design. Weekend rates start at £89 room only. **❼**

Roomzzz 12 Swinegate; also at 2 & 361 Burley Rd ⓣ0113/233 0400, ⓦ www.roomzzz.co.uk. Self-catering, one- and two-bedroom apartments in contemporary style, at three locations, Swinegate being the most central, the others a mile or so east of the centre. All come with great kitchens, memory foam beds, leather sofas, widescreen TVs and free Internet. Good weekend deals. Parking. **❺**

The City

The city's revitalized commercial life is most apparent in the packed pedestrianized streets south of **The Headrow**, where the Victorian and Edwardian buildings glitter with brand names and designer labels, while down along the **Leeds–Liverpool Canal** and **River Aire** a kind of post-industrial chic has infused the converted warehouses and railway arches. Most places – including the Art Gallery, Royal Armouries, markets and shopping arcades – are an easy walk apart, though you'll need transport for the outlying attractions – notably specialist museums of medicine and industry and Kirkstall Abbey, Leeds' most important medieval relic.

City Square to The Headrow

Opposite the train station, a prancing statue of Edward, the Black Prince, welcomes you to **City Square**, a smartened-up space that still retains its bronze nymph gas lamps. It's a short walk to the top of East Parade where you can't miss **Leeds Town Hall**, one of the finest expressions of nineteenth-century civic pride in the country and the masterpiece of local architect Cuthbert Broderick. Further up Calverley Street, to the side of the Town Hall and past the City Library, the city's turn-of-the-twenty-first-century contribution is **Millennium Square**, handsome enough in its landscaped, contemporary way, but not a patch on nearby **Park Square**. This graceful Georgian ensemble, southwest of the Town Hall, is a peaceful place for a sit-down among the rose bushes, where you can contemplate the flanking bulk of St Paul's House (1878), a red-brick Neo-Gothic former warehouse and cloth-cutting workshop.

East from the Town Hall and you're on **The Headrow**, the city's central spine, with the Art Gallery (see below) the major draw. At the junction with Cookridge Street, the former headquarters of the Leeds Permanent Building Society and adjacent buildings have been remodelled as **The Light**, a shopping, cinema, health club, hotel and bar-restaurant complex.

City Art Gallery and Henry Moore Institute

Leeds' **City Art Gallery** (Mon & Tues 10am–8pm, Wed noon–8pm, Thurs–Sat 10am–5pm, Sun 1–5pm; free; ⓦ www.leeds.gov.uk/artgallery) on The Headrow presents changing selections from the permanent collection of nineteenth- and twentieth-century art and sculpture, with an understandable bias towards pieces by Henry Moore and Barbara Hepworth, both former students at the Leeds School of Art; Moore's *Reclining Woman* lounges at the top of the steps outside the gallery. Local painter Atkinson Grimshaw also has a guaranteed showing, along with the founder of the Camden Town Group, Walter Sickert, his younger disciple Spencer Frederick Gore and later artists such as Stanley Spencer and Wyndham Lewis. There's a café in the restored Victorian tiled hall, and direct access to the **Craft Centre and Design Gallery** below (Tues–Fri 10am–5pm, Sat 10am–4pm; free), where changing displays of contemporary jewellery, ceramics and applied art are on show.

▲ Victoria Quarter, Leeds

From the City Art Gallery, a slender bridge connects to the adjacent **Henry Moore Institute** (daily 10am–5.30pm, Wed until 9pm; free; ⓦ www .henry-moore-fdn.co.uk), which has its own entrance on The Headrow. It's devoted to showcasing temporary exhibitions of sculpture from all periods and nationalities, and not, as you might imagine, pieces by the masterful Moore himself – for those, best visit the Yorkshire Sculpture Park (see p.786).

Most visitors make a beeline for the brimming, shop-filled arcades on either side of pedestrianized **Briggate**. These nineteenth-century palaces of marble, mahogany, stained glass and mosaics have been magnificently restored and perhaps the most splendid of all is the light-flooded **Victoria Quarter** (⊛www.vqleeds.com) – dubbed the "Knightsbridge of the North" – with Harvey Nichols (107–111 Briggate) as its designer lodestone. Compatriots in style include Gieves & Hawkes (38–40 Queen Victoria St), Vivienne Westwood (15–17 County Arcade) and Luis Vuitton (98–99 Briggate), while stylish *Anthony's Patisserie* (37 Queen Victoria St) is the favoured place to take the weight off your arms and muse on exactly how much those shoes just cost.

Across Vicar Lane, **Kirkgate Market** (⊛www.leedsmarket.com; closes 2pm Wed & all Sun) is the largest market in the north of England. Housed in a superb Edwardian building, it's a descendant of the medieval woollen markets that were instrumental in making Leeds the early focus of the region's textile industry – if you're after tripe, haberdashery or big knickers, there's no better place. The **open market** behind here (closed Wed & Sun), incidentally, is where Michael Marks set up stall in 1884 with the slogan "don't ask the price, it's a penny" – an enterprise that blossomed into the present-day retail giant Marks & Spencer. There's also a farmers' market here on the first and third Sunday of the month.

At the bottom of the street, on the corner of Vicar Lane and Duncan Street, the elliptical, domed **Corn Exchange** (open daily) was built in 1863, also by Cuthbert Broderick, whose design leaned heavily on his studies of Paris's corn exchange. This is now a hip market for jewellery, retro clothes, furnishings, music and other bits and bobs – extra craft stores open up at weekends.

Granary Wharf to the Royal Armouries

The biggest transformation in Leeds has been along both sides of the **Leeds–Liverpool Canal** and **River Aire**, formerly a stagnant relic of industrial decline. At **Granary Wharf**, a couple of minutes' walk from the train station, specialist shops fill the extensive cobbled, vaulted arches (the "Dark Arches"), while every weekend and bank holiday a market with stalls, bands and entertainers spills out onto the canal basin. **Brewery Wharf**, on the south side (or "Left Bank" as Leeds would like it to be known), sports a welter of bars and brasseries, while further east along the river beckons the glass turret and gun-metal grey bulk of the **Royal Armouries** (daily 10am–5pm; free; ⊛www.armouries.org.uk). Purpose-built to house the arms and armour collection from the Tower of London, it's a hugely adventurous museum that requires a leap of faith – discard the notion that all you'll see are casefuls of weapons because you're in for a treat. Themed galleries cover concepts such as "War" and "Hunting", with displays – ranging from gun emplacements to Mughal Indian elephant armour – backed up by intelligent commentary, video exhibits and documentary evidence. Interpretations and demonstrations take place throughout the day, so you might learn smallsword techniques from a Georgian swordsmaster or sixteenth-century javelin skills in the outdoor Tiltyard. It's an easy ten-minute walk along the river to the museum from the centre; there's parking outside.

Outlying attractions

The **Thackray Museum** on Beckett Street (daily 10am–5pm, last admission 3pm; £5.50; ⊛www.thackraymuseum.org), next to St James' Hospital, is sited in a former workhouse a mile east of the city centre; take bus #41 or #50 from

The Headrow or #42 from Infirmary Street (off City Square). Essentially a medical history museum, it's a hugely entertaining place with displays on subjects as diverse as the history of the hearing aid and the workings of the human intestine. It's gruesome, too, with film of a Victorian limb amputation in a gallery called "Pain, pus and blood". Needless to say, children love it.

For Leeds' industrial past, visit the vast **Leeds Industrial Museum**, two miles west of the centre off Canal Road (Tues–Sat 10am–5pm, Sun 1–5pm; £3; ☎0113/263 7861, ⓦwww.leeds.gov.uk/armleymills), which runs between Armley and Kirkstall Road – take bus #5, #14 or #67. There's been a mill on the site since at least the seventeenth century, and the present building was one of the world's largest woollen mills until its closure in 1969.

You should also see the bucolic ruins and cloisters of **Kirkstall Abbey** (dawn to dusk; free), which was built between 1152 and 1182 by Cistercian monks from Fountains Abbey. The former gatehouse now provides the setting for the family-friendly **Abbey House Museum** (Tues–Fri & Sun 10am–5pm, Sat noon–5pm; £3.50; ⓦwww.leeds.gov.ukabbeyhouse), where two floors take a look at Victorian Leeds. The abbey lies about three miles northwest of the city centre on Abbey Road; take the first turning right after the abbey, or bus #33, #33A or #670.

Four miles east of the city, the Tudor-Jacobean house of **Temple Newsam** (Tues–Sun 10.30am–4/5pm; £3.50; ☎0113/264 7321, ⓦwww.leeds.gov.uk /templenewsam) shows many of the paintings and much of the decorative art owned by Leeds City Art Gallery. There are over 1500 acres on the estate (park open daily dawn to dusk; free), which also contains Europe's largest **rare-breeds farm** (closed Mon; £3). There's an hourly Sunday bus service to the house; otherwise, parking costs £3.50.

Eating, drinking and nightlife

Eating out in Leeds has been transformed in recent years, with many old warehouses and grain mills converted into up-to-the-minute **restaurants and brasseries**. Late-opening **café-bars** infest the centre and exploit the city's relaxed licensing laws to the full. The best of the city's **pubs** are the ornate Victorian ale-houses in which Leeds specializes, and when these close you can move on to one of the city's DJ bars or **clubs**, many of which have a nationwide reputation – not least because Leeds lets you dance until 5 or 6am most weekends. For information about **what's on**, your best bets are the fortnightly listings magazine *The Leeds Guide* (ⓦwww.leedsguide.co.uk) or the daily *Yorkshire Evening Post*.

Café-bars and restaurants

Anthony's 19 Boar Lane ☎0113/245 5922. The foodie's choice – earthy flavours and ingredients dominate in the city's hottest restaurant, so expect squab (baby pigeon), offal and innovative combinations, immaculately presented. It's pricey, but lunch (3 courses for under £25) is a steal, while at *Anthony's at Flannel's* (68–78 Vicar Lane ☎0113/242 8732; closed Mon) there's moderately priced brunch, lunch and afternoon tea with all the flair of its big brother. Very expensive.

Art's Café 42 Call Lane ☎0113/243 8243. *Art's* kickstarted the Call Lane scene and it's still a relaxed hangout for drinks, dinner or a lazy

Sunday brunch. Mediterranean flavours dominate the well-priced menu, and the wine list is excellent. Moderate.

Brasserie 44 44 The Calls ☎0113/234 3232. Informal Modern British bar and brasserie, serving everything from pan-fried mackerel to fancied-up duck confit. Closed Sun. Expensive.

Little Tokyo 24 Central Rd ☎0113/243 9090. Leeds' favourite Japanese restaurant has an enormous menu – sushi, noodles, curries, grills and salads – with main courses around £7, or bento box set meals from £12. Moderate.

Norman Bar 36 Call Lane ☎0113/234 3988. A boho-chic interior – cast-iron girders to cuckoo clock – plus juice bar, Asian noodle/stir-fry/dim sum menu, and varied club nights, add up to one of the city's unique spots. The "Daily Norman" deal (all day Mon & Tues–Fri noon–3pm) provides a meal for a fiver. Moderate.

Restaurant Bar and Grill The Old Post Office, 3 City Square ☎0113/244 9625. The bank of wine bottles in the huge window draws you into this classy post office makeover. The menu ranges from Old Spot sausages, calves' liver and grills to Italian, Thai and North African dishes. Expensive.

Salvo's 115 Otley Rd, Headingley ☎0113/275 5017, ⓦwww.salvos.co.uk. Pizza in Leeds to a local means *Salvo's* – as authentic as they come – though there's a classy menu covering other Italian dishes as well and a choice list of daily specials. It really is worth the trek out from the centre. A daytime café-deli a couple of doors down offers lighter bites. Closed Sun. Expensive.

Sous le Nez en Ville Quebec House, 9 Quebec St ☎0113/244 0108. Housed in the splendid red-brick building of the former Liberal Club, this basement wine bar/restaurant is particularly strong on fish – there are always half a dozen special starters and mains, plus a wide bistro-style menu. Closed Sun. Expensive.

Bars and pubs

Bar Fibre 168 Lower Briggate ☎0870/120 0888, ⓦwww.barfibre.com. Leeds' finest gay bar comes with plenty of attitude, plus outside balcony, DJs most nights and dancing until midnight, 2am at weekends. It's also the pre-club bar for Leeds' most dramatic club night, Federation (first Sat of month) at *Mission*, 8–13 Heaton's Court.

Boutique 11-5 Hirsts Yard, Briggate. Small, perfectly formed venue with outdoor glass-topped tables revealing jelly babies, tennis balls, petals and the like. Expect equally diverse cocktails. Closed Sun.

Elbow Room 64 Call Lane. Funk and food, and a very cool place to play pool.

Milo 10–12 Call Lane ☎0113/245 7101. Unpretentious, offbeat bar with DJs most evenings, ringing the changes from old soul and reggae to indie and electronica.

🏃 **Mojo** 18 Merrion St. A great bar, pure and simple, with classic tunes ("music for the people") and a classy drinks menu to match.

North 24 New Briggate. The city's beer specialist is more new Leeds than old, but the basics are familiar: a massive selection of guest beers (more Belgian than bitter) plus cold meats and cheeses to nibble on.

Sandinista 5 Cross Belgrave St. Relaxed and unpretentious Latin American bar that suits an older crowd. Eclectic music, good champagne and rum cocktails, breakfasts, lunches and a great tapas menu.

🏃 **Whitelocks** Turk's Head Yard, off Briggate. Leeds' oldest and most atmospheric pub (tucked up an alley) retains its traditional decor and a good choice of beers.

Clubs and live music

Cockpit Bridge House, Swinegate ☎0113/244 1573, ⓦwww.thecockpit.co.uk. The city's best live music venue, plus assorted indie/new wave club nights.

Creation 55 Cookridge St ☎0113/242 7272, ⓦwww.creation-leeds.co.uk. Hosts high-profile live bands as well as club nights, chart to cheese, in the city's largest club.

Hifi 2 Central Rd ☎0113/242 7353, ⓦwww .thehificlub.co.uk. Small, relaxed club, playing everything from Stax and Motown to hip-hop or drum'n'bass, and with live music on selected days. Also check out the indie/alternative associate club *Wire* at 2-8 Call Lane (ⓦwww.wireclub.co.uk).

Mint Club 8 Harrison St ☎0113/244 3168. Up-to-the-minute beats (there's a "no-cheese" policy) and the best chill-out space in the city.

Oceana 16–18 Woodhouse Lane ☎0113/243 8229, ⓦwww.oceanaclubs.com. You've got the choice of dance, chart, R&B and indie in the Venetian Grand Ballroom, 70s and 80s disco on Europe's largest illuminated dance floor, or bars in the style of a Parisian boudoir or Aspen lodge. What's keeping you?

The Wardrobe St Peter's Sq ☎0113/383 8800, ⓦwww.thewardrobe.co.uk. Self-styled "café, bar, kitchen, club" with live jazz and soul acts, and DJs playing the best funk, soul, jazz and hip-hop.

The Warehouse 19–21 Somers St ☎0113/246 8287. House, electro and techno sounds bring in clubbers from all over the country, especially for Saturday's Technique.

Arts, festivals and entertainment

Temple Newsam hosts numerous concerts and events, from plays to rock gigs and opera, while at Kirkstall Abbey every summer there's a Shakespeare Festival (ⓦwww.britishshakespearecompany.com/leeds) with open-air productions of the Bard's works. Roundhay Park is the other large outdoor venue for concerts, while **Millennium Square** hosts gigs, festivals, markets and other events, including the annual Ice Cube, a temporary outdoor ice rink and café (mid-Jan to end-Feb). Bramham Park, ten miles east of the city, hosts the annual Leeds Festival (@www.leedsfestival.com) over the August bank holiday weekend with rock/indie music on five stages. The same weekend heralds the **West Indian Carnival** in Chapeltown, beaten in size only by Notting Hill.

Venues

City Varieties Swan St, Briggate @0845/644 1881, @www.cityvarieties.co.uk. One of the country's last surviving music halls, though these days it's more tribute bands, comedians and cabaret – great building and bar though.

Grand Theatre and Opera House 46 New Briggate @0870/121 4901, @www.leeds.gov.uk /grandtheatre. The regular base of Opera North (@www.operanorth.co.uk) and Northern Ballet (@www.northernballettheatre.co.uk) also puts on a full range of theatrical productions.

Hyde Park Picture House Brudenell Rd, Headingley @0113/275 2045,

@www.hydeparkpicturehouse.co.uk. The place to come for classic cinema with independent and art-house shows alongside more mainstream films; bus #56.

Leeds Town Hall The Headrow @0113/224 3801, @www.leedsconcertseason.com. Supports an annual international concert season of great distinction and is the venue for Leeds' internationally renowned piano competition (next in 2009).

West Yorkshire Playhouse Quarry Hill @0113/213 7700, @www.wyp.org.uk. The city's most innovative theatre has two stages, plus bar, restaurant and café, and hosts a wide range of productions and premieres of local works.

Listings

Airport Information and flight enquiries @0113/250 9696, @www.lbia.co.uk.

Hospital Leeds General Infirmary, Great George St @0113/243 2799.

Internet There's free access at the Central Library, Calverley St @0113/247 8274 (call for hrs).0

Laundry Woodsley Launderette, 6 Woodsley Rd @0113/242 0238.

Pharmacy Boots, Leeds Station Concourse @0113/242 1713 (6am–midnight).

Police Millgarth Police Station, Millgarth St @0845/606 0606.

Post office Branches on New York St, opposite Kirkgate market, and on Albion St, junction Merrion St.

Taxis Taxis are available 24hr at the train station, outside the bus station, and on New Briggate.

Out of the city

Give yourself another couple of days in Leeds and you can do justice to the region's major draws, though they're also all easily seen en route to your next destination – **Harewood** lies on the Harrogate road, while the **National Coal Mining Museum** and **Yorkshire Sculpture Park**, both south of Leeds, are easily reached from the M1. Only Harewood can straightforwardly be accessed by public transport from Leeds.

Harewood House

The stately home of **Harewood**, seven miles north of Leeds (mid-March to Oct daily 11am–4.30pm, grounds & bird garden 10am–5pm; July, Aug & bank hol weekends £13.15, otherwise £11.30; grounds & bird garden only £10.90/£8.80; @0113/218 1010, @www.harewood.org), was designed and decorated by one of the greatest architectural teams ever assembled. Conceived in 1759 by York architect John Carr, the building was finished by Robert Adam, the furniture made by Thomas Chippendale and the landscaped gardens laid out by Capability Brown. To cap it all, a sweeping terrace designed by Sir Charles Barry (architect of the Houses of Parliament) overlooks the gardens. It's still the home of the Earl and Countess of

Harewood, who let in the great unwashed in return for nothing more than a sizeable chunk of money. To be fair, there's an enormous amount to see and do, with daily tours and talks, and current exhibitions, included in the entrance fee. As well as the grand state and private rooms, the old kitchen and servants' quarters can be viewed, while outside in the magnificent **grounds** is an adventure playground and renowned **bird garden**. Here, four acres of aviaries cage over 150 species – the penguins get fed at 2pm.

There are frequent buses to Harewood from Leeds (including the #36, every 20min, 30min on Sun), and if you come by bus or bike you'll get a fifty-percent discount on admission (keep your bus ticket). The house is near the junction of the A659 and the A61 Leeds to Harrogate road, and parking is free.

National Coal Mining Museum

While the gentry enjoyed the comforts of life in grand houses like Harewood, generations of Yorkshiremen sweated out a living underground just a few miles distant. Mining is now little more than a memory in most parts of Yorkshire – the industry crushed by government policy in the 1980s – but visitors can get all too vivid an idea of pit life through the ages at the excellent **National Coal Mining Museum** (daily 10am–5pm; free; Ⓦ www.ncm.org .uk), about ten miles south of Leeds at Overton, halfway between Wakefield and Huddersfield (on the A642, signposted from the M1). Based in a former pit, Caphouse Colliery, the highlight is an underground mine tour (90min, warm clothes required; arrive early in school hols; last tour 3.15pm) with a former miner as your guide, though the museum has no shortage of other attractions, from machinery demonstrations to a stableful of retired pit ponies.

Yorkshire Sculpture Park

Another Yorkshire country estate, at West Bretton outside Wakefield, now serves as the **Yorkshire Sculpture Park** (daily 10am–5/6pm; free, but parking £4; Ⓦ www.ysp.co.uk), a mile from the M1 (junction 38). Trails and paths run across 500 acres of eighteenth-century parkland, past open-air "gallery spaces" for

▲ Yorkshire Sculpture Park

some of Britain's most famous sculptors. The two big local names represented here are Henry Moore (1898–1986), born in nearby Castleford, and his contemporary Barbara Hepworth (1903–75), from Wakefield, but the works of other artists also rise to the grandeur of the surroundings – in particular the large figurative granite sculptures of Ronald Rae, which adorn the Access Sculpture Trail (possible for wheelchairs/prams). The **Visitor Centre** near the car park is the place to check on current exhibitions and pick up a park map – the restaurant here has views over Moore's monumental pieces. There's direct access from the centre to the New Gallery – a concrete, glass and sandstone space with a turf roof that blends in with the gardens' formal terrace. Other exhibitions are held in the Longside Gallery (during exhibitions 11am–3/4pm; free), a former indoor riding arena on the estate, used by London's Hayward Gallery to present displays from the Arts Council's collection – catch the shuttle bus from the YSP car park or it's a two-kilometre walk through the park.

Bradford and around

First and foremost, **BRADFORD** has always been a working town, booming in tandem with the Industrial Revolution, when it changed in decades from a rural seat of woollen manufacture to a polluted metropolis. In its Victorian heyday it was the world's biggest producer of worsted cloth, its skyline etched black with mill chimneys, and its hills clogged with some of the foulest back-to-back houses of any northern city. Contemporary Bradford is valiantly rinsing away its associations with urban decrepitude, and while it can hardly yet be compared with neighbouring Leeds as a visitor attraction it might ultimately succeed on its own distinct terms – plans are in place to restyle the entire city centre as an urban park and cultural quarter. In the meantime, in the **National Museum of Photography, Film and Television** and the nearby **model village of Saltaire**, Bradford has two of West Yorkshire's most compelling attractions. You should also hang around at least long enough to sample one of Bradford's famous curry houses – legacy of the city's large population with roots in the Indian subcontinent. Bradford and its textile industry has always been a lure for immigrants: German and Jewish merchants, and Irish workers in the nineteenth century, and significant numbers of men from India, Pakistan and Bangladesh in the 1950s and 1960s. They later sent for their families, making Bradford perhaps the most multicultural centre in the UK outside London, with people of south Asian origin accounting for around 18 percent of the conurbation's total population.

The City

The focal point of the city centre is **Centenary Square**, commemorating not the founding of the original town – the "broad ford" was known before the arrival of the Romans – but the hundredth anniversary of the granting of its city charter by Queen Victoria in 1897. The **City Hall** behind shouts its Victorian credentials, the work of local architects Lockwood and Mawson, who also provided Bradford with **St George's Hall**, a Neoclassical extravaganza on Bridge Street still in use as a concert hall. Edwardian audiences later flocked to the minaret-topped **Alhambra Theatre**, across Princes Way, also splendidly restored.

Just across from here, on the rise, is the **National Museum of Photography, Film and Television** (Tues–Sun 10am–6pm; free; ☎0870/701 0200; ⊛www.nationalmediamuseum.org.uk), one of the most visited national museums outside London, which wraps itself around one of Britain's largest cinema screens showing daily **IMAX** and 3D film screenings (£6.95). The museum itself is crammed with memorabilia and hardware, including the world's biggest lens, the first example of a moving picture and other superlatives. Exhibitions are devoted to every nuance of film and television, including topics like digital imaging, light and optics, and computer animation, while there are detours into the mechanics of advertising and news-gathering – even a searchable archive of classic British TV. The **Pictureville** cinema at the museum has a year-round repertory programme (films from £5) and hosts several major film festivals, notably the Bradford Film Festival in March and Bite the Mango in September.

Back across Centenary Square, a walk past the Venetian-Gothic **Wool Exchange** building on Market Street provides ample evidence of the wealth of nineteenth-century Bradford. The building is now almost entirely taken up by a Waterstone's, its main hall stacked with books and overlooked by a statue of Richard Cobden, the statesman and economist who led the 1838–46 campaign against the restrictive Corn Laws. Over to the east, north of Leeds Road, the tight grid of streets that is **Little Germany** retains an enclave of warehouse and office buildings in which transplanted German and Jewish merchants once plied their wool trade.

For further insights into what once made the city tick, visit the **Bradford Industrial Museum** (Tues–Sat 10am–5pm, Sun noon–5pm; free; ⓦwww .bradfordmuseums.org/industrialmuseum) in the old Victorian Moorside Mills, on Moorside Road in Eccleshill, three miles northeast of the centre. Exhibitions and special events document the city's industrial heritage, alongside working textile machinery, surviving examples of the former workers' cottages, and shire horses hauling a selection of vintage trams and buses. Bus #896 from the Interchange runs to the museum (not Sun).

Practicalities

Trains and buses both arrive at **Bradford Interchange** off Bridge Street, a little to the south of the city-centre grid. There's also a smaller station at **Forster Square**, across the city, for trains to Keighley (for Haworth). The tourist office (Mon 10am–5pm, Tues–Sat 9.30am–5pm; ☎01274/433678, ⓦwww .visitbradford.com), located in Centenary Square's City Hall, is three minutes' signposted walk from the Interchange or five minutes from Forster Square. The major annual event is the **Bradford Mela** (ⓦwww.bradfordmela.org.uk), a two-day celebration of the arts, culture, food and sports of the Indian subcontinent, held in June or July.

Restaurants

Akbar's 1276–1278 Leeds Rd ☎01274/773311. A buzzing, upmarket balti house located east of Bradford, on the Leeds Road in Thornbury, a short drive away. Moderate.

Kashmir 27 Morley St ☎01274/726513. Two minutes up the road that runs between the Alhambra and the National Museum, this claims to have been Bradford's first curry house. Like many others in town it's unlicensed, though you can take your own booze. Open until 3am. Inexpensive.

Mumtaz 386–400 Great Horton Rd ☎01274/571861. Spacious contemporary restaurant where you buy your dish by weight – 220g or 440g, the larger portion serving two – and the sweet *lassi* is legendary. There's no alcohol allowed, and it's a twenty-minute walk up towards the university, but you won't be disappointed. Open until midnight. Inexpensive.

Saltaire

Three miles out of Bradford towards Keighley, along the A650 to the north, no one should pass up the chance to drop in on **SALTAIRE**, a model industrial village and textile mill built by the industrialist Sir Titus Salt. Trains to Saltaire Station run from Bradford Forster Square, or take bus #679 from the Interchange, which stops in Saltaire village.

The village (still lived in today) is a perfectly preserved 25-acre realization of one man's vision of an industrial utopia. Saltaire was built between 1851 and 1876, modelled on buildings of the Italian Renaissance, a period evoked because of its perceived similarities with nineteenth-century Britain, insofar as the cultural and social advances of both eras were made possible by the commercial acumen of textile barons. **Salt's Mill**, larger than St Paul's Cathedral in London, was the biggest factory in the world when it opened in 1853. It was surrounded by schools, hospitals, a train station, parks, baths and wash-houses, plus 45 almshouses and around 850 homes. For all Salt's philanthropic vigour, the scheme was highly paternalistic: of the village's 22 streets, for example, all – bar Victoria and Albert streets – were named after members of his family. Further to the master's whim, the church was the first public building to be finished and, most tellingly of all, the village contained not a single pub.

Salt's Mill remains the fulcrum of the village, the focus of which is the **1853 Gallery** (daily 10am–5.30/6pm; free; Ⓦ www.saltsmill.org.uk), three floors given over to the world's largest retrospective collection of the works of Bradford-born **David Hockney**. There are art, craft and furniture shops to browse in, plus *Salt's Diner* on the second floor with its Hockney-designed logo, menu and crockery, and the posher *Café Opera* on the third.

Haworth

Of English literary shrines, probably only Stratford sees more visitors than the quarter of a million who swarm annually into the village of **HAWORTH** to tramp the cobbles once trodden by the Brontë sisters. During the summer the village's steep, cobbled Main Street is lost under huge crowds, herded by multilingual signs around the various stations on the Brontë trail.

Of these, the **Brontë Parsonage Museum**, at the top of the main street (daily 10/11am–5/5.30pm; £5.50, Ⓦ www.bronte.info), is the obvious focus, a modest Georgian house bought by Patrick Brontë in 1820 to bring up his family. After the tragic early loss of his wife and two eldest daughters, the surviving four children – Anne, Emily, Charlotte and their dissipated brother, Branwell – spent most of their short lives in the place, which is furnished as it was in their day, and filled with the sisters' pictures, books, manuscripts and personal treasures. You can see the sofa on which Emily is said to have died in 1848, aged just 28, for example, and the footstool on which she sat outside on fine days writing *Wuthering Heights*.

The bluff **parish church** in front of the parsonage – substantially rebuilt since the Brontës lived here – contains the family vault; Charlotte was married here in 1854. At the **Sunday School**, between the parsonage and the church, Charlotte, Anne and even Branwell did weekly teaching stints; Branwell, however, was undoubtedly more at home in the **Black Bull**, a pub within staggering distance of the parsonage near the top of Main Street. He got his opium at the pharmacist's over the road (now a lace shop).

Patrick Prunty or Bronty (it's unclear which) was born in Ireland and became a schoolmaster at the age of 16. He later won a place at St John's, Cambridge, where he changed his name to **Brontë**, perhaps influenced by naval hero Lord Nelson, who was made the Duke of Brontë. Later ordained, the Reverend Brontë, and his Cornish wife Maria, took up a living at Thornton, just outside Bradford, where the four youngest of their six children – Maria, Elizabeth, Charlotte, Branwell, Emily and Anne – were born between 1816 and 1820. The house, at 72–74 Market St, still stands. Later that year, the Brontë family moved into the draughty **parsonage** in nearby Haworth.

Mrs Brontë died within the year and her sister was despatched to help look after the children. The four oldest girls were sent away to school, but withdrawn after first Maria, then Elizabeth, died after falling ill. The surviving daughters, and the cosseted Branwell, were kept at home, where they amused themselves by making up convoluted stories and writing miniature books. As they successively came of age, the girls took up short-lived jobs as governesses at various local schools; Charlotte and Emily even spent a year in Brussels, learning French. **Branwell**, meanwhile, was already sowing the dissolute seeds of his disappointing future: he had a certain talent for art, but failed to apply to study at the Royal Academy, got into debt, and then spent two years as a junior stationmaster near Halifax but was later dismissed in disgrace. He then took a tutor's job but was dismissed again after developing what was darkly referred to as an "unwise passion" for his employer's wife. He retreated to Haworth, made himself overly familiar with the beer in the *Black Bull* and began experimenting with drugs.

Charlotte's, Emily's and Anne's continuing attempts to amuse themselves with their writings led to the private publication, in 1846, of a series of poems. They used the (male) pseudonyms Currer, Ellis and Acton Bell – corresponding to their own initials – and though few copies of the collection were ever sold, the little volume acted as a catalyst. Keeping the pseudonym, **Charlotte** wrote a novel the same year, which was rejected by various publishers; but her *Jane Eyre*, submitted in 1847, was an instant success. **Emily**'s *Wuthering Heights* and **Anne**'s *Agnes Grey* received similar acclaim the same year; Anne's second novel, the better-known *Tenant of Wildfell Hall*, was published in 1848. As far as the public was concerned, the brilliant Bell brothers were a publishing sensation.

But the next two years destroyed the family, as it was ravaged by consumption. First Branwell, who had sunk ever deeper into addictive misery and ill health, died in September 1848, followed by Emily in December of that year, and Anne in May of the following year. Charlotte lived on for another six years, writing two more novels – *Shirley* (1849) and *Villette* (1853) – and becoming something of a literary figure once she had revealed her identity, making friends with fellow author Elizabeth Gaskell, who later wrote Charlotte's biography. Charlotte finally **married** Reverend Brontë's curate, Arthur Bell Nicholls, who moved into the parsonage, but she died after nine months of marriage in the early stages of pregnancy. The Reverend Brontë lived on until 1861 – the entire family, except Anne (who is buried in Scarborough), lies in the **Brontë vault** in the village church, next to the house.

The most popular local walk runs to **Brontë Falls** and **Bridge**, reached via West Lane and a track from the village, and to **Top Withens**, a mile beyond, a ruin fancifully (but erroneously) thought to be the model for Wuthering Heights (allow 3hr for the round trip). The moorland setting, however, beautifully evokes the flavour of the book, and to enjoy it further you could walk on another two and a half miles to **Ponden Hall**, perhaps the Thrushcross Grange of *Wuthering Heights* (this section of path, incidentally, forms part of the Pennine Way).

The **Keighley and Worth Valley Railway** runs steam trains (Easter week, school hols, July & Aug daily; rest of the year Sat & Sun) along a five-mile stretch of track between Keighley and Oxenhope, stopping at Haworth en route. The restored stations are a delight, with sections of the line etched into the memory of those who recall the film of E. Nesbit's *The Railway Children*, which was shot here in 1970. Valley footpaths run between the stations at Oakworth, Haworth and Oxenhope, allowing you to make a day of your reminiscences. Regular trains from Leeds or Bradford's Forster Square run to Keighley, where you change onto the branch line for the **steam services** (day rover ticket £12; ☎01535/645214, recorded information ☎01535/647777, ⓦwww.kwvr.co.uk).

Practicalities

Haworth is eight miles northwest of Bradford. To get here by bus, take the #662 from Bradford Interchange to Keighley (every 10min), and change there for the #663, #664 or #665 (every 20min), which drop at various points in the streets immediately below the cobbled Main Street. On Sundays, only the #663 and #665 operate (every 30min). However, the nicest way of getting here is by **train**, using the steam trains of the **Keighley and Worth Valley Railway** (see box above); the station is half a mile from the upper village – cross the footbridge from the station and follow Butt Lane up the side of the park to the bottom of **Main Street**. Steep Main Street and its continuation, **West Lane**, form one long run of gift and teashops, cafés and guest houses, with the busy Haworth **tourist office** at the top at 2–4 West Lane (daily 9.30am–5/5.30pm; ☎01535/642329, ⓦwww.haworth-village.org.uk).

Accommodation and eating

Aitches 11 West Lane ☎01535/642501, ⓦwww .aitches.co.uk. This stone-built Victorian house offers five stylish rooms with plenty of drapery, and has an attached restaurant that serves meals to residents (set menu £18). ❸

Apothecary 86 Main St ☎01535/643642, ⓦwww.theapothecaryguesthouse.co.uk. Traditional guest house opposite the church, whose rear rooms, breakfast room and attached café have splendid moorland views. ❷

Haworth YHA Longlands Hall ☎0870/770 5858, ⓔhaworth@yha.org.uk. The former mansion of a Victorian mill owner, overlooking the village a mile from the centre at Longlands Drive, Lees Lane, off the Keighley road. Bradford buses stop on the main road nearby. Weekends only Nov to mid-Feb. Dorm beds from £8.95, though summer up to £17.95.

Old Registry 4 Main St ☎01535/646503, ⓦwww .theoldregistryhaworth.co.uk. Flower-bedecked and picturesque old building at the bottom of Main Street, with tastefully presented accommodation – there's a four-poster bed in every room and co-ordinated furnishings throughout. Two-night minimum stay at weekends. ❻

Weaver's 15 West Lane ☎01535/643822, ⓦwww.weaversmallhotel.co.uk. A renowned restaurant-with-rooms operation housed in a converted row of weavers' cottages. Meals are served Tues–Sat dinner, plus Wed, Thurs, Fri & Sun lunch – good modern northern cuisine using local ingredients; dinner from around £25 a head, plus drinks. It's essential to book ahead. ❺

The Yorkshire Dales

The **Yorkshire Dales** – "dales" from the Viking word *dalr* (valley) – form a varied upland area of limestone hills and pastoral valleys at the heart of the Pennines. Protected as a national park since 1954, there are over twenty main dales covering 680 square miles, crammed with opportunities for outdoor

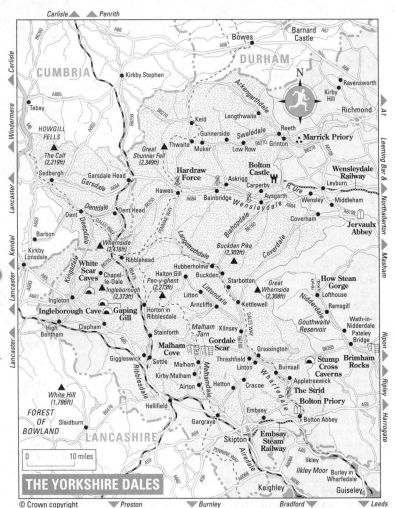

THE YORKSHIRE DALES

© Crown copyright

activities, including local hikes and long-distance footpaths, a specially designated cycle way, plus caving, pony-trekking and other more specialist pursuits.

Most approaches are from the industrial towns to the south, via the superbly engineered **Settle–Carlisle Railway**, or along the main A65 road from towns such as **Skipton**, **Settle** and **Ingleton**. This makes southern dales like **Wharfedale** the most visited, while neighbouring **Malhamdale** is also immensely popular, thanks to the fascinating scenery squeezed into its narrow confines around **Malham**, perhaps the single most visited village in the region. **Ribblesdale**, approached from Settle, is more sombre, its villages popular with hikers intent on tackling the Dales' famous **Three Peaks** – the mountains of Pen-y-ghent, Ingleborough and Whernside. To the northwest lies the more remote **Dentdale**, one of the least known but most beautiful of the valleys. Moving north, there are two parallel dales, **Wensleydale** and **Swaledale**, the latter pushing Dentdale as the most rewarding overall target. Both flow east, with Swaledale's lower stretches encompassing **Richmond**, an appealing historic town with a terrific castle. Finally, outside the national park boundary, to the east, is **Nidderdale**, which is relatively seldom visited, even though its beautiful upper reaches stand comparison with its more famous neighbours.

Public transport throughout the Dales is good, though bus services are limited in winter. However, countless special summer weekend and bank holiday services (usually May–Sept, peaking in school holidays) connect almost everywhere. Pick up the free **timetables** (Ⓦ www.dalesbus.org) available at tourist offices across the region, or consult Ⓦ www.traveldales.org.uk. Keep your bus ticket and you'll be able to claim discounts at businesses across the Dales – look for "Dales Bus Discount" window stickers. Many seasonal weekend bus services also offer **Dales Rover** tickets for unlimited travel, from £5 per day – buy on board the bus.

There are useful **National Park Centres** (Ⓦ www.yorkshiredales.org.uk) at Grassington, Aysgarth Falls, Malham, Reeth and Hawes. In addition, there are national park **information points** in shops, post offices and cafés throughout the area. For a different view of the Dales, consult Ⓦ www.outofoblivion.org .uk, which looks in depth at the archeology and history of the national park, and from which you can download walking trails ("podwalks").

The Pennine Way cuts right through the heart of the Dales, and the region is crossed by the Coast-to-Coast Walk, but the principal local route is the **Dales Way** (Ⓦ www.dalesway.org.uk), an 84-mile footpath from Ilkley to Bowness-on-Windermere in the Lake District. Shorter **guided walks** (5–13 miles, every Sun & bank hol Mon, April–Oct) are organized by the National Park Authority and Dalesbus Ramblers (Ⓦ www.dalesbusramblers.org.uk). The Dales also has a network of over 500 miles of bridleways, byways and other routes for **mountain bikers** to explore (Ⓦ www.mtbthedales.org.uk). The main touring cycle route is the circular 130-mile **Yorkshire Dales Cycle Way** (Ⓦ www.cyclethedales .org.uk), which starts and finishes in Skipton.

Skipton

SKIPTON, southernmost town of the Dales, is best visited to coincide with one of its four weekly **market days** (Mon, Wed, Fri & Sat), when the streets and pubs are filled with what seems like half the Dales' population. There's a farmers' market on the first Sunday of the month, and even a Mart Theatre on the outskirts of town (Ⓦ www.themarttheatre.org.uk), the only theatre to operate in a working auction market. Medieval and Christmas markets in December are an enjoyable feature, too.

Sceptone, or "Sheeptown" – the annual Sheep Day (first Sun in July) celebrates its ovine heritage – was a thriving agricultural settlement long before the arrival of the battling Normans. Their **castle**, at the top of the High Street (Mon–Sat 10am–4/6pm, Sun noon–4/6pm; £5.60; Ⓦ www.skiptoncastle.co.uk), is among England's best preserved, thanks mainly to the efforts of Lady Anne Clifford, who rebuilt much of her family seat between 1650 and 1675 following the pillage of the Civil War. A self-guided tour leads you through the original Norman gateway into the beautiful Conduit Court, where the yew tree was supposedly planted by Lady Anne herself. Further down the High Street, on the first floor of the town hall, don't miss the entertaining **Craven Museum** (April–Sept Mon & Wed–Sat 10am–4pm, Sun noon–4pm; Oct–March Mon & Wed–Fri noon–4pm, Sat 10am–4pm; free), whose collection runs the gamut from boneshaker bicycles to policemen's helmets, by way of flints, fossils, snuff boxes, grandfather clocks and a hippopotamus skull. The alleys on the western side of the High Street emerge on to the banks of the **Leeds–Liverpool Canal**, which runs right through the centre of Skipton; a one-hour signposted trail follows the towpath. Pennine Boat Trips at Waterside Court, off Coach Street, offers daily **canal cruises** (Easter–Oct & Dec; £5, ☎01756/790829, ⓦwww.canaltrips.co.uk) that last around an hour.

Practicalities

The **train** station is on Broughton Road, a ten-minute walk from the centre. The **bus** station is closer in, on Keighley Road, at the bottom of the High Street. Local services run from Skipton to Settle (not Sun) for connections on to Ingleton and Horton, to Malham (not Sun), and to Grassington. The main **car parks** are behind the town hall (off High Street) or on Coach Street nearer the canal, while the **tourist office** is at 35 Coach St (Mon–Sat 10am–4/5pm, Sun 11am–3pm; ☎01756/792809, ⓦwww.skiptononline.co.uk).

   Accommodation is plentiful, with a host of central pubs offering rooms, as well as several B&Bs a few minutes' walk out of the centre, either on Gargrave (west) or Keighley (south) roads.

Accommodation

Chinthurst Otley Rd ☎01756/799264, ⓦwww
.chinthurst.co.uk. Run by very amenable owners,
this elegant detached Victorian house features
spacious bathrooms, lovely bed linen and
contemporary art on the walls. ❹
Craven Heifer Grassington Rd ☎01756/792521,
ⓦwww.cravenheifer.co.uk. Stone-built Dales inn, a
mile out of town (2min drive), with rooms fashioned
from an old barn. Buffet continental breakfast
included, plus bar, restaurant and parking. No
single Saturday-night bookings. ❸
Woolly Sheep Inn 38 Sheep St, bottom of High
St ☎01756/700966, ⓦwww.timothytaylor.co.uk
/woollysheep. Some of the pine-furnished rooms
are a bit tight on space, but have decent beds,
good showers, and cafetieres supplied.
Downstairs in the public bar there are
Timothy Taylor's beers and meals served daily.
Parking. ❹

Restaurants

Aagrah Devonshire Place, off Keighley Rd
☎01756/790807. Reminiscent of a snake
charmer's boudoir, but this Indian restaurant has a
loyal local following. Dinner only. Moderate.
Bizzie Lizzies 36 Swadford St ☎01756/701131.
The town's award-winning fish-and-chip shop, with
the restaurant side of the operation (dining over the
canal) open until 9pm every night. Inexpensive.
Nosh 1 Devonshire Place ☎01756/700060.
Modern bar-brasserie (opposite *Aagrah*) serving
fashionable food. Closed Tues. Moderate.

Pub

The Narrow Boat 38 Victoria St
☎01756/797922. All you want from a pub – not
just varied cask ales and a multitude of Belgian
and German beers, but good, inexpensive food
(lunch daily, dinner Tues–Sat until 8.30pm), and
no piped music. It's the recipe for coming for one
drink and staying put.

Wharfedale

Wharfedale really starts just south and east of Skipton, with **Ilkley** and **Bolton Abbey**, and then continues north in a broad, pastoral sweep scattered with villages as picture-perfect as any in northern England. The popular walking centre of **Grassington** is the main village, while upland roads lead from the head of the valley up minor dales to cross the watershed into Wensleydale. However, the most attractive itinerary would take you up lonely Littondale to **Arncliffe**, a village almost too good to be true, and then over the tops to either Malham or Ribblesdale. Throughout the year, **buses** run roughly hourly (not Sun in winter) to Grassington from Skipton, and then half a dozen times a day on up the B6160 to Kettlewell, Starbotton and Buckden.

Bolton Abbey

BOLTON ABBEY, five miles east of Skipton, is the name of a whole village rather than an abbey, a confusion compounded by the fact that the place's main monastic ruin is known as **Bolton Priory** (daily 9am to dusk; free). Turner painted the site, and Ruskin described it as the most beautiful in England, though only the nave, which was incorporated into the village church in 1170, has survived in almost its original state. The priory is the starting point for several popular riverside walks, including a section of the **Dales Way** footpath that follows the river's west bank to take in Bolton Woods and the **Strid** (from "stride"), an extraordinary piece of white water two miles north of the abbey, where softer rock has allowed the river to funnel into a cleft just a few feet wide. Beyond the Strid, the path emerges at **Barden Bridge**, four miles from the priory, where the fortified **Barden Tower** shelters a tearoom.

Perhaps the nicest approach to the priory is on the **Embsay and Bolton Abbey Steam Railway** – the Bolton Abbey station is a mile and a half by footpath from the priory ruins. The trains (roughly hourly in summer; rest of year weekends and some other days; ☏01756/710614 or 795189, ⓦwww.embsayboltonabbeyrailway.org.uk; £7 return) start from Embsay, two miles east of Skipton. Alternatively, it costs £5.50 to park in any of the three estate **car parks**. There's local **information** from the estate office (☏01756/718009, ⓦwww.boltonabbey.com) and an information point at **Cavendish Pavilion**, a mile north of the priory, where there's also a riverside restaurant and café.

At Bolton Abbey the main **hotel** is the sumptuous *Devonshire Arms* (☏01756/718111, ⓦwww.thedevonshirearms.co.uk; ⓞ), owned by the Duchess of Devonshire and furnished with antiques from the ancestral pile at Chatsworth; there's a good brasserie and bar open to the public.

Grassington and around

GRASSINGTON is the dale's main village, nine miles from Bolton Abbey. It has a good Georgian centre, albeit one tempered by dollops of fake rusticity, and the surroundings are at their best by the river, where the shallow Linton Falls thunder after rain. The cobbled **Market Square** is home to several inns, a few gift shops and a small local museum. Traditional rural pursuits, as well as music and arts, are celebrated in the annual **Grassington Festival** (ⓦwww.grassington-festival.org.uk), held every June.

The **National Park Centre** is on Hebden Road (April–Oct daily 10am–5pm; Nov–March Fri–Sun 10am–4pm; ☏01756/751690), across from the bus stop; there's a huge pay-and-display **car park** here. Grassington also has the bulk of the dale's **services**, including a bank with ATM.

In summer you should book **accommodation** in advance. There's a fair amount in the village, but even so, at busy times you may have to look further afield – no hardship since Grassington is surrounded by tiny scenic villages, all connected by minor country roads and footpaths. Tearooms and **cafés** abound, and there are a couple of independent restaurants that might appeal, but Grassington's best places to eat – a series of country **inns** known for their food – are all slightly out of the centre.

Hotels, inns and B&Bs

Angel Barn Lodgings/Angel Inn Hetton, 4 miles southwest ☎01756/730263, ⓦwww.angelhetton.co.uk. This Dales' gastropub par excellence has five immaculate rooms and suites. Over the road in the inn, Modern British food is served either in the bar-brasserie (lunch & dinner) or more formal restaurant (Mon–Sat dinner & Sun lunch); they're expensive, and reservations advised for both. ❼, Sat night ❽

Ashfield House Summers Fold, Grassington ☎01756/752584, ⓦwww.ashfieldhouse.co.uk. Lovely seventeenth-century house, 50yd off the square (behind the *Devonshire Hotel*), boasting a walled garden, good breakfasts and some special weekend deals. ❺

Devonshire Fell Burnsall, 3 miles southeast ☎01756/729000, ⓦwww.devonshirefell.co.uk. Rooms here have been given the designer treatment – country house retreat, but definitely not "country" in feel. Views are either of garden and village or fells and river, while a classy bar and bistro complete the experience. Guests can use Bolton Abbey's *Devonshire Arms'* leisure facilities. Weekend two-night minimum. ❼

Grassington Lodge 8 Wood Lane, Grassington ☎01756/752518, ⓦwww.grassingtonlodge.co.uk. A splash of contemporary style – co-ordinated fabrics, hardwood floors, specially commissioned Dales photography – enhances this comfortable village guest house. The top two rooms, in the eaves, have the most space, while a great breakfast sets you up for the day. Parking available. No credit cards. ❺

Red Lion Burnsall, 3 miles southeast ☎01756/720204, ⓦwww.redlion.co.uk. A real old country inn, with log fires, oak beams, a cosy bar, and river views from its comfortable, traditionally furnished rooms. Inventive meals (in the bar or restaurant) use local ingredients (both expensive; restaurant reservations advised). ❼

Eating and drinking

Fountaine Inn Linton, 1 mile southwest of Grassington ☎01756/752210. The old pub on the green makes a nice target for a walk across the river from Grassington. The food's excellent, with daily specials (local meat, fresh fish and veggie options) that take some beating. Moderate.

Old Hall Inn Threshfield, 1 mile west of Grassington ☎01756/752441. Stone-flagged inn where you can expect to have to wait for a table before tucking into the likes of salmon, steaks and sausages, all locally sourced. Closed Mon lunch. Moderate.

Littondale, Kettlewell and upper Wharfedale

Wharfedale's scenery above Grassington grows still more impressive, starting a mile north with a tract of ancient woodland, Grass Wood, and followed two miles later by Kilnsey Crag, a dramatic, glacially carved overhang which attracts its fair share of climbers. Just beyond Kilnsey Crag, a minor road branches off left into **Littondale**, whose stunning scenery is best appreciated from **Arncliffe**, halfway up the dale, with a pub on the green that attracts walkers from far and wide. The valley-floor footpath from Arncliffe on to **Litton** (2–3 miles) is a delight, ending at the ancient and unspoilt *Queen's Arms* (☎01756/770208; ❺).

Kettlewell (Norse for "bubbling spring") is the main centre for the upper dale, with plenty of local B&B accommodation plus a youth hostel in the village centre (☎0870/770 5896; Ⓔkettlewell@yha.org.uk). The pubs, the *Bluebell* and the *King's Head*, are both cosy places for a drink. Incidentally, the village was one of the major locations for the film *Calendar Girls*, the true story of doughty Yorkshire ladies who bared all for a charity calendar.

It's lovely country north of Kettlewell, accessed either via the dale's single lonely road (B6160) or the Dales Way path. There's a good pub at **Starbotton**, two miles away, the *Fox & Hounds* (closed Mon & all Jan) which has ancient flagged floors and a huge fire in winter. Further upstream, the river flows through Langstrothdale to **Hubberholme** and the stone-flagged, whitewashed *George* (☎01756/760223, ⊚www.thegeorge-inn.co.uk; ❹), the favourite pub of archetypal Yorkshireman J.B. Priestley, who revelled in visiting a hamlet he thought "one of the smallest and pleasantest places in the world". His ashes are buried outside the church of St Michael and All Angels, over the stone bridge from the pub.

Malhamdale

A few miles west of Wharfedale lies **Malhamdale** (⊚www.malhamdale.com), one of the national park's most heavily visited regions, thanks to its three outstanding natural features of Malham Cove, Malham Tarn and Gordale Scar. It is classic limestone country, dominated by a mighty escarpment topped by a fractured pavement, and cut through with sheer walls, tumbling waterfalls and dry valleys. All three attractions are within easy hiking distance of **Malham village**, reached by bus from Skipton (Mon–Fri year-round) or on the seasonal **Malham Tarn shuttle** which runs between Settle (Easter–Oct, weekends & bank hols only, several daily departures) and the National Park Centre.

Malham village

MALHAM village is home to barely a couple of hundred people, who inhabit the huddled stone houses on either side of a bubbling river, but this microscopic gem attracts around half a million visitors a year. Provided you're prepared to do some walking you can escape the worst of the crowds, and something of the village's charm can be enjoyed in the evening when most of the trippers have gone home. The village is at its most traditional at the annual agricultural country fair, the **Malham Show** (August bank holiday Saturday).

The car park is by the **National Park Centre**, at the southern edge of the village (April–Oct daily 10am–5pm; Nov–March Sat & Sun 10am–4pm; ☎01969/652380). There are several good village **B&Bs**, plus many others dotted up and down dale, while the two **pubs** in Malham also have rooms. The *Buck Inn* has a popular walkers' back bar, but food is better at the fancier *Lister Arms* over the bridge. As well as the YHA hostel, there are also local campsites and bunk-barns – details from the National Park Centre.

The **Yorkshire Dales Trekking Centre** (☎01729/830352, ⊚www.ydtc .net) at Holme Farm in the village centre is the place to enquire about saddling up. Thirty-minute beginners' treks (minimum age 8) on hardy Dales ponies start at £12.

Accommodation

Beck Hall ☎01729/830332, ⊚www .beckhallmalham.com. Extended Dales cottage set in streamside gardens, 200yd from the fork in the village centre. A varied mix of en-suite rooms – some with panelling and four-posters, others with stream and field views – plus a cosy lounge and fire, Wi-Fi access, and all-year daytime café (closed Mon). Parking. ❹

Malham YHA ☎0870/770 5946, ⊚malham@yha .org.uk. Purpose-built hostel that's well-known as a walking and cycling centre. Dorms from £13.95; Nov & Dec usually weekends only; closed Jan.
Miresfield Farm ☎01729/830414, ⊚www .miresfield-farm.com. The first house in the village, by the river, means lovely rural views. Country-pine-style rooms vary in size, and there's also a small campsite with toilet and shower, with breakfast available. ❹

Malham Cove, Malham Tarn and Gordale Scar

Appearing in spectacular fashion a mile north of Malham, **Malham Cove** is a white-walled limestone amphitheatre rising three hundred feet above its surroundings. A broad track leads to the cove, passing some of England's most visible prehistoric field banks en route. After a breath-sapping haul to the top, the rewards are fine views and the famous limestone pavement, an expanse of clints (slabs) and grykes (clefts) created by water seeping through weaker lines in the limestone rock.

A simple walk (or summer shuttle bus ride) over the moors brings **Malham Tarn** abruptly into sight, a lake created by an impervious layer of glacial debris. Its waterfowl are protected by a nature reserve on the west bank, visible from a nature trail which forms part of the Pennine Way. Meanwhile, at **Gordale Scar** (also easily approached direct from Malham village), the cliffs are if anything more spectacular than at Malham Cove, complemented by a deep ravine to the rear caused by the collapse of a cavern roof. A little to the south of the scar, off the road, lies **Janet's Foss**, a peach of a waterfall set amidst green–damp rocks and overarching trees. The classic **circuit** takes in cove, tarn and scar in a clockwise walk from Malham (8 miles; 3hr 30min).

Ribblesdale

Ribblesdale, to the west of Malhamdale, is entered from Settle, starting point of the **Settle–Carlisle Railway**, among the most scenic rail routes in the country. The valley's only village of any size is **Horton in Ribblesdale**, a focus not only for the Ribble Way and Pennine Way, but also for those starting the **Three Peaks Walk**, an arduous hike around the Dales' highest peaks.

The Settle to Carlisle Railway

The **Settle–Carlisle** line is a feat of Victorian engineering that has few equals in Britain. In the six years between 1869 and 1875, when the 72-mile line opened, herculean efforts were made by thousands of navvies to blast a route through the unforgiving Dales mountainsides. Living in squalid shanty towns by the sides of the track, and even in the newly opened railway tunnels themselves, six thousand men built twenty viaducts and bored fourteen tunnels. Over two hundred workers died, some of smallpox and other diseases, others in horrific accidents; many now lie buried in the village churches that line the route.

The railway itself was an immediate success, forming a popular route to Scotland and later used as a freight and troop carrier during World War II. By the 1970s, though, services had been severely reduced and in 1983 it was announced that the line was to close. A vociferous local campaign kept the line open, ensuring the future of what the operators – with no hint of hype – dub **"England's most scenic railway"**. Between Horton and Ribblehead the line climbs two hundred feet in five miles, before crossing the famous 24-arched Ribblehead viaduct and then disappearing into the 2629 yards of the Blea Tunnel. Ribblehead station has an exhibition on the history of the line (closed Mon), while the remote *Station Inn* (ⓦ www.thestationinn.net), right by the Ribblehead rail bridge, serves pub grub daily. Meanwhile, the station at Dent Head is the highest, and bleakest, main-line station in England.

The journey from Settle to Carlisle only takes an hour and forty minutes, so it's easy to make a **return trip** (day return £18) along the whole length of the line. If you only have time for a short rail trip, the best section is that between Settle and Garsdale (30min). Walkers can access the Dales, Ribble and Pennine ways from the B6255 (Hawes road), just a mile or so east of the line at Ribblehead. There are connections to Settle from Skipton (20min) and Leeds (1hr); full **timetable** details are available from National Rail Enquiries, ☎0845/748 4950, or from the website, ⓦ www.settle-carlisle.co.uk.

Settle is the transport junction for Ribblesdale, with daily **trains** heading north through Horton to Carlisle and south to Skipton, Keighley and Leeds. Regular **buses** connect Skipton with Settle, from where there are services three or four times daily (not Sun) north through Stainforth to Horton, and northwest via Clapham to Ingleton in the western Dales.

Settle

Nestled under the wooded knoll of Castleberg, **SETTLE** has a typical seventeenth-century market square, still sporting its split-level arcaded shambles, which once housed butchers' shops. Other than on Tuesdays, when the market is in full swing, there's not much to see in the few streets behind the square and you might as well make the ten-minute climb up through the woods to the top of Castleberg for views over the town.

The **tourist office** in the town hall, just off Market Place (daily 9.30am–4.30pm; ☎01729/825192), has hiking maps and pamphlets. A seasonal weekend and bank holiday **shuttle bus** (Easter–Oct) runs over the tops to Malham in an hour. The **train station** is less than five signposted minutes' walk from Market Place, down Station Road. As for accommodation, two old **inns**, the *Royal Oak* on Market Place (☎01729/822561, ⓦwww .royaloaksettle.co.uk; ❹), and the *Golden Lion*, just off Market Place along Duke Street (☎01729/822203, ⓦwww.goldenlionhotel.net; ❺), are the most atmospheric places to stay. Best of the **B&Bs** is *Settle Lodge* on Duke Street (☎01729/823258, ⓦwww.settlelodge.co.uk; no credit cards; ❹), a Victorian house with spacious rooms in contemporary style.

Both the inns serve reasonable **food** and decent beer. The *Royal Oak* gets the nod by virtue of its extraordinary carved oak-panelled bar and dining room. During the day, however, it's hard to see anyone resisting the lure of ⓧ *Ye Olde Naked Man Café* on Market Place (☎01729/823230), serving breakfasts, proper coffee and good homemade food; a former undertakers, the café's name refers to the old adage that "you bring now't into the world and you take now't out".

Horton in Ribblesdale and the Three Peaks

The noted walking centre of **HORTON IN RIBBLESDALE** dates from Norman times – its church, St Oswald's, retains its original proportions in the fine nave – but the village gained a new lease of life in the nineteenth century when the arrival of the Settle–Carlisle Railway allowed it to expand its age-old quarrying operations. Mine workings old and new slightly spoil the west side of the village, but they don't mar the views from the surrounding walking trails.

The village is most convenient for the ascent of sphinx-shaped **Pen-y-ghent** (3–4hr round trip), the most dramatic of the three summits just to the east on the Pennine Way; the other peaks are more easily climbed from Ingleton, Chapel-le-Dale or Dentdale. The celebrated ⓧ *Pen-y-ghent Café* in the village has filling meals, and doubles as a **tourist office** (daily except Tues 8/9am–5.30pm; ☎01729/860333) and an unofficial headquarters for the famous **Three Peaks Walk** (see box, p.800). The café also operates a "safety service" for walkers, enabling anyone undertaking a long hike to register in and out (not Tues).

Horton straggles along an L-shaped mile of the Settle–Ribblehead road (B6479), with the **train station** at the northern end and the church at the southern end. In between are the café, a post office/store and a campsite. The *Crown Hotel* (☎01729/860209, ⓦwww.crown-hotel.co.uk; ❹), by the bridge, has plain but cosy rooms (some, without attached bath, a bit cheaper) and good bar food. The *Golden Lion* (☎01729/860206, ⓦwww.goldenlionhotel.co.uk), at the other end of the road by the church, has both B&B rooms (③) and bunk-house beds (from £10; breakfast and packed lunches available).

The western Dales

The **western Dales** is a term of convenience for a couple of tiny dales running north from **Ingleton**, a village perfectly poised for walks up **Ingleborough** and **Whernside**, and for **Dentdale**, one of the loveliest valleys in the national park. (Much of this region has been hived off into Cumbria, to the disgust of its erstwhile Yorkshire population.) Ingleton has the most accommodation, but **Dent** is by far the best target for a quiet night's retreat, with a cobbled centre barely altered in centuries. **Sedbergh** to the northwest has an interesting arts and crafts centre while just outside the park and county boundary, to the southwest, the pretty market town of **Kirby Lonsdale** features a graceful medieval bridge spanning the River Lune.

Ingleton is linked by **bus** to Kirby Lonsdale, Clapham, Settle (for Skipton) and Horton, while the Settle–Carlisle Railway offers access to scenic upper Dentdale and Garsdale (though it does drop you in the middle of nowhere). Sedbergh is actually easiest to reach from Kendal in the Lake District, and also has the only regular (but fairly limited) bus services to Dent.

Clapham and its caves

CLAPHAM, a seductive little riverside village at the southern foot of Ingleborough, is the starting point for the mile-long (30min) walk to **Ingleborough Cave** (mid-Feb to Oct daily 10am–4/5pm; £6; ☎01524/251242, ⓦwww.ingleboroughcave.co.uk), the Pennines' oldest show cave, discovered in 1837. There's a signposted public footpath to the cave, though most visitors actually follow the adjacent nature trail (50p) through Clapdale Woods.

To make a real walk of it you can continue on the footpath beyond the cave, through the narrow canyon walls of **Trow Gill** and up to the fenced site of **Gaping Gill**, 365ft deep and 450ft long, and the most famous of the Dales' many potholes. It's the largest underground chamber in Britain and though there's no public access, the local caving club winches down intrepid visitors every May and August bank holiday. Gaping Gill is 2.5 miles from Clapham, with the summit of Ingleborough just another mile beyond, up a clearly defined path – this is a far more interesting approach than the main route usually walked from Ingleton, in total a three to four-hour return walk from Clapham via the cave.

Clapham is equidistant from Settle and Ingleton, just off the A65, around four miles from either; its **train station** (on the Leeds/Skipton–Lancaster line) offers another entry to the Dales, but lies over a mile south of the village. The village has a couple of tearooms and a pub, while a mile or so to the east

in **Austwick**, the charms of the *Austwick Traddock* (℡01524/251224, Ⓦwww
.austwicktraddock.co.uk; ❼, minimum 2-night stay at weekends) are obvious:
an elegant Georgian country-house hotel with a cheery demeanour, agreeable
rooms with plump beds, and refined food.

Ingleton

The straggling slate-grey village of **INGLETON** sits upon a ridge at the
confluence of two streams, the Twiss and the Doe, whose beautifully wooded
valleys are easily the area's best features. The four-and-a-half mile **Falls' Walk**
(daily 9am–dusk; entrance fee £4; ℡01524/241930, Ⓦwww
.ingletonwaterfallswalk.co.uk) is a lovely circular walk (2hr 30min) taking in
both valleys, and providing viewing points over its waterfalls. Serious hikers
also tackle both **Ingleborough** and **Whernside** from Ingleton, two of the
Three Peaks.

   There are a dozen local **B&Bs and guest houses**, most lying along
Main Street. *Riverside Lodge*, 24 Main St (℡01524/241359, Ⓦwww
.riversideingleton.co.uk; ❸), is the pick of them, not so much for the rooms,
but for its valley-view conservatory, terraced garden and sauna. The centrally
located **youth hostel** (℡0870/770 5880, Ⓔingleton@yha.org.uk; from
£15) is an old stone house set in its own gardens, while *Stackstead Farm*, a
mile south off the minor road to High Bentham (℡01524/241386, Ⓦwww
.stacksteadfarm.co.uk), has a **bunkhouse barn** (from £10, groups only at
weekends). The *Inglesport Café* on the first floor of the hiking store on Main
Street (daily 9am–6pm) provides hearty soups and potatoes with everything.
In the evening there's *La Tavernetta*, 23 Main St (℡01524/242465; closed
Sun & Mon) serving inexpensive Italian meals and pizza. None of the **pubs**
in the village is up to much, though you can drive five miles up the Hawes
road (B6255), beyond the hamlet of Chapel-le-Dale, to the *Old Hill Inn*
(℡01524/241256; ❹; closed Mon), one of the lonelier pubs in England, but
worth the diversion for the cosily restored interior, good beers and posh pub
food, and the amazing sugar sculptures on display.

White Scar Caves

Just one and a half miles out of Ingleton on the Ribblehead/Hawes road
(B6255) is the entrance to the **White Scar Caves** (daily 10am–5pm;
weekends only Nov-Jan, weather permitting; £7.50; ℡01524/241244,
Ⓦwww.whitescarcave.co.uk), the longest show cave in England. Don't be put
off by the steep price – it's worth every penny for the eighty-minute tour of
dank underground chambers, contorted cave formations and glistening
stalactites. The system was discovered in 1923 by a student, one Christopher
Long, who crawled into a fissure in the hillside pushing a candle wedged in
a bowler hat ahead of him to light his way. It's now lined with steel-grid
walkways along which you edge, the thundering of the internal waterfall
becoming ever louder the further in you venture. The **Battlefield Cavern**
is a remarkable 330 feet long and 100 feet high; to get this far you'll have
had to negotiate natural features like the "Squeeze" (where the walkway
between two rock faces is little over a foot wide) and the "Gorilla Walk"
(several hundred yards where you need to hunch your way along a low-
roofed tunnel). Tours run every hour or so, and there's a café on site.

Dent

When travel writers turn out clichés like "stepping back in time", they mean to
describe places like **DENT** – the main road gives way to grassy cobbles, while

the huddled stone cottages sport blooming window-boxes trailing over ancient lintels, and have tiny windows to keep in the warmth. In the seventeenth and eighteenth centuries, **Dentdale** (Ⓦwww.dentdale.com) supported a flourishing hand-knitting industry, later ruined by mechanization. These days, the hill-farming community supplements its income through tourism and craft ventures, including the independent Dent Brewery.

You can stay at either of the village's two **pubs**, the *Sun Inn* (Ⓣ01539 /625208; ❶) and the *George & Dragon* (Ⓣ01539/625256, Ⓦwww.thegeorge anddragondent.co.uk; ❸), which are virtually next to each other in the centre. The *Sun* is the nicer, welcoming to walkers and with a great traditional feel; that said, the en-suite rooms at the *George & Dragon* have been modernized and are more comfortable. There are a handful of **B&Bs**, most notably *Stone Close Guest House* (Ⓣ01539/625231, Ⓔstoneclose@btinternet.com; no credit cards; ❷, en-suite ❸), which has a good café (noon–5pm all year; closed Mon & Fri). Both the pubs serve bar **meals**, nicest at the *Sun* where you can eat and drink in front of a log fire. The only other facilities in the village are a post office, small store and half a dozen craft shops.

Dent's **train station** (on the Settle–Carlisle line) is not in Dent at all, but four miles to the east, so be warned.

Sedbergh

A few miles northwest of Dent, up on the A684, the small stone-built market town of **SEDBERGH** is tucked under the brooding Howgill Fells. Historically, it's best known for its public school, established in 1525, and its Quaker meeting house of 1675 at nearby Briggflatts, but the **Dales Way** passes through, making it something of a hiking centre, while current plans are to boost its character as a "book town", along the lines of Hay-on-Wye; a festival of books and drama every August helps make the case. Otherwise, call in at Farfield Mill (mid-Feb to Dec daily 10am–5pm; £2.50; Ⓦwww.farfieldmill .org), a mile east of town on the Garsdale/Hawes road (A684 – follow the signs). The former woollen mill is now an enterprising arts and heritage centre – the admission fee allows you to view the historic exhibits, galleries, Victorian weaving looms and artists at work, though there's no charge for the excellent riverside café.

Kirkby Lonsdale

Close to the point where Yorkshire, Cumbria and Lancashire meet, the flint and limestone houses of quaint **KIRKBY LONSDALE** sit on a rise above the River Lune. Ten minutes' walk south of town on the A683, the three-arched **Devil's Bridge** once formed the main route into Yorkshire from the Lakes. There's parking by the bridge and a path from here follows the river to the base of a steep flight of steps that re-enters the town behind St Mary's Church at a point called **Ruskin's View**. Turner painted the famous view of the Lune Valley from here but it was John Ruskin who, with typical overstatement, declared that, "I do not know in all my own country, still less in France or Italy, a place more naturally divine."

Technically Kirkby Lonsdale is in Cumbria, but that doesn't stop it from being a very handy base for the western Yorkshire Dales, with both Dent (no public transport) and Ingleton only around eight miles away. The **tourist office** is at 24 Main St (Ⓣ01524/271437, Ⓦwww.kirkbylonsdale.co.uk), and posts a list of B&Bs in the window when closed, or stay at either the *Snooty Fox* on Main Street (Ⓣ01524/271308, Ⓦwww.snootyfoxhotel.co.uk; ❺) or the nearby *Sun Hotel*, 6 Market St (Ⓣ01524/271965, Ⓦwww.sunhotelkirkbylonsdale.co.uk; ❼), which backs onto the churchyard. Both are also decent places for a drink, and have brasserie-style menus. However, the real gourmet experience is to be found a couple of miles out of town, at the very lovely *Hipping Hall*, Cowan Bridge (℡01524/271187, ⓦwww.hippinghall.com; ❾, weekends ❾), a country house with fifteenth-century banqueting hall, where the cuisine is thoroughly contemporary.

Wensleydale

Best known of the Dales, if only for its cheese, **Wensleydale** (ⓦwww .wensleydale.org) is the largest and most serene of the national park's dales. Known in medieval times as Yoredale, after its river (the Ure), the dale takes its present name from an easterly village, and while there are towns to detain you – including one of the area's biggest in **Hawes**, to the west – it's Wensleydale's rural attractions that linger longest in the mind. Many will be familiar to devotees of the **James Herriot** books and TV series, set and filmed in the dale; elsewhere, there are several well-known waterfalls – notably **Aysgarth Falls** – and, as the dale opens into the Vale of York, a variety of historic buildings that range from **castles** at Bolton and Middleham to **abbeys** at Jervaulx and Coverham.

The dale is traversed by the national park's only east–west **main road** (the A684), and linked by high moor roads to virtually all the park's other dales of note. Year-round **public transport** is provided by a combination of post and service buses from Hawes on varied routes via Bainbridge, Askrigg, Aysgarth and Castle Bolton to Leyburn (for Richmond); and the #159 between Masham, Leyburn and Richmond. There are also summer weekend and bank holiday services connecting Hawes to Wharfedale (#800/805).

Hawes

HAWES is Wensleydale's chief town, main hiking centre, and home to its tourism, cheese and rope-making industries. It also claims to be Yorkshire's highest market town, and received its market charter in 1699; the weekly Tuesday market – crammed with farmers and market traders – is still going strong. If you haven't yet bought any **cheese**, the groaning stalls will doubtless persuade you otherwise. The cheese trail invariably leads to the **Wensleydale Creamery** on Gayle Lane (Mon–Sat 10am–5pm, Sun 10am–4.30pm; £2.50; ℡01969/667664, ⓦwww.wensleydale.co.uk), a few hundred yards south of the centre. The first cheese in Wensleydale was made by medieval Cistercian monks from ewes' milk, and after the Dissolution local farmers made a version from cows' milk which, by the 1840s, was being marketed as "Wensleydale" cheese. The Creamery doesn't make cheese every day, so call first to guarantee a viewing. On the Aysgarth side of town, in the former train station and warehouses, the **Dales Countryside Museum** (daily 10am–5pm; £3) embraces lead-mining, farming, peat-cutting, knitting (hand-knitted hosiery was a speciality) and all manner of rustic minutiae. Alongside it, in a long shed, the **Hawes Ropemakers** (Mon–Fri 9am–5.30pm, plus July–Oct Sat 10am–5.30pm; free) shows present-day rope-makers at work.

The **National Park Centre** (daily 10am–5pm; ℡01969/666 210) shares the same building as the Dales Countryside Museum. **Buses** stop in Market Place except for the summer-only services, which pull up outside the museum, and the post buses, which depart from outside the post office (over the road from the information centre car park). **Accommodation** is plentiful in local B&Bs, while all the pubs on and around the market square – the *Board*, *Crown*,

Fountain, Bull's Head and *White Hart* – have rooms, too. Traditional **tearooms and cafés** cluster around Market Place – *Beckindales*, by the Ropemakers Museum, has a more contemporary air and an outdoor terrace. **Pub** dining is best at the *Crown* – which has a raised rear garden with valley views; otherwise, you're limited to a couple of hotel dining rooms, an Indian restaurant and a fish-and-chip café.

Accommodation and food

Hawes YHA Lancaster Terrace ☎0870/770 5854, ✉hawes@yah.org.uk. Modern hostel on the edge of town, at the junction of the main A684 and B6255. Some twin and family rooms available (❶), otherwise dorm beds from £12.95. Closed Nov–Feb.

Herriot's Main St ☎01969/667536, ⓦwww .herriotsinhawes.co.uk. Small hotel, just off Market Place, where a couple of the rooms have fell views. The restaurant here is the best place to eat in town, offering hearty Dales dishes. ❹

The Old Dairy Farm Widdale, 3 miles west of Hawes ☎01969/667 070,

ⓦwww.olddairyfarm.co.uk. Farmhouse accommodation, but of the luxurious and contemporary kind, with fine dining available (dinner £28). ❼

Rose & Crown Bainbridge, 5 miles east of Hawes ☎01969/650225, ⓦwww.theprideofwensleydale .com. Fifteenth-century coaching inn with restaurant and bar, overlooking an emerald village green. ❺

Steppe Haugh Town Head ☎01969/667645, ⓦwww.steppehaugh.co.uk. Plenty of pine gives a cottagey feel to this traditional B&B, at the Ingleton road turn-off at the top of town. Five rooms available (four en-suite, one with private shower-room), plus parking. ❹

Askrigg, Aysgarth and Castle Bolton

The mantle of "Herriot country" lies heavy on **ASKRIGG**, six miles east of Hawes, as the TV series *All Creatures Great and Small* was filmed in and around the village. Nip into the King's Arms – a cosy old haunt with wood panelling, good beer and bar meals – and you can see stills from the TV series. For a rural retreat, you can't beat *Helm* (☎01969/650443, ⓦwww.helmyorkshire.com; ❺), a seventeenth-century farmhouse a mile west with magnificent views, open fires and oak beams.

The ribbon-village of **AYSGARTH**, straggling along and off the A684, is the vortex that sucks in Wensleydale's largest number of visitors, courtesy of the **Aysgarth Falls**, half a mile below the village. A marked nature trail runs through the surrounding woodlands and there's a big car park and excellent **National Park Centre** on the north bank (April–Oct daily 10am–5pm; Nov–March Fri–Sun 10am–4pm; ☎01969/662 910). The **Upper Falls** and picnic grounds lie just back from here, by the bridge and church; the more spectacular **Middle** and **Lower Falls** are a ten-minute stroll to the east through shaded woodland. The ice cream is good at the park centre **café**; otherwise, the two local **pubs** – the *Palmer Flatts* by the falls turn-off and the *George & Dragon* in the village – both have bar meals and outdoor tables, though the main A684 road does neither of them a favour.

There's a superb **circular walk** northeast from Aysgarth via Bolton Castle (6 miles; 4hr) – or you can simply drive to the castle in about ten minutes. The walk starts at the falls themselves and climbs up through Thoresby, with the foursquare battlements of **Bolton Castle** (March–Nov daily 10am–5pm; restricted winter opening, call for details; ☎01969/623981, ⓦwww.boltoncastle.co.uk; £5) themselves a magnetic lure from miles away. It's a massive defensive structure in which Mary, Queen of Scots was imprisoned for six months in 1568. The Great Chamber, a few adjacent rooms and the castle gardens have been restored, and there's also a café (free to enter) that's a welcome spot if you've just trudged up from Aysgarth.

A few miles east of Aysgarth, Wensleydale broadens into a low-hilled pastoral valley, the border of the national park marking the end of classic Dales scenery. The church of the **Holy Trinity** at **WENSLEY** ranks as one of the Dales' finest, founded in the thirteenth century but with fabric dating from the five centuries that followed, the most impressive being an extravagant box pew and a sixteenth-century rood-screen removed from Richmond's Easby Abbey. The market town of **LEYBURN** – a couple of miles east of Wensley and eleven miles southwest of Richmond – occupies almost the last piece of straggling high ground on the valley's north edge, a handsome place set around three open squares, replete with buildings from its eighteenth-century heyday. Market day is Friday, when Market Place puts out its fruit, veg, hard goods and bric-a-brac stalls. Trains have returned to Wensleydale, with the reopening of the scenic **Wensleydale Railway** (℗0845/450 5474, Ⓦ www.wensleydalerailway.com; £12 day rover) between Leyburn and Leeming Bar, 12 miles to the east (on the A1).

Two miles southeast of Leyburn, the tiny town of **MIDDLEHAM** is approached over an impressive early-nineteenth-century castellated bridge. A well-to-do place set around a sloping cobbled square, it's dominated by the imposing ruins of **Middleham Castle** (Easter–Sept daily 10am–4/6pm; £3.50; EH), built by the Normans to guard the route from Skipton to Richmond. Racehorses clip-clopping through the centre are a common sight, with over five hundred trained locally at more than a dozen stables. Several **pubs** vie for custom around the square – the *White Swan*, *Black Swan*, *Richard III* and *Black Bull* all have rooms available; the best food is at the *White Swan*.

Wensleydale all but peters out with the overgrown ruins of **Jervaulx Abbey** (daily dawn to dusk; £2; Ⓦ www.jervaulxabbey.com), four miles southeast of Middleham on the A6108 road to Ripon. Founded in 1156, it is the least prepossessing of the great trio of Cistercian abbeys completed by Fountains and Rievaulx, but makes an enjoyable stop for a ramble amid the wild flowers.

Masham

If you're a beer fan, the handsome market town of **MASHAM** (pronounced Mass'm) is an essential point of pilgrimage. It's home to **Theakston brewery** (tours daily 11am–3pm; reservations advised; ℗01765/680000; £4.95, Ⓦ www.theakstons.co.uk), sited here since 1827, where you can learn the arcane intricacies of the brewer's art and become familiar with the legendary Old Peculier ale. In the early 1990s one of the Theakston family brewing team left to set up the **Black Sheep Brewery**, also based in Masham and offering tours (daily 11am–4pm, but call for availability; £5.25; ℗01765/680100, Ⓦ www.blacksheepbrewery.com). Both breweries are just a few minutes' signposted walk out of the centre.

Masham itself is one of the most attractive small towns in Yorkshire, with a huge central market place (market days are Wednesday and Saturday), a handsome church and a smattering of local shops and galleries. There's no more agreeable **accommodation** – here, or for many miles around – than ⚹ *Swinton Park* (℗01765/680900, Ⓦ www.swintonpark.com; ❽), a stunning stately home with elegant rooms that overlook the sweeping grounds and curving river. There's a fine-dining restaurant, and the cookery school (day courses available) is also increasingly popular. The hotel is also only a gentle mile's stroll from Masham, where the *King's Head*, 42 Market Place (℗01765/689295, Ⓦ www.kingsheadmasham.com; ❹, breakfast not included),

▲ Black Sheep Brewery, Masham

is the best **place to eat** in town, more restaurant than pub. There's also a bistro inside the Black Sheep Brewery (open when the brewery's open and also for dinner most nights). The local beer's at its best in the *White Bear* (☏01765/689319), the **brewery pub** attached to Theakston's, which is very popular for bar meals.

Swaledale

Narrow and steep-sided in its upper reaches, **Swaledale** emerges rocky and rugged in its central tract before more typically pastoral scenery cuts in at the main village of Reeth, the dale's best overnight stop. From Richmond, **bus #30** (not Sun) runs up the valley along the B6270 as far as Keld. It's worth noting the Swaledale Festival (Ⓦwww.swaledale-festival.org.uk) every June, a widespread music and arts bash at villages up and down the dale.

Keld, eight miles north of Hawes and at the crossroads of the Pennine Way and the Coast-to-Coast Path, is no more than a straggle of hardy buildings surrounded by relics of the lead-mining industry that once brought a prosperity of sorts to much of the valley. The Pennine Way shadows the very minor Stonesdale road for the three or four miles across **Stonesdale Moor** to the *Tan Hill Inn* (Ⓣ01833/628246, Ⓦwww.tanhillinn.co.uk; ❹), reputedly the highest pub in Britain (1732ft above sea level). **Thwaite** is the first hamlet south of Keld, just a two-mile walk away, while some of the loveliest scenery follows beyond the little village of **Muker**, a mile or so to the east, where there are a couple of teashops and a decent pub, the *Farmers Arms*.

A couple of miles east, **REETH** is set in a dramatic moorland bowl. It's the dale's main village and market centre – market day is Friday – and its desirable cottages are gathered around a triangular green, where you'll find the **National Park Centre** (April–Oct daily 10am–5pm; Nov–March Fri–Sun 10am–4pm; Ⓣ01748/884059). Reeth has the biggest range of facilities in the dale, including several B&Bs, a petrol station, two ATMs and a post office, as well as several craft workshops. The three central **pubs** also have rooms, most notably the *King's Arms* (Ⓣ01748/884259, Ⓦwww.thekingsarms.com; ❺; weekend 2-night minimum), or for superior old-fashioned comforts there's the *Burgoyne Hotel* (Ⓣ01748/884292, Ⓦwww.theburgoyne.co.uk; no single Sat night reservations; ❼), lording it over the top of the green. Reeth Bakery is known for its great chocolate cake; and there's good food at *Overton House Café* (Ⓣ01748/884332; open daytime Mon & Wed–Sat, plus Thurs–Sat dinner), especially for fish.

East of Reeth lie the romantic ruins of **Marrick Priory** and **Ellerton Priory**, the latter visible from the B6270, while there are also numerous paths across the fields on the south side of the river, letting you complete a circular walk from Reeth via **Grinton**, whose attractive bridge, church and riverside inn are just a mile away by road.

Richmond

RICHMOND is the Dales' single most tempting historical town, thanks mainly to its magnificent castle, whose extensive walls and colossal keep cling to a precipice above the River Swale. Indeed, the entire town is an absolute gem, centred on a huge cobbled market square backed by Georgian buildings, hidden alleys and gardens. The town was first dubbed *Riche-Mont* ("noble hill") by the Normans who first built a castle here in 1071. That heritage is also celebrated in local street names such as Frenchgate and Lombard's Wynd (a "wynd" being a narrow alley).

There's no better place to start than **Richmond Castle** (April–Sept daily 10am–6pm; Oct–March Mon & Thurs–Sun 10am–4pm; £4; EH), which retains many features from its earliest incarnation, principally the gatehouse, curtain wall and Scolland's Hall, the oldest Norman great hall in the country. There are prodigious views from the fortified keep, which is over a hundred feet high, and from the Great Court, now an open lawn which ends in a sheer fall to the river below. Most of medieval Richmond sprouted around the castle, but much of the town now radiates from the **Market Place**, with the Market Hall alongside; market day is Saturday, augmented by a farmers' market on the third Saturday of the month. The defunct **Holy Trinity Church** on the square now houses the **Green Howards Museum** (Mon–Sat 10am–4pm; £3.50), honouring North Yorkshire's Green Howards regiment. For local history, visit the charming **Richmondshire Museum** (April–Oct daily 10.30am–4.30pm; £2.50), down Ryder's Wynd, off King Street on the northern side of the square.

The keenest interest of all, however, is in the town's **Theatre Royal** (1788), a fine piece of Georgian architecture that is one of England's oldest extant theatres. It's open for both **performances** (box office ☏01748/825252, ⓦwww.georgiantheatreroyal.co.uk) and **tours** (mid-Feb to mid-Dec Mon–Sat 10am–4pm, on the hour; £3.50), while a museum at the rear gives an insight into eighteenth-century theatrical life.

A signposted walk runs along the north bank of the **River Swale** out to the beautifully situated church of St Agatha, noted for its fine thirteenth-century wall paintings, and the golden stone walls of adjacent **Easby Abbey** (dawn to dusk; free; EH), a mile southeast of the town. The evocative ruins are extensive, and in places – notably the thirteenth-century refectory – still remarkably intact.

Practicalities

Buses stop in the Market Place; there are regular services into Wensleydale and Swaledale, and to Darlington, ten miles to the northeast, on the main east coast train line. There's free two-hour **parking** in Market Place (pick up a disc from local shops), or aim for the pay-and-display Nunn's Close car park on Hurgill Road, off Victoria Road. The **tourist office**, at Friary Gardens, Victoria Road (daily 9.30am–5.30pm; winter closed Sun; ☏01748/850252, ⓦwww.richmond .org.uk), is helpful in finding accommodation, and also organizes **guided walking tours** around the town in summer (free, donations welcome). The big events each year are the Richmond Meet (May, Spring Bank Holiday), with floats, parades and carnival, the free Richmond Live music festival (August), and September's Walking Festival.

By far the best option for eating out is the restaurant in the *Frenchgate Hotel* (see below), though *A Taste of Thailand* at 15 King St (☏01748/829696) has its strong points, and the *Black Lion* pub on Finkle Street is good for daytime food or an evening pint. Alternatively you can drive out into the gentle country to the north where prettily sited pubs like the *Shoulder of Mutton* (☏01748/822772) at **Kirby Hill** (3 miles) or the *Bay Horse Inn* (☏01325/718328) at **Ravensworth** (5 miles) make for a decent night out.

Accommodation

Aislabeck Natural Retreats Hurgill Rd, Aislabeck, 1 mile north of Richmond ☏0161/242 2970, ⓦwww.naturalretreats.com. Contemporary wood lodges sleeping up to six, built on sustainable lines and set in a beautifully secluded location. Minimum two-night stay, from £250.
Frenchgate Hotel 59–61 Frenchgate ☏01748/822087, ⓦwww.thefrenchgate.co.uk. Georgian town house hotel, with eight individually furnished rooms, lots of local art work and walled gardens. Its food (meals around £30; restaurant closed Mon) has an excellent reputation. Parking. ⓖ
Frenchgate House 66 Frenchgate ☏01748/823421, ⓦwww.66frenchgate.co.uk. The reward for staying in one of the three immaculately presented rooms is breakfast with the best panoramic view in town. ④
Millgate House Millgate ☏01748/823571, ⓦwww.millgatehouse .com. Shut the big green door of this

Georgian house and enter a world of books, antiques, embroidered sheets, oil paintings in the bathroom, hand-made toiletries, scrumptious breakfasts and the finest (and least precious) hosts you could wish for. If this is not enough, there's a haven of a walled garden too. No credit cards. ⑤, en-suite ⑥

Whashton Springs Near Whashton, 3 miles north, Ravensworth road ☎01748/822884, Ⓦwww.whashtonsprings.co.uk. This working Dales farm offers a peaceful night in the country in rooms (in the main house or round the courtyard) filled with family furniture. A farmhouse breakfast sets you up for the day, while nearby country pubs are a short drive (or even a walk) away. ④

Nidderdale

Nidderdale (Ⓦwww.nidderdale.co.uk), the easternmost and probably least known of the Yorkshire Dales, stretches for around twenty miles from the source of the River Nidd on Great Whernside to the village of **Ripley** in the lower dale, just four miles from Harrogate. The main approach is along the east–west B6265 between Grassington in Wharfedale and Ripon, with the only available route north being along the wild road from **Pateley Bridge**, the dale's main village, to Masham and, ultimately, Wensleydale.

RIPLEY (bus #36A from Ripon or Harrogate) is an impeccably kept village whose bizarre appearance is due to a whim of the Ingilby family, who between 1827 and 1854 rebuilt it in the manner of an Alsace-Lorraine village, for no other reason than they liked the style. Summer crowds pile in for the cobbled square, stocks, twee cottages and shops, not to mention the Ingilby house, parkland and **castle** (April–Oct daily 10.30am–3pm; March & Nov closed Mon, Wed & Fri; Dec–Feb Sat & Sun only; gardens daily all year 9am–4.30/5pm; £7, gardens only £4; Ⓦwww.ripleycastle.co.uk). The attractive *Boar's Head* (☎01423/771888, Ⓦwww.boarsheadripley.co.uk; ⑦) has a lovely bar and beer garden, and a high-class restaurant.

The characterful little town of **PATELEY BRIDGE** (**bus** #24 from Harrogate) serves as the dale's focus, acting as a base for campers, cavers and visitors of every kind. Make time for the **Panorama Walk** (2 miles; 1hr), signposted from the top of the High Street, and then refuel in one of the tearooms, pubs and restaurants along the High Street. Several local guest houses and hotels provide **accommodation**, one of the nicest places being the *Sportsmans Arms* (☎01423/711306, Ⓦwww.sportsmans-arms.co.uk; ⑦), a couple of miles out off the Nidderdale road at Wath-in-Nidderdale – there's really good food served here. Five miles west of the village on the Grassington road lie the **Stump Cross Caverns** (March–Nov daily 10am–6pm; Dec–Feb Sat & Sun 10am–4.45pm; £6; Ⓦwww.stumpcrosscaverns.co.uk), one of England's premier show caves, complete with massive stalagmites. About the same distance east of the village, signposted off the B6265, are the extraordinary **Brimham Rocks**, nearly four hundred acres of strangely eroded millstone grit outcrops scattered over one-thousand-foot-high moors. Views from here are superlative, stretching over the Vale of York, with York Minster visible on clear days.

North of Pateley Bridge, above the **Gouthwaite Reservoir**, Nidderdale closes in and the scenery is superb. At **Ramsgill**, at the northern end of the reservoir, the *Yorke Arms* (☎01423/755243, Ⓦwww.yorke-arms.co.uk; ⑧) is a renowned restaurant-with-rooms operation. A couple of miles further up the road, seven miles from Pateley Bridge, **How Stean Gorge** (Easter–Sept daily 10am–6pm; Oct–Easter Wed–Sun 10am–dusk, except Jan weekends only; £5; Ⓦwww.howstean.co.uk) is an ice-gouged ravine of surging waters and overhanging rocks.

Ripon

The attractive market town of **RIPON**, eleven miles north of Harrogate, is centred upon its small **Cathedral** (daily 8am–6.30pm; donation requested, ⓦwww.riponcathedral.org.uk), which can trace its ancestry back to its foundation by St Wilfrid in 672; the original crypt below the central tower can still be reached down a stone passage. The town's other focus is its **Market Place**, linked by narrow Kirkgate to the cathedral; market day is Thursday, with a farmers' market on the third Sunday of the month. A ninety-foot obelisk built in 1780 dominates the square, topped by a horned weather vane. This is an allusion to the "Blowing of the Wakeman's Horn", a ceremony which may date from 886, when Alfred the Great reputedly granted Ripon a charter and an ox's horn was presented for the setting of the town's watch. The horn is still blown nightly at 9pm in the square's four corners and outside the house of the incumbent mayor.

The town makes for an agreeable stroll – unlike many, the Market Square isn't entirely submerged under traffic and Ripon retains many traditional and independent shops. Three restored buildings show a different side of the local heritage, under the banner of the Yorkshire Law and Order Museums (all open April–Oct daily: July, Aug & school hols 11am–4pm, other times 1–4pm; combined ticket £6; ⓦwww.riponmuseums.co.uk). At the **Prison and Police Museum** on St Marygate behind the cathedral, the old cells serve as the backdrop for an informative and engaging exhibition on policing since Anglo-Saxon times. Cases were heard at the 1830s **Courthouse** on Minster Road, with guilty prisoners packed off to the cells or, in the early days at least, transported to Australia. Law-abiding locals often fared little better, with the "undeserving" poor incarcerated in the nearby **Ripon Workhouse**, on Allhallowgate, for such heinous crimes as being unable to pay their bills.

One of England's most splendid Queen Anne houses, **Newby Hall** (April–Sept Tues–Sun, plus Mon in July & Aug: noon–5pm, gardens 11am–5.30pm; £9.50, gardens only £7; ⓦwww.newbyhall.com), lies five miles southeast of Ripon near Skelton, south of the B6265. It contains some outstanding decorative plasterwork, lashings of Chippendale furniture and rich eighteenth-century tapestries. The grounds, sculpture park and gardens offer plenty for children, and there's also a tearoom and picnic area.

Practicalities

The **bus station** (#36 from Harrogate, or Leeds) is just off Market Place, while the town's **tourist office** is on Minster Road opposite the cathedral (April–Sept Mon–Sat 9.30/10am–5/5.30pm, Sun 1–4pm; Oct Mon–Sat 10am–4pm; Nov–March Thurs & Sat 10am–4pm; ☎01765/604625, ⓦwww.visitripon.org). There's no pressing need to stay the night, though Ripon is the nearest town to Fountains Abbey (see opposite). For **B&B**, a longstanding favourite is *Bishopton Grove House*, Bishopton (☎01765/600888, ⓦwww.bishoptongrovehouse.co.uk; no credit cards; ❸), a Georgian house in a peaceful corner of the town. Top honours, though, go to *The Old Deanery* on Minster Road (☎01765/600003, ⓦwww.theolddeanery.co.uk; ❻), just across from the cathedral, completely refurbished in contemporary fashion, with excellent rooms and food (reservations advised for dinner; expensive).

Fountains Abbey and Studley Royal

It's tantalizing to imagine how the English landscape might have appeared had Henry VIII not dissolved the monasteries, with all the artistic ruin precipitated by that act. **Fountains Abbey**, four miles southwest of Ripon off the B6265, gives a good idea of what might have been, and is the one Yorkshire monastic ruin you should make a point of seeing. Linked to it are the elegant water gardens of **Studley Royal**, landscaped in the eighteenth century to form a setting for the abbey. The estate is owned by the National Trust, which organizes an ambitious range of activities and events – from opera and firework displays to **free guided tours** (April–Oct daily; ☎01765/608888, ⓦwww .fountainsabbey.org.uk). Public transport to the abbey is limited, though summer Sunday and bank holiday **bus** services operate from York/Ripon/ Grassington (#812 and #132) – call ☎0871/200 2233 for details.

The Abbey

Beautifully set in a narrow, wooded valley, **Fountains Abbey** (daily 10am–4/5pm; closed Fri Nov–Jan; £7.15 including Studley Royal and Fountains Hall; NT) was founded in 1133 by thirteen dissident Benedictine monks and formally adopted by the Cistercian order two years later. Within a hundred years, Fountains had become the wealthiest Cistercian foundation in England and the three main phases of the abbey's development – nave and transepts, the domestic buildings, and the church's east end – all date from this thirteenth-century period. After the Dissolution the abbey ultimately became a source of building stone for the nearby Fountains Hall, though further desecration was avoided when in 1768 it became part of Studley Royal under William Aislabie, who extended the landscaping exploits of his father to bring the ruined abbey within the estate's orbit.

The Cistercians

The **Cistercian** movement was founded at Cîteaux in Burgundy, in reaction to the arrogant affluence of the Cluniacs, who themselves had earlier reacted against the same perceived fault in the Benedictines. Dressed in rough **habits** of undyed sheep's wool, the so-called "White Monks" lived a frugal and mostly silent existence. Besides this core of priest-monks, whose obligatory presence at choir seven times daily (starting with matins at 2.30am) left little time for work outside the cloister, the Cistercians uniquely had a second tier of lay brethren known as **conversi**, or "bearded ones". At Fountains, around forty monks were complemented by two hundred such *conversi*. Not ordained, and with fewer religious demands, the new recruits – often skilled farmers and masons – could venture far from the mother house, returning only for major festivals and feast days. They were organized into **granges** (farms) to run flocks of sheep, clear pasture, mine stone, lead or iron – even, in a couple of cases, to run a stud farm and sea-fishing business.

The Cistercians' success prompted the Augustinians (Kirkham and Guisborough) and Benedictines (York and Whitby) to promote similar economic ventures though within a hundred years much of their early vigour had been lost, partly as a result of an economic downturn which followed the Black Death. Granges were broken into smaller units and leased to a new class of tenant farmer, as the Cistercians joined the older orders in living off rents rather than actively developing their own estates. The resulting greed and complacency of the monasteries was ultimately used by Henry VIII as an excuse for their dissolution in the 1530s.

Most immediately eye-catching is the **abbey church**, in particular the **Chapel of the Nine Altars** at its eastern end, whose delicacy is in marked contrast to the austerity of the rest of the nave. A great sixty-foot-high window rises over the chapel, complemented by a similar window at the nave's western doorway, over 370ft away. The **Perpendicular Tower**, almost 180ft high, looms over the whole ensemble, added by the eminent early-sixteenth-century Abbot Marmaduke Huby, who presided over perhaps the abbey's greatest period of prosperity. Equally grandiose in scale is the undercroft of the **Lay Brothers' Dormitory** off the cloister, a stunningly vaulted space over 300ft long that was used to store the monastery's annual harvest of fleeces. Its sheer size gives some idea of the abbey's entrepreneurial scope, some thirteen tons of wool a year being turned over, most of it sold to Venetian and Florentine merchants who toured the monasteries.

The size of the lay buildings – including a substantial **Lay Brothers' Infirmary** – gives an idea of the number of lay brothers at the abbey. All are considerably larger than the corresponding monks' buildings, of which the most prepossessing are the **Chapter House** and **Refectory** – notice the huge fireplace of the tiny **Warming Room** alongside the refectory, the only heated space in the entire complex. Outside the abbey perimeter, between the gatehouse and the bridge, are the Abbey Mill and **Fountains Hall**, the latter a fine example of early-seventeenth-century domestic architecture.

Studley Royal

A bucolic riverside walk, marked from the visitor centre car park, takes you from Fountains Hall through the abbey to a series of ponds and ornamental gardens, harbingers of **Studley Royal** (same times as the abbey; NT). It can also be entered via the village of Studley Roger, where there's a separate car park. This lush medley of lawns, lake, woodland and **Deer Park** (daily dawn to dusk; free) was laid out in 1720. There are some scintillating views of the abbey from the gardens, though it's the cascades and water gardens that command most attention, framed by several small temples positioned for their aesthetic effect. You could easily spend an afternoon whiling away time in the gardens: the full circuit, from visitor centre to abbey and gardens and then back, is a good couple of miles' walk.

Harrogate

HARROGATE – the very picture of genteel Yorkshire respectability – owes its landscaped appearance and early prosperity to the discovery of Tewit Well in 1571. This was the first of over eighty ferrous and sulphurous springs that, by the nineteenth century, were to turn the town into one of the country's leading spas. By the mid-twentieth century, however, taking the waters had become a less popular pastime, and since the early 1970s Harrogate has instead concentrated on hosting conferences, exhibitions and festivals. Monuments to its past splendours still stand dotted around town and Harrogate manages to retain its essential Victorian and Edwardian character. Much of its appeal lies in the splendid parks and gardens – "England's floral town" keeps admirable pace with the changing seasons, and if you pick up a free "Floral Trail" leaflet from the tourist office you'll be guided around the best of the current blooms.

Harrogate's spa heritage begins with the **Royal Baths**, facing Crescent Road, first opened in 1897 and now restored to their late-Victorian finery. You can

The small town of Knaresborough, four miles east of Harrogate, rises spectacularly above the River Nidd's limestone gorge. It was home to a sixteenth-century sooth-sayer known as Mother Shipton (ⓦ www.mothershiptonscave.com), who dwelled in a river cave while predicting the defeat of the Armada, the Great Fire of London, world wars, cars, planes and iron ships – only falling short with her claim that "The world to an end will come, in eighteen hundred and eighty one." You can visit the cave today, while close by is the **Petrifying Well**, where dripping, lime-soaked waters coat everyday objects – gloves, hats, coats, toys – in a brownish veneer that sets rock-hard in a few weeks. Regular **trains** and **buses** (every 10min) from Harrogate make Knaresborough an easy side trip.

experience the beautiful Moorish-style interior during a session at the **Turkish Baths and Health Spa** (hours vary; call ☎01423/556746; from £14). The public entrance is on Parliament Street; allow two hours for the full treatment. Just along Crescent Road from the Royal Baths stands the **Royal Pump Room**, built in 1842 over the sulphur well that feeds the baths. The town's earliest surviving spa building, the old Promenade Room of 1806, is just 100 yards from the Pump Room on Swan Road; it now houses the **Mercer Art Gallery** (Tues–Sat 10am–5pm, Sun 2–5pm; free), which hosts regularly changing fine-art exhibitions.

Harrogate deserves much credit for the preservation of its green spaces, most prominent of which is **The Stray**, a jealously guarded green belt that curves around the south of the town centre. To the southwest (entrance opposite the Royal Pump Room), the 120-acre **Valley Gardens** are a delight, while many visitors also make for the botanical gardens at **Harlow Carr** (daily 9.30am–4/6pm; £6; ⓦ www.rhs.org.uk), the northern showpiece of the Royal Horticultural Society. These lie one and a half miles out, on the town's western edge – the nicest approach is to walk (30min) through the Valley Gardens and pine woods, but bus #106 (every 20min) will get you there as well. Although laid out with a scientific purpose – breeding fruit and vegetable stock suited to northern climates – the gardens are a year-round floral extravaganza, with especially wonderful rose displays and a notable exhibit of seven historical "Gardens Through Time". The tea-and-cake specialists *Bettys* of Harrogate provide the meals and drinks at Harlow Carr's excellent café and tea-house.

Practicalities

Bus and **train** stations are on Station Parade, just a few minutes from all the central sights. There's limited-hours **parking** along and around West Park, on the way into town, and there are signposted central car parks on Oxford Street and near the train station. Harrogate's **tourist office** (April–Sept Mon–Sat 9am–6pm, Sun 10am–1pm; Oct–March Mon–Fri 9am–5pm, Sat 9am–4pm; ☎01423/537300, ⓦ www.enjoyharrogate.com) is in the Royal Baths on Crescent Road.

There are scores of **accommodation** options, starting with the B&Bs on King's Road and Franklin Road, north of the centre. Side streets like Studley Road, off King's Road beyond the conference centre, are quieter. Despite this the town fills up quickly when major conferences and festivals take place. Of these the most famous are the **flower shows** (late April and mid-Sept; ⓦ www.flowershow.org.uk), but there's also the three-day **Great Yorkshire Show** (second week in July; ⓦ www.greatyorkshireshow.com) and various book and antique fairs, music festivals and craft shows.

Accommodation

Alexander 88 Franklin Rd ☎01423/503348. Victorian-era guest house on a residential street, less than 10min walk from the centre. No credit cards. ④

The Bijou 17 Ripon Rd ☎01423/567974, ⓦwww.thebijou.co.uk. The mellow lounge with wood-burning stove sets the tone for this small family-run boutique hotel, close to the centre. Good fresh choices for breakfast. Parking. ⑤

Brookfield 5 Alexandra Rd ☎01423/506646, ⓦwww.brookfieldhousehotel.co.uk. High-class Victorian B&B with period features and contemporary flourishes, just a few minutes from the centre. Parking. ⑤

Fountains 27 King's Rd ☎01423/530483, ⓦwww.thefountainshotel.co.uk. Family-run house a minute or two from the conference centre. Rooms have trim little bathrooms, and it's quieter at the side, where the rooms look over a shady copse. Parking. ④

General Tarleton Ferrensby, 5 miles northeast of Harrogate ☎01423/340284, ⓦwww .generaltarleton.co.uk. This gastropub with rooms, a couple of miles north of Knaresborough, is well worth the drive for excellent meals in either the restaurant or bar-brasserie. Fourteen pretty rooms are all furnished in up-to-the-minute style. ⑦

🏃 **Hotel du Vin** Prospect Place ☎01423/856800, ⓦwww.hotelduvin.com. Beautiful boutique-style rooms overlooking The Stray (including four stunning "loft suites") featuring trademark enormous beds and lavish bathrooms. The handsome bistro is sensibly priced, while public areas – champagne bar, lounge and snooker room, courtyard garden – are stylishly turned out. Breakfast not included; parking available. ⑦, loft suites ⑨

Ruskin 1 Swan Rd ☎01423/502045, ⓦwww .ruskinhotel.co.uk. Appealing Victorian villa with seven spacious en-suite rooms (one a four-poster), terraced bar and charming garden. Parking. ⑤

Restaurants and pubs

Bettys 1 Parliament St ☎01423/502746. Very much a Harrogate institution, established by a Swiss emigrant in the 1920s. The cakes and tarts are to die for (takeaway available), but full meals are also served – Alpine macaroni or *rösti*, say, or changing seasonal specialities. Closes at 9pm. Moderate.

🏃 **Drum and Monkey** 5 Montpellier Gardens ☎01423/502650. Outstanding fish and seafood restaurant, a firm favourite with locals and out-of-towners alike. Choose the best of the daily catch grilled, or go cheaper (seafood pie, fish brochette) more expensive (shellfish platter), or just go for a lunchtime sandwich or salad. Expensive.

Old Bell Tavern 6 Royal Parade ☎01423/507930. Treat it as a pub – it's the best in town – or come to eat, since there are bar meals and sandwiches served daily (lunchtime and 6–7pm, Sun from noon) and a brasserie upstairs dispensing braised lamb shank, steaks, smoked haddock and so on. Moderate.

Orchid 28 Swan Rd ☎01423/560425. Wok-wielding chefs conjure up specialities from all corners of Southeast Asia, tempura to Shanghai noodles. There's *dim sum* at lunch, and sushi and sashimi sets every Tuesday. Closed Sat lunch. Moderate.

Salsa Posada 4 Mayfield Grove ☎01423/565151. Funky Mexican restaurant with good-natured staff churning out reasonably authentic nachos, burritos, fajitas and the rest. Eves only. Moderate.

York and around

YORK is the north's most compelling city, a place whose history, said George VI, "is the history of England". This is perhaps overstating things a little, but it reflects the significance of a metropolis that stood at the heart of the country's religious and political life for centuries, and until the Industrial Revolution was second only to London in population and importance. These days a more provincial air hangs over the city, except in summer when York feels like a heritage site for the benefit of tourists. That said, no trip to this part of the country is complete without a visit to York, and the city's former importance means there are good road and rail connections and plenty of accommodation. York is also well placed for any number of **day-trips**: the coast is only an hour away by car or train (longer by bus), while Harrogate, Knaresborough, Ripon and Fountains Abbey are all easily accessible, too. However, if you've only time for one day-trip, it should probably be to **Castle Howard**, the gem amongst English stately homes.

A brief history of York

The Romans first chose the site of modern-day York for a military camp in 71 AD, and in time this fortress became a city – Eboracum, capital of the empire's northern European territories and the base for Hadrian's northern campaigns. Much fought over after the decline of Rome, the city later became the fulcrum of Christianity in northern England. It was here, on Easter Day in 627, that Bishop Paulinus, on a mission to establish the Roman Church, baptized King Edwin of Northumbria in a small timber chapel. Six years later the church became the first minster and Paulinus the first archbishop of York. In 867 the city fell to the **Danes**, who renamed it **Jorvik**, and later made it the capital of eastern England (Danelaw). Later Viking raids culminated in the decisive **Battle of Stamford Bridge** (1066), six miles east of the city, where English King Harold defeated Norse King Harald – a pyrrhic victory in the event, for his weakened army was defeated by the Normans just a few days later at the Battle of Hastings, with well-known consequences for all concerned.

The **Normans** devastated much of York's hinterland in their infamous "Harrying of the North". Stone walls were thrown up during the thirteenth century, when the city became a favoured Plantagenet retreat and commercial capital of the north, its importance reflected in the new title of Duke of York, bestowed ever since on the monarch's second son. The 48 **York Mystery Plays**, one of only four surviving such cycles, date from this era, created by the powerful guilds that rose with the city's woollen industry.

Although Henry VIII's Dissolution of the Monasteries took its toll on a city crammed with religious houses, York remained strongly wedded to the Catholic cause, and the most famous of the Gunpowder Plot conspirators, **Guy Fawkes**, was born here. During the **Civil War** Charles I established his court in the city, which was strongly pro-Royalist, inviting a Parliamentarian siege. Royalist troops, however, were routed by Cromwell and Sir Thomas Fairfax at the **Battle of Marston Moor** in 1644, another seminal battle in England's history, which took place just six miles west of York. It's said that only the fact that Fairfax was a local man saved York from destruction.

The city's eighteenth-century history was marked by its emergence as a social centre for Yorkshire's landed elite. Whilst the Industrial Revolution largely passed it by, the arrival of the **railways** brought renewed prosperity, thanks to the enterprise of pioneering "Railway King" George Hudson, lord mayor during the 1830s and 1840s. The railway is gradually losing its role as a major employer, as is the traditional but declining confectionery industry; incomes are now generated by new service and bioscience industries – not forgetting, of course, the four million annual tourists.

Arrival, information, transport and tours

Trains arrive at York Station, just outside the city walls, a 750-yard walk from the historic core. National Express **buses** and most other regional bus services drop off and pick up on Rougier Street, 200 yards north of the train station, just before Lendal Bridge, though some services, including the hourly service from Leeds Bradford Airport (Ⓦwww.yorkaircoach.com), call at the train station, too.

Frequent **park-and-ride** services operate into the city centre from sites adjacent to the A64, A19, A1079 and A166. Otherwise, drivers should park in

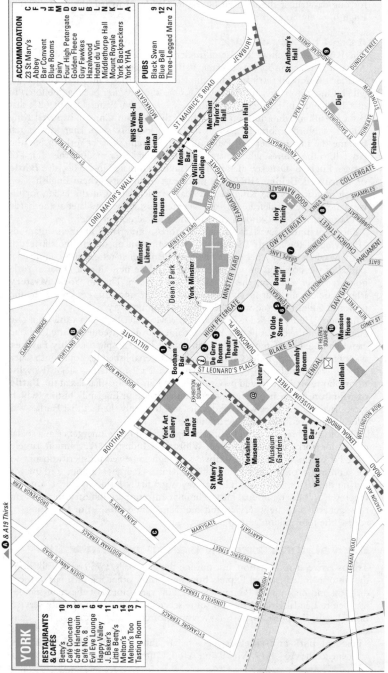

YORK

RESTAURANTS & CAFÉS

Betty's	10
Café Concerto	3
Café Harlequin	8
Café No. 8	1
Evil Eye Lounge	6
Happy Valley	4
J. Baker's	11
Little Betty's	5
Melton's	14
Melton's Too	13
Tasting Room	7

ACCOMMODATION

23 St Mary's	C
Abbey	F
Bar Convent	J
Blue Rooms	H
Dairy	M
Four High Petergate	D
Golden Fleece	G
Guy Fawkes	E
Hazelwood	B
Hotel du Vin	L
Middlethorpe Hall	N
Mount Royale	K
York Backpackers	I
York YHA	A

PUBS

Black Swan	9
Blue Bell	12
Three-Legged Mare	2

▲ A1036 Malton

▲ & A19 Thirsk

▲ A & A19 Thirsk

St John Street

Lord Mayor's Walk

Claremont Terrace

Portland Street

Gillygate

Bootham Row

Bootham

Marygate

Grosvenor Terr

Queen Anne's Road

Bootham Terrace

Sycamore Terrace

Saint Mary's

Marygate

Frederic Street

Longfield Terrace

Earlsborough T.

Monkgate

St Maurice's Road

Jewbury

Peasholme Green

Dundas Street

Hungate

St Saviourgate

Spen Lane

Aldwark

Bedern

St Andrewgate

Colliergate

Shambles

Swinegate

King's Sq

Church Street

Davygate

Coney St

New Street

Parliament St

Low Petergate

High Petergate

Stonegate

Deangate

Goodramgate

Minster Yard

College Street

Ogleforth

Museum Street

Blake St

Lendal

St Leonard's Place

St Helen's Square

Little Stonegate

Grape Lane

Jubbergate

Lendal Bridge

Wellington Row

Station Ave

Leeman Road

York Minster

Dean's Park

Minster Library

Treasurer's House

St William's College

Monk Bar

NHS Walk-In Centre

Bike Rental

Merchant Taylor's Hall

Bedern Hall

Digi!

Fibbers

St Anthony's Hall ❾

Holy Trinity ❹

Barley Hall ❼

Ye Olde Starre ❺

Mansion House ❿

Assembly Rooms

Guildhall

Bootham Bar ❶ ❷ ❸

De Grey Rooms

Theatre Royal

ⓘ

York Art Gallery

King's Manor

St Mary's Abbey

Yorkshire Museum

Museum Gardens

Lendal Bar

York Boat

Library @

Exhibition Square

❽

❻

Ⓔ

Ⓓ

Ⓑ

Ⓒ

Ⓕ

▼ National Railway Museum (100yds)

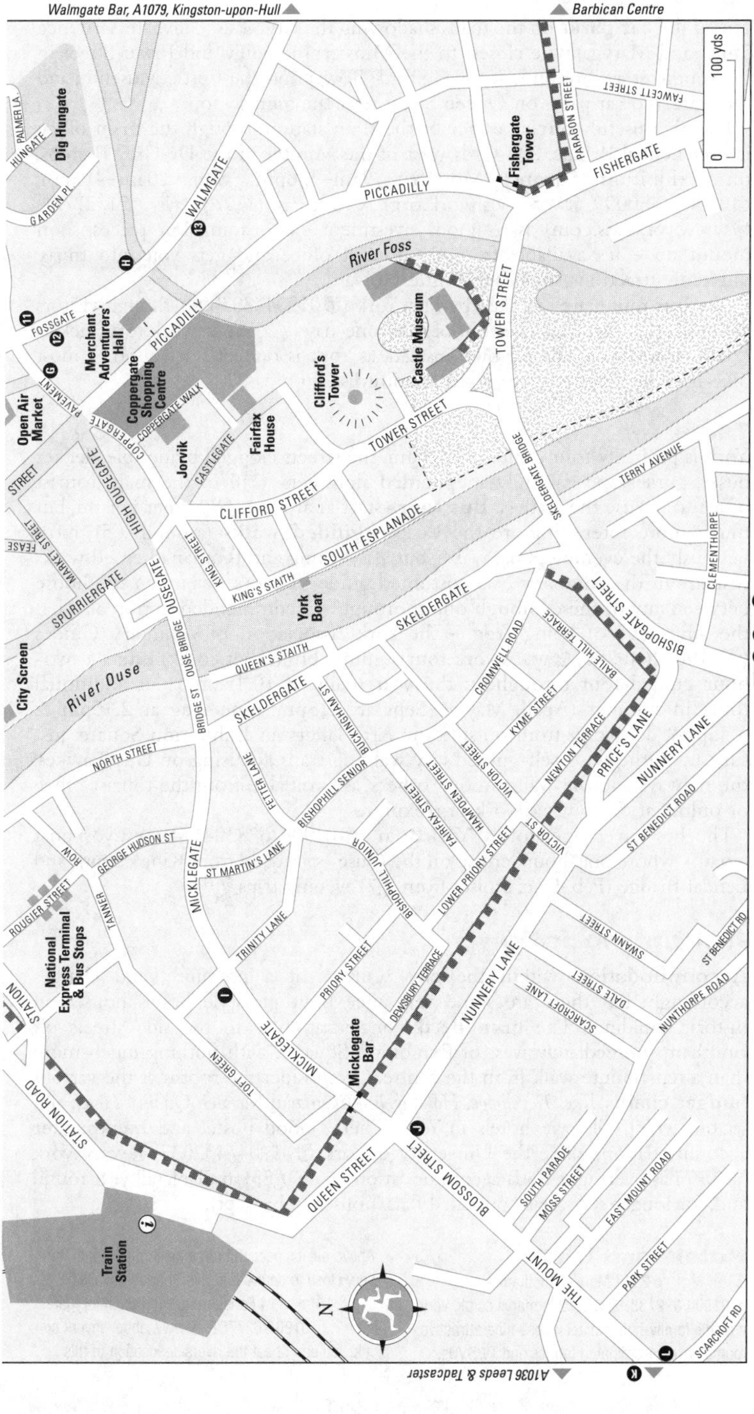

© Crown copyright

0   100 yds

12

YORKSHIRE

▶ ⑫ ⑬ ⑭

817

HUNGATE
PALMER LA
Dig Hungate
GARDEN PL
WALMGATE
PICCADILLY
River Foss
FISHERGATE
Fishergate Tower
PARAGON STREET
FAWCETT STREET
FISHERGATE
TOWER STREET
Castle Museum
Clifford's Tower
TOWER STREET
SKELDERGATE BRIDGE
TERRY AVENUE
CLEMENTHORPE
FOSSGATE
⑪ ⑫
Merchant Adventurers' Hall
PAVEMENT
⑬
H
PICCADILLY
Coppergate Shopping Centre
COPPERGATE
COPPERGATE WALK
Jorvik
CASTLEGATE
Fairfax House
KING STREET
Open Air Market
⑮
FEASE
MARKET STREET
STREET
HIGH OUSEGATE
OUSEGATE
SPURRIERGATE
CLIFFORD STREET
SOUTH ESPLANADE
KING'S STAITH
York Boat
SKELDERGATE
BISHOPGATE STREET
City Screen
River Ouse
NORTH STREET
QUEEN'S STAITH
SKELDERGATE
BRIDGE ST
OUSE BRIDGE
FETTER LANE
BUCKINGHAM ST
CROMWELL ROAD
BAILE HILL TERRACE
NEWTON TERRACE
PRICE'S LANE
KYME STREET
NUNNERY LANE
ST BENEDICT RD
ROUGIER STREET
STATION
National Express Terminal & Bus Stops
TANNER ROW
GEORGE HUDSON ST
MICKLEGATE
ST. MARTIN'S LANE
TRINITY LANE
BISHOPHILL SENIOR
BISHOPHILL JUNIOR
FETTER LANE
PRIORY STREET
FAIRFAX STREET
HAMPDEN STREET
VICTOR STREET
LOWER PRIORY STREET
VICTOR ST
NUNNERY LANE
SWANN STREET
DALE STREET
SCARCROFT LANE
ST BENEDICT RD
NUNTHORPE ROAD
ⅈ
MICKLEGATE
DEWSBURY TERRACE
TOFT GREEN
Micklegate Bar
QUEEN STREET
BLOSSOM STREET
SOUTH PARADE
MOSS STREET
EAST MOUNT ROAD
THE MOUNT
PARK STREET
SCARCROFT RD
STATION ROAD
Train Station
ⅈ
N
⑫
⑬
ⓚ
ⓛ

one of the **car parks** on the roads shadowing the city walls: Gillygate, Clarence Street and Marygate are closest to the Minster; Piccadilly and Tower Street in the southeast are convenient for Clifford's Tower and the Castle Museum; and there are also car parks on Queen Street near the train station.

There's a useful **tourist office** at the train station, though the main office is over Lendal Bridge, 200 yards west of the Minster in the De Grey Rooms, on Exhibition Square (Mon–Sat 9am–5/6pm; Sun 10am–4/5pm; ℡01904/550099, ⓦwww.visityork.org). A York Pass (1/2/3 days, £21/27/34; ⓦwww.yorkpass.com) is a good investment since admission prices soon mount up – it's available from the tourist office and gets you into thirty different attractions, including Castle Howard.

City **bus** routes are operated by First York (℡01904/883000), though visitors are unlikely to get much use out of their one-day (£3.50) or week rover tickets (£13). Consider renting a bike instead, as York is one of the country's most bike-friendly cities – there's a rental outfit listed on p.827.

Tours

York is probably tour capital of Britain, the streets clogged by double-decker buses, guides and carefully shepherded sightseers. Call in the main tourist office to peruse the leaflets. **Bus tours** start at around £8.50 per person, but much more interesting are the various **guided walks** (around £5), most famously the evening ghost walks, but also Viking and Roman-themed walks (usually in the company of a costumed guide). There's not much to choose between any of these, though one thoroughly recommended option also has the advantage of being **free** – the York Association of Voluntary Guides (℡01904/640780, ⓦwww.york.touristguides.btinternet.co.uk) offers a two-hour guided tour throughout the year (daily at 10.15am), plus additional tours in summer (April, May & Sept at 2.15pm; June–Aug at 2.15pm & 6.45pm), departing from outside the Art Gallery in Exhibition Square; just turn up. Otherwise, self-guided city walking trails, focusing on Guy Fawkes, the railways and the walls, among others, are available from the tourist office or online at ⓦwww.visityork.org/explore.

The best river operator is **YorkBoat** (℡01904/628324, ⓦwww.yorkboat.co.uk), whose one-hour "cruise on the Ouse" sails daily from King's Staith and Lendal Bridge (Feb–Dec; cruises from £7, evening trips £9).

Accommodation

Accommodation within the city walls is at a premium, and charges accordingly, but there are some very nice boutique-style hotels housed in historic buildings. The main **B&B** concentration is in the side streets off Bootham (immediately west of Exhibition Square), with nothing much more than a ten-minute walk from the centre. Or consider the rooms at the various **budget chains**, like *Travelodge*, *Holiday Inn*, *Ramada*, *Novotel*, *Quality Hotel*, and so on, which all have hotels in York. There's good hostel and **backpacker** accommodation, while the University of York ℡01904/432037, ⓦwww.york.ac.uk) has overnight B&B accommodation (from £55) available all year round and, for longer stays, self-contained flats/houses (July–Sept).

Hotels and B&Bs

23 St Mary's 23 St Mary's, Bootham ℡01904/622738, ⓦwww.23stmarys.co.uk. Very amiable family-house hotel whose nine attractive rooms have co-ordinated fabrics and TV/DVDs.

Above all, it's peaceful (on a no-through road), but very close to centre and river; parking available. ❺

Abbey 14 Earlsborough Terrace, Marygate ℡01904/627782, ⓦwww.abbeyghyork.co.uk. You can't beat the riverside location of this pretty terraced guest house. The five rooms are styled with flair, and there are river views at the front (where you pay the most) and from the nice, light dining room. Parking. ④, river view ⑤

Bar Convent 17 Blossom St ☎01904/643238, ⓦwww.bar-convent.org.uk. Grand Georgian building housing a museum and café as well as nine single rooms (£30 each), five twins, two double and a family room, self-catering kitchen and guest lounge. Pay-and-display parking over the road. Continental breakfast included. ③, en-suite ④

🕵 **Blue Rooms** Franklin's Yard ☎01904/673990, ⓦwww.thebluebicycle .com. The four one- and two-bedroom self-catering *Blue Rooms* apartments (available by the night), behind the *Blue Bicycle* restaurant, are enhanced by a quiet riverside situation. Two have balconies, one a 25ft lounge, and all are furnished in best contemporary style. Breakfast, fruit and champagne are included in the price. Parking. ⑦

Dairy 3 Scarcroft Rd ☎01904/639367, ⓦwww .dairyguesthouse.co.uk. Charming Victorian house half a mile south of the station, retaining its pine doors, cast-iron fireplaces, stained glass and pretty courtyard; six cottage-style rooms available. Closed Jan. ⑤

🕵 **Four High Petergate** 4 High Petergate ☎01904/658516, ⓦwww .fourhighpetergateyork.co.uk. Town-house hotel with private garden right by Bootham Bar and the walls, just seconds from the Minster. Rooms vary in size and aspect but have been given a classy shot-in-the-arm – teak beds, DVD players, power showers – while the adjacent bistro is one of the best places to eat in York. Parking available nearby. ⑥

Golden Fleece 16 Pavement ☎01904/625171, ⓦwww.goldenfleece.yorkwebsites.co.uk. Just four rooms available in this historic pub, but what a collection – one overlooks the Shambles, one has views to the Minster towers, and all are haunted (well, maybe). Decor is antique, the atmosphere unique. The pub itself is one of the oldest in the city and has a nice beer garden. ⑤

Guy Fawkes 25 High Petergate ☎01904/671001, ⓦwww.theguyfawkeshotel .com. You can virtually touch the Minster from the front door of this small town-house hotel, so no doubting the location (more dubious is the claim to be on the site of Guy Fawkes' birthplace). It's a contemporary place, though only the courtyard four-poster room, with a clawfoot bath, has any sense of space. ⑤, four-poster ⑥

Hazelwood 24–25 Portland St, Gillygate ☎01904/626548, ⓦwww.thehazelwoodyork.com.

This conversion of two Victorian houses offers elegant accommodation, just a minute from the walls in a quiet residential street. Rooms – antique pine, rich fabrics – are spacious, some with ornate fireplaces, and there's a handsome lounge and walled garden. ⑤

Hotel du Vin 89 The Mount ☎01904/557350, ⓦwww.hotelduvin.com. The slick boutique-hotel-and-bistro chain now has a new York address, close to the centre of town. The 44 rooms feature the trademark style, while the courtyard offers alfresco dining. There's also a vast selection of malts for whisky drinkers and a smokers' bothy in the garden. ⑦

Middlethorpe Hall Bishopsthorpe Rd ☎01904/641241, ⓦwww.middlethorpe.com. A grand eighteenth-century mansion a couple of miles south of the city, next to the racecourse. Antiques, wood panelling, superb rooms (some set in a private courtyard), gardens, parkland, pool and spa, and fine dining in the formal *Oak Room* restaurant. Courtyard ⑧, main house ⑨

Mount Royale The Mount ☎01904/628856, ⓦwww.mountroyale.co.uk. Antique-filled retreat with superb garden-suites set around a private garden, together with a heated outdoor pool (open summer only) and hot tub, sauna and steam room. Some less exalted standard rooms are also available. The contemporary restaurant here is well-regarded. ⑥, garden suites ⑧

Hostels

🕵 **York Backpackers** Micklegate House, 88–90 Micklegate ☎01904/627720, ⓦwww.yorkbackpackers.co.uk. Handsome building (the 1752 former home of the High Sheriff of Yorkshire) for an amiable hostel with good facilities – kitchen, laundry, Internet, TV and games room, café and cellar bar. High-ceilinged dorms (sleeping 8 to 18) from £14, cheaper for multi-night stays, plus private rooms (①); prices include continental breakfast.

York YHA Water End, Clifton ☎0870/770 6102, ⓔyork@yha.org.uk. Large Victorian mansion, 20min walk along Bootham from the tourist office and then a left turn at Clifton Green; or follow the riverside footpath. Beds are mostly in four-bedded dorms, though variously priced private rooms also available; book well in advance for these. Facilities include a licensed café, Internet, large garden, parking and discounted tickets for attractions. Buffet breakfast included in price. From £13.95 per person, up to £26.95 at peak times.

The City

Although there are around sixty churches, museums and historic buildings crammed within York's walls, in fact the tally of essential sights is surprisingly limited. Even so, it's hard to get round everything in less than two days, and equally difficult to stick to any rigid itinerary. The **Minster** is the obvious place to start, and you won't want to miss a walk around the walls, though after that it very much depends on your interests. The medieval city is at its most evocative around the streets known as Stonegate and the **Shambles**, while the earlier Viking city is entertainingly presented at **Jorvik**, perhaps the city's favourite family attraction. Stand-out historic buildings include the Minster's Treasurer's House, Georgian **Fairfax House**, the **Merchant Adventurers' Hall**, and the stark remnants of York's **Castle**. The two major museum collections are the incomparable **Castle Museum** and the **National Railway Museum**, where the appeal goes way beyond railway memorabilia, while the evocative ruins and gardens of St Mary's Abbey house the family-friendly **Yorkshire Museum**.

York Minster

York Minster (Mon–Sat 9/9.30am to last entry at 5pm, Sun noon–3.45pm, though times vary depending on season and services; Minster only £5.50, all attractions £9; ☎01904/557216, ⓦwww.yorkminster.org) ranks as one of the country's most important sights. Seat of the Archbishop of York, it is Britain's largest Gothic building and home to countless treasures, not least of which is an estimated half of all the medieval stained glass in England. In addition to the main body of the church, any complete tour of the building, which took 250 years to complete, should also include the foundations, crypt, chapter house and an ascent of the great central tower.

The first significant foundations were laid around 1080 by the first Norman archbishop, Thomas of Bayeux, and it was from the germ of this Norman church that the present structure emerged. The oldest surviving fabric, in the south transept, dates from 1220 during the reign of Archbishop Walter de Grey, who also began work on a new north transept in 1260. A new chapter house, in the Decorated style, appeared in 1300, and a new nave in the same style was completed in 1338. The Perpendicular (ie late Gothic) choir was realized in 1450 and the western towers in 1472. In 1480, the thirteenth-century central tower, which had collapsed in 1407, was rebuilt, thereby bringing the Minster to more or less its present state.

Nothing else in the Minster can match the magnificence of the **stained glass** in the nave and transepts. The **West Window** (1338) contains distinctive heart-shaped upper tracery (the "Heart of Yorkshire"), whilst in the nave's north aisle, the second bay window (1155) contains slivers of the oldest stained glass in the country. Moving down to the crossing, the north transept's **Five Sisters Window** is named after the five fifty-foot lancets, each glazed with thirteenth-century grisaille, a distinctive frosted, silvery-grey glass. Opposite, the south transept contains a sixteenth-century, 17,000-piece **Rose Window**, commemorating the marriage in 1486 of Henry VII and Elizabeth of York, an alliance which marked the end of the Wars of the Roses. The greatest of the church's 128 windows, however, is the majestic **East Window** (1405), at 78ft by 31ft the world's largest area of medieval stained glass in a single window. Its themes are the beginning and the end of the world, the upper panels showing scenes from the Old Testament, the lower sections mainly episodes from the Book of Revelation.

The foundations, or **undercroft** (Mon–Sat 9am–5pm, Sun 12.30–5pm; £4, including audioguide), have been turned into a museum, displaying fragments of the Roman fort which once stood on this site, as well as capitals, sculpture and fabric from the present Minster and its Norman predecessor. Amongst precious relics in the adjoining **treasury** is the eleventh-century Horn of Ulf, presented to the Minster by a relative of the tide-turning King Canute. There's also access from the undercroft to the **crypt**, the spot that transmits the most powerful sense of antiquity, as it contains sections of the original eleventh-century church, including pillars with fine Romanesque capitals. A small illuminated doorway opens onto the base of a pillar belonging to the guardhouse of the original Roman camp. Access to the undercroft, treasury and crypt is from the south transept, also the entrance to the **central tower** (£4), which you can climb for rooftop views over the city.

Around the Minster

The **Treasurer's House** in Chapter House Street (April–Oct Mon–Thurs, Sat & Sun 11am–3/4.30pm; £5.10; cellar £2.05; NT) is a glorious seventeenth-century town house, restored to reflect four centuries of styles by local industrialist Frank Green, who lived here from 1897 to 1930. His collection adorns the various period rooms – including an authentically kitted-out eighteenth-century kitchen and medieval hall. The cellar tour recounts the tale of the famed ghostly Roman legionaries; for recuperation there's a walled garden and nice café.

Just around the corner in College Street stands **St William's College**, an eye-catching half-timbered building, erected in 1467 for the Minster's priests. Nearby Goodramgate features even earlier constructions, in the form of the houses along **Our Lady's Row**, the oldest in the city (1316). These back onto the quiet churchyard of the delightful church of **Holy Trinity** (April–Sept Mon–Sat 10am–5pm, Sun noon–5pm; Oct–March Tues–Sat 10am–4pm; free), first built in the twelfth century but much altered since. It's worth going inside to see the medieval stained glass and Georgian woodwork, notably the jumbled box pews that have subsided with the slabbed floor.

Around the walls

Although much restored, the city's superb **walls** date mainly from the fourteenth century, though fragments of Norman work survive, particularly in the gates (known as "bars"), whilst the northern sections still follow the line of the Roman ramparts. The only break in the walls is along the eastern side, a few hundred yards along from Monk Bar, where the city was first protected by the marshes of the River Foss and later by the deliberately flooded area known as King's Pool.

Monk Bar is as good a point of access as any, tallest of the city's four main gates and host to the small **Richard III Museum** (daily 9/9.30am–4/5pm; £2.50; Ⓦ www.richardiiimuseum.co.uk), where you're invited to decide on the guilt or innocence of England's most maligned king. For just a taste of the walls' best section – with great views of the Minster and acres of idyllic-looking gardens – take the ten-minute stroll west from Monk Bar to Exhibition Square and **Bootham Bar**, the only gate on the site of a Roman gateway and marking the traditional northern entrance to the city. A stroll round the walls' entire two-and-a-half-mile length will also take you past the southwestern **Micklegate Bar**, long considered the most important of the gates since it marked the start of the road to London. The gate was built to a Norman design, reputedly using ancient stone coffins as building stone, and was later used to exhibit the heads of executed criminals and rebels. At the **Micklegate Bar Museum** (daily 9am–5pm; £2.50) – housed in a surviving

fortified tower – you can explore the story by way of old lithographs, models, paintings and the odd gruesome skull. Finally, **Walmgate Bar** in the east is the best preserved and the only one with its barbican intact.

Exhibition Square, Art Gallery and Yorkshire Museum

Exhibition Square, outside Bootham Bar, is the site of the refurbished **York Art Gallery** (daily 10am–5pm; free; ⓦ www.yorkartgallery.org.uk), housing an extensive collection of early Italian, British and northern European paintings. It's fun to pick out the smattering of York scenes, which include L.S. Lowry's take on Clifford's Tower. Otherwise, the gallery puts on a year-round series of special exhibitions and events, and is noted for its collections of British studio pottery and twentieth-century British painters.

South of Exhibition Square on Museum Street stands the entrance to the **Yorkshire Museum** (daily 10am–5pm; £5; ⓦ www.yorkshiremuseum.org.uk), which lies within the beautifully laid-out grounds of ruined St Mary's Abbey. It's one of York's better museums, with changing temporary exhibitions aimed largely at families, but otherwise strong on Roman archeological remains – grave effects, cooking utensils in a reconstructed kitchen, glassware, farming equipment and jewellery all illustrate the sophistication of life in the provincial capital of "Lower Britain". There are impressive displays of Viking and Anglo-Saxon artefacts, too, such as the richly decorated Coppergate Helmet, though chief exhibit is the fifteenth-century Middleham Jewel, found in 1985 – a diamond-shaped jewel with an oblong sapphire, acclaimed as the finest piece of Gothic jewellery in England.

Part of the museum basement incorporates the fireplace and chapter house of **St Mary's Abbey** (dawn to dusk; free), the ruins of which lie within the attractive museum gardens. Founded around 1080, the abbey later became an important Benedictine foundation – it was from here that disenchanted monks fled to found Fountains Abbey. The fact that the abbey controlled the city's brothels at the time can hardly have helped the Benedictine cause.

Stonegate, the Shambles and around

The two most photographed streets in York – if not the country – lie south of the Minster. **Stonegate** is as ancient as the city itself. Originally the Via Praetoria of Roman York, it's now paved with thick flags of York stone, which were once carried along here to build the Minster, hence the street name. Guy Fawkes' parents lived on Stonegate (there's a plaque opposite Mulberry Hall) and its Tudor buildings retain their considerable charm – **Ye Olde Starre** at no. 40, one of York's original inns, is on every tourist itinerary (you can't miss the sign straddling the street). Look up at the shop under the inn sign for the little red devil – the medieval sign for a printer's premises. Step through an alley known as Coffee Yard (by the Old Starre) to find **Barley Hall** (Tues–Sun 10am/noon–4pm; £3.50, @www.barleyhall.org.uk), a fine restoration of a late-medieval town-house given a hands-on twist – you can learn about fifteenth-century life here by touching the exhibits, playing period games, trying on costumes or attending other special events and festivals.

The **Shambles**, further to the south, could be taken as the epitome of medieval York. Almost impossibly narrow and lined with perilously leaning timber-framed houses, it was the home of York's butchers (the word "shambles" derives from the Old English for slaughterhouse), and old meat hooks still adorn the odd house. A little way further south, off Fossgate, the **Merchant Adventurers' Hall** (April–Sept Mon–Thurs 9am–5pm, Fri & Sat 9am–3.30pm, Sun noon–4pm; Oct–March Mon–Sat 9am–3.30pm; £2.50; @www .theyorkcompany.co.uk) is one of the finest medieval timber-framed halls in Europe. The beautiful building was raised by the city's most powerful guild: dealers in wool from the Wolds, woollens from the Dales and lead from the Pennines, commodities that were traded for exotica from far and wide.

Jorvik

The city's blockbuster historic exhibit is **Jorvik** (daily 10am–4/5pm; £7.95; ☎01904/543402, @www.vikingjorvik.com), located by the Coppergate shopping centre; you can avoid queuing by pre-booking your entrance ticket (though a surcharge applies). This multi-million-pound affair propels visitors in "time capsules" on a ride through the tenth-century city of York, presenting not just the sights but the sounds and even the smells of a riverside Viking city. This was a period when York was expanding rapidly, and most of the sites (blacksmiths' to bedrooms) and artefacts (leather shoes to wooden combs) were discovered during the 1976 excavations of Coppergate's real Viking settlement, now largely buried beneath the shopping centre outside. Jorvik shows how the artefacts were used, complete with live-action market and domestic scenes on actual Viking-age streets, with constipated villagers, axe-fighting, and other singular attractions.

Where Jorvik shows what was unearthed at Coppergate, the associated attraction that is **Dig!** (daily 10am–4/5pm; £5.50, joint ticket with Jorvik £11.20, pre-booking advised) illustrates the science involved. Housed five minutes' walk away from Jorvik, in the medieval church of St Saviour, on St Savioursgate, a simulated dig allows you to take part in a range of excavations in the company of archeologists, using authentic tools and methods. Tours (£1) to visit Dig Hungate, York's latest major archeological excavation, start from here.

Fairfax House

Fairfax House on Castlegate (Mon–Thurs & Sat 11am–4.30pm, Sun 1.30–4.30pm; guided tours only on Fri at 11am & 2pm; closed Jan & Feb; £5;

Ⓦ www.fairfaxhouse.co.uk) celebrates the wealth of the city's Georgian period. The elegant town house, decorated with superb stucco work, was restored to house the collection of fine arts left by Noel Terry, scion of one of the city's chocolate dynasties. The bulk of the collection consists of eighteenth-century furniture and clocks, though seasonal exhibitions showcase other arts, while every December the popular "Keeping of Christmas" exhibition recreates a Georgian Christmas in the house.

York Castle and the Castle Museum

Despite the rich architectural heritage elsewhere in the city, there's precious little left of **York Castle**, one of two established by William the Conqueror. Only the perilously leaning **Clifford's Tower** (daily 10am–4/6pm; £3; EH) remains, a stark stone keep built between 1245 and 1262. The old Norman keep was destroyed in 1190 during one of the city's more shameful historical episodes, when 150 Jews were put inside the tower for their own protection during an outburst of anti-Semitic rioting. The move did little to appease the mob, however, and faced with starvation or slaughter the Jews committed mass suicide by setting the tower on fire.

Immediately east of the tower lies the outstanding **Castle Museum** (daily 9.30/10am–5pm; £6.50, though prices may rise; Ⓦ www.yorkcastlemuseum .org.uk), a remarkable "collection of bygones" instigated by a Dr Kirk of Pickering, who in the 1920s realized that many of the everyday items used in rural areas were in danger of disappearing. He took the unusual step of accepting bric-a-brac from his patients in lieu of fees. When the pile of miscellanea grew too large for his own home it was housed in the city's old Debtors' Prison where, incidentally, the infamous highwayman Dick Turpin spent his last night on earth – you can still see his cell. A whole range of early craft, folk and agricultural ephemera is complemented by costumes, toys, machinery, domestic implements and show workshops, plus special exhibitions on subjects as diverse as swimming costumes through the ages and fire engines. Two entire reconstructed Victorian and Edwardian streets are perhaps the highlight, though Kirk's fetishistic collections of truncheons and biscuit moulds are surely unsurpassed. The extensive military displays, rambling dungeons and Sixties gallery are well worth seeing, too.

The National Railway Museum

The **National Railway Museum** on Leeman Road (daily 10am–6pm; free; Ⓦ www.nrm.org.uk) is a must if you have even the slightest interest in railways, history, engineering or Victoriana – allow at least two hours, though you could spend all day. The Great Hall alone features some fifty restored locomotives dating from 1829 onwards, among them the *Mallard*, at 126mph the world's fastest steam engine. By way of contrast, there's a Japanese bullet train on display, while the museum has also acquired the *Flying Scotsman*, the world's most famous locomotive, presently undergoing an overhaul, but due to be taking passengers again in 2009 (check for updates at the museum or call ℡0870/421 4472). The major permanent exhibitions include the plush splendour of the **royal carriages** ("Palaces on Wheels"), while dotted around the main hall is a welter of miscellaneous memorabilia: posters, models, paintings and period photographs, even a lock of George Stephenson's hair. A separate wing, "**The Works**", provides access to: the engineering workshop where conservation work is undertaken; a walk-round backstage warehouse area, showcasing the museum's reserve collection; and a track-and-signal viewing area over the East Coast main line. Finally, there's also the 54-metre-high Yorkshire Wheel at the

It would be hard to find a better caricature of a Victorian business baron than the portly and bewhiskered "Railway King" **George Hudson** (1800–71). Apprenticed to a York draper, he married the boss's daughter and then quickly inherited the business when his father-in-law was found drowned in mysterious circumstances. He ploughed his newfound wealth into railway shares, the basis of his subsequent empire, and a stepping stone to a career in local politics which eventually saw him become Lord Mayor of York. By 1844 he controlled 1016 miles of track, the largest network under single ownership until rail nationalization: in one typical move he managed to buy the Whitby and Pickering Railway for less than it had cost to build. However, lawsuits brought by disgruntled investors revealed untold dubious deals and in 1849 Hudson was ruined, and committed to York's Debtors' Prison. York, for its part, shunned its former hero until 1968, when a street and offices near the station were given his name.

museum (daily 10am–6pm; £6), which offers panoramic city and countryside views on a thirteen-minute pod ride. The museum and wheel are ten minutes' walk from the train station, or you can get there on a road train (Easter–Oct, every 30min, 11.15am–4.15pm) from Duncombe Place, near the Minster.

Eating and drinking

It's impossible to walk more than fifty yards in central York without coming across either a pub, teashop, café or restaurant – Daniel Defoe put it down to the "abundance of good company… and good families", though these days it's the tourist and student pound which fires the commercial engines. In keeping with much else in the city, many establishments are self-consciously old-fashioned, though there are some real highlights – truly **historic pubs**, the ultimate **teashop** experience that is *Bettys*, and a scattering of well-regarded **restaurants**. Riverside terraces between the Lendal and Ouse bridges have opened up the city for alfresco drinking, and there's a flourishing **café-bar** scene, with some honourable independents alongside the main chains. Every September, the city hosts the UK's biggest **food and drink festival** (www.yorkfestivaloffoodanddrink.com), with ten days of cookery demonstrations, promotions and events.

Tearooms, cafés and café-bars

Bettys/Little Bettys 6–8 St Helen's Sq ☏01904/659142. If there are tearooms in heaven they'll be like *Bettys*. Tea, cakes and pastries are the stock-in-trade (pikelets and Yorkshire fat rascals to name just a couple of specials), but there are a dozen or so hot dishes, great puddings, and a shop where you can buy fine-grade teas and coffees. Meanwhile, *Little Bettys*, 46 Stonegate, also serves fish and chips, bangers and *rösti*, and an all-day grilled breakfast. *Bettys* open daily until 9pm, *Little Bettys* until 5.30pm.

Café Concerto 21 High Petergate. Independent bistro, wallpapered with sheet music, boasting a good reputation and a relaxed atmosphere. Daily until 10pm.

Café Harlequin 2 Kings Square. Family run café overlooking the square, serving salads and snacks, accompanied by quality coffee, teas, frappés and smoothies. Closes 4/5pm.

Café No. 8 8 Gillygate ☏01904/653074. This wainscotted little café-bar, just outside Bootham Bar, has a great summer garden, while the food ranges from inventive wraps and sandwiches to more substantial mains (Moroccan meatballs, say, or chicken with ginger and tamarind). No dinner Sun or Mon nights. Closes 10pm.

Evil Eye Lounge 42 Stonegate. Colourful café-bar, where cosmopolitan reigns supreme. Tibetan dumplings and Japanese chicken vie with traditional Sunday roasts, Peruvian beers with Lindisfarne mead. Closes 11.30pm/12.30am.

Melton's Too 25 Walmgate
☎01904/629222. York's best and most relaxed café-bar – superior tapas, pasta, salads, steaks and more, with an emphasis on regional food. The food's very tasty and you're never rushed.

Restaurants

Happy Valley 70 Goodramgate ☎01904/654745. Housed in York's oldest row of houses, this half-timbered café certainly doesn't look like a Chinese restaurant, but pulls in Asian tourists for authentic, homestyle food. Most dishes are £5–8 making this a bargain not to miss. Inexpensive.

J. Baker's 7 Fossgate ☎01904/622688. Jeff Baker adds exquisite presentation to his drop-dead-gorgeous food. Experience his take on the best of Yorkshire produce in the seven-course dinner (£35) or the lunchtime grazing menu (a plate a snip at £10) There's catering for children too, who might steer you to the Chocolate Room upstairs. Reservations essential. Closed Sun & Mon. Expensive.

Melton's 7 Scarcroft Rd ☎01904/634341. You're assured of simple, classy cooking, including very good fish dishes, and imaginative vegetarian food

at *Melton's*. Closed Mon lunch & Sun dinner. Reservations advised. Expensive.

Tasting Room 13 Swinegate Court East, off Grape Lane ☎01904/627879. The city's sunniest courtyard makes a great lunch destination (smoked salmon on potato cakes, rocket-and-crayfish sandwiches); dinner in the pretty pastel restaurant shifts up a gear and the Modern British menu has plenty of choice. Closed certain days, call for details. Expensive.

Pubs

Black Swan Peasholme Green. York's oldest (sixteenth-century) pub has some superb stone flagging and wood panelling. The beer's good – you can get the local York Brewery stuff here – and it's also home of the city's folk club (🌐www.bsfc.org.uk for details of gigs).

Blue Bell Fossgate. A tiny, no-frills traditional pub – oak-panelling, real ales, no mobile phones, non-tourist clientele.

Three-Legged Mare 15 High Petergate. York Brewery's cosy outlet for its own quality beer and definitely a pub for grown-ups – no juke box, no video games and no kids.

Nightlife, culture and entertainment

Cultural entertainment is wide and varied, with the city supporting several theatres, cinemas and live music venues. Classical music recitals and concerts are often held in the city's churches and York Minster. For what's on listings see the local *Evening Press* (and its useful website, 🌐www.thisisyork.co.uk), and the monthly *What's On York* leaflet (🌐www.whatsonyork.com), while 🌐www.yorkfestivals.com gives the lowdown on the annual festivals and events.

The famous **York Mystery Plays** are traditionally held every four years, with the next planned for 2010 (🌐www.yorkmysteryplays.co.uk). Major annual events include York's **Viking Festival** (🌐www.vikingjorvik.com) every February and the **Early Music Festival** (🌐www.ncem.co.uk), held in July, perhaps the best of its kind in Britain. There are also noteworthy **Roman** (October) and **Christmas** (December) festivals, with plenty to see and do.

Venues

City Screen 13–17 Coney St ☎0870/758 3219, 🌐www.picturehouses.co.uk. The city's independent cinema is the art-house choice, with three screens, riverside café-bar, and *Basement Bar* with regular live music and a comedy club.

Fibbers Stonebow House, Stonebow ☎01904/651250, 🌐www.fibbers.co.uk. Inventive venue which puts on indie, guitar-pop, jazz, punk, rock and acoustic gigs.

Grand Opera House 4 Cumberland St ☎0870/606 3595, 🌐www.grandoperahouseyork.org.uk. Musicals, ballet, pop gigs and family entertainment in all its guises.

The National Centre for Early Music St Margaret's Church, Walmgate ☎01904/658338, 🌐www.ncem.co.uk. Not just early music, but also folk, world and jazz.

Theatre Royal St Leonard's Place ☎01904/623568, 🌐www.yorktheatreroyal.co.uk. Musicals, panto and mainstream theatre.

York delights in its independent, stylish and quirky shops – if there's anywhere else in England you can buy a Gothic nesting box and a Ford Capri coal sculpture on the same day, we've yet to find it. For special guidance, the *5 Routes to Shopping Heaven* shopping trail **leaflet** (Ⓦwww.york-tourism.co.uk/distinctiveshopping) is available from the tourist office, and you can check out the bargains at Ⓦwww.thesalesbible4york.co.uk.

Otherwise, for **brand and designer names** under one roof start at department stores Browns (Davygate; Ⓦwww.brownsyork.co.uk) or Fenwicks (Coppergate Centre), or, a little out of town at Fulford (buses every 10min from the train station), the York Designer Outlet (Ⓦwww.yorkdesigneroutlet.com), which houses 120 stores.

The Blue Ballroom (36 Gillygate) stocks **vintage and retro clothing**, and Porta Dextra (1 High Petergate) specializes in innovative contemporary jewellery. **Foodies** can choose their own curry mix from Rafi's Spicebox (17 Goodramgate; Ⓦwww.spicebox.co.uk), and bread, Italian-style, from La Via Vecchia (6 Shambles), a shop so good it doesn't even need a sign. Parliament Street, off the Shambles, sees numerous **outdoor markets** throughout the year, including the daily Newgate market, and a farmers' market on the last Friday of the month.

Booklovers will find a wealth of **secondhand/antiquarian bookshops**; favourites include the Barbican Bookshop (24 Fossgate; Ⓦwww.barbicanbookshop.co.uk) and the Minster Gate Bookshop (Minster Gate, off High Petergate; Ⓦwww.minstergatebooks.co.uk). The **York National Book Fair** every September (Ⓦwww.yorkbookfair.com) is one of the best for antiquarian books in the UK.

⑫

YORKSHIRE | York and around

Listings

Bike rental Bob Trotter, 13–15 Lord Mayor's Walk, at Monkgate ☏01904/622868. Rates from £12 per day, £50 per week. You can get a free city cycle map here.

Bus information National Express ☏0870/580 8080; East Yorkshire ☏01482/222222 (for Hull, Beverley and Bridlington); Yorkshire Coastliner ☏01653/692556 (for Leeds, Castle Howard, Pickering, Scarborough and Whitby).

Car rental Avis ☏01904/610460; Budget ☏01904/644919; Europcar ☏01904/656161; Hertz ☏01904/612586; Practical ☏01904/780500.

Hospital York District Hospital, Wigginton Road (24hr emergency number ☏01904/631313); bus #2, #5 or #6. The NHS Walk-in Centre, 31 Monkgate (daily 7am–10pm) offers care, advice and treatment without an appointment.

Internet City Library, off Museum St (Mon–Wed & Fri 9am–8pm, Thurs 9am–5.30pm, Sat 9am–4pm).

Laundry Walmgate Bar Laundromat, 39 Huby Court ☏01904/628588.

Pharmacy Boots, Kings Square ☏01904/671204.

Police Fulford Rd ☏0845/606 0247.

Post office 22 Lendal.

Racing York Racecourse ☏01904/620911, Ⓦwww.yorkracecourse.co.uk. One of Britain's finest, York Racecourse has regular meetings during the season (May–Sept), including the John Smith's Cup, the highlight of the annual calendar each July.

Taxis Ranks at Rougier Street, Duncombe Place, Exhibition Square, and the train station; or call Station Taxis ☏01904/623332.

Castle Howard

Immersed in the deep countryside of the Howardian Hills, fifteen miles northeast of York off the A64, **Castle Howard** (house March–Oct & late Nov to mid-Dec daily 11am–5pm; gardens open all year from 10am; £10; grounds only £7.50; Ⓦwww.castlehoward.co.uk) is the seat of one of England's leading aristocratic families and among the country's grandest stately homes. It's a pricey visit, but there's no question that it's worth seeing, the grounds especially, and you could easily spend the best part of a day here. The parking, at least, is free, though arriving by public transport is more problematic. The summer Moorsbus (see p.836) comes out here from Helmsley, while some Yorkshire Coastliner buses run from York, Malton or Pickering – it's best to call Traveline (℡0871/200 2233) to check schedules, or consider taking a bus tour from York.

The colossal main house was designed by **Sir John Vanbrugh** in 1699 and was almost forty years in the making – remarkable enough, even were it not for the fact that Vanbrugh was, at the start of the commission at least, best known as a playwright. He had no formal architectural training and seems to have been chosen by Charles Howard, third Earl of Carlisle, for whom the house was built, purely on the strength of his membership of the same London gentlemen's club. Shrewdly, Vanbrugh recognized his limitations and called upon the assistance of **Nicholas Hawksmoor**, who had a major part in the house's structural design – the pair later worked successfully together on Blenheim Palace. If Hawksmoor's guiding hand can be seen throughout, Vanbrugh's influence is clear in the very theatricality of the building, notably in the palatial **Great Hall**. This was gutted by fire in the 1940s, but has subsequently been restored from old etchings and photographs to something approaching its original state. Other rooms and chambers in endless succession are filled with Dutch porcelain, Roman statuary, furniture by Sheraton and Chippendale, paintings by Gainsborough, Veronese, Rubens and Van Dyck, not to mention trinkety objets d'art, gaudy friezes and monumental pilasters – vulgar in their excess if not provenance.

Vanbrugh also turned his attention to the estate's thousand-acre **grounds**, where he could indulge his playful inclinations – the formal gardens, clipped parkland, towers, obelisks and blunt sandstone follies stretch in all directions, sloping gently to two artificial lakes. The whole is a charming artifice of grand, manicured views – an example of what three centuries, skilled gardeners and pots of money can produce.

Daily outdoor **tours** (call for times; free) concentrate on aspects of the house and garden, and the annual outdoor Proms concert every August is very popular. There are **cafés** in the main house and by the larger lake, though the courtyard café at the main entrance has the nicest food. Facilities round off with a children's playground, nature trails, plant centre, gift shop and even a **camping and caravan** park (℡01653/648316; March–Oct).

Hull, the Humber and the East Yorkshire coast

The character of the historic "**East Riding**" has been shaped by a strong seafaring tradition, boosted by Hull's advantageous position on the **River Humber** estuary. Beyond **Hull**, up the East Yorkshire coast, lonely beaches, wild foreshores and forgotten seafront villages draw curious tourists keen to get off the beaten track. The bucket-and-spade resorts of **Bridlington** and **Filey** are the traditional draws, while the cliffs of **Flamborough Head** provide one of the best places in Britain for birdwatching. Inland, historic **Beverley**, with its marvellous minster, is plonked amid the flatlands that stretch northwards from Hull to meet the **Yorkshire Wolds**, a crescent-shaped ridge of hills that falls to the sea at Flamborough. Drivers approaching from Lincolnshire and the south will cross the **Humber Bridge**, an immense single-span suspension bridge opened in 1981; a viewing area allows you to stop and gasp.

Hull

HULL – officially Kingston upon Hull – has a maritime pre-eminence that dates back to 1299, when it was laid out as a seaport by Edward I. It quickly became England's leading harbour, and was still a vital garrison when the gates were closed against Charles I in 1642, the first serious act of rebellion of what was to become the English Civil War. Fishing and seafaring have always been important here, and today's city maintains a firm grip on its heritage while bolstering its attractions for visitors – the dramatic aquarium known as **The Deep**, a superior set of free local **museums** and a revived **Old Town** area – which together provide scope for a good couple of days' worth of sightseeing. Hull's most famous adopted son, the poet and university librarian Philip Larkin, was being typically curmudgeonly when he wrote, "I wish I could think of just one nice thing to tell you about Hull, oh yes ... it's very nice and flat for cycling". This is too harsh – museums aside, he might have mentioned the city's excellent historic pubs, its unique white telephone boxes, or the various **festivals** and fairs that Hull arranges with great flair, notably the colossal travelling funfair that is the Hull Fair (October), plus the Hull Literature Festival (June; ⓦwww.humbermouth .org.uk) and the Hull Jazz Festival (August).

The City

The central **Princes Dock** sets the tone for Hull's modern refurbishment, the waters now lined by landscaped brick promenades and café-bars, and overlooked by **Princes Quay**, a multi-tiered, glass-spangled shopping centre, with the marina beyond. To the north, the massive St Stephen's development, housing the new transport interchange and shopping complex, leads off Ferensway.

The city's maritime legacy is covered in the **Maritime Museum** (Mon–Sat 10am–5pm, Sun 1.30–4.30pm; free), housed in the Neoclassical headquarters of the former Town Docks Offices, on Queen Victoria Square. The main boost to the town's coffers in the eighteenth and nineteenth centuries was whaling, and here you can view a whale skeleton, a blubber pot cauldron, and a fine collection of scrimshaw (items made from whale bones and teeth) alongside model ships, old photographs, and Inuit relics.

Leave Queen Victoria Square by pedestrianized Whitefriargate and, after about 200 yards, turn right down Trinity House Lane for **Holy Trinity** (Tues 11am–2pm, Wed & Fri noon–3pm, Thurs 1–3pm, Sat 9am–noon; free; ⓦwww .holytrinityhull.co.uk), among the most pleasing parish churches in the country, notable for its early brick transepts and chancel. Trinity Square has long been the place for **markets**: there's the indoor Trinity Market (Mon–Sat 7.30am–5pm) and a farmers' market in the square on the second and fourth Friday of the month. Close by on South Church Side is one of Hull's most revered relics – the **Old Grammar School**, a red-brick edifice built in 1583, which for 120 years doubled as the town's Merchant Adventurers' Hall.

Two blocks east, over towards the River Hull, you reach the **Museums Quarter** (all attractions Mon–Sat 10am–5pm, Sun 1.30–4.30pm; free) and **High Street**, which has been designated an "Old Town" conservation area thanks to its crop of former merchants' houses and narrow cobbled alleys. At its northern end stands **Wilberforce House**, the former home of William Wilberforce, containing some fascinating exhibits on slavery and its abolition,

▲ The Deep, Hull

the cause to which he dedicated much of his life. Next door is **Streetlife**, devoted to the history of transport in the region and centred on a 1930s street scene of reconstructed shops, railway goods yard, and cycle and motor works. This is as much about social as transport history, with a (simulated) ride on a nineteenth-century coach, recorded conversations on a Hull Tram, and the rules of bicycle polo vying for your attention. If this is good, then the adjoining **Hull and East Riding Museum** is even better, full of inventive displays. A life-size mammoth and a walk-through Iron Age village set you up for the showpiece attractions, namely vivid displays of Celtic burials, the unique Bronze Age wooden figures from Roos Carr (complete with appendages the Victorians thought too rude to display) and spectacular Roman mosaics. Dredged from a river, meanwhile, came the Hasholme boat, an oak cargo boat 41 feet long and 2300 years old – now confined within a see-through conservation chamber.

Protruding from a promontory overlooking the River Humber looms **The Deep** (daily 10am–6pm, last entry 5pm; £8.50; Ⓦwww.thedeep.co.uk), ten minutes' walk from the old town. Its educational displays and videos wrap around an immense thirty-foot-deep, 2.3-million-gallon viewing tank filled with sharks, rays and octopuses. You see into the tank at every level on the ramped walk down – while diverting off to a deep-sea research station or the ice-cold Polar Gallery – and then return by underwater lift. Meanwhile the Twilight Zone extension takes you even further into the ocean's depths – and face-to-face with its deepwater inhabitants.

Finally, from the pier off Nelson Street, opposite the *Minerva* pub, **speedboat trips** (Ⓣ01964/603018 or 07815/629367, Ⓦwww.humberparascending.co.uk) whisk you along the Humber to the docks or under the Humber Bridge on a variety of tours (£3.50–15 per person) or parascending trips (£30). Departures are every weekend, bank holiday and school holiday weekdays, though it's best to call first.

Practicalities

Hull's **train station** is on the west side of town, on the main drag of Ferensway, with the **bus station** just to the north. Drivers should aim for the **car parks** in the St Stephen's development or Princes Quay shopping centre.

The **tourist office** is on Paragon Street at Queen Victoria Square (Mon–Sat 10am–5pm, Sun 11am–3pm; ☏01482/223559, ⊛www.hullcc.gov.uk/visithull). They co-ordinate richly anecdotal **guided tours** around the old town (April–Oct Mon–Sat at 2pm, Sun 11am; £3) departing from their office, or you can pick up the entertaining "Fish Trail" leaflet, a self-guided trail that kids will love. There's a fair choice of **accommodation** on offer, including several central small hotels and the budget chains *Ibis*, *Campanile* and *Holiday Express*. The tourist office can help – and through them you can get special weekend hotel rates (from around £25 per person per night).

Hull has dozens of city-centre **pubs and café-bars**, the best of which are picked out in a *Hull Ale Trail* leaflet available from the tourist office. The upcoming nightlife area is centred on Pearson Park, just north of the centre (take a taxi), where Princes Avenue has a line of popular café-bars and restaurants. Meanwhile, the excellent **Hull Truck Theatre Company** (☏01482/323638, ⊛www.hulltruck.co.uk) is where, among others, many of the plays of award-winning John Godber first see light of day. It's currently in its original premises on Spring Street, though by autumn 2008 will move to a new home in the St Stephen's development.

Accommodation

Holiday Inn Hull Marina Castle St ☏0870/400 9043, ⊛www.holiday-inn.co.uk. The trim, light rooms at the city's best central hotel overlook the marina, and there's parking, a restaurant and bar, plus indoor pool, gym and sauna. Good buffet breakfast served. ❺

Kingston Theatre Hotel 1-2 Kingston Sq ☏01482/225828, ⊛www.kingstontheatrehotel .com. Straightforward, but good-value hotel rooms on the city's prettiest square, across from Hull New Theatre. It's quiet for the city centre, and for a bit more money you can upgrade to one of the more spacious attached "Victorian Suites". ❹, suites ❺

Quality Hotel Royal 170 Ferensway ☏01482/325087, ⊛www.hotels-hull.com. Original Victorian hotel, by the station, that has been fully refurbished and incorporates a good leisure centre and pool. ❺

Cafés-bars and restaurants

Cerutti's 10 Nelson St ☏01482/328501. Down at the end of the east side of the marina, this leads the way in local seafood. Closed Sun lunch. Expensive.

Mimosa 406–408 Beverley Rd ☏01482/474748. Friendly Turkish restaurant with an open charcoal grill – it's around a mile and a half out of the centre – very regular buses run up Beverley Rd from the stations. Real value for money. Moderate.

Pave Café-Bar 16–20 Princes Ave ☏01482/333181. The best of the Pearson Park options is a contemporary watering hole with some outdoor tables, reasonably priced food (until 7pm) and live jazz sessions on Sun afternoons. Moderate.

Studio 10½ King St ☏01482/224625. Take the stairs above the gift shop, opposite Holy Trinity Church, and enter a trompe l'oeil painted walled garden, where a handsome range of lunches and snacks awaits. Vegans and special diets catered for. Daytime only; closed Sun. Inexpensive.

Taman Ria Tropicana 45-47 Princes Ave ☏01482/345640. Sort out your *rendang* from your *laksa* at this agreeable, authentic Malaysian/Indonesian restaurant, where all the main dishes cost under a tenner. Closed Mon. Moderate.

Pubs

George The Land of Green Ginger. Venerable pub found on Hull's most curiously named street – and featuring, if you can find it, England's smallest window.

Minerva Corner of Nelson St and Humber Dock St. Classic marina pub with cosy nooks, outdoor tables and cheap food.

Ye Olde White Harte 25 Silver St. Has a very pleasant courtyard beer garden and a history going back to the seventeenth century – witness the huge fireplaces and the skull behind the bar, found during renovations.

Beverley

BEVERLEY, nine miles north of Hull, ranks as one of northern England's premier towns, its minster the superior of many an English cathedral, its tangle of old streets, cobbled lanes and elegant Georgian and Victorian terraces the very picture of a traditional market town. Over 350 buildings are listed as possessing historical or architectural merit, and though you could see its first-rank offerings in a morning, this is one of a handful of places in this part of the world where you might want to stay.

Approaches to the town are dominated by the twin towers of **Beverley Minster** (Mon–Sat 9am–4/5.30pm, Sun noon–4/4.30pm; donation requested; ⓦ www.beverleyminster.org), visible for miles around. An early monastery stood on the site but a series of fires, and the collapse of the central tower in 1213, paved the way for two centuries of rebuilding. The result was one of the finest Gothic creations in the country. The **west front**, which crowned the work in 1420, is widely considered without equal, its survival due in large part to architect Nicholas Hawksmoor, who restored much of the church in the eighteenth century. Similar outstanding work awaits in the interior, most notably the fourteenth-century **Percy Tomb** on the north side of the altar, its sumptuously carved canopy one of the master-pieces of medieval European ecclesiastical art. Nearby stands the **Fridstol**, a Saxon "sanctuary chair", which provided a safe haven for men on the run. Other incidental carving throughout the church is magnificent, particularly the 68 misericords of the oak **choir** (1520–24), one of the largest and most accomplished in England. Much of the decorative work here and elsewhere is on a musical theme. Beverley had a renowned guild of itinerant minstrels, who provided funds in the sixteenth century for the carvings on the transept aisle capitals, where you'll be able to pick out players of lutes, bagpipes, horns and tambourines.

Cobbled Highgate runs from the minster through town, along the pedestrian-ized shopping streets and past the main Market Square, to Beverley's other great church, **St Mary's** (Mon–Sat 9.30/10am–4/4.30pm, Sun 2–4pm; Oct–March closed Sat; free), which nestles alongside the **North Bar**, sole survivor of the town's five medieval gates. Inside, the chancel's painted panelled ceiling (1445) contains portraits of English kings from Sigebert (623–37) to Henry VI (1421–71), while among the carvings, the favourite novelty is the so-called "Pilgrim's Rabbit", said to have been the inspiration for the White Rabbit in Lewis Carroll's *Alice in Wonderland*.

Practicalities

Beverley's **train station** on Station Square is just a couple of minutes' walk from the minster. The **bus station** is at the junction of Walkergate and Sow Hill Road, with the main street just a minute's walk away. The **tourist office** is at 34 Butcher Row in the main shopping area (Mon–Fri 9.30am–5.15pm, Sat 10am–4.45pm, plus Sun in July & Aug 11am–3pm; Ⓣ 01482/391672, ⓦ www.visiteastyorkshire.com).

There's plenty of local **accommodation**, including *Number One*, 1 Woodlands (Ⓣ 01482/862752, ⓦ www.number-one-bedandbreakfast-beverley.co.uk; no credit cards; ❷), a small B&B in a quiet Victorian house two minutes' walk from the market place. The top town-centre hotel is the *Beverley Arms*, North Bar Within (Ⓣ 01482/869241, ⓦ www.brook-hotels.co.uk; ❻), though there are several other less expensive choices. The **youth hostel** (Ⓣ 0870/770 5696, Ⓔ beverleyfriary@yha.org.uk; from £13.95; closed Nov–March) occupies one of the town's finer buildings, a restored Dominican friary that was mentioned in the Canterbury Tales. It's located in Friar's Lane, off Eastgate, just a hundred yards southeast of the minster.

Cerutti 2, in Station Square (☎01482/866700; closed Sun & Mon), is a sister **brasserie** to the restaurant of the same name in Hull and serves fresh fish; there's also a good deli next door. Otherwise, there's a full complement of tearooms and cafés, or you can eat in the **pubs** – the celebrated *White Horse* (also known as Nellie's) on Hengate, near St Mary's, is a thoroughly atmospheric traditional drinking den with folk music nights. The **Beverley Folk Festival** (Ⓦwww.beverleyfestival.com) takes place each June, featuring music, song and dance, while if you fancy a day at the races, contact **Beverley Races** (☎01482/867488, Ⓦwww.beverley-racecourse.co.uk).

The East Yorkshire coast

The **East Yorkshire coast** curves south in a gentle arc from the mighty cliffs of Flamborough Head to Spurn Head, a hook-shaped promontory formed by the constant erosion and shifting currents. There are few parts of the British coast as dangerous – indeed, the Humber lifeboat station at Spurn Point is the only one in Britain permanently staffed by a professional crew. Between the two points lie a handful of tranquil villages and miles of windswept dunes and mudflats, noted bird sanctuaries, and superbly lonely retreats accessible to anyone prepared to cycle or walk the paths that fan out amidst the dunes.

The two main resorts, **Bridlington** and **Filey** are linked by the regular **train** service between Hull and Scarborough. There's also an hourly bus service between Bridlington, Filey and Scarborough, while the seasonal Sunday **Spurn Ranger** service (Easter–Oct; ☎01482/222222) gives access to the isolated Spurn Head coastline.

Bridlington

The southernmost resort on the Yorkshire coast, **BRIDLINGTON** has maintained its harbour for almost a thousand years, though for much of that time it remained a small-scale place of little consequence. Like many coastal stations, it flourished in Edwardian times as a resort, but has spent recent decades in the same decline as other English bucket-and-spade holiday destinations. Renovations have smartened up the seafront promenade, which looks down upon the town's best asset – its sweeping sandy **beach**. It's an out-and-out family resort, which means plenty of candy-floss, fish and chips, rides, boat trips and amusement arcades.

Bridlington's largely Georgian Old Town is a mile inland, and home to the **Bayle Museum** (April–Sept Mon–Fri 10am–4pm, Sun 11am–4pm; £2), which presents local history in a building that once served as the gateway to a fourteenth-century priory. The Old Town's High Street is a narrow thoroughfare of antique shops and traditional stores – the *Georgian Tea Rooms* at no.56 has several floors of antiques and a tea garden at the rear.

In late October, the Spa Bridlington on the promenade is home to the renowned **Musicport World Music Festival** (Ⓦwww.musicport.fsnet.co.uk).

Flamborough Head and Bempton Cliffs

Around fourteen miles of precipitous four-hundred-foot cliffs gird **Flamborough Head**, just to the northeast of Bridlington. The best of the seascapes are visible on the peninsula's north side, accessible by road from Flamborough village. The **lighthouse** just a mile beyond (tours every 30min:

July–Oct Wed & Sun 11am/1pm–4/5pm; Aug also Thurs–Sat; £2.75; ☎01262/673769, ⓦwww.trinityhouse.co.uk) is the latest in a line of warning beacons here that date back to the seventeenth century, but which, in earlier times at least, manifestly failed to do their job: between 1770 and 1806, 174 ships went down in the hazardous waters off the headland.

From **Bempton**, two miles north of Bridlington, you can follow the grassy cliff-top path all the way round to Flamborough Head or curtail by cutting up paths to Flamborough village. The *Seabirds*, at the junction of the roads to the two villages, is a nice pub with a good line in fresh-fish bar meals. The RSPB sanctuary at **Bempton Cliffs**, reached along a quiet lane from Bempton, is the best single place to see the area's thousands of cliff-nesting birds. It's also the only mainland gannetry in England and you'll see gannets diving from fifty feet in the air to catch mackerel and herring. Bempton also boasts the second-largest **puffin colony** in the country, with several thousand returning to the cliffs between March and August. Late March and April is the best time to see the puffins, but the **Visitor Centre** (daily 9.30/10am–4/5pm; parking £3.50; ☎01262/851179, ⓦwww.rspb.org .uk) can advise on other breeds' activities and rent you a pair of binoculars. RSPB puffin and seabird **cruises** (mid-May to Sept, various times, usually on Sat & Sun; £11; ☎01262/850959) are a spectacular way to see the Bempton and Flamborough Head cliffs. They last three to four hours and depart from Bridlington.

Filey

FILEY, half a dozen miles further north up the coast, is at the very edge of the Yorkshire Wolds (and technically in North Yorkshire). It has a good deal more class as a resort than Bridlington, retaining many of its Edwardian features, including some splendid panoramic gardens. It, too, claims miles of wide sandy beach, stretching most of the way south to Flamborough Head and north the mile or so to the jutting rocks of **Filey Brigg**, where a nature trail wends for a couple of miles through the surroundings. **Bus** and **train** stations are just west of the centre on Station Avenue; there's a **car park** behind the bus station. Walk down Station Avenue and Murray Street to **Filey Visitor Centre** on John Street (May–Sept daily 10am–5pm; Oct–April Sat & Sun 10am–4.30pm; ☎01723/383637). You'll find a clutch of standard **B&Bs** on Rutland Street, off West Avenue, which runs from the church in the centre of town. A few pricier **hotels** sit amongst the holiday flats down on the beachfront. *Downcliffe House* (☎01723/513310, ⓦwww .downcliffehouse.com; ⑨) is the pick of them, with a sea-view restaurant with outdoor terrace serving a decent menu of fresh fish.

The North York Moors

Virtually the whole of the **North York Moors** (ⓦwww.moors.uk.net), from the Hambleton and Cleveland hills in the west to the cliff-edged coastline to the east, is protected as one of the country's finest national parks. The heather-covered, flat-topped hills are cut by deep, steep-sided valleys, and views here stretch for miles, interrupted only by giant cultivated forests, pale shadows of the woodland that covered the region before it was cleared by Neolithic and later peoples. Barrows and ancient forts provide memorials of these early settlers, mingling on the high moorland with the **Roman remains** of Wades

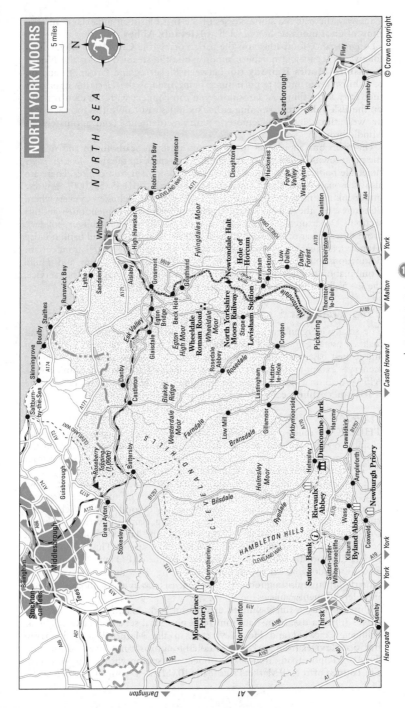

© Crown copyright

NORTH YORK MOORS

N O R T H   S E A

Filey
Hunmanby
Scarborough
Cloughton
Hackness
Forge Valley
West Ayton
Snainton
A170
Low Dalby
Dalby Forest
Ebberston
Thornton le-Dale
A169
Pickering
Cropton
Hutton-le-Hole
Lastingham
Gillamoor
Kirkbymoorside
A170
Harome
Oswaldkirk
Ampleforth
B1257
Coxwold
Newburgh Priory
Fylingdales Moor
Hole of Horcum
Newtondale Halt
Levisham
Lockton
Stape
North Yorkshire Moors Railway
Levisham Station
Newtondale
Robin Hood's Bay
Ravenscar
CLEVELAND WAY
A171
High Hawsker
Whitby
Grosmont
Goathland
A169
Beck Hole
Egton
Egton Bridge
Wheeldale Roman Road
Wheeldale Moor
Rosedale Abbey
Rosedale
Low Mill
Bransdale
Runswick Bay
Lythe
Sandsend
Aislaby
A171
Glaisdale
Esk Valley
Danby
Castleton
Egton High Moor
Blakey Ridge
Westerdale Moor
Farndale
Helmsley Moor
Helmsley
Duncombe Park
Rievaulx Abbey
Ryedale
Bilsdale
C L E V E L A N D   H I L L S
Staithes
Boulby
Skinningrove
Saltburn-by-the-Sea
A174
CLEVELAND WAY
Guisborough
A173
Great Ayton
A172
Roseberry Topping (1,050ft)
Battersby
Stokesley
B1257
HAMBLETON HILLS
Osmotherley
Sutton Bank
Sutton-under-Whitestonecliffe
Kilburn
Byland Abbey
Wass
CLEVELAND WAY
Mount Grace Priory
A684
Northallerton
Thirsk
A168
Asenby
A167
A19
A170
A1
A67
A66
Stockton-on-Tees
Middlesbrough
Billingham
Tees
A19

0   5 miles

0

▶ Darlington   ▼ A1   ▲ Harrogate ▶   ▼ York   ▼ York   ▲ Castle Howard   ▼ York   ▼ Malton   ▼ A64

835

Causeway, the battered stone crosses of the first Christian inhabitants and the ruins of great monastic houses such as **Rievaulx Abbey**.

Long-distance footpaths cross the park, notably the **Cleveland Way**, which follows the coast and northern moor, while the steam trains of the **North Yorkshire Moors Railway** run between Pickering and Grosmont and on to Whitby (even more popular since being used as the *Hogwarts Express* in the *Harry Potter* films). At Grosmont you can connect with the regular trains on the **Esk Valley** line, running either six miles east to Whitby and the coast, or west through more remote country settlements (and ultimately to Middlesbrough).

The main **bus** approaches to the moors are from Scarborough and York to the main towns of **Helmsley** and **Pickering** – pick up the free *Moors Explorer* timetable booklet from tourist offices and park information centres. There are also seasonal **Moorsbus** services (April–Oct; ☎01845/597000, ⓦwww.moors.uk.net/moorsbus), connecting Pickering and Helmsley to everywhere of interest in the national park (including everywhere mentioned in this section). Departures are several times daily in the school summer holidays, more restricted at other times (though at least every Sunday and bank holiday Monday), and get-on-get-off day tickets are a bargain £4, or £7 from certain destinations outside the park (like York, Thirsk, Scarborough and Hull). Combination tickets are also available for the Yorkshire Coastliner bus service, the Esk Valley train line and the North York Moors Railway.

The western moors

The small Georgian market town of **Thirsk** lies just outside the park and makes a useful gateway, but it's **Helmsley** that is by far the area's nicest town and its best base for explorations. Most outings are likely to centre less on the scenery – except for the walks and staggering views from **Sutton Bank** on the A170 – than on a cluster of historic buildings, of which the most prepossessing is **Rievaulx Abbey**, easily seen from Helmsley.

Thirsk

THIRSK, 23 miles north of York, made the most of its strategic crossroads position on the ancient drove road between Scotland and York and on the historic east–west route from dales to coast. Its medieval prosperity is clear from the large, cobbled **Market Place** (market days are Monday and Saturday), while well-to-do citizens later endowed the town with fine Georgian houses and halls, like those still standing on Kirkgate, which runs off the square. However, Thirsk's main draw is its attachment to the legacy of local vet Alf Wight, better known as James Herriot. Despite the confusing claims of various Yorkshire Dales villages, Thirsk was the "Darrowby" of the Herriot books, not least because the town was where the vet had his actual surgery. This building, at 23 Kirkgate, is now the **World of James Herriot** (daily 10/11am–4/5pm; £5.20; ⓦwww.worldofjamesherriot.org), an entertaining re-creation of the vet's 1940s surgery, dispensary, sitting room and kitchen, each crammed with period pieces and Herriot memorabilia.

Thirsk is only a thirty-minute drive from York, making an easy day-trip. **Buses** (three a day, Mon–Sat, from York, plus local services between Thirsk, Kilburn, Coxwold and Helmsley) stop in the Market Place. The **train station** (services from York and Middlesbrough) is a mile west of town on the A61 (Ripon road); minibuses connect the station with the town centre. The **tourist office**, 49 Market Place (daily 10/11am–4/5pm; ☎01845/522755,

@ www.hambleton.gov.uk), can help with **accommodation**. There are B&Bs on Kirkgate, on the road up to the parish church, while the Market Place is ringed by old-fashioned pubs, cafés and tearooms. Four miles to the south, down the A168 at **Asenby**, *Crab Manor* (℗01845/577286, @www .crabandlobster.co.uk; ❾) is something of a local curiosity – its lavish rooms are all styled in the fashion of famous hotels from around the world (the *Waldorf Astoria*, Barbados' *Sandy Lane* and so on), while its *Crab & Lobster* restaurant is a renowned for its fish.

Osmotherley

Eleven miles north of Thirsk, the little village of **OSMOTHERLEY** huddles around its green, proud of its ancient market cross and curious adjacent stone table from on top of which it's said John Wesley preached during one of his sermon tours. Having seen agriculture and industry come and go, the pretty settlement now gets by as a hiking centre, since it's a key stop on the **Cleveland Way** as well as starting point for the brutal 42-mile **Lyke Wake Walk** to Ravenscar, south of Robin Hood's Bay (see box below). It's one of England's more macho long-distance paths, and a highly popular route, so hikers and their back-up teams tend to pack both village youth hostel and campsite year round. For more comfort make for the *Three Tuns* (℗01609/883301, @www.threetunsrestaurant.co.uk; ❺), on the green, a renovated **pub** brimming with awards and serving classy meals.

Mount Grace Priory

Two miles from Osmotherley, the fourteenth-century **Mount Grace Priory** (April–Sept Mon & Thurs–Sun 10am–6pm; Oct–March Thurs–Sun 10am–4pm; £4; NT & EH), the most important of England's nine Carthusian ruins, provides a striking contrast to its more grandiose and worldly Cistercian counterparts. The Carthusians took a vow of silence and lived, ate and prayed alone in their two-storey cells, each separated from its neighbour by a privy, small garden and high walls. The foundations of the cells are still clearly visible, together with one that has been reconstructed to suggest its original layout and the monks' way of life. Other substantial remains include the ruins of the gatehouse and the walls and tower of the priory church, which divides the site's two main courtyards.

Road access to the priory is straight up the busy A19 from Thirsk, eleven miles to the south; it's reached off a signposted minor road just after the Osmotherley turn-off. Or it's an easy walk from Osmotherley, via Chapel Wood Farm.

The corpse walk

The **Lyke Wake Walk** takes its name from a dialect poem telling the story of a journey along the moorland "burial route" linking the moors' ancient burial mounds, and recalls the practice of waking (keeping vigil) over a dead body (the lyke). The route was conceived in 1955 as something of a joke: anyone who completed the 42-mile walk in under 24 hours became a member of the Lyke Wake Club and qualified for a badge in the shape of a coffin. As word spread, the walk became something of a cult – it still isn't marked on most maps. Provided you're completely fit, used to long-distance walking, have been in training and have a support team, first-timers can complete the walk in around 16 hours – some people have run it in less than five, though they are, of course, completely mad.

Sutton Bank and Kilburn

The main A170 road enters the national park from Thirsk as it climbs five hundred feet in half a mile to **Sutton Bank** (960ft), a phenomenal viewpoint from where the panorama extends across the Vale of York to the Pennines on the far horizon. At the top of the climb stands a huge car park and a North York Moors National Park **Visitor Centre** (Jan & Feb weekends only 10.30am–3.30pm; March–Dec daily 10/10.30am–3.30/5pm; ℡01845/597426, Ⓦwww.moors.uk.net), full of background on the short waymarked walks and off-road bike rides you can make from here. It has a cafe, too.

To the south of the A170, the **White Horse Nature Trail** (2–3 miles; 1hr 30min) skirts the crags of Roulston Scar en route to the **Kilburn White Horse**, northern England's only turf-cut figure, 314 feet long and 228 feet high. You could make a real walk of it by dropping a couple of miles down to pretty **KILBURN** village (a minor road also runs from the A170, passing the White Horse car park). The village has been synonymous with woodcarving since the days of "Mouseman" Robert Thompson (1876–1955), whose woodcarvings are marked by his distinctive mouse motif and can be found throughout Yorkshire – in York Minster and Trinity Church, Hull for instance, and beyond, even in Westminster Abbey. The **Mouseman Visitor Centre** (daily 10am–5pm; closed Mon in Oct and Mon & Tues in Nov & Dec; £3.50; Ⓦwww.robertthompsons .co.uk) displays examples of Thompson's personal furniture, and you can recuperate in the village's *Forresters Arms*.

Coxwold and around

Most of the many visitors to the attractive little village of **COXWOLD** come to pay homage to the novelist **Laurence Sterne**, who is buried by the south wall (close to the porch) in the churchyard of **St Michael's**, where he was vicar from 1760 until his death in 1768. The church, with its odd octagonal tower, is worth closer scrutiny – particularly the three-decker pulpit and medieval stained glass – before heading for **Shandy Hall**, 150 yards further up the road beyond the church (May–Sept Wed 2–4.30pm, Sun 2.30–4.30pm; gardens May–Sept daily except Sat 11am–4.30pm; also by appointment; house & gardens £4.50, gardens only £2.50; ℡01347/868465, Ⓦwww.shandean.org), Sterne's home, now a museum crammed with literary memorabilia. It was here that he wrote *A Sentimental Journey through France and Italy* and the wonderfully eccentric *The Life and Opinions of Tristram Shandy, Gentleman*.

The village pub, the *Fauconberg Arms*, is named after the viscount who married Mary, the daughter of Oliver Cromwell. He brought her to live in **Newburgh Priory**, half a mile south of the village (April–June Wed & Sun

---

The mysterious fate of Laurence Sterne

After a sojourn in France and Italy, gathering material for *A Sentimental Journey* (1768), Laurence Sterne later died of pleurisy in London, where he was buried. Immediate rumours surfaced that Sterne's body had been appropriated by **body-snatchers** and sold for medical experimentation – a story given credence when Sterne's body was finally exhumed in 1969 for reburial in Coxwold. Various bones and no fewer than five skulls were uncovered in the grave, one of which – after comparison with contemporary busts – is thought to have been Sterne's. Presumably, the eighteenth-century doctors who illegally bought the body were horrified to learn of its identity and hurriedly reburied it in its grave together with other human bits and pieces they had lying around. Sterne – or at least part of him – now lies at rest in Coxwold churchyard.

2.30–4.45pm; also Easter & May bank hols 2.30–4.45pm; £5.50, grounds only £2.50; Ⓦwww.newburghpriory.co.uk), which was originally raised on the site of an Augustinian monastery founded in 1150. The story goes that Mary brought her father's body here, after it was exhumed from Westminster Abbey in readiness to be "executed" at Tyburn in revenge for Cromwell's part in the Civil War.

Laurence Sterne talked of "A delicious Walk of Romance" from Coxwold to twelfth-century **Byland Abbey** (April–July & Sept Mon & Thurs–Sun 11am–6pm; Aug daily 11am–6pm; £3.50; EH), a mile and a half northeast of the village. His description captures the appeal of the ruins – seen from the distance as a mere finger of stone. The *Abbey Inn,* opposite the priory entrance (Ⓣ01347/868204; Ⓞ), has three intimate rooms, and serves coffee and meals (closed Sun eve & Mon lunch), or you can press on the half a mile to **Wass**, where the *Wombwell Arms* is known for its food and beer.

Helmsley

One of the moors' most appealing towns, **HELMSLEY** makes a perfect base for visiting the western moors and Rievaulx Abbey. Local life revolves around a large cobbled market square, dominated by a boastful monument to the second earl of Feversham, whose family was responsible for rebuilding most of the village in the nineteenth century. The old **market cross** now marks the start of the 110-mile Cleveland Way.

Signposted from the square, it's easy to find **Helmsley Castle** (March–Oct daily 10am–5/6pm; Nov–Feb Mon & Thurs–Sun 10am–4pm; £4; EH), its unique twelfth-century D-shaped keep ringed by massive earthworks. After a three-month siege during the Civil War it was "slighted" by Sir Thomas Fairfax, the Parliamentary commander, and much of its stone was plundered by towns-people for local houses. A visitor centre, castle exhibition and audioguide fill you in on the full history.

To the southwest of the town, overlooking a wooded meander of the Rye, stands the Feversham' country seat, **Duncombe Park** (May–Oct Mon–Thurs & Sun: house tours 12.30–3.30pm; garden, parkland & visitor

---

The Cleveland Way

The 110-mile **Cleveland Way**, one of England's premier long-distance national trails, starts at Helmsley in the North York Moors and follows a route that embraces both the northern rim of the moors and Cleveland Hills and the cliff scenery of the North Yorkshire coast. The path hits the sea at Saltburn and then runs south, terminating at Filey, south of Scarborough – though an unofficial "Missing Link" joins Scarborough to Helmsley, through the Tabular Hills, thus completing a circular walk.

Most people complete the Cleveland Way in around nine or ten days, though it's easy to walk short stages instead, particularly on the **coastal section**, where towns, villages and services are closer together. The outstanding high-cliff sections are (from south to north): Hayburn Wyke, near Ravenscar, to Robin Hood's Bay (7 miles); Robin Hood's Bay to Whitby (6 miles); Sandsend to Runswick Bay to Staithes (7 miles); and Staithes to Skinningrove, the section with the highest cliffs (5 miles).

The **Cleveland Way Project** (Ⓣ01439/770657) produces an annual accommodation guide, which you can download from Ⓦwww.nationaltrail.co.uk. The *National Trail Guide: Cleveland Way* by Ian Sampson (Aurum Press) and *Walking the Cleveland Way and The Missing Link* by Malcolm Boyes (Cicerone Press) cover the ground in detail.

centre 11am–5.30pm; house, gardens & parkland £7.25, gardens £4, parkland £2; ⓦwww.duncombepark.com), built for the Fevershams' ancestor Sir Thomas Duncombe in 1713. The building is by gentleman-architect William Wakefield, though he was probably influenced by Vanbrugh who was working on Castle Howard at about the same time. The grounds are perhaps more appealing than the house (which was extensively rebuilt after a fire in 1879), boasting acres of landscaped gardens including a brace of artfully sited temples.

Practicalities

Buses all stop on or near the Market Place. The useful **tourist office** is at the castle visitor centre (March–Oct daily 9.30am–5pm; Nov–Feb Fri–Sun 10am–4pm; ⓣ01439/770173, ⓦwww.ryedale.gov.uk), and has information on both the **Cleveland Way** and the **Ebor Way**, the latter a gentle seventy-mile route to Ilkley that links with the Dales Way.

Market day in Helmsley is Friday, when the town centre is filled with traders. The *Feathers* on the Market Place is the best place for a drink and a **pub** meal, while also on Market Place are two excellent delis, Hunters and Perns, the latter associated with the excellent *Star Inn* at Harome (see below). Borogate has several fine little **shops** in ancient houses, including a working smithy and a good secondhand bookshop in the old fire station. At **Helmsley Arts Centre** in the Old Meeting House, off Bridge Street (ⓣ01439/771700, ⓦwww.helmsleyarts.co.uk), there's a full programme of theatre, film, music and other events.

Accommodation and food

Crown Market Place ⓣ01439/770297, ⓦwww .tchh.co.uk. Of the inns ringing Market Place, this is the best mid-range (two-star) option, a comfortable, old-fashioned (in the best sense), family-run hotel. The restaurant (open to all) serves good-value lunches and evening meals. ❺

Feversham Arms 1 High St, behind the church ⓣ01439/770766, ⓦwww.fevershamarmshotel .com. Combines hip styling with comfort in its spacious rooms and Modern British brasserie. It's favoured by the country pursuits crowd, but there's also an outdoor pool, gym, tennis court and garden-terrace, while a spa and new poolside suites will be available in 2008. If you're not eating at the *Star Inn*, then lunch (under £20) or dinner (mains around £20) here is the next best bet. ❼

Helmsley YHA ⓣ0870/770 5860, ⓔhelmsley @yha.org.uk. A few hundred yards east of the Market Place – follow Bondgate to Carlton Rd and turn left. Open daily April–Sept. Dorm beds from £14.95.

No. 54 54 Bondgate ⓣ01439/771533, ⓦwww.no54.co.uk. A delightful cottage-style B&B offering three superior courtyard rooms just 500 yards from the Market Place. Power showers, fresh flowers, sheltered terrace and garden add up to a relaxing night, and breakfast (free-range eggs, proper bacon, kedgeree) is excellent. Picnics and evening meals also available. ❺

Star Inn Harome, 2 miles south of the A170 ⓣ01439/770397, ⓦwww.thestaratharome .co.uk. A thatched pub where Michelin-rated food awaits. Should you wish to make a night of it, eight very nice rooms in the adjacent lodge are individually furnished, some with spa baths, a couple with a private garden, and one with its own snooker table. No food Sun eve & Mon. ❼

Rievaulx Abbey and Terrace

From Helmsley you can easily walk across country to **Rievaulx Abbey** (April–Sept daily 10am–6pm; Oct–March Mon & Thurs–Sun 10am–4/5pm; £4.30; EH), once one of England's greatest Cistercian abbeys. The signposted path follows the opening two miles of the Cleveland Way, plus another mile's diversion off the Way, and takes around ninety minutes – a trail leaflet is available from the tourist office in Helmsley.

Founded in 1132, the abbey quickly developed from a series of rough shelters on the wooded banks of the River Rye to become a flourishing community with interests in fishing, mining, agriculture and the woollen industry. At its height, 140 monks and up to 500 lay brothers lived and worked at the abbey, though numbers fell dramatically once the Black Death (1348–49) had done its worst. The end came with the Dissolution, when many of the walls were razed and the roof lead stripped – the beautiful ruins, however, still suggest the abbey's former splendour. A **visitor centre** mounts exhibitions pertaining to the ruins and to monastic life in the valley.

Although it forms some sort of ensemble with the abbey, there's no direct access from the ruins to **Rievaulx Terrace** (daily 11am–5/6pm; £4; NT), a site entered from the B1257, a couple of miles northwest of Helmsley. This half-mile stretch of grass-covered terraces and woodland was laid out as part of Duncombe Park in the 1750s, and was engineered partly to enhance the views of the abbey. The resulting panorama over the ruins and the valley below is superb, making it a great spot for a picnic.

The central moors

The highest and wildest terrain in the North York Moors is in the **central moors**, bounded by Ryedale in the west and by **Rosedale** in the east. Purple swathes of summer heather carpet the tops, where ancient crosses and standing stones provide hints of the moorland's distant past.

Lying eight miles northeast of Helmsley, one of Yorkshire's quaintest villages, **HUTTON-LE-HOLE**, has become so great a tourist attraction that you'll have to come off-season to get much pleasure from its stream-crossed village green and the sight of sheep wandering freely through the lanes. Apart from the sheer photogenic quality of the place, the big draw is the family-oriented **Ryedale Folk Museum** (daily mid-Jan to mid-Dec 10am–dusk; £4.80; Ⓦwww.ryedalefolkmuseum.co.uk), where local life is explored in a series of reconstructed buildings, notably a sixteenth-century house, a glass furnace, a crofter's cottage and a nineteenth-century blacksmith's shop. Special events and displays throughout the season mean there's always something going on.

The museum also houses a **National Park information centre** (same hours as museum; Ⓣ01751/417367), while the nearby car park fills quickly in summer as walkers disperse from the village. The information centre has a list of local **B&Bs**, or make for *Burnley House* (Ⓣ01751/417548, Ⓦwww.burnleyhouse.com; ⑨), a hospitable Georgian house on the green with streamside garden. The *Forge Tea Shop* (closed weekdays Nov–Feb) is a renowned stop for tea and cakes, while if you stay the night you'll have plenty of time to become acquainted with the *Crown*, the local **pub**.

A mile and a half east of Hutton-le-Hole don't miss a look inside the church of **St Mary's** (daily 9am–dusk; free) in the hamlet of **Lastingham**. It preserves its early Norman crypt, one of Yorkshire's great ecclesiastical treasures. Its heavy vaults and carved columns still shelter the head of an ninth-century Anglo-Saxon cross, a Viking "hogsback" tombstone and the original doorposts of the Saxon monastery first built here in 654 AD.

A little to the northwest of Hutton-le-Hole the country lanes of **Farndale** are packed in spring as visitors arrive to see the area's wild daffodils, protected by the two-thousand-acre **Farndale nature reserve**. The Moorsbus runs a special "Daffodil" service every Sunday in April and over Easter, shuttling visitors from Hutton-le-Hole. The best area for the flowers is north of **Low Mill**, where roads from Gillamoor and Hutton-le-Hole meet, about four miles north of the latter.

Rosedale Abbey, four miles northeast of Hutton-le-Hole, preserves only a few fragments of the Cistercian priory (1158) that gave it its name, most of them incorporated into **St Lawrence's** parish church. The rooms at the *Milburn Arms* (☎01751/417312, ⓦwww.milburnarms.co.uk; ❾) overlook the small green, and there's a beer garden out front. Otherwise, north of Rosedale Abbey is the *Lion Inn* (☎01751/417320, ⓦwww.lionblakey.co.uk; ❹) on **Blakey Ridge**, a couple of miles south of the junction with the Hutton-le-Hole–Castleton road. A truly windswept local (at over 1300ft), the inn has an unbeatable location for an isolated night's stay – though come Sunday lunchtime the car park soon fills up.

Pickering and the eastern moors

The biggest centre for miles around, **Pickering** takes for itself the title "Gateway to the Moors", which is pushing it a bit, though it's certainly a handy halt if you're touring the villages and dales of the **eastern moors**. Its undoubted big pull is the **North Yorkshire Moors Railway** (NYMR; see box opposite), which provides a beautiful way of travelling up (and walking from) **Newtondale**, the Moors' most immediately spectacular dale, and of connecting with the Esk Valley line in Esk Dale, and with Whitby and the Yorkshire coast.

East of Pickering, **Dalby Forest** features a superb forest drive and a large number of specially marked trails. Villages are few and far between, though in **Thornton-le-Dale** the region has a high-ranking contender for prettiest village in Yorkshire. By far the best itinerary is to see Thornton-le-Dale and then drive or bike through Dalby Forest to rejoin the main A170 Pickering–Scarborough road at one of several points just outside Scarborough.

Pickering

A thriving market town at the junction of the A170 and the transmoor A169 (Whitby road), **PICKERING** rather fancies itself, yet a couple of hours is enough to show you its charms, certainly if you've already seen the best of the North York Moors to the west. Its most attractive feature is its motte and bailey **Castle** on the hill north of the Market Place (April–Sept daily 10am–6pm; Oct Mon & Thurs–Sun 10am–5pm; £3; EH), reputedly used by every English monarch up to 1400 as a base for hunting in nearby Blandsby Park. The other spot worth investigating is the Beck Isle Museum of Rural Life on Bridge Street (March–Oct daily 10am–5pm; Nov to mid-Dec Fri–Sun 10am–4pm; £3.50; ⓦwww.beckislemuseum.co.uk), which has reconstructions of a gents' outfitters and a barber's shop, a case full of knickers, and two giant Welsh guardsmen painted by Rex Whistler for a children's party.

Buses stop outside the library and **tourist office** (March–Oct Mon–Sat 9.30am–5pm, Sun 9.30am–4pm; Nov–Feb Mon–Sat 9.30am–4.30pm; ☎01751/473791, ⓦwww.ryedale.gov.uk), opposite the Co-op on The Ropery in the centre of town; the **NYMR train station** is less than five minutes' signposted walk away. The tourist office can help with **B&Bs**, though Whitby, only twenty minutes' drive away on the coast, is the better overnight destination. A couple of the **pubs** also have rooms, top choice easily being the *White Swan*, on Market Place (☎01751/472288, ⓦwww.white-swan.co.uk; ❼), with both contemporary and traditional bedrooms. There are cafés and tearooms throughout town, and a couple of Indian **restaurants**, though it's the *White Swan* that's most serious about its cooking – fine Modern British food at moderate prices. **Market** day in town is Monday, and there's a farmers' market on the first Thursday of the month.

The **North Yorkshire Moors Railway** (NYMR; ☎01751/472508, talking timetables ☎01751/473535, ⓦwww.nymr.co.uk) connects **Pickering** with the Esk Valley (Middlesbrough–Whitby) line at **Grosmont**, 18 miles to the north. The line was completed by George Stephenson in 1835, just ten years after the opening of the Stockton and Darlington Railway, making it one of the earliest lines in the country. Scheduled **services** operate year-round (limited to weekend and school hols service Nov–Feb), and a **day-return ticket** costs £14. Part of the line's attraction are the **steam trains**, though be warned that diesels are pulled into service when the fire risk in the forests is high. Steam services have also been extended from the end of the NYMR line at Grosmont to the nearby seaside resort of Whitby – departures are usually during school and bank holidays, with a return fare from Pickering of £20.

Along the North Yorkshire Moors Railway

The first stop is Levisham, perfect for walks to the village of **LEVISHAM**, a mile and a half to the east, where the *Horseshoe Inn* is a favourite target, especially for Sunday lunch. A steep winding road continues another mile beyond Levisham, down across the beck and then up to **LOCKTON**, where there's a youth hostel and a path due north to the **Hole of Horcum**, a bizarre natural hollow gouged by the glacial meltwaters that carved out Newtondale. The paths run back to Levisham Station from here, and the entire seven-mile circuit is one of the Moors' best short walks – take the short detour halfway round to the *Saltersgate Inn*, on the A169, which has good-value food (and a fire that hasn't been allowed to go out for a couple of centuries).

The second train stop, **Newtondale Halt**, is only a couple of miles southwest of the Hole of Horcum, or you can head off through the extensive woods of **Cropton Forest** to the west on trails specially marked by the Forestry Commission. At Stape – three miles southwest through the forest – you're just two miles south of the best-preserved stretch of Roman road in Europe, **Wheeldale Roman Road**, a mile of Wade's Causeway that ran from York to bases on the coast: the remains show a twenty-foot-wide stretch of sand and gravel studded by sandstone slabs and edged with kerbs and ditches.

The third NYMR station is at **GOATHLAND**, a highly attractive village set in open moorland beneath the great expanses of Wheeldale and Goathland moors. If it seems oddly familiar – and if it seems unduly crowded – it's because it's widely known as "Aidensfield", the fictional village at the centre of the *Heartbeat* TV series, while the station doubled as "Hogsmeade" in *Harry Potter and the Philosopher's Stone*. Outside summer weekends, when it's packed to distraction, Goathland can still be a joy to wander, with signposts pointing you to the local sight, the **Mallyan Spout**, a seventy-foot-high waterfall.

A gentle path from Goathland runs the mile through the fields down to **BECK HOLE**, an idyllic bridgeside hamlet focused on the 🍴 *Birch Hall Inn*, one of the finest rural pubs in all England – tiny to the point of claustrophobic, still doubling as a sweet shop and store as it has for a century, and serving great slabs of sandwiches with local ham and pies. It also serves as a focus for the summer game of quoits, played on the nearby green.

Thornton-le-Dale and Dalby Forest

THORNTON-LE-DALE, two miles east of Pickering, hangs onto its considerable charm despite the main A170 Scarborough road scything through its centre. Most of the houses, pubs and shops are fairly alluring, none more so than the thatched cottage near the parish church, which features in so many ads, magazine covers, chocolate boxes and calendars that it's been described as the most photographed house in Britain.

Minor roads from Thornton-le-Dale and from the A169 (Whitby road) lead into **Dalby Forest**: drivers pay a toll (£7; road closed 9pm–7am) to join the start of a nine-mile forest drive that emerges close to Hackness, just four miles from Scarborough. It's best to make first for the **visitor centre** (daily 10am–4.30/6pm; ☎01751/460295, ⊛www.forestry.gov.uk) at **Low Dalby**, which has information on the wildlife, picnic spots and the range of marked trails. This is also a great place for mountain biking, and there's high-wire fun and Tarzan swings at the **Go Ape** adventure course (April–Oct daily 9am–5pm, closed Mon in term time; Nov Sat & Sun 9am–5pm; £25; ☎0870/444 5562, ⊛www.goape.co.uk), across the road from the visitor centre, where the Moorsbus stops in summer.

The best walks are from a car park about three miles north of Low Dalby at Low Staindale, which include the one-and-a-half mile (1hr) **Bridestones Trail** – to the two great sandstone tors rising out of the heather that have been eroded into unearthly shapes. Similarly named outcrops are found all over the moors, and may be named for their connections with ancient fertility rites, or derive from a Norse word meaning "brink", or "boundary" stones.

The Esk Valley

The northernmost reaches of the national park are crossed by the east–west **Esk Valley**, whose pretty river flows into the sea at Whitby. It's a part of the North York Moors overlooked by many visitors – partly, one suspects, because its very attractions, at least in the eastern stretches, are its valley characteristics: there's not much moorland tramping to be done until you reach the isolated stone village of **DANBY**, one of the finest of all moorland villages. Here, you're within striking distance of some excellent walks, all detailed on trail leaflets available from the **Moors Centre** (March–Dec daily 10/10.30am–3.30/5pm; Jan & Feb Sat & Sun only 10.30am–3.30pm; ☎01439/772737, ⊛www.moors.uk.net), where there's also a good tearoom. Danby's pub is the *Duke of Wellington*, while the *Stonehouse Bakery & Tea Shop* is great for daytime snacks. A mile out of the village at **Ainthorpe**, the *Fox & Hounds* (☎01287/660218, ⊛www.foxandhounds-ainthorpe.com; ●) looks out over the moors.

You can reach Danby by road (from Whitby via the A169 through Sleights) or by **train**: the North York Moors Railway connects at **Grosmont**, where you're on the **Esk Valley line**, which runs between Whitby and Middlesbrough, stopping at **GREAT AYTON**. Here, the North York Moors give way to the **Cleveland Hills**, whose scattered peaks provide the buffer between the rural east of the region and the encroaching industry of Teesside to the west. It is Great Ayton's **Captain Cook** connections, though, that draw most visitors: the town was the boyhood home of England's greatest seaman and explorer, James Cook, between 1736 (when he was 8) and 1745. The young Cook lived at Aireyholme Farm (no public access) on the outskirts of town, though after James left to go to sea his father built a family **cottage** on Bridge Street, which was later dismantled and shipped to Melbourne, Australia in 1934; its site is marked by an obelisk of Australian granite near Low Green. Other Cook-related sights include **All Saints' Church**, also at Low Green, which the family attended and where Cook's mother Grace is buried;

Cook's school on the High Street, now the **Schoolroom Museum** (Ⓦwww
.captaincookschoolroommuseum.co.uk); and a **sculpture** of a youthful
Cook on High Green which depicts him – bare-chested, long-locked – in
Leonardo DiCaprio mode.

A waymarked path runs northeast out of Great Ayton, up to the summit of
Roseberry Topping (1050ft), the queerly shaped conical peak visible from all
over the locality – beacons were lit on top of here during the threat by the
Spanish Armada. It's a reasonably stiff climb, followed by a tramp across Easby
Moor to the south to the fifty-foot-high **Cook Monument** (1827) for more
amazing views, before circling back to Great Ayton.

The North Yorkshire coast

The **North Yorkshire coast** (Ⓦwww.discoveryorkshirecoast.com) is the
southernmost stretch of a cliff-edged shore that stretches almost unbroken to
the Scottish border. **Scarborough** is the biggest town and resort, with a full set
of attractions and a terrific beach. Cute **Robin Hood's Bay** is the most
popular of the coastal villages, with fishing and smuggling traditions, while bluff
Staithes – a fishing harbour on the far edge of North Yorkshire – has yet to tip
over into full-blown tourist mode. **Whitby**, in between the two, is the best
stopover, its fine sands and resort facilities tempered by its abbey ruins, cobbled
streets, Georgian buildings and maritime heritage – more than any other local
place Whitby celebrates Captain Cook as one of its own. **Walkers** should note
that two of the best parts of the **Cleveland Way** depart from Whitby: southeast
to Robin Hood's Bay (six miles) and northwest to Staithes (eleven miles), both
along thrilling high-cliff sections.

Scarborough

The oldest resort in the country, **SCARBOROUGH** first attracted early
seventeenth-century visitors to its newly discovered mineral springs. By the
1730s, the more enterprising spa-goers were also venturing onto the
sweeping local sands and dipping themselves in the bracing North Sea,
popularizing the racy pastime of sea-bathing. Still fashionable in Victorian
times – when it was "the Queen of the Watering Places" – Scarborough saw
its biggest transformation after World War II, when it (and many other
resorts) became a holiday haven for workers from the industrial heartlands.
In the 1950s, three million visitors a year thronged the beaches, rode on the
donkeys and paddled in the rock pools. All the traditional ingredients of a
beach resort are still here in force, from superb, clean sands, kitsch amusement
arcades to the more refined pleasures of its tight-knit old-town streets and a
genteel round of quiet parks and gardens.

Arrival, information and accommodation

The **train station** is at the top of town facing Westborough; **buses** pull up
outside or in the surrounding streets, though the National Express services
(direct from London) stop in the car park behind the station. Scarborough's
tourist offices are located inside the Brunswick Shopping Centre on
Westborough (Mon–Sat 9/9.30am–4.30/5pm, plus April–Sept Sun
11am–4.30pm; ℡01723/383637) and on Sandside by the harbour (April–Oct
daily 9.30/10am–5.30pm; Nov–March Sat & Sun 10am–4.30pm). To reach the
harbour and castle, walk straight down Westborough, Newborough and

Eastborough, through the main shopping streets. Open-top **seafront buses** (Easter–Sept daily from 9.30am, March weekends only; £1.60), meanwhile, run from North Bay to the Spa Complex in South Bay.

Scarborough is crammed with inexpensive **hotels and guest houses**. Happy hunting grounds include North Bay's Queen's Parade, where most of the guest houses have sweeping bay views and parking, and Blenheim Terrace, which is closer to the castle. The cheapest places in town are those without the sea views – try along central Aberdeen Walk (off Westborough), or on North Marine Road and Trafalgar Square, behind Queen's Parade. Above South Bay, hotels tend to be pricier, though there's a clutch of B&Bs along and around West Street. If you're stuck, call the tourist office's **accommodation hotline** (☎01723/383636).

Crown Spa Esplanade ☎01723/357400, Ⓦwww.crownspahotel.com. In a Regency terrace built in 1847 above South Bay, the *Crown* makes the most of its period features, views and genteel feel. There's a gym, pool and brasserie. ❼

Helaina 14 Blenheim Terrace ☎01723/375191, Ⓦwww.hotelhelaina.co.uk. Victorian terraced house on North Bay; bedrooms are on the small side, but beautifully furnished in contemporary style. Great sea views, and ample breakfasts. Parking. ❸

Interludes 32 Princess St ☎01723/360513, Ⓦwww.interludeshotel.co.uk. Quiet Georgian town house in the old-town streets behind the harbour. Bay views from the upper floors, and theatre memorabilia, antiques, fresh flowers and traditional English decor throughout; call for details of Stephen Joseph Theatre breaks. It's a gay-friendly place, though all (except children) are welcome. ❸

Riviera St Nicholas Cliff ☎01723/372277, Ⓦwww.riviera-scarborough.co.uk. Restored Victorian hotel opposite the *Grand* with bay views and refurbished rooms with crisp white bedding and colourful cushions. ❺

Scarborough YHA Burniston Rd, Scalby Mills, 2 miles north of town ☎0870/770 6022, Ⓔscarborough@yha.org.uk. Occupies a converted watermill, off the A165, 10min walk from the sea; the Cleveland Way passes close by. Closed Nov–Easter. Dorm beds from £13.

Windmill Mill St, off Victoria Rd ☎01723/372735, Ⓦwww.windmill-hotel .co.uk. Eighteenth-century windmill sited incongruously in the town centre with its country-style rooms (upper-floor ones with veranda) ranged around a cobbled courtyard; you take breakfast inside the mill dining room amid the owner's amazing toy collection. Two family rooms available, plus two self-catering flats within the windmill tower. Parking. ❸

The Town

There's no better place to acquaint yourself with the local layout than from the walls of **Scarborough Castle** (April–Sept daily 10am–6pm; Oct–March Mon & Thurs–Sun 10am–4/5pm; £4; EH), mounted on a jutting headland between two golden-sanded bays east of the town centre. Bronze and Iron Age relics have been found on the wooded castle crag, together with fragments of a fourth-century Roman signalling station, Saxon and Norman chapels and a Viking camp, reputedly built by a Viking with the nickname of Scardi (or "harelip"), from which the town's name derives. As you leave the castle, drop into the **church of St Mary** (1180), immediately below on Castle Road, whose graveyard contains the tomb of Anne Brontë, who died here in 1849.

The town's museums are currently undergoing reorganization (latest details on Ⓦwww.scarboroughmuseums.org.uk), but the collections at both the Art Gallery and Rotunda Museum (for geological displays) are definitely worth seeing. Otherwise, the chief cultural distraction is the unexpected concentration of Pre-Raphaelite art in the **church of St-Martin-on-the-Hill** (1863) on Albion Road. The Victorian-Gothic pile has a roof by William Morris, a triptych by Burne-Jones, a pulpit with four printed panels by Rossetti, stained glass by Morris, Burne-Jones and Ford Madox Brown, and an east wall whose tracery provides the frames for angels by Morris and *The Adoration of the Magi* by Burne-Jones.

The bays

The miniature North Bay Railway (daily Easter–Sept) runs up to the main attraction on the **North Bay** side, namely the **Sea Life Centre and Marine Sanctuary** at Scalby Mills (daily 10am–4.30/5.30pm; £11.95), distinguished by its white pyramids. The most enjoyable **amusements and rides** are the old-fashioned ones on the harbour, where creaky dodgems, helter-skelter and shooting galleries compete for custom. From the harbourside you'll be able to take one of the short **cruises and speedboat trips** that shoot off throughout the day in the summer. For unique entertainment, head for Peasholm Park, where naval warfare, in the shape of miniature man-powered naval vessels, battle it out on the lake (Mon, Thurs & Sat in July and Aug; full details from the tourist office).

The **South Bay** is more refined, backed by the pleasant Valley Gardens and the Italianate meanderings of the South Cliff Gardens, and topped by an esplanade from which a **hydraulic lift** (April–Sept daily 10am–5pm) chugs down to the beach. Here, Scarborough's Regency and Victorian glories are still in evidence, most impressively of all in the six million bricks and fifty-two chimneys of the **Grand Hotel**, built in 1867. Views from its gargantuan, neglected terrace are the best in town.

Eating, drinking and entertainment

Cafés, fish-and-chip shops and **tearooms** are thick on the ground: those down by the harbour are of variable quality and popularity, serving up fried food as fast as the punters can get it down. There's a more discerning selection when it comes to **restaurants**, not least because the town has a fair-sized Italian population – including the descendants of several POWs who settled in Scarborough after the war. Virtually every street has a **pub**, though few pass muster as the sort of place you might want to spend the entire evening.

Whatever the posters and advertising suggest, the cultural heart of Scarborough is neither the Spa Complex nor the Futurist Theatre, with their end-of-pier summer shows, but the renowned **Stephen Joseph Theatre** on Westborough (℡01723/370541, ᴡwww.sjt.uk.com), a real North Yorkshire gem. Housed in a former Art Deco cinema, the theatre premieres every new work of local playwright Alan Ayckbourn and promotes strong seasons of theatre and film; there's also a good café/restaurant (moderate prices) and the bar is open daily except Sunday. Finally, the annual free **Beached Festival** (ᴡwww.beached.net), on the South Bay beach over a weekend in mid-August, always has a good line-up of bands (in the past including the likes of the Kaiser Chiefs, Libertines and the Fratellis).

Cafés and restaurants

Café Fish 19 York Place, at Somerset Terrace ℡01723/500301. For a more sophisticated way with fish than most Scarborough restaurants – like sole Boursin or Cajun-style salmon. Dinner only. Expensive.

Café Italia 36 St Nicholas Cliff. Utterly charming, microscopic Italian coffee bar next to the *Grand*, where good coffee, focaccia slices and ice cream keep a battery of regulars happy. Closes 4pm. Closed Sun. Inexpensive.

Gianni's 13 Victoria Rd ℡01723/507388. The most immediately welcoming of the town's Italian restaurants, where the good-natured staff bustle up and down stairs, delivering quality pizzas, pastas and quaffable wine by the carafe. Dinner only; closed Sun & Mon. Moderate.

▲ Robin Hood's Bay

Golden Grid 4 Sandside. The harbourside's choicest fish-and-chip establishment, "catering for the promenader since 1883". Offers grilled fish, crab and lobster, a *fruits-de-mer* platter and a wine list alongside the standard crispy-battered fry-up. Closed Mon–Thurs dinner in winter. Moderate.
Lanterna 33 Queen St ☎01723/363616. Long-established, special-night-out destination, featuring traditional, seasonal Italian cooking in quiet, formal surroundings. Dinner only; closed Sun. Expensive.

Pubs
The Alma 1 Alma Parade, at the top of Westborough. A thoroughly decent local, just right for a quiet pint.
Indigo Alley 4 North Marine Rd ☎01723 381900. Guest ales, Belgian beers and live music a couple of times a week.

Robin Hood's Bay

Although known as Robbyn Huddes Bay as early as Tudor times, there's nothing except half-remembered myth to link **ROBIN HOOD'S BAY** with Sherwood's legendary bowman – locals anyway prefer the old name, Bay Town or simply Bay. The best-known and most heavily visited spot on the coast, the village fully lives up to its reputation, with narrow streets and pink-tiled cottages toppling down the cliff-edge site, evoking the romance of a time when this was both a hard-bitten fishing community and smugglers' den par excellence. So packed together are the houses, legend has it, that ill-gotten booty could be passed up the hill from cottage to cottage without the pursuing king's men being any the wiser.

From the upper village, lined with Victorian villas, now mostly B&Bs, it's a very steep walk down the hill to the harbour. The **Old Coastguard Station** (June–Sept Tues–Sun 10am–5pm; Oct–May weekends and school hols only; free; ☎01947/885900; NT) has been turned into a visitor centre with displays relating to the area's geology and sealife. When the tide is out, the massive rock beds below are exposed, split by a geological fault line and studded with fossil remains. There's an easy circular walk (2.5 miles) to **Boggle Hole** and its youth hostel, a mile south, returning inland via the path along the old Scarborough–Whitby railway line.

Practicalities

Drivers will have to leave their cars in one of two **car parks** in the upper part of the village, which is also where the buses stop. Whitby has the nearest train station, and the nearest tourist office; **walkers** can make Whitby to Robin Hood's Bay in around three hours.

Many people see the village as a day-trip from Whitby, and you can check on Bay accommodation in the tourist office there, or simply stroll the streets of the old part of the village to see if any of the small cottage **B&Bs** has vacancies. There are also three good **pubs** in the lower village, two of which have rooms: the tiny *Laurel*, on Main Street (℡01947/880400; ❸; two-night minimum), whose small self-catering flat sleeps two; and the *Bay Hotel*, right on the harbour (℡01947/880278; ❹), which is the traditional start or end of the Coast-to-Coast Walk. As well as a score of **guest houses** in the upper village, there's the late-Victorian *Victoria Hotel*, Station Road (℡01947/880205; ⓦwww.thevictoriahotel.info; ❺), at the top of the hill, with fine views from some of its rooms, and a cliff-top beer garden.

You'll probably end up **eating** in the pubs – food at the *Bay Hotel* is the best – though the *Swell Café* in the Old Chapel, Chapel Street (℡01947/880180; closes 4.30pm), serves a good range of dishes and has great coastal views from its terrace tables; you can catch family cinema shows in summer here too. The other pub, the eighteenth-century *Dolphin* in King Street, is the oldest in the village, and has folk nights every Friday.

Boggle Hole's **youth hostel** is one of Yorkshire's most popular, a former mill located in a wooded ravine about a mile south of Robin Hood's Bay at Mill Beck (℡0870/770 5704, ⓔbogglehole@yha.org.uk; from £12.95). Note that a torch is essential after dark, and that you can't access the hostel along the beach once the tide is up.

A couple of miles northwest of Robin Hood's Bay at Hawsker, on the A171, Trailways (℡01947/820207, ⓦwww.trailways.fsnet.co.uk) is a **bike-rental** outfit based in the old Hawsker train station, perfectly placed for day-trips in either direction along the disused railway line. They'll deliver or pick up from local addresses (including *Boggle Hole* youth hostel); there's also a refreshments kiosk at the station, and a small campsite and bunkhouse (call for details).

Whitby

If there's one essential stop on the North Yorkshire coast it's **WHITBY**, whose historical associations, atmospheric ruins, fishing harbour and intrinsic charm make it many people's favourite northern resort. The seventh-century clifftop abbey here made Whitby one of the key foundations of the early Christian period, and a centre of great learning. Below, for a thousand years the local herring boats landed their catch on the harbour banks of the River Esk, until the great whaling boom of the eighteenth century transformed the fortunes of the town. Melville's *Moby Dick* makes much of Whitby whalers such as William Scoresby, while James Cook took his first seafaring steps from the town in 1746, on his way to becoming a national hero. All four of Captain Cook's ships of discovery – the *Endeavour*, *Resolution*, *Adventure* and *Discovery* – were built in Whitby.

Divided by the River Esk, the town splits into two distinct halves joined by a swing bridge: the cobbled **old town** to the east, and the newer (though mostly eighteenth- and nineteenth-century) town across the bridge, generally known as **West Cliff**, which is home to the quayside, most of the hotels and shops, and the few arcades, amusements and souvenir stalls that have been

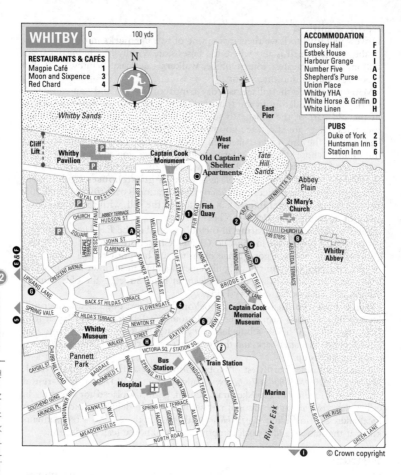

The map labels include:

WHITBY — 0 · 100 yds · N

RESTAURANTS & CAFÉS
Magpie Café · 1
Moon and Sixpence · 3
Red Chard · 4

ACCOMMODATION
Dunsley Hall · F
Estbek House · E
Harbour Grange · I
Number Five · A
Shepherd's Purse · C
Union Place · G
Whitby YHA · B
White Horse & Griffin · D
White Linen · H

PUBS
Duke of York · 2
Huntsman Inn · 5
Station Inn · 6

Whitby Sands · Cliff Lift · Whitby Pavilion · Captain Cook Monument · West Pier · East Pier · Old Captain's Shelter Apartments · Tate Hill Sands · Abbey Plain · St Mary's Church · 199 STEPS · Whitby Abbey · Fish Quay · Captain Cook Memorial Museum · Whitby Museum · Pannett Park · Hospital · Bus Station · Train Station · Marina · River Esk

allowed to proliferate. Virtually everything you want to see is in or above the old town on the east side, principally the **abbey ruins** and the **Captain Cook Memorial Museum**.

Arrival, information and accommodation

The **train station** is a couple of hundred yards south of the bridge to the old town. Special school- and bank-holiday steam train services also stop here, departing from the NYMR station at Grosmont. The bus station is adjacent and there's a **Travel Centre** (Mon–Fri 8.30am–4pm; ☎01947/602146) in the train station for all local transport enquiries. Whitby's **tourist office** (daily; May–Sept 9.30am–6pm; Oct–April 10am–12.30pm & 1–4.30pm; ☎01723/383637, ⓦwww.visitwhitby.com, www.whitbyonline.co.uk) is on the corner of Langborne Road and New Quay Road.

The main **B&B** concentrations are on West Cliff, in the streets stretching back from the elegant Royal Crescent. Across the river in the old town, several pubs have rooms, as does the *Moon and Sixpence* (see p.854), while if you're prepared to travel a couple of miles out of Whitby you can find some pleasant inns and

For a moment or two I could see nothing, as the shadow of a cloud obscured St Mary's Church. Then as the cloud passed I could see the ruins of the Abbey coming into view; and as the edge of a narrow band of light as sharp as a sword-cut moved along, the church and churchyard became gradually visible… [It] seemed to me as though something dark stood behind the seat where the white figure shone, and bent over it. What it was, whether man or beast, I could not tell.

Dracula, Bram Stoker

It was, of course, the figure of the voracious Count, feasting upon the blood of Lucy. Her friend Mina Murray – despite "flying along the fish-market to the bridge" and "toiling" up the endless steps to the Abbey – failed to save her. The story of *Dracula* is well known, but it's this exact attention to the geographical detail of Whitby – little changed since Bram Stoker first wrote the words – which has proved a huge attraction to visitors on the Dracula trail.

Using first-hand observation of a town he knew well – he stayed at a house on the West Cliff, now marked by a plaque – Stoker built a story which mixed real locations, legend, myth and historical fact: the grounding of Count Dracula's ship on Tate Hill Sands was based on an actual event reported in the local papers. The novel was published in 1897 and became synonymous with Stoker's name; it's been filmed, with varying degrees of faithfulness, dozens of times since, though no film version has yet used Whitby as a backdrop.

With many of the early chapters recognizably set in Whitby, it's hardly surprising that the town has cashed in on its **Dracula Trail**. The various sites – Tate Hill Sands, the abbey, church and steps, the graveyard, Stoker's house – can all be visited, while down on the harbourside the Dracula Experience attempts to pull in punters to its rather lame horror-show antics. Keen interest has also been sparked amongst the **Goth** fraternity, who now come to town en masse a couple of times a year (in late spring and around Halloween) for a vampire's ball, concerts and readings; at these times the streets are overrun with pasty-faced characters in Regency dress, wedding gowns, top hats and capes, meeting and greeting at their unofficial headquarters, the otherwise sedate *Elsinore* pub on Flowergate.

---

hotels in relaxed country surroundings. *The Old Boatman's Shelter Apartments* (℡01947/811089, ⊛www.oldboatmansshelter.co.uk; ❺) are superior **holiday apartments** right by the waterside, available nightly.

Hotels, B&Bs and guest houses

Dunsley Hall Dunsley ℡01947/893437, ⊛www .dunsleyhall.com. This stately oak-panelled pile (the choice of visiting celebs) has fine gardens, pool, sauna and leisure club, and very cosy bar. It's a couple of miles inland (west) of town. ❼

Estbek House Sandsend ℡01947/893424, ⊛www.estbekhouse.co.uk. Georgian house overlooking the stream at Sandsend, 2 miles from Whitby and just yards from the beach. There are four pretty double/twin rooms, while the relaxed restaurant (expensive; reservations recommended) is well known for its meals of fresh fish and seafood. ❼

Number Five 5 Havelock Place ℡01947/606361. Amiable West Cliff B&B that provides a good breakfast (veggie options available). There are five doubles and three singles, with small but smart shower rooms. No credit cards. ❷

Shepherd's Purse 95 Church St ℡01947/820228. Popular wholefood store combined with clothes and gift shop. Its best rooms (with brass bedsteads and pine furniture) are set around a galleried courtyard; the two pricier doubles on the upper level are nicest, and one has its own balcony. ❸

Union Place 9 Upgang Lane ℡01947/605501. The Pottas' elegant Georgian house – featured in *Ideal Home* magazine no less – offers genial B&B in two spacious double rooms, sharing a luxurious bathroom. Breakfast is locally sourced and there's a fine choice, from kedgeree to smoked salmon. Parking available. No credit cards. ❷

White Horse & Griffin 87 Church St ☏01947/604857, ⓦwww .whitehorseandgriffin.co.uk. A welcoming eighteenth-century coaching inn with stylishly decorated en-suite rooms (some have antique panelling, others a rooftop view), open fires and a good bistro restaurant serving local fish, meat and game. They also have self-catering cottages in the old town. ❹

White Linen 24 Bagdale ☏01947/603635, ⓦwww.whitelinenguesthouse.co.uk. Superior B&B in a restored Georgian house – ten individually styled rooms with contemporary colours and

furnishings and good shower rooms. Garden at the front, courtyard out back. ❺

Hostels

Harbour Grange Spital Bridge, Church St ☏01947/600817, ⓦwww.whitbybackpackers.co. uk. Backpackers' hostel right on the river (eastern side) with 24 beds in five small dorms (£14, plus £1 for bedding if required). Self-catering kitchen and lounge; curfew at 11.30pm.

Whitby YHA Abbey House, East Cliff ☏0870/770 6088, ⓔwhitby@yha.org.uk. Spanking new flagship hostel, located in a Grade 1 listed building right next to the Abbey Visitor Centre. Stunning views, Victorian conservatory, tearoom and restau-rant, and every facility. Rates include breakfast and entry to the Abbey. Dorm beds from £16.50, though more expensive in summer, double rooms ❸.

The old town

Cobbled **Church Street** is the old town's main thoroughfare, barely changed in aspect since the eighteenth century, though now lined with tearooms and gift shops, many selling jewellery and ornaments made from jet. This hard, black natural carbon, found locally, was worn first by the Romans but received its greatest boost after being shown at the Great Exhibition of 1851, after which it was popularized as mourning wear. Parallel Sandgate has more of the same, the two streets meeting at the small marketplace where souvenirs and trinkets are sold; there's a farmer's market here every Thursday.

Whitby, understandably, likes to make a fuss of Captain Cook who served an apprenticeship here from 1746–49 under John Walker, a Quaker ship-owner. The **Captain Cook Memorial Museum** (March–Oct daily 9.45am–3pm; £3; ⓦwww.cookmuseumwhitby.co.uk), housed in Walker's rickety old house in Grape Lane (on the east side of the swing bridge), contains an impressive amount of memorabilia, including ships' models, letters and paintings by artists seconded to Cook's voyages. The 18-year-old Cook assisted on the coal runs between Newcastle and London, learning his seafaring skills in flat-bottomed craft called "cats". Designed for inshore and river work their specifications were to prove perfect for Cook's later surveys of the South Sea Islands and the Australian coast. When he wasn't at sea, Cook, together with the other apprentices, slept in Walker's attic.

At the north end of Church Street, you climb the famous **199 steps** of the Church Stairs – now paved, but originally a wide wooden staircase built for pallbearers carrying coffins to the church of St Mary above. The views over the harbour and town are magnificent, while a little searching reveals the grave of William Scoresby Snr, master whaler, and inventor of the crow's nest.

The bizarre parish **church of St Mary** at the top of the steps is an architectural amalgam dating back to 1110, boasting a Norman chancel arch, a profusion of eighteenth-century panelling, box pews unequalled in England and a triple-decker pulpit – note the built-in ear trumpets, added for the benefit of a nineteenth-century rector's deaf wife.

Whitby Abbey

The cliff-top ruins of **Whitby Abbey** (April–Oct daily 10am–5/6pm; Nov–Easter Mon & Thurs–Sun 10am–4pm; £4.20; EH), beyond St Mary's, are some of the most evocative in England, the nave, soaring north transept and lancets of the east end giving a hint of the building's former delicacy and splendour. Its monastery was founded in 657 by St Hilda of Hartlepool, daughter of King Oswy of Northumberland, and by 664 had become important enough to host the **Synod of Whitby**, an event of seminal importance in the development of English Christianity. It settled once and for all the question of determining the date of Easter, and adopted the rites and authority of the Roman rather than the Celtic Church. **Caedmon**, one of the brothers at the abbey during its earliest years, has a twenty-foot cross to his memory which stands in front of St Mary's, at the top of the steps. His nine-line *Song of Creation* is the earliest surviving poem in English, making the abbey not only the cradle of English Christianity, but also the birthplace of English literature. The original abbey was destroyed by the Danes in 867 and refounded by the Benedictines in 1078, though most of the present ruins – built slightly south of the site of the Saxon original – date from between 1220 and 1539. You'll discover all this and more in the **visitor centre** (hours as above), housed in the shell of the adjacent mansion, built after the Dissolution using material from the plundered abbey. Ongoing archeological work on the headland has yielded finds dating back to Anglo-Saxon times, while audio-visual displays concentrate both on life at the medieval abbey and at the house, whose seventeenth-century geometric "hard" garden has been restored.

West Cliff

Whitby developed as a holiday resort in the nineteenth century, partly under the influence of York railway entrepreneur George Hudson, who brought the railway to town. Wide streets, elegant crescents, boarding houses and hotels were laid on the heights of **West Cliff**, topped by a whalebone arch, commemorating Whitby's former industry, and a statue of Captain Cook. The small **harbour front** below, along Pier Road, sports an active fish market and a run of arcades and chip shops, leading to the twin, pincered piers and lighthouses. Various short boat trips and cruises depart from Pier Road throughout the day. When the tide's out, the broad, clean sands to the west stretch for three miles to **Sandsend** (where the beer garden of the *Hart Inn* makes a tempting target).

Final port of call should be the gloriously eclectic **Whitby Museum** in Pannett Park (Tues–Sun 9.30am–4.30pm, plus bank hols; £3; ⓦwww .whitbymuseum.org.uk), up the hill from the train station. There's more Cook memorabilia, including various objects and stuffed animals brought back as souvenirs by his crew, as well as casefuls of exhibits devoted to Whitby's seafaring tradition, its whaling industry in particular. Some of the best and largest fossils of Jurassic period reptiles unearthed on the east coast are also preserved here.

Eating, drinking and entertainment

Unsurprisingly, Whitby is well known for its freshly caught fish. A multitude of **cafés** around town – especially along Pier Road and Bridge Street – serve fish and chips, bread and tea for around £5; the same thing in most of the **restaurants** costs a few pounds more.

Whitby has a strong local **music scene**, with especially good folk nights in some of its pubs – English folk's first family, the Waterson/Carthys, are from nearby Robin Hood's Bay. First fest of the year is the **Moor and Coast** (ⓦwww.moorandcoast.co.uk), a weekend over the May bank holiday; this is eclipsed by the annual **Whitby Folk Week** (ⓦwww.whitbyfolk.co.uk) in August (the week immediately preceding the bank holiday), when the town is filled day and night with singers, bands, traditional dancers, storytellers and music workshops. Best place to find out more is at *The Port Hole*, 16 Skinner St (☎01947/603475), a fair trade craft shop that's also the HQ of local collective **Musicport** (🌐www.musicport.fsnet.co.uk) who put on weekly gigs from big names in the world/folk scene.

Finally, the **Regatta** every August (moveable dates) is a noisy weekend of fairground rides, spectacular harbourside fireworks and boat races.

Restaurants

Magpie Café 14 Pier Rd ☎01947/602058. The traditional fish-and-chip choice in town for over forty years, and with a wide-ranging menu in case you don't want something battered and fried. In summer you'll have to queue to eat in or even for the takeaways. Closes 9pm. Moderate.

Moon and Sixpence 5 Marine Parade ☎01947/821071. Fish is outstanding here, but this contemporary spot on the quayside dishes up lots more besides, such as local game; champagne cocktails are on offer too. There's also a luxury room above the restaurant, with Jacuzzi and double shower (with television) from £120. Expensive.

Red Chard 22 Flowergate ☎01947/606660. Relaxed place for coffee or glass of wine, or dig into dishes ranging from prawn cocktail and bubble-and-squeak to saffron pappardelle. Closed Mon, and Sat lunch. Expensive.

Pubs and live music

Duke of York Church St. Classic Whitby pub, at the bottom of the 199 steps, with harbour views and a mixed clientele of tourists and locals who come for the good-value food and occasional music.

Huntsman Inn Aislaby. It's well worth driving (or cabbing) out the couple of miles to Aislaby for the home-cooked pub food here – steaks a speciality.

Station Inn New Quay Rd. The town's real-ale haunt, with a changing selection of guest beers and live music on Fri.

Staithes

Beyond the beach at Sandsend, a fine coastal walk through pretty Runswick Bay leads in around four hours to the fishing village of **STAITHES**. At first sight, it's an improbably beautiful grouping of huddled stone houses around a small harbour, backed by the severe outcrop of Cowbar Nab, a sheer cliff face which protects the northern flank of the village. Any time spent here, especially out of season, soon reveals its gruffer side – crumbling houses on either side of the beck, the fierce winter wind whistling down the cobbled main street, and the tenacious last gasp of a declining fishing fleet which once employed 300 men in 120 boats. James Cook first worked here in a draper's shop before moving to Whitby and he's remembered in the **Captain Cook and Staithes Heritage Centre**, on the High Street (daily 10am–5pm, weekends only Jan & Feb; £2.75), which recreates an eighteenth-century street among other interesting exhibits. Other than this, you'll have to content yourself with pottering about the rocks near the harbour – there's no beach to speak of – or clambering the nearby cliffs for spectacular views; at **Boulby**, a mile and a half's trudge up the coastal path (45min), you're walking on the highest cliff (670ft) on England's east coast.

Practicalities

The road into Staithes, off the A174, puts drivers into a **car park** at the top of the hill leading down into the old village; don't ignore the signs and drive down, since there's nowhere to park and it's hard work turning round again.

You could stay at one of the B&Bs in the houses at the top of the village, but better **accommodation** is available down below, specifically at the *Endeavour Restaurant* (☎01947/840825, 🌐www.endeavour-restaurant.co.uk; ❺). This is the best place to eat for miles around, with superb (but pricey) fresh fish meals (dinner only; closed Sun & Mon, except bank hols).

Alternatively, drive the three miles south (back towards Whitby) to **Runswick Bay**, a tiny little one-pub-village-and-beach, where the *Cliffemount Hotel* (℡01947/840103, ⓦwww.cliffemounthotel.co.uk; ❺) glories in its elevated position. It has a good sea-facing restaurant too, specializing in locally caught seafood.

Travel details

Buses

Details of minor and seasonal local bus services are frequently given in the text. It's essential to pick up either the *Dales Explorer* or *Moors Explorer* timetable booklets from a local tourist office if visiting those parts of the county. For details of the Moorsbus in the North York Moors National Park see p.836. For information on all other local and national bus services, contact Traveline ℡0871/200 2233, ⓦwww.yorkshiretravel.net.

Harrogate to: Knaresborough (every 10min; 15–25min); Leeds (every 30min–1hr; 40min); Pateley Bridge (hourly; 50min); Ripon (every 30min; 30min).

Helmsley to: Pickering (hourly; 40min); Scarborough (hourly; 1hr 30min); York (Mon–Sat 3–5 daily; 1hr 30min).

Pickering to: Helmsley (hourly; 40min); Scarborough (hourly; 1hr); Whitby (4–6 daily; 55min); York (hourly; 1hr 15min).

Richmond to: Masham (Mon–Sat hourly; 55min); Ripon (Mon–Sat hourly; 1hr 15min).

Scarborough to: Bridlington (hourly; 1hr 15min); Filey (hourly; 30min); Helmsley (hourly; 1hr 30min); Hull (hourly; 2hr 50min); Leeds (hourly; 2hr 40min); Pickering (hourly; 1hr); Robin Hood's Bay (hourly; 45min); Whitby (hourly; 1hr); York (hourly; 1hr 35min).

Skipton to: Grassington (Mon–Sat hourly; 30min); Malham (4 daily; 40min); Settle (Mon–Sat hourly; 40min).

Whitby to: Robin Hood's Bay (hourly; 25min); Staithes (hourly; 30min); York (4–6 daily; 2hr).

York to: Beverley (Mon–Sat hourly; Sun 7 daily; 30min); Hull (Mon–Sat hourly; Sun 7 daily; 1hr 45min); Leeds Bradford Airport (hourly; 55min); Pickering (hourly; 1hr 15min); Scarborough (hourly; 1hr 35min); Whitby (4–6 daily; 2hr).

Trains

Main routes and services are given below, and check timetables on ⓦwww.nationalrail.co.uk. For more detailed information about specific lines, see the boxes on the Settle to Carlisle Railway (p.798), North Yorkshire Moors Railway (p.843) and Keighley and Worth Valley Railway (p.791).

Harrogate to: Knaresborough (every 30min; 10min); Leeds (every 30min–1hr; 35min); York (hourly; 30min).

Hull to: Beverley (Mon–Sat hourly, Sun 6 daily; 15min); Leeds (hourly; 1hr); London (6 daily; 2hr 45min); Scarborough (every 2hr; 1hr 30min); York (9 daily; 1hr).

Knaresborough to: Harrogate (every 30min; 10min); Leeds (every 30min–1hr; 45min); York (hourly; 30min).

Leeds to: Bradford (every 15min; 20min); Carlisle (3–7 daily; 2hr 40min); Harrogate (every 30min–1hr; 35min); Hull (hourly; 1hr); Knaresborough (every 30min–1hr; 45min); Lancaster (4 daily; 2hr); Liverpool (hourly; 1hr 50min); London (every 30min; 2hr 20min); Manchester (every 30min; 1hr); Scarborough (every 30min–1hr; 1hr 20min); Settle (3–8 daily; 1hr); Sheffield (every 30min; 40min–1hr 25min); Skipton (every 30min; 40min–1hr 25min); York (every 30min; 30min).

Pickering to: Grosmont (April–Oct 5–8 daily, plus limited winter service; 1hr 5min).

Scarborough to: Bridlington (5–9 daily; 35min); Filey (5–9 daily; 15min); Hull (every 2hr; 1hr 30min); Leeds (hourly; 1hr 20min); York (hourly; 50min).

Sheffield to: Leeds (every 30min; 40min–1hr 25min); London (hourly; 2hr 20min); York (every 30min–1hr; 1hr).

Whitby to: Danby (4–5 daily; 35min); Egton Bridge (4–5 daily; 20min); Great Ayton (4–5 daily;

1hr 5min); Grosmont (4–5 daily; 15min); Middlesbrough (4–5 daily; 1hr 30min).
York to: Bradford (hourly; 1hr); Durham (every
30min; 50min); Harrogate (hourly; 30min); Hull
(9 daily; 1hr); Leeds (every 30min; 30min);

London (every 30min; 2hr 15min); Manchester
(hourly; 1hr 30min); Newcastle (every 30min;
1hr); Scarborough (hourly; 50min); Sheffield
(every 30min–1hr; 1hr).

13

The Northeast

CHAPTER 13

Highlights

* **Durham Cathedral** Awe-inspiring Romanesque church towering above the River Wear. See p.865

* **Beamish Museum** The northeast's industrial past poignantly recreated. See p.869

* **Killhope Lead Mining Museum** An excellent family day out – put the kids to work down t'pit. See p.873

* **Newcastle nightlife** Lock up your inhibitions, leave your coat at home and hit the Toon. See p.888

* **Bede's World** Fascinating evocation of the life and times of one of Europe's greatest scholars. See p.892

* **Hadrian's Wall Path** Put on your walking boots to make the most of this extraordinary monument. See p.897

* **Chillingham Wild Cattle** Don't get too close – this herd of cows has been seeing off intruders for over 800 years. See p.906

* **Holy Island** Cradle of early Christianity, with a brooding, isolated atmosphere. See p.914

▲ Holy Island

The Northeast

England's **northeast** (principally the counties of Durham and Northumberland) contains some of the country's biggest historic and natural attractions. In many ways a land apart from the rest of England – more remote, less affluent, its accents often impenetrable to outsiders – it also has the very stuff of English history etched across its landscapes. Romans, Vikings and Normans all left dramatic evidence of their colonization, while the Industrial Revolution exploited to the limit the northeast's natural resources and its people. Consequently, heritage centres, wildlife tours, national park hikes, stately homes and gardens, all vie with the standard "castles and coast" itinerary that most tourists follow.

Getting around the northeast

Frequent **trains** run up the coast on the London–Scotland route (calling principally at Darlington, Durham, Newcastle and Berwick-upon-Tweed), while numerous **buses** link the main towns and villages. A car is useful for exploring rural and coastal areas easily, but there are also bus services into the heart of the Northumberland National Park, while **Hadrian's Wall** has its own bus service.

The **Northeast Explorer Pass** (£7; ⓦwww.explorernortheast.co.uk), valid after 9am on weekdays and all day at weekends, gives one-day's unlimited travel on local buses (as far south as Scarborough in North Yorkshire or west to Carlisle), plus free travel on the Tyne and Wear metro and Shields ferries. The **Arriva Day Ticket** (£5) covers one-day Arriva bus travel over the same area. Useful **train passes** include the Northeast Regional Rover (7 days; £78.50) and the North Country Rover (any 4 days out of 8; £68), which is also valid in parts of Yorkshire and Lancashire.

The main long-distance footpath is the **Pennine Way**, which cuts up from the Yorkshire Dales, runs parallel to Hadrian's Wall from Greenhead to Housesteads, and then climaxes in a climb through the Northumberland National Park. The **Hadrian's Wall Path** (see p.897) provides access along the whole of Hadrian's Wall; less well known is the 63-mile pilgrim's route, **St Cuthbert's Way**, which links Melrose, where St Cuthbert started his ministry just across the border in Scotland, with Holy Island. Other major waymarked routes include the 100-mile **Teesdale Way** from Middleton-in-Teesdale to Teesmouth (just beyond Middlesbrough); and the 78-mile **Weardale Way**, from Cowshill at the head of the valley to the coast at Sunderland.

The 140-mile **Sea to Sea (C2C) cycle route** from Whitehaven/Workington to Sunderland/Newcastle drops into the northeast just beyond Alston and links Allenheads, Stanhope and Consett with either city. A second cross-country route, **Walney to Wear (W2W)**, diverges at Barnard Castle northwards to Durham city and Sunderland (150 miles) or southwards through Darlington to Whitby (170 miles), while **Hadrian's Cycleway** runs the length of Hadrian's Wall.

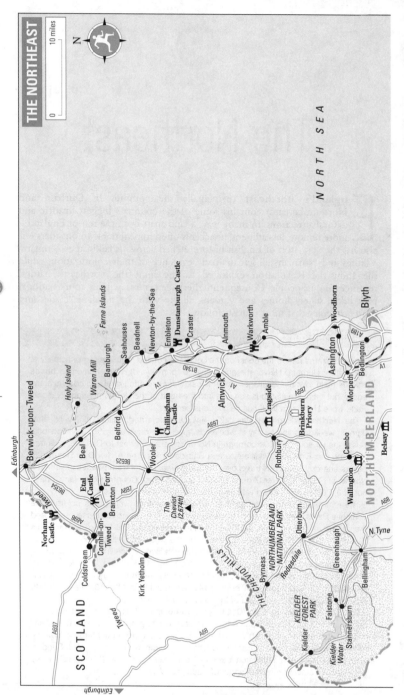

THE NORTHEAST

N

0   10 miles

Edinburgh

SCOTLAND

Tweed

A697

Coldstream

Kirk Yetholm

A698

Norham
Castle

Cornhill-on-
Tweed

B6354

Branxton

Ford

Etal
Castle

B6525

A697

Wooler

The Cheviot
(2,674ft)

THE CHEVIOT HILLS

The Byness

Redesdale

Otterburn

NORTHUMBERLAND
NATIONAL PARK

Greenhaugh

Bellingham

A68

KIELDER
FOREST
PARK

Kielder

Falstone

Stannersburn

Kielder
Water

N. Tyne

Berwick-upon-Tweed

Edinburgh

Beal

Holy Island

Waren Mill

Belford

Chillingham
Castle

A697

A1

Farne Islands

Bamburgh

Seahouses

Beadnell

Newton-by-the-Sea

Embleton

Craster

Dunstanburgh Castle

B1340

Alnmouth

Alnwick

A1

Cragside

A697

Brinkburn
Priory

Rothbury

Wallington

Cambo

Belsay

NORTHUMBERLAND

A68

Warkworth

Amble

Ashington

Woodhorn

Morpeth

Bedlington

A189

A1

Blyth

NORTH SEA

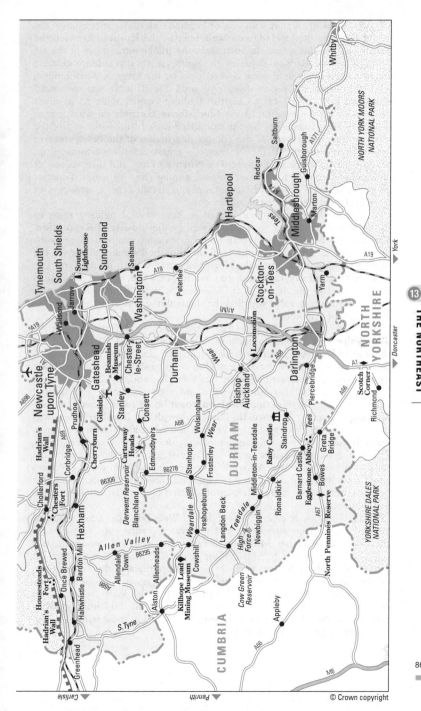

© Crown copyright

The essential sights start with one of England's most evocative ruins – the World Heritage site of **Hadrian's Wall**, built by the **Romans** between the North Sea and the west coast to contain the troublesome tribes of the far north. When the Romans departed, the northeast was divided into unstable Saxon principalities until order was restored by the kings of Northumbria, who dominated the region from 600 until the 870s. It was they who nourished the region's early Christian tradition, which achieved its finest flowering with the creation of the **Lindisfarne Gospels** on what is now known as Holy Island. The monks abandoned their island at the end of the ninth century, in advance of the Vikings' destruction of the Northumbrian kingdom, and only after the Norman Conquest did the northeast again become part of a greater England. The **Norman** kings and their successors repeatedly attempted to subdue Scotland, passing effective regional control to powerful local lords, whose authority is recalled by a sequence of formidable fortresses dotted along the coast.

Long after the northeast had ceased to be a critical military zone, its character and appearance were transformed by the **Industrial Revolution**. Towards the end of the eighteenth century two main coalfields were established – one dominating County Durham from the Pennines to the sea, the other stretching north along the Northumberland coast from the Tyne. The **world's first railway**, the Darlington and Stockton line, was opened in 1825 to move coal to the nearest port for export, while local coal and ore also fuelled the foundries that supplied the shipbuilding and heavy-engineering companies of Tyneside.

Most tourists dodge the industrial areas, bypassing the towns along the **Tees Valley** – Darlington, Stockton, Middlesbrough and Hartlepool – on the way to **Durham**, a handsome university city dominated by its magnificent twelfth-century cathedral. From Durham it's a short hop to **Newcastle upon Tyne**, distinguished by some fine Victorian buildings, the revitalized Quayside, and a vibrant cultural scene and nightlife. North, past the old colliery villages, the **Northumberland coast** boasts some superb castles – most impressively at **Warkworth**, **Dunstanburgh** and **Bamburgh** – as well as a string of superb dune-backed beaches and a handful of offshore islands. **Holy Island** is the best known, and the only one you can stay the night on, though the **Farne Islands** nature reserve makes a great day-trip from the small resort of Seahouses. **Alnwick**, four miles inland from the sea, features another stunning castle and northern England's finest new garden, while the extravagant ramparts of **Berwick-upon-Tweed** signal the imminence of the Scottish border.

Inland, the Durham dales of **Teesdale** and **Weardale** offer a mix of scenic countryside, heritage attractions, stately homes and rural pubs. However, it's the open-air **Beamish Museum**, between Durham and Newcastle, that soaks up most of the regional visitor traffic. To the north and west lies **Hadrian's Wall**, which can be easily visited from the appealing abbey town of **Hexham** – though the whole line of the Wall can also be followed along the long-distance Hadrian's Wall Path. Beyond the Wall are the harsh moorland, tree plantations, country towns, hiking trails and leisure opportunities of the **Northumberland National Park** – at its most remote around the reservoir and forest of **Kielder**.

Durham

The view from **DURHAM** train station is one of the finest in northern England – a panoramic prospect of Durham Cathedral, its towers dominating the skyline from the top of a steep sandstone bluff within a narrow bend of the River Wear. This dramatic site has been the resting place of St Cuthbert since 995, when his body was moved here from nearby Chester-le-Street, over one hundred years after his fellow monks had fled from Lindisfarne in fear of the Vikings, carrying his coffin with them. Cuthbert's hallowed remains made Durham a place of pilgrimage for both the Saxons and the Normans, who began work on the present cathedral at the end of the eleventh century.

Subsequently, the bishops of Durham were granted extensive powers to control the troublesome northern marches of the kingdom, ruling as semi-independent **Prince Bishops**, with their own army, mint and courts of law. The bishops were at the peak of their power in the fourteenth century, but thereafter the office went into decline, especially in the wake of the Reformation, yet they clung to the vestiges of their authority until 1836, when they ceded them to the Crown. They abandoned Durham Castle for their palace in Bishop Auckland and transferred their old home to the fledgling **Durham University**, England's third oldest seat of learning after Oxford and Cambridge. And so matters rest today, cathedral and university monopolizing a city centre that remains an island of privilege in what is otherwise a moderately sized, working-class town at the heart of the old Durham coalfield. It's well worth a night or two, and while there are attractions other than the cathedral and castle it's more the overall atmosphere that captivates, enhanced by the ever-present golden stone, slender bridges and glint of the river.

Arrival and information

From either Durham **train station,** or the **bus station** on North Road, it's a ten-minute walk to the city centre, across the river. The "Cathedral" **bus** links train and bus stations with the Market Place (for the tourist office) and the cathedral (every 20min; 50p for all-day ticket). Drivers should note that the peninsula road (to the castle and cathedral) is a toll road (Mon–Sat 10am–4pm; £2).

The **tourist office** (Mon–Sat 9.30am–5.30pm, Sun 11am–4pm; ☏0191/384 3720, ⓦ www.durhamtourism.co.uk) is located at **Millennium Place**, off Claypath, a development that also incorporates a theatre, cinema, public library, bar and café. To get out onto the river, either rent a **rowing boat** (£3.50 per person; 1hr) from Brown's Boathouse, Elvet Bridge, or take a **cruise** aboard the *Prince Bishop* (☏0191/386 9525; £5; 1hr), which has regular summer departures, again from Elvet Bridge.

Accommodation

Durham's varied city-centre **accommodation** now includes a budget *Premier Travel Inn* in the Walkergate development, adjacent to Millennium Place, and a *Radisson SAS* on the opposite side of the River Wear. Private rooms are offered at the colleges of **Durham University** (Christmas, Easter and July–Sept; from £28.50 per person, or £39.50 in en-suite rooms, breakfast included), all within walking distance of the centre; contact the Conference and Tourism Office (☏0800/289970, ⓦ www.dur.ac.uk/conference_tourism). Of the dozen colleges, University College has rooms inside the castle, while St Chad's, next to the cathedral, accepts **YHA bookings** in the same periods (☏0191/334 3358; from £19.50).

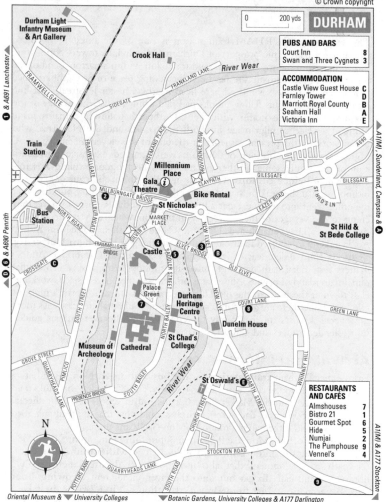

DURHAM

0 | 200 yds

Durham Light Infantry Museum & Art Gallery

Crook Hall

River Wear

FRANKLAND LANE

1 & A691 Lanchester

FRAMWELLGATE

SIDEGATE

Train Station

FREEMANS PLACE

PROVIDENCE ROW

FRAMWELLGATE

Millennium Place

Gala Theatre

Bike Rental

St Nicholas'

CLAYPATH

GILESGATE

GILESGATE

LEAZES ROAD

ST HILD'S LN

MILLBURNGATE BRIDGE

MILLBURNGATE

NORTH ROAD

Bus Station

MARKET PLACE

St Hild & St Bede College

D, 6 & A690 Penrith

CROSSGATE

FRAMWELLGATE BRIDGE

SILVER ST

Castle

NEW ELVET

ELVET BRIDGE

OLD ELVET

SADDLER STREET

SOUTH STREET

Palace Green

Durham Heritage Centre

Dunelm House

COURT LANE

GREEN LANE

NORTH BAILEY

NEW ELVET

Museum of Archeology

Cathedral

St Chad's College

River Wear

GROVE STREET

QUARRYHEADS LANE

PIMLICO

SOUTH BAILEY

PREBENDS BRIDGE

St Oswald's

CHURCH STREET

HALLGARTH STREET

WHINNEY HILL

A1(M), Sunderland, Campsie & A

A690

A1(M) & A177 Stockton

N

STOCKTON ROAD

SOUTH ROAD

POTTERS BANK

QUARRYHEADS LANE

Oriental Museum & ▼ University Colleges ▼Botanic Gardens, University Colleges & A177 Darlington

THE NORTHEAST | Durham

13

Hotels and guesthouses

Castle View Guest House 4 Crossgate ☎0191/386 8852, Ⓦwww.castle-view .co.uk. Pretty townhouse on a cobbled terrace next to St Margaret's Church, with six rooms and a quiet courtyard-garden. Plus, of course, great castle views. **⑤**

Farnley Tower The Avenue ☎0191/384 2796, Ⓦwww.farnley-tower.co.uk. A fine stone Victorian house, high on a hill, 10min walk from the centre. All 13 rooms feature co-ordinated fabrics and there's plenty of space, especially in the superior rooms, the best of which have sweeping city views. Parking. **⑥**

Marriott Royal County Old Elvet ☎0191/386 6821, Ⓦwww.marriotthotels.com. Durham's top hotel has its own riverside leisure centre with pool, while the rooms have plump beds and marble-trimmed bathrooms. Also restaurant, brasserie, bar and parking. Breakfast not included except with special/weekend rate. Parking. **⑦**

Seaham Hall Lord Byron's Walk, Seaham, 10 miles northeast of Durham ☎0191/516 1400, Ⓦwww .seaham-hall.com. Hip, holistic spa hotel that makes a great coastal base for city sightseeing - Durham is only a 20min drive away. Breakfast in bed is standard, there are amazing spa facilities, a well-regarded restaurant, and beaches and coastal walks nearby. ⑨

![icon] **Victoria Inn** 86 Hallgarth St ☎0191/386 5269, ⓦwww.victoriainn-durhamcity.co.uk. Six light and pretty rooms with iron bedsteads, above a family-run pub just a few minutes from the centre. The pub itself is a cracker - a quiet, Victorian-era local with half-a-dozen well-kept ales, coal fires, no food and no music, just like pubs used to be (and closed between 2 and 6pm, 7pm on Sun). Parking available. ④

The City

Surrounded on three sides by the River Wear, Durham's compact centre is approached by two road bridges that lead from the western, modern part of town across the river to the spur containing castle and cathedral. The commercial heart of this "old town" area is the triangular **Market Place**, flanked by the Guildhall and St Nicholas' Church. The Victorian **Market Hall** (closed Sun), buried in the vaults of the buildings that line the west side of the square, hosts a lively outdoor market every Saturday, as well as farmers' markets on the third Thursday of the month.

Durham Cathedral

From Market Place, it's a five-minute walk up cobbled Saddler Street to **Durham Cathedral** (Mon–Sat 9.30am–6/8pm, Sun 12.30–5.30/8pm; guided tours 3 daily Easter week & mid-July to mid-Sept; access sometimes restricted, call ☎0191/386 4266 to check; £4 suggested donation; tours £4; ⓦwww .durhamcathedral.co.uk), facing the castle across the manicured Palace Green. Standing on the site of an early wooden Saxon cathedral, built to house the remains of St Cuthbert, the present cathedral – a supreme example of the Norman-Romanesque style – was completed in 1133, and has survived the centuries pretty much intact. The awe-inspiring **nave**, completed in 1128, used pointed arches for the first time in England, raising the vaulted ceiling to new and dizzying heights. The weight of the stone is borne by massive pillars, their heaviness relieved by striking Moorish-influenced geometric patterns. A door gives access to the **tower** (Mon–Sat 10am–3/4pm; £3), from where there are fine views of the city.

Separated from the nave by a Victorian marble screen is the **choir**, where the dark-stained Restoration stalls are overshadowed by the vainglorious **bishop's throne**, reputedly the highest in medieval Christendom, built on the orders of the fourteenth-century Bishop Hatfield, whose militaristic alabaster tombstone lies just below. Beyond, the **Chapel of the Nine Altars** dates from the thirteenth century, its Early English stonework distinguished by its delicacy of detail. Here, and around the adjoining **Shrine of St Cuthbert**, much of the stonework is of local Weardale marble, each dark shaft bearing its own fancy pattern of fossils. Cuthbert himself lies beneath a plain marble slab, his presence and shrine having gained a reputation over the centuries for their curative powers. The legend was given credence in 1104, when the saint's body was exhumed for reburial here, and was found to be completely uncorrupted, more than four hundred years after his death on Lindisfarne. Almost certainly, this was the result of his fellow monks having (unintentionally) preserved the body by laying it in sand containing salt crystals.

Back near the entrance, at the west end of the church, the **Galilee Chapel** was begun in the 1170s, its light and exotic decoration in imitation of the Great Mosque of Córdoba. The chapel contains the simple tombstone of the **Venerable Bede**, the Northumbrian monk credited with being England's first historian. Bede died at the monastery of Jarrow in 735, and his remains were first transferred to the cathedral in 1020.

▲ Durham Cathedral

An ancient wooden doorway opposite the main entrance leads into the spacious **cloisters**, which are flanked by what remains of the monastic buildings. These include an oak-beamed **monks' dormitory** (Mon–Sat 10am–4pm, Sun 2–4.30pm; £1) containing fine Anglo-Saxon carved stones, and the **Treasures of St Cuthbert** exhibition in the undercroft (Mon–Sat 10am–4.30pm, Sun 2–4.30pm; £2.50), where you can see some striking relics of St Cuthbert. The cathedral's original twelfth-century lion-head Sanctuary Knocker is displayed here (the one on the main door is a replica), and there's also a splendid facsimile copy of the Lindisfarne Gospels (the originals are in the British Library in London).

The rest of the city

Across Palace Green from the cathedral, **Durham Castle** (Easter & July–Sept daily 10am–12.30pm & 2–4.30pm; rest of the year Mon, Wed, Sat & Sun 2–4pm; £5; ☎0191/334 3800, ⓦwww.durhamcastle.com) lost its medieval appearance long ago, and the university subsequently renovated the old keep as a hall of residence. It's only possible to visit the castle on a 45-minute guided tour, highlights of which include visits to the fifteenth-century kitchen, a climb up the enormous hanging staircase and the jog down to the Norman chapel, notable for its lively Romanesque carved capitals.

Below the castle and the cathedral are the wooded banks of the **River Wear**, where a pleasant footpath runs right round the peninsula. It takes about thirty minutes to complete the circuit. **Framwellgate Bridge** originally dates from the twelfth century, though it was widened to its present proportions in the mid-nineteenth century. Just along from here, on the riverbank, the university's **Museum of Archeology** (April–Oct daily 11am–4pm; Nov–March Mon & Fri–Sun 11.30am–3.30pm; £1; ⓦwww.dur.ac.uk/fulling.mill) occupies an old stone fulling mill. Eighteenth-century **Prebends Bridge** boasts celebrated views of the cathedral, and the path then continues round to the handsome **Elvet Bridge**, again widened far beyond its medieval course, though still retaining traces of both its erstwhile bridge-houses and the chapel, St Andrew's, which once stood at its eastern end.

The university's **Oriental Museum** (Mon–Fri 10am–5pm, Sat & Sun noon–5pm; £1.50; @www.dur.ac.uk/oriental.museum) is set among college buildings a couple of miles south of the city centre on Elvet Hill Road (take bus #5 or #6 to South Rd). Highlights of its wide-ranging collection include outstanding displays of Chinese jade and ceramics, Arabic calligraphy, a magnificent Chinese bed and Japanese wood-block prints. After the museum, you may as well continue to the nearby **Botanic Garden** (daily 10am–4/5pm; £2), whose glasshouses, café and visitor centre are set in eighteen acres of woodland, grassland and gardens near Collingwood College; buses run back to the centre from either Elvet Hill Road or South Road.

Heading north of the centre, at **Crook Hall** (Easter weekend & late May to mid-Sept Wed–Sun 11am–5pm; £4.50; @www.crookhallgardens.co.uk) at Frankland Lane, Sidegate, just above the river, a series of rambling, small enclosed gardens radiate from the medieval hall, a perfect spot for afternoon tea. From here it's a ten minute walk to the **Durham Light Infantry Museum and Art Gallery**, at Aykley Heads (daily 10am–4/5pm; £3.25; @www .durham.gov.uk/dli), whose temporary art exhibitions are bolstered by fascinating galleries telling the story of the DLI regiment, from World War I (when it lost 12,000) to its last parade in 1968.

Eating, drinking and entertainment

Durham is not a city for gourmets, with only a few town-centre **restaurants** that really cut the mustard. However, as a student and tourist haven you don't have to look far for inexpensive pizza, pasta or bar meals. Check out the Walkergate Complex next to the Gala Theatre, where new **bars** and restaurants vie with each other for a piece of the action. Regular **classical concerts** are held at venues around the city, including the cathedral, while the Gala Theatre on Millennium Place (℡0191/332 4041, @www.galadurham.co.uk) hosts music of all kinds, plus theatre, cinema, dance and comedy.

Cafés

Almshouses Palace Green. Bistro meals for around £5–6, served in a historic building in the shadow of the cathedral. July and Aug open until 8pm.

Vennel's Saddler's Yard, Saddler St. Named after the skinny alley or "vennel" where it stands – near the junction with Elvet Bridge – this self-service café dispenses appetizing sandwiches, salads, quiche and pastas in its sixteenth-century courtyard. Closes 5pm.

Restaurants

Bistro 21 Aykley Heads ℡0191/384 4354. Excellent Modern British cuisine in a converted farmhouse north of the centre, 10min walk from the DLI Museum and Art Gallery; courtyard seating in summer and good-value set menus at lunchtime. Closed Sun. Expensive.

Gourmet Spot The Avenue ℡0191/384 6655. Fun and innovation are the watchwords here. Expect balloons and liquid nitrogen, salmon with cauliflower foam, venison with chocolate paint and sensational puddings. The

Festival time

After the **Durham Regatta** in June, July sees a clutch of other festivals, starting on the first weekend with the **Durham Summer Festival**, encompassing musical entertainment and historical re-enactments on Palace Green. On the following Saturday, the **Miners' Gala** – when the traditional lodge banners are paraded through the streets – celebrates the international labour movement, while the **International Brass Band Festival** plays acid and gypsy brass as well as the more customary stuff during the first two weeks of the month.

most adventurous can opt for the Surrealism menu (£42.50, Mon–Thurs only). Closed Sun. Expensive.
Hide 39 Saddler St ☎0191/384 1999. The best of the café-bars with foodie pretensions, *Hide* serves a pizza, salad or brunch-style menu during the day, with prices rising at night for a Modern British tour of world cuisine. It's a buzzy place, with the music cranked up high. Moderate.
Numjai 19 Millburngate Centre ☎0191/386 2020. Authentic Thai restaurant that dishes up plenty of seafood and veggie options, with a river terrace and great views of the cathedral. Expensive.
The Pumphouse Farm Rd, Houghall ☎0191/386 9189. A few minutes' taxi ride southeast of the centre brings you to this Victorian pumphouse, where best use is made of locally sourced produce in imaginative and contemporary dishes. There's an excellent grill menu as well. Expensive.

Bars and pubs

Court Inn Court Lane. Best pub dining in town, a favourite with students and locals, with a classic pub menu and plenty of chips, plus dip-and-share tapas and some intriguing blackboard specials.
Swan & Three Cygnets Elvet Bridge. Town and gown converge in this popular riverside pub with a full-to-the-brim outdoor terrace.

Listings

Bike rental Cycle Force 2000, 87 Claypath ☎0191/384 0319. Closed Sun.
Hospital University Hospital, North Rd ☎0191/333 2333.
Internet Free access at the Claypath Library, opposite the tourist office, Millennium Place.
Pharmacy Boots, 2–5 Market Place ☎0191/384 2213.

Police HQ, Aykley Heads; also on New Elvet ☎0845/606 0365.
Post office Silver St.
Shopping At Fowlers Yard, Back Silver St, behind Market Place (Thurs–Sat 11am–4pm), watch artists and craftspeople at work in a series of creative studios – good for browsing or buying.

The rest of County Durham

In the 1910s, **County Durham** produced 41 million tons of coal each year, raised from three hundred pits by 170,000 miners. This was the heyday of an industry that since the 1830s had transformed the county's landscape, spawning scores of pit villages that matted the rolling hills from the Pennines to the North Sea. The miners, waging a long struggle against serf-like pay and conditions, achieved a gradual improvement of their lot, but could not prevent the slow decline of the Durham coalfield from the 1920s: just 127 mines were left when the industry was nationalized in 1947, only 34 in 1969, and today not a single pit remains. As a consequence, the old colliery villages have lost their sense of purpose and structure, some becoming godforsaken terraces in the middle of nowhere, others being swallowed up by neighbouring towns. For a taste of the old days, most people visit the reconstructed colliery village at the open-air **Beamish Museum**, north of Durham, while for the region's considerable railway heritage you shouldn't miss **Locomotion**, south of Durham, near Bishop Auckland – a fascinating outpost of the National Railway Museum.

Away from the old coalfields and railway works the rest of County Durham's attractions form a neat triangle. The two main towns are the ecclesiastical residence of **Bishop Auckland** and the well-to-do market town of **Barnard Castle**, beyond which – to the west – lie the isolated Pennine valleys of **Teesdale** and **Weardale**. It's easy to construct a circuit by car to see both, calling in at the valleys' small heritage centres, Methodist chapels and natural highlights; onward routes are then west via nearby Alston into Cumbria or north across the moors on minor roads from Weardale – the latter direction dropping into Northumberland, either through the bucolic **Allen Valley** or via the delightful stone village of **Blanchland**, tucked away in the Derwent River valley.

Beamish Museum

The open-air **Beamish Museum** (April–Oct daily 10am–5pm; Nov–April Tues–Thurs, Sat & Sun 10am–4pm; last admission 3pm; admission £16, £6 in winter; ☎0191/370 4000, ⓦwww.beamish.org.uk) spreads out over three hundred acres beside the A693, about ten miles north of Durham. It's the one County Durham attraction you really shouldn't miss, as popular with locals as it is with tourists. Come to chew the fat with the costumed guides, many of whom are recruited for their real-life experience – the collier who takes you down the drift mine may once have been a miner.

Buildings from all over the region have been painstakingly reassembled in six main sections, linked by restored trams and buses. Shopkeepers, workers and householders in period dress can answer your questions, and you can walk through many of the buildings and workshops to find out about daily life a century or two ago. Four of the sections show life in 1913, before the upheavals brought about by World War I: a pint-sized **colliery village**, complete with drift mine (regular tours throughout the day), cottages, Methodist chapel and school; a **farm** inhabited by breeds of livestock that were popular in the period; a **train station** and goods shed; and a large-scale recreation of a market **town**, its High Street lined by shops, offices, garage, stables, sweet factory and Masonic Hall. Two areas date to 1825, at the beginning of the northeast's industrial development: a **manor house**, with horse yard, formal gardens, vegetable plots and orchards; and the **Pockerley Waggonway**, where you can ride behind a replica of George Stephenson's *Locomotion*, the first passenger-carrying steam train in the world. There's a great deal to see, and what with the summertime Victorian funfair, the *Sun Inn* pub and tea rooms, and **special events** (from ploughing matches to leek shows), most people make a day of it – reckon on at least four hours to get round the lot in summer, two in winter when only the town and train station are usually open.

To **get there**, drivers should follow signs to the museum off the A1(M) Chester-le-Street exit, then follow the signs along the A693 to Stanley. Direct **buses** from Newcastle drop you close to the main entrance, though from Durham you'll need to change at Chester-le-Street – get up-to-date details from Traveline (☎0871/200 2233).

Bishop Auckland

Eleven miles southwest of Durham city, **BISHOP AUCKLAND** has been the country home of the bishops of Durham since the twelfth century and their official residence for more than a hundred years. Their palace, the gracious **Auckland Castle** (Easter–June & Sept Sun & Mon 2–5pm; July & Aug Sun 2–5pm, Mon & Wed 11–5pm; £4; ⓦwww.auckland-castle.co.uk), standing in eight-hundred-acre grounds, is approached through an imposing gatehouse just off the town's large Market Place. Most rooms are rather sparsely furnished, save the splendid seventeenth-century marble and limestone chapel and the long dining room, with its thirteen paintings of Jacob and his sons by Francisco de Zurbarán, commissioned in the 1640s for a monastery in South America. After you've seen the castle stroll into the adjacent **Bishop's Deer Park** (daily dawn–dusk; free), where an eighteenth-century deer house survives.

The town itself plays second fiddle to the castle, though don't leave until you've followed the mile-long lane from behind the Town Hall (signposted by the *Sportsman Inn*) to the remains of **Binchester Roman Fort** (daily: April–Sept 10/11am–5pm; £2.25). Only a small portion of Roman Vinovia has been excavated (with most of the finds displayed in the Bowes Museum at Barnard Castle), but a stretch of cobbled Dere Street has been uncovered (a fortified supply route stretching from York to Corbridge on Hadrian's Wall) and so has the country's best example of a **hypocaust**, built to warm the private bath suite of the garrison's commanding officer. The fort was abandoned in the fifth century and many of its stones found their way to the hamlet of **Escomb**, two miles west of Bishop Auckland (bus #86 from town), where they were used to build a seventh-century **Saxon church** (daily 9am–4/8pm; free; Ⓦ www.escombsaxonchurch.com).

Locomotion

The first passenger train (as opposed to freight) in the world left from the station at Shildon in 1825 – making the small County Durham town, around five miles southeast of Bishop Auckland, the world's oldest railway town. It's a heritage explored in the magnificently realized **Locomotion**, otherwise known as the **National Railway Museum at Shildon** (April–Oct daily 10am–5pm; Nov–March Wed–Sun 10am–4pm; free; Ⓣ 01388/777999, Ⓦ www .locomotion.uk.com); follow the signs off the B6282 (from Bishop Auckland) or the A6072 (from the A68/A1(M)). This regional outpost of York's National Railway Museum traces two hundred years of railway history, linking it directly to the growth of the works at Shildon – the town's own locomotive, *Non-Pareil* ("Without Compare"), competed in the Rainhill trials (held to provide transport on the fledgling Liverpool to Manchester railway), eventually losing out to George Stephenson's famous *Rocket*.

Locomotion is less a museum and more an experience, spread out around a kilometre-long site, the attractions linked by free bus from the reception building (where there's parking). The house of the first railway works' manager, Timothy Hackworth, presents more site interpretation, while depots, sidings, junctions and coal drops lead ultimately to the heart of the museum, **Collection** – a gargantuan steel hangar containing an extraordinary array of sixty locomotives, dating from the very earliest days of steam. Accompanied by an intoxicating aroma of oil and grease, you're free to explore Britain's rail heritage up close. With interactive children's exhibits, summer steam rides, rallies and shows, it makes an excellent family day out.

Barnard Castle and around

Fifteen miles southwest of Bishop Auckland, the attractive town of **BARNARD CASTLE** is overlooked by the skeletal remains of its **castle** (April–Oct daily 10am–4/6pm; Nov–March Mon & Thurs–Sun 10am–4pm; £4; EH), poking out from a cliff high above the River Tees. First fortified in the eleventh century, the castle was long a stronghold of the Balliols, a Norman family interminably embroiled in the struggle for the Scottish crown. However, by the seventeenth century the castle had outlived its usefulness and the Vanes of nearby Raby Castle were quarrying its stone to repair their premises.

The town, however, continued to thrive as a market centre (Wednesday is still market day) and it's pleasant to potter around the wide, well-kept streets of what the locals call "Barney". Castle aside, the prime attraction is the grand French-style chateau that constitutes the **Bowes Museum** (daily 11am–5pm; £6.35;

The precociously talented, 26-year-old **Charles Dickens**, already a hugely successful author with his *Pickwick Papers* and *Oliver Twist*, produced his third novel in serial form in 1838. *Nicholas Nickleby* presented the usual panoply of comic and grotesque figures, none more so than Wackford Squeers, the "villainous", one-eyed headmaster of Dotheboys Hall who, memorably, "appeared ill at ease in his clothes, and as if he were in a perpetual state of astonishment at finding himself so respectable". As throughout his career, Dickens did his homework assiduously. On a trip north in early 1838 he visited various of the so-called "Yorkshire Schools" in the area around Barnard Castle – established, more often than not, by unscrupulous businessmen who cared little for their charges. In these schools, illegitimate or awkward children, or simply those of unsuspecting parents, were destined for years of neglect, abuse or worse. Dickens stayed at the *King's Head* (now the *Charles Dickens*) on Market Place in **Barnard Castle**, spied on a local watchmaker's shop (giving him the idea for *Master Humphrey's Clock*) and visited nearby **Bowes**, where the Bowes Academy was run by the notorious William Shaw, earlier prosecuted for neglect of his schoolboys, several of whom had gone blind in his care. Dickens took careful note and modelled Squeers on Shaw and Dotheboys Hall on Bowes Academy. The school, along with others in the locality, was later closed, after the novel prompted parents and authorities finally to take action. The school building – "a long cold-looking house" – still stands at the west end of the village; Shaw is buried in the churchyard. As is the way with notoriety, several teachers soon claimed to be the original Wackford Squeers and Dickens himself, in print at least, remained vague about his identity, claiming in the novel's preface that Squeers was "representative of a class, and not of an individual".

(13)

Ⓦ www.bowesmuseum.org.uk), half a mile east of the centre, signposted along Newgate. Begun in 1869, the chateau was commissioned by John and Josephine Bowes, a local businessman and MP and his French actress wife, who spent much of their time in Paris collecting the ostentatious treasures and antiques. They shipped the whole lot back to County Durham and, in an early show of arts patronage, turned the house into a museum for the enlightenment of the Teesdale public (though neither lived to see its formal opening in 1892). It's a hugely rewarding collection, highlighting English period furniture, French decorative and religious art, and one of the most important Spanish collections in the UK, including El Greco's *The Tears of St Peter*. There are also tapestries, lace, ceramics and incidental curiosities, notably a late eighteenth-century mechanical silver swan in the lobby which still performs a couple of times daily (2pm and 3pm), preening to a brief forty-second melodic burst.

Practicalities

Buses stop on either side of central Galgate – once the road out to the town gallows, hence the name. The **tourist office** (daily 10/11am–4/6pm; Nov–March closed Sun; ☎01833/690909) is on Flatts Road, at the end of Galgate by the castle. Among several convenient **B&Bs** along the upper reaches of Galgate, the welcoming *Homelands*, 85 Galgate (☎01833/638757, Ⓦ www.homelandsguesthouse.co.uk; ❸), is the choice pick, offering pretty bedrooms and good breakfasts. The town has plenty of **cafés**, while the *Old Well Inn*, 21 The Bank, has a beer garden backing onto the castle walls. Barney's top **restaurant** is *Blagraves House*, 30–32 The Bank (☎01833/637668; closed Sun & Mon; meals from around £20), sporting low-beamed ceilings and large open fires.

Around Barnard Castle

From the town centre, it's a fine mile-and-a-half walk from the castle, southeast (downriver) through the fields above the banks of the Tees, to the glorious shattered ruins of **Egglestone Abbey** (dawn–dusk; free; EH), a minor foundation dating from 1195. Turner painted here on one of his three visits to Teesdale, and also at nearby **Rokeby Park** (bank hols & June–Aug Mon & Tues 2–5pm; £5; ℗01609/748612), a Palladian country house where Walter Scott wrote his ballad *Rokeby*. You can get to the hall directly on bus #79 from Barnard Castle, which also runs to Abbey Bridge End, for Egglestone Abbey.

Around seven miles northeast of town, up the A688, the splendid, sprawling battlements of **Raby Castle** (Easter week, May & Sept Wed & Sun 1–5pm; June–Aug Mon–Fri & Sun 1–5pm; gardens same days 11am–5.30pm; £9, park & gardens only £4; ⓦwww.rabycastle.com) mostly date from the fourteenth century, reflecting the power of the Neville family, who ruled the local roost until 1569. It was then that Charles Neville helped plan the "Rising of the North", the abortive attempt to replace Elizabeth I with Mary Queen of Scots. The revolt was a dismal failure, and Neville's estates were confiscated, with Raby subsequently passing to the Vane family in 1626. On the first floor, the spectacular octagonal drawing room reflects the elaborate taste of the 1840s. Outside, are the walled gardens, where peaches, apricots and pineapples once flourished under the careful gaze of forty gardeners.

Teesdale

Extending twenty-odd miles northwest from Barnard Castle, **Teesdale** begins calmly enough, though the pastoral landscapes of its lower reaches are soon replaced by wilder Pennine scenery. There's a regular bus service as far as Middleton-in-Teesdale, the valley's main settlement, with infrequent (Mon–Sat) services on to the spectacular High Force waterfall and Langdon Beck (for the youth hostel).

MIDDLETON-IN-TEESDALE was once the archetypal "company town", owned lock, stock and barrel by the Quaker-run London Lead Company, which began mining here in 1753. The firm built stone cottages for its workforce, who in return were obliged to send their children to Sunday school and keep off the booze. Not that the Quakers were over-mindful of working conditions: lead miners suffered bronchial complaints brought on by the contaminated air in the mines, illnesses compounded by long hours and an early start – "washerboys", who sorted the lead ore from the rock for ten hours a day and more, began at eight years old. For local information, call in at the **tourist office** (restricted hours, though usually daily 10am–1pm; ℗01833/641001) in the central Market Place. Otherwise, head three miles back down the road towards Barnard Castle, to the charming village of **Romaldkirk**, where the ⚓ *Rose & Crown* (℗01833/650213, ⓦwww.rose-and-crown.co.uk; ❼), an ivy-clad eighteenth-century inn, has lovely rooms in dusky colours and highly accomplished modern British cooking in the bar (moderate) or restaurant (expensive).

Past Middleton, the countryside becomes harsher and the Tees more vigorous as the B6277 travels the three miles on to **Bowlees Visitor Centre** (April–Sept daily 11.30am–4pm; ℗01833/622292), the halt for the short walk to the rapids of **Low Force**. A mile further up the road is the altogether more compelling **High Force**, a seventy-foot cascade that rumbles over an outcrop of the Whin Sill ridge. The waterfall is on private Raby land, and visitors must pay £1 to view the falls and £1.50 to use the nearby car park, by the B6277. The *High Force Hotel* by the car park brews its own beer to accompany the bar meals.

Six miles upstream is **Cauldron Snout**, near the source of the Tees, where the river rolls 200ft down a rock stairway as it leaves **Cow Green Reservoir**. To reach the reservoir by car, turn off the main road at **Langdon Beck** and follow the three-mile-long lane to the car park, which is a mile's walk from the Snout. The eco-friendly **youth hostel** is back on the B6277 at Forest-in-Teesdale (℡0870/770 5910, ℮langdonbeck@yha.org.uk; from £9).

Weardale

Weardale is an easy day out in a car from Durham, though seeing the dramatic high-dale scenery by public transport can be a frustrating business. Bus #101 runs roughly hourly between Bishop Auckland and **Stanhope**, the main village; however, to get the bus to take you to the fascinating lead-mining museum at **Killhope**, at the head of the valley, you'll have to ask the driver (or arrange it in advance with the bus company; ℡01388/528235) – and don't forget to request a pick-up for the way back. There's B&B accommodation in Stanhope and elsewhere in the dale, but the better overnight stop is actually Alston (see p.760), just over the border in Cumbria, six or seven miles from Killhope.

Stanhope and around

Weardale's main settlement, **STANHOPE**, lies about halfway up the valley. It's an elongated village that makes a useful halt for hikes on the local moors, including the enjoyable five-mile circuit from the town centre, up through the woods of **Stanhope Dene**, after which in summer you can cool off with a splash in the open-air heated swimming pool. The village has a castle (closed to the public), built for a local MP in 1798, whose walled gardens now house the **Durham Dales Centre** – on the main road through Stanhope – in which you'll find the **tourist office** (daily 10/11am–4/5pm; ℡01388/527650, ⓦwww.durhamdalescentre.co.uk) and a café. Before you go, take a quick look at the 250-million-year-old **fossilized tree trunk** in the grounds of St Thomas' Church, on the main road near the Dales Centre.

Nine miles upstream at Ireshopeburn, the **Weardale Museum** (Easter, May–July & Sept Wed–Sun 2–5pm, Aug daily 2–5pm; £2) tells the story of the dale, in particular its lead-mining and Methodism (the faith of most of County Durham's lead-miners). In a region dotted with Methodist chapels from the very earliest Wesleyan days, there's something of an unseemly scramble for the title of "world's oldest" – **High House Chapel** (1760), adjacent to the museum (entry included), hedges its bets with a claim to be the world's oldest Methodist chapel in continuous weekly use. If it's closed, you can at least peek through the window – parking is a hundred yards away at the *Weardale Inn* (where there's a beer garden and bar meals).

Killhope Lead Mining Museum

Lead and iron-ore mining flourished in and around Weardale from the 1840s to the 1880s, leaving today's landscape scarred with old workings. One of the bigger mines, situated about five miles west of Ireshopeburn, at the head of the valley and a windy 1500 feet above sea level, is now the **Killhope Lead Mining Museum** (April–Oct daily 10.30am–5pm; £4.50, £6.50 including mine visit; ⓦwww.durham.gov.uk/killhope), where industrial debris lies scattered across a large open-air site. This is a terrific attraction, presenting the nineteenth-century buildings and machinery in a way that really brings home the hardships of a mining life – investigating the cramped mineshop, where the workers lived away from their families all week, visiting the huge clanking

▲ Killhope Lead Mining Museum

waterwheel, or trying your hand as a washerboy on the old washing floor. The highlight, and not to be missed, is descending Park Level Mine (1hr tour; 01388/537505 call for times) with wellies, hard-hat and lamp in the company of a guide who expounds entertainingly about the realities of life underground, notably the perils of the "Black Spit", a lung disease which killed many men by their mid-forties. Expect to spend at least a couple of hours at the museum; there's a café on site.

The Allen Valley

The B6295 climbs north out of Weardale into Northumberland, soon dropping into the **Allen Valley**, where heather-covered moorland shelters small settlements that once made their living from lead mining. The dramatic surroundings are still easily viewed today from a series of river walks accessible from either of the main settlements.

At **ALLENHEADS**, at the top of the valley, twelve miles from Stanhope, handsome stone buildings stand close to the river. A heritage centre details the village's erstwhile industry, while a short nature trail guides you through the woodland around the East Allen River. The *Allenheads Inn* (☎01434 /685200; ❸), a popular stop for cyclists on the C2C route, provides beer and bar meals, and has seven rooms which get booked up quickly in summer.

ALLENDALE TOWN, another four miles north, also goes about its quiet, rural way – New Year's Eve excepted (see box opposite) – and claims to be at the exact centre of the British Isles. This is a good place to base yourself for the local walking, with a small supermarket and several friendly pubs and small hotels, all centred on the market square. A very good path connects **Allenheads to Allendale** (around nine miles one way), leaving or crossing the river on occasion, though connoisseurs rate higher the northern section, **from Allendale to the River Tyne** (eight miles one way), which is at its most dramatic when passing through the beautiful, tree-clad **Allen Gorge**, watched over by Staward Peel, a medieval fortified tower-house; there's road access at

Plankey Mill, around which the river becomes full of splashing families on summer weekends.

Blanchland and around

The other trans-moorland route into Northumberland is the B6278 which cuts north from Weardale at Stanhope for ten wild miles to **BLANCHLAND**, a handful of lichen-stained stone cottages huddled round an L-shaped square that was once the outer court of a twelfth-century abbey. The village has been preserved since 1721, when Lord Crewe bequeathed his estate to trustees on condition that they restored the old buildings, as Blanchland had slowly fallen into disrepair after the abbey's dissolution. Nothing but the faintest whiff of subsequent centuries has been allowed to intrude, the last concession being the construction of a pint-sized shelter in celebration of Queen Victoria's Diamond Jubilee. It's the *Lord Crewe Arms Hotel* (℡01434/675251, ⓦwww.crewearms .freeserve.co.uk; ⓞ) that now steals the show. Once the abbot's lodge, the hotel's nooks and crannies are an enticing mixture of medieval and eighteenth-century Gothic, including the dark vaulted basements, two big fireplaces left over from the canons' kitchen and a priest's hideaway stuck inside the chimney. You can eat in the restaurant (mains £12–15), or more cheaply in the fine public bar in the undercroft.

East of Blanchland, just past the **Derwent Reservoir**, at the junction with the A68, at **Carterway Heads**, the ⚲ *Manor House Inn* (℡01207/255268, ⓦwww .manorhouse-a68.co.uk; ⓞ) has rooms overlooking the reservoir and posh pub food at around £20 a head, though there's a cheaper lunchtime menu too.

The Tees Valley: Darlington to the coast

That the **River Tees** is so far off the contemporary tourist map as to be invisible is hardly the fault of towns whose livelihood largely disappeared once iron- and steel-making and shipbuilding became things of the past in England. But this area was one of the great engines of British economic power in the late nineteenth century. It was from **Darlington**, twenty miles south of Durham city, that George Stephenson's *Locomotion* made its inaugural run and where it is now on permanent display. The railway line ran first to Stockton-on-Tees and was then extended to ports at **Middlesbrough** and **Hartlepool**, to enable ever-increasing amounts of Durham coal to be unloaded and exported. Iron from the local Cleveland Hills supported a shipbuilding industry, which in Hartlepool at least had been flourishing since the eighteenth century.

In truth, few people are going to stop at any of these towns. But, for those that do, Darlington is the most surprisingly attractive, and you'd have to be hard-hearted not to derive some pleasure from Middlesbrough's fine new art gallery or Hartlepool's historic quay. Once out on the coast at the Victorian resort of **Saltburn**, or inland beyond Guisborough, you're very quickly in the heart of the North York Moors. In particular, note the Esk Valley train line from Middlesbrough to Whitby, which runs via Grosmont, northern terminal point of the North Yorkshire Moors Railway (see p.843).

Darlington

DARLINGTON hit the big time in 1825, when George Stephenson's "Number 1 Engine", later called *Locomotion*, hurtled from here to nearby Stockton-on-Tees, with the inventor at the controls and flag-carrying horsemen riding ahead to warn of the onrushing train, at the terrifying speed of fifteen miles per hour. This novel form of transport soon proved popular with passengers, an unlooked-for bonus for Edward Pease, the line's instigator: he had simply wanted a fast and economical way to transport coal from the Durham pits to the docks at Stockton. Subsequently, Darlington grew into a rail-engineering centre, and didn't look back till the closure of the works in 1966.

It's little surprise, then, that all signs in town point to the **Darlington Railway Centre and Museum** (Ⓦ www.drcm.org.uk), housed in Darlington's North Road Station, which was completed in 1842; it's a twenty-minute walk up Northgate from the central Market Place. The museum's pride and joy is the original *Locomotion*, actually built in Newcastle, which continued in service until 1841, while a special events programme throughout the year offers train rides and other family diversions.

The origins of the rest of Darlington lie deep in Saxon times. The monks carrying St Cuthbert's body from Ripon to Durham stopped here, the saint lending his name to the graceful riverside church of **St Cuthbert**. One of England's largest market squares spreads beyond the church up to the restored Victorian covered **market** (Mon–Sat 8am–5pm, with a large outdoor market Mon & Sat), next to the clocktower, both designed by Alfred Waterhouse, the architect responsible for Manchester's town hall and London's Natural History Museum. The pedestrianized **Market Place** has been given back to the people and while it may not be Rome, you can sip a cappuccino at one of several cafés and pubs that spill tables outside at the first hint of sunshine.

Practicalities

Darlington's **train station** is on the main line from London to Scotland (via Durham and Newcastle) and there are also services to Middlesbrough, Saltburn and Bishop Auckland. From the station, walk up Victoria Road to the roundabout and turn right down Feethams for the central Market Place. The Town Hall is on Feethams, opposite which most **buses** stop.

The **tourist office** (Mon–Fri 9am–5pm, Sat 9am–3pm; ℡01325/388666, Ⓦ www.visitdarlington.com) on the south side of Market Place at 13 Horsemarket has free **town trail** leaflets (on its railway or Quaker heritage, for example) and can help with **accommodation**. *Hotel Bannatyne* (℡01325/365858; Ⓦ www.bannatyne.co.uk; ⑤) on Southend Avenue, off the A66, offers spacious, elegant rooms in a Georgian townhouse, while the eighteenth-century *George Hotel* (℡01325/374576; ⑤), at **Piercebridge**, five miles west of Darlington, off the A67, has rooms and restaurant looking across the gentle banks of the River Tees.

There are several **cafés** on and around Market Place, while the traditional *Hole in the Wall* pub here serves authentic Thai meals (not Sun). *Number Twenty 2*, 22 Coniscliffe Rd, is a self-professed "alehouse" with plenty of guest beers on tap, wine by the glass and pub lunches (Mon–Sat). The more contemporary *Oven*, 30 Duke St (℡01325/466668, closed Sun dinner), puts a French slant on its dishes. For entertainment, check out the enterprising **Arts Centre** (Vane Terrace) and its affiliated **Civic Theatre** (Parkgate, between the Market Place and the train station), which together offer a year-round programme of theatre, film, comedy, exhibitions and live music (℡01325/486555, ⓦwww.darlingtonarts.co.uk).

Middlesbrough

MIDDLESBROUGH, Teesside's largest town, fifteen miles east of Darlington, is entirely a product of the early industrial age, with nineteenth-century iron and steel barons throwing up factories and housing almost as fast as they could ship their products out of the docks. What was a hamlet at the turn of the nineteenth century was a thriving industrial town of 100,000 people by the turn of the twentieth. When iron and steel declined in importance and the local shipbuilding industry collapsed (the last shipyard closed in 1986), Middlesbrough took to light engineering and the chemical industry, the belching plants of which still surround the outskirts. For visitors, none of this is as easily celebrated as the "heritage industry" of the coalfields further west, though in the stunning new **Middlesbrough Institute of Modern Art** (Tues–Sat & bank hols 10am–5pm, Sun noon–4pm; free; ⓦwww.visitmima.com), in Centre Square, the town finally has a major tourist draw. Bringing together its municipal art collections for the first time, changing exhibitions concentrate on fine arts and crafts (ceramics and jewellery in particular) from the early twentieth century to the present day. Coming here is also a good excuse to ride on Middlesbrough's famous **Transporter Bridge** (80p per car), built in 1911 and the sole working example left in the country. The **Newport Bridge** (1934), the first vertical lift bridge built in England, also recalls past feats of engineering.

The town also considers itself the "Gateway to Captain Cook Country", fair enough given that he was born a mile and a half south of the centre in Marton in 1728. Here, the **Captain Cook Birthplace Museum** in Stewart Park (Tues–Sun 9/10am–4/5.30pm; free; ⓦwww.captcook-ne.co.uk) entertainingly covers the life and times of Britain's greatest seaman and explorer. As well as displays of artefacts brought back from the South Seas on Cook's three main eighteenth-century voyages, you'll find touch-screen terminals providing contemporary testimony by his botanist Sir Joseph Banks, while a series of short films fill in the background about Cook's life and a sailor's lot at sea. Buses run from the bus station every fifteen minutes or so to Marton – ask the driver for the stop. For more on the captain and the local area, see ⓦwww.captaincook.org.uk, or call the town **tourist office** (℡01642/729700, ⓦwww.middlesbrough.gov.uk).

Hartlepool

HARTLEPOOL, ten miles north of Middlesbrough, was England's third-largest port in the nineteenth century and once a noted shipbuilding centre. After years in the doldrums, its image has been transformed by the renaissance of its once decaying dockland area, now spruced up as **Hartlepool's Maritime Experience** (daily 10am–5pm; £7.50; ⓦ www.hartlepoolsmaritimeexperience .com). The entrance fee gets you on to the bustling eighteenth-century quayside where active attractions based around press gangs, the Royal Navy, seaport life and fighting ships stir the senses. There are also period shops, a replica eighteenth-century maritime pub, games and play area, coffee shop and market, plus a tour of **HMS Trincomalee**, a navy training ship built in 1817 and now berthed here. On the edge of the quay in the **Museum of Hartlepool** at Jackson Dock (daily 10am–5pm; free), you can board a restored paddle-steamer and trace the town's history, including its most notorious episode, which to this day earns Hartlepudlians the nickname "monkey hangers": legend has it that when a French ship sank off the coast during the Napoleonic Wars, the locals mistook the sole survivor, a monkey, for a Frenchman, and tried and hanged it as a spy.

Saltburn

On the coast to the south of the Tees estuary, it's not a difficult decision to bypass the kiss-me-quick tackiness of Redcar in favour of **SALTBURN**, twelve miles east of Middlesbrough, a graceful Victorian resort in a dramatic setting overlooking extensive sands and mottled red sea-cliffs. Soon after the railway arrived in 1861 to ferry Teessiders out to the seaside on high days and holidays, Saltburn became a rather fashionable spa town boasting a hydraulic **inclined tramway**, complete with stained-glass windows, that still connects upper town to pier and promenade, and ornate **Italian Gardens** that run beneath the eastern side of town. The **Smugglers Heritage Centre** (April–Sept Wed–Sun 10am–6pm; £2), set in fishermen's cottages to the east of the pier, is a vivid recreation of Saltburn's darker past.

There are regular **train** services from Newcastle and Durham, via Darlington and Middlesbrough, while frequent **buses** from Middlesbrough (with connections from Newcastle) stop outside the train station. If you want to stay in summer it's best to call first at the **tourist office** (Tues–Sat 9am–5pm, closes lunch hour; ☎ 01287/622422, ⓦ www.redcar-cleveland .gov.uk) in the railway station buildings and find out about **accommodation** vacancies.

Newcastle upon Tyne

At first glance **NEWCASTLE UPON TYNE** – virtual capital of the area between Yorkshire and Scotland – may appear to be just another northern industrial conurbation, but the banks of the Tyne have been settled for nearly two thousand years and the city consequently has a greater breadth of attractions than many of its rivals. The Romans were the first to bridge the river here, and the "new castle" appeared as long ago as 1080. In the seventeenth century a regional monopoly on coal export brought wealth and power to Newcastle and – as well as giving a new expression to the English language – engendered its other great industry, shipbuilding. At one time, 25 percent of the world's shipping was built here, and the first steam train and steam turbine also emerged from local factories. In its nineteenth-century heyday, Newcastle's engineers and builders gave the city an elegance that has survived today in the impressive buildings of Grainger Town – indeed, only London and Bath have more listed classical buildings.

Tyneside and Newcastle's native inhabitants are known as **Geordies**, the word probably derived from a diminutive of the name "George" – there are various explanations of who George was (King George II, railwayman George Stephenson), all plausible, none now verifiable. Geordies speak a largely impenetrable dialect and accent, heavily derived from Old English, and locals can derive hours of innocent amusement by asking tourists for a "tab" (cigarette), requesting directions to the nearest "nettie" (toilet) or confusing a female visitor with a non-gender-specific greeting ("haway man!"). They evince a partisan pride in their city and an endearing, if self-delusional, optimism, most obviously manifested in their fanatical support for the perennially underachieving **Newcastle United** football team. It's difficult to overstate the team's importance – everyone in Newcastle has a black-and-white replica shirt, worn at all special occasions (football matches, weddings, funerals, etc), while the "Toon's" most revered sons (Jackie Milburn, Bobby Robson, Peter Beardsley, Paul Gascoigne, Alan Shearer) long ago shed the mantle of mere mortals and ascended to the Geordie pantheon.

Industrial decline hit Newcastle early, as highlighted by the Jarrow Crusade of 1936 (see p.892), but the extraordinary revival has meant that the city has shed its dowdy provincial coat and has emerged as a vibrant European arts and nightlife destination. The pre-eminent artistic symbol of this renewal is Antony Gormley's **Angel of the North**, a magnificent steel sculpture the size of a jumbo jet that welcomes anyone approaching from the south by rail or road. Newcastle's city centre has been transformed, particularly along the banks of the River Tyne, where the famous bridges act as a backdrop to the ever-developing cultural and entertainment scene. Both Newcastle and Gateshead sides of the river have seen dramatic change – indeed, these days visitors are encouraged to think of the city not as Newcastle upon Tyne but as "Newcastle Gateshead". On **Gateshead Quays** are the BALTIC contemporary arts centre and Norman Foster's Sage music centre, while Newcastle's **Quayside** is scene of much of the city's contemporary nightlife. Add to these the lure of some impressive **museums and galleries** – including the unique Life Science Centre, the Laing Art Gallery and Seven Stories, the Centre for Children's Books – and there's a case for taking whatever time you were going to spend in the city and doubling it.

Arrival

Central Station, on Neville Street, is a five-minute walk from the city centre or Quayside and has a useful Metro station. National Express services arrive at the **coach station** on St James's Boulevard, not far from Central Station, while most regional bus services use the **Haymarket bus station** (Haymarket Metro). Many other city and local bus services arrive at and depart from the bus station in **Eldon Square Shopping Centre**. There are **car parks** signposted all over the city (including on the Quayside, under the High Level and Swing bridges); street parking is usually free between 6.30pm and 8am.

Newcastle's **airport**, six miles north of the city, is linked by Metro to Central Station (5.50am–11.10pm, every 7–15min; 23min; £2.70) and beyond. Alternatively, take a taxi into the centre (around £15). **Ferry arrivals** from Scandinavia and Holland dock at Royal Quays, North Shields, seven miles east of the city – there are connecting bus services or a taxi to the city costs around £15.

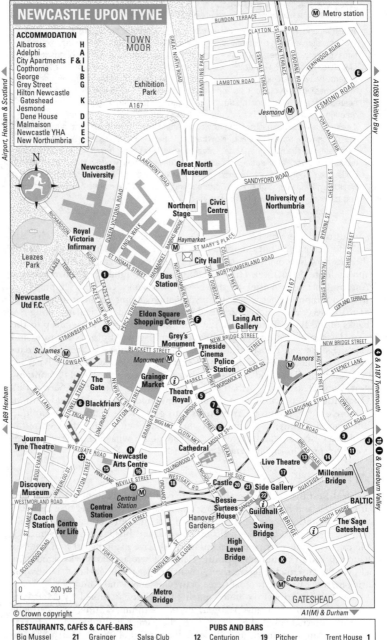

NEWCASTLE UPON TYNE

Ⓜ Metro station

ACCOMMODATION
Albatross	H
Adelphi	A
City Apartments	F & I
Copthorne	L
George	B
Grey Street	G
Hilton Newcastle	
Gateshead	K
Jesmond	
Dene House	D
Malmaison	J
Newcastle YHA	E
New Northumbria	C

▲ B1318 Morpeth   ▲ Ⓐ,Ⓑ,Ⓒ&Ⓓ

◄ Airport, Hexham & Scotland

A1058 Whitley Bay ►

◄ A69 Hexham

◄ 4 & A187 Tynemouth

10 & A1 Ouseburn Valley ►

BALTIC

GATESHEAD

© Crown copyright

A1(M) & Durham ▼

0   200 yds

RESTAURANTS, CAFÉS & CAFÉ-BARS
Big Mussel	21	Grainger	Salsa Club	12
Byker Vista Café	4	Rooms	2	Secco Ristorante	8
Café 21	14	Mangos	6	Salentino	
Caffe Vivo	13	Pani Café	5	Uno's	
El Coto	3	Paradiso	7	Vujon	17

PUBS AND BARS
Centurion	19	Pitcher		Trent House	1
Crown Posada	20	and Piano	11		
Forth Hotel	15	Popolo	7		
Free Trade	10	Stereo	9		
Head of Steam	16	Tokyo	18		

Information, city transport and tours

There are tourist offices at **Central Arcade**, Market St (Mon–Fri 9.30am–5.30pm, Sat 9am–5.30pm; ☎0191/277 8000, ⓦwww .visitnewcastlegateshead.com); in the **Guildhall** (Mon–Fri 10am–5pm, Sat 9am–5pm, Sun 9am–4pm; same phone) on Newcastle Quayside; and on the Gateshead side in **St Mary's Church**, Oakwellgate, next to the Sage (Mon–Fri 9am–5pm, Sat 10am–5pm, Sun & bank hols 11am–5pm; ☎0191/478 4222). All hand out maps, city guides and brochures, including the free *Walking Guide* and *Public Art Walks* leaflets.

Bright yellow **Quaylink** buses link Newcastle and Gateshead centres (daily 7am–midnight; 80p). The region also has an efficient commuter rail system, the **Metro** (daily 5.15am–11.30pm, services every 3–15min; ⓦwww .tyneandwearmetro.co.uk), with the landmark Grey's Monument marking the city centre and the site of **Monument**, the main interchange for the Metro's two lines: the green line for South Shields, Jarrow, Gateshead, Jesmond and the airport; and the yellow line for Wallsend, Tynemouth and Whitley Bay, plus a southern branch to Gateshead and Sunderland. The most useful discount pass is the **Metro Day Saver** for unlimited rides (£3.50 after 9am Mon, Tues, Thurs & Fri, all day Sat & Sun; £2.50 after 9am Wed; or £2 after 6pm any day), available from ticket machines at every station. For all public transport enquiries, contact **Nexus Traveline** (☎0871/200 2233, ⓦwww.nexus.org.uk) or visit the Nexus Travelshops at the Central Station, Haymarket, Monument or Gateshead Metro stations.

River Escapes Cruises' two- and three-hour **sightseeing cruises** (£10/12; ☎0167/078 5666, ⓦwww.riverescapes.co.uk) depart most weekends throughout the year, and other days in summer, from Newcastle's Quayside. Finally, a hop-on, hop-off, open-top **sightseeing bus** departs from Central Station (Easter–Dec daily 10am–4/5pm, departures every 30min–1hr; £7; ⓦwww.city-sightseeing.com).

Accommodation

Budget **hotel chains** offer plenty of good-value rooms in the city centre and down by the Quayside – *Premier Travel Inn, Jury's, Quality, Travelodge* and *Holiday Inn* all have hotels in the city centre. The biggest concentration of small hotels and **guesthouses** is a mile north of the centre in Jesmond, along and off Osborne Road: take bus #30B, #31B or #80 from Central Station or Haymarket. Save yourself time and effort by using the free **room-booking service** available at the tourist offices to personal callers. In addition, both the University of Newcastle (☎0191/222 6318) and University of Northumbria (☎0191/227 4499) have hundreds of **student rooms** available at various locations from July to September, from around £25 per person.

Hotels and guesthouses

Adelphi 63 Fern Ave, off Osborne Rd, Jesmond ☎0191/281 3109, ⓦwww.adelphihotelnewcastle .co.uk. Cheery and neat family-run B&B, in a quiet residential street. Five of the seven rooms are en-suite, and there are a couple of family rooms. ❹
Copthorne The Close, Quayside ☎0191/222 0333, ⓦwww.millenniumhotels.com. This stylish four-star hotel has Tyne views from most of its well-appointed rooms. Breakfast not included except for weekend packages. ❽, weekend ❼

George 88 Osborne Rd, Jesmond ☎0191/281 4442. Victorian town-house hotel with a dozen of the city's least expensive en-suite rooms. There's a patio, restaurant, bar with open fire and secure parking. ❹
Grey Street 2 Grey St ☎0191/230 6777, ⓦwww.greystreethotel.com. The city's sharpest designer digs retain the lofty proportions and original tiling of the Victorian bank building, but have added minimalist rooms with huge windows, flat-screen TVs and power-showers. Only space is

at a premium, though upgrading to a suite solves that. Pay parking nearby. **7**

Hilton Newcastle Gateshead Bottle Bank, Gateshead Quays ☎0191/490 9700, @www .hilton.co.uk/newcastlegateshead. The prominently sited *Hilton* has a fine location near the Tyne Bridge and Sage, though you'll want a river-facing room for the full effect. Comforts and facilities are four-star – pool, gym, health club, bar and fancy *Windows on the Tyne* restaurant. Pay parking at the hotel. **7**

Jesmond Dene House Jesmond Dene Rd, Jesmond ☎0191/212 3000, @www .jesmonddenehouse.co.uk. An imposing Arts and Crafts house in a wooded valley with big beds, big bathrooms and bold decoration. Bedrooms all have digital radios, flat-screen TVs and Wi-Fi, and service is impeccable. There's fine dining in the garden room restaurant. Parking. **8**

Malmaison Quayside ☎0191/245 5000, @www .malmaison.com. Chic lodgings in the former Co-op building, right on the Quayside. Rooms come with great beds, CD players, power showers, cable TV and modems. Jazzy sounds, crushed velvet sofas, brasserie, bar and gym provide the signature backdrop. Breakfast not included. **7**

New Northumbria 61–69 Osborne Rd, Jesmond ☎0191/281 4961, @www.newnorthumbria.com.

Contemporary boutique-style lodgings offering spacious rooms, big beds, warm decor and lovely panelled bathrooms with power showers. Café-bar and Italian restaurant attached. **6**

Hostels and apartments

Albatross 51 Grainger St ☎0191/233 1330, @www.albatrossnewcastle.co.uk. This award-winning 170-bed backpackers' hostel has a great central location and is immaculate throughout (bathrooms especially). It's a very welcoming place, with 24/7 reception, parking and Internet, and a free tea-and-toast breakfast. Dorm beds from £16.50. Double/twin rooms **3**.

City Apartments Jackson House, Northumberland St ☎0191/255 1660, and Walker Rd, Quayside ☎0191/276 4296; @www.mckeverhotels.co.uk. These very sleek one and two-bedroom apartments provide everything you need for a DIY stay, with loads of space to boot. Quayside apartments have balconies and parking. **6**.

Newcastle YHA 107 Jesmond Rd, near Jesmond Metro ☎0870/770 5972, @newcastle@yha.org .uk. The traditional hostel choice in the city, the YHA has fifty beds available in a converted townhouse. Breakfast and cheap evening meals served, though no laundry facilities. Closed Christmas to mid-Jan. Dorm beds from £16.50.

The City

The city splits into several distinct areas, though it's only a matter of minutes to walk between them. **Castle** and **cathedral** occupy the heights immediately above the River Tyne, whose Newcastle and Gateshead **quaysides** now form the biggest single attraction in the city. North of the cathedral lies **Grainger Town**, the city-centre district of listed Victorian buildings that is at its most dramatic along Grey Street. West of the centre is Chinatown and the two big draws of the Discovery Museum and Life Science Centre; east is the renowned Laing Gallery; and north the university and open parkland known as Town Moor. Further east along the river, the old industrial **Ouseburn Valley** district is gradually emerging as a cultural quarter, focusing on the Seven Stories children's books centre.

Castle and cathedral

Anyone arriving by train from the north will get a sneak preview of the **castle** (daily 9.30am–4.30/5.30pm; £1.50), as the rail line splits the keep from its gatehouse, the **Black Gate**, on St Nicholas' Street. A wooden fort was built here over an Anglo-Saxon cemetery by Robert Curthose, illegitimate eldest son of William the Conqueror, but the present keep dates from the twelfth century. Down in the garrison room, prisoners were incarcerated during the sixteenth to eighteenth centuries, while locals rushed to its deep shelter in World War II to sit out German bombing. There's a great view from the rooftop over the river and city.

Further along St Nicholas' Street stands the **cathedral** (Mon–Fri 7am–6pm, Sat 8.30am–4pm, Sun 7.30am–noon & 4–7pm; free), dating mainly from the fourteenth and fifteenth centuries and remarkable chiefly for its tower – erected in 1470, it is topped with a crown-like structure of turrets and arches supporting a lantern. Inside, behind the high altar, is one of the largest funerary brasses in England; it was commissioned by Roger Thornton, the Dick Whittington of Newcastle, who arrived in the city penniless and died its richest merchant in 1430.

Along the River Tyne

From between the castle and the cathedral a road known simply as The Side – formerly the main road out of the city – descends to Newcastle's **Quayside**. There have been fixed river crossings here since Roman times and today the Tyne is spanned by seven bridges in close proximity, the most prominent being the looming **Tyne Bridge** of 1928, symbol of the city, which bears a striking resemblance to the roughly contemporaneous Sydney Harbour Bridge – not surprising really, as both were built by Dorman Long of Middlesbrough. Immediately west is the hydraulic **Swing Bridge**, erected in 1876 by Lord Armstrong so that larger vessels could reach his shipyards upriver, while modern road and rail lines cross the river on the adjacent **High Level Bridge**, built by Robert Stephenson in 1849 – Queen Victoria was one of the first passengers to cross, promoting the railway revolution.

Beyond the Tyne Bridge, the modern-day regeneration of the Quayside is in full swing. Riverside apartments, a landscaped promenade, public sculpture and pedestrianized squares have paved the way for a series of fashionable bars and restaurants, centred on the graceful **Gateshead Millennium Bridge**, the world's first tilting span, designed to pivot to allow ships to pass. For tilting times see the information boards at either side of the bridge or visit ⓦ www.gateshead.gov.uk/bridge.

The bridge allows pedestrians to cross the Tyne to the **Gateshead Quays**, to visit **BALTIC**, the dramatic Centre for Contemporary Art (Mon–Sun 10am–6pm; free; ⓦ www.balticmill.com), fashioned from a brick flour mill built in the 1940s. This has been converted into a huge visual "art factory", second only in scale to London's Tate Modern. There's no permanent

▲ The Tyne Bridge and Sage Gateshead

collection here, though the galleries display a robust series of specially commissioned or invited art exhibitions, local community projects and other displays. Alongside the galleries, the BALTIC accommodates artists' studios, education workshops, an art performance space and cinema, plus a restaurant on the roof with uninterrupted views of the Newcastle skyline. The ground-floor café-bar is a handy spot for a drink, too.

The BALTIC is complemented on the Gateshead side by **The Sage Gateshead** (Ⓦwww.thesagegateshead.org), an extraordinary billowing steel, aluminium and glass concert hall complex, best seen at night when it glows with many colours. It's home to the Northern Sinfonia orchestra and Folkworks, an organization promoting British and international traditional music. The public concourse provides marvellous river and city views.

Grainger Town and the city centre

By the mid-nineteenth century, Newcastle's centre of balance had shifted away from the river, uphill to the rapidly expanding Victorian town. In a few short years, businessmen-builders and architects such as Richard Grainger, Thomas Oliver and John Dobson fashioned the best-designed Victorian town in England, with classical facades of stone lining splendid new streets, most notably **Grey Street** – "that descending, subtle curve", as John Betjeman described it. The street takes its name from the Northumberland dynasty of political heavyweights whose most illustrious member was the second Earl Grey (he of the tea), prime minister from 1830 to 1834. In the middle of his term in office he carried the Reform Bill through parliament, an act commemorated by **Grey's Monument** at the top of the street.

Today, Grey Street shows off much of its Victorian elegance, best exemplified by the **Theatre Royal**, halfway down. Other streets fell to the municipal butchers in the 1960s and 1970s – Eldon Square, once a model of Victorian balance, now a shopping centre, a case in point – though not all was lost. The restored **Grainger Market** (Mon–Sat 8am–5pm) near Grey's Monument, was Europe's largest undercover market when built in the 1830s, while John Dobson's nearby **Central Station**, facing Neville Street, trumpets the confidence of the railway age with its soaring interior spaces and curved ironwork.

West of here, behind Gallowgate, is the most complete stretch of the old **city walls**, leading down to Westgate Road. These once encircled the whole of medieval Newcastle, but were plundered for building stone after the sixteenth century. However, several towers remain, including the **Morden Tower** (once the haunt of Beat poets) alongside Stowell Street, where the outer defensive ditch has been restored. Stowell Street is Newcastle's **Chinatown**, lined with restaurants and supermarkets. Across Stowell Street from the tower, at Friar's Green, is the tranquil courtyard of **Blackfriars**, a thirteenth-century stone

Weighing up the goods

There's been a **weigh house** inside Grainger Market since it was first built, where shoppers could take their meat and other produce to check they weren't being cheated by unscrupulous traders. Nowadays, it's mainly used by curious shoppers who divest themselves of their outer garments and pay 10p to stand on the huge old-fashioned scales. An attendant writes down your weight on a piece of paper, which is then discreetly passed to you. Coat back on, and off you go, worrying about where those extra pounds came from.

monastery with ruined cloistered grounds, now lovingly restored to house a crafts centre and restaurant.

Discovery Museum

On the south side of Westgate Road, the **Discovery Museum** in Blandford Square (Mon–Sat 10am–5pm, Sun 2–5pm; free; ⓦwww.twmuseums.org.uk) puts into context the city's history in a series of impressive displays housed in the former headquarters of the Co-operative Wholesale Society. You are confronted on arrival by the hundred-foot-long *Turbinia*, the world's first steam-turbine-powered ship, built by a brilliant local engineer, Charles Parsons. Galleries on three floors surround the *Turbinia*, with standout attractions including the "Newcastle Story", a walk through the city's past with tales from animated characters along the way, and the interactive "Science Maze" which focuses on Newcastle's pioneering inventors (including one Joseph Swan who, according to locals at least, beat Edison to the invention of the light bulb). There's plenty to participate in, particularly in the "Science Maze" but also in the "Tyne Story" galleries, where the role of the river in the development of the city is investigated. Elsewhere in the museum, there are walk-through fashion galleries, displaying some of the eight thousand costume items in the collection, and old favourites like the talking regimental horse and barking drill-sergeant in "The Soldier's Life" exhibition.

Centre for Life

Heading back towards the Central Station along Westmorland Road, you can't miss the **Centre for Life** (Mon–Sat 10am–6pm, Sun 11am–6pm, last admission 4pm; £6.95; ☎0191/243 8210, ⓦwww.lifesciencecentre.org.uk), whose sleek buildings reach around the sweeping expanse of Times Square. This ambitious "science village" project combines bioscience and genetics research centres with a science visitor centre which aims to convey the secrets of life using the latest entertainment technology. Highlights include 3D motion-simulator rides, a sound-and-light "Big Brain" show and a block-buster exhibit on the history of human life. The centre is always adding new attractions and in winter an open-air **ice rink** is unveiled (mid-Nov to mid-Feb; £5.95). Children find the whole thing enormously rewarding – expect to spend a good three hours here, if not more.

Laing Art Gallery

The northeast's premier art collection is the **Laing Art Gallery** on New Bridge St (Mon–Sat 10am–5pm, Sun 2–5pm; free; ⓦwww.twmuseums.org.uk), off John Dobson Street, behind the library. Local pottery, glassware, costume and sculpture all play their part, while on permanent display is a sweep through British art from Reynolds to John Hoyland, with a smattering of Pre-Raphaelites, so admired by English industrial barons.

The real treat here is the work of **John Martin** (1789–1854), a self-taught Northumberland painter with a penchant for massive biblical and mythical scenes. He came from a rather dysfunctional family – his elder brother wore a tortoiseshell hat, another brother set fire to York Minster – and with the benefit of twenty-first-century psychological hindsight, it's easy to imagine what demons drove him in his work. The other must-see in the gallery is the **Art on Tyneside** exhibition, which romps through the history of art and applied art in the region since the seventeenth century with considerable gusto. There are digressions on such matters as eighteenth-century coffee houses and contem-porary city architecture, and investigations of clothes and materials, glassware and wood engraving. Outside the Laing's front door don't miss a stroll over the notorious **Blue Carpet** – a public art installation whose tiles fold back on themselves to form unusual benches, lit from underneath.

The Great North Museum, Hancock Museum and Town Moor

The **Great North Museum** (Wwww.twmuseums.org.uk), due to open in 2009, will bring together the major natural history and archeological collections previously housed in the university's Hancock Museum, Museum of Antiquities, and Shefton (Greek) Museum. However, the university's celebrated **Hatton Gallery** (Mon–Fri 10am–5.30pm, Sat 10am–5pm; free) will be maintained as a separate gallery – this is most famous for housing the only surviving example of German Dadaist Kurt Schwitters' *Merzbau* (a sort of architectural collage), though it also hosts a wide variety of temporary exhibitions.

Beyond the University of Newcastle, through the landscaped **Exhibition Park**, you reach the **Town Moor**, 1200 acres of common land where freemen of the city, including Jimmy Carter, Nelson Mandela and Bob Geldof, are entitled to graze their cattle. It's the site of the annual "Hoppings" in the last week of June, a huge week-long fair of rides, stalls and other attractions which keeps the cows awake until well after dark.

Ouseburn Valley and Seven Stories

Ten minutes' walk up the River Tyne from Millennium Bridge, the now sluggish Ouse Burn tributary was once at the heart of Newcastle's industry. Old Victorian mills and warehouses in the **Ouseburn Valley** are gradually being given a new lease of life by businesses like the Biscuit Factory (Europe's biggest commercial art space), 36 Lime Street (artists' studio group) and *The Cluny* (innovative music bar), a regeneration cemented by **Seven Stories**, 30 Lime St (Mon–Sat 10am–5pm, Sun 11am–5pm; £5; T0845/271 0777, Wwww .sevenstories.org.uk). This national centre for children's literature spreads across seven floors of a beautifully converted riverside mill, showcasing a unique collection of original manuscripts, documents and artwork – including Phillip Pullman's early books, manuscripts by Michael Rosen, material from Nina Bawden, the drawings from Noel Streatfeild's *Ballet Shoes*, and illustrations from *Charlie and the Chocolate Factory*, among much else. Changing exhibitions explore every facet of children's literature, with plenty of interactive engagement and events thrown in; weekends and school holidays see the most activity. There's also a café and an excellent children's bookshop.

Angel of the North

For over a decade Antony Gormley's **Angel of the North** has stood sentinel over the A1 at Gateshead. Situated on what used to be a colliery's pithead baths, it has become the symbol of Tyneside and the country's most viewed sculpture. Gormley himself wanted to remind people that miners worked underground here for two centuries, and to him the angel symbolizes an embracing celebration of industry. The sheer scale of its 175-foot wingspan, which inclines slightly forward, makes the most impact and it's even more imposing close up, when the ribbed structure of the body and rough, rusty texture gradually become apparent. An information board at the site fills you in on all the technical background. The Angel is accessible by car from the A167 (signed Gateshead South; there's a parking layby), and by frequent buses (#21 or #21A) that run from Pilgrim Street in Newcastle and from the Gateshead Interchange bus station.

Eating

Newcastle's tastes have moved a long way from the traditional gargantuan bread rolls called "stottie cakes" – you're more likely to find them drizzled with olive oil and stuffed with Parma ham and chargrilled vegetables these days. At the budget end of the market Italian, Indian and Chinese food dominates the scene, while at the top end of the scale the city has attracted some inventive chefs. The very cheapest places are found around Bigg Market, while in Stowell Street in Chinatown there are plenty of all-you-can-eat buffets as well as more refined Cantonese restaurants. Many city centre restaurants offer **early bird/happy hour** deals before 7pm, while others serve **set lunches** at often ludicrously low prices.

Café-bars

Byker Vista Café Biscuit Factory, 16 Stoddart St ☏0191/261 1103. Best place for a view of the Tyne and landmark Byker Wall, while tucking into enormous soups, salads and sandwiches, or taking a coffee on the terrace. Open daily until 5pm.

Pani Café 61–65 High Bridge St, off Grey St ☏0191/232 4366. Just up a side-street below the Theatre Royal, this buzzy Sardinian café has a loyal clientele, who come day and night (open until 10pm) for authentic, good-value stuffed sandwiches, antipasti, pasta and salads. Closed Sun.

Paradiso 1 Market Lane ☏0191/221 1240. Mellow café-bar hidden down an alley off Pilgrim Street – snacky food during the day, more substantial at night (like home-made pasta or the house special risotto). The sun-deck's a popular hangout. Live jazz on Sun afternoons.

Restaurants

Big Mussel 15 The Side ☏0191/232 1057. Mussels, chips and mayo served seven ways, though there are lots of other fish and seafood choices on the menu (and some meat). A £6 lunch and "clock saver" dinner (5.30–7pm) provide value for money. Moderate.

Café 21 Trinity Gardens ☏0191/222 0755. The Quayside's finest – a stylish Parisian-influenced bistro with a classic menu – confit of duck, fish cakes, beef in red wine – and slick service. Blackboard specials ring the changes, and the set lunches are a bargain for the quality. Expensive.

El Coto 21 Leazes Park Rd ☏0191/261 0555. The city's best tapas place makes a good lunch stop (there's a pretty courtyard) or night out – most dishes cost around £4, though you can spend more at the upstairs grill-house where pork, lamb, steaks and mixed grills (£11–16) are offered. Moderate.

Grainger Rooms 7 Higham Place ☏0191/232 4949. This place is making a name for itself for its locally sourced, seasonal and organic menu, served in what used to be a gentlemen's club. Service is unstuffy and amiable, and there are good deals at lunchtime. Expensive.

Mangos 43 Stowell St ☏0191/232 6522. A bit more stylish and authentic than most Chinatown eateries, *Mangos* offers traditional and new-wave Cantonese dishes, from *dim sum* and country-style hotpots to sizzling-plate specials. Meals every night until 2am. Moderate.

Salsa Club 89 Westgate Rd ☏0191/221 1022. A cosy, bare-boards place for a coffee, sandwich and tapas, or a great range of salsas. There's San Miguel on draught and DJs some nights. Closed Sun lunch. Inexpensive.

Secco Ristorante Salentino 86 Pilgrim St ☏0191/230 0444. The food mixes melt-in-the-mouth southern Italian dishes and Northumbrian ingredients (mains around £15), while the city's beautiful people congregate in the inordinately handsome top floor bar (until 2am). The wines, imported exclusively from Salento, are excellent. Closed Sun & Mon. Expensive.

Uno's 18 Sandhill ☏0191/261 5264. There are loads of budget Italian places in town but none quite so adept at delivering good food at decent prices (come weekdays before 7pm or Sat before 5pm and pizzas or pastas are £4.50). The party (and price) picks up at night, when this can prove to be a loud, packed, but fun place to eat. Moderate.

Vujon 29 Queen St ☏0191/221 0601. The city's classiest Indian restaurant with dishes a cut above the ordinary, from Rajasthani-style rack of lamb to *bhuna*-style salmon. You pay for the experience but it's worth it. Moderate.

Drinking, nightlife and music

Newcastle's boisterous pubs, bars and clubs are concentrated in several distinct areas: between Grainger Street and the cathedral in the area called the **Bigg Market** (spiritual home of Sid the Sexist and the Fat Slags from *Viz* magazine); around the **Quayside**, where the bars tend to be slightly more sophisticated; and in the mainstream leisure-and-cinema complex known as **The Gate** (Newgate St). There's really no getting away from the weekend mayhem, though the style bars around **Central Station** and nearby **Pink Lane** at least start off the evening with more civilised intent, while in **Jesmond**, there's a thriving strip of café-bars along Osborne Road. The "**Gay Quarter**" centres on the Centre for Life, spreading out to Waterloo Street and Westmorland and Scotswood roads.

There's something going on most nights in the city, with gigs, club nights and the gay scene reviewed exhaustively in *The Crack* (monthly; free; ⓦwww.thecrackmagazine.com), a **listings magazine** available in shops, pubs and bars. Specific recommendations are a little beside the point as everyone simply moves from pub to bar in the biggest (and largely good-natured) cattle market in Western Europe. Expect beefy security men on every door, queues at the more popular places and to have your clothes/appearance/attitude scrutinized. To fit in, wear as little as possible, whatever the weather. Top drinking brew is, of course, **Newcastle Brown** – an ale known locally as "Dog" – produced here since 1927.

Pubs and bars

Centurion Central Station, Neville St. The station's former first-class waiting rooms, now revived as an extraordinary bar. Victorian tiling, soaring ceiling and an impressive mural – and draught Newcastle Brown Ale.

Crown Posada 31 The Side. Local beers and guest ales in a small wood-and-glass-panelled Victorian pub. Music, not ear-splittingly loud for a change, comes courtesy of the gramophone and a stack of well-worn LPs.

Forth Hotel Pink Lane. Honest city-centre boozer with a fine juke box, a varied crowd, good lunchtime food and a decent range of wines by the glass.

Free Trade St Lawrence Rd. Walk along the Newcastle Quayside past the Millennium Bridge and look for the shabby pub on the hill, where you are invited to "drink beer, smoke tabs" with the city's pub *cognoscenti*. Cask beer from local micro-breweries, a great juke box and superb river views from the beer garden.

Head of Steam 2 Neville St. In a modern building opposite the *Royal Station Hotel* (but a whole lot better-looking inside), this relaxed drinking den has good sounds and big sofas. Live gigs every night (not Sun) in the basement from 8pm.

Pitcher & Piano 108 Quayside. The riverfront's most spectacular bar – sinuous roof, huge plate-glass walls, by the Millennium Bridge.

Popolo 82–84 Pilgrim St. Fewer youths, less noise, more style – this casual American-style bar is a firm city favourite with a slightly older crowd.

Stereo Sandgate, Quayside. Sharp designer style, plus an outdoor deck with Quayside views.

Tokyo 17 Westgate Rd. The dark main bar's handsome enough, but follow the tea-lights up the stairs for the outdoor "garden" bar, where there's at least a breath of fresh air. A pre-club favourite for Shindig.

Trent House 1–2 Leazes Lane. Many people's favourite pub, run by the WHQ people (see "Clubs" below), which means the jukebox is great – not to mention the surviving Space Invaders machine.

Clubs

Digital Centre for Life, Times Sq ⓦwww.yourfutureisdigital.com. The city's showpiece dance venue (currently Thurs, Fri & Sat nights), with amazing sound system – the big draw is Saturday's Shindig (ⓦwww.shindiguk.com).

Tuxedo Princess Hillgate Quay, Gateshead ☎0191/477 8899. A floating nightclub (aka "The Boat"), on the south side of the river, serving up scantily clad dancers in six bars to a raucous 18–25-year-old set. Closed Sun.

World Headquarters Carliol Sq ☎0191/261 7007, ⓦwww.theworldheadquarters.com. Newcastle's mellowest bar and club ("no sponsors, no corporates, no sell-out"), playing funk, soul and hip-hop every Friday and Saturday, plus regular DJ slots, indie to electro.

Live music venues

Black Swan Newcastle Arts Centre, 69 Westgate Rd ☎0191/261 9959. Cellar bar with live music up to five nights a week – rock, folk, world and jazz – and a rollicking Friday-night salsa session. Late bar until 2am.

Carling Academy Westgate Rd ☎0191/260 2020, ⓦ www.newcastle-academy.co.uk. The city's latest purpose-built music venue hosts big name bands, plus wannabees. DJs pound out rock on Fri nights.

 The Cluny 36 Lime St, Ouseburn Valley ☎0191/230 4474,

ⓦ www.theheadofsteam.co.uk. The best small venue in the city is out in the eastern sticks (20min walk from Quayside or take the yellow bus), with gigs almost every night from 8pm, real ales and a great bar courtesy of the *Head of Steam*.

Jazz Café 23 Pink Lane ☎0191/232 6505. Intimate jazz club with a late licence and live music from 9.30pm; salsa nights Thurs–Sat. Closed Sun.

Trillians Rock Bar Princess Sq ☎0191/232 1619, ⓦ www.trilliansrockbar.com. Headbangers of the world unite – local and national rock acts play this pub venue, plus rock DJ nights (Thurs–Sat) until 1am.

Arts, culture and festivals

There's a hugely varied theatrical and cultural life in the city, from the offerings at the splendid Victorian Theatre Royal to those of smaller contemporary **theatre** companies and local **arts centres**. The Sage and City Hall are the main classical music **concert venues**, but you'll also find performances throughout the year at Newcastle University's King's Hall and in St Nicholas' Cathedral and St Mary's Catholic Cathedral and other churches around town. There's a full **festival calendar** (details from the tourist office), with particular emphasis on outdoor concerts and sports – in October, Europe's biggest half-marathon, the Great North Run, sees 50,000 competitors running across the Tyne Bridge. Undoubted highlight is the New Year's Eve celebration on the Quayside, an exuberantly good-natured rival to the traditional gathering in London.

Arts centres

BALTIC South Shore Rd, Gateshead ☎0191/478 1810, ⓦ www.balticmill.com. As well as the four contemporary art galleries, there are studio sessions and classes, films, artists' talks, community projects, dance and concerts.

Newcastle Arts Centre 69 Westgate Rd ☎0191/261 5618, ⓦ www.newcastle-arts-centre .co.uk. Art gallery, workshops, and concert, drama and club venue.

Cinemas

Star and Shadow Cinema Stepney Bank, Ouseburn ☎0191/261 0066, ⓦ www. starandshadow.org.uk. Independent programme of art, classic and political films as well as exhibitions, bands and live art.

Tyneside Cinema 10 Pilgrim St ☎0191/232 8289, ⓦ www.tynecine.org. The city's premier art-house cinema, newly revamped, with a wide-ranging international programme. There's coffee, light meals and movie talk in the Art Deco cinema café (closes 9pm).

Concert venues

City Hall Northumberland Rd ☎0191/261 2606, ⓦ www.newcastle.gov.uk/cityhall. Orchestras from around the world, as well as mainstream rock, pop and comedy acts.

Journal Tyne Theatre 111 Westgate Rd ☎0870/145 1200, ⓦ www.tynetheatre.co.uk. Beautifully restored Victorian theatre with a wide range of shows (including children's performances and pantomime), comedy and gigs.

The Sage Gateshead South Shore Rd, Gateshead Quays ☎0191/443 4661, ⓦ www .thesagegateshead.org. Stunning international music centre, home of the Northern Sinfonia and Folkworks, hosting a full programme of classical, folk, world and jazz music. Tickets from £6.

Galleries

The Biscuit Factory Stoddart St ☎0191/261 1103, ⓦ www.thebiscuitfactory.com. Europe's biggest centre for original art has free entry and there's a good café and restaurant too.

Shopping in Newcastle

The advertising would have you believe that the be-all-and-end-all of city shopping is the **MetroCentre** at Gateshead (Ⓦ www.metrocentre-gateshead.co.uk), Europe's largest shopping and leisure venue, with its 330 shops, fifty restaurants and cafés, multi-screen cinema and indoor theme park. However, traditional city-centre shopping starts with Fenwick's venerable **department store** in Northumberland Street (with its own café and sushi bar), while for **streetwear** and **designer** labels, check out the trio of Cruise shops in Princess Square or Vivienne Westwood, 1 Hood St (off Market St). For **vintage clothing** head for the Period Clothing Warehouse at 29 Highbridge. The Ouseburn area is good for **affordable art**: cruise the Biscuit Factory and Mushroom Works (see "Galleries", p.889 & below) as well as the Art Works Galleries at Stepney Bank, which showcases local artists. Markets include the Sunday morning **Quayside market**, under the Tyne Bridge; the covered **Grainger Market** (daily except Sun; plus arts and crafts market on 2nd Sat of month) – where there are great bargains at the country's smallest Marks and Spencer store; and Jesmond's **Armstrong Bridge market** (Sun from 10am) for arts and crafts. A **farmers' market** is held on the first Friday of each month at Grey's Monument, while at **Tynemouth market** (Tynemouth metro, every weekend) there are antiques, crafts and household goods, with a farmers' market on the third Saturday of every month.

⑬

THE NORTHEAST | Newcastle upon Tyne

Globe Gallery Curtis Mayfield House, Carliol Sq ☎ 0191/222 1666, Ⓦ www.globegallery.org. Fashionable warehouse gallery, with regular exhibitions and one-off events.

Mushroom Works St Lawrence Rd, Ouseburn Valley ☎ 0191/224 4011, Ⓦ www.mushroomworks .com. Interesting artist-led gallery and studio space – open first weekend of every month (and other times for shows) for a stroll around and a chat with the artists.

Theatre, dance and comedy

The Hyena Leazes Lane ☎ 0191/232 6030, Ⓦ www.thehyena.com. Stand-up comedy with visiting national and international acts every Fri and Sat night from 7pm.

Live Theatre 27 Broad Chare ☎ 0191/232 1232, Ⓦ www.live.org.uk. Enterprising theatre company promoting local actors and writers (Lee Hall gave his boy-ballet movie, *Billy Elliot*, its first reading here). The attached *Caffe Vivo* is good for coffee by day and pre-theatre meal deals by night.

Northern Stage Barras Bridge, Haymarket ☎ 0191/230 5151, Ⓦ www.northernstage.co.uk. The company stages its own "visually driven" productions here as well as co-producing innovative work from Europe and beyond.

Theatre Royal 100 Grey St ☎ 0870/905 5060, Ⓦ www.theatreroyal.co.uk. Drama, opera, dance, musicals and comedy; also hosts the annual RSC season in Nov.

Listings

Airport Newcastle International Airport ☎ 0871/882 1121, Ⓦ www.newcastleinternational .co.uk.

Bike hire Tyne Bridge Bike Hire ☎ 0191/277 2441, Ⓦ www.tynebridgebikehire.co.uk, rents bikes for £15 per day, £60 per week, either for use in the city, or there's a pick-up and drop-off Hadrian's Wall service.

Football Newcastle United play at St James' Park (ticket office ☎ 0191/261 1571, Ⓦ www.nufc.co .uk) in front of the country's most long-suffering supporters. You're unlikely to get a ticket for the big matches against major rivals, but seats do go on

general sale for some games. Don't, under any circumstances, wear anything red (the colour of hated local rivals Sunderland).

Hospital Newcastle General Hospital, Westgate Rd ☎ 0191/233 6161.

Internet Access Available at the City Library and at the Live Wires Centre in the Discovery Museum.

Pharmacy Boots, Eldon Square ☎ 0191/232 4423.

Police Corner of Market and Pilgrim streets ☎ 0191/214 6555.

Post office St Mary's Place, near the Civic Centre, at Haymarket.

Around Newcastle

The Metro runs east along both banks of the **River Tyne**, connecting Newcastle with several historic attractions, and with the sandy beaches at Tynemouth and Whitley Bay – the beaches are fine if you just want to see the sea, though anyone intending to head further north up the Northumberland coast will find there's no comparison. To make a round trip of it, you can cross the river between North Shields and South Shields on the **Shields Ferry** (Mon–Sat 7am–10.50pm, Sun 10.30am–6pm; every 30min; 7min; £1 one way); there are Metro stations on either side, a short walk from the ferry terminals. A **Metro Day Saver ticket** is valid for most buses in the county of Tyne and Wear and for the Shields ferry.

Wallsend and Segedunum

As the name tells you, **WALLSEND**, four miles east of Newcastle, was the last outpost of Hadrian's great border defence. **Segedunum**, the "strong fort" a couple of minutes' signposted walk from the Metro station (daily 10am–3.30/5.30pm; £3.50; ⍟www.twmuseums.org.uk/segedunum), has been admirably developed as one of the prime attractions along the Wall. A range of activities takes place year-round (including summer re-enactments of Roman drill and equipment) and the grounds contain a fully recon-structed bathhouse, complete with heated pools and colourful frescoes. The cleverly conceived museum combines excavated finds with interactive computer displays to give a strong flavour of life at the fort, as well as bringing the history of the site up to the present day with displays on coalmining and shipbuilding. To complete the picture, climb the 110-foot tower for a spectacular overview of the remains and the adjacent ship-repair yards. The "wall's end" itself is visible at the edge of the site, close to the river and Swan Hunter shipyard, and it's from here that the **Hadrian's Wall Path** (see p.897) runs for 84 miles to Bowness-on-Solway in Cumbria; you can get your walk "passport" stamped inside the museum.

Jarrow

JARROW, five miles east of Newcastle, and south of the Tyne, has been ingrained on the national consciousness since the 1936 march (see p.892), though the town made a mark much earlier, as the seventh-century St Paul's church and monastery was one of the region's early cradles of Christianity. It was here that the **Venerable Bede** (673–735 AD) came to live as a boy, growing to become one of Europe's greatest scholars and England's first historian – his *History of the English Church and People*, describing the struggles of the island's early Christians, was completed at Jarrow in 731. His other writings were many and varied – poetry, scientific works on chronology and the calendar, lives of St Cuthbert, historical and geographical treatises – and his influence was immense, prompting a European-wide revival in monastic learning. Yet astonishingly Bede rarely left the monastery and probably never travelled further than York, relying on visitors and friends for

Jarrow owed its growth in the nineteenth century to the success of the steelworks and shipyard owned by local MP Charles Palmer. Producer of the world's first oil tanker, the Jarrow production line was a phenomenal organization, at one stage employing ten thousand men. However, demand for steel and ships went into decline after World War I, and eighty percent of the workforce had been laid off by 1934, the year Palmers was sold off and broken up. On October 5, 1936, two hundred men left Jarrow to walk the 290 miles to London under the "**Jarrow Crusade**" banner. They gathered sympathy and support all along the road to the capital, becoming the most potent image of the hardships of 1930s Britain. Some charitable aid was forthcoming after the marchers presented their petition to Parliament, but real recovery only came about through the re-armament of Britain in the build-up to World War II.

much of his information. After he died in 735, St Paul's soon became a site of pilgrimage, though church and monastery were later sacked by Viking raiding parties.

The years have been kind to **St Paul's** (Mon–Sat 10am–4pm, Sun 2–4.30pm), a tranquil stone church framed by the industrial clutter of the Tyneside docks. The original seventh-century dedication stone (dated 23 April, 685 AD, the earliest in England) can be seen inside, set in the arch above the chancel. Outside are the bare ruins of the buildings, cloister and burial ground of the monastery. Most of the standing walls and ruins date from the later eleventh-century refoundation.

Access to the church and monastery ruins is free, although they stand within the wider development that is **Bede's World** (Mon–Sat 10am–4.30/5.30pm, Sun noon–4.30/5.30pm; £4.50; Ⓦwww.bedesworld.co.uk), a fascinating exploration of early medieval Northumbria, centred on a museum and an Anglo-Saxon farm site and featuring an annual array of events and activities. The striking Mediterranean-style **museum** traces the development of Northumbria and England through the use of extracts from Bede's writings, set alongside archeological finds and vivid recreations of monastic life. After this you can take a turn through Gyrwe (pronounced "Yeerweh"), the eleven-acre demonstration **farm** which features reconstructed timber buildings from the early Christian period, as well as rare breeds and demonstrations of contemporary agricultural methods.

St Paul's and Bede's World are a signposted fifteen-minute walk through an industrial estate from **Bede Metro station**. Alternatively, buses #526 or #527 run roughly every thirty minutes from Neville Street (Central Station) in Newcastle or Jarrow Metro station, and stop in front of the church. The site is a little way off the A185, at the south end of the Tyne tunnel; follow the signs at the A185/A19 roundabout junction.

South Shields and the South Tyneside coast

Beyond Jarrow, it's impossible to miss the fact that South Tyneside is officially designated **Catherine Cookson Country**: the prolific author was born in **SOUTH SHIELDS**, the small town that guards the south side of the entrance to the Tyne. Although her childhood homes have since been demolished, South Shields **tourist office** (Mon–Sat 10am–5.30pm, Sun 1–5pm; Oct–April closed Sun; ☎0191/454 6612, Ⓦwww.visitsouthtyneside.co.uk), at the museum and art gallery on Ocean Road, a five-minute walk from the Metro station, can provide details of the "Catherine Cookson Trail" – plaques, sites and buildings associated with her life and novels, which romanticize the grittier industrial corners of South Tyneside.

Of more general interest is **Arbeia Roman Fort** (April–Sept Mon–Sat 10am–5.30pm, Sun 1–5pm; Oct–March Mon–Sat 10am–3.30pm; free; Ⓦwww.twmuseums.org.uk/arbeia) on Baring Street, off River Drive, five minutes' signposted walk north from the tourist office. It was built in 120–160 AD as a supply depot for Hadrian's Wall, and now gives a good indication of what life was like on the Wall through its reconstructions (on the original foundations) of a commanding officer's house, complete with furniture and frescoes, barrack blocks and gateway.

The A183 runs south down the coast from South Shields towards Sunderland, with a nice sandy beach at **Marsden Bay**. Just beyond, near Lizard Point, five miles north of Sunderland, you'll pass **Souter Lighthouse** (April–Oct Mon–Thurs, Sat & Sun 11am–5pm; £4; NT), opened in 1871 and the first lighthouse in the world to use electric light.

Wearside

There is an intense rivalry between Newcastle and Sunderland, twelve miles to the southeast: both cities outraged about being lumped together in the municipal appellation Tyne *and* Wear; both Geordies (from Newcastle) and Mackems (from Sunderland) indignant at being taken for the other by know-nothing southerners; supporters of both local football teams jubilant at the old enemy's misfortunes. To an outsider it can seem at times a bewildering argument over nothing at all, but whisper in **Wearside** at your peril the obviously superior charms of Newcastle as a city. Yet **Sunderland** and the River Wear do have their attractions, and in the adjacent new town of **Washington** stands one of the more intriguing historic sites of the northeast.

Sunderland

SUNDERLAND, bisected by the River Wear and elevated in 1992 to the ranks of Britain's cities, shares Newcastle's long history, river setting and indus-trial heritage but cannot match its architectural splendour. Formed from three medieval villages flanking the Wear, it was one of the wealthiest towns in England by 1500 and later supported the Parliamentary cause in the Civil War. The twentieth century made and broke the town: from being the largest shipbuilding centre in the world, Sunderland slumped after ferocious bombing during World War II. Depression and recession did the rest.

However, it's worth a trip to visit the **Sunderland Museum** (Mon–Sat 10am–5pm, Sun 2–5pm; free; Ⓦwww.twmuseums.org.uk/sunderland), easily accessible by Metro from Newcastle. It does a very good job of telling the city's history, while its **Winter Gardens**, housed in a steel-and-glass hot-house, invite a tree-top walk to view the impressive polished steel column of a water sculpture. Inside the museum, "Launched on Wearside" relates how Sunderland ships were once sent around the world – a trade, incidentally, which gave the city inhabitants their "Mackem" nickname, derived from a stage in the shipbuilding process. In "Coal", the roll call of closed collieries is sobering – one of the last to go, Wearmouth, has since been reclaimed as the site of Sunderland Football Club's ground, the Stadium of Light.

▲ National Glass Centre, Sunderland

The museum also has much to say about the city's other major trades, notably its production of lusterware (shown in the excellent Pottery Gallery) and particularly its glass industry, traditional since the seventh century, when workshops turned out stained glass for the north's monastic houses. It's a theme you can pursue across the River Wear, whose landscaped Riverside is actually the oldest settled part of the city (walk up Fawcett Street and then Bridge Street from the centre and across Wearmouth Bridge, around twenty minutes). Along the north bank of the river, in front of the university buildings, the early Christian Church of St Peter (674 AD) is the elder sibling of St Paul's Church at Jarrow and displays fragments of the oldest stained glass in the country. Then walk down to the waterside to find the city's National Glass Centre (daily 10am–5pm; free; Ⓦwww.nationalglasscentre .com), which tells the story of British glass and glass-making – there are daily demonstrations in the on-site workshop.

The main stop for Metros from Newcastle is in the central train station opposite the Bridges Shopping Centre, but get off at the previous stop, St Peter's, to walk along the north side of the river to the National Glass Centre or St Peter's Church. The tourist office (Mon–Sat 9am–5pm, bank hols 10am–4pm; ℡0191/553 2000, Ⓦwww.visitsunderland.com) is behind the central station on the main shopping drag at 50 Fawcett St.

Washington

Five miles west of Sunderland, the River Wear keeps to the south of the new town of **WASHINGTON**, focus of much of the area's contemporary investment and manufacture. Split into planned, numbered districts and organized on American lines, it's not an obvious stop, although the original **old village** has been zealously preserved as a conservation area.

Just off the village green stands the ancestral home of the family that spawned the first US president. The "de Wessyngtons" – later the Washingtons – originally came over with William the Conqueror and by 1183 were based at the

Old Hall (April–Oct Mon–Wed & Sun 11am–5pm; £4.65; NT), where they lived until 1613. Carefully preserved as a Jacobean showpiece, the stone-flagged house has a fine kitchen, Great Hall and garden, and some exemplary wood panelling, and although none of the furniture is original to the Washington family, it is contemporaneous. Every Fourth of July, the raising of the US flag at the house heralds Independence Day celebrations and entry to the Old Hall is free for the occasion. Washington himself probably knew little of his family's northeast English origins – the Old Hall had passed into other hands well before the future president's great-grandfather emigrated to Virginia in 1656, an exile after the English Civil War. Yet it seems too much of a coincidence that the old Washington family coat-of-arms (three stars and three horizontal red-and-white stripes) found its echo more than a century later in the earliest version of the new country's Stars and Stripes.

The other main attraction in the area is the **Washington Wildfowl and Wetlands Centre** (daily 9.30am–4.30/5.30pm; £6, ⓦ www.wwt.org.uk), east of town and north of the River Wear in District 15, its hundred acres designed by Sir Peter Scott and acting as a winter habitat for migratory birds, including geese, ducks, herons and flamingoes. It's signposted off most local roads, four miles from the A1(M), one mile from the A19.

Hadrian's Wall and Hexham

In 55 and 54 BC, Julius Caesar launched two swift invasions of southeast England from his base in Gaul, his success proving that Britain lay within the Roman grasp. The full-scale assault began under Claudius in 43 AD and, within forty years, Roman troops had reached the Firth of Tay in modern Scotland. In 83 AD, the Roman governor Agricola ventured farther north, but Rome subsequently transferred part of his army to the Danube, and the remaining legions withdrew to the frontier that was marked by the **Stanegate**, a military roadway linking Carlisle and Corbridge.

Emperor Hadrian, who toured Roman Britain in 122 AD, found this informal arrangement unsatisfactory. His imperial policy was quite straightforward – he wanted the empire to live at peace within stable frontiers, most of which were defined by geographical features. In northern Britain, however, there was no natural barrier and so Hadrian decided to create his own by constructing a 76-mile **wall** from the Tyne to the Solway Firth – "to separate the Romans from the barbarians", according to his biographer. It was not intended to be an impenetrable fortification, but rather a base for patrols that could push out into hostile territory and a barrier to inhibit movement. Built up to a height of fifteen feet in places, it was punctuated by **milecastles**, which served as gates, depots and mini-barracks, and by observation **turrets**, two of which stood between each pair of milecastles. Before the Wall was even completed, major modifications were made: the bulk of the garrison had initially been stationed along the Stanegate, but they were now moved up to the Wall, occupying a chain of new **forts**, which straddled the Wall at six- to nine-mile intervals. Simultaneously, a military zone was defined by the digging of a broad ditch, or **vallum**, on the south side of the Wall, crossed by causeways to each of the forts, turning them into the main points of access and rendering the milecastles, in this respect, largely redundant. The revised structure remained in operation until the late fourth century AD, though centralized Roman rule in Britain had broken down by then.

Most of Hadrian's Wall disappeared centuries ago, yet walking or cycling its length remains a popular pastime, following the waymarked Hadrian's Wall Path that partly shares its route with Hadrian's Cycleway. Approached from Newcastle along the valley of the Tyne, via the Roman museum and site at **Corbridge**, the prosperous-looking market town of **Hexham** makes a good base. Most visitors stick to the best-preserved portions of the Wall, which are concentrated between **Chesters Roman Fort**, four miles north of Hexham, and **Haltwhistle**, sixteen miles to the west. Scattered along this section are a variety of key archaeological sites and museums, notably the remains of **Housesteads Fort** and that of **Vindolanda**, the milecastle remains at **Cawfields** and, further west, the **Roman Army Museum** near Greenhead.

Visiting the Wall

Corbridge, Hexham and Haltwhistle have the best choice of **accommodation** along the Wall, augmented by B&Bs in the dramatic countryside between Hexham and Greenhead, and **youth hostels** at Once Brewed (near Haltwhistle) and Greenhead. Drivers use the A69 (Hexham to Carlisle) to flit between major towns, though it's the narrower B6318 that actually follows the line of the Wall from Chollerford to Greenhead.

A special **Hadrian's Wall bus**, the cutely tagged #AD122, runs from Newcastle to Corbridge, Hexham and all the Wall sites and villages, and then on to Carlisle and Bowness-on-Solway (the end of the Hadrian's Wall Path). This operates between Easter and October, up to five times a day in each direction; a typical one-way ticket, from Hexham to Vindolanda, costs £2.90, though **Day Rover** tickets (1/3/7 days, £7/14/28) are better value. There's also a year-round hourly service on the #685 bus between Newcastle and Carlisle, and other local services from Carlisle and Hexham, which provide access to various points on the Wall. The nearest **train** stations are on the Newcastle–Carlisle line at Corbridge, Hexham, Bardon Mill and Haltwhistle – a combination rail rover ticket with the Hadrian's Wall bus allows travel between Newcastle and Carlisle. The best place to **park and ride** is at Once Brewed visitor centre, where there's all-day parking and a bus stop for the Hadrian's Wall bus.

You can pick up a comprehensive Hadrian's Wall **public transport timetable** from Newcastle, Hexham, Carlisle and Haltwhistle tourist offices and the Once Brewed visitor centre. Or contact the **Hadrian's Wall information line** on ℡01434/322002, Ⓦwww.hadrians-wall.org.

Corbridge and East Tynedale

CORBRIDGE is a quiet and well-heeled commuter town overlooking the River Tyne from the top of a steep ridge. This spur of land was first settled by the Saxons, and their handiwork survives in parts of the **church of**

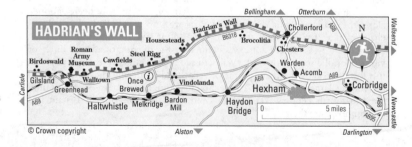

© Crown copyright

The **Hadrian's Wall Path** (🌐www.nationaltrail.co.uk/hadrianswall), an 84-mile waymarked National Trail, runs from Wallsend in the east to Bowness-on-Solway in the west, shadowing the line of the Wall, with over forty other linear or circular walks accessible en route. You could walk the main route in four days, but that's allowing little or no time to explore the archeological sites, towns and villages on the way, so a week is a more realistic timescale. To prove you made it, a "path passport" is available, which you get stamped at six locations along the way. Contact the Hadrian's Wall information line (☎01434/322002) for an official free **walking and accommodation guide**; there's also the *Hadrian's Wall Path: National Trail Guide* (Aurum Press), which details the route in exhaustive detail. Accommodation en route is not abundant – at least not on the Wall itself – so it's essential to book ahead and be prepared to be flexible. You may have to spend some nights a few miles from the end of your day's walk, though the Hadrian's Wall bus service is a boon in this respect. The best time to do the walk is between May and October, as the wet winter months are not only heavier going but also contribute to erosion and archeological damage. For the same reason, keep off the Wall itself at all times.

St Andrew, on the central Market Place, but it's the adjacent **Vicar's Pele** that catches the eye, an unusually well-preserved late-medieval fortified tower-house in which the priest could hole up in times of strife.

There's plenty of **accommodation** in and around town, though nearby Hexham makes the livelier overnight stop. *Priorfield* on Hippingstones Lane (☎01434/633179, 🌐www.priorfieldbedandbreakfast.co.uk; ●) has a couple of rooms (one with whirlpool bath) in an Edwardian family house, while the town's finest choice, the ★ *Angel Inn* on Main Street (☎01434/632119, 🌐www.theangelofcorbridge.co.uk; ●), serves classy lunches and dinners (not Sun eve). The creeper-covered station house, right on the railway line, is now home to the *Valley Restaurant* (☎01434/633434; closed Sun), where you'll get an excellent Indian meal.

Corbridge Roman Site

One mile west of the Market Place, accessible either by road or along the riverside footpath, lies **Corbridge Roman Site** (April–Oct daily 10am–4/5.30pm; Nov–March Sat & Sun 10am–4pm; £4.10; EH). This was first established as a supply base for the Roman advance into Scotland in 80 AD, thus predating the Wall itself. It remained in regular military use until the end of the second century, after which it became surrounded by a fast-developing town – most of the visible archeological remains date from this period, when "Corstopitum" served as the nerve centre of Hadrian's Wall, guarding the bridge at the intersection of Stanegate and Dere Street. The extensive remains provide an insight into the layout of the civilian town, showing the foundations of temples, public baths, garrison headquarters, workshops and houses as well as the best-preserved **Roman granaries** in Britain. In the site **museum** the celebrated *Lion and Stag* fountainhead – the so-called "Corbridge Lion" – gets pride of place; to the Romans, the lion and its prey symbolized the triumph of life over death.

Cherryburn, Prudhoe and Wylam

The local Roman remains are the big draw, but it's also an easy drive from Corbridge to three small-scale attractions along the eastern Tyne valley (A695 road), which can make a good half-day's outing by car.

Around six miles east of Corbridge, close to the south bank of the Tyne and signposted off the A695 at Mickley Square, **Cherryburn** (Easter–Oct Mon, Tues & Thurs–Sun 11am–5pm; £3.60; NT) is the birthplace museum of Thomas Bewick, England's greatest engraver (1753–1828). Still offering beautiful views of the rolling landscape that inspired Bewick, the simple birthplace cottage sits below a farmhouse-gallery, which contains displays that tell the story of his far-reaching legacy. Sunday is the big day here, with afternoon demonstrations of printing and woodblock engraving, and traditional Northumbrian music in the garden.

Back on the A695 through Prudhoe, moated **Prudhoe Castle** (April–Sept Mon & Thurs–Sun 10am–5pm; £3.50; EH) is worth a quick stop. Occupied continuously since the twelfth century – and the only castle in Northumberland never to have been taken by the Scots – its handsome grounds make a nice place for a picnic. Finally, a couple of miles beyond Prudhoe at **Wylam**, a whitewashed miner's cottage near the old Wylam Colliery is preserved as the **Birthplace of George Stephenson** (April–Oct Thurs–Sun noon–5pm; £2.20; NT), the celebrated railway engineer. He was born here in 1781 and furnishings inside reflect the period – the whole family living in one room.

Hexham

In 671, on a bluff above the Tyne, four miles west of Corbridge, St Wilfrid founded a Benedictine monastery whose church was, according to contemporary accounts, the finest to be seen north of the Alps. Unfortunately, its gold and silver proved irresistible to the Vikings, who savaged the place in 876, but the church was rebuilt in the eleventh century as part of an Augustinian priory and the town of **HEXHAM** grew up in its shadow. It's a handsome market town of some interest – the only significant stop between Newcastle and Carlisle – and however focused you are on seeing the Wall, you'd do well to give Hexham a night or even make it your base.

Arrival, information and accommodation

The **bus station** is off Priestpopple, a few minutes' stroll east of the abbey, while the **train station** sits on the northeastern edge of the town centre, a ten-minute walk from the abbey; the **tourist office** (Mon–Sat 9am–5pm, Sun 10am–5/6pm; Nov–March closed Sun, ☏01434/652220, ⒲www .hadrianswallcountry.org) is halfway between the two, in the main Wentworth **car park** near the Safeway superstore.

Guesthouses and hotels

Hallbank Hallgate, behind the Old Gaol ☏01434/605567, ⒲www.hallbankguesthouse .com. A restored house in a quiet town-centre location, with eight rooms with big beds, and an associated coffee shop/restaurant where you take breakfast. Parking. ❺

Kitty Frisk House Corbridge Rd ☏01434/601533, ⒲www.kittyfriskhouse.co.uk. Welcoming Edwardian retreat, half a mile from the centre down the Corbridge road (past the hospital) in a residential area. No credit cards. ❹

Matfen Hall Matfen, 10 miles northeast of Hexham ☏01661/886500, ⒲www.matfenhall.com. The northeast's ritziest golf-and-spa hotel presents a stylish take on country-house living, with modish rooms, compact pool and gym, and renowned Modern British restaurant. ❽

West Close House Hextol Terrace, off B6305, Allendale Rd ☏01434/603307. Quiet and secluded, with a delightful garden and wholefood continental breakfasts alongside the typical fry-up. No credit cards. ❸

The Town

The stately exterior of **Hexham Abbey** (daily 9.30am–5pm; free), properly the Priory Church of St Andrew, still dominates the west side of the Market Place. Entry is through the south transept, where there's a bruised but impressive first-century tombstone honouring Flavinus, a standard-bearer in the Roman cavalry, who's shown riding down his bearded enemy. The memorial lies at the foot of the broad, well-worn steps of the canons' **night stair**, one of the few such staircases – providing access from the monastery to the church – to have survived the Dissolution. Beyond, most of the high-arched nave dates from an Edwardian restoration and it's here that you gain access to the **crypt**, a Saxon structure made out of old Roman stones, where pilgrims once viewed the abbey's reliquaries. At the end of the nave is the splendid sixteenth-century **rood-screen**, whose complex tracery envelops the portraits of local bishops. Behind the screen, the chancel displays the inconsequential-looking **frith-stool**, an eighth-century stone chair that was once believed to have been used by St Wilfrid, rendering it holy enough to serve as the medieval sanctuary stool.

The rest of Hexham's large and irregularly shaped **Market Place** (main market day is Tuesday, farmers' market second and fourth Sunday of the month) is peppered with remains of its medieval past. The massive walls of the fourteenth-century **Moot Hall** were built to serve as the gatehouse to "The Hall", a well-protected enclosure that was garrisoned against the Scots. Nearby, the archbishops also built their own prison, a formidable fortified tower dating from 1330 and constructed using stones plundered from the Roman ruins at Corbridge. Known as the **Old Gaol**, this accommodates Hexham's local history museum (March–Oct daily 10am–4.30pm, Feb & Nov Tues & Sat 10am–4.30pm; £3.80).

Eating, drinking and entertainment

There are plenty of daytime **cafés**, four Indian and a couple of Italian **restaurants** in town, but the only place that really stands out is *The Green Room*, Station Rd (℡01434/608800; closed Sun night & Mon), an unpretentious Modern British restaurant in the old railway station waiting room. If you don't mind heading out of town, you can try one of the local **country pubs** instead. On Dipton Mill Road, two miles south of the centre (a 45min walk), *Dipton Mill Inn* (℡01434/606577) serves wholesome bar meals and own-brewed beer, in a lovely streamside setting. A similar distance to the northeast is the *Rat Inn* (℡01434/602814) at Anick (pronounced Ay-nick), on a glorious hillside location, with sweeping views, a pretty garden and fine food.

The main focus of entertainment in town is the **Queen's Hall Arts Centre** on Beaumont Street (℡01434/652477), which puts on a year-round programme of theatre, dance, music and art exhibitions. The centre has information about the **Hexham Gathering**, a folk festival held at various venues at the end of May, and the **Hexham Abbey Festival**, which presents classical and world music concerts in the abbey during the first week in September.

Chesters Roman Fort

Four miles north of Hexham – and half a mile west of present-day Chollerford – **Chesters Roman Fort** (daily 9.30/10am–4/6pm; £4.10; EH), otherwise known as Cilurnum, was built to guard the Roman bridge over the river. Enough remains of the original structure to pick out the design of the fort, and each section has been clearly labelled, but the highlight is down by the river where the vestibule, changing room and steam range of the garrison's **bath house** are still visible, along with the furnace and the latrines. The **museum** at the entrance has an excellent collection of Roman stonework – in particular, look out for Juno (now headless) in a delicately pleated dress standing on a cow, one of the finest pieces of statuary found along the Wall.

Next door to the site is the beautiful **Chesters Walled Garden** (Easter–Oct daily 10am–5pm; Nov–March variable hours, call ☎01434/681483, ⊛www.chesterswalledgarden.co.uk; £3), which shelters a fragrant display of herbs, including national collections of thyme and marjoram and a Roman herb section.

Housesteads to Cawfields

Overlooking the bleak Northumbrian moors from the top of the Whin Sill, **Housesteads Roman Fort** (daily 10am–4/6pm; £4.50; EH & NT), eight miles west of Chesters, has long been the most popular site on the Wall. The fort is of standard design but for one enforced modification – forts were supposed to straddle the line of the Wall, but here the original stonework tracked along the very edge of the cliff, so Housesteads was built on the steeply sloping ridge to the south. Access is via the tiny **museum**, from where you stroll across to the south gate, beside which lie the remains of the civilian settlement that was dependent on the one thousand infantrymen stationed within.

You don't need to pay for entrance to Housesteads if you simply intend to walk west along the Wall from here. The three-mile hike past the lovely wooded **Crag Lough** to **Steel Rigg** (car park) offers the most fantastic views, especially when you spy the course of the Wall as it threads over the crags ahead. Leaving the Wall at Steel Rigg, it's roughly half a mile south to the main road (B6318) and the visitor centre at **Once Brewed**, where there's also a youth hostel, pub and access road to the Vindolanda excavations. Otherwise, wall-walkers can continue another three miles west from Steel Rigg to **Cawfields** (free access), where the remains of another milecastle are perched on one of the most rugged crags on this section. There's a car park and picnic site at Cawfields, while if you make your way the mile or so south to the main B6318 you can recuperate at the *Milecastle Inn* (see opposite).

Practicalities

The very informative **Once Brewed National Park Visitor Centre** (March–Sept daily 9.30am–5/5.30pm; Nov–Feb Sat & Sun 10am–3pm; ☎01434/344396) has exhibitions on both the Wall and the national park. The side road beyond the centre continues for half a mile down to Vindolanda and then runs on to the A69, where you turn left for Haydon Bridge and Hexham or right for Haltwhistle.

Accommodation

Gibbs Hill Farm Once Brewed ☎01434/344030, ⊛www.gibbshillfarm.co.uk. Working farm with pretty rooms and great views of the Wall, two miles north of Steel Rigg. Also a hay-barn bunkhouse with shower rooms and kitchen (beds £12, breakfast available). ❸

Hadrian's Wall Camping and Caravan Site 2 miles north of Melkridge, just south of B6318 ☎01434/320495, ⊛www.romanwallcamping.co .uk. Friendly, family-run site half a mile from the Wall, with showers, washing machine and dryer and bike storage; breakfast available. Open all year.

Langley Castle A686, 2 miles south of Haydon Bridge ☎01434/688888, ⊛www.langleycastle .com. You don't get many chances to spend the night in a genuine medieval castle. The cheaper rooms are in the grounds, looking onto the castle, but all are spacious, some with four-posters, saunas and spa baths. There's also an atmospheric restaurant, cocktail bar, lounge and gardens. ❼, castle rooms ❾

Old Repeater Station Military Road (B6318), Grindon, 4 miles east of Once Brewed ⓣ01434/688668. ⓦwww.hadrians-wall -bedandbreakfast.co.uk. Remote location close to Hadrian's Wall, with a choice of simple en-suite rooms or rooms with bunk beds. The obliging host cooks breakfasts and dinners and offers an airport/rail/bus connection service. Dorm beds £20, rooms ❸

Once Brewed YHA Military Rd, B6318, Once Brewed ⓣ0870/770 5980, ⓔoncebrewed@yha .org.uk. Next to the visitor centre, providing walking leaflets, packed lunches, three-course dinners, kitchen and lounge. Dorms (from £11.95) are small (mostly four-bed), with modern facilities. Closed Dec & Jan.

Twice Brewed Inn Military Rd, B6318 ⓣ01434/344534. Friendly community pub, 50 yards up from Once Brewed visitor centre and hostel, with simple rooms, food served all day, beer-garden, local beers on tap and Internet access. ❷, en-suite ❸

Vallum Lodge Military Rd, B6318 ⓣ01434/344248, ⓦwww.vallum-lodge.co.uk. Cheery small hotel, a mile or so west down the main road from the visitor centre. Closed Nov–Feb. ❹

Eating and drinking

Cart's Bog Inn Langley ⓣ01434/684338. Just a quick drive from the Wall (and only around 10min from Hexham) is this welcoming middle-of-nowhere pub with real ales and good food.

General Havelock Inn A69, Haydon Bridge ⓣ01434/684376. Serves fine Modern European cuisine either in the bar (closed Mon) or grand rear restaurant (closed Sun eve & Mon). Bar meals are reasonably priced; three-course set dinners in the restaurant cost £25.

Milecastle Inn Military Rd, B6318 ⓣ01434/320682, ⓦwww.milecastle-inn .co.uk. A cosy pub on the Wall road that specializes in great home-cooked pies, from fish to wild boar.

Vindolanda

The excavated garrison fort of **Vindolanda** actually predates the Wall itself, though most of what you see today dates from the second to third century AD, when the fort was a thriving metropolis of five hundred soldiers with its own civilian settlement attached. The site (mid-Feb to mid-Nov daily 10am–5/6pm; winter reduced hours; £4.95, joint admission with Roman Army Museum £7.50; ⓣ01434/344277, ⓦwww.vindolanda.com) is operated by the private Vindolanda Trust, which has done an excellent job of imaginatively presenting its finds.

The ongoing **excavations** at Vindolanda are spread over a wide area, with civilian houses, inn, guest quarters, administrative building, commander's house and main gates all clearly visible. The path through the excavations descends to what's termed the **open-air museum**, where you can walk into reconstructions of a shrine of the water nymphs, a shop and a house, all with lively sound commentaries. Beyond lies the café, shop and **museum**, the latter housing the largest collection of Roman leather items ever discovered on a single site – dozens of shoes, belts, even a pair of baby boots – which were preserved in the black silt of waterlogged ditches. The most intriguing sections are concerned with the excavated hoard of **writing tablets**, now in the British Museum. Between 1973 and 1992, two hundred significant texts were discovered on the site, dealing with subjects as diverse as clerical filing systems and children's schoolwork. Then, in 1993, final excavations from a bonfire site revealed more tablets, apparently discarded when the garrison received orders in 103–104 AD to move to the Danube to participate in Emperor Trajan's Second Dacian War. The writings depict graphically the realities of military life in Northumberland: soldiers' requests for more beer, birthday party invitations, court reports, even letters from home containing gifts of underwear for freezing frontline troops.

Haltwhistle

There's not much to the small town of **HALTWHISTLE** and it's a couple of miles off the Wall itself, but it makes a useful overnight stop. The town features the only full set of amenities (ATMs, supermarket, shops and cafés) this side of Hexham and has a lively **market** each Thursday. It also claims to be the very centre of Britain, something you could debate with the **tourist office** (Easter–Oct Mon–Sat 9.30am–1pm & 2–5/5.30pm, Sun 1–5pm; Nov to Easter Mon–Sat 9.30am–noon & 1–3.30pm; ⊕01434/322002) in the train station, on the western edge of town, close to the A69. From here, walk up to Westgate, which becomes Main Street.

The best **hotel**, the *Centre of Britain* (⊕01434/322422, ⓦwww.centre -of-britain.org.uk; ❸–❺), is on Main Street, right in the middle of town. Built around a fifteenth-century fortified tower are a variety of tasteful bedrooms (some with spa bath and sauna) and lounges with wooden beams and stone fireplaces. **B&Bs** include *Ashcroft*, an elegant former vicarage on Lantys Lonnen (⊕01434/320213, ⓦwww.ashcroftguesthouse.co.uk; ❹) – a turn off Main Street near the *Centre of Britain*. Two or three of the pubs along Main Street also offer accommodation, while a couple of miles south of town the *Wallace Arms* at Rowfoot, near Featherstone, is a nice place for a **bar meal** and a country walk.

Roman Army Museum and Greenhead

A further four-mile trek west from Cawfields takes you past the remains of **Great Chesters Fort** before reaching a spectacular section of the Wall, known as the **Walltown Crags**. The views from here are marvellous and there's a handy nearby car park, picnic site and simple tea-and-ice-cream café. Very near the crags, at Carvoran, you can call into the Vindolanda Trust's **Roman Army Museum** (mid-Feb to mid-Nov daily 10am–5/6pm; winter reduced hours; £3.95, ⊕01697/747485, ⓦwww.vindolanda.com; joint ticket with Vindolanda £7.50), which tells you everything there is to know about life in the Roman army by way of exhibits, dioramas, reconstructions and games. There's also a virtual-reality aerial "flight" along the Wall.

Push on just a mile southwest, and you're soon in minuscule **GREENHEAD**, with a tearoom, pub and **youth hostel** (⊕0169/747411, ⓔdougsandragreenh@btconnect.com; £13), the latter located in a converted Methodist chapel. ⌖ *Holmhead Guest House* (⊕01697/747402, ⓦwww .holmhead.com; ❹), an old stone farmhouse sporting exposed beams and partly built with stones taken from the Wall itself, is up a track behind the hostel. There are only four rooms and guests should reserve in advance for the set-menu dinner (£25). There are also two **camping** spaces here and a small bunk-barn (£12 per person), handy for Wall walkers. Heading west, the next section of Hadrian's Wall worth exploring is at Birdoswald, in Cumbria, a four-mile walk or ten-minute ride on the bus.

Northumberland National Park

Northwest Northumberland, the great triangular chunk of land between Hadrian's Wall and the coastal plain, is dominated by the wide-skied landscapes of **Northumberland National Park** (ⓦwww.northumberland-national -park.org.uk), whose four hundred windswept square miles rise to the Cheviot Hills on the Scottish border. These uplands are interrupted by great slabs of forest, mostly the conifer plantations of the Forestry Commission, and a string of river valleys, of which Coquetdale, Tynedale and Redesdale are the longest. Remote from lowland law and order, these dales were once the homelands of the **Border Reivers**, turbulent clans who ruled the local roost from the thirteenth to the sixteenth century. The Reivers took advantage of the struggles between England and Scotland to engage in endless cross-border rustling and general brigandage, activities recalled by the ruined bastles (fortified farmhouses) and peels (defensive tower-houses) that lie dotted across the landscape.

The most popular hiking trail is the **Pennine Way**, which, entering the national park at Hadrian's Wall, cuts up through Bellingham on its way to **The Cheviot**, the park's highest peak at 2674ft, finishing at Kirk Yetholm, over the border in Scotland. As an introduction, it's hard to beat the lovely moorland scenery of the fifteen-mile stretch from Housesteads at Hadrian's Wall to **Bellingham**, a pleasant town on the banks of the North Tyne. Bellingham is also the gateway to **Kielder Water**, a massive pine-surrounded reservoir, water-sports centre and nature reserve. Further north, Victorian **Rothbury**, in Coquetdale, is convenient for walks in the Simonside Hills and for visits to the country estates of **Cragside** and **Wallington**, whilst at the hiking centre of **Wooler**, footpaths lead into the Cheviot Hills. Idiosyncratically restored **Chillingham** offers a different view of a stately home; the estate also accommodates an equally unusual herd of wild cattle.

Bellingham

The stone terraces of **BELLINGHAM** (pronounced Bellinjum) slope up from the banks of the Tyne on the eastern edge of the Northumberland National Park. There's nothing outstanding about the place, but it is a restful spot set in rural surroundings, and it does contain the medieval **church of St Cuthbert**, which has an unusual stone-vaulted roof – designed (successfully) to prevent raiding Border Reivers from burning the church to the ground.

Buses from Hexham stop on Market Place, a few hundred yards down from the helpful **tourist office** on Main Street (April–Oct Mon–Sat 9.30am–1pm & 2–5.30pm, Sun 1–5pm; Nov–March Mon–Fri 1–4pm; ☎01434/220616), housed in Bellingham's former Poor House building. The village's location on the Pennine Way means that there's a fair choice of **B&B** accommodation. Bellingham's **pubs** – the *Rose & Crown*, the *Black Bull* and the *Cheviot* – all have a few rooms, too, though the best choice hereabouts is *Riverdale Hall Hotel* (☎01434/220254, ⓦ www.riverdalehallhotel.co.uk; ⓞ), a country house on the village's western edge, with an indoor swimming pool and extensive grounds. Bellingham has a bank with an ATM, small supermarket and a couple of **cafés**, though otherwise you're dependent on the bar meals served at the pubs.

Kielder Water and Forest

The road from Bellingham follows the North Tyne River west and skirts the forested edge of **Kielder Water** (ⓦ www.kielder.org), passing the assorted visitor centres, waterside parks, picnic areas and anchorages that fringe its southern shore. The reservoir – England's largest by volume – and surrounding forest make a good day out, particularly for cyclists and hikers; you can really get off the beaten track here and there's some reasonable local accommodation if you fancy extending your stay.

First stop is the visitor centre at **Tower Knowe** (daily April–Oct 10am–4/6pm; ☎0870/240 3549), eight miles from Bellingham, with a café and an exhibition on the history of the valley and reservoir. Built to service the needs of a now largely defunct steel industry, the reservoir is gaining a second function as a leisure and tourism destination. Another four miles west, the **Leaplish** waterside park, bar and restaurant (opening hours vary;

℡0870/240 3549) is the focus of most of Kielder's outdoor activities and accommodation: there's also a heated indoor pool and sauna. The **Bird of Prey Centre** (daily 10.30am–4.30pm; £5; ℡01434/250400) here lays on entertaining daily flying displays and "hawk walks". Otherwise, an hour-and-a-half's cruise on the **Osprey ferry** (5 daily; April–Oct; £6) is always a pleasure; departures are from the piers at either Tower Knowe or Leaplish and you can be dropped off on the isolated north shore to make a day's walk of it.

Five miles from Leaplish at the top of the reservoir and just three miles from the Scottish border, the forestry settlement of **Kielder Village** is dominated by Kielder Castle, built in 1775 as the hunting lodge of the Duke of Northumberland and now the **Kielder Castle Visitor Centre** (April–Oct daily 10am–5pm; Nov Sat & Sun 11am–4pm; Dec daily 11am–4pm; closed Jan–March; ℡01434/250209), where free exhibitions praise the work of the Forestry Commission as well as focusing on the birds of the area. There's also a café and a full programme of events and activities throughout the year.

The castle is at the heart of **Kielder Forest Park**, Britain's largest forest, comprising several million spruce trees, criss-crossed by trails and home to red squirrels, deer, otters and countless birds, including goshawks, merlins and ospreys. Several clearly marked footpaths and bike trails lead from the castle into the forest, or you can explore some of the contemporary sculptures that Kielder is increasingly known for – like the **Minotaur Maze**, near the castle, or the **Skyspace** (1.5 miles from the castle), a light-and-space chamber you're encouraged to experience at dawn or dusk.

Practicalities

You really need your own transport to see much of Kielder, especially on a short visit. Otherwise, you're dependent on the local bus **from Bellingham**, which calls at Tower Knowe, Leaplish and Kielder, and less regularly at Stannersburn and Falstone. You'll pass a couple of pubs on the way, while **facilities** in Kielder village include a general store, garage, post office, tearoom and pub (May–June daily; Oct–April closed Mon). There's **mountain-bike rental** available from The Bike Place (℡01434/250457; £20 per day), signposted in the village, with advice given on waymarked trails and off-road routes through the forest.

As well as the **accommodation** options listed below, there are several other B&Bs in Kielder village and the surrounding area – the visitor centres can assist. The forest also has fourteen very basic **campsites** (℡01434/220242, no facilities, no vehicle access) for those who really want to walk the wild side – bring plenty of midge repellent.

Accommodation and food

Blackcock Inn Falstone ℡01434/240200. Small inn (closed Tues in winter) located in a pretty riverside hamlet. You can eat here, or at the excellent eco-friendly tearooms opposite (summer daily, winter closed Tues & Wed), located in the former village school. ③

Hollybush Inn Greenhaugh ℡01434/240391, ⓦwww.thehollybushinn.co.uk. Rustic old inn that's been given a makeover, in a hamlet about halfway between Kielder and Bellingham. Three nice rooms available, plus bar meals and a more elaborate weekend restaurant menu – hours tend to be limited, so call first, especially if you want to eat. ③

Kielder Lodges Leaplish Waterside Park ℡0870/240 3549, also available through Hoseasons ℡01502/502588, ⓦwww.hoseasons.co.uk. Extremely nice Scandinavian-style self-catering lodges available, £270–725 per week depending on size and season (cheaper 3-night stays available all year) – all have access to the park's pool, sauna, bar and restaurant.

Kielder YHA Kielder village ℡0870/770 5898, ⓔkielder@yha.org.uk. Well-equipped activity-based hostel, with some two- and three-bedded rooms plus small dorms, only 200 yards from the pub. Dorm beds from £14. Ring ahead in winter.

Pheasant Inn Stannersburn ℡01434/240382,

@www.thepheasantinn.com. On the road in from Bellingham, a couple of miles before the water, this early-seventeenth-century inn has eight comfortable rooms in a modern extension and decent meals (mains £9-13) served in the bar or restaurant. ⑤

Snabdough Farm Tarset, 5 miles west of Bellingham ☎01434/240239. Traditional farmhouse B&B – remote and quiet – on the minor road to Kielder from Bellingham. Breakfast on farm-fresh eggs to the strains of Mantovani or Lloyd-Webber; the *Hollybush* or *Pheasant* inns are your closest places for dinner. Call for directions. No credit cards. ③

Rothbury and around

ROTHBURY, straddling the River Coquet thirty miles northeast of Hexham, prospered as a late Victorian resort because it gave ready access to the forests, burns and ridges of the Simonside Hills. In the centre, where the High Street widens to form a broad triangle, there are hints of past pretensions in the assertive facades overlooking the Rothbury Cross, erected in 1902. The small town remains a popular spot for walkers, with several of the best local trails beginning from the **Simonside Hills** car park, a couple of miles southwest of Rothbury. Rothbury is also a handy base for visiting two of the northeast's most interesting landed estates, while each July a renowned **traditional music festival** (@www.rothbury-traditional-music.co.uk) brings folk into town from all over the region for Northumbrian pipe music, dancing and story-telling.

The **Tourist Information and National Park Visitor Centre** (April–Oct daily 10am–5pm; Nov–March Sat & Sun 10am–5pm; ☎01669/620887, @www.visit-rothbury.co.uk) is near the cross on Church Street. There's no pressing need to stay, even if you're walking for the day, with Alnwick (12 miles) and the coast so close, but the tourist office does have an informative folder of local **B&Bs**. Most of the places to eat and drink – two or three cafés, a deli and a couple of pubs – are strung out along the High Street, but the better move is to drive the two miles west to **Thropton** village (Otterburn road), where the *Three Wheat Heads* and the *Cross Keys Inn* soak up the local dining trade – the *Cross Keys* is excellent for fresh fish.

Cragside

Victorian Rothbury was dominated by Sir William, later the first **Lord Armstrong**, the immensely wealthy nineteenth-century arms manufacturer, shipbuilder and engineer who built his country home at **Cragside** (April–Oct Tues–Sun & bank hols 1–4.30/5.30pm; £10.50, gardens only £7; NT), a mile to the east of the village. He hired Richard Norman Shaw, one of the period's top architects, who produced a grandiose Tudor-style mansion that is entirely out of place in the Northumbrian countryside. The interior is stuffed with Armstrong's dark furnishings and fittings, enlivened by the William Morris stained glass in the library and the dining-room inglenook. Later extensions catered for Armstrong's numerous hobbies and diversions – his natural history and shell collection was placed in the gallery, a billiard room was added, while the marble-decked drawing room was completed in time for the visit of the Prince and Princess of Wales in 1884. Doubtless, they were too well brought up to comment on Shaw's "masterpiece", the spectacularly hideous Renaissance-style marble chimneypiece, which uses ten tons of the stuff to overly sentimental effect. Armstrong was also an avid innovator, and in 1880 he managed to make Cragside the first house in the world to be lit by hydroelectric power. The remains of the original pumping system are still visible in the **grounds**, which, together with the splendid **formal gardens**, have longer opening hours (mid-March to Oct Tues–Sun 10.30am–5.30pm; Nov to mid-Dec Wed–Sun 11am–4pm). Over at the visitor centre there's a **café/restaurant**, and an explanatory video and other displays in the adjacent Armstrong Energy Centre.

Wallington

Around 13 miles south of Rothbury, down the B6342 and a mile out of Cambo, stands **Wallington** (April–Oct daily except Tues 1–4.30/5.30pm; £8.40, gardens only £5.80; NT), an ostentatious mansion rebuilt by Sir Walter Blackett, the coal- and lead-mine owner, in the 1740s. The house is known for its Rococo plasterwork and William Bell Scott's Pre-Raphaelite murals of scenes from Northumbrian history. Children will love the collection of dolls' houses, one of which has 36 rooms and was originally fitted with running water and a working lift. However, it's the magnificent **gardens and grounds** (daily all year dawn–dusk) that are the real delight, with lawns, woods and lakes that are traced by easy-to-follow footpaths. A leisurely circuit of the estate might take you a couple of hours, depending on how long you spend in the magical **walled garden** (daily from 10am), exploring its terracing, conservatories, arbours and water features. There are events, concerts and activities throughout the year, as well as a café and farm shop on site.

Wooler

Stone-terraced **WOOLER**, a grey one-street market town twenty miles north of Rothbury, was wholly rebuilt after a calamitous fire in the 1860s, though its hillside setting high above Harthope Burn and its proximity to the Cheviot Hills do much to lift the spirits. For the most extensive views you'll have to tackle the trek to **The Cheviot** (2674ft) itself, seven miles to the southwest, which is the highest point in the Cheviot Hills. Starting out from Wooler youth hostel, count on four hours up, a little less back – from Hawsen Burn, the nearest navigable point, it's still two hours walking there and back. Wooler is also a staging-post on **St Cuthbert's Way**, the trans-Cheviot route, which runs west from the town to Kirk Yetholm and beyond or northeast to Holy Island.

Frequent buses link Wooler with Berwick-upon-Tweed and Alnwick, the two nearest towns, and the **bus station** is set back off the High Street. At the other end of the High Street, off Burnhouse Road (by the free **car park**), you'll find the **tourist office** (April–Oct Mon–Sat 10am–1.30pm & 2–5pm, Sun 10am–1.30pm & 2–6pm; ☎01668/282123) in the Cheviot Centre at Padgepool Place, which can provide local walking information.

B&Bs abound – there's a full list posted in the tourist office window – or for a bit more comfort try the *Tankerville Arms* (☎01668/281581, ⊛www .tankervillehotel.co.uk; ❻), a seventeenth-century coaching inn just off the A697 below town, which has a restaurant overlooking the attractive garden. But for complete remoteness, ⚘ *Hethpool House* ☎01668/216232, ⊛www .hethpoolhouse.co.uk; ❹) at Hethpool, seven miles west of Wooler, fits the bill. The turreted Edwardian manor house offers four charming rooms, dinner using home-grown produce (£15/20) and the Cheviots on the doorstep.

Chillingham

Six miles southeast of Wooler, **Chillingham Castle** (May–Sept daily except Sat 1–5pm, gardens and tearooms from noon; £6.75; ⊛www.chillingham-castle .com) provides a refreshing counterpoint to the high-minded tidiness of most stately homes. Starting life as an eleventh-century tower, the castle was augmented at regular intervals until the nineteenth century, but then from 1933 was largely left to the elements for fifty years, until the present owner set about restoring it in his own individualistic – all right, eccentric – way: bedrooms, living rooms and even a grisly torture chamber (designed to "cause maximum shock") are decorated with all manner of historical paraphernalia to give an idea of how the place would have looked through the ages, while chatty guides in each room tell tall tales of the castle and its visitors. In the **grounds** you can look around a small Elizabethan topiary garden, with its intricately clipped hedges of box and yew, and take a mile-long walk through the woods to the lake. Several self-catering **apartments** within the castle are available, either by the night (℡01668/215359; ❸) or by the week.

In 1220, the adjoining 365 acres of parkland were enclosed to protect the local wild cattle for hunting and food. And so the **Chillingham Wild Cattle** (visits April–Oct Mon & Wed–Sat 10am–noon & 2–5pm, Sun 2–5pm; winter by appointment; £4.50; ℡01668/215250, ⓦwww.chillingham-wildcattle.org.uk) – a fierce, primeval herd with white coats, black muzzles and black tips to their horns – have remained to this day, cut off from mixing with domesticated breeds. It's possible to visit these unique relics, who number about seventy, but only in the company of a warden, as the animals are potentially dangerous and need to be protected from outside infection. The visit takes up to an hour and a half and involves a short country walk before viewing the cattle at a safe distance, as the warden expands upon their history, heritage and even their DNA – all fascinating stuff, and the closest you're likely to get to big-game viewing in England. The site is signposted from the A1 and A697; bring strong shoes or walking boots if it's wet.

North to Berwick

North of Wooler, the B6525 leads straight to Berwick-upon-Tweed, but if you're in no hurry you can meander northwestwards up the A697 towards Coldstream. You're soon into rich, flat farmland, watered by the tributaries of the **River Tweed**, which marks the border with Scotland at this point. The views behind you are of the Cheviots, while detours off the main roads put you on country lanes presided over here and there by stately mansions with gatehouses.

Ten miles southwest of Berwick, on the B6354, **Etal Castle** (April–Sept daily 10am–4pm; £3.50; EH) was built in 1340 on the banks of the quiet River Till. The *Black Bull* in the pretty little village is the only thatched pub in Northumberland, while from Heatherslaw Mill, halfway back down the road to Ford, the narrow-gauge **Heatherslaw Light Railway** (hourly service, Easter–Oct daily 11am–3pm; extra trains during school holidays; £5.50 return, takes 40min) runs up the banks of the River Till to the foot of Etal Castle.

Back on the A697 just beyond Crookham, a minor road leads a mile west to the hamlet of **BRANXTON**, just above which, on the slopes of Branxton Hill, is the site of the English victory at the **Battle of Flodden** (1513). It was one of the most decisive of sixteenth-century conflicts: up to ten thousand Scots died in battle, including James IV and most of the contemporary Scottish nobility. The bodies were dumped in pits in Branxton churchyard, their passing now remembered by a simple granite memorial on the hill inscribed "To the brave of both nations".

The A697 runs four miles west of Branxton to reach the **border**, marked by Cornhill-on-Tweed on the English side and Coldstream in Scotland across the River Tweed. The ruins of **Norham Castle** (April–Oct Sun & bank hols only 10am–5pm; free; EH) overlook the tumbling Tweed (signposted off the A698), its pink sandstone walls and foursquare keep celebrated in paint by J.M.W. Turner and in verse in Sir Walter Scott's *Marmion*.

The Northumberland coast

The low-lying **Northumberland coast**, stretching 64 miles north from Newcastle to the Scottish border, boasts many of the region's principal attractions. In its heyday at the beginning of the twentieth century this area employed a quarter of Britain's colliers, but the mines closed years ago and entire local communities were devastated. Attempts have been made to clean up the southern part of this coast and its hinterland: at Ashington, once a huge pit village (birthplace of the footballing Charlton brothers and the great Jackie Milburn), a country park has been created from a former slag heap, while at neighbouring **Woodhorn** the colliery has been reborn as part of a museum complex.

Beyond Amble and its marina, you emerge into the best part of the coast, a pastoral, gently wooded landscape that spreads over the thirty-odd miles to Berwick-upon-Tweed. On the way there's a succession of mighty fortresses, beginning with **Warkworth Castle** and **Alnwick Castle**, former and present strongholds of the Percys, the county's biggest landowners. Further along, there's the formidable fastness of **Bamburgh** and then, last of all, the magnificent Elizabethan ramparts surrounding **Berwick-upon-Tweed**. In between you'll find splendid sandy beaches – notably at Warkworth, Bamburgh and the tiny seaside resort of **Alnmouth** – as well as the site of the Lindisfarne monastery on **Holy Island** and the seabird and nature reserve of the **Farne Islands**, reached by boat from Seahouses.

Public transport connections are good – only Holy Island is tricky to reach, an infrequent bus from Berwick-upon-Tweed being the sole connection. **By car**, the A1 from Alnwick (and, before that, from Newcastle) provides the fastest route to Berwick, though it runs well inland of the major coastal attractions. For these, the B1340 from Alnwick and its offshoots – signposted "Coastal Route" – are the ones to follow.

Woodhorn

Although mining in Woodhorn stopped in 1981, you can still visit the old colliery buildings as part of the **Woodhorn Northumberland Museum** (Wed–Sun 10am–4/5pm; free; £2 parking; ⓦ www.experiencewoodhorn.com). Within the main museum, identifiable by the halo of shards that forms the roofline, you can trace the lot of a miner, down the pit or in his pigeon loft, while a display in the East Gallery shows intimate and touching paintings of daily life by the **Ashington Art Group** – miners who learned to paint at night school in the 1930s. The museum is fifteen miles north of Newcastle, signposted off the A189.

Warkworth

WARKWORTH, a coastal hamlet set in a loop of the River Coquet a couple of miles from Amble, is best seen from the north, from where the grey stone terraces of the long main street slope up towards the commanding remains of **Warkworth Castle** (April–Oct daily 10am–4/6pm; Nov–March Mon, Sat & Sun 10am–4pm; £3.50; EH). Enough remains of the outer wall to give a clear impression of the layout of the medieval bailey, but nothing catches your attention as much as the three-storeyed keep. Mostly built in the fourteenth century, it's a fine example of the designs developed by the castle-builders of Plantagenet England. It was here that most of the Percy family, earls of Northumberland, chose to live throughout the fourteenth and fifteenth centuries.

A path from the village churchyard heads along the right bank of the Coquet to the little boat that shuttles visitors (weather permitting, April–Sept Wed, Sun and bank hols 11am–5pm; fee charged) across to **Warkworth Hermitage**, a series of simple rooms and a claustrophobic chapel that were hewn out of the cliff above the river sometime in the fourteenth century, but abandoned by 1567. The last resident hermit, one George Lancaster, was charged by the sixth earl of Northumberland to pray for his noble family, for which lonesome duty he received around £15 a year and a barrel of fish every Sunday.

The main street sweeps down into the attractive village, flattening out at Dial Place and the Church of St Lawrence before curving right to cross the River Coquet; just over the bridge, a signposted quarter-mile lane leads to the **beach**, which stretches for five miles from Amble to Alnmouth.

Alnmouth

It's just three miles north from Warkworth to the seaside resort of **ALNMOUTH**, whose narrow centre is strikingly situated on a steep spur of land between the sea and the estuary of the Aln. It's a lovely setting and there's a wide sandy beach and rolling dunes. Alnmouth was a prosperous port up until 1806, when the sea, driven by a freakish gale, broke through to the river and changed its course, moving the estuary from the south to the north side of Church Hill and rendering the original harbour useless. Alnmouth never really recovered, though it has been a low-key holiday spot since Victorian times, as attested by the elegant seaside villas at the south end of town. Many come for the golf: the village's splendid nine-hole course, right on the coast, was built in 1869 (it's claimed to be the second oldest in the country) and dune-strollers really do have to heed the "Danger – Flying Golf Balls" signs that adorn Marine Road.

The resort is a convenient interlude on the journey up or down the coast. There are local **bus services** from Alnwick and Warkworth, while the regular Newcastle to Alnwick bus also passes through Alnmouth and calls at its **train station** at Hipsburn, a mile and a half west of the centre. Most of the **accommodation** lies along or just off the main Northumberland Street. At no. 56, the friendly ♣ *Beaches* (℡01665/830006, ⓦwww.beachesbyo.co.uk; no credit cards; ❹) has a variety of highly individual en-suite rooms attached to a good **restaurant** (Mon–Sat dinner only), where meals of local cod, Northumbrian game casserole and the like go for around £15 a head; you can take your own wine.

Alnwick

The unassuming town of **ALNWICK** (pronounced "Annick"), thirty miles north of Newcastle and four miles inland from Alnmouth, is renowned for its castle and gardens – seat of the dukes of Northumberland – which overlook the River Aln. You'll need a full day to do these justice and Alnwick, as the biggest town between Hadrian's Wall and the Scottish border, itself warrants an overnight stop in any case. It's an appealing market town of cobbled streets and Georgian houses, centred on the old cross in Market Place, site of weekly markets (Thursdays and Saturdays) since the thirteenth century (and a farmers' market on the last Friday of the month).

Alnwick Castle and Garden

The Percys – who were raised to the dukedom of Northumberland in 1750 –
have owned **Alnwick Castle** (April–Oct daily 11am–5pm; £9; ⓦwww
.alnwickcastle.com) since 1309. In the eighteenth century, the castle was badly
in need of a refit, so the first duke had the interior refurbished by Robert Adam

▲ Alnwick Garden treehouse

in an extravagant Gothic style – which in turn was supplanted by the gaudy Italianate decoration preferred by the fourth duke in the 1850s. As you enter, look up to the sturdy battlements, which sport a number of stone soldiers – a piece of eighteenth-century flummery replacing the figurines of medieval times – set up there to ward off the evil eye.

There's plenty to see inside, though the **interior** is not to everyone's taste and it can be crowded at times – not least with families on the *Harry Potter* trail, since the castle doubled as Hogwarts School in the first two films. The most lavish decoration is in the red drawing room, where the rich polygonal panels of the ceiling bear down on damask-covered walls and some magnificent ebony cabinets rescued from Versailles during the French Revolution. Three of the perimeter towers contain **museum** collections – the Regimental Museum of the Royal Northumberland Fusiliers in the Abbot's Tower, early British and Roman finds in the Postern Tower and an exhibition dedicated to the Percy Tenantry Volunteers, a private force raised by the second duke during the Napoleonic Wars, in the Constable's Tower – but the bucolic garden walks and Capability Brown-designed **grounds** are a more profitable use of time once you've seen the main rooms.

Signs lead you out of the grounds for the short walk to the **Alnwick Garden** (April–Oct 10am–6/7pm; Nov–March 10am–4pm; £6; Ⓦ www.alnwickgarden .com), which draws crowds to marvel at its sheer scale and invention. At its heart is the computerized Grand Cascade, which shoots water jets in a regular synchronized display, while special features include a bamboo labyrinth maze and the popular Poison Garden – filled with the world's deadliest plants, on which volunteers are happy to expound. Superior ices, teas and snacks are available from the *Garden Café*, while Europe's biggest **treehouse** (opened in 2005) also houses a café and restaurant.

The rest of town

Other than castle and gardens, the main sight in Alnwick is the small-scale **Bailiffgate Museum**, 14 Bailiffgate (Easter–Oct daily 10am–5pm, Nov–Easter Tues–Sun 10am–4pm; £2.75; Ⓦ www.bailiffgatemuseum.co.uk), housed in the former church of St Mary, just around the corner from the castle's main entrance. This tells the history of the town and its trades, mixing in archive film and traditional music. The principal remains of the medieval town walls are on view at the **gatehouses** on Pottergate and Bondgate, while you can't miss the grandiose **Percy Tenantry Column** just to the southeast of the centre along Bondgate Without. A little further on, housed in the Victorian train station, **Barter Books** (Ⓦ www.barterbooks.co.uk), one of the largest secondhand bookshops in England, is definitely worth a call – not just books, but sofas, murals, open fire, coffee and biscuits, and a model railway that runs on top of the stacks.

Practicalities

Drivers should park in the **car park** around the back of the castle and gardens on Greenwell Road, a right turn just before the Bondgate arch as you come in from the A1. There are regular bus services to and from Alnmouth, Warkworth and Newcastle, as well as inland to Wooler and up the coast to Bamburgh. Alnwick **bus station** is on Clayport Street, a couple of minutes' walk west of the Market Place, where you'll find the **tourist office** (April–Oct Mon–Fri 9am–5/6pm, Sat 9/10am–4/5pm, Sun 10am–4pm; Nov–March Mon–Fri 9.30am–4.30pm, Sat 10am–4pm; ☏ 01665/510665, Ⓦ www.alnwick.gov.uk), in the arcaded Shambles.

Alnwick Playhouse, just through the arch on Bondgate Without (☎01665/510785, ⓦwww.alnwickplayhouse.co.uk), is a venue for theatre, music and film throughout the year. It's also host to concerts during the town's annual **International Music Festival** every August and the **Alnwick Northumbrian Gathering** of traditional music in November.

Accommodation and food

Masons' Arms Rennington, 5 miles northeast of town on the Seahouses (B1340) road ☎01665/577275, ⓦwww.masonsarms.net. An old coaching inn with good bar food, as well as eleven bedrooms, two with private sitting rooms. ❺, suites. ❻

Tower Restaurant & Accommodation 10 Bondgate Within ☎01665/603888, ⓦwww.tower-alnwick.co.uk. Just inside the gate, this place stands out for its bright, tasteful rooms and

hearty breakfasts; the pine-furnished restaurant below serves licensed meals, but closes at 8pm. Parking around the back. ❹

White Swan Bondgate Within ☎01665/602109, ⓦwww.classiclodges.co.uk. Alnwick's main hotel, where you might want to pop in at least for coffee or a meal – there's a comfortable lounge and restaurant, while the hotel's fine oak-panelled dining room was swiped from an old ocean liner, the *Olympic*, the twin of the *Titanic*. Parking. ❽

Craster, Dunstanburgh, Newton and Beadnell

Heading northeast out of Alnwick along the B1340, it's a six-mile hop to the region's kipper capital, the tiny fishing village of **CRASTER**. Half a dozen buses a day run here from Alnwick; the service continues to Seahouses and Bamburgh. You can buy wonderful kippers and oak-smoked salmon at Robson's factory, while the *Jolly Fisherman*, the **pub** above the harbour, features sea views from its back window and garden and famously good crabmeat, whisky and cream soup, crab sandwiches and kipper pâté.

Most spectacularly, however, Craster provides access to **Dunstanburgh Castle** (April–Oct daily 10am–4/5pm; Nov–March Mon & Thurs–Sun 10am–4pm; £2.90; NT & EH), whose shattered medieval ruins occupy a magnificent promontory about thirty minutes' windy walk up the coast – there's a car park in Craster. Originally built in the fourteenth century, parts of the surrounding walls survive – offering heart-stopping views down to the crashing sea below – though the dominant feature is the massive keep-gatehouse, which stands out from miles around on the bare coastal spur.

Many think that the coastline beyond Dunstanburgh is as good as Northumberland gets. Long sandy beaches backing Embleton and Beadnell bays are windswept and deserted in winter, busier in summer though rarely overly so. A minor road cuts down to the beachside hamlet of **NEWTON-BY-THE-SEA**, where the rustic *Ship Inn* (☎01665/576262; dinner reservations advised), on a square of old cottages, just yards from the beach, serves terrific fresh fish meals.

A couple of miles north around the next bay, **BEADNELL** also has a pub and fine beaches, which offer the best windsurfing on the northeast's coast. If you had to pick just one place to stay on the coast here it would be at welcoming 🏕 *Beach Court* (☎01665/720225, ⓦwww.beachcourt.com; ❻), a distinctive guest house right next to the harbour, with glorious bay views, an oak-panelled drawing room and three lovely rooms with big bathrooms – the most expensive of which is a "turret" suite with a crow's nest observatory; breakfast is continental. You can walk from the front door along the beach to the *Ship* at Newton (2 miles) or even on to Dunstanburgh (7 miles).

Seahouses and the Farne Islands

From Beadnell, it's three miles north to the fishing port of **SEAHOUSES**, the only place on the local coast that could remotely be described as a resort. Arrive in poor weather, with the rain lashing against the windows of the fish-and-chip shops, and you might wonder why you had bothered. But clear skies above the dunes to the north – Bamburgh castle a distant viewpoint – changes perspectives, as does the exciting possibility of a boat trip out to the windswept **Farne Islands**, a rocky archipelago lying a few miles offshore. Owned by the National Trust and maintained as a nature reserve, the Farnes are the summer refuge of hundreds of thousands of migrating seabirds, notably puffins, guillemots, terns, eider ducks and kittiwakes, and home to a grey seal colony.

Weather permitting, several operators run daily **boat trips** (around 2–3hr; from £10) from Seahouses quayside usually starting at around 10am. You can just wander down to the quayside and pick a departure, or contact either the **National Trust Shop**, 16 Main St (℡01665/721099), by the Seahouses traffic roundabout, or the **tourist office** (April–Oct daily 10am–5pm; ℡01665/720884, ⓦwww.seahouses.org), in the nearby main car park. During the bird breeding season (May–July) landings are restricted to morning trips to **Staple Island** and afternoons to **Inner Farne** – landing on either in the breeding season incurs a separate National Trust landing fee of £5.40. At all other times, bird-viewing trips normally land only on Inner Farne (NT fee £4.40), the largest of the Farne islands where you can also visit a restored fourteenth-century chapel built in honour of St Cuthbert, who spent much of his life and died here. Most operators also offer "sailaround" cruises, which get close to the birds and seals without landing, or you can take a trip to **Longstone Island** (not a bird sanctuary, so no landing fee) whose single attraction is the lighthouse from where Grace Darling (see p.914) launched her daring rescue.

It's unlikely you'd choose to stay the night in Seahouses, and there are regular buses to both Alnwick and Berwick-upon-Tweed. **Eating** is no problem, provided fish and chips is the solution, though at both the *Olde Ship* and the neighbouring *Bamburgh Castle Hotel*, just above the harbour, you'll also get something a bit more sophisticated. For the local catch, the *Fisherman's Kitchen*, 2 South St, sells smoked kippers, shellfish and salmon from its traditional smokehouse.

Bamburgh

Flanking a triangular green in the lee of its castle, three miles north of Seahouses, the tiny village of **BAMBURGH** is only a five-minute walk from two splendid sandy beaches, backed by rolling, tufted dunes. From the sands – in fact from everywhere – **Bamburgh Castle** (April–Oct daily 11am–5pm; £6.50; parking £1; ⓦwww.bamburghcastle.com) is a spectacular sight, its elongated battlements crowning a formidable basalt crag high above the beach. As an early Anglo-Saxon stronghold, it was one-time capital of Northumbria and the protector of the preserved head and hand of St Oswald, the seventh-century king who invited St Aidan over from Iona to convert his subjects. To the Normans, however, Bamburgh was just one of many border fortresses administered by second-rank vassals. In centuries-long decline – rotted by seaspray and buffeted by winter storms – the castle struggled on until 1894, when it was bought by Lord Armstrong (of Rothbury's Cragside, see p.905), who demolished most of the structure to replace it with a hybrid castle-mansion. The focal point of the new building was the King's Hall, a teak-ceilinged affair of colossal dimensions,

Bamburgh is the burial place of the widely celebrated English heroine **Grace Darling**, who rests beneath a Gothic Revival memorial in the churchyard of thirteenth-century St Aidan's. In September, 1838, a gale dashed the steamship *Forfarshire* against the rocks of the Farne Islands. Nine passengers struggled onto a reef, where they were subsequently saved by Grace and her lighthouseman father, William, who left the safety of the Longstone lighthouse to row out to them. *The Times* trumpeted Grace's bravery, offers of marriage and requests for locks of her hair streamed into the Darlings' lighthouse home and for the rest of her brief life Grace was plagued by unwanted visitors – she died of tuberculosis aged 26 in 1842. The story is told on any Farne islands boat trip from Seahouses (see p.913), while a RNLI Grace Darling Museum opposite the church in Bamburgh (under renovation) goes into more detail.

whose main redeeming feature is an exquisite collection of Fabergé glass animals. In the ground floor of the keep, the stone-vaulted ceiling maintains its Norman appearance; here the huge chains which once pulled wrecked ships ashore make the most impact.

Practicalities

A regular **bus** service links Alnwick and Berwick-upon-Tweed with Bamburgh, stopping on Front Street by the green. There's a public **car park** on the road below the castle and another at the castle itself for visitors. It's relatively easy to find **accommodation**, though booking ahead in summer is wise. At the top of the village green, there are smart, boutique-style rooms at the *Victoria Hotel* (℡01668/214431, ⓦwww.victoriahotel.net; ⓪), which also operates a couple of relaxing bars (meals, lunch and dinner) and a more expensive brasserie (dinner only) with a good Modern British menu. *The Greenhouse* (℡01668/214513, ⓦwww.thegreenhouseguesthouse.co.uk; ④), a few doors down at 5 Front St, has four contemporary rooms with flat-screen TVs, or further down still there's the traditional *Lord Crewe Hotel* (℡01668/214243, ⓦwww.lordcrewe.co.uk; ⑥; closed Jan), a comfortable old inn with oak beams, open fires, public bar and restaurant. Other moderate B&Bs are found on Lucker Road, beyond the top of the village green. **Eating and drinking** is best done at the places mentioned above – the *Victoria* is classiest, though there are also a couple of tearooms, a small deli, a butcher's selling homemade pies, and a bucket-and-spade general store. Romantics should head out to **Waren Mill**, a couple of miles to the west on the B1342 (Belford/A1 road), where the charming *Waren House Hotel* (℡01668/214581, ⓦwww.warenhousehotel.co.uk; ⑦) is set in its own quiet grounds on the edge of Budle Bay. Eating well here is no trouble whatsoever, with a refined four-course dinner served nightly.

Holy Island

There's something rather menacing about the approach to **Holy Island**, past the barnacle-encrusted marker poles that line the causeway. The danger of drowning is real enough if you ignore the safe crossing times posted at the start of the three-mile trip across the tidal flats. (The island is cut off for about five hours every day, so to avoid a tedious delay it's best to consult the **tide timetables** at one of the region's tourist offices or in the local newspapers.) Once on the island, the ancient remains of the priory and the brooding castle conjure yet more fantasies, not all pleasant. Small (just one and a half miles by one), sandy, flat and bare, it's easy to picture the furious Viking hordes sweeping across Holy Island, giving no quarter to the monks at this quiet outpost of early Christianity. Summer day-trippers clog the car parks as soon as the causeway is open, but Holy Island has a distinctive and isolated atmosphere. Give the place time and, if you can, stay overnight, when you'll be able to see the historic remains without hundreds of others cluttering the views.

Once known as **Lindisfarne**, it was here that St Aidan of Iona founded a monastery at the invitation of King Oswald of Northumbria in 634. The monks quickly established a reputation for scholarship and artistry, the latter exemplified by the **Lindisfarne Gospels**, the apotheosis of Celtic religious art, now kept in the British Library. The monastery had sixteen bishops in all, the most celebrated being the reluctant **St Cuthbert**, who never settled here – within two years, he was back in his hermit's cell on the Farne Islands (see p.913), where he died in 687. His colleagues rowed the body back to Lindisfarne, which became a place of pilgrimage until 875, when the monks abandoned the island in fear of marauding Vikings, taking Cuthbert's remains with them. In 1082 Lindisfarne was colonized by Benedictines from Durham, but the monastery was a shadow of its former self, a minor religious house with only a handful of attendant monks, the last of whom was evicted at the Dissolution.

The island

There's not much to the **village**, just a couple of streets radiating out from a small green and church cross, everything within a five-minute walk of everything else. You'll have to **park** in one of the large signposted car parks – keep an eye on the time and tide if you're not intending to stay. A shuttle bus runs every twenty minutes from the main car park to the castle.

Just off the green, the pinkish sandstone ruins of **Lindisfarne Priory** (Feb & March daily 10am–4pm; April–Oct daily 9.30am–4/5pm; Nov–Jan Sat, Sun & Mon 10am–2pm; £3.90; EH) are from the Benedictine foundation. Behind lie the scant remains of the monastic buildings while adjacent is the mostly thirteenth-century **Church of St Mary the Virgin**, whose delightful churchyard overlooks the ruins. The **museum** (same times as priory; entrance included in priory fee) features a collection of incised stones that constitute all that remains of the first monastery. The finest of them is a round-headed tombstone showing armed Northumbrians on one side and kneeling figures before the Cross on the other – presumably a propagandist's view of the beneficial effects of Christianity.

Stuck on a small pyramid of rock half a mile away from the village, past the dock and along the seashore, **Lindisfarne Castle** (April–Oct Tues–Sun, hours vary according to tide but always include noon–3pm; £5.80; NT; ☎01289/389244) was built in the middle of the sixteenth century to protect the island's harbour from the Scots. It was, however, merely a decaying shell when Edward Hudson, the founder of *Country Life* magazine, stumbled across it in 1901. Hudson bought the castle and turned it into a holiday home to designs by Edwin Lutyens, who used the irregular levels of the building to create the L-shaped living quarters that survive today. Lutyens kept the austere spirit of the castle alive in the great fireplaces, stone walls, columns and rounded arches that dominate the main rooms. He regularly collaborated with the garden designer Gertrude Jekyll, whose charming walled **garden** (90p) makes a pleasant place for contemplation.

The historic sites are all that most people bother with, but a **walk** around the island's perimeter is a fine way to spend a couple of hours. Most of the northwestern portion of the island is maintained as a **nature reserve**: from a bird hide you can spot terns and plovers and then plod through the dunes and grasses to your heart's content. The island even supports a seal colony, though sightings by visitors are rare – legend rather touchingly has it that the seals kept vigil with St Cuthbert as he prayed at the water's edge of his new domain.

Practicalities

The #477 **bus** from Berwick-upon-Tweed to Holy Island is something of a law unto itself given the interfering tides, but basically service is daily in August and twice-weekly the rest of the year. Departure times (and sometimes days) vary with the tides, and the journey takes thirty minutes. **Information** is available from Berwick-upon-Tweed tourist office, or consult the local community website, ⓦwww.lindisfarne.org.uk, which also posts bus and tide times.

The island is short on accommodation and you should make an advance booking, whenever you visit. Straightforward **B&B** is on offer at *Rose Villa* (☏01289/389268; ⓔbarbarakyle2@aol.com; ❸), just by the green, or there are a couple of traditional **hotels**, the *Lindisfarne* (☏01289/389273; ❻; closed Jan) and the *Manor House* (☏01289/389207; ❻ includes dinner; closed Jan), the latter backing on to the priory. Otherwise, you might have to stay just off the island – there's B&B (shared bathrooms) at the peaceful *Brock Mill Farmhouse* (☏01289/381283; ❷) at Beal, just off the A1 down the island road and on the left. The best pub on the island is the *Ship* (☏01289/389311, ⓦwww .theshipinn-holyisland.co.uk; ❺; closed Nov to early Dec & Jan) on Marygate, down from the green. Options for **eating and drinking** are limited to a couple of tearooms and the hostelries, of which the *Ship* is the pick.

Berwick-upon-Tweed

Before the union of the English and Scottish crowns in 1603, **BERWICK-UPON-TWEED**, twelve miles north of Holy Island, was the quintessential frontier town, changing hands no fewer than fourteen times between 1174 and 1482, when the Scots finally ceded the stronghold to the English. Interminable cross-border warfare ruined Berwick's economy, turning the prosperous Scottish port of the thirteenth century into an impoverished English garrison town. By the late sixteenth century, Berwick's fortifications were in a dreadful state of repair and Elizabeth I, apprehensive of the resurgent alliance between France and Scotland, had the place rebuilt in line with the latest principles of military architecture. Berwick's ramparts – one and a half miles long and still in pristine condition – are no more than twenty feet high but incredibly thick: a facing of ashlared stone protects ten to twelve feet of rubble, which, in turn, backs up against a vast quantity of earth.

The ramparts are now the town's major attraction, and it warrants a night's stay, especially as Berwick is a useful staging post between England and Scotland. It's not a large place but there's a fair choice of accommodation and services, and its quality-of-life charms have been recognized with its recent "cittaslow" (slow town) designation, a movement that has strong links with the Slow Food network.

Arrival, information and tours

From Berwick **train station** it's ten minutes' walk down Castlegate and Marygate to the town centre. Most regional **buses** stop closer in on Golden Square (where Castlegate meets Marygate), on the approach to the Royal Tweed Bridge, though some may also stop in front of the station. Drivers should use the main **car parks**, just outside the walls off Castlegate and down below the quay walls at the bottom of Sandgate.

The helpful **tourist office** (April–Sept Mon–Sat 10am–5/6pm, Sun 11am–3pm; Oct–March Mon–Sat 10am–noon & 1–4/5pm; ☎01289/330733, ⓦ www.exploreberwick.co.uk) at 106 Marygate can book you onto informative one-hour **walking tours** of town (Easter–Oct Mon–Fri 3 daily; £4). For **bike rental**, contact Wilson Cycles, 17a Bridge St (☎01289/331476) – you can get details of a scenic route to Holy Island (24 miles return) either here or from the tourist office.

Accommodation

Berwick has plenty of **accommodation** – local hotels and B&Bs post pictures and adverts inside the tourist office. Apart from our choices below, you'll find others ranged along Church Street and Ravensdowne (off Woolmarket, the continuation of Marygate); or head north up Castlegate, past the station, to North Road. Other concentrations are found in **Tweedmouth**, just on the other side of the bridge (10min walk), or near the beach at **Spittal** (bus from Golden Square).

Berwick Backpackers 56–58 Bridge St ☎01289/331481, ⓦwww .berwickbackpackers.co.uk. Not so much a backpackers' (though there's a small six-bed dorm, beds £14.95) as a self-styled "superior budget B&B". The rambling place (part once a shoe factory) has simple but smartly decorated en-suite rooms (available as single/double/triple), one with a gallery, another with a private kitchen, all tastefully done. There's a fully equipped kitchen/lounge, plus Internet access; prices include continental breakfast. No credit cards. ❷

Coach House Crookham, 10 miles southwest of Berwick ☎01890/820293, ⓦwww .coachhousecrookham.com. Has a range of rooms in converted farm buildings sporting exposed beams – some are priced a category higher. Guests are pampered with tasty home-made breakfasts and four-course dinners (£20). ❹

Clovelly House 58 West St ☎01289/302337, ⓦwww.clovelly53 .freeserve.co.uk. A really nice B&B, centrally located on a steep cobbled street by the Arts Centre (free parking provided nearby). Rooms are very smart with lots of little touches – fresh milk, DVD library, fruit and chocolates, posh toiletries – that elevate them out of the ordinary, while breakfast is superb. No credit cards. ❸

No.1 Sallyport Bridge St ☎01289/308827, ⓦwww.sallyport.co.uk. Berwick's most luxurious B&B, with six sensational rooms in a seventeenth-century house next to the city walls (by the Bridge Street Bookshop). Two spacious rooms and four lavish suites are elegantly furnished, retro to contemporary, and breakfast is terrific. Reservations essential; minimum 2-night weekend stays. ❻, suites ❼

Old Vicarage Guest House 24 Church Rd, Tweedmouth ☎01289/306909, ⓦwww .oldvicarageberwick.co.uk. The finest choice in Tweedmouth, a delightful Victorian villa with spacious rooms. No credit cards. ❷

Pot-a-Doodle-Do Wigwam Village Borewell, Scremerston, 3 miles south of Berwick ☎01289/307107, ⓦwww .northumbrianwigwams.com. Wooden wigwams sleeping four, with fridge, heating and light, provide a comfortable alternative to camping. In summer, tepees are available too. Good facilities and activities on hand, plus a Finnish barbecue hut with reindeer skins. Closed Mon & Tues Nov–March, and all Jan. Tepees ❷, wigwams. ❶

Queen's Head 6 Sandgate ☎01289/307852, ⓦwww.queensheadberwick.co.uk. Old Berwick inn that's gone for the gastropub look – rooms are good for the price, and it's a handy location (with nearby parking), while the daily changing black-board menu (mains £9–18, crab and seabass to Northumbrian lamb and venison) is the best in town. ❺

Whyteside House 46 Castlegate ☎01289/331019, ⓦwww.whyteside.co.uk. Victorian splendour at the top end of Castlegate – the house retains many original features, including the oak panelling, rooms are spacious and prettily furnished, and there's private parking. ❹

The Town

Berwick's **walls** – protected by ditches on three sides and the Tweed on the fourth – are strengthened by immense bastions, whose arrowhead-shape ensured that every part of the wall could be covered by fire. Begun in 1558, the defences were completed after eleven years at a cost of £128,000, more than Elizabeth I paid for all her other fortifications put together. And, as it turned out, it was all a waste of time and money: the French didn't attack and, once England and Scotland were united, Berwick was stuck with a white elephant. Today, the easy mile circuit along the top of the walls and ramparts (allow an hour) offers a succession of fine views out to sea, across the Tweed and over the orange-tiled rooftops of a town that's distinguished by its elegant **Georgian mansions**. These, dating from Berwick's resurgence as a seaport between 1750 and 1820, are the town's most attractive feature, with the tapering **Lions' House** on Windmill Hill and the daintily decorated facades of **Quay Walls**, beside the river, of particular note. The three bridges spanning the Tweed are worth a look, too – the huge arches of the **Royal Border Railway Bridge**, built in the manner of a Roman aqueduct by Robert Stephenson in the 1840s, contrasting with the desultory concrete of the **Royal Tweed**, completed in 1928, and the modest seventeenth-century **Berwick Bridge**.

Within the ramparts, the Berwick skyline is punctured by the stumpy spire of the eighteenth-century **Town Hall** (April–Sept Mon–Fri tours at 10.30am & 2pm; £2) at the bottom of Marygate, right at the heart of the compact centre. This retains its original jailhouse on the upper floor, now housing the **Cell Block Museum**, entertaining tours of which dwell on tales of crime and punishment in Berwick. Unruly visitors can spend a reflective minute or two locked in the condemned cell. From here, it's a couple of minutes' walk along Church Street to **Holy Trinity Church**, one of the few churches built during the Commonwealth, the absence of a tower supposedly reflecting the wishes of Cromwell, who found them irreligious.

Opposite the church, the finely proportioned **Barracks** (April–Sept Wed–Sun 10am–5pm; £3.40; EH), designed by Nicholas Hawksmoor (1717), were in use until 1964, when the King's Own Scottish Borderers regiment decamped. Inside, there's a regimental museum, as well as the *By Beat of Drum* exhibition, which in a series of picture boards and dioramas traces the life of the British infantryman from the sixteenth to the nineteenth century. These are of rather specialist interest, though most will warm to the temporary exhibitions of contemporary art in the **Gymnasium Gallery** and the borough museum and art gallery, sited in the **Clock Block**. Geared up for school parties, the museum features imaginative displays of local traditional life, even a model of a local clergyman haranguing visitors from his pulpit.

Eating, drinking and entertainment

Berwick has plenty of daytime **cafés and tearooms**, including one on the ground floor of the historic Town Hall, though fine **restaurant** dining is a bit limited – the *Queen's Head* (see p.917; reservations advised) is the out-and-out winner. In 1799 there were 59 **pubs** and three coaching inns in town – today only one really stands out from the crowd, though between that and the local **arts centre** you should be able to spend quite a happy evening. Berwick's arts centre, The Maltings, Eastern Lane (☎01289/330999, ⓦwww.maltingsberwick.co.uk), has a year-round programme of music, theatre, comedy, film and dance, and river views from its licensed café.

Restaurants and pubs

Amaryllis 7 West St ☎01289/331711.
Contemporary, spacious brasserie with great
dishes, like smoked lamb or pesto-stuffed chicken.
Closed Sun and dinner Mon–Wed. Dinner
reservations advised. Expensive.

Barrels Ale House 59–61 Bridge St
☎01289/308013, ⓦwww.thebarrelsalehouse.com.

Chilled-out independent pub at the foot of the
Berwick Bridge, with funky furniture, guest beers,
and an interesting programme of live music and
DJs.

Foxton's 26 Hide Hill ☎01289/303939. This
amiable town-centre bar-brasserie serves a varied
English- and Mediterranean-style menu. Closed
Sun. Moderate.

Travel details

Buses

For more information on all local and
national bus services, contact Traveline
☎0871/200 2233, ⓦwww.traveline
.org.uk.

Alnwick to: Bamburgh (Mon–Sat 5 daily; 1hr);
Berwick-upon-Tweed (Mon–Sat 5 daily; 1hr).

Bamburgh to: Alnwick (Mon–Sat 5 daily; 1hr);
Craster (Mon–Sat 5 daily; 30–40min); Seahouses
(Mon–Sat 5 daily, 10min).

Barnard Castle to: Bishop Auckland (Mon–Sat 7
daily, Sun 4; 50min); Darlington (hourly; 40min);
Middleton-in-Teesdale (Mon–Sat hourly; Sun 4
daily; 35min); Raby Castle (9 daily; 15min)

Berwick-upon-Tweed to: Holy Island (Aug 2 daily,
rest of the year 2 weekly; 35min); Newcastle
(Mon–Sat 6 daily, Sun 3; 2hr 15min); Wooler
(Mon–Sat 10 daily; 55min).

Darlington to: Barnard Castle (hourly; 40min);
Bishop Auckland (Mon–Sat every 30min; Sun
hourly; 50min); Durham (every 30min; 1hr 10min);
Middleton-in-Teesdale (Mon–Sat 9 daily, Sun 4;
1hr 20min).

Durham to: Bishop Auckland (every 30min;
35min); Chester-le-Street (every 30min; 25min);
Darlington (every 30min; 1hr 10min); Newcastle
(Mon–Sat every 30min, Sun 4–6; 50min).

Haltwhistle to: Alston (Mon–Sat 4 daily; 40min);
Hexham (hourly; 35min).

Hexham to: Allendale (Mon–Sat 6 daily; 25min);
Allenheads (Mon–Sat 6 daily; 45min); Bellingham
(Mon–Sat 8 daily; 45min); Haltwhistle (hourly;
35min).

Middlesbrough to: Newcastle (Mon–Sat every
30min; 1hr); Saltburn (Mon–Sat every 30min; 40min).

Newcastle to: Alnmouth (hourly; 1hr 40min);
Alnwick (hourly; 1hr 20min–1hr 50min);
Bamburgh (4 daily; 2hr 30min); Beamish (daily
every 30min; 1hr); Berwick-upon-Tweed
(Mon–Sat 6 daily, Sun 5; 2hr 30min); Carlisle
(Mon–Sat hourly, Sun 4; 2hr 10min); Durham
(Mon–Sat every 30min, Sun 4–6; 50min); Hexham
(hourly; 50min); Middlesbrough (Mon–Sat every
30min; 1hr); Rothbury (Mon–Sat 5 daily; 1hr
20min); Seahouses (4 daily; 2hr 10min);
Warkworth (hourly; 1hr 20min).

Wooler to: Alnwick (Mon–Sat 5 daily; 45min);
Berwick-upon-Tweed (Mon–Sat 7 daily; 50min).

Trains

For information on all local and
national rail services, contact National
Rail Enquiries ☎0845/748 4950,
ⓦwww.rail.co.uk.

Darlington to: Bishop Auckland (7 daily; 25min);
Durham (every 30min; 20min); Newcastle (every
30min; 35min).

Durham to: Darlington (every 30min; 20min);
London (hourly; 3hr); Newcastle (every 30min;
15min); York (every 30min; 50min).

Hexham to: Carlisle (hourly; 50min); Haltwhistle
(hourly; 20min); Newcastle (hourly; 40min).

Middlesbrough to: Durham (hourly; 50min);
Grosmont, for North York Moors Railway (see p.843:
5 daily; 1hr 5min); Newcastle (hourly; 1hr 30min);
Saltburn (hourly; 25min); Whitby (5 daily; 1hr
30min).

Newcastle to: Alnmouth (9 daily; 30min);
Berwick-upon-Tweed (hourly; 45min); Carlisle
(hourly; 1hr 30min); Corbridge (hourly; 35min);
Darlington (every 30min; 35min); Durham (every
30min; 15min); Haltwhistle (hourly; 1hr); Hexham
(hourly; 40min); London (hourly; 2hr 45min–3hr
30min); York (hourly; 1hr).

⑬

THE NORTHEAST | Travel details

Contexts

Contexts

History

E ngland's history is long and densely woven, and events within this small nation have had an influence far outweighing the country's modest size. Its protagonists have been influential figures in Western Europe from Anglo-Saxon times and more latterly, with the expansion of the British Empire, the whole globe. What follows is therefore a necessarily brief introduction to a complex subject: for some recommendations for more detailed accounts, see our "Books and literature" section on p.961.

Stone and Bronze Age England

England has been inhabited for the best part of half a million years, though the earliest archeological evidence of human life dates from about **250,000 BC**. These meagre remains, found just east of London across the Thames from Tilbury, belong to one of the migrant communities whose comings and goings were dictated by the fluctuations of the several Ice Ages. Renewed glaciation then created a longer break and the next traces – mainly roughly worked flint implements – were left around **40,000 BC** by cave-dwellers at Creswell Crags in Derbyshire, Kent's Cavern near Torquay and Cheddar Cave in Somerset. The last spell of intense cold began about 17,000 years ago, and it was the final thawing of this **last Ice Age** around 5000 BC that caused the British Isles to separate from the European mainland.

The **sea barrier** did nothing to stop further migrations of nomadic hunters, drawn by the rich forests that covered ancient Britain. In about 3500 BC a new wave of colonists arrived from the continent, probably via Ireland, bringing with them a **Neolithic culture** based on farming and the rearing of livestock. These tribes were the first to make some impact on the environment, clearing forests, enclosing fields, constructing defensive ditches around their villages and digging mines to obtain flint used for tools and weapons. Fragments of Neolithic pottery have been found near Peterborough and at Windmill Hill, near Avebury in Wiltshire, but the most profuse relics of this culture are their graves, usually stone-chambered, turf-covered mounds (called **long barrows**). These are scattered throughout the country – the most impressive ones are at Belas Knap in Gloucestershire and at Wayland's Smithy in Berkshire.

The transition from the Neolithic to the **Bronze Age** began around 2000 BC, with the immigration from northern Europe of the so-called **Beaker People** – named from the distinctive cups found at their burial sites. Originating in the Iberian peninsula and bringing with them bronze-workers from the Rhineland, these newcomers had a comparatively well-organized social structure with an established aristocracy and they quickly intermixed with the native tribes. Many of Britain's stone circles were completed at this time, including **Avebury** and **Stonehenge** in Wiltshire, while many others belong entirely to the Bronze Age – for example, the Hurlers and the Nine Maidens on Cornwall's Bodmin Moor. Large numbers of earthwork forts were also built in this period, suggesting endemic tribal warfare, but none were able to withstand the Celtic invaders from central Europe, who began sweeping over Britain around 600 BC.

The Celts and the Romans

Skilled in battle, the **Celts** soon intermingled with the local inhabitants of Britain, establishing a sophisticated farming economy and a social hierarchy that was dominated by a druidic priesthood. Familiar with Mediterranean artefacts through their far-flung trade routes, they introduced superior methods of metal-working that favoured iron rather than bronze, from which they forged not just weapons but also coins and ornamental works, thus creating the first recognizable English art. The principal Celtic contribution to the landscape was a network of hillforts and other defensive works stretching over the entire country, the greatest of them at **Maiden Castle** in Dorset, a site first fortified almost 2500 years earlier.

Maiden Castle was also one of the first British fortifications to fall to the **Roman** legions in 43 AD. Coming at the end of a long period of commercial probing, the Roman invasion had begun hesitantly, with small cross-Channel incursions led by **Julius Caesar** in 55 and 54 BC. Britain's rumoured mineral wealth was a primary motive, but the immediate spur to the eventual conquest that came nearly a century later was anti-Roman collaboration between the British Celts and their fiercely independent cousins in France. The sub-text was that the **Emperor Claudius**, who led the invasion, owed his power to the army and needed a military triumph. The death of the king of southeast England, Cunobelin – Shakespeare's Cymbeline – presented Claudius with a golden opportunity and in **August 43 AD** a substantial Roman force landed in Kent, from where it fanned out, soon establishing a base along the estuary of the Thames. Joined by a menagerie of elephants and camels for the major battle of the campaign, the Romans soon reached Camulodunum (Colchester) – the region's most important city – and within four years were dug in on the frontier of south Wales.

Some determined resistance did occur, notably from the Catuvellauni chief, **Caractacus**, who conducted a guerrilla campaign from Wales until he was captured in about 50 AD. This was, however, nothing compared with the revolt of the East Anglian Iceni, under their queen **Boudicca** (or Boadicea) in 60 AD. The Iceni sacked Camulodunum and Verulamium (St Albans), and even reached the undefended new port of Londinium (London), but the Romans rallied and exacted a terrible revenge. In the event, the rebellion turned to be an isolated act of resistance, and it would seem that most of the southern tribes were content – or at least resigned – to their absorption into the empire. In the next decades, the Romans extended their control, subduing Wales and the north of England by 80 AD. They did not, however, manage to conquer Scotland and eventually gave up – as signified by the construction of **Hadrian's Wall** in 130 AD. Running from the Tyne to the Solway, the wall marked the northern limit of the Roman Empire, and stands today as England's most impressive remnant of the Roman occupation.

The written history of England begins with the Romans, whose rule lasted nearly four centuries. For the first time, the country began to emerge as a clearly identifiable entity with a defined political structure. Peace also brought prosperity. Commerce flourished and cities prospered, including the most northerly Roman town of Eboracum (York), the garrison of Isca Dumnoniorum (Exeter), the leisure resort of Aquae Sulis (Bath), and of course **Londinium**, which immediately assumed a pivotal role in the commercial and administrative life of the colony. Although Latin became the language of the Romano-British ruling elite, local traditions were allowed to coexist alongside imported customs, so that Celtic gods were often worshipped at the same time as Roman ones, and sometimes merged with them. Perhaps the most important legacy of the

Roman occupation, however, was the introduction of **Christianity** from the third century on, becoming firmly entrenched after its official recognition by the Emperor Constantine in 313.

Anglo-Saxon England and the Danes

As early as the reign of Constantine, Roman England was being **raided** by Germanic Saxons, and by the middle of the fourth century – with the Romans on the run – Picts from Scotland and Scots from northern Ireland were harrying inland areas in the north and west. As economic life declined and rural areas became depopulated, individual military leaders began to usurp local authority. Indeed, by the start of the fifth century England had become irrevocably detached from what remained of the Roman Empire and within fifty years the **Saxons** had begun settling England themselves. This marked the start of a gradual conquest that culminated in the defeat of the native Britons in 577 at the **Battle of Dyrham** (near Bath) and, despite the despairing efforts of such semi-mythical figures as King Arthur, the last independent Britons were driven deep into Cumbria, Wales and the southwest. The Saxons all but eliminated Romano-British culture and by the end of the sixth century the rest of England was divided into the Anglo-Saxon kingdoms of Northumbria, Mercia, East Anglia, Kent and Wessex. So complete was the Anglo-Saxon domination of England, through conquest and intermarriage, that some ninety percent of English place names today have an Anglo-Saxon derivation. Only in the westerly extremities of the country did the ancient Celtic traditions survive, as untouched by the new invaders as they had been by the Romans. Here also, Christian worship was kept alive, though the countrywide revival of Christianity was driven mainly by the arrival of **St Augustine**, who was despatched by Pope Gregory I and landed on the Kent coast in 597, accompanied by forty monks.

The missionaries were received by **Ethelbert**, the overlord of all the English south of the River Humber, whose marriage to a Christian princess from France made him sympathetic to Augustine's message. Ethelbert gave Augustine permission to found a monastery at Canterbury (on the site of the present cathedral), where the king himself was then baptized, followed by ten thousand of his subjects at a grand Christmas ceremony. Despite some reversals in the years that followed, the Christianization of England proceeded quickly, so that by the middle of the seventh century all of the Anglo-Saxon kings had at least nominally adopted the faith. Tensions and clashes between the Augustinian missionaries and the Celtic monks inevitably arose, to be resolved by the **Synod of Whitby** in 663, when it was agreed that the English Church should follow the rule of Rome, thereby ensuring a realignment with the European cultural mainstream.

The central English region of **Mercia** became the dominant Anglo-Saxon kingdom in the eighth century under kings Ethelbald and **Offa**. The latter was responsible for the greatest public work of the Anglo-Saxon period, **Offa's Dyke**, an earthwork marking the border with Wales from the River Dee to the River Severn. Yet, after Offa's death, **Wessex** gained the upper hand, and by 825 the Wessex kings had conquered or taken allegiance from all the other English kingdoms. Their triumph was, however, short-lived. Carried here by their remarkable longboats, the **Vikings** – in this case mostly **Danes** – had started to raid the east coast towards the end of the eighth century, one notable casualty being the great monastery of Lindisfarne, which was razed in 793. Emboldened by their success, these raids grew in size and then turned into a migration. In 865, a substantial Danish army landed in East Anglia, and within six years they had conquered Northumbria, Mercia and East Anglia. The Danes then set their sights on Wessex, whose new king was the formidable and exceptionally talented **Alfred the Great**. Despite the odds, Alfred successfully resisted the Danes and eventually the two warring parties signed a truce, which fixed an uneasy border between Wessex and Danish territory – the **Danelaw** – to the north. Ensconced in northern England and what is today the East Midlands, the Danes soon succumbed to Christianity and internal warfare, while Alfred modernized his kingdom and strengthened its defences.

Alfred died in 899, but his successor, **Edward the Elder**, capitalized on his efforts, establishing Saxon supremacy over the Danelaw to become the de facto overlord of all England. The relative calm continued under Edward's son, **Athelstan**, who extended his overlordship over much of Scotland and Wales, and his son, **Edgar**, who became the first ruler to be crowned **king of England** in 973. However, this was but a lull in the Viking storm. Returning in force, the Vikings milked Edgar's son **Ethelred the Unready** ("lacking counsel") for all the money they could, but the ransom (the Danegeld) paid brought only temporary relief and, in 1016, Ethelred hot-footed it to Normandy, leaving the Danes in command.

The first Danish king of England was **Canute**, a shrewd and gifted ruler, but his two disreputable sons quickly dismantled his carefully constructed Anglo-Scandinavian empire. Thereafter, the Saxons regained the initiative, restoring Ethelred's son, **Edward the Confessor**, to the throne in 1042. It was a poor choice. Edward was more suited to be a priest than a king and he allowed power to drift into the hands of his most powerful subject, Godwin, Earl of Wessex, and his son Harold. On Edward's death, the Witan – a sort of council of elders – confirmed **Harold** as king, ignoring several rival claims including that of William, Duke of Normandy. William's claim was a curious affair, but he always insisted – however improbable it may seem – that the childless Edward the Confessor had promised him his crown. Unluckily for Harold, his two main rivals struck at the same time. First up was his alienated brother **Tostig** and his ally King Harald of Norway, a giant of a man reliably reckoned to be seven feet tall. They landed with a Viking army in Yorkshire and Harold hurriedly marched north to meet them. Harold won a crushing victory at the battle of Stamford Bridge, but then he heard that William of Normandy had invaded the south. Rashly, Harold did not pause to muster more men, but dashed south, where William famously routed the Saxons – and killed Harold – at the **Battle of Hastings** in 1066. On Christmas Day, William the Conqueror was installed as king in Westminster Abbey.

The Normans and the Plantagenets

Making little attempt to reach any understanding with his new subjects, **William I** imposed a Norman aristocracy, reinforcing his rule with a series of strongholds, the grandest of which was the Tower of London. Initially, there was some resistance, but William crushed these sporadic rebellions with great brutality – Yorkshire and the north were ravished and the fenland resistance of Hereward the Wake was brought to a savage end. Nonetheless, perhaps the single most effective controlling measure was the compilation of the **Domesday Book** between 1085 and 1086. Recording land ownership, type of cultivation, the number of inhabitants and their social status, it afforded William an unprecedented body of information about his subjects, providing the framework for the administration of taxation, the judicial structure and ultimately feudal obligations.

In 1087, William died and was succeeded by his son **William Rufus**, an ineffectual ruler but a notable benefactor of religious foundations. Rufus died in mysterious circumstances – killed by an unknown assailant's arrow while hunting in the New Forest – and the throne passed to **Henry I**, William I's youngest son. Henry spent much of his time struggling with his unruly barons, but at least he proved to be more conciliatory in his dealings with the Saxons, even marrying into one of their leading families. On his death in 1135, William I's grandson Stephen of Blois contested the accession of Henry's daughter Mathilda and the result was a long-winded civil war. Matters were eventually resolved when both factions accepted Mathilda's son **Henry II**, the first of the **Plantagenets**, so-called after this branch of the family. Energetic and far-sighted, Henry kept his barons firmly in check and instigated profound administrative reforms, including the introduction of trial by jury. Neither was England Henry's only concern, his inheritance bequeathing him great chunks of France. This territorial entangle-ment was to create all sorts of problems for his successors, but Henry was brought low by his attempt to subordinate church to crown. This went terribly awry in 1170, when Henry sanctioned the murder in Canterbury Cathedral of his erstwhile drinking companion **Thomas à Becket**, whose canonization just three years later created an enduring Europe-wide cult.

The last years of Henry's reign were riven by quarrels with his sons, the eldest of whom, **Richard I** (or Lionheart), spent most of his ten-year reign crusading in the Holy Land. Neglected, England fell prey to the scheming of Richard's brother **John**, the villain of the Robin Hood tales, who became king in his own right after Richard died of a battle wound in France in 1199. Yet John's inability to hold on to his French possessions and his rumbling dispute with the Vatican alienated the English barons, who eventually forced him to consent to a charter guaranteeing their rights and privileges, the **Magna Carta**, which was signed in 1215 at Runnymede, on the Thames.

The power struggle with the barons continued into the reign of **Henry III**, who was defeated by their leader Simon de Montfort at Lewes in 1264, when both Henry and Prince Edward were taken prisoner. Edward escaped and promptly routed the barons' army at the battle of Evesham in 1265, killing de Montfort in the process. This was something of a watershed and Henry's successor, **Edward I**, who inherited the throne in 1272, was much more in control of his kingdom than his predecessor. Edward was also a great law-maker, but he became obsessed by military matters, spending years subduing Wales and imposing English jurisdiction over Scotland. Fortunately for the Scots – it was too late for Wales – the next king of England, **Edward II**, proved to be completely hopeless and in 1314 Robert the Bruce inflicted a huge defeat on his guileless army at the battle of **Bannockburn**. This reverse spelt the beginning of the end for Edward, who was ultimately murdered by his wife Isabella and her lover Roger Mortimer in 1327.

Edward III began by sorting out the Scottish imbroglio before getting stuck into his main preoccupation – his (essentially specious) claim to the throne of

France. Starting in 1337, the resultant **Hundred Years War** kicked off with several famous English victories, principally Crécy in 1346 and Poitiers in 1356, but was interrupted by the outbreak of the **Black Death** in 1349. The plague claimed about one and a half million English souls – some one third of the population – and the scarcity of labour that followed gave the peasantry more economic clout than they had ever had before. Predictably, the landowners attempted to restrict the concomitant rise in wages, but thereby provoked the widespread rioting that culminated in the **Peasants' Revolt** of 1381. The rebels marched on London under the delusion that they could appeal to the king – now **Richard II** – for fair treatment, but they soon learnt otherwise. The king did indeed meet a rebel deputation in person, but his aristocratic bodyguards took the opportunity to kill the peasants' leader, **Wat Tyler**, the prelude to the enforced dispersal of the crowds and mass slaughter.

Running parallel with this social unrest were the clerical reforms demanded by the scholar **John Wycliffe** (1320–1384), whose acolytes made the first translation of the Bible into English in 1380. Another sign of the elevation of the common language was the success enjoyed by **Geoffrey Chaucer** (c.1345–1400), a wine merchant's son, whose *Canterbury Tales* was the first major work written in the vernacular and one of the first English books to be printed.

The houses of Lancaster and York

In 1399, **Henry IV**, the first of the **Lancastrian** kings, supplanted the weak and indecisive Richard II. Henry died in 1413 to be succeeded by his son, the bellicose **Henry V**, who promptly renewed the Hundred Years War with vigour. Henry famously defeated the French at the battle of **Agincourt**, a comprehensive victory that forced the French king to acknowledge Henry as his heir in the Treaty of Troyes of 1420. However, he died just two years later and his son, **Henry VI** – or rather his regents – all too easily succumbed to a French counter-attack inspired by **Joan of Arc** (1412–1431); by 1454, only Calais was left in English hands.

It was soon obvious that **Henry VI** was mentally unstable, and consequently, as the new king drifted in and out of insanity, so two aristocratic factions attempted to squeeze control. These two factions were the Yorkists, whose emblem was the white rose, and the Lancastrians, represented by the red rose – hence the **Wars of the Roses**. At first, the Lancastrians had the better of things, but the Yorkist **Edward IV** seized the crown in 1461. Imprudently, Edward then attempted to shrug off his most powerful backer, Richard Neville, Earl of Warwick – aka "Warwick the Kingmaker" – and Warwick returned the favour by switching sides. Edward was driven into exile and Henry VI returned for a second term as king – but not for long. In 1471, Edward IV was back again, Warwick was killed and Henry was captured – and subsequently dispatched – when the Yorkists crushed the Lancastrians at the battle of Tewkesbury.

Edward IV proved to be a precursor of the great Tudor princes – licentious, cruel and despotic, but also a patron of Renaissance learning. In 1483, his 12-year-old son succeeded as **Edward V**, but his reign was cut short after only two months, when he and his younger brother were murdered in the Tower of London – probably at the behest of their uncle, the Duke of Gloucester, who was crowned **Richard III**. In 1485, Richard was famously toppled at Bosworth Field by Henry Tudor, Earl of Richmond, who took the throne as Henry VII.

The Tudors

The opening of the **Tudor** period brought radical transformations. A Lancastrian through his mother's line, **Henry VII** promptly reconciled the Yorkists by marrying Edward IV's daughter Elizabeth, thereby ending the Wars of the Roses at a stroke. It was a shrewd gambit and others followed. Henry married his daughter off to James IV of Scotland and his son to Catherine, the daughter of Ferdinand and Isabella of Spain – and by these means England began to assume the status of a major European power. There were economic stirrings too, with the burgeoning wool and cloth trades spawning an increasingly prosperous merchant class.

Henry's son, **Henry VIII** is best remembered for his separation of the English Church from Rome and his establishment of an independent Protestant church – the **Church of England**. This is not without its ironies. Henry was not a Protestant himself and such was his early orthodoxy that the pope even gave him the title "Defender of the Faith" for a pamphlet he wrote attacking Luther's treatises. In fact, the schism between Henry and the pope was triggered not by doctrinal issues but by the failure of his wife **Catherine of Aragon** – widow of his elder brother – to provide Henry with male offspring. Failing to obtain a decree of nullity from Pope Clement VII, he dismissed his long-time chancellor Thomas Wolsey and turned instead to Thomas Cromwell, who helped make the English Church recognize Henry as its head. One of the consequences was the **Dissolution of the Monasteries**, which conveniently gave both king and nobles the chance to get their hands on valuable monastic property. The Dissolution was completed in two stages in the late 1530s, though Henry was temporarily delayed by the **Pilgrimage of Grace**, a widespread rebellion that began in Louth, in Lincolnshire, and spread across the north buoyed by pro-Catholic sentiment amongst the peasantry and minor gentry.

In his later years Henry became a corpulent, syphilitic wreck, six times married but at last furnished with an heir, **Edward VI**, who was only nine years old when he ascended the throne in 1547. His short reign saw Protestantism established on a firm footing, with churches stripped of their images and Catholic services banned, yet on Edward's death most of the country readily accepted his half-sister **Mary**, daughter of Catherine of Aragon and a fervent Catholic, as queen. She returned England to the papacy and married the future Philip II of Spain, forging an alliance whose immediate consequence was war with France and the loss of Calais, the last of England's French possessions. The marriage was unpopular and so was Mary's foolish decision to begin persecuting Protestants, executing the leading lights of the English Reformation, Hugh Latimer, Nicholas Ridley and Thomas Cranmer, the archbishop of Canterbury who was largely responsible for the first **English prayer book**, published in 1549.

When she came to the throne in 1558 on the death of her half-sister, **Elizabeth I** looked very vulnerable. The country was divided by religion – Catholic against Protestant – and threatened from abroad by Philip II of Spain, the most powerful man in Europe. Famously, Elizabeth eschewed marriage and, although a Protestant herself, steered a delicate course between the two religious groupings. Her prudence rested well with the English merchant class, who were becoming the greatest power in the land, its members mostly opposed to foreign military entanglements. An exception was, however, made for the piratical activities of the great English seafarers of the day, sea captains like Walter Raleigh, Martin Frobisher, John Hawkins and Francis Drake, who made a fortune raiding Spain's American colonies. Inevitably, Philip II's irritation took a warlike turn, but the **Spanish Armada** he sent in 1588 was defeated, thereby establishing England as a major European sea power. Elizabeth's reign also saw the efflorescence of a specifically English Renaissance – **William Shakespeare** (1564–1616) is the obvious name – the only major snag being the queen's reluctant execution of her cousin and rival **Mary Queen of Scots** in 1587.

Kings and queens

House of Wessex
Egbert 802–39
Ethelwulf 839–55
Ethelbald 855–60
Ethelbert 860–66
Ethelred I 866–71
Alfred the Great 871–99
Edward the Elder 899–924
Athelstan 924–39
Edmund I 939–46
Eadred 946–55
Eadwig 955–59
Edgar 959–75
Edward the Martyr 975–78
Ethelred II (Ethelred the Unready)
   978–1016
Edmund II (Edmund Ironside) 1016

House of Skjoldung
Canute 1016–35
Harold I 1035–40
Harthacanute 1040–42

House of Wessex
Edward the Confessor 1042–66
Harold II 1066

House of Normandy
William I (William the Conqueror)
   1066–87
William II (William Rufus) 1087–1100
Henry I 1100–35
Stephen 1135–54

House of Plantagenet
Henry II 1154–89
Richard I (Richard the Lionheart)
   1189–99
John 1199–1216
Henry III 1216–72
Edward I 1272–1307
Edward II 1307–27
Edward III 1327–77
Richard II 1377–99

House of Lancaster
Henry IV 1399–1413
Henry V 1413–22
Henry VI 1422–61 & 1470

House of York
Edward IV 1461–70 & 1471–83
Edward V 1483
Richard III 1483–85

House of Tudor
Henry VII 1485–1509
Henry VIII 1509–47
Edward VI 1547–53
Mary I 1553–58
Elizabeth I 1558–1603

House of Stuart
James I 1603–25
Charles I 1625–49
Commonwealth and Protectorate
   1649–60
Charles II 1660–85
James II 1685–88
William III and Mary II 1688–94
William III 1694–1702
Anne 1702–14

House of Hanover
George I 1714–27
George II 1727–60
George III 1760–1820
George IV 1820–30
William IV 1830–37
Victoria 1837–1901

House of Saxe-Coburg
Edward VII 1901–10

House of Windsor
George V 1910–36
Edward VIII 1936
George VI 1936–52
Elizabeth II 1952–

The early Stuarts and the Commonwealth

The son of Mary Queen of Scots, James VI of Scotland, succeeded Elizabeth as **James I** of England in 1603, thereby uniting the English and Scottish crowns. James quickly moved to end hostilities with Spain and adopted a policy of toleration towards the country's Catholics. Inevitably, both initiatives offended many Protestants, whose worst fears were confirmed in 1605 when **Guy Fawkes** and a group of Catholic conspirators were discovered preparing to blow up king and Parliament in the so-called **Gunpowder Plot**. During the ensuing hue and cry, many Catholics met an untimely end and Fawkes himself was hung, drawn and quartered. Nevertheless, despite the purges, many Protestants felt the English state was irredeemably corrupt and some of the more dedicated **Puritans** fixed their eyes on establishing a "New Jerusalem" in North America following the foundation of the first permanent **colony** in Virginia in 1608. Twelve years later, the **Pilgrim Fathers** landed in New England, establishing a colony that would absorb about a hundred thousand Puritan immigrants by the middle of the century.

Meanwhile, James was busy alienating his landed gentry. He clung to an absolutist vision of the monarchy – the divine right of kings – that was totally out of step with the Protestant leanings of the majority of his subjects and he also relied heavily on court favourites, especially the much reviled George Villiers, Duke of Buckingham. It was a recipe for disaster, but it was to be his successor, **Charles I**, who reaped the whirlwind. Charles inherited James's dislike of the Protestants and liking for absolutism, ruling without Parliament from 1629 to 1640. But he over-stepped himself when he tried to impose a new Anglican prayer book on the Scots, who rose in revolt, forcing Charles to recall Parliament to raise the money for an army. This was Parliament's chance and they were not going to let it slip. The **Long Parliament**, as it became known, impeached several of Charles's allies – most notably Archbishop Laud, who was hung out to dry by the king and ultimately executed – and compiled its grievances in the Grand Remonstrance of 1641.

Facing the concerted hostility of Parliament, the king withdrew to Nottingham where he raised his standard, the opening act of the **Civil War**. The Royalist forces ("Cavaliers") were initially successful, winning the battle of Edgehill, but afterwards key regiments of the Parliamentarian army ("Roundheads") were completely overhauled by **Oliver Cromwell**. The **New Model Army** Cromwell created was something quite unique: singing psalms as they went into battle and urged on by preachers and "agitators", this was an army of believers whose ideological commitment to the parliamentary cause made it truly formidable. Cromwell's revamped army cut its teeth at the battle of Naseby and thereafter simply brushed the Royalists aside. Attempting to muddy the political waters, Charles surrendered himself to the Scots, but they finally handed him over to the English Parliament, by whom – after prolonged negotiations, endless royal shenanigans and more fighting – he was ultimately executed in January 1649.

For the next eleven years England was a **Commonwealth** – at first a true republic, then, after 1653, a **Protectorate** with Cromwell as the Lord Protector and commander in chief. Cromwell reformed the government, secured advantageous commercial treaties with foreign nations and used his New Model Army to put the fear of God into his various enemies. The turmoil of the Civil War and the pre-eminence of the army unleashed a furious legal, theological

▲ Oliver Cromwell

and political debate in every corner of the country. This milieu spawned a host of leftist sects, the most notable of whom were the **Levellers**, who demanded wholesale constitutional reform, and the more radical **Diggers**, who proposed common ownership of all land. **Nonconformist** religious groups also flourished, prominent among them the pacifist **Quakers**, led by the much persecuted George Fox (1624–91), and the **Dissenters**, to whom the most famous writers of the day, John Milton (1608–74) and John Bunyan (1628–88), both belonged.

Cromwell died in 1658 to be succeeded by his son **Richard**, who ruled briefly and ineffectually and, while the leftists squabbled among themselves and the army remained unpaid for month after month, more conservative Protestants, led by General Monk, rallied to restore the monarchy. Charles II, the exiled son of the previous king, entered London in triumph in May 1660.

The Restoration and the later Stuarts

A Stuart was back on the English throne, but **Charles II** had few absolutist illusions – the terms of the **Restoration** were closely negotiated and included a general amnesty for all those who had fought against the Stuarts, with the exception of the regicides: those who had signed Charles I's death warrant. Nonetheless, there was a sea-change in public life with the re-establishment of a royal court, a new exuberance in art, literature and theatre, and the foundation of the **Royal Society**, whose scientific endeavours were furthered by Isaac Newton (1642–1727). The low points of Charles's reign were the **Great Plague** of 1665 and the 1666 **Great Fire of London**, though the London that rose from the ashes was an architectural showcase for Christopher Wren (1632–1723) and his fellow classicists. Politically, there were still underlying tensions between the monarchy and Parliament, but the latter was more concerned with the struggle between the **Whigs** and **Tories**, political factions representing, respectively, the low-church gentry and the high-church aristocracy. There was a degree of religious toleration too, but its brittleness was all too apparent in the anti-Catholic riots of 1678.

James II, the brother of Charles II, came to the throne in 1685. He was a Catholic, which made the bulk of his subjects uneasy, but there was still an indifferent response when the Protestant **Duke of Monmouth**, the favourite among Charles II's illegitimate sons, raised a rebellion in the West Country. Monmouth was defeated at Sedgemoor, in Somerset, in July 1685, and was beheaded for his pains; his followers received summary treatment at the hands of the notorious Judge Jeffreys in the aptly named **Bloody Assizes**. However, if James felt secure he was mistaken. A foolish man, James showed all the traditional weaknesses of his family, from his enthusiasm for the divine right of kings to an over-reliance on sycophantic favourites. Even worse, as far as the Protestants were concerned, he built up a massive standing army, officered it with Roman Catholics and proposed a **Declaration of Indulgence**, removing anti-Catholic restrictions. When James's queen gave him a son, securing a Catholic succession, the most powerful Protestants in the land begged **William of Orange**, the Dutch husband of Mary, the Protestant daughter of James II, to save them from Catholic tyranny – and that was precisely what he did. William landed in Devon and, as James's forces simply melted away, he speedily took control of London in the **Glorious Revolution** of 1688. This was the final postscript to the Civil War – although it was a couple of years before James and his Jacobite army was finally defeated in Ireland at the **Battle of the Boyne**.

William and Mary were made joint sovereigns after they agreed a **Bill of Rights** defining the limitations of the monarchy's power and the rights of its subjects. This, together with the **Act of Settlement of 1701** – among other things, barring Catholics or anyone married to one from succession to the English throne – made Britain a **constitutional monarchy**, in which the roles of legislature and executive were separate and interdependent. The model was broadly consistent with that outlined by the philosopher and political thinker John Locke (1632–1704), whose essentially Whig doctrines of toleration and social contract were gradually embraced as the new orthodoxy.

Ruling alone after Mary's death in 1694, William regarded England as a prop in his defence of Holland against France, a stance that defined England's political alignment in Europe for the next sixty years. In the reign of **Anne**, second daughter of James II, English armies won a string of remarkable victories on the continent, beginning with the Duke of Marlborough's triumph at Blenheim in 1704, followed the next year by the capture of Gibraltar, establishing a British presence in the Mediterranean once and for all. These military escapades were part of the Europe-wide **War of the Spanish Succession**, which rumbled on until the Treaty of Utrecht in 1713 – a treaty which all but settled the European balance of power for the rest of the eighteenth century. Otherwise Anne's reign was distinguished mainly for the 1707 **Act of Union**, uniting the English and Scottish parliaments.

With none of her children surviving into adulthood, Anne was the last of the Stuarts and, when she died in 1714, the succession passed – in accordance with the terms of the Act of Settlement – to the Duke of Hanover, a non-English-speaking, Protestant German who became **George I** of England.

The Hanoverians

As power leaked away from the monarchy into the hands of the Whig oligarchy, the king ceased to attend Cabinet meetings, his place being taken by his chief minister. Most prominent of these ministers was **Robert Walpole** (1676–1745), regarded as England's **first prime minister**. To all intents and purposes, Walpole governed from 1721 to 1742, a tranquil period politically, with the country standing aloof from foreign affrays. The financial world, however, was prey to a mania for speculation and subjected to numerous fraudulent or at least ill-conceived financial ventures. The most dramatic was the fiasco of the South Sea Company, which in 1720 sold shares in its monopoly of trade in the Pacific and along the east coast of South America. The "**bubble**" burst when the shareholders took fright at the extent of their own investments and the value of the shares dropped through the floor, reducing many to penury and almost bringing down Walpole and his government.

Peace ended in the reign of **George II**, when England declared war on Spain in 1739 at the start of yet another dynastic squabble, the eight-year War of the Austrian Succession. Then, in 1745, the **Young Pretender**, **Charles Stuart** invaded England and Scotland in the second and most dangerous of the Jacobite rebellions (the first had failed dismally in 1715). So-called Bonnie Prince Charlie and his Highland army managed to reach Derby, just 120 miles from London, creating pandemonium in the capital, but their lines of supply were over-extended and they were obliged to retreat north. It all ended in Jacobite tears, when a Hanoverian army under the brutal Duke of Cumberland caught up with them and hacked them to pieces at Culloden, in Scotland. Otherwise, the **Seven Years War** harvested England further overseas territory in India and Canada at the expense of France and, in 1768, **Captain James Cook** sailed to New Zealand and Australia, thereby netting another chunk of the globe.

In 1760, **George III** succeeded his father. The early years of his sixty-year reign saw a revived struggle between king and Parliament, enlivened by the intervention of John Wilkes, first of a long and increasingly vociferous line of parliamentary radicals. The contest was exacerbated by the deteriorating relationship with the thirteen colonies of North America, a situation brought to a head by the **American Declaration of Independence** and Britain's subsequent defeat in the Revolutionary War. Chastened by this disaster, Britain chose not to interfere in the momentous events taking place across the Channel, where France, long its most consistent foe, was convulsed by revolution. Out of the turmoil emerged the most daunting of enemies, **Napoleon** (1769–1821), whose stunning military progress was interrupted by Nelson at **Trafalgar** in 1805 and finally stopped ten years later by the Duke of Wellington at **Waterloo**.

The Industrial Revolution

England's triumph over Napoleon was underpinned by its financial strength, which was itself born of the **Industrial Revolution**, the switch from an agricultural to a manufacturing economy that completely changed the face of the country in the space of a hundred years. The earliest mechanized production lines were in the Lancashire **cotton mills**, where cotton-spinning was transformed from a cottage industry into a highly productive factory-based system. Initially, river water powered the mills, but the technology changed after James Watt patented his **steam engine** in 1781. Watt's engines needed **coal**, which made it convenient to locate mills and factories near coal mines, a tendency that was accelerated as **ironworks** took up coal as a smelting fuel, vastly increasing the output from their furnaces. Accordingly, there was a shift of population towards the Midlands and north of England, where the great coal reserves were located, and as the industrial economy boomed and diversified, so these regions' towns mushroomed at an extraordinary rate. There were steel towns like Sheffield, huge cotton warehouses in Manchester, pottery in Stoke-on-Trent and vast dock facilities in Liverpool, where raw materials from India and the Americas came in and manufactured goods went out. Commerce and industry were also served by improving transport facilities, such as the building of a network of **canals** in the wake of the success of the Bridgewater Canal in 1765, which linked the Worsley coal mines with Manchester and the River Mersey. But the great leap forward came with the arrival of the **railway**, heralded by the Stockton–Darlington line in 1825 and followed five years later by the Liverpool–Manchester railway, as travelled by George Stephenson's *Rocket*.

Boosted by a vast influx of Jewish, Irish, French and Dutch workers, the country's population rose from about seven and a half million at the beginning of George III's reign to more than fourteen million by its end. As the factories and their attendant towns expanded, so the rural settlements of England declined, inspiring the elegiac pastoral yearnings of Samuel Taylor Coleridge and William Wordsworth, the first great names of the **Romantic movement**. Later Romantic poets such as Percy Bysshe Shelley and Lord Byron took a more socially engaged position, but much more dangerous to the ruling class were the nation's factory workers, who grew restless when machines put thousands of them out of work. The discontent coalesced in the **Chartists**, a broadly based popular movement that demanded parliamentary reform – the most important of the industrial boom towns were still unrepresented in Parliament – and the repeal of the hated **Corn Laws**, which kept the price of bread artificially high to the advantage of the large landowners. In 1819, there was a mass demonstration in Manchester, but the protestors were cut down by troops in what became known as the **Peterloo Massacre**.

The following year, a weak, blind and insane George III finally died to be succeeded, in fairly rapid succession, by two of his sons, **George IV** and then **William IV**. Tensions continued to run high throughout the 1820s, and in retrospect it seems that the country may have been saved from a French-style revolution by a series of judicious parliamentary acts: the **Reform Act** of 1832 established the principle (if not actually the practice) of popular representation; the **Poor Law** of 1834 did something to alleviate the condition of the most destitute; and the repeal of the Corn Laws in 1846 cut the cost of bread. Furthermore, there was such a furore after five Dorset labourers – the **Tolpuddle Martyrs** – were transported to Australia in 1834 for joining an agricultural trade union, that the judiciary decided it was prudent to overturn the judgement six years later. Significant sections of the middle classes were just as eager to see progressive reform as the working classes, as evidenced by the immense popularity of **Charles Dickens** (1812–70), whose novels railed against poverty and injustice. Dickens's social concerns had been anticipated in the previous century by John Wesley (1703–91) and his Methodists, who – along with other Nonconformist Christians – led the anti-slavery campaign. As a result of their efforts, **slavery** was banned throughout the British Empire in 1833 – long after the seaports of Bristol and Liverpool had grown rich on the backs of the trade.

Victorian England

In 1837, William IV was succeeded by his niece, **Victoria**, whose long reign witnessed the zenith of British power. For much of the period, the economy boomed – typically the nation's cloth manufacturers boasted that they supplied the domestic market before breakfast, the rest of the world thereafter. The British trading fleet was easily the mightiest in the world and it underpinned an empire upon which, in that famous phrase of the time, "the sun never set", with Victoria herself becoming the symbol of both the nation's success and the imperial ideal. There were extraordinary intellectual achievements too – as typified by the publication of Charles Darwin's *On the Origin of Species* in 1859 – and the country came to see itself as both a civilizing agent and, on occasion, the hand of (a very Protestant) God on earth. Britain's industrial and commercial prowess was best embodied by the great engineering feats of Isambard Kingdom Brunel (1806–1859) and by the **Great Exhibition** of 1851, a display of manufacturing achievements without compare.

With trade at the forefront of the agenda, much of the political debate crystallized into a conflict between the **Free Traders** – led by the Whigs, who formed the Liberal Party – and the **Protectionists** under Bentinck and **Disraeli**, guiding light of the Conservatives, descended from the Tories. Parliament itself was long dominated by the duel between Disraeli and the Liberal leader **Gladstone**, the pre-eminent statesmen of the day. It was Disraeli who eventually passed the Second Reform Bill in 1867, further extending the electoral franchise, but it was Gladstone's first ministry of 1868–74 that ratified some of the century's most far-reaching legislation, including compulsory education, the full legalization of trade unions and an Irish Land Act.

There were foreign entanglements, too. In 1854 troops were sent to protect the Ottoman empire against the Russians in the **Crimea**, an inglorious debacle whose horrors were relayed to the public by the first ever press coverage of a military campaign and by the revelations of Florence Nightingale (1820–1910), who was appalled by the lack of medical care for wounded and sick soldiers. The **Indian Mutiny** of 1857 was a further shock to the imperial system, exposing the fragility of Britain's hold on the Asian subcontinent, but the status quo was eventually restored and Victoria took the title Empress of India after 1876. Thereafter, the British army was flattered by a series of minor wars against poorly armed Asian and African opponents, but promptly came unstuck when it faced the Dutch settlers of South Africa in the **Boer War** (1899–1902). The British ultimately fought their way to a sort of victory, but the discreditable conduct of the war prompted a military shake-up at home that was to be of significance in the coming European war.

From World War I to World War II

Victoria died in 1901, to be succeeded by her son, **Edward VII**, whose leisurely lifestyle has sometimes been seen as the epitome of the complacent era to which he gave his name. This complacency came to an abrupt end on August 4, 1914, when the Liberal government, honouring the Entente Cordiale signed with France in 1904, declared war on Germany. Hundreds of thousands volunteered for the British army, but their enthusiastic nationalism was not enough to ensure a quick victory and **World War I** dragged on for four miserable years, its key engagements fought in the trenches that zigzagged across northern France and west Belgium. Britain and her allies eventually prevailed, but the number of dead beggared belief, undermining the authority of the British ruling class, whose generals had shown a particularly lethal combination of incompetence and indifference to the plight of their men. Many looked admiringly at the Soviet Union, where the workers had rid themselves of the Tsar and seized control in 1917.

At the war's end in 1918 the political fabric of England was changed dramatically when the sheer weight of public opinion pushed Parliament into extending the **vote** to all men over 21 and to women over 30. This tardy liberalization of women's rights owed much to the efforts of the radical **Suffragettes**, led by Emmeline Pankhurst and her daughters Sylvia and Christabel, but the process was only completed in 1929 when women were at last granted the vote at 21, on equal terms with men.

During this period, the **Labour Party** supplanted the Liberals as the main force on the left wing of British politics, its strength built on an alliance between the working-class trade unions and middle-class radicals. Labour formed its first government in 1923 under Ramsay MacDonald (1866–1937), but the publication of the **Zinoviev Letter**, a forged document that purported to be a letter from the Soviets urging British leftists to promote revolution, undermined MacDonald's position and the Conservatives were returned with a large parliamentary majority in 1924. Two years later, in a time of acute economic difficulty, a bitter dispute between the nation's colliers and the owners of the coal mines spread to the railways, the newspapers and the iron and steel industries, escalating into a **General Strike**. The strike lasted nine days and involved half a million workers, provoking the government into draconian action – the army was called in, and the strike was broken. The economic situation deteriorated even further after the crash of the New York Stock Exchange in 1929, which precipitated a worldwide depression. Unemployment reached over 2.8 million in 1931, generating a series of mass demonstrations, which peaked with the **Jarrow March** from the northeast to London in 1936. The same year, economist John Maynard Keynes argued in his *General Theory of Employment, Interest and Money* for a greater degree of state intervention in the management of the economy, though the whole question was soon overshadowed by international events.

Abroad, the structure of the **British Empire** had undergone profound changes since World War I. The status of **Ireland** had been partly resolved following the electoral gains of the nationalist Sinn Fein in 1918. Their success led to the establishment of the Irish Free State in 1922, though (and this was to cause endless problems thereafter) the six counties of the mainly Protestant North (Ulster) chose to "contract out" and stay part of the United Kingdom. Four years later, the **Imperial Conference** recognized the autonomy of the British dominions, comprising all the major countries that had previously been part of the Empire. This agreement was formalized in the 1931 Statute of Westminster, whereby each dominion was given an equal footing in a Commonwealth of Nations, though each still recognized the British monarch. The royal family itself was shaken in 1936 by the **abdication of Edward VIII**, following his decision to marry a twice-divorced American, Wallis Simpson. In the event, the succession passed smoothly to his brother **George VI**, but the royals had to play catch-up to regain their popularity among the population as a whole.

Non-intervention in both the Spanish Civil War and the Sino–Japanese War was paralleled by a policy of appeasement towards **Adolf Hitler**, who began to rearm Germany in earnest in the mid-1930s. This policy was epitomized by the antics of Prime Minister Neville Chamberlain, who returned from meeting Hitler at Munich in 1938 with an assurance of good intentions that he took at face value. Consequently, when **World War II** broke out in September 1939, Britain was seriously unprepared. In May 1940 the discredited Chamberlain stepped down in favour of a national coalition government headed by the charismatic **Winston Churchill** (1874–1965), whose bulldog persistence and heroic speeches provided the inspiration needed in the backs-against-the-wall mood of the time. Partly through Churchill's manoeuvrings, the United States became a supplier of foodstuffs and munitions to Britain and this, combined with the US breaking trade links with Japan in June (in protest at their attacks on China), may have helped precipitate the Japanese bombing of Pearl Harbor on December 7, 1941. Once attacked, the US immediately joined the war, declaring against both Japan and Germany, and its intervention, combined with the heroic efforts of the Soviet Red Army, swung the military balance. In terms of the number of casualties, World War II was not as calamitous as World War I, but its impact upon the civilian population of Britain was much greater. In its first wave of **bombing** on the UK, the Luftwaffe caused massive damage to industrial and supply centres such as London, Coventry, Manchester, Liverpool, Southampton and Plymouth. In later raids, intended to shatter morale rather than factories and docks, the cathedral cities of Canterbury, Exeter, Bath, Norwich and York all took a battering too. At the end of the fighting, nearly one in three of all the houses in the nation had been destroyed or damaged, nearly a quarter of a million members of the British armed forces and over 58,000 civilians had lost their lives.

Postwar England

The end of the war in 1945 was quickly followed by a general election. Hungry for change (and demobilization), the electorate replaced Churchill with a Labour government under **Clement Attlee** (1883–1967), who, with a large parliamentary majority, set about a radical programme to **nationalize** the coal, gas, electricity, iron and steel industries, as well as the inland transport services. Building on the plans for a social security system presented in Sir William Beveridge's report of 1943, the **National Insurance Act** and the **National Health Service Act** were both passed early in the Labour administration, giving birth to what became known as the **welfare state**. But despite substantial American aid, the huge problems of rebuilding the economy made austerity the keynote, with the rationing of food and fuel remaining in force long after 1945. This cost the Labour Party dear in the general election of 1951, which returned the Conservatives to power with a modest majority under the leadership of an ageing Churchill.

Meanwhile, in April 1949, Britain, the United States, Canada, France and the Benelux countries signed the **North Atlantic Treaty** as a counterbalance to Soviet power in Eastern Europe, thereby defining the country's postwar international commitments. Yet confusion regarding Britain's post-imperial role was shown up by the **Suez Crisis** of 1956, when Anglo-French and Israeli forces invaded Egypt to secure control of the Suez Canal, only to be hastily recalled following international (American) condemnation. Revealing severe limitations on the country's capacity for independent action, the Suez incident resulted in the resignation of Churchill's successor as Conservative prime minister, Anthony Eden, who was now replaced by the more pragmatic **Harold Macmillan** (1894–1986). Nonetheless, Macmillan maintained a nuclear policy that suggested a continued desire for an international role, and nuclear testing went on against a background of widespread marches under the auspices of the Campaign for Nuclear Disarmament.

The 1960s, dominated by the Labour premiership of **Harold Wilson** (1916–1995), saw a boom in consumer spending, some pioneering social legislation (primarily on the legalization of homosexuality and abortion), and a corresponding cultural upswing, with London becoming the hippest city on the planet. The good times lasted barely a decade. Though Tory prime minister Edward Heath led Britain into the brave new world of the **European Economic Community** (EEC), the 1970s were a decade of recession and industrial strife. A succession of public-sector strikes and mis-timed decisions by James Callaghan's Labour government handed the 1979 general election to the Conservatives and **Margaret Thatcher** (b.1925), who four years earlier had ousted Heath to become the first woman to lead a major political party in Britain.

The 1980s and 1990s

Thatcher went on to win three general elections, but pushed the UK into a period of sharp social polarization. While taxation policies and easy credit fuelled a consumer boom for the professional classes, the erosion of manufacturing industry and the weakening of the welfare state impoverished a great swathe of the population. Thatcher won an increased majority in the 1983 election, largely thanks to the successful recapture of the **Falkland Islands**, a remote British dependency in the south Atlantic, retrieved from the occupying Argentine army in 1982. Her electoral domination was also assisted by the fragmentation of the Labour opposition, particularly following the establishment of the short-lived Social Democratic Party, which had split in panic at what it perceived as the radicalization of the Labour Party.

Social and political tensions surfaced in sporadic urban rioting and the year-long **miners' strike** (1984–85) against colliery closures, a bitter industrial dispute in which the police were given unprecedented powers to restrict the movement of citizens, while the media perpetrated some immensely misleading coverage of events. The violence in Northern Ireland also intensified, and in 1984 the bombing campaign of the IRA came close to killing the entire Cabinet when they blew up the Brighton hotel where the Conservatives were staying during their annual conference.

The divisive politics of Thatcherism reached their apogee with the introduction of the **Poll Tax**, a desperately unpopular tax scheme that led ultimately to Thatcher's overthrow by Conservative colleagues who feared annihilation should she lead them into another general election. The beneficiary was **John Major** (b.1943), a notably uninspiring figure who nonetheless managed to win the Conservatives a fourth term of office in 1992, albeit with a much reduced Parliamentary majority. While his government presided over a steady growth in economic performance, they gained little credit amid allegations of mismanagement, incompetence and feckless leadership, and were also engulfed by endless tales of Tory "sleaze", with revelations of extramarital affairs, cover-ups and financial deceit gleefully blazed by the British press. The Conservatives were also ideologically split over Europe: one part of the party was pro the European Union (formerly the EEC), the other – a vocal right-wing group of **Eurosceptics** – insisted Britain should keep a safe distance from the EU in general and the proposed common currency – the euro – in particular.

Also in trouble by the mid-1990s was the **Royal Family**, whose credibility fissured with the break-up of the marriage of Prince Charles and Diana. Revelations about the cruel treatment of Diana by both the prince and his family badly damaged the royals' reputation and suddenly the institution itself seemed an anachronism, its members stiff, old-fashioned and dim-witted. By contrast, **Diana**, who was formally divorced from Charles in 1994, appeared warm-hearted and glamorous, so much so that her death in a car accident in Paris in 1997 may actually have saved the royal family as an institution. In the short term, Diana's death had a profound impact on the British, who joined in a media-orchestrated exercise in public grieving unprecedented in modern times.

Meanwhile, the **Labour Party**, which had been wracked by factionalism in the 1980s, regrouped under Neil Kinnock and then John Smith, but the two never reaped the political rewards. These dropped into the lap of a new and dynamic young leader, **Tony Blair** (b.1953), who soon began to push the party further and further away from traditional left-wing socialism. Blair's mantle of idealistic, media-friendly populism worked to devastating effect, sweeping the Labour Party to power in the **general election of May 1997** on a wave of genuine popular optimism. There were immediate rewards in enhanced relations with Europe and progress in the Irish peace talks, and Blair's electoral touch was soon repeated in Labour-sponsored **devolution referenda**, whose results semi-detached Scotland and Wales from their larger neighbour. There was also much Labourite tub-thumping about the need to improve **public services**, but Blair only set about the task in earnest during his second term in office.

The 2000s

Labour won the **general election of June 2001** with another parliamentary landslide. This second victory was, however, little of the optimism of before and voter turnout was lower than any time since World War II. Few voters fully trusted Blair and his administration had an unenviable reputation for laundering of events to present the government in the best possible light. As a result, although there was a massive and much-needed investment in public services, with education and health being the prime beneficiaries, and a concerted attempt to lift (many of) the country's poorer citizens out of poverty, these achievements did not secure the recognition they deserved. Nonetheless, the ailing Conservative Party failed to capitalize on the situation, leaving Blair streets ahead of his political rivals in the opinion polls when the hijacked planes hit New York's World Trade Center on **September 11, 2001**. Blair rushed to support President Bush, joining in the attack on Afghanistan and then, to the horror of millions of Brits, sending British forces into **Iraq** alongside the Americans in 2003. Saddam Hussein was deposed with relative ease, but neither Bush nor Blair seemed to have a coherent exit strategy, and back home Blair was widely seen as having spun Britain into the war by exaggerating the danger Saddam presented with his supposed **WMDs** (Weapons of Mass Destruction). No WMDs were ever found and for a moment Blair looked acutely vulnerable, but his political opponents – both within the party and without – failed to deliver the coup de grace and Blair soon recovered his power and poise. In the event Blair won a **third general election in May, 2005**, though not before he had promised to step down before the next general election thereafter – by any standard, a rather odd way to secure victory. After the election, Blair teased and tormented his many political enemies with promises of his imminent departure, but finally, in June 2007, he did indeed move on, and was succeeded uncontested by his arch-rival, **Gordon Brown**.

Brown has made a hesitant start as leader of the country and seems to have little of the sure-footed nous of the early Blair. Whether or not the other political parties – primarily the Conservatives and Liberal Democrats – can make up the necessary electoral ground to unseat the Labour Party in the **next general election** is, however, a moot point. At Blair's behest, New Labour's great skill was to occupy the centre of British politics with such consummate ease that its opponents have been obliged to compete in the same narrow political space with precious little to separate any and all of them: this is hardly scheduled to fire up the British electorate, and whoever wins next time will almost certainly be on a lower poll than for a century.

England today

England is a querulous, quarrelsome country – it always has been – but the arguments change and move on at a rattling pace. The focus of much of the debate today is to do with external threat, principally **immigration**, both legal and illegal, as well as **Islamic terrorism** – the first fuelled by an influx of eastern Europeans following the widening of the European Union, the second by the war in Iraq and the London bombings of 2005. There are perceived internal threats too, principally **street crime** and **political corruption**, and just about everything is served up with liberal dollops of celebrity chit-chat. The mass newspapers – the tabloids – usually set the populist agenda, stirring up irrational fears in their search for sales, but more considered voices follow in their slipstream, stretching the debate into agonized (sometimes agonizing) discussions on everything from the breakdown of the family unit to the corrosive banalities of **reality TV**, which has taken the English by storm.

Running alongside has been a long debate about the nature of "**Englishness**". The immediate prompt was political: in 1999, the UK Parliament devolved many of its powers to a Scottish Parliament and a Welsh Assembly, a reconfiguration that seemed to some to herald the break-up of the United Kingdom. It may yet, but ever since a fair chunk of England's cultural elite have been rambling on about Englishness, musings that have rolled into a larger debate about **multiculturalism** – and whether England should be a "melting pot" of peoples, along the lines of the American model, or a divergent "fruit cake", with individual cultures retaining a strong sense of separate identity. The political right – in both the ruling Labour Party and the Conservative opposition – has been energized by this sprawling discussion, but, much to their credit, the English as a whole have proved largely indifferent. Indeed, attempts to instil a sense of local or regional identity through political tinkering ended in high farce in 2002 when, in one of the earliest elections to the newly upgraded post of town mayor, the good citizens of Hartlepool voted into office the monkey mascot of their football team under the slogan "Free bananas for schoolchildren".

In truth, the most damaging change in England in the last decade has nothing to do with identity, but more to do with money. In the UK, the top ten percent of adult earners now take home forty percent of all the income earned and the top one percent – just 470,000 people – earn an average of £222,000 per year. Even worse, the **gap between the rich and the poor** is accelerating and neither is there any concerted opposition to it: spasmodic protests about the obscenely huge wages paid to footballers and TV presenters have, for example, just been brushed aside or ignored. Put simply, this is the triumph of greed, a crass **consumerism** that was promulgated by Margaret Thatcher and her Conservative government in the 1980s and adopted willingly by her successors in the Labour Party. As never before, the English have become obedient consumers rather than active citizens, with brand loyalty the nearest thing to religious/spiritual belief. In the flight to consumption, many of those organizations that have long glued the English together – trade unions, churches, political parties – have declined steeply in membership, whilst the paroxysms of protest that marked the 1980s – the Miners' Strike, Greenham Common – have, with the notable exception of the mass march against the war in Iraq in 2003, simply melted away.

Of course, not all the English have bent to the prevailing wind and the country's multitude of special interest groups – from pigeon fanciers to anglers and ramblers – continue to flourish, but these are perturbing times and many English people do indeed feel perturbed. The English may have more material goods than they ever have had before, but they also swallow antidepressants by the bucket-load. Perhaps it would help if they gave themselves enough credit for their achievements: the xenophobic country of yesteryear has become probably the least racist country in Europe and, with homophobia in retreat, same-sex civil partnerships were legalized in the UK in 2004. It's hard to see where the country will go next, but wherever it is there will always be a chorus of self-mockery. "Make Tea, not War" should become the national motto.

Architecture

I f England sometimes seems like a historic theme park, jam-packed with **monuments** and **buildings** recalling a fascinating past, then it's because physical evidence of its long history is so easily accessible. Despite the best efforts of Victorian modernizers, the Luftwaffe and twentieth-century town planners, every corner of the country has some landmark worthy of attention, whether it be a Neolithic burial site or a postmodern addition to a world-famous gallery.

Prehistoric England

The oldest traces of building in England date from the **fourth millennium BC**, when **Neolithic** peoples, who practised rudimentary agriculture, succeeded the earlier hunter-gatherers, who had inhabited cave-dwellings and hide-covered camps. The remains of round stone huts have been excavated on Carn Brea, outside Redruth in Cornwall, but the major surviving habitations are entrenched sites found throughout southern England. These consist of concentric rings of ditches and banks, the largest being at Windmill Hill in Wiltshire. Neolithic peoples were also responsible for the numerous **long barrows** (burial mounds) that lie dotted all over England. These featureless, pear-shaped hummocks of earth are concentrated along the southern chalk downs from Sussex to Dorset, with others sprinkled around Lincolnshire, Yorkshire and the Cotswolds, where the barrows are noteworthy for holding stone chambers for collective family burials.

One of the largest and most elaborate Neolithic burial sites is **Woodhenge**, on Salisbury Plain, comprising a network of banks and ditches enclosing no fewer than six concentric ovals of wooden posts, arranged along the axis of the midsummer sunrise. Woodhenge is also near the most famous of all English prehistoric monuments, **Stonehenge**, a remarkable megalithic stone circle started around 3000 BC and subsequently added to over the next thousand years by the early Bronze Age Beaker People. Stonehenge probably had an astronomical and sacred significance, as did **Avebury**, on the other side of Salisbury Plain, which is even more extensive than Stonehenge, though is neither so large nor so well preserved. The size and complexity of both imply a highly organized communal effort, though they were undoubtedly embellished over the centuries – in much the same way as medieval cathedrals. Less grandiose **stone circles and rows** survive up and down the country, from Castlerigg, near Keswick in the Lake District, to the Hurlers of Cornwall's Bodmin Moor. **Hut circles** on the moors of the West Country bear testimony to the presence of later Bronze Age peoples; Grimspound, on Dartmoor, is one of the best examples – dating from around 1200 BC, its round stone houses with beehive roofs are ringed by a protective wall.

The Celtic and Roman periods

Around 700 BC, **Celtic** invaders brought the Iron Age to the British Isles. Their chief contribution to the English landscape was a series of **hilltop forts** and other defensive works, often adapted from earlier constructions. At their simplest, these strongholds consisted of a circular earthwork within which the inhabitants dwelt in timber-built round huts – a good example is Castle Dore, near Fowey in Cornwall. At **Maiden Castle** in Dorset, however, a whole town was enclosed within a multiple system of ramparts, a formidable enlargement of a much older hill-fort of modest proportions. The best preserved of all Iron Age villages, however, is the stronghold of **Chysauster**, near Zennor in Cornwall, consisting of stone houses arranged in pairs, each with a courtyard and garden plot. The settlement was inhabited until well into the Roman era, preserved thanks to its distance from the most westerly Roman outpost.

The **Romans** imposed order and peace, the prerequisites for the construction of those **public buildings** that appeared in every part of the empire. There were several types, including amphitheatres, like the one in Chester, theatres as in York, and baths, the most famous of which were at Bath. No Roman temples remain standing, but Colchester and St Albans have revealed impressive remains, as befits two of Roman Britain's principal towns. Other important settlements – such as London, Gloucester, Leicester and Lincoln – were all planned according to the classic chessboard pattern favoured by the Romans, but have yielded little, the Roman remains obliterated by later occupants. In general terms, the architecture of Roman Britain was, as one might anticipate, thoroughly provincial – and not a patch on that of Rome – but none the less it certainly proclaimed imperial power and wealth. A prime example is the palace at **Fishbourne** in West Sussex, built around 75 AD, probably for a Romanized British chieftain. Fishbourne's columned entrance prefaces an interior whose decorative details were as carefully elaborated as the ground plan, with lavish use of mosaics, a feature also exemplified by private houses excavated at St Albans and Cirencester. Most of the great Roman villas reached their peak of comfort and artistic excellence during the first half of the fourth century, when even relatively modest farmhouses were equipped with heating systems.

Anglo-Saxon England

The **Anglo-Saxons** who followed the Romans had little interest in their predecessors' architectural achievements and certainly didn't try to emulate them. Initially, the newcomers stuck to mud, wattle and thatch before moving on to **timber**, a specialization in which the English were to excel throughout the Middle Ages, though the perishability of timber has meant that little remains from this period. What fragments have survived were the product of the new Christian ideology, expressed in **stone-built churches** that were the chief medium of architectural innovation until the Reformation. But even stone churches were vulnerable to the Vikings and those that did survive were subject to constant modifications and accretions. Such was the case with two of the earliest English churches, both in **Canterbury** – St Peter and St Paul, dating from 597, and the town's first cathedral, erected about five years later. In general terms, Anglo-Saxon churches were modelled on churches in Rome, with round apses at the eastern end, unlike the square ends that are evident in some churches showing Celtic inspiration – remnants of the earlier partial Christianization of Britain under the Romans, for the most part eradicated by the incoming Saxons – or in the seventh-century Christian revival churches of **Northumbria**. In the latter case, the ascetic Celtic tradition of the Scottish and Irish monks who led the movement did not encourage refined architecture, and the three churches built by Benedict Biscop in County Durham – Monkwearmouth, Escomb and the Venerable Bede's own church at Jarrow – are small and roughly built. The most impressive of all Saxon churches, however, lies in the Midlands, at **Brixworth** in Northamptonshire, erected around 670, and distinguished by the systematic use of arches.

In the eighth and ninth centuries, the Vikings despoiled the richest of the country's churches and pretty much put a stop to new construction work. However, a revival came with the installation of Dunstan as bishop of Glastonbury around 940, which led to the foundation of monasteries all over the country. Much of the work was undertaken by churchmen who had spent time in the great European monasteries. Yet, far from showing the influence of continental styles, the sparse remains demonstrate instead a penchant for quirky decoration, visible today in the spiral columns in the crypt at St Wystan's Church in Repton, Derbyshire.

Norman architecture

England's architectural insularity faded away in the early eleventh century. Continental influences wafted across the Channel and when Edward the Confessor rebuilt **Westminster Abbey** (1050–65) he followed the Norman – or Romanesque – style in imitation of the great French abbey churches of Caen and Jumièges. French architectural styles became the dominant influence under the Normans, who seized control of the country under William the Conqueror in 1066. To subdue his new subjects, William built dozens of castles. The earliest types followed a "motte and bailey" design, consisting of a central tower (or keep) placed on a mound (the motte), and encircled by one or more courts (the baileys). Most such castles were built of wood until the time of Henry II, though some were stone-constructed from the beginning, including those at **Rochester** and **Colchester** and the **White Tower** at the **Tower of London**, the most formidable of all the Norman strongholds. **Dover Castle** (1168–85), built by the Plantagenet Henry II, introduced the refinement of a double row of outer walls with towers at intervals, a design probably influenced by the fortresses encountered by Crusaders in the Holy Land.

Once the country had been secured, the Normans set about transforming the English Church, filling its key positions with imported clergy, all of whom proved keen to introduce the lofty architectural conceptions then current in mainland Europe. Many of the major churches of the country – for example at **Canterbury**, **York**, **St Albans**, **Winchester**, **Worcester** and **Ely** – were rebuilt along Romanesque lines, with cruciform ground plans and massive cylindrical columns topped by semicircular arches. The finest Norman church was **Durham Cathedral**, begun in 1093 and boasting Europe's first example of large-scale ribbed vaulting. Also incorporated were spectacular zigzag and diamond patterns on its colossal piers, a strong and immediately influential contrast to the austerity of the first generation of Norman churches. Furthermore, an increasing love of decoration was evident in the elaborately carved capitals and blind arcading in Canterbury Cathedral and the beakhead moulding in Lincoln Cathedral. Neither were the Normans idle when it came to the country's parish churches, though the newly intricate ornamental features on dozens of these often owe more to the creative vigour of the Anglo-Saxon masons than they do to the influence of the Normans.

Incidentally, it's characteristic of the English Church that **bishoprics** were often given to the heads of monastic houses. Thus, many English cathedrals were also monastic churches, which explains the prevalence of **cloisters**, **chapter houses** and other monastic structures within the precincts of English cathedrals.

The Transitional and Early English Styles

In common with the rest of Europe, the twelfth century brought a dramatic increase in the wealth and power of England's **monastic houses**, a process which had begun with the Benedictines before the Conquest. The **Cistercians** were responsible for some of the most splendid foundations, establishing an especially grand group of self-sufficient monasteries in Yorkshire – **Fountains**, **Rievaulx** and **Jervaulx**. These all featured examples of the pointed arch, an idea imported from northern France, where it may have been introduced by Crusaders returning from the Middle East. The reforming Cistercians favoured a plain style, but the native penchant for decoration gradually infiltrated their buildings – for instance at Kirkstall Abbey (c.1152), near Leeds – while other orders had a preference for greater elaboration from the very beginning. Amongst the latter was the **Cluniac** order, whose extravagantly ornate west front of Norfolk's Castle Acre priory (1140–50) is typical.

Profuse carved decoration and pointed arches were distinctive elements in the evolution of a **Transitional style**, which, from the middle of the twelfth century, represented a shift away from purely Romanesque forms. The pointed arch permitted a far greater flexibility in the relation of the height of a building to its span than the round arch. It also allowed the introduction of highly scientific systems of vaulting and buttressing, which in turn led to a significant increase of window area in the walls between the buttresses, since these walls no longer had to carry the main weight of the roof. Improvements in masonry techniques also meant that walls could be reduced in thickness, and the cylindrical columns of the Normans replaced by more slender piers.

In England, the first phase of **Gothic** architecture began in earnest in the last quarter of the twelfth century, when Gothic motifs were used at Roche Abbey and **Byland**, both in Yorkshire. However, it was the French-designed **choir** at **Canterbury Cathedral**, built in 1175–84, which really established the new style, though admittedly the Gothic themes were somewhat compromised here by being grafted onto the remains of the earlier Anglo-Norman building. This first phase of English Gothic, lasting through most of the thirteenth century, is known as **Early English** (or Pointed or Lancet), and was given its full expression in what is regarded as the first truly Gothic cathedral in England, **Wells**, largely completed by 1190.

Begun shortly afterwards, **Lincoln Cathedral** takes the process of vertical emphasis further, substituting Wells' three-tier nave, which was subdivided horizontally, with wall-shafts that soar all the way to the ceiling. The decoration was also more profuse than anything anywhere in France, never mind England. The influence of Lincoln remained strong in English architecture, though it was resisted by the builders of **Salisbury Cathedral**, which is one of the most homogeneous of the Early English churches, most of it being built in the comparatively short period 1220–65.

A transitional phase in the evolution of Gothic architecture is represented by the **rebuilding of Westminster Abbey** in 1220, when the abbey became the most French of English churches. There was French influence at work in the flying buttresses that were added to support its greater height, and in the lavish use of **window tracery**, whereby geometric patterns were created by subdividing each window with moulded ribs (or mullions), a device first seen at Reims in 1211.

The Decorated and Perpendicular styles

The development of complicated **tracery** is one of the chief characteristics of the **Decorated** style, ushered in by Westminster Abbey and by the Angel Choir at Lincoln and the nave of Lichfield, both designed in the late 1250s. The fully blown Decorated style emerged around the end of the thirteenth century and at the beginning of the fourteenth, when the cathedral at **Exeter** was almost completely rebuilt, with a dense exuberance of rib vaulting and multiple moulding on the arches and piers. **York Minster**, rebuilt from 1225 and the largest of all English Gothic churches, introduced another innovation associated with this period – **lierne vaulting**, whereby a subsidiary, mainly ornamental, rib is added to the roof complex. Intricately carved roof bosses and capitals are other common features of Decorated Gothic, as is the use of the organic **ogee curve** – a curve with a double bend in it. One-off experiments are also characteristic of this period, the most striking examples being the octagonal lantern tower at **Ely** (1320s), and the rebuilding of **Bristol Cathedral** (1298–1330), which shows many of the features of the continental hall-church style, with nave and aisles of roughly the same height.

The style that came to prevail in the second half of the fourteenth century, the **Perpendicular**, was the first post-Conquest architecture unique to England. This new-found insularity was partly due to the loss of England's French territories towards the end of the Hundred Years War, though another contributing factor was the Black Death, which decimated the number of craftsmen and made the abandonment of elaborate design almost inevitable. Thus, whereas French architecture progressed to an emphatically curvilinear or "Flamboyant" style, the emphasis in England was on rectilinear design, anticipated in the rebuilding of **Gloucester Cathedral** (1337–57). Here the cloister features the first fully developed **fan vault** while the massive east window is a good example of the new window design, in which the maximization of light is paramount and the tracery organized in vertical compartments. Edward II's tomb – the focal point of Gloucester Cathedral – also exemplifies the wave of **memorial building** common in the Perpendicular period, as do the chantry tombs at **Winchester Cathedral** and **Tewkesbury Abbey**. Other resplendent monuments from this period include the tomb of the Black Prince in **Canterbury Cathedral**, where the Norman nave was rebuilt after 1379, though it was the addition of the Bell Harry Tower and tracery in the aisle windows that injected the most strongly Perpendicular elements. Henry Yevele, who was responsible for this work, and his contemporary at Winchester, William Wynford, were forerunners of the modern architect, reflecting the gradual elevation of the master-mason into the creative designer-cum-overseer.

The Wars of the Roses meant that few new "prestige" buildings were commissioned in the second half of the fifteenth century, though parish churches eagerly embraced the new Perpendicular style, most notably in East Anglia, Somerset and the Cotswolds. Thereafter, the restoration of strong government saw a resurgence of royal patronage and the construction of three splendid chapels during the reign of Henry VII – **St George's Chapel**, Windsor, **King's College Chapel**, Cambridge, and **Henry VII's Chapel** in Westminster Abbey. By now, walls had become panelled screens filled mostly with stained glass, the weight transmitted from stone ribs onto bold buttresses that were usually capped with tall pinnacles. At King's College, the fan vaulting extended over the whole nave and harmonized with the windows and wall panelling, but it was the densely sculptured Chapel of Henry VII that took such vaulting to the limit, the complexity heightened by a lavish use of decorative pendants – a rare element in English design.

The Renaissance

The Perpendicular style held sway throughout the Tudor era and the impact of **Renaissance** architecture was largely confined to small decorative features. Such were the terracotta busts of Roman emperors at the otherwise conventionally Tudor **Hampton Court Palace**, to which Henry VIII added a Great Hall with a superb hammer-beam roof similar to that in Westminster Hall (1397–99), albeit here embellished with Italianate details.

The dissemination of the latest ideas in design and decoration came about chiefly through commissions from high-ranking courtiers and statesmen. These nobles demonstrated their acquaintance with the sophisticated classical canons in such mansions as **Burghley House**, Lincolnshire (1552–87), and **Longleat**, Wiltshire (1568–80), projects which mingled the Gothic and the Renaissance while also heralding a taste for landscaped parklands in preference to enclosed courtyards. These projects were made much easier by Henry VIII's Dissolution of the Monasteries, whereby some twenty to thirty percent of England's land was released into private hands. The mason at Longleat, Robert Smythson, was probably also the designer of **Hardwick Hall** in Derbyshire (1591–96), celebrated in local rhyme as "Hardwick Hall, more glass than wall" – words which sum up the predilection for huge glazed areas displayed in Elizabethan great houses.

Hatfield House in Hertfordshire, rebuilt 1607–11 by the chief minister of Elizabeth and James I, Robert Cecil, represents a bridge between Elizabethan and **Jacobean** architecture, the latter being characterized by a greater infusion of classical ideas. Classicism, at the time, was primarily decorative, as exemplified in the Tower of the Five Orders (1613–18) at the **Bodleian Library** in Oxford, where the Classical Orders as defined by Vitruvius were applied as appendages to a building with mullioned windows, battlements and pinnacles. The full spirit of the Renaissance did not find full expression in England until **Inigo Jones** (1573–1652) began to apply the lessons learned from his visits to Italy, and in particular from his familiarity with Palladio's rules of proportion and symmetry, as laid out in the *Quattro Libri dell'Architettura* of 1570. Appointed Royal Surveyor to James I in 1615 (a position he held also under Charles I), Jones changed the direction of English architecture with only a handful of works, in each one of which he adapted Palladian ideals to English requirements. Three of his most prominent projects were built in London: the **Banqueting House** in Whitehall (1619–22), the first truly classical building to be completed in England since Roman times; the **Queen's House** at Greenwich (1617–35); and **St Paul's Church**, Covent Garden (1630s), the focal point of the first planned city square in England.

Wren and Baroque

Despite Jones's promulgation of classical architecture, Gothic endured well into the seventeenth century, especially in Oxford, where **Christ Church** was given a magnificent fan-vaulted staircase hall as late as 1640. Oxford's first classical construction, the **Sheldonian Theatre**, was also the first building designed by the artistic heir of Inigo Jones, **Christopher Wren** (1632–1723), who established himself as a notable mathematician and astronomer before turning to architecture shortly after the Restoration of 1660. As far as is known, Wren never visited Italy (though he met Bernini, the greatest architect of the day, in Paris), and as a result his work was never so wholeheartedly Italianate as that of Inigo Jones. Instead, Wren developed an eclectic style that combined orthodox classicism with **Baroque** inventiveness, all underpinned by the dual influences of French and Dutch architecture.

Wren's work in Oxford was quickly followed by Pembroke College Chapel, Cambridge, but the bulk of his achievement is to be seen in London, where the **Great Fire of 1666** led to a commission for the building of no less than 53 churches. The most striking of these buildings display a remarkable elegance and harmony: they include **St Bride** in Fleet Street, **St Mary-le-Bow** in Cheapside, **St Vedast** in Foster Lane, and, perhaps the finest of all, the domed **St Stephen Walbrook** alongside Mansion House – though all were partly rebuilt after World War II bomb damage. Most monumental of all was Wren's rebuilding of **St Paul's Cathedral** (1675–1710) in a cruciform shape very different from his original radical design, though its principal feature – the massive central dome – was retained.

As Surveyor-General, Wren also rebuilt, extended or altered several royal palaces, including the south and east wings of **Hampton Court** (1689–1700). Other secular works include **Chelsea Hospital** (1682–92), **Trinity College Library**, Cambridge (1676–84), the **Tom Tower of Christ Church**, Oxford (1681–82) – a rare work in the Gothic mode – and, grandest of all, **Greenwich Hospital** (1694–98), a magnificent foil to the Queen's House built by Inigo Jones, and to Wren's own Royal Observatory (1675).

Work at Greenwich Hospital was continued by Wren's only major pupil, **Nicholas Hawksmoor** (1661–1736), whose distinctively muscular form of the Baroque is seen to best effect in his London churches. Most of these are in the East End with the pick being **St George-in-the-East** (1715–23) and **Christ Church**, Spitalfields (1723–29). His exercises in Gothic pastiche included the western towers of **Westminster Abbey** (1734) and **All Souls College**, Oxford (1716–35), while the mausoleum at **Castle Howard** in Yorkshire (1729) shows close affinities with the Roman Baroque.

The third great English architect of the Baroque era was **John Vanbrugh** (1664–1726), who was famed as a dramatist but lacked any architectural training when he was commissioned by the Earl of Carlisle to design a new country seat at **Castle Howard** (1699–1726). More flamboyant than either Hawksmoor or Wren – with both of whom he worked – Vanbrugh went on to design numerous other grandiose houses, of which the outstanding examples are the gargantuan **Blenheim Palace** (1705–20), the culminating point of English Baroque, and the fortress-like **Seaton Delaval**, not far from Newcastle upon Tyne (1720–28), a building which harks back to the architecture of medieval England.

Gibbs and Palladianism

In the field of church architecture, the most influential architect of the eighteenth century was **James Gibbs** (1682–1754), whose masterpiece, **St Martin-in-the-Fields** in London (1722–26), with its steeple sprouting above a pedimented portico, was widely imitated as a model of how to combine the classical with the Gothic. Gibbs was barred from royal commissions on account of his Catholic and Jacobite sympathies, but he worked at the two universities, designing Cambridge's **Senate House** (1722–30) and the **Fellows' Building** at King's College (1723–49), and Oxford's **Radcliffe Camera** (1737–49), a beautifully sited construction drawing heavily on his knowledge of Roman styles. Gibbs was one of the very few architects of his generation to have studied in Italy, but this situation changed when the Treaty of Utrecht (1713) brought peace to Europe, opening it up to English aristocrats on the Grand Tour, as the self-educating long holiday on the continent became known. For architecture in England, the immediate result was a rebirth of the **Palladianism** introduced by Inigo Jones a century before, an orthodoxy that was to dominate the secular architecture of the eighteenth century.

The Palladian movement was championed by a Whig elite led by **Lord Burlington** (1694–1753), an enthusiastic patron of the arts whose own masterpiece was **Chiswick House** in London (1725), a domed villa closely modelled on Palladio's Villa Rotonda. Burlington collaborated with the decorator, garden designer and architect **William Kent** (1685–1748) on such stately piles as **Holkham Hall** in Norfolk (1734), whose imposing portico and ordered composition typify the break with Baroque dramatics. The third chief player in the return to Renaissance simplicity was **Colen Campbell** (1673–1729), author of the influential *Vitruvius Britannicus* (1715), a compilation of designs from which architects freely borrowed. Campbell worked closely with Burlington on such works as **Burlington House** in London (1718–19), though his best achievements were two country homes, Houghton Hall, Norfolk (1722), and Mereworth Castle, Kent (1723).

The Palladian idiom was further disseminated by such men as **John Wood** (1704–54), designer of Liverpool Town Hall (1749–54) but better known for the work he did in his native **Bath**, helping to transform the city into a paragon of town planning. His showpieces there are **Queen Square** (1729–36) and the **Circus** (1754), the latter completed by his son, **John Wood the Younger** (1728–81), who went on to design Bath's **Royal Crescent** (1767–74). The embellishment of Georgian Bath was further developed by **Robert Adam** (1728–92), a Palladian who designed the city's **Pulteney Bridge** (1769–74). Adam's forte, however, was in the field of domestic architecture, especially in the designing of decorative interiors, where he showed himself to be the most versatile and refined architect of his day. His elaborate concoctions are best displayed in **Syon House** (1762–69) and **Osterley Park** (1761–80), both on the western outskirts of London, and **Kenwood** (1767–79) on the edge of Hampstead Heath, all epitomizing his scrupulous attention to detail as well as his dexterity at large-scale planning. Adam's chief rival was the more fastidious **William Chambers** (1723–96), whose masterpiece, **Somerset House** on London's Strand (1776–98), is an academic counterpoint to Adam's dashing originality.

Adam and Chambers competed in a highly active market whose chief patrons regarded themselves as belonging to the most cultivated class in the island's history. Undoubtedly they were among the wealthiest, spending vast sums of money not just on their houses but also on the grounds in which these houses stood. **Landscape gardening** was the quintessential English contribution to European culture in the eighteenth century, and its greatest exponent was **Capability Brown** (1716–83) – so-called because of his custom of assessing the "capabilities" of a landscape. All over England, Brown and his acolytes modified the estates of the landed gentry into "Picturesque" landscapes, an idealization of nature along the lines of the paintings of Poussin and Lorrain, often enhancing the view with a romantic "ruin" or some exotic structure such as a Chinese pagoda or Indian temple.

The nineteenth century

The greatest architect of the late eighteenth and early nineteenth centuries was **John Nash** (1752–1835), whose Picturesque country houses, built in collaboration with the landscapist Humphrey Repton (1752–1818), represented just one part of his diverse repertoire. In this versatility Nash was typical of his time, though he is associated above all with the style favoured during the **Regency** of his friend and patron the Prince of Wales (afterwards George IV), a decorous style that owed much to Chambers and Adam, making plentiful use of stucco. His strangest and best-known building was also a commission from the Prince – the orientalized Gothic palace known as the **Brighton Pavilion**. A prolific worker, Nash was responsible for much of the present-day appearance of such **resorts** as Brighton, Weymouth, Cheltenham, Clifton and Tunbridge Wells, as well as numerous parts of central **London**, including the **Haymarket Theatre** (1820), the church of **All Souls**, Langham Place (1822–25), **Clarence House** (1825) and **Carlton House Terrace** (1827). He also planned the layout of **Regent's Park** and **Regent Street** in London (from 1811), and remodelled **Buckingham Palace** (1826–30), a project that foundered at the death of his patron. Nash's contemporary, **Sir John Soane** (1753–1837), was more of an inventive antiquarian, his pared-down classical experiments presenting a serious-minded contrast to Nash's extrovert creations. Very little remains of his greatest masterpiece, the **Bank of England** (1788–1833), but his idiosyncratic style is well illustrated by two other buildings in London – his own home, **Sir John Soane's Museum** on Lincoln's Inn Fields (1812–13) and **Dulwich Art Gallery** (1811–14).

Classicism was, however, soon challenged. As early as 1753, the connoisseur Horace Walpole built an ornate villa, **Strawberry Hill** near Twickenham, in an ornate Gothic style. Nash and other exponents of the Picturesque also dabbled in the Gothic, as a passion for romance and medievalism gained ground in literary and intellectual circles. In 1818, when Parliament voted a million pounds for the construction of new Anglican churches, the **Gothic Revival** got properly under way – two-thirds of the churches built under this Act were in a Gothic or near-Gothic style. Many public buildings continued to draw on Renaissance, Greek or Roman influences – notably the town halls of Birmingham and Leeds (1832–50 & 1853–58) – but the pre-eminence of neo-Gothic was confirmed when the Houses of Parliament were rebuilt in that style after the fire of 1834. The contract was given to **Charles Barry** (1795–1860), the designer of the classical Reform Club, but his collaborator, **Augustus Welby Pugin** (1812–52), was to become the unswerving apostle of the neo-Gothic. None the less, it wasn't all one-way traffic: the eminent architect **George Gilbert Scott** (1811–78) submitted a Gothic design for the new government offices (now the Foreign Office) in **Whitehall** (1855–72), but was told to go back to the drawing board and prepare an Italian Renaissance design instead. On the other hand, Scott was able to give rein to his personal tastes in the extravaganzas of **St Pancras Station** (1868–74) and the **Albert Memorial** (1863–72), both based on his preferred Flemish and north Italian Gothic models. When the first English cathedral to be consecrated outside London since the Middle Ages was built at Truro (1880–1910), the approved design was a scholarly exercise in French-influenced Gothic; yet when it came to commissioning the Catholic **Westminster Cathedral** (1895–1903), the design chosen was neo-Byzantine.

This architectural stew was further enriched by a string of engineer-architects, who employed cast iron and other industrial materials in works as diverse as Isambard Kingdom Brunel's **Clifton Suspension Bridge** in Bristol (1829–64) and Joseph Paxton's glass and iron **Crystal Palace** (1851), which was subsequently transferred from London's Hyde Park to the suburb of Sydenham, where it burned down in 1936. The potential of iron and glass was similarly exploited in **Newcastle Central Station** (1846–55), the first of a generation of monumental railway stations incorporating classical motifs and rib-vaulted iron roofs.

John Ruskin (1819–1900) and his disciple **William Morris** (1834–96), leader of the Arts and Crafts Movement, rejected these industrial technologies in favour of traditional materials – such as brick, stone and timber – worked in traditional ways. Morris was not an architect himself, but he did plan the interior of his own home, the **Red House** in Bexley, Kent (1854), from designs by Philip Webb (1831–1915). Unusually, Morris took responsibility for every aspect of the work, as did **Richard Norman Shaw** (1831–1912), whose red-brick, heavily gabled constructions – in a Dutch style reminiscent of the Queen Anne period – were widely imitated in central London. His best work is displayed in Swan House, Chelsea (1875), Albert Hall Mansions, Kensington (1879) – one of England's earliest apartment blocks – and in Bedford Park, west London (1877), the first of the capital's "garden suburbs".

Another architect to fall under the sway of the Arts and Crafts Movement was **Charles Voysey** (1851–1941), whose clean-cut cottages and houses eschewed all ostentation, depending instead on the meticulous and subtle use of local materials for their effect. The originality of Voysey's work and that of his contemporaries M.H. Baillie Scott (1865–1945) and Ernest Newton (1856–1922) was later debased by scores of speculative suburban builders, though not before their refreshingly simple style had found recognition first in Germany and then across the rest of Europe.

The twentieth century to the present

At the turn of the twentieth century, English architecture was rooted in a nostalgic aesthetic, whose precepts were typified by **Edwin Lutyens** (1869–1944). Most of Lutyens's early works were country houses in the Arts and Crafts style, but later he moved onto virtuoso classicized structures, such as the elegant Baroque of what he himself termed "Wrenaissance" and a more sober neo-Georgianism, which, in its turn, initiated a widespread Georgian Revival. However, perhaps his most striking achievements in England are the one-off **Castle Drogo** on Dartmoor (1910–30), the last of the great country houses, and the **Cenotaph** on London's Whitehall (1918), a masterpiece of stripped-down monumentalism.

Revivalist tendencies prevailed in England throughout the early decades of the twentieth century, but an awareness of more radical trends surfaced in isolated projects in the 1930s. One of these was **Senate House** in London's Bloomsbury (1932), designed by **Charles Holden** (1875–1960), who was also responsible for some of London's Underground stations, notably **Arnos Grove** (1932). The **Tecton group**, led by the Russian immigrant Lubetkin, also made several successful examples of the austere International Modern style, most notably London Zoo's **Penguin Pool** (1934), a witty demonstration of the plastic possibilities of concrete. The UK's first public building built in the modernist style was the sleek, streamlined **De La Warr Pavilion** in Bexhill-on-Sea, Sussex, designed by Erich Mendelsohn and Serge Chermayeff in 1935, and described by Mendelsohn as a "horizontal skyscraper". Nonetheless, these were the exceptions rather than the rule despite developments on the continent, where the modernist ideas (and reinforced concrete) of architects such as Le Corbusier, Walter Gropius and the Bauhaus group were increasingly dominant, and in North America, which was in thrall to high-rise, steel-frame buildings.

In England, a general acceptance of modern style had to wait for the reforming atmosphere that followed World War II and more particularly the 1951 **Festival of Britain** on London's South Bank, which showcased the latest technological marvels. Many of the festival pavilions were designed by **Basil Spence** (1907–76), whose best-known work was the replacement of the bombed **Coventry Cathedral**, incorporating defiantly modernist detail into a neo-Gothic structure (1951–59). The only architectural survivor of the Festival of Britain is the **Royal Festival Hall** (1949–51), a triumphant modernist departure from the traditional model for classical music venues. The site was later augmented by the addition of the far less attractive **National Theatre** (1967–77) by **Denys Lasdun** (1914–2001), a Tecton architect who remained true to the principles of the group. Prestige projects apart, the bombs of World War II had helped create a national **housing crisis** of immense proportions and in every city across the land there was a determination to clear the rubble and demolish the slums which had been a hallmark of prewar industrial Britain. The problem was that speed of construction – rather than quality – was too often the key criterion and the consequent use of **prefabricated units** produced generally dire results. **Tower blocks** sprouted up by the score, creating the desolate urban wastelands that are a characteristic feature of English cities today, while the wholesale restructuring of scores of city centres led to roads being ploughed through willy-nilly, to service yet more concrete office blocks and shopping centres.

The general situation might have been desperate, but some interesting 1960s architecture was created at the new "redbrick" universities, notable examples being Spence's **Sussex University** at Brighton (1961) and Lasdun's **University of East Anglia** at Norwich (1963). The universities were also where a string of younger architects cut their teeth, most notably **James Stirling** (1926–92) and **Norman Foster** (b. 1935), who, along with **Richard Rogers** (b. 1933), initially found greater scope working abroad than in Britain. That said, Stirling's postmodern extension for London's Tate Gallery (1989) was one of the more controversial projects of recent times, and Rogers' Lloyd's Building (1978–86) in London is a bold high-tech display along the lines of his Pompidou Centre in Paris. Factory sites have provided Foster with several English contracts, though the building which first raised his profile is the glass-tent terminal at London's **Stansted Airport** (1991).

In the early to mid-1990s, the architectural scene was stranded between a popular dislike for the modern and a general reluctance amongst architects to return to the architectural past. Prince Charles also entered the debate,

The ten best buildings in England from the last hundred years

Liverpool Anglican Cathedral, Liverpool, 1904–78 (see p.692)
Senate House, Bloomsbury, London, 1932
De La Warr Pavilion, Bexhill-on-Sea, East Sussex, 1935
Tate Modern, London, 1948–63 & 2000 (see p.121)
Coventry Cathedral, 1951–59 (see p.548)
Shri Swaminarayan Mandir, Neasden, London, 1995 (see p.135)
Eden Project, Cornwall, 2001 (see p.434)
Imperial War Museum North, Manchester, 2002 (see p.674)
30 St Mary Axe, London ("The Gherkin"), 2004 (see p.115)
The Sage Gateshead, 2004 (see p.884)

campaigning against architectural modernism: one of the results was a countrywide rash of modern office buildings with peculiar pastel-painted gables and other retrospective accoutrements. The most obvious repercussion, however, was in regard to the **Sainsbury Wing** (1991) at London's National Gallery, a commission whose original winning design was notoriously condemned by the prince as "a monstrous carbuncle on the face of a much-loved and elegant friend". Hastily withdrawn, the proposal was replaced by a safe pastiche of Neoclassicism that blended with the 1838 design of the main building by William Wilkins, despite being the work of postmodernist supremos Robert Venturi and Denise Scott-Brown. On the whole, however, the general public have taken kindly to modern buildings that exhibit some wit and/or sinuosity, such as **Michael Hopkins**' eye-catching Mound Stand for the Lord's Cricket Ground, his wood-panelled auditorium at the **Glyndebourne Opera House** (1994), and his **Inland Revenue Headquarters** (1995) in Nottingham.

The century finished with a rush to regenerate inner-city brown-field sites. Rogers' **Millennium Dome** (1999, now the O2 arena), in a rundown part of Greenwich, was heavily criticized – though more for its content than the space itself – while a Foster-dominated London scene produced the **Millennium Bridge** and **British Museum Great Court** (both 2000), the **Greater London Assembly** (2002) and the **30 St Mary Axe** (2004) in the City, nicknamed the "Gherkin". Most spectacular of all London's redevelopments, however, was the transformation of Giles Gilbert Scott's South Bank power station into the world's largest modern art gallery, **Tate Modern** (2000), by Herzog & de Meuron.

Not to be outdone by the capital, the resurgence of formerly industrial cities saw such eye-catching developments as Gateshead's **BALTIC** arts centre (Ellis Williams Architects, 2002) and **Sage Gateshead** (Foster and Partners, 2004); the striking modernism of Manchester's **Imperial War Museum North** (Libeskind, 2002); and Birmingham's new **Selfridges** department store (Future Systems, 2003), shimmering with its sequin coat. In the rush to market and re-brand themselves, smaller towns and cities have commissioned iconic works, for example Brighton's **Jubilee Library** and Portsmouth's **Spinnaker Tower** (both 2005). The first of these also embodies the green principles that are a trumpeted feature of almost all high-profile projects in recent years, with their increasing emphasis on sustainable design. Probably the most successful of these in terms of sheer popularity has been Cornwall's **Eden Project** (2001), a stylish exercise in eco-awareness which in 2007 was voted best building of the last 20 years by the UK construction industry.

▲ The Gherkin

According to all indications, British architecture is in a healthy state, even if its most original practitioners often get most commissions abroad. Exciting and fresh work can appear in the unlikeliest of places, as within the hallowed Victorian frontage of **St Pancras Station**, overhauled and expanded and reopened to grand acclaim in 2007. Eulogized by the public and critics alike, the building is a heartening demonstration that twenty-first century fizz and panache can co-exist with Neo-Gothic exuberance and High Victoriana, in the organic, incremental tradition of English architecture.

Books and literature

A tour of literary England could take many lifetimes. Many of the world's most famous writers were born, lived and died here, leaving footprints that reach into every corner of the country. Writers' birth-places, houses, libraries and graves are a staple of the local tourist industry, while in places like Stratford-upon-Avon or Grasmere literature and tourism have formed an unbreakable symbiosis. England even has one quintessential bookish destination, Hay-on-Wye, the town on the Anglo–Welsh border that is entirely devoted to the buying, selling and enjoyment of books – its annual literary festival (every May) is the nation's biggest book-related jamboree.

Literary England

For readers and book-lovers of all ages, there's something deeply satisfying about immersing yourself in English literature's natural fabric, whether it's tramping the Yorkshire moors with the Brontë sisters or exploring the streets of Dickens' Rochester. And for every over-trumpeted sight in "Shakespeare Country" or "Beatrix Potter's Lakeland" there are dozens of other locales that a contemporary English writer has made unquestionably their own, from Martin Amis' London to P.D. James' East Anglia. Here's our pick of the best places to follow in the footsteps of your favourite author.

Shakespeare Country

Warwickshire in the West Midlands is – as the road signs attest – "Shakespeare Country", though to all intents and purposes it's a county with just one destination – **Stratford-upon-Avon**, birthplace in 1564 of England's greatest writer. So few facts about Shakespeare's life are known that Stratford can be a disappointment for the serious literary pilgrim, its buildings and sights hedged with "reputedlys" and "maybes" – after 500 years, still the only incontrovertible evidence is that he was born in Stratford, and lived, married, had children and died there. Real Shakespeare country could just as easily be London, where his plays were written and performed (there was no theatre in Stratford in Shakespeare's day). But, from the house where he was born (probably) to the church in which he's buried (definitely), Stratford at least provides a coherent centre for England's Shakespeare industry – and it's certainly the most atmospheric place to see a production by the Royal Shakespeare Company.

Wordsworth's Lake District

William Wordsworth and the **Lake District** are inextricably linked, and in the streets of Cockermouth (where he was born), Hawkshead (where he went to school) and Grasmere (where he lived most of his life), you're never very far from a sight associated with the poet and his circle. Wordsworth's views on nature and the natural world stood at the very heart of all his poetry, and it's still a jolt to encounter the very views that inspired him – from his carefully tended garden at Rydal Mount to the famous daffodils of Gowbarrow Park. It wasn't just Wordsworth either. The "Lake Poets" of popular description – Wordsworth, Samuel Taylor Coleridge and Robert Southey – formed a clique of fluctuating friendships with a shared passion for the Lakes at its core.

Poetic England

From the *Canterbury Tales* onwards, English poets have taken inspiration from the country's people and landscape. Traditionally, much was made of England's rural lives and trades, by poets as diverse as Northamptonshire "peasant poet" John Clare and A.E. Houseman, whose nostalgic *A Shropshire Lad* is one of English poetry's most favoured works. But with Yorkshire-born (and later Devon resident) Ted Hughes, savage English nature found a unique voice, while for poets like Cumbria's Norman Nicholson it was working people, their dialect and industry that inspired. Perhaps there's something about the north in particular that engages and enrages poets: Philip Larkin, famously, spent the last 30 years of his life in Hull; the self-proclaimed "bard of Salford", John Cooper Clarke, skewered Manchester in his early machine-gun-style punk poems; and Huddersfield-born Simon Armitage continues to report "from the long, lifeless mud of the River Colne". Meanwhile, dub poet Linton Kwesi Johnson uses Jamaican patois in devastating commentaries on the English social condition ("Inglan is a bitch").

Haworth and the Brontës

Quite why the sheltered life of the Brontë sisters, Charlotte, Emily and Anne, should exert such a powerful fascination is a puzzle, though the contrast of their pinched provincial existence in the Yorkshire village of **Haworth** with the brooding moors and tumultuous passions of their novels may well form part of the answer. Their old home in the village parsonage and the family vault in the parish church only tell half the story. As Charlotte later recalled, "resident in a remote district . . . we were wholly dependent on ourselves and each other, on books and study, for the enjoyments and occupations of life". Charlotte's *Jane Eyre*, the harrowing story of a much put-upon governess, sprang from this domestic isolation, yet it was out on the bleak moors above Haworth that inspiration often struck, and where works like Emily's *Wuthering Heights* and Anne's *The Tenant of Wildfell Hall* progressed from mere parlour entertainments to melodramatic studies of emotion and obsession.

Dickensian England

Charles Dickens' name has passed into the language as shorthand for a city's filthy stew of streets and gallery of grotesques. But although any dark alley or old curiosity shop in London might still be considered "Dickensian", it's a different matter trying to trace the author through his works. He was born in Portsmouth, though spent his younger years in **Rochester** and **Chatham**, in Kent (and set most of his last book, *The Mystery of Edwin Drood*, there). Is this Dickensian England? Perhaps only if you succumb to the pull of "Dickens World", Chatham's "themed entertainment in-house visitor attraction" where Scrooge's house and Fagin's den are offered up as "a new and entertaining way to enjoy Dickens". Many of the most famous books – including *Oliver Twist*, *David Copperfield*, *Bleak House* and *Little Dorrit* – are set or partly set in a **London** that Dickens unquestionably made his own. His unhappy early experiences of the city – the boot-blacking factory at the age of twelve, his father's spell in a debtors' prison, working as a law clerk – form the basis of many of

Dickens' most trenchant pieces of social analysis. Yet only one of his London houses survives (Dickens House in Bloomsbury), and he only lived in that for two years. To the north then, finally, for Dickensian England, to the fictional "Coketown" of *Hard Times*. Dickens went to Preston and other Lancashire mill towns to gather material for his "state-of-the-nation" satire about the social and economic conditions of factory workers, while in Barnard Castle (County Durham) he found a heartbreaking neglect of schoolchildren that underpinned the magnificent *Nicholas Nickleby*.

Criminal England

Contemporary crime writers have moved well beyond the enclosed country-house mysteries of Agatha Christie. Colin Dexter's morose Inspector Morse flits between town and gown in university **Oxford** in a cerebral series of whodun-nits, while in the elegantly crafted novels of P.D. James it's the remote coast and isolated villages of **East Anglia** that often provide the backdrop. The other English "Queen of Crime", Ruth Rendell, sets her long-running Inspector Wexford series in "Kingsmarkham" – inspired by Midhurst in **West Sussex**, surely the most crime-ridden town in the country after twenty Wexford novels. **London**, of course, preoccupies many writers, from Derek Raymond or Jake Arnott recreating Sixties villainy to Rendell again, writing as Barbara Vine, at home with the capital's suburban misfits, drop-outs and damaged. Val McDermid, and her sassy private eye, Kate Brannigan, nail contemporary **Manchester**, and the seedier side of the city also gets a good kicking in the noir novels of Nicholas Blincoe. **Yorkshire** of the 1970s and 1980s is dissected in David Peace's majestic Red Riding quartet about corrupt police; Reginald Hill's popular Dalziel and Pascoe series portrays a more traditional pair of Yorkshire detectives, but in his Joe Sixsmith private-eye novels it's a re-imagined **Luton** that forms the backdrop. Graham Greene gave us seedy **Brighton** first; Peter James' policeman, Roy Grace, digs further into its underbelly, while in

---

Writers at home

Brantwood, Cumbria. There's no more finely sited writer's house in Britain than John Ruskin's Victorian home set high above Coniston Water. See p.738.

Chawton, Hampshire. The modest house where Jane Austen lived and wrote most of her celebrated classics on manners, society and the pursuit of the happy ever after. See p.252.

Fleet Street, London. Dr Johnson, England's most renowned man of letters, put together his famous pioneer dictionary in his London town house. See p.113.

Hill Top, Cumbria. Sheep-farmer Mrs Heelis (aka Beatrix Potter) and her beloved lakeland farmhouse suck in thousands of tourists from all over the world. See p.730.

Jarrow, Tyneside. England's first historian, the Venerable Bede, wrote his *Ecclesiastical History of the English People* at the seventh-century Saxon monastery. See p.891.

Nether Stowey, Somerset. Visit the crucible of English Romanticism, the cottage where Samuel Taylor Coleridge, and William and Dorothy Wordsworth, forged a new age of poetry. See p.379.

Thirsk, North Yorkshire. It shouldn't happen to a vet – but it invariably did in James Herriott's "Darrowby", where his former surgery is now a major tourist attraction. See p.836.

Portsmouth it's Graham Hurley's Joe Faraday charged with keeping the peace. Britain's rural areas don't escape the escalating body count either. Peter Robinson's Inspector Banks series is set in the **Yorkshire Dales**, and for Stephen Booth and his Derbyshire detective Ben Cooper it's the wilds of the **Peak District**.

Recommended books

Whether you're looking for light holiday reading, historical background, classic literature or an insight into what it is to be English, you should find something appealing in the list of books reviewed below. It's necessarily selective, and entirely subjective – feel free to disagree. Most of the books reviewed are currently in print, though if local bookshops can't help then the online bookseller Amazon almost certainly can (Ⓦ www.amazon.co.uk; Ⓦ www.amazon.com).

Travels and places

Peter Ackroyd *London: The Biography; Albion.* London is integral to many of Ackroyd's works, novels to biographies, and here the great city itself is presented as a living organism, with themed chapters covering its fables, follies and foibles. Meanwhile, in the massively erudite *Albion*, Ackroyd traces the very origins of English culture and imagination.

Bill Bryson *Notes From A Small Island.* After twenty years living and working in England, Bryson set off on one last tour of Britain before returning to the States – his snort-with-laughter observations set the tone for his future travel, popular science and language best-sellers.

Stuart Maconie *Pies and Prejudice.* The north of England explained, wittily and engagingly, by a Lancastrian exile. Find out where the north starts (Crewe station, apparently) and unravel the arcane mysteries of northern dialect, dress and delicacies – just take the unflattering Rough Guide references with a pinch of salt, as Maconie relies on a very old edition.

Ian Marchant *The Longest Crawl.* The pub – so central to English life and landscape – is dissected in this highly entertaining account of a month-long crawl across the country, involving pork scratchings, funny beer names and lots of falling over.

Harry Pearson *Racing Pigs and Giant Marrows; The Far Corner.* The subtitles tell you all you need to know about content – "Travels Around North Country Fairs" and "A Mazy Dribble Through North-East Football" respectively – though they don't tell you that you'll laugh until you're sick.

J.B. Priestley *English Journey.* The Bradford-born playwright and author's record of his travels around England in the 1930s say nothing about contemporary England, but in many ways its quirkiness, and eye for English eccentricity, formed the blueprint for the later Brysons and Therouxs.

W.G. Sebald *Rings of Saturn.* Intriguing, ruminative book that is a heady mix of novel, travel and memoir, focusing ostensibly on the author's walking tour of Suffolk.

Windows onto England's past

In his celebrated diary, **Samuel Pepys** recorded an eyewitness account of daily life in London from 1660 until 1669, covering momentous events like the Great Plague and the Great Fire. The plague of 1665 also takes centre stage in *Journal of a Plague Year* by **Daniel Defoe** (author of *Robinson Crusoe*), a fictional "observation" of London's trials actually written sixty years later, while the same author's *Tour Through the Whole Island of Great Britain* (1724) was an early sort of economic guide to the country in the years immediately before the Industrial Revolution. Later, the changing seasons in a Hampshire village were recorded by **Gilbert White**, whose *Natural History of Selborne* (1788) is still seen as a masterpiece of nature writing. By 1830, **William Cobbett** was bemoaning the death of rural England and its customs in *Rural Rides*, while decrying both the growth of cities and the iniquities suffered by the exploited urban poor. These last were given magnificent expression in *The Condition of the Working Class in England*, an unforgettable portrait of life in England's hellish industrial towns, published in 1844 as **Friedrich Engels** worked in his father's Manchester cotton mills. Journalist **Henry Mayhew** would later do something similar for the Victorian capital's downtrodden in his mighty *London Labour and the London Poor* (1851). **George Orwell** was therefore following in a well-worn path when he published his dissections of 1920s and 1930s' working-class and under-class life, *Down and Out in Paris and London* (1933) *and The Road to Wigan Pier* (1937), giving respectively a tramp's-eye view of the world and the brutal effects of the Great Depression on the industrial communities of Lancashire and Yorkshire. A later period of English transformation was recorded in *Akenfield* (1969), the surprising best-seller by **Ronald Blythe** that presented life in a rural Suffolk village on the cusp of change – **Craig Taylor**'s update, *Return to Akenfield* (2006), shows that interest in ordinary English life endures today.

Iain Sinclair *London Orbital*. After spending a couple of years walking around the "concrete necklace" of the M25, the erudite Sinclair delves into the dark and mysterious heart of suburban London.

Paul Theroux *The Kingdom By The Sea*. Travelling around the British coast in its entirety in 1982, to find out what the British are really like, leaves Theroux thoroughly bad tempered. No change there then.

Guidebooks

Simon Jenkins *England's Thousand Best Churches*; *England's Thousand Best Houses*. A lucid, witty pick of England's churches and houses, divided by county and with a star rating – for the houses book Jenkins includes all sorts of curiosities, from caves in Nottingham to prefabs in Buckinghamshire.

Sam Jordison and Dan Kieran *The Idler Book of Crap Towns*; *Crap Towns II*. The books that made local councils all over England as mad as hell – utterly prejudiced but hilarious accounts of the worst

places to live in the country. We daren't even repeat the names of the "winners", we'll only get letters of complaint.

Nikolaus Pevsner *The Buildings of England*. If you want to know who built what, when, why and how, look no further than this popular architectural series, in 46 county-by-county volumes. The magisterial project was initially a one-man show, but after Pevsner died in 1983 later authors revised his text, inserting newer buildings but generally respecting the founder's personal tone.

A. Wainwright *A Pictorial Guide to the Lakeland Fells* (7 vols); *A Coast to Coast Walk*. More than mere guidebooks could ever be, the beautifully produced small-format volumes of handwritten notes and sketches (produced between 1952 and 1966) have led generations up the Lake District's mountains. The originals are now being revised to take account of changing routes and landscapes.

History, society and politics

Antonia Fraser *The Weaker Vessel*; *The Six Wives of Henry VIII*; *Warrior Queens*. The women of England tend to get short shrift in mainstream history books, but not so with Fraser – *The Weaker Vessel* is a tour de force exploring the lives of women in seventeenth-century England, *The Six Wives* shifts the emphasis firmly away from the corpulent Henry, while *Warrior Queens* celebrates Boudicca and Elizabeth I among others.

Lynsey Hanley *Estates*. The story of social housing (the council "estates" of the title) hardly sounds like a winning topic, but Hanley's "intimate history" brilliantly reveals how class structure is built into the very English landscape (albeit a land that tourists rarely see).

Christopher Hill *The World Turned Upside Down*. Britain's foremost Marxist historian is the most interesting writer on the English Civil War and Commonwealth period. *Upside Down* explores the radical groups – the Diggers, Ranters and Levellers – though many other works trace the history of the Civil War and its personalities, including *God's Englishman* on Oliver Cromwell.

Francis Pryor *Britain BC; Britain AD; Britain in the Middle Ages.* The sometimes arcane field discoveries of working archeologists are given fascinating new exposure in Pryor's lively archeological histories of Britain. Everything from before the Romans to the sixteenth century is examined through the archeologist's eye, unearthing a more sophisticated native culture than was formerly thought along the way.

Diane Purkiss *The English Civil War: A People's History.* The English story of revolution, given a human face – the clue is in the subtitle, as Purkiss gets away from battles and armies, focusing instead on the men who fought and the women who had to feed and tend them.

Simon Schama *A History of Britain* (3 vols). British history, from 3000 BC to 2001, delivered by the country's major TV historical popularizer (the books followed the series). Schama's the best at this kind of stuff, though plenty of others have weighed in recently with similar TV-and-book history tie-ins, notably Andrew Marr (*A History of Modern Britain*) and David Dimbleby (*How We Built Britain*).

W.C. Sellar and R.J. Yeatman *1066 And All That.* The classic alternative history of England was first published in 1930, and subsequent generations have rejoiced in its parodic litany of "Good Things" and "Bad Kings". Not, under any circumstances, to be used for exam revision purposes.

James Sharpe *Remember Remember the Fifth of November.* Sharpe's crisp retelling of the Gunpowder Plot of 1605 also helps put the English phenomenon that is Bonfire Night into context – and explains why Guy Fawkes (not even the leader of this "failed act of terrorism") is the plotter remembered still each year.

E.P. Thompson *The Making of the English Working Class.* A seminal text – essential reading for anyone who wants to understand the fabric of English society – tracing the birth of England's working-class society between 1780 and 1832.

Michael Wood *In Search of England: Journeys into the English Past.* Historian Wood was also an early TV historical popularizer and consequently his books are highly readable. *In Search of England* delves into the myths and historical record behind the notion of England and Englishness, while other "In search of..." titles shed new light on the Dark Ages and the Domesday Book.

People

David Beckham *My Side.* The world's most famous living Englishman tells his own story (well, to a ghost writer anyway). This takes you up to his move from England to Madrid, though expect updates on the American adventure any time soon. And, as Amazon kindly suggests, how can you possibly read this without the companion piece, the lovely Victoria's *Learning to Fly*?

Alan Clark *Diaries: In Power; Into Politics; The Last Diaries.* Political diaries and memoirs a yawn? Not these – former minister Clark's candid (ie downright rude), conceited and cutting insights into governmental power trace his rise from becoming an MP in 1974 to a place at the heart of Margaret Thatcher's administration, and beyond. Controversial, often unpleasant, and scabrously funny.

David Horspool *Why Alfred Burned the Cakes.* Little is known of the life of Alfred the Great, king of Wessex and arguably the first king of what would become "England", but Horspool adds a welcome new dimension to the myths and legends. And in case you were wondering about the cakes, Alfred probably didn't.

Roy Jenkins *Churchill: A Biography.* Churchill biographies abound (and the man himself, of course, wrote up his own life), but politician and statesman Jenkins adds an extra level of understanding. Jenkins specialized in political biogs of men of power, so you can also read his take on Gladstone, Asquith, various Chancellors of the Exchequer and others.

Andrew Morton *Diana: Her True Story.* The biography of the "People's Princess" that started all the hulla-baloo – and now they won't let it lie. Morton's is still the one they all

aspire to join in mega-sales nirvana, but if he won't do there are always books by the butler (Paul Burrell), the bodyguard (Trevor Rees-Jones), the feminist (Beatrix Campbell), the magazine editor (Tina Brown), Uncle Tom Cobbley and all.

Katie Price *Being Jordan.* If you don't know who Jordan is, you're not English, don't watch reality television or never read the tabloids, simple as that.

James Sharpe *Dick Turpin.* Subtitled "The myth of the English highwayman", Sharpe stands and delivers a broadside to the commonly accepted notion of Turpin and his ilk – not romantic robbers but brutal villains after all.

Lytton Strachey *Queen Victoria.* Strachey is often credited with establishing a warmer, wittier, more all-encompassing form of biography, with his *Queen Victoria* (1921) following on from the ground-breaking *Eminent Victorians.* Many others have followed in trying to understand Britain's longest reigning monarch – Christopher Hibbert and Elizabeth Longford two of the most recent and respected – but few match Strachey's economy and wit.

Being English

Julian Baggini *Welcome to Everytown: A Journey into the English Mind.* Baggini's "Everytown" is Rotherham, South Yorkshire, supposedly containing the most typical mix of household types in the country. As a philosopher, his six-month stay there wasn't in search of the English character, but rather their "folk philosophy" (ie, what they think). The result? A surprising, illuminating view of mainstream English life.

Michael Collins *The Likes of Us.* Baggini's main finding – "England's

culture remains predominantly working class" – is underpinned by this celebration of the white working class, as Collins weaves family history into the story of England's urban development.

A.A. Gill *The Angry Island.* Gill's self-confessed "collection of prejudice" seeks to explain what England and the English like. Not everyone will like his conclusions ("They have a unique national habit of bringing out the worst in each other"), but you'll certainly keep reading.

Sarfraz Manzoor *Greetings From Bury Park.* You have to know your Springsteen to appreciate fully the title, though journalist Manzoor's memoir of "race, religion and rock and roll" in Bury Park, Luton, is a terrific introduction to the second-generation immigrant experience.

Jeremy Paxman *The English: A Portrait of a People.* The acerbic journalist and newsman presents the character of the English as he sees it – from attitudes to sex and sport to the emotionalism of Princess Diana's funeral.

England in fiction

Julian Barnes *England, England; Metroland.* One of England's most intelligent contemporary writers satirizes the role of tourism, with the entire country recreated as a theme park on the Isle of Wight. *Metroland* meanwhile is a coming-of-age story set in London's stifling suburbs.

George Eliot *Middlemarch.* Eliot (real name Mary Ann Evans) wrote mostly about the county of her birth, Warwickshire, notably in her gargantuan portrayal of English provincial life prior to the Reform Act of 1832.

John Fowles *The French Lieutenant's Woman.* Fowles' most famous novel – a tricksy neo-Victorian love story with a notorious DIY ending – is set in Lyme Regis on the Dorset coast, where the novelist lived.

Elizabeth Gaskell *North and South; Mary Barton.* Gaskell excelled in nineteenth-century "condition of England" novels. *North and South* defines precisely her preoccupations with the emergent differences between the rural south and new industrial north, while *Mary Barton* is about a Manchester factory worker's daughter in the 1840s, a time of industrial unrest and grinding poverty.

William Golding *The Spire.* Atmospheric novel centred on the building of a cathedral spire, taking place in a thinly disguised medieval Salisbury. Also, if you ever wondered what it was like to be at sea in an early nineteenth-century British ship, try

the splendid *Rites of Passage* trilogy.

Graham Greene *Brighton Rock.* The dysfunctional, seedy, morally decadent backdrop to much of Greene's work – critics called it "Greeneland" – was echoed in his choice of place, from Haiti (*The Comedians*) to West Africa (*The Heart of the Matter*), but in the gang wars and criminal underworld of 1930s Brighton the author found a domestic setting that was just as unsettling.

Jerome K. Jerome *Three Men in a Boat.* An instant hit with its late-Victorian readers, the light-hearted tale of an accident-prone paddle on the River Thames has never been out of print since.

D.H. Lawrence *Sons and Lovers.* Before he got his funny ideas about sex and became all messianic, Lawrence wrote magnificent prose on daily working-class life in Nottinghamshire's pit villages – or rather his vision of it, as in this fraught, autobiographical novel. His interpretation never went down well with the locals and even now his name can raise a snarl or two.

Laurie Lee *Cider with Rosie.* Ever-popular reminiscences of adolescent frolics in the rural Cotswolds of the 1920s.

Daphne du Maurier *Frenchman's Creek; Jamaica Inn; Rebecca.* Nail-biting, swashbuckling romantic novels set in the author's adopted home of

Cornwall – they've probably done more for West Country tourism than anything else since.

Graham Swift *Waterland*; *Last Orders*. The first is a family saga set in East Anglia's fenlands – excellent on the history and appeal of this superficially drab landscape – while Booker-Prize-winning *Last Orders* reminisces with four old folk on a trip to Margate to scatter a friend's ashes.

Adam Thorpe *Ulverton*. Hugely imaginative recreation of life in a fictional village on the Wessex Downs, in southwest England, following the generations over the course of three centuries.

Anthony Trollope *The Warden*. The "Chronicles of Barsetshire" novels (1855–67) made Trollope's name as a novelist – the first in the series of six, *The Warden*, was his first major success as a writer, though it's the second, *Barchester Towers*, that's the best known. Comic yet socially penetrating, they deal in Victorian clerical politics, and are set in and around a fictional version of Salisbury.

P.G. Wodehouse *The Jeeves Omnibus*; *Life at Blandings Omnibus*. For many, Wodehouse (1881–1975) is the quintessential English humorist and his memorable characters (principally the nice-but-dim Bertie Wooster, his valet Jeeves, and the eccentric upper-crust set at Blandings Castle) are much adored. Wodehouse's deftly crafted stories spanned a seventy-year career, reflecting an unchanging, carefree, between-the-wars England that never really existed at all.

Pop Britannia: A regional history of English music

ngland's fifty-year heritage as a source of inspirational rock'n'roll is indisputable: the country is sufficiently influential to attract talent from all over the world, but small enough for minority tastes to make it into the mainstream. England's historic role as the hub of the British Empire, absorbing immigrants from around the world into its numberless ports, has helped it assimilate styles and rhythms that have shaken the planet, and bred a sturdy domestic brand of popular music strengthened by regular injections from abroad. At the same time, in many musical genres – jazz, blues, ska, Northern Soul and reggae – England has provided a haven for foreign beats under threat at home. And as a small, but densely populated market in which to break a band, it's become almost traditional for American rockers to make it big in England before they take on their hometown stadium. It means that even after half a century, the country is still punching above its weight in the pop business.

England's best music has come from its cities, nourished by fashions from the urban stews and flavoured from the cultural melting pot. Here is a brief survey of some of its major cities, and the musical legacies they have created.

London

Inevitably, **London** has the bulk of the history and is home to the widest range of international influences; local acts soaked up the delicious musical juices seeping out of the shebeens, developing, for example, a taste for ska matched only in Kingston, Jamaica, and a white audience for US black music that Tamla Motown would envy. Until the rise of the post-punk indie labels in the late 1970s – typified by Manchester's Factory Records – artists on the way up had to make the trek to the capital to perform, to record and to sign a contract. Management and publishing companies lurked on the cheaper outskirts of the West End theatre and entertainment district, within easy reach of the BBC, record companies and recording studios; even though it never matched the US hit factories in scale, there was certainly a domestic "Tin Pan Alley", centred on **Denmark Street** in London's West End.

In the 1950s, US rock'n'rollers could sing along with Chuck Berry about "motorvatin' over the hill", but with the UK still gripped by austerity, and car ownership an impossible dream, English kids were more likely to blow their wages on music. In London, entrepreneurs such as Larry Parnes created menacing-sounding stage personae (**Tommy Steele**, **Marty Wilde** and **Billy Fury** for example) and stalked the cappuccino bars of Soho to find compliant star material they could reshape as the ideal "all-round entertainer". The whole sordid scene was spoofed in the 1959 film, *Espresso Bongo*, starring **Cliff Richard**.

The Sixties: Swinging London and psychedelia

As the industry blossomed in the early 1960s, the demonic **Rolling Stones** made their base in London and provided contrast and foil to The Beatles' thumbs-up attitude, bringing shade and cool to the otherwise permanent sunshine of pop music. Acts formed in London by native-born Londoners such as **The Who** and **The Small Faces** were merely the noisiest and most successful "**beat groups**" who terrified the locals before heading to the USA, following in the wake of The Beatles, in a "British Invasion". At its forefront were the archetypal Sixties' London band, **The Kinks**, led by brothers Ray and Dave Davies. They took their front-room brawling and musical rivalries worldwide, recording some of the most thoughtful, poignant and enduring pop charmers of the era, in between bouts of breaking equipment and scrapping onstage.

Swinging London was still the place to be when a wave of hippy lifestyles and free love washed over England from sunny California. This mid-Sixties tsunami upturned a lot of English pop furniture too: The **Bonzo Dog Doo-Dah Band** stirred up acid-jazz, **Pink Floyd** started out playing Chicago-style blues in Cambridge pubs before the acid kicked in and took them to the "Big Smoke". The *UFO* – downstairs at the now-demolished *Blarney's Club* on Tottenham Court Road – kick-started British psychedelia, booking the Floyd and **Soft Machine** in as house bands, hosting the first "light show" and promoting the **14 Hour Technicolor Dream** at Alexandra Palace in 1967 – London's most notorious gig of the decade.

The Seventies: Glitter, Bowie and the Pistols

When the beautiful dreams wore off, English rock became too heavy to bear, and English pop shouldered some weight itself in a return to the primitive stomping of **glam rock** and its pop-oriented offspring, **glitter**. For a while, East-End-boy-turned-bopping-elf **Marc Bolan** – the only one of the glittery pop stars of the 1970s who could really carry off the make-up and sparkle – ruled the roost. Then **Bowie** appeared – part glittery pop act, part all-round entertainer, part serious musician, 100 percent alien from another planet – to mess with minds around the world. Superficially at least, English pop had always been über-straight, and it's difficult today to convey just how shocking David's sexual "confession" of gayness/bisexuality was to an audience accustomed to sliced white bread and vanilla sex from its entertainers.

Bowie's flirtation with Weimar Republic decadence in the mid-Seventies extended to some of the era's more obnoxious political ideas. These, filtered through the airhead suburban minds of late-teen **Roxy Music** or Kraftwerk kids, mutated almost beyond recognition into **punk**. Typically those swastika-toting, bondage-clad rockers had no interest in politics at all, however, and would just as happily have worn a hammer and sickle if the Cold War enemy had been as potent a bogeyman and tool for baiting the bourgeoisie.

There's no denying that punk started off in New York, but it found its spiritual home among the arty end of London's student community before spreading to infect the dispossessed, disillusioned and downright snotty. Once **The Sex Pistols** – latest in a long line of iconoclastic West London bands that stretched back to The Who – had been associated by the media with **The Clash** and their satellite town peers including **The Damned**, **The Jam** and **Siouxsie & The Banshees**, a bandwagon was built and rolling, and for a few ecstatic months, punk rock ruled.

It mutated rapidly into a confusing mix of **post-punk** scenes pulling in different directions, from a brief rockabilly revival that swept across the south attempting to dance away the depression of a country in recession, to

Manchester's horde of grey-raincoated intelligentsia bellowing gloomy sagas of industrial apocalypse. **Sham 69**'s punky/skinhead crowd moved almost en masse into a smart-suited rudeboy look with a taste for high-speed **ska**.

The Eighties and beyond: from glamour to grime

Those left unmoved by the lack of glamour or style shown by most of these new movements turned by default back to the superficial fashion wars of nightclubs on the outskirts of Covent Garden (then still known only as the unused, dilapidated chunk of real estate that used to be the capital's fruit and veg market). London-formed acts such as **Duran Duran**, **Spandau Ballet**, **Culture Club** and **Adam & The Ants** (a one-time punk band reinvented as a crew of pirates) headed a squadron of **New Romantics** out of the nightlife and into the spotlight. Chart success led to world-cracking tours, with Duran Duran in particular going on to an apparently never-ending career in the US. George Michael even took **Wham!** from London to Beijing in 1985, becoming the first western pop act to gig in Red China.

England's pop shrines

Alley of love, Brighton Hometown of some of England's finest pop stars, Brighton was also the location of the main beachfront action in the movie of The Who's mod opera, *Quadrophenia*. Meanwhile, in an alley off East Street, Jimmy gets lucky with Leslie Ash and escapes from the cops by tumbling through a doorway and into a shop's back yard.

Glastonbury Home to the country's biggest festival (which however takes place on a farm some miles away), Glasto is England's mystic omphalos and consequently subject of far too many hippy-dippy tributes in song. One of the few places where you can still see people busking on the sackbut for spare change.

Town & Country Club, Leeds The city's best-loved major venue for the final years of the last millennium.

Eric's, Liverpool Crucible of the alternative and underground scene from the Seventies onward.

Abbey Road Studios, London The Beatles' permanent recording HQ in the capital, and birthplace to countless classic recordings from Pink Floyd to Radiohead.

Soho, London Stand in the centre of Soho Square, throw a brick in any direction and you'll hit a revered institution, recording company office, musicians' unlicensed club or aspiring superstar. Soho is where every facet of English pop finally comes together in an evil glitter. Seek out 23 Heddon St for that essential Ziggy Stardust tribute pic.

Hacienda Club, Manchester Now demolished, with a trendy urban apartment block development dancing on its grave, "The Hassy" was a traditional nightclub as envisioned by Tony Wilson, the city's most famous distracted, anarchistic musical entrepreneur.

Salford Lads' Club, Manchester Featured on the cover of The Smiths' album *The Queen Is Dead*, the club once boasted Allan Clarke of The Hollies among its members.

Twisted Wheel Club, Manchester Northern Soul venue par excellence, the Twisted Wheel played it fast, loud, heavy and all night long. The list of visiting bands reads like a Motown/Stax greatest hits set.

Leadmill Club, Sheffield Boasting more than 25 years as the city's top venue, the Leadmill has been an A-listed must-play gig for acts as diverse as Cabaret Voltaire, Killing Joke and The Fall in the Eighties to today's sleek young turns such as New Young Pony Club and Reverend & The Makers.

As usual in pop history though, the frills and ruffles eventually gave way to a search for "roots" and a "back to basics" movement in which the substance of lyrics and melody were considered more important than looks. As the Eighties' "me generation" attitude faded, the quest for authenticity in music in the Nineties threw up big names, including **Blur**, **Suede** and **Elastica** in London, and saw Camden reinvented as the capital of "**Britpop**". Elsewhere, the rise of ecstasy and the affection of a few DJs for the **house** and **techno** scenes of Chicago and Detroit laid the roots of the UK's enduring dance music culture, which for many began at Danny Rampling's euphoric *Shoom* night in Southwark in the last years of the 1980s.

The Camden school endures in reduced form to the present day, recent graduates including **The Libertines** (and their offshoots **Dirty Pretty Things** and **Babyshambles**), but it's still producing nothing more exciting than re-heated rock music. Arguably, the most vital of today's music centres on the harsh, hectic East London **grime** sound and South London's more minimal **dubstep**, both bastardized fusions of hip-hop, R&B and the weirder end of the dance spectrum.

Liverpool: Beatles to Zutons

As one of England's major port cities, **Liverpool** was home to substantial immigrant populations – of Chinese, Irish and West Indian in particular – with strong commercial links to the New York pop scene owing to the volume of maritime traffic between the two cities. Liverpool's post-war club scene scoured any softness from acts on stage, either through heckling or by throwing bottles, with the effect that any band that lasted a week's residency at *The Cavern* could do a 200-date US tour standing on its head.

When they hit big in 1963, **The Beatles** brought moptops, R&B and genuine passion to a pop scene stuffed with fake tough guys, insipid novelty tunes and crooning balladry. From *Please Please Me* to *Hey Jude*, their music furnished a constant reassuring backing track to the rest of the decade. Their success put the whole Merseyside music scene into the glare of a short-lived country-wide spotlight of interest: **Cilla Black** took shop-assistant naiveté to the top of the charts, while **Billy J. Kramer** led his **Dakotas** on screaming raids on the nation's dancehalls in a last gasp burst of old-school rock'n'roll. When The Beatles made the long drive down to London and became, save for a few lyrical memories, independent of Liverpool, the media attention moved away.

With so much cultural detritus washing up on the city's streets, however, it should come as no surprise Liverpudlian pop should rise again. **The Teardrop Explodes** and **Echo And The Bunnymen** played *Eric's* (on the same street as *The Cavern*) in the late Seventies, while throughout the Eighties and Nineties, kids would hook up at Probe Records before moving on for a night raving at local superclub, *Cream*. Meanwhile, Beatle-style melodic pop echoed back to the singalong romanticism much enjoyed in the Irish side of the community, and lived on long after the boys had split up. In the Nineties, **The La's**, love songs to heroin and **The Lightning Seeds'** tinkly prettinesses were bolstered by the more robust galloping beauties of **The Boo Radleys**, living on today in such flavours as **The Zutons** and **The Coral**.

Manchester: Morrissey, Madchester and Take That

At the other end of the M62 motorway, **Manchester**'s contribution to English pop music is even more impressive than Liverpool's. The city boasts Wigan Casino – home of Northern Soul – Morrissey's beloved Salford Lads Club, The Factory, Granada TV and the BBC's main northern studios, though it's the hedonistic nights at *The Hacienda* that excite the most wistful smiles. Furthermore, the list of Manchester bands is endless: from Sixties pop success stories such as **Herman's Hermits** to more recent heroes such as **Badly Drawn Boy**, the city's role as musical capital of the north continues unchallenged.

Manchester was the second city of English punk, and it nurtured a more sardonic, thoughtful crop of post-punk acts, including **Buzzcocks**, **The Fall** and **Joy Division** (who morphed into New Order on the death of singer Ian Curtis), that showed more genuine artistry and greater resilience than the perhaps more fashion-led London bands. From the Eighties, two bands, **The Smiths** and **New Order**, despite coming from opposite ends of the pop spectrum, stand out in particular. Morrissey's gentle meditations on confused sexuality, shyness and solitude gave a voice to a generation left cold by the mainstream pop world of the mid-80s, but if anything it was New Order that had the more far-reaching effect. Having embraced the new hedonism of synth-powered dance music, their music inspired an ecstasy-driven dance-all-night lifestyle that ultimately created local superclub **The Hacienda**. From this developed the "**Madchester**" scene that threw up **The Happy Mondays**, **The Stone Roses**, **The Charlatans** and **James**, and even lumped in straightforward guitar bands such as **Inspiral Carpets** and dime-a-dozen soul artists like **Lisa Stansfield**.

After "Madchester", the Manchester scene seemed to lose some of its energy – the early Nineties' most successful Mancunian act was manufactured boy band, **Take That**. But the city retained its swagger in the soap opera squabbles of **Oasis**'s Gallagher brothers, and its taste for downbeat realism with bands such as **The Verve**, and more recently, **Doves** and **Elbow**.

Birmingham and the west

Whilst **Brumbeat** donated its fair share of acts to the early to mid-Sixties scenes – with **Spencer Davis Group** and **Traffic** deserving special attention for pushing basic beat music forward to the edge of psychedelia – it was not till the era of **Black Sabbath** and **Led Zeppelin**, at the end of the decade, that Brummie pop came alive. Psychedelia couldn't last forever, and in the traditional metal-bashing areas of Birmingham and the West Midlands, it was soon stamped out of existence. Chart pop grew to thrive on hairstyles, glitter and dinosaur stomp delivered by unlikely-looking journeymen rock'n'rollers from an earlier generation. Local boy **Roy Wood** escaped The Move and Electric Light Orchestra to emerge as front man to **Wizzard** in the most extreme make-up ever seen on *Top Of The Pops*; **Slade**'s Noddy Holder sported trousers even more raucous than his gravelly voice; and **Edgar Broughton** was strident enough to stop a pint glass hurled at his head by sheer force of larynx. At the tail-end of the

Ray Davies, **Waterloo Sunset** (1967). Epic and timeless, The Kinks' greatest hit eulogizes that rarest of pleasures – a warm, sunny, romantic evening out in the capital.

Roy Harper, **One Of Those Days In England** (1977). A bowdlerized bucolic vision of a country on its way down the pan, Harper's classic tune is boosted by backing vocals from Paul and Linda McCartney, input from half of The Faces and some of the country's best session musicians. The full, ten-part version of the song is among the most profound "rock" memoirs ever recorded.

Elvis Costello, **I Don't Wanna Go To Chelsea** (1977). An oblique, if still obviously uncomplimentary, lyrical lashing of one of the capital's most divided quarters.

The JAMs, **It's Grim Up North** (1991). Pounding, industrial-strength, guitar-driven frenzy provides the ideal backing track to a list of dour-sounding towns and locations yelled into the roaring throat of a moorland storm. The video, apparently filmed at dead of night in the middle of a hurricane on a stretch of abandoned motorway, says it even better.

Cat Stevens, **Matthew & Son** (1967). English pop's favourite convert to Islam recorded this hate-filled tribute to the grinding conformism and exploitation of the proletariat, and took it high in the charts.

Morrissey, **Piccadilly Palare** (1990). Whether it be Piccadilly in London, in Manchester or wherever, there has to be a place in any top ten for one of England's great contributions to gay culture.

Julie Driscoll, **Vauxhall To Lambeth Bridge** (1969). One of the great Sixties psychedelic London songs (Big Ben gives our Jools a smile and a wink as she passes, for example) and based on a solid knowledge of the riverside walk it describes.

Kevin Coyne, **Eastbourne Ladies** (1978). Beautiful, rambling, backhanded tribute to a blue-rinsed generation that perhaps exists no more.

Babyshambles, **Albion** (2005). Winsome ballad to a mythical England of past and present – "violence in dole queues" – extolling the virtues of such exotic destinations as Catford and Oldham.

Billy Bragg, **A13, Trunk Road To The Sea** (1983). Essex's answer to Route 66 – the road to coastal resort Southend – as espoused by the Bard of Barking.

C

Seventies, **The Beat** and Coventry's **The Specials** were at the forefront of a ska revival, while a decade later, all the best "Grebo" (a term coined by **Pop Will Eat Itself**'s Clint Mansell, for a brand of pop aimed at wannabe motorcycle outlaws) bands talked like they had day jobs as Brummie diesel mechanics.

Along the M5 from Birmingham, **Bristol** is another of England's great ports. Its most recent heyday came with trip-hop, a catch-all term encompassing artists as diverse as **Portishead**, **Tricky** and **Massive Attack**, who rejected the guitar-led Britpop scene of the mid-Nineties in favour of a spacier, more downtempo sound. In truth, though, England's southwest has always had a reputation for left-field mavericks, from Dorset's **PJ Harvey** to Cornwall's **Aphex Twin**.

Yorkshire and the northeast

Newcastle gave us Sting, but had earned the right to one screw up after so many right moves: in the 1960s **The Animals** started here before growling their way to transatlantic success; a decade later punk heroes **Penetration** narrowly avoided moving beyond local-hero status. **Durham** sent us the mixed charm and cynicism of **Prefab Sprout**, but the area is best known for heavy metal and wild drunken misbehaviour from local mavericks such as **Lindisfarne** (who recorded *Fog On The Tyne*) and Ginger of **The Wildhearts**.

Magic dropped from the skies of **Hull** when Mick Ronson and Mick Woodmansey agreed to become the linchpins of Bowie's **Spiders From Mars** and took the first train south in the early Seventies. Having developed a taste for **Scritti Politti**'s silken balladry, Eighties' pop took a big boost from local darlings **Everything But The Girl** and **The Housemartins**, both acts who delighted in depressing realities normally scorned by chart acts.

When post-punk provided a gloomy context to match the prevailing dismal climate, **Leeds** responded with bands such as **The Mekons**, **Gang of Four** and **Chumbawamba** (one-hit anarcho-syndicalist wonders who struck gold fifteen years later with *Tubthumping*), each of whom happily churned up a subversive storm of their own. Elsewhere in Leeds, **Soft Cell** and **Sisters of Mercy** provided a suitably evil backdrop to the era's pop cheeriness, paving the way for **The Wedding Present**'s guitar onslaught.

Dave Berry and **Joe Cocker** led **Sheffield**'s steel city invasion in the Sixties, with the punishing stylings of **Def Leppard**, **Cabaret Voltaire** and others maintaining the city's metal-bashing traditions long after the cutlery factories had closed down. The city has also given us a more stylish brand of pop than other regional conurbations, with **Human League**'s glossy magazine tunes giving way to the elegant sophistication of **ABC**. **Pulp**'s domination of the thinking-teen's playlist kept the city in the limelight in the 1990s, while **Warp Records** championed an eclectic selection of techno, ambient and rock music, giving an early home to dance iconoclast, Aphex Twin. By the mid-2000s, though, the baton of elegant sneering, backed up by solid musicianship, had been passed to current favourites, **Arctic Monkeys**.

The music industry today

With such a rich history, live music is alive and well across England in the twenty-first century, finding a forum in an ever-expanding glut of clubs, venues and summer festivals. The record business however is in trouble, with stores closing in cities all across the country, big name labels in decline and the death of the *NME* predicted in several quarters. Bands such as Arctic Monkeys, The Libertines and Babyshambles generated enough word-of-mouth via the Internet that they were able to dispense with the kind of crippling contractual agreement that hobbled so many artists in earlier years. In 2007, **Radiohead**, consistently the most influential band of their era, made history by releasing their seventh album initially through digital download only, with fans able to choose their own price. The Biz has responded to these changes of direction in the industry, as usual, by leaping on dimly perceived traces of a new bandwagon whenever it appears. Women behaving badly are always popular – where once it was the **Spice Girls**, these days it's **Girls Aloud**, **Amy Winehouse**, **Lily Allen** and their pals proudly carrying the torch of mischief – but looking at the whole dismal spread it's plain that today's music business is as bloodthirsty as ever. It's so cutthroat that a lot of promising ideas and genuinely exciting talents have been drowned in a wash of advance payments and overexposure. Reality TV shows draw out undeniably talented but bloodless performers whose records still hit the charts, but the best English music is still to be found in the clubs where the coolest kids hang out.

Al Spicer

Film

F or much of its history, the British **film industry** has been pretty much an English affair, with its major studios (Ealing, Pinewood and Shepperton) not far from central London and its stars drawn from the ranks of the capital's stage actors. However, unlike the Hollywood star system, the English film industry tended – and still significantly relies on – strong ensemble playing. As for the particulars, **Ealing's films** were a by-word for social comedy, the **Hammer horror series** (usually featuring Christopher Lee and Peter Cushing) stuck to Dracula, Frankenstein and so forth, whereas costume dramas were typified by the **Gainsborough** company's productions. There were also the **James Bond** films and the **Carry On** series, which kept a generation of comedy actors in work long past their sell-by date. In the 1960s, English films developed a justifiable reputation for social realism, which has been maintained in more recent times by directors such as Ken Loach and Mike Leigh.

Today's film industry is in a healthier state than perhaps at any point since the 1930s with a diversity and vitality that reflects the dominance of independent productions. Some film fans might argue that the influence of television means that many such productions are essentially small-screen ventures, but in recent years a host of English pictures – *Atonement* for one – have enjoyed great international success.

The films listed below are all set in England. They are not exclusively greats – though some rank amongst the best movies ever made – but all depict a particular aspect of English life, whether reflecting the experience of immigrant communities, exploring the country's history, or depicting its richly varied landscapes.

The 1930s and 1940s

Brief Encounter (David Lean, 1945). Wonderful weepie as Trevor Howard and Celia Johnson teeter on the edge of adultery at a commuter railway station. Noël Coward was responsible for the clipped dialogue, Rachmaninov for the flushed, dreamy score.

Brighton Rock (John Boulting, 1947). A fine adaptation of Graham Greene's novel, featuring a young, genuinely scary Richard Attenborough as the psychopathic hood Pinkie, who marries a witness to one of his crimes to ensure her silence. Beautiful cinematography and good performances, with a real sense of *film noir* menace.

A Canterbury Tale (Michael Powell and Emeric Pressburger, 1944). Set in a wartime Kent village, where a plucky Land Girl, a small-town GI and a sardonic English sergeant are billeted. Overseen by a mysterious local magistrate, they make their own pilgrimage to Canterbury, the cathedral glowing high over bomb-damaged streets. A mystical vision of English history is fused with bucolic images of rural life, a restrained exploration of the characters' personal suffering underlying a truly magical masterpiece.

Fires Were Started (Humphrey Jennings, 1943). One of the best films to come out of the British documentary tradition, this is the story of the experiences of a group of firemen through one night of bombing during the Blitz. The use of real firemen as performers rather than professional actors, and the avoidance of formulaic heroics, gives the film great power as an account of the courage of ordinary people who fought on the home front.

Great Expectations (David Lean 1946). Early film by one of England's finest directors – *Lawrence of Arabia*, *Bridge on the River Kwai* – this superb rendition of the Dickens novel features magnificent performances by John Mills (as Pip) and Finlay Currie (as Abel Magwitch). The scene in the graveyard will make your hair stand on end.

Henry V (Laurence Olivier, 1944). Featuring glowing Technicolor backdrops, this rousing piece of wartime propaganda is emphatically "theatrical", the action spiralling out from the Globe Theatre itself. Olivier is a brilliantly charismatic king, the pre-battle scene where he goes disguised amongst his men being delicately muted and atmospheric.

Jane Eyre (Robert Stevenson, 1943). Joan Fontaine does a fine job of portraying Jane, and Orson Welles is a suavely sardonic Rochester – the scene in which he is thrown from his horse in the mist hits the perfect melodramatic pitch. With the unlikely tagline "A Love Story Every Woman Would Die a Thousand Deaths to Live!", it briefly features a young Elizabeth Taylor as a dying Helen Burns.

Kind Hearts and Coronets (Robert Hamer, 1949). As with the best of the Ealing movies, this is a savage comedy on the cruel absurdities of the British class system. With increasing ingenuity, Dennis Price's suave and ruthless anti-hero murders his way through the D'Ascoyne clan (all brilliantly played by Alec Guinness) to claim the family title.

The Life and Death of Colonel Blimp (Michael Powell and Emeric Pressburger, 1943). An epic if somewhat sentimental celebration of the romantic spirit of the English, personified by the wonderful Roger Livesey. We follow him through the actual and emotional duels of his youth, against his equally dashing German foe, to crusty old age in World War II. A daring and visually stunning story of love and friendship, it was hated by Churchill for supposedly being unpatriotic.

Rebecca (Alfred Hitchock, 1940). Hitchcock does du Maurier: Laurence Olivier is wonderfully enigmatic as Maxim de Winter, and Joan Fontaine glows as his meek second wife, living in the shadow of her mysterious predecessor. Perfectly paced and beautifully shot, Hitch's first Hollywood picture is a classic.

The Thirty-Nine Steps (Alfred Hitchcock, 1935). Hitchcock's best-loved British movie, full of wit and acts of derring-do. Robert Donat stars as innocent Richard Hannay, inadvertently caught up in a mysterious spy ring and forced to flee both the spies and the agents of Scotland Yard. In a typically perverse Hitchcock touch, he spends a generous amount of time handcuffed to Madeleine Carroll, fleeing across the Scottish countryside, before the action returns to London for the film's great music-hall conclusion.

The Wicked Lady (Leslie Arliss, 1945). One of the best of Gainsborough Studios' series of escapist romances, this features a magnificently amoral and headstrong Margaret Lockwood, wooed into a criminal double life by James Mason's quintessentially dashing highwayman. Its opulent recreation of eighteenth-century England is terribly appealing, as are the tempestuous entanglements of its two wayward stars.

Billy Liar (John Schlesinger, 1963).
Tom Courtenay is stuck in a dire job
as an undertaker's clerk in a northern
town, and spends his time creating
extravagant fantasies. His life is lit up
by the appearance of Julie Christie,
who holds out the glamour and
promise of swinging London.
Touching and amusing in equal
measure.

Carry On Screaming (Gerald
Thomas, 1966). One of the better
efforts from the Carry On crew, with
most of the usual suspects (Kenneth
Williams, Charles Hawtrey, Joan
Sims) hamming it up in a Hammer
Horror spoof and serving up a few
scares along with the usual single-
entendre jokes.

Dracula (Terence Fisher, 1958).
Classic Hammer Horror flick, loosely
based on Bram Stoker's original
book and pairing Christopher Lee as
the blood-sucking count with Peter
Cushing's vampire-staking Van
Helsing.

Far From the Madding Crowd
(John Schlesinger, 1967). A largely
successful and imaginative adaptation
of Hardy's doom-laden tale of the
desires and ambitions of wilful
Bathsheba Everdene. Julie Christie is
a radiant and spirited Bathsheba,
Terence Stamp flashes his blade to
dynamic effect, Alan Bates is quietly
charismatic as dependable Gabriel
Oak, and the West Country setting is
sparsely beautiful.

I'm Alright Jack (John and Roy
Boulting, 1959). The best of the
Boulting Brothers' comic explorations of English social mores explores
the class system in the context of
industrial unrest. Peter Sellers is on
top form as the shop steward, while
management is represented by a
hapless Ian Carmichael (brought in
to cause disruption through his own

ineptitude) who, naturally, falls in
love with Sellers' daughter. Very
reactionary, but intriguing all the
same.

Kes (Kenneth Loach, 1969). This is
the unforgettable story of a neglected
Yorkshire schoolboy who finds solace
and liberation in training his kestrel.
As a still pertinent commentary on
poverty and an unsympathetic school
system, it's bleak but idealistic, and
pale and pinched David Bradley who
plays Billy Casper is hugely affecting.

The Ladykillers (Alexander
Mackendrick, 1955). Alec Guinness is
fabulously toothy and malevolent as
"Professor Marcus", a murderous
conman who lodges with a sweet
little old lady, Mrs Wilberforce. The
professor and his ragbag of criminal
accomplices – their sinister intent a
hilarious counterpoint to Mrs
Wilberforce's genteel tea parties – try
to pass themselves off as musicians,
while, thanks to her innocent
interventions, the body count
inexorably mounts.

A Man For All Seasons (Fred
Zinnemann, 1966). Sir Thomas More
versus Henry VIII in one of British
history's great moral confrontations,
following a skilful, tactile script by
Robert Bolt. Muted, atmospheric
visuals and a heavenly host of
theatrical talent (including a cheering
appearance by Orson Welles as
Cardinal Wolsey) add to the spectacle,
if not the tension, which is where
the film dithers.

Night and the City (Jules Dassin,
1950). Great *film noir*, with Richard
Widmark as an anxious nightclub
hustler on the run. Gripping and
convincingly sleazy, the London
streetscapes have an expressionist
edge of horror.

Performance (Nicolas Roeg/
Donald Cammell, 1970). Credited

C

with precipitating James Fox's breakdown and subsequent retirement from the movies, this shape-shifting tale of gangsters and pop culture is the best account of the hedonistic end to Britain's psychedelic 1960s. Well known for its strange drug-hazed second half, the film is also brilliantly funny in parts and should be cherished for its sharp-witted destruction of the myth of Kray-style criminals.

Saturday Night and Sunday Morning (Karel Reisz, 1960). Reisz's monochrome captured all the grit and dead-end grind of Albert Finney's work in a Nottingham bicycle factory and his attempts to find spice and romance in the city's pubs and on its canal banks.

This Sporting Life (Lindsay Anderson, 1963). One of the key British films of the 1960s, *This Sporting Life* tells the story of a northern miner turned star player for his local rugby league team. The young Richard Harris gives a great performance as the inarticulate anti-hero, able only to express himself through physical violence, and the film is one of the best examples of the gritty "kitchen sink" genre it helped to usher in.

The War Game (Peter Watkins, 1965). Watkins' astonishing documentary approach to the effects of a Russian nuclear attack on southeast England, using both local people and various official "talking heads", shocked its commissioner, the BBC, into refusing to show it – hardly surprising, since its overall effect was to question our trust in authority. Much-dated in comparison to modern computer-driven special effects, it still retains the power to alarm.

The 1970s and 1980s

Akenfield (Peter Hall, 1974). A powerfully involving evocation of English rural life whose ingredients include glowing cinematography and Michael Tippett's wonderful music. Past and present are skilfully contrasted, but the heart of the film lies in its ecstatic but still unsentimental rendering of the past.

Babylon (Franco Rosso, 1980). A moving account of black, working-class London life. We follow the experiences of young Blue through a series of encounters that reveal the insidious forces of racism at work in Britain. Good performances and a great reggae soundtrack; an all too rare example of Black Britain taking centre stage in a British movie.

Chariots of Fire (Hugh Hudson, 1981). Based around the 1924 Olympics, this hugely successful movie tells the true story of two runners, the Scottish missionary Eric Liddell (Ian Charleson) and repressed Cambridge student Harold Abrahams (Ben Cross). Oscar-winning and a tad overblown, it's distinguished by Charleson's quiet performance, and some great locations.

A Clockwork Orange (Stanley Kubrick, 1971). Famously banned in the UK by director Kubrick himself, this is a genuinely disturbing if now slightly dated depiction of violence and society's reaction to it, in which young droog Alex – played with charm and menace by Malcolm McDowell – finds himself first the perpetrator and then the victim, all to a rousing Beethoven soundtrack.

Comrades (Bill Douglas, 1986). In 1830s England, a group of farm workers decide to stand up to the exploitative tactics of the local landowner, and find themselves prosecuted and transported to

Australia. Based on the true story of the Tolpuddle Martyrs, this combines political education (the founding of the modern trade union movement) with a moving and visually stunning celebration of working lives.

Distant Voices, Still Lives (Terence Davies, 1988). Beautifully realized autobiographical tale of growing up in Forties and Fifties Liverpool. The mesmeric pace is punctuated by astonishing moments of drama, and the whole is a very moving account of how a family survives and triumphs, in small ways, against the odds.

Frenzy (Alfred Hitchcock, 1972). Hitchcock comes back to Blighty in top form, with the story of a man on the run, under suspicion for the vicious "neck tie" murders carried out in Covent Garden. Trademark sly black humour combines with a disturbing exploration of sexual immaturity.

Get Carter (Mike Hodges, 1971). Although not the masterpiece some claim, this is still one of the most vivid and interesting British gangster movies, featuring a monumentally savage outing for Michael Caine as the eponymous villain, returning to his native Newcastle to avenge his brother's death. Great use of northeast locations and a fine turn by playwright John Osborne as the local godfather, though the misogyny can be wearisome.

Hope and Glory (John Boorman, 1987). A glorious autobiographical feature about the Blitz seen through the eyes of nine-year-old Bill, who revels in the liberating chaos of bomb-site playgrounds, tumbling barrage balloons and shrapnel collections. His older sister's unfettered romps with a Canadian soldier and the adults' privation and occasional despair are an additional source of amusement for Bill and his sister.

The Last of England (Derek Jarman, 1987). Derek Jarman was a genuine maverick presence in Eighties Britain and this is his most abstract account of the state of the nation. Composed of apparently unrelated shots of decaying London landscapes, rent boys and references to emblematic national events such as the Falklands War, this may not be to all tastes, but it is a fitting testament to a unique talent in British film-making.

The Long Good Friday (John MacKenzie, 1979). Bob Hoskins is in top form as a maniacal East End gang boss threatened by powerful, mysterious new arrivals – the IRA. However, the film's vision of East End villains can seem more than a touch self-indulgent, and the plodding TV visual style doesn't help to raise the level.

Made in Britain (Alan Clarke, 1982). One of Alan Clarke's series of incisive dissections of Eighties Britain, featuring a 17-year-old Tim Roth as skinhead Trevor on a downbeat odyssey of job-centre visits, drug-taking and racist explosions. The energy of the central performance delivers a film of real force, and a very powerful indictment of Thatcher's Britain.

Mona Lisa (Neil Jordan, 1986). This fine London-based thriller has powerful performances from Bob Hoskins, Michael Caine and then-newcomer Cathy Tyson, the latter playing a high-class prostitute who recruits Hoskins to help find her lost friend. This takes him, and us, on a nightmarish exploration of the dark side of Eighties London, lightened only slightly by an utterly convincing, poignant love story, as Bob begins to fall for his beautiful employer.

My Beautiful Laundrette (Stephen Frears, 1985). A slice of Thatcher's Britain, with Omar, a young Asian on the make, opening a ritzy laundrette. His lover, Johnny (Daniel Day-Lewis), is an ex-National Front glamour boy, angry and inarticulate when forced by the acquisitive Omar into a menial role in the laundrette. The racial, sexual and class dynamics of their relationship are closely observed, and mirror the tensions engendered by the Asian presence in an unforgiving London.

Withnail and I (Bruce Robinson, 1986). Richard E. Grant is superb as the raddled, drunken Withnail, an out-of-work actor with a penchant for drinking lighter fluid. Paul McGann is the "I" of the title – a bemused and beautiful spectator of Withnail's wild excesses, as they abandon an astonishingly grotty London flat for the wilds of a remote cottage, and the attentions of Withnail's randy uncle Monty.

The 1990s

Bhaji on the Beach (Gurinder Chadha, 1993). An Asian women's group takes a day-trip to Blackpool in this issue-laden but enjoyable picture. A lot of fun is had contrasting the seamier side of British life with the mores of the Asian aunties, though the male characters are cartoon villains one and all.

East is East (Damien O'Donnell, 1999). Seventies Salford is the setting for this lively comedy, with a Pakistani chip-shop owner struggling to keep control of his seven children as they rail against the strictures of Islam and arranged marriages. Inventively made, with some pleasing performances.

Elizabeth (Shekhar Kapur, 1998). Visually stunning, if historically dubious, account of Elizabeth I's early years as queen. Amidst the swirling cloaks and echoing corridors, Cate Blanchett carries all before her, ably supported by Kathy Burke (Queen Mary), Geoffrey Rush (Walsingham) and Joseph Fiennes (Robert Dudley). Try not to notice the bit part by one-time footballing star Eric Cantona.

Four Weddings and a Funeral (Richard Curtis, 1994). Standard rom-com that used an American actress and gags based on English eccentricities to pull in big audiences worldwide. Hugh Grant and his middle-class chums maybe entirely unfamiliar to most contemporary Brits, but there are some very funny set-pieces.

The Full Monty (Peter Cattaneo, 1997). Six Sheffield ex-steel workers throw caution to the wind and become male strippers, their boast being that all will be revealed – the "full monty". Unpromising physical specimens all, they score an unlikely hit with the local lasses. The film was itself an unlikely hit worldwide, largely because the theme of manhood in crisis is sensitively explored. The long-awaited striptease is a joy to behold.

Lock, Stock and Two Smoking Barrels (Guy Ritchie, 1998). Four lads attempt to pay off gambling debts by making a drug deal in this highly stylized picture, which, though it has a modern setting, pays dubious homage to the London of the Kray twins. However, the suits are sharp, the production is slick and football's hard man turned actor Vinnie Jones turns in a surprisingly solid debut performance.

The Madness of King George (Nicholas Hytner, 1994). Adapted from an Alan Bennett play, this royal romp is handsomely staged with the king's loopy antics played out against a cartoon-like court and its acolytes. An endearing, witty script.

Nil by Mouth (Gary Oldman, 1997). With strong performances by Ray Winstone (Ray) as a boorish south Londoner and Kathy Burke (Valery) as his battered wife, this brave and bleak picture depicts Ray as a victim of his own violence, as well as the devastatingly vulnerable Valery. Brace yourself.

The Remains of the Day (James Ivory, 1993). Kazuo Ishiguro's masterly study of social and personal repression translates beautifully to the big screen. Anthony Hopkins is the overly decorous butler who gradually becomes aware of his master's fascist connections, Emma Thompson the housekeeper who struggles to bring his real, deeply suppressed feelings to the surface.

Richard III (Richard Loncraine, 1995). A splendid film version of a renowned National Theatre production, which brilliantly transposed the action to a fascist state in the 1930s. The infernal political machinations of a snarling Ian McKellen as Richard are heightened by Nazi associations, and the style of the period imbues the film with the requisite glamour – as does languorously drugged Kristin Scott-Thomas as Lady Anne.

Secrets and Lies (Mike Leigh, 1995). Much-loved Mike Leigh slice-of-life drama, with wonderful Timothy Spall at the head of a spectacularly dysfunctional London family. His sister Cynthia (Brenda Blethyn), her heart of gold buried in boozy, cloying unhappiness, is reunited with the black daughter she gave up for adoption at birth. Overlong improvised sequences and a depiction of suburban vulgarity which comes close to parody are lifted by stunning ensemble performances and sustained by the simple strength of its central tenet: that secrets and lies in a family will only cause unnecessary pain.

Sense and Sensibility (Ang Lee, 1995). Jane Austen's sprightly essay on the merits of well-modified behaviour is nicely realized by Lee, and neatly scripted by Emma Thompson. Both Kate Winslet and Thompson are charming as the downtrodden Dashwood sisters: Winslet is a brilliantly over-wrought, romantic Marianne, while Thompson turns in a perfect performance as prudent Elinor.

Shakespeare in Love (John Madden, 1998). An irresistible homage to life, love and Shakespeare has an energetic Joseph Fiennes as the quill-chewing bard and Gwyneth Paltrow as his sparky love interest. Sharply scripted by Tom Stoppard, it skips a dainty line between parody and over-reverence, and has fun sending up the British fondness for cameos, with Rupert Everett as melancholy Kit Marlowe, off on a one-way trip for a drink in Deptford.

The 2000s

Atonement (Joe Wright, 2007). Critically acclaimed film, based on the eponymous Ian McEwan novel, in which a young girl's accusations against her older sister's lover sets in motion a series of events that follows them right through World War II. Some great set-piece scenes – not least of the Dunkirk evacuation in 1940 – and a fine evocation of 1930s England with its clipped mores and tight class system.

Bend It like Beckham (Gurinder Chadha, 2003). Immensely successful film focusing on the coming of age of a football-loving Punjabi girl in a suburb of London. Both socially acute and comic.

Bridget Jones's Diary (Sharon Maguire, 2001). American Renée Zellweger put on a plummy English accent and several pounds to play the lead in this *Pride and Prejudice* for the new millennium. Ably assisted by deliciously nasty love-interest Hugh Grant, the film stands out as one of the better British romantic comedies of the last ten years.

Children of Men (Alfonso Cuaron, 2006). Set in a seedy, futuristic London, where gangs run wild and foreign refugees are imprisoned in cages, this explosive sci-fi film eschews high-tech gadgetry to focus on what London might become if the worst comes to the worst. The (semi-) optimistic ending is a surprise. Riveting stuff.

Control (Anton Corbijn, 2007). Ian Curtis, the lead singer of Joy Division, committed suicide in 1980 at the age of 23. This biopic tracks his life in and around Manchester and Macclesfield based on the account provided by his wife, Deborah. Some have raved over Sam Riley's portrayal of Curtis, others have been less convinced, but as an evocation of the early days of Factory Records it's hard to beat.

Dirty Pretty Things (Stephen Frears, 2003). A tumbling mix of melodrama, social criticism and black comedy, this forceful, thought-provoking film explores the world of Britain's illegal immigrants.

Eastern Promises (David Cronenberg, 2007). Russian gangsters in London is the theme – and the Canadian horror specialist, Cronenberg, is the practitioner. Full of vim and verve, blood and guts.

Elizabeth: The Golden Age (Shekhar Kapur, 2007). Presses all the same buttons as Kapur's earlier *Elizabeth* (see p.978), with Blanchett taking centre stage once again.

Enigma (Michael Apted, 2001). This blockbuster, scripted by playwright Tom Stoppard, is a fictional tale depicting Britain's wartime efforts to crack the Germans' Enigma encrypting machine, with Kate Winslet excelling amongst a generally fine cast.

Gosford Park (Robert Altman, 2001). Astutely observed upstairs-downstairs murder mystery set in class-ridden 1930s England. The multi-layered plot is typical of Altman while the who's who of great British actors is led by the superb Maggie Smith – and only let down by Stephen Fry's bumbling police inspector who looks like he's wandered in from an entirely different film.

Harry Potter and the Philosopher's Stone (Chris Columbus, 2001). The first of the Harry Potter films did wonders for the English tourist industry, pulling punters to its key locations – Alnwick Castle for one. The subsequent films are also darkly enjoyable, with excellent ensemble casts – Spall, Gambon, Thompson et al.

London to Brighton (Paul Andrew Williams, 2006). Urgent, compelling film set amidst the sleazy violence of gangster England. Two women – one a prostitute, the other an under-age runaway – hot-foot it to Brighton to escape a brutal pimp, in the process establishing a tender (but never sentimental) friendship that transcends their situation.

Sexy Beast (Jonathan Glazer, 2000). Gangster thriller distinguished by the performances of Ray Winstone (Gary Dove) and more especially Ben Kingsley (Don Logan), who plays one of the hardest, meanest criminals ever.

Shaun Of The Dead (Edgar Wright, 2004). Horror-romp in which Simon Pegg (Shaun), the hapless hero, and his band of chums, struggle to escape the clutches of the army of flesh-eating zombies that have taken over north London. Juicy script too.

This Is England (Shane Meadows, 2007). British cinema rarely ventures out into the Midlands, but this is where Shane Meadows is at home. Set in the early 1980s, this thoughtful and thought-provoking film deals with a young working-class lad who falls in with skinheads – the good-hearted ones to begin with, the racists thereafter. If it gives you a taste for Meadows, try also his *Dead Man's Shoes* (2004), a tale of revenge for the cruel murder of the protagonist's brother; again, there's a Midlands setting.

24 Hour Party People (Michael Winterbottom, 2002). Steve Coogan plays the entrepreneurial/inspirational Tony Wilson in this fast-moving recreation of the early days of Manchester's Factory Records. Stunning soundtrack too.

Vera Drake (Mike Leigh, 2004). Moving story of a 1950s working-class woman, Vera Drake, who performs illegal abortions from the goodness of her heart and without thought for either money or the legal consequences, which eventually threaten to destroy her and her close-knit family. A powerful counter-blast to the anti-abortion lobby.

Glossary of architectural terms

Aedicule Small decorative niche formed by two columns or pilasters supporting a pediment.

Aisle Clear space parallel to the nave, usually with lower ceiling than the nave.

Altar Table at which the Eucharist is celebrated, at the east end of the church.

Ambulatory Covered passage around the outer edge of the choir of a church.

Apse The curved or polygonal east end of a church.

Arcade Row of arches on top of columns or piers, supporting a wall.

Art Deco Geometrical style of art and architecture popular in the 1930s.

Art Nouveau Style of art, architecture and design based on highly stylized vegetal forms. Especially popular in the early part of the twentieth century.

Ashlar Dressed building stone worked to a smooth finish.

Bailey Area enclosed by castle walls.

Balustrade An ornamental rail, running, almost invariably, along the top of a building.

Barbican Defensive structure built in front of a main gate.

Barrel vault Continuous rounded vault, like a semi-cylinder.

Boss A decorative carving at the meeting point of the lines of a vault.

Box pew Form of church seating in which each row is enclosed by high, thin wooden panels.

Broach spire Octagonal spire rising straight out of a square tower.

Buttress Stone support for a wall; some buttresses are wholly attached to the wall, others take the form of an outer support with a connecting half-arch, known as a "flying buttress".

Capital Upper section of a column, usually carved.

Chancel The eastern part of a church, often separated from the nave by a screen (see "rood-screen" p.984). Contains the choir and ambulatory.

Chantry Small chapel in which masses were said for the soul of the person who financed its construction; none built after the Reformation as Protestants rejected the doctrine of prayers for the dead.

Choir Area in which the church service is conducted; next to or the same as the chancel.

Classical Architectural style incorporating Greek and Roman elements – pillars, domes, colonnades etc – at its height in the seventeenth century and revived, as Neoclassical (see opposite), in the nineteenth.

Clerestory Upper story of a church, with windows.

Coffering Regular recessed spaces set into a ceiling.

Crenellations Battlements with square indentations.

Crossing (church) The intersection of the nave, choir and transepts.

Decorated Middle Gothic style; about 1280–1380.

Dogtooth Form of early Gothic decorative stonework, looking like raised teeth.

Dormer Window raised out of the main roof.

Early English First phase of Gothic architecture in England; about 1150–1280.

Fan vaulting Late Gothic form of vaulting, in which the area between the walls and ceiling is covered with stone ribs in the shape of an open fan.

Finial Any decorated tip of an architectural feature.

Flushwork Kind of surface decoration in which tablets of white stone alternate with pieces of flint; very common in East Anglia.

Fresco Wall painting – durable through application to wet plaster.

Gargoyle Grotesque exterior carving, usually a decorative form of water spout.

Gothic Architectural style of the thirteenth to sixteenth centuries, characterized by pointed arches, rib vaulting, flying buttresses and a general emphasis on verticality. See also "Decorated", "Early English" and "Perpendicular".

Hammer beam Type of ceiling in which horizontal brackets support vertical struts that connect to the roof timbers.

Jesse Tree Christian legend asserts that Jesse, the father of King David, was the ancestor of Jesus, and Jesse windows trace the genealogical tree by means of their stained-glass pictures.

Keep Main structure of a castle.

Lady Chapel Chapel dedicated to the Virgin, often found at the east end of major churches.

Lancet Tall, narrow and plain window.

Lantern Upper part of a dome or tower, often glazed.

Misericord Ledge on choir stall on which the occupant can be supported while standing; often carved with secular subjects (bottoms were not thought worthy of religious subject matter – quite right too).

Motte Mound on which a castle keep stands.

Mullion Vertical post between the panes of a window.

Nave Main body of a church.

Neoclassical A style of classical architecture (see opposite) revived in the nineteenth century.

Neo-Gothic Revived Gothic style of architecture popular in the late eighteenth and nineteenth centuries.

Ogee Double curve; distinctive feature of Decorated style.

Oriel Projecting window.

Palladian Seventeenth- and eighteenth-century classical style adhering to the principles of Andrea Palladio.

Pediment Triangular space above a window or doorway.

Perpendicular Late Gothic style; about 1380–1550.

Pier A massive column, often consisting of several fused smaller columns.

Pilaster Flat Column set against a wall.

Renaissance The period of European history, begun in Italy, marking the end of the medieval period and the rise of the modern world. Defined, amongst many criteria, by an increase in classical scholarship, geographical discovery, the rise of secular values and the growth of individualism.

Reredos Painted or carved panel behind an altar.

Retable Altarpiece.

Romanesque Early medieval architecture distinguished by squat, heavy forms, rounded arches and naive sculpture.

Rood-loft Gallery (or space) on top of a rood-screen.

Rood-screen Decorative screen separating the nave from the chancel.

Rose window Large circular window, divided into vaguely petal-shaped sections.

Sedilia Seats for the participants in the church service, usually on the south side of the choir.

Stalls Seating for clergy in the choir area of a church.

Tracery Pattern formed by narrow bands of stone in a window or on a wall surface.

Transept Arms of a cross-shaped church, placed at ninety degrees to nave and chancel.

Triforium Arcade above the nave or transept in a church.

Triptych Carved or painted work on three panels. Often used as an altarpiece.

Tympanum Sculpted, usually recessed, panel above a door.

Vault An arched ceiling or roof.

Travel store

D: Rough Guide
DIRECTIONS for
short breaks

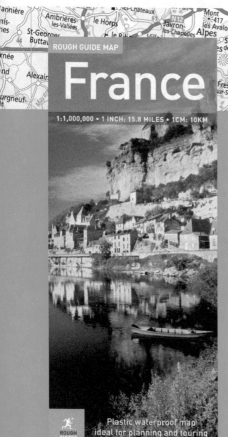

www.roughguides.com

Information on over 25,000 destinations around the world

- **Read** Rough Guides' trusted travel info
- **Access** exclusive articles from Rough Guides authors
- **Update** yourself on new books, maps, CDs and other products
- **Enter** our competitions and win travel prizes
- **Share** ideas, journals, photos & travel advice with other users
- **Earn** points every time you contribute to the Rough Guide
  community and get rewards

Avoid Guilt Trips

Buy fair trade coffee + bananas ✓

Save energy - use low energy bulbs ✓

- don't leave tv on standby ✓

Offset carbon emissions from flight to Madrid ✓

Send goat to Africa ✓

Join Tourism Concern today ✓

Slowly, the world is changing.
Together we can, and will, make a difference.

Tourism Concern is the only UK registered charity fighting exploitation in one of the largest industries on earth: people forced from their homes in order that holiday resorts can be built, sweatshop labour conditions in hotels and destruction of the environment are just some of the issues that we tackle.

Sending people on a guilt trip is not something we do. We know as well as anyone that holidays are precious. But you can help us to ensure that tourism always benefits the local communities involved.

Call 020 7133 3330
or visit **tourismconcern.org.uk** to find out how.

A year's membership of Tourism Concern costs just £20 (£12 unwaged)
- that's 38 pence a week, less than the cost of a pint of milk, organic of course.

Fighting
Exploitation
in Tourism

TourismConcern

NOTES

NOTES

Small print and
Index

A Rough Guide to Rough Guides

Published in 1982, the first Rough Guide – to Greece – was a student scheme that became a publishing phenomenon. Mark Ellingham, a recent graduate in English from Bristol University, had been travelling in Greece the previous summer and couldn't find the right guidebook. With a small group of friends he wrote his own guide, combining a highly contemporary, journalistic style with a thoroughly practical approach to travellers' needs.

The immediate success of the book spawned a series that rapidly covered dozens of destinations. And, in addition to impecunious backpackers, Rough Guides soon acquired a much broader and older readership that relished the guides' wit and inquisitiveness as much as their enthusiastic, critical approach and value-for-money ethos.

These days, Rough Guides include recommendations from shoestring to luxury and cover more than 200 destinations around the globe, including almost every country in the Americas and Europe, more than half of Africa and most of Asia and Australasia. Our ever-growing team of authors and photographers is spread all over the world, particularly in Europe, the USA and Australia.

In the early 1990s, Rough Guides branched out of travel, with the publication of Rough Guides to World Music, Classical Music and the Internet. All three have become benchmark titles in their fields, spearheading the publication of a wide range of books under the Rough Guide name.

Including the travel series, Rough Guides now number more than 350 titles, covering: phrasebooks, waterproof maps, music guides from Opera to Heavy Metal, reference works as diverse as Conspiracy Theories and Shakespeare, and popular culture books from iPods to Poker. Rough Guides also produce a series of more than 120 World Music CDs in partnership with World Music Network.

Visit www.roughguides.com to see our latest publications.

Rough Guide travel images are available for commercial licensing at www.roughguidespictures.com

SMALL PRINT

Rough Guide credits

Text editors: Edward Aves, Emma Gibbs
Layout: Anita Singh
Cartography: Ed Wright, Miles Irving, Katie Lloyd-Jones
Picture editor: Mark Thomas
Production: Rebecca Short
Proofreaders: Elaine Pollard, Anne Burgot
Cover design: Chloë Roberts
Photographer: Tim Draper
Editorial: London Ruth Blackmore, Alison Murchie, Karoline Thomas, Andy Turner, Keith Drew, Alice Park, Lucy White, Jo Kirby, James Smart, Natasha Foges, Róisín Cameron, Emma Traynor, Kathryn Lane, Christina Valhouli, Monica Woods, James Rice, Mani Ramaswamy, Joe Staines, Peter Buckley, Matthew Milton, Tracy Hopkins, Ruth Tidball; **New York** Andrew Rosenberg, Steven Horak, AnneLise Sorensen, April Isaacs, Ella Steim, Anna Owens, Sean Mahoney, Courtney Miller, Paula Neudorf; **Delhi** Madhavi Singh, Karen D'Souza
Design & Pictures: London Scott Stickland, Dan May, Diana Jarvis, Nicole Newman, Sarah Cummins, Emily Taylor; **Delhi** Umesh Aggarwal,

Ajay Verma, Jessica Subramanian, Ankur Guha, Pradeep Thapliyal, Sachin Tanwar, Nikhil Agarwal
Production: Vicky Baldwin
Cartography: **London** Maxine Repath; **Delhi** Jai Prakash Mishra, Rajesh Chhibber, Ashutosh Bharti, Rajesh Mishra, Animesh Pathak, Jasbir Sandhu, Karobi Gogoi, Amod Singh, Alakananda Bhattacharya, Swati Handoo
Online: Narender Kumar, Rakesh Kumar, Amit Verma, Rahul Kumar, Ganesh Sharma, Debojit Borah, Saurabh Sati, Ravi Yadav
Marketing & Publicity: **London** Liz Statham, Niki Hanmer, Louise Maher, Jess Carter, Vanessa Godden, Vivienne Watton, Anna Paynton, Rachel Sprackett, Libby Jellie; **New York** Geoff Colquitt, Katy Ball; **Delhi** Ragini Govind
Manager India: Punita Singh
Reference Director: Andrew Lockett
Operations Manager: Helen Phillips
PA to Publishing Director: Nicola Henderson
Publishing Director: Martin Dunford
Commercial Manager: Gino Magnotta
Managing Director: John Duhigg

Publishing information

This eighth edition published May 2008 by
Rough Guides Ltd,
80 Strand, London WC2R 0RL
345 Hudson St, 4th Floor,
New York, NY 10014, USA
14 Local Shopping Centre, Panchsheel Park,
New Delhi 110017, India
Distributed by the Penguin Group
Penguin Books Ltd,
80 Strand, London WC2R 0RL
Penguin Group (USA)
375 Hudson Street, NY 10014, USA
Penguin Group (Australia)
250 Camberwell Road, Camberwell,
Victoria 3124, Australia
Penguin Books Canada Ltd,
10 Alcorn Avenue, Toronto, Ontario,
Canada M4V 1E4
Penguin Group (NZ)
67 Apollo Drive, Mairangi Bay, Auckland 1310,
New Zealand
Cover concept by Peter Dyer.

Typeset in Bembo and Helvetica to an original design by Henry Iles.

Printed in Italy by Legoprint S.p.A

© Robert Andrews, Jules Brown, Rob Humphreys and Phil Lee 2008

No part of this book may be reproduced in any form without permission from the publisher except for the quotation of brief passages in reviews.

1016pp includes index

A catalogue record for this book is available from the British Library

ISBN: 978-1-85828-498-9

Help us update

We've gone to a lot of effort to ensure that the eighth edition of **The Rough Guide to England** is accurate and up to date. However, things change – places get "discovered", opening hours are notoriously fickle, restaurants and rooms raise prices or lower standards. If you feel we've got it wrong or left something out, we'd like to know, and if you can remember the address, the price, the hours, the phone number, so much the better.

Please send your comments with the subject line "**Rough Guide England Update**" to ✉ mail@roughguides.com. We'll credit all contributions and send a copy of the next edition (or any other Rough Guide if you prefer) for the very best emails.

Have your questions answered and tell others about your trip at ⊛ community.roughguides.com

Acknowledgements

Robert Andrews would like to thank heartily Jo Morgan and Quinn Andrews for excellent contributions, and Ed Aves for thorough and sympathetic editing.

Phil Lee would like to thank his editor, Ed Aves, for his enthusiastic help and close attention to detail during the preparation of this new edition of the *Rough Guide to England*.

Readers' letters

Thanks to all the readers who took the trouble to write in with their comments and suggestions (and apologies if we've inadvertently omitted or misspelt anyone's name):

Kate Abbot; Margaret Anderson; H. Anderton; Josie Aston; Philip Barstow; Holly Bathie; Bethany de Bont & Johnathan Cain; Jason Borthwick; John Brayton; Dave Cross; Patrick Debacker; Lisa Delaney-Galal; Colin Duncan; Luke Dunstan; B.N. Evans; Rolf Fruin; Steve Gillon; Verity Gorry; Sean Gostage; Bob & Clare Griffiths; Vladimir Grishechkin; Allison Hahn; Duncan Hamilton; Bert & Jane Hansen; Lian Hazewinkel; Meera Hindocha; Colin Hood; Graham Hoyland; Fiona Humphreys; Sue Jenden; Dean Jennings; Margaret Kemp; Arnelle Kendall; Harmony Kirtley; John D. Landstreet; Jenny Leighton; Jonas Ludvigsson; Roger Manser; Lynn Marshall; Susan Mears; Martin Miller; John and Carole Moore; Colin Morrison; Paul Nelson; T. Okamoto; Charlie Pearson; Jim Vander Putten; Jen Randall; Katherine Rich; Noel Richardson; Rob M. Romano; Pamela Rumbell; Anna Ryan; Hermann Schoenecker; Nicola Shelton; Odette Smith; Gary Spinks; Daphne Stanley; Sian Thomas; Michelle Wales; Paul Wales; Jim Walker; Kate Watson; Eva Weber; Helen Welsh; Nicola Weston; Susanne Wild; Chris Woodcock; Jonathan Worrell; Mel Wreford; Kate Wright-Morris.

SMALL PRINT

Photo credits

All photos © Rough Guides except the following:

Full page
Bamburgh Castle © Mark Thomas

Introduction
p.7 Tin mine, Bodmin Moor © Mark Thomas
p.9 Exchange Square, Manchester © Paul Quayle/Axiom
p.9 Stained-glass window, Canterbury Cathedral © Mark Thomas
p.11 Pub, Eastbourne © Roger Bamber/Alamy

Things not to miss
02 Shopping in Leeds © Diana Jarvis
11 Houses of Parliament © Mark Thomas
13 Snaefell Mountain Railway © David Newham/ Alamy
14 Eden Project © Mark Thomas
15 Liverpool © Suzanne & Nick Geary/Getty Images
21 Canterbury Cathedral © Mark Thomas
22 Surfing in Newquay © Steve Allen Travel/ Alamy
26 Tate Modern © Mark Thomas/Axiom
32 Scilly Isles © Sarah Cummins

Coastal England colour section
Par Beach © Sarah Cummins

Festivals and events colour section
Glastonbury Festival © Mark Thomas
Accordionist at the Padstown Obby Oss © Roger Cracknell/Alamy

Swan Upping on the River Thames © Homer Sykes/Alamy
Cheese rolling at Brockworth © Carl de Souza/ AFP/Getty Images

Black and whites
p.72 British Museum © Mark Thomas/Axiom
p.119 The London Eye © Mark Thomas
p.173 Oysters, Whitstable © Chloë Roberts
p.228 Cowes Week © Patrick Eden/Alamy
p.278 Longleat © Chloë Roberts
p.290 Christ Church College, Oxford © David Bell/Alamy
p.300 The White Horse © Hideo Kurihara/Alamy
p.334 The Falkland Arms, Great Tew © Chloë Roberts
p.410 Clapper bridge © Rob Andrews
p.460 Tintagel Castle © Mark Thomas
p.638 Stoke Bruerne © Travelshots.com
p.755 Ravenglass and Eskdale Railway © Imagebroker/Alamy
p.786 The Yorkshire Sculpture Park © Martin Mayer/Alamy
p.830 The Deep, Hull © Less Gibon/Alamy
p.858 Holy Island © Mark Thomas/Axiom
p.866 Durham Cathedral © Mark Thomas/Axiom
p.883 Tyne Bridge and Sage Gateshead © Mark Thomas
p.932 Statue of Oliver Cromwell © Mark Thomas
p.955 The Gherkin © Mark Thomas

SMALL PRINT

Selected images from our guidebooks are available for licensing from:

ROUGHGUIDESPICTURES.COM

Index

Map entries are in colour.

INDEX

INDEX

Map symbols

▬▬	Motorway	♛	Castle
▦▦▦	Toll motorway	▟	Tower
═══	Major road	🏛	Monument
───	Minor road	⊙	Memorial/statue
▬▬▬	Pedestrianized street	⋔	Abbey
-----	Path	♰	Church (regional maps)
▥▥▥	Steps	✡	Synagogue
┗┗┗┗	Wall	⊠–⊠	Gate
━━━	Railway	🅿	Parking
— —	Ferry route	⊖	London Underground station
───	River	Ⓜ	Metro/light rail/tram station
─·─	National boundary	✈	Airport
─·─	County boundary	★	Bus stop
─ ─	Chapter boundary	@	Internet access
▲	Mountain peak	ⓘ	Tourist information
🗻	Rocks	✉	Post office
🌿	Gorge	⊞	Hospital
🌿	Waterfall	🏊	Swimming pool
⚓	Lighthouse	◉	Accommodation
⌂	Caves	▬	Building
♦	Point of interest	✚	Church/cathedral
∴	Ruin	🏞	Park/national park
✂	Battlefield	🪦	Cemetery
♟	Museum	🌲	Forest
🏛	Stately/historic house	🌾	Marshland
🌴	Public gardens	░	Beach

MAP SYMBOLS